2 0 1 8   E D I T I O N   |   P R I D E   &   F E R R E L L

# MARKETING

## W I L L I A M   M .   P R I D E

Texas A & M University

## O . C .   F E R R E L L

Auburn University

CENGAGE
Learning®

Australia • Brazil • Mexico • Singapore • United Kingdom • United States

**Marketing, 2018**
**William M. Pride, O.C. Ferrell**

Vice President, General Manager, Social
    Science & Qualitative Business: Erin Joyner

Product Director: Jason Fremder

Product Manager: Heather Mooney

Content Developer: Megan Fischer

Product Assistant: Allie Janneck

Marketing Manager: Charisse Darin

Content Project Manager: Megan Guiliani

Manufacturing Planner: Ron Montgomery

Production Service: SPi Global

Sr. Art Director: Bethany Casey

Internal Designer: Mike Stratton & Lou Ann
    Thesing

Cover Designer: Studio Montage

Cover Image: Leigh Prather/Shutterstock.com

Intellectual Property
    Analyst: Diane Garrity

    Project Manager: Sarah Shainwald

Library of Congress Control Number: 2016953429

ISBN: 978-1-337-27289-6

**Cengage Learning**
20 Channel Center Street
Boston, MA 02210
USA

Unless otherwise noted, all items © Cengage Learning.

Cengage Learning is a leading provider of customized learning solutions with employees residing in nearly 40 different countries and sales in more than 125 countries around the world. Find your local representative at **www.cengage.com**.

Cengage Learning products are represented in Canada by Nelson Education, Ltd.

To learn more about Cengage Learning Solutions, visit **www.cengage.com**

Purchase any of our products at your local college store or at our preferred online store **www.cengagebrain.com**

Printed in the United States of America
Print Number: 01    Print Year: 2018

To Nancy, Allen, Carmen, Gracie, Mike, Ashley, Charlie, J.R.,
and Anderson Pride

To James Collins Ferrell and George Collins Ferrell

# brief contents

# contents

## Part 2: Environmental Forces and Social and Ethical Responsibilities 63

## Part 3: Marketing Research and Target Market Analysis 129

## Part 4: Buying Behavior, Global Marketing, and Digital Marketing 193

## Part 6: Distribution Decisions 419

# Part 8: Pricing Decisions 595

# Preface

## MARKETING: A KEY TO SUCCESS

This edition of *Marketing* has been completely revised and updated to reflect dynamic changes in marketing and its environment. Marketing knowledge is important to every student's success, regardless of their career path. There is significant evidence that marketing is becoming a more important function in organizations, and students will need to be prepared to understand opportunities and challenges from a marketing perspective. This new edition provides the concepts, frameworks, and engagement in decision-making experiences that will prepare students for their careers. It is not enough to learn terminology and memorize concepts. To support success we provide a portfolio of learning devices to advance learning and critical thinking skills.

Active learning requires a holistic understanding with examples, exercises, and cases facilitated by MindTap, our online teaching experience. MindTap provides relevant assignments that guide students to analyze, apply, and improve thinking, allowing them to measure skills and outcomes with ease. This means that students using this book should develop respect for the importance of marketing and understand that the learning of marketing requires in-depth knowledge and the mastering of essential concepts. We have made the learning experience as fresh as possible with available research, new examples and boxes, as well as illustrations.

We address how technology is changing the marketing environment. As students prepare for the new digital world, they will also need to practice developing communication skills, especially teamwork, that go beyond their personal interaction with digital devices. Digital media can lower costs, generate awareness, build better relationships with customers, and achieve improved marketing research. Apps that connect consumers with products are creating opportunities for closer relationships. Buyers and sellers are entering zones of interdependency and co-creation of products. The sharing economy, defined as an economic concept harnessing peer-to-peer power and sharing underutilized resources such as automobiles, boats, and houses to earn income, is exploding. For example, Airbnb—a website that links people with renters of lodging accommodations—now has significantly more bookings each evening than Hilton.

We also provide numerous ancillary materials to aid in student comprehension of marketing concepts as well as to increase instructor resources for teaching this important material. Online materials include quizzes, PowerPoint presentations, videos, and flashcards. Our marketing video case series enables students to learn how real-world companies address marketing challenges. Our video series has been expanded to include YouTube videos that can bring engagement and excitement to the classroom. Our Interactive Marketing Plan Worksheets and video program provide students with practical knowledge of the challenges and the planning process of launching a new product. Together these revisions and additional materials will assist students in gaining a full understanding of pertinent marketing practices.

Online social networking has become an increasingly powerful tool for marketers. Most discussions about marketing today bring up issues such as how digital media can lower costs, improve communications, provide better customer support, and achieve improved marketing research. All elements of the marketing mix should be considered when using digital media and social networking. We discuss how digital media and social networking tools can create effective digital marketing strategies that can enhance marketing efforts. In addition, the entire book integrates important digital marketing concepts and examples where appropriate.

We have paid careful attention to enhancing all key concepts in marketing and have built this revision to be current and to reflect important changes in marketing. Our book is a market leader because students find it readable and relevant. Our text reflects the real world of marketing and provides the most comprehensive coverage possible of important marketing topics.

Specific details of this extensive revision are available in the transition guide in the *Instructor's Manual*. We have also made efforts to improve all teaching ancillaries and student learning tools. PowerPoint presentations continue to be a very popular teaching device, and a special effort has been made to upgrade the PowerPoint program to enhance classroom teaching. The *Instructor's Manual* continues to be a valuable tool, updated with engaging in-class activities and projects. The authors and publisher have worked together to provide a comprehensive teaching package and ancillaries that are unsurpassed in the marketplace.

The authors have maintained a hands-on approach to teaching this material and revising the text and its ancillaries. This results in an integrated teaching package and approach that is accurate, sound, and successful in reaching students. The outcome of this involvement fosters trust and confidence in the teaching package and in student learning outcomes. Student feedback regarding this textbook is highly favorable.

# WHAT'S NEW TO THIS EDITION?

Our goal is to provide the most up-to-date content—concepts, examples, cases, exercises, and data—possible. Therefore, in this revision there are significant changes that make learning more engaging and interesting to the students. The following highlight the types of changes that were made in this revision.

**MARKETING INSIGHTS**

**Airbnb Facilitates the Sharing Lodging Experience**

Airbnb has come far in the eight years it has been in business. The company started when founders Brian Chesky and Joe Gebbia turned their apartment into a bed and breakfast. They could afford to present. and Airbnb takes 3 percent of the booking price when the property is rented out.

Despite its immense success, Airbnb believes it can create more value for more customers for instance, it has to

- **Boxed features.** Each chapter includes two new or updated boxed features that highlight green marketing, marketing entrepreneurs, emerging trends in marketing, or controversial issues in marketing. The majority of the boxed features are new to this edition; a few have been significantly updated and revised to fit the themes of this edition.
- **New Snapshot features.** The Snapshot features are new and engage students by highlighting interesting, up-to-date statistics that link marketing theory to the real world.

- **Foundational content.** Each chapter has been updated with the latest knowledge available related to frameworks, concepts, and academic research. These additions have been seamlessly integrated into the text. Many examples are new and a review of footnotes at the ends of chapters will reveal where new content has been added. Many of the new examples and content changes have been updated to 2016.
- **Opening vignettes:** *Marketing Insights*. All of the chapter-opening vignettes are new or updated. They are written to introduce the theme of each chapter by focusing on actual entrepreneurial companies and how they deal with real-world situations.

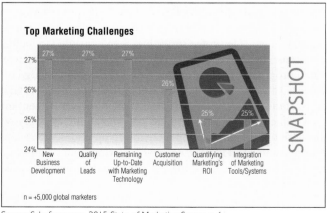

**Top Marketing Challenges**

SNAPSHOT

n = +5,000 global marketers

Source: Salesforce.com, 2015 State of Marketing Survey, p. 6.

- **New research.** Throughout the text we have updated content with the most recent research that supports the frameworks and best practices for marketing.
- **New illustrations and examples.** New advertisements from well-known firms are employed to illustrate chapter topics. Experiences of real-world companies are used to exemplify marketing concepts and strategies throughout the text. Most examples are new or updated to include digital marketing concepts as well as several new sustainable marketing illustrations.
- **End-of-chapter cases.** Each chapter contains two cases, including a video case, profiling firms to illustrate concrete application of marketing strategies and concepts. Many of our video cases are new to this edition and are supported by current and engaging videos.

# FEATURES OF THE BOOK

As with previous editions, this edition of the text provides a comprehensive and practical introduction to marketing that is both easy to teach and to learn. *Marketing* continues to be one of the most widely adopted introductory textbooks in the world. We appreciate the confidence that adopters have placed in our textbook and continue to work hard to make sure that, as in previous editions, this edition keeps pace with changes. The entire text is structured to excite students about the subject and to help them learn completely and efficiently.

- An *organizational model* at the beginning of each part provides a "road map" of the text and a visual tool for understanding the connections among various components.
- *Objectives* at the start of each chapter present concrete expectations about what students are to learn as they read the chapter.
- Every chapter begins with an *opening vignette*. This feature provides an example of the real world of marketing that relates to the topics covered in the chapter. After reading the vignette, the student should be motivated to want to learn more about concepts and strategies that relate to the varying topics. Students will be introduced to such companies as Airbnb, Primark, Farmgirl Flowers, and Dressbarn.
- Boxed features—*Emerging Trends in Marketing* and *Going Green*— capture dynamic changes in marketing. These changes are influencing marketing strategies and customer behavior. Strong feedback from adopters indicated the need for coverage in these areas.

## EMERGING **TRENDS IN MARKETING**

**Making Trade Fair**

Fair Trade–certified organizations require factories to meet different conditions. They must pay their workers a minimum wage in the country in which they are employed, with the intention of working toward a "livable wage." A livable wage allows workers to afford basic necessities. Additionally, brands must pay a premium to factory workers. These premiums are placed in a collective bank account and are used for bonuses or to address community needs.

The Fair Trade trend is gaining traction among fashion and home furnishings. After the Bangladesh factory collapsed in 2013, many apparel and home furnishing brands made a commitment to improve factory conditions. Twenty brands have chosen to become Fair Trade certified.

Consumers are embracing Fair Trade apparel and home goods as well. For instance, Bed Bath & Beyond quickly sold out of back-to-school supplies labeled as Fair Trade–certified. This demonstrates consumers' increased concern for how goods are manufactured. In particular, Fair Trade certification focuses on improving the labor conditions of factory workers.

Although fair trade certification costs brands 1–5 percent of what companies pay to factories, it is clear that demand is on the rise. Fair trade apparel and home furnishings have increased fivefold in the past few years, spurring more factories to work toward achieving certification. Marketers monitoring the environment are finding the costs of Fair Trade well worth the benefits.[a]

© Stockphoto.com/CTR design LLC

- The *Emerging Trends* boxes cover such marketing phenomena as fair trade, marketing analytics, and shopping tourism. Featured companies include Harley-Davidson, USAA, Marvel, and Netflix.

## MARKETING DEBATE

### ISSUE: Should Drugstores Sell Tobacco Products?

When CVS announced it would stop selling tobacco products in 2014, the company acknowledged that this change in policy would cost it $2 billion in annual revenues. Still, CVS wanted to highlight its commitment to helping customers stay healthy—and, in fact, it renamed the company CVS Health to spotlight that mission. Some health advocates and state attorneys general praised the move and called on CVS's competitors to follow suit by dropping cigarettes, cigars, and other tobacco products.

However, Walgreens and other drug retailers have not followed CVS's lead. According to a Walgreen's statement: "We believe that if the goal is to truly reduce tobacco use in America, then the most effective thing retail pharmacies can do is address the root causes and help smokers quit." Walgreen's and other drug stores sell numerous smoking-cessation products, but they also tend to display packs of cigarettes near checkout counters, where they can catch the eye of shoppers.

Even if CVS's competitors decide to stop selling tobacco products, the change in policy might not make a huge difference in smoking rates because more cigarettes are sold at gas stations and convenience stores than in drug stores. Still, should stores that specialize in health-related goods and services continue to market tobacco products, which are legal but proven to be unhealthy?[a]

© Stockphoto.com/CTR design LLC

- The *Marketing Debate* marginal feature discusses controversial issues related to drugstores selling tobacco products, banning trans fat from food products, facial recognition and privacy, the truthfulness of native advertising, and surge pricing.

- The *Going Green* boxes introduce students to such topics as bio-plastics, algae biofuels, and natural claims on cigarette packaging. Featured companies include Campbell's, Walmart, and 1 Hotel.

## GOING GREEN

### Lego: Building with Bio-Plastics

The Lego Company has announced its most daring move yet in its sustainability efforts: getting rid of plastic. The Lego Company makes 60 billion blocks a year using the oil-based plastic ABS. It is estimated that Lego goes through 6,000 tons of plastic annually. The company has made a strategic decision toward sustainability in its products.

Lego has set the strategic goal of eliminating ABS plastics by 2030. The company estimates that about 75 percent of its carbon emissions come from extracting and refining oil for its toys. Eliminating this type of plastic would there-

million toward developing the Lego Sustainable Materials Centre in Denmark. In particular, Lego is looking for a substitute for oil-based plastics and believes bio-based plastics may be the key.

Unfortunately, not everyone is confident Lego will succeed. ABS plastic is easily moldable, and it is an ideal composition for ensuring that each Lego piece fits together. Early forays into plant-based plastics show that this type of bio-plastic has difficulty clicking, sticking, and maintaining its shape. However, Lego is confident that it

© Stockphoto.com/CTR design LLC

## Entrepreneurship in Marketing

### Protein Bar Restaurant: Satisfying Consumers

**Founder:** Matt Matros
**Business:** Protein Bar Restaurant
**Founded:** 2009, in Chicago, IL
**Success:** The Protein Bar restaurant has been featured in numerous newspapers and has expanded to four cities.

At 22, entrepreneur Matt Matros decided to drastically change his life. He lost 50 pounds through a strong regimen of exercise and a high-protein diet. Afterward, he decided to start the Chicago-based restaurant Protein Bar.

To be successful, Matros had to select the right mix of product, distribution, promotion, and price. Matros conceived of a casual dining restaurant that would offer

include burritos, salads, breakfast items, raw juices, and side dishes. Matros chose prices for these products that would be reasonable for on-the-go consumers who did not want to spend time making their own protein shakes.

The company has created publicity by recently teaming up with Chicago Bears wide receiver Brandon Marshall to promote a new Protein Bar drink called Crazy Stigma Green. For every drink purchased, $1 is donated to the Project 375 Foundation. Protein Bar has also received coverage in newspapers such as *Washington Post* and *Chicago Tribune*. The restaurant has expanded to Washington D.C., Denver, and Boulder, Colorado. Matros has

© Stockphoto.com/CTR design LLC

- The *Entrepreneurship in Marketing* feature focuses on the role of entrepreneurship and the need for creativity in developing successful marketing strategies by featuring successful entrepreneurial companies like Protein Bar, Second City, Instacart, Honest Company, Counter Culture Coffee, and Scentsy.
- *Key term definitions* appear in the margins to help students build their marketing vocabulary.
- Figures, tables, photographs, advertisements, and Snapshot features increase comprehension and stimulate interest.

- A complete *chapter summary* reviews the major topics discussed, and the list of important terms provides another end-of-chapter study aid to expand students' marketing vocabulary.
- *Discussion and review questions* at the end of each chapter encourage further study and exploration of chapter content.
- Two *cases* at the end of each chapter help students understand the application of chapter concepts. One of the end-of-chapter cases is related to a video segment. Some examples of companies highlighted in the cases are Dollar Shave Club, Alibaba, Blue Bell Creameries, Mattel, Hilton Worldwide, Zappos, Theo Chocolate, and CVS.
- A *strategic case* at the end of each part helps students integrate the diverse concepts that have been discussed within the related chapters. Examples include REI, IKEA, Patagonia, Sseko Designs, and Eaton. *Appendices* discuss marketing career opportunities, explore financial analysis in marketing, and present a sample marketing plan.
- A comprehensive *glossary* defines more than 625 important marketing terms.

# TEXT ORGANIZATION

We have organized the eight parts of *Marketing* to give students a theoretical and practical understanding of marketing decision making.

**Part 1**  **Marketing Strategy and Customer Relationships**

In *Chapter 1*, we define marketing and explore several key concepts: customers and target markets, the marketing mix, relationship marketing, the marketing concept, and value-driven marketing. In *Chapter 2*, we look at an overview of strategic marketing topics, such as the strategic planning process; corporate, business-unit, and marketing strategies; the implementation of marketing strategies; performance evaluation of marketing strategies; and the components of the marketing plan.

**Part 2**  **Environmental Forces and Social and Ethical Responsibilities**

We examine competitive, economic, political, legal and regulatory, technological, and sociocultural forces that can have profound effects on marketing strategies in *Chapter 3*. In *Chapter 4*, we explore social responsibility and ethical issues in marketing decisions.

**Part 3**  **Marketing Research and Target Market Analysis**

In *Chapter 5*, we provide a foundation for analyzing buyers with a look at marketing information systems and the basic steps in the marketing research process. We look at elements that affect buying decisions to better analyze customers' needs and evaluate how specific marketing strategies can satisfy those needs. In *Chapter 6*, we deal with how to select and analyze target markets—one of the major steps in marketing strategy development.

**Part 4**  **Buying Behavior, Global Marketing, and Digital Marketing**

We examine consumer buying decision processes and factors that influence buying decisions in *Chapter 7*. In *Chapter 8*, we explore business markets, business customers, the buying center, and the business buying decision process. *Chapter 9* focuses on the actions, involvement, and strategies of marketers that serve international customers. In *Chapter 10*, we discuss digital marketing, social media, and social networking.

**Part 5**  **Product Decisions**

In *Chapter 11*, we introduce basic concepts and relationships that must be understood to make effective product decisions. Also, we discuss a number of dimensions associated with branding and packaging. We analyze a variety of topics regarding product management in *Chapter 12*, including line extensions and product modification, new-product development, and product deletions. *Chapter 13* discusses services marketing.

**Part 6**  **Distribution Decisions**

In *Chapter 14*, we look at supply-chain management, marketing channels, and the decisions and activities associated with the physical distribution of products, such as order processing, materials handling, warehousing, inventory management, and transportation. *Chapter 15* explores retailing and wholesaling, including types of retailers and wholesalers, direct marketing and selling, and strategic retailing issues.

**Part 7     Promotion Decisions**

We discuss integrated marketing communications in *Chapter 16*. The communication process and major promotional methods that can be included in promotion mixes are described. In *Chapter 17*, we analyze the major steps in developing an advertising campaign. We also define public relations and how it can be used. *Chapter 18* deals with personal selling and the role it can play in a firm's promotional efforts. We also explore the general characteristics of sales promotion and describe sales promotion techniques.

**Part 8     Pricing Decisions**

In *Chapter 19*, we discuss the importance of price and look at some characteristics of price and nonprice competition. We explore fundamental concepts such as demand, elasticity, marginal analysis, and break-even analysis. We then examine the major factors that affect marketers' pricing decisions. In *Chapter 20*, we look at the six major stages of the process marketers use to establish prices.

# A COMPREHENSIVE INSTRUCTIONAL RESOURCE PACKAGE

For instructors, this edition of *Marketing* includes an exceptionally comprehensive package of teaching materials.

## Instructor's Manual

The *Instructor's Manual* has been revamped to meet the needs of an engaging classroom environment. It has been updated with diverse and dynamic discussion starters, classroom activities, and group exercises. It includes such tools as:

- Quick Reference Guides
- Purpose Statements
- Integrated Lecture Outlines
- Discussion Starter recommendations that encourage active exploration of the in-text examples
- Class Exercises and Semester Project Activities
- Suggested Answers to end-of-chapter exercises, cases, and strategic cases
- Guides to teaching Role-Play Team Exercises

## Test Bank

The test bank provides more than 4,000 test items, including true/false, multiple choice, and essay questions. In this edition, you will find several new questions for each learning objective. Each objective test item is accompanied by the correct answer, appropriate Learning Objective, level of difficulty, Bloom's level of thinking, Program Interdisciplinary Learning Outcomes, and Marketing Disciplinary Learning Outcomes. Cengage Learning Testing powered by Cognero is a flexible, online system that allows you to:

- Author, edit, and manage test bank content from multiple Cengage Learning solutions
- Create multiple test versions in an instant
- Deliver tests from your LMS, your classroom, or wherever you want

## American Marketing Association Professional Certified Marketer®

The American Marketing Association has recently started offering marketing graduates the opportunity of adding the AMA PCM® credentials to their undergraduate or MBA degree, which can serve as a symbol of professional excellence that affirms mastery of marketing knowledge and commitment to quality in the practice of marketing. Certification, which is voluntary, requires passing a rigorous and comprehensive exam and then maintaining the certification through continuing education. Earning an AMA PCM certification demonstrates to employers, peers, and clients that the holer:

- Has mastered essential marketing knowledge and practices
- Goes the extra mile to stay current in the marketing field
- Follows the highest professional standards

The AMA recommends Pride and Ferrell's *Marketing* as a suggested resource for AMA PCM students to utilize as they prepare for taking the AMA PCM certification exam, and the text was used as a source to design the course and as a source for suitable examination questions. Now, more than ever, you need to stand out in the marketplace. AMA's Professional Certified Marketer (PCM®) program is the perfect way to showcase your expertise and set yourself apart.

To learn more about the American Marketing Association and the AMA PCM exam, visit **www.marketingpower.com/Careers/Pages/ ProfessionalCertifiedMarketer.aspx**

## PowerPoint Slides

PowerPoint continues to be a very popular teaching device, and a special effort has been made to upgrade the PowerPoint program to enhance classroom teaching. Premium lecture slides, containing such content as advertisements, and unique graphs and data, have been created to provide instructors with up-to-date, unique content to increase student application and interest.

## Marketing Video Case Series

This series contains videos specifically tied to the video cases found at the end of the book. The videos include information about exciting companies such as New Belgium Brewing, Theo Chocolate, Alibaba, Louis Vuitton, and Luxottica. MindTap video exercises provide students with opportunities to use the videos to test and expand their knowledge. New to this edition are YouTube videos that have been selected by the authors specifically to be used in the classroom to engage students and illustrate marketing concepts.

## Online Role-Play Exercises

The eight role-play exercises, available online, highlight key chapter concepts. These exercises involve team participation where students engage in a discussion of a marketing dilemma and provide a solution. The class breaks into teams and reaches decisions that relate to the short term, intermediate term, and long term. Each team member is assigned a role and should take on that role in team decision making. The case dilemmas are disguised but are based on real-world marketing situations. All information, including a background section and the roles, are online. See the *Instructor's Manual* for more guidance on these exercises.

## MindTap for *Marketing*

MindTap is a personalized teaching experience with relevant assignments that guide students to analyze, apply, and improve thinking, allowing them to measure skills and outcomes with ease.

- Personalized Teaching: Becomes yours with a learning path that is built with key student objectives. Control what students see and when they see it. Use it as-is or match to your syllabus exactly—hide, rearrange, add, and create your own content.

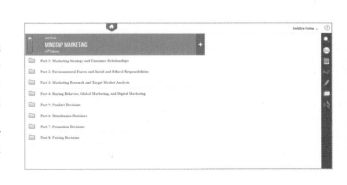

- Guide Students: A unique learning path of relevant readings, multimedia, and activities that move students up the learning taxonomy from basic knowledge and comprehension to analysis and application.
- Promote Better Outcomes: Empower instructors and motivate students with analytics and reports that provide a snapshot of class progress, time in course, and engagement and completion rates.

## Author's Website

The authors also maintain a website at *http://prideferrell.net* to provide additional video resources that can be used as supplements and class exercises. The videos have been developed as marketing labs with worksheets for students to use after observing the videos. Some of the videos are accessible through links, and there is also information on where some of the videos can be obtained. These videos are in addition to the new set of YouTube videos described earlier.

## Building a Marketing Plan

New in this edition, the marketing plan has been expanded into eight parts that walk students through the steps of building a marketing plan as they finish relevant content in the book. Online worksheets guide students through the steps to build a marketing plan and end with a place for them to upload their work on their marketing plan for each section. Sections of Building a Marketing Plan can be assigned individually or as an entire ongoing project throughout the course.

# SUPPLEMENTS TO MEET STUDENT NEEDS

The complete package available with *Marketing* includes support materials that facilitate student learning. To access additional course materials, please visit *www.cengagebrain.com*. At the CengageBrain.com home page, search for the ISBN of your textbook (from the back cover of your book) using the search box at the top of the page. This will take you to the product page, where the following resources can be found:

- Interactive teaching and learning tools, including:
  - Full-color e-book—Allows you to highlight and search for key terms
  - Quizzes
  - Flashcards
  - Videos
  - An Interactive Marketing Plan
  - And more!

# YOUR COMMENTS AND SUGGESTIONS ARE VALUED

As authors, our major focus has been on teaching and preparing learning materials for introductory marketing students. We have traveled extensively to work with students and to understand the needs of professors of introductory marketing courses. We both teach this marketing course on a regular basis and test the materials included in the book, test bank, and other ancillary materials to make sure they are effective in the classroom.

Through the years, professors and students have sent us many helpful suggestions for improving the text and ancillary components. We invite your comments, questions, and criticisms. We want to do our best to provide materials that enhance the teaching and learning of marketing concepts and strategies. Your suggestions will be sincerely appreciated. Please write us, or e-mail us at **w-pride@tamu.edu** or **ocferrell@gmail.com**, or call 979-845-5857 (Bill Pride).

# ACKNOWLEDGMENTS

Like most textbooks, this one reflects the ideas of many academicians and practitioners who have contributed to the development of the marketing discipline. We appreciate the opportunity to present their ideas in this book. A number of individuals have made helpful comments and recommendations in their reviews of this or earlier editions.

Zafar U. Ahmed
*Lebanese American University*

Thomas Ainscough
*University of South Florida*

Sana Akili
*U.S. Department of Commerce*

Katrece Albert
*Southern University*

Joe F. Alexander
*Belmont University*

Mark I. Alpert
*University of Texas at Austin*

David M. Ambrose
*University of Nebraska*

David Andrus
*Kansas State University*

George Avellano
*Central State University*

Emin Babakus
*University of Memphis*

Julie Baker
*Texas Christian University*

Siva Balasubramanian
*Illinois Institute of Technology*

Joseph Ballenger

*Stephen F. Austin State University*

Frank Barber
*Cuyahoga Community College*

Thomas E. Barry
*Southern Methodist University*

Richard C. Becherer
*University of Tennessee–Chattanooga*

Walter H. Beck, Sr.
*Reinhardt College*

Russell Belk
*York University*

John Bennett
*University of Missouri–Columbia*

W. R. Berdine
*California State Polytechnic Institute*

Karen Berger
*Pace University*

Roger Blackwell
*Blackwell Business Advisors*

Peter Bloch
*University of Missouri–Columbia*

Nancy Bloom
*Nassau Community College*

Paul N. Bloom
*Duke University*

James P. Boespflug
*Arapahoe Community College*

Joseph G. Bonnici
*Central Connecticut State University*

Peter Bortolotti
*Johnson & Wales University*

Chris D. Bottomley
*Ocean County College*

Jenell Bramlage
*University of Northwestern Ohio*

James Brock
*Pacific Lutheran University*

John R. Brooks, Jr.
*Houston Baptist University*

John Buckley
*Orange County Community College*

Pat J. Calabros
*University of Texas–Arlington*

Linda Calderone
*State University of New York College of Technology at Farmingdale*

Joseph Cangelosi
*University of Central Arkansas*

William J. Carner
*University of Texas–Austin*

Nancy M. Carr
*Community College of Philadelphia*

James C. Carroll
*University of Central Arkansas*

Terry M. Chambers
*Westminster College*

Lawrence Chase
*Tompkins Cortland Community College*

Larry Chonko
*Baylor University*

Ernest F. Cooke
*Loyola College–Baltimore*

Robert Copley
*University of Louisville*

Robert Corey
*West Virginia University*

Deborah L. Cowles
*Virginia Commonwealth University*

William L. Cron
*Texas Christian University*

Gary Cutler
*Dyersburg State Community College*

Bernice N. Dandridge
*Diablo Valley College*

Sally Dibb
*Open University*

Katherine Dillon
*Ocean County College*

Ralph DiPietro
*Montclair State University*

Paul Dishman
*Utah Valley University*

Casey L. Donoho
*Northern Arizona University*

Todd Donovan
*Colorado State University*

Kent Drummond
*University of Wyoming*

Tinus Van Drunen
*University Twente (Netherlands)*

Robert F. Dwyer
*University of Cincinnati*

Roland Eyears
*Central Ohio Technical College*

Cheryl A. Fabrizi
Broome Community College, State University of New York

Kathleen Ferris-Costa
*Bridgewater State University*

James Finch
*University of Wisconsin–La Crosse*

Renée Florsheim
*Loyola Marymount University*

Charles W. Ford
*Arkansas State University*

John Fraedrich
*Southern Illinois University, Carbondale*

Terry Gabel
*Monmouth College*

Robert Garrity
*University of Hawaii*

Geoffrey L. Gordon
*Northern Illinois University*

Sharon F. Gregg
*Middle Tennessee University*

Charles Gross
*University of New Hampshire*

John Hafer
*University of Nebraska at Omaha*

David Hansen
*Texas Southern University*

Richard C. Hansen
*Ferris State University*

Nancy Hanson-Rasmussen
*University of Wisconsin–Eau Claire*

Robert R. Harmon
*Portland State University*

Michael Hartline
*Florida State University*

Salah S. Hassan
*George Washington University*

Manoj Hastak
*American University*

Dean Headley
*Wichita State University*

Esther Headley
*Wichita State University*

Debbora Heflin-Bullock
*California State Polytechnic University–Pomona*

Tony Henthorne
*University of Nevada, Las Vegas*

Charles L. Hilton
*Eastern Kentucky University*

Elizabeth C. Hirschman
*Rutgers, State University of New Jersey*

Deloris James
*Howard University*

Ron Johnson
*Colorado Mountain College*

Theodore F. Jula
*Stonehill College*

Peter F. Kaminski
*Northern Illinois University*

Jerome Katrichis
*University of Hartford*

Garland Keesling
*Towson University*

James Kellaris
*University of Cincinnati*

Alvin Kelly
*Florida A&M University*

Sylvia Keyes
*Bridgewater State College*

William M. Kincaid, Jr.
*Oklahoma State University*

Hal Koenig
*Oregon State University*

Kathleen Krentler

*San Diego State University*

John Krupa, Jr.
*Johnson & Wales University*

Barbara Lafferty
*University of South Florida*

Patricia Laidler
*Massasoit Community College*

Bernard LaLonde
*Ohio State University*

Richard A. Lancioni
*Temple University*

Irene Lange
*California State University–Fullerton*

Geoffrey P. Lantos
*Stonehill College*

Charles L. Lapp
*University of Texas at Dallas*

Virginia Larson
*San Jose State University*

John Lavin
*Waukesha County Technical Institute*

Marilyn Lavin
*University of Wisconsin Whitewater*

Hugh E. Law
*East Tennessee State University*

Monle Lee
*Indiana University–South Bend*

Ron Lennon
*University of South Florida–Sarasota-Manatee*

Richard C. Leventhal
*Ashford University*

Marilyn L. Liebrenz-Himes
*George Washington University*

Terry Loe
*Kennesaw State University*

Mary Logan
*Global University*

Paul Londrigan
*Mott Community College*

Anthony Lucas
*Community College of Allegheny County*

George Lucas
*U.S. Learning, Inc.*

William Lundstrom
*Cleveland State University*

Rhonda Mack
*College of Charleston*

Stan Madden
*Baylor University*

Patricia M. Manninen
*North Shore Community College*

Gerald L. Manning
*Des Moines Area Community College*

Lalita A. Manrai
*University of Delaware*

Franklyn Manu
*Morgan State University*

Allen S. Marber
*University of Bridgeport*

Gayle J. Marco
*Robert Morris College*

Marilyn Martin Melchiorre
*College of Idaho*

Carolyn A. Massiah
*University of Central Florida*

James McAlexander
*Oregon State University*

Donald McCartney
*University of Wisconsin–Green Bay*

Jack McNiff
*State University of New York College of Technology at Farmington*

Lee Meadow
*Eastern Illinois University*

Jeffrey A. Meier
*Fox Valley Technical College*

James Meszaros
*County College of Morris*

Brian Meyer
*Minnesota State University*

Martin Meyers
*University of Wisconsin–Stevens Point*

Stephen J. Miller
*Oklahoma State University*

Carol Morris-Calder
*Loyola Marymount University*

David Murphy
*Madisonville Community College*

Keith Murray
*Bryant University*

Sue Ellen Neeley
*University of Houston–Clear Lake*

Carolyn Y. Nicholson
*Stetson University*

Francis L. Notturno, Sr.
*Owens Community College*

Terrence V. O'Brien
*Northern Illinois University*

James R. Ogden
*Kutztown University of Pennsylvania*

Shannon Ogden
*Black River Technical College*

Lois Bitner Olson
*San Diego State University*

Robert S. Owen
*Texas A&M University—Texarkana*

David P. Paul, III
*Monmouth University*

Terry Paul
*Ohio State University*

Teresa Pavia
*University of Utah*

John Perrachione
*Truman State University*

Lana Podolak
*Community College of Beaver County*

William Presutti
*Duquesne University*

Daniel Rajaratnam
*University of Texas at Dallas*

Mohammed Rawwas
*University of Northern Iowa*

James D. Reed
*Louisiana State University–Shreveport*

John Reed
*University of New Mexico*

William Rhey
*Florida Southern College*

Glen Riecken
*College of Charleston*

Ed Riordan
*Wayne State University*

Bruce Robertson
*San Francisco State University*

Robert A. Robicheaux
*University of Alabama–Birmingham*

Linda Rose
*Westwood College Online*

Bert Rosenbloom
*Drexel University*

Robert H. Ross
*Wichita State University*

Tom Rossi
*Broome Community College*

Vicki Rostedt
*The University of Akron*

Catherine Roster
*University of New Mexico*

Don Roy
*Middle Tennessee State University*

Catherine Ruggieri
*St. John's University*

Rob Salamida
*SUNY Broome Community College*

Ronald Schill
*Middlebury Institute of International Studies at Monterey*

Bodo Schlegelmilch
*Vienna University of Economics and Business Administration*

Edward Schmitt
*Villanova University*

Donald Sciglimpaglia
*San Diego State University*

Stanley Scott
*University of Alaska—Anchorage*

Beheruz N. Sethna
*University of West Georgia*

Abhay Shah
*Colorado State University—Pueblo*

Morris A. Shapero
*Eckerd College*

Mark Siders
*Southern Oregon University*

Carolyn F. Siegel
*Eastern Kentucky University*

Lyndon Simkin
*University of Reading*

Roberta Slater
*Cedar Crest College*

Paul J. Solomon
*University of South Florida*

Sheldon Somerstein
*City University of New York*

Eric R. Spangenberg
*University of Mississippi*

Rosann L. Spiro
*Indiana University*

William Staples
*University of Houston–Clear Lake*

Carmen Sunda
*University of New Orleans*

Crina Tarasi
*Central Michigan University*

Ruth Taylor
*Texas State University*

Steven A. Taylor
*Illinois State University*

Ira Teich
*Lander College for Men*

Debbie Thorne
*Texas State University*

Sharynn Tomlin
*Angelo State University*

James Underwood
*University of Louisiana–Lafayette*

Barbara Unger
*Western Washington University*

Dale Varble
*Indiana State University*

Bronis Verhage
*Georgia State University*

R. "Vish" Viswanathan Iyer
*University of Northern Colorado*

Kirk Wakefield
*Baylor University*

Harlan Wallingford
*Pace University*

Jacquelyn Warwick
*Andrews University*

James F. Wenthe
*Georgia College*

Sumner M. White
*Massachusetts Bay Community College*

Janice Williams
*University of Central Oklahoma*

Alan R. Wiman
*Rider College*

John Withey
*St. Edwards University*

We would like to thank Charlie Hofacker and Michael Hartline, both of Florida State University, for many helpful suggestions and insights in developing the chapter on digital marketing and social networking. Michael Hartline also assisted in the development of the marketing plan outline and provided suggestions throughout the text.

We thank Jennifer Sawayda and Gwyn Walters for their research and editorial assistance in the revision of the chapters. We appreciate the efforts of Marian Wood for developing and revising a number of boxed features and cases. We deeply appreciate the assistance of Clarissa Means, Megan Story, Fatima Wood, and Marilyn Ayala for providing editorial technical assistance and support.

We express appreciation for the support and encouragement given to us by our colleagues at Texas A&M University and Auburn University. We are also grateful for the comments and suggestions we received from our own students, student focus groups, and student correspondents who provided feedback through the website.

A number of talented professionals at Cengage Learning and SPi Global have contributed to the development of this book. We are especially grateful to Heather Mooney, Megan Fischer, Megan Guiliani, Allie Janneck, Bethany Casey, and Chandrasekar Subramanian. Their inspiration, patience, support, and friendship are invaluable.

*William M. Pride*
*O. C. Ferrell*

# ABOUT THE AUTHORS

**William M. Pride** is Professor of Marketing, Mays Business School, at Texas A&M University. He received his PhD from Louisiana State University. In addition to this text, he is the coauthor of Cengage Learning's *Business* text, a market leader. Dr. Pride teaches principles of marketing at both undergraduate and graduate levels and constantly solicits student feedback important to revising a principles of marketing text.

Dr. Pride's research interests are in advertising, promotion, and distribution channels. His research articles have appeared in major journals in the fields of marketing, such as the *Journal of Marketing*, the *Journal of Marketing Research*, the *Journal of the Academy of Marketing Science*, and the *Journal of Advertising*.

Dr. Pride is a member of the American Marketing Association, Academy of Marketing Science, Society for Marketing Advances, and the Marketing Management Association. He has received the Marketing Fellow Award from the Society for Marketing Advances and the Marketing Innovation Award from the Marketing Management Association. Both of these are lifetime achievement awards.

**O. C. Ferrell** is The James T. Pursell Sr. Eminent Scholar Chair in Ethics and Director of the Center for Ethical Organizational Cultures at Auburn University's Raymond Harbert College of Business. He was previously a University Distinguished Professor of Marketing at the Anderson School of Management, University of New Mexico. He has also been on the faculties of Belmont University, the University of Wyoming, Colorado State University, University of Memphis, Texas A&M University, Illinois State University, and Southern Illinois University. He received his PhD in marketing from Louisiana State University.

Dr. Ferrell is president-elect of the Academy of Marketing Science. He is past president of the Academic Council of the American Marketing Association and chaired the American Marketing Association Ethics Committee. Under his leadership, the committee developed the AMA Code of Ethics and the AMA Code of Ethics for Marketing on the Internet. In addition, he is a former member of the Academy of Marketing Science Board of Governors and is a Society of Marketing Advances and Southwestern Marketing Association Fellow and an Academy of Marketing Science Distinguished Fellow. He has served for nine years as the vice president of publications for the Academy of Marketing Science. In 2010, he received a Lifetime Achievement Award from the Macromarketing Society and a special award for service to doctoral students from the Southeast Doctoral Consortium. He received, from the Academy of Marketing Science, the Harold Berkman Lifetime Service Award and, more recently, the Cutco Vector Distinguished Marketing Educator Award.

Dr. Ferrell is the co-author of 20 books and more than 100 published articles and papers. His articles have been published in the *Journal of Marketing Research*, the *Journal of Marketing*, the *Journal of Business Ethics*, the *Journal of Business Research*, the *Journal of the Academy of Marketing Science, AMS Review*, and the *Journal of Public Policy & Marketing*, as well as other journals.

# part 1

## Marketing Strategy and Customer Relationships

**1:** An Overview of Strategic Marketing

**2:** Planning, Implementing, and Evaluating Marketing Strategies

**PART 1** introduces the field of marketing and offers a broad perspective from which to explore and analyze various components of the marketing discipline.

**CHAPTER 1** defines *marketing* and explores some key concepts, including customers and target markets, the marketing mix, relationship marketing, the marketing concept, and value.

**CHAPTER 2** provides an overview of strategic marketing issues, such as the effect of organizational resources and opportunities on the planning process; the role of the mission statement; corporate, business-unit, and marketing strategies; and the creation of the marketing plan.

# chapter 1     An Overview of Strategic Marketing

---

## OBJECTIVES

---

**1-1**   Define *marketing*.

**1-2**   Explain the different variables of the marketing mix.

**1-3**   Describe how marketing creates value.

**1-4**   Briefly explore the marketing environment.

**1-5**   Summarize the marketing concept.

**1-6**   Identify the importance of building customer relationships.

**1-7**   Explain why marketing is important to our global economy.

# MARKETING INSIGHTS

## Airbnb Facilitates the Sharing Lodging Experience

Letuve/Dreamstime.com

Airbnb has come far in the eight years it has been in business. The company started when founders Brian Chesky and Joe Gebbia turned their apartment into a bed and breakfast so they could afford to pay rent. The founders had identified an unmet customer need: the desire to stay in less expensive but homier lodgings. They launched the Airbnb website in 2007 to connect travelers to people in the area willing to rent out their couch or extra room. Like Uber, the car-sharing service, Airbnb embraces the sharing economy concept that promotes the renting of underutilized human and physical resources. It sells more rooms per night than Hilton.

The target market was initially conference attendees but soon expanded to all types of travelers. Today Airbnb connects travelers to lodgings in 34,000 cities across 190 countries. Those who wish to rent an extra room or house can set their own prices, and Airbnb takes 3 percent of the booking price when the property is rented out.

Despite its immense success, Airbnb believes it can create more value for more customers. For instance, it began to offer Business Travel on Airbnb to concentrate on corporate clients. Airbnb claims it has signed up 700 businesses including Google and Salesforce.com. It is especially popular among new employees who are being put up by an employer until they find a more permanent location.

Not all stakeholders are happy about Airbnb, however. Some cities and regulators believe Airbnb encourages owners of multiple properties to rent them in the short-term rather than turning them into long-term residences—thus causing a disruption in urban housing. However, Airbnb contends that it is creating customer value in the form of less-expensive lodging for travelers and additional income for renters.[1]

Like all organizations, Airbnb strives to provide products that customers want, communicate useful information about them to excite interest, make them available when and where customers want to buy them, and price them appropriately. Even if an organization does all these things well, however, competition from marketers of similar products, economic conditions, and other factors can affect the company's success. Such factors influence the decisions that all organizations must make in strategic marketing.

This chapter introduces the strategic marketing concepts and decisions covered throughout the text. First, we develop a definition of *marketing* and explore each element of the definition in detail. Next, we explore the importance of value-driven marketing. We also introduce the marketing concept and consider several issues associated with its implementation. Additionally, we take a look at the management of customer relationships and relationship marketing. Finally, we examine the importance of marketing in global society.

**marketing** The process of creating, distributing, promoting, and pricing goods, services, and ideas to facilitate satisfying exchange relationships with customers and to develop and maintain favorable relationships with stakeholders in a dynamic environment

## 1-1 DEFINING *MARKETING*

If you ask several people what *marketing* is, you are likely to hear a variety of descriptions. Although many people think marketing is advertising or selling, marketing is much more complex than most people realize. In this book we define **marketing** as the process of creating, distributing, promoting, and pricing goods, services, and ideas to facilitate satisfying exchange relationships with customers and to develop and maintain favorable relationships with stakeholders in a dynamic environment. Our definition is consistent with that of the American Marketing Association (AMA), which defines *marketing* as "the activity, set of institutions, and processes for creating, communicating, delivering, and exchanging offerings that have value for customers, clients, partners, and society at large."[2]

The essence of marketing is to develop satisfying exchanges from which both customers and marketers benefit. The customer expects to gain a reward or benefit greater than the costs incurred in a marketing transaction. The marketer expects to gain something of value in return, generally the price charged for the product. Through buyer–seller interaction, a customer develops expectations about the seller's future behavior. To fulfill these expectations, the marketer must deliver on promises made. Over time, this interaction results in relationships between the two parties. Fast-food restaurants such as Wendy's and Subway depend on repeat purchases from satisfied customers—many often live or work a few miles from these restaurants—whereas customer expectations revolve around tasty food, value, and dependable service.

The marketing mix variables—which include product, distribution, promotion, and price—are often viewed as controllable because they can be modified. However, there are limits to how much marketing managers can alter them. Competitive forces, economic conditions, political forces, laws and regulations, technology, and sociocultural forces shape the decision-making environment for

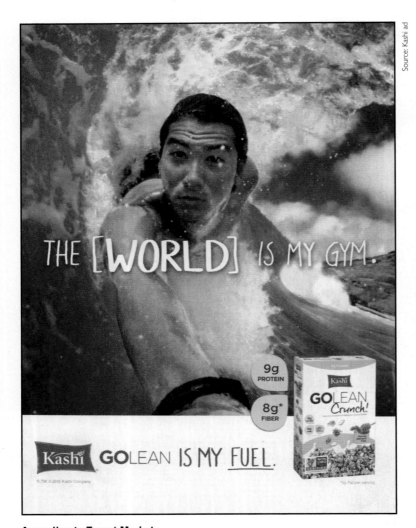

Source: Kashi ad

**Appealing to Target Markets**
Kashi appeals to consumers who desire a nutritious breakfast.

controllable variables. While some products are tangible goods, services are also products and represent a significant part of the economy. Entire industries such as health care, entertainment, sports, and hospitality and tourism provide services.

## 1-1a  Marketing Focuses on Customers

As the purchasers of the products that organizations develop, distribute, promote, and price, **customers** are the focal point of all marketing activities (see Figure 1.1). Organizations have to define their products not as what the companies make or produce but as what they do to satisfy customers. The Kashi brand, for example, creates products that satisfy customer needs, especially those who are looking for a nutritious alternative to more traditional cereals. The Kashi advertisement of a surfer emphasizes how the health benefits of Kashi cereal help active individuals live life to the fullest.

Organizations generally focus their marketing efforts on a specific group of customers, called a **target market**. Marketing managers may define a target market as a vast number of people or a relatively small group. For instance, marketers are increasingly interested in Hispanic consumers. Within the last decade, Hispanics made up more than half of the population gains in the United States. As a result, marketers are developing new ways to reach this demographic. For instance, Macy's has increased bilingual signage in its stores and launched a line of clothing by Mexican singer Thalia Sodi.[3] Often companies target multiple markets with different products, distribution systems, promotions, and prices for each one. Others focus on a smaller niche market. Lehman's Hardware, for example, originally targeted the Amish community with simple non-electric products. Today Lehman's markets "simple products for a simpler life" not only to Amish customers, but also to environmental advocates, Peace Corps volunteers, and even movie producers who have used Lehman's products in movies such as *Pirates of the Caribbean*.[4] Home Depot, on the other hand, targets a number of markets with thousands of product items. It provides home improvement products for both household consumers and contractors.

Figure 1.1  **Components of Strategic Marketing**

**customers** The purchasers of organizations' products; the focal point of all marketing activities

**target market** A specific group of customers on whom an organization focuses its marketing efforts

# 1-2 MARKETING DEALS WITH PRODUCTS, DISTRIBUTION, PROMOTION, AND PRICE

Marketing is more than simply advertising or selling a product; it involves developing and managing a product that will satisfy customer needs. It also requires promotion that helps customers to learn about the product and determine if the product will satisfy their needs. It focuses on communicating availability in the right place and at the right price. It also requires communicating information that helps customers determine if the product will satisfy their needs. These activities are planned, organized, implemented, and controlled to meet the needs of customers within the target market. Marketers refer to these activities—product, distribution, promotion, and pricing—as the **marketing mix** because they decide what type of each variable to use and how to coordinate the variables. Marketing creates value through the marketing mix. A primary goal of a marketing manager is to create and maintain the right mix of these variables to satisfy customers' needs for a general product type. Apple is well-known for its implementation of the marketing mix. It routinely engages in research and development to create new or upgraded products. It promotes these products through advertising, social media, and media events. Apple distributes the products through its own retail stores, AT&T, and other service providers, as well as through the Internet. It provides these products at a premium price to convey their quality and effectiveness. Note in Figure 1.1 that the marketing mix is built around the customer.

Marketing managers strive to develop a marketing mix that matches the needs of customers in the target market. Clothing retailer Billabong, for example, targets shoppers with an active lifestyle with snowboarding, surfing, and skateboarding clothing and accessories. The company distributes these products through stores in shopping malls at competitive prices and supports them with promotional activities such as advertising and social media. Additionally, marketing managers must constantly monitor the competition and adapt their products, distribution decisions, promotion, and pricing to foster long-term success.

Before marketers can develop an appropriate marketing mix, they must collect in-depth, up-to-date information about customer needs. Such information might include data about the age, income, ethnicity, gender, and educational level of people in the target market, their preferences for product features, their attitudes toward competitors' products, and the frequency with which they use the product. Billabong, for example, has to closely monitor fashion trends and adjust its marketing mix accordingly to continue to satisfy its target market. Armed with market information, marketing managers are better able to develop a marketing mix that satisfies a specific target market.

Let's look more closely at the decisions and activities related to each marketing mix variable.

## 1-2a  The Product Variable

Successful marketing efforts result in products that become part of everyday life. Consider the satisfaction customers have had over the years from Coca-Cola, Levi's jeans, Visa credit cards, Tylenol pain relievers, and professional sports such as baseball, basketball, hockey, and football. The product variable of the marketing mix deals with researching customers' needs and wants and designing a product that satisfies them. A **product** can be a good, a service, or an idea. A good is a physical entity you can touch. Oakley sunglasses, Ford F-150 trucks, and iPhones are all examples of products. A service is the application of human and mechanical efforts to people or objects to provide intangible benefits to customers. Air travel, education, insurance, banking, health care, and day care are examples of services. Ideas include concepts, philosophies, images, and issues. For instance, a marriage counselor, for a fee, gives spouses

**marketing mix** Four marketing activities—product, pricing, distribution, and promotion—that a firm can control to meet the needs of customers within its target market

**product** A good, a service, or an idea

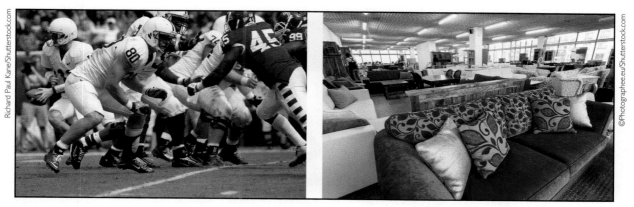

**Types of Products**
Sports events are intangible products that provide fans with a fun experience. Furniture represents a tangible good that consumers use for comfort and relaxation.

ideas to help improve their relationship. Other marketers of ideas include political parties, churches, and animal protection groups.

The product variable also involves creating or modifying brand names and packaging and may include decisions regarding warranty and repair services. For example, New Belgium Brewing introduced aluminum cans because they can be recycled easier than glass bottles and are safer to use in some environments. The company adapted its product's packaging to provide a healthier and "greener" offering.

Product variable decisions and related activities are important because they directly relate to customers' needs and wants. Apple continues to upgrade its iPhone using different model numbers such as 5, 6, and 7 to signal new modifications. To maintain an assortment of products that helps an organization achieve its goals, marketers must develop new products, modify existing ones, and eliminate those that no longer satisfy enough buyers or that yield unacceptable profits.

## 1-2b  The Distribution Variable

To satisfy customers, products must be available at the right time and in appropriate locations. Subway, for example, locates its restaurants not only in strip malls but also inside Walmarts, Home Depots, laundromats, churches, and hospitals, as well as inside Goodwill stores, car dealerships, and appliance stores. There are 44,489 Subways in 111 different countries, surpassing McDonald's as the world's largest chain.[5]

In dealing with the distribution variable, a marketing manager makes products available in the quantities desired to as many target-market customers as possible, keeping total inventory, transportation, and storage costs as efficient as possible. A marketing manager also may select and motivate intermediaries (wholesalers and retailers), establish and maintain inventory control procedures, and develop and manage transportation and storage systems. All companies must depend on intermediaries to move their final products to the market. The advent of the Internet and electronic commerce also has dramatically influenced the distribution variable. Consider Amazon's distribution system that is now integrating its own warehousing and transportation to deliver products—sometimes the same day they are ordered. Companies now can make their products available throughout the world without maintaining facilities in each country. For instance, Pandora and Spotify have benefitted from the ability to stream music over the Internet. Customers can listen to music for free with commercial interruptions, or they can pay to upgrade to listen without commercials. Pandora has 80 million active users, while Spotify has 60 million.[6]

endermasali/Shutterstock.com

**Distribution**
Spotify uses digital distribution to allow consumers to stream videos, podcasts, and music. For paid premiums, users can view entertainment uninterrupted by commercials.

## 1-2c  The Promotion Variable

The promotion variable relates to activities used to inform and persuade to create a desired response. Promotion can increase public awareness of the organization and of new or existing products. It can help create a direct response by including a link to access a website or order a product. Consider Geico's television and radio advertising that encourages people to spend 15 minutes "to save 15% or more on car insurance." Geico's tagline is meant to elicit a direct response from consumers, encouraging them to take 15 minutes to make a sales call to a Geico representative.

Promotional activities can inform customers about product features. The Purina advertisement, for instance, describes how its ONE® cat food is made from real poultry and fish and that its veterinarian-recommended formula is nutritious for all ages of cats. In addition, promotional activities can urge people to take a particular stance on a political or social issue, such as smoking or drug abuse. For example, the U.K. nonprofit Women's Aid released an experiential marketing campaign to draw attention to victims of domestic violence. The organization used a pro bono agency to install billboards depicting a bruised woman. The billboards were equipped with facial recognition software so that when people walked by and looked at the advertisement, the bruises would "heal" to demonstrate that ordinary people can work toward stopping domestic violence.[7]

Promotion can also help to sustain interest in established products that have been available for decades, such as Jell-O or Tide detergent. Many companies are using the Internet to communicate information about themselves and their products. Trader Joe's website provides a diverse array of recipes using ingredients that can be found in its stores.[8]

## 1-2d  The Price Variable

The price variable relates to decisions and actions associated with pricing objectives and policies and actual product prices. Price is a critical component of the marketing mix because customers are concerned about the value obtained in an exchange. Price is often used as a competitive tool, and intense price competition sometimes leads to price wars. Higher prices can be used competitively to establish a product's premium image. Seven 4 All Mankind jeans, for example, have an image of high quality and high price that has given them significant status. Other companies are skilled at providing products at prices lower than competitors (consider Walmart's tagline "Save Money, Live Better"). Amazon uses its vast network of partnerships and cost efficiencies to provide products at low prices. Brick-and-mortar retailers have not been able to offer comparable products with prices that low, providing Amazon with a considerable competitive advantage.

The marketing-mix variables are often viewed as controllable because they can be modified. However, there are limits to how much marketing managers can alter them. Economic conditions, competitive structure, and government regulations may prevent a manager from adjusting prices frequently or significantly. Making changes in the size, shape, and design of most tangible goods is expensive; therefore, such product features cannot be altered very often. In addition, promotional campaigns and methods used to distribute products ordinarily cannot be rewritten or revamped overnight.

## 1-3 MARKETING CREATES VALUE

Value is an important element of managing long-term customer relationships and implementing the marketing concept. We view **value** as a customer's subjective assessment of benefits relative to costs in determining the worth of a product (customer value = customer benefits – customer costs). Consumers develop a concept of value through the integration of their perceptions of product quality and financial sacrifice.[9] From a company's perspective, there is a trade-off between increasing the value offered to a customer and maximizing the profits from a transaction.[10]

Customer benefits include anything a buyer receives in an exchange. Hotels and motels, for example, basically provide a room with a bed and bathroom, but each firm provides a different level of service, amenities, and atmosphere to satisfy its guests. Motel 6 offers the minimum services necessary to maintain a quality, efficient, low-price overnight accommodation. In contrast, the Ritz-Carlton provides every imaginable service a guest might desire. The hotel even allows its staff members to spend up to $2,000 to settle customer complaints.[11] Customers judge which type of accommodation offers the best value according to the benefits they desire and their willingness and ability to pay for the costs associated with the benefits.

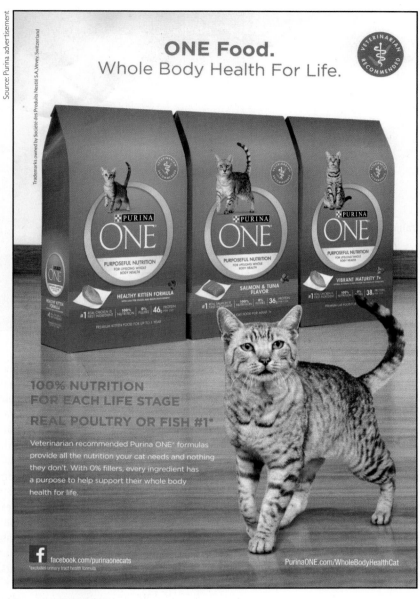

**Promotional Activities**
This Purina advertisement informs the audience about how its ONE® formula is full of nutritious ingredients for cats.

**value** A customer's subjective assessment of benefits relative to costs in determining the worth of a product

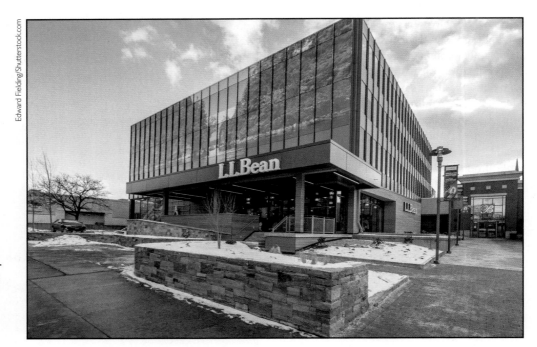

Edward Fielding/Shutterstock.com

**Value-Driven Marketing**
L.L.Bean creates value for customers with its product guarantees, liberal return policies, and strong customer service. The firm competes with Amazon.com as the number one customer service champion.

Customer costs include anything a buyer must give up to obtain the benefits the product provides. The most obvious cost is the monetary price of the product, but nonmonetary costs can be equally important in a customer's determination of value. Two nonmonetary costs are the time and effort customers expend to find and purchase desired products. To reduce time and effort, a company can increase product availability, thereby making it more convenient for buyers to purchase the firm's products. Another nonmonetary cost is risk, which can be reduced by offering good basic warranties or extended warranties for an additional charge.[12] Another risk-reduction strategy is the offer of a 100 percent satisfaction guarantee. This strategy is increasingly popular in today's Internet shopping environment. L.L. Bean, for example, uses such a guarantee to reduce the risk involved in ordering merchandise from its catalogs and website.

The process people use to determine the value of a product may differ widely. All of us tend to get a feel for the worth of products based on our own expectations and previous experience. We can, for example, compare the value of tires, batteries, and computers directly with the value of competing products. We evaluate movies, sporting events, and performances by entertainers on the more subjective basis of personal preferences and emotions. For most purchases, we do not consciously try to calculate the associated benefits and costs. It becomes an instinctive feeling that General Mills' Cheerios is a good value or that McDonald's is a good place to take children for a quick lunch. The purchase of an automobile or a mountain bike may have emotional components, but more conscious decision making also may figure in the process of determining value.

In developing marketing activities, it is important to recognize that customers receive benefits based on their experiences. For example, many computer buyers consider services such as fast delivery, ease of installation, technical advice, and training assistance to be important elements of the product. Each marketing activity has its own benefits and costs and must be adapted for its contribution to value.[13] For example, Amazon found that two-day delivery adds value, leading to the development of its Prime Shipping program. Prime now includes additional services such as streaming instant video, photo storage, music access, and discounts. Customers also derive benefits from the act of shopping and selecting products. These benefits can be affected by the atmosphere or environment of a store, such as Red Lobster's nautical/seafood theme. Even the ease of navigating a website can have a tremendous impact on perceived value. When the download and streaming music service GhostTunes was developed, co-owner country singer Garth Brooks had to ensure that the site was user-friendly. The site had to be easy so users could navigate through it and choose which music to stream or download.

Unlike iTunes, Brooks wants GhostTunes to allow copyright holders more freedom as to how their music should be sold on the site.[14] Different customers may view different songs or albums on the site as an exceptional value for their own personal satisfaction.

The marketing mix can be used to enhance perceptions of value. A product that demonstrates value usually has a feature or an enhancement that provides benefits. Promotional activities can also help to create image and prestige characteristics that customers consider in their assessment of a product's value. In some cases value may be perceived simply as the lowest price. Many customers may not care about the quality of the paper towels they buy; they simply want the cheapest ones for use in cleaning up spills because they plan to throw them in the trash anyway. On the other hand, more people are looking for the fastest, most convenient way to achieve a goal and therefore become insensitive to pricing. For example, many busy customers are buying more prepared meals in supermarkets to take home and serve quickly, even though these meals cost considerably more than meals prepared from scratch. In such cases the products with the greatest convenience may be perceived as having the greatest value. The availability or distribution of products also can enhance their value. Taco Bell wants to have its Mexican fast-food products available at any time and any place people are thinking about consuming food. It therefore has introduced Taco Bell products into supermarkets, vending machines, college campuses, and other convenient locations. Thus, the development of an effective marketing strategy requires understanding the needs and desires of customers and designing a marketing mix to satisfy them and provide the value they want.

## 1-3a Marketing Builds Relationships with Customers and Other Stakeholders

Marketing also creates value through the building of stakeholder relationships. Individuals and organizations engage in marketing to facilitate **exchanges**, the provision or transfer of goods, services, or ideas in return for something of value. Any product (good, service, or even idea) may be involved in a marketing exchange. We assume only that individuals and organizations expect to gain a reward in excess of the costs incurred.

For an exchange to take place, four conditions must exist. First, two or more individuals, groups, or organizations must participate, and each must possess something of value that the other party desires. Second, the exchange should provide a benefit or satisfaction to both

**exchanges** The provision or transfer of goods, services, or ideas in return for something of value

Turtix/Shutterstock.com

**Satisfying Stakeholder Needs**
Google continues to excel at creating products that satisfy customers, generate jobs, create shareholder wealth, and contribute to greater life enjoyment.

Figure 1.2    **Exchange between Buyer and Seller**

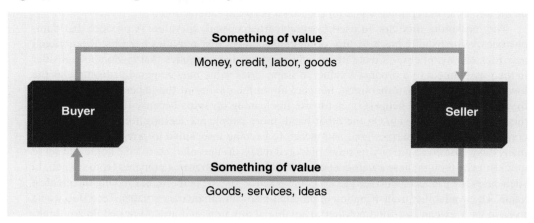

parties involved in the transaction. Third, each party must have confidence in the promise of the "something of value" held by the other. If you go to a Justin Timberlake concert, for example, you go with the expectation of a great performance. Finally, to build trust, the parties to the exchange must meet expectations.

Figure 1.2 depicts the exchange process. The arrows indicate that the parties communicate that each has something of value available to exchange. An exchange will not necessarily take place just because these conditions exist; marketing activities can occur even without an actual transaction or sale. You may see an ad for a Sub-Zero refrigerator, for instance, but you might never buy the luxury appliance. When an exchange occurs, products are traded for other products or for financial resources.

Marketing activities should attempt to create and maintain satisfying exchange relationships. To maintain an exchange relationship, buyers must be satisfied with the good, service, or idea obtained, and sellers must be satisfied with the financial reward or something else of value received. A dissatisfied customer who lacks trust in the relationship often searches for alternative organizations or products. The customer relationship often endures over an extended time period, and repeat purchases are critical for the firm.

Marketers are concerned with building and maintaining relationships not only with customers but also with relevant stakeholders. **Stakeholders** include those constituents who have a "stake," or claim, in some aspect of a company's products, operations, markets, industry, and outcomes; these include customers, employees, investors and shareholders, suppliers, governments, communities, competitors, and many others. While engaging in marketing activities, the firm should be proactive and responsive to stakeholder concerns. This engagement has been found to increase financial performance.[15] Therefore, developing and maintaining favorable relations with stakeholders is crucial to the long-term growth of an organization and its products. For example, employees directly influence customer satisfaction, and suppliers are necessary to make quality products. Communities can be a positive contributor to the firm's reputation and in turn they provide an opportunity to make a social and economic contribution. Customers and competitors are often considered to be core stakeholders in developing a marketing strategy.[16]

**stakeholders** Constituents who have a "stake," or claim, in some aspect of a company's products, operations, markets, industry, and outcomes

**marketing environment** The competitive, economic, political, legal and regulatory, technological, and sociocultural forces that surround the customer and affect the marketing mix

# 1-4 MARKETING OCCURS IN A DYNAMIC ENVIRONMENT

Marketing activities do not take place in a vacuum. The **marketing environment**, which includes competitive, economic, political, legal and regulatory, technological, and sociocultural forces, surrounds the customer and affects the marketing mix (see Figure 1.1). The effects of these forces on buyers and sellers can be dramatic and difficult to predict. Their impact on value can be extensive as market changes can easily influence how stakeholders perceive certain products. They can create threats to marketers but also can generate opportunities for new products and new methods of reaching customers.

The forces of the marketing environment affect a marketer's ability to facilitate value-driven marketing exchanges in three general ways. First, they influence customers by affecting their lifestyles, standards of living, and preferences and needs for products. Because a marketing manager tries to develop and adjust the marketing mix to satisfy customers, effects of environmental forces on customers also have an indirect impact on marketing-mix components. Second, marketing environment forces can determine whether and how a marketing manager can perform certain marketing activities. Third, environmental forces may shape a marketing manager's decisions and actions by influencing buyers' reactions to the firm's marketing mix.

Marketing environment forces can fluctuate quickly and dramatically, which is one reason why marketing is so interesting and challenging. Because these forces are closely interrelated, changes in one may cause changes in others. For example, evidence linking children's consumption of soft drinks and fast foods to health issues has exposed marketers of such products to negative publicity and generated calls for legislation regulating the sale of soft drinks in public schools. Some companies have responded to these concerns by voluntarily reformulating products to make them healthier or even introducing new products. For example, Pepsi reformulated its Diet Pepsi product by replacing the sweetener aspartame with sucralose. Although the Food and Drug Administration (FDA) has ruled aspartame as safe, many consumers view aspartame as having health risks. Despite Pepsi's attempt to appeal to changing consumer preferences, the initial reaction among Diet Pepsi loyalists after the company reformulated the product were often negative.[17] Changes in the marketing environment produce uncertainty for marketers and at times hurt marketing efforts, but they also create opportunities. For example, when oil and gasoline prices increase, consumers shift to potential alternative sources of transportation including bikes, buses, light rail, trains, carpooling, more energy-efficient vehicle purchases, or telecommuting when possible. When those prices decrease, consumers purchase more SUVs, drive more, and may have more money for other purchases.

Marketers who are alert to changes in environmental forces not only can adjust to and influence these changes but can also capitalize on the opportunities such changes provide. Marketing-mix variables—product, distribution, promotion, and price—are factors over which an organization has control; the forces of the environment, however, are subject to far less control. Even though marketers know that they cannot predict changes in the marketing environment with certainty, they must nevertheless plan for them. Because these environmental forces have such a profound effect on marketing activities, we explore each of them in considerable depth in Chapter 3.

# 1-5 UNDERSTANDING THE MARKETING CONCEPT

Firms frequently fail to attract customers with what they have to offer because they define their business as "making a product" rather than as "helping potential customers satisfy their needs and wants." For example, when digital music became popular, businesses had opportunities to develop new products to satisfy customers' needs. Firms such as Apple developed the iTunes music store and products like the iPod, iPhone, and iPad to satisfy consumers' desires for portable, customized music libraries. Even common household devices are changing. For instance, Nest Labs developed the Nest Learning Thermostat that is able to learn the types of temperatures consumers like. As the advertisement shows, the product adjusts the temperature as the seasons and weather change based on the preferences of the household. Companies that do not pursue such opportunities struggle to compete.

According to the **marketing concept**, an organization should try to provide products that satisfy customers' needs through a coordinated set of activities that also allows the organization

**marketing concept**
A managerial philosophy that an organization should try to satisfy customers' needs through a coordinated set of activities that also allows the organization to achieve its goals

Source: Nest Learning Thermostat

The new Nest
Learning Thermostat
Adjusts to your schedule
as the seasons change.

**The Marketing Concept**

Nest Labs developed the Nest Learning Thermostat that adapts its temperature depending upon the season and the customer.

to achieve its goals. Customer satisfaction is the major focus of the marketing concept. To implement the marketing concept, an organization strives to determine what buyers want and uses this information to develop satisfying products. It focuses on customer analysis, competitor analysis, and integration of the firm's resources to provide customer value and satisfaction, as well as to generate long-term profits.[18] Howard Schultz, founder and CEO of Starbucks, demonstrates the company's grasp on the marketing concept by explaining that Starbucks is not a coffee business that serves people, but rather a "people business serving coffee." Starbucks' leadership sees the company as being "in the business of humanity," emphasizing the fact that Starbucks is not only concerned about customers but society as well.[19] Thus, the marketing concept emphasizes that marketing begins and ends with customers. Research has found a positive association between customer satisfaction and shareholder value,[20] and high levels of customer satisfaction also tend to attract and retain high-quality employees and managers.[21]

The marketing concept is not a second definition of marketing. It is a management philosophy guiding an organization's overall activities. This philosophy affects all organizational activities, not just marketing. Production, finance, accounting, human resources, and marketing departments must work together. For example, at Procter & Gamble the marketing function coordinates research and development, distribution, and resource deployment to focus on providing consumer products for households.

The marketing concept is a strategic concept to achieve objectives. A firm that adopts the marketing concept must satisfy not only its customers' objectives but also its own, or it will not stay in business long. The overall objectives of a business usually relate to profits, market share, sales, or probably a combination of all three. The marketing concept stresses that an organization can best achieve these objectives by being customer oriented. Thus, implementing the marketing concept should benefit the organization as well as its customers.

It is important for marketers to consider not only their current buyers' needs but also the long-term needs of society. Striving to satisfy customers' desires by sacrificing society's long-term welfare is unacceptable. For instance, there is significant demand for large SUVs and trucks. However, environmentalists and federal regulators are challenging automakers to produce more fuel-efficient vehicles with increased miles-per-gallon standards. The question that remains is whether Americans are willing to give up their spacious SUVs for the good of the environment. Automakers are addressing environmental concerns with smaller, more fuel-efficient SUVs. Demand for these SUVs shows that these vehicles are not going away anytime soon. So implementing the marketing concept and meeting the needs of society is a balancing act.

# Entrepreneurship in Marketing

## Protein Bar Restaurant: Satisfying Consumers

**Founder:** Matt Matros
**Business:** Protein Bar Restaurant
**Founded:** 2009, in Chicago, IL
**Success**: The Protein Bar restaurant has been featured in numerous newspapers and has expanded to four cities.

At 22, entrepreneur Matt Matros decided to drastically change his life. He lost 50 pounds through a strong regimen of exercise and a high-protein diet. Afterward, he decided to start the Chicago-based restaurant Protein Bar.

To be successful, Matros had to select the right mix of product, distribution, promotion, and price. Matros conceived of a casual dining restaurant that would offer healthy food options high in protein. Product offerings include burritos, salads, breakfast items, raw juices, and side dishes. Matros chose prices for these products that would be reasonable for on-the-go consumers who did not want to spend time making their own protein shakes.

The company has created publicity by recently teaming up with Chicago Bears wide receiver Brandon Marshall to promote a new Protein Bar drink called Crazy Stigma Green. For every drink purchased, $1 is donated to the Project 375 Foundation. Protein Bar has also received coverage in newspapers such as *Washington Post* and *Chicago Tribune*. The restaurant has expanded to Washington D.C., Denver, and Boulder, Colorado. Matros has since become CEO of another company.[a]

## 1-5a Evolution of the Marketing Concept

The marketing concept may seem like an obvious approach to running a business. Yet while satisfied consumers are necessary for business success, historically not all firms were successful in implementing this concept. The evolution of marketing has gone through three time periods, including production, sales, and market orientation. While this is an oversimplification, these frameworks help to understand marketing over time. There have always been companies that embraced the marketing concept and focused on the interests of consumers.

### The Production Orientation

During the second half of the 19th century, the Industrial Revolution was in full swing in the United States. Electricity, rail transportation, division of labor, assembly lines, and mass production made it possible to produce goods more efficiently. With new technology and new ways of using labor, products poured into the marketplace, where demand for manufactured goods was strong. Although mass markets were evolving, firms were developing the ability to produce more products, and competition was becoming more intense.

### The Sales Orientation

While sales have always been needed to make a profit, during the first half of the 20th century competition increased and businesses realized that they would have to focus more on selling products to many buyers. Businesses viewed sales as the major means of increasing profits, and this period came to have a sales orientation. Businesspeople believed that the most important marketing activities were personal selling, advertising, and distribution. Today, some people incorrectly equate marketing with a sales orientation. On the other hand, some firms still use a sales orientation.

### The Market Orientation

Although marketing history reveals that some firms have always produced products that consumers desired, by the 1950s, both businesses and academics developed new philosophies and terminology to explain why this approach is necessary for organizational success.[22] This perspective emphasized that marketers first need to determine what customers want and then produce those products rather than making the products first and then trying to persuade customers that they need them. As more organizations realized the importance of satisfying customers' needs, U.S. businesses entered the marketing era, called market orientation.

A **market orientation** requires the "organizationwide generation of market intelligence pertaining to current and future customer needs, dissemination of the intelligence across departments, and organizationwide responsiveness to it."[23] Market orientation is linked to new product innovation by developing a strategic focus to explore and develop new products to serve target markets.[24] For example, consumers increasingly like environmentally responsible products offered at fair prices. To meet this demand, Method laundry detergent is eight times more concentrated and can clean 50 loads of laundry from a container the size of a small soft-drink bottle. Top managers, marketing managers, nonmarketing managers (those in production, finance, human resources, and so on), and customers are all important in developing and carrying out a market orientation. Trust, openness, honoring promises, respect, collaboration, and recognizing the market as the *raison d'etre* are six values required by organizations striving to become more market oriented.[25]

A market orientation should recognize the need to create specific types of value-creating capabilities that enhance organizational performance.[26] For example, a bank needs to use its resources to provide the desired level of customer service. Also, unless marketing managers provide continuous customer-focused leadership with minimal interdepartmental conflict, achieving a market orientation will be difficult. Nonmarketing managers must communicate with marketing managers to share information important to understanding the customer. Finally, a market orientation involves being responsive to ever-changing customer needs and wants. Keurig Green Mountain, for example, has released successful products such as coffee blends and flavors, brewing systems, and Keurig cups because it understands what consumers want. Today, businesses want to satisfy customers and build meaningful long-term buyer–seller relationships. Doing so helps a firm boost its own financial value.[27]

## 1-5b  Implementing the Marketing Concept

A philosophy may sound reasonable and look good on paper, but this does not mean that it can be put into practice easily. To implement the marketing concept, a market-oriented organization must accept some general conditions and recognize and deal with several problems. Consequently, the marketing concept has yet to be fully accepted by all businesses.

Management must first establish an information system to discover customers' real needs and then use the information to create satisfying products. SAP offers enterprise software to help clients manage their business operations and customer relationships. One of its clients, the German Football Association, used SAP software to improve communication with fans and personalize marketing activities.[28] Listening and responding to consumers' frustrations and appreciation is the key in implementing the marketing concept. An information system is usually expensive; management must commit money and time for its development and maintenance. Without an adequate information system, however, an organization cannot be market oriented.

To satisfy customers' objectives as well as its own, a company also must coordinate all of its activities. This may require restructuring its internal operations, including production, marketing, and other business functions. This requires the firm to adapt to a changing external environment, including changing customer expectations. Companies that monitor the external environment can often predict major changes and adapt successfully. For instance, Fanuc, a Japanese company that is a leader in robotics and numerical controllers, faced a major crisis when microelectronics began to dominate the field. Fanuc had been focusing its business on oil-based hydraulic controllers. However, the company recognized the shift toward microelectronics and took steps to adapt to changing conditions. It interviewed customers about how they used Fanuc's products and established global service centers. These actions not only helped Fanuc to survive, but it also thrived as a company.[29] If marketing is not included in the

**market orientation** An organizationwide commitment to researching and responding to customer needs organization's top-level management, a company could fail to address actual customer needs and desires. Implementing the marketing concept demands the support not only of top management but also of managers and staff at all levels of the organization.

# 1-6 CUSTOMER RELATIONSHIP MANAGEMENT

**Customer relationship management (CRM)** focuses on using information about customers to create marketing strategies that develop and sustain desirable customer relationships. Achieving the full profit potential of each customer relationship should be the fundamental goal of every marketing strategy. Marketing relationships with customers are the lifeblood of all businesses. At the most basic level, profits can be obtained through relationships in the following ways: (1) by acquiring new customers, (2) by enhancing the profitability of existing customers, and (3) by extending the duration of customer relationships. In addition to retaining customers, companies also should focus on regaining and managing relationships with customers who have abandoned the firm.[30] Implementing the marketing concept means optimizing the exchange relationship, otherwise known as the relationship between a company's financial investment in customer relationships and the return generated by customers' loyalty and retention.

## 1-6a Relationship Marketing

Maintaining positive relationships with customers is a crucial goal for marketers. The term **relationship marketing** refers to "long-term, mutually beneficial arrangements in which both the buyer and seller focus on value enhancement through the creation of more satisfying exchanges."[31] Relationship marketing continually deepens the buyer's trust in the company, and as the customer's confidence grows, this, in turn, increases the firm's understanding of the customer's needs. Buyers and marketers can thus enter into a close relationship in which both participate in the creation of value.[32] Successful marketers respond to customer needs and strive to increase value to buyers over time. Eventually, this interaction becomes a solid relationship that allows for cooperation and mutual dependency. Southwest Airlines has implemented relationship marketing with the view that customers are its most important stakeholder. The company's mission statement "is dedication to the highest quality Customer Service delivered with a sense of warmth, friendliness, individual pride, and Company Spirit."[33]

Relationship marketing strives to build satisfying exchange relationships between buyers and sellers by gathering useful data at all customer contact points and analyzing that data to better understand customers' needs, desires, and habits. It focuses on building and using databases and leveraging technologies to identify strategies and methods that will maximize the lifetime value of each desirable customer to the company. It is imperative that marketers educate themselves about their customers' expectations if they are to satisfy their needs; customer dissatisfaction will only lead to defection.[34]

To build these long-term customer relationships, marketers are increasingly turning to marketing research and information technology. By increasing customer value over time, organizations try to retain and increase long-term profitability through customer loyalty, which results from increasing customer value. The airline industry is a key player in CRM efforts with its frequent-flyer programs. Frequent-flyer programs enable airlines to track individual information about customers, using databases that can help airlines understand what different customers want, and treat customers differently depending on their flying habits. Relationship-building efforts like frequent-flyer programs have been shown to increase customer value.[35]

Through the use of Internet-based marketing strategies (e-marketing), companies can personalize customer relationships on a nearly one-on-one basis. A wide range of products, such as computers, jeans, golf clubs, cosmetics, and greeting cards, can be tailored for specific customers. Customer relationship management provides a strategic bridge between information

**customer relationship management (CRM)** Using information about customers to create marketing strategies that develop and sustain desirable customer relationships

**relationship marketing** Establishing long-term, mutually satisfying buyer-seller relationships technology and marketing strategies aimed at long-term relationships. This involves finding and retaining customers by using information to improve customer value and satisfaction. At the same time, ensuring customer satisfaction is not just a one way street. Customers themselves contribute to the relationship by their purchase behaviors and their use of resources to maximize customer satisfaction. For example, customers can do pre-purchase research and spend time experiencing or examining the product before purchasing it.[36]

## 1-6b  Customer Lifetime Value

Managing customer relationships requires identifying patterns of buying behavior and using that information to focus on the most promising and profitable customers.[37] Companies must be sensitive to customers' requirements and desires and must establish communication to build their trust and loyalty. **Customer lifetime value (CLV)** predicts the net value (profit or loss) for the future relationship with the customer. Pizza Hut, for example, is estimated to have a lifetime customer value of $8,000, whereas Cadillac estimates its lifetime customer's value at $332,000.[38] A customer's value over a lifetime represents an intangible asset to a marketer that can be augmented by addressing the customer's varying needs and preferences at different stages in his or her relationship with the firm.[39] In general, when marketers focus on customers chosen for their lifetime value, they earn higher profits in future periods than when they focus on customers selected for other reasons.[40]

The ability to identify individual customers allows marketers to shift their focus from targeting groups of similar customers to increasing their share of an individual customer's purchases. The emphasis changes from *share of market* to *share of customer*. Focusing on share of customer requires recognizing that all customers have different needs and that not all customers weigh the value of a company equally. The most basic application of this idea is the 80/20 rule: 80 percent of business profits come from 20 percent of customers. The goal is to assess the worth of individual customers and thus estimate their lifetime value to the company. The concept of customer lifetime value (CLV) may include not only an individual's tendency to engage in purchases but also his or her strong word-of-mouth communication about the company's products. Some customers—those who require considerable hand-holding or who return products frequently—may simply be too expensive to retain due to the low level of profits they generate. Companies can discourage these unprofitable customers by requiring them to pay higher fees for additional services.

**customer lifetime value (CLV)**
A key measurement that forecasts a customer's lifetime economic contribution based on continued relationship marketing efforts

CLV is a key measurement that forecasts a customer's lifetime economic contribution based on continued relationship marketing efforts. It can be calculated by taking the sum of the customer's present value contributions to profit margins over a specific time frame. For example, the lifetime value of a Lexus customer could be predicted by how many new automobiles Lexus could sell the customer over a period of years and a summation of the contribution to margins across the time period. Although this is not an exact science, knowing a customer's potential lifetime value can help marketers determine how best to allocate resources to marketing strategies to sustain that customer over a lifetime.

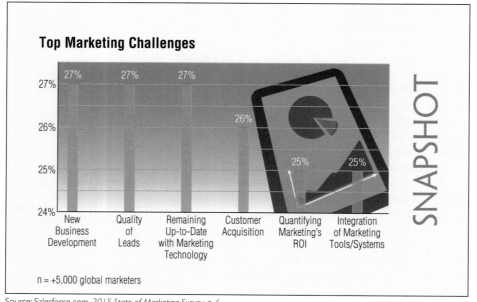

### Top Marketing Challenges

| | |
|---|---|
| New Business Development | 27% |
| Quality of Leads | 27% |
| Remaining Up-to-Date with Marketing Technology | 27% |
| Customer Acquisition | 26% |
| Quantifying Marketing's ROI | 25% |
| Integration of Marketing Tools/Systems | 25% |

SNAPSHOT

n = +5,000 global marketers

Source: Salesforce.com, *2015 State of Marketing Survey*, p. 6.

# 1-7 THE IMPORTANCE OF MARKETING IN OUR GLOBAL ECONOMY

Our definition of marketing and discussion of marketing activities reveal some of the obvious reasons the study of marketing is relevant in today's world. In this section we look at how marketing affects us as individuals and its role in our increasingly global society.

## 1-7a Marketing Costs Consume a Sizable Portion of Buyers' Dollars

Studying marketing will make you aware that many marketing activities are necessary to provide satisfying goods and services. Obviously, these activities cost money. About one-half of a buyer's dollar goes toward marketing costs. If you spend $200 on a new smartphone, more than half goes toward marketing expenses, including promotion and distribution, as well as profit margins. A family with a monthly income of $3,000 that allocates $600 to taxes and savings spends about $2,400 for goods and services. On average, $1,200 goes toward marketing activities. If marketing expenses consume that much of your dollar, you should know how this money is being used. Marketing costs have an impact on the economy and the standard of living for consumers.

## 1-7b Marketing is Used in Nonprofit Organizations

Although the term *marketing* may bring to mind advertising for Coca-Cola, BMW, and American Express, marketing is also important in organizations working to achieve goals other than ordinary business objectives (such as profit). Government agencies at the federal, state, and local levels engage in marketing activities to fulfill their mission and goals. Universities and colleges engage in marketing activities to recruit new students, as well as to obtain donations from alumni and businesses.

In the private sector, nonprofit organizations also employ marketing activities to create, distribute, promote, and price programs that benefit particular segments of society. The Red Cross provides disaster relief throughout the world and offers promotional messages to encourage donations to support their efforts. Nonprofits operate just like businesses in that they serve a client base and have to create revenue to meet their needs. Marketing activities are necessary to create effective exchange relationships with donors and those served by the nonprofit.

## 1-7c Marketing Is Important to Businesses and the Economy

Businesses must engage in marketing to survive and grow, and marketing activities are needed to reach customers and provide products. Marketing is the business function responsible for creating revenue to sustain the operations of the organization and to provide financial returns to investors. Innovation in operations and products drive business success and customer loyalty. Nonprofit businesses need to understand and use marketing to survive and provide services to their target market.

Marketing activities help to produce the profits that are essential to the survival of individual businesses. Without profits, businesses would find it difficult, if not impossible, to buy more raw materials, hire more employees, attract more capital, and create additional products that, in turn, make more profits. Without profits, marketers cannot continue to provide jobs and contribute to social causes. Companies promote their support of social causes through promotional activities such as the BP advertisement. In the advertisement, BP explains how the company is working with nonprofit organizations to find solutions toward deficiencies in

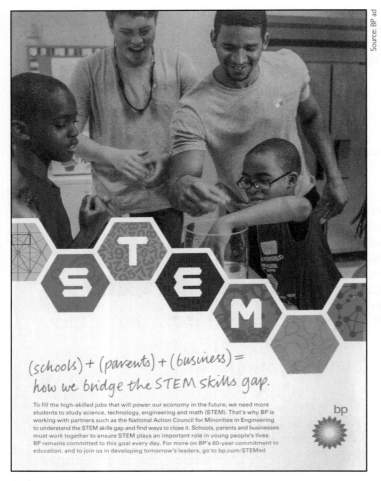

**Social Marketing**
Marketing is used by companies such as BP to create awareness of the social causes they support to improve society.

science, technology, engineering, and math (STEM) skills among young people—particularly among minorities. Therefore, marketing helps create a successful economy and contributes to the well-being of society.

### 1-7d Marketing Fuels Our Global Economy

Marketing is necessary to advance a global economy. Advances in technology, along with falling political and economic barriers and the universal desire for a higher standard of living, have made marketing across national borders commonplace while stimulating global economic growth. As a result of worldwide communications and increased international travel, many global brands have achieved widespread acceptance around the world. At the same time, customers in the United States have greater choices among the products they buy because foreign brands such as Toyota (Japan), Bayer (Germany), and Nestlé (Switzerland) sell alongside U.S. brands such as General Motors, Tylenol, and Google. People around the world watch CNN and MTV on Samsung and Sony televisions they purchased at Walmart. Social media and the Internet now enable businesses of all sizes to reach buyers worldwide. We explore the international markets and opportunities for global marketing in Chapter 9.

### 1-7e Marketing Knowledge Enhances Consumer Awareness

Besides contributing to the well-being of our global economy, marketing activities help to improve the quality of our lives. Studying marketing allows us to understand the importance of marketing to customers, organizations, and our economy. Thus, we can analyze marketing efforts that need improvement and how to attain that goal. Today the consumer has more power from information available through websites, social media, and required disclosure. As you become more knowledgeable, it is possible to improve career options as well as purchasing decisions. In general, you have more accurate information about a product before you purchase it than at any other time in history. Understanding marketing enables us to evaluate corrective measures (such as laws, regulations, and industry guidelines) that could stop unfair, damaging, or unethical marketing practices. Also, knowledge of marketing helps you to evaluate public policy toward marketing that could potentially affect economic well-being. Thus, understanding how marketing activities work can help you to be a better consumer, increase your ability to maximize value from purchases, and understand how marketing is a necessary function in all organizations.

### 1-7f Marketing Connects People through Technology

Technology, especially information technology, helps marketers to understand and satisfy more customers than ever before. Access to the Internet has changed the daily lives of consumers. Mobile devices, e-mails, and office management systems are almost universally used.

Facebook, Twitter, and Google have changed the way consumers communicate, learn about products, make purchases, and share their opinions with others. The global spread of mobile devices has enabled marketers and consumers to forge new relationships that challenge how the traditional marketing mix variables are implemented. Evolving software tools make it easy to create, store, share, and collaborate.[41]

Technology has also enabled firms like Uber and Airbnb to create successful new product concepts by harnessing peer-to-peer power and sharing underutilized resources such as automobiles, boats, and houses to earn income. This economic model is called the sharing economy. It is also referred to as the "gig economy" because firms specializing in peer-to-peer services are using independent contractors to provide services. These contractors essentially run their own businesses and take on service jobs, or "gigs," whenever they desire to earn income using their own resources. While some gig workers do this to earn extra income, more and more are pursuing this as a full-time job.[42] This has led to a rise in independent contracting; it is estimated that independent contractors grew by 2.1 million between 2010 and 2014.[43] This disruptive technology challenges traditional industries such as taxis and hotels.

Additionally, marketers have new methods to store, communicate, and share information through advanced platforms that access what has been termed as "big data." We define big data as massive data files that can be obtained from both structured and unstructured databases. Companies such as Salesforce.com have used big data to provide customer relationship management services. A new generation of consumers are using social networks and mobile messaging applications rather than e-mail.[44] Figure 1.3 shows some of the most common cell phone activities.

The Internet allows companies to provide tremendous amounts of information about their products to consumers and to interact with them through e-mail and websites as well as Instagram and Twitter. A consumer shopping for a new car, for example, can access automakers' webpages, configure an ideal vehicle, and get instant feedback on its cost. Consumers can visit Autobytel, Edmund's, and other websites to find professional reviews and obtain comparative pricing information on both new and used cars to help them find the best value. They can also visit a consumer review site, such as Yelp, to read other consumers' reviews of the products. They can then purchase a vehicle online or at a dealership. A number of companies employ social media to connect with their customers, utilizing blogs and social networking sites such as Facebook and Twitter. We consider social networking and other digital media in Chapter 10.

## 1-7g  Socially Responsible Marketing: Promoting the Welfare of Customers and Stakeholders

The success of our economic system depends on marketers whose values promote trust and cooperative relationships in which customers and other stakeholders are proactively engaged and their concerns are addressed through marketing activities. Social responsibility and ethical conduct are a part of strategic planning and the implementation of marketing activities. Although some marketers' irresponsible or unethical activities end up on the front pages of *USA Today* or *The Wall Street Journal*, more firms are working to develop a responsible approach to developing long-term relationships with customers and other stakeholders. Firms recognize that trust is built on ethical conduct.

In the area of the natural environment, companies are increasingly embracing the notion of **green marketing**, which is a strategic process involving stakeholder assessment to create meaningful long-term relationships with customers while maintaining, supporting, and enhancing the natural environment. For example, Greenpeace recognized Whole Foods, Wegmans, Hy-Vee, and Safeway for the sustainability of the seafood they sell. Whole Foods purchases most of its seafood from certified fisheries, uses third parties to verify that its fish come from eco-friendly aquaculture, and uses sustainability ratings to inform consumers about the seafood it sells.[45] Such initiatives not only reduce the negative impact that businesses have on the

**green marketing** A strategic process involving stakeholder assessment to create meaningful long-term relationships with customers while maintaining, supporting, and enhancing the natural environment

Figure 1.3    **Cell Phone Activities**

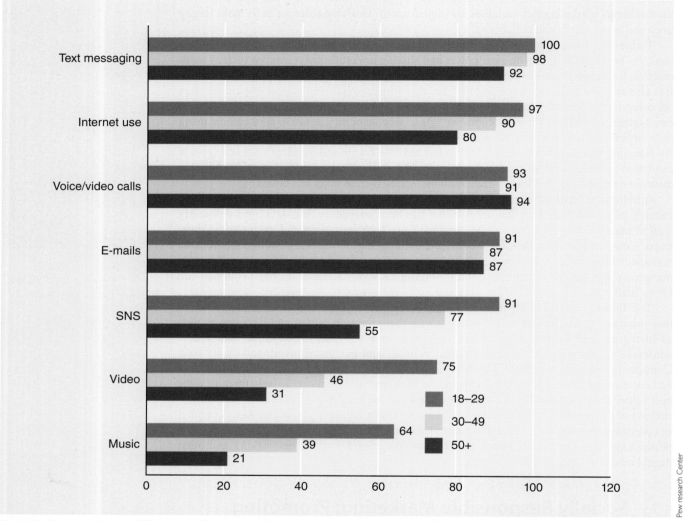

**Some Features are Popular With a Broad Spectrum of Smartphone Owners; Social Networking, Watching Video, and Music/Podcasts are Especially Popular Among Young Users**
*% of smartphone owners in each age group who used the following features on their phone at least once over the course of 14 surveys spanning a one-week period*
Pew Research Center American Trends Panel experience sampling survey, November 10–16, 2014
Respondents were contacted twice a day over the course of one week (14 total surveys) and asked how they had used their phone in the preceding hour (besides completing the survey). Only those respondents who completed 10 or more surveys over the course of the study period are included in this analysis

environment but also serve to enhance their reputations as sustainability concerns continue to grow.

By addressing concerns about the impact of marketing on society, a firm can contribute to society through socially responsible activities as well as increase its financial performance. For example, studies have revealed that market orientation combined with social responsibility improves overall business performance.[46] We examine these issues and many others as we develop a framework for understanding more about marketing in the remainder of this book.

## 1-7h Marketing Offers Many Exciting Career Prospects

From 25 to 33 percent of all civilian workers in the United States perform marketing activities. The marketing field offers a variety of interesting and challenging career opportunities throughout the world, such as personal selling, advertising, packaging, transportation, storage, marketing research, product development, social media management, wholesaling, and retailing. All industries have marketing positions, including health care, sports, consumer products, nonprofits, government, as well as agriculture and commodities such as the oil and gas industry. When unemployment is high, sales positions remain among the most attractive job opportunities. Marketing positions are among the most secure positions because of the need to manage customer relationships. In addition, many individuals working for nonbusiness organizations engage in marketing activities to promote political, educational, cultural, church, civic, and charitable activities.

**Marketing Connects People through Technology**
Consumers can now wear the Internet on the go in the form of smart watches. Smart watches allow users to make calls, receive notifications, search for directions, and surf the Internet.

It is a mistake to believe that the only way to contribute to society is to work for a nonprofit. Without businesses the economic system that supports jobs and contributes to a standard of living would not exist otherwise. Consider that 5 percent of charitable contributions are corporate donations from companies such as Walmart. Many large companies also form foundations to serve their communities. Foundations donate 15 percent of all charitable contributions in

# GOING GREEN

### Lego: Building with Bio-Plastics

The Lego Company has announced its most daring move yet in its sustainability efforts: getting rid of plastic. The Lego Company makes 60 billion blocks a year using the oil-based plastic ABS. It is estimated that Lego goes through 6,000 tons of plastic annually. The company has made a strategic decision toward sustainability in its products.

Lego has set the strategic goal of eliminating ABS plastics by 2030. The company estimates that about 75 percent of its carbon emissions come from extracting and refining oil for its toys. Eliminating this type of plastic would therefore make a significant impact on the firm's environmental footprint.

Lego realizes it will not be easy to completely redesign its most iconic product. That is why it is committing $150 million toward developing the Lego Sustainable Materials Centre in Denmark. In particular, Lego is looking for a substitute for oil-based plastics and believes bio-based plastics may be the key.

Unfortunately, not everyone is confident Lego will succeed. ABS plastic is easily moldable, and it is an ideal composition for ensuring that each Lego piece fits together. Early forays into plant-based plastics show that this type of bio-plastic has difficulty clicking, sticking, and maintaining its shape. However, Lego is confident that its commitment will pay off. It views its goal as customer-oriented because it will help create a more sustainable planet for future children.[b]

the United States.[47] Two major foundations formed by business founders include the Arthur M. Blank Family Foundation (founder of Home Depot) and the Bill and Melinda Gates Foundation (founder of Microsoft). Successful businesses provide the resources necessary to sustain nonprofits and governments. While most charitable contributions are from individuals, most of these people earned their wealth as entrepreneurs or corporate managers. Therefore, marketing plays a key role in supporting philanthropy. Whether a person earns a living through marketing activities or performs them voluntarily for a nonprofit group, marketing knowledge and skills are valuable personal and professional assets.

# Summary

## 1-1  Define *marketing*.

Marketing is the process of creating, pricing, distributing, and promoting goods, services, and ideas to facilitate satisfying exchange relationships with customers and to develop and maintain favorable relationships with stakeholders in a dynamic environment. The essence of marketing is to develop satisfying exchanges from which both customers and marketers benefit. Organizations generally focus their marketing efforts on a specific group of customers called a target market. A target market is the group of customers toward which a company directs a set of marketing efforts.

## 1-2  Explain the different variables of the marketing mix.

Marketing involves developing and managing a product that will satisfy customer needs, making the product available at the right place and at a price acceptable to customers, and communicating information that helps customers determine if the product will satisfy their needs. These activities—product, distribution, promotion, and price—are known as the marketing mix because marketing managers decide what type of each element to use and in what amounts. Marketing managers strive to develop a marketing mix that matches the needs of customers in the target market. Before marketers can develop a marketing mix, they must collect in-depth, up-to-date information about customer needs. The product variable of the marketing mix deals with researching customers' needs and wants and designing a product that satisfies them. A product can be a good, a service, or an idea. In dealing with the distribution variable, a marketing manager tries to make products available in the quantities desired to as many customers as possible. The promotion variable relates to activities used to inform individuals or groups about the organization and its products. The price variable involves decisions and actions associated with establishing pricing policies and determining product prices. These marketing mix variables are often viewed as controllable because they can be changed, but there are limits to how much they can be altered.

## 1-3  Describe how marketing creates value.

Individuals and organizations engage in marketing to facilitate exchanges—the provision or transfer of goods, services, and ideas in return for something of value. Four conditions must exist for an exchange to occur. First, two or more individuals, groups, or organizations must participate, and each must possess something of value that the other party desires. Second, the exchange should provide a benefit or satisfaction to both parties involved in the transaction. Third, each party must have confidence in the promise of the "something of value" held by the other. Finally, to build trust, the parties to the exchange must meet expectations. Marketing activities should attempt to create and maintain satisfying exchange relationships.

## 1-4  Briefly explore the marketing environment.

The marketing environment, which includes competitive, economic, political, legal and regulatory, technological, and sociocultural forces, surrounds the customer and the marketing mix. These forces can create threats to marketers, but they also generate opportunities for new products and new methods of reaching customers. These forces can fluctuate quickly and dramatically.

## 1-5  Summarize the marketing concept.

According to the marketing concept, an organization should try to provide products that satisfy customers' needs through a coordinated set of activities that also allows the organization to achieve its goals. Customer satisfaction is the marketing concept's major objective. The philosophy of the marketing concept emerged in the United States during the 1950s after the production and sales eras. Organizations that develop activities consistent with the marketing concept become market-oriented organizations. To implement the marketing concept, a market-oriented organization must establish an information system to discover customers' needs and use the information to create satisfying products. It must also coordinate all its activities and develop marketing mixes that create value for customers in order to satisfy their needs.

## 1-6  Identify the importance of building customer relationships.

Relationship marketing involves establishing long-term, mutually satisfying buyer–seller relationships. Customer relationship management (CRM) focuses on using information about customers to create marketing strategies that develop and sustain desirable customer relationships. Managing customer relationships requires identifying patterns of buying behavior and using that information to focus on the most promising and profitable customers. A customer's value over a lifetime represents an intangible asset to a marketer that can be augmented by addressing the customer's varying needs and preferences at different stages in his or her relationship with the firm. Customer lifetime value is a key measurement that forecasts a customer's lifetime economic contribution based on continued relationship marketing efforts. Knowing a customer's potential lifetime value can help marketers determine how to best allocate resources to marketing strategies to sustain that customer over a lifetime.

## 1-7 Explain why marketing is important to our global economy.

Marketing is important to our economy in many ways. Marketing costs absorb about half of each buyer's dollar. Marketing activities are performed in both business and nonprofit organizations. Marketing activities help business organizations to generate profits, and they help fuel the increasingly global economy. Knowledge of marketing enhances consumer awareness. New technology improves marketers' ability to connect with customers. Socially responsible marketing can promote the welfare of customers and society. Green marketing is a strategic process involving stakeholder assessment to create meaningful long-term relationships with customers while maintaining, supporting, and enhancing the natural environment. Finally, marketing offers many exciting career opportunities.

---

**Go to www.cengagebrain.com for resources to help you master the content in this chapter as well as for materials that will expand your marketing knowledge!**

---

## Important Terms

| | | |
|---|---|---|
| marketing  4 | exchange  11 | customer relationship management (CRM)  17 |
| customers  5 | stakeholders  12 | relationship marketing  17 |
| target market  5 | marketing environment  12 | customer lifetime value (CLV)  18 |
| marketing mix  6 | marketing concept  13 | green marketing  21 |
| product  6 | market orientation  16 | |
| value  9 | | |

## Discussion and Review Questions

1. What is *marketing*? How did you define the term before you read this chapter?
2. What is the focus of all marketing activities? Why?
3. What are the four variables of the marketing mix? Why are these elements known as variables?
4. What is value? How can marketers use the marketing mix to enhance the perception of value?
5. What conditions must exist before a marketing exchange can occur? Describe a recent exchange in which you participated.
6. What are the forces in the marketing environment? How much control does a marketing manager have over these forces?
7. Discuss the basic elements of the marketing concept. Which businesses in your area use this philosophy? Explain why.
8. How can an organization implement the marketing concept?
9. What is customer relationship management? Why is it so important to "manage" this relationship?
10. Why is marketing important in our society? Why should you study marketing?

# Video Case 1.1

## Cruising to Success: The Tale of New Belgium Brewing

In 1991 electrical engineer Jeff Lebesch and Kim Jordan began making Belgian-style ales in their basement. The impetus for the brewery occurred after Lebesch had spent time in Belgium riding throughout the country on his mountain bike. He believed he could manufacture high-quality Belgian beers in America. After spending time in the Colorado Rockies deciding the values and directions of their new company, the two launched New Belgium Brewing (NBB), with Kim Jordan as marketing director. The company's first beer was named Fat Tire in honor of Lebesch's Belgian mountain biking trek. Fat Tire remains one of NBB's most popular ales.

NBB has come far from its humble basement origins. Today, the Fort Collins–based brewery is the fourth-largest craft brewer in the country with products available in 39 states, as well as Sweden and the Canadian provinces Alberta and British Columbia. For years Kim Jordan has helmed the company as one of the few female CEOs of a large beer firm. "This entrepreneurial thing sneaks up on you," Jordan states. "And even after 20 years, I still have those pinch me moments where I think, wow, this is what we've created here together." While total beer sales remain flat, craft beer sales are growing. Today craft beers constitute 11 percent of the total beer market.

Tim Fleming/Alamy Stock Photo

Creating such success required a corporate culture that stressed creativity and an authentic approach to treating all stakeholders with respect. While the New Belgium product is a quality craft beer, just as important to the company is how it treats employees, the community, and the environment. Each variable of the marketing mix was carefully considered. The company spends a significant amount of time researching and creating its beers, even collaborating with other craft brewers to co-create new products. This collaboration has led to products such as Ranger IPA and Biere de Garde. NBB's culture is focused on making a quality product and satisfying

customers. It has even ventured into organic beer with its creation of Mothership Wit Organic Wheat Beer. The company has several product line varieties, including its more popular beers Fat Tire, 1554, Shift, Ranger IPA, Rampant Imperial IPA, Blue Paddle Lager, and Sunshine Wheat; seasonal beers such as Skinny Dip, Accumulation, and Long Table; and its Lips of Faith line, a series of experimental beers including La Folie, Barleywine, and Le Terroir.

The distribution element of the product mix was complex at the outset. In her initial role as marketing director, Jordan needed to convince distributors to carry their products. Often, new companies must work hard to convince distributors to carry their brands since distributors are fearful of alienating more established rivals. However, Jordan tirelessly got NBB beer onto store shelves, even delivering beer in her Toyota station wagon. As a craft brewer, NBB uses a premium pricing strategy. Its products are priced higher than domestic brands such as Coors or Budweiser and have higher profit margins. The popularity of NBB beers has prompted rivals to develop competitive products such as MillerCoors' Blue Moon Belgian White.

Perhaps the most notable dimension of NBB's marketing mix is promotion. From the beginning the company based its brand on its core values, including practicing environmental stewardship and forming a participative environment in which all employees can exert their creativity. "For me, brand is absolutely everything we are. It's the people here. It's how we interact with one another. And then there's the other piece of that creativity, obviously, which is designing beers," Kim Jordan said. NBB promotion has attempted to portray the company's creativity and its harmony with the natural environment. For instance, one NBB video features a tinkerer repairing a bicycle and riding down the road, while another features NBB "rangers" singing a hip-hop number to promote the company's Ranger IPA ale. The company has also heavily promoted its brand through Facebook and Twitter. This "indie" charm has served to position NBB as a company committed to having fun and being socially responsible.

NBB also markets itself as a company committed to sustainability. Sustainability has been a core value at NBB from day one. The company was the first fully wind-powered brewery in the United States. NBB recycles cardboard boxes, keg caps, office materials, and amber glass. The brewery stores spent barley and hop grains in an on-premise silo and invites local farmers to pick up the grains, free of charge, to feed their pigs. The company also provides employees with a cruiser bicycle after one year of employment so they can bike to work instead of drive.

NBB's popularity allowed it to open up a second brewery in Asheville, North Carolina. This new brewery will help as NBB expands throughout the Eastern United States. Amidst the changes, Kim Jordan announced she was turning the CEO position over to President and COO Christine Perch. Kim Jordan assumed the role of Executive Chair of the company's Board of Directors so she can continue to impact NBB on a strategic level and work with the New Belgium Family Foundation. The combination of a unique brand image, strong marketing mix, and an orientation that considers all stakeholders has turned NBB into a multi-million dollar success, and Kim Jordan wants this success to inspire other firms to adopt progressive and socially responsible business practices.[48]

### Questions for Discussion

1. How has New Belgium implemented the marketing concept?
2. What has Kim Jordan done to create success at New Belgium?
3. How does New Belgium's focus on sustainability as a core value contribute to its corporate culture and success?

# Case 1.2

## Dollar Shave Club: The Company for Men

For Dollar Shave Club (DSC), it's all about how to solve a problem for the customer—specifically, men. The idea of the firm emerged from a conversation that entrepreneur Michael Dubin was having with the father of his friend's fiancée, co-founder Mark Levine, about the annoyances of shaving. They found it inconvenient and costly to have to purchase multiple brand-name blades each month. This resulted in the concept for a subscription-based service headquartered in Venice, California. Consumers that become members of DSC would be mailed razor blades for as little as $1 per month.

To be successful the founders had to choose a strong marketing mix consisting of product, distribution, promotion, and price. They chose three types of razors with different numbers of blades priced at $1, $6, or $9 per month, depending on the product. Customers sign up through the company's website, and razors are packaged in cardboard envelopes featuring the DSC logo. Razor blades are delivered monthly through the mail.

The entrepreneurs had to find a low-cost way of promoting their new business. For $4,500 Michael Dubin developed and starred in a humorous video marketing the benefits of Dollar Shave razors (e.g., stainless steel blades, aloe vera lubricating strips, and a pivot head), while also poking fun at the extra bells-and-whistles that come with brand-name razors. Dubin wanted to tell a story and demonstrate how Dollar Shave could serve the audience.

The video was posted on YouTube, where it quickly went viral. Within six hours the company had run out of inventory, and the website had so much activity that the servers crashed. It took a day to get the servers up again. By that time DSC already had 12,000 members. Within one year the firm had sales valued at $4 million. Today the firm makes an estimated $140 million in sales, has 2 million subscribers, and ships 50 million cartridges per year.

DSC is a customer-focused organization with the goal to "own the men's bathroom." The secret to the firm's success is a market orientation that identifies customer needs and develops products to meet those needs. For instance, the company recognized that many men do not change their blades on a regular basis, likely due to the expense involved and having to buy them at stores. DSC encourages men to change their blades each week and makes it easy for them to do so with its low-cost subscription service.

While its razors are its most well-known product offering, Dubin is constantly on the lookout for new product ideas. DSC embraces the marketing concept by always considering other ways in which it can solve problems for guys. This led to personal grooming products including hair products, shaving butter, and butt wipes. To launch its One Wipe Charlies, Dubin released another video on YouTube titled "Let's Talk about #2." The company intends to use a market orientation to compete against corporate bigwigs Unilever and L'Oreal. In regards to their competition, Dubin claims that their competitors take a mass market approach with the assumption that customers do not care about what is in the products. DSC, on the other hand, uses natural botanicals in its grooming products to ensure quality.

The success of DSC has led to a number of competitors entering the market. Online competitors include 800Razors LLC and Harry's Razor Co., while Gillette has begun to compete more on product value. Gillette even filed a lawsuit against DSC claiming that it had infringed on its intellectual property. It continues to hold 60 percent of the retail market for shaving products but only one-fifth of the online market. On the other hand, razor sales in general have declined somewhat due to an increased preference for facial hair.

DSC remains undaunted by these challenges. It now releases commercials on broadcast television that continue to call out its rivals' higher prices. While razor sales may have declined, Web sales of men's shaving gear have doubled and are expected to grow. DSC has received $73 million in venture funding, placing its value at approximately $615 million. The company's strong customer focus, strategic marketing mix, and emphasis on value have turned it into a multi-million-dollar brand within the first few years of its existence.[49]

### Questions for Discussion

1. How has a market orientation contributed to Dollar Shave Club's rapid growth?
2. Describe how Dollar Shave Club embraces the marketing concept.
3. How is the marketing mix of Dollar Shave Club different from retail competitors like Gillette?

# NOTES

[1] Marco della Cava, "Airbnb Pushes Itself Further and Farther," *USA Today*, August 20, 2015, 3B; Eric Newcomer, "Airbnb Overhauls Service for Business Travelers," *Bloomberg*, July 20, 2015, http://www.bloomberg.com/news/articles/2015-07-20/airbnb-overhauls-service-for-business-travelers (accessed September 14, 2015); Airbnb, "About Us," https://www.airbnb.com/about/about-us (accessed September 14, 2015); Tomio Geron, "Airbnb and the Unstoppable Rise of the Share Economy," *Forbes*, January 23, 2013, http://www.forbes.com/sites/tomiogeron/2013/01/23/airbnb-and-the-unstoppable-rise-of-the-share-economy/ (accessed September 14, 2015); Christine Lagorio-Chafkin, "Brian Chesky, Joe Gebbia, and Nathan Blecharczyk, Founders of Airbnb," *Inc.*, July 19, 2010, http://www.inc.com/30under30/2010/profile-brian-chesky-joe-gebbia-nathan-blecharczyk-airbnb.html (accessed September 14, 2015).

[2] "Definition of Marketing," American Marketing Association, www.marketingpower.com/AboutAMA/Pages/DefinitionofMarketing.aspx (accessed December 9, 2015).

[3] Ashley Rodriguez, "Retailers Duke It Out for Hispanic Shoppers' Dollars," *Advertising Age*, April 6, 2015, http://adage.com/article/cmo-strategy/retailers-duke-hispanic-shoppers-dollars/297902/ (accessed December 8, 2015).

[4] Lehman's website, https://www.lehmans.com/ (accessed December 9, 2015); Lisa Girard, "At Ohio stores, sales are simple," *Home Channel News*, September 9, 2007, http://www.homechannelnews.com/article/ohio-store-sales-are-simple (accessed December 9, 2015); Linda Chojnacki, "Attend Lehman's 55th Anniversary Open House Next Weekend," *Cleveland.com*, April 11, 2010, http://www.cleveland.com/our-town/index.ssf/2010/04/attend_lehmans_55th_anniversary_open_house_next_weekend.html (accessed December 9, 2015).

[5] Julie Jargon, "Subway Runs Past McDonald's Chain," *The Wall Street Journal*, March 9, 2011, B4; Subway, "Store Locator," http://www.subway.com/storelocator/ (accessed December 8, 2015).

[6] John Patrick Pullen, "Streaming Showdown: Apple Music vs. Spotify vs. Pandora vs. Rdio," June 9, 2015, *Time*, June 9, 2015, http://time.com/3913955/apple-music-spotify-pandora-rdio-streaming/ (accessed January 7, 2016).

[7] Molly Soat, "Turning Heads," *Marketing News*, July 2015, pp. 12–13.

[8] "Recipes," *Trader Joe's*, http://www.traderjoes.com/recipes (accessed December 8, 2015).

[9] Rajneesh Suri, Chiranjeev Kohli, and Kent B. Monroe, "The Effects of Perceived Scarcity on Consumers' Processing of Price Information," *Journal of the Academy of Marketing Science* 35, 1 (2007): 89–100.

[10] Natalie Mizik and Robert Jacobson, "Trading Off Between Value Creation and Value Appropriation: The Financial Implications and Shifts in Strategic Emphasis," *Journal of Marketing* 67, 1 (January 2003): 63–76.

[11] Micah Solomon, "A Ritz-Carlton Caliber Customer Experience Requires Employee Empowerment and Customer Service Standards," *Forbes*, September 18, 2013, http://www.forbes.com/sites/micahsolomon/2013/09/18/empowered-employees-vs-brand-standards-the-customer-experience-needs-both/ (accessed January 7, 2016).

[12] O. C. Ferrell and Michael Hartline, *Marketing Strategy*, 5th ed. (Mason, OH: South-Western, 2011), 370.

[13] Sara Leroi-Werelds, Sandra Streukens, Michael K. Brady, and Gilbert Swinnen, "Assessing the value of commonly used methods for measuring customer value: A multi-setting empirical study," *Journal of the Academy of Marketing Science* 42, 4 (July 2014): 430–451.

[14] Randy Lewis, "Garth Brooks unveils iTunes alternative: GhostTunes," *Los Angeles Times*, September 4, 2014, http://www.latimes.com/entertainment/music/posts/la-et-ms-garth-brooks-ghost-tunes-itunes-alternative-competition-20140904-story.html (accessed December 9, 2015).

[15] Isabelle Maignan, Tracy Gonzalez-Padron, G. Tomas Hult, and O.C. Ferrell, "Stakeholder orientation: Development and testing of a framework for socially responsible marketing," *Journal of Strategic Marketing* 19, 4 (2011): 313–338.

[16] Vijay K. Patel, Scott. C. Manley, O.C. Ferrell, Torsten M. Pieper, and Joseph F. Hair, Jr. "Stakeholder Orientation: Proactive and Responsive Components and Firm Performance," Working paper, 2016.

[17] Mike Esterl, "New Diet Pepsi Leaves Some Loyalists with Bad Taste," *Wall Street Journal*, October 8, 2015, http://www.wsj.com/articles/new-diet-pepsi-leaves-some-loyalists-with-bad-taste-1444327691 (accessed December 9, 2015).

[18] Ajay K. Kohli and Bernard J. Jaworski, "Market Orientation: The Construct, Research Propositions, and Managerial Implications," *Journal of Marketing* 54, 2 (April 1990): 1–18; O. C. Ferrell, "Business Ethics and Customer Stakeholders," *Academy of Management Executive* 18, 2 (May 2004): 126–129.

[19] "Starbucks CEO Howard Schultz is all abuzz," *CBS News*, March 27, 2011, www.cbsnews.com/stories/2011/03/27/business/main20047618.shtml (accessed December 9, 2015).

[20] Eugene W. Anderson, Claes Fornell, and Sanal K. Mazvancheryl, "Customer Satisfaction and Shareholder Value," *Journal of Marketing* 68, 4 (October 2004): 172–185.

[21] Xeuming Luo and Christian Homburg, "Neglected Outcomes of Customer Satisfaction," *Journal of Marketing* 71, 2 (April 2007): 133–149.

[22] O.C. Ferrell, Joe F. Hair, Jr., Greg W. Marshall, and Robert D. Tamilia, "Understanding the History of Marketing Education to Improve Classroom Instruction," *Marketing Education Review* 25, 2 (2015): 159–175.

[23] Kohli and Jaworski, "Market Orientation: The Construct, Research Propositions, and Managerial Implications."

[24] Kwaku Atuahene-Gima, "Resolving the Capability-Rigidity Paradox in New Product Innovation," *Journal of Marketing* 69, 4 (October 2005): 61–83.

[25] Gary F. Gebhardt, Gregory S. Carpenter, and John F. Sherry Jr., "Creating a Market Orientation," *Journal of Marketing* 70 (October 2006): 37–55.

[26] James D. Doyle and Anahit Armenakyan, "Value-creating mechanisms within the market orientation—performance relationship: a meta-analysis," *Journal of Strategic Marketing* 22, 3 (2014): 193–205.

[27] Sunil Gupta, Donald R. Lehmann, and Jennifer Ames Stuart, "Valuing Customers," *Journal of Marketing Research* 41, 1 (February 2004): 7–18.

[28] SAP, "A Winning Team for College Football," SAP website, http://www.sap.com/customer-testimonials/sports-entertainment/dfb.html (accessed December 8, 2015).

[29] Nitin Pangarkar, "Survival of the Fittest: How Can Companies Adapt to Changing Upheavals," *International Business Times*, January 7, 2014, http://www.ibtimes.com/survival-fittest-how-can-companies-adapt-technological-upheavals-1529724 (accessed December 9, 2015).

[30] Jacquelyn S. Thomas, Robert C. Blattberg, and Edward J. Fox, "Recapturing Lost Customers," *Journal of Marketing Research* 41, 1 (February 2004): 31–45.

[31] Jagdish N. Sheth and Rajendras Sisodia, "More Than Ever Before, Marketing Is under Fire to Account for What It Spends," *Marketing Management* (Fall 1995): 13–14.

[32] Stephen L. Vargo and Robert F. Lusch, "Service-dominant logic: Continuing the evolution," *Journal of the Academy of Marketing Science* 36 (2008): 1–10.

[33] Southwest Airlines, "About Southwest," http://www.southwest.com/html/about-southwest/ (accessed December 9, 2015).

[34] Chezy Ofir and Itamar Simonson, "The Effect of Stating Expectations on Customer Satisfaction and Shopping Experience," *Journal of Marketing Research* XLIV (February 2007): 164–174.

[35] Robert W. Palmatier, Lisa K. Scheer, and Jan-Benedict E. M. Steenkamp, "Customer Loyalty to Whom? Managing the Benefits and Risks of Salesperson-Owned Loyalty," *Journal of Marketing Research* XLIV (May 2007): 185–199.

[36] Ruth M. Stock and Marei Bednareck, "As they sow, so shall they reap: Customers' influence on customer satisfaction at the customer interface," *Journal of the Academy of Marketing Science* 42, 4 (July 2014): 400–414.

[37] Werner J. Reinartz and V. Kumar, "On the Profitability of Long-Life Customers in a Noncontractual Setting: An Empirical Investigation and Implications for Marketing,"

*Journal of Marketing* 64, 4 (October 2000): 17–35.

[38] Customer Insight Group, Inc., "Program Design: Loyalty and Retention," www.customerinsightgroup.com/loyalty_retention.php (accessed January 4, 2011).

[39] V. Kumar and Morris George, "Measuring and Maximizing Customer Equity: A Critical Analysis," *Journal of the Academy of Marketing Science* 35 (2007): 157–171.

[40] Rajkumar Venkatesan and V. Kumar, "A Customer Lifetime Value Framework for Customer Selection and Resource Allocation Strategy," *Journal of Marketing* 68, 4 (October 2004): 106–125.

[41] Richard Waters and Hannah Kuchler, "Social networks now a staple of office life," *Financial Times*, November 19, 2014, pp. 15.

[42] Arun Sundararajan, "The 'gig economy' is coming. What will it mean for work?" *The Guardian*, July 25, 2015, http://www.theguardian.com/commentisfree/2015/jul/26/will-we-get-by-gig-economy (accessed December 15, 2015).

[43] Will Rinehart, "Independent Contractors and the Emerging Gig Economy," *American Action Forum*, July 29, 2015, http://americanactionforum.org/ research/independent-contractors-and-the-emerging-gig-economy (accessed December 15, 2015).

[44] Richard Waters and Hannah Kuchler, "Social networks now a staple of office life," *Financial Times*, November 19, 2014, pp. 15.

[45] David Pinsky, "Carting Away the Oceans 2015," *Greenpeace*, 2015, http://www.greenpeace.org/usa/research/carting-away-the-oceans-2015/ (accessed January 7, 2016).

[46] Anis Ben Brik, Belaid Rettab, and Kemel Mallahi, "Market Orientation, Corporate Social Responsibility, and Business Performance," *Journal of Business Ethics* 99 (2011): 307–324.

[47] "Charitable Giving Statistics," National Philanthropic Trust, http://www.nptrust.org/philanthropic-resources/charitable-giving-statistics/ (accessed Decem-ber 9, 2015).

[48] New Belgium website, newbelgium.com (accessed January 7, 2016); "New Belgium Brewing: Ethical and Environmental Responsibility," in O. C. Ferrell, John Fraedrich, and Linda Ferrell, *Business Ethics: Ethical Decision Making and Cases*, 9th ed. (Mason, OH: South-Western Cengage

Learning, 2013), 355–363; New Belgium, "The Tinkerer," *YouTube*, https://www.youtube.com/watch?v=8UfTzXhdz5Y (accessed January 7, 2016); Devin Leonard, "New Belgium and the Battle of the Microbrews," *Bloomberg Businessweek,* December 1, 2011, www.businessweek.com/magazine/new-belgium-and-the-battle-of-the-microbrews-12012011.html (accessed January 7, 2016); New Belgium, "Kim's Joy Ride: Fat Tire Ale," *YouTube*, https://www.youtube.com/watch?v=L94PE12VaFY (accessed January 7, 2016); "Case 15: New Belgium Brewing: Engaging in Sustainable Social Responsibility," in O.C. Ferrell, Debbie Thorne, and Linda Ferrell, *Business & Society: A Strategic Approach to Social Responsibility and Ethics*, 5th ed., (Chicago: Chicago Business Press, 2016), pp. 556-563; Eric Gorski, "U.S. craft brewers exporting beer – and ideas – around the world," *Denver Post*, April 8, 2014, http://www.denverpost.com/news/ci_25517990/u-s-craft-brewers-exporting-beer-and-ideas (accessed January 7, 2016); New Belgium, "New Belgium President and Christine Perich to Assume CEO

Position," August 10, 2015, http://www.newbelgium.com/community/Blog/new-belgium-brewing/2015/08/10/New-Belgium-President-and-COO-Christine-Perich-to-assume-CEO-position (accessed January 7, 2016); Charles Sizemore, "Why Big Beer Is Struggling in the Age of Craft Beer," *Forbes*, June 9, 2015, http://www.forbes.com/sites/moneybuilder/2015/06/09/why-big-beer-is-struggling-in-the-age-of-craft-beer/ (accessed January 7, 2016).

[49] Serena Ng and Paul Ziobro, "Razor Sales Move Online, Away From Gillette," *The Wall Street Journal*, June 23, 2015, B1; "How YouTube Crashed Our Website—And Why We Loved It," *Inc.*, July/August 2015, 98-100; Adam Lashinsky, "The Cutting Edge of Care," *Fortune*, March 15, 2015, 61-62; Dollar Shave Club website, http://www.dollarshaveclub.com/ (accessed July 14, 2015); Paresh Dave, "Up to 2 million members, Dollar Shave Club worth $615 million, investors say," *Los Angeles Times*, June 22, 2015, http://www.latimes.com/business/technology/la-fi-tn-dollar-shave-club-investment-20150622-story.

html (accessed July 14, 2015); "Meet the 2015 CNBC Disruptor 50 Companies," *CNBC*, May 12, 2015, http://www.cnbc.com/2015/05/12/dollar-shave-club-disruptor-50.html (accessed July 14, 2015); Dollar Shave Club, "DollarShaveClub.com – Our Blades Are F***ing Great," *YouTube*, March 6, 2012, https://www.youtube.com/watch?v=ZUG9qYTJMsI (accessed July 14, 2015); Dollar Shave Club, "Let's Talk About #2," *YouTube*, June 4, 2013, https://www.youtube.com/watch?v=3FOae1V1-Xg (accessed July 14, 2015); "Pay Up – TV Commercial," *YouTube*, November 10, 2014, https://www.youtube.com/watch?v=5Ds-82SYmLs&feature=iv&src_vid=JbsJPO-ZreM&annotation_id=annotation_2355018053 (accessed July 14, 2015); Dollar Shave Club, "Tranq Dart – TV Commercial," *YouTube*, November 10, 2014, https://www.youtube.com/watch?v=PWPkZH_UicU (accessed July 14, 2015); David Spiegel, "The nick in Gillette suit against upstart Dollar Shave Club," *CNBC*, December 18, 2015, http://www.cnbc.com/2015/12/18/ (accessed January 7, 2016).

## Feature Notes

[a] Mark Brandau, "Protein Bar," *Nation's Restaurant News*, June 27, 2011, http://www.theproteinbar.com/ftpprotein/ProteinBar_6.27.11_NationsRestaurantNews.pdf (accessed July 9, 2014); The Protein Bar website, http://www.theproteinbar.com/ (accessed July 9, 2014); Brigid Sweeney, "40 Under 40: 2012," *Crain's Chicago Business*, http://www.chicagobusiness.com/section/40under40-2012?p=Matros (accessed July 9, 2014); Luis Gomez, "Brandon Marshall, Protein Bar team up to sell 'Crazy Stigma Green' drink," *Chicago Tribune*, October 12,

2014, http://www.chicagotribune.com/sports/smackblog/chi-brandon-marshall-protein-bar-thresholds-20141011-column.html (accessed October 29, 2014).

[b] Adele Peters, "Why Lego Is Spending Millions to Ditch Oil-Based Plastic," *Fast Company*, July 1, 2015, http://www.fastcoexist.com/3048017/why-lego-is-spending-millions-to-ditch-oil-based-plastic (accessed September 15, 2015); "Lego puts big bucks behind push to go green," *CNN Money*, June 23, 2015, http://money.cnn.com/2015/06/23/news/companies/lego-sustainable-material/ (accessed September 15,

2015); Dominique Mosbergen, "Lego Saying 'No' to Plastic, Invests Millions Into Search for 'Sustainable' Material," *The Huffington Post*, June 24, 2015, http://www.huffingtonpost.com/2015/06/24/lego-plastic-sustainable-materials_n_7651190.html (accessed September 15, 2015); Katie M. Palmer, "Sorry, but the Perfect Lego Brick May Never Be Eco-Friendly," *Wired*, July 7, 2015, http://www.wired.com/2015/07/sorry-perfect-lego-brick-may-never-eco-friendly/ (accessed September 15, 2015).

cacaroot/iStock/Getty Images

# chapter 2

## Planning, Implementing, and Evaluating Marketing Strategies

### OBJECTIVES

**2-1** Explain the strategic planning process.

**2-2** Understand the importance of a firm's mission statement and corporate and business-unit strategy.

**2-3** Describe how analyzing organizational resources and the marketing environment can help identify opportunities and create competitive advantage.

**2-4** Explore how a firm develops marketing objectives and strategies that contribute to overall objectives.

**2-5** Identify what is necessary to effectively manage the implementation of marketing strategies.

**2-6** Describe the four major elements of strategic performance evaluation.

**2-7** Describe the development of a marketing plan.

# MARKETING INSIGHTS

## Dressbarn Dresses Up Its Strategy

Susan Montgomery/Shutterstock.com

What's in a name? For Dressbarn, it's more than 50 years of brand history and the name of the product that holds the key to the company's revamped marketing strategy. The first Dressbarn store opened in 1962, targeting working women who wanted good-looking, affordable clothing for the office and beyond. Today, the retailer does business in more than 800 stores coast to coast, as part of Ascena Retail Group, a corporation that operates apparel retailers such as Justice (targeting young teens), Ann Taylor (targeting style-conscious women), and Lane Bryant (targeting plus-size women).

In recent years, as competitors entered the market with edgier styles and flashier stores, Dressbarn's growth slowed. To reignite revenues and reinvigorate the brand, the CEO and the chief marketing officer took an unflinching look at the retailer's strengths and weaknesses, as well as the customers it targets. Although they considered changing the Dressbarn name, they discovered their customers care more about the styles on the racks than the name over the door. So they kept the name but signed more contemporary designers, expanded the dress department, dressed up the dressing rooms, and added specials. Next, they launched a high-profile ad campaign featuring supermodels in stylish dresses, surrounded by barnyard animals, with cheeky headlines like "Think you know Dressbarn? Think again."

Dressbarn also analyzed its customer base and discovered a segment of bargain-hunters who buy only during clearance sales. Now, instead of spending money all year to reach these customers, the retailer plans for just a few strategically timed communications to alert these customers when clothing is discounted for clearance. This frees up resources to spend on more high-value customers.[1]

Whether it's Dressbarn or your local print shop, an organization must be able to create customer value and achieve its goals. This occurs through successful strategic marketing management. **Strategic marketing management** is the process of planning, implementing, and evaluating the performance of marketing activities and strategies, both effectively and efficiently. Effectiveness and efficiency are key concepts to understanding strategic marketing management. *Effectiveness* is the degree to which long-term customer relationships help achieve an organization's objectives. *Efficiency* refers to minimizing the resources an organization uses to achieve a specific level of desired customer relationships. Thus, the overall goal of strategic marketing management is to facilitate highly desirable customer relationships and to minimize the costs of doing so.

We begin this chapter with an overview of the strategic planning process and a discussion of the nature of marketing strategy. These elements provide a framework for an analysis of the development, implementation, and evaluation of marketing strategies. We conclude with an examination of how to create a marketing plan.

# 2-1 THE STRATEGIC PLANNING PROCESS

Through the process of **strategic planning**, a company establishes an organizational mission and formulates goals, a corporate strategy, marketing objectives, and a marketing strategy.[2] A market orientation should guide the process of strategic planning to ensure that a concern for customer satisfaction is an integral part of the entire company, leading to the development of successful marketing strategies and planning processes.[3]

Figure 2.1 shows the various components of the strategic planning process, which begins with the establishment or revision of an organization's mission and goals. The corporation and

Figure 2.1   **Components of the Strategic Planning Process**

**strategic marketing management** The process of planning, implementing, and evaluating the performance of marketing activities and strategies, both effectively and efficiently

**strategic planning** The process of establishing an organizational mission and formulating goals, corporate strategy, marketing objectives, and marketing strategy

Source: Figure adopted from *Marketing Strategy*, 3rd ed., by O.C. Ferrell and Michael Hartline. Reprinted with permission of Cengage Learning.

individual business units then develop strategies to achieve these goals. The company performs a detailed analysis of its strengths and weaknesses and identifies opportunities and threats within the external marketing environment. Next, each functional area of the organization (marketing, production, finance, human resources, and so forth) establishes its own objectives and develops strategies to achieve them, which must support the organization's overall goals and mission and should be focused on market orientation. Because this is a marketing book, we are most interested in marketing objectives and strategies. We will examine the strategic planning process by taking a closer look at each component, beginning with organizational mission statements and goals.

# 2-2 ESTABLISHING MISSION, GOALS, AND STRATEGIES

The strategic planning process begins with deciding on the firm's organizational mission— its *raison d'etre*—and goals. These give meaning and direction to the organization.

## 2-2a Developing Organizational Mission and Goals

The goals of any organization should derive from its **mission statement**, a long-term view or vision of what the organization wants to become. For instance, Twitter's mission, "to give everyone the power to create and share ideas instantly, without barriers," speaks to the company's desire to transform the way the world communicates.[4] When an organization decides on its mission, it is answering two questions: *Who are our customers?* and *What is our core competency?* Although these questions appear very simple, they are two of the most important questions for any company to address. Defining customers' needs and wants gives direction to what the company must do to satisfy them.

Mission statements, goals, and objectives must be properly implemented to achieve the desired result. It is advantageous to broadcast them to the public, customers, employees, and other stakeholders so that they know what they may expect from the firm. Companies try to develop and manage a consistent *corporate identity*—their unique symbols, personalities, and philosophies—to support all corporate activities, including strategic planning and marketing. For example, Warby Parker established this mission: "Warby Parker was founded with a rebellious spirit and a lofty objective: to offer designer eyewear at a revolutionary price, while leading the way for socially conscious business."[5] This declaration guides the firm's corporate identity, strategic direction, connection with its customers, and even helps it recruit like-minded employees. Although many customers don't know that the bright blue color of the liner in every Warby Parker eyeglass case was inspired by the color of the feet of the rare blue-footed booby, that symbol of the firm's identity inspires Warby Parker executives and employees to value curiosity, stylish design, flair, and humor. The firm's mission also inspired it to donate one pair of glasses to a needy person in a developing country for every pair it sells—something that gives everyone who works there a reason to do what they do.[6]

Consider the advertisement for Delta, which conveys the corporate identity the company desires to project. Delta wants its target market to see the company as the go-to airline for flying to wherever they want to go. The company's advertisement, which features a Delta jet-liner flying above the clouds with the sun setting in the distance, highlights that the firm's 80,000 employees are there to help customers reach their destination and discover the potential there. The corporate identity is further reinforced by multiple appearances of the airline's logo, along with the tagline, "Keep Climbing." Delta's ad makes the statement that its corporate identity is in tune with on-the-go business and consumer fliers who travel frequently.

An organization's goals and objectives, derived from its mission statement, guide its planning efforts. Goals focus on the end results the organization seeks. Each level of management and department within the firm should have goals that stem from the mission statement and provide direction for the firm's activities.

**mission statement** A long-term view, or vision, of what the organization wants to become

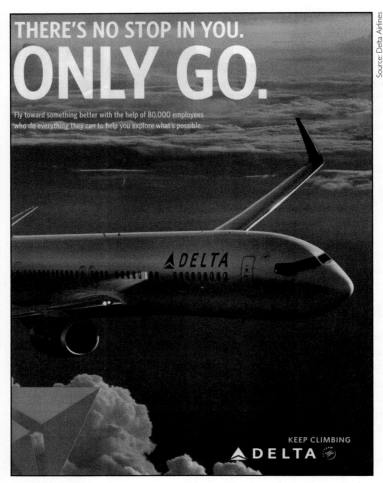

Source: Delta Airlines

**Corporate Identity**
Delta has established a corporate identity as a company that can get you where you want to go.

## 2-2b Developing Corporate and Business-Unit Strategies

In most organizations, strategic planning begins at the corporate level and proceeds downward to the business-unit and marketing levels. However, organizations are increasingly developing strategies and conducting strategic planning that moves in both directions. When conducting strategic planning, a firm is likely to seek out experts from many levels of the organization to take advantage of in-house expertise and a variety of opinions.

Figure 2.2 shows the relationships among three planning levels: corporate, business unit, and marketing. Corporate strategy is the broadest of the three levels and should be developed with the organization's overall mission in mind. Business-unit strategy should be consistent with the corporate strategy while also serving the unit's needs. Marketing strategy utilizes the marketing mix to develop a message that is consistent with the business-unit and corporate strategies.

### Corporate Strategies

**Corporate strategy** determines the means for utilizing resources in the functional areas of marketing, production, finance, research and development, and human resources to achieve the organization's goals. A corporate strategy outlines the scope of the business and such considerations as resource deployment, competitive advantages, and overall coordination of functional areas. Top management's level of marketing expertise and ability to deploy resources to address the company's markets can affect sales growth and profitability. Corporate strategy addresses the two questions posed in the organization's mission statement: *Who are our customers?* and *What is our core competency?* The term *corporate* in this case does not apply solely to corporations. In this context, it refers to the top-level (i.e., highest) strategy and is used by organizations of all sizes and types.

Corporate strategy planners are concerned with broad issues such as organizational culture, competition, differentiation, diversification, interrelationships among business units, and environmental and social issues. They attempt to match the resources of the organization with the opportunities and threats in the environment. Toyota and Honda, for example, recognized that elderly Japanese drivers seem to be getting into more accidents at the same time as younger Japanese drivers are less interested in driving and owning cars. Both companies have therefore invested in and are developing driver-assistance and autonomous-driving technologies and systems that may be especially appealing to the world's growing population of drivers over age 65. Both automakers expect to employ the first of these in 2020 vehicles in Japan and ultimately worldwide. Google and Tesla are testing similar technologies in the United States.[7]

Likewise, take a look at the Samsung Galaxy S6 edge advertisement. Samsung Electronics—a unit of Samsung Group—identified an opportunity in the marketing environment to target Apple iPhone customers who want a faster and more powerful mobile phone for business. This ad depicts a Galaxy S6 edge as an office building with people working into the night,

**corporate strategy** A strategy that determines the means for utilizing resources in the various functional areas to reach the organization's goals

Figure 2.2     **Levels of Strategic Planning**

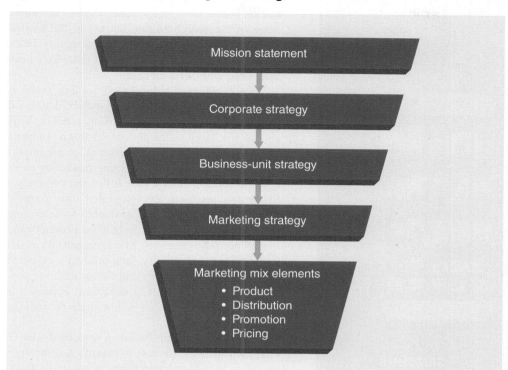

showing off the smartphone's ability to stay in contact 24/7, a necessity in today's connected global economy. The ad also informs how the features of the Galaxy S6 edge create a product that can keep up with the demands of any business team no matter the time of day. Samsung's promotion highlights its efforts to innovate in order to continue to satisfy the changing needs of its business customers. The proactive nature of a company's corporate strategy can affect its capacity to innovate.

## Business-Unit Strategies

After analyzing corporate operations and performance, the next step in strategic planning is to determine future business directions and develop strategies for individual business units. A **strategic business unit (SBU)** is a division, product line, or other profit center within the parent company. Nestlé, for example, has SBUs for Confectionaries and Beverages. Each SBU sells a distinct set of products to an identifiable group of customers, and each competes with a well-defined set of competitors. The revenues, costs, investments, and strategic plans of each SBU can be separated from those of the parent company and evaluated. SBUs face different market growth rates, opportunities, competition, and profit-making potential. Business strategy should seek to create value for the company's target markets and attain greater performance, which marketing research suggests requires implementing appropriate strategic actions and targeting appropriate market segments.[8]

Strategic planners should recognize the performance capabilities of each SBU and carefully allocate resources among them. Several tools allow a company's planners to classify and visually display its portfolio of SBUs, or even individual products, according to the attractiveness of markets and the business's relative market share. A **market** is a group of individuals and/or organizations that have needs for products in a product class and have the ability, willingness, and authority to purchase those products. The percentage of a market that actually buys a

**strategic business unit (SBU)** A division, product line, or other profit center within the parent company

**market** A group of individuals and/or organizations that have needs for products in a product class and have the ability, willingness, and authority to purchase those products

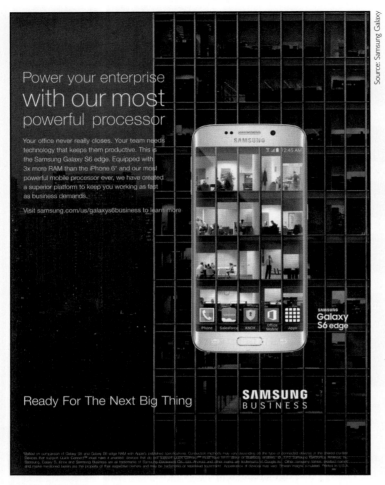

**Business-Unit Strategies**
Samsung targets business customers who want a powerful smartphone.

specific product from a particular company is referred to as that product's (or business unit's) **market share**. Google, for example, has a dominant share of the search engine market in the United States, at nearly 75 percent.[9] Product quality, order of entry into the market, and market share have been associated with SBU success.[10]

One of the most helpful tools for a marketer is the **market growth/market share matrix**, developed by the Boston Consulting Group (BCG). This approach is based on the philosophy that a product's market growth rate and its market share are important considerations in determining marketing strategy. To develop such a tool, all of the company's SBUs and products are integrated into a single matrix and compared and evaluated to determine appropriate strategies for individual products and overall portfolio strategies. Managers use this model to determine and classify each product's expected future cash contributions and future cash requirements. However, the BCG analytical approach is more of a diagnostic tool than a guide for making strategy prescriptions.

Figure 2.3, which is based on work by the BCG, enables a strategic planner to classify a company's products into four basic types: stars, cash cows, dogs, and question marks. *Stars* are products with a dominant share of the market and good prospects for growth. However, they use more cash than they generate to finance growth, add capacity, and increase market share. Microsoft's hybrid Surface Pro 3 tablet computers might be considered stars because they are gaining market share quickly but remain well behind Apple, the leader. *Cash cows* have a dominant share of the market, but low prospects for growth. They typically generate more cash than is required to maintain market share. Bounty paper towels represent a cash cow for Procter & Gamble because it is a product that consistently sells well. *Dogs* have a subordinate share of the market and low prospects for growth. Dogs are often found in established markets. The cathode ray tube television would probably be considered a dog by a company like Panasonic, as most customers prefer flat screens. *Question marks*, sometimes called "problem children," have a small share of a growing market and generally require a large amount of cash to build market share. The Chevrolet Bolt electric car, for example, is a question mark relative to General Motors' more established gasoline-powered cars and trucks.

The long-term health of an organization depends on having a range of products, some that generate cash (and generate acceptable profits) and others that use cash to support growth. The major indicators of a firm's overall health are the size and vulnerability of the cash cows, the prospects for the stars, and the number of question marks and dogs. Particular attention should be paid to products that require large cash flows, as most firms cannot afford to sponsor many such products. If resources are spread too thin, the company will be unable to finance promising new product entries or acquisitions. Procter & Gamble, for example, merged or divested a number of units and brands with lower growth or profit potential, including Duracell and Eukanuba, in order to focus its resources on its 70 to 80 best-performing brands of products. The company's chief financial officer said, "The brands we're exiting are not bad businesses. . . . Most simply do not play to our strengths."[11]

**market share** The percentage of a market that actually buys a specific product from a particular company

**market growth/market share matrix** A helpful business tool, based on the philosophy that a product's market growth rate and its market share are important considerations in determining its marketing strategy

Figure 2.3    **Growth Share Matrix Developed by the Boston Consulting Group**

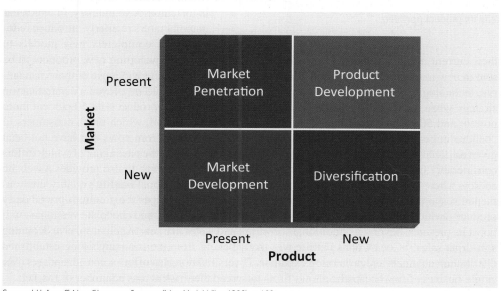

Source: *Perspectives*, No. 66, "The Product Portfolio." Reprinted by permission from The Boston Consulting Group, Inc., Boston, MA, Copyright © 1970.

## Competitive Growth Strategies

Based on analyses of each product or business unit, a firm may choose one or more competitive strategies. Figure 2.4 shows these competitive strategies on a product-market matrix. The matrix can help in determining growth that can be implemented through marketing strategies.

*Market penetration* is a strategy of increasing sales in current markets with current products. Coca-Cola, for example, boosted sales by 2 percent, thanks to a promotion that offered soft-drink bottles labeled with about 250 different personal names as well as phrases such as

Figure 2.4    **Competitive Growth Strategies**

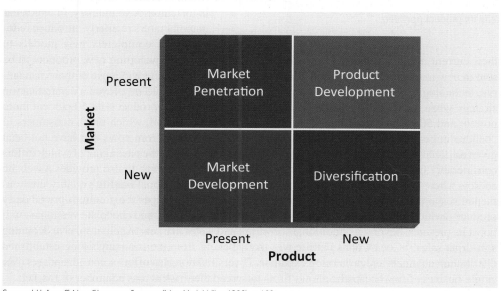

Source: H.I. Ansoff, *New C/orporate Strategy*, (New York: Wiley, 1988), p. 109.

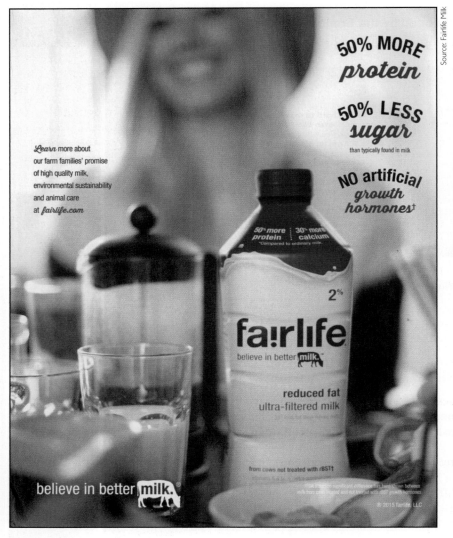

**Diversification**

The Coca-Cola Company created Fairlife Milk, which it hopes will appeal to increasingly health-conscious consumers, to diversify its product portfolio.

"Friends," "Family," and "BFF." The personalized labels were especially popular with younger consumers, and half a million photos of personalized bottles on Instagram included the hashtag #shareacoke. The temporary campaign was so successful that the firm brought it back the following year with even more personal names and phrases.[12] *Market development* is a strategy of increasing sales of current products in new markets. Arm & Hammer, for example, successfully introduced its baking soda, the firm's basic product, into new markets for use as carpet deodorizer, as freshener for litter boxes, as laundry detergent, as deodorant, and as a toothpaste. Market development also occurs when a company introduces its products into international markets for the first time. When Yum Brands opened Pizza Hut stores in South Africa, it paid special attention to local tastes for its toppings and used local slang on signs and napkins to appeal to residents.[13]

*Product development* is a strategy of increasing sales by improving present products or developing new products for current markets. Apple, for example, introduced a smartwatch that provides the functionality and style of its iconic iPhone with the wearability of a wristwatch and health benefits of a fitness band. Perhaps the most common example of product development occurs in the automotive industry, in which car manufacturers regularly introduce redesigned or completely new models to their current markets. Finally, *diversification* is a strategy of developing new products to be sold in new markets. Diversification allows firms to make better and wider use of their managerial, technological, and financial resources. Coca-Cola, for example, employed a diversification strategy when it developed Fairlife, a long-life, lactose-free milk product with 50 percent more protein and 50 percent less sugar than conventional milk. The ad, which urges consumers to "believe in better milk," also highlights that the product comes from cows that have not been given artificial growth hormones. It shows a bottle of the product, the packaging of which differs considerably from other Coke products as well as most milk brands. It also provides a website address where interested consumers can go for more information about Fairlife's quality, environmental sustainability, and animal care practices. The company hopes the premium-priced dairy product—which ultimately will come in whole, reduced fat, skim, and chocolate versions—will boost its presence beyond its traditional soft-drink and water markets to help it survive declining soft-drink sales.[14] Coca-Cola's Fairlife will likely benefit from the company's long-established distribution channels and promotion expertise. Diversification also offers some advantages over single-business firms because it allows firms to spread their risk across a number of markets.

# 2-3 ASSESSING ORGANIZATIONAL RESOURCES AND OPPORTUNITIES

The strategic planning process begins with an analysis of the marketing environment, including the industry in which the company operates or intends to sell its products. As we will see in Chapter 3, the marketing environment (which includes economic, competitive, political, legal and regulatory, sociocultural, and technological forces) can threaten an organization and influence its overall goals affecting the amount and type of resources the company can acquire. However, these forces can also create favorable opportunities that can help an organization achieve its goals and marketing objectives.

Any strategic planning effort must take into account the organization's available financial and human resources and capabilities and how these resources are likely to change over time, as changes may affect the organization's ability to achieve its mission and goals. Adequate resources can help a firm generate customer satisfaction and loyalty, goodwill, and a positive reputation, all of which impact marketing by creating well-known brands and strong financial performance. Coca-Cola, Apple, and Google all benefit from high levels of brand recognition and goodwill. Such strengths also include **core competencies**, things a company does extremely well—sometimes so well that they give the company an advantage over its competition.

Analysis of the marketing environment also includes identifying opportunities in the marketplace, which requires a solid understanding of the company's industry. When the right combination of circumstances and timing permits an organization to take action to reach a particular target market, a **market opportunity** exists. For example, Starbucks sees a market opportunity in the $90 billion tea market. CEO Howard Schultz believes that Starbucks can transform the tea market just as it transformed the coffee market. The company recently purchased retailer Teavana and partnered with Oprah Winfrey on new tea offerings.[15] Such opportunities are often called **strategic windows**, temporary periods of optimal fit between the key requirements of a market and the particular capabilities of a company competing in that market.[16] When a company matches a core competency to opportunities in the marketplace, it is said to have a **competitive advantage**. Some companies possess manufacturing, technical, or marketing skills that they can tie to market opportunities to create a competitive advantage. As shown in the ad, Fitbit has a significant advantage over competing brands—its name is effectively synonymous for fitness trackers. The company also offers a wide range of fitness trackers at varying price points to ensure that there is a device that meets every shopper's needs. In the ad, the Fitbit Surge is targeted at bicyclists who want to record every aspect of their rides—such as location, distance, and heart rate—in order to maximize their training and performance. The product's

**core competencies** Things a company does extremely well, which sometimes give it an advantage over its competition

**market opportunity** A combination of circumstances and timing that permits an organization to take action to reach a particular target market

**strategic windows** Temporary periods of optimal fit between the key requirements of a market and the particular capabilities of a company competing in that market

**competitive advantage** The result of a company matching a core competency to opportunities it has discovered in the marketplace

**Competitive Advantage**
Fitbit has a competitive advantage over other wearable fitness tracker brands because of its well-known name and extensive range of devices at different price points, such as the Fitbit Surge watch.

long battery life and ability to display caller ID, control music, and sync wirelessly make cycling long distances more fun and productive. The photo underscores the ease of use by showing two cyclists enjoying their ride.

## 2-3a  SWOT Analysis

A SWOT analysis can be helpful for gauging a firm's capabilities and resources relative to the industry. The **SWOT analysis** assesses an organization's strengths, weaknesses, opportunities, and threats. It can provide a firm with insights into such factors as timing market entry into a new geographic region or product category. Figure 2.5 depicts the SWOT analysis as a four-cell matrix and shows how marketers must seek to convert weaknesses into strengths, threats into opportunities, and match internal strengths with external opportunities to develop competitive advantages. Strengths and weaknesses are internal factors that can influence an organization's ability to satisfy target markets.

*Strengths* refer to competitive advantages, or core competencies, that give the company an advantage. *Weaknesses* are limitations a company faces in developing or implementing a marketing strategy. Consider Walmart, a company that was so dominant for decades that it almost did not need to worry about competitors. However, Amazon has grown into such a threat recently, with its low costs and high customer satisfaction, that Walmart has been forced to acknowledge it has a serious weakness in online sales and technological innovation. To respond to this threat, Walmart revamped its website to provide a better online shopping experience and offers same-day delivery when customers choose to pick up an item—including groceries—they've ordered online at their nearest Walmart store.[17] Both strengths and weaknesses should be examined from a customer perspective. Only those strengths that relate to satisfying customers should be considered true competitive advantages. Likewise, weaknesses that directly affect customer satisfaction should be considered disadvantages.

Opportunities and threats affect all organizations within an industry, market, or geographic region because they exist outside of and independently of the company. *Opportunities* refer to favorable conditions in the environment that could produce rewards for the organization if acted upon. Opportunities are situations that exist but must be exploited for the company to benefit from them. *Threats*, on the other hand, refer to barriers that could prevent the company

**SWOT analysis** Assessment of an organization's strengths, weaknesses, opportunities, and threats

Figure 2.5  **The Four-Cell SWOT Matrix**

Source: Adapted from Nigel F. Piercy, *Market-Led Strategic Change*. Copyright 1992, Butterworth-Heinemann Ltd., p. 371. Reprinted with permission.

## MARKETING DEBATE

### ISSUE: Should Drugstores Sell Tobacco Products?

When CVS announced it would stop selling tobacco products in 2014, the company acknowledged that this change in policy would cost it $2 billion in annual revenues. Still, CVS wanted to highlight its commitment to helping customers stay healthy—and, in fact, it renamed the company CVS Health to spotlight that mission. Some health advocates and state attorneys general praised the move and called on CVS's competitors to follow suit by dropping cigarettes, cigars, and other tobacco products.

However, Walgreens and other drug retailers have not followed CVS's lead. According to a Walgreen's statement: "We believe that if the goal is to truly reduce tobacco use in America, then the most effective thing retail pharmacies can do is address the root causes and help smokers quit." Walgreen's and other drug stores sell numerous smoking-cessation products, but they also tend to display packs of cigarettes near checkout counters, where they can catch the eye of shoppers.

Even if CVS's competitors decide to stop selling tobacco products, the change in policy might not make a huge difference in smoking rates because more cigarettes are sold at gas stations and convenience stores than in drug stores. Still, should stores that specialize in health-related goods and services continue to market tobacco products, which are legal but proven to be unhealthy?[a]

from reaching its objectives. Threats must be acted upon to prevent them from limiting the organization's capabilities. Opportunities and threats can stem from many sources within the environment. When a competitor's introduction of a new product threatens a company, a firm may require a defensive strategy. If the company can develop and launch a new product that meets or exceeds the competition's offering, it can transform the threat into an opportunity. It is important to use SWOT analysis to explore the internal organization and the marketing environment without judgment, focusing on issues that could lead to the greatest possibilities of success. This means using some resources for open-minded examination rather than looking for information to confirm current beliefs.[18]

## 2-3b First Mover and Late-Mover Advantage

An important factor that marketers must consider when identifying organizational resources and opportunities is whether the firm has the resources to cultivate a first-mover advantage, or is in a position to choose between developing a first-mover or late-mover advantage. A **first-mover advantage** is the ability of an innovative company to achieve long-term competitive advantages by being the first to offer a certain product in the marketplace. Being the first to enter a market helps a company build a reputation as a pioneer and market leader. Amazon and eBay were both first-mover start-ups that remain leaders as they grow and innovate ahead of the competition. For a first mover, the market is, for at least a short period, free of competition as potential competitors work to develop a rival product. Because consumers have no choice initially, being a first mover also helps establish customer brand loyalty in cases when switching to another brand later may be costly or difficult. The first to develop a new product can also protect secrets and technology through patents.

There are risks, however, of being the first to enter a market. There are usually high cost outlays associated with creating a new product, including market research, product development, production, and marketing—or buyer education—costs. Also, early sales growth may not match predictions if the firm overestimates demand or fails to target marketing efforts correctly. The company runs the risk that the product will fail due to market uncertainty, or that the product might not completely meet consumers' expectations or needs.

A **late-mover advantage** is the ability of later market entrants to achieve long-term competitive advantages by not being the first to offer a certain product in a marketplace.

**first-mover advantage** The ability of an innovative company to achieve long-term competitive advantages by being the first to offer a certain product in the marketplace

**late-mover advantage** The ability of later market entrants to achieve long-term competitive advantages by not being the first to offer a certain product in a marketplace

Competitors that enter the market later can benefit from the first mover's mistakes and have a chance to improve on the product design and marketing strategy. For example, Google was not the first search engine out there, but its ease-of-use and superior services soon made it the dominant player in the market. A late mover is also likely to have lower initial investment costs than the first mover because the first mover has already developed a distribution infrastructure and educated buyers about the product. By the time a late mover enters the market, there is also more data, and therefore more certainty, about product success. Case in point, the competition in the tablet computer market has become fierce. Although Nokia entered the market before Apple, the Apple iPad currently dominates the tablet computer market with a 27 percent share of the global market. Samsung, in second place with 17 percent, has capitalized on its late-mover advantage and is gaining market share, although the tablet market itself is slowing.[19]

There are disadvantages of being a late mover too, though. The company that entered the market first may have patents and other protections on its technology and trade secrets that prevent the late mover from producing a similar product. If customers who have already purchased the first mover's product believe that switching to the late mover's product will be expensive or time-consuming, it may be difficult for the late mover to gain market share.

It is important to note that the timing of entry into the market is crucial. Companies that are relatively quick to enter the market after the first mover have a greater chance of building market share and brand loyalty. Companies that enter the market later on, after many other companies have done so, face stronger competition and have more disadvantages.

## 2-4 DEVELOPING MARKETING OBJECTIVES AND MARKETING STRATEGIES

The next phase in strategic planning is the development of marketing objectives and marketing strategies, which are used to achieve marketing objectives. A **marketing objective** states what is to be accomplished through marketing activities. These objectives can be given in terms of product introduction, product improvement or innovation, sales volume, profitability, market share, pricing, distribution, advertising, or employee training activities. A marketing objective of Ritz-Carlton hotels, for example, is to have more than 90 percent of its customers indicate that they had a memorable experience at the hotel. Marketing objectives should be based on a careful study of the SWOT analysis, matching strengths to opportunities, eliminating weaknesses, and minimizing threats.

Marketing objectives should possess certain characteristics. First, a marketing objective should be expressed in clear, simple terms so all marketing and non-marketing personnel in the company understand exactly what they are trying to achieve. Second, an objective should be measurable, which allows the organization to track progress and compare outcomes against beginning benchmarks. For instance, if an objective is to increase market share by 10 percent in the United States, the company should be able to measure market share changes accurately to ensure that it is making gains toward that objective. Third, a marketing objective should specify a time frame for its accomplishment, such as six months or one year. Finally, a marketing objective should be consistent with both business-unit and corporate strategies. This ensures that the company's mission is carried out consistently at all levels of the organization by all personnel. Marketing objectives should be achievable and use company resources effectively, and successful accomplishment should contribute to the overall corporate strategy. A marketing strategy ensures that the firm has a plan in place to achieve its marketing objectives.

A **marketing strategy** is the selection of a target market and the creation of a marketing mix that will satisfy the needs of target-market members. A marketing strategy articulates the best use of the company's resources to achieve its marketing objectives. It also directs resource deployment so as to boost competitive advantage. Marketing strategy is the key variable in strengthening organizational competitiveness.[20]

**marketing objective**
A statement of what is to be accomplished through marketing activities

**marketing strategy** A plan of action for identifying and analyzing a target market and developing a marketing mix to meet the needs of that market

# GOING GREEN

## Campbell Soup's Recipe for Sustainability and Transparency

Famous for its iconic canned soups, the Campbell Soup Company now sees significant market opportunities in offering fresh foods and organic foods, as well as in being transparent about what's in its food products. The New Jersey–based company markets meals, soups, snacks, and beverages under such diverse brands as Campbell's, Swanson, V8, Prego, Pace, and Pepperidge Farm. Not only is the company aware that demographics are changing, it also recognizes that younger consumers are "shopping and thinking differently about food, and in a way that is influential."

Thus, after decades of focusing on processed foods, Campbell branched out into fresh foods by buying Bolthouse Farms, a leading producer of bagged carrots that also makes juices, smoothies, and salad dressings. Then Campbell made an even greener acquisition, buying

Plum Organics, which markets organic food products to parents who want healthy meals for their kids, "from the high chair to the lunch box." Plum, Bolthouse, and some other brands in the Campbell portfolio make sustainability a high priority, reducing the environmental footprint of their packaging and recycling as much as possible.

Campbell is also calling for federally mandated labeling of foods that contain genetically modified ingredients. The company isn't waiting for U.S. government action, nor is it waiting for other major food marketers to support GMO labeling in America. Campbell is already preparing labels to inform consumers about any of its foods made from genetically modified corn, soybeans, and other GMO crops. "We've always believed consumers have a right to know what's in their food," the CEO explains.[b]

Marketing strategies may need to be adapted as the environment changes. Some organizations fail to adapt their strategy in response to competition, consumer behavior, or other factors that may create the need for a new modified strategy.[21] For example, as tablet computers became popular, Microsoft had to adapt its strategy to compete in the market. Microsoft developed its Microsoft Surface tablet in response to competition and consumer demand.

## 2-4a Selecting the Target Market

Selecting an appropriate target market may be the most important decision a company makes in the strategic planning process and is crucial for strategic success. The target market must be chosen before the organization can adapt its marketing mix to meet the customers' needs and preferences. If a company selects the wrong target market, all other marketing decisions are likely to be in vain. The local U.K. TV channel London Live, for example, was launched with much fanfare and was targeted toward the youth market. Within five months of its launch, the station was struggling severely. The programs aired on London Live did not appear to resonate with younger audiences, prompting the network to try to reposition itself by changing its target market to focus on an older demographic.[22]

Careful and accurate target-market selection is crucial to productive marketing efforts. Products, and even whole companies, sometimes fail because marketers misidentify the best target market for their products. Organizations that try to be all things to all people rarely satisfy the needs of any customer group very well. Identification and analysis of a target market provide a foundation on which the company can develop its marketing mix.

When exploring possible target markets, marketing managers try to evaluate how entry could affect the company's sales, costs, and profits. Marketing information should be organized to facilitate a focus on the chosen target customers. Accounting and information systems, for example, can be used to track revenues and costs by customer (or customer group). The firm should offer rewards to managers and employees who focus efforts on profitable customers. Firms should develop teamwork skills that promote a flexible customer orientation that allows the firm to adapt to changes in the marketing environment.

Compare the target markets for the Aveeno and Skechers Sport products featured in the accompanying advertisements. Although both of these advertisements show personal products

**Target Market Selection**
Who are the target markets for Skechers and for Aveeno products? Are they targeting the same customers?

touted by celebrities, they are targeted at very different audiences. The ad for Skechers Sport shoes features boxing icon Sugar Ray Leonard lounging in a pair of Skechers Sport shoes. Shoes are a category of product that is more often targeted at women. However, this ad exhibits Skechers directly targeting male consumers by encouraging them to purchase athletic shoes endorsed by a famous athlete in a sport favored by men. The Aveeno ad also employs a celebrity to promote its gentle body lotion. The ad, which features a smiling Jennifer Anniston, conveys how Aveeno's lotion soothes sensitive skin and feels indulgent. The target market for this ad is women who have sensitive skin and prefer lotions that are effective, gentle, and not strongly scented.

Marketers should determine whether a selected target market aligns with the company's overall mission and objectives. If it does, they should assess whether the company has the appropriate resources to develop a marketing mix (product, price, promotion, and distribution) that meets the needs of that target market. The size and number of competitors already marketing products in potential target markets are concerns as well. For example, the market for mobile gaming has become so competitive that new entrants must carefully evaluate whether their products represent a new product that would be in demand by the target market or a genuine improvement over what already exists. This market is estimated to reach $60 billion by 2017.[23]

## 2-4b Creating the Marketing Mixes

Using all relevant information available to conduct in-depth research allows a firm to select the most appropriate target market, which is the basis for creating a marketing mix that satisfies the needs of that market. Tesla Motors selected a unique segment of the battery electric vehicle market and created a marketing mix of new technology that included not only a sleek electric automobile but also distribution direct from the manufacturer. It selected promotional methods and price points that suitably reflected the upper end of the electric car market.[24]

An organization should analyze demographic information, customer needs, preferences, and behaviors with respect to product design, pricing, distribution, and promotion. For example, research indicates that more men are engaging in grocery shopping than in years past, but they have different needs and preferences than women do. Food companies are taking advantage of this trend with new promotions and products targeting men. Kraft, for instance, has released more commercials featuring men (these commercials were traditionally dominated by women). Campbell's has introduced new product items such as Chunky Beer-n-cheese with Beef & Bacon flavor soup to appeal to millennial male shoppers.[25]

Marketing-mix decisions should have two additional characteristics: consistency and flexibility. All marketing-mix decisions should be consistent with the business-unit and corporate strategies. Such consistency allows the organization to achieve its objectives on all three levels of planning. Flexibility, on the other hand, permits the organization to alter the marketing mix in response to changes in market conditions, competition, and customer needs. Marketing strategy flexibility has a positive influence on organizational performance.

Utilizing the marketing mix as a tool set, a company can detail how it will achieve a sustainable competitive advantage. A **sustainable competitive advantage** is one that the competition cannot copy in the foreseeable future. Amazon maintains a sustainable competitive advantage in shipping because of its high-tech logistics system and extensive network of distribution centers (40 in the United States, with five more under construction), which allows the online giant to offer low prices and fast service. Many retailers struggle to compete with Amazon in terms of low-cost products and fast, reliable, and low-cost shipping.[26] Maintaining a sustainable competitive advantage requires flexibility in the marketing mix when facing uncertain competitive environments.

# 2-5 MANAGING MARKETING IMPLEMENTATION

**Marketing implementation** is the process of putting marketing strategies into action. Through planning, marketing managers provide purpose and direction for an organization's marketing efforts and are positioned to implement specific marketing strategies. The effective implementation of any and all marketing activities depends on a well-organized marketing department that is capable of motivating personnel, communicating effectively, employing good coordination efforts, and setting reasonable and attainable timetables for activity completion. Managers play a key role in creating desired outcomes through supervisory actions that provide rewards, reduce risks, and recognize behaviors that implement the marketing strategy.[27]

## 2-5a Organizing the Marketing Unit

The structure and relationships of a marketing unit—including lines of authority and communication that connect and coordinate individuals—strongly affect marketing activities. Companies that truly adopt the marketing concept develop an organizational culture that is based on a shared set of beliefs that places the customer's needs at the center of decisions about strategy and operations. Technology can help companies adopt the marketing concept. For example, firms increasingly use online tracking and related technology to gather and analyze information from every interaction with customers to improve their understanding of customers' needs and wants. Though some worry that such tracking may violate individual privacy, the "big data" generated and analyzed help marketers build detailed profiles for their target markets, which helps them identify and better satisfy the needs and wants of the target market.

**sustainable competitive advantage** An advantage that the competition cannot copy

**marketing implementation** The process of putting marketing strategies into action

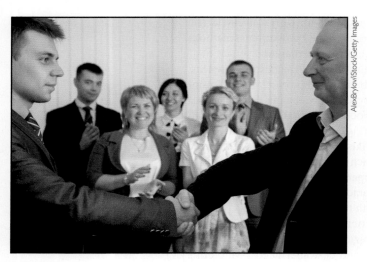

**Recognition**
Recognizing outstanding performance is one approach to motivating marketing personnel.

Firms must decide whether to centralize or decentralize operations, a choice that directly affects marketing decision making and strategy. In a **centralized organization**, top-level managers delegate little authority to lower levels. In a **decentralized organization**, decision-making authority is delegated as far down the chain of command as possible. In centralized organizations, marketing decisions are made at the top levels. However, centralized decision making may prove ineffective in firms that must respond quickly to fluctuations in customer demand. In these organizations, decentralized authority allows the company to adapt more rapidly to customer needs.

How effectively a company's marketing management can implement marketing strategies also depends on how the marketing unit is organized. Organizing marketing activities to align with the overall strategic marketing approach enhances organizational efficiency and performance. A marketing department should clearly outline the hierarchical relationships between personnel and who is responsible for performing certain activities and making decisions.

## 2-5b  Coordinating and Communicating

Marketing managers must coordinate diverse employee actions to achieve marketing objectives and work closely with management in many areas, including research and development, production, finance, accounting, and human resources to ensure that marketing activities align with other functions of the firm. They must also coordinate the activities of internal marketing staff with the marketing efforts of external organizations, including advertising agencies, resellers (wholesalers and retailers), researchers, and shippers. Marketing managers can improve coordination by making each employee aware of how his or her job relates to others and how his or her actions contribute to the achievement of marketing objectives. This requires effective communication and motivation of everyone involved in the marketing process.

Marketing managers must be in clear communication with the firm's upper-level management to ensure that they are aware of the firm's goals and achievements and that marketing activities are consistent with the company's overall goals and strategies. The marketing unit should also take steps to ensure that its activities are in sync with those of other departments, such as finance or human resources. For instance, marketing personnel should work with the production staff to design products that have the features that marketing research indicates are what customers desire.

It is important that communication flow up, from the front lines of the organization to upper management. Customer-contact employees are in a unique position to understand customers' wants and needs, and pathways should be open for them to communicate this knowledge to marketing managers. In this way, marketing managers can gain access to a rich source of information about what customers require, how products are selling, the effectiveness of marketing activities, and any issues with marketing implementation. Upward communication also allows marketing managers to understand the problems and requirements of lower-level employees, a critical group to keep satisfied, as they are the ones who interface with customers.

Training is an essential element of communicating with marketing employees. An effective training program provides employees with a forum to learn and ask questions, and results in employees who are empowered and can be held accountable for their performance. Many firms utilize a formalized, high-tech information system that tracks data and facilitates communication among marketing managers, sales managers, and sales personnel. Information systems expedite communications within and between departments and support other activities, such as allocating scarce organizational resources, planning, budgeting, sales analyses, performance evaluations, and report preparation.

**centralized organization**
A structure in which top-level managers delegate little authority to lower levels

**decentralized organization**
A structure in which decision-making authority is delegated as far down the chain of command as possible

To motivate marketing personnel, managers must address their employees' needs to maintain a high level of workplace satisfaction. Employee motivation and reward programs should be fair, ethical, and well understood to maintain a high level of workplace satisfaction. Employee rewards should also be tied to organizational goals. A firm can motivate its workers through a variety of methods, including by linking pay with performance, informing workers how their performance affects department and corporate results and their own compensation, providing appropriate and competitive compensation, implementing a flexible benefits program, and adopting a participative management approach.

Diversity in the workplace can complicate employee motivational strategies, as different generations and cultures may be motivated by different things. A specific employee might value autonomy or recognition more than a pay increase. Managers can compensate employees, not just with money and fringe benefits, but also with nonfinancial rewards, such as prestige or recognition, job autonomy, skill variety, task significance, increased feedback, or a more relaxed dress code. It is crucial for management to show that it takes pride in its workforce and to motivate employees to take pride in their company.

## 2-5c Establishing a Timetable for Implementation

Successful marketing implementation requires that employees know the specific activities for which they are responsible and the timetable for completing them. Establishing an implementation timetable involves several steps: (1) identifying the activities to be performed, (2) determining the time required to complete each activity, (3) separating the activities to be performed in sequence from those to be performed simultaneously, (4) organizing the activities in the proper order, and (5) assigning responsibility for completing each activity to one or more employees, teams, or managers. Completing all implementation activities on schedule requires tight coordination within the marketing unit and among other departments that contribute to marketing activities, such as production. Pinpointing which activities can be performed simultaneously will reduce the total amount of time needed to put a given marketing strategy into practice. Because scheduling can be a complicated task, some organizations use sophisticated computer programs to plan the timing of marketing activities. Even smaller businesses can use sophisticated software to help manage their marketing activities. San Francisco–based FruitGuys, for example, uses a software tool called Desk.com to monitor feedback, analyze trends, and respond in a timely manner. An estimated 9 percent of small businesses are using business intelligence tools to improve marketing and operations.[28]

## 2-6 EVALUATING MARKETING STRATEGIES

To achieve marketing objectives, marketing managers must evaluate marketing strategies effectively. **Strategic performance evaluation** consists of establishing performance standards, measuring actual performance, comparing actual performance with established standards, and modifying the marketing strategy, if needed.

## 2-6a Establishing Performance Standards

A **performance standard** is an expected level of performance against which actual performance can be compared. A performance standard might be a 20 percent reduction in customer complaints, a monthly sales quota of $150,000, or a 10 percent increase per month in new-customer accounts. Performance standards are derived from marketing objectives that are set while developing the marketing strategy. By establishing marketing objectives, a firm indicates what a marketing strategy is supposed to accomplish. Marketing objectives directly or indirectly set forth performance standards, usually in terms of sales, costs, or communication dimensions, such as brand awareness or product feature recall. Actual performance should be measured in similar terms to facilitate comparisons.

**strategic performance evaluation** Establishing performance standards, measuring actual performance, comparing actual performance with established standards, and modifying the marketing strategy, if needed

**performance standard** An expected level of performance against which actual performance can be compared

**Analyzing Actual Performance**
Products, such as services sold by Qlik, can help firms better analyze actual performance to improve their marketing plans.

## 2-6b Analyzing Actual Performance

The principal means by which a marketer can gauge whether a marketing strategy has been effective in achieving objectives is by analyzing the actual performance of the marketing strategy. Analyzing actual performance associated with communication dimensions is usually achieved by conducting customer research. Generally speaking, technological advancements have made it easier for firms to analyze actual performance. Firms such as Qlik, featured in the advertisement, can help companies analyze actual performance using high-tech tools. This ad states that Qlik's software models can help marketers discover relationships among data to find unexpected connections. The ad depicts a pencil with the iconic Big Ben as its writing point to symbolize a potential connection between tourism and education costs as an example of a connection that can be useful in marketing decision making. The ad emphasizes that the firm's data analytics solutions help marketers see "the whole story" and thus improve the quality of decision making and marketing implementation. In this section, we focus on two bases—sales and cost—for evaluating the actual performance of marketing strategies.

### Sales Analysis

**Sales analysis** uses sales figures to evaluate a firm's current performance. It is a common method of evaluation because sales data are readily available, at least in aggregate form, and can reflect the target market's reactions to a marketing mix. If sales spike after a particular marketing mix is implemented, marketers can be reasonably certain that the marketing mix was effective at reaching the target audience. Consider the sales spike that McDonald's experienced in the same quarter after it began selling its breakfast menu—including the much loved Egg McMuffin—all day long.[29] Information gleaned from sales data alone is not sufficient, however. To be useful, marketers must compare current sales data with forecasted sales, industry sales, specific competitors' sales, and the costs incurred from marketing efforts to achieve the sales volume. For example, knowing that a specialty store attained a $600,000 sales volume this year does not tell management whether its marketing strategy has succeeded. However, if managers know expected sales were $550,000, they are in a better position to determine the effectiveness of the firm's marketing efforts. In addition, if they know the marketing costs needed to achieve the $600,000 volume were 12 percent less than budgeted, they are in an even better position to analyze their marketing strategy precisely.

Although sales may be measured in several ways, the basic unit of measurement is the sales transaction. A sales transaction results in an order for a specified quantity of the organization's product sold under specified terms by a particular salesperson or sales team on a certain date. Organizations should record all information related to a transaction so that they can analyze sales in terms of dollar volume or market share. Firms frequently use dollar volume in their sales analyses because the dollar is a common denominator of sales, costs, and profits.

**sales analysis** Analysis of sales figures to evaluate a firm's performance

A marketing manager who uses dollar-volume analysis should factor out the effects of price changes, which can skew the numbers by making it seem that more or fewer sales have been made than is the actual case.

A firm's market share is the firm's sales of a product stated as a percentage of industry sales of competing products. Market share analysis lets a company compare its marketing strategy with competitors' strategies. The primary reason for using market share analysis is to estimate whether sales changes have resulted from the firm's marketing strategy or from uncontrollable environmental forces. When a company's sales volume declines but its share of the market stays the same, the marketer can assume that industry sales declined because of outside factors. However, if a company experiences a decline in both sales and market share, it should consider making changes to its marketing strategy to make it more effective.

Even though market share analysis can be helpful in evaluating the performance of a marketing strategy, the user must exercise caution when interpreting results. When attributing a sales decline to uncontrollable factors, a marketer must keep in mind that factors in the external marketing environment do not impact all firms equally because firms have varying strategies and objectives. Changes in the strategies of one company can affect the market shares of one or all companies in that industry. Within an industry, the entrance of new firms, the launch of new products by competing firms, or the demise of established products also affects a firm's market share. Market share analysts should attempt to account for these effects. In one case, Apple caused its competitors to reevaluate their marketing strategies when it introduced the iPad and iPhone, spurring competitor innovation and revised marketing strategies.

## Marketing Cost Analysis

Although sales analysis is critical for evaluating the performance of a marketing strategy, it provides only a partial picture. A marketing strategy that successfully generates sales may nevertheless be deemed ineffective if it is extremely costly. A firm must take into account the marketing costs associated with a strategy to gain a complete understanding of its effectiveness at achieving a desired sales level. **Marketing cost analysis** breaks down and classifies costs to determine which are associated with specific marketing efforts. Comparing costs of previous marketing activities with results allows a marketer to allocate the firm's marketing resources better in the future. Marketing cost analysis lets a company evaluate the performance of marketing strategy by comparing sales achieved and costs sustained. By pinpointing exactly where a company incurs costs, this form of analysis can help isolate profitable or unprofitable customers, products, and geographic areas.

A company that understands and manages its costs appropriately has a competitive advantage. Evidence shows that a low-cost provider is in a position to engage in aggressive price competition. The Internet offers low-cost marketing options, such as e-mail, social media, and viral videos. It is also the medium where it is easiest for consumers to compare prices, making it a suitable medium to engage in price competition. Bazaarvoice is a company that helps firms create more effective marketing strategies by utilizing social media, targeting key markets, and allowing customers to create and share information about products and brands. Firms like Bazaarvoice help companies efficiently use new technological tools in marketing to maximize impact and keep costs low, while also creating methods for marketers to track customer responses to marketing activities.[30]

One way to analyze costs is by comparing a company's costs with industry averages. Many companies check the amount of money they spend on marketing efforts and other operations against average levels for the industry to identify areas in need of improvement. For example, a business could compare its advertising costs as a percentage of its sales with the industry average. A company might determine it spends 6 percent of its sales on advertising, while the industry average is 2 percent. When looking at industry averages, however, a company should take into account its own unique situation. The company's costs can differ from the industry average for several reasons, including its own marketing objectives, cost structure, geographic location, types of customers, and scale of operations. When comparing its

**marketing cost analysis**
Analysis of costs to determine which are associated with specific marketing efforts

## How much do companies spend on marketing?

| Company | Total revenue | Percent of revenue spent on marketing |
|---|---|---|
| salesforce.com | $2,170,000,000 | 53% |
| Twitter | $614,110,000 | 44% |
| Linkedin | $774,410,000 | 35% |
| Tempur + Sealy | $619,900,000 | 21% |
| Microsoft | $51,810,000,000 | 18% |

SNAPSHOT

Source: Vital., "Content Marketing Strategy: What Percent of Revenue Do Publicly Traded Companies Spend on Marketing and Sales?" Infographic by Sarah Brady, https://vtldesign.com/inbound-marketing/content-marketing-strategy/percent-of-revenue-spent-on-marketing-sales/ (accessed February 1, 2016).

advertising costs with the industry average, for instance, the company just mentioned might be spending a larger proportion on advertising because it is a smaller company competing against industry giants. Or perhaps this firm's advertising objectives are much more aggressive than those of other firms in the industry.

Costs can be categorized in different ways when performing marketing cost analysis. One way is to identify which ones are affected by sales or production volume. Some costs are fixed, meaning they do not change between different units of time, regardless of a company's production or sales volume. Fixed costs are variables such as rent and employees' salaries, which are not affected by fluctuations in production or sales. Fixed costs are generally not very illuminating when determining how to use marketing funds more effectively. For example, it does little good to know that $80,000 is spent for rent annually. The marketing analyst must conduct additional research to determine that, of the $80,000 spent on rent, $32,000 is spent on facilities associated with marketing efforts.

Some costs are directly attributable to production and sales volume. These costs are known as variable costs and are stated as a per quantity (or unit) cost. Variable costs include the cost to produce or sell each unit of a specific product, such as the materials and labor, or the amount of commissions that are paid to salespeople when they sell products.

Another way to categorize costs is based on whether or not they can be linked to a specific business function. Costs that can be linked are allocated, using one or several criteria, to the functions that they support. If the firm spends $80,000 to rent space for production, storage, and sales facilities, the total rental cost can be allocated to each of the three functions using a measurement, such as square footage. Some costs cannot be assigned according to any logical criteria. These are costs such as interest paid on loans, taxes paid to the government, and the salaries of top management.

## 2-6c Comparing Actual Performance with Performance Standards and Making Changes, If Needed

When comparing actual performance with established performance standards, a firm may find that it exceeded or failed to meet performance standard benchmarks. When actual performance exceeds performance standards, marketers will likely be satisfied and a marketing strategy will be deemed effective. It is important that a firm seek to gain an understanding of why the strategy was effective, because this information may allow marketers to adjust the strategy tactically to be even more effective.

When actual performance does not meet performance standards, marketers should seek to understand why a marketing strategy was less effective than expected. Perhaps a marketing mix variable, such as price, was not ideally suited to the target market, which could result in lower performance. Both environmental changes and aggressive competitive behavior can both cause a marketing strategy to underperform.

When a marketer finds that a strategy is underperforming expectations, a question sometimes arises as to whether the marketing objective, against which performance is measured, is realistic. After studying the problem, the firm may find that the marketing objective is indeed unrealistic. In this case, marketers must alter the marketing objective to bring it in line with more sensible expectations. It is also possible that the marketing strategy is underfunded, which can result in lower performance.

## 2-7 CREATING THE MARKETING PLAN

The strategic planning process ultimately yields a marketing strategy that is the framework for a **marketing plan**, a written document that specifies the marketing activities to be performed to implement and evaluate the organization's marketing strategies. Developing a clear and well-written marketing plan, though time-consuming, is important. It provides a uniform marketing vision for the firm and is the basis for internal communications. It delineates marketing responsibilities and tasks and outlines schedules for implementation. The plan presents objectives and specifies how resources are to be allocated to achieve them. Finally, the marketing plan helps marketing managers monitor and evaluate the performance of a marketing strategy.

A single marketing plan can be developed and applied to the business as a whole, but it is more likely that a company will choose to develop multiple marketing plans, with each relating to a specific brand or product. Multiple marketing plans are part of a larger strategic business plan and are used to implement specific parts of the overall strategy.

Organizations use many different formats when producing a marketing plan. They may be written for strategic business units, product lines, individual products or brands, or specific markets. The key is to make sure that the marketing plan aligns with corporate and business-unit strategies and is accessible to and shared with all key employees. A marketing plan represents a critical element of a company's overall strategy development, and it should reflect the company's culture and be representative of all functional specialists in the firm.

Marketing planning and implementation are closely linked in successful companies. The marketing plan provides a framework to stimulate thinking and provide strategic direction. Implementation is an adaptive response to day-to-day issues, opportunities, and unanticipated situations—such as an economic slowdown that dampens sales—that cannot be incorporated into marketing plans.

Table 2.1 describes the major parts of a typical marketing plan. Each component builds on the last. The first component is the executive summary, which provides an overview of the entire marketing plan so that readers can quickly identify the key issues and their roles in the planning and implementation process. The executive summary includes an introduction, an explanation of the major aspects of the plan, and a statement about the costs.

The next component of the marketing plan is the environmental analysis, which supplies information about the company's current situation with respect to the marketing environment, the target market, and the firm's current objectives and performance. The environmental analysis includes an assessment of all the environmental factors—competitive, economic, political, legal, regulatory, technological, and sociocultural—that can affect marketing activities. It then examines the current needs of the organization's target markets. In the final section of the environmental analysis, the company evaluates its marketing objectives and performance to ensure that objectives are consistent with the changing marketing environment. The next component of the marketing plan is the SWOT analysis (strengths, weaknesses, opportunities, and threats), which uses the information gathered in the environmental analysis.

The marketing objectives section of the marketing plan states what the company wants to accomplish through marketing activities, using the SWOT analysis as a guide of where the firm stands in the market. The marketing strategies component outlines how the firm plans to achieve its marketing objectives and discusses the company's target market selection(s) and

**marketing plan** A written document that specifies the activities to be performed to implement and control the organization's marketing strategies

Table 2.1  **Components of the Marketing Plan**

| Plan Component | Component Summary | Highlights |
| --- | --- | --- |
| Executive Summary | One- to two-page synopsis of the entire marketing plan | 1. Stress key points<br>2. Include one to three key points that make the company unique |
| Environmental Analysis | Information about the company's current situation with respect to the marketing environment | 1. Assessment of marketing environment factors<br>2. Assessment of target market(s)<br>3. Assessment of current marketing objectives and performance |
| SWOT Analysis | Assessment of the organization's strengths, weaknesses, opportunities, and threats | 1. Strengths of the company<br>2. Weaknesses of the company<br>3. Opportunities in the environment and industry<br>4. Threats in the environment and industry |
| Marketing Objectives | Specification of the company's marketing objectives | 1. Qualitative measures of what is to be accomplished<br>2. Quantitative measures of what is to be accomplished |
| Marketing Strategies | Outline of how the company will achieve its objectives | 1. Target market(s)<br>2. Marketing mix |
| Marketing Implementation | Outline of how the company will implement its marketing strategies | 1. Marketing organization<br>2. Activities and responsibilities<br>3. Implementation timetable |
| Performance Evaluation | Explanation of how the company will evaluate the performance of the implemented plan | 1. Performance standards<br>2. Financial controls<br>3. Monitoring procedures (audits) |

marketing mix. The marketing implementation component of the plan outlines how marketing strategies will be implemented. The success of the marketing strategy depends on the feasibility of marketing implementation. Finally, the performance evaluation section establishes the standards for how results will be measured and evaluated, and what actions the company should take to reduce the differences between planned and actual performance. It is important to note that most organizations use their own unique formats and terminology to describe the marketing plan. Every marketing plan is, and should be, unique to the organization for which it was created. Creating and implementing a marketing plan allows the organization to achieve its marketing objectives and its business-unit and corporate goals. However, a marketing plan is only as good as the information it contains and the effort and creativity that went into its development. Therefore, the importance of having a good marketing information system that generates robust and reliable data cannot be overstated. Equally important is the role of managerial judgment throughout the strategic planning process. Although the creation of a marketing plan is an important milestone in strategic planning, it is by no means the final step. To succeed, a company must have a plan that is closely followed, yet flexible enough to allow for adjustments to reflect the changing marketing environment.

# Summary

## 2-1  Explain the strategic planning process.

Through the process of strategic planning, a company identifies or establishes an organizational mission and goals, corporate strategy, marketing objectives, marketing strategy, and a marketing plan. To achieve its marketing objectives, an organization must develop a marketing strategy, which includes identifying a target market and creating a plan of action for developing, distributing, promoting, and pricing products that meet the needs of customers in that target market. The strategic planning process ultimately yields the framework for a marketing plan, a written document that specifies the activities to be performed for implementing and controlling an organization's marketing activities.

## 2-2 Understand the importance of a firm's mission statement and corporate and business-unit strategy.

An organization's goals should align with its mission statement—a long-term view, or vision, of what the organization wants to become. A well-formulated mission statement gives an organization a clear purpose and direction, distinguishes it from competitors, provides direction for strategic planning, and fosters a focus on customers. An organization's goals, which focus on the end results sought, guide the remainder of its planning efforts.

Corporate strategy determines the means for using resources in the areas of production, finance, research and development, human resources, and marketing to reach the organization's goals. Business-unit strategy focuses on strategic business units (SBUs)—divisions, product lines, or other profit centers within the parent company used to define areas for consideration in a specific strategic marketing plan. The Boston Consulting Group's market growth/market share matrix integrates a company's products or SBUs into a single, overall matrix for evaluation to determine appropriate strategies for individual products and business units. Based on its analysis, a firm may choose one or more competitive strategies: market penetration, market development, product development, and/or diversification.

## 2-3 Describe how analyzing organizational resources and the marketing environment can help identify opportunities and create competitive advantage.

The marketing environment, including economic, competitive, political, legal and regulatory, sociocultural, and technological forces, can affect the resources available to a company to create favorable opportunities. Resources may help a firm develop core competencies, which are things that a company does extremely well, sometimes so well that it gives the company an advantage over its competition. When the right combination of circumstances and timing permits an organization to take action toward reaching a particular target market, a market opportunity exists. Strategic windows are temporary periods of optimal fit between the key requirements of a market and the particular capabilities of a company competing in that market. When a company matches a core competency to opportunities it has discovered in the marketplace, it is said to have a competitive advantage. A marketer can use SWOT analysis to assess a firm's ability to achieve a competitive advantage.

If marketers want to understand how the timing of entry into a marketplace can create competitive advantage, they can examine the comparative benefits of first-mover and late-mover advantages.

## 2-4 Explore how a firm develops marketing objectives and strategies that contribute to overall objectives.

The next phase of strategic planning involves the development of marketing objectives and strategies. Marketing objectives state what is to be accomplished through marketing activities, and should be consistent with both business-unit and corporate strategies. Marketing strategies, the most detailed and specific of the three levels of strategy, are composed of two elements: the selection of a target market and the creation of a marketing mix that will satisfy the needs of the target-market members. The selection of a target market serves as the basis for the creation of the marketing mix to satisfy the needs of that market. Marketing-mix decisions should also be consistent with business-unit and corporate strategies and be flexible enough to respond to changes in market conditions, competition, and customer needs. Different elements of the marketing mix can be changed to accommodate different marketing strategies.

## 2-5 Identify what is necessary to effectively manage the implementation of marketing strategies.

Marketing implementation is the process of executing marketing strategies. Through planning, marketing managers provide purpose and direction for an organization's marketing efforts. Marketing managers must understand the problems and elements of marketing implementation before they can effectively implement specific marketing activities.

The marketing unit must have a coherent internal structure in order to organize direct marketing efforts. In a centralized organization, top-level managers delegate very little authority to lower levels, whereas in decentralized organizations, decision-making authority is delegated as far down the chain of command as possible. Marketing managers must also be able to effectively coordinate marketing activities. This entails both coordinating the activities of the marketing staff within the firms and integrating those activities with the marketing actions of external organizations that are also involved in implementing the marketing strategies. Proper communication should move both down (from top management to the lower-level employees) and up (from lower-level employees to top management). Marketing managers learn marketing employees' needs and develop different methods to motivate those employees to help the organization meet its goals.

Finally, successful marketing implementation requires that a timetable be established. Establishment of an implementation timetable involves several steps and ensures that employees know the specific activities for which they are responsible and the timeline for completing each activity. Completing all activities on schedule requires tight coordination among departments. Many organizations use sophisticated computer programs to plan the timing of marketing activities.

## 2-6 Describe the four major elements of strategic performance evaluation.

Strategic performance evaluation consists of establishing performance standards, analyzing actual performance, comparing actual performance with established standards, and modifying the marketing strategy when needed. When actual performance is compared with performance standards, marketers must determine whether a discrepancy exists and, if so, whether it requires corrective action, such as changing the performance standard or improving actual performance.

Two possible ways to evaluate the actual performance of marketing strategies are sales analysis and marketing cost analysis. Sales analysis uses sales figures to evaluate a firm's current performance. It is the most common method of evaluation because sales data are a good indication of the target market's reaction to a marketing mix. Marketing cost analysis breaks down and classifies costs to determine which are associated with specific marketing efforts. Marketing cost analysis helps marketers decide how to best allocate the firm's marketing resources.

## 2-7 Describe the development of a marketing plan.

A key component of marketing planning is the development of a marketing plan, which outlines all the activities necessary to implement marketing strategies. The plan fosters communication among employees, assigns responsibilities and schedules, specifies how resources are to be allocated to achieve objectives, and helps marketing managers monitor and evaluate the performance of a marketing strategy.

---

**Go to www.cengagebrain.com for resources to help you master the content in this chapter as well as for materials that will expand your marketing knowledge!**

---

# Important Terms

strategic marketing
    management 34
strategic planning 34
mission statement 35
corporate strategy 36
strategic business
    unit (SBU) 37
market 37
market share 38

market growth/market
    share matrix 38
core competencies 41
market opportunity 41
strategic windows 41
competitive
    advantage 41
SWOT analysis 42
first-mover advantage 43

late-mover advantage 43
marketing objective 44
marketing strategy 44
sustainable competitive
    advantage 47
marketing
    implementation 47
centralized
    organization 48

decentralized
    organization 48
strategic performance
    evaluation 49
performance standard 49
sales analysis 50
marketing cost
    analysis 51
marketing plan 53

# Discussion and Review Questions

1. Identify the major components of strategic planning, and explain how they are interrelated.
2. Explain how an organization can create a competitive advantage at the corporate strategy level and at the business-unit strategy level.
3. How might a planner decide on competitive growth strategies using tools such as the market growth/market share matrix (Figure 2.3) and product-market matrix (Figure 2.4)?
4. What are some issues to consider in analyzing a company's resources and opportunities? How do these issues affect marketing objectives and marketing strategy?
5. What is SWOT analysis and why is it important?
6. How can an organization make its competitive advantages sustainable over time? How difficult is it to create sustainable competitive advantages?

7. How should organizations set marketing objectives?
8. What are the two major parts of a marketing strategy?
9. When considering the strategic planning process, what factors influence the development of a marketing strategy?
10. Identify and explain the major managerial actions that are a part of managing the implementation of marketing strategies.
11. Which element of the strategic planning process plays a major role in the establishment of performance standards? Explain.
12. When assessing actual performance of a marketing strategy, should a marketer perform marketing cost analysis? Why or why not?
13. Identify and explain the major components of a marketing plan.

# Video Case 2.1

## BoltBus Offers Affordable Transportation for Tech-Savvy Consumers

Bus service had a stodgy, old-fashioned image when BoltBus began developing a new marketing plan in 2007. Co-owned by Greyhound Lines and Peter Pan Bus Lines, BoltBus noticed that traditional full-fare bus companies were losing market share, and bus travel was on the decline. Time-pressured, price-conscious consumers simply didn't want to sit on a bus for hours or even days as it rattled from stop to stop along a lengthy route. Some of these consumers switched to discount airlines, searching hard for bargain fares to their destination. Others chose to hop on buses operated by a new breed of low-fare, city-to-city bus companies. Instead of operating from existing bus terminals, these bus companies kept costs low by picking up and dropping off passengers at designated street corners in each city.

The marketers at Bolt-Bus recognized a market opportunity in the making. They planned to shake off the outdated image of inter-city bus service and create a new premium express bus system for 21st century travelers on a budget. The brand they chose, BoltBus, conveyed the key benefit of point-to-point speed, contrasted with the old strategy of long routes connecting multiple cities and towns.

©iStockphoto.com/wdstock

Looking at the market, they recognized that college students, young professionals, and young families were interested in comfortable, affordable alternatives to long car trips or pricier air, rail, and bus transportation. These tech-savvy consumers were accustomed to using computers and smartphones for all kinds of daily tasks, including price comparisons. So BoltBus decided to sell tickets through a dedicated website, bypassing the more costly method of selling tickets at bus stations. And, like competitors, BoltBus planned to avoid city bus stations in favor of curbside service, both to keep costs down and to make travel more convenient for customers.

One of the most important decisions BoltBus's marketers made was to keep fares low. During promotions, a limited number of tickets are priced as low as $1 for a one-way trip, an eye-catching figure for travelers on a budget. BoltBus adjusts its prices depending on demand and other factors. In general,

the earlier customers buy their tickets, the lower the bus fare. Taking into account low promotional fares, the average Bolt-Bus fare is about $20, quite affordable compared with typical intercity rail and air fares.

The marketers also decided to differentiate BoltBus by upgrading the experience to counter the perception that using intercity bus service means riding dingy, noisy old vehicles. BoltBus's gleaming red deluxe buses feature generous leg room, electric plugs at every seat for powering laptops and phones, and Wi-Fi service to keep passengers connected throughout the trip. BoltBus drivers are professional and friendly, adding to the sociable atmosphere once the bus gets rolling. BoltBus also offers a rewards program to reinforce customer loyalty. For convenience, customers can use BoltBus's BusTracker app to see when a bus will arrive and track its progress in approaching each stop.

Originally, BoltBus targeted consumers traveling between major East Coast cities, routing buses through a few suburban areas at the suggestion of customers. After establishing a reputation for affordable, comfortable, and speedy bus service, BoltBus expanded to the West Coast, scheduling service to Los Angeles, San Francisco, Portland, Seattle, and other cities. It also began offering limited service to Las Vegas, part of the long-range plan to add routes to interior cities.

Meanwhile, BoltBus's competitors weren't standing still. Megabus, founded a year earlier than BoltBus, operates luxury double-decker express buses equipped with Wi-Fi and power plugs at every seat. Year after year, Megabus has added intercity routes. Today, it serves more than 120 U.S. cities, coast to coast. Other competitors focus on specific city pairs, such as New York and Boston or Philadelphia and New York.

Greyhound, one of BoltBus's owners, has started a premium discount service called Greyhound Express, featuring free Wi-Fi and power plugs on deluxe buses traveling point-to-point between more than a dozen U.S. cities. In addition, Greyhound operates Crucero Direct, a bus service targeting Hispanic-American consumers who travel between Los

Angeles, San Ysidro, and San Diego. It also operates special bus service from major cities to casinos in New Jersey, Connecticut, and Las Vegas.

BoltBus and its competitors have attracted so many customers that the bus ridership is no longer in decline. In fact, bus transportation is now the fastest-growing method of travel between U.S. cities. Watch for more growth as BoltBus drives ahead with future marketing plans.[31]

## Questions for Discussion

1. How would you describe BoltBus's strengths, weaknesses, opportunities, and threats?
2. Where does BoltBus fit within Greyhound's levels of strategic planning? What challenges does this pose for Greyhound?
3. Why was BoltBus's selection of a target market so vital to the success of its marketing strategy?

# Case 2.2

## Netflix Uses Technology to Change How We Watch Videos

When Netflix was founded in 1997, the movie rental giant Blockbuster had thousands of stores from coast to coast, filled to the rafters with videocassettes ready for immediate rental to customers. Netflix had a different vision from this well-established, well-financed competitor. Looking at the recent development of DVD technology, Netflix saw an opportunity to change the way consumers rent movies. The entrepreneurial firm built its marketing strategy around the convenience and low cost of renting DVDs by mail, for one low monthly subscription fee.

Instead of going to a local store to pick out a movie on videocassette, subscribers logged onto the Netflix website to browse the DVD offerings and click to rent. Within a day or two, the DVD would arrive in the customer's mailbox, complete with a self-mailer to return the DVD. And, unlike any other movie rental service, Netflix customers were invited to rate each movie, after which they'd see recommendations tailored to their individual interests.

Fast-forward to the 21st century. Videocassettes are all but obsolete, and Blockbuster, once the dominant brand in movie rentals, is no longer in business. By eliminating the need for brick-and-mortar stores, Netflix has minimized its costs and extended its reach to any place that has postal service and Internet access. The company still rents DVDs by mail, but it has also taken advantage of changes in technology to add video streaming on demand. Now customers can stream movies and television programs to computers, television sets, videogame consoles, DVD players, smartphones, and other web-enabled devices. One plus: Streaming a movie costs Netflix less per customer than paying the postage to deliver and return a DVD to that customer.

Netflix made technology a core competency from the very beginning. Because the business has always been web-based, it can electronically monitor customer activity and analyze everything that customers view or click on. With this data, it can fine-tune the website, determine which movies are most popular among which segments, prepare for peak periods of online activity, and refine the recommendations it makes based on each individual's viewing history and interests. The company also uses its technical know-how to be sure the website looks good on any size screen, from a tiny smartphone to a large-screen television.

A few years ago, planning for a significant rise in demand for streaming entertainment, Netflix decided against investing in expanded systems for this purpose. Instead, it arranged for Amazon Web Services to provide the networking power for streaming. Now, on a typical night, Netflix streaming occupies up to 20,000 servers in Amazon data centers. Demand is so strong, in fact, that Netflix streaming accounts for about one-third of *all* Internet traffic to North American homes during the evening.

Although Blockbuster is no longer a competitive threat, Netflix does face competition from Amazon's own video streaming service, as well as from Hulu, YouTube, and others that stream entertainment content. It also competes with other entertainment providers, including cable, satellite, and broadcast television. To differentiate itself, Netflix has commissioned exclusive programming such as *House of Cards, Arrested Development*, and *Orange Is the New Black*. The cost to produce such programs runs to hundreds of millions of dollars. Yet Netflix plans to continue pouring money into exclusive content because of the payoff in positioning, positive publicity, and customer retention.

In addition, the way Netflix releases its exclusive programming reflects its in-depth knowledge of customer behavior. The company found, through data analysis, that customers often indulge in "binge watching" for a series they like, viewing episodes one after another in a short time. Based on this research, Netflix launched all 13 episodes of the inaugural season of *House of Cards* at one time, an industry first. Executives gathered at headquarters to monitor the introduction, cheering as thousands of customers streamed episode after episode. By the end of the first weekend, many customers had watched the entire series and shared their excitement via social media, encouraging others to subscribe and watch. When Netflix won multiple Emmy Awards for *House of Cards* later that year, it was another first—the first time any Internet company had been honored for the quality of its original programming.

One key measure of Netflix's growth is change in the number of monthly subscribers. At the end of 2010, it had 20 million monthly subscribers. These days, it serves more than 75 million subscribers in 190 countries, many of whom only stream entertainment on demand. Looking ahead, the company is expanding the amount of original programming it offers and exploring opportunities to market its services in China.[32]

### Questions for Discussion

1. When Netflix originally entered the movie rental business, was it competing on the basis of a first-mover advantage or a late-mover advantage? Did it rely on the same advantage when it began streaming original content?
2. How does Netflix use its marketing mix to create a sustainable competitive advantage?
3. What performance standards do you think Netflix uses to evaluate the outcome of its marketing strategies?

# Strategic Case 1

## Sseko Designs: Using Marketing for Social Impact

Sseko Designs is a for-profit company that was founded to engage in social entrepreneurship. Social entrepreneurship occurs when an entrepreneur founds an organization with the purpose of creating social value. Sseko understands that to be successful, it has to create an effective marketing strategy to serve its target market and develop a marketing mix that provides value to consumers. Sseko's social mission is to create economic change through better income for Ugandan women. To be successful the company must earn profits in order to create economic opportunities in East Africa.

Sseko's story started when founder Liz Forkin-Bohannon quit her job at a global communications firm. Afterward, she traveled to Uganda and was stunned by the contrast between the five-star hotels and the poverty she saw on the streets. After some investigation, Liz learned that Ugandan women who finished schooling were given a nine-month break before college to go back to their villages and earn enough money to pay for tuition. Unfortunately, most women could not secure jobs with adequate wages. This means 98 percent of Ugandan women do not complete higher education.

After conferring with a Ugandan friend, Liz realized that what would make the biggest difference would be to provide the women with jobs that would allow them to earn their own money for college. What she needed next was not only a product that Ugandan women could develop and sell, but also a good marketing strategy that included opportunities for Ugandan women. During her college years, Liz disliked the flapping noise of traditional sandals, so she redesigned them by purchasing rubber flip-flop bottoms and tying them with ribbon. This was a low-cost way to reduce the flapping noise and allowed

adisa/iStock/Getty Images

Liz to use the ribbons to tie the sandals in creative ways. Her ribbon sandals quickly caught the eye of other students who viewed them as fashionable. This product was also unique and would give Liz's company the opportunity to benefit from first-mover advantages.

Liz believed she could improve upon her original design using materials obtained locally. She was mindful that to be successful, the product would have to be of interest to a target market. A few years earlier Toms Shoes had introduced a social enterprise using a one-to-one model in which for each pair of fashionable shoes a customer bought, another pair would be donated to children in need. The enterprise was successful, proving that these types of products could gain customer acceptance. After developing a step-by-step manual, Liz formulated a strategy for a work-study model for Ugandan women who showed college potential. She would offer women employment during the nine-month period they had to earn money for college. The women would make sandals and other products that could be sold to consumers in the United States. The organization would place 50 percent of the women's salaries into a university savings account. At the end of the nine months Sseko would match the savings collected 100 percent with a scholarship. Sseko Designs (pronounced say-ko from the Lugandan word for laughter) was officially born.

Now Liz and her husband had to convince buyers of their products' value and potential market acceptance. Together they traveled the nation for six months in their Honda Odyssey minivan to try and convince stores to purchase sandals from Sseko Designs. The Bohannons adopted the following organizational mission statement: *Sseko Designs uses fashion to provide employment and scholarship opportunities to women pursuing their dreams and overcoming poverty.*

## Marketing Strategy

The Bohannons began to zero in on a target market who were interested in fashionable sandals and were also concerned about supporting a social cause. Now that the Bohannons had a product, they needed to focus on other marketing mix variables. Their pricing strategy needed to cover the costs of sandals and tuition. The sandals themselves cost $47 for the rubber and leather bases and $8–$13 for the straps. What consumers seemed to like most about the shoes is that the straps are interchangeable and can be changed out to create new fashions. The shoes come with two sets of interchangeable ribbons and sell for approximately $65.

Within a year Sseko Designs obtained its first break when Martha Stewart included the sandals in her holiday gift guide. The target market sees value in the product not only for its unique design but for its ability to make a difference. This has been critical in the development of mutually beneficial relationships between Sseko Designs and its customers.

Retailers were also interested in the social enterprise. Two companies in Portland, Oregon, saw the sandals as a great opportunity. They display the products with a point-of-purchase card that users can scan with their smartphones. That connects customers to YouTube videos demonstrating the various ways the ribbons can be tied.

The success of Sseko Designs enabled the company to expand into other areas, including accessories and handbags. While the sandals and accessories are developed in the company's Uganda workshop, Sseko Designs has also partnered with different groups in East Africa to develop crafted goods. This has allowed it to extend its distribution network beyond Uganda into other East African countries. Workers are paid $200 to $250 monthly compared to an average wage of $60. With half of this money being saved in a college fund, Sseko Designs matches the savings at the end of the nine-month period so that enough funds are available to cover college tuition. Today Sseko Designs products are sold online and by 400 retailers in North America.

## Shark Tank

On February 13, 2015, Liz and Ben Bohannon presented Sseko to the panel of "sharks" on the reality television show *The Shark Tank*. The panel consisted of self-made billionaires including Dallas Mavericks owner Mark Cuban, real estate maven Barbara Corcoran, and venture capitalist Kevin O'Leary. The couple offered the sharks a 10 percent stake in the firm for a $300,000 investment. At the time of the episode, Sseko sales had surpassed $3 million. Company strengths included a committed workforce, strong consumer support for its mission, an established distribution network, and the unique and fashionable nature of its products. On the other hand, Sseko also had several weaknesses. The firm suffered losses in 2014 and 2015, and it was uncertain when profitability would be reached. The Bohannons explained that the reason for the loss is that they were putting more money into development and hiring more salespeople. They expressed their belief that as more Americans learn about Sseko, sales would increase and the firm would recoup its profits.

A negative cash flow often turns off investors. Of greatest concern to the sharks was the belief that the Bohannons had overvalued their business. The Bohannons explained they could not lower their valuation due to deals they had struck with four private investors. Kevin O'Leary told the couple he would require 50 percent equity for him to invest the full amount. The Bohannons rejected the deal.

Liz Forkin-Bohannon was not discouraged. She knew that 6 million people watch *Shark Tank*, and many would support their social mission. The exposure on the show resulted in a 500-fold increase in traffic on their website and a 1,000 percent increase in sales for the month of February.

The show also gave Liz the chance to defend their marketing model. She believes that the prevailing view among the sharks is that they should earn profit quickly and then use some of those profits to donate to charity. However, Liz claims they are not in the business of philanthropy. She points out that millennials (also known as Generation Y and born during the 1980s and 1990s) tend to be less concerned with big brand names and more concerned with the story behind the brand. Research shows that the millennial generation is more engaged with brands and have a more personal connection to them. Brands that support a cause consumers care about are viewed favorably.

## The Future

Sseko Designs has already had a major impact on Uganda. Not only is it the largest footwear manufacturer, it also serves to empower women. Those women that complete the nine-month program learn important skills such as quality control and design that could help them in their future careers. Sseko has sent 60 girls to college and employed another 120.

The trick for Sseko Designs is to maintain a strong marketing strategy that will allow it to remain profitable. While it is not easy to incorporate social impact into their marketing model, the Bohannons feel their venture will succeed. They hope to eventually build a production base for Sseko that would be able to produce products for both small and large brands.[33]

## Questions for Discussion

1. How would you define the target market for Sseko Design sandals?
2. Explain how the marketing mix that Liz developed helped reach her target market.
3. Are there any advantages to Sseko in being a for-profit company that is trying to engage in social entrepreneurship in building its brand?

# NOTES

[1] Caroline Winter, "Why Don't They Just Call It 'Clothing Pile'?" *Bloomberg Businessweek*, December 21, 2015, pp. 59–61; David Moin, "Dressbarn Campaign Plays on the Name," *Women's Wear Daily*, September 2, 2015, http://wwd.com/media-news/advertising/dressbarns-fun-farm-campaign-10209383/ (accessed January 28, 2016); "The Existing Power of Customer Lifetime Value," *Wharton Customer Analytics Initiative (University of Pennsylvania)*, December 17, 2015, http://wcai.wharton.upenn.edu/blog (accessed January 28, 2016).

[2] O. C. Ferrell and Michael Hartline, *Marketing Strategy*, 6th ed. (Mason, OH: South-Western Cengage Learning, 2014), 9.

[3] Christian Homburg, Karley Krohmer, and John P. Workman, Jr., "A Strategy Implementation Perspective of Market Orientation," *Journal of Business Research* 57, 12 (2004): 1331–1340.

[4] "About," Twitter, https://about.twitter.com/company (accessed January 11, 2016).

[5] "History," Warby Parker, https://www.warbyparker.com/history (accessed January 11, 2016).

[6] Jenni Avins, "Warby Parker Proves Customers Don't Have to Care About Your Social Mission," *Quartz*, December 29, 2014, http://qz.com/318499/warby-parker-proves-customers-dont-have-to-care-about-your-social-mission/ (accessed January 11, 2016); Richard Feloni, "How a Blue-Footed Boobie Helped Create the Warby Parker Brand," *Business Insider*, June 27, 2014, http://www.businessinsider.com/warby-parkers-blue-footed-boobie-2014-6 (accessed January 11, 2016).

[7] Ma Jie, Masatsugu Horie, and Yuki Hagiwara, "Japan's Carmakers Proceed with Caution on Self-Driving Cars," *BloombergBusiness*, October 27, 2015, http://www.bloomberg.com/news/articles/2015-10-28/japan-s-carmakers-proceed-with-caution-on-self-driving-cars (January 29, 2016).

[8] Stanley F. Slater, G. Tomas, M. Hult, and Eric M. Olson, "On the Importance of Matching Strategic Behavior and Target Market Selection to Business Strategy in High-Tech Markets," *Journal of the Academy of Marketing Science* 35, 1 (2007): 5–17.

[9] Brett Molina, "Google Search Slipping in U.S. Market Share," *USA Today*, February 13, 2015, http://www.usatoday.com/story/tech/2015/02/03/google-search/22787853/ (January 11, 2016).

[10] Robert D. Buzzell, "The PIMS Program of Strategy Research: A Retrospective Appraisal," *Journal of Business Research* 57, 5 (2004): 478–483.

[11] Jack Neff, "P&G Will Divest Duracell in Biggest Piece of Brand Culling," *Advertising Age*, October 24, 2014, http://adage.com/article/cmo-strategy/p-g-divest-duracell-biggest-piece-brand-culling/295559/ (accessed January 11, 2016); "P&G Brand Divestitures Will Be Bigger than Original Targets," *AdAge*, February 19, 2015, http://adage.com/article/cmo-strategy/p-g-brand-divestitures-bigger-original-targets/297240/ (accessed January 11, 2016).

[12] E. J. Schultz, "'Share a Coke' to Return, but Bigger," *AdAge*, April 10, 2015, http://adage.com/article/cmo-strategy/share-a-coke-return-bigger/297994/ (accessed January 11, 2016); Mike Esterl, "'Share a Coke' Credited with a Pop in Sales," *The Wall Street Journal*, September 25, 2014, http://www.wsj.com/articles/share-a-coke-credited-with-a-pop-in-sales-1411661519 (accessed April 9, 2015).

[13] Janice Kew and Christopher Spillane, "Pizza Hut Returns to Africa," *Bloomberg Business*, February 19, 2015, http://www.bloomberg.com/news/articles/2015-02-19/pizza-hut-returns-to-africa-with-new-strategy (accessed January 11, 2016).

[14] Bruce Horovitz, "Coke Gets Moo Juice with Premium-Price Milk," *USA Today*, February 5, 2015, http://www.usatoday.com/story/money/2015/02/03/coca-cola-coke-fairlife-milk-premium-milk-dairy-nutrition/22798261/ (accessed January 29, 2016).

[15] Jeff Morganteen, "Starbucks CEO: We're Going After the $90 Billion Tea Market," *CNBC*, April 25, 2014, http://www.cnbc.com/id/101614206# (accessed January 11, 2016).

[16] Derek F. Abell, "Strategic Windows," *Journal of Marketing* 42, 3 (1978): 21.

[17] Jacob Davidson, "3 Ways Walmart Is Trying to Out-Amazon Amazon," *Money*, August 4, 2014, http://time.com/money/3079546/walmart-out-amazon-amazonfresh/ (accessed January 11, 2016); Shelly Banjo, "Wal-Mart Matches Online Prices," *The Wall Street Journal*, October 31, 2014, http://online.wsj.com/articles/wal-mart-weighs-matching-online-prices-during-holidays-1414672782 (accessed January 29, 2016).

[18] Robert F. Everett, "A Crack in the Foundation: Why SWOT Might Be Less Than Effective in Market Sensing Analysis," *Journal of Marketing and Management*, Special Issues 1, 1 (2014): 58–78.

[19] Michael Endler, "Apple iPad Loses Tablet Market Share," *Information Week*, July 25, 2014, http://www.informationweek.com/mobile/mobile-devices/apple-ipad-loses-tablet-market-share/d/d-id/1297568 (accessed January 11, 2016).

[20] Jared M. Hansen, Robert E. McDonald, and Ronald K. Mitchell, "Competence Resource Specialization, Causal Ambiguity, and the Creation and Decay of Competitiveness: The Role of Marketing Strategy in New Product Performance and Shareholder Value," *Journal of the academy of Marketing Science*, 41, 3 (2013): 300–319.

[21] Tilottama G. Chowdhury, Sreedhar Madhavarm, S. Ratneshwar, and Rhetta Standifer, "The Appropriateness of Different Modes of Strategy from a Product-Market Perspective," *Journal of Strategic Marketing*, 22, 5 (2014): 442–468.

[22] Arif Durrani, "London Live to Move Closer to Evening Standard," *Campaign*, August 14, 2014, http://www.campaignlive.co.uk/news/1307558/london-live-move-closer-evening-standard/ (accessed January 11, 2016).

[23] Dean Takahashi, "Mobile Gaming Could Drive Entire Video Game Industry to $100B in Revenue by 2017," *VentureBeat*, January 14, 2014, http://venturebeat.com/2014/01/14/mobile-gaming-could-drive-entire-game-industry-to-100b-in-revenue-by-2017/ (accessed January 11, 2016); Keith Stuart, "Mobile Games Revenue to Overtake Consoles in 2015, says analyst," *The Guardian*, October 23, 2014, http://www.theguardian.com/technology/2014/oct/23/mobile-games-revenue-overtake-consoles-2015 (accessed January 11, 2016).

[24] Myles Edwin Mangram, "The Globalization of Tesla Motors: a Strategic Marketing Plan Analysis," *Journal of Strategic Marketing*, 20, 4 (2012): 289–312.

[25] Sarah Halzack, "Major Food Brands Go after a Once-Ignored Customer: Men," *The Washington Post*, September 25, 2014, http://www.washingtonpost.com/business/economy/major-food-brands-go-after-a-once-ignored-

customer-men/2014/09/25/6c0ebb6c-337b-11e4-9e92-0899b306bbea_story.html (accessed January 11, 2016); Anne Marie Chaker, "Groceries Be-come a Guy Thing," *The Wall Street Journal*, October 16, 2013, http://online.wsj.com/articles/SB10001424052702303680404579139422972891330 (accessed January 11, 2016).

26 Jose Pagliery, "Local Shops Fear Amazon's Expansion," *CNN Money*, September 4, 2013, http://money.cnn.com/2013/09/04/smallbusiness/amazon-expansion/ (accessed January 11, 2016).

27 Shikhar Sarin, Goutam Challagalla, and Ajay K. Kohli, "Implementing Changes in Marketing Strategy: The Role of Perceived Outcome- and Process-Oriented Supervisory Actions," *Journal of Marketing Research*, 49, 4 (2012): 564–580.

28 John Grossman, "Finding Ways to Use Big Data to Help Small Shops," *The New York Times*, July 9, 2014, http://www.nytimes.com/2014/07/10/business/smallbusiness/finding-affordable-ways-to-use-big-data.html?_r=0 (accessed January 11, 2016).

29 Paul R. LaMonica, "McDonald's Sales Soar Thanks to All Day Breakfast," CNN Money, January 25, 2016, http://money.cnn.com/2016/01/25/investing/mcdonalds-earnings/index.html (accessed January 25, 2016).

30 Bazaarvoice, www.bazaarvoice.com (accessed February 1, 2016).

31 "BusTracker Now Available On BoltBus.com and BoltBus Mobile App," BoltBus, news release, December 3, 2015, http://finance.yahoo.com/news/bustracker-now-available-boltbus-com-182500904.html (accessed January 28, 2016); Tim O'Reiley, "BoltBus Beginning LV-L.A. Service with Promotional Fares," *Las Vegas Review-Journal*, December 11, 2013, www.reviewjournal.com; Linda Zavoral, "BoltBus to Launch Bay Area-Los Angeles Service," *San Jose Mercury News*, October 18, 2013, www.mercurynews.com; Josh Sanburn, "Reinventing the Wheels," *Time*, November 15, 2012, http://business.time.com; Jeff Plungis, "Megabus, BoltBus Overcome U.S. Stigma with Cheap Travel," *Bloomberg*, January 7, 2013, www.bloomberg.com; "BoltBus" Cengage video.

32 Shalini Ramachandran and Maria Armental, "Netflix Adds More Subscribers Than Expected," *Wall Street Journal*, January 19, 2016, www.wsj.com; Julien Ponthus and Leila Ab-boud, "Netflix Meets with Officials on French Launch," *Reuters*, December 4, 2013, www.reuters.com; Brian Stelter, "Netflix Won't Release 'Turbo: Fast' for Binge Viewing," *CNN Money*, December 3, 2013, http://money.cnn.com; Ashlee Vance, "The Man Who Ate the Internet," *Bloomberg Businessweek*, May 9, 2013, pp. 56–62; Julia Boorstin, "Exclusive: Netflix CEO Reed Hastings Talks Strategy," *CNBC*, July 23, 2013, www.cnbc.com.

33 Hilary Burns, "A case study on social goodness: How 3 companies market to millennials," *BizWomen*, March 27, 2015, http://www.bizjournals.com/bizwomen/news/profiles-strategies/2015/03/a-case-study-on-social-goodness-how-3-companies.html?page=all (accessed November 16, 2015); Laura Dunn, "Women in Businesses: Liz Forkin Bohannon, Founder, Sseko Designs," *The Huffington Post*, May 6, 2015, http://www.huffingtonpost.com/laura-dunn/women-in-business-liz-for_b_7220286.html (accessed November 16, 2015); Liz Forkin Bohannon, "After the Shark Attack," *The Huffington Post*, February 24, 2015, http://www.huffingtonpost.com/liz-forkin-bohannon/after-the-shark-attack_b_6738426.html (accessed November 16, 2015); "How Millennials Are Changing the Face of Marketing Forever," *BCG Perspectives*, https://www.bcgperspectives.com/content/articles/marketing_center_consumer_customer_insight_how_millennials_changing_marketing_forever/?chapter=3 (accessed November 16, 2015); Katy Muldoon, "Sseko Designs fashions a footwear business, based in Portland and Uganda, to lift women out of poverty," *Oregon Live*, January 7, 2012, http://www.oregonlive.com/O/index.ssf/2012/01/sseko_designs_fashions_a_footw.html (accessed November 16, 2015); "Shark Tank—Sandals from Uganda—Sseko Designs [Recap]," *YouTube*, https://www.youtube.com/watch?v=4xkXWVhXKPQ (accessed November 16, 2015); Sseko Designs website, http://ssekodesigns.com/ (accessed November 16, 2015); Steph Bazzle, "Shark Tank: Sseko Designs Customizable Sandals a Poor Fit with Sharks," *Business 2 Community*, February 13, 2015, http://www.business2community.com/entertainment/shark-tank-sseko-designs-customizable-sandals-poor-fit-sharks-01156083#yjPEKE9wA42cX59S.99 (accessed November 16, 2015); Jaclyn Trop, "Why this company isn't worried it left Shark Tank empty-handed," *Fortune*, February 27, 2015, http://fortune.com/2015/02/27/shark-tank-empty-handed (accessed November 16, 2015).

## Feature Notes

a Phil Wahba, "How CVS Plans to Replace $2 Billion in Lost Tobacco Sales," *Fortune*, June 22, 2015, http://fortune.com/2015/06/22/cvs-retail-strategy-without-tobacco/ (accessed January 28, 2016); Tom Murphy, "CVS Launches Health, Beauty Makeover for Drugstores Hit by Slower Sales Since Tobacco Exit," *Associated Press*, June 17, 2015, http://www.startribune.com/cvs-health-launches-health-beauty-makeover-for-drugstores/307901331/ (accessed January 28, 2016); Kelly Gilblom and Michelle Fay Cortez, "CVS's Competitors Can't Afford to Quit Tobacco," *Bloomberg*, November 4, 2014, http://www.bloomberg.com/news/articles/2014-11-04/cvs-s-competitors-can-t-afford-to-quit-tobacco (accessed January 28, 2016).

b Mark Garrison, "Why Campbell Changed Its Mind on GMO Labeling," *Marketplace*, January 11, 2016, http://www.marketplace.org/2016/01/08/world/big-food-hates-gmo-labels-one-giant-company-disagrees (accessed January 28, 2016); Stephanie Strom, "Campbell Rethinks Its Soup Recipe as Consumer Tastes Change," *New York Times*, November 9, 2015, http://www.nytimes.com/2015/11/10/business/campbell-rethinks-its-recipe-as-consumer-tastes-change.html?_r=0 (accessed January 28, 2016); Stephanie Strom, "Campbell Labels Will Disclose G.M.O. Ingredients," *New York Times*, January 7, 2016, http://www.nytimes.com/2016/01/08/business/campbell-labels-will-disclose-gmo-ingredients.html (accessed January 28, 2016).

# part 2

# Environmental Forces and Social and Ethical Responsibilities

**PART 2** deals with the marketing environment, social responsibility, and marketing ethics.

**CHAPTER 3** examines competitive, economic, political, legal and regulatory, technological, and sociocultural forces in the marketing environment, which can have profound effects on marketing strategies.

**CHAPTER 4** explores the role of social responsibility and ethical issues in marketing decisions.

Photosebia/Shutterstock.com

# chapter 3     The Marketing Environment

---

## OBJECTIVES

---

**3-1**   Summarize why it is important to examine and respond to the marketing environment.

**3-2**   Explain how competitive factors affect an organization's ability to compete.

**3-3**   Articulate how economic factors influence a customer's ability and willingness to buy products.

**3-4**   Identify the types of political forces in the marketing environment.

**3-5**   Explain how laws, government regulations, and self-regulatory agencies affect marketing activities.

**3-6**   Describe how new technology impacts marketing and society.

**3-7**   Outline the sociocultural issues marketers must deal with as they make decisions.

# MARKETING INSIGHTS

## Pepsi: A Healthier Alternative

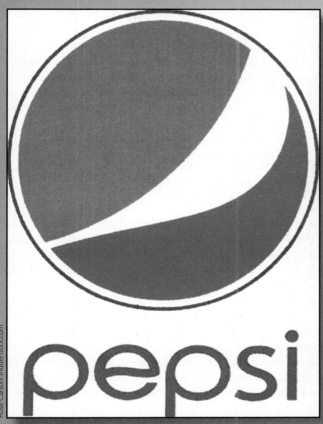

A key part of marketing is analyzing the marketing environment and predicting market trends. Indra Nooyi, CEO of PepsiCo, has skills in these areas. Although sales of soda have declined 14 percent in nine years, the past few years have seen an increase in PepsiCo revenue. Much of this is due to Nooyi's correct assumptions that consumers are becoming more interested in purchasing healthier foods.

When Nooyi took the helm, she made a surprising acknowledgement: Many of Pepsi-Co's most popular products were unhealthy. She therefore decided to cut marketing in certain areas and invest in healthier products. This move was not successful right away, and PepsiCo continued to struggle, particularly during the recession. Activist investors were calling on PepsiCo to separate its beverage business from its snacks business. Not only was Nooyi against splitting the company, she believed a key to success was to triple the sales of healthier products. She made the decision that Pepsi would pursue long-term growth and not worry as much about trying to gain one or two points in short-term market share. Under her leadership, Pepsi assumed a market orientation based upon customer preferences. For instance, because consumers perceive high-fructose corn syrup as unhealthy, Pepsi began offering products with real sugar.

Despite the naysayers, Nooyi's strategy appears to be paying off. PepsiCo stock is beating that of Coca-Cola, and revenue has grown. However, because PepsiCo works in an industry with intense monopolistic competition, Pepsi knows it must constantly innovate. For instance, Nooyi purchases carts full of competitor products and has her team analyze and evaluate them. Knowing the competition places Pepsi in a better position to compete.[1]

Companies like Pepsi are modifying marketing strategies in response to changes in the marketing environment. Because recognizing and addressing such changes in the marketing environment are crucial to marketing success, we will focus in detail on the forces that contribute to these changes.

This chapter explores the competitive, economic, political, legal and regulatory, technological, and sociocultural forces that constitute the marketing environment. First, we define the marketing environment and consider why it is critical to scan and analyze it. Next, we discuss the effects of competitive forces and explore the influence of general economic conditions: prosperity, recession, depression, and recovery. We also examine buying power and look at the forces that influence consumers' willingness to spend. We then discuss the political forces that generate government actions that affect marketing activities and examine the effects of laws and regulatory agencies on these activities. After analyzing the major dimensions of the technological forces in the environment, we consider the impact of sociocultural forces on marketing efforts.

## 3-1 EXAMINING AND RESPONDING TO THE MARKETING ENVIRONMENT

The marketing environment consists of external forces that directly or indirectly influence an organization's acquisition of inputs (human, financial, natural resources and raw materials, and information) and creation of outputs (goods, services, or ideas). As we saw in Chapter 1, the marketing environment includes six such forces: competitive, economic, political, legal and regulatory, technological, and sociocultural.

Whether fluctuating rapidly or slowly, environmental forces are always dynamic. Changes in the marketing environment create uncertainty, threats, and opportunities for marketers. Firms providing digital products such as software, music, and movies face many environmental threats as well as opportunities. Advancing technology provides digital delivery of these products, which is an efficient and effective way to reach global markets. On the other hand, technology has made it easier for file-sharing websites to infringe on others' intellectual property. Even streaming sites that operate legally have encountered controversy. Taylor Swift pulled her entire collection from the music streaming site Spotify over a royalty dispute. The issue is that the cost per stream is much less than the costs of a permanent download. On the other hand, studies show that sites such as Spotify and Pandora combat piracy by getting consumers to listen to music legally.[2] The marketing environment constantly fluctuates, requiring marketers to monitor it regularly.

Although the future is sometimes hard to predict, marketers try to forecast what may happen. We can say with certainty that marketers continue to modify their marketing strategies and plans in response to dynamic environmental forces. Consider how technological changes have affected the products offered by the mobile phone industry and how the public's growing concern with health and fitness has influenced the products of clothing, food, exercise equipment, and health-care companies. Wearable technology such as FitBit linked to a smartphone can monitor many vital signs of health and exercise. Marketing managers who fail to recognize changes in environmental forces leave their firms unprepared to capitalize on marketing opportunities or to cope with threats created by those changes. For instance, Kodak's failure to make the switch from film development to digital photos led to its downfall. Although Kodak helped to develop digital photography, its failure to capitalize on this new innovation led the firm to file for bankruptcy in 2012. It emerged from bankruptcy the next year and has since restructured to focus on packaging, printing, and graphic communications services. Monitoring the environment is crucial to an organization's survival and to the long-term achievement of its goals.

### 3-1a Environmental Scanning and Analysis

**environmental scanning**
The process of collecting information about forces in the marketing environment

To monitor changes in the marketing environment effectively, marketers engage in environmental scanning and analysis. **Environmental scanning** is the process of collecting information about forces in the marketing environment. Scanning involves observation; secondary

# EMERGING **TRENDS IN MARKETING**

## Making Trade Fair

Fair Trade–certified organizations require factories to meet different conditions. They must pay their workers a minimum wage in the country in which they are employed, with the intention of working toward a "livable wage." A livable wage allows workers to afford basic necessities. Additionally, brands must pay a premium to factory workers. These premiums are placed in a collective bank account and are used for bonuses or to address community needs.

The Fair Trade trend is gaining traction among fashion and home furnishings. After the Bangladesh factory collapsed in 2013, many apparel and home furnishing brands made a commitment to improve factory conditions. Twenty brands have chosen to become Fair Trade certified.

Consumers are embracing Fair Trade apparel and home goods as well. For instance, Bed Bath & Beyond quickly sold out of back-to-school supplies labeled as Fair Trade–certified. This demonstrates consumers' increased concern for how goods are manufactured. In particular, Fair Trade certification focuses on improving the labor conditions of factory workers.

Although fair trade certification costs brands 1–5 percent of what companies pay to factories, it is clear that demand is on the rise. Fair trade apparel and home furnishings have increased fivefold in the past few years, spurring more factories to work toward achieving certification. Marketers monitoring the environment are finding the costs of Fair Trade well worth the benefits.[a]

sources such as business, trade, government, and general-interest publications; and marketing research. The Internet has become a popular scanning tool because it makes data more accessible and allows companies to gather needed information quickly. Environmental scanning gives companies an edge over competitors in allowing them to take advantage of current trends. However, simply gathering information about competitors and customers is not enough; companies must know *how* to use that information in the strategic planning process. Managers must be careful not to gather so much information that sheer volume makes analysis impossible.

**Environmental analysis** is the process of assessing and interpreting the information gathered through environmental scanning. A manager evaluates the information for accuracy, tries to resolve inconsistencies in the data, and, if warranted, assigns significance to the findings. Evaluating this information should enable the manager to identify potential threats and opportunities linked to environmental changes. Understanding the current state of the marketing environment and recognizing threats and opportunities that might arise from changes within it help companies in their strategic planning. A threat could be rising interest rates or commodity prices. An opportunity could be increases in consumer income, decreases in the unemployment rate, or a sudden drop in commodity prices. The last-mentioned occurred during 2014–2016, when oil prices dropped more than 40 percent within a few months.

## 3-1b  Responding to Environmental Forces

Marketing managers take two general approaches to environmental forces: accepting them as uncontrollable or attempting to influence and shape them.[3] An organization that views environmental forces as uncontrollable remains passive and reactive toward the environment. Instead of trying to influence forces in the environment, its marketing managers adjust current marketing strategies to environmental changes. They approach with caution market opportunities discovered through environmental scanning and analysis. On the other hand, marketing managers who believe environmental forces can be shaped adopt a more proactive approach. If a market opportunity is blocked by environmental constraints, proactive marketing managers may use their political skills to overcome obstacles. For example, if a company decides to align itself with social interests, it should be proactive and disclose its social responsibility activities to maintain transparent communication with stakeholders.[4] Amazon, Intel, and Google have

**environmental analysis**
The process of assessing and interpreting the information gathered through environmental scanning

responded to political, legal, and regulatory concerns by communicating the value of their competitive approaches to stakeholders. British multinational Kingfisher Group communicates its belief that big businesses can make a big environmental difference. It proactively pursues reforestation, sustainable products, and waste-reduction initiatives to promote sustainable innovation while minimizing its environmental impact.[5]

A proactive approach can be constructive and bring desired results. To influence environmental forces, marketing managers seek to identify market opportunities or to extract greater benefits relative to costs from existing market opportunities. For instance, Subaru identified an opportunity to increase its reputation for sustainability. The company's advertisement uses a landfill to draw attention to the fact that the automaker became the first U.S. auto manufacturer to become zero-landfill. The advertisement further explains that Subaru is partnering with the National Park Service to share knowledge and increase the sustainability of the nation's national parks. Subaru is using a proactive approach not to sell a particular product but to generate goodwill toward the brand. Political action is another way to affect environmental forces. The pharmaceutical industry, for example, has lobbied very effectively for fewer restrictions on prescription drug marketing. However, managers must recognize that there are limits to the degree that environmental forces can be shaped. Although an organization may be able to influence legislation through lobbying—as the movie and music industries are doing to try and stop the piracy of their products—it is unlikely that a single organization can significantly change major economic factors such as recessions, interest rates, or commodity prices.

Whether to take a reactive or a proactive approach to environmental forces is a decision for a firm to make based on its strengths or weaknesses. For some organizations, the passive, reactive approach is more appropriate, but for others the aggressive approach leads to better performance. Selection of a particular approach depends on an organization's managerial philosophies, objectives, financial resources, customers, and human resources skills, as well as on the environment within which the organization operates. Both organizational factors and managers' personal characteristics affect the variety of responses to changing environmental conditions. Microsoft, for instance, can take a proactive approach because of its financial resources and the highly visible image of its founder, Bill Gates. However, Microsoft has also been the target of various lawsuits regarding anticompetitive practices, demonstrating that even Microsoft is limited in how far it can influence the business environment.

Source: Subaru landfill

**Responding to the Marketing Environment**
Subaru is marketing its zero-landfill policy and its partnership with the National Parks Service to enhance its positive reputation with consumers.

In the remainder of this chapter, we explore in greater detail the six environmental forces—competitive, economic, political, legal and regulatory, technological, and sociocultural—that interact to create opportunities and threats that must be considered in strategic planning.

# 3-2 COMPETITIVE FORCES

Few firms, if any, operate free of competition. In fact, for most goods and services, customers have many alternatives from which to choose. For instance, a customer in the market for a tablet computer could choose from Apple, Samsung, Lenovo, and more. The customer could also choose an alternative such as a Microsoft Surface. Thus, when marketing managers define the target market(s) their firm will serve, they simultaneously establish a set of competitors.[6] In addition, marketing managers must consider the type of competitive structure in which the firm operates. In this section, we examine types of competition and competitive structures, as well as the importance of monitoring competitors' actions.

## 3-2a  Types of Competitors

Broadly speaking, all firms compete with one another for customers' dollars. More practically, however, a marketer generally defines **competition** as other firms that market products that are similar to or can be substituted for its products in the same geographic area. These competitors can be classified into one of four types. **Brand competitors** market products with similar features and benefits to the same customers at similar prices. For instance, a thirsty, calorie-conscious customer may choose a diet soda such as Diet Coke or Diet Pepsi from the soda machine. However, these sodas face competition from other types of beverages. **Product competitors** compete in the same product class but market products with different features, benefits, and prices. The thirsty dieter might purchase iced tea, juice, a sports beverage, or bottled water instead of a soda.

**Generic competitors** provide very different products that solve the same problem or satisfy the same basic customer need. Our dieter might simply have a glass of water from the kitchen tap to satisfy her thirst. **Total budget competitors** compete for the limited financial resources

**competition** Other organizations that market products that are similar to or can be substituted for a marketer's products in the same geographic area

**brand competitors** Firms that market products with similar features and benefits to the same customers at similar prices

**product competitors** Firms that compete in the same product class but market products with different features, benefits, and prices

**generic competitors** Firms that provide very different products that solve the same problem or satisfy the same basic customer need

**total budget competitors** Firms that compete for the limited financial resources of the same customers

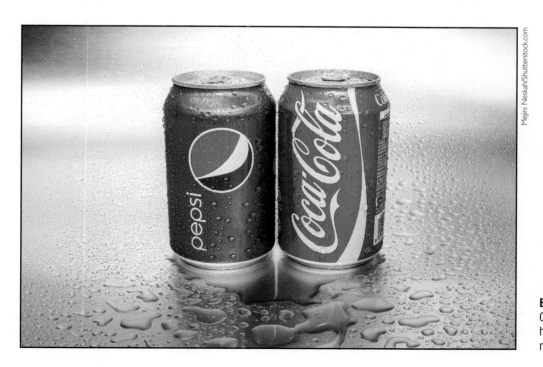

Mejini Neskah/Shutterstock.com

**Brand Competition**
Coke and Pepsi compete head-to-head in the soft-drink market

of the same customers.[7] Total budget competitors for Diet Coke, for example, might include gum, a newspaper, and bananas. Although all four types of competition can affect a firm's marketing performance, brand competitors are the most significant because buyers typically see the different products of these firms as direct substitutes for one another. Consequently, marketers tend to concentrate environmental analyses on brand competitors.

## 3-2b  Types of Competitive Structures

The number of firms that supply a product may affect the strength of competitors. When just one or a few firms control supply, competitive factors exert a different form of influence on marketing activities than when many competitors exist. Table 3.1 presents four general types of competitive structures: monopoly, oligopoly, monopolistic competition, and pure competition.

A **monopoly** exists when an organization offers a product that has no close substitutes, making that organization the sole source of supply. Because the organization has no competitors, it controls the supply of the product completely and, as a single seller, can erect barriers to potential competitors. In reality, most monopolies surviving today are local utilities, which are heavily regulated by local, state, or federal agencies. Regulators in a number of countries allege that Google is becoming a digital monopoly. It has almost 70 percent of the Web search-engine market in the United States and more than 90 percent in many European countries. The European Parliament has suggested that Google is too powerful and should be broken up by unbundling its search engine business.[8]

An **oligopoly** exists when a few sellers control the supply of a large proportion of a product. In this case, each seller considers the reactions of other sellers to changes in marketing activities. Products facing oligopolistic competition may be homogeneous, such as aluminum, or differentiated, such as packaged delivery services. The airline industry is an example of an oligopoly. However, even an industry dominated by a few companies must still compete and release promotional materials. Southwest Airlines releases advertising to demonstrate the great deals it offers to passengers. The Southwest ad uses "man's best friend" to show that passengers with small dogs or cats can bring them aboard Southwest flights. It also emphasizes its low pet fares. Southwest recognizes the importance consumers place on their pets and has found these benefits help differentiate it from rival airlines. Usually barriers of some sort make it difficult to enter the market and compete with oligopolies. For example, because of the enormous financial outlay required, few companies or individuals could afford to enter the oil-refining or steel-producing industry. Moreover, some industries demand special technical or marketing skills, a qualification that deters the entry of many potential competitors.

**monopoly** A competitive structure in which an organization offers a product that has no close substitutes, making that organization the sole source of supply

**oligopoly** A competitive structure in which a few sellers control the supply of a large proportion of a product

Table 3.1    **Selected Characteristics of Competitive Structures**

| Type of Structure | Number of Competitors | Ease of Entry into Market | Product | Examples |
|---|---|---|---|---|
| Monopoly | One | Many barriers | Almost no substitutes | Water utilities |
| Oligopoly | Few | Some barriers | Homogeneous or differentiated (with real or perceived differences) | UPS, FedEx, U.S. Postal Service (package delivery) |
| Monopolistic competition | Many | Few barriers | Product differentiation, with many substitutes | Wrangler, Levi Strauss (jeans) |
| Pure competition | Unlimited | No barriers | Homogeneous products | Vegetable farm (sweet corn) |

**Monopolistic competition** exists when a firm with many potential competitors attempts to develop a marketing strategy to differentiate its product. For example, Wrangler and True Religion have established an advantage for their blue jeans through well-known trademarks, design, advertising, and a reputation for quality. Wrangler is associated with a cowboy image, while True Religion tries to maintain a premium designer image. Although many competing brands of blue jeans are available, these firms have carved out market niches by emphasizing differences in their products, especially style and image.

**Pure competition**, if it existed at all, would entail an extremely large number of sellers, none of which could significantly influence price or supply. Products would be homogeneous, and entry into the market would be easy. The closest thing to an example of pure competition is an unregulated farmers' market, where local growers gather to sell their produce. Commodities such as soybeans, corn, and wheat have their markets subsidized or regulated by the government. Pure competition is an ideal at one end of the continuum, and a monopoly is at the other end. Most marketers function in a competitive environment somewhere between these two extremes.

### 3-2c  Monitoring Competition

Marketers need to monitor the actions of major competitors to determine what specific strategies competitors are using and how those strategies affect their own. Competitive intensity influences a firm's strategic approach to markets. Price is one marketing strategy variable that most competitors monitor. When Delta or Southwest Airlines lowers its fare on a route, most major airlines attempt to match the price. Monitoring guides marketers in developing competitive advantages and in adjusting current marketing strategies and planning new ones. When two large companies such as Time Warner Cable and Comcast merge, there is the potential for less competition.

In monitoring competition, it is not enough to analyze available information; the firm must develop a system for gathering ongoing information about competitors and potential competitors. Understanding the market and what customers want, as well as what the competition is providing, will assist in maintaining a market orientation.[9] Information about competitors allows marketing managers to assess the performance of their own marketing efforts and to recognize the strengths and weaknesses in their own marketing strategies. Data about market shares, product movement, sales volume, and expenditure levels can be useful. However, accurate information on these matters is often difficult to obtain.

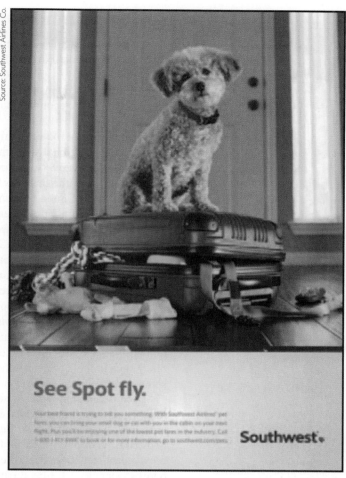

Source: Southwest Airlines Co.

**See Spot fly.**

Your best friend is trying to tell you something. With Southwest Airlines' pet fares, you can bring your small dog or cat with you in the cabin on your next flight. Plus you'll be enjoying one of the lowest pet fares in the industry. Call 1-800-I-FLY-SWA℠ to book or for more information, go to southwest.com/pets.

**Southwest.**

**Oligopoly**
The airline industry is an example of an oligopoly. In the United States, Southwest competes with only a few other major airlines. Its advertising emphasizes its superiority with its great deals for passengers—and their pets.

# 3-3  ECONOMIC FORCES

Economic forces in the marketing environment influence both marketers' and customers' decisions and activities. In this section, we examine the effects of general economic conditions as well as buying power and the factors that affect people's willingness to spend.

**monopolistic competition** A competitive structure in which a firm has many potential competitors and tries to develop a marketing strategy to differentiate its product

**pure competition** A market structure characterized by an extremely large number of sellers, none strong enough to significantly influence price or supply

## 3-3a **Economic Conditions**

The overall state of the economy fluctuates in all countries. Even downturns in large countries such as China can affect the global economy. Changes in general economic conditions affect (and are affected by) supply and demand, buying power, willingness to spend, consumer expenditure levels, and intensity of competitive behavior. Therefore, current economic conditions and changes in the economy have a broad impact on the success of organizations' marketing strategies.

Fluctuations in the economy follow a general pattern, often referred to as the **business cycle**. In the traditional view, the business cycle consists of four stages: prosperity, recession, depression, and recovery. From a global perspective, different regions of the world may be in different stages of the business cycle during the same period. Throughout much of the 1990s, for example, the United States experienced growth (prosperity). The U.S. economy began to slow in 2000, with a brief recession, especially in high-technology industries, in 2001, when many dot-com or Internet companies failed. Japan, however, endured a recession during most of the 1990s and into the early 2000s. Economic variation in the global marketplace creates a planning challenge for firms that sell products in multiple markets around the world. In 2008, the United States experienced an economic downturn due to higher energy prices, falling home values, increasing unemployment, the financial crisis in the banking industry, and fluctuating currency values. That recession was the longest since the Great Depression of the 1930s.

During **prosperity**, unemployment is low and total income is relatively high. Assuming a low inflation rate, this combination ensures high buying power. If the economic outlook remains prosperous, consumers generally are willing to buy. In the prosperity stage, marketers often expand their product offerings to take advantage of increased buying power. They can sometimes capture a larger market share by intensifying distribution and promotion efforts.

Because unemployment rises during a **recession**, total buying power declines. These factors, usually accompanied by consumer pessimism, often stifle both consumer and business spending. As buying power decreases, many customers may become more price and value conscious, and look for basic, functional products. When buying power decreased during the most recent recession, department store sales dropped. Consumers began shopping at off-price retailers such as T.J. Maxx and Ross. Macy's is trying to capitalize on T.J. Maxx's and other off-price stores' success by opening its own line of off-price stores called Macy's Backstage. At the same time, it is being forced to close a number of underperforming department store locations.[10] Online retailers such as Amazon also attract consumers desiring low prices.

During a recession, some firms make the mistake of drastically reducing their marketing efforts, thus damaging their ability to survive. Obviously, however, marketers should consider some revision of their marketing activities during a recessionary period. Because consumers are more concerned about the functional value of products, a company should focus its marketing research on determining precisely what functions buyers want and make sure those functions become part of its products. Promotional efforts should emphasize value and utility. Marketers must also carefully monitor the needs and expectations of their companies' target markets.

A prolonged recession may become a **depression**, a period in which unemployment is extremely high, wages are very low, total disposable income is at a minimum, and consumers lack confidence in the economy. A depression usually lasts for an extended period, often years, and has been experienced by Russia, Mexico, and Brazil in the 2000s. Although evidence supports maintaining or even increasing spending during economic slowdowns, marketing budgets are more likely to be cut in the face of an economic downturn.

During **recovery**, the economy moves from recession or depression toward prosperity. During this period, high unemployment begins to decline, total disposable income increases, and the economic gloom that reduced consumers' willingness to buy subsides. The U.S. economy went through a long recovery from a deep recession during 2011–2016. Both the ability and the willingness to buy rose slowly. Marketers face some problems during recovery, as it is difficult to ascertain how quickly and to what level prosperity will return. Large firms such as Procter & Gamble must try to assess how quickly consumers will increase their purchase of higher-priced brands versus economy brands. In this stage, marketers should maintain as much flexibility in their marketing strategies as possible so they can make the needed adjustments.

**business cycle** A pattern of economic fluctuations that has four stages: prosperity, recession, depression, and recovery

**prosperity** A stage of the business cycle characterized by low unemployment and relatively high total income, which together ensure high buying power (provided the inflation rate stays low)

**recession** A stage of the business cycle during which unemployment rises and total buying power declines, stifling both consumer and business spending

**depression** A stage of the business cycle when unemployment is extremely high, wages are very low, total disposable income is at a minimum, and consumers lack confidence in the economy

**recovery** A stage of the business cycle in which the economy moves from recession or depression toward prosperity

## 3-3b **Buying Power**

The strength of a person's **buying power** depends on economic conditions and the size of the resources—money, goods, and services that can be traded in an exchange—that enable the individual to make purchases. The major financial sources of buying power are income, credit, and wealth. For an individual, **income** is the amount of money received through wages, rents, investments, pensions, and subsidy payments for a given period, such as a month or a year. Normally this money is allocated among taxes, spending for goods and services, and savings. The median annual household income in the United States is approximately $53,657.[11] However, because of differences in people's educational levels, abilities, occupations, and wealth, income is not equally distributed in this country.

Marketers are most interested in the amount of money left after payment of taxes because this **disposable income** is used for spending or saving. Because disposable income is a ready source of buying power, the total amount available in a nation is important to marketers. Several factors determine the size of total disposable income. One is the total amount of income, which is affected by wage levels, the rate of unemployment, interest rates, and dividend rates. Because disposable income is income left after taxes are paid, the number and amount of taxes directly affect the size of total disposable income. When taxes rise, disposable income declines; when taxes fall, disposable income increases.

Disposable income that is available for spending and saving after an individual has purchased the basic necessities of food, clothing, and shelter is called **discretionary income**. People use discretionary income to purchase entertainment, vacations, automobiles, education, pets, furniture, appliances, and so on. Changes in total discretionary income affect sales of these products, especially automobiles, furniture, large appliances, and other costly durable goods. Montblanc—known for its luxury writing instruments—sells products that are often purchased with discretionary income. The advertisement depicts a model wearing sunglasses from its new eyewear collection to create an image of desirability and exclusivity for the product.

*Credit* enables people to spend future income now or in the near future. However, credit increases current buying power at the expense of future buying power. Several factors determine whether people use, acquire, or forgo credit. First, credit must be available. Interest rates also affect buyers' decisions to use credit, especially for expensive purchases such as homes, appliances, and automobiles. When interest rates are low, the total cost of automobiles and houses becomes more affordable. In the United States, low interest rates in the 2000s induced many buyers to take on the high level of debt necessary to own a home, fueling a tremendous boom in the construction of new homes and the sale of older homes. In contrast, when interest rates are high, consumers are more likely to delay buying such expensive items. Use of credit is also affected by credit terms, such as size of the down payment and amount and number of monthly payments.

**Wealth** is the accumulation of past income, natural resources, and financial resources. It exists in many forms, including cash, securities, savings accounts, gold, jewelry, and real estate. Global wealth is increasing, with 14.6 million millionaires worldwide.[12] Like income, wealth is unevenly

**buying power** Resources, such as money, goods, and services, that can be traded in an exchange

**income** For an individual, the amount of money received through wages, rents, investments, pensions, and subsidy payments for a given period

**disposable income** After-tax income

**discretionary income** Disposable income available for spending and saving after an individual has purchased the basic necessities of food, clothing, and shelter

**wealth** The accumulation of past income, natural resources, and financial resources

Source: Montblanc

MONT BLANC

Montblanc Eyewear Collection

Crafted for New Heights

Visit Montblanc.com

**Discretionary Income**
Montblanc has expanded its luxury products into eyewear. Montblanc sunglasses would be purchased using discretionary income.

distributed. A person can have a high income and very little wealth. It is also possible, but not likely, for a person to have great wealth but little income. The significance of wealth to marketers is that as people become wealthier, they gain buying power in three ways: They can use their wealth to make current purchases, to generate income, and to acquire large amounts of credit. Knowing that approximately 30 percent of the population of Brazil and India consists of Millennials would be useful for marketers selling high-end, electric sports cars to this target market because they might have less buying power than older consumers.[13]

Income, credit, and wealth equip consumers with buying power to purchase goods and services. Marketing managers must be aware of current levels and expected changes in buying power in their own markets because buying power directly affects the types and quantities of goods and services customers purchase. Information about buying power is available from government sources, trade associations, and research agencies. One of the most current and comprehensive sources of buying-power data is the *Sales & Marketing Management Survey of Buying Power*, published annually by *Sales & Marketing Management* magazine. Having buying power, however, does not mean consumers will buy. They must also be willing to use their buying power.

### 3-3c  Willingness to Spend

People's **willingness to spend**—their inclination to buy because of expected satisfaction from a product—is, to some degree, related to their ability to buy. That is, people are sometimes more willing to buy if they have the buying power. However, a number of other elements also influence willingness to spend. Some elements affect specific products; others influence spending in general. A product's price and value influence almost all of us. TAG Heuer, for instance, appeals to customers who are willing to spend more for watches even when lower-priced ones are readily available. The amount of satisfaction received from a product already owned may

**willingness to spend**
An inclination to buy because of expected satisfaction from a product, influenced by the ability to buy and numerous psychological and social forces

Figure 3.1    **National Customer Satisfaction Index**

Source: American Customer Satisfaction Index, "U.S. Overall Customer Satisfaction," http://www.theacsi.org/national-economic-indicator/us-overall-customer-satisfaction (accessed December 11, 2015).

also influence customers' desires to buy other products. Satisfaction depends not only on the quality of the currently owned product but also on numerous psychological and social forces. The American Customer Satisfaction Index, computed by the National Quality Research Center at the University of Michigan (see Figure 3.1), offers an indicator of customer satisfaction with a wide variety of businesses. The American Customer Satisfaction Index helps marketers to understand how consumers perceive their industries and businesses and adapt their marketing strategies accordingly.

Factors that affect consumers' general willingness to spend are expectations about future employment, income levels, prices, family size, and general economic conditions. Willingness to spend ordinarily declines if people are unsure whether or how long they will be employed, and it usually increases if people are reasonably certain of higher incomes in the future. Expectations of rising prices in the near future may also increase willingness to spend in the present. For a given level of buying power, the larger the family, the greater the willingness to spend. One reason for this relationship is that as the size of a family increases, more dollars must be spent to provide the basic necessities to sustain family members.

# 3-4 POLITICAL FORCES

Political, legal, and regulatory forces of the marketing environment are closely interrelated. Legislation is enacted, legal decisions are interpreted by courts, and regulatory agencies are created and operated, for the most part, by elected or appointed officials. Legislation and regulations (or the lack thereof) reflect the current political outlook. After the financial crisis caused a worldwide recession, the government passed the Dodd-Frank Wall Street Reform and Consumer Protection Act of 2010. This agency was created to increase accountability and transparency in the financial industry.[14] The legislation established a new Consumer Financial Protection Bureau to protect consumers from deceptive financial practices.[15] On the other hand, many political leaders blamed this legislation for slowing down the economic recovery and adding extra costs and uncertainty to business decision making. Consequently, the political forces of the marketing environment have the potential to influence marketing decisions and strategies.

Marketing organizations strive to maintain good relations with elected and appointed political officials for several reasons. Political officials well disposed toward particular firms or industries are less likely to create or enforce laws and regulations unfavorable to those companies. Consequently, political officials who believe oil companies are making honest efforts to control pollution are unlikely to create and enforce highly restrictive pollution-control laws. Government contracts can be very profitable, so understanding the competitive bidding process for obtaining contracts is important. Finally, political officials can play key roles in helping organizations secure foreign markets. Government officials will sometimes organize trade missions in which business executives go to foreign countries to meet with potential clients or buyers.[16]

Many marketers view political forces as beyond their control and simply adjust to conditions that arise from those forces. Some firms, however, seek to influence the political process. In some cases, organizations publicly protest the actions of legislative bodies. More often, organizations help elect individuals to political offices who regard them positively. Much of this help is in the form of campaign contributions. AT&T is an example of a company that has attempted to influence legislation and regulation over a long period of time. Since 1990, AT&T has made more than $62 million in corporate donations for use in supporting the campaign funds of political candidates.[17] Until recently, laws have limited corporate contributions to political campaign funds for specific candidates, and company-sponsored political advertisements could primarily focus only on topics (e.g., health care) and not on candidates. In the 2010 ruling for *Citizens United vs. Federal Election Commission*, the Supreme Court ruled that the government is not authorized to ban corporate spending in candidate elections.[18] This means that elections can be affected by large corporate donations to candidates. Marketers also can influence the political process through political action committees (PACs) that solicit donations from individuals and then contribute those funds to candidates running for political office.

Companies can also participate in the political process through lobbying to persuade public and/or government officials to favor a particular position in decision making. Many organizations concerned about the threat of legislation or regulation that may negatively affect their operations employ lobbyists to communicate their concerns to elected officials. Case in point, as the U.S. government debates whether to pass stricter laws regulating marketing activities over the Internet, social media firms such as Facebook are sending lobbyists to give their respective viewpoints regarding the proposed legislation.

# 3-5 LEGAL AND REGULATORY FORCES

A number of federal laws influence marketing decisions and activities. Table 3.2 lists some of the most important laws. In addition to discussing these laws, which deal with competition and consumer protection, this section examines the effects of regulatory agencies and self-regulatory forces on marketing efforts.

## 3-5a Procompetitive Legislation

Procompetitive laws are designed to preserve competition. Most of these laws were enacted to end various antitrade practices deemed unacceptable by society. The Sherman Antitrust Act, for example, was passed in 1890 to prevent businesses from restraining trade and monopolizing markets. Examples of illegal anticompetitive practices include stealing trade secrets or obtaining other confidential information from a competitor's employees, trademark and copyright infringement, price fixing, false advertising, and deceptive selling methods such as "bait and switch" and false representation of products. The Lanham Act (1946) and the Federal Trademark Dilution Act (1995), for instance, help companies protect their trademarks (brand names, logos, and other registered symbols) against infringement. The latter also requires users of names that match or parallel existing trademarks to relinquish them to prevent confusion among consumers. Antitrust laws also authorize the government to punish companies that engage in such anticompetitive practices. For instance, Teva Pharmaceuticals reached a $1.2 billion settlement with the Federal Trade Commission due to accusations that the pharmaceutical company Cephalon—which Teva had acquired—paid its generic competitors money so they would refrain from selling a generic version of its hit drug Provigil.[19]

Laws have also been created to prevent businesses from gaining an unfair advantage through bribery. The U.S. Foreign Corrupt Practices Act (FCPA) prohibits American companies from making illicit payments to foreign officials in order to obtain or keep business. To illustrate, Bristol-Meyers Squibb was fined $14 million to settle allegations that it used its joint venture in China to bribe state-owned hospitals to obtain prescription sales.[20] The FCPA does allow for small facilitation ("grease") payments to expedite routine government transactions. However, the passage of the U.K. Bribery Act does not allow for facilitation payments.[21] The U.K. Bribery Act is more encompassing than the FCPA and has significant implications for global business. Under this law companies can be found guilty of bribery even if the bribery did not take place within the U.K., and company officials without explicit knowledge about the misconduct can still be held accountable. The law applies to any business with operations in the U.K.[22] However, the U.K. Bribery Law does allow for leniency if the company has an effective compliance program and undergoes periodic ethical assessments.[23] In response to the

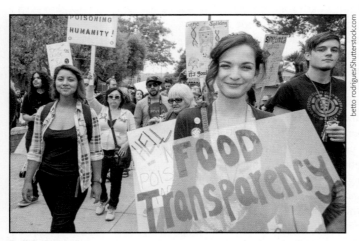

**Political Forces**

Protestors carry signs to protest genetically modified food and call for transparency.

betto rodrigues/Shutterstock.com

Table 3.2    **Major Federal Laws That Affect Marketing Decisions**

| Name and Date Enacted | Purpose |
|---|---|
| Sherman Antitrust Act (1890) | Prohibits contracts, combinations, or conspiracies to restrain trade; establishes as a misdemeanor monopolizing or attempting to monopolize |
| Clayton Act (1914) | Prohibits specific practices such as price discrimination, exclusive-dealer arrangements, and stock acquisitions whose effect may noticeably lessen competition or tend to create a monopoly |
| Federal Trade Commission Act (1914) | Created the Federal Trade Commission; also gives the FTC investigatory powers to be used in preventing unfair methods of competition |
| Robinson-Patman Act (1936) | Prohibits price discrimination that lessens competition among wholesalers or retailers; prohibits producers from giving disproportionate services or facilities to large buyers |
| Wheeler-Lea Act (1938) | Prohibits unfair and deceptive acts and practices regardless of whether competition is injured; places advertising of foods and drugs under the jurisdiction of the FTC |
| Lanham Act (1946) | Provides protections for and regulation of brand names, brand marks, trade names, and trademarks |
| Celler-Kefauver Act (1950) | Prohibits any corporation engaged in commerce from acquiring the whole or any part of the stock or other share of the capital assets of another corporation when the effect would substantially lessen competition or tend to create a monopoly |
| Fair Packaging and Labeling Act (1966) | Prohibits unfair or deceptive packaging or labeling of consumer products |
| Magnuson-Moss Warranty (FTC) Act (1975) | Provides for minimum disclosure standards for written consumer product warranties; defines minimum consent standards for written warranties; allows the FTC to prescribe interpretive rules in policy statements regarding unfair or deceptive practices |
| Consumer Goods Pricing Act (1975) | Prohibits the use of price maintenance agreements among manufacturers and resellers in interstate commerce |
| Foreign Corrupt Practices Act (1977) | Prohibits American companies from making illicit payments to foreign officials in order to obtain or keep business |
| Trademark Counterfeiting Act (1980) | Imposes civil and criminal penalties against those who deal in counterfeit consumer goods or any counterfeit goods that can threaten health or safety |
| Trademark Law Revision Act (1988) | Amends the Lanham Act to allow brands not yet introduced to be protected through registration with the Patent and Trademark Office |
| Nutrition Labeling and Education Act (1990) | Prohibits exaggerated health claims; requires all processed foods to contain labels with nutritional information |
| Telephone Consumer Protection Act (1991) | Establishes procedures to avoid unwanted telephone solicitations; prohibits marketers from using an automated telephone dialing system or an artificial or prerecorded voice to certain telephone lines |
| Federal Trademark Dilution Act (1995) | Grants trademark owners the right to protect trademarks and requires relinquishment of names that match or parallel existing trademarks |
| Digital Millennium Copyright Act (1996) | Refined copyright laws to protect digital versions of copyrighted materials, including music and movies |
| Children's Online Privacy Protection Act (2000) | Regulates the collection of personally identifiable information (name, address, e-mail address, hobbies, interests, or information collected through cookies) online from children under age 13 |
| Do Not Call Implementation Act (2003) | Directs the FCC and FTC to coordinate so their rules are consistent regarding telemarketing call practices including the Do Not Call Registry and other lists, as well as call abandonment; in 2008, the FTC amended its rules and banned prerecorded sales pitches for all but a few cases |
| Credit Card Act (2009) | Implements strict rules on credit card companies regarding topics such as issuing credit to youths, terms disclosure, interest rates, and fees |
| Dodd-Frank Wall Street Reform and Consumer Protection Act (2010) | Promotes financial reform to increase accountability and transparency in the financial industry, protects consumers from deceptive financial practices, and establishes the Bureau of Consumer Financial Protection |

law, companies have begun to strengthen their compliance programs related to bribery. For instance, Lockheed-Martin publicly changed its internal compliance procedures to ban facilitation payments in adherence to the new law.[24]

## 3-5b Consumer Protection Legislation

Consumer protection legislation is not a recent development. During the mid-1800s, lawmakers in many states passed laws to prohibit adulteration of food and drugs. However, consumer protection laws at the federal level mushroomed in the mid-1960s and early 1970s. A number of them deal with consumer safety, such as the food and drug acts, and are designed to protect people from actual and potential physical harm caused by adulteration or mislabeling. Other laws prohibit the sale of various hazardous products, such as flammable fabrics and toys that may injure children. Others concern automobile safety.

Congress has also passed several laws concerning information disclosure. Some require that information about specific products, such as textiles, furs, cigarettes, and automobiles, be provided on labels. Other laws focus on particular marketing activities: product development and testing, packaging, labeling, advertising, and consumer financing. Concerns about companies' online collection and use of personal information, especially about children, resulted in the passage of the Children's Online Privacy Protection Act (COPPA), which prohibits websites and Internet providers from seeking personal information from children under age 13 without parental consent. Fines for violating COPPA can be severe. The Federal Trade Commission charged online review website Yelp's mobile app with collecting information about children under the age of 13 without parental consent. Yelp claims this tracking occurred due to a problem in the system. The company paid $450,000 for violating COPPA.[25]

## 3-5c Encouraging Compliance with Laws and Regulations

Marketing activities are sometimes at the forefront of organizational misconduct, with fraud and antitrust violations the most frequently sentenced organizational crimes. Legal violations usually begin when marketers develop programs that unwittingly overstep legal bounds. Many marketers lack experience in dealing with complex legal actions and decisions. Some test the

**Consumer Credit Card Security**
Credit card theft has created the need for consumer vigilance and regulatory agencies' assistance in preventing fraud.

limits of certain laws by operating in a legally questionable way to see how far they can get with certain practices before being prosecuted. Other marketers interpret regulations and statutes very strictly to avoid violating a vague law. When marketers interpret laws in relation to specific marketing practices, they often analyze recent court decisions both to better understand what the law is intended to do and to predict future court interpretations.

The current trend is moving away from legally based organizational compliance programs. Instead, many companies are choosing to provide incentives that foster a culture of ethics and responsibility that encourages compliance with laws and regulations. Developing best practices and voluntary compliance creates rules and principles that guide decision making. Many companies are encouraging their employees to take responsibility for avoiding legal misconduct themselves. The New York Stock Exchange, for example, requires all member companies to have a code of ethics, and some firms try to go beyond what is required by the law. Many firms are trying to develop ethical cultures based on values and proactive assessments of risks to prevent misconduct.

## 3-5d  Regulatory Agencies

Federal regulatory agencies influence many marketing activities, including product development, pricing, packaging, advertising, personal selling, and distribution. Usually these bodies have the power to enforce specific laws, as well as some discretion in establishing operating rules and regulations to guide certain types of industry practices. Because of this discretion and overlapping areas of responsibility, confusion or conflict regarding which agencies have jurisdiction over which marketing activities is common.

Of all the federal regulatory units, the **Federal Trade Commission (FTC)** most heavily influences marketing activities. Although the FTC regulates a variety of business practices, it allocates a large portion of resources to curbing false advertising, misleading pricing, and deceptive packaging and labeling. For instance, the FTC opened a preliminary probe into whether Google was using its Android operating system to require handsets to prominently display its maps, search, and other features. The agency believed this requirement incentivized handsets to favor Google services on smartphones' home screens, placing Google's rivals at a disadvantage.[26] When it has reason to believe a firm is violating a law, the commission typically issues a complaint stating that the business is in violation and takes appropriate action. If, after it is issued a complaint, a company continues the questionable practice, the FTC can issue a cease-and-desist order demanding that the business stop doing whatever caused the complaint. The firm can appeal to the federal courts to have the order rescinded. However, the FTC can seek civil penalties in court, up to a maximum penalty of $10,000 a day for each infraction if a cease-and-desist order is violated. The commission can require companies to run corrective advertising in response to previous ads deemed misleading (see Figure 3.2).

**Federal Trade Commission (FTC)** An agency that regulates a variety of business practices and curbs false advertising, misleading pricing, and deceptive packaging and labeling

Figure 3.2   **Federal Trade Commission Enforcement Tools**

| Cease-and-desist order | Consent decree | Redress | Corrective advertising | Civil penalties |
|---|---|---|---|---|
| A court order to a business to stop engaging in an illegal practice | An order for a business to stop engaging in questionable activities to avoid prosecution | Money paid to customer to settle or resolve a complaint | A requirement that a business make new advertisement to correct misinformation | Court-ordered civil fines for up to $10,000 per day for violating a cease-and-desist order |

The FTC also assists businesses in complying with laws and evaluates new marketing methods every year. The agency has held hearings to help firms establish guidelines for avoiding charges of price fixing, deceptive advertising, and questionable telemarketing practices. It has also held conferences and hearings on electronic (Internet) commerce, identity theft, and childhood obesity. When general sets of guidelines are needed to improve business practices in a particular industry, the FTC sometimes encourages firms within that industry to establish a set of trade practices voluntarily. The FTC may even sponsor a conference that brings together industry leaders and consumers for this purpose.

Unlike the FTC, other regulatory units are limited to dealing with specific goods, services, or business activities. Consider the Food and Drug Administration (FDA), which enforces regulations that prohibit the sale and distribution of adulterated, misbranded, or hazardous food and drug products. After the Blue Bell ice cream recall—in which bacteria-contaminated ice cream led to three deaths—the FDA finalized rules to make it mandatory for food manufacturers to adopt detailed plans for how to prevent foodborne illnesses.[27] Table 3.3 outlines the areas of responsibility of seven federal regulatory agencies.

In addition, all states, as well as many cities and towns, have regulatory agencies that enforce laws and regulations regarding marketing practices within their states or municipalities. State and local regulatory agencies try not to establish regulations that conflict with those of federal regulatory agencies. They generally enforce laws dealing with the production and sale of particular goods and services. The utility, insurance, financial, and liquor industries are commonly regulated by state agencies. Among these agencies' targets are misleading advertising and pricing. Recent legal actions suggest that states are taking a firmer stance against perceived deceptive pricing practices and are using basic consumer research to define deceptive pricing.

State consumer protection laws offer an opportunity for state attorneys general to deal with marketing issues related to fraud and deception. Most states have consumer protection laws that are very general in nature and provide enforcement when new schemes evolve that injure consumers. The New York Consumer Protection Board, for instance, is proactive in monitoring consumer protection and providing consumer education. New York became the first state to implement an airline passenger rights law. In addition, New York City has banned trans fats and tried to ban large soft drinks.

**Table 3.3** **Major Federal Regulatory Agencies**

| Agency | Major Areas of Responsibility |
|---|---|
| Federal Trade Commission (FTC) | Enforces laws and guidelines regarding business practices; takes action to stop false and deceptive advertising, pricing, packaging, and labelling |
| Food and Drug Administration (FDA) | Enforces laws and regulations to prevent distribution of adulterated or misbranded foods, drugs, medical devices, cosmetics, veterinary products, and potentially hazardous consumer products |
| Consumer Product Safety Commission (CPSC) | Ensures compliance with the Consumer Product Safety Act; protects the public from unreasonable risk of injury from any consumer product not covered by other regulatory agencies |
| Federal Communications Commission (FCC) | Regulates communication by wire, radio, and television in interstate and foreign commerce |
| Environmental Protection Agency (EPA) | Develops and enforces environmental protection standards and conducts research on the adverse effects of pollution |
| Federal Power Commission (FPC) | Regulates rates and sales of natural gas producers, thereby affecting the supply and price of gas available to consumers; also regulates wholesale rates for electricity and gas, pipeline construction, and U.S. imports and exports of natural gas and electricity |
| Consumer Financial Protection Bureau (CFPB) | Regulates the offering and provision of consumer financial products and serves to protect consumers from deceptive financial practices |

Source: "Subtitle A—Bureau of Consumer Financial Protection," *One Hundred Eleventh Congress of the United States of America,* 589.

## 3-5e Self-Regulatory Forces

Various forms of self-regulation that promote cooperation, along with voluntary ethics and social responsibility standards, create accountability and transparency that go beyond government regulation.[28] In an attempt to be good corporate citizens and prevent government intervention, some businesses try to regulate themselves. Similarly, a number of trade associations have developed self-regulatory programs. Though these programs are not a direct outgrowth of laws, many were established to stop or stall the development of laws and governmental regulatory groups that would regulate the associations' marketing practices. Sometimes trade associations establish ethics codes by which their members must abide or risk censure or exclusion from the association. For instance, the National Association of Home Builders has adopted a code of ethics and guiding principles by which its members must abide.[29] The Direct Selling Association and the Direct Marketing Association also require compliance with detailed codes of ethics in order for member organizations to retain their membership.

Perhaps the best-known self-regulatory group is the **Better Business Bureau (BBB)**, which is a system of nongovernmental, independent, local regulatory agencies that are supported by local businesses. More than 110 bureaus help settle problems between consumers and specific business firms. Each bureau also acts to preserve good business practices in a locality, although it usually lacks strong enforcement tools for dealing with firms that employ questionable practices. When a firm continues to violate what the Better Business Bureau believes to be good business practices, the bureau warns consumers through local newspapers or broadcast media. If the offending organization is a BBB member, it may be expelled from the local bureau. Table 3.4 describes some of the major self-regulatory issues that often occur in the marketing industry.

The Council of Better Business Bureaus is a national organization composed of all local Better Business Bureaus. The National Advertising Division (NAD) of the council operates a self-regulatory program that investigates claims regarding alleged deceptive advertising. For instance, the NAD advised Sprint to discontinue its advertising that claimed its network was "brand new" or "all-new" because it felt there was no industry standard to measure the claim of "newest."[30]

Another self-regulatory entity, the **National Advertising Review Board (NARB)**, considers cases in which an advertiser challenges issues raised by the NAD about an advertisement. Cases are reviewed by panels drawn from NARB members that represent advertisers, agencies, and the public. In one case, the NARB recommended that personal care company Philosophy, Inc. modify its claims regarding "Time in a Bottle Age-Defying Serum." The claims had already been reviewed by the NAD, but Philosophy, Inc. took the case to the NARB. The NARB determined that the study Philosophy, Inc. had relied upon to make its claims was reliable, but still recommended it modify or discontinue certain claims that could potentially be misleading.[31] The NARB, sponsored by the Council of Better Business Bureaus and three advertising trade organizations, has no official enforcement powers. However, if a firm refuses to comply with its decision, the NARB may publicize the questionable practice and file a complaint with the FTC.

Self-regulatory programs have several advantages over governmental laws and regulatory agencies. Establishment and implementation are usually less expensive, and guidelines are generally more realistic and operational. In addition, effective self-regulatory programs reduce the need to expand government bureaucracy. However, these programs have several limitations. When a trade association creates a set of industry guidelines for its members, nonmember firms

**Better Business Bureau (BBB)** A system of nongovernmental, independent, local regulatory agencies supported by local businesses that helps settle problems between customers and specific business firms

**National Advertising Review Board (NARB)** A self-regulatory unit that considers challenges to issues raised by the National Advertising Division (an arm of the Council of Better Business Bureaus) about an advertisement

Table 3.4 **Self-Regulatory Issues in Marketing**

| | |
|---|---|
| 1 | Truthful Advertising Messages |
| 2 | Health and Childhood Obesity |
| 3 | Internet Tracking/User Privacy |
| 4 | Concern for Vulnerable Populations |
| 5 | Failure to Deliver on Expectations and Promises |
| 6 | Sustainable Marketing Practices and Greenwashing |
| 7 | Transparent Pricing |
| 8 | Understandable Labelling and Packaging |
| 9 | Supply Chain Relationships/Ethical Sourcing |
| 10 | Marketing of Dangerous Products |
| 11 | Product Quality Failures |
| 12 | Nonresponse to Customer Complaints |

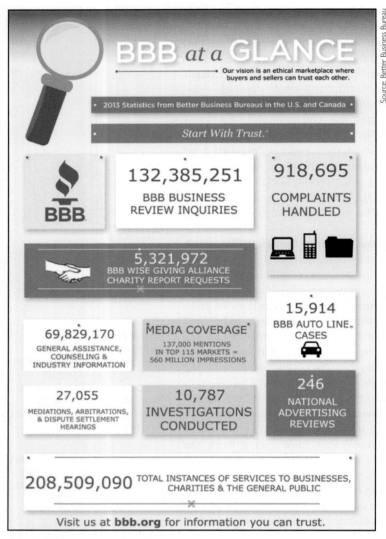

Source: Better Business Bureau

**Self-Regulatory Forces**
The Better Business Bureau is one of the best known self-regulatory organizations.

do not have to abide by them. Furthermore, many self-regulatory programs lack the tools or authority to enforce guidelines. Finally, guidelines in self-regulatory programs are often less strict than those established by government agencies.

## 3-6 TECHNOLOGICAL FORCES

The word *technology* brings to mind scientific advances such as electric vehicles, smartphones, drones, lifestyle drugs, radio-frequency identification tags, and more. Technology has revolutionized the products created and offered by marketers and the channels by which they communicate about those products. However, even though these innovations are outgrowths of technology, none of them *are* technology. **Technology** is the application of knowledge and tools to solve problems and perform tasks more efficiently. Technology grows out of research performed by businesses, universities, government agencies, and nonprofit organizations. More than half of this research is paid for by the federal government, which supports research in such diverse areas as health, defense, agriculture, energy, and pollution.

The rapid technological growth of the last several decades is expected to accelerate. It has transformed the U.S. economy into the most productive in the world and provided Americans with an ever-higher standard of living and tremendous opportunities for sustained business expansion. Disruptive technologies and innovations often create a new market or greater value for consumers. This new market often replaces older industry leaders. Uber and Airbnb are examples of firms using peer-to-peer Internet platforms to challenge existing markets. Technology and technological advancements clearly influence buyers' and marketers' decisions, so let's take a closer look at the impact of technology and its use in the marketplace.

### 3-6a Impact of Technology

Technology determines how we, as members of society, satisfy our physiological needs. In various ways and to varying degrees, eating and drinking habits, sleeping patterns, sexual activities, health care, and work performance are all influenced by both existing technology and changes in technology. Because of the technological revolution in communications, for example, marketers can now reach vast numbers of people more efficiently through a variety of media. Social networks, smartphones, and tablet computers help marketers stay in touch with clients, make appointments, and handle last-minute orders or cancellations. A growing number of U.S. households, as well as many businesses, have given up their land-lines in favor of using cell phones as their primary phones. Currently, about 43 percent of Americans have exchanged their land-lines for cell phones.[32]

**technology** The application of knowledge and tools to solve problems and perform tasks more efficiently

The growth of information technology (IT) is staggering. IT is changing the lives of consumers across the globe. Not only does it offer lucrative career opportunities, it also provides business opportunities for the entrepreneur. For instance, entrepreneur Marc Bernioff built an entire organization around the cloud computing industry. Today Salesforce.com continues to be listed among the world's most innovative companies.[33] The Internet also improves supply-chain management as it allows manufacturers, distributors, retailers, and other members of the supply chain to collaborate more closely and serve their customers more efficiently.[34] The importance of the Internet will only increase in the future. It is estimated that

Source: US edition, Deloitte Global Mobile Consumer Survey, May–Jun 2015
Base Graph 1: All respondents: 2015: 2,069

by the end of the decade, more than 50 billion things, including cars, refrigerators, medical devices, and more, will be hooked up to the Internet infrastructure. South Korea is making significant progress in this pursuit. This phenomenon—known as the Internet of Things—will greatly impact how we do business and live our daily lives.[35] However, it also requires significant investment in security systems to protect these devices from cybercriminals.

Computers have become a staple in American homes, but the type of computer has been changing drastically in this past decade. Traditional desktop computers appear to be on the decline. Laptops became immensely popular due to their mobility, but analysts estimate that laptops might be entering the maturity stage of the product life cycle. Tablet computers are in the growth stage of the product life cycle, but it seems that this growth is already slowing down. In response many companies are creating apps specifically made for the iPad and similar devices. The rapidly evolving state of technology requires marketers to familiarize themselves with the latest technological changes.

The Internet has become a major tool in most households for communicating, researching, shopping, and entertaining. It is estimated that U.S. adults spend an average of 1 hour and 16 minutes on digital devices watching videos per day.[36] Time spent on social networks also makes up a significant portion of a consumer's online activities. One study estimates that users worldwide spend 28 percent of their time online on social networking sites.[37]

Although technology has had many positive impacts on our lives, there are also many negative impacts to consider. We enjoy the benefits of communicating through the Internet; however, we are increasingly concerned about protecting our privacy and intellectual property. Hackers and those who steal digital property are also using advanced technology to harm others. Likewise, technological advances in the areas of health and medicine have led to the creation of new drugs that save lives; however, such advances have also led to cloning and genetically modified foods that have become controversial issues in many segments of society. Consider the impact of cell phones. The ability to call from almost any location has many benefits, but it also has negative side effects, including increases in traffic accidents, increased noise pollution, and fears about potential health risks.[38]

The effects of technology relate to such characteristics as dynamics, reach, and the self-sustaining nature of technological progress. The *dynamics* of technology involve the constant change that often challenges the structures of social institutions, including social relationships, the legal system, religion, education, business, and leisure. *Reach* refers to the broad nature of technology as it moves through society.

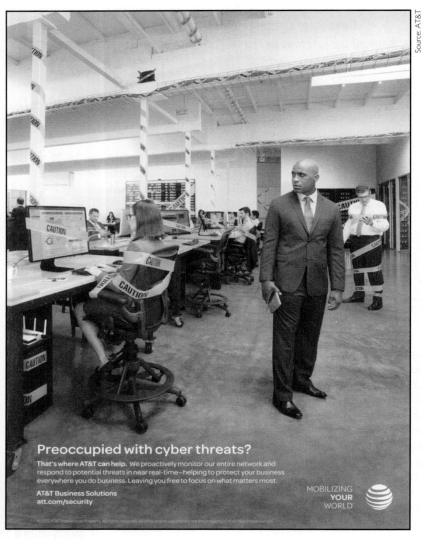

Source: AT&T

**Preoccupied with cyber threats?**

That's where AT&T can help. We proactively monitor our entire network and respond to potential threats in near real-time—helping to protect your business everywhere you do business. Leaving you free to focus on what matters most.

**AT&T Business Solutions**
att.com/security

MOBILIZING YOUR WORLD

**Impact of Technology**
AT&T uses technology to develop security services businesses can purchase that will enable AT&T to monitor their networks and respond to potential threats.

The *self-sustaining* nature of technology relates to the fact that technology acts as a catalyst to spur even faster development. As new innovations are introduced, they stimulate the need for more advancement to facilitate further development. Our increasing reliance on computer technology for business purposes has led to an increased risk of hacking or data theft. This in turn has caused more demand for Internet security services that combat hacking attempts. AT&T's advertisement uses caution tape to demonstrate how serious this issue can be and why AT&T has the right solution to address online threats as soon as they arise. Technology initiates a change process that creates new opportunities for new technologies in every industry segment or personal life experience that it touches. At some point, there is a multiplier effect that causes still greater demand for more change to improve performance.[39]

The expanding opportunities for e-commerce, the sharing of business information, the ability to maintain business relationships, and the ability to conduct business transactions via digital networks are changing the relationship between businesses and consumers.[40] Many people use the Internet to purchase consumer electronics, clothing, software, books, furniture, and music. Amazon.com has actually surpassed Walmart in market value to become the world's biggest retailer.[41] More people now opt to purchase music online or simply listen for free on social networking sites. As a result, CD sales have decreased over the years. In addition, consumers go online to acquire travel-related services, financial services, and information. The forces unleashed by the Internet are particularly important in business-to-business relationships, where uncertainties are being reduced by improving the quantity, reliability, and timeliness of information.

## 3-6b  Adoption and Use of Technology

Many companies lose their status as market leaders because they fail to keep up with technological changes. It is important for firms to determine when a technology is changing the industry and to define the strategic influence of the new technology. The Internet has created the need for ever-faster transmission of signals through 4G, cable broadband, satellite, Wi-Fi, or fiber optic technology. To remain competitive, companies today must keep up with and adapt to technological advances.

The extent to which a firm can protect inventions that stem from research also influences its use of technology. How secure a product is from imitation depends on how easily others can copy it without violating its patent. If groundbreaking products and processes cannot be protected through patents, a company is less likely to market them and make the benefits of its research available to competitors.

Through a procedure known as *technology assessment*, managers try to foresee the effects of new products and processes on their firm's operations, on other business organizations, and on society in general. With information obtained through a technology assessment, management tries to estimate whether benefits of adopting a specific technology outweigh costs to the firm and to society at large. The degree to which a business is technologically based also influences its managers' response to technology.

# 3-7 SOCIOCULTURAL FORCES

**Sociocultural forces** are the influences in a society and its culture(s) that bring about changes in people's attitudes, beliefs, norms, customs, and lifestyles. Profoundly affecting how people live, these forces help determine what, where, how, and when people buy products. Like the other environmental forces, sociocultural forces present marketers with both challenges and opportunities. For a closer look at sociocultural forces, we examine three major issues: demographic and diversity characteristics, cultural values, and consumerism.

## 3-7a Demographic and Diversity Characteristics

Changes in a population's demographic characteristics—age, gender, race, ethnicity, marital and parental status, income, and education—have a significant bearing on relationships and individual behavior. These shifts lead to changes in how people live and ultimately in their consumption of such products as food, clothing, housing, transportation, communication, recreation, education, and health services. We'll look at a few of the changes in demographics and diversity that are affecting marketing activities.

One demographic change that is affecting the marketplace is the increasing proportion of older consumers. According to the U.S. Bureau of the Census, the number of people age 65 and older is expected to more than double by the year 2050, reaching 83.7 million.[42] Consequently, marketers can expect significant increases in the demand for health-care services, recreation, tourism, retirement housing, and selected skin-care products. Even online companies are trying to take advantage of the opportunities baby boomers present. Several online dating sites directed toward boomers have been launched, such as BabyBoomerPeopleMeet.com and SeniorPeopleMeet.com.[43] To reach older customers effectively, of course, marketers must understand the diversity within the mature market with respect to geographic location, income, marital status, and limitations in mobility and self-care.

The number of singles is also on the rise. Singles currently comprise more than half of American households.[44] Single people have quite different spending patterns than couples and

**sociocultural forces** The influences in a society and its culture(s) that change people's attitudes, beliefs, norms, customs, and lifestyles

## MARKETING DEBATE

**ISSUE: Should the FDA ban trans fats from food products?**

A nationwide trend toward healthier food is growing not only among consumers but also regulators. The Food and Drug Administration mandated that food manufacturers have three years to phase out partially hydrogenated oils (PHO) from their products as it is a main source of unhealthy trans fat. Many food manufacturers have already eliminated trans fats from their products. Until the ban, food could be labeled as having 0 grams of trans fat if it contained less than 0.5 grams per serving. The government estimates the ban will prevent 20,000 heart attacks yearly.

However, it is estimated that it will cost food manufacturers $12–14 billion. PLO helps to preserve food longer, so companies must extensively research healthier alternatives that have the same benefits. Critics view the ban as unnecessary as consumption of trans fats fell 78 percent in less than a decade. They also believe the government is micromanaging people's lives by removing the right to make their own decisions. Additionally, 0.5 grams per serving is considered safe for consumption, although consumers often consume multiple servings.[b]

families with children. They are less likely to own homes and thus buy less furniture and fewer appliances. They spend more heavily on convenience foods, restaurants, travel, entertainment, and recreation. In addition, they tend to prefer smaller packages, whereas families often buy bulk goods and products packaged in multiple servings.

Despite these trends, the United States is facing a baby bust with its lowest fertility rate ever. This means that without immigration, the United States will fail to grow.[45] The U.S. population experienced the slowest rate of growth in the last decade since the Great Depression at 9.7 percent growth. Today the U.S. population is about 322 million. While the birth rate is declining, new immigrants help with population gains.[46] It is estimated that those in the U.S. population that were born in other countries has more than doubled since the 1960s, with more than 40 million foreign-born individuals.[47]

The number of immigrants into the United States has steadily risen during the last 40 years. In the 1960s, 3.3 million people immigrated to the United States; in the 1970s, 4.4 million immigrated; in the 1980s, 7.3 million arrived; in the 1990s, the United States received 9.1 million immigrants; and in the 2000s, more than 8.3 million people have immigrated to the United States.[48] In contrast to earlier immigrants, very few recent ones are of European origin. Another reason for the increasing cultural diversification of the United States is that most recent immigrants are relatively young, whereas U.S. citizens of European origin are growing older. These younger immigrants tend to have more children than their older counterparts, further shifting the population balance. By the turn of the 20th century, the U.S. population had shifted from one dominated by whites to one consisting largely of three racial and ethnic groups: whites, blacks, and Hispanics. The U.S. government projects that by the year 2060, approximately 119 million Hispanics, 59.7 million blacks or African Americans, and 39 million Asians will call the United States home.[49] Table 3.5 provides a glimpse into the multicultural nature of the U.S. population. Although the majority of the population still identify themselves as white, Hispanic and Asian ethnicities are expected to grow in the next 50 years, while white non-Hispanics ethnicities are estimated to decrease.

Marketers recognize that these profound changes in the U.S. population bring unique problems and opportunities. But a diverse population means a more diverse customer base, and marketing practices must be modified—and diversified—to meet its changing needs. For instance, Mattel has started releasing Barbie dolls with more average waistlines and individual style trends. This is in response to parents' desires to have dolls for their children that do not depict unrealistic standards (such as the impossible proportions of Barbie) and that stress individuality so children are encouraged to be themselves.[50]

## 3-7b Cultural Values

Changes in cultural values have dramatically influenced people's needs and desires for products. Although cultural values do not shift overnight, they do change at varying speeds. Marketers try to monitor these changes, knowing this information can equip them to predict changes in consumers' needs for products, at least in the near future. For instance, automakers are

Table 3.5   **The Multicultural Nature of the U.S. Population**

| Race | % Population 2014 | Estimated % 2060 |
| --- | --- | --- |
| White | 77.5 | 68.5 |
| Hispanic | 17.4 | 28.6 |
| Black or African American | 13.2 | 14.3 |
| Asian | 5.4 | 11.7 |
| American Indian or Alaska Native | 1.2 | 1.3 |
| Native Hawaiian or Pacific Islander | 0.2 | 0.3 |

Source: Sandra L. Colby and Jennifer M. Ortman, *Projections of the Size and Composition of the U.S. Population: 2014 to 2060* (Washington, D.C.: U.S. Census Bureau, March 2015), p. 9.

adapting their strategies to appeal to the younger demographic because fewer young adults are choosing to purchase vehicles or get their drivers' licenses. An alternative some teens are pursuing is opening up an Uber account so they can get where they want to go without their parents and without having to go through the hassle of obtaining a license.[51]

Starting in the late 1980s, issues of health, nutrition, and exercise grew in importance. People today are more concerned about the foods they eat and thus are choosing healthier products. Compared to those in the previous two decades, Americans today are more likely to favor smoke-free environments and to consume less alcohol. They have also altered their sexual behavior to reduce the risk of contracting sexually transmitted diseases. Marketers have responded with a proliferation of foods, beverages, and exercise products that fit this new lifestyle, as well as with programs to help people quit smoking and contraceptives that are safer and more effective. Americans are also becoming increasingly open to alternative medicines and nutritionally improved foods. As a result, sales of organic foods, herbs and herbal remedies, vitamins, and dietary supplements have escalated. In addition to the proliferation of new organic brands, such as Earthbound Farm, Horizon Dairy, and Whole Foods' 365, many conventional marketers have introduced organic versions of their products, including Orville Redenbacher, Heinz, and Walmart.

The major source of cultural values is the family. For years, when asked about the most important aspects of their lives, adults specified family issues and a happy marriage. Today, however, only one out of two marriages is predicted to last. Values regarding the permanence of marriage are changing. Because a happy marriage is prized so highly, more people are willing to give up an unhappy one and seek a different marriage partner or opt to stay single.

Children continue to be very important. Marketers have responded with safer, upscale baby gear and supplies, children's electronics, and family entertainment products. Marketers are also aiming more marketing efforts directly at children because children often play pivotal roles in purchasing decisions. A study in Austria reported that children influence twice as many purchase decisions in the supermarket than parents are aware of, and the majority of items children requested are products positioned at their eye level.[52]

Children and family values are also factors in the trend toward more eat-out and take-out meals. Busy families in which both parents work generally want to spend less time in the kitchen and more time together enjoying themselves. Beneficiaries of this trend have primarily been fast-food and casual restaurants like McDonald's, Taco Bell, and Applebee's, but most supermarkets have added more ready-to-cook and ready-to-serve meal components to meet the needs of busy customers. Some also offer dine-in cafés.

Green marketing helps establish long-term consumer relationships by maintaining, supporting, and enhancing the natural environment. One of society's environmental hurdles is proper disposal of waste, especially of nondegradable materials such as disposable diapers and polystyrene packaging. Companies have responded by developing more environmentally sensitive products and packaging. Procter & Gamble, for example, uses recycled materials in some of its packaging and sells environmentally friendly refills. Companies like Seventh Generation, which sells products like paper towels and bathroom tissue made from recycled paper as well as eco-friendly cleaning products, have entered the mainstream. Everything

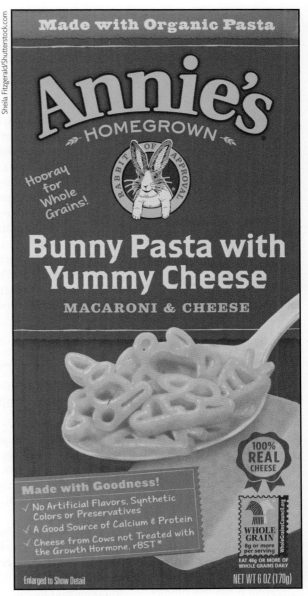

**Sociocultural Forces**

Consumers' busy schedules often require them to grab ready-to-cook meals, but there is also a growing shift toward eating more natural organic foods. Annie's Homegrown macaroni and cheese has turned both of these trends into opportunities.

the company produces is as environmentally friendly as it can be, in hopes of having as little impact on the next seven generations as possible.[53] A number of marketers sponsor recycling programs and encourage their customers to take part in them.

### 3-7c  Consumerism

**Consumerism** involves organized efforts by individuals, groups, and organizations to protect consumers' rights. The movement's major forces are individual consumer advocates, consumer organizations and other interest groups, consumer education, and consumer laws.

To achieve their objectives, consumers and their advocates write letters or send e-mails to companies, post on social media sites, lobby government agencies, broadcast public service announcements, and boycott companies whose activities they deem irresponsible. Consider that a number of consumers would like to eliminate telemarketing and e-mail spam, and some of them have joined organizations and groups attempting to stop these activities. Businesses that engage in questionable practices invite additional regulation. Several organizations, for instance, evaluate children's products for safety, often announcing dangerous products before Christmas so parents can avoid them. Other actions by the consumer movement have resulted in seat belts and air bags in automobiles, dolphin-friendly tuna, the banning of unsafe three-wheel motorized vehicles, and numerous laws regulating product safety and information. We take a closer look at consumerism in the next chapter.

**consumerism** Organized efforts by individuals, groups, and organizations to protect consumers' rights

# Summary

### 3-1  Summarize why it is important to examine and respond to the marketing environment.

The marketing environment consists of external forces that directly or indirectly influence an organization's acquisition of inputs (personnel, financial resources, raw materials, and information) and generation of outputs (goods, services, and ideas). The marketing environment includes competitive, economic, political, legal and regulatory, technological, and sociocultural forces.

Environmental scanning is the process of collecting information about forces in the marketing environment; environmental analysis is the process of assessing and interpreting information obtained in scanning. This information helps marketing managers predict opportunities and threats associated with environmental fluctuation. Marketing managers may assume either a passive, reactive approach or a proactive, aggressive approach in responding to these environmental fluctuations. The choice depends on the organization's structures and needs and on the composition of environmental forces that affect it.

### 3-2  Explain how competitive factors affect an organization's ability to compete.

All businesses compete for customers' dollars. A marketer, however, generally defines *competition* as other firms that market products that are similar to or can be substituted for its products in the same geographic area. These competitors can be classified into one of four types: brand competitors, product competitors, generic competitors, and total budget competitors. The number of firms controlling the supply of a product may affect the strength of competitors. The four

general types of competitive structures are monopoly, oligopoly, monopolistic competition, and pure competition. Marketers monitor what competitors are currently doing and assess changes occurring in the competitive environment.

### 3-3  Articulate how economic factors influence a customer's ability and willingness to buy products.

General economic conditions, buying power, and willingness to spend can strongly influence marketing decisions and activities. The overall state of the economy fluctuates in a general pattern known as the business cycle, which consists of four stages: prosperity, recession, depression, and recovery. Consumers' goods, services, and financial holdings make up their buying power, or ability to purchase. Financial sources of buying power are income, credit, and wealth. After-tax income used for spending or saving is disposable income. Disposable income left after an individual has purchased the basic necessities of food, clothes, and shelter is discretionary income. Factors affecting buyers' willingness to spend include product price; level of satisfaction obtained from currently used products; family size; and expectations about future employment, income, prices, and general economic conditions.

### 3-4  Identify the types of political forces in the marketing environment.

The political, legal, and regulatory forces of the marketing environment are closely interrelated. Political forces may determine what laws and regulations affecting specific marketers are enacted, how much the government purchases, and from which suppliers. They can also be important in helping organizations secure foreign markets. Companies influence political forces in several ways, including maintaining good relationships with political officials, protesting the actions of legislative bodies, helping elect individuals who regard them positively to public office through campaign contributions, and employing lobbyists to communicate their concerns to elected officials.

### 3-5 Explain how laws, government regulations, and self-regulatory agencies affect marketing activities.

Federal legislation affecting marketing activities can be divided into procompetitive legislation—laws designed to preserve and encourage competition—and consumer protection laws, which generally relate to product safety and information disclosure. Actual effects of legislation are determined by how marketers and courts interpret the laws. Federal guidelines for sentencing concerning violations of these laws represent an attempt to force marketers to comply with the laws.

Federal, state, and local regulatory agencies usually have power to enforce specific laws. They also have some discretion in establishing operating rules and drawing up regulations to guide certain types of industry practices. Industry self-regulation represents another regulatory force; marketers view this type of regulation more favorably than government action because they have more opportunity to take part in creating guidelines. Self-regulation may be less expensive than government regulation, and its guidelines are generally more realistic. However, such regulation generally cannot ensure compliance as effectively as government agencies.

### 3-6 Describe how new technology impacts marketing and society.

Technology is the application of knowledge and tools to solve problems and perform tasks more efficiently. Consumer demand, buyer behavior, product development, packaging, promotion, prices, and distribution systems are all influenced directly by technology. The rapid technological growth of the last few decades is expected to accelerate. Revolutionary changes in communication technology have allowed marketers to reach vast numbers of people; however, with this expansion of communication has come concern about privacy and intellectual property. And while science and medical research have brought many great advances, cloning and genetically modified foods are controversial issues in many segments of society. Home, health, leisure, and work are all influenced to varying degrees by technology and technological advances. The *dynamics* of technology involves the constant change that challenges every aspect of our society. *Reach* refers to the broad nature of technology as it moves through and affects society.

Many companies lose their status as market leaders because they fail to keep up with technological changes. The ability to protect inventions from competitor imitation is also an important consideration when making marketing decisions.

### 3-7 Outline the sociocultural issues marketers must deal with as they make decisions.

Sociocultural forces are the influences in a society and its culture that result in changes in attitudes, beliefs, norms, customs, and lifestyles. Major sociocultural issues directly affecting marketers include demographic and diversity characteristics, cultural values, and consumerism.

Changes in a population's demographic characteristics, such as age, income, race, and ethnicity, can lead to changes in that population's consumption of products. Changes in cultural values, such as those relating to health, nutrition, family, and the natural environment, have had striking effects on people's needs for products and therefore are closely monitored by marketers. Consumerism involves the efforts of individuals, groups, and organizations to protect consumers' rights. Consumer rights organizations inform and organize other consumers, raise issues, help businesses develop consumer-oriented programs, and pressure lawmakers to enact consumer protection laws.

---

**Go to www.cengagebrain.com for resources to help you master the content in this chapter as well as materials that will expand your marketing knowledge!**

---

## Important Terms

| | | | |
|---|---|---|---|
| environmental scanning  66 | oligopoly  70 | buying power  73 | Better Business Bureau (BBB)  81 |
| environmental analysis  67 | monopolistic competition  71 | income  73 | National Advertising Review Board (NARB)  81 |
| competition  69 | pure competition  71 | disposable income  73 | technology  82 |
| brand competitors  69 | business cycle  72 | discretionary income  73 | sociocultural forces  85 |
| product competitors  69 | prosperity  72 | wealth  73 | consumerism  88 |
| generic competitors  69 | recession  72 | willingness to spend  74 | |
| total budget competitors  69 | depression  72 | Federal Trade Commission (FTC)  79 | |
| monopoly  70 | recovery  72 | | |

# Discussion and Review Questions

1. Why are environmental scanning and analysis important to marketers?
2. What are the four types of competition? Which is most important to marketers?
3. In what ways can each of the business cycle stages affect consumers' reactions to marketing strategies?
4. What business cycle stage are we experiencing currently? How is this stage affecting business firms in your area?
5. Define *income, disposable income*, and *discretionary income*. How does each type of income affect consumer buying power?
6. How do wealth and consumer credit affect consumer buying power?
7. What factors influence a buyer's willingness to spend?
8. Describe marketers' attempts to influence political forces.
9. What types of problems do marketers experience as they interpret legislation?
10. What are the goals of the Federal Trade Commission? List the ways in which the FTC affects marketing activities. Do you think a single regulatory agency should

have such broad jurisdiction over so many marketing practices? Why or why not?
11. Name several nongovernmental regulatory forces. Do you believe self-regulation is more or less effective than governmental regulatory agencies? Why?
12. What does the term *technology* mean to you? Do the benefits of technology outweigh its costs and potential dangers? Defend your answer.
13. Discuss the impact of technology on marketing activities.
14. What factors determine whether a business organization adopts and uses technology?
15. What evidence exists that cultural diversity is increasing in the United States?
16. In what ways are cultural values changing? How are marketers responding to these changes?
17. Describe consumerism. Analyze some active consumer forces in your area.

# Video Case 3.1

## Apple vs. Samsung: Gloves Are Off

Both Apple and Samsung have been at the forefront of technology innovation. Technological forces are pushing for newer and better products, and tech companies must constantly pursue product development to compete effectively against each other. As a result, the tech environment has become highly aggressive with firms going to great lengths to protect their patents. A patent rewards an innovator for a new invention or technology by providing the innovator the sole rights to develop and sell that product for 20 years. Patents offer the owner legal protection. If during that time competitors try to sell the product, they can be sued for damages.

In the United States, whoever files a patent first gets legal protection. This can get complicated, however, when it is hard to determine which company obtained a patent first, or when a firm accuses another firm of violating their patent by copying certain product features protected under the patent. This was the case between Apple and Samsung, leading to a legal battle that would take multiple years to resolve. It started in 2011, when Apple accused Samsung of violating its iPhone patent by copying certain iPhone features for its Galaxy S. In

its allegations, Apple accused Samsung of copying the iPhone shape; color; tap-to-zoom, flip-to-rotate, and slide-to-scroll features; and more. It also claimed that Samsung violated the patent for its iPad.

Samsung claimed the opposite. It claimed that it had patented these components before Apple and that therefore Apple's iPhone violated Samsung's intellectual property rights. Samsung countersued. Soon the lawsuit had taken on global proportions as lawsuits were filed in the United States, South Korea, Germany, Japan, the United Kingdom, and other countries. Since the legal and regulatory environments differ in each country, the courts often came up with different verdicts. For instance, South Korea courts found that Apple had violated two of Samsung's patents, while Samsung violated one of Apple's. The United Kingdom ruled in favor of Samsung.

In the United States, Apple wanted more than $2 billion in damages from Samsung. In the original verdict, U.S. courts ruled that Samsung had violated Apple's patents and ordered Samsung to pay $1 billion in damages. Later appeals reduced this amount. In 2012 Apple filed a new lawsuit against

Samsung claiming it had copied five features protected under Apple's patent. Samsung sued Apple, claiming it had violated two of the patents it owned.

This time the jury issued a mixed verdict. "Among the popular features, it found Samsung copied the slide-to-unlock button on some of its phones and autocorrect," said Betty Yu, a reporter from KPIX 5 CBS who covered the outcome. "Samsung accused Apple of infringing two of its patents and in the end was found guilty of just one. It involves photo and video organization in folders."

As a result of the verdict, Samsung was ordered to pay $120 million in damages to Apple, whereas Apple was told to pay Samsung $158,000. Analysts see the legal battle as being a fight over dominance rather than a concern over money. Both companies hold a large share of the smartphone market, and neither is willing to give up market share.

For consumers the verdict is likely to have little impact. Sometimes legal battles over intellectual property can result in the losing company being ordered to stop selling the product within the country. However, this did not happen with the Apple vs. Samsung case.

"What does all this mean for you and me? Well, experts say that this really doesn't mean anything for us," Betty Yu says. "You can still use your phones involved in this case, and the newest devices aren't an issue."

As this case demonstrates, intellectual property is not always an easy path to navigate, especially for global companies who operate in countries with different laws. In China, for instance, intellectual property rights laws are more lax, and copying is more common. Although some might view Apple as being overly aggressive, maintaining control over intellectual property in the tech industry could mean the difference between company failure and success. Currently, Samsung overshadows Apple in the global smartphone market. However, newer competitors including Chinese firms Huawei, Lenovo, and Xiaomi are quickly gaining in market share.[54]

### Questions for Discussion

1. In what type of competitive environment do you think Apple and Samsung operate?
2. How do technological forces impact how Apple and Samsung operate when it comes to protecting their intellectual property?
3. Why is it important for international tech firms to be familiar with the laws and regulations of the countries in which they operate?

# Case 3.2

## Volkswagen Hits a Bump in the Road

Although the impact of technology has created benefits for businesses and consumers alike, it has also provided a greater opportunity to cheat ethical and legal requirements. Volkswagen, once lauded for its green reputation, experienced a devastating blow after it was discovered the company had purposefully fooled regulators and consumers with its emissions testing. Volkswagen used a "defeat device" in its software that changed the vehicle's performance depending upon the environment. For instance, the software was able to detect when vehicles were undergoing emissions testing. During this testing, the software made the vehicles run below performance, which released fewer emissions and met requirements. However, on the road the cars ran at maximum performance and gave off up to 40 times the allowable limit for emissions in the United States.

Thus far, Volkswagen estimates that 11 million vehicles in the United States and Europe have been affected by this defeat device. Until the scandal broke, VW had promoted itself as a more eco-friendly company. Its commercials featured Volkswagen rally driver and host on *Top Gear USA* Tanner Foust driving elderly women around town in a TDI Volkswagen to dispel the myth that diesel is slow. As a result of its marketing, Volkswagen made large in-roads in gaining acceptance for its clean diesel vehicles, even though many car buyers had a negative view of diesel previously. This green image was highly beneficial for Volkswagen as consumer values are changing to value greener products.

While technology allowed VW to cheat the system, it also played a large part in its downfall. Discovery began when European testers noticed that VW vehicles did not perform as well on emissions testing on the road as they did in the lab. They commissioned a team in West Virginia to conduct research on VW vehicles made for Americans because the United States has some of the toughest emissions standards in the world. The team in West Virginia used a portable emission system measurement to measure emissions on the road. They found that the measurements did not nearly match up with what was shown in lab tests. The results were reported to the Environmental Protection Agency, which confronted Volkswagen with the evidence. Volkswagen eventually admitted it had designed and installed a defeat device that could detect when the vehicle was being tested and modify its performance levels so that it would meet emissions requirements.

Source: http://www.istockphoto.com/photo/
volkswagen-golf-at-the-vw-stand-58967210?st=69c4b2a

As a result, Volkswagen's CEO resigned and governments are demanding answers. Such a fraud does not only violate ethical standards but also laws and regulation in Europe and the United States. The company will have to pay $10 billion to repair, retrofit, or buy back affected vehicles in the United States, and it will likely pay hefty fines for breaking the law. Those who knew about or were responsible for the defeat device's installation could face jail time.

Perhaps the worst impact the scandal has caused has been to VW's reputation. Many VW customers claim they purchased the cars because they believed them to be better for the environment and felt utterly betrayed by the company. Consumer rights were violated because consumers did not have accurate information, meaning they were not able to make informed purchasing decisions. Lawsuits are being filed against VW for the deception. Its reputation for sustainability has been shattered, and two awards it had been given for "Green Car of the Year" were pulled.

Volkswagen has begun to take steps to restore consumer trust. For instance, it recalled vehicles and offered a $1,000 goodwill package to its American car owners. Yet even with incentives, Volkswagen will have to face this loss of goodwill for years to come. It also faces the potential for massive fines from the United States for violating environmental regulations. Because it is the world's second-largest carmaker operating in an oligopoly, other global car companies may benefit from the scandal and gain market share from Volkswagen. At the same time, while they might benefit from a competitive standpoint, VW's conduct has caused problems for the industry as a whole. Consumers are now questioning the environmental claims of other car brands, and automakers will have to work harder to prove that their claims are accurate. Consumer trust is easily lost and is not restored overnight.[55]

### Questions for Discussion:

1. Describe some ways Volkswagen ignored the six forces in the marketing environment. How did it violate its responsibilities to competitors, consumers, and regulators?

2. What overall impact do you think the scandal will have for Volkswagen competitors? Will it help them or harm them? Why?

3. How should VW change its marketing strategies to cope with recovering from the environmental reputation disaster?

# NOTES

[1] Jennifer Reingold, "Indra Nooyi Was Right. Now What?" *Fortune*, June 15, 2015, pp. 246–253; Adi Ignatius, "How Indra Nooyi Turned Design Thinking Into Strategy: An Interview with PepsiCo's CEO," *Harvard Business Review*, September 2015, https://hbr.org/2015/09/how-indra-nooyi-turned-design-thinking-into-strategy (accessed October 6, 2015); Valerie Baurlein, "PepsiCo Chief Defends Her Strategy to Promote 'Good for You' Foods," *The Wall Street Journal*, June 28, 2011, http://www.wsj.com/articles/SB10001 424052702303627104576412232408827462

(accessed October 6, 2015); Duane Stanford, "Indra Nooyi Rediscovers the Joy of Pepsi," *Bloomberg Businessweek*, February 2, 2012, http://www.bloomberg.com/bw/magazine/indra-nooyi-rediscovers-the-joy-of-pepsi-02022012.html (accessed October 6, 2015).

[2] Jeffrey Sparshott, "Spotify, Downloads and Piracy: How Streaming Affects Music Sales," *The Wall Street Journal*, October 30, 2015, http://blogs.wsj.com/economics/2015/10/30/spotify-downloads-and-piracy-how-streaming-affects-music-sales/ (accessed December 14, 2015).

[3] P. Varadarajan, Terry Clark, and William M. Pride, "Controlling the Uncontrollable: Managing Your Market Environment," *Sloan Management Review* 33, 2 (Winter 1992): 39–47.

[4] MuiChing Carina Chan, John Watson, and David Woodliff, "Corporate Governance Quality and CSR Disclosures," *Journal of Business Ethics* 125, 1 (2014): 59–73.

[5] Lynn Beavis, "Kingfisher pioneers environmental philosophy," *The Guardian*, May 15, 2014, www.theguardian.com/sustainable-business/

sustainability-case-studies-kingfisher-environmental-philosophy (accessed December 9, 2015).

[6] O. C. Ferrell and Michael D. Hartline, *Marketing Strategy* (Mason, OH: Cengage Learning, 2008), 58.

[7] O. C. Ferrell and Michael D. Hartline, *Marketing Strategy* (Mason, OH: Cengage Learning, 2008), 58.

[8] Economist staff, "Should Digital Monopolies Be Broken Up?" *The Economist*, November 29-December 5, 2014, 11.

[9] O. C. Ferrell and Michael D. Hartline, *Marketing Strategy* (Mason, OH: Cengage Learning, 2008), 58.

[10] Phil Wahba, "Macy's takes on T.J. Maxx with new, smaller discount stores," *Fortune*, May 5, 2015, http://fortune.com/2015/05/05/macys-discount-stores/ (accessed December 14, 2015); Phil Wahba, "Macy's closing up to 40 stores as sales stall," *Fortune*, September 8, 2015, http://fortune.com/2015/09/08/macys-closing-stores/ (accessed December 14, 2015).

[11] Carmen DeNavas-Walt and Bernadette D. Proctor, *Income and Poverty in the United States*: 2014 (Washington, D.C.: U.S. Department of Commerce, 2015).

[12] Laura Lorenzetti, "Here's how many people became millionaires last year," *Fortune*, June 17, 2015, http://fortune.com/2015/06/17/millionaires-worldwide/ (accessed December 11, 2015).

[13] JWT Intelligence, *Meet the BRIC Millennials*, September 2013, https://www.jwt.com/en/worldwide/thinking/meetthebricmillennials/ (accessed January 19, 2016).

[14] Joshua Gallu, "Dodd-Frank May Cost $6.5 Billion and 5,000 Workers," *Bloomberg*, February 14, 2011, www.bloomberg.com/news/2011-02-14/dodd-frank-s-implementation-calls-for-6-5-billion-5-000-staff-in-budget.html (accessed February 22, 2011); Binyamin Appelbaum and Brady Dennis, "Dodd's Overhaul Goes Well Beyond Other Plans," *The Washington* Post, November 11, 2009, www.washingtonpost.com/wp-dyn/content/article/2009/11/09/AR2009110901935.html?hpid=topnews&sid=ST2009111003729 (accessed January 19, 2016).

[15] "Wall Street Reform: Bureau of Consumer Financial Protection (CFPB)," U.S. Treasury, www.treasury.gov/initiatives/Pages/cfpb.aspx (accessed January 19, 2016).

[16] "Trade Mission," BusinessDictionary.com, www.businessdictionary.com/definition/trade-mission.html (accessed January 19, 2016).

[17] OpenSecrets.org, "Top Organization Contributors," http://www.opensecrets.org/orgs/list.php (accessed December 11, 2015).

[18] "Campaign Finance," *The New York Times*, http://topics.nytimes.com/top/reference/timestopics/subjects/c/campaign_finance/index.html (accessed January 19, 2016).

[19] Rebecca R. Ruiz and Katie Thomas, "Teva Settles Cephalon Generics Case with F.T.C. for $1.2 Billion," *New York Times*, May 28, 2015, http://www.nytimes.com/2015/05/29/business/teva-cephalon-provigil-ftc-settlement.html?_r=0 (accessed December 15, 2015).

[20] Roger Yu, "Bristol-Meyers fined $14M over bribe claims," *USA Today*, October 6, 2015, 3B.

[21] Dionne Searcey, "U.K. Law on Bribes Has Firms in a Sweat," *The Wall Street Journal*, December 28, 2010, p. B1; Julius Melnitzer, "U.K. Enacts 'Far-Reaching' Anti-Bribery Act," *Law Times*, February 13, 2011, http://www.lawtimesnews.com/201102141679/headline-news/uk-enacts-far-reaching-anti-bribery-act (accessed January 19, 2016).

[22] Julius Melnitzer, "U.K. Enacts 'Far-Reaching' Anti-Bribery Act," *Law Times*, February 13, 2011, http://www.lawtimesnews.com/201102141679/headline-news/uk-enacts-far-reaching-anti-bribery-act (accessed January 19, 2016).

[23] Ibid.

[24] Samuel Rubenfeld, "Lockheed Martin Gets into Step with UK Bribery Act With New Policy," *The Wall Street Journal*, June 8, 2011, http://blogs.wsj.com/corruption-currents/2011/06/08/lockheed-martin-gets-into-step-with-uk-bribery-act-with-new-policy/ (accessed January 19, 2016).

[25] Kathleen Caulderwood, "FTC Says Yelp Violated COPPA Child Privacy Rules, Fined $450K," *International Business Times*, September 18, 2015, http://www.ibtimes.com/ftc-says-yelp-violated-coppa-child-privacy-rules-fined-450k-1691229 (accessed December 15, 2015).

[26] Diane Bartz, "Google faces renewed U.S. antitrust scrutiny, this time over Android," *Reuters*, September 25, 2015, http://www.reuters.com/article/google-antitrust-idUSL-1N11V0PJ20150925 (accessed December 15, 2015).

[27] Jesse Newman, "FDA Tightens Its Food-Safety Rules," *The Wall Street Journal*, September 11, 2015, B3.

[28] Anica Zeyen, Markus Beckmann, and Stella Wolters, "Actor and Institutional Dynamics in the Development of Multi-stakeholder Initiatives," *Journal of Business Ethics*, accepted November 11, 2014, DOI 10.1007/s10551-014-2468-1.

[29] Home Builders Association of Central Missouri, "Code of Ethics," http://www.hbacentralmo.com/about-us/code-of-ethics/ (accessed November 14, 2014).

[30] Council of Better Business Bureaus, "NAD Recommends Sprint Discontinue 'New' Network, Customer Satisfaction Claims, Following T-Mobile Challenge," *ASRC*, March 3, 2015, http://www.asrcreviews.org/2015/03/nad-recommends-sprint-discontinue-new-network-customer-satisfaction-claims-following-t-mobile-challenge/ (accessed December 1, 2015).

[31] Council of Better Business Bureaus, "National Advertising Review Board Recommends Philosophy Modify or Discontinue Certain Claims for 'Time in a Bottle'," *ASRC*, May 14, 2015, http://www.asrcreviews.org/2015/05/national-advertising-review-board-recommends-philosophy-modify-or-discontinue-certain-claims-for-time-in-a-bottle/ (accessed December 15, 2015).

[32] Scott Keeter and Kyley McGeeney, "Pew Research will call more cellphones in 2015," *Pew Research Center*, January 7, 2015, http://www.pewresearch.org/fact-tank/2015/01/07/pew-research-will-call-more-cellphones-in-2015/ (accessed December 11, 2015).

[33] "Salesforce.com," *Forbes*, May 2015, http://www.forbes.com/companies/salesforce/ (accessed January 19, 2016).

[34] William M. Pride and O. C. Ferrell, *Marketing: Concepts and Strategies*, 12th ed. (Boston: Houghton Mifflin, 2003), 493.

[35] Economist staff, "Home, Hacked Home," *The Economist: Special Report* on Cyber-Security, July 12, 2014, pp. 14–15; *Economist staff*, "Prevention is better than cure," *The Economist: Special Report on Cyber-Security*, July 12, 2014, 16.

[36] "US Adults Spend 5.5 Hours with Video Content Each Day," *eMarketer*, April 16, 2015, http://www.emarketer.com/Article/US-Adults-Spend-55-Hours-with-Video-Content-Each-Day/1012362 (accessed December 15, 2015).

[37] Shea Bennett, "28% of Time Spent Online is Social Networking," *AdWeek*, January 27, 2015, http://www.adweek.com/socialtimes/time-spent-online/613474 (accessed December 15, 2015).

[38] Debbie McAlister, Linda Ferrell, and O. C.Ferrell, *Business and Society* (Mason, OH: South-Western Cengage Learning, 2011), pp. 352–353.

[39] Ibid.

[40] Vladmir Zwass, "Electronic Commerce: Structures and Issues," *International Journal of Electronic Commerce* (Fall 2000): 3–23.

[41] Shannon Pettypiece, "Amazon Passes Wal-Mart as Biggest Retailer by Market Value," *Bloomberg Business*, July 23, 2015, http://www.bloomberg.com/news/articles/2015-07-23/amazon-surpasses-wal-mart-as-biggest-retailer-by-market-value (accessed January 8, 2016).

[42] Jennifer M. Ortman, Victoria A. Velkoff, and HowardHogan, "An Aging Nation: The Older Population in the United States (Washington, D.C.: U.S. Census Bureau, May 2014).

[43] SeniorPeopleMeet website, www.senior-peoplemeet.com (accessed December 15, 2015); BabyBoomerPeopleMeet, babyboomerpeople-meet.com (accessed December 15, 2015).

[44] Allison Schrager, "Most Americans Are Single, and They're Changing the Economy," *Bloomberg Business*, September 12, 2014, http://www.bloomberg.com/bw/articles/2014-09-12/most-americans-are-single-dot-what-does-it-mean-for-the-economy (accessed December 11, 2015).

[45] Neil Shah, "Baby Bust Threatens Growth," *The Wall Street Journal*, December 4, 2014, A3.

[46] Haya El Nasser, Gregory Korte, and PaulOverberg, "308.7 Million," *USA Today*, December 22, 2010, p. 1A; "U.S. and World Population Clocks," U.S. Census Bureau, http://www.census.gov/popclock/ (accessed December 15, 2015).

[47] CAP Immigration Team, "The Facts on Immigration Today," *American Progress*, October 23, 2014, www.americanprogress.org/issues/immigration/report/2014/10/23/59040/the-facts-on-immigration-today-3/ (accessed January 19, 2016).

[48] U.S. Census Bureau, Statistical Abstract of the United States, 2010, 58.

[49] Sandra L. Colby and Jennifer M. Ortman, *Projections of the Size and Composition of the U.S. Population: 2014 to 2060* (Washington, D.C.: U.S. Census Bureau, March 2015), p. 9.

[50] Anne Marie Chaker, "Even Barbie Wants a Makeover," *Wall Street Journal*, November 19, 2015, D1.

[51] Nick Bilton, "For Some Teenagers, 16 Candles Mean It's Time to Join Uber," *The New York Times*, April 8, 2015, http://www.nytimes.com/2015/04/09/style/for-some-teenagers-16-candles-mean-its-time-to-join-uber.html (accessed December 15, 2015).

[52] "Parents Grossly Underestimate the Influence Their Children Wield over In-Store Purchases," *Science News*, March 17, 2009, http://www.sciencedaily.com/releases/2009/03/090316075853.htm (accessed December 15, 2015).

[53] "About Seventh Generation," www.seventh-generation.com/about (accessed January 19, 2016).

[54] Kurt Eichenwald, "The Great Smartphone War," *Vanity Fair*, June 2014, http://www.vanityfair.com/business/2014/06/apple-samsung-smartphone-patent-war (accessed January 11, 2016); "Samsung Ordered to Pay Apple $120m for Patent Violation," *The Guardian*, May 2, 2014, http://www.theguardian.com/technology/2014/may/03/samsung-ordered-to-pay-apple-120m-for-patent-violation?CMP=EMCNEWEML6619I2 (accessed January 11, 2016); Dan Levine, "Apple, Google Agree to Settle Lawsuit Alleging Hiring Conspiracy," *Reuters*, April 24, 2014, http://www.reuters.com/article/2014/04/24/us-apple-google-settlement-idUSBRE-A3N1Y120140424 (accessed January 11, 2016); Ian Scerr, "Apple, Samsung Square off over Patent Damages," The Wall Street Journal, December 6, 2012, http://online.wsj.com/article/SB10001424127887323501404578164021886466686.html?mod=WSJ_article_comments#articleTabs%3Darticle (accessed January 11, 2016); Evan Ramstad, "Award to Apple Isn't Raised," *The Wall Street Journal*, June 30, 2012, http://online.wsj.com/article/SB10001424127887324329204578272870432069736.html?KEYWORDS=apple+samsung KEYWORDS%3Dapple+samsung (accessed January 11, 2016); Dino Grandoni, "How the Apple Samsung Lawsuit Hurt Consumers," *The Huffington Post*, July 31, 2012, http://www.huffingtonpost.com/2012/07/31/apple-samsung-lawsuit-consumers_n_1721623.html (accessed January 11, 2016); Paul Elias, "Apple's Samsung Verdict Nearly Cut in Half by Federal Judge," The Huffington Post, March 1, 2013, http://www.huffingtonpost.com/2013/03/01/half-of-billion-apple-samsung-settlement-invalidated_n_2792624.html (accessed January 11, 2016); Scott Bicheno, "Global smartphone market Q3 2015—Samsung strikes back," *Telecoms*, October 29, 2015, http://telecoms.com/450101/global-smartphone-market-q3-2015-samsung-strikes-back/ (accessed January 11, 2016); Based off a news clip from the BBC, May 2014, https://vimeo.com/album/3731955/video/151163184

[55] Sarah Sloat, "Volkswagen to Offer $1,000 Package to U.S. Customers Hit by Emissions Scandal," *The Wall Street Journal*, November 9, 2015, http://www.wsj.com/articles/volkswagen-to-offer-1-000-package-to-u-s-customers-hit-by-emissions-scandal-1447088254?alg=y (accessed November 9, 2015); Russell Hotten, "Volkswagen: The scandal explained," *BBC News*, November 4, 2015, http://www.bbc.com/news/business-34324772 (accessed November 9, 2015); Associated Press, "VW Scandal Widens: Vehicles Don't Meet Standard for Second Pollutant," NBC News, November 3, 2015, http://www.nbcnews.com/business/autos/vw-scandal-widens-vehicles-dont-meet-standard-second-pollutant-n456726 (accessed November 9, 2015); Chris Woodyard, "Volkswagen faces lawsuits over emissions deception," *USA Today*, September 22, 2015, http://www.usatoday.com/story/money/cars/2015/09/22/volkswagen-vw-emissions-lawsuits/72604396/ (accessed November 9, 2015); Sam Abuelsamid, "Does VW Diesel Cheating Threaten Consumer Trust of Automotive Software?" *Forbes*, October 21, 2015, http://www.forbes.com/sites/pikeresearch/2015/10/21/vw-diesel/ (accessed November 9, 2015); Jackie Wattles, "Volkswagen stripped of two 'Green Car of the Year' titles," *CNN-Money*, October 1, 2015, http://money.cnn.com/2015/10/01/news/companies/volkswagen-green-car-of-year-awards-rescinded/ (accessed December 10, 2015); Bourree Lam, "The Academic Paper that Broke the Volkswagen Scandal," *The Atlantic*, September 25, 2015, http://www.theatlantic.com/business/archive/2015/09/volkswagen-scandal-cheating-emission-virginia-epa/407425/ (accessed December 10, 2015);

David Morgan, "West Virginia engineer proves to be a David to VW's Goliath," *Reuters*, September 23, 2015, http://www.reuters.com/article/us-usa-volkswagen-researchers-idUSKCN0RM2D720150924#Cl2HkHXLgPtmsqeF.97 (accessed December 10, 2015); Jeff Plungis and Dana Hull, "VW's Emissions Cheating Found by Curious Clean-Air Group," *Bloomberg Businessweek*, September 19, 2015, http://www.bloomberg.com/news/articles/2015-09-19/volkswagen-emissions-cheating-found-by-curious-clean-air-group (accessed December 10, 2015); Sonari Glinton, "How a Little Lab in West Virginia Caught Volkswagen's Big Cheat," NPR, September 25, 2015, http://www.npr.org/2015/09/24/443053672/how-a-little-lab-in-west-virginia-caught-volkswagens-big-cheat (accessed December 10, 2015); Steve Innskeep, "The Volkswagen Scandal and Germany's Reputation," NPR, October 1, 2015, http://www.npr.org/2015/10/01/444912600/the-volkswagen-scandal-and-germanys-reputation (accessed December 10, 2015); Paul Argenti, "The biggest culprit in VW's emissions scandals," *Fortune*, October 13, 2015, http://fortune.com/2015/10/13/biggest-culprit-in-volkswagen-emissions-scandal/ (accessed December 10, 2015); "Volkswagen Using Creepy Old Ladies and Tanner Faust to Sell Diesel Cars," Car Buzz, http://www.carbuzz.com/news/2015/2/27/Volkswagen-Using-Creepy-Old-Ladies-And-Tanner-Faust-To-Sell-Diesel-Cars-7725671/ (accessed December 10, 2015); Julia Edwards and Georgina Prodhan, "VW faces billions in fines as U.S. sues for environmental regulations," Reuters, January 6, 2016, http://www.reuters.com/article/us-volkswagen-usa-idUSKBN0U-I1QP20160106 (accessed January 7, 2016).

## Feature Notes

[a] Andria Cheng, "'Fair Trade' Becomes a Fashion Trend," *The Wall Street Journal*, July 8, 2015, B7; Catherine Clifford, "First Coffee, Now Fashion: Apparel Brands Seek Fair Trade Certification Despite Challenges," *Entrepreneur*, October 17, 2013, http://www.entrepreneur.com/article/229444 (accessed October 5, 2015); Hayli Goode, "Ethical Vs Fair Trade Fashion, Because the Difference Definitely Matters," Bustle, April 30, 2015, http://www.bustle.com/articles/79529-ethical-vs-fair-trade-fashion-because-the-difference-definitely-matters (accessed October 5, 2015).

[b] Kimberly Leonard, "Say Goodbye to Popcorn and Pies as You Know Them," U.S. News, June 16, 2015, http://www.usnews.com/news/articles/2015/06/16/fda-bans-trans-fats-in-move-that-will-alter-us-food-landscape (accessed July 13, 2015); David Harsanyi, "Why the Trans Fat Ban Is Worse Than You Think," *The Federalist*, June 17, 2015, http://thefederalist.com/2015/06/17/why-the-trans-fat-ban-is-worse-than-you-think/ (accessed July 13, 2015); Liz Szabo, "FDA to trim trans fats out of food," *USA Today*, June 17, 2015, 1A; Hadley Malcolm, "Cutting trans fats could be expensive," *USA Today*, June 17, 2015, 1B-2B.

Onur Dongel/iStock / Getty Images Plus/Getty Images

## chapter 4

## Social Responsibility and Ethics in Marketing

---

### OBJECTIVES

---

**4-1** Define the four dimensions of social responsibility.

**4-2** State the importance of marketing ethics.

**4-3** Describe the three factors of ethical decision making.

**4-4** Comment on the requirements for improving ethical decision making.

**4-5** Critique the role of social responsibility and ethics in improving marketing performance.

# MARKETING INSIGHTS

## Starbucks Goes Grande on Job Opportunities

Starbucks has decided to embark upon a social responsibility initiative that involves 15 new store locations. Each of these stores will be in low-income, predominately minority neighborhoods. Starbucks has chosen these locations with a major goal in mind: to provide ways to improve communities through employment opportunities, job training, and education.

Starbucks's decision is part of the "100,000 Opportunities Initiative," a collaboration among companies that include Starbucks, Alaska Air, CVS, Walmart, Microsoft, and Lyft. The goal is to create 100,000 new jobs and internship opportunities for lower-income consumers between the ages of 16 and 24. The initiative was spearheaded by Starbucks CEO Howard Schultz, whose goal is to hire at least 10,000 young workers over the next three years.

Those employees who get jobs in the low-income areas will also qualify for the Starbucks partnership with Arizona State to earn a college degree. The Starbucks College Achievement Plan offers full tuition for the four years needed to obtain a bachelor's degree. Because the classes are online, employees from all across the nation can choose to participate.

Some people question whether it is a smart economic move to locate in lower-income locations. The distribution element of the marketing mix is difficult to change once locations are chosen. Starbucks's response is that the challenges have more to do with choosing appropriate vendors and collaborators near the stores. It is therefore partnering with local organizations. For instance, Starbucks's Ferguson location is partnering with African-American business owner Natalie DuBose to supply caramel cakes from her bakery to sell in-store. Starbucks believes that despite the challenges, it has a responsibility to create employment opportunities and give back to communities.[1]

Most businesses operate responsibly and within the limits of the law, but organizations often walk a fine line between acting ethically and engaging in questionable behavior. Research shows that ethical companies often have better stock performance, but too often companies are distracted by the short-term costs of implementing ethics programs and the fleeting benefits of cutting ethical corners. Another common mistake companies make is a tendency to believe that because an activity is legal, it is also ethical. In fact, ethics often goes above and beyond the law and should therefore be a critical concern of marketers.

Some of the most common types of unethical practices among companies include deceptive sales practices, bribery, price discrimination, deceptive advertising, misleading packaging, and marketing defective products. Deceptive advertising in particular causes consumers to become defensive toward all promotional messages and distrustful of all advertising, so it hurts not only consumers but marketers as well.[2] Practices of this kind raise questions about marketers' obligations to society. Inherent in these questions are the issues of social responsibility and marketing ethics.

Because social responsibility and ethics often have profound impacts on the success of marketing strategies, we devote this chapter to their role in marketing decision making. We begin by defining social responsibility and exploring its dimensions. We then discuss social responsibility issues, such as sustainability and the marketer's role as a member of the community. Next, we define and examine the role of ethics in marketing decisions. We consider ethical issues in marketing, the ethical decision-making process, and ways to improve ethical conduct in marketing. Finally, we incorporate social responsibility and ethics into strategic market planning.

## 4-1 THE NATURE OF SOCIAL RESPONSIBILITY

In marketing, **social responsibility** refers to an organization's obligation to maximize its positive impact and minimize its negative impact on society. Social responsibility thus deals with the total effect of all marketing decisions on society. In marketing, social responsibility includes the managerial processes needed to monitor, satisfy, and even exceed stakeholder expectations and needs.[3] Remember from Chapter 1 that stakeholders are groups that have a "stake," or claim, in some aspect of a company's products, operations, markets, industry, and outcomes. CEOs such as Denise Morrison, CEO of Campbell Soup, are increasingly recognizing that businesses must take their leadership roles and social responsibilities more seriously.[4]

Ample evidence demonstrates that ignoring stakeholders' demands for responsible marketing can destroy customers' trust and even prompt government regulation. Irresponsible actions that anger customers, employees, or competitors may not only jeopardize a marketer's financial standing but have legal repercussions as well. Corporate social responsibility can have a direct, observable effect on both employees and customers. If employees perceive that management and customers support social responsibility activities, they positively identify with the firm. This means social responsibility activities can improve employee performance and customer loyalty to the organization.[5]

Socially responsible activities can generate positive publicity and boost sales. Google, for example, developed a campaign to raise money for global refugees and migrants. Google invited visitors to the site to donate money to their campaign. For every dollar donated, Google would match it. The campaign ended up raising nearly $11 million. Although the program is costly, Google's efforts have likely improved its relationships with stakeholders and generated significant goodwill.[6]

Socially responsible efforts have a positive impact on local communities; at the same time, they indirectly help the sponsoring organization by attracting goodwill, publicity, and potential customers and employees. Thus, although social responsibility is certainly a

**social responsibility** An organization's obligation to maximize its positive impact and minimize its negative impact on society positive concept in itself, most organizations embrace it in the expectation of indirect long-term benefits. Gucci founded the Chime for Change movement to raise awareness about education, health, and justice for girls and women worldwide. Its advertisement features popular celebrity Beyoncé Knowles-Carter as an endorser for the movement. Because Beyoncé is a figure that many people admire, having her as an endorser encourages others to support the movement. Our own research suggests that an organizational culture that supports social responsibility generates greater employee commitment and improved business performance.[7] Table 4.1 provides a sampling of companies that have chosen to make social responsibility a strategic long-term objective.

## 4-1a The Dimensions of Social Responsibility

Socially responsible organizations strive for **marketing citizenship** by adopting a strategic focus for fulfilling the economic, legal, ethical, and philanthropic social responsibilities that their stakeholders expect of them. Companies that consider the diverse perspectives of stakeholders in their daily operations and strategic planning are said to have a *stakeholder orientation*, an important element of social responsibility.[8] A stakeholder orientation in marketing goes beyond customers, competitors, and regulators to include understanding and addressing the needs of all stakeholders, including communities and special-interest groups. As a result, organizations are now under pressure to undertake initiatives that demonstrate a balanced perspective on stakeholder interests.[9] For instance, Pfizer has secured stakeholder input on a number of issues including rising health-care costs and health-care reform.[10] As Figure 4.1 shows, the economic, legal, ethical, and philanthropic dimensions of social responsibility can be viewed as a pyramid.[11]

At the most basic level, all companies have an economic responsibility to be profitable so that they can provide a return on investment to their owners and investors, create jobs for the community, and contribute goods and services to the economy. How organizations relate to stakeholders affects the economy. When economic downturns or poor decisions lead companies to lay off employees, communities often suffer as they attempt to absorb the displaced employees. Customers may experience diminished levels of service as a result of fewer experienced employees. Stock prices often decline when layoffs are announced, reducing the value of shareholders' investment portfolios. An organization's sense of economic responsibility is especially significant for employees, raising such issues as equal job opportunities, workplace diversity, job safety, health, and employee privacy. Economic responsibilities require finding a balance in stakeholder interests while recognizing that a firm must make a profit to be sustainable in the long run.

Marketers also have an economic responsibility to engage in fair competition and build ethical customer relationships. Government regulatory agencies often define the activities that constitute fair competition along with unethical issues such as price fixing, deceptive sales practices, false advertising, bribery,

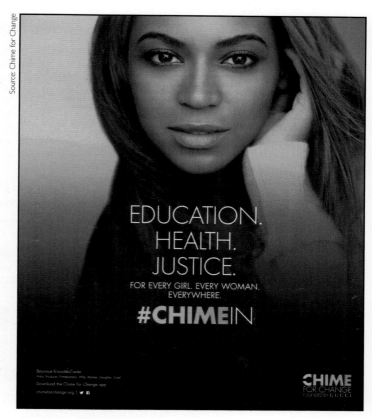

**Social Responsibility**
Chime for Change was founded by Gucci to generate funds and raise awareness about the challenges girls and women face across the world.

**marketing citizenship** The adoption of a strategic focus for fulfilling the economic, legal, ethical, and philanthropic social responsibilities expected by stakeholders

**Table 4.1  Best Corporate Citizens**

| 1 | Microsoft Corp. |
|---|---|
| 2 | Hasbro, Inc. |
| 3 | Johnson & Johnson |
| 4 | Xerox Corp. |
| 5 | Sigma-Aldrich Corp. |
| 6 | Bristol-Meyers Squibb Co. |
| 7 | Intel Corp. |
| 8 | Campbell Soup Co. |
| 9 | Ecolab, Inc. |
| 10 | Lockheed Martin Corp. |

Source:"CR's 100 Best Corporate Citizens 2015," CR, http://www.thecro.com/files/100%20Best%20List%202015.pdf (accessed December 15, 2015).

**Figure 4.1 The Pyramid of Corporate Social Responsibility**

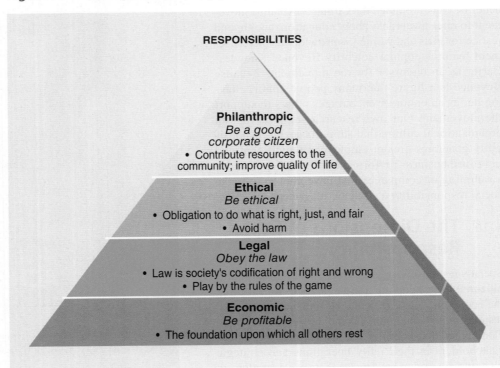

Source: From Archie B. Carroll, "The Pyramid of Corporate Social Responsibility: Toward the Moral Management of Organizational Stakeholders," adaption of Figure 3, p. 42. Reprinted from *Business Horizons*, July/August 1991, by the Foundation for the School of Business at Indiana University. Reprinted with permission.

and questionable distribution practices. This misconduct can be considered unfair competition that is also damaging to consumers. Companies that engage in questionable conduct damage their reputation and can destroy customer trust. On the other hand, the "World's Most Ethical Companies"—a designation given by the Ethisphere Institute—have a track record of avoiding these types of issues. Starbucks, Cummins, Johnson Controls, Adobe, and Waste Management are profitable and have excellent reputations with their customers. Marketers are also expected, of course, to obey laws and regulations. Laws and regulations are designed to keep U.S. companies' actions within the range of acceptable conduct and fair competition. When customers, interest groups, or businesses become outraged over what they perceive as misconduct on the part of a marketing organization, they may urge their legislators to draft new legislation to regulate the behavior or engage in litigation to force the organization to "play by the rules."

Economic and legal responsibilities are the most basic aspects of social responsibility for a good reason: Failure to consider them may mean that a marketer does not operate long enough to engage in ethical or philanthropic activities. Beyond these dimensions lies **marketing ethics**, principles and standards that define acceptable conduct in marketing as determined by various stakeholders, including the public, government regulators, private-interest groups, consumers, industry, and the organization itself. The most basic of these principles have been codified as laws and regulations to encourage marketers to conform to society's expectations for conduct. However, marketing ethics goes beyond legal issues. Ethical marketing decisions foster trust, which helps build long-term marketing relationships. Trust is a key part of developing customer relationships. It has been found that transparency about how products are produced, as well as how a firm's philanthropic activities give back to the community, creates trust and intentions to purchase. This also creates positive word-of-mouth communication about the firm.[12] We take a more detailed look at the ethical dimension of social responsibility later in this chapter.

**marketing ethics** Principles and standards that define acceptable marketing conduct as determined by various stakeholders

### The Nature of Social Responsibility

Whole Foods maintains high quality standards for its meat products. It will not buy from suppliers who treated the animals with antibiotics. Whole Foods is attempting to demonstrate its social responsibility to suppliers as well as adhere to its core values.

At the top of the pyramid of corporate responsibility (see Figure 4.1) are philanthropic responsibilities. These responsibilities, which go beyond marketing ethics, are not required of a company, but they promote human welfare or goodwill, as do the economic, legal, and ethical dimensions of social responsibility. That many companies have demonstrated philanthropic responsibility is evidenced by $17.8 billion in annual corporate donations and contributions to environmental and social causes.[13] Even small companies participate in philanthropy through donations and volunteer support of local causes and national charities, such as the Red Cross and the United Way. For example, Colorado Springs small business ShelfGenie, which designs, builds, and customizes shelving systems for cabinets, partners with nonprofit Homes for Our Troops in providing homes that are specially designed for disabled veterans. ShelfGenie realized that its shelving systems provide ease of access for disabled individuals and is using its expertise to give back to the community.[14]

More companies than ever are adopting a strategic approach to corporate philanthropy. Many firms link their products to a particular social cause on an ongoing or short-term basis, a practice known as **cause-related marketing**. Marketers like the programs because well-designed ones increase sales and create feelings of respect and admiration for the companies involved. After CVS announced it would no longer sell cigarettes, it partnered with the American Lung Association to sponsor an annual in-store fundraising campaign called LUNG FORCE. Customers could contribute at the check-out counters in CVS stores or online.[15] The campaign fits well with CVS's move to become more of a health-care firm by eliminating cigarettes and creates favorable impressions among consumers who sympathize with the cause. Indeed, research suggests that 91 percent of Millennials (those born between the early 1980s and 2000) are willing to switch to a brand associated with a cause.[16]

On the other hand, some companies are beginning to extend the concept of corporate philanthropy beyond financial contributions by adopting a **strategic philanthropy** approach, the synergistic use of organizational core competencies and resources to address key stakeholders' interests and achieve both organizational and social benefits. Strategic philanthropy involves employees, organizational resources and expertise, and the ability to link those assets to the concerns of key stakeholders, including employees, customers, suppliers, and social needs.

**cause-related marketing** The practice of linking products to a particular social cause on an ongoing or short-term basis

**strategic philanthropy** The synergistic use of organizational core competencies and resources to address key stakeholders' interests and achieve both organizational and social benefits

**Cause-Related Marketing**
CVS has partnered with the American Lung Association in an annual campaign to raise money and awareness for lung health.

Strategic philanthropy involves both financial and nonfinancial contributions to stakeholders (employee time, goods and services, company technology and equipment, etc.), while also benefiting the company.[17] Warby Parker, an American brand of prescription eyewear, donates one pair of eyeglasses to the nonprofit VisionSpring for each pair that is sold. This socially responsible initiative is a core part of Warby Parker's mission and business model.[18]

## 4-1b  Social Responsibility Issues

Although social responsibility may seem to be an abstract ideal, managers make decisions related to social responsibility every day. To be successful, a business must determine what customers, government regulators, competitors, and society want or expect in terms of social responsibility. Table 4.2 summarizes three major categories of social responsibility issues: sustainability, consumerism, and community relations.

### Sustainability

One of the more common ways marketers demonstrate social responsibility is through programs designed to protect and preserve the natural environment. **Sustainability** is the potential for the long-term well-being of the natural environment, including all biological entities, as well as the interaction among nature and individuals, organizations, and business strategies. Sustainability includes the assessment and improvement of business strategies, economic sectors, work practices, technologies, and lifestyles—all while maintaining the natural environment. New England and Mid-Atlantic–based supermarket Wegmans uses advertising to promote its Wild-Caught Shrimp and educate consumers about the company's sustainability projects. It describes the story behind the product by featuring one of its family-owned suppliers in the advertisement. Many companies are making contributions to sustainability by adopting more eco-friendly business practices and/or supporting environmental initiatives. Method has been largely successful in selling green cleaning supplies. Its success prompted other firms in the industry such as S.C. Johnson to begin their own green product lines. The company also has a Greenlist™ process by which it ranks the sustainability of ingredients it uses in its product formulas.[19] Such efforts generate positive publicity and often increase sales for the companies involved.

### Table 4.2  **Social Responsibility Issues**

| Issue | Description | Major Social Concerns |
|---|---|---|
| Sustainability | Consumers insisting not only on a good quality of life but also on a healthful environment so they can maintain a high standard of living during their lifetimes | Conservation<br>Water pollution<br>Air pollution<br>Land pollution |
| Consumerism | Activities undertaken by independent individuals, groups, and organizations to protect their rights as consumers | The right to safety<br>The right to be informed<br>The right to choose<br>The right to be heard |
| Community relations | Society eager to have marketers contribute to its well-being, wishing to know what marketers do to help solve social problems | Equality issues<br>Disadvantaged members of society<br>Safety and health<br>Education and general welfare |

**sustainability** The potential for the long-term well-being of the natural environment, including all biological entities, as well as the interaction among nature and individuals, organizations, and business strategies

The consumption of green products can be promoted by emphasizing the shared responsibility between the firm and consumers in protecting the environment.[20] For example, some retailers will assist consumers in recycling used electrical equipment.

Many products have been certified as "green" by environmental organizations such as Green Seal and carry a special logo identifying their organization as green marketers. Kimberly Clark became the first consumer-products company to become certified by the Forest Stewardship Council (FSC). Its tissues carry the FSC label to indicate that they were harvested from sustainable forests using environmentally friendly methods.[21] In Europe, companies can voluntarily apply for the EU Ecolabel to indicate that their products are less harmful to the environment than competing products, based on scientifically determined criteria (see Figure 4.2). On the other hand, consumers are becoming very skeptical of greenwashing, which occurs when firms claim to protect the environment but fail to demonstrate their commitment.[22]

Although demand for economic, legal, and ethical solutions to environmental problems is widespread, the environmental movement in marketing includes many different groups whose values and goals often conflict. Some environmentalists and marketers believe companies should work to protect and preserve the natural environment by implementing the following goals:

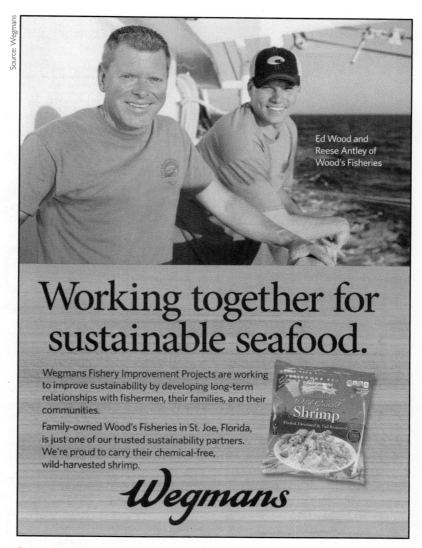

**Green Marketing**
Wegmans makes consumers aware of its chemical-free, wild-harvest shrimp as well as the story behind it.

1. *Eliminate the concept of waste.* Recognizing that pollution and waste usually stem from inefficiency, the question is not what to do with waste but how to make things without waste.

2. *Reinvent the concept of a product.* Products should be reduced to only three types and eventually just two. The first type is consumables, which are eaten or, when placed in the ground, turn into soil with few harmful side effects. The second type is durable goods—such as cars, televisions, computers, and refrigerators—that should be made, used, and returned to the manufacturer within a closed-loop system. Such products should be designed for disassembly and recycling. The third category is unsalables and includes such products as radioactive materials, heavy metals, and toxins. These products should always belong to the original makers, who should be responsible for the products and their full life-cycle effects. Reclassifying products in this way encourages manufacturers to design products more efficiently.

3. *Make prices reflect the cost.* Every product should reflect or at least approximate its actual cost—not only the direct cost of production but also the cost of air, water, and soil. To illustrate, the cost of a gallon of gasoline is higher when pollution, waste disposal, health effects, and defense expenditures are factored in. There have been tax credits for electric cars to reflect their positive impact on the environment.

Figure 4.2    **The EU Ecolabel**

© EU Ecolabel

4. *Make environmentalism profitable.* Consumers are beginning to recognize that competition in the marketplace should not occur between companies that are harming the environment and those that are trying to save it.[23]

## Consumerism

Another significant issue in socially responsible marketing is consumerism, which we defined in Chapter 3 as the efforts of independent individuals, groups, and organizations to protect the rights of consumers. A number of interest groups and individuals have taken action against companies they consider irresponsible by lobbying government officials and agencies, engaging in letter-writing campaigns and boycotts, and making public-service announcements. Some consumers choose to boycott firms and products out of a desire to support a cause and make a difference.[24] How a firm handles customer complaints affects consumer evaluations and in turn customer satisfaction and loyalty.[25]

The consumer movement has been helped by news-format television programs, such as *Dateline, 60 Minutes,* and *Prime Time Live*, as well as by 24-hour news coverage from CNN, MSNBC, and Fox News. The Internet too has changed the way consumers obtain information about companies' goods, services, and activities. Consumers can share their opinions about goods and services and about companies they see as irresponsible at consumer-oriented websites, such as epinions.com and ConsumerReview.com, and through blogs and social networking sites.

Ralph Nader, one of the best-known consumer activists, continues to crusade for consumer rights. Consumer activism by Nader and others has resulted in legislation requiring many features that make cars safer: seat belts, air bags, padded dashboards, stronger door latches, head restraints, shatterproof windshields, and collapsible steering columns. Activists' efforts have also facilitated the passage of several consumer protection laws, including the Wholesome Meat Act of 1967, the Radiation Control for Health and Safety Act of 1968, the Clean Water Act of 1972, and the Toxic Substance Act of 1976.

Also of great importance to the consumer movement are four basic rights spelled out in a consumer "bill of rights" that was drafted by President John F. Kennedy. These rights include the right to safety, the right to be informed, the right to choose, and the right to be heard.

# GOING GREEN

## The Walmart Supply Chain Goes Green

Ten years ago Walmart decided to increase its sustainability on a global scale. While it still has a long way to go, Walmart has made great strides in pursuing its goals. Twenty-six percent of its electricity is currently supplied by renewable energy sources, and it has increased fleet efficiency 84.2 percent since 2005. Walmart has also worked with suppliers to develop products and processes that are less wasteful.

These partnerships have benefited not only the environment but consumers as well. For instance, Walmart collaborated with consumer goods company Henkel to develop a detergent that is 50 percent more effective than its older version but sold at the same price. In sub-Sahara Africa, more water-efficient products have enabled consumers to reduce traveling long distances for water.

Walmart has also increased its sustainability criteria for suppliers. It ranks suppliers on sustainability in 700 categories. This pressure from Walmart has encouraged them to develop more sustainable products and packaging. Several years ago Procter & Gamble, a major Walmart supplier, agreed to sell detergent that was more concentrated. Since then P&G has made a number of sustainability improvements to its products, including using recyclable materials for its laundry bottles. As such a giant company, Walmart's commitment to sustainability will have a ripple effect on how businesses approach this important area.[a]

Ensuring consumers' *right to safety* means marketers are obligated not to market a product that they know could harm consumers. This right can be extended to imply that all products must be safe for their intended use, include thorough and explicit instructions for proper and safe use, and have been tested to ensure reliability and quality. Johnson & Johnson suspended sales of a surgical tool known as a power morcellator used to remove uterine fibroids in women. Although a minimally invasive surgical procedure, studies indicate that in patients with undetected uterine cancer, the morcellators can spread the cancer. The FDA is investigating how much Johnson & Johnson knew about potential hazards beforehand.[26] Continuing to a use a tool or product that could cause unnecessary harm is a violation to the consumer's right to safety.

Consumers' *right to be informed* means consumers should have access to and the opportunity to review all relevant information about a product before buying it. Many laws require specific labeling on product packaging to satisfy this right. In addition, labels on alcoholic and tobacco products must inform consumers that these products may cause illness and other problems.

The *right to choose* means consumers should have access to a variety of products at competitive prices. They should also be assured of satisfactory quality and service at a fair price. Activities that reduce competition among businesses in an industry might jeopardize this right.

The *right to be heard* ensures that consumers' interests will receive full and sympathetic consideration in the formulation of government policy. The right to be heard also promises consumers fair treatment when they complain to marketers about products. This right benefits marketers, too, because when consumers complain about a product, the manufacturer can use this information to modify the product and make it more satisfying.

The Federal Trade Commission provides a wealth of consumer information at its website (www.consumer.ftc.gov/) on a variety of topics ranging from automobiles and the Internet to diet, health, fitness, and identity theft.

## Community Relations

On the other hand, being a good community citizen also means avoiding harmful actions that could damage the community. Examples include pollution, urban sprawl, and exploitation of the workforce. A firm that participates in the economic viability of the community improves community relations. For example, Cutco Corp. in Olean, New York, gives its employees

**Corporate Contributions**

General Mills makes a positive contribution to society through its Box Tops for Education initiative. The Box Top logo can often be found on the upper right-hand corner of cereal boxes. Customers can clip the Box Tops and send them to the school of their choice. The schools are provided 10 cents for every Box Top.

gift certificates to local stores at Christmas. This supports local businesses and helps build good relationships with the community.

Although most charitable donations come from individuals, corporate philanthropy is on the rise. Samsung, for instance, holds a Samsung Day of Service. Samsung Electronics North America closes its offices for an entire day so employees have the chance to volunteer in their communities. Samsung also has a Hope for Children initiative in which the firm provides time, money, and resources to nonprofits for creating positive opportunities in children's lives.[27]

Smaller firms can also make positive contributions to their communities. California–based clothing company Patagonia donates 1 percent of its sales toward preserving and restoring the environment.[28] From a positive perspective, a marketer can significantly improve its community's quality of life through employment opportunities, economic development, and financial contributions to educational, health, cultural, and recreational causes.

## 4-2 MARKETING ETHICS

As noted earlier, marketing ethics is a dimension of social responsibility that involves principles and standards that define acceptable conduct in marketing. Acceptable standards of conduct in making individual and group decisions in marketing are determined by various stakeholders and by an organization's ethical climate. Marketers must also use their own values and knowledge of ethics to act responsibly and provide ethical leadership for others.

Marketers should be aware of stakeholders, including customers, employees, regulators, suppliers, and the community. When marketing activities deviate from accepted standards, the exchange process can break down, resulting in customer dissatisfaction, lack of trust, and lawsuits. In recent years, a number of ethical scandals have resulted in a massive loss of confidence in the integrity of U.S. businesses. About 60 percent of U.S. consumers trust businesses today.[29] Trust is an important concern for marketers because it is the foundation for long-term relationships. Consumer lack of trust has increased in recent years due to the financial crisis and deep recession. The questionable conduct of high-profile financial institutions and banks has caused many consumers to critically examine the conduct of all companies. Trust must be built or restored to gain the confidence of customers. Figure 4.3 describes the trust global consumers have for different institutions. Once trust is lost, it can take a lifetime to rebuild. The way to deal with ethical issues is proactively during the strategic planning process, not after major problems materialize.

Our focus here is on the ethical conduct of marketers. It is not our purpose to examine the conduct of consumers, although some do behave unethically (engaging, for instance, in coupon fraud, shoplifting, intellectual property piracy, and other abuses). We discuss consumer misbehavior and ethical issues associated with this misconduct in Chapter 7. Our goal in this chapter is to underscore the importance of resolving ethical issues in marketing and to help you learn about marketing ethics.

Figure 4.3   **Global Trust in Different Industries**

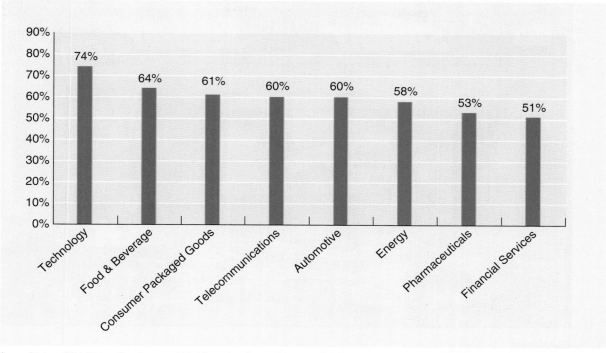

Source: Edelman, *2016 Edelman Trust Barometer Global Report*, http://www.edelman.com/insights/intellectual-property/2016-edelman-trust-barometer/global-results/ (accessed April 14, 2016).

## 4-2a  Ethical Issues in Marketing

An **ethical issue** is an identifiable problem, situation, or opportunity that requires an individual or organization to choose from among several actions that must be evaluated as right or wrong, ethical or unethical. Any time an activity causes marketing managers or customers in their target market to feel manipulated or cheated, a marketing ethical issue exists, regardless of the legality of that activity. For instance, fast-food chains have received criticism from activists who claim that their marketing to children contributes to the obesity epidemic. As a result, Burger King, Wendy's, and McDonald's have all eliminated soft drinks from kid's menus.[30]

Regardless of the reasons behind specific ethical issues, marketers must be able to identify those issues and decide how to resolve them. Doing so requires familiarity with the many kinds of ethical issues that may arise in marketing. Research suggests that the greater the consequences associated with an issue, the more likely it will be recognized as an ethics issue and the more important it will be in making an ethical decision.[31] Some examples of ethical issues related to product, distribution, promotion, and price (the marketing mix) appear in Table 4.3.

Product-related ethical issues generally arise when marketers fail to disclose risks associated with a product or information regarding the function, value, or use of a product. Pressures can build to substitute inferior materials or product components to reduce costs. Ethical issues also arise when marketers fail to inform customers about existing conditions or changes in product quality; such failure is a form of dishonesty about the nature of the product. *Product recalls* occur when companies ask customers to return products found to be defective. Companies that issue product recalls are often criticized for not having adequate quality controls to catch the defective product before it was released. For instance, Chipotle Grill suffered a major reputational blow after an E.coli outbreak forced it to temporarily close 43 of its restaurants in the Seattle and Portland areas. The failure to maintain product quality and integrity in

**ethical issue** An identifiable problem, situation, or opportunity requiring a choice among several actions that must be evaluated as right or wrong, ethical or unethical

Brendan Howard/Shutterstock.com

**Ethical Issue**
The use of antibiotics on animals used for food has become controversial because of the increase in drug-resistant bacteria. Subway announced it would no longer sell meat treated with antibiotics in light of this growing concern.

production is a significant ethical issue, and Chipotle Grill continues to work hard to improve food safety and handling procedures to reassure consumers.[32]

Promotion can create ethical issues in a variety of ways, among them false or misleading advertising and manipulative or deceptive sales promotions, tactics, and publicity. One controversial issue in the area of promotion is *greenwashing*, which occurs when products are promoted as being more environmentally friendly than they really are. As green products gain in popularity, companies are increasingly selling products that they claim to be "green." However, there are no formal criteria for what constitutes a green product, so it is hard to determine whether a company's product is truly green. Another major ethical issue is promoting products that might be construed as harmful, such as violent video games or fatty foods, to children.

Many other ethical issues are linked to promotion, including the use of bribery in personal selling situations. *Bribery* occurs when an incentive (usually money or expensive gifts) is offered in exchange for an illicit advantage. Even a bribe that is offered to benefit the organization is usually considered unethical. Because it jeopardizes trust and fairness, it hurts the organization in the long run. For this reason, sales promotion activities such as games, contests, and other sales attempts must be communicated accurately and transparently.

In pricing, common ethical issues are price fixing, predatory pricing, and failure to disclose the full price of a purchase. The emotional and subjective nature of price creates many situations in which misunderstandings between the seller and buyer cause ethical problems. Marketers have the right to price their products to earn a reasonable profit, but ethical issues may crop up when a company seeks to earn high profits at the expense of its customers. Some pharmaceutical companies, for example, have been accused of *price gouging*, or pricing products at exorbitant levels, and taking advantage of customers who must purchase the medicine to survive or to maintain their quality of life. Various forms of *bait and switch* pricing schemes attempt to gain consumer interest with a low-priced product, but then switch the buyer to a

Table 4.3    **Sample Ethical Issues Related to the Marketing Mix**

| | |
|---|---|
| Product Issue<br>*Product information* | Covering up defects that could cause harm to a consumer; withholding critical performance information that could affect a purchase decision. |
| Distribution Issue<br>*Counterfeiting* | Counterfeit products are widespread, especially in the areas of computer software, clothing, and audio and video products. The Internet has facilitated the distribution of counterfeit products. |
| Promotion Issue<br>*Advertising* | Deceptive advertising or withholding important product information in a personal-selling situation. |
| Pricing Issue<br>*Deceptive Pricing* | Indicating that an advertised sale price is a reduction below the regular price when in fact that is not the case. |

more expensive product or add-on service. One way companies do this is by telling customers that the lower-priced product they wanted is unavailable. Another issue relates to quantity surcharges that occur when consumers are effectively overcharged for buying a larger package size of the same grocery product.[33]

Ethical issues in distribution involve relationships among producers and marketing intermediaries. Marketing intermediaries, or middlemen (wholesalers and retailers), facilitate the flow of products from the producer to the ultimate customer. Each intermediary performs a different role and agrees to certain rights, responsibilities, and rewards associated with that role. For example, producers expect wholesalers and retailers to honor agreements and keep them informed of inventory needs. Serious ethical issues with regard to distribution include manipulating a product's availability for purposes of exploitation and using coercion to force intermediaries to behave in a specific manner. Several companies have been accused of *channel stuffing*, which involves shipping surplus inventory to wholesalers and retailers at an excessive rate, typically before the end of a quarter. The practice may conceal declining demand for a product or inflate financial statement earnings, which misleads investors.[34] Another ethical issue that has become a worldwide problem is *counterfeiting*. Counterfeit products not only cost the firm, but they can also be dangerous to the consumer. For instance, while legitimate sellers of pharmaceuticals are using call centers to sell to consumers, a number of call centers have arisen that sell counterfeit drugs—particularly in the Philippines, which employs the greatest number of call center employees. These counterfeits could seriously jeopardize public safety.[35]

As this section has shown, the nature of marketing ethics involves the ethics of all marketing channel members. However, the member managing the product is often held accountable for ethical conduct throughout the total supply chain. Party City was placed near the bottom of the list that ranks compliance with conflict mineral laws. Party City reported that some of its balloons might have utilized tin from areas that are involved in serious conflicts and/or civil wars. Although this violates conflict-minerals laws, Apple, General Electric, Microsoft, and Ford claim they also might have used tainted materials, demonstrating how difficult it is to trace all the materials used in a product throughout the supply chain.[36]

## 4-2b Ethical Dimensions of Managing Supply Chain Relationships

Managing supply chains responsibly is one of the greatest difficulties of marketing ethics and therefore needs some additional explanation. Supply chains require constant vigilance on the part of marketers as well as the need to anticipate unforeseen circumstances. Consider Costco, a well-known firm with a strong reputation. Lawsuits were filed against the firm alleging it had sold farmed prawns from Thailand that made use of slave labor. According to reports, there is concern that the food used to feed the prawns is caught at sea using unpaid labor. Costco claims that it does not tolerate human suffering and will work with the Thai government to get to the bottom of the issue.[37]

The issues that Costco has faced highlight the numerous risks that occur in global supply chains. Although companies often create a Supplier Code of Conduct, it requires regular audits to ensure that factories are following compliance standards—which in turn can incur significant costs to companies in both time and finances. Countries with lax labor laws, such as China and Russia, require even more diligent monitoring. Often suppliers hire subcontractors to do some of the work, which increases a company's network of suppliers and the costs of trying to monitor all of them. Finally, company compliance requirements may conflict with the mission of the procurement office. Because it is the procurement division's job to procure resources at the lowest price possible, the division may very well opt to source from less expensive suppliers with questionable ethical practices rather than from more expensive ethical suppliers. Nike faced this problem during the 1990s when it was highly criticized for worker abuses in its supplier factories.[38]

Managing supply chain ethical decision making is important because many stakeholders hold the firm responsible for all ethical conduct related to product availability. This requires the company to exercise oversight over all of the supplies used in producing a product. Developing good supply chain ethics is important because it ensures the integrity of the product and the firm's operations in serving customers. For instance, leading health-care supply company Novation has been recognized for its strong corporate governance and reporting mechanisms in its supply chain. To encourage its suppliers to report misconduct, the company has instituted a vendor grievance and feedback system. This allows vendors to report potential problems before they reach the next level of the supply chain, which reduces the damage such problems will cause if the products continue down the supply chain unchecked.[39]

Fortunately, organizations have been coming up with solutions to promote ethical sourcing practices. First, it is essential for all companies that work with global suppliers to adopt a Global Supplier Code of Conduct and ensure that it is effectively communicated to suppliers. Additionally, companies should encourage compliance and procurement employees to work together to find ethical suppliers at reasonable costs. Marketers must also work to make certain that their company's supply chains are diverse. This can be difficult because sometimes the best product manufacturers are located in a single country. Yet although it is expensive to diversify a company's supply chain, disasters can incapacitate a country.[40] Finally, and perhaps most importantly, companies must perform regular audits on its suppliers and, if necessary, discipline those found to be in violation of company standards.[41] More on supply chain management will be discussed in Chapter 14.

# 4-3 THE NATURE OF MARKETING ETHICS

To grasp the significance of ethics in marketing decision making, it is helpful to examine the factors that influence the ethical decision-making process. As Figure 4.4 shows, individual factors, organizational relationships, and opportunity interact to determine ethical decisions in marketing.

## 4-3a Individual Factors

When people need to resolve ethical conflicts in their daily lives, they often base their decisions on their own values and principles of right or wrong. People learn values and principles through socialization by family members, social groups, religion, and formal education. Because of different levels of personal ethics in any organization, there will be significant ethical diversity among employees. Most firms do not attempt to change an individual's personal ethics but try to hire employees with good character. Therefore, shared ethical values and compliance standards are required to prevent deviation from desired ethical conduct. In the workplace, however, research has established that an organization's culture often has more influence on marketing decisions than an individual's own values.[42]

Figure 4.4 **Factors That Influence the Ethical Decision-Making Process**

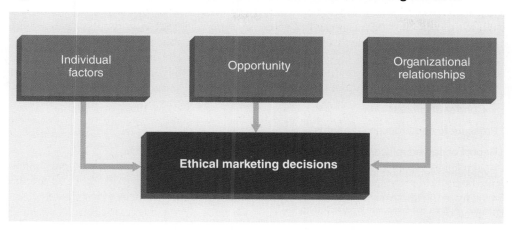

## 4-3b Organizational Relationships

Although people can and do make ethical choices pertaining to marketing decisions, no one operates in a vacuum.[43] Ethical choices in marketing are most often made jointly, in work groups and committees, or in conversations and discussions with coworkers. Marketing employees resolve ethical issues based not only on what they learned from their own backgrounds but also on what they learn from others in the organization. The outcome of this learning process depends on the strength of each individual's personal values, opportunity for unethical behavior, and exposure to others who behave ethically or unethically. Superiors, peers, and subordinates in the organization influence the ethical decision-making process. While individuals may have good ethics, they often face new and complex decisions in the business environment. Although people outside the organization, such as family members and friends, also influence decision makers, organizational culture and structure operate through organizational relationships to influence ethical decisions.

**organizational (corporate) culture** A set of values, beliefs, goals, norms, and rituals that members of an organization share

**Organizational**, or **corporate, culture** is a set of values, beliefs, goals, norms, and rituals that members of an organization share. These values also help shape employees' satisfaction with their employer, which may affect the quality of the service they provide to customers. A firm's culture may be expressed formally through codes of conduct, memos, manuals, dress codes, and ceremonies, but it is also conveyed informally through work habits, extracurricular activities, and stories. An organization's culture gives its members meaning and suggests rules for how to behave and deal with problems within the organization.

With regard to organizational structure, most experts agree that the chief executive officer or vice president of marketing sets the

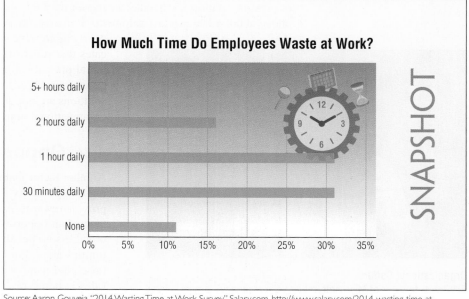

Source: Aaron Gouveia, "2014 Wasting Time at Work Survey," Salary.com, http://www.salary.com/2014-wasting-time-at-work/slide/2/ (accessed December 15, 2015).

Table 4.4    **Observed Ethical Conduct in the United States**

| Misconduct Facts | Percentages |
|---|---|
| Observed misconduct | 30% |
| *Abusive behavior* | 22% |
| *Lying to stakeholders* | 22% |
| *Conflict of interest* | 19% |
| Pressure to compromise standards | 22% |
| Report observed misconduct | 76% |
| Experience retaliation for reporting | 53% |

Source: Ethics and Compliance Initiative, *2016 Global Business Ethics Survey™: Measuring Risk and Promoting Workplace Integrity* (Arlington, VA: Ethics and Compliance Initiative, 2016), p. 43.

ethical tone for the entire marketing organization. Lower-level managers obtain their cues from top managers, but they too impose some of their personal values on the company. Top-performing sales representatives may influence the conduct of other salespersons as they serve as role models for success. This interaction between corporate culture and executive leadership helps determine the firm's ethical value system.

Coworkers' influence on an individual's ethical choices depends on the person's exposure to unethical behavior. Especially in gray areas, the more a person is exposed to unethical activity by others in the organizational environment, the more likely he or she is to behave unethically. Most marketing employees take their cues from coworkers in learning how to solve problems, including ethical problems.[44] The most recent Global Business Ethics Survey (GBES) found that 30 percent of employees in the United States observe some form of misconduct. About 24 percent choose not to report the misconduct.[45] Table 4.4 describes observed ethical conduct in the United States. Moreover, research suggests that marketing employees who perceive their work environment as ethical experience less role conflict and ambiguity, are more satisfied with their jobs, and are more committed to their employer.[46]

Organizational pressure plays a key role in creating ethical issues. For example, because of pressure to meet a schedule, a superior may ask a salesperson to lie to a customer over the phone about a late product shipment. Similarly, pressure to meet a sales quota may result in overly aggressive sales tactics. Research in this area indicates that superiors and coworkers can generate organizational pressure, which plays a key role in creating ethical issues. Nearly all marketers face difficult issues whose solutions are not obvious or that present conflicts between organizational objectives and personal ethics.

## 4-3c  Opportunity

Another factor that may shape ethical decisions in marketing is opportunity—that is, conditions that limit barriers or provide rewards. A marketing employee who takes advantage of an opportunity to act unethically and is rewarded or suffers no penalty may repeat such acts as other opportunities arise. For instance, a salesperson who receives a raise after using a deceptive sales presentation to increase sales is being rewarded and thus will probably continue the behavior. Indeed, opportunity to engage in unethical conduct is often a better predictor of unethical activities

**Organizational Culture**
Bill Gates, founder of Microsoft, reflects the company's organizational culture through his and his wife's personal convictions. Microsoft has been selected as one of the World's Most Ethical Companies.

Frederic Legrand - COMEO/Shutterstock.com

# Entrepreneurship in Marketing

## Second City Brings Ethics Training to Life

**Founders:** Paul Sills, Howard Alk, and Bernie Sahlins
**Business:** The Second City
**Founded:** 1959, in Chicago, Illinois
**Success:** Hundreds of global companies have used Second City Communication's RealBiz ethics shorts, which it created with the help of companies such as Dow Jones, Best Buy, and MasterCard

Second City Communications (SCC), a division of the Second City comedy theater company, seeks to bring comedy to ethics training. Second City was founded as a cabaret theater, and although the company never lost its theater roots, it has expanded into many different areas. SCC, for instance, focuses on the power of comedy to tackle important business issues.

In response to employee perceptions that business ethics training is dull, SCC has released videos called RealBiz shorts showing humorous scenarios of what *not* to do in business. For instance, in one video, the boss unveils the number of the company ethics hotline as 1-800-RAT-FINK. The videos introduce issues such as reporting misconduct, and it is assumed that the firm will address how reporting works within its own organization.

The purpose is to engage workers and encourage them to listen to what their businesses have to say. There may be a downside, however. Some businesses are wary of poking fun at issues that could have legal consequences. Despite this issue, RealBiz shorts have become so popular that SCC rolled out a cloud-based service to make the videos available on demand.[b]

---

than are personal values.[47] Beyond rewards and the absence of punishment, other elements in the business environment may create opportunities. Professional codes of conduct and ethics-related corporate policy also influence opportunity by prescribing what behaviors are acceptable. The larger the rewards and the milder the punishment for unethical conduct, the greater is the likelihood that unethical behavior will occur.

However, just as the majority of people who go into retail stores do not try to shoplift at each opportunity, most marketing managers do not try to take advantage of every opportunity for unethical behavior in their organizations. Although marketing managers often perceive many opportunities to engage in unethical conduct in their companies and industries, research suggests that most refrain from taking advantage of such opportunities. Moreover, most marketing managers do not believe that unethical conduct in general results in success.[48] Individual factors as well as organizational culture may influence whether an individual becomes opportunistic and tries to take advantage of situations unethically.

# 4-4 IMPROVING MARKETING ETHICS

It is possible to improve ethical conduct in an organization by hiring ethical employees and eliminating unethical ones, and by improving the organization's ethical standards. One way to approach improvement of an organization's ethical standards is to use a "bad apple–bad barrel" analogy. Some people always do things in their own self-interest, regardless of organizational goals or accepted moral standards; they are sometimes called "bad apples." To eliminate unethical conduct, an organization must rid itself of bad apples through screening techniques and enforcement of the firm's ethical standards. However, organizations sometimes become "bad barrels" themselves, not because the individuals within them are unethical but because the pressures to survive and succeed create conditions (opportunities) that reward unethical behavior. One way to resolve the problem of the bad barrel is to redesign the organization's image and culture so that it conforms to industry and societal norms of ethical conduct.[49]

Without ethics and compliance programs and uniform standards and policies regarding conduct, it is hard for employees to determine what conduct is acceptable within the company. In the absence of such programs and standards, employees will generally make decisions based on their observations of how coworkers and superiors behave. To improve ethics, many organizations have developed **codes of conduct** (also called *codes of ethics*) that consist of formalized rules and standards that describe what the company expects of its employees. Most large corporations have formal codes of conduct, but not all codes are effective if implemented improperly. Codes must be periodically revised to identify and eliminate weaknesses in the company's ethical standards and policies. Most codes address specific ethical risk areas in marketing. For instance, Pfizer's code of conduct has a bribery policy that prohibits both the bribing of foreign officials as well as commercial bribery. In its more detailed policy, Pfizer also prohibits facilitation payments, or small payments paid out to expedite an activity, and any type of gift or service of nominal value.[50] Codes of conduct promote ethical behavior by reducing opportunities for unethical behavior; employees know both what is expected of them and what kind of punishment they face if they violate the rules. Codes help marketers deal with ethical issues or dilemmas that develop in daily operations by prescribing or limiting specific activities.

Codes of conduct do not have to be so detailed that they take every situation into account, but they should provide guidelines that enable employees to achieve organizational objectives in an ethical manner. The American Marketing Association Code of Ethics, reprinted in Table 4.5, does not cover every possible ethical issue, but it provides a useful overview of what marketers believe are sound principles for guiding marketing activities. This code serves as a helpful model for structuring an organization's code of conduct.

**codes of conduct** Formalized rules and standards that describe what the company expects of its employees

If top management develops and enforces ethical and legal compliance programs to encourage ethical decision making, it becomes a force to help individuals make better decisions.

Table 4.5    **Code of Ethics of the American Marketing Association**

**Ethical Norms and Values for Marketers**

**PREAMBLE**

The American Marketing Association commits itself to promoting the highest standard of professional ethical norms and values for its members (practitioners, academics, and students). Norms are established standards of conduct that are expected and maintained by society and/or professional organizations. Values represent the collective conception of what communities find desirable, important and morally proper. Values also serve as the criteria for evaluating our own personal actions and the actions of others. As marketers, we recognize that we not only serve our organizations but also act as stewards of society in creating, facilitating and executing the transactions that are part of the greater economy. In this role, marketers are expected to embrace the highest professional ethical norms and the ethical values implied by our responsibility toward multiple stakeholders (e.g., customers, employees, investors, peers, channel members, regulators, and the host community).

**ETHICAL NORMS**

As Marketers, we must:

1. **Do no harm.** This means consciously avoiding harmful actions or omissions by embodying high ethical standards and adhering to all applicable laws and regulations in the choices we make.

2. **Foster trust in the marketing system.** This means striving for good faith and fair dealing so as to contribute toward the efficacy of the exchange process as well as avoiding deception in product design, pricing, communication, and delivery of distribution.

3. **Embrace ethical values.** This means building relationships and enhancing consumer confidence in the integrity of marketing by affirming these core values: honesty, responsibility, fairness, respect, transparency, and citizenship.

**Ethical Values**

**Honesty**—to be forthright in dealings with customers and stakeholders. To this end, we will:

- Strive to be truthful in all situations and at all times.

- Offer products of value that do what we claim in our communications.

- Stand behind our products if they fail to deliver their claimed benefits.

- Honor our explicit and implicit commitments and promises.

**Responsibility**—to accept the consequences of our marketing decisions and strategies. To this end, we will:

- Strive to serve the needs of customers.

- Avoid using coercion with all stakeholders.

- Acknowledge the social obligations to stakeholders that come with increased marketing and economic power.

- Recognize our special commitments to vulnerable market segments such as children, seniors, the economically impoverished, market illiterates and others who may be substantially disadvantaged.

- Consider environmental stewardship in our decision making.

**Fairness**—to balance justly the needs of the buyer with the interests of the seller. To this end, we will:

- Represent products in a clear way in selling, advertising, and other forms of communication; this includes the avoidance of false, misleading, and deceptive promotion.

- Reject manipulations and sales tactics that harm customer trust.
  Refuse to engage in price fixing, predatory pricing, price gouging, or "bait-and-switch" tactics.

- Avoid knowing participation in conflicts of interest.
  Seek to protect the private information of customers, employees, and partners.

**Respect**—to acknowledge the basic human dignity of all stakeholders. To this end, we will:

- Value individual differences and avoid stereotyping customers or depicting demographic groups (e.g., gender, race, sexual orientation) in a negative or dehumanizing way.

- Listen to the needs of customers and make all reasonable efforts to monitor and improve their satisfaction on an ongoing basis.

- Make every effort to understand and respectfully treat buyers, suppliers, intermediaries, and distributors from all cultures.

- Acknowledge the contributions of others, such as consultants, employees, and coworkers, to marketing endeavors.

- Treat everyone, including our competitors, as we would wish to be treated.

**Transparency**—to create a spirit of openness in marketing operations. To this end, we will:

- Strive to communicate clearly with all constituencies.

- Accept constructive criticism from customers and other stakeholders.

- Explain and take appropriate action regarding significant product or service risks, component substitutions or other foreseeable eventualities that could affect customers or their perception of the purchase decision.

- Disclose list prices and terms of financing as well as available price deals and adjustments.

**Citizenship**—to fulfill the economic, legal, philanthropic, and societal responsibilities that serve stakeholders. To this end, we will:

- Strive to protect the ecological environment in the execution of marketing campaigns.

- Give back to the community through volunteerism and charitable donations.
  Contribute to the overall betterment of marketing and its reputation.

- Urge supply chain members to ensure that trade is fair for all participants, including producers in developing countries.

### Implementation

We expect AMA members to be courageous and proactive in leading and/or aiding their organizations in the fulfillment of the explicit and implicit promises made to those stakeholders. We recognize that every industry sector and marketing sub-discipline (e.g., marketing research, e-commerce, Internet selling, direct marketing, and advertising) has its own specific ethical issues that require policies and commentary. An array of such codes can be accessed through links on the AMA Web site. Consistent with the principle of subsidiarity (solving issues at the level where the expertise resides), we encourage all such groups to develop and/or refine their industry and discipline-specific codes of ethics to supplement these guiding ethical norms and values.

Figure 4.5 **Retaliation against Whistle-Blowers**

At least one third of reporters experience
retaliation in most countries

| | |
|---|---|
| China | 29% |
| Mexico | 31% |
| France | 33% |
| Russia | 34% |
| Japan | 34% |
| Italy | 35% |
| South Korea | 36% |
| Brazil | 37% |
| Spain | 43% |
| Germany | 50% |
| United States | 53% |
| United Kingdom | 63% |
| India | 74% |
| Median value | 36% |

Source: Ethics and Compliance Initiative, *2016 Global Business Ethics Survey™: Measuring Risk and Promoting Workplace Integrity* (Arlington, VA: Ethics and Compliance Initiative, 2016), p. 18.

A company's ethical culture is the greatest determinant of future misconduct. Thus, a well-implemented ethics program and a strong corporate culture result in the greatest decrease in ethical risks for an organization. Companies that wish to improve their ethics, then, should implement a strong ethics and compliance program and encourage organization-wide commitment to an ethical culture.[51] Ethics programs that include written standards of conduct, ethics training, and hotlines increase the likelihood that employees will report misconduct observed in the workplace. When top managers talk about the importance of ethics and model ethical behavior themselves, employees observe significantly fewer instances of unethical conduct. When marketers understand the policies and requirements for ethical conduct, they can more easily resolve ethical conflicts. However, marketers can never fully abdicate their personal ethical responsibility in making decisions. Claiming to be an agent of the business ("the company told me to do it") is unacceptable as a legal excuse and is even less defensible from an ethical perspective.[52] It is also unacceptable for managers to punish those who do report ethical misconduct, although retaliation is still fairly prevalent. From a global perspective, the GBES study shows that approximately one-third of whistle blowers experience some type of retaliation.[53] Figure 4.5 shows the rate of retaliation whistle blowers face in different countries.

# 4-5 INCORPORATING SOCIAL RESPONSIBILITY AND ETHICS INTO STRATEGIC PLANNING

Although the concepts of marketing ethics and social responsibility are often used interchangeably, it is important to distinguish between them. *Ethics* relates to individual and group decisions—judgments about what is right or wrong in a particular decision-making situation—whereas *social responsibility* deals with the total effect of marketing decisions on society.

The two concepts are interrelated because a company that supports socially responsible decisions and adheres to a code of conduct is likely to have a positive effect on society. Because ethics and social responsibility programs can be profitable as well, an increasing number of companies are incorporating them into their overall strategic market planning. Ben & Jerry's, for instance, built socially responsible principles into its original business model. When company strategies are implemented, they must align with the organization's core beliefs and values. As the advertisement shows, Ben & Jerry's demonstrates its values and social responsibility in many different ways, including providing job-training programs, using non-genetically modified ingredients, participating in the Caring Dairy initiative, and using fair trade ingredients in products.

As we have emphasized throughout this chapter, ethics is one dimension of social responsibility. Being socially responsible relates to doing what is economically sound, legal, ethical, and socially conscious. One way to evaluate whether a specific activity is ethical and socially responsible is to ask other members of the organization if they approve of it. Contact with concerned consumer groups and industry or government regulatory groups may be helpful. A check to see whether there is a specific company policy about an activity may help resolve ethical questions. If other organizational members approve of the activity and it is legal and customary within the industry, chances are that the activity is acceptable from both an ethical and a social responsibility perspective.

A rule of thumb for resolving ethical and social responsibility issues is that if an issue can withstand open discussion that results in agreement or limited debate, an acceptable solution may exist. Nevertheless, even after a final decision is reached, different viewpoints on the issue may remain. Openness is not the end-all solution to the ethics problem. However, it creates trust and facilitates learning relationships.[54]

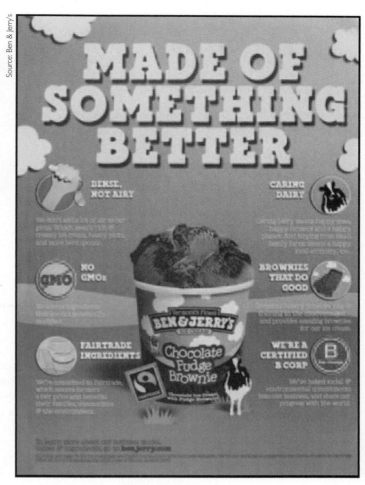

Source: Ben & Jerry's

**Social Responsibility and Strategic Planning**
Ben & Jerry's incorporates social responsibility into its strategies. Its advertisement explains that its ice cream is made with fair trade ingredients and does not contain GMOs. It also emphasizes its support for the humane treatment of cows and for job programs.

Many of society's demands impose costs. For example, society wants a cleaner environment and the preservation of wildlife and their habitats, but it also wants low-priced products. Consider the plight of the gas station owner who asked his customers if they would be willing to spend an additional 1 cent per gallon if he instituted an air filtration system to eliminate harmful fumes. The majority indicated they supported his plan. However, when the system was installed and the price increased, many customers switched to a lower-cost competitor across the street. Thus, companies must carefully balance the costs of providing low-priced products against the costs of manufacturing, packaging, and distributing their products in an environmentally responsible manner.

In trying to satisfy the desires of one group, marketers may dissatisfy others. Regarding the smoking debate, for instance, marketers must balance nonsmokers' desire for a smoke-free environment against smokers' desires, or needs, to continue to smoke. Some anti-tobacco crusaders call for the complete elimination of tobacco products to ensure a smoke-free world. However, this attitude fails to consider the difficulty smokers have in quitting (now that tobacco

**Ethical Treatment of Stakeholders**
Although some people believe that electronic cigarettes are a responsible alternative to smoking, e-cigarettes remain controversial due to continued health concerns.

marketers have admitted their product is addictive) and the impact on U.S. communities and states that depend on tobacco crops for their economic survival. Thus, this issue, like most ethical and social responsibility issues, cannot be viewed in black and white.

Balancing society's demands to satisfy all members of society is difficult, if not impossible. Marketers must evaluate the extent to which members of society are willing to pay for what they want. For instance, customers may want more information about a product but be unwilling to pay the costs the firm incurs in providing the data. Marketers who want to make socially responsible decisions may find the task a challenge because, ultimately, they must ensure their economic survival.

## 4-5a  Social Responsibility and Ethics Improve Marketing Performance

The challenges of ethical conduct are an important part of marketing success. Increasing evidence indicates that being socially responsible and ethical results in increased profits. Research suggests that a relationship exists between a stakeholder orientation and an organizational climate that supports marketing ethics and social responsibility. Marketing is often the most visible interaction that consumers have with a firm. Also, stakeholders observe marketing activities such as promotion and learn about their activities through the mass media. Anytime there is a product recall or potential unethical act, reputational damage can occur. On the other hand, firms that are highly ethical and build trust with customers are usually not headline stories in the mass media.

The evidence is strong that a broad stakeholder view of the firm can help improve marketing practices that contribute to improved financial, social, and ethical performance.[55] This relationship implies that being ethically and socially concerned is consistent with meeting the demands of customers and other stakeholders. By encouraging employees to understand their markets, companies can help them respond to stakeholders' demands.[56] A stakeholder orientation helps to broaden and redefine marketing beyond a market orientation that focuses on customers and competitors by considering primary stakeholders such as employees, suppliers, regulators, shareholders, customers, and the community. Marketers need to analyze stakeholder relationships to maximize value for specific target markets.

This creates a need to prioritize stakeholders, deal with conflicting demands, and respond with a marketing strategy to provide balance. For instance, utility company NiSource incorporates values and stakeholder needs into all facets of its operations. The company offers customers energy efficiency programs that allowed them to save $16 million in energy costs. It was listed on the Dow Jones Sustainability Index due to its sustainable business practices. NiSource also treats its employees well. The company stresses workplace safety as well as honesty and transparency. Not only did it earn a listing on Ethisphere's "World's Most Ethical Companies" list, it was recognized by *Business Insider*'s list of Happiest Companies in America.[57] By incorporating ethics into its marketing strategy, NiSource has balanced the needs of its stakeholders and developed a solid reputation of trust. All of these actions should be grounded in social responsibility and marketing ethics. The results should be positive relationships with customers and increased financial performance.[58]

**Social Responsibility Improves Marketing**
Patagonia has developed its entire reputation around its socially responsible and environmentally friendly activities.

A direct association exists between corporate social responsibility and customer satisfaction, profits, and market value.[59] In a survey of consumers, 90 percent indicated that when quality and price are similar among competitors, they would be more likely to buy from the company associated with a good cause. In addition, 57 percent of consumers indicated that they would purchase a product of lesser quality if the brand has demonstrated social and environmental responsibility.[60]

Thus, recognition is growing that the long-term value of conducting business in an ethical and socially responsible manner far outweighs short-term costs.[61] Companies that fail to develop strategies and programs to incorporate ethics and social responsibility into their organizational culture may pay the price with poor marketing performance and the potential costs of legal violations, civil litigation, and damaging publicity when questionable activities are made public. Because marketing ethics and social responsibility are not always viewed as organizational performance issues, many managers do not believe they need to consider them in the strategic planning process. Individuals also have different ideas as to what is ethical or unethical, leading them to confuse the need for workplace ethics and the right to maintain their own personal values and ethics. Although the concepts are undoubtedly controversial, it is possible—and desirable—to incorporate ethics and social responsibility into the planning process.

# Summary

## 4-1  Define the four dimensions of social responsibility.

Social responsibility refers to an organization's obligation to maximize its positive impact and minimize its negative impact on society. It deals with the total effect of all marketing decisions on society. Although social responsibility is a positive concept, most organizations embrace it in the expectation of indirect long-term benefits. Marketing citizenship involves adopting a strategic focus for fulfilling the economic, legal, ethical, and philanthropic social responsibilities expected of organizations by their stakeholders, those constituents who

have a stake, or claim, in some aspect of the company's products, operations, markets, industry, and outcomes.

At the most basic level, companies have an economic responsibility to be profitable so that they can provide a return on investment to their stockholders, create jobs for the community, and contribute goods and services to the economy. Marketers are also expected to obey laws and regulations. Marketing ethics refers to principles and standards that define acceptable conduct in marketing as determined by various stakeholders, including the public, government regulators, private-interest groups, industry, and the organization itself.

Philanthropic responsibilities go beyond marketing ethics; they are not required of a company, but they promote human welfare or goodwill. Many firms use cause-related marketing, the practice of linking products to a social cause on an ongoing or short-term basis. Strategic philanthropy is the synergistic use of organizational core competencies and resources to address key stakeholders' interests and achieve both organizational and social benefits.

Three major categories of issues that fit into the four dimensions of social responsibility are sustainability, consumerism, and community relations. One of the more common ways marketers demonstrate social responsibility is through programs designed to protect and preserve the natural environment. Sustainability is the potential for the long-term well-being of the natural environment, including all biological entities, as well as the interaction among nature and individuals, organizations, and business strategies. Consumerism consists of the efforts of independent individuals, groups, and organizations to protect the rights of consumers. Consumers expect to have the right to safety, the right to be informed, the right to choose, and the right to be heard. Many marketers view social responsibility as including contributions of resources (money, products, and time) to community causes such as the natural environment, arts and recreation, disadvantaged members of the community, and education.

## 4-2  State the importance of marketing ethics.

Whereas social responsibility is achieved by balancing the interests of all stakeholders in the organization, ethics relates to acceptable standards of conduct in making individual and group decisions. Marketing ethics goes beyond legal issues. Ethical marketing decisions foster mutual trust in marketing relationships.

An ethical issue is an identifiable problem, situation, or opportunity requiring an individual or organization to choose from among several actions that must be evaluated as right or wrong, ethical or unethical. A number of ethical issues relate to the marketing mix (product, distribution, promotion, and price).

## 4-3  Describe the three factors of ethical decision making.

Individual factors, organizational relationships, and opportunity interact to determine ethical decisions in marketing. Individuals often base their decisions on their own values and principles of right or wrong. However, ethical choices in marketing are most often made jointly, in work groups and committees, or in conversations and discussions with coworkers. Organizational culture and structure operate through organizational relationships (with superiors, peers, and subordinates) to influence ethical decisions. Organizational, or corporate, culture is a set of values, beliefs, goals, norms, and rituals that members of an organization share. The more a person is exposed to unethical activity by others in the organizational environment, the more likely he or she is to behave unethically. Organizational pressure plays a key role in creating ethical issues, as do opportunity and conditions that limit barriers or provide rewards.

## 4-4  Comment on the ways to improve ethical decisions in marketing.

It is possible to improve ethical behavior in an organization by hiring ethical employees and eliminating unethical ones, and by improving the organization's ethical standards. If top management develops and enforces ethics and legal compliance programs to encourage ethical decision making, it becomes a force to help individuals make better decisions. To improve company ethics, many organizations have developed codes of conduct—formalized rules and standards that describe what the company expects of its employees. To nurture ethical conduct in marketing, open communication is essential. Firms should also periodically monitor and audit their operations, including their supply chain, to ensure the integrity of the product and the firm's activities. Companies must consistently enforce standards and impose penalties or punishment on those who violate codes of conduct.

## 4-5  Critique the role of social responsibility and ethics in improving marketing performance.

An increasing number of companies are incorporating ethics and social responsibility programs into their overall strategic marketing planning. To promote socially responsible and ethical behavior while achieving organizational goals, marketers must monitor changes and trends in society's values. They must determine what society wants and attempt to predict the long-term effects of their decisions. Costs are associated with many of society's demands, and balancing those demands to satisfy all of society is difficult. However, increasing evidence indicates that being socially responsible and ethical results in valuable benefits: an enhanced public reputation (which can increase market share), costs savings, and profits.

---

**Go to www.cengagebrain.com for resources to help you master the content in this chapter as well as for materials that will expand your marketing knowledge!**

## Important Terms

social responsibility  98
marketing citizenship  99
marketing ethics  100
cause-related marketing  101

strategic philanthropy  101
sustainability  102
ethical issue  107

organizational (corporate)
  culture  111
codes of conduct  114

## Discussion and Review Questions

1. What is social responsibility? Why is it important?
2. What are stakeholders? What role do they play in strategic marketing decisions?
3. What are four dimensions of social responsibility? What impact do they have on marketing decisions?
4. What is strategic philanthropy? How does it differ from more traditional philanthropic efforts?
5. What are some major social responsibility issues? Give an example of each.
6. What is the difference between ethics and social responsibility?
7. Why is ethics an important consideration in marketing decisions?
8. How do the factors that influence ethical or unethical decisions interact?
9. What ethical conflicts may exist if business employees fly on certain airlines just to receive benefits for their personal frequent-flyer programs?
10. Give an example of how ethical issues can affect each component of the marketing mix.
11. How can the ethical decisions involved in marketing be improved?
12. How can people with different personal values work together to make ethical decisions in organizations?
13. What trade-offs might a company have to make to be socially responsible and responsive to society's demands?
14. What evidence exists that being socially responsible and ethical is worthwhile?

# Video Case 4.1

## Theo Chocolate Makes a Sweet Difference

"I want to build a model that other companies can look at and emulate. A model that's based on strong ethics and financial success," Joe Whinney, founder of Theo Chocolate, says when describing his company.

Seattle–based Theo Chocolate uses the cocoa bean to make the world a better place. The company has become known for its organic, Fair Trade bean-to-bar chocolate. Theo takes cocoa beans and manages the entire process to turn them into high-quality chocolate. The concept for Theo Chocolate came two decades ago when Whinney was traveling through Central America and Africa. He witnessed farmers being exploited by multinational companies and wanted to develop a firm that would sell a high-quality product and benefit the farmers that supplied the ingredients. In 2006 Whinney and his ex-wife Debra Music, who is now chief marketing officer, founded Theo Chocolate. They later relocated to Seattle and built a factory that began producing chocolate in 2006.

Originally, Theo wanted to develop flavors it was excited about, such as coconut curry. However, Whinney and Music realized that they also needed to listen to the consumer and develop more traditional flavors such as chocolate and mint. Their attention to consumer needs is not only ethical but is an important part of a successful marketing strategy.

The firm decided it wanted to do everything it could to ensure the quality and integrity of its products. This is why it not only sources Fair Trade products but also oversees the production of the chocolate from bean to bar. Its ability to oversee the entire process allows it to control for any disruptions that might compromise the chocolate's integrity.

"Just being organic and Fair Trade isn't enough. You will spark consumers' interest because of our certifications and the integrity of our product, but if it doesn't taste good, if people don't enjoy it, then it really doesn't matter," Whinney says. "So we put as much or more of an emphasis on quality because without that, then nothing else really matters."

Today the firm employs 100 people and produces a successful line of chocolate bars, confections, caramels, and specialty items. Although the chocolate bars are priced higher than competitors, consumers know that they are supporting fair trade and organic practices that benefit the farmers. One of Theo's greatest marketing tools is the tours it provides to visitors of its facilities. From the beginning, Theo's founders wanted to educate consumers about Fair Trade and tell the story behind its chocolate to give consumers an appreciation for the work that goes into it and the farmers who supply the beans.

These stories have become even more important with an initiative Theo has embarked upon to help farmers from the Democratic Republic of the Congo (DRC). Theo has launched a line of chocolate bars from the DRC. These bars cost a little bit extra at $5 a bar, but the extra money goes toward improving the farmers' lives. Whinney pays the farmers in the DRC from whom he sources chocolate two to three times the market rate.

Whinney was inspired to invest in the DRC by actor Ben Affleck, founder of the Eastern Congo Initiative. Affleck founded the initiative with the intent to create investment in the country. He learned that the DRC was a war-torn country in which 5 million people had died in the conflict. Affleck started out by leading a group of philanthropists to the DRC to invest in the communities. Investment is not necessarily easy. Affleck visited Theo Chocolate and asked it to partner with the initiative in improving the lives of Congolese cocoa farmers. Theo Chocolate has committed to buying 340 tons of cocoa from the region.

In addition to purchasing cocoa and paying farmers higher wages, the partnership has also provided education to 2,000 farmers on how to improve cocoa crop yields. Whinney is committed to developing trust and mutually beneficial relationships among suppliers, companies, and consumers.

Theo Chocolate embodies all four levels of social responsibility as it is profitable, obeys relevant laws, acts ethically, and engages in philanthropic activities. Although some believe that a company should focus on profits over community relations or stakeholder well-being, Theo Chocolate demonstrates that a firm can create positive change and be profitable at the same time.[62]

### Questions for Discussion

1. How has Theo Chocolate incorporated its model of philanthropy and social responsibility into a successful business concept?
2. Why is it important to create investment in the Congo and not just provide aid?
3. What advantages does Theo Chocolate have by sourcing cocoa from the Congo, even though the chocolate ends up costing consumers more?

# Case 4.2

## Blue Bell Creameries Moo'ves Ahead after Listeria Crisis

Blue Bell Creameries began as a small creamery in Brenham, Texas, in 1907. For more than 100 years the company was a success. By 2015 it was the third largest ice cream maker in the nation with more than $500 million in annual revenue. A major employer for the city of Brenham, Blue Bell sells products in 23 states and has four manufacturing plants in Texas, Oklahoma, and Alabama.

Despite the company's success, it faced perhaps its greatest challenge in 2015 when a listeria outbreak was traced to its ice cream products. Listeria is a bacterium that can be deadly to people with weakened immune systems as well as newborns, consumers 65 years and older, and pregnant women. In March, Kansas officials determined that five people who had contracted listeria in a hospital got the disease after eating Blue Bell ice cream products. Three of the five died from the illness.

Further investigations showed that 10 people are thought to have gotten sick from listeria contracted from Blue Bell products since 2010. Blue Bell reacted immediately to the news, issued a voluntary recall of all products, and shut down its plants. Its sales force consisting of more than 3,000 workers began calling grocery and convenience stores and asked them to pull their brands. Listeria was traced to three plants in Texas, Oklahoma, and Alabama.

Despite Blue Bell's quick actions, an ethical issue arose when it was revealed that its plant in Broken Arrow, Oklahoma had tested positively for listeria 16 times since 2013. This caused some to wonder whether Blue Bell should have known that an outbreak was likely to occur. Blue Bell claims that after inspectors found listeria bacteria in the plant, it implemented clean-up procedures to get rid of the listeria and thought it had worked. However, listeria can be hard to kill and can live on drains or pipes for over a year. After the outbreak federal inspectors determined that the clean-up attempts in 2013 were inadequate.

Blue Bell's contaminated products arose from deficiencies in supply-chain management. Because supply chains require constant vigilance, it can be difficult for companies to monitor everything going on. In the case of Blue Bell, the problem appeared to be a lack of sanitary conditions. Federal officials had witnessed workers touching products or packaging without washing their hands, wearing dirty clothing, and not monitoring the temperature of the water used to clean equipment. The Oklahoma plant also had leaks and condensation that dripped onto the products. Blue Bell believes that listeria from a drain contaminated buckets that were then used in the production area of its Oklahoma plant.

The company has adopted controls to increase its compliance with safety standards. Blue Bell improved policies and its testing procedures. After ceasing production, it implemented retraining for all employees and began a massive cleaning of its factories, including taking apart its equipment to clean thoroughly. A clothing policy was also adopted requiring employees to wear covers in the production area. To reduce contamination from condensation, Blue Bell added troughs and splash guards in its factories.

However, the public relations damage and cleanup costs were highly damaging to Blue Bell. The company was forced to recall and dispose of at least 8 million gallons of ice cream, losing significant profits in the process. The plant closures and cleanup forced Blue Bell to lay off 37 percent of its workforce and furlough many others. Those employees retained for clean-up saw their pay reduced. Blue Bell began seeking financing from owners when it realized it only had enough resources to run company operations for 30-45 days. An investment by Texas billionaire Sid Bass provided Blue Bell with a lifeline and allowed it to begin returning its products to store shelves. Six months after the listeria outbreak it re-opened its Brenham plant. It looks like Blue Bell will survive the crisis, but its close call demonstrates how a marketing ethics issue can spell disaster for even the most established of companies.[63]

### Questions for Discussion

1. What did the listeria outbreak reveal about the quality control processes at Blue Bell plants, and how is this an ethical issue?
2. Do you feel that the organizational culture of the factories contributed to the quality control and sanitation issues? Why or why not?
3. Assess how Blue Bell managed its ethical responsibilities after the listeria outbreak. Do you believe they were effective in containing the outbreak?

# Strategic Case 2

## REI: An Ethical Consumer Cooperative

Recreational Equipment Incorporated (REI) is a national retail cooperative famous for its outdoor apparel and equipment. A cooperative consists of individuals who have joined together to secure the benefits of a larger organization. In the case of REI, the company is organized as a consumer cooperative. Members of the cooperative receive a portion of the organization's profits annually based on a percentage of their eligible purchases, receive discounts on products and classes, and can vote for board members. REI has 5.1 million active members and generated revenues of $2.2 billion.

Customers are only the beginning of REI's stakeholder orientation. The company also values its communities and the issues that are important to them through philanthropic activities and advocacy efforts. It shows its concern for the environment by promoting and practicing environmentally-friendly behaviors. As a result, REI maintains a strong focus on all stakeholders, an emphasis that has encouraged the organization to offer superior goods and services in areas such as mountain climbing, camping, and other outdoor activities.

REI's values include authenticity, quality, service, respect, integrity, decency, and balance. These values are at the heart of the company's work environment and are reflected in each of their activities. The ethical culture of REI is not just about employees and customers, but includes all stakeholders. Ethical conduct is at the core of its culture.

The concept of REI originated during the 1930s when Lloyd Anderson, a member of the Pacific Northwest Mountaineers, was looking for a high-quality ice axe at a reasonable cost. After searching without success, Anderson found what he needed in an Austrian Alpine Gear catalog for $3.50. His find excited the climbing community around Seattle, prompting Anderson to envision a local business that would carry items for mountain climbers at reasonable prices. In 1938 Lloyd Anderson and his wife Mary, along with 21 fellow climbers, founded an outdoor gear consumer cooperative. At first the cooperative was focused specifically on mountain climbing. Its first full-time employee and eventual CEO was John Whittaker, the first American to successfully climb Mt. Everest. Yet over the years REI grew to include gear for camping and hiking, bicycling, fitness, paddling, and more. Today it is the largest consumer cooperative in the United States.

### REI Maintains Customer Satisfaction

REI operates more than 143 retail stores in 35 states. To help customers choose the right product, REI retail locations contain features like bike trails and rock climbing walls that allow customers to test the gear, as well as Internet kiosks to educate consumers about the brands and products it sells. In addition, to make sure that customers purchase products that meet their needs, REI offers a 100% Satisfaction Guarantee. In line with its ethical view of customer satisfaction, REI's return policy used to allow customers to return merchandise at any time and receive a refund. However, some of their cus-

to inspire and educate the younger generation about the outdoors. The company's Promoting Environmental Awareness in Kids (PEAK) program is one step toward youth engagement. This program teaches kids about outdoor ethics—such as cleaning up waste materials and respecting wildlife— while having fun outdoors. PEAK has two goals: to introduce youth to the wonders of the outdoors, and to

tomers engaged in misbehavior. They took advantage of REI's policy by either purposefully damaging products and returning them to the store or buying REI merchandise at yard sales and returning them for cash. This misconduct cut into company profits, and REI responded by maintaining its 100% Satisfaction Guarantee but instituting a year-long window for items to be returned.

In changing its policy, REI attempted to maintain fairness to all stakeholders. Its one-year return period gives customers a significant amount of time to decide if they are satisfied. It also helps curb consumer misconduct that could harm other stakeholders. REI learned that although it wants to be ethical to its customers, there are times when it must adopt controls to reduce the potential for unethical conduct.

REI's role in the competitive environment is largely based on quality products. Its competitors, L.L. Bean and Sports Authority, also offer quality products but at lower prices. REI has received some criticism over its higher-priced products, but many of its customers are willing to pay the higher prices because their values align with the company's. REI cooperative members tend to share similar values as well. They receive the added benefit of profiting from their purchases—the more they buy at the store, the more return they will receive in the annual dividends REI provides to members.

### REI Uses Marketing to Support Outdoor Initiatives

REI has become an expert in monitoring its environment to ensure that it continues to meet customer needs. For instance, the company uses social media outlets to gauge and address the sociocultural environment. In response to the change in people's desires to reduce their carbon footprint and maintain an active lifestyle, REI produces videos on YouTube and posts on Facebook and Twitter to educate customers about kayaking, road biking, and family camping.

Additionally, REI demonstrates social responsibility by supporting local programs to further conservation and outdoor recreation. A primary focus for REI is youth. REI seeks

practice responsible "No Trace" principles. REI also encourages employees to volunteer in improving and protecting the outdoors. In all of these efforts, REI's philanthropic initiatives contribute to its brand and customer loyalty. Consumers expect businesses to give back to the community, and REI goes beyond what is required.

### REI Cares for the Environment

Changing sociocultural trends have made the environment an important stakeholder for businesses. Stakeholders have begun to express an interest in how businesses affect the environment. For this reason, REI develops an annual environmental stewardship report. This not only generates goodwill among stakeholders but also fits well with REI's strategic emphasis on outdoor activities and product offerings. REI has benchmarked areas of sustainability concern in its stewardship report into four sections: (1) curate sustainable products, (2) create access, (3) catalyze experiences, and (4) core practices. The organization also considers its product stewardship responsibilities and has acted as a leader in this area.

REI has been reducing the impact of its greenhouse gas emissions through methods such as the purchase of carbon offsets. It uses solar to power 26 REI locations and has taken action to retrofit its buildings to reduce emissions. For instance, by retrofitting its data center REI experienced a 93 percent reduction in cooling costs.

In terms of its paper sourcing, REI wants to ensure that the paper it uses is sourced responsibly. It is impossible for REI to completely eliminate its use of paper, but the company's paper policy encourages the purchase of paper products sourced from post-consumer waste or virgin fiber harvested from forests certified by the Forest Stewardship Council (FSC). Certification implies that the paper-based products have been responsibly sourced. Although REI saw its paper usage increase in a one year period, 70.8 percent of its total paper footprint consisted of post-consumer recycled paper and third-party certified fiber.

Finally, REI recognizes that environmental stewardship does not stop after a company sells a product. REI makes product stewardship a key tenet of its sustainability goals. It advocates for a universal standard that can be used to judge a product's sustainability. To that end, REI partnered with Timberland to create the Eco Index. In 2012 the Eco Index was modified to form the HiGG Index, a tool used to measure the sustainability of apparel and footwear products. REI also supports the bluesign® system, a system to responsibly manage chemicals in the supply chain. Approximately 25 percent of materials that REI uses is bluesign-certified.

REI also takes its environmental concerns to the political level. Its advocacy efforts center on its desire to protect the environment and promote outdoor recreation. The company has lobbied and continues to lobby for public lands and environmental causes. More specifically, the organization has supported the Outdoor Industry Association. Additionally, REI sometimes partners its employees with nonprofits that support its environmental goals, such as the Outdoor Alliance and People for Bikes.

Because of REI's customer-based mission, it is able to generate loyalty and enthusiasm among stakeholders. Though some of the company's marketing activities are sales-related, much of it provides stakeholders with information directly related to their outdoor interests and environmental concerns. The marketing citizenship that the company embraces has proven to be a strong force in garnering stakeholder attention, generating profits, and advancing a stakeholder orientation.[64]

### Questions for Discussion

1. Describe stakeholder orientation at REI.
2. How does REI implement social responsibility?
3. How do REI's values relate to the development of an ethical culture?

# NOTES

[1] Aamer Madhani, "Starbucks to open stores in low-income areas," *USA Today*, July 16, 2015, http://www.usatoday.com/story/news/2015/07/16/starbucks-to-open-15-locations-in-low-income-minority-communities/30206071/ (accessed July 20, 2015); Julie Jargon, "Starbucks Leads Push to Boost Youth Jobs," *The Wall Street Journal*, July 14, 2015, B3; Micah Solomon, "Starbucks to Open Store, Customer Service Training Center in Ferguson, 14 Other Distressed Locations," *Forbes*, July 16, 2015, http://www.forbes.com/sites/micahsolomon/2015/07/16/starbucks-to-open-store-customer-service-training-center-in-ferguson-14-other-distressed-locations/ (accessed July 20, 2015); Starbucks, "Starbucks College Achievement Plan: Frequently Asked Questions," https://news.starbucks.com/views/starbucks-college-achievement-plan-frequently-asked-questions (accessed January 8, 2015).

[2] Peter R. Darke and Robin J. B. Ritchie, "The Defensive Consumer: Advertising Deception, Defensive Processing, and Distrust," *Journal of Marketing Research* 4, 1 (February 2007): 114–127.

[3] Isabelle Maignan and O. C. Ferrell, "Corporate Social Responsibility and Marketing: An Integrative Framework," *Journal of the Academy of Marketing Science* 32 (January 2004): 3–19.

[4] Ucilia Wang, "Campbell Soup CEO: 'You can lead the change or be a victim of change'," *The Guardian*, October 25, 2013, www.theguardian.com/sustainable-business/campbell-soup-ceo-business-social-responsibility (accessed January 19, 2016).

[5] Daniel Korschun, C.B. Bhattacharya, and Scott D. Swain, "Corporate Social Responsibility, Customer Orientation, and the Job Performance of Frontline Employees," *Journal of Marketing* 78 (May 2014): 20–37.

[6] "Thank You for Helping Us Reach Our Goal Together," *One Today*, https://onetoday.google.com/page/refugeerelief/ (accessed December 16, 2015).

[7] Isabelle Maignan and O. C. Ferrell, "Antecedents and Benefits of Corporate Citizenship: An Investigation of French Businesses," *Journal of Business Research* 51 (2001): 37–51.

[8] Debbie Thorne, Linda Ferrell, and O. C. Ferrell, *Business and Society: A Strategic Approach to Social Responsibility*, 4th ed. (Boston: Houghton Mifflin, 2011), pp. 38–40.

[9] O. C. Ferrell, "Business Ethics and Customer Stakeholders," *Academy of Management Executive* 18 (May 2004): 126–129.

[10] Academy of Managed Care Pharmacy, "Top 10 Emerging Health Care Trends Report Finds Opportunities to Achieve Triple Aim of Health Reform," October 9, 2014, http://www.amcp.org/uploadedFiles/Production_Menu/Functional_Navigation/Media_Room/Press_Releases/Media%20Release%20-%20AMCP%20Foundation%20October%209.pdf (accessed January 19, 2016).

[11] Archie Carroll, "The Pyramid of Corporate Social Responsibility: Toward the Moral Management of Organizational Stakeholders," *Business Horizons* (July/August 1991): 42.

[12] Jiyun Kang and Gwendolyn Hustvedt, "Building Trust Between Consumers and Corporations: The Role of Consumer Perceptions of Transparency and Social Responsibility," *Journal of Business Ethics* 125, 2 (2014): 253–265.

[13] Diane Cardwell, "Charitable Giving Rises Past Prerecession Mark," *The New York Times*, June 16, 2015, http://www.nytimes.com/2015/06/16/business/charitable-giving-rises-past-prerecession-mark.html?_r=0 (accessed December 16, 2015).

[14] AllBusiness Editors, "11 Heartwarming Ways Real Small Businesses Are Giving Back for the Holidays," *allBusiness*, http://www.allbusiness

.com/slideshow/11-heartwarming-ways-real-small-businesses-are-giving-back-for-the-holidays-16739378-1.html/9 (accessed December 16, 2015).

[15] CVS, "LUNG FORCE," https://www.cvshealth.com/social-responsibility/our-giving/corporate-giving/national-partners/lung-force (accessed December 17, 2015).

[16] Cone Communications, "Research & Insights," http://www.conecomm.com/research (accessed December 17, 2015).

[17] Thorne, Ferrell, and Ferrell, *Business and Society*, p. 335.

[18] Douglas MacMillan, "Warby Parker Adds Storefronts to Its Sales Strategy," *The Wall Street Journal*, November 17, 2014, http://online.wsj.com/articles/warby-parker-adds-storefronts-to-its-sales-strategy-1416251866 (accessed December 15, 2015); Warby Parker, "Buy a Pair, Give a Pair," www.warbyparker.com/buy-a-pair-give-a-pair (accessed December 15, 2015).

[19] Dinah Eng [interviewer], "Mopping Up with Green Cleaners," *Fortune*, October 28, 2013, pp. 47–48; SC Johnson, *The SC Johnson Greenlist™ Process*, 2014, http://fortune.com/2013/10/10/mopping-up-with-method/ (accessed August 22, 2016).

[20] Simona Romani, Silvia Grappi, and Richard P. Bagozzi, "Corporate Socially Responsible Initiatives and Their Effects on Consumption of Green Products," *Journal of Business Ethics*, accepted November 19, 2014, DOI: 10.1007/s10551-014-2485-0.

[21] Forest Stewardship Council, "Kimberly-Clark Grows Its Commitment to FSC," *Newsletter Stories*, January 23, 2014, https://us.fsc.org/newsletter.239.809.htm (accessed December 15, 2015).

[22] Gergely Nyilasy, Harsha Gangadharbatla, and Angela Paladino, "Perceived Greenwashing: The Interactive Effects of Green Advertising and Corporate Environmental Performance on Consumer Reactions," *Journal of Business Ethics*, 125, 4 (2014): 693–707.

[23] Paul Hawken and William McDonough, "Seven Steps to Doing Good Business," *Inc.* (November 1993): 79–90.

[24] Jill Gabrielle Klein, N. Craig Smith, and Andrew John, "Why We Boycott: Consumer Motivations for Boycott Participation," *Journal of Marketing* 68 (July 2004): 92–109.

[25] Christian Homburg and Andreas Fürst, "How Organizational Complaint Handling Drives Customer Loyalty: An Analysis of the Mechanistic and the Organic Approach," *Journal of Marketing* 69 (July 2005): 95–114.

[26] Jon Kamp and Jennifer Levitz, "Johnson & Johnson Pulls Hysterectomy Device from Hospitals," *The Wall Street Journal*, July 30, 2014, http://www.wsj.com/articles/johnson-johnson-to-call-for-voluntary-return-of-morcellators-1406754350 (accessed December 17, 2015); Jennifer Levitz, "FBI Is Investigating Hysterectomy Device Found to Spread Uterine Cancer," *The Wall Street Journal*, May 27, 2015, http://www.wsj.com/articles/fbi-is-investigating-surgical-device-1432746641 (accessed December 17, 2015).

[27] Samsung, "Samsung Hope for Children Program," http://www.samsung.com/us/aboutsamsung/citizenship/hopeforchildren/ (accessed December 17, 2015); Samsung, "Citizenship," http://www.samsung.com/us/corporate-citizenship/index.html (accessed December 17, 2015).

[28] "Environmentalism: What We Do," Patagonia, www.patagonia.com/us/patagonia.go?assetid=1960 (accessed December 15, 2015).

[29] Edelman, *Edelman Trust Barometer 2013 Annual Global Study*, www.slideshare.net/EdelmanInsights/global-deck-2013-edelman-trust-barometer-16086761 (accessed November 21, 2013).

[30] Bruce Horovitz, "Sorry, kids, no soda with your meal," *USA Today*, March 10, 2015, 1A.

[31] Tim Barnett and Sean Valentine, "Issue Contingencies and Marketers' Recognition of Ethical Issues, Ethical Judgments and Behavioral Intentions," *Journal of Business Research* 57 (2004): 338–346.

[32] Trefis Team, "Can Chipotle Mexican Grill Recover from the E.Coli Outbreak Impact?" *Forbes*, December 14, 2015, http://www.forbes.com/sites/greatspeculations/2015/12/14/can-chipotle-mexican-grill-recover-from-the-e-coli-outbreak-impact/ (accessed December 16, 2015).

[33] David E. Sprott, Kenneth C. Manning, and Anthony D. Miyazaki, "Grocery Price Setting and Quantity Surcharges," *Journal of Marketing* (July 2003): 34–46.

[34] Stephen Taub, "SEC Probing Harley Statements," *CFO.com*, July 14, 2005, http://ww2.cfo.com/accounting-tax/2005/07/

sec-probing-harley-statements (accessed January 19, 2016).

[35] Kathy Chu and Trefor Moss, "Call Centers: New Battle Front for Fake Drugs," *The Wall Street Journal*, June 7, 2015, http://www.wsj.com/articles/call-centers-new-battle-front-for-fake-drugs-1433712783 (accessed December 17, 2015).

[36] Lynnley Browning, "Companies Struggle to Comply with Rules on Conflict Minerals," *The New York Times*, September 7, 2015, http://www.nytimes.com/2015/09/08/business/dealbook/companies-struggle-to-comply-with-conflict-minerals-rule.html?_r=0 (accessed December 17, 2015).

[37] Ben Dipietro, "Slave Labor Concerns Give Companies More Supply Chain Worries," *The Wall Street Journal*, September 3, 2015, http://blogs.wsj.com/riskandcompliance/2015/09/03/slave-labor-concerns-give-companies-more-supply-chain-worries/ (accessed December 17, 2015).

[38] "Monitoring and Auditing Global Supply Chains Is a Must," *Ethisphere*, Q3, (2011): 38–45.

[39] "Health Care Supply Company Novation Earns Ethics Inside Certification," *Ethisphere*, November 8, 2011, https://ethisphere.com/novation-llc-again-earns-ethics-inside-certification/ (accessed August 22, 2016).

[40] Maxwell Murphy, "Reinforcing the Supply Chain," *The Wall Street Journal*, January 11, 2012, p. B6; "Monitoring and Auditing Global Supply Chains Is a Must," pp. 38–45.

[41] "Monitoring and Auditing Global Supply Chains Is a Must," **Ethisphere, Q3, (2011)**: pp. 38–45.

[42] Peggy H. Cunningham and O. C. Ferrell, "The Influence of Role Stress on Unethical Behavior by Personnel Involved in the Marketing Research Process" (working paper, Queens University, Ontario, 2004), p. 35.

[43] Joseph W. Weiss, *Business Ethics: A Managerial, Stakeholder Approach* (Belmont, CA: Wadsworth, 1994), p. 13.

[44] O. C. Ferrell, Larry G. Gresham, and John Fraedrich, "A Synthesis of Ethical Decision Models for Marketing," *Journal of Macromarketing* (Fall 1989): 58–59.

[45] Ethics and Compliance Initiative, *2016 Global Business Ethics Survey™: Measuring Risk and Promoting Workplace Integrity* (Arlington, VA: Ethics and Compliance Initiative, 2016), p. 43.

[46] Barry J. Babin, James S. Boles, and Donald P. Robin, "Representing the Perceived Ethical Work Climate Among Marketing Employees," *Journal of the Academy of Marketing Science* 28 (2000): 345–358.

[47] Ferrell, Gresham, and Fraedrich, "A Synthesis of Ethical Decision Models for Marketing."

[48] Lawrence B. Chonko and Shelby D. Hunt, "Ethics and Marketing Management: A Retrospective and Prospective Commentary," *Journal of Business Research* 50 (2000): 235–244.

[49] Linda K. Trevino and Stuart Youngblood, "Bad Apples in Bad Barrels: A Causal Analysis of Ethical Decision Making Behavior," *Journal of Applied Psychology* 75 (1990): 378–385.

[50] Pfizer, "Pfizer's International Anti-Bribery and Anti-Corruption Business Principles," https://www.pfizer.com/sites/default/files/corporate_citizenship/pfizer_antibribery_anticorruption91112.pdf (accessed December 17, 2015); Pfizer, *The Blue Book: Summary of Pfizer Policies on Business Conduct*, http://www.pfizer.com/files/investors/corporate/bluebook_english.pdf (accessed December 17, 2015).

[51] Ethics Resource Center, "The Ethics Resource Center's 2009 National Business Ethics Survey," p. 41.

[52] Ethics Resource Center, "The Ethics Resource Center's 2007 National Business Ethics Survey," p. ix.

[53] Ethics and Compliance Initiative, *2016 Global Business Ethics Survey™: Measuring Risk and Promoting Workplace Integrity* (Arlington, VA: Ethics and Compliance Initiative, 2016), p. 18.

[54] Sir Adrian Cadbury, "Ethical Managers Make Their Own Rules," *Harvard Business Review* (September/October 1987): 33.

[55] Isabelle Maignan, Tracy L. Gonzalez-Padron, G. Tomas M. Hult, and O. C. Ferrell, "Stakeholder Orientation: Development and Testing of a Framework for Socially Responsible Marketing," *Journal of Strategic Marketing*, vol. 19, 4 (July 2011): 313–338.

[56] Ferrell, Fraedrich, and Ferrell, *Business Ethics*, pp. 27-30.

[57] UNM Daniels Fund website, "NiSource and Columbia Gas of Kentucky Maintain a Values-Based Ethics Program," 2014, https://danielsethics.mgt.unm.edu/pdf/columbia-gas.pdf (accessed December 17, 2015); NiSource, "Our Accomplishments," 2015, https://www.nisource.com/about-us/our-accomplishments (accessed December 17, 2015).

[58] G. Thomas Hult, Jeannette Mena, O. C. Ferrell, and Linda Ferrell, "Stakeholder Marketing: A Definition and Conceptual Framework," *AMS Review* 1, 1 (2011): 44–65.

[59] Marjorie Kelly, "Holy Grail Found: Absolute, Definitive Proof That Responsible Companies Perform Better Financially," *Business Ethics*, Winter 2004: 4–5; Xueming Luo and C. B. Bhattacharya, "Corporate Social Responsibility, Customer Satisfaction, and Market Value," *Journal of Marketing* 70 (October 2006): 1–18; Isabelle Maignan, O.C. Ferrell, and Linda Ferrell, "A Stakeholder Model for Implementing Social Responsibility in Marketing," *European Journal of Marketing* 39 (September/October 2005): 956–977.

[60] Cone Communications, "Cone Releases the 2015 Cone Communications/Ebiquity Global CSR Study," May 27, 2015, http://www.conecomm.com/2015-global-csr-study-press-release (accessed December 17, 2015).

[61] Maignan, Ferrell, and Ferrell, "A Stakeholder Model for Implementing Social Responsibility in Marketing."

[62] Theo Chocolate, "Our Story," https://www.theochocolate.com/mission#story (accessed January 11, 2016); Eastern Congo Initiative, http://www.easterncongo.org/about (accessed January 11, 2016); Rebekah Denn, "From Theo, a book of love and chocolate," *Seattle Times*, September 23, 2015, http://www.seattletimes.com/life/food-drink/from-theo-a-book-of-love-and-chocolate/ (accessed January 11, 2016); Glenn Drosendahl, "Seattle's Theo Chocolate teams with Ben Affleck group to help Congolese farmers," *Puget Sound Business Journal*, February 12, 2013, http://www.bizjournals.com/seattle/blog/2013/02/seattles-theo-chocolate-teams-with.html (accessed January 11, 2016); CBS, "Chocolate that makes a difference," *YouTube*, December 2, 2012, https://www.youtube.com/watch?v=5x0PLZ6RzBQ (accessed May 18, 2016).

[63] Blue Bell Creameries website, http://cdn.bluebell.com/the_little_creamery/our_history.html (accessed June 26, 2015); Blue Bell Creameries, "Blue Bell Creameries Voluntarily Expands Recall to Include All of Its Products Due to Possible Health Risk," April 20, 2015, http://www.bluebell.com/the_little_creamery/press_releases/all-product-recall (accessed June 26, 2015); Centers for Disease Control and Prevention, "Multistate Outbreak of Listeriosis Linked to Blue Bell Creameries Products (Final Update)," June 10, 2015, http://www.cdc.gov/listeria/outbreaks/ice-cream-03-15/index.html (accessed June 26, 2015); CNN Money, "Blue Bell recall: Feds detail Listeria contamination and unsanitary conditions," *CNN*, May 7, 2015, http://money.cnn.com/2015/05/07/news/companies/blue-bell-ice-cream-listeria/index.html (accessed June 26, 2015); Alison Griswold, "Blue Bell's Listeria Crisis Will Cost 1,450 Employees Their Jobs," *Slate*, May 15, 2015, http://www.slate.com/blogs/moneybox/2015/05/15/blue_bell_creameries_layoffs_listeria_crisis_takes_jobs_from_1_450_employees.html (accessed June 26, 2015); Rick Harmon, "Blue Bell says its ice cream won't return soon," *USA Today*, May 8, 2015, http://www.usatoday.com/story/money/business/2015/05/07/blue-bell-says-ice-cream-return-soon/70965334/ (accessed June 26, 2015); KHOU-TV, "Listeria outbreak linked to a single Blue Bell machine," *USA Today*, March 16, 2015, http://www.usatoday.com/story/money/business/2015/03/16/blue-bell-deadly-listeria/24836935/ (accessed June 26, 2015); Terri Langford, "State Health Tests Prodded Blue Bell Recall," *Texas Tribune*, April 24, 2015, http://www.texastribune.org/2015/04/24/how-blue-bell-chose-recall/ (accessed June 26, 2015); Juan A. Lozano from Associated Press, "Blue Bell: Listeria likely linked to non-sanitary room at Oklahoma plant; unclear in Texas," *U.S. News & World Report*, June 10, 2015, http://www.usnews.com/news/business/articles/2015/06/10/blue-bell-listeria-source-likely-idd-at-oklahoma-plant (accessed June 26, 2015); Jesse Newman, "Texas Billionaire Bass Invests In Ice Cream Maker Blue Bell," *The Wall Street Journal*, July 15, 2015, B3; William Thornton, "Blue Bell recall: State gets 2 weeks' notice on ice cream restart," *AL.com*, June 3, 2015, http://www.al.com/news/anniston-gadsden/index.ssf/2015/06/blue_bell_recall_state_gets_2.html (accessed June 26, 2015); Reuters, "Ice cream maker Blue Bell restarts biggest plant shut for listeria," *Fox News*, November 19, 2015, http://www.foxnews.com/health/2015/11/19/ice-cream-maker-blue-bell-restarts-biggest-plant-shut-for-listeria.html (accessed December 15, 2015).

[64] Monte Burke, "A Conversation with REI Chief Executive Sally Jewell," *Forbes*, May 19, 2011, http://blogs.forbes.com/monteburke/2011/05/19/a-conversation-with-

rei-chief-executive-sally-jewell (accessed December 16, 2015); Fair Factories Clearinghouse, "Streamlining Business Practices," www.fairfactories.org/Main/Index.aspx (accessed October 17, 2013); O. C. Ferrell, Geoffrey A. Hirt, and Linda Ferrell, *Business: A Changing World*, 8th ed. (New York: McGraw-Hill Irwin, 2011), p. 138; Christine Frey, "Product-Testing REI Employees Take the Scrapes for Buyers," *Seattle PI*, October 18, 2002, www.seattlepi.com/default/article/Product-testing-REI-employees-take-the-scrapes-1098834.php (accessed December 16, 2015); FSC, "FSC Certification," https://ic.fsc.org/en (accessed December 16, 2015); International Labour Organization, "About the ILO," www.ilo.org/global/about-the-ilo/lang--en/index.htm (accessed December 16, 2015); Leave No Trace Website, www.lnt.org/programs/peak/index.html (accessed December 16, 2015); New York Job Source, "Recreation Equipment Inc.," December 8, 2015, http://nyjobsource.com/rei.html (accessed December 16, 2015); REI, "REI & Youth," www.rei.com/aboutrei/reikids02.html (accessed October 17, 2013); REI, "Being an

REI Member Just Got Better: REI Introduces Free Shipping Exclusively for Members," www.rei.com/aboutrei/releases/10free_shipping.html (accessed December 16, 2015); REI, "Overview," www.rei.com/aboutrei/business.html (accessed December 16, 2015); REI, "Workplace," www.rei.com/stewardship/rei_workplace (accessed December 16, 2015); REI Adventures, www.rei.com/adventures (accessed December 16, 2015); Giselle Tsirulnik, "REI App Ppurpose Is Twofold: Sales and Service," *Mobile Commerce Daily*, March 25, 2011, http://www.mobilecommercedaily.com/rei-app-purpose-is-twofold-sales-and-service (accessed December 16, 2015); REI, "Factory Fair Labor Compliance: 2011 Stewardship Report," www.rei.com/stewardship/report/2011/workplace/factory-fair-labor.html (accessed December 16, 2015); REI, "Return Policy," http://www.rei.com/help/return-policy.html (accessed December 16, 2015); Amy Martinez, "REI now limiting returns to one year," *Seattle Times*, June 3, 2013, http://www.seattletimes.com/business/rei-now-limiting-returns-to-one-year/ (accessed December 16, 2015); Ariel Webber,

"Recreational Equipment Inc. Ads Are Made for Outdoor Enthusiasts," *Trend Hunter Marketing*, February 18, 2013, www.trendhunter.com/trends/recreational-equipment-inc (accessed December 16, 2015); Elaine Porterfield, "How REI Became the Most Respected Private Company Brand in Washington," *Puget Sound Business Journal*, July 29, 2011, www.bizjournals.com/seattle/print-edition/2011/07/29/how-rei-became-the-most-respected.html?page=all (accessed December 16, 2015); Rachael King, "REI Appoints First CIO," *The Wall Street Journal*, September 1, 2015, http://blogs.wsj.com/cio/2015/09/01/rei-appoints-first-cio/ (accessed December 16, 2015); REI, "REI Promotes Craig Rowley to Vice President of Marketing, Welcomes Jed Paulson as Vice President of Digital Retail," REI Coop, December 9, 2015, http://newsroom.rei.com/news/rei-promotes-craig-rowley-to-vice-president-marketing-welcomes-jed-paulson-as-vice-president-digital-retail.htm (accessed December 16, 2015); REI, "2014 Stewardship Report," http://www.rei.com/stewardship/report/2014/stewardship-report.html (accessed December 16, 2015).

## Feature Notes

[a] "Change the World List: No. 4: Walmart," *Fortune*, September 1, 2015, 57–84; Steve Banker, "Walmart Has One of the World's Most Sustainable Supply Chains? Really?" *Logistics Viewpoints*, April 27, 2015, http://logisticsviewpoints.com/2015/04/27/walmart-has-one-of-the-worlds-most-sustainable-supply-chains-really/ (accessed October 6, 2015); "Wal-Mart and the Green Consumer," *The Wall Street Journal*, March 30, 2015, http://www

.wsj.com/articles/wal-mart-and-the-green-consumer-1427770855 (accessed October 6, 2015).

[b] Bill Briggs, "Business Ethics, with a Chuckle," MSNBC, June 11, 2010, www.msnbc.msn.com/id/37595722/ns/business-small_business/ (accessed July 20, 2015); "RealBiz Shorts," Second City Communications, www.realbizshorts.com/ (accessed July 20, 2015); Lauren Bloom, "Watch Second City's Ethics Shorts, Laugh, and Learn," Lauren Bloom's Blog, June 14, 2010,

www.thebusinessethicsblog.com/watch-second-citys-ethics-shorts-laugh-and-learn (accessed December 1, 2011); "History of The Second City," The Second City, www.secondcity.com/history/ (accessed July 20, 2015); "RealBiz Shorts Now Available On-Demand!" The Second City, February 26, 2015, http://www.secondcity.com/works/updates/news/article/realbiz-shorts-now-available-on-demand/ (accessed July 20, 2015).

# part 3
## Marketing Research and Target Market Analysis

**PART 3** examines how marketers use information and technology to better understand and reach customers.

**CHAPTER 5** provides a foundation for analyzing buyers through a discussion of marketing information systems and the basic steps in the marketing research process. Understanding elements that affect buying decisions enables marketers to better analyze customers' needs and to evaluate how specific marketing strategies can satisfy those needs.

**CHAPTER 6** deals with selecting and analyzing target markets, which is one of the major steps in marketing strategy development.

*big data*

# chapter 5

## Marketing Research and Information Systems

---

### OBJECTIVES

---

5-1    Define marketing research and its importance to decision makers.

5-2    Distinguish between exploratory and conclusive research.

5-3    Name the five basic steps in conducting marketing research, including the two types of data and four survey methods.

5-4    Describe the tools, such as databases, big data, marketing analytics, and decision support systems useful to marketing decision making.

5-5    Identify ethical and international issues in marketing research.

# MARKETING INSIGHTS

## SamplingLab: Marketing Research Goes Retail

martinedoucet/E+/Getty Images

Marketing consultant Jeff Davis knows that marketing research can be expensive. He wanted to create a type of test environment that would cost companies less while allowing consumers to try free samples without feeling the face-to-face pressures of in-store sampling.

Enter SamplingLab, a Portland-based store with shelves of free full-sized samples of food, household products, and more. To try the samples, consumers become a member of SamplingLab. Afterwards, they browse the store looking for a sample they would like to try, often sipping on free beer offered in the store. Instead of paying to try the product, consumers fill out online questionnaires of 15–20 mostly multiple-choice questions of their opinions of the product. Consumers are encouraged to share their opinions on social media for additional perks and special events. They must fill out a questionnaire before trying another product.

Davis founded SamplingLab with the belief that younger people reluctant to join a traditional focus group would be more willing to hang out in a lounge area and try free samples at their leisure. Thus far, his idea is on target: 7,600 consumers became members in six months, and three-fourths were aged 34 or younger. Davis plans to earn future revenue by charging client companies for consumer reviews.

While this seems like a great deal for consumers, do companies benefit? One company used SamplingLab to offer taste tests of its new beer. The results indicated that the packaging confused customers regarding the product's taste. The company responded by educating wholesalers and retailers on how to clearly describe the beer's taste to customers. It also made plans to change the packaging to better reflect the beer's taste in the upcoming year.[1]

Marketing research enables marketers to implement the marketing concept by helping them acquire information about whether and how their goods and services satisfy the desires of target market customers. When used effectively, such information facilitates relationship marketing by helping marketers focus their efforts on meeting and even anticipating the needs of their customers. Marketing research and information systems that can provide practical and objective information to help firms develop and implement marketing strategies are therefore essential to effective marketing.

In this chapter, we focus on how marketers gather information needed to make marketing decisions. First, we define marketing research and examine the individual steps of the marketing research process, including various methods of collecting data. Next, we look at how technology aids in collecting, organizing, and interpreting marketing research data. Finally, we consider ethical and international issues in marketing research.

## 5-1 THE IMPORTANCE OF MARKETING RESEARCH

**Marketing research** is the systematic design, collection, interpretation, and reporting of information to help marketers solve specific marketing problems or take advantage of marketing opportunities. As the word *research* implies, it is a process for gathering information that is not currently available to decision makers. The purpose of marketing research is to inform an organization about customers' needs and desires, marketing opportunities for products, and changing attitudes and purchase patterns of customers. Market information increases the marketer's ability to respond to customer needs, which leads to improved organizational performance. Detecting shifts in buyers' behaviors and attitudes helps companies stay in touch with the ever-changing marketplace. Some retail stores, for instance, are redesigning their selling floors to keep customers in the store longer. Studies have shown that slower shoppers tend to buy more, and offering amenities such as lounges are one way retailers can differentiate the shopping experience from purchasing items online.[2] Strategic planning requires marketing research to facilitate the process of assessing such opportunities or threats from competitors.

Marketing research can help a firm better understand market opportunities, ascertain the potential for success for new products, and determine the feasibility of a particular marketing strategy. It can also reveal some surprising trends. Characters on cereal boxes are designed to create eye contact with customers as they pass through supermarket aisles in order to increase brand loyalty. Although more studies must be conducted to determine the effect on sales, this "eye contact" between customers and cereal box characters has been found to create positive feelings for the consumer.[3] Failing to conduct research can prevent companies from maintaining a competitive advantage.

Many types of organizations use marketing research to help them develop marketing mixes to match the needs of customers. Supermarkets have learned from marketing research that roughly half of all Americans prefer to have their dinners ready in 15 to 30 minutes. Such information highlights a tremendous opportunity for supermarkets to offer high-quality "heat-and-eat" meals to satisfy this growing segment of the food market. Political candidates also depend on marketing research to understand the scope of issues their constituents view as important. National political candidates may spend millions surveying voters to better understand issues and craft their images accordingly.

Changes in the economy have dramatically changed marketers' decision-making strategies. Increasingly, businesses need speed and agility to survive and to react quickly to changing consumer behaviors. Understanding the market is crucial for effective marketing strategies. Evidence shows that automakers use information about consumer vehicle preferences to determine what features are important in the development of new vehicles. Marketing research has shifted its focus toward smaller studies like test marketing, small-scale surveys, and short-range

**marketing research** The systematic design, collection, interpretation, and reporting of information to help marketers solve specific marketing problems or take advantage of marketing opportunities forecasting in order to learn about changing dynamics in the marketplace. However, large, high-value research projects remain necessary for long-term success. Though it is acceptable to conduct studies that take six months or more, many companies need real-time information to help them make good decisions. Firms may benefit from historical or secondary data, but due to changes in the economy and buyer behavior, such data are not as useful in today's decision-making environment. As we discuss in this chapter, online research services and the use of big data are helping to supplement and integrate findings in order to help companies make tactical and strategic decisions. In the future, the marketing researcher will need to be able to identify the most efficient and effective ways of gathering information.[4]

The real value of marketing research is measured by improvements in a marketer's ability to make decisions. IKEA, for instance, is testing out products that are suitable for small, cramped homes. In order to test the products, the company refurbished a small apartment and invited several families to stay there. The families were provided with iPads so they could write down their impressions of what it was like to live there. IKEA hopes to use this information to expand into a wider market for furniture.[5] Marketers should treat information the same way as other resources, and they must weigh the costs and benefits of obtaining information. Information should be considered worthwhile if it results in marketing activities that better satisfy the firm's target customers, lead to increased sales and profits, or help the firm achieve some other goal. Take a look at the advertisement for SAP's HANA system, a computing platform and data management system that offers a range of services. The advertisement targeted toward businesses stresses the importance of knowing one's customers and anticipating their needs before anyone else does—including the customers themselves. SAP HANA uses big data to predict future trends. This type of marketing research can be crucial in developing and adapting marketing strategies to connect with customers.

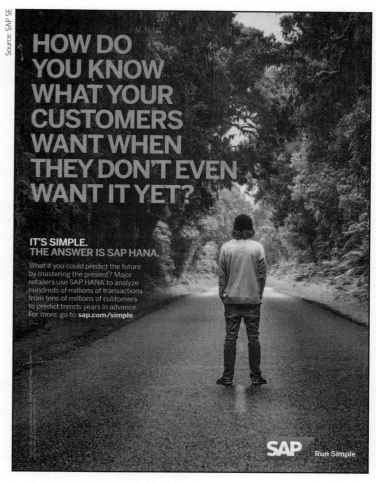

Source: SAP SE

**Importance of Marketing Research**
SAP HANA is used to analyze data that would be impossible for a single marketing researcher. The insights gleaned from this data can be used to predict future consumer trends, which would provide businesses using this platform with a competitive advantage.

## 5-2 **TYPES OF RESEARCH**

The nature and type of research vary based on the research design and the hypotheses under investigation. Marketing research can involve two forms of data. *Qualitative data* yields descriptive non-numerical information. *Quantitative data* yields empirical information that can be communicated through numbers. Marketers may choose to collect either depending upon the research required.

To collect this data, marketers conduct either exploratory research or conclusive research. Although each has a distinct purpose, the major differences between them are formalization and flexibility rather than the specific research methods used. Table 5.1 summarizes the differences.

Table 5.1   **Differences between Exploratory and Conclusive Research**

| Research Project Components | Exploratory Research | Conclusive Research |
|---|---|---|
| Research purpose | General: to generate insights about a situation | Specific: to verify insights and aid in selecting a course of action |
| Data needs | Vague | Clear |
| Data sources | Ill-defined | Well-defined |
| Data collection form | Open-ended, rough | Usually structured |
| Sample | Relatively small; subjectively selected to maximize generalization of insights | Relatively large; objectively selected to permit generalization of findings |
| Data collection | Flexible; no set procedure | Rigid; well-laid-out procedure |
| Data analysis | Informal; typically nonquantitative | Formal; typically quantitative |
| Inferences/ recommendations | More tentative than final | More final than tentative |

Source: A. Parasuraman, *Marketing Research*, Second Edition. © 2007 Cengage Learning, Inc. Reproduced by permission www.cengage.com/permissions.

## 5-2a  Exploratory Research

When marketers need more information about a problem or want to make a tentative hypothesis more specific, they may conduct **exploratory research**. The main purpose of exploratory research is to better understand a problem or situation and/or to help identify additional data needs or decision alternatives.[6] Consider that until recently, there was no research available to help marketers understand how consumers perceive the terms *clearance* versus *sale* in describing a discounted price event. An exploratory study asked one group of 80 consumers to write down their thoughts about a store window sign that said "sale" and another group of 80 consumers to write about a store window sign that read "clearance." The results revealed that consumers expected deeper discounts when the term *clearance* was used, and they expected the quality of the clearance products to be lower than that of products on sale.[7] This type of exploratory research helped marketers better understand how consumers view these terms and opened up the opportunity for additional research hypotheses about options for retail pricing.

More organizations are starting **customer advisory boards**, which are small groups of actual customers who serve as sounding boards for new product ideas and offer insights into their feelings and attitudes toward a firm's products, promotion, pricing, and other elements of marketing strategy. Though these advisory boards help companies maintain strong relationships with valuable customers, they can also provide great insight into marketing research questions. Oracle maintains customer advisory boards that allow customers to use the products, engage in collaborative sessions with Oracle executives and product experts, and offer feedback.[8]

One common method for conducting exploratory research is through a focus group. A **focus group** brings together multiple people to discuss a certain topic in a group setting led by a moderator. For example, CVS maintains a mock-up store where it not only tests new products but also conducts focus groups with consumers.[9] Focus groups are often conducted informally, without a structured questionnaire. They allow customer attitudes, behaviors, lifestyles, needs, and desires to be explored in a flexible and creative manner. Questions are open-ended and stimulate respondents to answer in their own words. A traditional focus group session consists of approximately 8 to 12 individuals and is led by a moderator, an independent

**exploratory research** Research conducted to gather more information about a problem or to make a tentative hypothesis more specific

**customer advisory boards** Small groups of actual customers who serve as sounding boards for new-product ideas and offer insights into their feelings and attitudes toward a firm's products and other elements of its marketing strategy

**focus group** An interview that is often conducted informally, without a structured questionnaire, in small groups of 8 to 12 people, to observe interaction when members are exposed to an idea or a concept

**Focus Groups**
Focus groups consist of multiple people discussing a certain topic in a group setting. Usually, focus groups are led by a moderator who encourages group discussion.

individual hired by the research firm or the company. The moderator encourages group discussion among all of the participants and can direct the discussion by occasionally asking questions.

Focus groups can provide companies with ideas for new products or be used for initial testing of different marketing strategies for existing products. Illustrative of this, Ford may use focus groups to determine whether to change its advertising to emphasize a vehicle's safety features rather than its style and performance. The less-structured format of focus groups, where participants can interact with one another and build on each other's comments, is beneficial to marketers because it can yield more detailed information to researchers, including information that they might not have necessarily thought to ask participants about beforehand.

A current trend for researchers is online focus groups. In this method, participants sign in to a website and type their comments and responses there. Online focus groups can gather data from large and geographically diverse groups in a less intensive manner than focus-group interviews. Online focus groups are also more convenient for the participants than traditional focus groups. However, this method makes it more difficult to ask participants about a product's smell or taste, if that is relevant to the product being tested. Researchers also cannot observe the participants' nonverbal cues and body language in this setting, which can often reveal "gut" reactions to questions asked or topics discussed.

Focus groups do have a few disadvantages for marketers. Sometimes, the focus group's discussion can be hindered by overly talkative, confrontational, or shy individuals. Some participants may be less than honest in an effort to be sociable or to receive money and/or food in exchange for their participation.[10] For these reasons, focus groups provide only qualitative, not quantitative, data and are thus best used to uncover issues that can then be explored using quantifiable marketing research techniques.

## 5-2b Conclusive Research

**Conclusive research** is designed to verify insights through an objective procedure to help marketers make decisions. It is used when the marketer has one or more alternatives in mind and needs assistance in the final stages of decision making. Consider exploratory research that has revealed that the terms *clearance* and *sale* send different signals to consumers. To make a decision about how to use this information, marketers would benefit from a well-defined and

**conclusive research** Research designed to verify insights through objective procedures and to help marketers in making decisions structured research project that will help them decide which approach is best for a specific set of products and target consumers. The typically quantitative study should be specific in selecting a course of action and using methods that can be verified. Two such types of conclusive research are descriptive research and experimental research.

If marketers need to understand the characteristics of certain phenomena to solve a particular problem, **descriptive research** can aid them. Descriptive studies may range from general surveys of customers' education, occupations, or ages to specifics on how often teenagers consume sports drinks or how often customers buy new pairs of athletic shoes. For example, if Nike and Reebok want to target more young women, they might ask 15- to 35-year-old females how often they work out, how frequently they wear athletic shoes for casual use, and how many pairs of athletic shoes they buy in a year. Such descriptive research can be used to develop specific marketing strategies for the athletic-shoe market. Descriptive studies generally demand much prior knowledge and assume that the problem or issue is clearly defined. Some descriptive studies require statistical analysis and predictive tools. The marketer's major task is to choose adequate methods for collecting and measuring data.

Descriptive research is limited in providing evidence necessary to make causal inferences (i.e., that variable $X$ causes a variable $Y$). **Experimental research** allows marketers to make causal deductions about relationships. Such experimentation requires that an independent variable (one not influenced by or dependent on other variables) be manipulated and the resulting changes in a dependent variable (one contingent on, or restricted to, one value or set of values assumed by the independent variable) be measured. For instance, McDonald's has been testing a number of new menu items in its restaurants as part of a turnaround strategy, including sales of energy drinks, breakfast at all hours, and chef-crafted sandwiches.[11] To truly determine whether these products are successful, McDonald's will have to hold other variables such as promotion constant. Manipulation of the causal variable and control of other variables are what make experimental research unique. As a result, they can provide much stronger evidence of cause and effect than data collected through descriptive research.

# 5-3 **THE MARKETING RESEARCH PROCESS**

We will examine a generalized approach to the research process that should be adapted to a specific project. Marketing research should be customized to use methods that provide the best information for the marketing decision. Analytical approaches provide flexible and insightful information.[12]

**descriptive research** Research conducted to clarify the characteristics of certain phenomena to solve a particular problem

**experimental research** Research that allows marketers to make causal inferences about relationships

To maintain the control needed to obtain accurate information, marketers approach marketing research as a process with logical steps: (1) locating and defining problems or issues, (2) designing the research project, (3) collecting data, (4) interpreting research findings, and (5) reporting research findings (see Figure 5.1). These steps should be viewed as an overall approach to conducting research rather than as a rigid set of rules to be followed in each project. In planning research projects, marketers must consider each step carefully and determine how they can best adapt the steps to resolve the particular issues at hand.

Figure 5.1    **The Five Steps of the Marketing Research Process**

1 Locating and defining issues or problems → 2 Designing the research project → 3 Collecting data → 4 Interpreting research findings → 5 Reporting research findings

## 5-3a Locating and Defining Problems or Research Issues

The first step in launching a research study is problem or issue definition, which focuses on uncovering the nature and boundaries of a situation or question related to marketing strategy or implementation. The first sign of a problem is typically a departure from some normal function, such as the failure to attain objectives. If a corporation's objective is a 12 percent sales increase and the current marketing strategy resulted in a 6 percent increase, this discrepancy should be analyzed to help guide future marketing strategies. A decrease in sales is a symptom of the problem, not the problem itself. Declining sales, increasing expenses, and decreasing profits also signal problems that could merit research. Customer relationship management (CRM) is frequently based on analysis of existing customers. Armed with this knowledge, a firm could define a problem as finding a way to adjust for biases stemming from existing customers when gathering data or to develop methods for gathering information to help find new customers. Conversely, when an organization experiences a dramatic rise in sales or some other positive event, it may conduct marketing research to discover the reasons and maximize the opportunities stemming from them. Often, the discrepancy relates to marketing-related issues.

Marketing research often focuses on identifying and defining market opportunities or changes in the environment. When a firm discovers a market opportunity, it may need to conduct research to understand the situation more precisely so it can craft an appropriate marketing strategy. Such market research is quite common in the film industry. Market research is performed in the movie industry both to see how the audience will respond to the movie as well as the best ways to promote it. One challenge these firms face is how to adapt their methods to the increasingly tech-savvy consumer. Today word-of-mouth through digital forums including Twitter and Facebook are considered to be integral mediums in the promotion of upcoming movies.[13]

To pin down the specific boundaries of a problem or an issue through research, marketers must define the nature and scope of the situation in a way that requires probing beneath the superficial symptoms. The interaction between the marketing manager and the marketing researcher should yield a clear definition of the research needed. Researchers and decision makers should remain in the problem or issue definition stage until they have determined precisely what they want from marketing research and how they will use it. Deciding how to refine a broad, indefinite problem or issue into a precise, researchable statement is a prerequisite for the next step in the research process.

## 5-3b Designing the Research Project

Once the problem or issue has been defined, the next step is to create a **research design**, an overall plan for obtaining the information needed to address it. This step requires formulating a hypothesis and determining what type of research is most appropriate for testing the hypothesis to ensure the results are reliable and valid. The project should not be limited to a small set of research approaches or methods. Marketers should recognize that a large diversity of approaches is available and should be customized to address the most important research questions.[14]

## Developing a Hypothesis

The objective statement of a marketing research project should include a hypothesis based on both previous research and expected research findings. A **hypothesis** is an informed guess or assumption about a certain problem or set of circumstances. It is based on all the insight and knowledge available about the problem or circumstances from previous research studies and other sources. So, since data suggest that salsa sales have surpassed ketchup sales in the United States, a food marketer at H. J. Heinz might develop a hypothesis that consumers perceive salsa to be a healthier alternative. As information is gathered, the researcher can test the hypothesis.

**research design** An overall plan for obtaining the information needed to address a research problem or issue

**hypothesis** An informed guess or assumption about a certain problem or set of circumstances

For example, a marketer at a cosmetics company might propose the hypothesis that the fragrance of its scented beauty products will influence in-store purchase patterns. A marketing researcher would then gather data, perhaps through testing scents in the store and seeing whether sales change. The researcher would then analyze the data and draw conclusions as to whether the hypothesis is correct. Sometimes, several hypotheses are developed over the course of a research project. The hypotheses that are accepted or rejected become the study's conclusions.

## Research Reliability and Validity

In designing research, marketing researchers must ensure that research techniques are both reliable and valid. A research technique has **reliability** if it produces almost identical results in repeated trials. However, a reliable technique is not necessarily valid. To have **validity**, the research method must measure what it is supposed to measure, not something else. For example, although a group of customers may express the same level of satisfaction based on a rating scale, as individuals they may not exhibit the same repurchase behavior because of different personal characteristics. If the purpose of rating satisfaction was to estimate potential repurchase behavior, this result may cause the researcher to question the validity of the satisfaction scale.[15] A study to measure the effect of advertising on sales would be valid if advertising could be isolated from other factors or from variables that affect sales. The study would be reliable if replications of it produced the same results.

## 5-3c **Collecting Data**

The next step in the marketing research process is collecting data to help prove (or disprove) the research hypothesis. The research design must specify what types of data to collect and how they will be collected.

## Types of Data

Marketing researchers have two types of data at their disposal. **Primary data** are observed and recorded or collected directly from respondents. This type of data must be gathered by observing phenomena or surveying people of interest. **Secondary data** are compiled both inside and outside the organization for some purpose other than the current investigation. Secondary data include general reports supplied to an enterprise by various data services and internal and online databases. Such reports might concern market share, retail inventory levels, and customers' buying behavior. Commonly, secondary data are already available in private or public reports or have been collected and stored by the organization itself. Due to the opportunity to obtain data via the Internet, more than half of all marketing research now comes from secondary sources.

## Sources of Secondary Data

**reliability** A condition that exists when a research technique produces almost identical results in repeated trials

**validity** A condition that exists when a research method measures what it is supposed to measure

**primary data** Data observed and recorded or collected directly from respondents

**secondary data** Data compiled both inside and outside the organization for some purpose other than the current investigation

Marketers often begin the data-collection phase of the marketing research process by gathering secondary data. They may use available reports and other information from both internal and external sources to study a marketing problem.

Internal sources of secondary data can contribute tremendously to research. An organization's own database may contain information about past marketing activities, such as sales records and research reports, which can be used to test hypotheses and pinpoint problems. From sales reports, a firm may be able to determine not only which product sold best at certain times of the year but also which colors and sizes customers preferred. Such information may have been gathered using customer relationship management tools for marketing, management, or financial purposes.

Accounting records are also an excellent source of data but, surprisingly, are often overlooked. The large volume of data an accounting department collects does not automatically flow to other departments. As a result, detailed information about costs, sales, customer accounts, or profits by product category may not be easily accessible to the marketing area. This condition develops particularly in organizations that do not store marketing information on a systematic basis. A third source of internal secondary data is competitive information gathered by the sales force.

External sources of secondary data include trade associations, periodicals, government publications, unpublished sources, and online databases. Trade associations, such as the American Marketing Association, offer guides and directories that are full of information. Periodicals such as *Bloomberg Businessweek, The Wall Street Journal, Sales & Marketing Management, Advertising Age, Marketing Research*, and *Direct Selling News* publish general information that can help marketers define problems and develop hypotheses. *Survey of Buying Power*, an annual supplement to *Sales & Marketing Management*, contains sales data for major industries on a county-by-county basis. Many marketers also consult federal government publications such as the *Statistical Abstract of the United States*, the *Census of Business*, the *Census of Agriculture*, and the *Census of Population*; most of these government publications are available online. Although the government still conducts its primary census every 10 years, it also conducts the American Community Survey, an ongoing survey sent to population samples on a regular basis.[16] This provides marketers with a more up-to-date demographic picture of the nation's population every year. A company might use survey census data to determine whether to construct a shopping mall in a specific area.[17]

**Sources of Secondary Data**
Newspapers such as *USA Today* are important sources of secondary data.

In addition, companies may subscribe to services such as ACNielsen or Information Resources Inc. (IRI) that track retail sales and other information. For example, IRI tracks consumer purchases using in-store, scanner-based technology. Marketing firms can purchase information from IRI about a product category, such as frozen orange juice, as secondary data.[18] Small businesses may be unable to afford such services, but they can still find a wealth of information through industry publications and trade associations.

Companies such as TiVo are challenging services like ACNielsen by offering year-round second-by-second information about the show and advertising viewing habits of consumers who own the company's DVRs. The data are anonymous and are recorded by the TV viewers' boxes. ACNielsen only measures local program viewing for four months a year. However, TiVo's data gathering is limited. Its privacy-protection policies prevent the company from collecting information that Nielson can provide, such as demographic breakdowns and the number of people watching each TV set. On the other hand, TiVo information can aid local TV news programs in their programming decisions by helping them choose when to air sports and weather and how much time to devote to each segment.[19]

The Internet can be especially useful to marketing researchers. Search engines such as Google can help marketers locate many types of secondary data or to research topics of interest. Of course, companies can mine their own websites for useful information by using CRM tools. Amazon.com, for instance, has built a relationship with its customers by tracking the types of books, music, and other products they purchase. Each time a customer logs on to the website, the company can offer recommendations based on the customer's previous purchases. Such a marketing system helps the company track the changing desires and buying habits of its most valued customers. Furthermore, marketing researchers are increasingly monitoring blogs to discover what consumers are saying about their products—both positive and negative. Some, including yogurt maker Stonyfield Farms, have even established their own blogs as a way to monitor consumer dialogue on issues of their choice. There are many reasons people go online, which can make the job of using the Internet complicated for marketers. Table 5.2 summarizes the external sources of secondary data, excluding syndicated services.

Table 5.2   **Examples of Secondary Sources**

| Government Sources | |
| --- | --- |
| Economic census | www.census.gov/econ/census |
| Export.gov—country and industry market research | www.export.gov/mrktresearch/index.asp |
| National Technical Information Services | www.ntis.gov |
| Industry Canada | http://www.ic.gc.ca/eic/site/icgc.nsf/eng/home |
| **Trade Associations and Shows** | |
| American Society of Association Executives | www.asaecenter.org |
| Directory of Associations | www.marketingsource.com/associations |
| Trade Show News Network | www.tsnn.com |
| **Magazines, Newspapers, Video, and Audio News Programming** | |
| Resource Library | http://findarticles.com |
| Google Video Search | www.video.google.com |
| Google News Directory | www.google.com/news/directory |
| Yahoo! Video Search | www.video.search.yahoo.com |
| **Corporate Information** | |
| Annual Report Service | www.annualreportservice.com |
| Bitpipe | www.bitpipe.com |
| Business Wire—press releases | www.businesswire.com |
| Hoover's Online | www.hoovers.com |
| Open Directory Project | www.dmoz.org |
| PR Newswire—press releases | www.prnewswire.com |

Source: Adapted from "Data Collection: Low-Cost Secondary Research," *KnowThis.com*, www.knowthis.com/principles-of-marketing-tutorials/data-collection-low-cost-secondary-research (accessed December 21, 2015).

## Methods of Collecting Primary Data

Collecting primary data is a lengthier, more expensive, and more complex process than collecting secondary data. To gather primary data, researchers use sampling procedures, survey methods, and observation. These efforts can be handled in-house by the firm's own research department or contracted to a private research firm such as ACNielsen, Information Resources Inc., or IMS International. Consider the advertisement for marketing research firm FocusVision. FocusVision uses an image of a multitool to describe its suite of products that can be used to collect both quantitative and qualitative data. For instance, FocusVision clients can use its Decipher platform to collect primary data through mobile and web surveys.

**population** All the elements, units, or individuals of interest to researchers for a specific study

**sample** A limited number of units chosen to represent the characteristics of a total population

**sampling** The process of selecting representative units from a total population

**Sampling** Because the time and resources available for research are limited, it is almost impossible to investigate all the members of a target market or other population. A **population**, or "universe," includes all the elements, units, or individuals of interest to researchers for a specific study. Consider a Gallup poll designed to predict the results of a presidential election. All registered voters in the United States would constitute the population. By systematically choosing a limited number of units—a **sample**—to represent the characteristics of a total population, researchers can project the reactions of a total market or market segment. (In the case of the presidential poll, a representative national sample of several thousand registered voters would be selected and surveyed to project the probable voting outcome.) **Sampling** in marketing research, therefore, is the process of selecting representative units from a total population. Sampling techniques allow marketers to predict buying behavior fairly accurately on the basis of the responses from a representative portion of the population of interest. Most types of marketing research employ sampling techniques.

There are two basic types of sampling: probability sampling and nonprobability sampling. With **probability sampling**, every element in the population being studied has a known chance of being selected for study. Random sampling is a form of probability sampling. When marketers employ **random sampling**, all the units in a population have an equal chance of appearing in the sample. The various events that can occur have an equal or known chance of taking place. For instance, a specific card in a regulation deck should have a 1 in 52 probability of being drawn at any one time. Sample units are ordinarily chosen by selecting from a table of random numbers statistically generated so that each digit, 0 through 9, will have an equal probability of occurring in each position in the sequence. The sequentially numbered elements of a population are sampled randomly by selecting the units whose numbers appear in the table of random numbers.

Another type of probability sampling is **stratified sampling**, in which the population of interest is divided into groups according to a common attribute, and a random sample is then chosen within each group. The stratified sample may reduce some of the error that could occur in a simple random sample. By ensuring that each major group or segment of the population receives its proportionate share of sample units, investigators avoid including too many or too few sample units from each group. Samples are usually stratified when researchers believe there may be variations among different types of respondents. As an example, many political opinion surveys are stratified by gender, race, age, and/or geographic location.

The second type of sampling, **nonprobability sampling**, is more subjective than probability sampling because there is no way to calculate the likelihood that a specific element of the population being studied will be chosen. Quota sampling, for example, is highly judgmental because the final choice of participants is left to the researchers. In **quota sampling**, researchers divide the population into groups and then arbitrarily choose participants from each group. In quota sampling, there are some controls—usually limited to two or three variables, such as age, gender, or race—over the selection of participants. The controls attempt to ensure that representative categories of respondents are interviewed. A study of people who wear eyeglasses, for instance, may be conducted by interviewing equal numbers of men and women who wear eyeglasses. Because quota samples are not probability samples, not everyone has an equal chance of being selected and sampling error therefore cannot be measured statistically. Quota samples are used most often in exploratory studies, when hypotheses are being developed.

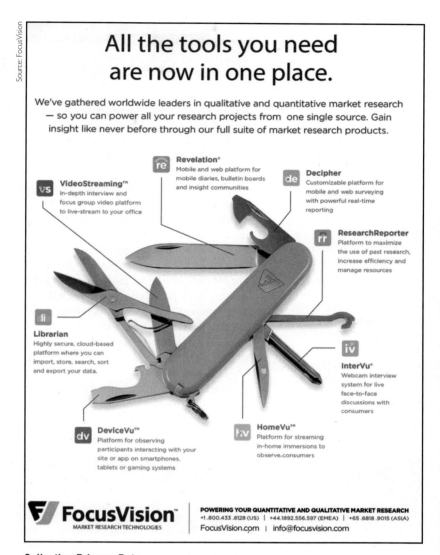
**Collecting Primary Data**
FocusView offers a number of tools companies can use to collect both primary qualitative and quantitative market research.

**probability sampling** A type of sampling in which every element in the population being studied has a known chance of being selected for study

**random sampling** A form of probability sampling in which all units in a population have an equal chance of appearing in the sample, and the various events that can occur have an equal or known chance of taking place

**stratified sampling** A type of probability sampling in which the population is divided into groups with a common attribute and a random sample is chosen within each group

Often a small quota sample will not be projected to the total population, although the findings may provide valuable insights into a problem. Quota samples are useful when people with some common characteristic are found and questioned about the topic of interest. Consequently, a probability sample used to study people who are allergic to cats would be highly inefficient.

**Survey Methods** Marketing researchers often employ sampling to collect primary data through mail, telephone, personal interview, online, or social networking surveys. The results of such surveys are used to describe and analyze buying behavior. The survey method chosen depends on the nature of the problem or issue; the data needed to test the hypothesis; and the resources, such as funding and personnel, available to the researcher. Marketers may employ more than one survey method depending on the goals of the research. Surveys can be quite expensive (Procter & Gamble spends about $400 million on consumer research and conducts more than 15,000 research studies annually),[20] but small businesses can turn to sites such as SurveyMonkey.com[21] and zoomerang.com for inexpensive or even free online surveys. Table 5.3 summarizes and compares the advantages of the various survey methods.

Gathering information through surveys is becoming increasingly difficult because fewer people are willing to participate. Many people believe responding to surveys requires too much scarce personal time, especially as surveys become longer and more detailed. Others have concerns about how much information marketers are gathering and whether their privacy is being invaded. The unethical use of selling techniques disguised as marketing surveys has also led to decreased cooperation. These factors contribute to nonresponse rates for any type of survey.

In a **mail survey**, questionnaires are sent to respondents, who are encouraged to complete and return them. Mail surveys are used most often when the individuals in the sample are spread over a wide area and funds for the survey are limited. A mail survey is less expensive

**nonprobability sampling**
A sampling technique in which there is no way to calculate the likelihood that a specific element of the population being studied will be chosen

**quota sampling** A nonprobability sampling technique in which researchers divide the population into groups and then arbitrarily choose participants from each group

**mail survey** A research method in which respondents answer a questionnaire sent through the mail

**Table 5.3   Comparison of the Four Basic Survey Methods**

|  | Mail Surveys | Telephone Surveys | Online Surveys | Personal Interview Surveys |
|---|---|---|---|---|
| Economy | Potentially lower in cost per interview than telephone or personal surveys if there is an adequate response rate. | Avoids interviewers' travel expenses; less expensive than in-home interviews. | The least expensive method if there is an adequate response rate. | The most expensive survey method; shopping mall and focus-group interviews have lower costs than in-home interviews. |
| Flexibility | Inflexible; questionnaire must be short and easy for respondents to complete. | Flexible because interviewers can ask probing questions, but observations are impossible. | Less flexible; survey must be easy for online users to receive and return; short, dichotomous, or multiple-choice questions work best. | Most flexible method; respondents can react to visual materials; demographic data are more accurate; in-depth probes are possible. |
| Interviewer bias | Interviewer bias is eliminated; questionnaires can be returned anonymously. | Some anonymity; may be hard to develop trust in respondents. | Interviewer bias is often eliminated with e-mail, but e-mail address on the return eliminates anonymity. | Interviewers' personal characteristics or inability to maintain objectivity may result in bias. |
| Sampling and respondents' cooperation | Obtaining a complete mailing list is difficult; nonresponse is a major disadvantage. | Sample limited to respondents with telephones; devices that screen calls, busy signals, and refusals are a problem. | The available e-mail address list may not be a representative sample for some purposes. Social media surveys might be skewed as fans may be more likely to take the survey. | Not-at-homes are a problem, which may be overcome by focus-group and shopping mall interviewing. |

than a telephone or personal interview survey as long as the response rate is high enough to produce reliable results. The main disadvantages of this method are the possibility of a low response rate and of misleading results if respondents differ significantly from the population being sampled. One method of improving response rates involves attaching a brief personal message on a Post-it® Note to the survey packet. Response rates to these surveys are higher, and the quality and timeliness of the responses are also improved.[22] As a result of these issues, companies are increasingly moving to Internet surveys and automated telephone surveys.

Premiums or incentives that encourage respondents to return questionnaires have been effective in developing panels of respondents who are interviewed regularly by mail. Such mail panels, selected to represent a target market or market segment, are especially useful in evaluating new products and providing general

**Mail Survey**
Mailing surveys to consumers to fill out and send back can be highly useful for reaching a widespread sample over a large geographic area. However, this survey method often has a low response rate, prompting some marketers to offer some sort of incentive for taking the survey.

information about customers, as well as records of their purchases (in the form of purchase diaries). Mail panels and purchase diaries are much more widely used than custom mail surveys, but both panels and purchase diaries have shortcomings. People who take the time to fill out a diary may differ from the general population based on income, education, or behavior, such as the time available for shopping activities. Internet and social networking surveys have also greatly gained in popularity, although they are similarly limited as well—given that not all demographics utilize these media equally.

In a **telephone survey**, an interviewer records respondents' answers to a questionnaire over a phone line. A telephone survey has some advantages over a mail survey. The rate of response is higher because it takes less effort to answer the telephone and talk than to fill out and return a questionnaire. If enough interviewers are available, a telephone survey can be conducted very quickly. Thus, political candidates or organizations that want an immediate reaction to an event may choose this method. In addition, a telephone survey permits interviewers to gain rapport with respondents and ask probing questions. Automated telephone surveys, also known as interactive voice response or "robosurveys," rely on a recorded voice to ask the questions while a computer program records respondents' answers. The primary benefit of automated surveys is the elimination of any bias that might be introduced by a live researcher.

Another option is the **telephone depth interview**, which combines the traditional focus group's ability to probe with the confidentiality provided by a telephone survey. This type of interview is most appropriate for qualitative research projects among a small targeted group that is difficult to bring together for a traditional focus group because of members' professions, locations, or lifestyles. Respondents can choose the time and day for the interview. Many companies are using Skype so that interviewers can have personal interaction with respondents and show products. Although this method is difficult to implement, it can yield revealing information from respondents who otherwise would be unwilling to participate in marketing research.

However, only a small proportion of the population likes to participate in telephone surveys or interviews. This can significantly limit participation and distort representation. Moreover, surveys and interviews conducted over the telephone are limited to oral communication; visual aids or observation cannot be included. Interpreters of results must make adjustments for individuals who are not at home or do not have telephones. Many households are excluded from telephone directories by choice (unlisted numbers) or because the residents moved after the

**telephone survey** A research method in which respondents' answers to a questionnaire are recorded by an interviewer on the phone

**telephone depth interview** An interview that combines the traditional focus group's ability to probe with the confidentiality provided by telephone surveys directory was published. Potential respondents often use telephone answering machines, voice mail, or caller ID to screen or block calls; additionally, millions have signed up for "Do Not Call Lists." Moreover, an increasing number of Americans are giving up their fixed telephone lines in favor of cellular or wireless phones. These issues have serious implications for the use of telephone samples in conducting surveys or interviews.

In a **personal interview survey**, participants respond to questions face-to-face. Various audiovisual aids—pictures, products, diagrams, or prerecorded advertising copy—can be incorporated into a personal interview. Rapport gained through direct interaction usually permits more in-depth interviewing, including probes, follow-up questions, or psychological tests. In addition, because personal interviews can be longer, they may yield more information. Respondents can be selected more carefully, and reasons for nonresponse can be explored. One such research technique is the **in-home (door-to-door) interview**. The in-home interview offers a clear advantage when thoroughness of self-disclosure and elimination of group influence are important. In an in-depth interview of 45 to 90 minutes, respondents can be probed to reveal their true motivations, feelings, behaviors, and aspirations. Door-to-door interviewing is increasingly difficult due to respondent and interviewer security and safety issues. This method is particularly limited in gated communities such as condos or apartments.

The nature of personal interviews has changed. In the past, most personal interviews, which were based on random sampling or prearranged appointments, were conducted in the respondent's home. Today, many personal interviews are conducted in shopping malls. **Shopping mall intercept interviews** involve interviewing a percentage of individuals who pass by an "intercept" point in a mall. Like any face-to-face interviewing method, mall intercept interviewing has many advantages. The interviewer is in a position to recognize and react to respondents' nonverbal indications of confusion. Respondents can view product prototypes, videotapes of commercials, and the like, and provide their opinions. The mall environment lets the researcher deal with complex situations. In taste tests, for instance, researchers know that all the respondents are reacting to the same product, which can be prepared and monitored from the mall test kitchen. In addition to the ability to conduct tests requiring bulky equipment, lower cost and greater control make shopping mall intercept interviews popular.

An **on-site computer interview** is a variation of the shopping mall intercept interview in which respondents complete a self-administered questionnaire displayed on a computer monitor. A computer software package can be used to conduct such interviews in shopping malls. After a brief lesson on how to operate the software, respondents proceed through the survey at their own pace. Questionnaires can be adapted so that respondents see only those items (usually a subset of an entire scale) that may provide useful information about their attitudes.

### Online and Social Media Surveys

We give online surveys and Internet research its own section because as more and more consumers gain Internet access, Internet surveys are likely to become the predominate tool for general population sampling. In an **online survey**, questionnaires can be transmitted to respondents either through e-mail or through a website. Marketing researchers often send these surveys to online panel samples purchased from professional brokers or put together by the company. Marketing research firms that specialize in Internet research can also be used to conduct digital research for their client organizations. Many offer tools that help to complement or enhance online surveys. SurveyMonkey

**personal interview survey** A research method in which participants respond to survey questions face-to-face

**in-home (door-to-door) interview** A personal interview that takes place in the respondent's home

**Shopping mall intercept interviews** A research method that involves interviewing a percentage of individuals passing by "intercept" points in a mall

**on-site computer interview** A variation of the shopping mall intercept interview in which respondents complete a self-administered questionnaire displayed on a computer monitor

**online survey** A research method in which respondents answer a questionnaire via e-mail or on a website

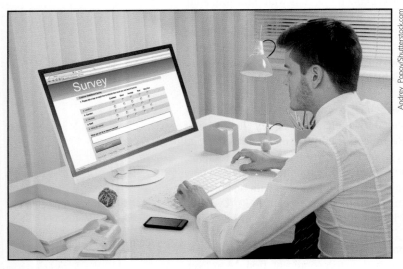

Andrey_Popov/Shutterstock.com

**Online Surveys**
Online surveys are becoming increasingly common as they offer a low-cost and convenient way to survey a large number of customers over vast geographic areas.

is an online cloud-based company that allows marketers to create free online surveys or questionnaires or upgrade to a paid plan that offers more advanced features and analysis.

Because e-mail is semi-interactive, recipients can ask for clarification of specific questions or pose questions of their own. The potential advantages of online surveys are quick response and lower cost than traditional mail, telephone, and personal interview surveys if the response rate is adequate. More firms are using their websites to conduct surveys. They may include a premium, such as a chance to win a prize, to encourage participation. In addition, online surveys can be completed via mobile devices. For example, apps on smartphones can collect online information without active moment-to-moment participation by respondents.[23]

Social networking sites can also be used to conduct surveys. Marketers can use digital media forums such as chat rooms, blogs, newsgroups, social networks, and research communities to identify trends in interests and consumption patterns. However, using these forums for conducting surveys has some limitations. Often consumers choose to go to a particular social media site or blog and then take the survey; this eliminates randomness and makes it more difficult to obtain a representative sample size. On the other hand, they can provide a general idea of consumer trends and preferences. Movies, consumer electronics, food, and computers are popular topics in many online communities. Indeed, by "listening in" on these ongoing conversations, marketers may be able to identify new product opportunities and consumer needs. Moreover, this type of online data can be gathered at little incremental cost compared to alternative data sources.

**Crowdsourcing** combines the words *crowd* and *outsourcing* and calls for taking tasks usually performed by a marketer or researcher and outsourcing them to a crowd, or potential market, through an open call. In the case of digital marketing, crowdsourcing is often used to obtain the opinions or needs of the crowd (or potential markets). Consider Lego's crowdsourcing platform Lego Ideas. Lego Ideas is a site that invites consumers to submit ideas for Lego sets. Those ideas that get 10,000 votes are reviewed by the firm for possible development. If the Lego set is chosen for development, the creator gets 1 percent of the product's total net sales.[24] Crowdsourcing is a way for marketers to gather input straight from willing consumers and to actively listen to people's ideas and evaluations on products. It is also important for organizations to harness all of their internal information, and internal social networks can be helpful for that. On the other hand, results appear to show that internal social networks are not very popular with employees. A major reason is thought to be that top executives do not use internal collaboration platforms, which convinces employees that they are not necessary. It is therefore important to have top management's support and participation for companies that want to adopt strong digital internal social networks.[25]

One Internet system that uses crowdsourcing to connect people from across the world is Amazon's Mechanical Turk (MTurk). MTurk is an online marketplace that connects requesters for tasks with workers willing to complete them. MTurk operates on the premise that there are still various tasks that only humans, and not computers, can complete. Based on this idea, MTurk allows companies and entrepreneurs to crowdsource human intelligence tasks (HITs) to workers worldwide. Workers who are equipped to complete these tasks have the flexibility to work their own hours from their homes. Money for the tasks is deposited into MTurk accounts.[26] Some have found the data generated from these crowdsourcing processes to be just as reliable as data gathered through more traditional methods.[27] However, others have criticized MTurk because it is sometimes impossible to determine if respondents are representing themselves accurately. There has been a tendency for more respondents to be from countries outside of the United States. Freelancers who use MTurk have also complained that they are seen as little more than algorithms rather than skilled workers.[28]

Marketing research will likely rely heavily on online panels and surveys in the future. Furthermore, as negative attitudes toward telephone surveys render that technique less representative and more expensive, the integration of e-mail and voice mail functions into one computer-based system provides a promising alternative for survey research. However, there are some ethical issues to consider when using the Internet for marketing research, such as

**crowdsourcing** Combines the words *crowd* and *outsourcing* and calls for taking tasks usually performed by a marketer or researcher and outsourcing them to a crowd, or potential market, through an open call unsolicited e-mail, which could be viewed as "spam," and privacy, as some potential survey respondents fear their personal information will be given or sold to third parties without their knowledge or permission. Additionally, as with direct mail, Internet surveys have a good chance of being discarded, particularly with users who receive dozens of e-mails every day.

Another challenge for researchers is obtaining a sample that is representative of the desired population. Although Internet surveys allow respondents to retain their anonymity and flexibility, they can also enable survey takers to abuse the system. For instance, some survey takers take multiple surveys or pose as other people to make more money. To get around this problem, companies are developing screening mechanisms and instituting limits on how many surveys one person can take.[29] Survey programs such as Qualtrics can also delete surveys that appear suspicious.

**Questionnaire Construction** A carefully constructed questionnaire is essential to the success of any survey. Questions must be clear, easy to understand, and directed toward a specific objective; that is, they must be designed to elicit information that meets the study's data requirements. Researchers need to define the objective before trying to develop a questionnaire because the objective determines the substance of the questions and the amount of detail. A common mistake in constructing questionnaires is to ask questions that interest the researchers but do not yield information useful in deciding whether to accept or reject a hypothesis. Finally, the most important rule in composing questions is to maintain impartiality. The questions are usually of three kinds: open-ended, dichotomous, and multiple-choice. Problems may develop in the analysis of dichotomous or multiple-choice questions when responses for one outcome outnumber others. For example, a dichotomous question that asks respondents to choose between "buy" or "not buy" might require additional sampling from the disproportionately smaller group if there were not enough responses to analyze.[30] Researchers must also be very careful about questions that a respondent might consider too personal or that might require an admission of activities that other people are likely to condemn. Questions of this type should be worded to make them less offensive.

**Observation Methods** In using observation methods, researchers record individuals' overt behavior, taking note of physical conditions and events. Direct contact with them is avoided; instead, their actions are examined and noted systematically. For instance, researchers might use observation methods to answer the question, "How long does the average McDonald's restaurant customer have to wait in line before being served?" Observation may include the use of ethnographic techniques, such as watching customers interact with a product in a real-world environment. Interestingly, many online retailers are starting to open physical stores, not simply to extend their reach but also as a way of observing customers in ways that cannot be done online. Being able to observe how customers interact with products in-store helps marketers of online firms like Bonobos understand consumer likes and dislikes—information that is integral to improving its product offering both in-store and online. Even online maverick Amazon.com opened a physical store in Seattle.[31] Observation may also be combined with interviews. For instance, during a personal interview, the condition of a respondent's home or other possessions may be observed and recorded. The interviewer can also directly observe and confirm such demographic information as race, approximate age, and gender.

Data gathered through observation can sometimes be biased if the subject is aware of the observation process. However, an observer can be placed in a natural market environment, such as a grocery store, without influencing shoppers' actions. If the presence of a human observer is likely to bias the outcome or if human sensory abilities are inadequate, mechanical means may be used to record behavior. Mechanical observation devices include cameras, recorders, counting machines, scanners, and equipment that records physiological changes. A special camera can be used to record the eye movements of people as they look at an advertisement. Tracking the eye movements of online shoppers has revealed that function and non-functionality product characteristics result in greater eye movement and intensity,[32] suggesting that using these attributes in product descriptions could engage viewers more thoroughly. The camera detects the sequence of reading and the parts of the advertisement that receive the greatest attention. The electronic scanners used in supermarkets are very useful in marketing research: They provide accurate data on sales and customers' purchase patterns, and marketing researchers may buy such data from the supermarkets.

Observation is straightforward and avoids a central problem of survey methods: motivating respondents to state their true feelings or opinions. However, observation tends to be descriptive. When it is the only method of data collection, it may not provide insights into causal relationships. Another drawback is that analyses based on observation are subject to the observer's biases or the limitations of the mechanical device.

## 5-3d **Interpreting Research Findings**

After collecting data to test their hypotheses, marketers need to interpret the research findings. Interpretation of the data is easier if marketers carefully plan their data analysis methods early in the research process. They should also allow for continual evaluation of the data during the entire collection period. Marketers can then gain valuable insights into areas that should be probed during the formal analysis. Table 5.4 shows that interpreting analytics and implementing insights—as well as research and data collection—are among the top 10 marketing challenges.

The first step in drawing conclusions from most research is to display the data in table format. If marketers intend to apply the results to individual categories of the things or people being studied, cross-tabulation may be useful, especially in tabulating joint occurrences. Using the two variables of gender and purchase rates of automobile tires, for instance, a cross-tabulation could show how men and women differ in purchasing automobile tires. The advertisement promoting marketing research firm NPD Group's Checkout Tracking service emphasizes the need to understand the customer. Checkout Tracking tracks consumer purchases online and in-store. By linking these purchases to consumer patterns and demographics, Checkout Tracking aids businesses in both collecting and interpreting purchase data.

After the data are tabulated, they must be analyzed. **Statistical interpretation** focuses on what is typical and what deviates from the average. It indicates how widely responses vary and how they are distributed in relation to the variable being measured. When marketers interpret statistics, they must take into account estimates of expected error or deviation from the true

**statistical interpretation**
Analysis of what is typical and what deviates from the average

---

Table 5.4    **Biggest Marketing Challenges**

| Marketing Challenge |
| --- |
| 1. Data and analytics |
| 2. Content marketing |
| 3. Business growth |
| 4. Metrics/performance measurement |
| 5. Lead generation |
| 6. Website/digital |
| 7. Customer engagement/loyalty |
| 8. Budget |
| 9. Brand management |
| 10. Targeting/segmentation/personalization |

Source: Melody Udell, "Business Growth and Content Marketing Biggest 'Pain Points' in 2016, AMA Study Shows," *Marketing News*, 2015, https://www.ama.org/publications/MarketingNews/Pages/what-lies-ahead.aspx (accessed December 21, 2015).

Source: NPD Group, Inc

**Interpreting Research Findings**
NPD Group uses the image of a man with a black bar covering his eyes to symbolize how its Checkout Tracking service can help businesses interpret customer purchase data to truly know their customers.

values of the population. The analysis of data may lead researchers to accept or reject the hypothesis being studied. Data require careful interpretation by the marketer. If the results of a study are valid, the decision maker should take action; if a question has been incorrectly or poorly worded, however, the results may produce poor decisions. Consider the research conducted for a food marketer that asked respondents to rate a product on criteria such as "hearty flavor," as well as how important each criterion was to the respondent. Although such results may have had utility for advertising purposes, they are less helpful in product development because it is not possible to discern each respondent's meaning of the phrase "hearty flavor." Managers must understand the research results and relate them to a context that permits effective decision making.

### 5-3e Reporting Research Findings

The final step in the marketing research process is to report the research findings. Before preparing the report, the marketer must take a clear, objective look at the findings to see how well the gathered facts answer the research question or support or negate the initial hypotheses. In most cases, it is extremely doubtful that the study can provide everything needed to answer the research question. Thus, the researcher must point out the deficiencies in the research and their causes in the report. Research should be meaningful to all participants, especially top managers who develop strategy. Therefore, researchers must try to make certain that their findings are relevant and not just interesting. Research is not useful unless it supports the organization's overall strategy objectives. The more knowledge researchers have about the opportunities and challenges facing an organization, the more meaningful their research report will be. If an outside research agency conducts research, it is even more important to understand the client's business. After conducting research, a research report is the next step. Those responsible for preparing the report must facilitate adjusting the findings to the environment, as elements change over time. Most importantly, the report should be helpful to marketers and managers on an ongoing basis.[33]

The report of research results is usually a formal, written document. Researchers must allow time for the writing task when they plan and schedule the project. Because the report is a means of communicating with the decision makers who will use the research findings, researchers need to determine beforehand how much detail and supporting data to include. They should keep in mind that corporate executives prefer reports that are short, clear, and simply expressed. Researchers often give their summary and recommendations first, especially if decision makers do not have time to study how the results were obtained. A technical report allows its users to analyze data and interpret recommendations because it describes the research methods and procedures and the most important data gathered. Thus, researchers must recognize the needs and expectations of the report user and adapt to them.

Marketing researchers want to know about behavior and opinions, and they want accurate data to help them in making decisions. Careful wording of questions is very important because a biased or emotional word can dramatically change the results. Marketing research and marketing information systems can provide an organization with accurate and reliable customer feedback,

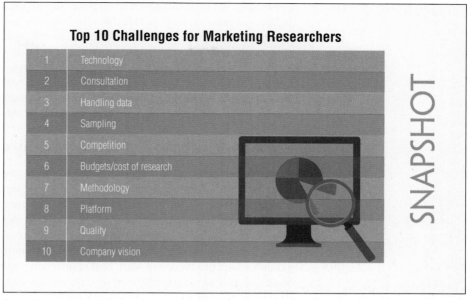

**Top 10 Challenges for Marketing Researchers**

| 1 | Technology |
| 2 | Consultation |
| 3 | Handling data |
| 4 | Sampling |
| 5 | Competition |
| 6 | Budgets/cost of research |
| 7 | Methodology |
| 8 | Platform |
| 9 | Quality |
| 10 | Company vision |

SNAPSHOT

Source: GreenBook, "The Top 10 Challenges in the Market Research Industry," June 26, 2015, http://www.greenbookblog. org/2015/06/26/the-top-10-challenges-in-the-market-research-industry/ (accessed December 22, 2015).

which a marketer must have to understand the dynamics of the marketplace. As managers recognize the benefits of marketing research, they assign it a much larger role in decision making.

## 5-4 USING TECHNOLOGY TO IMPROVE MARKETING INFORMATION GATHERING AND ANALYSIS

Technology makes information for marketing decisions increasingly accessible. The ability of marketers to track customer buying behavior and to better discern what buyers want is changing the nature of marketing. Information technology permits internal research and quick information gathering to help marketers better understand and satisfy customers. The use of data is helping marketers discover customer insights that would have been hard to discover through traditional methods. Company responses to e-mail complaints—as well as to communications through mail, telephone, and personal contact—can be used to improve customer satisfaction, retention, and value. Armed with such information, marketers can fine-tune marketing mixes to satisfy their customers' needs.

Consumer feedback is an important aspect of marketing research, and new technology such as digital media is enhancing this process. Online retailers such as Amazon, Netflix, and Priceline are capitalizing on these ratings and reviews by allowing consumers to post comments on their sites concerning books, movies, hotels, and more. Marketers can use these social media forums to closely monitor what their customers are saying. In the case of negative feedback, marketers can communicate with consumers to address problems or complaints more easily than with traditional marketing channels. In one survey, it was noted that a business has the opportunity to turn 18 percent of negative reviewers into loyal customers by responding to their negative feedback. In addition, more than 60 percent of those who receive a reply will replace their negative comments with positive ones.[34] By researching what consumers are saying about their products, companies can understand what features of their product mixes should be promoted or modified.

Finally, the integration of telecommunications and computer technologies allows marketers to access a growing array of valuable information sources related to industry forecasts, business trends, and customer buying behavior. Electronic communication tools can be effectively used to gain accurate information with minimal customer interaction. Most marketing researchers have electronic networking at their disposal. In fact, many firms use marketing information systems and CRM technologies to network all these technologies and organize all the marketing data available to them. In this section, we look at marketing information systems and specific technologies that are helping marketing researchers obtain and manage marketing research data.

## 5-4a Marketing Information Systems

A **marketing information system (MIS)** is a framework for the day-to-day management and structuring of information gathered regularly from sources both inside and outside the organization. As such, an MIS provides a continuous flow of information about prices, advertising expenditures, sales, competition, and distribution expenses. Marketing information systems can be an important asset for developing effective marketing strategies. Procter & Gamble managers, for instance, search through P&G's proprietary MIS for data to help the company predict which products will work best in different countries.[35] The main focus of the MIS is on data storage and retrieval, as well as on computer capabilities and management's information requirements. Regular reports of sales by product or market categories, data on inventory levels, and records of salespeople's activities are examples of information that is useful in making decisions. In the MIS, the means of gathering data receive less attention than do the procedures for expediting the flow of information. Most firms develop a dashboard display where data can be integrated into useful management reports for strategic and tactical decisions.

An effective MIS starts by determining the objective of the information—that is, by identifying decision needs that require certain information. The firm can then specify an information system for continuous monitoring to provide regular, pertinent information on both the external and internal environment. FedEx, for instance, has interactive marketing systems that provide instantaneous communication between the company and customers. Customers can track their packages and receive immediate feedback concerning delivery via the Internet. The company's website provides information about customer usage and allows customers to convey what they think about company services. The evolving telecommunications and computer technologies allow marketers to use information systems to cultivate one-to-one relationships with customers.

## 5-4b Databases

Most marketing information systems include internal databases. A **database** is a collection of information arranged for easy access and retrieval. Databases allow marketers to tap into an abundance of information useful in making marketing decisions: internal sales reports, newspaper articles, company news releases, government economic reports, bibliographies, and more, often accessed through a computer system. Information technology has made it possible to develop databases to guide strategic planning and help improve customer services. Information technology has made it possible for firms to develop databases that are vastly enhanced in their speed and storage capacity to guide strategic planning and improve customer service.

Customer relationship management employs database marketing techniques to identify different types of customers and develop specific strategies for interacting with each customer. CRM incorporates these three elements:

1. Identifying and building a database of current and potential consumers, including a wide range of demographic, lifestyle, and purchase information.
2. Delivering differential messages according to each consumer's preferences and characteristics through established and new media channels.
3. Tracking customer relationships to monitor the costs of retaining individual customers and the lifetime value of their purchases.[36]

**marketing information system (MIS)** A framework for managing and structuring information gathered regularly from sources inside and outside the organization

**database** A collection of information arranged for easy access and retrieval

Many commercial websites require consumers to register and provide personal information to access the site or to make a purchase. Frequent-flyer programs permit airlines to ask loyal customers to participate in surveys about their needs and desires and to track their best customers' flight patterns by time of day, week, month, and year. Also, supermarkets gain a significant amount of data through checkout scanners tied to store discount cards.

Marketing researchers can also use databases, such as LexisNexis, to obtain useful information for marketing decisions. Many commercial databases are accessible online for a fee. Sometimes, they can be obtained in printed form or digitally. With most commercial databases, the user typically conducts a computer search by keyword, topic, or company, and the database service generates abstracts, articles, or reports that can then be printed out.

Information provided by a single firm on household demographics, purchases, television viewing behavior, and responses to promotions such as coupons and free samples is called **single-source data**. For example, BehaviorScan Rx ad testing, offered by IRI, allows different TV advertisements to be played in the same market. It is also able to discover important links between TV viewing behaviors and consumer activities.[37] It is important to gather longitudinal (long-term) information on customers to maximize the usefulness of single-source data.

## 5-4c  Big Data

Big data has the potential to revolutionize the way businesses gather marketing research and develop tailored marketing campaigns. **Big data** involves massive data files that can be obtained from both structured and unstructured databases. Big data often consists of high-volume data that marketers can use to discover unique insights and make more knowledgeable marketing decisions.[38] Big data can include mountains of data collected from social networks, RFID, retailer scanning, purchases, logistics, and production.[39] The amount of data that can be gleaned from consumer activities and purchase patterns yields significant insights for marketers. The complexity of big data requires sophisticated software to store and analyze it.[40] It also requires marketers to identify and understand how to use this data to develop stronger customer relationships. Many firms like Walmart, Whole Foods, and General Electric are adopting centralized systems to integrate disparate data and glean the most insights about consumers.[41]

Big data presents a new opportunity to use IT-enabled information to assist in marketing decision making. The amount of data is rapidly increasing through an array of generating sources, including mobile devices, Internet searches, behavioral observations, and tracking of purchase behavior. Marketers want to use this data to create competitive advantages that will help them discover new insights into customer behavior. Many companies are optimistic that increasingly advanced methodologies for analyzing and interpreting big data will lead to the development of new innovations with major impacts for society.[42]

The positive impact that big data has had upon marketing is undeniable. A McKinsey study showed that companies that incorporate big data into their marketing decisions saw their return on investment improve between 15 and 20 percent. Big data is also important in giving firms a competitive advantage. Organizations that effectively utilize big data as well as marketing analytics tend to have productivity and profitability that surpass their rivals by 5–6 percent.[43] Unlike other forms of marketing research, using big data can reveal specific details about consumers that would be hard to discover in other ways. The marketing vice president at DataSift—an organization that analyzes social data—has determined that his company's software can mine 400 pieces of data from a 140-word tweet.[44] For these reasons, Whole Foods is working with software maker Infor Inc. to develop a new retail management system that will be able to collect data sets from multiple stores so it can derive more insights about customers and its supply chain.[45]

Big data is important because marketers can look at patterns of consumption behavior and discover trends that predict future buying behaviors. Not all of these patterns would be as visible through traditional marketing research methods. It is obvious, for instance, that a woman buying baby supplies is likely pregnant or has a new baby. However, other consumption patterns

**single-source data** Information provided by a single marketing research firm

**big data** Massive data files that can be obtained from both structured and unstructured databases

Source: Qlik

**Big Data Generation**
Qlik is able to take large quantities of data, identify unexpected connections among the data, and deliver these insights to client organizations to improve their marketing strategies.

are less obvious. Target has found that purchases of larger quantities of unscented lotions, cotton balls, scent-free soap, and supplements are also predictors of pregnancy. Target discovered these trends through analyzing its collection of data on consumer purchases. These discoveries have allowed the firm to accurately predict pregnancy. As a result, it has been able to send out marketing materials, such as coupons for diapers, to this demographic in the hopes that they will become future loyal customers.[46] Big data can therefore improve the relationship between company and consumer.

Despite the benefits of big data to marketing research, the challenge for marketers is to figure out how to use pieces of data to develop more targeted marketing strategies. Marketers must know what data to examine, which analytical tools to use, and how to translate this data into customer insights.[47] Big data is useless if an organization's marketers do not know how to use it. Mining big data for customer insights takes much time and energy. In one research study surveying marketers, a little more than half indicated that their organizations had a good understanding of big data. A major reason is that many marketers do not understand the definition of big data or its benefits.[48] Additionally, as with marketing research, big data can still be subject to bias, projection error, and sampling issues.[49]

Although big data yields tremendous insights into consumer preferences, lifestyles, and behaviors, it also creates serious privacy issues. Many consumers do not like to have their purchases or behaviors tracked, and sometimes using big data for marketing purposes creates conflict. President Obama requested that a report be conducted investigating how big data affects consumer privacy. Of particular concern is the possibility of infringing on consumer privacy or using big data to discriminate among customers. Theft of customer data is becoming more common as hackers break into company databases.[50] This concern led to a serious backlash against a data analytics initiative involving student data. The initiative was meant to collect data from students so that schools could tailor assignments to meet students' individual needs. However, parents were concerned that this data would be hacked and pressured the schools to back out.[51] A consumer privacy bill of rights and legislation mandating how companies should report data breaches are two recommendations for legislation dealing with this issue.[52]

Although the benefits of big data for marketing are numerous, and many consumers appreciate the added benefits of receiving marketing materials specifically targeted toward their needs, others feel uncomfortable with companies knowing so much about them. At the same time, companies that ignore big data miss out on the opportunity to develop stronger marketing strategies and customer relationships. As the Qlik advertisement demonstrates, research data can be hard to organize, leading marketers to miss important information. Firms such as Qlik claim to be able to interpret big data to help their clients find unexpected connections that could yield important insights for improving marketing strategies. The image of a gasoline Jerry Can turning into a flamingo is meant to demonstrate how Qlik can identify hard-to-see connections that other analytics firms cannot see. Avoiding big data could cause a business to sacrifice a competitive advantage. Although there is no easy solution to this issue, consumers can do one thing if they do not want their store purchases tracked: pay in cash. However, some stores still track purchases by recording customer account numbers for frequent purchase awards.

## 5-4d Marketing Analytics

Big data is of little use without tools to measure and interpret the data to glean insights and develop better-targeted marketing campaigns. As digital marketing has become more popular, adding more complexity to the field of marketing, organizations have found the need to focus more extensively on how to measure the effectiveness of their marketing strategies. **Marketing analytics** uses tools and methods to measure and interpret the effectiveness of a firm's marketing activities. The purpose of marketing analytics is to evaluate the company's return on investment (ROI) on their marketing strategies and make adjustments when necessary. This usually involves investing in software that can track, store, and analyze data. Big data and tools such as marketing decision support systems (described in the next section) are important to the success of marketing analytics. Investing in marketing analytics involves the following four steps: 1) defining what to measure and which tools to use; 2) collecting data; 3) developing reporting capabilities; and 4) implementing the campaign and analyzing the results.[53] Having the right data and the right methods is necessary in our data-rich business environment.[54]

Marketing analytics is becoming an increasingly important part in companies' marketing activities, even among mid-sized and smaller organizations. More than 30 percent of companies have integrated marketing analytics into the daily activities of the marketing function, and marketing professionals believe that an increasing percentage of the marketing budget should go toward analytics. Web analytics have become highly important for measuring marketing effectiveness. More than 82 percent of marketers that use analytics tools measure their website traffic and performance.[55] Google Analytics is the most popular web analytics software and can be helpful for small businesses without a large marketing budget because its basic functions are free to use. Marketers use Google Analytics to measure website visitors, page views, the percentage of new visits, the average amount of time spent during a visit, and more.[56] Even more sophisticated marketing analytics software is available for marketers who want a more in-depth look at the effectiveness of their marketing activities.

**marketing analytics** Use of and methods to measure and interpret the effectiveness of a firm's marketing activities

# EMERGING **TRENDS IN MARKETING**

## Marketing Research Embraces Analytics

The field of marketing research is changing. Where it was once dominated by focus groups and surveys, today's marketers are increasingly turning to marketing analytics to glean customer insights. A report found that large business-to-consumer firms are planning to increase their spending on marketing analytics by almost 100 percent in the next three years. Eighty-three percent of business leaders pursue big data projects in the belief that it will provide their firms with a competitive advantage.

It is not enough simply to record big data. The hard part is determining which small bits of information among massive data files will reveal significant customer insights. However, interpreting big data correctly can help marketers recognize trends they never would have realized otherwise. For instance, one analytics firm helped a mobile phone manufacturer determine that the major reason consumers bought its phone was not because of the camera, which is what the firm thought, but because of a certain app built into the phone.

Marketing analytics is not just for large firms, either. Family-owned business Sykes Cottages used big data to analyze why people make travel bookings. It used what it gleaned from this information to maximize its promotional campaigns, increasing its Internet conversion rate by 19 percent. There is no doubt that marketing analytics has begun to revolutionize marketers' understanding of customer trends and preferences.[a]

The highest goal marketers appear to have with marketing analytics is identifying how to develop better-targeted marketing campaigns.[57] British Airways, for example, has successfully used marketing analytics to increase activities geared toward forming relationships with customers. It adopted a marketing analytics program that combined information on customer loyalty with information on the online behavior and buying patterns of the company's 20 million customers. The software has enabled the company to target thank-you messages to their most loyal customers and offer incentives.[58] The successful deployment of marketing analytics positively relates to favorable and sustainable marketing performance. Research shows that a one-unit increase in marketing analytics deployment results in an 8 percent increase in a company's return on assets.[59] It is therefore imperative that marketers investigate which marketing analytics metrics would best work for their companies to improve marketing performance and maintain competitive advantages.

### 5-4e  Marketing Decision Support Systems

A **marketing decision support system (MDSS)** is a customized computer software that aids marketing managers in decision making by helping them anticipate the effects of certain decisions. MDSS is linked to the availability of big data and marketing analytics. An MDSS has a broader range and offers greater computational and modeling capabilities and advanced marketing analytics that lets managers explore a wide range of alternatives. For instance, an MDSS can determine how sales and profits might be affected by higher or lower interest rates or how sales forecasts, advertising expenditures, production levels, and the like might affect overall profits. For this reason, MDSS software is often a major component of a company's marketing information system. Some decision support systems incorporate artificial intelligence and other advanced computer technologies.

## 5-5 ISSUES IN MARKETING RESEARCH

Marketers should identify concerns that influence the integrity of research. Ethical issues are a constant risk in gathering and maintaining the quality of information. International issues relate to environmental differences, such as culture, legal requirements, level of technology, and economic development.

### 5-5a  The Importance of Ethical Marketing Research

Marketing managers and other professionals are relying more and more on marketing research, marketing information systems, and new technologies to make better decisions. Therefore, it is essential that professional standards be established by which to judge the reliability of marketing research. Such standards are necessary because of the ethical and legal issues that develop in gathering marketing research data. In the area of online interaction, for example, consumers remain wary of how the personal information collected by marketers will be used, especially whether it will be sold to third parties. In addition, the relationships between research suppliers, such as marketing research agencies, and the marketing managers who make strategy decisions require ethical behavior. Organizations such as the Marketing Research Association have developed codes of conduct and guidelines to promote ethical marketing research. To be effective, such guidelines must instruct marketing researchers on how to avoid misconduct. Table 5.5 provides sample steps researchers should follow when introducing a questionnaire to a customer in order to ensure respondent cooperation and satisfaction.

Consumer privacy has also become a significant issue. Firms now have the ability to purchase data on customer demographics, interests, and more personal matters such as bankruptcy filings and past marriages. This information has allowed companies to predict customer behavior or current life changes more accurately but may also infringe upon consumer privacy.[60] Videotaping customers in retail stores or tracking shoppers' mobile phones helps retailers

**marketing decision support system (MDSS)** Customized computer software that aids marketing managers in decision making

Table 5.5   **Guidelines for Questionnaire Introduction**

- Allow interviewers to introduce themselves by name.
- State the name of the research company.
- Indicate that this questionnaire is a marketing research project.
- Explain that no sales will be involved.
- Note the general topic of discussion (if this is a problem in a "blind" study, a statement such as "consumer opinion" is acceptable).
- State the likely duration of the interview.
- Assure the anonymity of the respondent and the confidentiality of all answers.
- State the honorarium, if applicable (for many business-to-business and medical studies, this is done up-front for both qualitative and quantitative studies).
- Reassure the respondent with a statement such as, "There are no right or wrong answers, so please give thoughtful and honest answers to each question" (recommended by many clients).

Source: The Marketing Research Association

understand store traffic, repeat customers, and eye movement. It also raises serious concerns about whether the stores are violating the rights of "honest shoppers."[61] The popularity of the Internet has enabled marketers to collect data on Internet users who visit their websites. Many companies have been able to use this to their advantage. For instance, Amazon, Netflix, and eBay use data to make customized recommendations based on their customers' interests, ratings, or past purchases. Although such data enable companies to offer more personalized services, policy makers fear that it could also allow them to discriminate among consumers who do not appear to make "valuable" customers.[62]

## 5-5b International Issues in Marketing Research

As we shall see in Chapter 9, sociocultural, economic, political, legal, and technological forces vary in different regions of the world. These variations create challenges for the organizations that are attempting to understand foreign customers through marketing research. The marketing

# MARKETING DEBATE

## Anonymous Data Can Still Find You

**ISSUE: Should marketers use information from anonymous credit card transactions since they can so easily be tracked to individual shoppers?**

Anonymous shopping data is not really anonymous. A Massachusetts Institute of Technology study determined that an analysis of credit-records combined with four types of information—such as the location and date of purchase—can be used to identify the individual purchasing patterns of more than 90 percent of consumers. How can this happen without names or credit card numbers? Social media may be partially to blame. Many individuals post photos or information about their locations publicly on Facebook, Instagram, and Foursquare. Even with names and credit card numbers removed, a few bits of additional information could help pinpoint your transactions from millions of others.

With over 60 percent of transactions in the United States made by credit card, this offers opportunities for marketers to tailor their promotions to appeal to the individual customer. However, many consumers do not want their information tracked so precisely, believing it to be an invasion of their privacy. Interestingly, it is easier to identify higher-income individuals from the data, possibly because they use credit cards more.[b]

Table 5.6    **Top U.S. Marketing Research Firms**

| Company Rank | Global Revenues (in Millions of U.S. Dollars) | Percent of Revenues from Outside the United States |
|---|---|---|
| 1 The Nielsen Co. | $6,288.0 | 45.7% |
| 2 Kantar | 3,785.0 | 74.5 |
| 3 IMS Health Inc. | 2,600.0 | 63.0 |
| 4 Ipsos S.A. | 2,219.0 | 75.2 |
| 5 IRI | 954.0 | 44.1 |

Source: Diane Bowers, "The 2015 AMA Gold Top 50 Report," *Marketing News*, June 2015, 36-93.

research process we describe in this chapter is used globally, but to ensure the research is valid and reliable, data-gathering methods may have to be modified to allow for regional differences. To make certain that global and regional differences are satisfactorily addressed, many companies retain a research firm with experience in the country of interest. The advertisement from Lionbridge describes how the firm can take its client's marketing content and adapt it to local customs to reach consumers in different countries. Lionbridge claims its services will help its client engage with global consumers and increase global efficiency.

Most of the largest marketing research firms derive a significant share of their revenues from research conducted outside the United States. As Table 5.6 indicates, Kantar, one of the largest marketing research firms in the world, is a U.S. company but has a market presence in 100 different countries. About 74.5 percent of its revenue is generated from outside of the country.[63]

Experts recommend a two-pronged approach to international marketing research. The first phase involves a detailed search for and analysis of secondary data to gain a greater understanding of a particular marketing environment and to pinpoint issues that must be taken into account in gathering primary research data. Secondary data can be particularly helpful in building a general understanding of the market, including economic, legal, cultural, and demographic issues, as well as in assessing the risks of doing business in that market and in forecasting demand. Marketing researchers often begin by studying country trade reports from the U.S. Department of Commerce, as well as country-specific information from local sources, such as a country's website, and trade and general business publications such as *The Wall Street Journal*. These sources can offer insights into the marketing environment in a particular country and can even indicate untapped market opportunities abroad.

The second phase involves field research using many of the methods described earlier, including focus groups and telephone surveys, to refine a firm's understanding of specific customer needs and preferences. Specific differences among countries can have a profound influence on data gathering. In-home (door-to-door) interviews are illegal in some countries. In developing countries, few people have land-line telephones as many opt for cell phones,

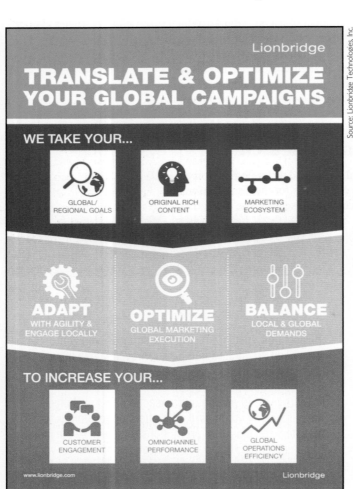

Source: Lionbridge Technologies, Inc.

**International Marketing Research**
Lionbridge provides services to help firms adapt their marketing strategies so that they effectively reach consumers with various backgrounds and cultures.

making telephone surveys less practical and less representative of the total population. Primary data gathering may have a greater chance of success if the firm employs local researchers who better understand how to approach potential respondents and can do so in their own languages.[64] Regardless of the specific methods used to gather primary data, whether in the United States or abroad, the goal is to recognize the needs of specific target markets to craft the best marketing strategy to satisfy the needs of customers in each market, as we will see in the next chapter.

# Summary

## 5-1 Define marketing research and its importance to decision makers.

Marketing research is the systematic design, collection, interpretation, and reporting of information to help marketers solve specific marketing problems or take advantage of marketing opportunities. It is a process for gathering information not currently available to decision makers. Marketing research can help a firm better understand market opportunities, ascertain the potential for success for new products, and determine the feasibility of a particular marketing strategy. The value of marketing research is measured by improvements in a marketer's ability to make decisions.

## 5-2 Distinguish between exploratory and conclusive research.

There are two types of marketing research: exploratory research and conclusive research. When marketers need more information about a problem or want to make a tentative hypothesis more specific, they may conduct exploratory research. The main purpose of exploratory research is to better understand a problem or situation and/or to help identify additional data needs or decision alternatives. More organizations are starting customer advisory boards, small groups of actual customers who serve as sounding boards for new product ideas and offer insights into their feelings and attitudes toward a firm's products, promotion, pricing, and other elements of marketing strategy. Another common method for conducting exploratory research is through a focus group. A focus group brings together multiple people to discuss a certain topic in a group setting led by a moderator.

Conclusive research is designed to verify insights through an objective procedure to help marketers make decisions. It is used when the marketer has one or more alternatives in mind and needs assistance in the final stages of decision making. Conclusive research can be descriptive or experimental. If marketers need to understand the characteristics of certain phenomena to solve a particular problem, descriptive research can aid them. Experimental research allows marketers to make causal deductions about relationships. Such experimentation requires that an independent variable (one not influenced by or dependent on other variables) be manipulated and the resulting changes in a dependent variable (one contingent on, or restricted to, one value or set of values assumed by the independent variable) be measured.

## 5-3 Name the five basic steps in conducting marketing research, including the two types of data and four survey methods.

To maintain the control needed to obtain accurate information, marketers approach marketing research as a process with logical steps: (1) locating and defining problems or issues, (2) designing the research project, (3) collecting data, (4) interpreting research findings, and (5) reporting research findings.

The first step in launching a research study, the problem or issue definition, focuses on uncovering the nature and boundaries of a situation or question related to marketing strategy or implementation. When a firm discovers a market opportunity, it may need to conduct research to understand the situation more precisely so it can craft an appropriate marketing strategy. In the second step, marketing researchers design a research project to obtain the information needed to address it. This step requires formulating a hypothesis and determining what type of research to employ to test the hypothesis so the results are reliable and valid. A hypothesis is an informed guess or assumption about a problem or set of circumstances. Marketers conduct exploratory research when they need more information about a problem or want to make a tentative hypothesis more specific; they use conclusive research to verify insights through an objective procedure. Research is considered reliable if it produces almost identical results in repeated trials; it is valid if it measures what it is supposed to measure.

For the third step of the research process, collecting data, two types of data are available. Primary data are observed and recorded or collected directly from respondents; secondary data are compiled inside or outside the organization for some purpose other than the current investigation. Sources of secondary data include an organization's own database and other internal sources, periodicals, government publications, unpublished sources, and online databases. Methods of collecting primary data include sampling, surveys, observation, and experimentation. Sampling involves selecting representative units from a total population. In probability sampling, every element in the population being studied has a known chance of being selected for study. Nonprobability sampling is more subjective than probability sampling because there is no way to calculate the likelihood that a specific element of the population being studied will be chosen. Marketing researchers employ sampling to collect primary data through mail, telephone, online, or personal interview surveys. A carefully constructed questionnaire is essential to the success of any survey. In using observation methods, researchers record respondents' overt behavior and take note of physical conditions and events. In an experiment, marketing researchers attempt to maintain certain variables while measuring the effects of experimental variables.

To apply research data to decision making, marketers must interpret and report their findings properly—the final two steps in the marketing research process. Statistical interpretation focuses on what is typical or what deviates from the average. After interpreting the research findings, the researchers must prepare a report on the findings that the decision makers can understand and use. Researchers must also take care to avoid bias and distortion.

## 5-4  Describe the tools, such as databases, big data, marketing analytics, and decision support systems useful to marketing decision making.

Many firms use computer technology to create a marketing information system (MIS), a framework for managing and structuring information gathered regularly from sources both inside and outside the organization. A database is a collection of information arranged for easy access and retrieval. Big data involves massive data files that can be obtained from both structured and unstructured databases. Marketing analytics is the use of tools and methods to measure and interpret the effectiveness of a firm's marketing activities. A marketing decision support system (MDSS) is a customized computer software that aids marketing managers in decision making by helping them anticipate the effects of certain decisions. Online information services and the Internet also enable marketers to communicate with customers and obtain information.

## 5-5  Identify ethical and international issues in marketing research.

Eliminating unethical marketing research practices and establishing generally acceptable procedures for conducting research are important goals of marketing research. Both domestic and international marketing use the same marketing research process, but international marketing may require modifying data-gathering methods to address regional differences.

---

**Go to www.cengagebrain.com for resources to help you master the content in this chapter as well as materials that will expand your marketing knowledge!**

---

## Important Terms

marketing research   132
exploratory research   134
customer advisory boards   134
focus group   134
conclusive research   135
descriptive research   136
experimental research   136
research design   137
hypothesis   137
reliability   138
validity   138
primary data   138
secondary data   138

population   140
sample   140
sampling   140
probability sampling   141
random sampling   141
stratified sampling   141
nonprobability sampling   141
mail survey   141
quota sampling   142
telephone survey   143
telephone depth interview   143
personal interview survey   144
in-home (door-to-door) interview   144

shopping mall intercept interviews   144
on-site computer interview   144
online survey   144
crowdsourcing   145
statistical interpretation   147
marketing information
   system (MIS)   150
database   150
single-source data   151
big data   151
marketing analytics   153
marketing decision support system
   (MDSS)   154

## Discussion and Review Questions

1. What is marketing research? Why is it important?
2. Describe the five steps in the marketing research process.
3. What is the difference between defining a research problem and developing a hypothesis?
4. Describe the different types of approaches to marketing research, and indicate when each should be used.

5. Where are data for marketing research obtained? Give examples of internal and external data.
6. What is the difference between probability sampling and nonprobability sampling? In what situation would random sampling be best? Stratified sampling? Quota sampling?
7. Suggest some ways to encourage respondents to cooperate in mail surveys.

8. If a survey of all homes with listed telephone numbers is to be conducted, what sampling design should be used?

9. Describe some marketing problems that could be solved through information gained from observation.

10. What is a marketing information system, and what should it provide?

11. Define a database. What is its purpose, and what does it include?

12. What is big data? Why is it important to marketing research?

13. How can marketers use online services and the Internet to obtain information for decision making?

14. What role do ethics play in marketing research? Why is it important that marketing researchers be ethical?

15. How does marketing research in other countries differ from marketing research in the United States?

# Video Case 5.1

## Big Boom Theory: Marketing Research Targets Baby Boomers

For many years, marketers have focused upon consumers between the ages of 18 and 34 to promote products. Marketers feel that wooing consumers early in life will ensure that they become lifetime loyal customers. While this seems logical, research is revealing that Baby Boomers might be a more profitable demographic. Statistics show that although spending for Millennials is actually shrinking, Baby Boomer spending has been increasing. Baby Boomers and older Americans are estimated to own 63 percent of all American financial assets.

The Baby Boomer generation is vastly different from the generations preceding it. Baby Boomers desire to have a variety of products available to them. Many of the products traditionally thought to belong to the younger generation, such as cars and technical products, are actually bought the most by older generations. With approximately 111 million Americans 50 years or older, marketers are beginning to research better ways for marketing to Baby Boomers.

In one study researchers attempted to understand how older consumers shop and interact in stores. Because store marketers often target younger generations of consumers, little thought has been given to how accessible these stores are for older generations. The research design involved equipping a person with gloves, neck braces, helmets, blurry goggles, and other equipment to simulate how a person in his or her 70s with arthritis is feeling. Researchers would then observe how the person takes items off of shelves, gets into his or her car, and gets up from chairs.

This research has been shared with many businesses that have interpreted the findings to create a retail environment better suited to this demographic. CVS, for instance, has lowered its shelves, made its store lighting softer, and installed magnifying glasses for hard-to-read labels. Other businesses are using this information to redesign their products. Diamond Foods Inc., for example, has designed the packaging of its Emerald snack nuts to be easier to open, a great help for older consumers whose hands become less mobile as they age. The company also studied consumers with arthritis and decreased the time it takes to rotate the caps to open its products. In-store customer service is also much more important to Baby Boomers than the Millennial generation.

Additionally, Baby Boomers have created an opportunity for businesses to market entirely new products. Baby Boomers tend to embrace fitness and exercise regimens as a way to stay fit and prolong their lives. Technology firms are seeing an opportunity to develop products to be installed in the homes of older consumers. These products monitor the movements of the inhabitants and alert family or experts if there are any changes in the inhabitants' movements. A decrease in mobility could signal a change in the person's physical and mental state, which may require medical attention. Although these devices might otherwise seem intrusive, Baby Boomers' desires to stay healthy and prolong life are increasing their demand. Many Baby Boomers are also concerned with preserving their more youthful appearance. Lingerie maker Maidenform has created shapewear, or clothes that help to "tone" the body, targeted toward those aged 35 to 54.

There is one description that marketers must avoid when marketing to Baby Boomers: any words or phrases that make them feel old. Marketing research has revealed that Baby Boomers do not like to be reminded that they are aging. Therefore, many marketing initiatives aimed at older consumers must be subtle. For this reason, Diamond Foods does not market the fact that its packages are easier to open because it does not want to make Baby Boomers feel aged. Even marketers of products that are for older people have overhauled their promotional campaigns to focus less on the concept of aging. Kimberly-Clark's Depend brand for incontinence was widely regarded as "adult diapers." This negative connotation led many to avoid them. To try to counteract this view, Kimberly-Clark released commercials that discussed the benefits of the product but also tried to "de-myth" the brand by discussing its similarity in look and feel to underwear. Many other businesses that sell similar products are following suit.

Although marketers have long focused on Millennials, the demand for products by Baby Boomers is changing the ways that businesses market to consumers. Marketing research is key to understanding the Baby Boomer demographic and creating the goods and services that best meet their needs.[65]

**Questions for Discussion**

1. Why are Baby Boomers such a lucrative market?
2. How has the marketing research process been used to understand how Baby Boomers shop and interact in stores?
3. How have stores used marketing research findings to tailor their stores and products to appeal to Baby Boomers?

# Case 5.2

## Largest Toymaker in the World: Lego Builds on Past Success

If the number of Lego bricks were averaged out among the world's population, each person would own approximately 86 bricks. These simple blocks have propelled the family-owned LEGO Group to the world's largest global toymaker. The company manufactures approximately 86,667 Legos per minute. Traditionally geared more toward young boys, Lego used market research to expand its target market toward girls with new product lines. It also uses crowdsourcing to elicit new ideas for Lego sets.

The LEGO Group is a Denmark-based company founded in 1932 by carpenter Ole Kirk Kristiansen. In 1947 the firm decided to produce plastic toys after purchasing an injection-molding machine. Among these toys were plastic bricks aimed toward young children. Kristiansen's son Godtfred, who would head the company after his father's death, began investigating ways to design these plastic bricks. He conceived of an interlocking system design that would allow children to connect the bricks together easily. In 1958 he patented the stud-and-tube coupling system, a system that would popularize Lego toys on a global dimension.

Although Godfred Kristiansen considered Lego products to be for both genders, this was not the case at the beginning of the 21st century. Legos were considered to be more of a boy's toy. However, this began to change a few years ago when Lego made a strategic decision to develop product lines for girls. This decision was not taken lightly. Lego spent four years interviewing this demographic and their families to understand the preferences and desires of young girls. Researchers observed girls at play to note the differences between

hxdbzxy/Shutterstock.com

girls and boys. One of the biggest observations that Lego discovered is that young girls tend to like to role-play, making Lego mini-figures an important part of the Lego experience. They also discovered that girls tend to pay more attention to color. In all, 3,500 girls were interviewed or observed.

This type of market research has paid off for Lego in the development of a highly successful product line. Based on their observations, Lego developed Lego Friends sets. These sets consist of five female mini-figures living in the fictional city of Heartlake City. These sets were developed in a variety of colors that young girls seem to prefer, including pink, turquoise, and lavender. The colors were not without controversy as some consumers were concerned that Lego Friends reinforced gender stereotypes. However, they became a hit among young girls. Lego Friends sold twice as well as expected and has helped The LEGO Group triple its revenue since 2007.

One reason for Lego's recent success might be due to its tendency to step outside of the box. A decade ago, the future of Lego as an independent firm was threatened, forcing the CEO to revamp operations and re-position the firm. Lego's emphasis on adults and young girls—as well as its strong partnerships with companies like Marvel—have come far in rejuvenating the firm. Another way that Lego is able to solicit creative ideas is by getting fans actively involved. Lego has a crowdsourcing platform through a Japanese partner called Lego Ideas. The platform solicits consumer-generated ideas for new play sets. Consumers can submit their ideas and vote for the sets they think should be developed into new products. Lego reviews those ideas that receive 10,000 or more votes for possible development. If an idea is chosen for development, the creator of the idea receives one percent of the product's total net sales. This is a benefit for Lego because it helps generate new product ideas that it might not have considered on its own. Lego also ensures that its employees are creative contributors. Job applicants interested in design jobs with Lego are invited to sketch and build Lego sets that will be reviewed by the firm to see if the applicant is a good fit.

Lego continues to use marketing research to determine new opportunities for product lines. The firm has even used MRI scans of children at play to examine which parts of the brain light up during interactions with specific toys. This use of new and advanced tools for marketing research is integral for Lego to maintain its top spot as the world's largest toymaker.[66]

## Questions for Discussion

1. Describe the marketing research process Lego undertook to develop Lego Friends. Why do you think this was important to the product's success?
2. How does Lego get consumers involved in marketing research?
3. Why is it important for Lego to use new tools to continually gather market research from its target markets?

# NOTES

[1] Katy Muldoon, "But How Will It Play in Portland?" *The Wall Street Journal*, July 16, 2015, D1, D4; SamplingLab, "About Us," http://www.samplinglab.com/#about-us (accessed July 20, 2015); Reggie Aqui, "Everything's free at the new Portland 'Sampling Lab'," *KGW*, May 5, 2015, http://www.kgw.com/story/money/business/2015/05/05/everythings-free-at-the-new-portland-sampling-lab/26932501/ (accessed July 20, 2015); Molly Woodstock, "Inside North Portland's SamplingLab, Where Everything Is Free," *Portland Monthly Magazine*, December 17, 2014, http://www.portlandmonthlymag.com/articles/2014/12/17/amplinglab-where-everything-is-free-december-2014 (accessed July 20, 2015).

[2] Ellen Byron, "The Slower You Shop, the More You Spend," *The Wall Street Journal*, October 20, 2015, http://www.wsj.com/articles/the-slower-you-shop-the-more-you-spend-1445359614 (accessed December 21, 2015).

[3] Mary Bowerman, "Cereal aisle psychology: All eyes on the consumer," *USA Today*, April 3, 2014, 5B.

[4] Allison Enright, "Surviving 2010," *Marketing News*, February 28, 2010, pp. 30–33.

[5] Jens Hansegard, "IKEA Slides Into Cramped Quarters," *The Wall Street Journal*, October 1, 2015, B1, B6.

[6] Dhruv Grewal Parasuraman and R. Krishnan, *Marketing Research* (Boston: Houghton Mifflin, 2007).

[7] Ken Manning, O. C. Ferrell, and Linda Ferrell, "Consumer Expectations of Clearance vs. Sale Prices," University of New Mexico, working paper, 2013.

[8] Oracle, "About the Customer Advisory Board," Oracle Communications, https://www.oracle.com/communications-customer-advisory-board/about.html (accessed December 22, 2015).

[9] Phil Wahba, "The change agent inside CVS," *Fortune*, September 11, 2015, http://fortune.com/2015/09/11/cvs-health-helena-foulkes/ (accessed December 21, 2015).

[10] Daniel Gross, "Lies, Damn Lies, and Focus Groups," *Slate*, October 10, 2003, www.slate.com/articles/business/moneybox/2003/10/lies_damn_lies_and_focus_groups.html (accessed July 9, 2012).

[11] Peter Frost, "Here's the next step in McDonald's turnaround plan," *Chicago Business*, October 21, 2015, http://www.chicagobusiness.com/article/20151021/NEWS07/151029955/heres-the-next-step-in-mcdonalds-turnaround-plan (accessed December 21, 2015); Lori Weisberg, "McDonald's tests new menu in SD," *The San Diego Union-Tribune*, September 25, 2015, http://www.sandiegouniontribune.com/news/2015/sep/25/mcdonalds-launches-customized-sandwich-test/ (accessed December 21, 2015).

[12] Andreas Persson and Lynette Ryals, "Making customer relationship decisions: Analytics v rules of thumb," *Journal of Business Research*, 67( 8), August 2014, 1725–1732.

[13] Laura J. Nelson, "Hollywood market research evolves to reflect tech-savvy moviegoers," *Los Angeles Times*, March 4, 2014, http://articles.latimes.com/2013/mar/04/business/la-fi-ct-market-research-20130305 (accessed December 21, 2015).

[14] Donna F. Davis, Susan L. Golicic, Courtney N. Boerstler, Sunny Choi, and Hanmo Oh, "Does marketing research suffer from methods myopia?" *Journal of Business Research*, 66(9), 1245–1250.

[15] Vikas Mittal and Wagner A. Kamakura, "Satisfaction, Repurchase Intent, and Repurchase Behavior: Investigating the Moderating Effects of Customer Characteristics," *Journal of Marketing Research* (February 2001): 131–142.

[16] U.S. Census Bureau, *American Community Survey*, www.census.gov/acs/www (accessed January 20, 2011).

[17] Aaron Gilchrist, "Census Forms Confusion: 'American Community Survey' Is Legit," *nbc12.com*, January 27, 2010, www.nbc12.com/Global/story.asp?S=11890921 (accessed January 21, 2011).

[18] Symphony IRI Group, "About Us," http://symphonyiri.com/About/History/tabid/60/Default.aspy (accessed January 21, 2011).

[19] David Lieberman, "TiVo to Sell Data on What People Watch, Fast-Forward," *USA Today*, April 20, 2010, www.usatoday.com/tech/news/2009-04-20-tivo-data-new-plan_N.htm (accessed March 19, 2010).

[20] Kelly Tay, "Marketing in a Digital Age," *Business Intelligence*, September 25, 2013, www.businesstimes.com.sg/specials/forward-thinkers/marketing-digital-age-20130925 (accessed November 26, 2013); Brian Terran, "Insights Key to Sustainability Cause, Says P&G Chief Executive," *Research*, September 27, 2012, www.research-live.com/news/news-headlines/insights-key-to-sustainability-cause-says-pg-chief-executive/4008338.article (accessed November 25, 2013).

[21] Procter & Gamble 2009 Annual Report, February 24, 2010, p. 3, http://annualreport.pg.com/annualreport2009/index.shtml (accessed March 20, 2010).

[22] Warren Davies, "How to Increase Survey Response Rates Using Post-it Notes," *GenerallyThinking.com*, August 3, 2009, http://generallythinking.com/blog/how-to-increase-survey-response-rates-using-post-it-notes (accessed March 9, 2010); Randy Garner, "Post-it Note Persuasion: A Sticky Influence," *Journal of Consumer Psychology* 15 (2005): 230–237.

[23] Ray Poynter, "Mobile Market Research, 2014," *International Journal of Market Research*, 56(6), 705–707.

[24] David Robertson, "Building Success: How Thinking 'Inside the Brick' Saved Lego," *Wired*, October 9, 2013, www.wired.co.uk/magazine/archive/2013/10/features/building-success (accessed November 19, 2014); Lego Ideas website, https://ideas.lego.com/ (accessed November 19, 2014).

[25] Charlene Li, "Why No One Uses the Corporate Social Network," *Harvard Business Review*, April 7, 2015, https://hbr.org/2015/04/why-no-one-uses-the-corporate-social-network (accessed December 21, 2015).

[26] Amazon Mechanical Turk website, http://aws.amazon.com/mturk/ (accessed December 16, 2014).

[27] Michael Buhrmester, Tracy Kwang, and Samuel B. Gosling, "Amazon's Mechanical Turk: A New Source of Inexpensive, Yet High-Quality Data?" *Perspectives on Psychological Science*, doi: 10.1177/1745691610393980.

[28] James Vincent, "Amazon's Mechanical Turkers want to be recognized as 'actual human beings'," *The Verge*, December 4, 2014, http://www.theverge.com/2014/12/4/7331777/amazon-mechanical-turk-workforce-digital-labor (accessed January 11, 2016); Utpal Dholakia, "My Experience as an Amazon Mechanical Turk (MTurk) Worker," July 20, 2015, https://www.linkedin.com/pulse/my-experience-amazon-mechanical-turk-mturk-worker-utpal-dholakia (accessed January 11, 2016).

[29] Sue Shellenbarger, "A Few Bucks for Your Thoughts?" *The Wall Street Journal*, May 18, 2011, http://online.wsj.com/news/articles/SB10001424052748703509104576329110724411724 (accessed March 28, 2014).

[30] Bas Donkers, Philip Hans Franses, and Peter C. Verhoef, "Selective Sampling for Binary Choice Models," *Journal of Marketing Research* (November 2003): 492–497.

[31] Elizabeth Weise, "Online retailers getting physical," *USA Today*, November 6, 2015, http://www.usatoday.com/story/tech/2015/11/06/amazon-brick-and-mortar-bonobos-modcloth/75235308/ (accessed December 21, 2015).

[32] Hsin-Hui Lin and Shu-Fei Yang, "An eye movement study of attribute framing in online shopping," *Journal of Marketing Analytics*, 2(2), June 2014, 72–80.

[33] Piet Levy, "10 Minutes with . . . Gregory A. Reid," *Marketing News*, February 28, 2010, p. 34.

[34] *Reputation.com*, "How to Make a Negative Review Work in Your Favor," www.reputation.com/reputationwatch/articles/how-make-negative-review-work-your-favor (accessed November 25, 2013).

[35] Lauren Coleman-Lochner, "Why Procter & Gamble Needs to Shave More Indians," *Bloomberg Buinessweek*, June 9, 2011, www.businessweek.com/magazine/content/11_25/b4233021703857.htm (accessed April 15, 2016).

[36] David Aaker, V. Kumar, George Day, and Robert Lane, *Marketing Research*, 10th ed. (New York: Wiley & Sons, 2010).

[37] "BehaviorScan Rx," IRI, http://www.iriworldwide.com/default.aspx?TabId=159&0026;productid=75 (accessed November 19, 2014).

[38] Douglas Laney, "The Importance of 'Big Data': A Definition," Gartner, June 2012.

[39] Peter Daboll, "5 Reasons Why Big Data Will Crush Big Research," *Forbes*, December 3, 2013, www.forbes.com/sites/onmarketing/2013/12/03/5-reasons-why-big-data-will-crush-big-research (accessed December 5, 2013).

[40] Danny Bradbury and Tim Anderson, "Big Data and Marketing: An Inevitable Partnership," *The Guardian*, October 16, 2013, www.theguardian.com/technology/2013/oct/16/big-data-and-marketing-an-inevitable-partnership (accessed December 5, 2013).

[41] Steven Norton, "Big Companies Rein In Data Sprawl," *The Wall Street Journal*, October 22, 2015, B4.

[42] Paula B. Goes, "Editor's Comments: Big Data and IS Research," *MIS Quarterly*, *38*(3), September 2014, iii–viii.

[43] Jonathan Gordon, "Big Data, Analytics and the Future of Marketing and Sales," *Forbes*, July 22, 2015, http://www.forbes.com/sites/mckinsey/2013/07/22/big-data-analytics-and-the-future-of-marketing-sales/ (accessed December 21, 2015).

[44] Bradbury and Anderson, "Big Data and Marketing: An Inevitable Partnership."

[45] Steven Norton, "Big Companies Rein in Data Sprawl," *The Wall Street Journal*, October 22, 2015, B4.

[46] Kashmir Hill, "How Target Figured Out a Teen Girl Was Pregnant Before Dad Did," *Forbes*, February 16, 2012, www.forbes.com/sites/kashmirhill/2012/02/16/how-target-figured-out-a-teen-girl-was-pregnant-before-her-father-did (accessed December 5, 2013).

[47] SAS, "Big Data, Bigger Marketing," www.sas.com/software/customer-intelligence/big-data-marketing.html (accessed December 5, 2013).

[48] James Rubin, "Survey Demonstrates the Benefits of Big Data," *Forbes*, November 15, 2013, www.forbes.com/sites/forbesinsights/2013/11/15/survey-demonstrates-the-benefits-of-big-data (accessed December 5, 2013).

[49] Peter Daboll, "5 Reasons Why Big Data Will Crush Big Research."

[50] Aamer Madhani, "White House raises concerns about 'big data'," *USA Today*, May 2, 2014, 5A.

[51] Olga Kharif, "Big Data Stops Here," *Bloomberg Businessweek*, May 5-11, 2014, pp. 37–38.

[52] Madhani, "White House raises concerns about 'big data'."

[53] Jayson DeMers, "2014 Is The Year Of Digital Marketing Analytics: What It Means For Your Company," *Forbes*, February 10, 2014, http://www.forbes.com/sites/jaysondemers/2014/02/10/2014-is-the-year-of-digital-marketing-analytics-what-it-means-for-your-company/ (accessed December 15, 2014).

[54] Marketing Science Institute, "MSI closes knowledge gap on marketers' top concerns," *Marketing Science Institute Review*, Fall 2014, pp. 1–2.

[55] Elisabeth A. Sullivan, "Marketing Analytics," *Marketing News*, December 2014, pp. 24–33.

[56] Regina Pefanis Schlee and Katrin R. Harich, "Teaching Students How to Integrate and Assess Social Networking Tools in Marketing Communications," *Marketing Education Review*, 23(3), Fall 2013, 209–223.

[57] Elisabeth A. Sullivan, "Marketing Analytics," *Marketing News*, December 2014, pp. 24–33.

[58] Doug Henschen, "Big Data Success: 3 Companies Share Secrets," *InformationWeek*, October 4, 2013, http://www.informationweek.com/big-data/big-data-analytics/big-data-success-3-companies-share-secrets/d/d-id/1111815? (accessed December 15, 2014).

[59] Frank Germann, Gary L. Lilien, and Arvind Rangaswamy, "Performance implications of deploying marketing analytics," *International Journal of Research in Marketing*, 30 (2), June 2013, 114–128.

[60] Chares Duhigg, "How Companies Learn Your Secrets," *The New York Times*, February 15, 2012, www.nytimes.com/2012/02/19/magazine/shopping-habits.html?_r=1&pagewanted=all (accessed February 28, 2012).

[61] "We Snoop to Conquer," *The Economist*, February 9, 2013, p. 64.

[62] Emily Steel and Julia Angwin, "The Web's Cutting Edge, Anonymity in Name Only," *The Wall Street Journal*, August 4, 2010, http://online.wsj.com/article/SB10001424052748703294904575385532109190198.html (accessed February 7, 2012).

[63] Diane Bowers, "The 2015 AMA Gold Top 50 Report," *Marketing News*, June 2015, 36–93.

[64] Reprinted with permission of The Marketing Research Association, P.O. Box 230, Rocky Hill, CT 06067-0230, 860-257-4008.

[65] Ellen Byron, "From Diapers to 'Depends': Marketers Discreetly Retool for Aging Boomers," *The Wall Street Journal*, February 5, 2011, http://online.wsj.com/article/SB10001424052748704013604576104394209062996.html (accessed March 30, 2012); Bruce Horovitz, "Big-Spending Baby Boomers Bend the Rules of Marketing," *USA Today*, November 16, 2010, www.usatoday.com/money/advertising/2010-H-16-1Aboomerbuyers16_CV_N.htm (accessed March 30, 2012); Mark Bradbury, "The 7 Incredible Facts about Boomers' Spending Power," *The Huffington Post*, March 17, 2015, http://www.huffingtonpost.com/mark-bradbury/the-7-incredible-facts-about-boomers-spending_b_6815876.html (accessed January 21, 2016); Synchrony Financial, "These findings about how millennials and baby boomers shop may surprise you," *Business Insider*, April 22, 2015, http://www.businessinsider.com/sc/how-millennials-and-baby-boomers-shop-2015-4 (accessed January 21, 2016).

[66] Jens Hansegard, "Lego Shrugs Off Toy-Market Blues," *The Wall Street Journal*, February 21, 2013, http://online.wsj.com/news/articles/SB10001424127887323549204578317603729616028 (accessed December 14, 2015); Jens Hansegard, "Winning a Job at Lego," *The Wall Street Journal*, November 13, 2013, http://online.wsj.com/news/articles/SB10001424052702303460004579193901642418812 (accessed December 14, 2015); William Harvey, "Block Party!" *St. Petersburg Times (Florida)*, October 27, 2011, 8; "Lego becomes world's second-biggest toy maker," *BBC News*, September 5, 2013, http://www.bbc.co.uk/news/business-23968860 (accessed December 14, 2015); "Lego Facts," Lego Education, http://education.lego.com/en-us/about-us/lego-education-worldwide/lego-facts (accessed December 14, 2015); "LEGO History Timeline," Lego website, http://aboutus.lego.com/en-us/lego-group/the_lego_history (accessed December 14, 2015); Lego website, Lego.com, http://www.lego.com/en-us/ (accessed December 14, 2015); "Legos for Girls Sell at Twice the Expected Volume," *New Haven Register*, January 5, 2013, http://nhregister.com; Melinda Mahaffey Icden, "Building Lego," *Spirit*, February 2014, pp. 65-69; Dan Milmo, "Lego's 'sexist' Friends range for girls spurs 35% profit rise," *The Guardian*, August 31, 2012, http://www.theguardian.com/lifeandstyle/2012/aug/31/lego-friends-profit-rise (accessed December 14, 2015); David Robertson, "Building success: how thinking 'inside the brick' saved Lego," *Wired*, October 9, 2013, http://www.wired.co.uk/magazine/archive/2013/10/features/building-success (accessed December 14, 2015); Brad Wieners, "Lego is for Girls," *Bloomberg Businessweek*, December 19-25, 2011, 68-73; Jens Hansegard, "Lego Bucks Industry Trend with Profit Growth," *The Wall Street Journal*, February 25, 2015, http://www.wsj.com/articles/lego-reports-2014-profit-growth-1424857331 (accessed December 14, 2015); Matthew Heller, "Lego's Research of Kids' Play Pays Off," *Financial Times*, March 30, 2015, http://www.ft.com/cms/s/0/f03d0188-513d-11e5-9497-c74c95a1a7b1.html#axzz3uJtaYenZ (accessed December 14, 2015); Lego, http://shop.lego.com/en-US/Ideas-ByTheme (accessed December 14, 2015).

## Feature Notes

[a] Danny Bradbury, "Small Business, Big Data: How to Boost Your Marketing with Analytics," *Forbes*, June 5, 2015, http://www.forbes.com/sites/ramcommercial/2015/06/05/small-business-big-data-how-to-boost-your-marketing-with-analytics/ (accessed September 10, 2015); Kimberly A. Whitler, "How the Best Marketers are Using Analytics to Create Competitive Advantage," *Forbes*, July 18, 2015, http://www.forbes.com/sites/kimberlywhitler/2015/07/19/how-some-of-the-best-marketers-are-using-analytics-to-create-a-competitive-advantage/ (accessed September 10, 2015); Louis Columbus, "Roundup of Analytics, Big Data & Business Intelligence Forecasts and Market Estimates, 2015," *Forbes*, May 25, 2015, http://www.forbes.com/sites/louiscolumbus/2015/05/25/roundup-of-analytics-big-data-business-intelligence-forecasts-and-market-estimates-2015/ (accessed September 10, 2015).

[b] Robert Lee Hotz, "Even Nameless Data Can Reveal Identity, Study Finds," *The Wall Street Journal*, January 29, 2015, A3; Rebecca Jacobson, "Your 'anonymous' credit card is not so anonymous, study find," *PBS*, January 29, 2015, http://www.pbs.org/newshour/rundown/anonymous-credit-card-data-anonymous-study-finds/ (accessed October 5, 2015); Larry Hardesty, "Privacy challenges," *MIT News*, January 29, 2015, http://news.mit.edu/2015/identify-from-credit-card-metadata-0129 (accessed October 5, 2015).

Monkey Business Images/Shutterstock.com

# chapter 6

## Target Markets: Segmentation and Evaluation

---

### OBJECTIVES

---

**6-1** Explain what markets are and how they are generally classified.

**6-2** Identify the five steps of the target market selection process.

**6-3** Describe the differences among three targeting strategies.

**6-4** Identify the major segmentation variables.

**6-5** Explain what market segment profiles are and how they are used.

**6-6** Explain how to evaluate market segments.

**6-7** Identify the factors that influence the selection of specific market segments for use as target markets.

**6-8** Discuss sales forecasting methods.

# MARKETING INSIGHTS

## Carnival's Ten-Brand Targeting Strategy

Ruth Peterkin/Shutterstock.com

With 100 cruise ships sailing under 10 different cruise brands, Carnival Corporation rings up $16 billion worldwide and serves more than 10 million passengers every year. Competition is intense, so the company will continue to grow only if it is effective in targeting vacationers of different ages, backgrounds, and interests, including first-time cruisers.

For example, its Carnival Cruise brand targets families with accommodations and activities for both adults and children. Its staterooms are spacious enough for parents and children to room together. Splash-park rides, Drive-In Movies, preteen camps, and teen events entertain kids between ports of call. Meanwhile, educational programs and nostalgic themes such as 1980s "Throwback Sea Day" cater to adult tastes.

Other Carnival cruise brands are also geared toward specific customer groups. Seabourn targets high-income adults who desire luxurious suites, gourmet meals, and personalized service aboard smaller ships that dock in exciting destinations. Cunard offers "legendary British elegance" with the tradition of formal dinners, ballrooms, and other amenities appreciated by affluent vacationers. AIDA targets young, active German-speaking vacationers who prefer a casual shipboard atmosphere.

The newest Carnival brand, Fathom, is marketed as "travel with heart," for Millennials and other young, active consumers who want to make a difference by volunteering while on vacation. Fathom customers who cruise to the Dominican Republic can choose to help local children improve their English skills or distribute water filters, for instance. As they cruise, passengers receive Spanish lessons and learn about Dominican Republic culture. Social responsibility may be just the ticket to attract first-time cruisers in their 20s and 30s who are drawn to "voluntourism."[1]

Like most organizations that are trying to compete effectively, Carnival Cruise must identify specific customer groups, such as families and active Millennials, toward which they will direct marketing efforts. This process includes developing and maintaining marketing mixes that satisfy the needs of those customers. In this chapter, we define and explore the concepts of markets and market segmentation. First, we discuss the major requirements of a market. Then, we examine the steps in the target market selection process, including identifying the appropriate targeting strategy, determining which variables to use for segmenting consumer and business markets, developing market segment profiles, evaluating relevant market segments, and selecting target markets. We conclude with a discussion of the various methods for developing sales forecasts.

# 6-1 WHAT ARE MARKETS?

In Chapter 2, we defined a *market* as a group of individuals and/or organizations that have a desire or need for products in a product class and have the ability, willingness, and authority to purchase those products. You, as a student, are part of the market for textbooks. You are part of other markets as well, such as for computers, clothes, food, and music. To truly be a market, consumers must possess all four characteristics. For instance, teenagers are not part of the market for alcohol. They may have the desire, willingness, and ability to buy liquor, but they do not have the authority to do so because teenagers are prohibited by law from buying alcoholic beverages.

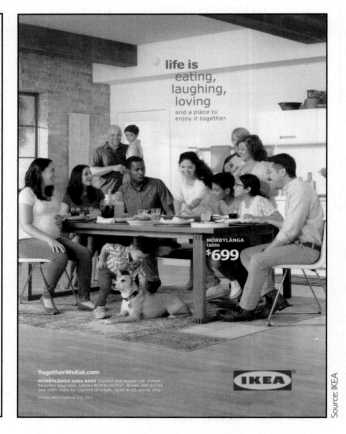

**Types of Markets**
Dropbox targets a business market by showing how the product can be used to share documents, while IKEA focuses on a consumer market by emphasizing how its furniture can help bring families and friends together.

Markets fall into one of two categories: consumer markets and business markets. These categories are based on the characteristics of the individuals and groups that make up a specific market and the purposes for which they buy products. A **consumer market** consists of purchasers and household members who intend to consume or benefit from the purchased products and do not buy products to make a profit. Consumer markets are sometimes referred to as *business-to-consumer (B2C) markets*. Each of us belongs to numerous consumer markets for all the purchases we make in categories such as housing, food, clothing, vehicles, personal services, appliances, furniture, recreational equipment, and other products.

A **business market** consists of individuals or groups that purchase a specific kind of product for one of three purposes: resale, direct use in producing other products, or use in general daily operations. For instance, a producer that buys electrical wire to use in the production of lamps is part of a business market for electrical wire. Some products can be part of either the business or consumer market, depending on their end use. For instance, if you purchase a chair for your home, that chair is part of the consumer market. However, if an office manager purchases the same chair for use in a business office, it is part of the business market. Business markets may be called *business-to-business (B2B), industrial,* or *organizational markets* and can be sub-classified into producer, reseller, government, and institutional markets, as we shall see in Chapter 8.

The advertisements show a product targeted at the consumer market and one targeted at the business market. Dropbox Business allows business people to share and work on various types of documents across platforms and devices with members of their team. As shown in the ad, Dropbox allows for businesses to control who can view and change documents, which team members can access from wherever they might be to review content or make changes. The IKEA ad, on the other hand, is targeted to a consumer market. The photo in this advertisement shows a diverse group of family and friends gathered together for a meal set on an IKEA dining set. Although the ad describes the table and provides its price, the emphasis is on the satisfaction to be derived from the consumer product. You can see from these two advertisements that the one for Dropbox focuses on the practical application of the product in the business world, while the advertisement for IKEA furniture highlights how it will make the consumer feel good about togetherness, emphasizing how marketers will have different objectives depending on which market they target.

## 6-2 TARGET MARKET SELECTION PROCESS

As indicated earlier, the first of two major components of developing a marketing strategy is to select a target market. Although marketers may employ several methods for target market selection, generally they follow a five-step process. This process is shown in Figure 6.1, and we discuss it in the following sections.

**consumer market** Purchasers and household members who intend to consume or benefit from the purchased products and do not buy products to make profits

**business market** Individuals, organizations, or groups that purchase a specific kind of product for resale, direct use in producing other products, or use in general daily operations

Figure 6.1  **Target Market Selection Process**

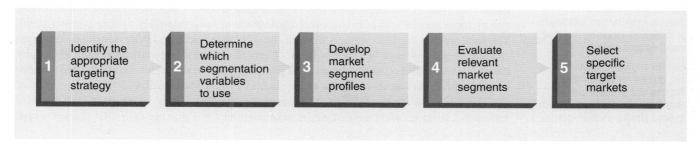

1. Identify the appropriate targeting strategy
2. Determine which segmentation variables to use
3. Develop market segment profiles
4. Evaluate relevant market segments
5. Select specific target markets

# 6-3 STEP 1: IDENTIFY THE APPROPRIATE TARGETING STRATEGY

A target market is a group of people or organizations for which a business creates and maintains a marketing mix specifically designed to satisfy the needs of group members. The strategy used to select a target market is affected by target market characteristics, product attributes, and the organization's objectives and resources. Figure 6.2 illustrates the three basic targeting strategies: undifferentiated, concentrated, and differentiated.

## 6-3a Undifferentiated Targeting Strategy

An organization sometimes defines an entire market for a product as its target market. When a company designs a single marketing mix and directs it at the entire market for a particular product, it is using an **undifferentiated targeting strategy**. As Figure 6.2 shows, the strategy assumes that all customers in the target market have similar needs, and thus the organization can satisfy most customers with a single marketing mix with little or no variation. Products marketed successfully through the undifferentiated strategy include commodities and staple food items, such as sugar, salt, and conventionally raised produce.

The undifferentiated targeting strategy is effective under two conditions. First, a large proportion of customers in a total market must have similar needs for the product, a situation termed a **homogeneous market**. A marketer using a single marketing mix for a total market of customers with a variety of needs would find that the marketing mix satisfies very few people. For example, marketers would have little success using an undifferentiated strategy to sell a "universal car" because different customers have varying needs. Second, the organization must have the resources to develop a single marketing mix that satisfies customers' needs in a large portion of a total market and the managerial skills to maintain it.

The reality is that although customers may have similar needs for a few products, for most products their needs are different enough to warrant separate marketing mixes. In such instances, a company should use a concentrated or a differentiated strategy.

## 6-3b Concentrated Targeting Strategy through Market Segmentation

Although most people will be satisfied with the same white sugar, not everyone wants or needs the same car, furniture, or clothes. A market comprised of individuals or organizations with diverse product needs is called a **heterogeneous market**. Some individuals, for instance, want a Ford truck because they have to haul heavy loads for their work, while others live in the city and enjoy the ease of parking and good gas mileage of a Smart car. The automobile market thus is heterogeneous.

For heterogeneous markets, market segmentation is the best approach. **Market segmentation** is the process of dividing a total market into groups, or segments, that consist of people or organizations with relatively similar product needs. The purpose is to enable a marketer to design a marketing mix that more precisely matches the needs of customers in the selected market segment. A **market segment** consists of individuals, groups, or organizations that share one or more similar characteristics that cause them to have relatively similar product needs. The total market for blue jeans is divided into multiple segments. Price-sensitive customers can buy bargain jeans at Walmart or Ross. Others may need functional jeans, like the Carhartt brand, for work. Still other customers wear jeans as a fashion statement and are willing to spend hundreds of dollars on an exclusive brand such as 7 for All Mankind.

The rationale for segmenting heterogeneous markets is that a company will be most successful in developing a satisfying marketing mix for a portion of a total market whose

**undifferentiated targeting strategy** A strategy in which an organization designs a single marketing mix and directs it at the entire market for a particular product

**homogeneous market** A market in which a large proportion of customers have similar needs for a product

**heterogeneous market** A market made up of individuals or organizations with diverse needs for products in a specific product class

**market segmentation** The process of dividing a total market into groups with relatively similar product needs to design a marketing mix that matches those needs

**market segment** Individuals, groups, or organizations sharing one or more similar characteristics that cause them to have similar product needs

Figure 6.2  **Targeting Strategies**

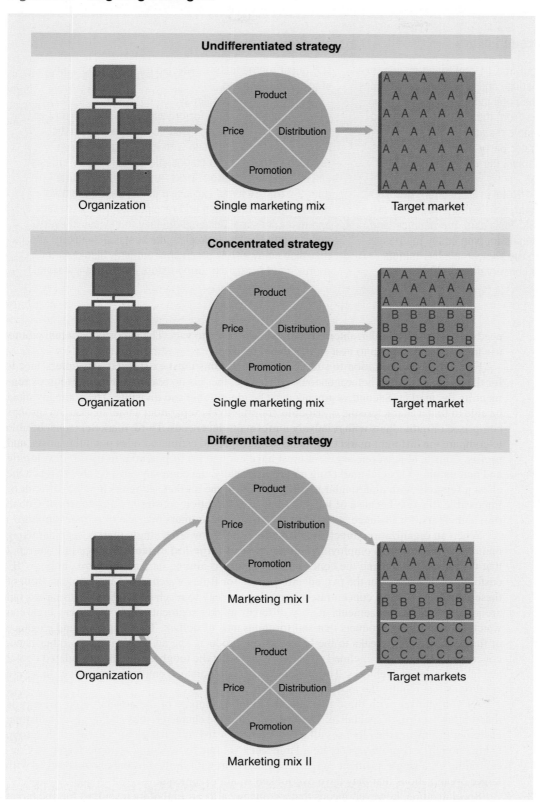

*The letters in each target market represent potential customers. Customers with the same letters have similar characteristics and similar product needs.*

# GOING GREEN

## 1 Hotel Stands for Green Luxury

From check-in to check-out, the 1 Hotel brand stands for "nature-inspired" sustainability and luxury. The upscale startup is a standout in the hotel industry because green is built into every element, from the building design and the décor to the farm-to-table restaurant meals. The target market, according to founder Barry Sternlicht, is sophisticated consumers who "travel the world and also care about it."

Guests who stay in a 1 Hotel in Manhattan, Brooklyn, or Miami are pampered in an eco-friendly way. They are driven around in all-electric Tesla cars, for instance, and sleep on organic-cotton linens topping cushy mattresses made from hemp. Next to the shower is a five-minute timer to encourage water conservation. Lobby areas

and guest rooms feature recycled materials and energy-efficient LED lighting.

Instead of hanging flimsy "do not disturb" signs, guests signal their wish for privacy using rocks inscribed with "Now" or "Not Now." Traditional wire and plastic hangers are gone, replaced with hangers made from recycled cardboard. No disposable slippers here—guests can slip into cozy cotton socks, and take them home after the trip. To avoid excessive use of paper, the hotel offers digital registration and receipts. Even newspapers and magazines are delivered digitally to devices in every guest room. Guests appreciate the sustainable luxury and they also enjoy a truly green environment, thanks to the profusion of plants that bring nature inside every 1 Hotel.[a]

needs are relatively similar, since customers' needs tend to vary. The majority of organizations use market segmentation to best satisfy their customers.

For market segmentation to succeed, five conditions must exist. First, customers' needs for the product must be heterogeneous. Otherwise, there is no reason to waste resources segmenting the market. Second, segments must be identifiable and divisible. The company must be able to find a characteristic, or variable, for effectively separating a total market into groups comprised of individuals with relatively uniform product needs. Third, marketers must be able to compare the different market segments with respect to estimated sales potential, costs, and profits. Fourth, at least one segment must have enough profit potential to justify developing and maintaining a special marketing mix for it. Finally, the company must be able to reach the chosen segment with a particular marketing mix. Some market segments may be difficult or impossible to reach because of legal, social, or distribution constraints. Producers of Cuban rum and cigars, for instance, cannot market to U.S. consumers because of a trade embargo.

When an organization directs its marketing efforts toward a single market segment using one marketing mix, it is employing a **concentrated targeting strategy**. Notice in Figure 6.2 that the organization using the concentrated strategy is aiming its marketing mix only at "B" customers. Take a look at the two advertisements for Rolex watches and Yeti coolers. Both of these brands are using a concentrated marketing strategy to reach a specific target market, but are aiming their advertisements at very different market segments. Rolex is a very high-end watch company with products that sell for thousands of dollars. The simplicity and elegance of the advertisement speaks to the luxury of the product. The ad for Yeti, on the other hand, concentrates on outdoor-inclined consumers who want the toughest and most insulated cooler available for their adventures. The ad depicts two outdoorsmen enjoying themselves in severe conditions that require the most durable cooler.

As you can see with these two ads, the chief advantage of the concentrated strategy is that it allows a firm to specialize. The firm analyzes the characteristics and needs of a distinct customer group and then focuses all its energies on satisfying that group's needs. If the group is big enough, a firm may generate a large sales volume by reaching a single segment. Concentrating on a single segment can also permit a firm with limited resources to compete with larger organizations that may have overlooked smaller segments.

**concentrated targeting strategy**
A market segmentation strategy in which an organization targets a single market segment using one marketing mix

Specialization, however, means that a company allocates all of its resources for one target segment, which can be hazardous. If a company's sales depend on a single segment and the segment's demand for the product declines, the company's financial health also deteriorates.

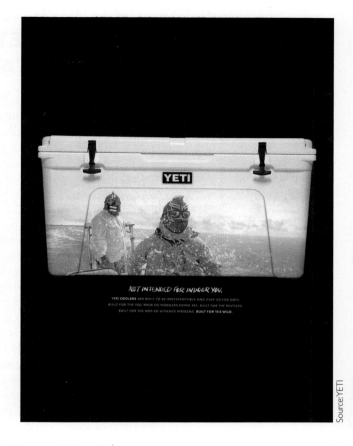

**Concentrated Targeting Strategy**
Both Rolex and Yeti use a concentrated targeting strategy, each aiming at different single market segments.

The strategy can also prevent a firm from targeting other segments that might be successful, because when a firm penetrates one segment, its popularity may keep it from extending its marketing efforts into other segments.

## 6-3c Differentiated Targeting Strategy through Market Segmentation

With a **differentiated targeting strategy**, an organization directs its marketing efforts at two or more segments by developing a marketing mix for each segment (See Figure 6.2). After a firm uses a concentrated targeting strategy successfully in one market segment, it may expand its efforts to include additional segments. Enterprise Rent-A-Car is piloting Harley Davidson motorcycle rentals in Las Vegas to satisfy a demand for rental motorcycles among a more thrill-seeking segment of the tourist market. After conducting market research, Enterprise learned that motorcycle riders frequently wish they had more options to ride even when away from home and that they are not satisfied with renting a car. The company anticipates strong demand, especially from foreign tourists who want to visit nearby Southwest attractions like the Grand Canyon. If successful, the company will expand the availability to additional markets in the region.[2]

A benefit of a differentiated approach is that a firm may increase sales within the total market because its marketing mixes are aimed at more customers. For this reason, a company with excess production capacity may find a differentiated strategy advantageous because the sale of products to additional segments can help to absorb excess capacity. On the other hand, a differentiated strategy often demands more production processes, materials, and people because the different ingredients in each marketing mix will vary. Thus, production costs for a differentiated strategy may be higher than with a concentrated strategy.

**differentiated targeting strategy** A strategy in which an organization targets two or more segments by developing a marketing mix for each segment

# 6-4 STEP 2: DETERMINE WHICH SEGMENTATION VARIABLES TO USE

**Segmentation variables** are the characteristics of individuals, groups, or organizations used to divide a market into segments. Location, age, gender, and rate of product usage can all be bases for segmenting markets. Marketers may use several variables in combination when segmenting a market. For example, Cheerwine is a type of soda manufactured in North Carolina and distributed in the southern and mid-Atlantic states. It is targeted at soda drinkers in its distribution area and at young people through heavy use of online and social media for advertising and promotional efforts. Because of its limited availability, the soda has maintained a desirability among fans of cool, regional products.[3]

To select a segmentation variable, markets consider several factors. The segmentation variable should relate to customers' needs for, uses of, or behavior toward the product. It is likely a television marketer will segment television viewers for primetime television by income and age but not by religion, for example, because television viewing does not vary much because of religion. Marketers must select measurable segmentation variables, such as age, location, or gender, if individuals or organizations in a total market are to be classified accurately.

There is no best way to segment markets, and the approach will vary depending on a number of factors. A company's resources and capabilities affect the number and size of segment variables used. The type of product and degree of variation in customers' needs also dictate the number and size of segments targeted. No matter what approach is used, choosing one or more segmentation variables is a critical step in effectively targeting a market. Selecting an inappropriate variable limits the chances of developing a successful marketing strategy. To help you better understand potential segmentation variables, we next examine the differences between the major variables used to segment consumer and business markets.

## 6-4a Variables for Segmenting Consumer Markets

A marketer that is using segmentation to reach a consumer market can choose one or several variables. As Figure 6.3 shows, segmentation variables can be grouped into four major categories: demographic, geographic, psychographic, and behavioristic.

**segmentation variables**
Characteristics of individuals, groups, or organizations used to divide a market into segments

Figure 6.3    **Segmentation Variables for Consumer Markets**

**Demographic variables**
- Age
- Gender
- Race
- Ethnicity
- Income
- Education
- Occupation
- Family size
- Family life cycle
- Religion
- Social class

**Geographic variables**
- Region
- Urban, suburban, rural
- City size
- County size
- State size
- Market density
- Climate
- Terrain

**Psychographic variables**
- Personality attributes
- Motives
- Lifestyles

**Behavioristic variables**
- Volume usage
- End use
- Benefit expectations
- Brand loyalty
- Price sensitivity

## Demographic Variables

Demographers study aggregate population characteristics such as the distribution of age and gender, fertility rates, migration patterns, and mortality rates. Demographic characteristics that marketers commonly use include age, gender, race, ethnicity, income, education, occupation, family size, family life cycle, religion, and social class. Marketers segment markets by demographic characteristics because they are often closely linked to customers' needs and purchasing behaviors and can be readily measured.

Age is a common variable for segmentation purposes. A trip to the shopping mall highlights the fact that many retailers, including Zara, Forever 21, and American Eagle Outfitters, target teens and very young adults. If considering segmenting by age, marketers need to be aware of age distribution, how that distribution is changing, and how it will affect the demand for different types of products. The proportion of consumers under age 55 is expected to continue to decrease over time as Baby Boomers (born between 1946 and 1964) age. In 1970, the median age of a U.S. citizen was 27.9. It is currently 37.3.[4] Because of the increasing average age of Americans, many marketers are searching for ways to market their products to older adults. As Figure 6.4 shows, Americans in different age groups have different product needs because of their different lifestyles and health situations. Citizens age 65 and older, for instance, spend the most on health care, while those under age 35 spend the most on entertainment and transportation.

Figure 6.4   **Spending Levels by Age Groups for Selected Product Categories**

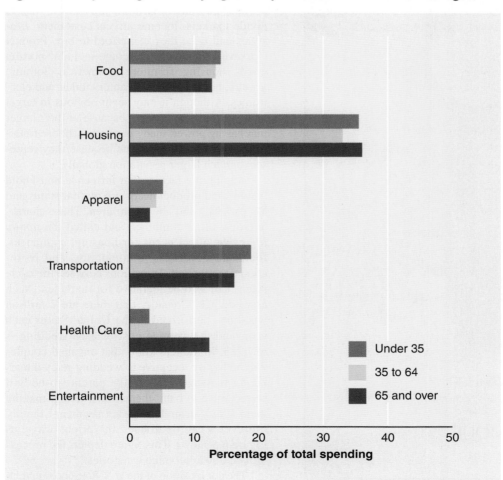

Source: Derived from Ann C. Foster, "Consumer Expenditures by Age," Beyond the Numbers (U.S. Department of Labor, Bureau of Labor Statistics), December 2015, Table 2, http://www.bls.gov/opub/btn/volume-4/consumer-expenditures-vary-by-age.htm (accessed February 4, 2016).

Gender is another demographic variable that is commonly used to segment markets, including clothing, soft drinks, nonprescription medications, magazines, some food items, and personal care products. The U.S. Census Bureau reports that females account for 50.8 percent, and males for 49.2 percent, of the total U.S. population.[5] Although they represent only slightly more than half of the population, women disproportionately influence buying decisions. It is estimated that women account for 85 percent of all consumer purchases, causing many marketers to consider female customers when making marketing decisions.[6] Consider the advertisement for Clinique. Because marketers know that women do the majority of household shopping and do more housework than men, this ad is clearly targeted at females. The ad depicts the Clinique Sonic Cleansing brush and touts that the device can promote clear, fresh, and glowing skin. The colors of the ad are predominantly bright pink, yellow, and orange—all very feminine colors. Even the background in the ad contains modern floral motifs that suggest the spinning brush head.

Marketers also use race and ethnicity as variables for segmenting markets for such products as food, music, clothing, cosmetics, banking, and insurance. Cosmetics, for example, is an industry where it is important to match the shade of the products with the skin colors of the target market to maintain customer satisfaction and loyalty. Iman Cosmetics is a line created by the Ethiopian supermodel Iman, with deeper colors designed to flatter the skin tones of women of color, be they Black, Hispanic, or Asian. These products are not made for, nor marketed to, light-skinned women.[7]

Because income strongly influences people's product purchases, it often provides a way to divide markets. Income affects customers' lifestyles and what they can afford to buy. Product markets segmented by income include sporting goods, housing, furniture, cosmetics, clothing, jewelry, home appliances, automobiles, and electronics. Although it may seem obvious to target higher-income consumers because of their larger purchasing power, many marketers choose to target lower-income segments because they represent a much larger population globally.

Among the factors that influence household income and product needs are marital status and the presence and age of children. These characteristics, often combined and called the *family life cycle*, affect needs for housing, appliances, food and beverages, automobiles, and recreational equipment. Transitions between life cycle stages can also be lucrative for marketers, such as weddings. Consider that there are 2 million weddings performed in the United States each year, and the average cost of each wedding is $31,213. Marketers know that engaged couples will be highly receptive to wedding-related marketing messages, much like parents-to-be will be receptive to baby-themed marketing, making them a very desirable market segment.[8] Family life cycles can be divided in various ways, as Figure 6.5 shows. This figure depicts the process broken down into nine categories.

The composition of the U.S. household in relation to the family life cycle has changed considerably over the last several decades. Single-parent

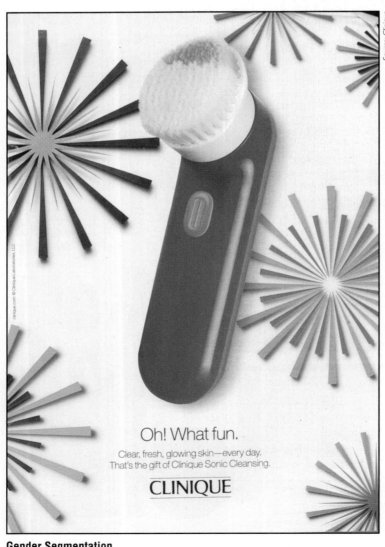

**Gender Segmentation**
Clinique targets its marketing efforts at women for this product.

Figure 6.5 **Family Life Cycle Stages as a Percentage of All Households**

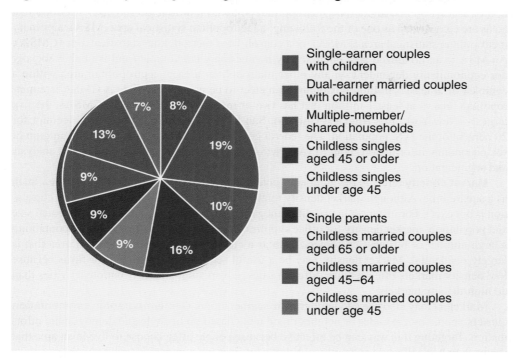

families are on the rise, meaning that the "typical" family no longer necessarily consists of a married couple with children. In fact, husband-and-wife households only account for 48.4 percent of all households in the United States, whereas they used to account for a majority of living arrangements. An estimated 26.7 percent of Americans live alone. Recently, previously small groups have risen in prominence, prompting an interest from marketers. Unmarried households represent 6.6 percent of the total, an increase of 41 percent since 2000. Same-sex partners represent 0.6 percent of households, which is a small proportion of the total population of households, but an increase of more than 81 percent since 2000.[9] People live in many different situations, all of which have different requirements for goods and services. Tracking demographic shifts such as these helps marketers be informed and prepared to satisfy the needs of target markets through new marketing mixes that address their changing lifestyles.

## Geographic Variables

Geographic variables—climate, terrain, city size, population density, and urban/rural areas—also influence consumer product needs. Markets may be divided using geographic variables because differences in location, climate, and terrain will influence consumers' needs. Consumers in the South, for instance, rarely have a need for snow tires. A company that sells products to a national market might divide the United States into Pacific, Southwest, Central, Midwest, Southeast, Middle Atlantic, and New England regions. A firm that is operating in one or several states might regionalize its market by counties, cities, zip code areas, or other units.

City size can be an important segmentation variable. Many firms choose to limit marketing efforts on cities above a certain size because small populations have been calculated to generate inadequate profits. Other firms actively seek opportunities in smaller towns. A classic example is Walmart, which initially was located only in small towns and even today can be found in towns where other large retailers stay away. If a marketer chooses to divide by a geographic variable, such as by city size, the U.S. Census Bureau provides reporting on population and demographics that can be of considerable assistance to marketers.

Because cities often cut across political boundaries, the U.S. Census Bureau developed a system to classify metropolitan areas (any area with a city or urbanized area with a population of at least 50,000 and a total metropolitan population of at least 100,000). Metropolitan areas are categorized as one of the following: a metropolitan statistical area (MSA), a primary metropolitan statistical area (PMSA), or a consolidated metropolitan statistical area (CMSA). An MSA is an urbanized area encircled by nonmetropolitan counties and is neither socially nor economically dependent on any other metropolitan area. A metropolitan area within a complex of at least 1 million inhabitants can elect to be named a PMSA. A CMSA is a metropolitan area of at least 1 million that has two or more PMSAs. Of the 20 CMSAs, the five largest—New York, Los Angeles, Chicago, San Francisco, and Philadelphia—account for 20 percent of the U.S. population. The federal government provides a considerable amount of socioeconomic information about MSAs, PMSAs, and CMSAs that can aid in market analysis and segmentation.

**market density** The number of potential customers within a unit of land area

**geodemographic segmentation** An approach to market segmentation that clusters people by zip codes or neighborhood units based on lifestyle and demographic information

**micromarketing** An approach to market segmentation in which organizations focus precise marketing efforts on very small geographic markets

**Market density** refers to the number of potential customers within a unit of land area, such as a square mile. Although market density relates generally to population density, the correlation is not exact. For instance, in two different geographic markets of approximately equal size and population, market density for office supplies would be much higher in an area containing a large number of business customers, such as a city downtown, than in another area that is largely residential. Market density may be a useful segmentation variable for firms because low-density markets often require different sales, advertising, and distribution activities than do high-density markets.

Marketers may also use geodemographic segmentation. **Geodemographic segmentation** clusters people by zip codes or neighborhood units based on lifestyle and demographic information. Targeting this way can be effective because people often choose to live in an area that shares their basic lifestyle and political beliefs. Information companies such as Nielsen provide geodemographic data services and products. PRIZM, for example, classifies zip code areas into 66 different cluster types, based on demographic information of residents.[10]

Geodemographic segmentation allows marketers to engage in micromarketing. **Micromarketing** involves focusing precise marketing efforts on very small geographic markets, such as community and even individual neighborhoods. Providers of financial and health-care services, retailers, and consumer product companies use micro marketing. Many retailers use

# MARKETING DEBATE

## Facial Recognition and Privacy

### ISSUE: Should facial recognition be used for marketing?

Facial recognition is an increasingly familiar technology. Facebook uses it to suggest names when users want to tag faces in the photos they post. On Disney cruises, facial-recognition software allows ship photographers to group images according to families traveling together, so passengers can easily preview and buy the photos of their choice. The coffee company Douwe Egberts recently tested facial recognition in an airport promotion, looking for people who were yawning as they walked by the coffee machine—and dispensing a free cup to yawners. Some hotels have tested the technology for alerting employees when VIP guests are approaching so they can be greeted by name.

Despite the potential for convenience and personalization, privacy advocates worry that facial-recognition data can be gathered, used, and shared without consumers' knowledge or consent. "What's unique about face recognition is the fact that you can do it surreptitiously, from a distance, and continually," observes a pioneer in this technology. Consumers are understandably wary. In one study, 75 percent of those responding said they would not shop in a store that uses facial recognition for marketing. Only a handful of states are currently looking at requiring companies to obtain the consumer's permission before using facial recognition, as a way to safeguard individual privacy and anonymity. So should marketers be using facial-recognition technology?[b]

micromarketing to determine the merchandise mix for individual stores. Increasingly, firms can engage in micromarketing in online retailing, given the Internet's ability to target precise interest groups. Unlike traditional micromarketing, online micromarketing is not limited by geography. The wealth of consumer information available online allows marketers to appeal efficiently and effectively to very specific consumer niches.

Climate is commonly used as a geographic segmentation variable because of its broad impact on people's behavior and product needs. Product markets affected by climate include air-conditioning and heating equipment, fireplace accessories, clothing, gardening equipment, recreational products, and building materials.

## Psychographic Variables

Marketers sometimes use psychographic variables, such as personality characteristics, motives, and lifestyles, to segment markets. A psychographic variable can be used by itself or in combination with other types of segmentation variables.

Personality characteristics can be a useful means of segmentation when a product resembles many competing products and consumers' needs are not significantly related to other segmentation variables. However, segmenting a market according to personality traits can be risky. Although marketing practitioners have long believed consumer choice and product use vary with personality, marketing research has generally indicated only a weak relationship. It is difficult to measure personality traits accurately, especially because most personality tests were developed for clinical use, not for segmentation purposes.

When appealing to a personality characteristic, a marketer almost always selects one that many people view positively. Individuals with this characteristic, as well as those who aspire to have it, may be influenced to buy that marketer's brand. Marketers taking this approach do not worry about measuring how many people have the positively valued characteristic. They assume a sizable proportion of people in the target market either have it or aspire to have it.

When motives are used to segment a market, the market is divided according to consumers' reasons for making a purchase. Personal appearance, affiliation, status, safety, and health are examples of motives affecting the types of products purchased and the choice of stores in which they are bought. Marketing efforts based on particular motives can be a point of competitive advantage for a firm. Look at the advertisement for Vicks ZzzQuil, a night-time sleep aid, which targets consumers who are motivated by their desire for a good night's sleep. The ad emphasizes the fact that ZzzQuil is made by the same firm that produces NyQuil, a cold-care product often used as a sleep aid, to convey the product's ability to help users fall asleep easily, sleep soundly, and wake refreshed. The picture of a soundly sleeping man dressed in the ZzzQuil brand's purple color further reinforces the idea of a good night's sleep, which should appeal to those who haven't been sleeping well.

Lifestyle segmentation groups individuals according to how they spend their time, the importance of things in their surroundings (homes or jobs, for example), beliefs about themselves and broad issues, and some demographic characteristics, such

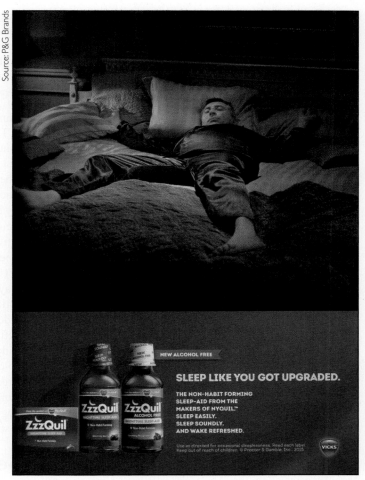

Source: P&G Brands

**Segmentation Based on Motives**
Consumers who buy ZzzQuil are motivated to get a better night's sleep.

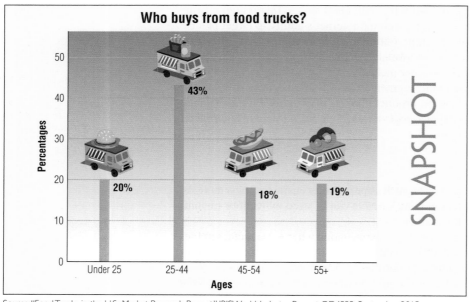

**Who buys from food trucks?**

SNAPSHOT

Source: "Food Trucks in the U.S.: Market Research Report," IBISWorld, Industry Report OD4322, September 2015, http://ibisworld.com (accessed December 15, 2015).

as income and education.[11] Lifestyle analysis provides a broad view of buyers because it encompasses numerous characteristics related to people's activities (e.g., work, hobbies, entertainment, sports), interests (e.g., family, home, fashion, food, technology), and opinions (e.g., politics, social issues, education, the future).

PRIZM, by Nielsen, is commonly used by marketers to segment by demographic variables. It can also be used to segment by lifestyles. PRIZM combines demographics, consumer behavior, and geographic data to help marketers identify, understand, and reach their customers and prospects, resulting in a highly robust tool for marketers.[12] PRIZM divides U.S. households into demographically and behaviorally distinct segments that take into account such factors as likes, dislikes, lifestyles, and purchase behaviors. Used by thousands of marketers, including many within Fortune 500 companies, PRIZM provides marketers with a common tool for understanding and reaching customers in a highly diverse and complex marketplace.

## Behavioristic Variables

Firms can divide a market according to consumer behavior toward a product, which commonly involves an aspect of product use. Therefore, a market may be separated into users—classified as heavy, moderate, or light—and nonusers. To satisfy a specific group, such as heavy users, marketers may create a distinctive product and price or initiate special promotion and distribution activities. Per capita consumption data help determine different levels of usage by product category. To satisfy customers who use a product in a certain way, some feature—packaging, size, texture, or color—may be designed precisely to make the product easier to use, safer, or more convenient.

**Benefit segmentation** is the division of a market according to benefits that consumers want from the product. Although most types of market segmentation assume a relationship between the variable and customers' needs, benefit segmentation differs in that the benefits customers seek *are* their product needs. Consider that a customer who purchases over-the-counter cold relief medication may be specifically interested in two benefits: stopping a runny nose and relieving chest congestion. Thus, individuals are segmented directly according to their needs. By determining the desired benefits, marketers can divide people into groups by the benefits they seek. The effectiveness of such segmentation depends on three conditions: (1) the benefits sought must be identifiable, (2) using these benefits, marketers must be able to divide people into recognizable segments, and (3) one or more of the resulting segments must be accessible to the firm's marketing efforts.

Marketers can segment consumer markets using many characteristics. They do not, however, use the same variables to segment business characteristics. We will learn about business market segmentation in the next section.

## 6-4b Variables for Segmenting Business Markets

Like consumer markets, business markets are frequently segmented for marketing purposes. Marketers segment business markets according to geographic location, type of organization, customer size, and product use.

**benefit segmentation** The division of a market according to benefits that consumers want from the product

## Geographic Location

Earlier we noted that the demand for some consumer products can vary considerably among geographic areas because of differences in climate, terrain, or regional customer preferences. Demand for business products also varies according to geographic location. For instance, producers of lumber may divide their markets geographically because customers' needs vary by region. Geographic segmentation may be especially appropriate for producers seeking to reach industries concentrated in certain locations, such as furniture and textile producers concentrated in the Southeast.

## Type of Organization

A company sometimes segments a market by types of organizations within that market because they often require different product features, distribution systems, price structures, and selling strategies. Given these variations, a firm may either concentrate on a single segment with one marketing mix (a concentration targeting strategy) or focus on several groups with multiple mixes (a differentiated targeting strategy). A carpet producer could segment potential customers into several groups, such as automobile makers, commercial carpet contractors (firms that carpet large office buildings), apartment complex developers, carpet wholesalers, and large retail carpet outlets.

## Customer Size

An organization's size may affect its purchasing procedures and the types and quantities of products it wants. Size can thus be an effective variable for segmenting a business market. To reach a segment of a particular size, marketers may have to adjust one or more marketing mix ingredients. For instance, marketers may want to offer customers who buy in large quantities a discount as a purchase incentive. Personal selling is common and expected in business markets, where a higher level of customer service may be required—larger customers may require a higher level of customer service because of the size and complexity of their orders. Because the needs of large and small buyers tend to be distinct, marketers frequently use different marketing practices to reach target customer groups. Examine the advertisement for the Capital One Spark Business credit card, for example. Credit cards are a product that can be used for a variety of purposes and targeted at many different markets. In this ad, Capital One is targeting its Spark Business credit card at small businesses. The ad depicts a woman working in a small industrial setting pondering some detail. The ad informs small business owners that they can get cash back for purchases they make on the Spark card, something every small business owner could use. The ad also refers small business owners to a webpage for additional information relevant to their needs.

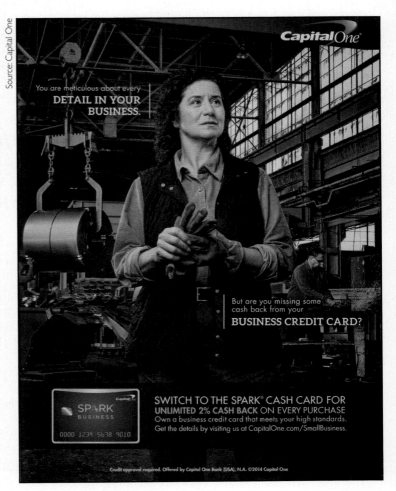

**Segmenting Business Markets**
Capital One markets credit cards that can be used for a variety of purposes and targeted at different business markets. The Spark Business card is targeted at small businesses and earns cardholders cash back on every purchase.

## Product Use

Certain products, particularly raw materials like steel, petroleum, plastics, and lumber, can be used in numerous ways in the production of goods. These variations will affect the types and amounts of products purchased, as well as the purchasing method. An industrial paint manufacturer, for example, might target different paint products at construction companies for painting bridges and at automakers for painting vehicles.

## 6-5 STEP 3: DEVELOP MARKET SEGMENT PROFILES

A market segment profile describes the similarities among potential customers within a segment and explains the differences among people and organizations in different segments. A profile may cover aspects such as demographic characteristics, geographic factors, product benefits sought, lifestyles, brand preferences, and usage rates. Individuals and organizations within segments should be relatively similar with respect to several characteristics and product needs and differ considerably from those within other market segments. Marketers use market segment profiles to assess the degree to which their products fit potential customers' product needs. Market segment profiles help marketers understand how a business can use its capabilities to serve potential customer groups.

Market segment profiles help a marketer determine which segment or segments are most attractive relative to the firm's strengths, weaknesses, objectives, and resources. Although marketers may initially believe certain segments are attractive, a market segment profile may unveil new information that makes a segment less attractive than previously thought. Market segment profiles can be useful in helping a firm make marketing decisions relating to a specific market segment or segments.

## 6-6 STEP 4: EVALUATE RELEVANT MARKET SEGMENTS

After analyzing the market segment profiles, a marketer should be able to narrow his or her focus to several promising segments that warrant further analysis. Marketers should examine sales estimates, competition, and estimated costs associated with each of these segments.

### 6-6a  Sales Estimates

Potential sales for a market segment can be measured along several dimensions, including product level, geographic area, time, and level of competition.[13] With respect to product level, potential sales can be estimated for a specific product item (e.g., Diet Coke) or an entire product line (e.g., Coca-Cola Classic, Diet Coke, and Coke Zero comprise goods in a product line). A manager must also determine the geographic area to include in the estimate. In relation to time, sales estimates can be short range (one year or less), medium range (one to five years), or long range (longer than five years). The competitive level specifies whether sales are being estimated for a single firm or for an entire industry.

**market potential** The total amount of a product that customers will purchase within a specified period at a specific level of industry-wide marketing activity

**Market potential** is the total amount of a product that customers will purchase within a specified period at a specific level of industry-wide marketing activity. Market potential can be stated in terms of dollars or units. A segment's market potential is affected by economic, sociocultural, and other environmental forces. The specific level of marketing effort will vary from one firm to another, and each firm's marketing activities together add up to the industry-wide marketing effort total. A marketing manager must also estimate whether and to what extent industry marketing efforts will change over time.

**company sales potential** The maximum percentage of market potential that an individual firm within an industry can expect to obtain for a specific product

**Company sales potential** is the maximum percentage share of a market that an individual firm within an industry can expect to capture for a specific product. Several factors influence company sales potential for a market segment. First, the market potential places absolute limits on the size of the company's sales potential—a firm cannot exceed the market potential. Second, the magnitude of industry-wide marketing activities has an indirect but definite impact on the company's sales potential. When Domino's Pizza advertises home-delivered pizza, for instance, it indirectly promotes pizza in general. Maybe you see the ad and it sparks a craving for pizza, but you call the Pizza Hut down the street because it is more familiar to you. Third, the intensity and effectiveness of a company's marketing activities relative to competitors' activities affect the size of the company's sales potential. If a company spends twice as much as any of its competitors on marketing efforts, and if each dollar spent is more effective in generating sales, the firm's sales potential will be high relative to competitors' sales potential.

Two general approaches that measure company sales potential are breakdown and buildup. In the **breakdown approach**, the marketing manager first develops a general economic forecast for a specific time period. Next, the manager estimates market potential based on this forecast. The manager derives the company's sales potential from the forecast and an estimate of market potential. In the **buildup approach**, the marketing manager begins by estimating how much of a product a potential buyer in a specific geographic area, such as a sales territory, will purchase in a given period. The manager then multiplies that amount by the total number of potential buyers in that area. The manager performs the same calculation for each geographic area in which the firm sells products and then adds the totals for each area to calculate market potential. To determine company sales potential, the manager must estimate, based on planned levels of company marketing activities, the proportion of the total market potential the company can reasonably attain.

**breakdown approach**
Measuring company sales potential based on a general economic forecast for a specific period and the market potential derived from it

**buildup approach** Measuring company sales potential by estimating how much of a product a potential buyer in a specific geographic area will purchase in a given period, multiplying the estimate by the number of potential buyers, and adding the totals of all the geographic areas considered

## 6-6b **Competitive Assessment**

Besides obtaining sales estimates, it is crucial to assess competitors that are already operating in the segments being considered. A market segment that initially seems attractive based on sales estimates may turn out to be much less so after a competitive assessment. Such an assessment should ask several questions about competitors: How many exist? What are their strengths and weaknesses? Do several competitors already have major market shares and together dominate the segment? Can our company create a marketing mix to compete effectively against competitors' marketing mixes? Is it likely that new competitors will enter this segment? If so, how will they affect our firm's ability to compete successfully? Answers to such questions are important for proper assessment of the competition in potential market segments.

The market for hot sauces, for instance, has many competitors. Cholula, featured in the advertisement, competes against these other brands by highlighting how its products are unique. The ad underscores this distinctiveness by informing the reader that Cholula uses a recipe handed down through the generations as well as unique peppers and spices. The eye-catching bottle with the traditional label reinforces the idea that Cholula is an authentic and unique sauce. The ad also refers interested consumers to its website where there is more information about each flavor and its uses.

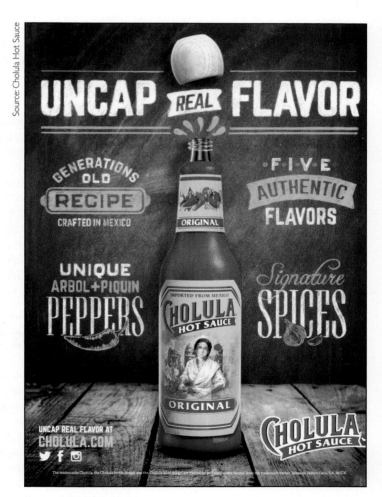

Source: Cholula Hot Sauce

**Competitive Assessment**
Marketers conducted an assessment and determined that Cholula hot sauce can maintain an advantage in a market filled with competing brands by offering an authentic sauce with unique peppers and spices.

### 6-6c  Cost Estimates

To fulfill the needs of a target segment, an organization must develop and maintain a marketing mix that precisely meets the wants and needs of that segment, which can be expensive. Distinctive product features, attractive package design, generous product warranties, extensive advertising, attractive promotional offers, competitive prices, and high-quality personal service use considerable organizational resources. In some cases, marketers may conclude that the costs to reach some segments are so high that they are essentially inaccessible. Marketers also must consider whether the organization can reach a segment at costs equal to or below competitors' costs. If the firm's costs are likely to be higher, it will be unable to compete in that segment in the long run.

## 6-7 STEP 5: SELECT SPECIFIC TARGET MARKETS

An important initial consideration in selecting a target market is whether customers' needs differ enough to warrant the use of market segmentation. If segmentation analysis shows customer needs to be homogeneous, the firm's management may decide to use the undifferentiated approach, discussed earlier. However, if customer needs are heterogeneous, which is more likely, marketers must select one or more target markets.

Assuming one or more segments offer significant opportunities to achieve organizational objectives, a marketer must decide which offers the most potential at reasonable costs. Ordinarily, information gathered in the previous step—concerning sales estimates, competitors, and cost estimates—requires careful review in this final step to determining long-term marketing opportunities. At this time, the firm's management must investigate whether the organization has sufficient financial resources, managerial skills, employee expertise, and facilities to compete effectively in selected segments. The firm must also consider the possibility that the requirements of some market segments are at odds with the firm's overall objectives, and that possible legal problems, conflicts with interest groups, and technological advancements will render certain segments unattractive. Finally, marketers must consider long-term versus short-term growth. If long-term prospects look poor, a marketer may ultimately choose not to target a segment because it would be difficult to recoup expenses.

Selecting appropriate target markets is important to an organization's effective adoption and use of the marketing concept philosophy. Identifying the right target market is the key to implementing a successful marketing strategy. Failure to do so can lead to low sales, high costs, and severe financial losses. A careful target market analysis places an organization in a strong position to serve customers' needs and achieve its objectives.

## 6-8 DEVELOPING SALES FORECASTS

After a company selects a target market or markets, it must develop a **sales forecast**—the amount of a product the company expects to sell during a specific period at a specified level of marketing activity. The sales forecast differs from the company sales potential in that it concentrates on what actual sales will be at a certain level of company marketing effort. The company sales potential assesses what sales are possible at various levels of marketing activities, assuming certain environmental conditions exist. Businesses use the sales forecast for planning, organizing, implementing, and controlling activities. The success of numerous activities depends on this forecast's accuracy. Common problems in failing companies are improper planning and lack of realistic sales forecasts. Overly ambitious sales forecasts can lead to overbuying, overinvestment, and higher costs that weaken a firm's strength and position.

To forecast sales, a marketer can choose from a number of forecasting methods, some arbitrary and quick and others more scientific, complex, and time-consuming. A firm's choice of

**sales forecast** The amount of a product a company expects to sell during a specific period at a specified level of marketing activities method or methods depends on the costs involved, type of product, market characteristics, time span and purpose of the forecast, stability of the historical sales data, availability of required information, managerial preferences, and forecasters' expertise and experience.[14] Common forecasting techniques fall into five categories: executive judgment, surveys, time series analysis, regression analysis, and market tests.

## 6-8a  Executive Judgment

**Executive judgment** is the intuition of one or more executives. This is an unscientific but expedient and inexpensive approach to sales forecasting. It is not a very accurate method, but executive judgment may work reasonably well when product demand is relatively stable and the forecaster has years of market-related experience. However, because intuition is heavily influenced by recent experience, the forecast may weight recent sales booms or slumps excessively. Another drawback to executive judgment is that the forecaster has only past experience as a guide for deciding where to go in the future.

## 6-8b  Surveys

Another way to forecast sales is to question customers, sales personnel, or experts regarding their expectations about future purchases. In a **customer forecasting survey**, marketers ask customers what types and quantities of products they intend to buy during a specific period. This approach may be useful to a business with relatively few customers. Consider Lockheed Martin, the U.S. government's largest contractor. Because most of its contracts come from the same customer, the government, Lockheed Martin could conduct customer forecasting surveys effectively. PepsiCo, by contrast, has millions of customers and could not feasibly use a customer survey to forecast future sales.

In a **sales force forecasting survey**, the firm's salespeople estimate anticipated sales in their territories for a specified period. The forecaster combines these territorial estimates to arrive at a tentative forecast. A marketer may survey the sales staff for several reasons, the most important being that the sales staff is the company personnel closest to customers on a daily basis. They, therefore, have first-hand knowledge about customers' product needs. Moreover, when sales representatives assist in developing the forecast, they are invested in the process and are more likely to work toward its achievement. Forecasts can be prepared for single territories, divisions consisting of several territories, regions made up of multiple divisions, and the total geographic market.

When a company wants an **expert forecasting survey**, it hires professionals to help prepare the sales forecast. These experts are usually economists, management consultants, advertising executives, college professors, or other individuals outside the firm with experience in a specific market. Drawing on this experience and their analyses of available information about the company and the market, experts prepare and present forecasts or answer questions. Using experts is a quick way to get information and is relatively inexpensive. However, because they work outside the firm, these forecasters may be less motivated than company personnel to do an effective job.

A more complex form of the expert forecasting survey incorporates the Delphi technique. In the **Delphi technique**, experts create initial forecasts, submit them to the company for averaging, and have the results returned to them so they can make individual refined forecasts. When making calculations using the Delphi technique, experts use the averaged results to eradicate outliers and to refine predictions. The procedure can be repeated several times until the experts, each working separately, reach a consensus. Because this technique gets rid of extreme data, the ultimate goal in using the Delphi technique is to develop a highly reliable sales forecast.

## 6-8c  Time Series Analysis

With **time series analysis**, the forecaster uses the firm's historical sales data to discover a pattern or patterns in sales over time. If a pattern is found, it can be used to forecast sales. This forecasting method assumes that past sales patterns will continue into the future. The accuracy, and thus usefulness, of time series analysis hinges on the validity of this assumption.

**executive judgment** A sales forecasting method based on the intuition of one or more executives

**customer forecasting survey** A survey of customers regarding the types and quantities of products they intend to buy during a specific period

**sales force forecasting survey** A survey of a firm's sales force regarding anticipated sales in their territories for a specified period

**expert forecasting survey** Sales forecasts prepared by experts outside the firm, such as economists, management consultants, advertising executives, or college professors

**Delphi technique** A procedure in which experts create initial forecasts, submit them to the company for averaging, and then refine the forecasts

**time series analysis** A forecasting method that uses historical sales data to discover patterns in the firm's sales over time and generally involves trend, cycle, seasonal, and random factor analyses

In a time series analysis, a forecaster usually performs four types of analyses: trend, cycle, seasonal, and random factor. **Trend analysis** focuses on aggregate sales data, such as the company's annual sales figures, covering a period of many years to determine whether annual sales are generally rising, falling, or staying about the same. Through **cycle analysis**, a forecaster analyzes sales figures (often monthly sales data) for a three- to five-year period to ascertain whether sales fluctuate in a consistent, periodic manner. When performing a **seasonal analysis**, the analyst studies daily, weekly, or monthly sales figures to evaluate the degree to which seasonal factors, such as climate and holiday activities, influence sales. In a **random factor analysis**, the forecaster attempts to attribute erratic sales variations to random, nonrecurring events, such as a regional power failure, a natural disaster, or political unrest in a foreign market. After performing each of these analyses, the forecaster combines the results to develop the sales forecast. Time series analysis is an effective forecasting method for products with reasonably stable demand, but not for products with erratic demand.

### 6-8d Regression Analysis

Like time series analysis, regression analysis requires the use of historical sales data. In **regression analysis**, the forecaster seeks to find a relationship between past sales (the dependent variable) and one or more independent variables, such as population, per capita income, or gross domestic product. Simple regression analysis uses one independent variable, whereas multiple regression analysis includes two or more independent variables. The objective of regression analysis is to develop a mathematical formula that accurately describes a relationship between the firm's sales and one or more variables. However, the formula indicates only an association, not a causal relationship. Once an accurate formula is established, the analyst plugs the necessary information into the formula to derive the sales forecast.

Regression analysis is useful when a precise association can be established. However, a forecaster seldom finds a perfect correlation. Furthermore, this method can be used only when available historical sales data are extensive. Thus, regression analysis is futile for forecasting sales of new products.

### 6-8e Market Tests

A **market test** involves making a product available to buyers in one or more test areas and measuring purchases and consumer responses to the product, distribution, promotion, and price. Test areas are often midsized cities with populations of 200,000 to 500,000, but they can be towns or small cities with populations of 50,000 to 200,000. Test areas are chosen for their representativeness of a firm's target markets.

A market test provides information about consumers' actual, rather than intended, purchases. In addition, purchase volume can be evaluated in relation to the intensity of other marketing activities such as advertising, in-store promotions, pricing, packaging, and distribution. Forecasters base their sales estimates for larger geographic units on customer response in test areas. McDonald's is partnering with Monster Beverage to test-market Monster Energy drinks at select McDonald's restaurants. The high-caffeine drinks are available for an extra $1.50 with value meals at those outlets. McDonald's will use data from the market tests in Michigan, Ohio, Georgia, Florida, and Illinois to determine whether to offer Monster Energy drinks at all McDonald's restaurants. The decision to test-market energy drinks was a result of actively collecting customer feedback and conducting product tests in McDonald's outlets.[15]

Because it does not require historical sales data, a market test is effective for forecasting sales of new products or of existing products in new geographic areas. A market test also gives a marketer an opportunity to test the success of various elements of the marketing mix. However, these tests are often time-consuming and expensive. In addition, a marketer cannot be certain that consumer response during a market test represents the total market response or that such a response will continue in the future.

**trend analysis** An analysis that focuses on aggregate sales data over a period of many years to determine general trends in annual sales

**cycle analysis** An analysis of sales figures for a 3- to 5-year period to ascertain whether sales fluctuate in a consistent, periodic manner

**seasonal analysis** An analysis of daily, weekly, or monthly sales figures to evaluate the degree to which seasonal factors influence sales

**random factor analysis** An analysis attempting to attribute erratic sales variations to random, nonrecurrent events

**regression analysis** A method of predicting sales based on finding a relationship between past sales and one or more independent variables, such as population or income

**market test** Making a product available to buyers in one or more test areas and measuring purchases and consumer responses to marketing efforts

## 6-8f  Using Multiple Forecasting Methods

Although some businesses depend on a single sales forecasting method, most firms use several techniques. Sometimes a company is forced to use multiple methods when marketing diverse product lines, but even a single product line may require several forecasts, especially when the product is sold to different market segments. Thus, a producer of automobile tires may rely on one technique to forecast tire sales for new cars and on another to forecast sales of replacement tires. Variation in the length of forecasts may call for several forecasting methods as well. A firm that employs one method for a short-range forecast may find it inappropriate for long-range forecasting. Sometimes a marketer verifies results of one method by using one or more other methods and comparing outcomes.

# Summary

### 6-1  Explain what markets are and how they are generally classified.

A market is a group of people who, as individuals or as organizations, have needs for products in a product class and have the ability, willingness, and authority to purchase such products. Markets can be categorized as consumer markets or business markets, based on the characteristics of the individuals and groups that make up a specific market and the purposes for which they buy products. A consumer market, also known as a *business-to-consumer (B2C) market*, consists of purchasers and household members who intend to consume or benefit from the purchased products and do not buy products for the main purpose of making a profit. A business market, also known as *business-to-business (B2B), industrial*, or *organizational market*, consists of individuals or groups that purchase a specific kind of product for one of three purposes: resale, direct use in producing other products, or use in general daily operations.

### 6-2  Identify the five steps of the target market selection process.

In general, marketers employ a five-step process when selecting a target market. Step one is to identify the appropriate targeting strategy. Step two is determining which segmentation variables to use. Step three is to develop a market segment profile. Step four is evaluating relevant market segments. Finally, step five is selecting specific target markets. Not all marketers will follow all of these five steps in this order, but this process provides a good general guide.

### 6-3  Describe the differences among three targeting strategies.

Step one of the target market selection process is to identify the appropriate targeting strategy. When a company designs a single marketing mix and directs it at the entire market for a particular product, it is using an undifferentiated targeting strategy. The undifferentiated strategy is effective in a homogeneous market, whereas a heterogeneous market needs to be segmented through a concentrated targeting strategy or a differentiated targeting strategy. Both of these strategies divide markets into segments consisting of individuals, groups, or organizations that have one or more similar characteristics and can be linked to similar product needs. When using a concentrated strategy, an organization directs marketing efforts toward a single market segment through one marketing mix. With a differentiated targeting strategy, an organization directs customized marketing efforts at two or more segments.

Certain conditions must exist for market segmentation to be effective. First, customers' needs for the product should be heterogeneous. Second, the segments of the market should be identifiable and divisible. Third, the total market should be divided so segments can be compared with respect to estimated sales, costs, and profits. Fourth, at least one segment must have enough profit potential to justify developing and maintaining a special marketing mix for that segment. Fifth, the firm must be able to reach the chosen segment with a particular marketing mix.

### 6-4  Identify the major segmentation variables.

The second step is determining which segmentation variables to use, which are the characteristics of individuals, groups, or organizations used to divide a total market into segments. The segmentation variable should relate to customers' needs for, uses of, or behavior toward the product. Segmentation variables for consumer markets can be grouped into four categories: demographic (e.g., age, gender, income, ethnicity, family life cycle), geographic (e.g., population, market density, climate), psychographic (e.g., personality traits, motives, lifestyles), and behavioristic (e.g., volume usage, end use, expected benefits, brand loyalty, price sensitivity). Variables for segmenting business markets include geographic location, type of organization, customer size, and product use.

## 6-5    Explain what market segment profiles are and how they are used.

Step three in the target market selection process is to develop market segment profiles. Such profiles describe the similarities among potential customers within a segment and explain the differences among people and organizations in different market segments. They are used to assess the degree to which the firm's products can match potential customers' product needs. Segments, which may seem attractive at first, may be shown to be quite the opposite after a market segment profile is completed.

## 6-6    Explain how to evaluate market segments.

Step four is evaluating relevant market segments. Marketers analyze several important factors, such as sales estimates, competition, and estimated costs, associated with each segment. Potential sales for a market segment can be measured along several dimensions, including product level, geographic area, time, and level of competition. Besides obtaining sales estimates, it is crucial to assess competitors that are already operating in the segments being considered. Without competitive information, sales estimates may be misleading. The cost of developing a marketing mix that meets the wants and needs of individuals in that segment must also be considered. If the firm's costs to compete in that market are very high, it may be unable to compete in that segment in the long run.

## 6-7    Identify the factors that influence the selection of specific market segments for use as target markets.

The final step involves the actual selection of specific target markets. In this step, the company considers whether customers' needs differ enough to warrant segmentation and which segments to target. If customers' needs are heterogeneous, the decision of which segment to target must be made, or whether to enter the market at all. Considerations such as the firm's available resources, managerial skills, employee expertise, facilities, the firm's overall objectives, possible legal problems, conflicts with interest groups, and technological advancements must be considered when deciding which segments to target.

## 6-8    Discuss sales forecasting methods.

A sales forecast is the amount of a product the company actually expects to sell during a specific period at a specified level of marketing activities. To forecast sales, marketers can choose from a number of methods. The choice depends on various factors, including the costs involved, type of product, market characteristics, and time span and purposes of the forecast. There are five categories of forecasting techniques: executive judgment, surveys, time series analysis, regression analysis, and market tests. Executive judgment is based on the intuition of one or more executives. Surveys include customer, sales force, and expert forecasting. Time series analysis uses the firm's historical sales data to discover patterns in the firm's sales over time and employs four major types of analysis: trend, cycle, seasonal, and random factor. With regression analysis, forecasters attempt to find a relationship between past sales and one or more independent variables. Market testing involves making a product available to buyers in one or more test areas and measuring purchases and consumer responses to the product, distribution, promotion, and price. Many companies employ multiple forecasting methods.

---

**Go to www.cengagebrain.com for resources to help you master the content in this chapter as well as for materials that will expand your marketing knowledge!**

---

# Important Terms

consumer market  167
business market  167
undifferentiated targeting
    strategy  168
homogeneous market  168
heterogeneous market  168
market segmentation  168
market segment  168
concentrated targeting
    strategy  170
differentiated targeting
    strategy  171
segmentation variables  172

market density  176
geodemographic
    segmentation  176
micromarketing  176
benefit segmentation  178
market potential  180
company sales potential  180
breakdown approach  181
buildup approach  181
sales forecast  182
executive judgment  183
customer forecasting
    survey  183

sales force forecasting
    survey  183
expert forecasting
    survey  183
Delphi technique  183
time series analysis  183
trend analysis  184
cycle analysis  184
seasonal analysis  184
random factor analysis  184
regression analysis  184
market test  184

# Discussion and Review Questions

1. What is a market? What are the requirements for a market?
2. In your local area, identify a group of people with unsatisfied product needs who represent a market. Could this market be reached by a business organization? Why or why not?
3. Outline the five major steps in the target market selection process.
4. What is an undifferentiated strategy? Under what conditions is it most useful? Describe a present market situation in which a company is using an undifferentiated strategy. Is the business successful? Why or why not?
5. What is market segmentation? Describe the basic conditions required for effective segmentation. Identify several firms that use market segmentation.
6. List the differences between concentrated and differentiated strategies, and describe the advantages and disadvantages of each.
7. Identify and describe four major categories of variables that can be used to segment con-sumer markets. Give examples of product markets that are segmented by variables in each category.
8. What dimensions are used to segment business markets?
9. Define *geodemographic segmentation*. Identify several types of firms that might employ this type of market segmentation, and explain why.
10. What is a market segment profile? Why is it an important step in the target market selection process?
11. Describe the important factors that marketers should analyze to evaluate market segments.
12. Why is a marketer concerned about sales potential when trying to select a target market?
13. Why is selecting appropriate target markets important for an organization that wants to adopt the marketing concept philosophy?
14. What is a sales forecast? Why is it important?
15. What are the two primary types of surveys a company might use to forecast sales? Why would a company use an outside expert forecasting survey?
16. Under what conditions are market tests useful for sales forecasting? What are the ad-vantages and disadvantages of market tests?
17. Under what conditions might a firm use multiple forecasting methods?

# Video Case 6.1

## Family-Owned Ski Butternut Targets Family Skiers

Located in the picturesque Berkshire Mountains of Western Massachusetts, Ski Butternut has been a family-owned, family-oriented ski destination for more than 50 years. The resort includes 22 trails for downhill skiing and snowboarding, two terrain parks for riding, and a dedicated area for snow tubing. Although Ski Butternut hosts some non-ski events during summer and fall, its business goes into high gear when snowy weather arrives, bringing skiers and riders from across Massachusetts, Connecticut, New York, and New Jersey.

Matt Sawyer, Ski Butternut's director of marketing, says the primary target market has always been families with young children who are seeking affordable skiing. Everything from the snack-bar menus to the ski-shop merchandise is presented with families in mind. So that parents can have fun in the snow without worry, the resort has a Children's Center for children who are too young to ski or have no interest. Fifth-graders are invited to ski for free when accompanied by an adult who buys an adult lift ticket. The resort also created two terrain parks for young snowboarders who were clamoring for a more

exciting riding experience. Without the terrain parks, Sawyer says, these boarders would have asked their parents to take them to competing mountains in Vermont.

Ski Butternut's research shows that first-timers are a particularly important segment, because they tend to have a strong allegiance to the resort where they learn to ski. First-timers typically visit the resort seven times before seeking out more challenging mountains. As a result, Ski Butternut has made teaching first-timers to ski or snowboard one of its specialties. For this market, the resort bundles ski or board rentals, lift tickets, and also offers a wide range of individual and group lessons for all ages and abilities at a value price. Because Ski Butternut has trails for different skill levels, beginners can challenge themselves by changing trails within the resort once they feel confident.

Ski Butternut also targets seniors and college students. Knowing that weekends are the busiest period, the resort offers special midweek prices to attract seniors who have free time to ski on weekdays. College students are particularly value-conscious, and they often travel to ski resorts as a group. As a result, Ski Butternut offers weekend and holiday discounts to bring in large numbers of students who would otherwise ski elsewhere. Thanks to Facebook, Twitter, and other social media, students quickly spread the word about special pricing, which enhances Ski Butternut's ability to reach this key segment. In addition, the resort highlights discount pricing for families when targeting specific segments, such as scout troops, military personnel, emergency services personnel, and members of local ski clubs.

Another segment Ski Butternut has selected for marketing attention is ski racers. The resort features professional coaching, lessons, and programs for ski racers in the age group of 8 to 20. Sawyer notes that these ski racers are extremely dedicated to training, which means they're on the slopes as often as possible, a positive for the resort's attendance and revenue. To stay in touch with racers, Ski Butternut has a special website and a dedicated Facebook page.

Sawyer conducts up to 1,200 customer surveys every year to better understand who his customers are and what they need. He also compares the results with skiers who visit mountains of a similar size in other areas. Digging deeper, he analyzes data drawn from the ski shop's rental business to build a detailed picture of customers' demographics,

abilities, and preferences. Based on this research, he knows that the typical family at Ski Butternut consists of two children under age 18 who ski or ride, and at least one parent who skis.

Because they can obtain so much information from and about their customers, Sawyer and his team are able to make better decisions about the marketing mix for each segment. By better matching the media with the audience, they get a better response from advertising, e-mail messages, and other marketing communications. As one example, they found that 15 percent of the visitors to Ski Butternut's website were using a smartphone to access the site. Sawyer has now created a special version of the site specifically for mobile use and created a text-message contest to engage skiers who have smartphones.[16]

### Questions for Discussion

1. Of the four categories of variables, which one seems to be the most central to Ski Butternut's segmentation strategy, and why?
2. How is Ski Butternut applying behavioristic variables in its segmentation strategy? Explain your answer.
3. What role do geographic variables play in Ski Butternut's segmentation and targeting?

# Case 6.2

## Mattel Uses Market Segmentation to Stay on Top

In Mattel's toy chest, Barbie and Draculaura share space with Max Steel, Hot Wheels, American Girl, and Barney. The $6 billion company is the number-two toy maker in the world, trailing Lego and ahead of Hasbro. Mattel has enjoyed success with *Star Wars* toy cars, but it also lost the license to make Disney Princess dolls (now made by Hasbro). To regain momentum and combat competition, Mattel is applying savvy marketing based on careful targeting and segmentation.

For example, Mattel sees significant revenue potential in targeting boys between the ages of 6 and 11, a customer group that's fascinated with superheroes. Mattel's research indicates that boys in this segment like watching videos, reading graphic novels, and playing videogames featuring favorite superheroes. These boys also like discovering new things about their superheroes and figuring out why and how these characters fight their foes.

Mattel targeted this group when it planned a U.S. relaunch of the action figure Max Steel, a superhero toy it has successfully marketed in South America for more than a

decade. Max is a high school student who uses his superhero powers to save the world from monsters like Toxcon and Dredd. Months before the new toy appeared in U.S. stores, a Max Steel cartoon premiered on Disney cable channels and a Max Steel website began offering online tournaments, downloadable accessories, and other extras. By the time Max Steel figures and play sets arrived in stores for holiday gift-giving, boys were familiar with the superhero and his background—and were ready to put Max Steel on their wish lists.

The Monster High line of toys and accessories was created for the target market of girls between the ages of 6 and 12 who like vampire romances, zombie stories, and other trendy monster myths. Through research, Mattel learned that these girls can be self-conscious about their looks. They're also thinking ahead to high school and to the fun but sometimes stressful school-related social activities.

For this target market, Mattel created a line of unconventional-looking dolls, the children of monsters like Frankenstein. Each has her own personality and personal style, embodying the idea that girls can be attractive even when they don't fit the standard definition of beauty. Instead of Barbie's perfect face and dainty fashions, a Monster High doll has monster features (a were-wolf's daughter has wolf ears, a vampire's daughter has prominent canine teeth) and dresses in appealing yet off-beat styles (monster-platform shoes, Goth-style clothing). The target market responded so enthusiastically that Monster High products blossomed into a $1 billion business in less than three years.

Barbie's popularity peaked a few years ago, but the brand still has a lot of life left as Mattel refines its targeting to boost worldwide sales. In China, for example, Mattel originally emphasized Barbie's glamour when communicating with the target market of preteen girls. It opened a glitzy flagship store in Shanghai to showcase Barbie's fashions and accessories—and closed the store when sales fell short of expectations.

As a result of this experience, Mattel decided to take a fresh look at the other target market for dolls, parents and grandparents who buy toys for cherished girls in one-child families. This time, Mattel focused on gift-givers who have high educational aspirations for their daughters and granddaughters. It created new

products like Violin Soloist Barbie and Baby Panda Care Barbie, dolls that are good-looking but also have a serious side (musical achievements, saving pandas). Combined with marketing changes to other Mattel brands and products, the company's new targeting strategy helped it to triple sales in China within three years.

Mattel recently decided to target Hispanic-American mothers, a fast-growing, increasingly affluent market for all kinds of toys. Its research revealed that these mothers either make the buying decisions or are instrumental in the buying decisions for most household purchases. Furthermore, these mothers spend more than non-Hispanic-American consumers when they shop for toys—and they tend to be brand-loyal.

Instead of simply translating its English advertisements into Spanish, Mattel dug deeper for cultural insights such as the importance of family and the celebration of Three Kings Day on the twelfth day after Christmas. Based on this research, Mattel created the marketing theme of "'Toy Feliz," meaning "Toy Happy," a twist on the Spanish phrase "Estoy feliz," meaning "I'm happy." Mattel tested the theme in cities with large Hispanic-American populations. After the test produced positive results, Mattel began using the theme in television and print ads featuring Barbie, Hot Wheels cars, and other products in its portfolio. It also invited parents to download discount coupons from a special website. Based on the response, Mattel will give this high-potential target market even more marketing attention in the future.[17]

### Questions for Discussion

1. Is Mattel using an undifferentiated, concentrated, or differentiated targeting strategy? How do you know?
2. Identify the categories of variables used by Mattel to segment the market for Max Steel action figures. Can you suggest additional variables that Mattel might use in this market?
3. What factors do you think were particularly influential in Mattel's decision to select Hispanic-American mothers as a target market?

# Strategic Case 3
## Home Depot Builds on Research, Segmentation, and Targeting

Nearly 40 years after Home Depot opened its first two stores, the Atlanta-based company is the U.S. market leader in one-stop shopping for home-improvement tools and materials. It rings up $83 billion in annual sales, mainly through more than 2,260 North American stores but also through its online store and mobile-ready website.

Before the rise of Home Depot and its big-box competitors, consumers shopped at small hardware stores where the owners would offer advice and order any obscure tool or odd-sized nail that wasn't in stock. Although do-it-your-selfers (DIYers) might have to wait for out-of-stock or specially ordered items to be delivered to the store, it was the best option available at the time. Today, however, consumers and contractors all around the country have convenient access to hundreds of thousands of everyday and hard-to-find products stacked on floor-to-ceiling shelves under one giant, warehouse-sized roof.

Over the years, Home Depot has expanded its merchandise selection and service extras to address the needs of specific target markets. One key target market has always been do-it-yourselfers who tackle home projects on their own. Within this market, Home Depot has been giving special marketing attention to women who want to learn how to tackle house repairs or improvements. The retailer is also targeting construction professionals who use Home Depot as a local source of lumber and other building supplies.

## Getting to Know DIYers

Counting in-store and online purchases, Home Depot completes more than one billion transactions every year. This fills the company's database with all kinds of details concerning who buys what, when, where, and how. Analyzing the data enables Home Depot to keep products in stock where and when they're needed. It also helps the retailer to plan the proper merchandise assortment for each store in each season.

To learn more about its customers, the company regularly conducts shopper surveys and other marketing research studies. Its marketing managers visit stores to hear first-hand from local employees about what their customers like, dislike, return, and request. Reading the reviews of products that customers post on HomeDepot.com also helps the company understand what its customers want and expect.

In addition, its marketers use observation to identify particular customer problems and needs that can be addressed through marketing. For example, the company recently hired a designer to create a new kind of bucket exclusively for the Home Depot. Even though the humble bucket is a mainstay for many household uses, Home Depot wanted to develop something new to showcase its customer-centered innovation. The designer began by observing how people use buckets in and around their homes and gardens. He noticed that women, in particular, have difficulty lifting, carrying, and unloading a conventional bucket full of soil or other contents.

Based on this insight, he redesigned the plastic bucket by forming an indented "grip pocket" on the underside. He also added a large, comfortable handle in addition to a secondary

grip opening on one side of the rim. These features make it easier to hold the Big Gripper bucket steady while moving and unloading it, solving a problem experienced by millions of homeowners. The Big Gripper is made in America, adding to the appeal for customers who use their purchases to support U.S. manufacturers.

## Watch It, Try It, Do It Yourself

Research shows that some Home Depot customers are first-timer DIYers, and others may have more experience but want to brush up their skills before they undertake a project. To meet these diverse needs, Home Depot offers a variety of free how-to workshops and videos. Consumers can visit the local store for weekly lessons and demonstrations showing everything from how to install closet organizers to how to tile bathroom floors. In "do it herself" workshops, women can test out different power tools, learn how to clean and care for equipment, and get a hands-on feel for common repair techniques. Home Depot even has free children's workshops to teach basic woodworking skills. Participants go home with a handcrafted item such as a racing car, as well as a workshop apron and a special pin. Feedback from these workshops and inquiries about future workshops help Home Depot plan ahead to support customers' informational and instructional needs, which in turn encourages store visits and brand loyalty.

Knowing that many customers can't get to a store workshop or prefer to watch a process several times before trying it themselves at home, Home Depot has also posted dozens of YouTube videos for consumers and professionals. The retailer's free step-by-step demonstrations and product-specific videos have already attracted more than 34 million views. Its thousands of Pinterest pins give customers ideas and inspiration for home improvement, decorating, gardening, and craft projects. By checking the number of views on YouTube and Pinterest, Home Depot can quickly spot the most popular topics and prepare additional videos and posts that fit viewers' interests.

## Targeting Online and Mobile Customers

Although online sales are currently a tiny percentage of Home Depot's overall revenues, research indicates that time-pressured customers are increasingly interested in browsing online or by cell phone and ordering with a click. Some customers like the ability to buy online and pick up their purchases at the nearest Home Depot store, avoiding any shipping delays. Others are looking for same-day delivery to home or work site, so they can start or finish a project on time.

Home Depot is investing heavily to improve its back-office technology and expedite shipping so customers receive their orders quickly. Today, 90 percent of its customers who buy online receive their orders within two days, or even sooner. And, instead of opening hundreds and hundreds of new stores, Home Depot plans to increase its revenues by expanding its online inventory and adding new distribution centers to fulfill online orders quickly and efficiently.

For customers on the go, Home Depot's smartphone apps allow convenient access to product specifications, pricing, and customers' reviews. Customers can set up a wish list for products they want from Home Depot. When these customers visit a Home Depot store, sensors detect the app and offer directions to the aisle and shelf where wish-list products are located. The retailer also uses the app to offer coupons on certain products as customers walk through the store. Customers who are not DIYers can find a professional installer or contractor using Home Depot's RedBeacon app.

### Targeting the Pros

Purchases and equipment rentals by building professionals account for more than one-third of Home Depot's revenues. The retailer's research reveals that these customers are mainly small contractors with no more than five employees and less than $500,000 in annual revenues. For these customers, product availability and price are top concerns. Contractors who buy from Home Depot can schedule delivery at a job site on any day of the week, not just on a week-day. If they run low on lumber or nails, they can use the retailer's Pro app to locate what they need in stock at a nearby Home Depot store, make

the purchase, and drive there for immediate pickup. Customers can also consult the app or call Home Depot's experts when they have questions about tools or supplies. If contractors submit an order in advance, the Pro Desk in each store can have all merchandise ready to load when these customers arrive.

The better its contractor customers do, the more they can buy from Home Depot. So to help contractors serve their customers, the retailer offers a number of handy online tools. For example, the retailer has web-based software that contractors can use to prepare estimates and proposals, select specific materials for each job, and calculate costs. Contractors who enroll in the Pro Xtra loyalty program receive special discounts and exclusive offers, among other benefits.

Looking ahead, Home Depot will continue to use marketing research, segmentation, and targeting to increase its customer base, keep customers loyal, and build sales year after year.[18]

### Questions for Discussion

1. What hypothesis do you think the product designer formulated before he began researching how consumers use buckets? Do you agree with his decision to use observation rather than another method of collecting primary data? Why?

2. Is Home Depot using differentiated targeting, undifferentiated targeting, or concentrated targeting? How do you know?

3. Which segmentation variables does Home Depot appear to be using to reach consumer markets? Why are these appropriate?

4. Do you think Home Depot is segmenting the contractor market using only business variables or a combination of business and consumer variables? Explain your answer.

# NOTES

[1] Christopher Palmeri, "Carnival Rocks the Boat," *Bloomberg Businessweek*, November 12, 2015, www.bloomberg.com/news/articles/2015-11-12/carnival-rocks-the-boat (accessed January 20, 2016); Fran Golden, "Will Carnival's Volunteerism Cruise Line Fathom Do Good?" *USA Today*, January 20, 2016, http://experience.usatoday.com/cruise/story/best-of-cruising/2015/09/16/carnival-volunteerism-line-fathom-activities-dominican-republic/72309350/ (accessed January 20, 2016); Kenrya Rankin Naasel, "Take a Deep Dive into Fathom, Carnival's New Cruise Line for Volunteers," *Fast*

*Company*, September 14, 2015, www.fastcompany.com/3050575/behind-the-brand/take-a-deep-dive-into-fathom-carnivals-new-cruise-line-for-volunteers (accessed January 20, 2016).

[2] A. Powlowski, "Enterprise Lets 'Easy Rider' Wannabes Rent Motorcycles in Vegas," *NBC News*, October 21, 2013, www.nbcnews.com/business/enterprise-lets-easy-rider-wannabes-rent- motorcycles-vegas-8C11417912 (accessed February 3, 2016)

[3] Cheerwine, www.cheerwine.com (accessed February 3, 2016).

[4] American Community Survey, U.S. Census Bureau, 2014, http://factfinder.census.gov/faces/tableservices/jsf/pages/productview.xhtml?pid=PEP_2014_PEPAGESEX&prodType=table (accessed February 3, 2016).

[5] American Community Survey, U.S. Census Bureau, 2014, http://factfinder.census.gov/faces/tableservices/jsf/pages/productview.xhtml?pid=ACS_14_5YR_S0101&prodType=table (accessed February 3, 2016).

[6] "Marketing to Women—Quick Facts," She-Conomy, http://she-conomy.com/report/

marketing-to-women-quick-facts (accessed February 3, 2016).

[7] "FAQ," Iman Cosmetics, www.imancosmetics.com/faq (accessed February 4, 2016).

[8] Molly Soat, "Inside the Mind of a Wedding Consumer," *Marketing News*, November 2015, https://www.ama.org/publications/Marketing-News/Pages/inside-mind-wedding-consumer.aspx (accessed February 4, 2016).

[9] "Households and Families: 2010," U.S. Census Briefs, www.census.gov/prod/cen2010/briefs/c2010br-14.pdf (accessed February 4, 2016).

[10] "My Best Segments," Nielsen, https://segmentationsolutions.nielsen.com/mybestsegments/Default.jsp?ID=70&menuOption=learnmore (accessed February 4, 2016).

[11] Joseph T. Plummer, "The Concept and Application of Life Style Segmentation," *Journal of Marketing*, 38, 1 (1974): 33.

[12] Nielsen PRIZM, https://segmentationsolutions.nielsen.com/mybestsegments/Default.jsp?ID=70&menuOption=learnmore (accessed February 5, 2016).

[13] Philip Kotler and Kevin Keller, *Marketing Management*, 14th ed. (Englewood Cliffs, NJ: Prentice Hall, 2012).

[14] Charles W. Chase, Jr., "Selecting the Appropriate Forecasting Method," *Journal of Business Forecasting*, 16, 3 (1997): 2, 23, 28–29.

[15] "McDonald's Testing Monster Energy Drinks," *Crain's Chicago Business*, October 21, 2015, http://www.chicagobusiness.com/article/20151021/NEWS07/151029969/mcdonalds-testing-monster-energy-drinks (accessed February 8, 2016).

[16] Jeanette DeForge, "Skiing Areas Spending Millions to Upgrade Snowmaking," *The Republican (Springfield, MA)*, December 4, 2013, www.masslive.com; Kathleen Mitchell, "Great Barrington Has Become a True Destination," *BusinessWest*, August 26, 2013, www.business-west.com; Ski Butternut website, www.skibutternut.com (accessed February 9, 2016); "Ski Butternut" Cengage video.

[17] Kara Yorio, "Disney's Princess Dolls Get a Makeover," *The Record (Bergen county, New Jersey)*, January 14, 2016, www.northjersey.com/news/business/shopping/disney-dolls-break-the-mold-1.1491520 (accessed January 20, 2016); Shareen Pathak, "Competition from Everywhere Has Hasbro, Mattel in Toyland Showdown," *Advertising Age*, December 2, 2013, www.adage.com; Tanzina Vega, "Spanish Message with One Word That Needs No Translation," *The New York Times*, October 31, 2013, www.nytimes.com; Mark J. Miller, "Mattel Localizes Barbie for Education-Focused China Market," *Brand Channel*, November 8, 2013, www.brandchannel.com; Abram Brown, "Life After Barbie," *Forbes*, May 6, 2013, www.forbes.com.

[18] Sarah Halzack, "Home Depot Looks to Adapt For Baby Boomers Who Aren't So into 'Do-It-Yourself' Anymore," *Washington Post*, December 9, 2015, www.washington-post.com/news/business/wp/2015/12/09/home-depot-looks-to-adapt-for-baby-boomers-who-arent-so-into-do-it-yourself-anymore/ (accessed January 20, 2016); Joseph Flaherty, "How Home Depot Copied Apple to Build an Ingenious New Bucket," *Wired*, December 31, 2013, www.wired.com/design/2013/12/home-depot-reinvents-buckets; Shelly Banjo, "Home Depot Looks to Offer Same-Day hipping," *The Wall Street Journal*, December 11, 2013, http://online.wsj.com/news/articles/SB10001424052702303932504579251782609141934; Elizabeth Dwoskin and Greg Bensinger, "Tracking Technology Sheds Light on Shopper Habits," *The Wall Street Journal*, December 9, 2013, http://online.wsj.com/news/articles/SB10001424052702303332904579230401308; Shelly Banjo, "Home Depot Beats Wal-Mart, Target Online," *The Wall Street Journal*, November 6, 2013, http://blogs.wsj.com/corporate-intelligence/2013/11/06/home-depot-beats-wal-mart-target-online; Geoff Colvin, "Housing Is Back—and So Is Home Depot," *Fortune*, September 26, 2013, http://money.cnn.com/2013/09/19/leadership/home-depot-blake.pr.fortune; Chantal Tode, "Home Depot's Redbeacon Escalates App Marketing to Drive Mobile Business," *Mobile Commerce Daily*, August 6, 2013, http://www.mobilecommercedaily.com/home-depot%E2%80%99s-redbeacon-escalates-app-marketing-to-drive-mobile-business.

## Feature Notes

[a] Shivani Vorajan, "New York Hotels Make a Green Pledge," *New York Times*, January 19, 2016, www.nytimes.com/2016/01/24/travel/green-hotels-new-york-city.html (accessed January 20, 2016); Nancy Trejos, "Eco-Friendly 1 Hotel Central Park Debuts in New York City," *USA Today*, August 5, 2015, www.usatoday.com/story/travel/hotels/2015/08/05/1-hotels-central-park-new-york-barry-sternlicht/31073943/ (accessed January 20, 2016); Juliana Shallcross, "This Hotel Wants to Time Your Shower," *Conde Nast Traveler*, October 13, 2015, www.cntraveler.com/stories/2015-10-13/1-hotel-central-park-wants-to-time-your-shower (accessed January 20, 2016).

[b] "Who's Tracking You in Public?" *Consumer Reports*, February 2016, pp. 41–45; E. J. Schultz, "Facial-Recognition Lets Marketers Gauge Consumers' Real Responses to Ads," *Advertising Age*, May 18, 2015, http://adage.com/article/digital/facial-recognition-lets-marketers-gauge-real-responses/298635/ (accessed January 20, 2016); Harmon Leon, "How 5 Brands Have Used Facial Recognition Technology," *Digiday*, September 7, 2015, http://digiday.com/brands/5-campaigns-used-facial-recognition-technology/ (accessed January 20, 2016).

# part 4

# Buying Behavior, Global Marketing, and Digital Marketing

**PART 4** continues our focus on the customer. Understanding elements that affect buying decisions enables marketers to analyze customers' needs and evaluate how specific marketing strategies can satisfy those needs.

**CHAPTER 7** examines consumer buying behavior, the decision processes, and factors that influence buying decisions.

**CHAPTER 8** stresses business markets, organizational buyers, the buying center, and the organizational buying decision process.

**CHAPTER 9** looks at how marketers can reach global markets and the actions, involvement, and strategies that marketers employ internationally.

**CHAPTER 10** examines how online social networking and digital media have affected marketing strategies with the creation of new communication channels and the consumer behavior related to these emerging technologies and trends.

Monkey Business Images/Shutterstock.com

# chapter 7     **Consumer Buying Behavior**

---

## O B J E C T I V E S

**7-1**   Recognize the stages of the consumer buying decision process.

**7-2**   Describe the types of consumer decision making and the level of involvement.

**7-3**   Explain how situational influences may affect the consumer buying decision process.

**7-4**   Identify the psychological influences that may affect the consumer buying decision process.

**7-5**   Describe the social influences that may affect the consumer buying decision process.

**7-6**   Discuss consumer misbehavior.

# MARKETING INSIGHTS

## Need Another Holiday? Marketers at Amazon and Alibaba Think So

Jeramey Lende/Shutterstock.com

Make room, Black Friday and Cyber Monday: Amazon and Alibaba, the world's leading online retailers, have created their own multi-billion-dollar "shopping holidays." Amazon launched its initial Amazon Prime Day on July 15, 2015, as part of its twentieth-anniversary celebration. The idea was to stimulate buying with a mid-summer sale, attract new customers for its Prime fee-based membership program, and create an "in-crowd" feeling with members-only bargains.

Amazon posted thousands of special deals throughout the day, providing free two-day delivery for Prime members, and used the hashtag #primeday for online promotion. The shopping holiday gained momentum from social media comments as consumers visited Amazon's site to see the discounts and, if not members, to sign up for a free 30-day Prime trial. During the 24 hours of Amazon Prime Day, the company sold more than 34 million items and generated more revenue than it had on the previous Black Friday, which is usually the busiest shopping day of the year.

Alibaba, China's top online retailer, introduced Singles' Day on November 11, 2009. In a play on the number *one* in the date 11–11, Alibaba wanted to encourage single consumers to buy for themselves or for friends. Every year since, Alibaba has smashed one-day revenue records as its deeply discounted merchandise attracts shoppers by the millions. In 2015, Alibaba sold $14.3 billion worth of products on Singles' Day, including more than 3 million cell phones. Looking ahead, Alibaba expects to keep up the sales momentum as word spreads and more consumers log on for Singles' Day bargains.[1]

Amazon, Alibaba, and many other online, digital, and traditional marketers go to great lengths to understand their customers' needs and gain a better grasp of customers' **buying behavior**, which is the decision processes and actions of people involved in buying and using products. **Consumer buying behavior** refers to the buying behavior of ultimate consumers—those who purchase products for personal or household use and not for business purposes. Marketers attempt to understand buying behavior for several reasons. First, customers' overall opinions and attitudes toward a firm's products have a great impact on the firm's success. Second, as we saw in Chapter 1, the marketing concept stresses that a firm should create a marketing mix that meets customers' needs. To find out what satisfies consumers, marketers must examine the main influences on what, where, when, and how they buy. Third, by gaining a deeper understanding of the factors that affect buying behavior, marketers are better-positioned to predict how consumers will respond to marketing strategies.

In this chapter, we first examine the major stages of the consumer buying decision process, beginning with problem recognition, information search, and evaluation of alternatives, and proceeding through purchase and postpurchase evaluation. We follow this with an investigation into how the customer's level of involvement affects the type of decision making they use and discuss the types of consumer decision-making processes. Next, we explore situational influences—surroundings, time, purchase reason, and buyer's mood and condition—that affect purchasing decisions. We go on to consider psychological influences on purchasing decisions: perception, motives, learning, attitudes, personality and self-concept, and lifestyles. Next, we discuss social influences that affect buying behavior, including roles, family, reference groups and opinion leaders, social classes, and culture and subcultures. We conclude with a discussion of consumer misbehavior.

**buying behavior** The decision processes and actions of people involved in buying and using products

**consumer buying behavior** The decision processes and purchasing activities of people who purchase products for personal or household use and not for business purposes

**consumer buying decision process** A five-stage purchase decision process that includes problem recognition, information search, evaluation of alternatives, purchase, and postpurchase evaluation

# 7-1 CONSUMER BUYING DECISION PROCESS

The **consumer buying decision process**, shown in Figure 7.1, includes five stages: problem recognition, information search, evaluation of alternatives, purchase, and postpurchase evaluation. Before we examine each stage, consider these important points. First, as shown in

Figure 7.1    **Consumer Buying Decisions Process and Possible Influences on the Process**

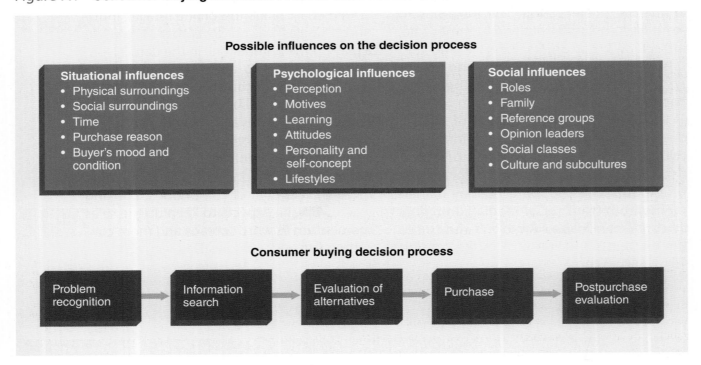

Possible influences on the decision process

**Situational influences**
- Physical surroundings
- Social surroundings
- Time
- Purchase reason
- Buyer's mood and condition

**Psychological influences**
- Perception
- Motives
- Learning
- Attitudes
- Personality and self-concept
- Lifestyles

**Social influences**
- Roles
- Family
- Reference groups
- Opinion leaders
- Social classes
- Culture and subcultures

**Consumer buying decision process**

Problem recognition → Information search → Evaluation of alternatives → Purchase → Postpurchase evaluation

Figure 7.1, this process can be affected by numerous influences, which are categorized as situational, psychological, and social. Second, the actual act of purchasing is usually not the first stage of the process. Third, not all decision processes lead to a purchase—individuals can end the process at any stage. Finally, not all consumer decisions include all five stages.

## 7-1a  Problem Recognition

*Problem recognition* occurs when a buyer becomes aware of a difference between a desired state and an actual condition. For example, a person may recognize a desire for clean floors, but lack a working vacuum cleaner to fulfill that need. The speed of consumer problem recognition can be quite rapid or rather slow. Sometimes a person has a problem or need but is unaware of it. Marketers use sales personnel, advertising, and packaging to help trigger recognition of such needs or problems. Consider this advertisement for Seirus Heattouch gloves. The gloves can provide heating for up to six hours with the touch of a button, which may appeal to someone experiencing cold hands while working or playing outdoors in cold weather conditions. The straightforward ad presents a pair of thick gloves, each with a glowing red button, on a background that seems to radiate warmth. The ad informs potential buyers that they can stay warmer longer with Seirus products and refers them to a website to find just the right pair of gloves.

## 7-1b  Information Search

After recognizing the problem or need, a buyer will decide whether to pursue satisfying that need. If the consumer chooses to move forward, he or she will next search for product information to help resolve the problem or satisfy the need. If, for example, a consumer realizes that he needs to back up the files on his computer, he will conduct a search on different products that could fulfill this need.

An information search has two aspects. In an **internal search**, buyers search their memories for information about products that might solve their problem. If they cannot retrieve enough information from memory to make a decision, they seek additional information from outside sources in an **external search**. The external search may focus on communication with friends or relatives, comparison of available brands and prices, marketer-dominated sources, and/or public sources. An individual's personal contacts—friends, relatives, and coworkers—often are influential sources of information because the person trusts and respects them. However, consumers should take care not to overestimate the product knowledge of family and friends. Consumers may also use marketer-dominated sources of information, such as salespeople, advertising, websites, package labeling, and in-store demonstrations and displays because they typically require little effort.

The Internet has become a major resource during the consumer buying decision process, with its many sources for product descriptions and reviews and the ease of comparing prices. Buyers can also obtain information from independent sources: government reports, news presentations, publications such as *Consumer Reports*, and reports from product-testing organizations, for instance. Consumers frequently view information from these sources as credible because of their factual and unbiased nature. For services that are hard to evaluate even after

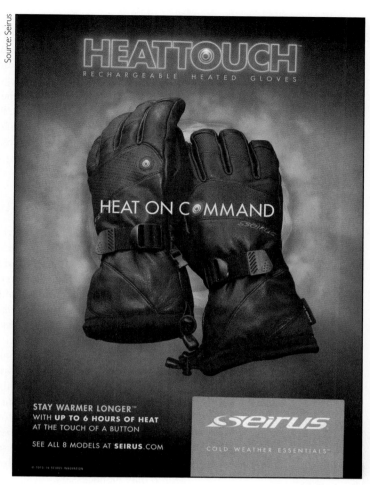

Source: Seirus

**Problem Recognition**
This advertisement is attempting to stimulate problem recognition by showing off a warm pair of gloves.

**internal search** An information search in which buyers search their memories for information about products that might solve their problem

**external search** An information search in which buyers seek information from sources other than their memories consumption (e.g., legal advice), consumers rely more on salespeople, friends and family, and independent consumer reports.[2] Buyers today routinely turn to user review sites and apps such as Yelp, Zagat, TripAdvisor, and Angie's List for insights into both goods and services. Increasingly, consumers begin their information search on a mobile device.

Repetition, a technique well-known to advertisers, increases consumers' information retention and recall. When they see or hear an advertising message for the first time, recipients may not grasp all its important details, but they recall more particulars as the message is repeated. However, marketers should be wary not to repeat a message too many times, as consumers can grow tired of it and begin to respond unfavorably. Information can be presented verbally, numerically, or visually. Marketers pay great attention to the visual components of their advertising materials.

## 7-1c  Evaluation of Alternatives

A successful information search within a product category yields a group of brands that a buyer views as possible alternatives. This group of brands is sometimes called a **consideration set** (or an *evoked set*). Consumers assign a greater value to a brand they have heard of than to one they have not—even when they do not know anything else about the brand other than the name. For example, a consideration set of tablet computers might include devices from Apple, Microsoft, Dell, and Lenovo. A consumer will probably lean initially toward the one with which he or she is most familiar, or that his or her friends prefer, before conducting any additional searches.

To assess the products in a consideration set, the buyer uses **evaluative criteria**: objective characteristics (such as the size, speed, capacity) and subjective characteristics (such as style and color) that are important to him or her. Consider that one tablet buyer may want a large display, whereas another may want one with a lot of memory. The buyer assigns a certain level of importance to each criterion. However, some features and characteristics carry more weight than others, depending on consumer preferences. The buyer rates, and eventually ranks, brands in the consideration set using the selected evaluative criteria. It is possible that the evaluation stage may yield no brand the buyer is willing to purchase. In that case, a further information search may be necessary.

Marketers may influence consumers' evaluations by *framing* the alternatives—that is, describing the alternatives and their attributes in a certain manner. Framing can make a characteristic seem more important to a consumer and facilitate its recall from memory. For instance, by stressing a car's superior comfort and safety features over those of a competitor's, a carmaker can direct consumers' attention toward these points. Framing can also be used with items that carry more risk. For products such as gambling or contests, consumers are less willing to pay when they are framed as "lottery ticket," "gamble," or "raffle" than when framed more positively, such as "gift certificate" or "voucher."[3] You have experienced the framing effect if you have ever walked into a gourmet grocery or high-end clothing store where the displays make the products seem so appealing that you feel you just have to buy them, only to return home and be less satisfied than you were in the store. Framing has a stronger influence on the decision processes of inexperienced buyers. If the evaluation of alternatives yields one or more brands that the consumer is willing to buy, he or she is ready to move on to the next stage of the decision process: the purchase.

## 7-1d  Purchase

**consideration set** A group of brands within a product category that a buyer views as alternatives for possible purchase

**evaluative criteria** Objective and subjective product characteristics that are important to a buyer

In the purchase stage, the consumer chooses to buy the product or brand yielded by the evaluation of alternatives. However, product availability may influence which brand is ultimately purchased. If the brand that ranked highest in evaluation is unavailable and the buyer is unwilling to wait until it is available again, the buyer may choose to purchase the brand that ranked second. So, if a consumer is at the mall shopping for jeans and the preferred Levis in her size are out of stock but the Lucky brand jeans are not, the consumer may opt to purchase the Lucky brand to save another trip to the mall later.

During this stage, buyers also pick the seller from which they will buy the product—it could be a specific retail shop, chain, or online retailer. The choice of seller may affect final product selection and, therefore, the terms of sale, which, if negotiable, are determined at this stage. Consumers also settle other issues, such as price, delivery, warranties, maintenance agreements, installation, and credit arrangements, at this time. Finally, the actual purchase takes place (although the consumer can still decide to terminate the buying decision process even at this late stage).

## 7-1e  Postpurchase Evaluation

After the purchase, the buyer evaluates the product to ascertain if its actual performance meets expected levels. Many criteria used in evaluating alternatives are applied again during postpurchase evaluation in order to make a comparison. The outcome of this stage is either satisfaction or dissatisfaction, which influences whether the consumer will repurchase the brand or product, complain to the seller, or communicate positively or negatively with other possible buyers. Postpurchase intent may differ between consumers. For example, the perceived value of the purchase has a weaker effect on the repurchase intent for women than for men. On the other hand, the costs and efforts of switching to a new store affect men's repurchase decisions much more than women.[4]

The postpurchase evaluation stage is especially important for high-priced items. Shortly after the purchase of an expensive product, evaluation may result in **cognitive dissonance**, which involves doubts in the buyer's mind about whether purchasing the product was the right decision. Cognitive dissonance is most likely to arise when a person recently bought an expensive, high-involvement product that is found to be lacking some of the desirable features of competing brands. A buyer who is experiencing cognitive dissonance may attempt to return the product or may seek out positive information, such as reviews, to justify choosing it. For instance, a person would likely experience cognitive dissonance if he or she bought a pair of Nike shoes for full price and then found them on sale a week later. Marketers sometimes attempt to reduce cognitive dissonance by having salespeople telephone or e-mail recent purchasers to make sure they are satisfied with their new purchases. Salespeople may send recent buyers results of studies showing that other consumers are very satisfied with the brand.

As Figure 7.1 shows, three major categories of influences are believed to affect the consumer buying decision process: situational, psychological, and social. In the remainder of this chapter, we focus on these influences. Although we discuss each major influence separately, their effects on the consumer decision process are interrelated.

# 7-2 TYPES OF CONSUMER DECISION MAKING AND LEVEL OF INVOLVEMENT

To acquire products that satisfy their current and future needs, consumers engage in different types of decision-making processes that vary depending on the nature of the product. The amount of effort, both mental and physical, that buyers expend in solving problems also varies considerably with the cost and type of product.

## 7-2a  Consumer Decision Making

There are three types of consumer decision making, which vary in involvement level and other factors: routinized response behavior, limited decision making, or extended decision making (Table 7.1).

A consumer uses **routinized response behavior** when buying frequently purchased, low-cost items that require very little search-and-decision effort. A consumer may have a brand preference, but will be satisfied with several brands in the product class. Typically, low-involvement products are bought through routinized response behavior—that is, almost

**cognitive dissonance**
A buyer's doubts shortly after a purchase about whether the decision was the right one

**routinized response behavior**
A consumer decision-making process used when buying frequently purchased, low-cost items that require very little search-and-decision effort

Table 7.1    **Consumer Decision Making**

| | Routinized Response | Limited | Extended |
|---|---|---|---|
| Product cost | Low | Low to moderate | High |
| Search effort | Little | Little to moderate | Extensive |
| Time spent | Short | Short to medium | Lengthy |
| Brand preference | More than one is acceptable, although one may be preferred | Several | Varies, usually many |

automatically. For example, buyers spend little time or effort selecting most supermarket items such as soft drinks or batteries. If the preferred brand is out of stock, they will select a competing product with little thought.

Buyers engage in **limited decision making** when they buy products occasionally, or from unfamiliar brands in a familiar product category. This type of decision making requires slightly more time for information gathering and deliberation. For instance, if Procter & Gamble introduces a new Pantene brand shampoo, interested buyers will seek additional information about the product, perhaps by asking a friend who has used it, watching a commercial about it, or visiting the company's website, before making a trial purchase.

The most complex type of decision making, **extended decision making**, occurs with high-involvement, unfamiliar, expensive, or infrequently purchased items—for instance, a computer, car, or the services of a doctor or lawyer. The buyer uses many criteria to evaluate alternative brands or choices and spends much time seeking information and deciding before making the purchase.

Purchase of a particular product does not elicit the same type of decision-making process every time. We may engage in extended decision making the first time we buy a product, but find that limited decision making suffices when we buy it again. If a routinely purchased brand is discontinued or no longer satisfies us, we may use limited or extended decision making to switch to a new brand. Thus, if we notice that the brand of pain reliever we normally buy is no longer working well, we may seek out a different brand through limited decision making.

It is important to note that consumer decision making is not always rational. Most consumers occasionally make purchases solely on impulse and not on the basis of any of these three decision-making processes. **Impulse buying** involves no conscious planning and stems from a

**limited decision making**
A consumer decision-making process used when purchasing products occasionally or needing information about an unfamiliar brand in a familiar product category

**extended decision making** A consumer decision-making process employed when purchasing unfamiliar, expensive, or infrequently bought products

**impulse buying** An unplanned buying behavior resulting from a powerful urge to buy something immediately

**Low-Involvement Products**
Soft drinks, such as Pepsi, are low-involvement products because they are inexpensive and purchased frequently. When buying soft drinks, consumers usually employ routinized response behavior.

powerful urge to buy something immediately. Research indicates that 75 percent of U.S. shoppers have purchased something impulsively, and half regretted doing so.[5] Retailers set up gum, beef jerky, peanuts, and magazines close to the cash registers to encourage impulse buying.

## 7-2b Consumer Level of Involvement

A major factor in the type of decision-making process employed depends on the customer's **level of involvement**, which is the degree of interest in a product and the importance the individual places on that product. As an example, involvement with wine can be used to segment consumers who will visit a winery. Those consumers with high involvement with wine differ significantly in visitation motives and patterns than those identified as low involvement.[6] High-involvement products tend to be those that are visible to others (e.g., real estate, high-end electronics, or automobiles) and are more expensive. High-importance issues, such as health care, are also associated with high levels of involvement. Low-involvement products are much less expensive and have less associated social risk (e.g., grocery or drugstore items).

A person's interest in a product or product category that is ongoing and long-term is referred to as *enduring involvement*. Most consumers have an enduring involvement with very few activities or items—the product categories in which they have the most interest. Many consumers, for instance, have an enduring involvement with Apple products, a brand that inspires loyalty and trust. Consumers will expend a great deal of effort to purchase and learn about Apple products, such as waiting in line for the latest iPhone release and reading articles about the various features of the newest iPad. In contrast, *situational involvement* is temporary and dynamic, and results from a particular set of circumstances, such as the sudden need to buy a new laptop after the current one starts malfunctioning right before a research project is due. For a short period of time the consumer will research computer types, brands, models, retailers, and prices, but will settle on a choice relatively quickly because the consumer needs a functional computer as soon as possible. Once the purchase is made, the consumer's interest and involvement wane quickly. Consumer involvement may be attached to product categories (e.g., sports), loyalty to a specific brand, interest in a specific advertisement (e.g., a funny commercial) or a medium (e.g., a television show), or to certain decisions and behaviors (e.g., a love of shopping). Interest, such as finding an advertisement entertaining, does not necessarily mean the consumer will become involved with the brand. It may not satisfy a need the customer currently has, or he or she may be loyal to another brand.

There are several factors that influence a buyer's level of involvement. The most significant is the perceived risk of a purchase. In particular, high-priced items have greater risk of financial loss of future purchasing power. Buying a new car, for example, generally requires a monthly payment that will significantly reduce your purchasing power for other items in your monthly budget. Thus, high-priced products tend to be associated with a higher level of involvement. On the other hand, previous experience with a product is usually associated with lower levels of involvement because buyers do not need to engage in extensive decision making for a product they have purchased several times before. Finally, a buyer who is highly interested in something is likely to have a higher level of involvement than someone who is not. Consider an avid runner who likes to compete in marathons; he is more likely than most to be interested in running shoes and sports drinks, as well as magazines and blogs devoted to running and marathons. His level of involvement in a pair of running shoes is likely to be higher than for a college student who is just buying shoes to wear around campus.

## 7-3 SITUATIONAL INFLUENCES ON THE BUYING DECISION PROCESS

**Situational influences** result from circumstances, time, and location that affect the consumer buying decision process. Imagine buying an automobile tire after noticing, while washing your car, that the current tire is badly worn. This is a different experience from buying a tire right after a blowout on the highway spoils your road trip because in the prior scenario you can take

**level of involvement**
An individual's degree of interest in a product and the importance of the product for that person

**situational influences**
Influences that result from circumstances, time, and location that affect the consumer buying decision process

the time to conduct research and select the best product and supplier for your needs. Situational factors can influence the buyer during any stage of the consumer buying decision process and may cause the individual to shorten, lengthen, or terminate the process. Situational factors can be classified into five categories: physical surroundings, social surroundings, time perspective, reason for purchase, and the buyer's momentary mood and condition.[7]

Physical surroundings include location, store atmosphere, scents, sounds, lighting, weather, and other factors in the physical environment in which the decision process occurs. A sports stadium, for example, includes not only the playing field and seats but also concession stands, souvenir shops, entertainment, music, and the energy of the audience. Retail chains try to design their store environment and layout in a way that makes shopping as enjoyable and easy as possible, so consumers are more inclined to linger and make purchases. Marketers at banks, department stores, and specialty stores go to considerable effort and expense to create physical settings that are conducive to making purchase decisions. Restaurant chains, such as Olive Garden and Chili's, invest heavily in facilities, often building from the ground up, to provide surroundings that are distinctive to the chain and that enhance customers' experiences. Even remodeling the physical surroundings of a store can directly affect sales. Remodeling tends to increase the sales to new customers, who will spend more per visit and return to the store more frequently than existing customers.[8]

Consider the advertisement for TAG Heuer watches. TAG Heuer is an exclusive Swiss watch brand, with products selling for thousands of dollars in high-end jewelry stores. The ad features football champion Tom Brady to signify the idea that TAG Heuer watches never crack under pressure. Retail outlets where TAG Heuer products are sold are likely to encourage purchases through situational influences, such as appealing displays, highly-attentive salespeople, lighting calculated to enhance the look of the watches, and strategic positioning of products to catch consumers' eyes.

However, dimensions such as weather, traffic sounds, and odors are clearly beyond the marketers' control in some settings. General climatic conditions, for example, may influence a customer's decision to buy a specific type of vehicle (e.g., an SUV) with certain features (e.g., a four-wheel drive). Current weather conditions, or other external factors, may be either encouraging or discouraging to consumers when they seek out specific products. Such factors may be favorable to retailers, as when forecasted bad weather causes customers to stock up and even hoard staples.

Social surroundings include characteristics and interactions of others who are present during a purchase decision, such as friends, relatives, salespeople, and other customers. Buyers may feel pressured to behave in a certain way because they are in a public place such as a restaurant, store, or sports arena. Warmer temperatures have been found to increase a consumer's social closeness to other decision makers in the environment, resulting in higher conformity with the product preferences of the crowd.[9] Thoughts about who will be around when the product is used or consumed are another dimension of

Source: TAG Heuer

**Situational Influences**
TAG Heuer watches are sold at high-end jewelry stores, where situational influences are likely to affect your purchase decision.

the social setting. Negative elements of physical surroundings, such as an overcrowded store or an argument between a customer and a salesperson, may cause consumers to leave the store before purchasing anything.

The time dimension influences the buying decision process in several ways. It takes varying amounts of time to progress through the steps of the buying decision process, including learning about, searching for, purchasing, and using a product. Time also plays a major role when consumers consider the frequency of product use, the length of time required to use it, and the overall product life. Other time dimensions that can influence purchases include time of day, day of the week or month, seasons, and holidays. Thus, a customer under time constraints is likely to either make a quick purchase decision or delay a decision. On the other hand, consumers may be willing to wait longer to purchase certain products depending upon their desire for them. An Apple enthusiast might spend a considerable time waiting for the newest iPhone to be released.

The reason for purchase involves what exactly the product purchase should accomplish and for whom. Generally, consumers purchase an item for their own use, for household use, or as a gift. Purchase choices are likely to vary depending on the reason. For example, you will likely choose a nicer product brand for a gift than you would for yourself. If you own a Mont Blanc pen, which is a very expensive brand, it is likely that you received it as a gift from someone very close to you.

The buyer's moods (e.g., anger, anxiety, or contentment) or conditions (e.g., fatigue, illness, or having cash on hand) may also affect the consumer buying decision process. Such moods or conditions are momentary and occur immediately before the situation where a buying decision will be made. They can affect a person's ability and desire to search for or receive information, or seek and evaluate alternatives. Moods can also significantly influence a consumer's postpurchase evaluation. If you are happy immediately after purchase, you may be more likely to attribute the mood to the product and will judge it favorably.

# 7-4 **PSYCHOLOGICAL INFLUENCES ON THE BUYING DECISION PROCESS**

**Psychological influences** partly determine people's general behavior and thus influence their behavior as consumers. Primary psychological influences on consumer behavior are perception, motives, learning, attitudes, personality and self-concept, and lifestyles. Even though these psychological factors operate internally, they are affected strongly by external social forces.

## 7-4a **Perception**

People perceive the same event or thing at the same time in different ways. When you first look at the illustration, for instance, do you see columns or women? Similarly, the same individual may perceive an item in different ways at different times. **Perception** is the process of selecting, organizing, and interpreting information inputs to produce meaning. **Information inputs** are sensations received through sight, taste, hearing, smell, and touch. When we hear an advertisement on the radio, see a friend, smell food cooking at a restaurant, or touch a product, we receive information inputs. Some inputs are more effective in attracting attention than others. For instance, research has shown that advertisements for food items that appeal to multiple senses at once are more effective than ones that focus on taste alone.[10] Cinnabon has recognized the power of its cinnamon roll flavor and aroma, and even lends its signature scent and brand to non-food items, such as car fresheners. Most people have positive associations with the warm scent of cinnamon, sugar, and butter, and marketers have found that the brand's scent can successfully sell a wide variety of products.[11]

**psychological influences** Factors that in part determine people's general behavior, thus influencing their behavior as consumers

**perception** The process of selecting, organizing, and interpreting information inputs to produce meaning

**information inputs** Sensations received through sight, taste, hearing, smell, and touch

**Perception?**
Do you see two women or three columns?

Selection is the first step in the perceptual process. Perception can be interpreted different ways because, although we constantly receive pieces of information, only some reach our awareness. We would be completely overwhelmed if we paid equal attention to all sensory inputs, so we select some and ignore others. This process is called **selective exposure** because an individual selects (mostly unconsciously) which inputs will reach awareness. If you are concentrating on this paragraph, you probably are not aware that cars outside are making noise, that the room light is on, that a song is playing in the background, or even that you are touching the page. Even though you receive these inputs, they do not reach your awareness until they are brought to your attention. An individual's current set of needs affects selective exposure. Information inputs that relate to one's strongest needs are more likely to reach conscious awareness. It is not by chance that many fast-food commercials are aired near mealtimes. Customers are more likely to pay attention to these advertisements at times when they are hungry.

The selective nature of perception may also result in two other conditions: selective distortion and selective retention. **Selective distortion** is changing or twisting received information. It occurs when a person receives information inconsistent with personal feelings or beliefs and he or she selectively interprets the information, changing its meaning to align more closely with expectations. Selective distortion explains why people will reject logical information, even when presented with supporting evidence. Selective distortion can both help and hurt marketers. For instance, a consumer may become loyal to a brand and remain loyal, even when confronted with evidence that another brand is superior. However, selective distortion can also lessen the impact of the message on the individual substantially. In **selective retention**, a person remembers information inputs that support personal feelings and beliefs and forgets inputs that do not. After hearing a sales presentation and leaving a store, for example, a customer may quickly forget many selling points if they contradict personal beliefs or preconceived notions about a product.

The second step in the process of perception is perceptual organization. Information inputs that reach awareness are not received in an organized form. To produce meaning, an individual must organize and integrate new information with what is already stored in memory. People use several methods to achieve this. One method is called *figure-ground*. When an individual uses figure-ground, a portion of the information inputs that reach awareness stands out as the figure and others become the background. For example, when looking back at the image of the columns or women, when you mentally allow the women to stand out as the figure, the columns become the background. If you allow the columns to stand out as the figure, the women become the background. Another method, called *closure*, occurs when a person fills in missing information in a way that conforms to a pattern or statement. In an attempt to draw attention to its brand, a marketer may capitalize on closure by using incomplete images, sounds, or statements in advertisements.

Interpretation, the third step in the perceptual process, is the assignment of meaning to what has been organized. A person interprets information according to what he or she expects or what is familiar. For this reason, a manufacturer who changes a product or its package may face consumer backlash from customers looking for the old, familiar product or package and who do not recognize, or do not like, the new one. PepsiCo, for example, faced a significant backlash after it redesigned the look of the packaging for its popular Tropicana Pure Premium orange juice. The new juice cartons featured cleaner text and simple graphics, but consumers quickly rejected—or simply failed to recognize—them. After sales fell 20 percent, the company

**selective exposure** The process by which some inputs are selected to reach awareness and others are not

**selective distortion** An individual's changing or twisting of information that is inconsistent with personal feelings or beliefs

**selective retention** Remembering information inputs that support personal feelings and beliefs and forgetting inputs that do not hastily returned to its more familiar packaging.[12] Unless a product or package change is accompanied by a promotional program that makes people aware of the change, an organization may suffer a sales decline.

Although marketers cannot control buyers' perceptions, they often try to influence them. Several problems may arise from such attempts, however. First, a consumer's perceptual process may operate such that a seller's information never reaches the target. For example, a buyer may block out and not notice an advertisement in a magazine. Second, a buyer may receive information but perceive it differently from what was intended, as occurs in selective distortion. For instance, when a toothpaste producer advertises that "35 percent of the people who use this toothpaste have fewer cavities," a customer could potentially infer that 65 percent of users have more cavities. Third, a buyer who perceives information inputs to be inconsistent with prior beliefs is likely to forget the information quickly, as is the case with selective retention.

## 7-4b Motives

A **motive** is an internal energizing force that directs a person's activities toward satisfying needs or achieving goals. Buyers are affected by a set of motives rather than by just one. At any point in time, certain motives will have a stronger influence on the person than others will. For example, the sensation of being cold is a strong motivator on the decision to purchase a new coat, making the motivation more urgent in the winter than it is in the summer. Motives can be physical feelings, states of mind, or emotions. Some motives may help an individual achieve his or her goals, whereas others create barriers to achievement. Motives also affect the direction and intensity of behavior.

With online shopping increasing annually, marketers have increasingly found a need to understand the motives of online shoppers and how the new shopping medium affects their buying behavior. One research project divided online shoppers by two basic motivations: utilitarian (or functional) shoppers and hedonic (or nonfunctional) shoppers. Utilitarian consumers shop online because it is a useful and fast way to purchase certain items, whereas hedonic consumers shop online because it is a fun and enjoyable way to find bargains. The research found that hedonic consumers spent more time on the Internet for each purchase and shopped online more often than utilitarian consumers. Hedonic consumers were also more likely to make impulse buys online and engage in bidding wars on sites like eBay.[13]

Abraham Maslow, an American psychologist, conceived a theory of motivation based on a hierarchy of needs. According to Maslow, humans seek to satisfy five levels of needs, from most to least basic to survival, as shown in Figure 7.2. This pyramid is known as **Maslow's hierarchy of needs**. Maslow proposed that people are constantly striving to move up the hierarchy, fulfilling one level of needs, then aspiring to fulfill the next.

**motive** An internal energizing force that directs a person's behavior toward satisfying needs or achieving goals

**Maslow's hierarchy of needs** The five levels of needs that humans seek to satisfy, from most to least important

Figure 7.2 **Maslow's Hierarchy of Needs**

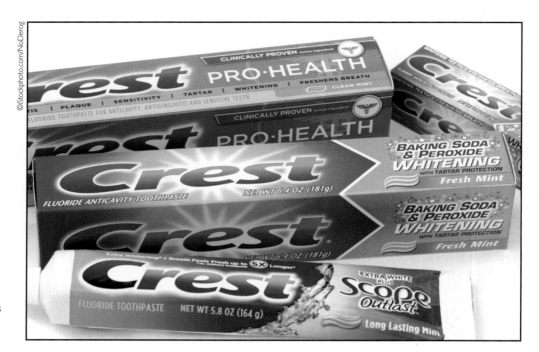

**Safety Needs**
Crest brand toothpaste appeals to safety needs because it fights tooth decay, resulting in better health for the user.

At the most basic level are *physiological needs*, requirements for survival such as food, water, sex, clothing, and shelter, which people try to satisfy first. Food and beverage marketers often appeal to physiological needs, such as sex appeal or hunger. Carl's Jr. is famous for its commercials of lingerie models eating burgers, appealing to two physiological needs at once—hunger and sex. Crest toothpaste appeals to the physiological need to have a healthy mouth.

At the next level are *safety needs*, which include security and freedom from physical and emotional pain and suffering. Life insurance, automobile air bags, carbon monoxide detectors, vitamins, and decay-fighting toothpastes are products that consumers purchase to ensure their safety needs are met.

Next are *social needs*—the human requirements for love and affection and a sense of belonging. Advertisements for beauty products, jewelry, and even cars often suggest that purchasing these products will bring love and social acceptance. Certain types of clothing, such as items emblazoned with logos or slogans, appeal to the customer's need to belong by displaying his or her affinity for popular brands.

At the level of *esteem needs*, people require respect and recognition from others as well as self-esteem, a sense of one's own worth. Owning a Lexus automobile, purchasing a Michael Kors handbag, or flying first class can satisfy esteem needs. Many consumers are more willing to purchase products, even if they cost more, from firms that have a reputation for being charitable. Purchasing products from firms that have reputations for being socially responsible can be motivated by a customer's desire to be perceived as a caring individual, thus contributing to satisfying esteem needs.

At the top of the hierarchy are *self-actualization needs*. These refer to people's needs to grow and develop and to become all they are capable of becoming. Many people never reach this level of the hierarchy, but it can be motivating to try. Some products that may send messages that they satisfy these needs include fitness center memberships, education, and self-improvement workshops.

**patronage motives** Motives that influence where a person purchases products on a regular basis

Motives that influence which establishments a customer frequents are called **patronage motives**. A buyer may shop at a specific store because of such patronage motives as price, service, location, product variety, or friendliness of salespeople. To capitalize on patronage motives, marketers try to determine why regular customers frequent a particular store and to emphasize these characteristics in the store's marketing mix.

## 7-4c Learning

**Learning** refers to changes in a person's thought processes and behavior caused by information and experience. Consequences of behavior strongly influence the learning process. Behaviors that result in positive consequences tend to be repeated. For instance, a consumer who buys a Kind snack bar, enjoys the taste, and feels satisfied after eating it is more likely to buy a Kind bar again. The individual will probably continue to purchase that product until it no longer provides satisfaction. When outcomes of the behavior are no longer satisfying or stand in the way of achieving a desired goal, such as weight loss, the person may switch to a less fattening brand or stop eating snack bars altogether.

Purchasing decisions require customers to process information, an ability that varies by individual. The type of information inexperienced buyers use may differ from the type used by experienced shoppers who are familiar with the product and purchase situation. Thus, two potential buyers of an antique desk may use different types of information in making their purchase decisions. The inexperienced buyer may judge the desk's value by price and appearance, whereas the more experienced buyer may look at the construction and condition of the desk and seek information about the manufacturer, period, and place of origin to assess the desk's quality and value. Consumers who lack experience may seek information from others when making a purchase and even take along an informed friend with experience. Experienced buyers have greater self-confidence and more knowledge about the product and can recognize which product features are reliable cues to quality.

Marketers help customers learn about their products by facilitating opportunities to gain experience with them, which makes customers feel more comfortable. They engage in *shaping* potential buyers' early experience through free samples, sometimes coupled with coupons, to encourage product trial and reduce purchase risk. For instance, because some consumers may be wary of trying new products outside of their routine, Costco, HEB's Central Market, and Whole Foods permit consumers to sample their products in the stores' aisles. Personal-care products sometimes include a sample of another product in the package. In-store demonstrations foster knowledge of product uses. A software producer may use point-of-sale product demonstrations to introduce a new product. Test drives give potential new-car purchasers some experience with the automobile's features.

Consumers also learn by experiencing products indirectly through information from salespeople, advertisements, websites, Internet videos, social media, friends, and relatives. Through sales personnel and advertisements, marketers offer information before (and sometimes after) purchases that can create favorable consumer attitudes toward the product. However, marketers may encounter problems in attracting and holding consumers' attention, providing them with information for making purchase decisions and convincing them to try the product.

## 7-4d Attitudes

An **attitude** is an individual's enduring evaluation of feelings about and behavioral tendencies toward an object or idea. The objects toward which we have attitudes may be tangible or intangible, living or nonliving. For example, we have attitudes toward sex, religion, politics, and music, just as we do toward cars, football, and breakfast cereals. Although attitudes can change over time, they tend to remain stable and do not vary, particularly in the short term. A person's attitudes toward different things do not have equal impact at any one time, and some are stronger than others. Individuals acquire attitudes through experience and interaction with other people.

An attitude consists of three major components: cognitive, affective, and behavioral. The cognitive component is the person's knowledge and information about the object or idea. For example, as consumers have become more knowledgeable about heath, obesity, and quality ingredients, their attitudes toward soft drinks and fast food have declined along with the sales of companies like McDonald's and Coca-Cola. The affective component comprises the individual's feelings and emotions toward the object or idea. Emotions involve both psychological and biological elements. They relate to feelings and can create visceral responses related to

**learning** Changes in an individual's thought processes and behavior caused by information and experience

**attitude** An individual's enduring evaluation of feelings about and behavioral tendencies toward an object or idea behavior. Love, hate, anger, and fear are emotions that can influence behavior. Consumers who feel fear while in the presence of a brand tend to feel a greater emotional attachment to that brand compared with those who feel sadness, joy, or excitement.[14] For some people, certain brands, such as Apple, Starbucks, or REI, elicit an emotional response. Firms that successfully create an emotional experience or connection with customers establish a positive brand image that can result in customer loyalty. Apple, for example, has forged a deep emotional connection with many of its customers through creative pre-product launch "leaks" and hype, grandly staged presentations, and enjoyable shopping experiences at its Apple stores that all stoke anticipation of the next release of the iPhone, Apple Watch, or latest innovation.[15] This means it is important for marketers to generate authentic messages that consumers can relate to on an emotional level. The behavioral component manifests itself in the person's actions regarding the object or idea. Changes in cognitive, affective, or behavioral components may possibly affect other components.

Consumer attitudes toward a company and its products greatly influence success or failure of the firm's marketing strategy. When consumers have strong, negative attitudes toward one or more aspects of a firm's marketing practices, they may not only stop using its products but also urge relatives and friends to do likewise. Because attitudes play an important part in determining consumer behavior, marketers should regularly measure consumer attitudes toward prices, package designs, brand names, advertisements, salespeople, repair services, store locations, features of existing or proposed products, and social responsibility efforts.

Efforts to understand attitudes has resulted in two major academic models: the attitude toward the object model (known as the Fishbein model) and the behavioral intentions model (also known as the Theory of Reasoned Action). These models provide an understanding of the role of attitudes in decision making. The attitude toward the object model can be used to understand, and possibly predict, a consumer's attitude. It consists of three elements: beliefs about product attributes, the strength of beliefs, and the evaluation of beliefs. These elements combine to form what is called the overall attitude toward the object.[16]

The behavioral intentions model, rather than focusing on attributes, focuses on intentions to act or purchase. This model considers consumer perceptions of what other people, particularly peers, believe is the best choice among a set of alternatives. As its name indicates, this model focuses on attitudes toward the buying behavior, not toward the object. The subjective norm component is important in recognizing that individuals live in an inherently social environment and are influenced by what others think and believe. Consider attitudes toward personal appearance (e.g., what clothes people wear, hairstyles, or body modifications such as piercings or tattoos). Consumers will take into account what others may think of their decisions before committing to products that alter appearance. Many people are motivated to comply with what others hold to be an acceptable norm and stay in close communication through word-of-mouth, traditional, and digital media.

Several methods help marketers gauge consumer attitudes. One of the simplest ways is to question people directly. The Internet and social networking sites are useful tools for marketers seeking to garner information on attitudes directly from consumers. Using sites such as Facebook, companies can ask consumers for feedback and product reviews.

Marketers also evaluate attitudes through attitude scales. An **attitude scale** usually consists of a series of adjectives, phrases, or sentences about an object. Respondents indicate the intensity of their feelings toward the object by reacting to the adjectives, phrases, or sentences. For example, a marketer who is measuring people's attitudes toward shopping might ask respondents to indicate the extent to which they agree or disagree with a number of statements, such as "shopping is more fun than watching television."

When marketers determine that a significant number of consumers have negative attitudes toward an aspect of a marketing mix, they may try to change those attitudes. This task is generally lengthy, expensive, and difficult and can require extensive promotional efforts. To alter responses so that more consumers purchase a certain brand, a firm might launch an information-focused campaign to change the cognitive component of a consumer's attitude, or a persuasive (emotional) campaign to influence the affective component. Distributing free samples might help change the behavioral component.

**attitude scale** A means of measuring consumer attitudes by gauging the intensity of individuals' reactions to adjectives, phrases, or sentences about an object

Both business and nonbusiness organizations try to change people's attitudes about many things, from health and safety to prices and product features. Look at the advertisement for CapriSun juice, for instance. As more consumers grow concerned about the ingredients in their food, many parents have cut back on purchasing packaged cookies and juices—for fear of artificial ingredients and preservatives and other ingredients they perceive as unhealthy. CapriSun seeks to overcome negative attitudes about juice in this ad by prominently pointing out that its products contain no high fructose corn syrup. The ad also pictures children playing in a backyard, while reminding parents that they can control what their kids drink. The ad targets parents who want their kids to use their imaginations and consume products without potentially harmful ingredients.

## 7-4e Personality and Self-Concept

**Personality** is a set of internal traits and distinct behavioral tendencies that result in consistent patterns of behavior in certain situations. An individual's personality is a unique combination of hereditary characteristics and personal experiences. Personalities typically are described as having one or more characteristics, such as compulsiveness, ambition, gregariousness, dogmatism, authoritarianism, introversion, extroversion, and competitiveness. Marketing researchers look for relationships between such characteristics and buying behavior. Even though a few links between several personality traits and buyer behavior have been determined, studies have not proven a definitive link. However, weak association between personality and buying behavior may be the result of unreliable measures, rather than a true lack of a relationship.

A number of marketers are convinced that consumers' personalities do indeed influence types and brands of products purchased. Because of this believed relation, marketers aim advertising at specific personality types. For example, truck commercials often highlight rugged, all-American individualism. Marketers generally focus on positive personality characteristics, such as security consciousness, sociability, independence, or competitiveness, rather than on negatively valued ones, such as insensitivity or timidity. The PRIZM program, owned by Nielsen, is one consumer framework that takes into account individual personality differences. (See the following "Lifestyles" section.)

A person's self-concept is closely linked to personality. **Self-concept** (sometimes called *self-image*) is one's perception or view of oneself. Individuals develop and alter their self-concepts based on an interaction between psychological and social dimensions. Research shows that buyers purchase products that reflect and enhance their self-concepts and that

Source: Kraft Foods Groups, Inc.

CAPRISUN.COM

YES TO BASKHEADBALL
NO TO HIGH FRUCTOSE CORN SYRUP.

PUSH PLAY
YOU DECIDE WHAT THEY DRINK.     LEAVE THE REST UP TO THEM.

NOW WITH NO HIGH FRUCTOSE CORN SYRUP

**Communication to Influence Attitudes**
CapriSun seeks to overcome negative consumer attitudes about juice products with this ad.

**personality** A set of internal traits and distinct behavioral tendencies that result in consistent patterns of behavior in certain situations

**self-concept** A perception or view of oneself

# Entrepreneurship in Marketing

## What's a "Glam Bag?" Ipsy Knows

**Founder:** Michelle Phan
**Business:** Ipsy
**Founded:** 2011, in San Mateo, California
**Success:** In the short time it has been in business, Ipsy already has 1.5 million subscribers.

YouTube star Michelle Phan has used her popularity as a makeup guru to develop a thriving business marketing cosmetics products and know-how. Phan's path to entrepreneurship began in 2007, when she filmed herself applying cosmetics and posted the videos on YouTube. As her how-to videos attracted millions and millions of views, she cofounded a business selling sample-sized beauty products by monthly subscription. For $10 per month, customers receive a "Glam Bag" with five different samples of eye shadow, lipstick, nail color, or other beauty items supplied by leading brands such as Urban Decay, Smashbox, and OPI. Customers can watch Phan and other Ipsy beauty experts using these products and learn new techniques as they get the latest tips about beauty trends.

Already, more than 1.5 million subscribers have joined Ipsy to take advantage of the opportunity to try new products without spending a fortune. To continue growing the business and to compete even more aggressively against Birchbox and other rivals, Ipsy is investing in state-of-the-art studios for use by its ever-expanding roster of beauty experts. With its marketers posting new videos day after day, and selecting the latest products for Glam Bag shipments, Ipsy is a great source of beauty ideas and advice for every age, every personality, every lifestyle, and every occasion. "The one-size-fits-all look no longer really exists in this new paradigm," explains Michelle Phan.[a]

purchase decisions are important to the development and maintenance of a stable self-concept.[17] Consumers who feel insecure about their self-concept may purchase products that help them bolster the image of themselves that they would like to project. Consumers' self-concepts may influence whether they buy a product in a specific product category and may affect brand selection as well as the retailers they frequent. The outfitting company Patagonia appeals to consumers with a self-concept of being outdoor enthusiasts. Many consumers are loyal to the brand because its products and values represent their lifestyle. Patagonia is committed to its mission of sustainability so that people can continue to enjoy nature. It reincorporated under a new organizational structure, a benefit corporation, which further signals that it values doing good as much as making profits.[18]

## 7-4f Lifestyles

Many marketers attempt to segment markets by lifestyle. A **lifestyle** is an individual's pattern of living expressed through activities, interests, and opinions. Lifestyle patterns include the ways people spend time, the extent of their interaction with others, and their general outlook on life and living. People partially determine their own lifestyles, but lifestyle is also affected by personality and by demographic factors such as age, education, income, and social class. Lifestyles have a strong impact on many aspects of the consumer buying decision process, from problem recognition to postpurchase evaluation. Lifestyles influence consumers' product needs and brand preferences, types of media they use, and how and where they shop.

One of the most popular frameworks for understanding consumer lifestyles and their influences on purchasing behavior is a product called PRIZM (see also Chapter 6). Originally developed by Claritas, PRIZM was acquired by Nielsen, one of the leading research companies in the world. It divides consumers in the United States into 66 distinct groups based on numerous variables such as education, income, technology use, employment, and social groups.[19] These groups can help marketers understand consumers and how things like lifestyle and education

**lifestyle** An individual's pattern of living expressed through activities, interests, and opinions will impact their purchasing habits. Because technology is increasingly important to marketers and plays a huge role in many consumers' lives, Nielsen also released another product, ConneXions, which uses the same lifestyle groups as PRIZM to analyze consumer communications behavior. This information can be valuable to marketers, as it reveals how consumers choose to access information.[20]

## 7-5 SOCIAL INFLUENCES ON THE BUYING DECISION PROCESS

Forces that other people exert on buying behavior are called **social influences**. As Figure 7.1 shows (located near the beginning of this chapter), they are divided into five major groups: roles, family, reference groups and opinion leaders, social classes, and culture and subcultures.

### 7-5a Roles

All of us occupy positions within groups, organizations, and institutions. In these positions, we play one or more **roles**, which are sets of actions and activities a person in a particular position is supposed to perform based on the expectations of both the individual and surrounding people. Because every person occupies numerous positions, they have many roles. A man may perform the roles of son, husband, father, employee, employer, church member, civic organization member, and student in an evening college class. Thus, multiple sets of expectations are placed on each person's behavior.

An individual's roles influence both general behavior and buying behavior. The demands of a person's many roles may be diverse, and even at times inconsistent or at odds. Consider the various types of clothes that you buy and wear depending on whether you are going to class, to work, to a party, or to the gym. You and others in these settings have expectations about what is acceptable attire for these activities. Thus, the expectations of those around us affect our purchases of many different types of products.

**social influences** The forces other people exert on one's buying behavior

**roles** Actions and activities that a person in a particular position is supposed to perform based on expectations of the individual and surrounding persons

**consumer socialization** The process through which a person acquires the knowledge and skills to function as a consumer

### 7-5b Family Influences

Parents teach children how to cope with a variety of problems, including those that help with purchase decisions. Thus, family influences have a direct impact on the consumer buying decision process. **Consumer socialization** is the process through which a person acquires the knowledge and skills to function as a consumer. Often, children gain this knowledge and set of skills by observing parents and older siblings in purchase situations. Children observe brand preferences and buying practices in their families and, as adults, will retain some of these brand preferences and buying practices as they

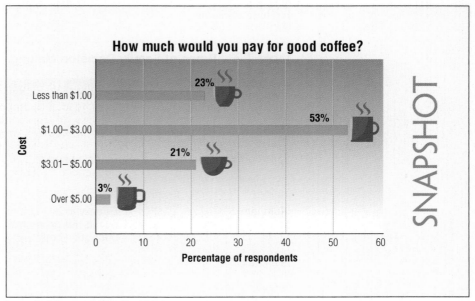

SNAPSHOT

**How much would you pay for good coffee?**

Less than $1.00 — 23%
$1.00–$3.00 — 53%
$3.01–$5.00 — 21%
Over $5.00 — 3%

Cost

Percentage of respondents

Source: PayPal survey of 610 coffee drinkers.

establish and raise their own families. Buying decisions made by a family are a combination of group and individual decision making.

The extent to which family members take part in family decision making varies among families and product categories. Traditionally, family decision-making processes have been grouped into four categories: autonomic, husband dominant, wife dominant, and syncratic, as shown in Table 7.2. Although female roles have changed over time, women still make the majority of purchase decisions in households. Indeed, research indicates that women remain the primary decision makers for 85 percent of all consumer buying decisions.[21]

When two or more family members participate in a purchase, their roles may dictate that each is responsible for performing certain purchase-related tasks, such as initiating the idea, gathering information, determining if the product is affordable, deciding whether to buy the product, or selecting the specific brand. The specific purchase tasks performed depend on the types of products being considered, the kind of family purchase decision process typically employed, and the presence and amount of influence children have in the decision process. Thus, different family members may play different roles in the family buying process.

Within a household, an individual may perform one or more roles related to making buying decisions. The gatekeeper is the household member who collects and controls information, including price and quality comparisons, locations of sellers, and assessment of which brand best suits the family's needs. For example, if a family is planning a summer vacation, the gatekeeper might compare prices for hotels and airfare to determine the best deal. The influencer is a family member who expresses his or her opinions. In the vacation example, an influencer might be a child who wants to go to Disney World or a teenager who wants to go snowboarding. The decider is a member who makes the buying choice. This role switches based on the type and expense of the product being purchased. In the case of a vacation, the decider will more likely be the adults, who possess information, influence, and their own preferences. The buyer is a member who actually makes the purchase. The user is a household member who consumes or uses the product. In this Disney World example, all members of the family are users.

The family lifecycle stage affects individual and joint needs of family members and therefor buying behavior. Family lifecycle stage influences purchases ranging from housing, clothing, and personal-care items to entertainment and investment products. For example, consider how the car needs of recently married "twenty-somethings" compare to those of the same couple when they are "thirty-somethings" with a baby or "forty-somethings" with teenagers. Family lifecycle changes can affect which family members are involved in purchase decisions and the types of products purchased. Children also have a strong influence on many household purchase decisions.

## Table 7.2    Types of Family Decision Making

| Decision-Making Type | Decision Maker | Types of Products |
|---|---|---|
| Husband dominant | Male head of household | Lawnmowers, hardware and tools, stereos, automobile parts |
| Wife dominant | Female head of household | Children's clothing, women's clothing, groceries, household furnishings |
| Autonomic | Equally likely to be made by the husband or wife, but not by both | Men's clothing, luggage, toys and games, sporting equipment, cameras |
| Syncratic | Made jointly by husband and wife | Vacations, TVs, living room furniture, carpets, financial planning services, family cars |

**Family Influences**
The consumer decision processes related to the purchase of numerous products are influenced by both parents and children. Children learn about buying many products from their families, which they apply when making similar decisions when they are adults.

## 7-5c  Reference Groups

A **reference group** is a group, either large or small, with which a person identifies so strongly that he or she adopts the values, attitudes, and behavior of group members. Most people have several reference groups, such as families, work-related groups, fraternities or sororities, civic clubs, professional organizations, or church-related groups.

In general, there are three major types of reference groups: membership, aspirational, and disassociative. A membership reference group is one to which an individual actually belongs. The individual identifies intensely enough with this group to take on the values, attitudes, and behaviors of people in that group. An aspirational reference group is one to which a person aspires to belong. The aspiring member desires to be like group members. This is why companies may partner with celebrities to market their brands or products. A group that a person does not wish to be associated with is a disassociative, or negative, reference group. The individual does not want to take on the values, attitudes, and behavior of group members.

A reference group may serve as an individual's point of comparison and source of information. A customer's behavior may change to be more in line with actions and beliefs of group members. For instance, a person may switch to a different brand of shirt based on reference group members' advice and preferences. An individual may also seek information from the reference group about other factors regarding a prospective purchase, such as where to buy a certain product.

Reference groups can affect whether a person does or does not buy a product at all, buys a type of product within a product category, or buys a specific brand. The extent to which a reference group affects a purchase decision depends on the product's conspicuousness and on the individual's susceptibility to reference group influence. Generally, the more conspicuous a product, the more likely that reference groups will influence a consumer's purchase decision. A product's conspicuousness is determined by whether others can see it and whether it attracts attention. A marketer sometimes tries to use reference group influence in advertisements by suggesting that people in a specific group buy a product and are satisfied with it. Whether this kind of advertising succeeds depends on three factors: how effectively the advertisement communicates the message, the type of product, and the individual's susceptibility to reference group influence. In this type of appeal, the advertiser hopes that many people will accept the suggested group as a reference group and buy (or react more favorably to) the product.

**reference group**  A group that a person identifies with so strongly that he or she adopts the values, attitudes, and behavior of group members

## 7-5d  Opinion Leaders

An **opinion leader** is a member of an informal group who provides information about a specific topic, such as smartphones, to other group members seeking information. The opinion leader is in a position, or has knowledge or expertise, that makes him or her a credible source of information about a few topics. Opinion leaders are easily accessible and are viewed by other group members as being well informed about one or multiple topics. Opinion leaders are not the foremost authority on all topics, but because such individuals know they are opinion leaders, they feel a responsibility to remain informed about specific topics, and thus seek out advertisements, manufacturers' brochures, salespeople, and other sources of information. Opinion leaders have a strong influence on the behavior of others in their group, particularly relating to product adoption and purchases.

An opinion leader is likely to be most influential when consumers have high product involvement but low product knowledge, when they share the opinion leader's values and attitudes, and when the product details are numerous or complicated. Possible opinion leaders and topics are shown in Table 7.3.

## 7-5e  Social Classes

In all societies, people rank others into higher or lower positions of respect. This ranking process, called social stratification, results in social classes. A **social class** is an open aggregate of people with similar social rank. A class is referred to as *open* because people can move into and out of it. Criteria for grouping people into classes vary from one society to another. In the United States, we take into account many factors, including occupation, education, income, wealth, race, ethnic group, and possessions. A person who is ranking someone into a class does not necessarily apply all of a society's criteria. Sometimes, too, the role of income tends to be overemphasized in social class determination. Although income does help determine social class, the other factors also play a role. Within social classes, both incomes and spending habits differ significantly among members.

Analyses of social class in the United States commonly divide people among three to seven categories. Social scientist Richard P. Coleman suggests that, for purposes of consumer analysis, the population is best divided into the three major status groups (shown in Table 7.4), which are upper, middle, and lower classes. However, he warns marketers that considerable diversity exists in people's life situations within each status group.

To some degree, individuals within social classes develop and assume common behavioral patterns. They may have similar attitudes, values, language patterns, and possessions. Social class influences many aspects of people's lives. Because people most frequently interact with others within their own social class, people are more likely to be influenced by others within their own class than by those in other classes. Social class can influence choice of religion, financial planning decisions, and access to education, occupation, and leisure-time activities.

**opinion leader** A member of an informal group who provides information about a specific topic to other group members

**social class** An open group of individuals with similar social rank

Table 7.3    **Examples of Opinion Leaders and Topics**

| Opinion Leader | Possible Topics |
| --- | --- |
| Local religious leader | Charities to support, political ideas, lifestyle choices |
| "Movie buff" friend | Movies to see in theaters, rent, or buy; television programs to watch |
| Family doctor | Prescription drugs, vitamins, health products |
| "Techie" acquaintance | Computer and other electronics purchases, software purchases, Internet service choices, video game purchases |

Table 7.4     **Social Class Behavioral Traits and Purchasing Characteristics**

| Class (Percent of Population) | Behavioral Traits | Buying Characteristics |
|---|---|---|
| **Upper Americans** | | |
| Upper-upper (0.5) | Social elite<br>Of aristocratic, prominent families<br>Inherited their position in society | Children attend private preparatory schools and best colleges<br>Do not consume ostentatiously<br>Spend money on private clubs, various causes, and the arts |
| Lower-upper (3.8) | Newer social elite<br>Successful professionals earning very high incomes<br>Earned their position in society | Purchase material symbols of their status, such as large, suburban houses and expensive automobiles<br>Provide a substantial market for luxury product offerings<br>Visit museums and attend live theater<br>Spend money on skiing, golf, swimming, and tennis |
| Upper-middle (13.8) | Career-oriented, professional degree holders<br>Demand educational attainment of their children | Provide a substantial market for quality product offerings<br>Family lifestyle characterized as gracious yet careful<br>Spend money on movies, gardening, and photography |
| **Middle Americans** | | |
| Middle class (32.8) | "Typical" Americans<br>Work conscientiously and adhere to culturally defined standards<br>Average-pay white-collar workers<br>Attend church and obey the law<br>Often very involved in children's school and sports activities | Greatly value living in a respected neighborhood and keep their homes well furnished<br>Generally price sensitive<br>Adopt conventional consumption tastes and consult category experts<br>Spend on family-oriented physical activities, such as fishing, camping, boating, and hunting |
| Working class (32.3) | Average-pay blue-collar workers<br>Live a routine life with unchanging day-to-day activities<br>Hold jobs that entail manual labor and moderate skills<br>Some are union members<br>Socially not involved in civic or church activities; limit social interaction to close neighbors and relatives | Reside in small houses or apartments in depressed areas<br>Impulsive as consumers yet display high loyalty to national brands<br>Seek best bargains<br>Enjoy leisure activities like local travel and recreational parks |
| **Lower Americans** | | |
| Upper-lower (9.5) | Low-income individuals who generally fail to rise above this class<br>Reject middle-class morality | Living standard is just above poverty<br>Seek pleasure whenever possible, especially through impulse purchases<br>Frequently purchase on credit |
| Lower-lower (7.3) | Some are on welfare and may be homeless<br>Poverty stricken<br>Some have strong religious beliefs<br>Some are unemployed<br>In spite of their problems, often good-hearted toward others<br>May be forced to live in less-desirable neighborhoods | Spend on products needed for survival<br>Able to convert discarded goods into usable items |

Sources: Roger D. Blackwell, Paul W. Miniard, and James F. Engel, *Consumer Behavior*, 10th ed. (Mason, OH: South-Western, 2005); "The Continuing Significance of Social Class Marketing," *Journal of Consumer Research* 10 (December 1983): 265–280; Eugene Sivadas, George Mathew, and David J. Curry, "A Preliminary Examination of the Continued Significance of Social Class in Marketing," *Journal of Consumer Marketing* 14, no. 6 (1997): 463–469.

Social class also influences people's spending, saving, and credit practices. It can determine the type, quality, and quantity of products a person buys and uses. For instance, it affects purchases of clothing, foods, financial and health-care services, travel, recreation, entertainment, and home furnishings. Behaviors within a social class can influence others as well. Most common is the "trickle-down" effect, in which members of lower classes attempt to emulate members of higher social classes, such as purchasing desirable automobiles, large homes, and even selecting certain names for their children. Couture fashions designed for the upper class influence the clothing sold in department stores frequented by the middle class, which eventually is sold to the working class who shop at discount clothing stores. Less often, status float will occur, when a product that is traditionally associated with a lower class gains status and popularity among upper classes. Blue jeans, for example, were originally worn exclusively by the working class. Youth of the 1950s began wearing them as a symbol of rebellion against their parents. By the 1970s and 1980s, jeans had also been adopted by upper-class youth when they began to acquire designer labels. Today, blue jeans are acceptable attire for all social classes and cost anywhere from a few dollars to thousands of dollars, depending on the brand.

Social class also affects an individual's shopping patterns and types of stores patronized. In some instances, marketers attempt to focus on certain social classes through store location and interior design, product design and features, pricing strategies, personal sales efforts, and advertising. Many companies focus on the middle and working classes because they account for such a large portion of the population. Outside the United States, the middle class is growing rapidly in places such as India, China, and Brazil, making these consumers desirable targets for marketing messages. For example, Kellogg Company acquired Egyptian cereal maker Mass Food Group, largely to give it a competitive advantage in emerging markets. Mass Food Group's breakfast cereals and bars are more established in desirable markets, particularly in the Middle East and North Africa. Rather than developing products to compete, Kellogg acquired the company.[22]

Some firms target different classes with a range of products at different price points. Even designers who previously only made clothing for the wealthy have learned about the benefits of offering items at different price points. For instance, luxury fashion designer Lilly Pulitzer created a limited-edition collection of women's wear and home goods to be sold at Target.[23]

## 7-5f  Culture and Subcultures

**Culture** is the accumulation of values, knowledge, beliefs, customs, objects, and concepts that a society uses to cope with its environment and passes on to future generations. Culture permeates most things you do and objects you interact with, from the style of buildings in your town, to the type of education you receive, to the laws governing your country. Culture also includes society-specific core values and the degree of acceptability of a wide range of behaviors. For example, in U.S. culture, customers as well as business people are expected to behave ethically.

Culture influences buying behavior because it permeates our daily lives. Our culture determines what we wear and eat and where we reside and travel. Society's interest in the healthfulness of food affects food companies' approaches to developing and promoting their products. Culture also influences how we buy and use products and the satisfaction we get from them.

When U.S. marketers sell products in other countries, they must be aware of the tremendous impact specific cultures have on product purchases and use. Global marketers will find that people in other regions of the world have different attitudes, values, and needs, which call for different methods of doing business and different marketing mixes. Some international marketers fail because they do not or cannot adjust to cultural differences.

A culture consists of various subcultures. A **subculture** is a group of individuals whose characteristics, values, and behavioral patterns are similar within the group and different from those of people in the surrounding culture. Subcultural boundaries are usually based on geographic designations and demographic characteristics, such as age, religion, race, and ethnicity. U.S. culture is marked by many different subcultures. Among them are punk, rocker, gamer, biker, endurance sports enthusiast, cowboy, and business professional. Within subcultures,

**culture** The accumulation of values, knowledge, beliefs, customs, objects, and concepts that a society uses to cope with its environment and passes on to future generations

**subculture** A group of individuals whose characteristics, values, and behavioral patterns are similar within the group and different from those of people in the surrounding culture greater similarities exist in people's attitudes, values, and actions than within the broader culture. Relative to other subcultures, individuals in one subculture may have stronger preferences for specific types of clothing, furniture, food, or consumer electronics. Take a look at the advertisement for Clairol Beautiful Collection line of hair relaxers, for example. Women of color who like to wear their hair straight are the subculture targeted by this advertisement. Marketers underscore the long tradition of relaxing hair by showing a women dressed up to look like she is from the 1950s facing the same women wearing contemporary clothing. This ad is clearly appealing to a subculture because most other potential consumers do not have the hair texture to require this product.

Subcultures can play a significant role in how people respond to advertisements, particularly when pressured to make a snap judgment. It is important for marketers to understand that a person can be a member of more than one subculture and that the behavioral patterns and values attributed to specific subcultures do not necessarily apply to all group members.

The percentage of the U.S. population consisting of ethnic and racial subcultures has grown and is expected to continue to grow. By 2050, about one-half of the U.S. population will be members of racial and ethnic minorities. The three largest and fastest-growing ethnic U.S. subcultures are African Americans, Hispanics, and Asians.[24] More than 50 percent of children under the age of five are now minorities.[25] The population growth of these racial and ethnic subcultures represents a large potential opportunity

**Subcultures**
Clairol is appealing to the subculture of African American women who like to straighten their hair with its line of Beautiful Collection hair products.

for marketers because of cultural-specific tastes and desires. Businesses recognize that, to succeed, their marketing strategies have to take into account the values, needs, interests, shopping patterns, and buying habits of these various subcultures. McDonald's, for example, has separate marketing directors to focus on the key market segments of African Americans, Hispanics, and Asian Americans. The company's efforts to target these lucrative segments have been rewarded with the company being named Marketer of the Year by the AHAA: The Voice of Hispanic Marketing.[26]

## African American Subculture

In the United States, the African American subculture represents 13.2 percent of the population.[27] African American consumers are more likely to shop online and interact with brands via social media. Younger African Americans have become trendsetters for all young American consumers regardless of race or ethnicity. The combined buying power of African American consumers is estimated to be approximately $1.4 trillion by 2020, up 275 percent since 1990.[28]

With so much buying power and growing influence of young African Americans, it's no surprise that companies are increasing their focus on the African American community. Allstate, for example, launched a national campaign on its YouTube, Instagram, and Facebook pages to highlight the contributions of ten prominent African Americans. The images and videos celebrate the positive impact these individuals have had on fields such as education, health, science, and entrepreneurship and strive to connect with black consumers with regard to insurance products.[29] Apple targeted its Apple Music streaming service at multiple segments with different ads. An ad targeted at African Americans featured actresses Kerry Washington and Taraji P. Henson hanging out with Mary J. Blige listening and dancing to music put together by Apple's playlist service. The well-received ad was designed to educate about the service and to connect with African American consumers.[30]

## Hispanic Subculture

Hispanics represent 17.1 percent of the U.S. population, but that figure is projected to grow to 28 percent by 2050.[31] Hispanic buying power is estimated to be approximately $1.6 trillion by 2018.[32] Hispanics represent a large and powerful subculture, and are an attractive consumer group for marketers. Four clusters of the Hispanic market have been identified based upon language preferences, classified as retainers (those who speak Spanish as their main language), biculturals (alternate between Spanish and English), assimilators (speak English but acknowledge Hispanic background), and non-identifiers.[33]

When considering the buying behavior of Hispanics (or any ethnic or racial subculture, for that matter), marketers must keep in mind that this subculture is really composed of many diverse cultures coming from a huge geographic region that encompasses nearly two dozen nationalities, including Cuban, Mexican, Puerto Rican, Caribbean, Spanish, and Dominican. Each has its own history and unique culture that affect consumer preferences and buying behavior. Marketers should also recognize that the terms *Hispanic* and *Latino* refer to an ethnic category rather than a racial distinction. In spite of its complexity, because of the group's growth and purchasing power, understanding the Hispanic subculture is critical to marketers.

The buying power and diversity of the Hispanic population represents a huge opportunity for firms large and small. Target, for example, created its "Sin Traducción," ("Without Translation") campaign solely for its Hispanic customers to forge deeper connections. The retailer spends about 3 percent of its total advertising campaign funds on Hispanic media. Macy's is reaching out to Latino customers in a variety of ways, but particularly through mobile media. The retailer has also introduced a collection of clothing, shoes, and jewelry from popular singer and telenova star Thalia Sodi. The line features trendy items and includes colors and patterns designed to appeal to Latinas of different cultures.[34] Marketers should recognize that simply translating an English-speaking ad into Spanish may not resonate with Hispanic consumers—and may even backfire. Consider that when the California Milk Processing Board sought to translate its popular and long-running "Got Milk?" campaign into Spanish, it did not consult with actual Spanish speakers, and the resulting campaign, "Are You Lactating?" failed.[35]

## Asian American Subculture

The term *Asian American* includes Filipinos, Chinese, Japanese, Asian Indians, Koreans, and Vietnamese, encompassing people from more than 15 highly diverse ethnic groups. Asian Americans tend to identify strongly with their culture of origin; most prefer to refer to themselves by their country of origin (e.g., Japanese or Japanese American) rather than being referred to as Asian American.[36] This group represents 5.3 percent of the U.S. population.[37] The individual language, religion, and value system of each group influences its members' purchasing decisions. The combined buying power of Asian American consumers is projected to reach $1 trillion by 2018.[38] Though they represent a smaller proportion of the overall population, Asian Americans are the fastest-growing demographic and are projected to increase by 50 percent in a decade. As a group, Asian Americans are also more educated and have household incomes that are 29 percent higher than the median income[39]—making them an appealing target market.

Although Asian Americans are a smaller subculture than African Americans and Hispanics in the United States, their higher household income makes them a lucrative

# EMERGING **TRENDS IN MARKETING**

## How Global Brands Mark the Lunar New Year

More brands are using marketing to say "Happy Lunar New Year" to people in China and to those with Chinese roots who live in other countries. This important holiday kicks off a period of gift-giving, travel, and celebration that brings families and friends together. From Pepsi to Burberry, basketball, and beyond, brands are marking the Lunar New Year with culturally-appropriate marketing that resonates with the target market locally and overseas.

Every year, PepsiCo releases a special limited-edition holiday can of Pepsi in China, backed up by marketing that connects the soft-drink brand to New Year's symbols. During the Year of the Monkey in 2016, when Pepsi's can featured a monkey, the firm posted a video about a boy who trains to portray the legendary "Monkey King," following his family's heritage. The video reflected positive cultural traditions and attracted millions of views worldwide.

The apparel brand Burberry recently teamed up with the Chinese social-media app WeChat to create a digital "unwrapping" app featuring special new-year's products and messages. Users swiped and tapped their phones to digitally remove the gift-wrapping and view holiday-edition Burberry products like scarves and trench coats as suggestions for gift-giving. Then users could send free, personalized greetings to friends and family through the app and have the opportunity to win Burberry products.

Even the National Basketball Association builds on holiday goodwill (and the growing popularity of basketball in China) by having stars such as Stephen Curry and Jeremy Lin make personal appearances and videos specifically for the Lunar New Year.[b]

segment to marketers. However, Asian Americans appear to lack the recognition in marketing that other subcultures have gained. For instance, advertisers spend less to reach this important segment.[40] However, ignoring such an important segment represents missed opportunities for marketers. Although values differ between Asian ethnicities, common values include interest in savings, long-term planning, respect for elders, and education.[41] Marketers who create campaigns around these values are more likely to resonate with their Asian American audience.

# 7-6 **CONSUMER MISBEHAVIOR**

Approaching the topic of inappropriate consumer behavior requires some caution because of varying attitudes and cultural definitions of what comprises misbehavior. However, it is generally agreed that some conduct, such as shoplifting or purchasing illegal drugs, falls under the category of activities that are not accepted by established norms. Therefore, we will define **consumer misbehavior** as behavior that violates generally accepted norms of a particular society. Shoplifting is one of the most obvious misconduct areas. U.S. retailers lose more than $32 billion annually due to individuals shoplifting grocery items, electronics, and more, as well as employee thefts, and the cost of these losses is passed on to consumers as higher prices.[42] Organized retail crime—where criminal groups engage in large-scale theft from retail and online stores—has become a major threat, not only to retailers, but to all organizations including governments. Experts estimate that organized retail crime alone costs businesses about $30 billion annually.[43] Aside from selling goods on the black market, consumer motivation for shoplifting includes the low risk of being caught, a desire to be accepted by a group of peers (particularly among young people), and the excitement associated with the activity.

Consumer fraud includes purposeful actions to take advantage of and/or damage others during a transaction. Using fraudulently obtained credit cards, debit cards, checks, or bank accounts falls into this category, as does making false insurance claims. Although few realize it, purchasing

**consumer misbehavior**
Behavior that violates generally accepted norms of a particular society

Table 7.5 **Motivations for Unethical or Illegal Misbehavior**

| | |
|---|---|
| Justification/rationalization | The thrill of getting away with it |
| Economic reasons | There is little risk of getting caught |
| It is accepted by peers | People think they are smarter than others |

Source: Kevin J. Shanahan and Michael J. Hyman, "Motivators and Enablers of Scouring: A Study of Online Piracy in the US and UK," *Journal of Business Research* 63 (September–October 2010): 1095–1102.

a dress for a special event, wearing it once with the tags hidden, and then returning it is also fraud. Returning items for cash when those items were actually received as gifts or even stolen is another example of fraud. Retailers lose an estimated $9.1 billion annually to return fraud.[44] Some consumers engage in identity theft, which is a serious and growing legal problem—particularly as more shopping is conducted online, where regulations and security are more difficult to enforce.

Piracy is copying computer software, video games, movies, or music without paying the producer for them. It is estimated that global businesses spend approximately $500 billion to fix issues associated with pirated software. Global consumers spend approximately $25 billion and waste 1.2 billion hours to fix problems resulting from downloaded pirated software.[45] The recording industry broadcasts messages explaining why sharing music is not acceptable, but it remains a serious problem. Understanding motivations for piracy can be helpful in developing a plan to combat the issue (see Table 7.5).

Yet another area of concern with consumer misbehavior is abusive consumers. Rude customers engage in verbal or physical abuse, can be uncooperative, and may even break policies. Airlines remove abusive customers if they represent a threat to employees and other passengers. Belligerently drunk customers, especially in environments such as bars and restaurants, have to be removed in order to protect others. Understanding the psychological and social reasons for consumer misconduct can be helpful in preventing or responding to the problem.

# Summary

### 7-1 Recognize the stages of the consumer buying decision process.

The consumer buying decision process includes five stages: problem recognition, information search, evaluation of alternatives, purchase, and postpurchase evaluation. Not all decision processes culminate in a purchase, nor do all consumer decisions include all five stages. Problem recognition occurs when buyers become aware of a difference between a desired state and an actual condition. After recognizing the problem or need, buyers search for information about products to help resolve the problem or satisfy the need. In the internal search, buyers search their memories for information about products that might solve the problem. If they cannot retrieve from memory sufficient information to make a decision, they seek additional information through an external search. A successful search yields a group of brands, called a consideration set, which a buyer views as possible alternatives. To evaluate the products in the consideration set, the buyer establishes

certain criteria by which to compare, rate, and rank different products. Marketers can influence consumers' evaluations by framing alternatives. In the purchase stage, consumers select products or brands on the basis of results from the evaluation stage and on other dimensions. Buyers also choose the seller from whom they will buy the product. After the purchase, buyers evaluate the product to determine if its actual performance meets expected levels.

### 7-2 Describe the types of consumer decision making and the level of involvement.

Buying behavior consists of the decision processes and acts of people involved in buying and using products. Consumer buying behavior is the buying behavior of ultimate consumers. An individual's level of involvement—the importance and intensity of interest in a product in a particular situation—affects the type of decision-making process used. Enduring involvement is an ongoing interest in a product class because of personal relevance, whereas situational involvement is a temporary interest that stems from the particular circumstance or environment in which buyers find themselves. There are three kinds of consumer decision making: routinized response behavior, limited decision making, and extended decision making. Consumers rely on routinized response behavior when buying frequently purchased, low-cost items requiring little search-and-decision effort. Limited decision making is used for products purchased occasionally or when buyers need to acquire information about an unfamiliar brand in a familiar product category. Consumers engage in extended decision making when purchasing an unfamiliar, expensive, or infrequently bought product. Purchase of a certain product does not always elicit the same type of decision making. Impulse buying is not a consciously planned buying behavior but involves a powerful urge to buy something immediately.

### 7-3 Explain how situational influences may affect the consumer buying decision process.

Three major categories of influences affect the consumer buying decision process: situational, psychological, and social. Situational influences are external circumstances or conditions existing when a consumer makes a purchase decision. Situational influences include surroundings, time, reason for purchase, and the buyer's mood and condition.

### 7-4 Identify the psychological influences that may affect the consumer buying decision process.

Psychological influences partly determine people's general behavior, thus influencing their behavior as consumers. The primary psychological influences on consumer behavior are perception, motives, learning, attitudes, personality and self-concept, and lifestyles. Perception is the process of selecting, organizing, and interpreting information inputs (sensations received through sight, taste, hearing, smell, and touch) to produce meaning. The three steps in the perceptual process are selection, organization, and interpretation. Individuals have numerous perceptions of packages, products, brands, and organizations that affect their buying decision processes. A motive is an internal energizing force that orients a person's activities toward satisfying needs or achieving goals. Learning refers to changes in a person's thought processes and behavior caused by information and experience. Marketers try to shape what consumers learn to influence what they buy. An attitude is an individual's enduring evaluation, feelings, and behavioral tendencies toward an object or idea and consists of three major components: cognitive, affective, and behavioral. Personality is the set of traits and behaviors that make a person unique. Self-concept, closely linked to personality, is one's perception or view of oneself. Researchers have found that buyers purchase products that reflect and enhance their self-concepts. Lifestyle is an individual's pattern of living expressed through activities, interests, and opinions. Lifestyles influence consumers' needs, brand preferences, and how and where they shop.

### 7-5 Describe the social influences that may affect the consumer buying decision process.

Social influences are forces that other people exert on buying behavior. They include roles, family, reference groups and opinion leaders, social class, and culture and subcultures. Everyone occupies positions within groups, organizations, and institutions, and each position involves playing a role—a set of actions and activities that a person in a particular position is supposed to perform based on expectations of both the individual and surrounding persons. Consumer socialization is the process through which a person acquires the knowledge and skills to function as a consumer. The consumer socialization process is partially accomplished through family influences.

A reference group is a group that a person identifies with so strongly that he or she adopts the values, attitudes, and behavior of group members. The three major types of reference groups are membership, aspirational, and disassociative. An opinion leader is a member of an informal group who provides information about a specific topic to other group members.

A social class is an open group of individuals with similar social rank. Social class influences people's spending, saving, and credit practices. Culture is the accumulation of values, knowledge, beliefs, customs, objects, and concepts that a society uses to cope with its environment and passes on to future generations. A culture is made up of subcultures, groups of individuals whose characteristic values and behavior patterns are similar to one another but different from those of the surrounding culture. U.S. marketers focus on three major ethnic subcultures: African American, Hispanic, and Asian American.

### 7-6 Discuss consumer misbehavior.

Consumer misbehavior is defined as behavior that violates generally accepted norms of a particular society. One form of consumer misbehavior involves shoplifting, or stealing goods from retail stores. Another form of consumer misbehavior is consumer fraud, which involves purposeful actions to take advantage of and/or damage others. Piracy, the copying or sharing of music, movies, video games, and computer software, is another form of misbehavior. One final area of concern with regard to consumer misbehavior is abusive consumers, which include customers who are rude, verbally or physically abusive, and/or uncooperative, which may violate some companies' policies. To respond to or even prevent these growing problems, organizations need to understand the psychological and social reasons for consumer misbehavior.

Go to www.cengagebrain.com for resources to help you master the content in this chapter as well as for materials that will expand your marketing knowledge!

## Important Terms

buying behavior  196
consumer buying
    behavior  196
consumer buying decision
    process  196
internal search  197
external search  197
consideration set  198
evaluative criteria  198
cognitive dissonance  199
routinized response
    behavior  199

limited decision
    making  200
extended decision
    making  200
impulse buying  200
level of involvement  201
situational influences  201
psychological
    influences  203
perception  203
information inputs  203
selective exposure  204

selective distortion  204
selective retention  204
motive  205
Maslow's hierarchy of
    needs  205
patronage motives  206
learning  207
attitude  207
attitude scale  208
personality  209
self-concept  209
lifestyle  210

social influences  211
roles  211
consumer
    socialization  211
reference group  213
opinion leader  214
social class  214
culture  216
subculture  216
consumer
    misbehavior  219

## Discussion and Review Questions

1. What are the major stages in the consumer buying decision process? Are all these stages used in all consumer purchase decisions? Why or why not?
2. How does a consumer's level of involvement affect his or her choice of decision-making process?
3. Name the types of consumer decision-making processes. List some products you have bought using each type. Have you ever bought a product on impulse? If so, describe the circumstances.
4. What are the categories of situational factors that influence consumer buying behavior? Explain how each of these factors influences buyers' decisions.
5. What is selective exposure? Why do people engage in it?
6. How do marketers attempt to shape consumers' learning?
7. Why are marketers concerned about consumer attitudes?
8. In what ways do lifestyles affect the consumer buying decision process?

9. How do roles affect a person's buying behavior? Provide examples.
10. What are family influences, and how do they affect buying behavior?
11. What are reference groups? How do they influence buying behavior? Name some of your own reference groups.
12. How does an opinion leader influence the buying decision process of reference group members?
13. In what ways does social class affect a person's purchase decisions?
14. What is culture? How does it affect a person's buying behavior?
15. Describe the subcultures to which you belong. Identify buying behavior that is unique to one of your subcultures.
16. What is consumer misbehavior? Describe the various forms of consumer misbehavior.

# Video Case 7.1

## How Ford Drives Future Innovation

What do consumers care about today, what will they think about tomorrow, and what does it all mean for automotive manufacturers? Sheryl Connelly, Ford's manager of global consumer trends—the company's chief trend-watcher—has been studying consumer behavior worldwide, with an eye toward determining what consumers will want and need long before they know. By

surveying consumers, and analyzing emerging social trends, technological developments, political issues, environmental concerns, and economic changes, Connelly provides Ford's marketers with insights that shape and refine the company's future innovations.

For example, when Connelly looked at technological trends, she found that medical advances are allowing seniors to lead active lifestyles far longer than ever before. Yet as they age, drivers will need vehicles with features that help them adapt to changes in their physical and mental capabilities. Based on Connelly's conclusions, Ford has been adding features such as automated parking assistance systems and ergonomic seats that enable drivers—old and young—to stay safe and comfortable behind the wheel.

Zoran Karapancev/Shutterstock.com

Another trend Connelly recently identified is growing demand for products that are "more anticipatory and self-sufficient" in fulfilling consumers' needs. Self-driving cars will do this by steering themselves and maintaining a safe distance between other vehicles, freeing drivers from having to concentrate on the road as they travel. The company plans to have a self-driving car on the market within a few years, with a popular price tag. According to Connelly's research, buyers in the United States and the United Kingdom have less-positive attitudes about self-driving cars than buyers in China and India. Why? Because commuters in India and China battle more traffic congestion and face more challenging road conditions than drivers in the Western nations. Ford is also working on a voice-command system that will allow drivers to handle specific tasks such as opening a garage door simply by speaking, instead of using their hands.

Increasingly, consumers want the benefits of mobility without the expense and responsibility of owning and maintaining vehicles individually. Especially in urban areas, consumers are flocking to alternatives such as hailing a ride to be driven somewhere or hiring a car to drive themselves for a few hours or a few days. In response, Ford has created a suite of mobility services branded "Ford Pass" to give customers and non-customers alike more alternatives when they're deciding how to get

where they want to go. For example, consumers who install the Ford Pass app can use it to locate a parking lot or spot, pay for parking, and arrange to share a ride with other people.

In addition, Connelly has noticed how many consumers are interested in environmental issues, such as conserving natural resources. Showcasing its sustainability initiatives, Ford looks carefully at its impact from raw materials to finished products and beyond. For example, the manufacturer is experimenting with ways to incorporate recycled materials as car parts.

Finally, Connelly's research has revealed a strong emphasis on self-reliance, which in turn means that buyers place a high value on product quality, versatility, and durability. Research shows that 76 percent of U.S. adults expect to keep and drive the same car for a decade or longer. As a result, Ford must be sure its cars, sport-utility vehicles, vans, and pickup trucks will deliver dependable transportation for years and years to first-time buyers, adults with families, seniors, and other consumer segments.[46]

### Questions for Discussion

1. How does Ford take into account the diversity of consumer roles as it plans its future marketing? Explain Ford's approach in understanding two or more roles that can affect the buying decision process for vehicles.
2. In terms of psychological influences on buying, why would Ford make its "Ford Pass" app available to both customers and non-customers?
3. Ford widely publicizes Sheryl Connelly's research findings about the broad trends affecting consumer behavior. During which stages of the consumer buying decision process is this publicity likely to prove influential, and why?

# Case 7.2

## Disney Markets to the Young and the Young at Heart

Walt Disney Company, the corporate home of Mickey and Minnie Mouse, is also home to such well-known characters as the Little Mermaid, Buzz Lightyear, and Iron Man. Disney theme parks and resorts host millions of families every year in Florida, California, Tokyo, Hong Kong, Paris, and beyond. Millions of youngsters log onto the company's Club Penguin website or use its app to play in a unique virtual

world. Disney's media empire includes the Disney Channel, ABC, ESPN, and the A&E channels. Its studios turn out hit movies like *Star Wars: The Force Awakens, The Avengers*, and *Frozen*. In short, with $52.5 billion in annual revenues, Disney knows how to use its understanding of consumer buying behavior to market to the young and the young at heart.

Disney's movie studios aim to attract a varied audience, including families with young children, adults, teens, seniors, and everyone in between. Positive attitudes toward its hit movies and a high level of consumer involvement in key movie brands combine to create demand for other Disney products at the same time. Consider *Star Wars: The Force Awakens*, which appeals to fans of the original 1977 movie as well as to younger consumers who are just being introduced to this brand. The 2015 movie set box-office records and led to high ongoing demand for related toys and videogames. Given the enduring consumer interest in *Star Wars*, Disney began offering *Star Wars* theme days aboard its cruise ships and opening new *Star Wars* attractions in its theme parks. In addition, the company profited from *Star Wars* mania by charging cable providers millions of dollars for the rights to air the movies.

Families with young children are a particular target market for Walt Disney World in Orlando and other Disney theme parks. During peak periods, however, families may face long waits for popular rides. To address this inconvenience, Disney introduced the FastPass reservation system, allowing customers to bypass the long lines and "reserve" a spot at a top attraction later in the day. More recently, Disney began testing MagicBand, a wristband intended to streamline the park experience even further. MagicBand serves as an admission ticket and an easy way to make FastPass reservations in advance or on the spot. It can also unlock the user's room in a Disney hotel or resort and, when linked with a credit card, lets the user pay for food or souvenirs with a simple flip of the wrist. And because wristbands are set up individually, Disney can use the data gathered by each band to analyze where users go, and when, and to personalize the park experience by, for example, having employees greet MagicBand users by name.

Disney is expanding into graphic novels for preteen boys. In the past, parents and educators often had negative attitudes toward comic books. These days, however, graphic novels with engaging artwork, complex plots, and interesting characters are perceived as another way to encourage children to read. Libraries and schools have begun to welcome graphic novels, and some book stores now dedicate significant shelf space to graphic novels. For the *Space Mountain* line of graphic novels, Disney built on broad awareness of its Space Mountain theme-park ride to tell the story of space cadets on a time-travel adventure. Knowing that the reading habits of this target market are evolving, Disney released the graphic novels in both printed and electronic form.

Disney has a long line of princess characters designed to appeal to girls from toddlers through teenagers. It created Sofia the First, an ordinary preteen girl turned princess, with the attitudes, interests, and aspirations of preschool children and kindergartners in mind. As shown in her popular Disney Junior cable-television program, Sofia's life changes overnight when her mother marries a king. Sofia has to adjust to being part of a step-family, living in a castle, going to a new school, and acting like a princess—challenges that combine the familiar and the magical. Little girls are drawn to Sofia's unique situation and growing self-reliance. Sofia's story also contains elements geared to adults, such as music reminiscent of famous jazz and Motown songs. No wonder parents are buying books, soundtracks, dolls, and other merchandise for their young Sofia fans.[47]

### Questions for Discussion

1. Which psychological influences on the buying decision process does Disney address with its marketing efforts?
2. Which social influences on the buying decision process do Disney marketing activities take into account?
3. Which situational influences on the buying decision process are particularly important to Disney's marketing efforts?

# NOTES

[1] David Jones, "In the Shadow of the Amazon Prime Juggernaut," *E-Commerce Times*, January 19, 2016, www.ecommercetimes.com/story/82998.html (accessed January 29, 2016); Neal Ungerleider, "Amazon Creates Its Own Sales Holiday, 'Amazon Prime Day,'" *Fast Company*, July 6, 2015, www.fastcompany.com/3048275/fast-feed/amazon-creates-its-own-sales-holiday-amazon-prime-day (accessed January 29, 2016); Larry Dignan, "Amazon Prime Day Post Mortem: 7 Takeaways," *ZDNet*, July 16, 2015, www.zdnet.com/article/amazon-prime-day-post-mortem-7-takeaways (accessed January 29, 2016); Paul Carsten, "Alibaba's Singles' Day Sales Surge 60 percent to $14.3 Billion," *Reuters*, November 11, 2015, www.reuters.com/article/us-alibaba-singles-day-idUSKCN0SZ34J20151112 (accessed January 29, 2016); Wataru Kodaka, "Alibaba Group Holding Profit Scores 33% Gain on Singles' Day Success," *Nikkei Asian Review*, January 29, 2016, http://asia.nikkei.com/Business/AC/Profit-scores-33-gain-on-Singles-Day-success (accessed January 29, 2016).

[2] Kathleen Mortimer and Andrew Pressey, "Customer Information Search and Credence Services: Implications for Service Providers," *Journal of Services Marketing*, 27, 1 (2013): 49–58.

[3] Yang Yang, Joachim Vosgerau, and George Loewenstein, "Framing Influences Willingness to Pay but Not Willingness to Accept," *Journal of Marketing Research*, 50, 6 (2013): 725–738.

[4] Björn Frank, Takao Enkawa, and Shane J. Schvaneveldt, "How Do the Success Factors Driving Repurchase Intent Differ between Male

and Female Customers?" *Journal of the Academy of Marketing Science*, 42, 2 (2014): 171–185.

5 Nancy Hellmich, "Put Down that Shiny Object; Most Have Made Impulse Buys," *USA Today*, November 26, 2014, www.usatoday.com/story/money/personalfinance/2014/11/24/impulse-purchases-holiday-shopping/19477369/ (accessed February 10, 2016).

6 Athina Nella and Christou Evangelos, "Segmenting Wine Tourists on the Basis of Involvement with Wine," *Journal of Travel & Tourism Marketing*, 31, 7 (2014): 783–798.

7 Russell W. Belk, "Situational Variables and Consumer Behavior," *Journal of Consumer Research 2*, 3 (1975): 157–164.

8 Tracey S. Dagger and Peter J. Danaher, "Comparing the Effect of Store Remodeling on New and Existing Customers," *Journal of Marketing*, 78, 3 (2014): 62–80.

9 Xun Huang, Meng Zhang, Michael K. Hui, and Robert S. Wyer, "Warmth and Conformity: The Effects of Ambient Temperature on Product Preferences and Financial Decision," *Journal of Consumer Psychology*, 24, 2 (2014): 241–250.

10 Ryan S. Elder and Ariadna Krishna, "The Effects of Advertising Copy on Sensory Thoughts and Perceived Taste," *Journal of Consumer Research 36*, 5 (2010): 748–756.

11 Tom Bara, "The Force Behind Cinnabon's 'Almost Pornographic' Global Appeal," *The Wall Street Journal*, September 27, 2013, http://blogs.wsj.com/corporate-intelligence/2013/09/27/the-force-behind-cinnabons-almost-pornographic-global-appeal/?KEYWORDS=sensory+marketing (accessed February 11, 2016); Sarah Nassauer, "Using Scent as a Marketing Tool, Stores Hope It—and Shoppers—Will Linger," *The Wall Street Journal*, May 20, 2014, http://www.wsj.com/articles/SB10001424052702303468704579573953132979382 (accessed February 11, 2016).

12 "What to Learn from Tropicana's Packaging Redesign Failure," *The Branding Journal*, May 2015, http://www.thebrandingjournal.com/2015/05/what-to-learn-from-tropicanas-packaging-redesign-failure/ (accessed February 11, 2016).

13 Sojung Kim and Matthew S. Eastin, "Hedonic Tendencies and the Online Consumer: An Investigation of the Online Shopping Process," *Journal of Internet Commerce* 10, 1 (2011): 68–90.

14 Lea Dunn and Joandrea Hoegg, "The Impact of Fear on Brand Attachment," *Journal of Consumer Research*, *41, 1* (2014): 152–168.

15 Robin Lewis and Michael Dart, "How Apple Neurologically Hooked Its Customers," *Forbes*, September 2, 2014, http://www.forbes.com/sites/robinlewis/2014/09/02/how-apple-neurologically-hooked-its-customers/ (accessed February 11, 2016).

16 Barry J. Babin and Eric G. Harris, *CB3* (Mason, OH: South-Western Cengage Learning, 2012), p. 130.

17 Aric Rindfleisch, James E. Burroughs, and Nancy Wong, "The Safety of Objects: Materialism, Existential Insecurity, and Brand Connection," *Journal of Consumer Research* 36, 1 (2009): 1–16.

18 Patagonia, www.patagonia.com (accessed February 12, 2016); James Surowiecki, "Companies with Benefits," *The New Yorker*, August 4, 2014, http://www.newyorker.com/magazine/2014/08/04/companies-benefits (accessed February 12, 2016).

19 Nielsen PRIZM, https://segmentationsolutions.nielsen.com/mybestsegments/Default.jsp?ID=70&menuOption=learnmore (accessed February 12, 2016).

20 Nielsen ConneXions, https://segmentationsolutions.nielsen.com/mybestsegments/Default.jsp?ID=90&menuOption=learnmore (accessed February 12, 2016).

21 "Marketing to Women—Quick Facts," She-Conomy, http://she-conomy.com/report/marketing-to-women-quick-facts (accessed February 3, 2016).

22 "Kellogg Company Acquires Mass Food Group, Egypt's Leading Cereal Company," Kellogg Company, press release September 28, 2015, http://newsroom.kelloggcompany.com/2015-09-28-Kellogg-Company-Acquires-Mass-Food-Group-Egypts-Leading-Cereal-Company (accessed February 12, 2016).

23 Charlotte Wilder, "The Haters Were Wrong, Lilly Pulitzer for Target Killed It," Boston.com, April 23, 2015, http://www.boston.com/life/fashion/2015/04/23/the-haters-were-wrong-lilly-pulitzer-for-target-killed/f4un68xngWqBrVCcyW6k0H/story.html (accessed February 12, 2016).

24 Sandra L. Colby and Jennifer M. Ortman, "Projections of the Size and Composition of U.S. Population: 2014 to 2060," United States Census Bureau, March 2015, https://www.census.gov/content/dam/Census/library/publications/2015/demo/p25–1143.pdf (accessed February 12, 2016).

25 D'Vera Cohn, "Falloff in Births Slows Shift to a Majority-Minority Youth Population," *Pew Research Center*, June 26, 2014, http://www.pewresearch.org/fact-tank/2014/06/26/falloff-in-births-slows-shift-to-a-majority-minority-youth-population/.

26 Laurel Wentz, "McDonald's Is Marketer of the Year at AHAA's Hispanic Conference," Advertising Age, May 1, 2014, http://adage.com/article/hispanic-marketing/mcdonald-s-marketer-year-ahaa-conference/292979/ (accessed February 12, 2016).

27 United States Census Bureau, "State & Country QuickFacts," December 2, 2015, http://quickfacts.census.gov/qfd/states/00000.html (accessed February 16, 2016).

28 Janie Boschma, "Black Consumers Have 'Unprecedented Impact' in 2015," The Atlantic, February 2, 2016, http://www.theatlantic.com/politics/archive/2016/02/black-consumers-have-unprecedented-impact-in-2015/433725/ (accessed February 16, 2016).

29 "Allstate Black History Month Campaign Spotlights Modern African-American Inspirational Stories," Allstate, press release, February 1, 2016, http://finance.yahoo.com/news/allstate-black-history-month-campaign-140000349.html (accessed February 16, 2016).

30 Ann-Christine Diaz, "How Apple Music's Star-Studded Emmy Ad Came Together," *Advertising Age*, September 21, 2015, http://adage.com/article/advertising/apple-s-star-studded-emmy-s-ad/300463/ (accessed February 16, 2016).

31 Laurel Wentz, "Tipping Point: The Majority Will Become the Minority by 2044," *Advertising Age*, April 6, 2015, http://adage.com/article/hispanic-marketing/tipping-point-majority-minority-2044/297911/ (accessed February 16, 2016); United States Census Bureau, "State & Country QuickFacts."

32 Krystina Gustafson, "These Consumers Can Make or Break Sales Growth," *CNBC*, February 20, 2015, http://www.cnbc.com/2015/02/20/hispanic-consumers-driving-growth-in-beauty.html (accessed February 16, 2016).

33 Cecilia M.O. Alvarez, Peter R. Dickson, and Gary K. Hunter, "The Four Faces of the Hispanic Consumer: An Acculturation-Based Segmentation," *Journal of Business Research*, *67, 2* (2014): 108–115.

34 Rick Wartzman, How Macy's Found Its Fit in the Hispanic Market," *Fortune*, April 17, 2015,

http://fortune.com/2015/04/17/macys-diversity-hispanic-consumers/ (accessed February 16, 2016); Ashley Rodriguez, "Retailers Duke It Out for Hispanic Shoppers' Dollars," *Advertising Age*, April 6, 2015, http://adage.com/article/cmo-strategy/retailers-duke-hispanic-shoppers-dollars/297902/ (accessed February 16, 2016).

35 Eli Bishop, "6 Brands That Succeed at Understanding Hispanic Marketing," Business 2 Community, October 7, 2014, http://www.business2community.com/marketing/6-brands-succeed-understanding-hispanic-market-ing-01030311 (accessed February 16, 2016).

36 "Asian-Americans Are Not One Big Group," *Washington Examiner*, March 16, 2015, http://www.washingtonexaminer.com/asian-amer-icans-are-not-one-big-group/article/2561445 (accessed February 16, 2016).

37 United States Census Bureau, "State & Country QuickFacts."

38 "Nielsen: Asian-American Buying Power Increased by More than $50 Billion in One Year—Expected to Hit $1 Trillion by 2018," Nielsen.com, June 11, 2015, press release, http://www.nielsen.com/us/en/press-room/2015/nielsen-asian-ameri-can-buying-power-increased-by-more-than-50B-in-one-year.html (accessed February 16, 2016).

39 Ben Casselman, "Five Years of Recovery Haven't Boosted the Median Household Income," Fivethirtyeight, September 16, 2014, http://fivethir-tyeight.com/datalab/five-years-of-recovery-havent-boosted-the-median-household-income/ (accessed February 16, 2016); Cass Sunstein, "Asian-Amer-icans Will Soon Be the Wealthiest Americans," *Chicago Tribune*, March 3, 2015, http://www.chicagotribune.com/news/opinion/commentary/chi-asian-americans-wealthiest-20150303-story.html (accessed February 16, 2016).

40 Amy Jo Coffey, "Understanding the Invisibil-ity of the Asian-American Television Audience:

Why Marketers Often Overlook an Audience of 'Model' Consumers," *Journal of Advertising Research*, 53 (1, 2013): 101–118.

41 Christine Birkner, "Asian-Americans in Focus," *Marketing News*, March 2013, p. 14.

42 Phil Wahba, "Shoplifting, Worker Theft Cost Retailers $32 Billion Last Year," *Fortune*, June 24, 2015, http://fortune.com/2015/06/24/shop-lifting-worker-theft-cost-retailers-32-billion-in-2014/ (accessed February 16, 2016).

43 Kathy Grannis Allen, "National Retail Federation Survey Finds ORC Still Prevalent Across Industry," *National Retail Federation*, September 14, 2015, https://nrf.com/media/press-releases/national-retail-federation-survey-finds-orc-still-prevalent-across-the-industry (accessed February 16, 2016).

44 Kathy Grannis Allen, "Retailers Estimate Hol-iday Return Fraud Will Cost Them $2.2 Billion in 2015," *National Retail Federation,* December 17, 2015, https://nrf.com/media/press-releases/retailers-estimate-holiday-return-fraud-will-cost-22-billion-2015 (accessed February 16, 2016).

45 Don Reisinger, "Microsoft Touts Study Show-ing the Cost of Pirated Software," *CNET*, March 19, 2014, http://www.cnet.com/news/microsoft-touts-study-showing-the-cost-of-pirated-soft-ware/ (accessed February 16, 2016).

46 "Ford's 'Futurist' Predicts Upcoming Trends," *CBS This Morning*, December 12, 2014, www.cbsnews.com/videos/fords-futurist-predicts-upcoming-trends (accessed February 2, 2016); Melissa Wylie, "What It Means to Be Ford's 'Futurist'—No Crystal Ball," *Business Journals*, December 14, 2015, www.bizjournals.com/bizwomen/news/profiles-strategies/2015/12/what-it-means-to-be-fords-futurist-no-crystal-ball.html?page=all (accessed February 2, 2016); Dale Buss, "Ford Futurist Sheryl Connelly Issues 2016 Trends Report," *Brand Channel*, December 9,

2015, http://brandchannel.com/2015/12/09/ford-future-trends-sheryl-connelly-120915/ (accessed February 2, 2016); Michael Martinez, "Ford at CES: Dramatic Change on Way," *Detroit News*, January 5, 2016, www.detroitnews.com/story/business/autos/ford/2016/01/04/ford-tout-drones-driverless-cars-ces/78289104 (accessed February 2, 2016); Bradley Berman, "Big Auto Searches for Meaning Beyond Selling Cars," *MIT Technology Review*, January 21, 2016, www.technologyreview.com/s/545646/big-auto-searches-for-meaning-beyond-selling-cars/ (accessed February 2, 2016).

47 Subrat Patniak, "'Star Wars' Toys Gener-ate More than $700 Million in Sales in 2015," *Reuters*, January 20, 2016, www.reuters.com/article/us-star-wars-toys-idUSKCN0UY2D7 (accessed January 29, 2016); Sandra Pedicini, "Disney Theme-Park Division Reports Strong Gains," *Orlando Sentinel,* November 5, 2015, www.orlandosentinel.com/business/os-disney-earnings-20151105-story.html (accessed January 29, 2016); Jon Waterhouse, "'Star Wars' Days, Other New Treats Await on Disney Cruise Line," *Atlanta Journal Constitution*, January 25, 2016, www.ajc.com/news/travel/star-wars-days-other-new-treats-await-on-disney-cr/np8T6/ (accessed January 29, 2016); Dean Takahashi, "Disney Takes Its Club Penguin Virtual World to the iPad," *Venture Beat*, December 12, 2013; Steve Smith, "Building the Perfect Princess," *Media-post*, November 18, 2013, www.mediapost.com; Heidi MacDonald, "Disney Expands Its Comics Program," *Publishers Weekly*, November 13, 2013, www.publishersweekly.com; Brad Tuttle, "Why Vacationers Will Soon Spend Even More Time and Money at Disney World," *Time*, January 10, 2013, http://business.time.com; Katherine Rosman, "Test-Marketing a Modern Princess," *Wall Street Journal*, April 9, 2013, www.wsj.com; www.thewaltdisneycompany.com.

## Feature Notes

a Nicole LaPorte, "Serious Beauty," *Fast Com-pany*, February 2016, pp. 27–29; Geoff Weiss, "How Ipsy, Michelle Phan's Million-Member Sampling Service, Is Giving Birchbox a Run for Its Money," *Entrepreneur*, March 31, 2015, www.entrepreneur.com/article/244536 (accessed February 1, 2016); Susan Adams, "30 Under 30 All-Star Updates: Michelle Phan," *Forbes*, January 4, 2016, www.forbes.com/sites/susanadams/2016/01/04/30-under-30-all-

star-updates-michelle-phan/#c78d5216ef3c (accessed February 1, 2016).

b Renee Hartman, "Chinese New Year Dos and Don'ts for Luxury Brands and Retailers," *Lux-ury Daily*, January 26, 2016, www.luxurydaily.com/chinese-new-year-dos-and-donts-for-lux-ury-brands-and-retailers (accessed February 1, 2016); Be On, "Pepsi Rings in the Chinese New Year with the Monkey King Family," *Marketing*

*Magazine*, January 15, 2016, www.marketingmagazine.co.uk/article/1379437/pepsi-rings-chinese-new-year-monkey-king-family (accessed February 1, 2016); "WeChat Campaign Spotlight: Burberry Gets Festive for Chinese New Year," *Jing Daily*, January 7, 2016, https://jingdaily.com/wechat-campaign-spot-light-burberry-gets-festive-for-chinese-new-year (accessed February 1, 2016).

Dmitry Kalinovsky/Shutterstock.com

# chapter 8

## Business Markets and Buying Behavior

# MARKETING INSIGHTS

## Why Live Oak Bank Targets Small Businesses

Wavebreakmedia/iStock/Getty Images Plus/Getty Images

What bank would want to lend money to an independent funeral parlor, a poultry processor, a self-storage facility, or a brewery? Those are only some of the dozen industries targeted by Live Oak Bank of Wilmington, North Carolina. Founded in 2008, the bank specializes in loans to small and independent businesses operating in industries that Live Oak regards as flourishing but underserved by banking institutions. Other targeted industries: pharmacies, veterinary practices, health-care groups, dental groups, hotels, family entertainment centers, investment advisors, and insurance firms.

By lending to a limited number of industries, Live Oak's experts can immerse themselves in the details and learn what businesses in each industry need to succeed. For their part, small business owners are put at ease by dealing with bankers who understand their industry's special challenges and terminology. Live Oak's bankers not only have to stay up-to-date on industry developments, they also must examine the performance and potential of businesses that seek loans to determine whether the money they borrow is likely to be repaid.

When the co-owners of HenHouse Brewing Company wanted to expand craft beer production, they asked local banks about a loan. Those banks showed little interest, because the firm was only four years old and not very big. Then the owners approached Live Oak Bank, which had a new office in Santa Rosa, California, where HenHouse wanted to relocate. After analyzing HenHouse's business plan and loan application, Live Oak's industry experts agreed to lend more than $1 million so the brewery could increase its output and outfit a tasting room to show off its beers.[1]

Marketers are just as concerned with meeting the needs of business customers as they are of meeting those of consumers. Marketers at Live Oak Bank, for instance, go to considerable lengths to understand their customers so they can provide better, more satisfying products and develop and maintain long-term customer relationships.

In this chapter, we look at business markets and business buying decision processes. We first discuss various kinds of business markets and the types of buyers that comprise those markets. Next, we explore several dimensions of business buying, such as the characteristics of transactions, attributes and concerns of buyers, methods of buying, and distinctive features of demand for business products. We then examine how business buying decisions are made and who makes the purchases. Finally, we consider how businesses rely on technology and the Internet when marketing and building relationships with business customers.

# 8-1 BUSINESS MARKETS

As defined in Chapter 6, a business market (also called a *business-to-business market* or *B2B market*) consists of individuals, organizations, or groups that purchase a specific kind of product for one of three purposes: resale, direct use in producing other products, or use in general daily operations. Marketing to businesses employs the same concepts—defining target markets, understanding buying behavior, and developing effective marketing mixes—as marketing to ultimate consumers. However, there are important structural and behavioral differences in business markets. A company that markets to another company must be aware of how its product will affect other firms in the marketing channel, such as resellers and other manufacturers. Business products can also be technically complex, and the market often consists of sophisticated buyers.

Because the business market consists of relatively smaller customer populations, a segment of a market could be as small as a few customers—or even just one. The market for railway equipment in the United States, for example, is limited to a few major carriers, such as CSX. Some products can be both business and consumer products, especially commodities like corn, bolts, or screws, or supplies like light bulbs or furniture. An Apple iPad might customarily be thought of as a consumer product, but some restaurants are using them to list menu items or take orders. Salespeople at many car dealerships have also begun to use iPads for personal selling purposes. However, the quantity purchased and the buying methods differ significantly between the consumer and business markets, even for the same products. Business marketing is often based on long-term mutually profitable relationships across members of the marketing channel based on cooperation, trust, and collaboration. Manufacturers may even co-develop new products, with business customers sharing marketing research, production, scheduling, inventory management, and information systems. Business marketing can take a variety of forms, ranging from long-term buyer–seller relationships to quick exchanges of basic products at competitive market prices. For most business marketers, the goal is to understand customer needs and provide a value-added exchange that shifts from attracting customers to keeping customers and developing relationships.

The four categories of business markets are producer, reseller, government, and institutional. In the remainder of this section, we discuss each of these types of markets.

## 8-1a Producer Markets

Individuals and business organizations that purchase products for the purpose of making a profit by using them to produce other products or using them in their operations are classified as **producer markets**. Producer markets include buyers of raw materials, as well as purchasers of semi-finished and finished items, used to make other products. Producer markets include a broad array of industries, including agriculture, forestry, fisheries, mining, construction, transportation, communications, and utilities. As Table 8.1 indicates, the number of business establishments in national producer markets is enormous. For instance, manufacturers buy raw materials and component parts for direct use in product creation. Grocery stores and

**producer markets** Individuals and business organizations that purchase products to make profits by using them to produce other products or using them in their operations

Table 8.1 **Number of Establishments in Industry Groups**

| Industry | Number of Establishments |
|---|---|
| Agriculture, forestry, fishing, and hunting | 22,111 |
| Mining, quarrying, and oil/gas extraction | 28,720 |
| Construction | 658,483 |
| Manufacturing | 292,094 |
| Transportation and warehousing | 215,547 |
| Utilities | 18,004 |
| Finance and insurance | 472,242 |
| Real estate | 302,374 |

Source: "Statistics of U.S. Businesses (SUSB) Main," all industries, U.S. Bureau of the Census, www.census.gov/econ/susb (accessed February 17, 2016).

supermarkets are part of producer markets for numerous support products, such as paper and plastic bags, shelves, counters, and scanners. Farmers are part of producer markets for farm machinery, fertilizer, seed, and livestock. Chemical manufacturing plants are also part of producer markets, as they produce materials and ingredients that other firms use in the production of other goods. Service providers such as delivery services, banks, and airlines are also an important part of producer markets.

## 8-1b  Reseller Markets

**Reseller markets** consist of intermediaries, such as wholesalers and retailers, which buy finished goods and resell them for a profit. Aside from making minor alterations, resellers do not change the physical characteristics of the products they handle. Resellers also exist for services and intangible products. For instance, there are reseller markets for financial products such as stocks and bonds. Priceline, Orbitz, and Kayak act as resellers for hotel services. Except for items producers sell directly to consumers, all products sold to consumer markets are first sold to reseller markets.

**reseller markets** Intermediaries that buy finished goods and resell them for a profit

**Producer Markets**
Chemical plants are part of the producer market because they produce goods that organizations purchase to use as ingredients in the production of other goods.

Wholesalers purchase products for resale to retailers, other wholesalers, producers, governments, and institutions. Like manufacturers, wholesalers can also be geographically concentrated. Of the 419,648 wholesale establishments in the United States, a large number are located in New York, California, Illinois, Texas, Ohio, Pennsylvania, New Jersey, and Florida.[2] Although some products are sold directly to end users, many manufacturers sell their products to wholesalers, which then sell the products to other firms in the distribution system. Seafood, for example, goes through a number of intermediaries, including producer, processor, and wholesaler or distributor all the way down to the retailer and final customer. Thus, wholesalers play a very important role in helping producers get their products to customers.

Retailers purchase products and resell them to final consumers. There are more than 1 million retailers in the United States, employing 15 million people and generating approximately $5 trillion in annual sales.[3] The United States continues to be a powerful force in retailing. Half of the top 10 largest retail companies in the world are based in the United States: Walmart, Costco, The Kroger Co., The Home Depot Inc., and Walgreens.[4] Some retailers—Home Depot, PetSmart, and Staples, for example—carry a large number of items. Supermarkets may handle as many as 50,000 different products. In small, individually-owned retail stores, owners or managers make purchasing decisions. In chain stores, a central office buyer or buying committee frequently decides whether store managers will stock a product on their shelves. For many products, however, local managers make the actual buying decisions for a particular store.

When making purchase decisions, resellers consider several factors. They evaluate the level of demand for a product to determine the quantity and the price at which the product can be resold. Retailers assess the amount of space required to handle a product relative to its potential profit, sometimes on the basis of sales per square foot of selling area. Because customers often depend on resellers to have products available when needed, resellers typically appraise a supplier's ability to provide adequate quantities when and where they are needed. Colgate Palmolive, for example, has an oral care division that helps retail customers such as Target assess their space and merchandise involving toothpaste, mouthwash, and other oral care products. Resellers also take into account the ease of placing orders and whether producers offer technical assistance or training programs. Before resellers buy a product for the first time, they will try to determine whether the product competes with or complements products they currently handle. These types of concerns distinguish reseller markets from other markets.

### 8-1c  Government Markets

Federal, state, county, and local governments make up **government markets**. These markets spend billions of dollars annually for a wide range of goods and services—from office supplies and health-care services to vehicles, heavy equipment, and weapons—to support their internal operations and provide citizens with such products as highways, education, water service, energy, and national defense. Government spending accounts for about 36 percent of the U.S. total gross domestic product (GDP).[5] The government also purchases services such as hotel rooms, food services, vehicle rentals, and legal and consulting services. The amount spent by federal, state, and local governments over the decades has gone up on average because the total number of government units and the services they provide have both increased. Costs of providing these services have also risen.

Because government agencies spend public funds to buy the products needed to provide services, they are accountable to the public. This accountability explains their relatively complex buying procedures. Some firms choose not to sell to government buyers because of the additional time and expense the red tape costs them. However, many marketers benefit enough from government contracts that they do not find these procedures to be a stumbling block. For certain products, such as defense-related items, the government may be the only customer.

Governments advertise their product needs through releasing bids or negotiated contracts. Although companies may be reluctant to approach government markets because of

**government markets** Federal, state, county, or local governments that buy goods and services to support their internal operations and provide products to their constituencies the complicated bidding process, once they understand the rules of this process, firms can routinely penetrate government markets. To make a sale under the bid system, firms must apply and be approved for placement on a list of qualified bidders. When a government unit wants to buy, it sends out a detailed description of the products to qualified bidders. Businesses whose products fit with the needs described will submit bids. The government unit is usually required to accept the lowest bid. When buying nonstandard or highly complex products, a government unit often uses a negotiated contract. Under this procedure, the government unit selects only a few firms and then negotiates specifications and terms. It eventually awards the contract to one of the negotiating firms.

## 8-1d  Institutional Markets

Organizations with charitable, educational, community, or other nonbusiness goals comprise **institutional markets**. Members of institutional markets include churches, some hospitals, fraternities and sororities, charitable organizations, and private colleges. Institutions purchase millions of dollars' worth of products annually to support their activities and provide goods, services, and ideas to various audiences. Because institutions often have different goals and fewer resources than other types of organizations, firms may use special marketing efforts to serve them. For example, Aramark provides a variety of products to institutional markets, including schools, hospitals, and senior living centers. It frequently ranks as one

**Institutional Markets**
This pipe organ producer supplies products mainly to churches, which are a part of institutional markets.

of the most admired companies in its industry. For areas like university food service, Aramark aims its marketing efforts directly at students. [6] Another example is the pictured pipe organ manufacturer. Because most businesses or individuals have no need for pipe organs, the producer mainly targets its marketing efforts at churches.

## 8-2  USING THE NORTH AMERICAN INDUSTRY CLASSIFICATION SYSTEM TO IDENTIFY AND ASSESS BUSINESS CUSTOMERS

Marketers have access to a considerable amount of information about potential business customers through government and industry publications and websites. Marketers use this information to identify potential business customers and to estimate their purchase potential. The **North American Industry Classification System (NAICS)** is a single industry classification system used by the United States, Canada, and Mexico to generate comparable statistics among

**institutional markets**
Organizations with charitable, educational, community, or other non-business goals

**North American Industry Classification System (NAICS)**
An industry classification system that generates comparable statistics among the United States, Canada, and Mexico

the three North American Free Trade Agreement partners. The NAICS classification is based on production activities. NAICS is also similar to the International Standard Industrial Classification (ISIC) system used in Europe and many other parts of the world.

NAICS divides industrial activity into 20 sectors with 1,170 industry classifications. NAICS is comprehensive and up-to-date, and it provides considerable information about service industries and high-tech products.[7] Table 8.2 shows some NAICS codes for Apple Inc. and AT&T Inc. Industry classification systems provide a consistent means of categorizing organizations into groups based on such factors as the types of goods and services provided. Although an industry classification system is a vehicle for segmentation, it is best used in conjunction with other types of data to determine exactly how many and which customers a marketer can reach.

A business marketer can identify and locate potential customers in specific groups by using state directories or commercial industrial directories, such as *Standard & Poor's Register* and Dun & Bradstreet's *Million Dollar Database*. These sources contain information about a firm, including its name, NAICS classification, address, phone number, and annual sales. By referring to one or more of these sources, marketers locate potential business customers by industry classification numbers, determine their locations, and develop lists of prospective customers by desired geographic area. A more expedient, although more expensive, approach is to use a commercial data service. Dun & Bradstreet, for example, can provide a list of organizations that fall into a particular industry classification group. For each company on the list, Dun & Bradstreet provides the name, location, sales volume, number of employees, type of products handled, names of chief executives, and other pertinent information. Either method can identify and locate effectively a group of potential customers by industry and location. Because some companies on the list will have greater potential than others, marketers must conduct further research to determine which customer or customer group to pursue.

To estimate the purchase potential of business customers or groups of customers, a marketer must find a relationship between the size of potential customers' purchases and a variable available in industrial classification data, such as the number of employees. Thus, a paint manufacturer might attempt to determine the average number of gallons purchased by a type of potential customer relative to the number of employees. Once this relationship is established, it can be applied to customer groups to estimate the size and frequency of potential purchases. After deriving these estimates, the marketer is in a position to select the customer groups with the most sales and profit potential.

Table 8.2   **Examples of NAICS Classification**

| NAICS Hierarchy for AT&T Inc. | | NAICS Hierarchy for Apple Inc. | |
|---|---|---|---|
| Sector 51 | Information | Sector 31-33 | Manufacturing |
| Subsector 517 | Telecommunications | Subsector 334 | Computer and Electronic Manufacturing |
| Industry Group 5171 | Wired Telecommunication Carriers | Industry Group 3341 | Computer and Peripheral Equipment Manufacturing |
| Industry Group 5172 | Wireless Telecommunications Carriers | | |
| Industry 51711 | Wired Telecommunication Carriers | Industry 33411 | Computer and Peripheral Equipment Manufacturing |
| Industry 51721 | Wireless Telecommunications Carriers | | |
| Industry 517110 | Wired Telecommunication Carriers | U.S. Industry 334111 | Electronic Computer Manufacturing |
| Industry 517210 | Wireless Telecommunications Carriers | | |

Source: "North American Industry Classification System," U.S. Census Bureau, http://www.census.gov/eos/www/naics/ (accessed February 17, 2016).

# 8-3 DIMENSIONS OF MARKETING TO BUSINESS CUSTOMERS

Now that we have considered different types of business customers and how to identify them, we look at several dimensions of marketing related to them, including transaction characteristics, attributes of business customers and some of their primary concerns, buying methods, major types of purchases, and the characteristics of demand for business products (see Figure 8.1).

## 8-3a Characteristics of Transactions with Business Customers

Transactions between businesses differ from consumer sales in several ways. Orders by business customers tend to be much larger than individual consumer sales. Major government contractor Booz Allen Hamilton is sometimes awarded contracts worth up to half a billion dollars to supply medical and IT support assessments and services to various government agencies.[8] Suppliers of large, expensive, or complex goods often must sell products in large quantities to make profits. Consequently, they may prefer not to sell to customers who place small orders.

Some business purchases involve expensive items, such as complex computer systems. For instance, aerospace and defense technology firm Northrop Grumman signed a $1.7 billion contract with the North Atlantic Treaty Organization (NATO) to provide a five-drone surveillance and intelligence system by 2017. Company executives hope that the deal will lead to additional orders throughout Europe.[9] Other products, such as raw materials and component items, are used continuously in production, and their supply may need frequent replenishing. The contract regarding terms of sale of these items is likely to be a long-term agreement.

Discussions and negotiations associated with business purchases can require considerable marketing time and selling effort. Purchasing decisions are often made by committee,

Figure 8.1    **Dimensions of Marketing to Business Customers**

orders are frequently large and expensive, and products may be custom built. Several people or departments in the purchasing organization are often involved. For instance, one department expresses a need for a product, a second department develops the specifications, a third stipulates maximum expenditures, and a fourth places the order.

Business customers look for solutions to reach their objectives. Therefore, suppliers need to identify and promote their competencies to position their products so as to indicate how they provide customer value. Staples recognized this need when it ran a television and radio advertising campaign illustrating how the office-supply retailer can help small businesses succeed in affordable ways.[10] To be successful, suppliers also have to differentiate their products from competitors. Building a brand reputation is an effective way to develop long-term relationships.[11] For instance, Federal Express develops long-term relationships with business customers by integrating customer solutions as a provider of many tracking, transportation, and delivery services.

One practice unique to business markets is **reciprocity**, an arrangement in which two organizations agree to buy from each other. Reciprocal agreements that threaten competition are illegal. The Federal Trade Commission and the Justice Department monitor and take actions to stop anticompetitive reciprocal practices, particularly among large firms. Nonetheless, a certain amount of reciprocal activity occurs among small businesses and, to a lesser extent, among larger companies. Because reciprocity influences purchasing agents to deal only with certain suppliers, it can lead to less-than-optimal purchases.

## 8-3b **Attributes of Business Customers**

Business customers also differ from consumers in their purchasing behavior because they are generally better informed about the products they purchase. They typically demand detailed information about a product's functional features and technical specifications to ensure that it meets their needs. Personal goals, however, may also influence business buying behavior. Most purchasing agents seek the psychological satisfaction that comes with organizational advancement and financial rewards. Agents who consistently exhibit rational business buying behavior are likely to attain their personal goals because they help their firms achieve organizational objectives. Suppliers need to take into account organizational behavior in the form of individual-level decisions. Often the reaction of an individual buyer triggers the purchase of products and affects the broader organizational acceptance of them.[12]

Today, many suppliers and their customers build and maintain mutually beneficial relationships, sometimes called *partnerships*. Researchers find that even in a partnership between a small vendor and a large corporate buyer, a strong partnership can exist because high levels of interpersonal trust can lead to higher levels of commitment to the partnership by both organizations.[13] Consider JetBlue Airways' program to mentor small food businesses and prepare them for success, hopefully as future JetBlue suppliers of sustainable food items. The BlueBud program connects promising small firms with resources and opportunities to work with its leaders to develop business strategies aligned with JetBlue's.[14]

## 8-3c **Primary Concerns of Business Customers**

When making purchasing decisions, business customers take into account a variety of factors. Among their chief considerations are price, product quality, service, and supplier relationships. Price is an essential consideration for business customers because it influences operating costs and costs of goods sold, which affects selling price, profit margin, and ultimately the ability to compete. A business customer is likely to compare the price of a product with the benefits the product will yield to the organization, often over a period of years. When purchasing major equipment, a business customer views price as the amount of investment necessary to obtain a certain level of return or savings on business operations. On the other hand, excellent service and product quality also enter into the decision. A product with a higher price could yield lower operating costs for the buyer in terms of service and quality.

**reciprocity** An arrangement unique to business marketing in which two organizations agree to buy from each other

For instance, Caterpillar construction equipment may be sold at a higher price with superior service and parts availability.

Most business customers try to maintain a specific level of quality in the products they buy. To achieve this goal, most firms establish standards (usually stated as a percentage of defects allowed) for these products and buy them on the basis of a set of expressed characteristics. These standards, commonly called **product specifications**, are written statements describing a product's necessary characteristics, standards of quality, and other information essential to identifying the best supplier for the needed product. The auto industry, for instance, is turning toward aluminum to build vehicles because it is a lighter metal, which can help boost fuel efficiency. Metal companies wanting to sell aluminum to automakers must meet certain specifications in strength and lightness. Alcoa developed a way of creating a stronger type of aluminum sheet that it plans to market to automakers.[15] A customer evaluates the quality of the products being considered to determine whether they meet specifications. In Alcoa's case, its success will depend on how automakers view the price and quality of its metal sheets. If a product fails to meet specifications or malfunctions for the ultimate consumer, the customer may drop that product's supplier and switch to a different one. On the other hand, customers are ordinarily cautious about buying products that exceed specifications because such products often cost more, which increases the organization's overall costs. As a result, business customers must strike a balance between quality and price when making purchasing decisions. Specifications are designed to meet a customer's wants, and anything that does not contribute to meeting those wants may be considered wasteful.

Because their purchases tend to be large and sometimes complicated, business buyers value service. Services offered by suppliers directly and indirectly influence customers' costs, sales, and profits. Typical services business customers desire from suppliers are market information, inventory maintenance, on-time delivery, and repair services. Business buyers may need technical product information, data regarding demand, information about general economic conditions, or supply and delivery information. Purchasers of machinery are especially concerned about obtaining repair services and replacement parts quickly because inoperable equipment is costly, in terms of both repairs and lost productivity. Offering quality customer service can be a means of gaining a competitive advantage over other firms, which leads some businesses to seek out ways to improve their customer service. Long known for its quality customer service and strong customer devotion, Bain & Company targets these businesses with programs to improve their clients' service operations in retail establishments, call centers, and a variety of other service situations. For example, it has developed multiple frameworks of different steps their clients can take to become customer-centered service providers.[16]

**product specifications** Written statements describing a product's necessary characteristics, standards of quality, and other information essential to identifying the best supplier for the needed product

Source: Saia LTL Freight

**Concerns of Business Customers**
No matter what the shipping needs are, Saia promises to deliver a high level of service and customer satisfaction through its shipping services.

Maintaining adequate inventory is critical to quality, customer service, customer satisfaction, and managing inventory costs and distribution efficiency. Furthermore, on-time delivery is crucial to ensuring that products are available as needed. Reliable on-time delivery saves business customers money because it enables them to carry only the inventory needed at any given time. Consider the advertisement for Saia Freight. The ad shows an eager looking truck driver with his paperwork all ready to go to illustrate Saia's commitment to reliable performance and on-time delivery. The ad also describes how Saia's systems can help its customers achieve their goals and have confidence that their shipments will be delivered properly and on time.

Customer expectations about quality of service have increased and broadened over time. Using traditional service quality standards based only on traditional manufacturing and accounting systems is not sufficient. Customers also expect to have access to communication channels that allow them to ask questions, voice complaints, submit orders, and track shipments. Increasingly, they expect to be able to do that on the fly through their cell phone or other mobile device. Marketers should develop customer service objectives and monitor customer service programs, striving for uniformity of service, simplicity, truthfulness, and accuracy. Firms can observe service by formally surveying customers or informally calling on customers and asking questions about the service they receive. Spending the time and effort to ensure that customers are satisfied can greatly benefit marketers by increasing customer retention.

Businesses are also increasingly concerned about ethics and social responsibility. Sustainability in particular is rising as a consideration among customers making purchases. Managers are playing a key role in green marketing strategies through the integration of environmental values into the organizational culture.[17] This results in purchase decisions that favor sustainable and environmentally friendly products. In fact, improvement of environmental performance can indirectly improve financial performance. For instance, the government places a high priority on sustainable purchasing. The Environmental Protection Agency created an Environmentally Preferable Purchasing program to help the federal government comply with green purchasing guidelines and support suppliers selling eco-friendly products.[18]

Finally, business customers are concerned about the costs of developing and maintaining relationships with their suppliers. By building trust with a particular supplier, buyers can reduce their search efforts and uncertainty about prices. Business customers have to keep in mind the

## GOING GREEN

### Government Buyers Go-Go-Go for Greener Buses

Buyers for government agencies are on the go, seeking clean, reliable buses for public transportation that will not only lower fuel costs but also spare the planet and people from harmful emissions. Across the country, more than 40 percent of public-transit buses run on alternative fuels or are powered by hybrid or all-electric engines. Buyers spend considerable time evaluating their needs and their options before making such expensive purchases.

Before the Chicago Transit Authority decided to buy up to 30 all-electric buses, it took a year to test two such buses on city routes. Agency officials looked at the initial cost and fuel savings, as well as other factors. They concluded that each all-electric bus would save the city $25,000 in yearly fuel costs. Just as important, they found that the buses were quiet, delivered a smooth ride, and

contributed to cleaner air that reduced the occurrence of respiratory ailments. Therefore, although all-electric buses have higher price tags than diesel buses, Chicago's buyers chose all-electric models.

When Maryland allocated funds for 172 new buses in 2016, the Maryland Transit Administration set a tight deadline for delivery because it needed replacements quickly for Baltimore's aging bus fleet. After considering buses with hybrid gas-electric engines and buses that run on alternative fuels, officials decided on clean diesel buses because they fit the state's performance and emissions specifications. Maryland established specific bus length requirements and wanted only vehicles made in America, which limited the number of eligible suppliers. In the end, only one supplier bid on that contract.[a]

overall fit of a supplier and its products with marketing objectives, including distribution and inventory-maintenance costs and efficiency.

## 8-3d  Methods of Business Buying

Although no two business buyers do their jobs the same way, most use one or more of the following purchase methods: *description*, *inspection*, *sampling*, and *negotiation*. The most straightforward is description. When products are standardized and graded according to certain characteristics such as size, shape, weight, and color, a business buyer may be able to purchase simply by describing or specifying quantity, grade, and other attributes. Commodities and raw materials may be purchased this way. Sometimes buyers specify a particular brand or its equivalent when describing the desired product. Purchases based on description are especially common between a buyer and seller with an ongoing relationship built on trust.

Certain products, such as industrial equipment, used vehicles, and buildings, have unique characteristics and may vary with regard to condition. Depending on how they were used and for how long, two products may be in very different conditions, even if they look identical on paper. Consequently, business buyers of such products should base purchase decisions on inspection.

Sampling entails evaluating a portion of the product on the assumption that its characteristics represent the entire lot. This method is appropriate when the product is homogeneous—for instance, grain—and examining the entire lot is not physically or economically feasible.

**new-task purchase**
An organization's initial purchase of an item to be used to perform a new job or solve a new problem

Some purchases by businesses are based on negotiated contracts. In certain instances, buyers describe exactly what they need and ask sellers to submit bids. They then negotiate with the suppliers that submit the most attractive bids. This approach is generally used for very large or expensive purchases, such as commercial vehicles. This is frequently how government departments conduct business. In other cases, the buyer may be unable to identify specifically what is to be purchased and can provide only a general description, as might be the case for a piece of custom-made equipment. A buyer and seller might negotiate a contract that specifies a base price and provides for the payment of additional costs and fees. These contracts are most commonly used for one-time projects such as buildings, capital equipment, and special projects.

## 8-3e  Types of Business Purchases

Most business purchases are one of three types: new-task, straight rebuy, or modified rebuy. Each type is subject to different influences and require business marketers to modify their selling approaches appropriately. For a **new-task purchase**, an organization makes an initial purchase of an item to be used to perform a new job or solve a new problem. A new-task purchase may require development of product specifications, vendor specifications, and procedures for future product purchases. To make the initial purchase, the business buyer usually needs to acquire a lot of information. New-task purchases are important to suppliers because they can result in a long-term buying relationship if customers are satisfied.

Source: Dell.

**Less wait. More work.**

Reduce downtime by 50%, get 4X faster performance and gain 3X battery life.

Your employees want to do their best work. Refresh your business and increase productivity with powerfully performing Dell technology and Intel® Core™ processors.

Make work beautiful again at Dell.com/business or 1-877-414-Dell

Intel Inside®.
Powerful Solution
Outside.

**Types of Business Purchases**
When purchasing equipment, such as Dell laptops, business customers are likely to use a modified rebuy strategy as business needs change over time.

A **straight rebuy purchase** occurs when buyers purchase the same products routinely under approximately the same terms of sale. Buyers require little information for routine purchase decisions and tend to use familiar suppliers that have provided satisfactory service and products in the past. These marketers may set up automatic systems to make reordering easy and convenient for business buyers. A supplier may even monitor the business buyer's inventories and communicate to the buyer what should be ordered and when.

For a **modified rebuy purchase**, a new-task purchase is altered after two or three orders, or requirements associated with a straight rebuy purchase are modified. A business buyer might seek faster delivery, lower prices, or a different quality level of product specifications. Retaining existing customers should receive more attention than attracting new customers. If a long-term purchase contract does not exist, a firm should use all information available to develop retention strategies.[19] This means knowing what customers are likely to purchase and how their purchases might change over time. For example, business customers of Dell computers, featured in the advertisement, probably use modified rebuy purchases as their computing needs change. For instance, a business might choose to upgrade to the Dell XPS 13 because it can reduce downtime, speed up performance, and last longer, thereby boosting productivity and minimizing downtime in the workplace. Orders are likely to be similar over time, but demand for specific business products and supplies may fluctuate in cycles that mirror periods of higher and lower customer demand. A modified rebuy situation may cause regular suppliers to compete to keep the account. When a firm changes the terms of a service contract, such as modifying the speed or comprehensiveness of a telecommunication services package, it has made a modified rebuy purchase.

## 8-3f   Demand for Business Products

Demand for business products (also called *industrial demand*) can be characterized as (1) derived, (2) inelastic, (3) joint, or (4) fluctuating.

### Derived Demand

Because business customers, especially producers, buy products for direct or indirect use in the production of goods and services to satisfy consumers' needs, the demand for business products derives from the demand for consumer products—it is therefore called **derived demand**. In the long run, no demand for business products is totally unrelated to the demand for consumer products. The derived nature of demand is usually multilevel in that business marketers at different levels are affected by a change in consumer demand for a product. For example, demand for Intel processors derives from the demand for computers. The "Intel Inside" sticker featured on many computers is meant to stimulate derived demand by encouraging customers to choose a brand of computer with an Intel processor. Change in consumer demand for a product affects demand for all firms involved in the production of that product.

### Inelastic Demand

With **inelastic demand**, a price increase or decrease does not significantly alter demand for a business product. A product has inelastic demand when the buyer is not sensitive to price or when there are no ready substitutes. Because many business products are more specialized

**straight rebuy purchase**
A routine purchase of the same products under approximately the same terms of sale by a business buyer

**modified rebuy purchase**
A new-task purchase that is changed on subsequent orders or when the requirements of a straight rebuy purchase are modified

**derived demand**  Demand for business products that stems from demand for consumer products

**inelastic demand**  Demand that is not significantly altered by a price increase or decrease

**Derived Demand**
The demand for Intel processors derives from the sale of computers that are constructed with Intel processors. The "Intel Inside" message in advertisements and on computer packaging aims at stimulating derived demand.

# EMERGING **TRENDS IN MARKETING**

## LP Revival Boosts Vinyl Record Manufacturers

Decades before downloadable music and compact discs, vinyl long-playing records were the musical medium of choice. Although collectors and music buffs still appreciated the colorful album covers and richer sound of vinyl, record companies released fewer and fewer LPs after the 1970s, because consumers were more interested in newer music technology.

These days, vinyl is back in vogue, and strong consumer demand is boosting demand for vinyl-pressing equipment that can churn out LPs by the thousands. GZ Media, a vinyl-record producer in the Czech Republic, pressed only 300,000 LPs in 1994. By 2014, however, the LP revival meant that GZ Media's old-fashioned machinery was working overtime to press more than 14 million records. The company is still growing so rapidly that it

is scouring the world in search of used vinyl-pressing equipment that it can restore and put into service.

Third Man Records in Detroit is launching its own LP production center adjacent to its record store so consumers can watch as melted vinyl is poured into a mold and pressed with a metal plate to form the record shape and cut its grooves. Cofounded by Jack White of the White Stripes, Third Man Records is buying machinery based on older vinyl-pressing methods but updated with electronic controls and new power supplies. Still, the company had to wait for delivery of its equipment because so many businesses are clamoring to make LPs. Meanwhile, United Record Pressing, based in Nashville, has 30 vinyl-pressing machines working around the clock—and, like most record manufacturers, it remains overwhelmed by demand. Will the vinyl revival last?[b]

than consumer products, buyers will continue to make purchases even as the price goes up. Because some business products contain many different parts, price increases that affect only one or two parts may yield only a slightly higher per-unit production cost. Because some business products contain a large number of parts that each comprise a small portion of the overall cost, price increases that affect only one or two parts may yield only a slightly higher per-unit production cost. However, when a sizable price increase for a component represents a large proportion of the product's cost, demand may become more elastic because the price increase in the component causes the price at the consumer level to rise sharply. If manufacturers of a key part of solar panels, for instance, substantially increase their prices, forcing the cost of solar photovoltaic panel units to skyrocket, the demand for that source of renewable energy will decrease (or become more elastic) as businesses and consumers reconsider whether there will be a return on investment in installing a solar energy system.

Inelasticity of demand in the business market applies at the industry level, while demand for an individual firm's products may fluctuate. Suppose a spark plug producer increases the price of spark plugs sold to small-engine manufacturers, but its competitors continue to maintain lower prices. The spark plug company that raised its prices will experience reduced unit sales because most small-engine producers will switch to lower-priced brands. A specific firm, therefore, remains vulnerable to elastic demand, while demand across the industry as a whole will not fluctuate drastically.

## Joint Demand

Certain business products, especially raw materials and components, are subject to joint demand. **Joint demand** occurs when two or more items are used in combination to produce a product. Consider the advertisement for Patron tequila, which emphasizes the quality of the ingredients that go into the products, even the material used in its corks. Demand for the special material Patron uses will increase or decrease jointly with tequila sales, as it is a required component of every bottle of tequila sold. Understanding the effects of joint demand is particularly important for a marketer that sells multiple jointly demanded items. Such a marketer realizes that when a customer begins purchasing one of the jointly demanded items, a good opportunity exists to sell related products.

**joint demand** Demand involving the use of two or more items in combination to produce a product

**Joint Demand**

The demand for the high-quality cork used in Patron's tequila bottle stoppers increases or decreases jointly as demand for the bottles used for the tequila increases or decreases.

## Fluctuating Demand

Because the demand for business products is derived from consumer demand, it is subject to dramatic fluctuations. In general, when consumer products are in high demand, producers buy large quantities of raw materials and components to ensure that they meet long-run production requirements. These producers may expand production capacity to meet demands as well, which entails acquiring new equipment and machinery, more workers, and more raw materials and component parts. Conversely, a decline in demand for certain consumer goods reduces demand for business products used to produce those goods.

Sometimes, price changes lead to surprising temporary changes in demand. A price increase for a business product initially may cause business customers to buy more of the item in an attempt to stock up because they expect the price to continue to rise. Similarly, demand for a business product may decrease significantly following a price cut because buyers are waiting for further price reductions. Fluctuations in demand can be substantial in industries in which prices change frequently.

## 8-4 BUSINESS BUYING DECISIONS

**Business (organizational) buying behavior** refers to the purchase behavior of producers, government units, institutions, and resellers. Although several factors that affect consumer buying behavior (discussed in Chapter 7) also influence business buying behavior, a number of factors are unique to businesses. In this section, we analyze the buying center to learn who participates in business buying decisions. Then we focus on the stages of the buying decision process and the factors that affect it.

### 8-4a The Buying Center

Relatively few business purchase decisions are made by just one person. Often purchases are made through a buying center. The **buying center** is the group of people within the organization who make business buying decisions. They include users, influencers, buyers, deciders, and gatekeepers.[20] One person may perform several roles within the buying center, and participants share goals and risks associated with their decisions.

*Users* are the organizational members who will actually use the product. They frequently initiate the purchase process and/or generate purchase specifications. After the purchase, they evaluate product performance relative to the specifications.

*Influencers* are often technical personnel, such as engineers, who help develop product specifications and evaluate alternatives. Technical personnel are especially important influencers when the products being considered involve new, advanced technology.

*Buyers* select suppliers and negotiate terms of purchase. They may also be involved in developing specifications. Buyers are sometimes called purchasing agents or purchasing managers. Their choices of vendors and products, especially for new-task purchases, are heavily

**business (organizational) buying behavior** The purchase behavior of producers, government units, institutions, and resellers

**buying center** The people within an organization who make business purchase decisions influenced by others in the buying center. For straight rebuy purchases, the buyer plays a major role in vendor selection and negotiations.

*Deciders* actually choose the products. Although buyers may be deciders, it is not unusual for different people to occupy these roles. For routinely purchased items, buyers are commonly deciders. However, a buyer may not be authorized to make purchases that exceed a certain dollar limit, in which case higher-level management personnel are deciders.

Finally, *gatekeepers*, such as administrative assistants and technical personnel, control the flow of information to and among the different roles in the buying center. Buyers who deal directly with vendors also may be gatekeepers because they can control information flows. The flow of information from a supplier's sales representatives to users and influencers is often controlled by personnel in the purchasing department.

The number and structure of an organization's buying centers are affected by the organization's size and market position, the volume and types of products being purchased, and the firm's overall managerial philosophy on who should make purchase decisions. The size of a buying center is influenced by the stage of the buying decision process and by the type of purchase (new task, straight rebuy, or modified rebuy). The size of the buying center is generally larger for a new-task purchase than for a straight rebuy. A marketer attempting to sell to a business customer should first determine who the people in the buying center are, the roles they play, and which individuals are most influential in the decision process. Although it may not be feasible to contact all those involved in the buying center, marketers should contact a few of the most influential people.

## 8-4b Stages of the Business Buying Decision Process

Like consumers, businesses follow a buying decision process. This process is summarized in the lower portion of Figure 8.2.

---

**Figure 8.2**    **Business (Organizational) Buying Decision Process and Factors That May Influence It**

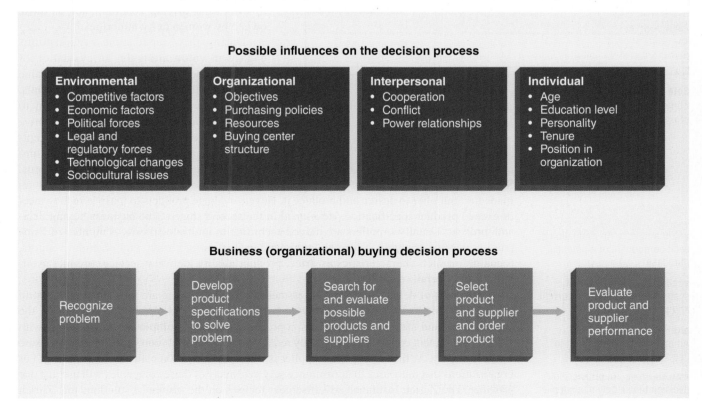

**Possible influences on the decision process**

**Environmental**
- Competitive factors
- Economic factors
- Political forces
- Legal and regulatory forces
- Technological changes
- Sociocultural issues

**Organizational**
- Objectives
- Purchasing policies
- Resources
- Buying center structure

**Interpersonal**
- Cooperation
- Conflict
- Power relationships

**Individual**
- Age
- Education level
- Personality
- Tenure
- Position in organization

**Business (organizational) buying decision process**

Recognize problem → Develop product specifications to solve problem → Search for and evaluate possible products and suppliers → Select product and supplier and order product → Evaluate product and supplier performance

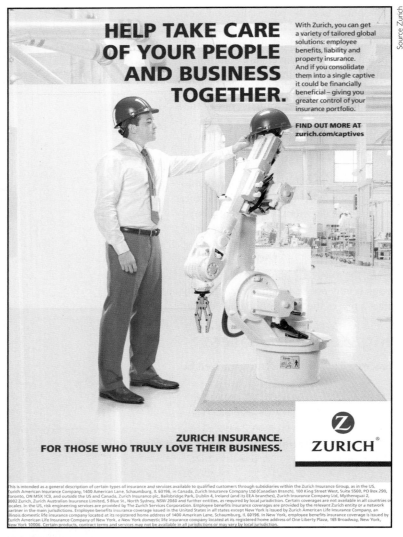

**Sole Sourcing**
Some organizations use just one source to help them manage certain kinds of risks.

In the first stage, one or more individuals recognize that a problem or need exists. *Problem recognition* may arise under a variety of circumstances—for instance, when machines malfunction or a firm modifies an existing product or introduces a new one. It may be individuals in the buying center or other individuals in the firm who initially recognize that a problem exists.

The second stage of the process, *development of product specifications*, requires that buying center participants assess the problem or need and determine what is necessary to resolve or satisfy it. During this stage, users and influencers, such as engineers, provide information and advice for developing product specifications. By assessing and describing needs, the organization should be able to establish product specifications.

*Searching for and evaluating potential products and suppliers* is the third stage in the decision process. Search activities may involve looking in company files and trade directories, looking at websites, contacting suppliers for information, soliciting proposals from known vendors, and examining various online and print publications. It is common for organizations, particularly those with a reputation for having open hiring policies, to specify a desire to work with diverse vendors, such as those owned by women or by minorities.

During this stage, some organizations engage in **value analysis**, an evaluation of each component of a potential purchase. Value analysis examines quality, design, materials, and possibly item reduction or deletion to acquire the product in the most cost-effective way. Some vendors may be deemed unacceptable because they are not large enough to supply needed quantities. Others may be excluded because of poor delivery and service records. Sometimes the product is not available from any vendor and the buyer will work with an innovative supplier to design and produce it. Buyers evaluate products to make sure they meet or exceed product specifications developed in the second stage of the business buying decision process. Usually suppliers are judged according to multiple criteria. A number of firms employ **vendor analysis**, a formal, systematic evaluation of current and potential vendors, focusing on such characteristics as price, product quality, delivery service, product availability, and overall reliability.

**value analysis** An evaluation of each component of a potential purchase

**vendor analysis** A formal, systematic evaluation of current and potential vendors

**multiple sourcing** An organization's decision to use several suppliers

**sole sourcing** An organization's decision to use only one supplier

The results of deliberations and assessments in the third stage are used during the fourth stage of the process to *select the product to be purchased and the supplier*. In some cases, the buyer selects and uses several suppliers, a process known as **multiple sourcing**. Firms with federal government contracts are generally required to have several sources for an item to ensure a steady supply. At times, only one supplier is selected, a situation called **sole sourcing**. For organizations that outsource their insurance services, many of these companies will use just one provider. The Zurich Insurance advertisement focuses on the insurance solutions that Zurich can provide businesses—ranging from employee benefits to liability and property insurance. The ad shows an employee placing a hard hat on an industrial robot to symbolize reducing risk for all aspects of a company's business. Sole sourcing has historically been discouraged except in the cases where a product is only available from one company. Though still not common, more organizations now choose sole sourcing, partly because the arrangement often means better communications between buyer and supplier, greater stability and higher profits for suppliers, and lower prices for buyers. However, multiple sourcing remains preferable for most firms because it lessens the possibility of disruption caused by strikes, shortages, or bankruptcies. The actual product is ordered in this fourth stage, and specific details regarding terms, credit arrangements, delivery dates and methods, and technical assistance are finalized.

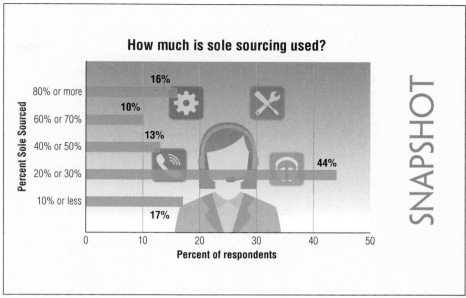

**How much is sole sourcing used?**

Source: A Report by the Supply Chain Management Faculty at the University of Tennessee Managing Risk in the Global Supply Chain (page 11)
http://globalsupplychaininstitute.utk.edu/publications/documents/Risk.pdf.

In the final stage, members of the buying center *evaluate the supplier's and product's performance by comparing it with specifications*. Sometimes the product meets the specifications, but its performance fails to adequately solve the problem or satisfy the need recognized in the first stage. In that case, product specifications must be adjusted. The supplier's performance is also evaluated during this stage. If supplier performance is inadequate, the business purchaser seeks corrective action from the supplier or searches for a new one. Results of the evaluation become useful feedback in future business purchase decisions.

This business buying decision process is used in its entirety primarily for new-task purchases. Several stages, but not necessarily all, are used for modified rebuy and straight rebuy situations.

## 8-4c Influences on the Business Buying Decision Process

Figure 8.2 also lists the four major factors that influence business buying decisions: environmental, organizational, interpersonal, and individual. Environmental factors include competitive and economic factors, political forces, legal and regulatory forces, technological changes, and sociocultural issues. These factors can generate considerable uncertainty for an organization, including in buying decisions. Changes in one or more environmental forces, such as new government regulations or increased competition, can create opportunities and threats that affect purchasing decisions.

Organizational factors that influence the buying decision process include the company's objectives, purchasing policies, resources, and the size and composition of its buying center. An organization may also have certain buying policies to which buying center participants must conform that limit buying decisions. For instance, a firm's policies may mandate contract lengths that are undesirable to many sellers. An organization's financial resources may require special credit arrangements. Any of these conditions could affect purchase decisions.

Interpersonal factors are the relationships among people in the buying center. Trust is crucial in collaborative partnerships. This is especially true when customized products are involved—the buyer may not see the product until it is finished and must trust that the producer is creating it to specifications. Trust and clear communication will ensure that all parties are satisfied with the outcome. Interpersonal dynamics and varying communication abilities within the buying center may complicate processes.

Individual factors are the personal characteristics of participants in the buying center, such as age, education level, personality, and tenure and position in the organization. Consider a 55-year-old manager who has been in the organization for 25 years. This manager is likely to have a greater influence and power over buying center decisions than a 30-year-old employed at the firm only two years. The influence of various factors, such as age and tenure, on the buying decision process depends on the buying situation, the type of product, and the type of purchase (new task, modified rebuy, or straight rebuy). Employees' negotiating styles will vary, as well. To be effective, marketers must know customers well enough to be aware of these individual factors and their potential effects on purchase decisions.

Promotion targeted to individuals in the buying center can influence individual decision making as well. Most trade publications carry advertising to influence buyers. Cintas, for example, launched its first-ever national advertising campaign using television, radio, print, and online ads to show how the commercial laundry and uniform provider can help a variety of businesses be "ready."[21] Trade shows are very popular when products can be demonstrated and samples provided. Personal selling is by far the most important influence of trust in maintaining strong relationships. Interestingly, business-to-business marketers seem to hesitate in embracing social media as a relationship marketing tool. When they use social media, they tend to focus on emotional appeals rather than on functional or rational appeals for purchases.[22] When using Twitter or other social media sites, business-to-business marketers should try to craft messages to convey useful information and develop trust rather than close the sale.

# 8-5 RELIANCE ON THE INTERNET AND OTHER TECHNOLOGY

Whereas in the past, an organization seeking a type of product might contact product suppliers, speak with someone on the sales force, and request a catalog or brochure, business customers today first turn to the Internet to search for information and find sources. The Internet has become a major channel in organizational buying, accounting for $780 billion in sales.[23] Indeed, 62 percent of business buyers now purchase products online, and 30 percent of them researched at least 90 percent of products online before making a purchase. Moreover, 94 percent of B2B buyers engaged in online research prior to purchasing a product, and 55 percent report researching at least half their organizations' purchases online.[24] In many cases, business buyers' needs and wants have been shaped by their experiences as consumers shopping at sites such as Amazon.com, LandsEnd.com, and Walmart.com.

Organizational buyers often begin searching for a product after recognizing a need or problem. The Internet allows buyers to research potential solutions, talk with peers about their experiences with those products, read blogs, consult webinars and watch YouTube videos, examine specifications, and even find reviews of potential products long before beginning a formal buying process. Interactions with a sales representative now may occur much later in the process than in the past. For this reason, marketers should ensure that they post informative content through blogs, webinars, videos, eBooks, white papers, and even responses to forum queries with a variety of information about how their products might solve customers' problems or address their needs.[25] John Deere, for example, uses its comprehensive website to showcase its products so that business buyers can research product details and find the right one to match their needs. The screenshot for John Deere's backhoe loaders offers general information about the features of its backhoe loaders as well as detailed specifications for different models. It also highlights a quote from a user who appreciated being asked for input when Deere designed new machines with improvements to boost productivity.

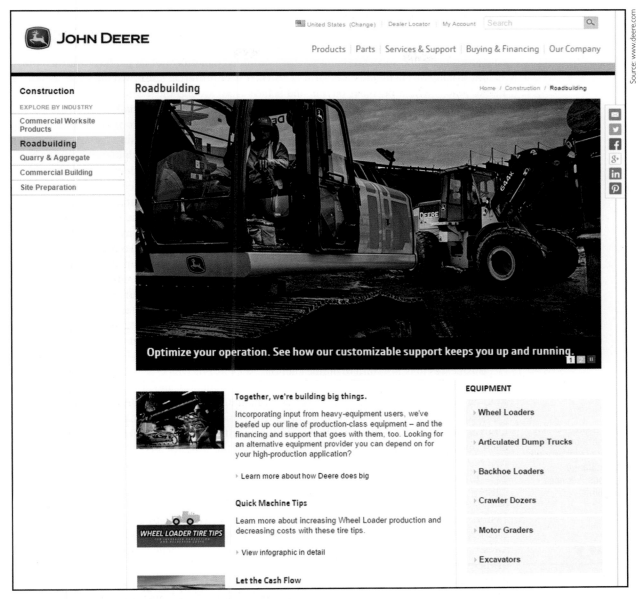

**Technology Facilitates the Buying Decision Process**
Astute B2B marketers ensure that they provide detailed information about their products on their websites to streamline the research process for potential buyers.

For most firms, online marketing efforts make the buying process far more efficient because it saves time and reduces costs. Boga Paddle and Surf Company processes 80 percent of its dealer customers' orders online. The company, which relies on TradeGecko e-commerce software, has been able to capitalize on the growing trend of stand-up paddle-boarding to grow 55 percent a year since its inception. The software allows Boga's sales representatives to access the firm's entire catalog on their smartphones in the field so that retailers know exactly what the firm has in stock and where their orders are.[26] As we shall see in Chapter 14, Internet technology has streamlined physical distribution and other supply chain activities, resulting in significant cost savings.

Organizations can make purchases directly from a firm's website, such as computers from dell.com or hp.com. Like many larger companies, Dell and Hewlett Packard offer special access through a password-protected portal to B2B customers where they can track orders, see past orders, and access relevant information. Organizations can also purchase supplies from a retailer's website. Amazon Business, for example, offers business buyers 2.2 million products in 17 categories using the successful and secure e-commerce platform of its parent, Amazon.com.[27]

Increasingly, businesses are turning to **B2B e-commerce sites**, which serve as online marketplaces where business buyers and sellers from around the world can exchange information, goods, services, ideas, and payments. Variously known as trading exchanges, B2B exchanges, and ehubs, B2B e-commerce sites may be independent or private. Independent sites act as a neutral third party and charge a fee for providing a trading forum. Some sites may be focused on a specific industry, while others may offer products and attract businesses from many industries. AutoWurld.com, for example, is an independent e-commerce site for wholesale and retail buying and selling of motor vehicles. Dealers pay a flat fee of $395/month to gain access to unlimited vehicle listings and sales transactions.[28] Alibaba, on the other hand, connects buyers from all over the world with Chinese manufacturing firms offering products for many industries and purposes. The Chinese e-marketer now handles thousands of industrial orders amounting to millions of dollars a day from millions of buyers around the world.[29] Such exchanges are especially beneficial for small businesses because they allow them to expand their customer base while reducing the costs of marketing to and buying from other companies. Private B2B exchanges connect member firms, who typically share supply chains or complex customers, through a secure system that permits all the organizations to share significant information as well as facilitate exchanges. Exostar, for example, serves as a private exchange for companies in the aerospace, defense, health care, pharmaceutical, and financial markets.

Businesses may also turn to online auctions, such as FreeMarkets, to find products. As with a traditional auction, a seller posts an item to an online auction, and potential buyers bid on the item against each other; the highest bidder wins the right to buy the item. Such auctions are especially popular for liquidating unsold, returned, and used merchandise. In a reverse auction, a buyer invites businesses to bid to supply the specified good or service in competition with each other; the lowest bidder wins the right to sell the product. FedBid, for example, offers reverse online auctions for government agencies; the federal government alone awarded $1.8 billion in government contracts through FedBid, saving those agencies an estimated $160 million by bidding the prices down.[30]

**B2B e-commerce sites** Online marketplaces where business buyers and sellers from around the world can exchange information, goods, services, ideas, and payments

# Summary

## 8-1 Distinguish among the four types of business markets.

Business (B2B) markets consist of individuals, organizations, and groups that purchase a specific kind of product for resale, direct use in producing other products, or use in day-to-day operations. Producer markets include those individuals and business organizations that purchase products for the purpose of making a profit by using them to produce other products or as part of their operations. Intermediaries that buy finished products and resell them to make a profit are classified as reseller markets. Government markets consist of federal, state, county, and local governments, which spend billions of dollars annually for goods and services to support internal operations and to provide citizens with needed services. Organizations with charitable, educational, community, or other nonprofit goals constitute institutional markets.

## 8-2 Describe the North American Industry Classification System and how it can be used to identify and analyze business markets.

Business marketers have a considerable amount of information available for use in planning marketing strategies. The North American Industry Classification System (NAICS) replaced the earlier Standard Industrial Classification (SIC) system and is used by the United States, Canada, and Mexico. It provides marketers with information needed to identify business customer groups. It can best be used for this purpose in conjunction with other information. After identifying target industries, a marketer can obtain the names and locations of potential customers by using government and commercial data sources. Marketers then must estimate potential purchases of business customers by finding a relationship between a potential customer's purchases and a variable available in industrial classification data.

## 8-3 Identify the major characteristics of business customers and transactions.

Transactions that involve business customers differ from consumer transactions in several ways. Business transactions tend to be larger and negotiations occur less frequently, though they are often lengthy. They may involve more than one person or department in the purchasing organization. They may also involve reciprocity, an arrangement in which two organizations agree to buy from each other. Business customers are usually better informed than ultimate consumers and are more likely to seek information about a product's features and technical specifications.

Business customers are particularly concerned about quality, service, price, and supplier relationships. Quality is important because it directly affects the quality of products the buyer's firm produces. To achieve an exact level of quality, organizations often buy products on the basis of a set of expressed characteristics, called specifications. Because services have such a direct influence on a firm's costs, sales, and profits, factors such as market information, on-time delivery, and availability of parts are crucial to a business buyer. Although business customers do not depend solely on price to decide which products to buy, price is of primary concern because it directly influences profitability.

Business buyers use several purchasing methods, including description, inspection, sampling, and negotiation. Most organizational purchases are new-task, straight rebuy, or modified rebuy. In a new-task purchase, an organization makes an initial purchase of items to be used to perform new jobs or solve new problems. A straight rebuy purchase occurs when a buyer purchases the same products routinely under approximately the same terms of sale. In a modified rebuy purchase, a new-task purchase is changed the second or third time it is ordered or requirements associated with a straight rebuy purchase are modified.

Industrial demand differs from consumer demand along several dimensions. Industrial demand derives from demand for consumer products. At the industry level, industrial demand is inelastic. If an industrial item's price changes, product demand will not change as much proportionally. Some industrial products are subject to joint demand, which occurs when two or more items are used in combination to make a product. Finally, because organizational demand derives from consumer demand, the demand for business products can fluctuate significantly.

## 8-4 Describe the buying center, the stages of the business buying decision process, and the factors that affect this process.

Business (or organizational) buying behavior refers to the purchase behavior of producers, resellers, government units, and institutions. Business purchase decisions are made through a buying center, the group of people involved in making such purchase decisions. Users are those in the organization who actually use the product. Influencers help develop specifications and evaluate alternative products for possible use. Buyers select suppliers and negotiate purchase terms. Deciders choose the products. Gatekeepers control the flow of information to and among individuals occupying other roles in the buying center.

The stages of the business buying decision process are problem recognition, development of product specifications to solve problems, search for and evaluation of products and suppliers, selection and ordering of the most appropriate product, and evaluation of the product's and supplier's performance.

Four categories of factors influence business buying decisions: environmental, organizational, interpersonal, and individual. Environmental factors include competitive forces, economic conditions, political forces, laws and regulations, technological changes, and sociocultural factors. Business factors include the company's objectives, purchasing policies, and resources, as well as the size and composition of its buying center. Interpersonal factors are the relationships among people in the buying center. Individual factors are personal characteristics of members of the buying center, such as age, education level, personality, and tenure and position in the organization.

## 8-5 Explore how the Internet facilitates business buying and marketing.

The Internet has become a major facilitator of business transactions, with business buyers often beginning the buying process informally by searching online for information to solve a problem or address a need. They may find useful information in online catalogs, blogs, videos, webinars, white papers, and peer reviews to help them find the best products and suppliers. Online marketing efforts make the buying process more efficient by saving time and reducing costs. Organizational buyers can purchase directly from a company's website, from an online retailer, from a B2B e-commerce site, or through an online auction. A B2B e-commerce site is an online marketplace where buyers and sellers from around the world can exchange information, goods, services, ideas, and payments.

---

**Go to www.cengagebrain.com for resources to help you master the content in this chapter as well as for materials that will expand your marketing knowledge!**

# Important Terms

producer markets 230
reseller markets 231
government markets 232
institutional markets 233
North American Industry
   Classification System
   (NAICS) 233
reciprocity 236

product specifications 237
new-task purchase 239
straight rebuy purchase 240
modified rebuy purchase 240
derived demand 240
inelastic demand 240
joint demand 241

business (organizational) buying
   behavior 242
buying center 242
value analysis 244
vendor analysis 244
multiple sourcing 244
sole sourcing 244
B2B e-commerce sites 248

# Discussion and Review Questions

1. Identify, describe, and give examples of the four major types of business markets.
2. What function does an industrial classification system help marketers perform?
3. Why might business customers generally be considered more rational in their purchasing behavior than ultimate consumers?
4. What are the primary concerns of business customers?
5. List several characteristics that differentiate transactions involving business customers from consumer transactions.
6. What are the commonly used methods of business buying?
7. Why do buyers involved in straight rebuy purchases require less information than those making new-task purchases?
8. How does demand for business products differ from consumer demand?
9. What are the major components of a firm's buying center?
10. Identify the stages of the business buying decision process. How is this decision process used when making straight rebuys?
11. How do environmental, business, interpersonal, and individual factors affect business purchases?
12. How has the Internet facilitated the organizational buying process?

# Video Case 8.1

## Will Apple Pay Pay Off for Retailers?

When Apple introduced its mobile payment system in 2014, the company was looking to leverage the popularity of its iPhone by adding more functionality and convenience for millions of customers. With Apple Pay, iPhone owners (and Apple Watch wearers) first enter their credit- or debit-card information, which Apple confirms with the banks. Once this information is on file, Apple creates a digital "token" that will be electronically transmitted to the retailer when an iPhone owner pays for something. To complete a purchase, the customer simply waves the phone or taps it at the checkout, uses the iPhone's built-in fingerprint security to activate Apple Pay, and the phone instantly transfers the token as payment.

Even though Apple Pay offers consumers the benefits of convenience and security, Apple knew it wouldn't succeed without a large network of retailers, restaurants, and other businesses agreeing to accept its mobile payments. Among the earliest businesses to sign up with Apple was

McDonald's, which agreed to honor Apple Pay in its 14,000 U.S. restaurants and drive-through locations. "We serve 27 million customers every day. This is a clear and compelling business opportunity for us," explained McDonald's chief information officer. Compared with cash transactions, Apple Pay transactions cost McDonald's a few pennies more to process because of bank fees. Yet the fast-food giant was willing to sign on because it saw competitive advantage and profit potential in wooing iPhone users interested in speedy checkout.

Another early business supporter was Walgreens, the nationwide drugstore chain with 85 million customers enrolled in its frequent-buyer rewards program. Walgreens sells snacks, household products, and health and beauty items in addition to health-care products. Not only did Walgreens agree to accept Apple Pay at its checkout counters, it was also the first U.S. retailer to add its rewards program to Apple

Denys Prykhodov/Shutterstock.com

Pay's easy sign-on system. As a result, Walgreens' customers tap twice at the checkout, once to activate the rewards account and display their savings, the second time to process the actual payment. By deciding to honor Apple Pay, Walgreens said it was "enabling a simple and convenient customer experience."

Several hundred thousand businesses had signed on to participate by the time Apple Pay launched in October 2014. Apple's ongoing efforts to increase business participation paid off: Eighteen months later, the network of participating businesses topped two million, and major companies like Starbucks, Dominos, and Crate & Barrel were preparing to participate. Eyeing international expansion, Apple also initiated talks with banks in China to bring Apple Pay to millions of iPhone users there.

Even though more consumers are making more mobile payments year after year, not every U.S. retailer is willing or able to work with Apple Pay. Some aren't satisfied with the amount of consumer information that Apple Pay shares with participating merchants. Others would have to upgrade to new checkout technology for Apple Pay. Still others are locked into exclusive mobile payment deals with competing services.

Today, mobile payments represent a tiny fraction of all purchase transactions, dwarfed by cash as well as by credit and debit payments. And Apple Pay faces strong competition from Google, Samsung, and others operating in the mobile-payment market. To remain a leader, Apple will have to keep signing more participating businesses and showing consumers the benefits of paying by iPhone or Apple Watch whenever they make a purchase.[31]

### Questions for Discussion

1. When a retailer is considering whether to participate in Apple Pay, is the decision process like a new-task purchase, a straight rebuy purchase, or a modified rebuy purchase? Explain your answer.
2. Which of the four categories of business markets is Apple Pay best suited for, and why?
3. Which environmental influences on the decision process seem to have been most important to McDonald's when it decided to honor Apple Pay?

## Case 8.2

## General Electric Goes Social to Reach Business Buyers

With more than $120 billion in annual revenue, General Electric (GE) is a global leader in sophisticated equipment, software, and services for transportation, health care, energy, and other industries. Both Boeing and Airbus buy GE jet engines for their commercial aircraft. Hospitals and clinics on nearly every continent buy GE's ultrasound imaging equipment and GE's power management systems. In recent years, GE has sold off its consumer appliance business and its television network interests, and slimmed down its finance division to focus more closely on business buyers. One of its more recent initiatives is GE Digital, which develops software to keep GE's industrial machinery running smoothly and to speed service support to GE's business customers.

Knowing that businesses, institutions, and government agencies need factual data about product features and usage, especially during the early stages of the business buying decision process, GE has put a tremendous amount of information online for quick and easy access. Whether users are thinking about upgrading existing machinery or purchasing agents are researching a product's exact specifications, they can find plenty of details, diagrams, and case studies on GE's websites, available at any hour with just a click or two. In addition, GE's sales and technical personnel are ready to help evaluate a business customer's needs on-site or by phone and suggest solutions tailored to each customer's unique situation.

Another reason for GE's ongoing success in business marketing is that it does not view members of the buying center as mere cogs in the buying process. In the words of GE's chief marketing officer, "customers are people too." GE's marketing experts work hard to make a human connection with both business customers and consumers through marketing communications that polish its image as an innovator in many fields of science and technology.

The social-media-based "Six Second Science Fair" is a good example. Company marketers posted a few six-second Vine videos of fun experiments to launch a virtual science fair on a special Tumblr page, inviting members of the public to submit their own six-second experiment videos. GE posted these videos on Tumblr and promoted them on Twitter using the hashtag #6SecondScience. The project quickly attracted hundreds of thousands of viewers. Individual videos went viral as viewers retweeted and revined their favorites, giving the GE brand even wider exposure in the business community and the media world.

GE's marketers launched another social-media campaign, "Gravity Day," as a low-key, fun celebration of how Newton got the idea for the principle of gravity by seeing an apple fall from the tree. Once again, GE invited businesses and consumers to submit six-second Vine videos, this time with the theme of dropping an apple in some creative way. Edited together, the segments formed a fun video in which an apple is tossed or juggled or otherwise moved from one video frame to the next. GE promoted "Gravity Day" on its social-media sites and, as before, was rewarded with media coverage and extensive social-media sharing.

Being a big company, GE has jumped into social media in a big way. "Gravity Day" and other Vine video projects are posted on GE's YouTube channel, along with corporate commercials and hundreds of videos demonstrating goods and services. GE's main Facebook page has 1.5 million likes, its corporate Twitter account has 400,000 followers, and its Pinterest account has 25,000 followers. The company

Philip Scalia/Alamy Stock Photo

also maintains separate Twitter accounts for individual divisions, such as @GEAviation and @GELighting. Similarly, in addition to a corporate YouTube channel, GE posts videos on channels for each division, such as GE Power and GE Digital. The company uses its MRI and X-ray equipment to capture engaging visuals of insects and other living things for posting on its medical imaging division's Tumblr account. No matter where businesspeople click on social media, GE has a presence, offering opportunities for customers to learn more about the company, its products, its people, and its principles.

GE's marketers demonstrate the company's technical capabilities and social responsibility by providing a wide range of goods and services for the Olympic games. Only a tiny fraction of the Olympics' worldwide viewing audience is in a position to buy energy generation systems, industrial lighting, medical imaging equipment, or jet engines. But seeing GE put its best foot forward during this high-profile event is sure to make a positive impression on those who can sign a purchase order or recommend a supplier.[32]

## Questions for Discussion

1. Why is GE's involvement with the Olympics a good way to show that the company understands the primary concerns of business customers?
2. How does derived demand apply to the demand for passenger-jet engines? What are the implications for GE's marketing efforts?
3. In which stage of the business buying decision process is GE's reputation likely to have the most influence on a railroad that is considering the purchase of new locomotives?

# NOTES

[1] Bill Swindell, "New Bank Makes Big Entrance into Sonoma County Beer Industry," *The Press Democrat (Sonoma county, CA)*, October 25, 2015, www.pressdemocrat.com/business/4637123-181/ new-bank-makes-big-entrance?artslide=0 (accessed February 3, 2016); Jenny Callison, "2015 Top Stories: No. 3: Live Oak Bank Bancshares Goes Public," *WilmingtonBiz (Wilmington, N.C.)*, December 18, 2015, www.wilmingtonbiz. com/more_news/2015/12/18/2015_top_stories_ no_3_-_live_oak_bank_bancshares_goes_ public/14186 (accessed February 3, 2016); James Sterngold, "An Online Bank with a Personal Touch," *Wall Street Journal*, September 3, 2015,

www.wsj.com/articles/an-online-bank-with-a-personal-touch-1441322491?cb=logged0.8615003043621547 (accessed February 3, 2016); www.liveoakbank.com.

2 "Statistics of U.S. Businesses (SUSB), Main," all industries, U.S. Bureau of the Census, www.census.gov/econ/susb (accessed February 17, 2016).

3 "Statistics of U.S. Businesses (SUSB) Main," all industries, U.S. Bureau of the Census; "US Retail Sales to Near $5 Trillion in 2016," eMarketer, December 21, 2015, http://www.emarketer.com/Article/US-Retail-Sales-Near-5-Trillion-2016/1013368 (accessed February 17, 2016).

4 Deloitte, "Global Powers of Retailing 2016: Navigating the New Digital Divide," January 2016, http://www2.deloitte.com/content/dam/Deloitte/global/Documents/Consumer-Business/gx-cb-global-powers-of-retailing-2016.pdf, p. 11.

5 Total Government Spending, 2015, http://www.usgovernmentspending.com/percent_gdp (accessed February 17, 2016).

6 Aramark, "Aramark Named as a 2015 World's 'Most Ethical' Company by the Ethisphere Institute for the Fifth Time," press release, March 9, 2015, http://www.aramark.com/PressRoom/PressReleases/Ethisphere2015.aspx (accessed February 17, 2016).

7 "North American Industry Classification System," U.S. Census Bureau, http://www.census.gov/eos/www/naics/ (accessed February 17, 2016).

8 "Notable Contract Awards," Booz Allen Hamilton, www.boozallen.com/media-center/company-news/notable-contract-awards (accessed February 18, 2016).

9 Sarah Young, "Northrop Grumman Sees European Interest in Hawk Surveillance Drone," Reuters, August 20, 2014, http://www.reuters.com/article/2014/08/20/us-northropgrumman-drones-europe-idUSKBN0GK1T420140820 (accessed February 18, 2016); Robert Wall, "Drone Maker Northrop Grumman Eyes Europe Order," *The Wall Street Journal*, August 20, 2014, http://www.wsj.com/articles/grumman-sees-nato-drone-use-spurring-european-orders-1408543976 (accessed March 26, 2015).

10 Kate Maddox, "Staples to Launch New Campaign Aimed at Small Businesses," *Advertising Age*, February 6, 2015, http://adage.com/article/btob/staples-launch-campaign-aimed-small-businesses/297043/ (accessed March 26, 2015).

11 Anne Maarit Jalkala and Joona Keränen, "Brand Positioning Strategies for Industrial Firms Providing Customer Solutions," *Journal of Business & Industrial Marketing*, 29, 3 (2014): 253–264.

12 Hannu Sakari Makkonen and Wesley J. Johnston, "Innovation Adoption and Diffusion in Business-to-Business Marketing," *Journal of Business & Industrial Marketing*, 29, 4 (2014): 324–331.

13 Das Narayandas and V. Kasturi Rangan, "Building and Sustaining Buyer-Seller Relationships in Mature Industrial Markets," *Journal of Marketing* (July 2004): 63.

14 "JetBlue's New Mentoring Program Helping Small, Responsible Food Businesses Get off the Ground," *Brand Innovation*, March 16, 2015, http://www.sustainablebrands.com/news_and_views/brand_innovation/sustainable_brands/jetblues_new_mentoring_program_helping_small_resp (accessed February 18, 2016).

15 John W. Miller, "Alcoa Targets Auto Industry with New Aluminum Process," *The Wall Street Journal*, December 4, 2014, http://www.wsj.com/articles/alcoa-targets-auto-industry-with-new-aluminum-process-1417734874 (accessed April 3, 2015).

16 Bain & Company, "Service Operations," http://www.bain.com/consulting-services/performance-improvement/service-operations.aspx (accessed February 18, 2016); Oliver Straehle, Michael Fuellemann, and Oliver Bendig, "Service Now! Time to Wake up the Sleeping Giant," November 27, 2012, http://www.bain.com/Images/Bain%20study_Service_Now.pdf (accessed April 3, 2015).

17 Elena Fraj, Eva Martinez, and Jorge Matute, "Green Marketing in B2B Organisations: an Empirical Analysis from the Natural-Resource-Based View of the Firm," *Journal of Business & Marketing*, 28, 5 (2013): 396–410.

18 United States Environmental Protection Agency, "Environmentally Preferable Purchasing," http://www.epa.gov/epp/pubs/about/about.htm (accessed April 3, 2015).

19 Ali Jahromi Tamaddoni, Stanislav Stakhovych, and Michael Ewing, "Managing B2B Customer Churn, Retention and Profitability," *Industrial Marketing Management*, 43, 7 (2014): 1258–1268.

20 Frederick E. Webster, Jr., and Yoram Wind, "A General Model for Understanding Organizational Buyer Behavior," *Marketing Management* (Winter/Spring 1996): 52–57.

21 Kate Maddox, "Cintas Launches First National Brand Campaign in Its 87-Year History," *Advertising Age*, January 26, 2016, http://adage.com/article/btob/cintas-launches-national-brand-campaign-history/302356/ (accessed February 19, 2016).

22 Kunal Swani, Brian P. Brown, and George R. Milne, "Should Tweets Differ for B2B and B2C? An Analysis of Fortune 500 Companies' Twitter Communications," *Industrial Marketing Management*, 43, 4 (2014): 873–881.

23 Paul Demery, "B2B e-commerce Sales Will Top $1.13 Trillion by 2020," *Internet Retailer*, April 2, 2015, https://www.internetretailer.com/2015/04/02/new-report-predicts-1-trillion-market-us-b2b-e-commerce (accessed February 19, 2016).

24 Acquity Group, "2014 State of B2B Procurement Study: Uncovering the Shifting Landscape in B2B Commerce," https://www.accenture.com/us-en/insight-state-b2b-procurement-study-uncovering-shifting-landscape.aspx (accessed February 19, 2016).

25 Aseem Badshah, "How Technology Is Disrupting the B2B Sales Process," *Information Week*, April 8, 2014, http://www.informationweek.in/informationweek/perspective/288235/technology-disrupting-b2b-sales-process (accessed February 19, 2016).

26 Nona Tepper, "Paddleboard Manufacturer Boga Makes a Splash Through E-commerce," *Internet Retailer*, March 9, 2015, https://www.internetretailer.com/2015/03/09/paddleboard-manufacturer-boga-makes-splash-through-e-commerce (accessed February 19, 2016).

27 "About Us," Amazon Business, http://www.amazon.com/b?ie5UTF8&node511261610011 (accessed February 19, 2016); Clare O'Connor, "Amazon's Wholesale Slaughter: Jeff Bezos' $8 Trillion B2B Bet," *Forbes*, May 26, 2014, http://www.forbes.com/sites/clareoconnor/2014/05/07/amazons-wholesale-slaughter-jeff-bezos-8-trillion-b2b-bet/ (accessed February 19, 2016).

28 Paul Demery, "AutoWurld.com Launches as a Wholesale and Retail Marketplace," *Internet Retailer*, March 9, 2015, https://www.internetretailer.com/2015/03/09/autowurldcom-launches-wholesale-and-retail-marketplace (accessed February 19, 2016).

[29] Mai P. Tran, "Buy or Sell on Alibaba, the World's Largest E-Commerce B2B Marketplace," *CPCStrategy*, May 19, 2015 http://www.cpcstrategy.com/blog/2015/05/buy-sell-alibaba-worlds-largest-e-commerce-b2b-marketplace/ (accessed February 19, 2016).

[30] Danielle Ivory, "'Reverse Auctions' Draw Scrutiny," *New York Times*, April 6, 2014, http://www.nytimes.com/2014/04/07/business/reverse-auctions-draw-scrutiny.html?_r=0 (accessed April 3, 2015).

[31] Menchie Mendoza, "Apple Pay Availability Tops 2 Million Locations, Soon Adding Chains Like Chick-Fil-A," *Tech Times*, February 4, 2016, www.techtimes.com/articles/130671/20160204/apple-pay-availability-tops-2-million-locations-soon-adding-chains-like-chick-fil-a.htm (accessed February 4, 2016); Caitlin McGarry, "Why Your Favorite Stores Still Don't Support Apple Pay," *Mac-World*, June 5, 2015, www.macworld.com/article/2932356/ios/why-your-favorite-stores-still-dont-support-apple-pay.html (accessed February 4, 2016); James F. Peltz, "Mobile-Payment Systems Draw More Shoppers and Merchants," *Los Angeles Times*, January 18, 2016, www.latimes.com/business/la-fi-agenda-mobile-payments-20160118-story.html (accessed February 4, 2016); Bill Snyder, "McDonald's CIO on Why It's Supporting Apple Pay on Launch Day," *CIO*, October 16, 2014, www.cio.com/article/2834502/consumer-technology/mcdonalds-cio-on-why-its-supporting-apple-pay-on-launch-day.html (accessed February 4, 2016); Sarah Perez, "Walgreens Becomes First Retailer to Integrate Its Loyalty Program with Apple Pay," *Tech Crunch*, November 5, 2015, http://techcrunch.com/2015/11/05/walgreens-becomes-first-retailer-to-integrate-its-loyalty-program-with-apple-pay (accessed February 4, 2016).

[32] John Dodge, "GE Focusing on Planes, Trains, and . . . Software," *Boston Globe*, January 24, 2016, www.bostonglobe.com/business/2016/01/24/focusing-planes-trains-and-software/g6rfqfWCUqO2VDiUfzFEDM/story.html (accessed February 2, 2016); Steve Olenski, "Social Media for Health Care, Who's Doing It Right," *Forbes*, November 27, 2015, www.forbes.com/sites/steveolenski/2015/11/27/social-media-for-health-care-whos-doing-it-right/#619e33e81b16 (accessed February 2, 2016); Kate Maddox, "BtoB's Best Marketers: Linda Boff, General Electric," *BtoB*, October 15, 2013, www.btobonline.com; Lisa Lacy, "GE Hosts World's First Science Fair on Vine," *ClickZ*, August 13, 2013, www.clickz.com; E. J. Schultz, "GE Tells the Secret of Making Geeky Cool," *Advertising Age*, October 5, 2013, www.adage.com; Christopher Heine, "GE Gets 30% Better Returns through Smart Content Marketing," *AdWeek*, October 4, 2013, www.adweek.com; www.ge.com.

## Feature Notes

[a] Brianna Gurciullo, "CTA to Buy More Electric Buses," *Chicago Tribune*, January 22, 2016, www.chicagotribune.com/news/local/breaking/ct-cta-electric-buses-met-20160122-story.html (accessed February 3, 2016); Rick Seltzer, "Maryland Is Spending $97.8 Million Toward New Baltimore Buses," *Baltimore Business Journal*, January 27, 2016, www.bizjournals.com/baltimore/news/2016/01/27/maryland-is-spending-97-8-million-toward-new.html (accessed February 3, 2016); "41% of U.S. Public Transit Buses Use Alt Fuels, Hybrid Technology," *Metro*, April 17, 2015, www.metro-magazine.com/sustainability/news/293950/41-of-u-s-public-transit-buses-use-alt-fuels-hybrid-technology (accessed February 3, 2016).

[b] Ben Sisario, "Vinyl LP Frenzy Brings Record-Pressing Machines Back to Life," *New York Times*, September 14, 2015, www.nytimes.com/pages/business/media/index.html (accessed February 3, 2016); Rick Lyman, "Czech Company, Pressing Hits for Years on Vinyl, Finds It Has Become One," *New York Times*, August 6, 2015, www.nytimes.com/2015/08/07/world/europe/vinyl-records-gz-media-lodenice.html?_r=0 (accessed February 3, 2016); Catherine Kavanaugh, "Vinyl Record Presses Hit the Market After a 30-Year Break," *Plastics News*, December 4, 2015, www.plasticsnews.com/article/20151204/NEWS/151209890/vinyl-record-presses-hit-the-market-after-a-30-year-break (accessed February 3, 2016).

Viasin Lee/Shutterstock.com

# chapter 9    **Reaching Global Markets**

## OBJECTIVES

**9-1**   Define *international marketing*.

**9-2**   Differentiate between the environmental forces that affect international marketing efforts.

**9-3**   List important international trade agreements.

**9-4**   Identify methods of international market entry.

**9-5**   Examine various forms of global organizational structures.

**9-6**   Describe the use of the marketing mix internationally.

# MARKETING INSIGHTS

## Developing Countries Prove Lucrative for Unilever

360b/Shutterstock.com

Not so long ago, Unilever—a British–Dutch company—was hit by a weakened world economy. Less than a year later, however, the company rebounded by beating sales expectations. One factor in this rebound is Unilever's actions of raising prices in emerging economies.

When first entering emerging markets, companies like Unilever introduced simpler products at lower prices. Now those prices are rising as the middle class has begun to desire more advanced products. As the middle classes increase in countries such as India and China, Unilever is seeing an opportunity to woo these consumers with more sophisticated packaging and upgraded products. It hopes that consumers have become so brand loyal to its products that they will be willing to pay the additional cost.

Unilever's predictions have so far come true. Many consumers in emerging markets are willing to pay more for their favorite brands, especially shampoos and deodorants. Unilever is also introducing products with improved features, such as a more concentrated version of its laundry detergent in Brazil.

Despite the initial success, there is the risk that Unilever's price increases will cause it to alienate customers. Consumers in emerging markets tend to be highly price sensitive, with some markets—such as Hong Kong and South Korea—more price sensitive than others. However, consumers in emerging economies also tend to pay more for products that they perceive as having more value. Therefore, Unilever's introduction of premium products perceived as having additional value is generating interest from these countries. This is important for Unilever as 60 percent of its revenue comes from emerging markets.[1]

Technological advances and rapidly changing political and economic conditions are making it easier than ever for companies to market their products overseas as well as at home. With most of the world's population and two-thirds of total purchasing power outside the United States, international markets represent lucrative opportunities for growth. For instance, Levi Strauss sees major opportunities for expansion into Indonesia as it is the fastest-growing market in Asia.[2] Accessing international markets can promote innovation, while intensifying competition can spur companies to develop global strategies.

Due to the increasingly global nature of marketing, we devote this chapter to the unique aspects of global markets and international marketing. We begin by considering the nature of global marketing strategy and the environmental forces that create opportunities and threats for international marketers. Next, we explore several regional trade alliances, markets, and agreements. Then we examine the modes of entry into international marketing and companies' degree of involvement in it, as well as some of the structures that can be used to organize multinational enterprises. Finally, we examine how firms may alter their marketing mixes when engaging in international marketing efforts. All of these factors must be considered in any marketing plan that includes an international component.

# 9-1 THE NATURE OF GLOBAL MARKETING STRATEGY

**international marketing**
Developing and performing marketing activities across national boundaries

**International marketing** involves developing and performing marketing activities across national boundaries. Global marketing strategies require knowledge about the marketing environment and customers. For the United States, with just 7 percent of the world's population, tremendous opportunities exist globally. For instance, Walmart has approximately 2.2 million employees and operates 11,598 units in 28 countries outside the United States.[3] General Motors sells more cars in China than it does in the United States. Consider the advertisement for Australia. The advertisement is trying to attract business to the continent by portraying Australia as a good place to hold business events. It emphasizes the uniqueness of Australia and how it offers the perfect setting for team meetings or business gatherings. Clearly, the advertisement is meant for an international audience.

Firms are finding that international markets provide strong prospects for growth. To encourage international growth, many countries offer practical assistance and valuable research to help their domestic firms become more competitive globally. One example is Export.gov, a website managed by the U.S. Department of Commerce's International Trade Administration, which collects a variety of resources to help businesses that want to export to other countries.[4] A major element of the assistance that government organizations can provide for firms (especially small and medium-sized firms) is knowledge of the internationalization process.

Traditionally, most companies have entered the global marketplace gradually and incrementally as they gained knowledge and experience about various markets and opportunities. However, some firms—such as eBay, Google, and Twitter—were founded with the knowledge and resources to accelerate their participation and investment in the global marketplace. These "born globals"—typically small technology-based firms earning as much as 70 percent of their sales outside the domestic home market—export their products almost immediately after being established in market niches in which they compete with larger, more established firms.[5] Whether a firm chooses

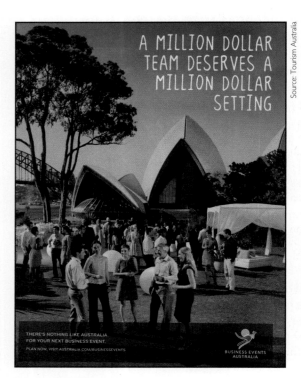

Source: Tourism Australia

A MILLION DOLLAR TEAM DESERVES A MILLION DOLLAR SETTING

THERE'S NOTHING LIKE AUSTRALIA FOR YOUR NEXT BUSINESS EVENT.
PLAN NOW, VISIT AUSTRALIA.COM/BUSINESSEVENTS

BUSINESS EVENTS AUSTRALIA

**International Marketing**
Australia uses advertisements such as this one to attract the interest of global businesses planning their next event.

to adopt the traditional approach, the born global approach, or an approach that merges attributes of both, international marketing strategy is a critical element of a firm's global operations. Today, global competition in most industries is intense and becoming increasingly fierce with the addition of newly emerging markets and firms.

# 9-2 ENVIRONMENTAL FORCES IN GLOBAL MARKETS

Firms that enter international markets must often make significant adjustments to their marketing strategies. The environmental forces that affect foreign markets may differ dramatically from those that affect domestic markets, and failure to understand them can result in significant costs. Thus, a successful international marketing strategy requires a careful environmental analysis. Conducting research to understand the needs and desires of international customers is crucial to global marketing success. Many firms have demonstrated that such efforts can generate tremendous financial rewards, increase market share, and heighten customer awareness of their products around the world. In this section, we explore how differences in the sociocultural; economic; political, legal, and regulatory; social and ethical; competitive; and technological forces in other countries can profoundly affect marketing activities.

## 9-2a Sociocultural Forces

Cultural and social differences among nations can have profound effects on marketing activities. Because marketing activities are primarily social in purpose, they are influenced by beliefs and values regarding family, religion, education, health, and recreation. By identifying, understanding, and respecting sociocultural deviations among countries, marketers lay the groundwork for effective adjustments of marketing strategy. When McDonald's expanded into Vietnam, the company offered not only its regular meal options but also introduced McPork sandwiches. These sandwiches are meant to appeal to local tastes since pork is very popular in Vietnam.[6]

Local preferences, tastes, and idioms can prove complicated for international marketers. For example, although football is a popular sport in the United States and a major opportunity for many television advertisers, soccer is the most popular televised sport in Europe and Latin America. Indeed, outside of the United States, the term "football" actually refers to soccer. Additionally, while middle-class consumers in some countries prefer to create their own unique fashion styles to demonstrate their individuality, in Turkey middle-class consumers accept fashion themes and demonstrate their creativity by "rotating" items in their wardrobe.[7] And, of course, marketing communications often must be translated into other languages. Sometimes, the true meaning of translated messages can be misinterpreted or lost. Consider some translations that went awry in foreign markets: KFC's long-running slogan "Finger lickin' good" was translated in China as "Eat your fingers off," while Coors' "Turn it loose" campaign was translated into Spanish as "Drink Coors and get diarrhea."[8]

It can be difficult to transfer marketing symbols, trademarks, logos, and even products to international markets, especially if these are associated with objects that have profound religious or cultural significance in a particular culture. Consider the problem Kellogg had with its Corn Flakes brand in South Africa. Because South Africans are used to hot porridge for breakfast, many of them were boiling Kellogg's corn flakes and ruining the meal. To adapt to this cultural expectation, Kellogg's reformulated the product and released Corn Flakes Instant Porridge to the South African market.[9]

Cultural differences may also affect marketing negotiations and decision-making behavior. Differences in the emphasis placed on personal relationships, status, and decision-making styles have been known to complicate dealings between Americans and businesspeople from other countries. In many parts of Asia, a gift may be considered a necessary introduction before negotiation, whereas in the United States or Canada, a gift may be misconstrued as an illegal bribe.

Buyers' perceptions of other countries can influence product adoption and use. Consumers that have a global orientation tend to have a positive attitude toward purchasing global brands. On the other hand, when consumers think local and are ethnocentric, they are more negative toward global brands.[10] Multiple research studies have shown that consumer preferences for products depend on both the country of origin and the product category of competing products.[11] When people are unfamiliar with products from another country, their perceptions of the country as a whole may affect their attitude toward the product and influence whether they will buy it. If a country has a reputation for producing quality products and therefore has a positive image in consumers' minds, marketers of products from that country will want to make the country of origin well known. BMW is a respected German brand that manufactures many of its vehicles in the United States, Mexico, and South Africa. In the case of BMW, the brand is more important than the country of origin to most consumers. On the other hand, marketers may want to distance themselves from a particular country in order to build a brand's reputation as truly global or because that country does not have a good reputation for quality. Traditionally, Chinese brands have been viewed as being of low quality. However, the global success of companies such as Lenovo, Xiaomi, and Alibaba are not only increasing China's brand reputation but are also challenging top competitors such as Hewlett-Packard, Apple, and Amazon. The extent to which a product's brand image and country of origin influence purchases is subject to considerable variation based on national culture characteristics.

When products are introduced from one nation into another, acceptance is far more likely if similarities exist between the two cultures. In fact, many similar cultural characteristics exist across countries. For international marketers, cultural differences have implications for product development, advertising, packaging, and pricing. When Walmart expanded into China, for instance, it quickly found that it had to adapt its stores' seafood section because Chinese shoppers like to select their own seafood. This required the stores to build large tanks containing live fish so customers could choose which ones they wanted to purchase.

# GOING GREEN

## A Recipe for Biofuels: Algae

If Euglena has its way, algae will become the fuel of the future. The name of this Tokyo-based company comes from the product it sells: the algae *Euglena gracilis*. Euglena's business is focused on five key areas: food, fiber, feed, fertilizer, and fuel. The company has been successful in developing food and cosmetics using algae and is now making its mark in the biofuel industry.

As carbon emissions become an increasing problem—particularly for countries like the United States, China, and India—governments are looking toward biofuels as an alternative fuel source. Research has shown that the algae in which Euglena specializes has strong potential for biofuel production. Euglena oversees all aspects of the process, including cultivation of the algae and the refining and marketing of the fuel. A partnership with Isuzu Motors has allowed Euglena to successfully mix its algae biofuel with light oil to power city buses. However, Euglena is determined to create its own algae biofuel that will not require oil so it can completely eliminate carbon emissions. The company is also working with ANA Holdings to develop algae-based jet fuel.

Euglena has certainly attracted the attention of investors, but any promising breakthrough brings competition. ExxonMobil has partnered with Synthetic Genomics to investigate algae biofuels, and others are trying to create biofuels from garbage. The biofuel industry is growing globally, requiring firms like Euglena to remain innovative as competition heats up.[a]

## 9-2b Economic Forces

Global marketers also need to understand the international trade system, particularly the economic stability of individual nations, as well as trade barriers that may stifle marketing efforts. Economic differences among nations—differences in standards of living, credit, buying power, income distribution, national resources, exchange rates, and the like—dictate many of the adjustments firms must make in marketing internationally. Country-specific factors such as economic wealth and national culture have a direct influence on the success of a new product in specific countries.[12]

Instability is a constant in the global business environment. The

SNAPSHOT

**Top 15 Happiest Countries**

| Ranking | Country |
|---------|---------|
| 1 | Switzerland |
| 2 | Iceland |
| 3 | Denmark |
| 4 | Norway |
| 5 | Canada |
| 6 | Finland |
| 7 | Netherlands |
| 8 | Sweden |
| 9 | New Zealand |
| 10 | Australia |
| 11 | Israel |
| 12 | Costa Rica |
| 13 | Austria |
| 14 | Mexico |
| 15 | United States |

Source: John F. Helliwell, Richard Layard, and Jeffrey Sachs (eds.), *World Happiness Report 2015* (New York: Sustainable Development Solutions Network, 2015).

United States and the European Union are more stable economically than many other regions of the world. However, even these economies have downturns in regular cycles. In recent years, a number of countries, including Greece, Russia, Spain, and Thailand, have experienced economic hardships, such as recessions, high unemployment, corporate bankruptcies, banking failures, instabilities in banking systems, and trade imbalances. Fluctuating economic conditions in different countries require that marketers carefully monitor the global environment and adjust their marketing strategies accordingly. Economic instability can also disrupt the markets for U.S. products in places that otherwise might be excellent marketing opportunities. On the other hand, competition from the sustained economic growth of countries like China and India can disrupt markets for U.S. products.

An important economic factor in the global business environment is currency valuation. The value of the dollar, euro, and yen has a major impact on the prices of products in many countries. Many countries have a floating exchange rate, which means the currencies of those countries fluctuate, or float, according to the foreign exchange market. Table 9.1 compares the value of the dollar, euro, yen, and yuan. China has been criticized for devaluing its currency, or setting its currency's value below market value. This gives it an advantage in selling exports, since the Chinese yuan has a lower value than other nations' currencies. It also decreases demand for manufacturers and exporters from other countries.

Table 9.1  **Exchange Rates of Global Currencies**

|        | 1 USD (U.S. dollars) | 1 EUR (euro) | 1 JPY (Japanese yen) | 1 CNY (China yuan renminbi) |
|--------|----------------------|--------------|----------------------|------------------------------|
| 1 USD  | 1.00   | 0.92   | 119.42 | 119.42 |
| 1 EUR  | 1.08   | 1.00   | 129.27 | 7.07   |
| 1 JPY  | 0.0084 | 0.0077 | 1.00   | 0.055  |
| 1 CNY  | 0.15   | 0.14   | 18.27  | 1.00   |

**Floating Currency**

Although China has increased the value of its currency in recent years, it is still criticized for failing to float its currency according to the foreign exchange market rate.

Devaluing currency worries investors because it suggests that China's economy is slowing down.[13] The value of the U.S. dollar is also important. In the last few years, the value of the dollar has been strong relative to other currencies. This means that U.S. exports cost more if purchased using euros or yen. Because many countries float their exchange rates around the dollar, too much or too little U.S. currency in the economy could create inflationary effects or harm exports.[14]

In terms of the value of all products produced by a nation, the United States has the largest gross domestic product in the world at more than $18 trillion.[15] **Gross domestic product (GDP)** is an overall measure of a nation's economic standing; it is the market value of a nation's total output of goods and services for a given period. However, it does not take into account the concept of GDP in relation to population (GDP per capita). The United States has a GDP per capita of $54,400. Switzerland is roughly 230 times smaller than the United States—a little larger than the state of Maryland—but its population density is six times greater than that of the United States. Although Switzerland's GDP is much smaller than the size of the United States' GDP, its GDP per capita is slightly higher. On the other hand, Canada, which is comparable in size to the United States, has a lower GDP and GDP per capita.[16] Table 9.2 provides a comparative economic analysis of 15 countries, including the United States. Knowledge about per capita income, credit, and the distribution of income provides general insights into market potential.

Opportunities for international trade are not limited to countries with the highest incomes. The countries of Brazil, Russia, India, China, and South Africa (BRICS) have attracted attention as their economies are rapidly advancing. Relationship marketing has proven to be a highly effective tool in reaching these emerging markets. This is because businesses in these countries value long-term and close interactions with marketers that they can trust. Relationship marketing has been shown to be 55 percent more effective in the growing economies of Brazil, Russia, India, and China than in the United States.[17] Other nations are progressing at a much faster rate than they were a few years ago, and these countries—especially in Latin America, Africa, eastern Europe, and the Middle East—have great market potential. Myanmar offers significant expansion opportunities for global firms, including Gap, Coca-Cola, and General Electric. Until recently U.S. sanctions against the country prohibited the United States from shipping goods into or out of the country. A temporary removal of sanctions increases opportunities for other U.S. companies to engage in trade with the country.[18] Marketers must also understand the political and legal environments before they can convert buying power of customers in these countries into actual demand for specific products.

**gross domestic product (GDP)** The market value of a nation's total output of goods and services for a given period; an overall measure of economic standing

**BRICS**
Although it started off in Sweden, today IKEA stores can be found worldwide. This IKEA store is located in Russia. BRICS countries consisting of Brazil, Russia, India, China, and South Africa offer lucrative opportunities for businesses like IKEA to expand globally.

Table 9.2    **Comparative Analysis of Selected Countries**

| Country | Population (in Millions) | GDP (U.S.$ in Billions) | Exports (U.S.$ in Billions) | Imports (U.S.$ in Billions) | Internet Users (in Millions) | Cell Phones (in Millions) |
|---|---|---|---|---|---|---|
| Brazil | 204.3 | $ 1,903.93 | $ 224.6 | $108.2 | 108.2 | 280.7 |
| Canada | 35.1 | $ 1,592 | $ 478.4 | $ 473.8 | 32.4 | 29.5 |
| China | 1,367.5 | $11,383.03 | $2,343 | $1,960 | 626.6 | 1,300 |
| Honduras | 8.7 | $ 18.55 | $ 8.1 | $ 11.1 | 1.7 | 7.7 |
| India | 1,251.7 | $ 2,288.72 | $ 329.6 | $ 472.8 | 237.3 | 944 |
| Japan | 126.9 | $ 4,412.60 | $ 669.5 | $ 798.6 | 109.3 | 152.7 |
| Jordan | 8.1 | $ 33.68 | $ 8.4 | $ 20.2 | 3.6 | 11.1 |
| Kenya | 45.9 | $ 76.46 | $ 6.2 | $ 17.6 | 16.5 | 33.6 |
| Mexico | 121.7 | $ 1,291 | $ 398.3 | $ 400.4 | 49.5 | 102.2 |
| Russia | 142.4 | $ 1,178.92 | $ 497.8 | $ 308 | 84.4 | 221 |
| South Africa | 53.7 | $ 323.81 | $ 92.5 | $ 98.9 | 24.8 | 79.5 |
| Switzerland | 8.1 | $ 685.4 | $ 327.6 | $ 272.6 | 7.1 | 11.5 |
| Turkey | 79.4 | $ 806.11 | $ 168.9 | $ 232.5 | 36.6 | 71.9 |
| Thailand | 68.0 | $ 417.8 | $ 224.8 | $ 200.2 | 19.5 | 97.1 |
| U.S. | 321.4 | $18,558.13 | $1,633 | $2,374 | 276.6 | 317.4 |

Source: Central Intelligence Agency, "Guide to Country Comparisons," World Factbook, https://www.cia.gov/library/publications/the-world-factbook/rankorder/rankorderguide.html (accessed January 8, 2016); International Monetary Fund, http://www.imf.org/external/index.htm (accessed July 1, 2016).

### 9-2c **Political, Legal, and Regulatory Forces**

The political, legal, and regulatory forces of the environment are closely intertwined in the United States. To a large degree, the same is true in many countries internationally. Typically, legislation is enacted, legal decisions are interpreted, and regulatory agencies are operated by elected or appointed officials. A country's legal and regulatory infrastructure is a direct reflection of its political climate. In some countries, this political climate is decided by the people via elections, whereas in other countries leaders are appointed or have assumed leadership based on certain powers. Although laws and regulations have direct effects on a firm's operations in a country, political forces are indirect and often not clearly known in all countries.

Additionally, businesses from different countries might be similar in nature but operate differently based on legal, political, or regulatory conditions in their home countries. For instance, in the United States airlines operate as private companies. Emirates airlines is owned by the government of Dubai, although it operates as a commercial enterprise that does not receive government financial support.[19] This advertisement for Emirates airlines stresses the choices that consumers have when they choose to fly with Emirates airlines. It is the largest airline in the Middle East with 120 destinations across the world. On the other hand, some countries have political climates that make it easier for international entrepreneurs to start their own businesses. Table 9.3 lists some of the best countries in which to start a business, according to *Forbes*. The United States is not in the top ten, possibly due to fewer incentives, regulations, and taxes.

**import tariff** A duty levied by a nation on goods bought outside its borders and brought into the country

The political climate in a country or region, political officials in a country, and political officials in charge of trade agreements directly affect the legislation and regulations (or lack thereof). Within industries, elected or appointed officials of influential industry associations also set the tone for the regulatory environment that guides operations in a particular industry. Consider the American Marketing Association, which has one of the largest professional associations for marketers with 30,000 members worldwide in every area of marketing. It has established a statement of ethics, called "Ethical Norms and Values for Marketers," that guides the marketing profession in the United States.[20]

A nation's political system, laws, regulatory bodies, special-interest groups, and courts all have a great impact on international marketing. Laws regarding competition may serve as trade barriers. For example, the European Union has stronger antitrust laws than in the United States. Being found guilty of anticompetitive behavior has cost companies like Intel billions of dollars. Because some companies do not have the resources to comply with more stringent laws, this can act as a barrier to trade.

Some countries have established import barriers, such as tariffs. An **import tariff** is any duty levied by a nation on goods bought outside its borders and brought into the country. Because they raise the prices of foreign goods, tariffs impede free trade between nations. Tariffs are usually designed either to raise revenue for a

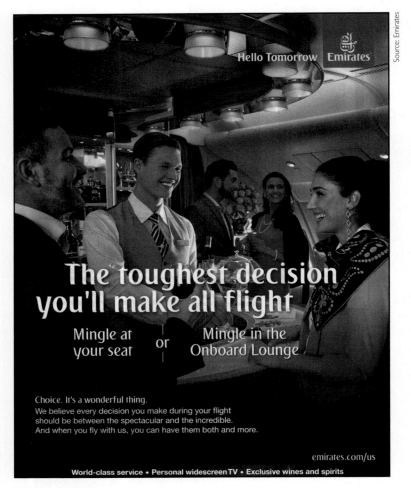

Source: Emirates

**Emirates Airlines**
Emirates airlines is quickly growing. This advertisement features individuals in First and Business class to highlight the comfort of Emirates and the many choices passengers have when they choose to fly with the airline.

Table 9.3　**The Best Countries for Starting a Business**

| Rank | Country |
|------|---------|
| 1 | Denmark |
| 2 | New Zealand |
| 3 | Norway |
| 4 | Ireland |
| 5 | Sweden |
| 6 | Finland |
| 7 | Canada |
| 8 | Singapore |
| 9 | Netherlands |
| 10 | United Kingdom |

Source: Kurt Badenhausen, "The Best Countries for Business 2015," *Forbes*, December 16, 2015, http://www.forbes.com/sites/kurtbadenhausen/2015/12/16/the-best-countries-for-business-2015/ (accessed January 4, 2015).

country or to protect domestic products. In the United States, tariff revenues account for a small percentage of total federal revenues, down from about 50 percent of total federal revenues in the early 1900s.

Nontariff trade barriers include quotas and embargoes. A **quota** is a limit on the amount of goods an importing country will accept for certain product categories in a specific period of time. The United States maintains tariff-rate quotas on imported raw cane sugar, refined and specialty sugar, and sugar-containing products. An **embargo** is a government's suspension of trade in a particular product or with a given country. Embargoes are generally directed at specific goods or countries and are established for political, health, or religious reasons. An embargo may be used to suspend the purchase of a commodity like oil from a country that is involved in questionable conduct, such as human rights violations or terrorism. Products that were created in the United States or by U.S. companies or those containing more than 20 percent of U.S.-manufactured parts cannot be sold to Cuba. Until recently, most Americans were banned from visiting Cuba because of the embargo. However, diplomatic relations between the U.S. and Cuba have resumed, and the Obama administration supported an end to the embargo.[21] As the advertisement shows, access to Cuba is increasing, and cruise companies like Pearl Seas Cruises are offering trips to the island.

**Exchange controls**, government restrictions on the amount of a particular currency that can be bought or sold, may also limit international trade. They can force businesspeople to buy and sell foreign products through a central agency, such as a central bank. On the other hand, to promote international trade, some countries have joined to form free trade zones, multinational economic communities that eliminate tariffs and other trade barriers. Such regional trade alliances are discussed later in the chapter. As mentioned earlier, foreign currency exchange rates also affect the prices marketers can charge in foreign markets. Fluctuations in the international monetary market can change the prices charged across national boundaries on a daily basis. Thus, these fluctuations must be considered in any international marketing strategy.

Countries may establish barriers to limit imports in order to maintain a favorable balance of trade. The **balance of trade** is the difference in value between a nation's exports and its imports. When a nation exports more products than it imports, a favorable balance of trade exists because money is flowing into the country. The United States has a negative balance of trade for goods and services of more than $700 billion.[22] A negative balance of trade is considered harmful, because it means U.S. dollars are supporting foreign economies at the expense of U.S. companies and workers. At the same time, U.S. citizens benefit from the assortment of imported products and their typically lower prices.

**quota** A limit on the amount of goods an importing country will accept for certain product categories in a specific period of time

**embargo** A government's suspension of trade in a particular product or with a given country

**exchange controls** Government restrictions on the amount of a particular currency that can be bought or sold

**balance of trade** The difference in value between a nation's exports and its imports

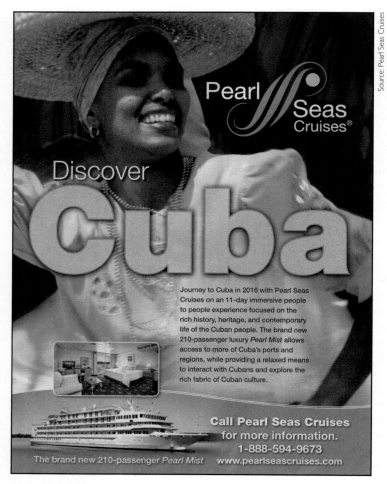

**Relations with Cuba**
With the reestablishment of diplomatic relations with Cuba, more U.S. consumers are having the opportunity to visit the country. Pearl Seas Cruises has seized upon this opportunity to promote an 11-day cruise to Cuba.

Many nontariff barriers, such as quotas and minimum price levels set on imports, port-of-entry taxes, and stringent health and safety requirements, still make it difficult for U.S. companies to export their products. For instance, the collectivist nature of Japanese culture and the high-context nature of Japanese communication make some types of direct marketing messages through the Internet and mass media less effective and may predispose many Japanese to support greater regulation of direct marketing practices.[23] Because of their collectivist culture, direct selling involving face-to-face communication may be more acceptable. A government's attitude toward importers has a direct impact on the economic feasibility of exporting to that country.

### 9-2d Ethical and Social Responsibility Forces

Differences in national standards are illustrated by what the Mexicans call *la mordida*: "the bite." The use of payoffs and bribes is deeply entrenched in many parts of the world. Because U.S. trade and corporate policy, as well as U.S. law, prohibits direct involvement in payoffs and bribes, it may be difficult for U.S. companies to compete with foreign firms that engage in these practices. Some U.S. businesses that refuse to make payoffs are forced to hire local consultants, public relations firms, or advertising agencies, which results in indirect payoffs that are also illegal under U.S. law. The ultimate decision about whether to give small tips or gifts where they are customary must be based on a company's code of ethics. However, under the Foreign Corrupt Practices Act (FCPA) of 1977, it is illegal for U.S. firms to attempt to make large payments or bribes to influence policy decisions of foreign governments. Nevertheless, facilitating payments, or small payments to support the performance of standard tasks, are often acceptable. The FCPA also subjects all publicly held U.S. corporations to rigorous internal controls and record-keeping requirements for their overseas operations.

Many other countries have outlawed bribery. As we discussed in Chapter 3, the U.K. Bribery Act redefined what many companies consider to be bribery versus gift-giving. Companies with operations in the United Kingdom could still face penalties for bribery, even if the bribery occurred outside the country and managers were not aware of the misconduct. In this case, the U.K. Bribery Act might be considered stricter than the U.S. Foreign Corrupt Practices Act. It is thus essential for global marketers to understand the major laws in the countries in which their companies operate.

Differences in ethical standards can also affect marketing efforts. In China and Vietnam, for example, standards regarding intellectual property differ dramatically from those in the United States, creating potential conflicts for marketers of computer software, music, and books. Pirated and counterfeit goods consume $1 trillion from the world's economy.[24] This influx of counterfeit goods is presenting a hurdle for Chinese Internet firm Alibaba as it expands globally. Although Alibaba claims it is building systems that allow it to more effectively detect counterfeit goods, it has been heavily criticized for the number of counterfeit goods found through its site.[25] The enormous amount of counterfeit products available worldwide, the time it takes to track them down, and legal barriers in certain countries make the pursuit of counterfeiters challenging for many companies.

When marketers do business abroad, they sometimes perceive that other business cultures have different modes of operation. This sensitivity is especially pronounced in marketers who have not traveled extensively or interacted much with foreigners in business or social settings. For example, a perception exists among many in the United States that U.S. firms are different from those in other countries. This implied perspective of "us" versus "them" is also common in other countries. In business, the idea that "we" differ from "them" is called the self-reference criterion (SRC). The SRC is the unconscious reference to one's own cultural values, experiences, and knowledge. When confronted with a situation, we react on the basis of knowledge we have accumulated over a lifetime, which is usually grounded in our culture of origin. Our reactions are based on meanings, values, and symbols that relate to our culture but may not have the same relevance to people of other cultures.

Many companies try to conduct global business based on the local culture. These business-people adapt to the cultural practices of the country they are in and use the host country's cultural practices as the rationalization for sometimes straying from their own ethical values when doing business internationally. For instance, by defending the payment of bribes or "greasing the wheels of business" and other questionable practices in this fashion, some businesspeople are resorting to **cultural relativism**—the concept that morality varies from one culture to another and that business practices are therefore differentially defined as right or wrong by particular cultures. Table 9.4 indicates the countries that business people, risk analysts, and the general public perceive as having the most and least corrupt public sectors. Most global companies are recognizing that they must establish values and standards that are consistent throughout the world.

**cultural relativism** The concept that morality varies from one culture to another and that business practices are therefore differentially defined as right or wrong by particular cultures

---

Table 9.4   **Ranking of Countries Based Upon Corruption of Public Sector**

| Country Rank | CPI Score* | Least Corrupt | Country Rank | CPI Score* | Most Corrupt |
|---|---|---|---|---|---|
| 1 | 91 | Denmark | 167 | 8 | Somalia |
| 2 | 90 | Finland | 167 | 8 | North Korea |
| 3 | 89 | Sweden | 166 | 11 | Afghanistan |
| 4 | 88 | New Zealand | 165 | 12 | Sudan |
| 5 | 87 | Netherlands | 163 | 15 | South Sudan |
| 5 | 87 | Norway | 163 | 15 | Angola |
| 7 | 86 | Switzerland | 161 | 16 | Libya |
| 8 | 85 | Singapore | 161 | 16 | Iraq |
| 9 | 83 | Canada | 158 | 17 | Venezuela |
| 10 | 81 | Germany | 158 | 17 | Guinea-Bissau |
| 10 | 81 | Luxembourg | 158 | 17 | Haiti |
| 10 | 81 | United Kingdom | 154 | 18 | Yemen |
| 13 | 79 | Australia | 154 | 18 | Turkmenistan |
| 13 | 79 | Iceland | 154 | 18 | Syria |
| 15 | 77 | Belgium | 154 | 18 | Eritrea |

\* CPI score relates to perceptions of the degree of public sector corruption as seen by business people and country analysts and ranges between 10 (highly clear) and 0 (highly corrupt). The United States is perceived as the 16th least-corrupt nation.

Source: © Transparency International, *Corruption Perceptions Index 2015* (Berlin, Germany, 2016). All rights reserved.

Because of differences in cultural and ethical standards, many companies work both individually and collectively to establish ethics programs and standards for international business conduct. Levi Strauss's code of ethics, for example, bars the firm from manufacturing in countries where workers are known to be abused. Many firms, including Texas Instruments, Coca-Cola, DuPont, Hewlett-Packard, and Walmart, endorse following international business practices responsibly. These companies support a globally based resource system called Business for Social Responsibility (BSR). BSR tracks emerging issues and trends, provides information on corporate leadership and best practices, conducts educational workshops and training, and assists organizations in developing practical business ethics tools.[26]

## 9-2e Competitive Forces

Competition is often viewed as a staple of the global marketplace. Customers thrive on the choices offered by competition, and firms constantly seek opportunities to outmaneuver their competition to gain customers' loyalty. Firms typically identify their competition when they establish target markets worldwide. Customers who are seeking alternative solutions to their product needs find the firms that can solve those needs. However, the increasingly interconnected international marketplace and advances in technology have resulted in competitive forces that are unique to the international marketplace.

Each country has unique competitive aspects—often founded in the other environmental forces (i.e., sociocultural, technological, political, legal, regulatory, and economic forces)—that are often independent of the competitors in that market. The most globally competitive countries are listed in Table 9.5. Although competitors drive competition, nations establish the infrastructure and the rules for the types of competition that can take place. For example, the privacy laws in the European Union are stricter than those in the United States. A wide-sweeping EU privacy law is much more stringent than U.S. privacy laws and is expected to change how Internet companies collect information. The new law will limit how companies can use the online information they collect. Instead of using a blanket statement to seek permission, companies collecting online information from EU consumers may now have to gain specific consent for each instance where they would like to use the collected data. Fines for violating the law could total up to 4 percent of a company's global revenue.[27] However, like the United States, other countries allow some monopoly structures to exist. In Sweden, for example, all alcoholic beverage sales are made through the government store Systembolaget, which is legally supported by the Swedish Alcohol Retail Monopoly. According to Systembolaget, the

Table 9.5    **Ranking of the Most Competitive Countries in the World**

| Rank | Country | Rank | Country |
|------|---------|------|---------|
| 1 | Switzerland | 11 | Norway |
| 2 | Singapore | 12 | Denmark |
| 3 | United States | 13 | Canada |
| 4 | Germany | 14 | Qatar |
| 5 | Netherlands | 15 | Chinese Taipei |
| 6 | Japan | 16 | New Zealand |
| 7 | Hong Kong SAR | 17 | United Arab Emirates |
| 8 | Finland | 18 | Malaysia |
| 9 | Sweden | 19 | Belgium |
| 10 | United Kingdom | 20 | Luxembourg |

Source: World Economic Forum, "Competitiveness Rankings," 2015–2016, http://reports.weforum.org/global-competitiveness-report-2015–2016/competitiveness-rankings/ (accessed January 4, 2016).

Swedish Alcohol Retail Monopoly exists for one reason: "to minimize alcohol-related problems by selling alcohol in a responsible way."[28]

A new breed of customer—the global customer—has changed the landscape of international competition drastically. In the past, firms simply produced goods or services and provided local markets with information about the features and uses of their goods and services. Customers seldom had opportunities to compare products from competitors, know details about the competing products' features, and compare other options beyond the local (country or regional) markets. Now, however, not only do customers who travel the globe expect to be able to buy the same product in most of the world's 200 countries, but they also expect that the product they buy in their local store in Miami will have the same features as similar products sold in London or even in Beijing. If either the quality of the product or the product's features are more advanced in an international market, customers will soon demand that their local markets offer the same product at the same or lower prices.

## 9-2f  Technological Forces

Advances in technology have made international marketing much easier. Interactive websites, instant messaging, and podcast downloads (along with the traditional vehicles of voice mail, e-mail, and smart phones) make international marketing activities more affordable and convenient. Internet use and social networking activities have accelerated dramatically within the United States and abroad. In Japan 109.3 million have Internet access, and 84.4 million Russians, 237.3 million Indians, and 626.6 million Chinese are logging on to the Internet (refer back to Table 9.1).[29]

In many developing countries that lack the level of technological infrastructure found in the United States and Japan, marketers are beginning to capitalize on opportunities to leapfrog existing technology. For example, cellular and wireless phone technology is reaching many countries at a more affordable rate than traditional hard-wired telephone systems. Consequently, opportunities for growth in the cell phone market remain strong in Southeast Asia, Africa, and the Middle East. One opportunity created by the rapid growth in mobile devices in Africa is mobile banking. Africa tends to have low infrastructure for physical banks, providing unique opportunities to encourage the growth of electronic banking. Kenya-based mobile phone operator Safaricom runs a money-transfer system called M-PESA that has been adopted by 14 million adult Kenyans.[30]

Despite the enormous benefits of digital technology, however, the digital economy may actually be increasing the divide between skilled wealthy workers and the rest of the labor force. Instead of increasing wages overall, wages have remained relatively flat. There is also the fear that technology will take over people's jobs. At a Foxconn factory in China, automation replaced many workers to reduce the risk of injury. However, technology also leads to the hire of skilled individuals to work on the automation. Despite the labor imbalance that some technologies are causing, they offer a great opportunity for entrepreneurs in developing countries to reach the rest of the world.[31]

# 9-3 REGIONAL TRADE ALLIANCES, MARKETS, AND AGREEMENTS

Although many more firms are beginning to view the world as one huge marketplace, various regional trade alliances and specific markets affect companies engaging in international marketing; some create opportunities, and others impose constraints. In fact, while trade agreements in various forms have been around for centuries, the last century can be classified as the trade agreement period in the world's international development. Today, there are nearly 200 trade agreements around the world compared with only a select handful in the early 1960s. In this section, we examine several of the more critical regional trade alliances, markets, and changing conditions affecting markets. These include the North American Free Trade Agreement, European Union, Southern Common Market, Asia-Pacific Economic Cooperation, Association of Southeast Asian Nations, and World Trade Organization.

## 9-3a The North American Free Trade Agreement (NAFTA)

The **North American Free Trade Agreement (NAFTA)**, implemented in 1994, effectively merged Canada, Mexico, and the United States into one market of nearly 454 million consumers. NAFTA eliminated virtually all tariffs on goods produced and traded among Canada, Mexico, and the United States to create a free trade area. The estimated annual output for this trade alliance is more than $17 trillion.[32]

NAFTA makes it easier for U.S. businesses to invest in Mexico and Canada; provides protection for intellectual property (of special interest to high-technology and entertainment industries); expands trade by requiring equal treatment of U.S. firms in both countries; and simplifies country-of-origin rules, hindering Japan's use of Mexico as a staging ground for further penetration into U.S. markets. Although most tariffs on products coming to the United States were lifted, duties on more sensitive products, such as household glassware, footwear, and some fruits and vegetables, were phased out over a 15-year period.

Canada's more than 35 million consumers are relatively affluent, with a per capita GDP of $45,000.[33] Trade between the United States and Canada totals approximately $575 billion.[34] Canada is the single largest trading partner of the United States, which in turn supports millions of U.S. jobs. NAFTA has also facilitated additional trade between Canada and Mexico. Mexico is Canada's fifth largest export market and third largest import market.[35]

With a per capita GDP of $18,000, Mexico's more than 121 million consumers are less affluent than Canadian consumers.[36] However, they buy more than $236 billion worth of U.S. products.[37] Many U.S. companies, including Hewlett-Packard, IBM, and General Motors, have taken advantage of Mexico's low labor costs and close proximity to the United States to set up production facilities, sometimes called *maquiladoras*. Production at the *maquiladoras*, especially in the automotive, electronics, and apparel industries, has grown rapidly as companies as diverse as Ford, John Deere, Motorola, Kimberly-Clark, and VF Corporation set up facilities in north-central Mexican states. Although Mexico suffered financial instability throughout the 1990s—as well as the more recent drug cartel violence—privatization of some government-owned firms and other measures instituted by the Mexican government and businesses have helped Mexico's economy. Moreover, increasing trade between the United States and Canada constitutes a strong base of support for the ultimate success of NAFTA.

Mexico's membership in NAFTA links the United States and Canada with other Latin American countries, providing additional opportunities to integrate trade among all the nations in the Western Hemisphere. Indeed, efforts to create a free trade agreement among the 34 nations of North and South America are under way. A related trade agreement—the Dominican Republic–Central American Free Trade Agreement (CAFTA-DR)—among Costa Rica, the Dominican Republic, El Salvador, Guatemala, Honduras, Nicaragua, and the United States has also been ratified in all those countries except Costa Rica. The United States exports $30 billion to the CAFTA-DR countries annually.[38]

## 9-3b The European Union (EU)

The **European Union (EU)**, sometimes also referred to as the *European Community* or *Common Market*, was established in 1958 to promote trade among its members, which initially included Belgium, France, Italy, West Germany, Luxembourg, and the Netherlands. Today the Euro Zone (countries that have adopted the euro as their currency) consists of 28 separate countries with varying political landscapes.[39] In 1991, East and West Germany united, and by 2015, the EU included the United Kingdom, Spain, Denmark, Greece, Portugal, Ireland, Austria, Finland, Sweden, Republic of Cyprus, Poland, Hungary, the Czech Republic, Slovenia, Estonia, Latvia,

**North American Free Trade Agreement (NAFTA)** An alliance that merges Canada, Mexico, and the United States into a single market

**European Union (EU)** An alliance that promotes trade among its member countries in Europe

Lithuania, Slovakia, Malta, Romania, Bulgaria, and Croatia. The Former Yugoslav Republic of Macedonia and Turkey are candidate countries that hope to join the European Union in the near future.[40] However, in 2016 the United Kingdom voted by a slim margin to exit the EU. Known as 'Brexit,' this vote means the U.K. will become the first country to exit the trade bloc. Some U.K. consumers are calling for another vote because of the impact this could have on the economy. Even if the vote stands, exiting the EU will likely take years. The European Union consists of more than half a billion consumers and has a combined GDP of nearly $18 trillion.[41] In recent years, a worldwide recession has slowed Europe's economic growth and created a debt crisis. Several members have budget deficits and are struggling to recover. Exiting the EU could have an even greater impact on the economy. For instance, economists are predicting that Brexit will slow growth in the U.K., create barriers to trade, and lead to conflict among the U.K. and other countries in the EU.

The EU is a relatively diverse set of democratic European countries. It is not a state that is intended to replace existing country states, nor is it an organization for international cooperation. Instead, its member states have common institutions to which they delegate some of their sovereignty to allow specific matters of joint interest to be decided at the European level. The primary goals of the EU are to establish European citizenship; ensure freedom, security, and justice; promote economic and social progress; and assert Europe's role in world trade.[42] To facilitate free trade among members, the EU is working toward standardizing business regulations and requirements, import duties, and value-added taxes; eliminating customs checks; and creating a standardized currency for use by all members. Many European nations (Austria, Belgium, Finland, France, Germany, Ireland, Italy, Luxembourg, the Netherlands, Portugal, Greece, and Spain) are linked to a common currency, the *euro*, but several EU members have rejected the euro in their countries (e.g., Denmark, Sweden, and the United Kingdom). Although the common currency may necessitate that marketers modify their pricing strategies and subjects them to increased competition, it also frees companies that sell products among European countries from the complexities of exchange rates. The European Central Bank is committed to supporting the value of the euro, even in countries in the Euro Zone like Greece that required financial support. The long-term goals are to eliminate all trade barriers within the EU, improve the economic efficiency of the EU nations, and stimulate economic growth, thus making the union's economy more competitive in global markets, particularly against Japan and other Pacific Rim nations and North America.

In Green/Shutterstock.com

**European Union**
While the economies of Spain, Italy, and Greece have struggled in recent years, other countries such as Poland have prospered. Poland has the sixth-largest economy in the European Union.

As the EU nations attempt to function as one large market, consumers in the EU may become more homogeneous in their needs and wants. Marketers should be aware, however, that cultural differences among the nations may require modifications in the marketing mix for customers in each nation. Differences in tastes and preferences in these diverse markets are significant for international marketers. But there is evidence that such differences may be diminishing, especially within the younger population that includes teenagers and young professionals. Gathering information about these distinct tastes and preferences is likely to remain a very important factor in developing marketing mixes that satisfy the needs of European customers.

Although the United States and the EU do not always agree, partnerships between the two have been profitable and the two entities generally have a positive relationship. Much of this success can be attributed to the shared values of the United States and EU. The EU is mostly democratic and has a strong commitment to human rights, fairness, and the rule of law. As a result, the United States and EU have been able to collaborate on mutually beneficial projects with fewer problems than partnerships with other trade alliances that do not share similar values.[43] There have been discussions about the possibility of a trade agreement between the two entities. In many respects, the United States, the EU, and Asia have become largely interdependent in trade and investment. For instance, the United States and the EU have adopted the "Open Skies" agreement to remove some of the restrictions on transatlantic flights, and the two often collaborate on ways to prevent terrorist attacks, cyber hacking, and crime. The United States and the EU hope that by working together, they can create mutually beneficial relationships that will provide benefits to millions of their citizens.[44]

## 9-3c The Southern Common Market (MERCOSUR)

The **Southern Common Market (MERCOSUR)** was established in 1991 under the Treaty of Asunción to unite Argentina, Brazil, Paraguay, and Uruguay as a free trade alliance. Venezuela and Bolivia joined in 2006 and 2015, respectively.[45] Currently, Chile, Colombia, Ecuador, and Peru are associate members. The alliance represents two-thirds of South America's population and has a combined GDP of more than $2.9 trillion, making it the fourth-largest trading bloc behind NAFTA, the EU, and ASEAN. Like NAFTA, MERCOSUR promotes "the free circulation of goods, services, and production factors among the countries" and establishes a common external tariff and commercial policy.[46]

South America and Latin America are drawing the attention of many international businesses. The region is advancing economically with an estimated growth rate of four to five percent. Another trend is that several of the countries, including some of the MERCOSUR alliance, are starting to experience more stable democracies. Even Cuba, one of the traditionally harshest critics of capitalism in Latin America, is accepting more privatization. Cuba has become more open to privatization, fueling 10 percent of GDP.[47]

## 9-3d The Asia-Pacific Economic Cooperation (APEC)

The **Asia-Pacific Economic Cooperation (APEC)**, established in 1989, promotes open trade and economic and technical cooperation among member nations, which initially included Australia, Brunei Darussalam, Canada, Indonesia, Japan, South Korea, Malaysia, New Zealand, the Philippines, Singapore, Thailand, and the United States. Since then, the alliance has grown to include China, Hong Kong, Taiwan, Mexico, Papua New Guinea, Chile, Peru, Russia, and Vietnam. The 21-member alliance represents approximately 2.8 billion people, 57 percent of world GDP, and 47 percent of global trade. APEC differs from other international trade alliances in its commitment to facilitating business and its practice of allowing the business/private sector to participate in a wide range of APEC activities.[48] Companies of the APEC have become increasingly competitive and sophisticated in global business in the last few decades. Moreover, the markets of the APEC offer tremendous opportunities to marketers who understand them. In fact, the APEC region has consistently been one of the most economically dynamic parts of the world.

Japanese firms in particular have made tremendous inroads on world markets for automobiles, motorcycles, watches, cameras, and audio and video equipment. Products from Sony, Sanyo, Toyota, Mitsubishi, Canon, Suzuki, and Toshiba are sold all over the world and have

**Southern Common Market (MERCOSUR)** An alliance that promotes the free circulation of goods, services, and production factors, and has a common external tariff and commercial policy among member nations in South America

**Asia-Pacific Economic Cooperation (APEC)** An alliance that promotes open trade and economic and technical cooperation among member nations throughout the world set standards of quality by which other products are often judged. Despite the high volume of trade between the United States and Japan, the two economies are less integrated than the U.S. economy is with Canada and the European Union. If Japan imported goods at the same rate as other major nations, the United States would sell billions of dollars more each year to Japan.

The most important emerging economic power in APEC is China, which has become one of the most productive manufacturing nations. China, which is now the United States' second-largest trading partner, has initiated economic reforms to stimulate its economy by privatizing many industries, restructuring its banking system, and increasing public spending on infrastructure. Many foreign companies, including Apple and Samsung, have opened factories in China to take advantage of its low labor costs, and China has become a major global supplier in virtually every product category. For international businesses, the potential of China's consumer market is so vast that it is almost impossible to measure. However, doing business in China entails many risks. Political and economic instability—especially inflation, corruption, and erratic policy shifts—have undercut marketers' efforts to stake a claim in what could become the world's largest market. Piracy, in particular, is a major issue, and protecting a brand name in China is difficult. Because copying is a tradition in China, and laws that protect copyrights and intellectual property are weak and minimally enforced, the country is flooded with counterfeit media, computer software, furniture, and clothing. However, there are signs that piracy laws are beginning to be more greatly enforced in China. China's National Copyright Administration is taking an active role in combating music piracy, removing 2.2 million songs from online music platforms deemed to be unlicensed.[49]

Pacific Rim regions like South Korea, Thailand, Singapore, Taiwan, and Hong Kong are also major manufacturing and financial centers. Even before Korean brand names, such as Samsung, Daewoo, and Hyundai, became household words, these products prospered under U.S. company labels, including GE, GTE, RCA, and JCPenney. Singapore boasts huge global markets for rubber goods and pharmaceuticals. Hong Kong is still a strong commercial center after being transferred to Chinese control. Vietnam is one of Asia's fastest-growing markets for U.S. businesses, and more businesses are choosing to open factories in Vietnam as China's labor costs continue to grow.[50] Taiwan, given its stability and high educational attainment, has the most promising future of all the Pacific Rim nations as a strong local economy and low import barriers draw increasing imports. The markets of APEC offer tremendous opportunities to marketers who understand them.

Another important trade agreement involving countries bordering the Pacific is the Trans-Pacific Partnership (TPP), a proposed trade agreement between Singapore, Brunei, Chile, New Zealand, Vietnam, Malaysia, Japan, Peru, the United States, Canada, Mexico, and Australia.[51] The agreement would create standards for state-owned enterprises, labor, international property, and the environment.[52] Supporters of the partnership believe it will increase the overall global competitiveness of member countries, bring the United States closer to some Asian countries, and could act as a standard for future trade agreements. Opponents fear the plan would increase competition for U.S. companies by eliminating tariffs. The Obama administration supported the agreement, and the United States is working with the other countries on how to implement the TPP.[53] If approved by Congress, the TPP will eliminate tariffs on thousands of items traded among the countries.[54]

## 9-3e Association of Southeast Asian Nations (ASEAN)

The **Association of Southeast Asian Nations (ASEAN)**, established in 1967, promotes trade and economic integration among member nations in Southeast Asia. The trade pact includes Malaysia, the Philippines, Indonesia, Singapore, Thailand, Brunei Darussalam, Vietnam, Laos, Myanmar, and Cambodia.[55] The region is home to over 600 million people with a combined GDP of $2.4 trillion.[56] With its motto "One Vision, One Identity, One Community," member nations have expressed the goal of encouraging free trade, peace, and collaboration between member countries.[57] ASEAN's three pillars are sociocultural, political, and economic. The ASEAN Economic Community (AEC) attempts to unite the regional economy.[58]

Despite the positive growth potential, ASEAN faces many obstacles in becoming a unified trade bloc. There have been conflicts among members themselves and concerns over issues

**Association of Southeast Asian Nations (ASEAN)** An alliance that promotes trade and economic integration among member nations in Southeast Asia

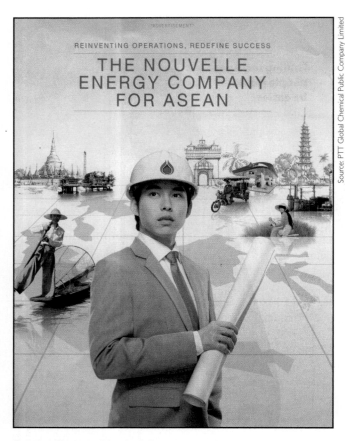

**Growing Opportunities in Asia**
Thailand's state-owned energy company PPT Chemical is likely to benefit from its inclusion in the ASEAN trade bloc as the energy needs of Southeast Asia increase.

such as human rights and disputed territories.[59] Therefore, there are great opportunities but also substantial risk. The state-owned oil and gas company in Thailand, PTT Chemical Company, is one organization that looks to prosper from growth in the ASEAN trade bloc. With the population of Southeast Asia estimated to hit 690 million by 2020, the growing need for energy bodes well for PPT Chemical.[60] As the advertisement shows, the organization is trying to affiliate itself with the ASEAN trade bloc by referring to itself as the *Nouvelle Energy Company of the ASEAN*.

While many choose to compare ASEAN with the European Union, ASEAN members are careful to point out their differences. Although members hope to increase economic integration, they expressed that there will be no common currency or fully free labor flows between members. In this way, ASEAN plans to avoid some of the pitfalls that occurred among nations in the EU during the latest worldwide recession.[61]

### 9-3f The World Trade Organization (WTO)

The **World Trade Organization (WTO)** is a global trade association that promotes free trade among 162 member nations. The WTO is the successor to the **General Agreement on Tariffs and Trade (GATT)**, which was originally signed by 23 nations in 1947 to provide a forum for tariff negotiations and a place where international trade problems could be discussed and resolved. Rounds of GATT negotiations reduced trade barriers for most products and established rules to guide international commerce, such as rules to prevent **dumping**, the selling of products at unfairly low prices. The WTO came into being in 1995 as a result of the Uruguay Round (1988–1994) of GATT negotiations. Broadly, WTO is the main worldwide organization that deals with the rules of trade between nations; its main function is to ensure that trade flows as smoothly, predictably, and freely as possible between nations.[62]

Fulfilling the purpose of the WTO requires eliminating trade barriers; educating individuals, companies, and governments about trade rules around the world; and assuring global markets that no sudden changes of policy will occur. At the heart of the WTO are agreements that provide legal ground rules for international commerce and trade policy. Based in Geneva, Switzerland, the WTO also serves as a forum for dispute resolution.[63] For example, the WTO ruled against the United States regarding country-of-origin labels for meat products that required information on where the animals were born, raised, and slaughtered. Canada and Mexico argued that these laws discriminated against their livestock. The WTO agreed, which authorized Mexico and Canada to seek retaliatory measures against the United States if the law continues.[64]

**World Trade Organization (WTO)** An entity that promotes free trade among member nations by eliminating trade barriers and educating individuals, companies, and governments about trade rules around the world

**General Agreement on Tariffs and Trade (GATT)** An agreement among nations to reduce worldwide tariffs and increase international trade

**dumping** Selling products at unfairly low prices

## 9-4 MODES OF ENTRY INTO INTERNATIONAL MARKETS

Marketers enter international markets and continue to engage in marketing activities at several levels of international involvement. Traditionally, firms have adopted one of four different modes of entering an international market; each successive "stage" represents different degrees of international involvement.

Figure 9.1 **Levels of Involvement in Global Marketing**

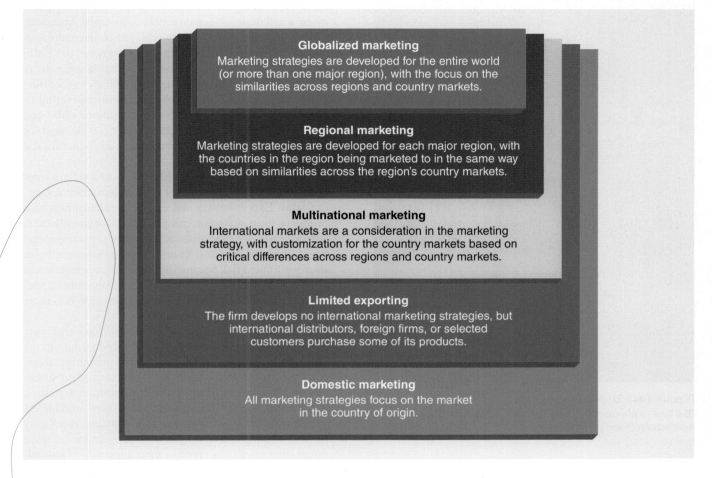

- Stage 1: No regular export activities
- Stage 2: Export via independent representatives (agents)
- Stage 3: Establishment of one or more sales subsidiaries internationally
- Stage 4: Establishment of international production/manufacturing facilities[65]

As Figure 9.1 shows, companies' international involvement today covers a wide spectrum, from purely domestic marketing to global marketing. Domestic marketing involves marketing strategies aimed at markets within the home country; at the other extreme, global marketing entails developing marketing strategies for the entire world (or at least more than one major region of the world). Many firms with an international presence start out as small companies serving local and regional domestic markets and expand to national markets before considering opportunities in foreign markets (the born global firm, described earlier, is one exception to this internationalization process). Limited exporting may occur even if a firm makes little or no effort to obtain foreign sales. Foreign buyers may seek out the company and/or its products, or a distributor may discover the firm's products and export them. The level of commitment to international marketing is a major variable in global marketing strategies. In this section, we examine importing and exporting, trading companies, licensing and franchising, contract manufacturing, joint ventures, direct ownership, and some of the other approaches to international involvement.

## 9-4a  Importing and Exporting

Importing and exporting require the least amount of effort and commitment of resources. **Importing** is the purchase of products from a foreign source. **Exporting**, the sale of products to foreign markets, enables firms of all sizes to participate in global business. The

**importing** The purchase of products from a foreign source

**exporting** The sale of products to foreign markets

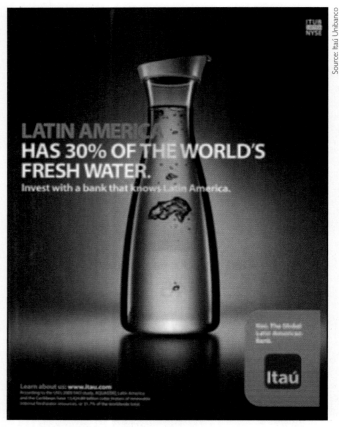

**Importing and Exporting**
Itaú bank encourages businesses to invest with it because it knows the Latin American market.

advertisement for Itaú bank in Latin America highlights the fact that 30 percent of the world's fresh water is in Latin America. This means that trade is a major—and often challenging—activity between Latin American regions and other parts of the world. The bank encourages businesses to invest with it because it knows the Latin American market and can provide valuable insights. A firm may also find an exporting intermediary to take over most marketing functions associated with marketing to other countries. This approach entails minimal effort and cost. Modifications in packaging, labeling, style, or color may be the major expenses in adapting a product for the foreign market.

Export agents bring together buyers and sellers from different countries and collect a commission for arranging sales. Export houses and export merchants purchase products from different companies and then sell them abroad. They are specialists at understanding customers' needs in global markets. Using exporting intermediaries involves limited risk because no foreign direct investment is required. For example, China has an insatiable appetite for pork and pork imports, while Poland exports more apples than any other country.

Buyers from foreign companies and governments provide a direct method of exporting and eliminate the need for an intermediary. These buyers encourage international exchange by contacting overseas firms about their needs and the opportunities available in exporting to them. Indeed, research suggests that many small firms tend to rely heavily on such native contacts, especially in developed markets, and remain production-oriented rather than market-oriented in their approach to international marketing.[66] Domestic firms that want to export with minimal effort and investment should seek out export intermediaries. Once a company becomes involved in exporting, it usually develops more knowledge of the country and becomes more confident in its competitiveness.[67]

## 9-4b Trading Companies

Marketers sometimes employ a **trading company**, which links buyers and sellers in different countries but is not involved in manufacturing and does not own assets related to manufacturing. Trading companies buy products in one country at the lowest price consistent with quality and sell them to buyers in another country. For instance, WTSC offers a 24-hour-per-day online world trade system that connects 20 million companies in 245 countries, offering more than 60 million products.[68] A trading company acts like a wholesaler, taking on much of the responsibility of finding markets while facilitating all marketing aspects of a transaction. An important function of trading companies is taking title to products and performing all the activities necessary to move the products to the targeted foreign country.

Trading companies reduce risk for firms that want to get involved in international marketing. A trading company provides producers with information about products that meet quality and price expectations in domestic and international markets. Additional services a trading company may provide include consulting, marketing research, advertising, insurance, product research and design, legal assistance, warehousing, and foreign exchange.

**trading company** A company that links buyers and sellers in different countries

## 9-4c Licensing and Franchising

When potential markets are identified across national boundaries, and when production, technical assistance, or marketing know-how is required, **licensing** is an alternative to direct investment. The licensee (the owner of the foreign operation) pays commissions or royalties on sales or supplies used in manufacturing. The licensee may also pay an initial down payment or fee when the licensing agreement is signed. Exchanges of management techniques or technical assistance are primary reasons for licensing agreements. Yoplait, for example, is a French yogurt that is licensed for production in the United States; the Yoplait brand tries to maintain a French image. Similarly, sports organizations like the International Olympic Committee (IOC), which is responsible for the Olympic Games, typically concentrate on organizing their sporting events while licensing the merchandise and other products that are sold.

Licensing is an attractive alternative when resources are unavailable for direct investment or when the core competencies of the firm or organization are not related to the product being sold (such as in the case of Olympics merchandise). Licensing can also be a viable alternative when the political stability of a foreign country is in doubt. In addition, licensing is especially advantageous for small manufacturers wanting to launch a well-known brand internationally.

Franchising is a form of licensing in which a company (the franchiser) grants a franchisee the right to market its product, using its name, logo, methods of operation, advertising, products, and other elements associated with the franchiser's business, in return for a financial commitment and an agreement to conduct business in accordance with the franchiser's standard of operations. This arrangement allows franchisers to minimize the risks of international marketing in four ways: (1) the franchiser does not have to put up a large capital investment; (2) the franchiser's revenue stream is fairly consistent because franchisees pay a fixed fee and royalties; (3) the franchiser retains control of its name and increases global penetration of its product; and (4) franchise agreements ensure a certain standard of behavior from franchisees, which protects the franchise name.[69]

**licensing** An alternative to direct investment that requires a licensee to pay commissions or royalties on sales or supplies used in manufacturing

**contract manufacturing** The practice of hiring a foreign firm to produce a designated volume of the domestic firm's product or a component of it to specification; the final product carries the domestic firm's name

## 9-4d Contract Manufacturing

**Contract manufacturing** occurs when a company hires a foreign firm to produce a designated volume of the firm's product (or a component of a product) to specification and the final product carries the domestic firm's name. The Gap, for example, relies on contract manufacturing for some of its apparel; Nike uses contract manufacturers in Vietnam to produce many of its athletic shoes. Marketing may be handled by the contract manufacturer or by the contracting company.

**Franchising**
McDonald's has franchises in a number of countries, including Jerusalem, Israel and Moscow, Russia.

Three specific forms of contract manufacturing have become popular in the last decade: outsourcing, offshoring, and offshore outsourcing. **Outsourcing** is defined as the contracting of noncore operations or jobs from internal production within a business to an external entity that specializes in that operation. For example, outsourcing certain elements of a firm's operations to China and Mexico has become popular. The majority of all footwear is now produced in China, regardless of the brand name on the shoe you wear.

**Offshoring** is defined as moving a business process that was done domestically at the local factory to a foreign country, regardless of whether the production accomplished in the foreign country is performed by the local company (e.g., in a wholly owned subsidiary) or a third party (e.g., subcontractor). Typically, the production is moved to reap the advantages of lower cost of operations in the foreign location. **Offshore outsourcing** is the practice of contracting with an organization to perform some or all business functions in a country other than the country in which the product will be sold. Today, some manufacturers that previously engaged in offshore outsourcing are moving production back to the United States to maintain quality and tighter inventory control, a process known as reshoring. However, offshoring still outpaces reshoring for U.S. manufacturers.[70]

## 9-4e  Joint Ventures

In international marketing, a **joint venture** is a partnership between a domestic firm and a foreign firm or government. Joint ventures are especially popular in industries that require large investments, such as natural resources extraction or automobile manufacturing. Control of the joint venture may be split equally, or one party may control decision making. Joint ventures are often a political necessity because of nationalism and government restrictions on foreign ownership. Qualcomm formed a joint venture with Chinese chip maker Semiconductor Manufacturing International Corporation to produce semiconductors. It is believed that this joint venture will allow Qualcomm to gain a foothold in selling chips in the Chinese market.[71] Joint ventures may also occur when acquisition or internal development is not feasible or when the risks and constraints leave no other alternative.

Joint ventures also provide legitimacy in the eyes of the host country's citizens. Local partners have firsthand knowledge of the economic and sociopolitical environment and the workings of available distribution networks, and they may have privileged access to local resources (raw materials, labor management, and so on). However, joint venture relationships require trust throughout the relationship to provide a foreign partner with a ready means of implementing its own marketing strategy. Joint ventures are assuming greater global importance because of cost advantages and the number of inexperienced firms that are entering foreign markets. They may be the result of a trade-off between a firm's desire for completely unambiguous control of an enterprise and its quest for additional resources.

**Strategic alliances** are partnerships formed to create a competitive advantage on a worldwide basis. They are very similar to joint ventures, but while joint ventures are defined in scope, strategic alliances are typically represented by an agreement to work together (which can ultimately mean greater involvement than a joint venture). In an international strategic alliance, the firms in the alliance may have been traditional rivals competing for the same market. They may also be competing in certain markets while working together in other markets where it is beneficial for both parties. One such strategic alliance was formed between accounting firm Ernst & Young and career networking site LinkedIn. The purpose of the relationship is to help companies in their ability to use technology, social networking, and sales.[72] Whereas joint ventures are formed to create a new identity, partners in strategic alliances often retain their distinct identities, with each partner bringing a core competency to the union.

The success rate of international alliances could be higher if a better fit between the companies existed. A strategic alliance should focus on a joint market opportunity from which all partners can benefit. In the automobile, computer, and airline industries, strategic alliances are becoming the predominant means of competing internationally. Competition in these industries is so fierce and the costs of competing on a global basis are so high that few firms have all the

**outsourcing** The practice of contracting noncore operations with an organization that specializes in that operation

**offshoring** The practice of moving a business process that was done domestically at the local factory to a foreign country, regardless of whether the production accomplished in the foreign country is performed by the local company (e.g., in a wholly owned subsidiary) or a third party (e.g., subcontractor)

**offshore outsourcing** The practice of contracting with an organization to perform some or all business functions in a country other than the country in which the product will be sold

**joint venture** A partnership between a domestic firm and a foreign firm or government

**strategic alliances** A partnership that is formed to create a competitive advantage on a worldwide basis resources needed to do it alone. Firms that lack the internal resources essential for international success may seek to collaborate with other companies. A shared mode of leadership among partner corporations combines joint abilities and allows collaboration from a distance. Focusing on customer value and implementing innovative ways to compete create a winning strategy.

## 9-4f  Direct Ownership

Once a company makes a long-term commitment to marketing in a foreign country that has a promising market as well as a suitable political and economic environment, **direct ownership** of a foreign subsidiary or division is a possibility. Most foreign investment covers only manufacturing equipment or personnel because the expenses of developing a separate foreign distribution system can be tremendous. The opening of retail stores in Europe, Canada, or Mexico can require a staggering financial investment in facilities, research, and management.

The term **multinational enterprise**, sometimes called *multinational corporation (MNC)*, refers to a firm that has operations or subsidiaries in many countries. Often, the parent company is based in one country and carries on production, management, and marketing activities in other countries. The firm's subsidiaries may be autonomous so they can respond to the needs of individual international markets, or they may be part of a global network led by the headquarters' operations.

At the same time, a wholly owned foreign subsidiary may be allowed to operate independently of the parent company to give its management more freedom to adjust to the local environment. Cooperative arrangements are developed to assist in marketing efforts, production, and management. A wholly owned foreign subsidiary may export products to the home country, its market may serve as a test market for the firm's global products, or it may be a component of the firm's globalization efforts. Some U.S. automobile manufacturers, for example, import cars built by their foreign subsidiaries. A foreign subsidiary offers important tax, tariff, and other operating advantages. Table 9.6 lists some major multinational companies across the world.

One of the greatest advantages of a multinational enterprise is the ability to adopt a cross-cultural approach. A subsidiary usually operates under foreign management so it can develop a local identity. In particular, the firm (i.e., seller) is often expected to adapt, if needed, to the buyer's culture. This may become less of an advantage over time as the cultural values

**direct ownership** A situation in which a company owns subsidiaries or other facilities overseas

**multinational enterprise** A firm that has operations or subsidiaries in many countries

Table 9.6  **Multinational Corporations**

| Company | Country | Description |
|---|---|---|
| Royal Dutch Shell | Netherlands | Oil and gas |
| Toyota | Japan | Automobiles |
| Walmart | United States | Retail |
| Siemens | Germany | Electronics and engineering |
| Nestlé | Switzerland | Nutritional, snack-food, and health-related consumer goods |
| Samsung | South Korea | Subsidiaries specializing in electronic components, telecommunications equipment, medical equipment, and more |
| Unilever | United Kingdom | Consumer goods including cleaning and personal care, foods, beverages |
| Boeing | United States | Aerospace and defense |
| Lenovo | China | Computer technology |
| Subway | United States | Largest fast-food chain |

of younger consumers (under 30 years of age) are becoming increasingly similar around the world. Today, a 20-year-old in Russia is increasingly similar in mindset to a 20-year-old in China and a 20-year-old in the United States, especially with regard to their tastes in music, clothes, cosmetics, and technology. This makes marketing goods and services to the younger population easier today than it was only a generation ago. Nevertheless, there is still great danger involved in having a wholly owned subsidiary in some parts of the world due to political uncertainty, terrorism threats, and economic instability. After the terrorist attacks in Paris, France, for instance, many large firms, including Coca-Cola Enterprises and Priceline Group, became more concerned about geopolitical risk since they receive 30 percent or more of their revenue from Europe.[73]

Whereas the most well-known multinational corporations come from developed countries, the world is seeing a rise in MNCs from emerging economies as well. Brazil's Embraer (an aircraft company) and South Africa's MTN (a mobile phone company) are two examples. India's Tata Group is even beginning to rival more established MNCs. Tata owns several firms that qualify as MNCs, specializing in such diverse products as cars, hotels, steel, and chemicals.

# 9-5 **GLOBAL ORGANIZATIONAL STRUCTURES**

Firms develop their international marketing strategies and manage their marketing mixes (i.e., product, distribution, promotion, and price) by developing and maintaining an organizational structure that best leverages their resources and core competencies. This organizational structure is defined as the way a firm divides its operations into separate functions and/or value-adding units and coordinates its activities. Most firms undergo a step-by-step development in their internationalization efforts of the firm's people, processes, functions, culture, and structure. The pyramid in Figure 9.2 symbolizes how deeply rooted the international operations and values are in the firm, with the base of the pyramid—structure—being the most difficult to change (especially in the short term). Three basic structures of international organizations exist: export departments, international divisions, and internationally integrated structures (e.g., product division structures, geographic area structures, and matrix structures). The existing structure of the firm, or the structure that the firm chooses to adopt, has implications for international marketing strategy.

## 9-5a **Export Departments**

As we described earlier, the early stages of international development for most firms are often informal and not fully planned. During this early stage, sales opportunities in the global marketplace motivate a company to engage internationally. For instance, born global firms make exporting a primary objective from their inceptions. For most firms, however, very minimal, if any, organizational adjustments take place to accommodate international sales. Foreign sales are typically so small that many firms cannot justify allocating structural or other resources to the internationalization effort in the infancy of internationalization. Exporting, licensing, and using trading companies are preferred modes of international market entry for firms with an export department structure.

Some firms develop an export department as a subunit of the marketing department, whereas others organize it as a separate department at an equal level with the other functional units. Some companies choose to hire outside export departments to handle their international operations. Lone Star Distribution, a distributor for sports and nutritional supplements, has an export department that helps its clients transport their goods internationally.[74] Another unique case of developing a successful export operation early after its inception is the born global firm of Logitech International. Founded in 1981, Logitech is a Swiss company that designs

Figure 9.2 **Organizational Architecture**

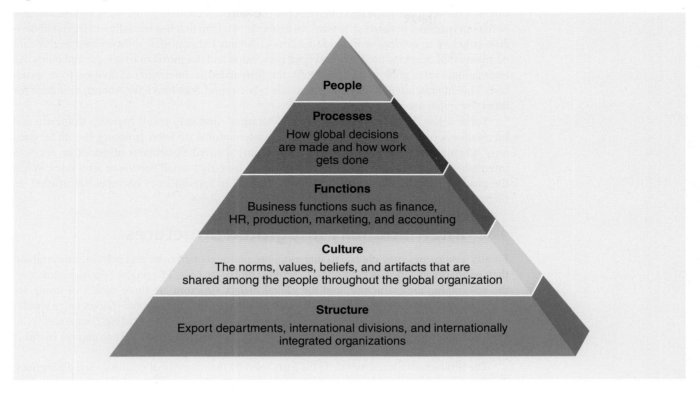

personal computer peripherals that enable people to effectively work, play, and communicate in the digital world.

As demand for a firm's goods and services grows or its commitments increase due to its internationalization efforts, it develops an international structure. Many firms evolve from using their export department structure to forming an international division.

## 9-5b International Divisions

As a company gains greater international exposure and sales, it may centralize all of the responsibility for international operations and all international activities into an international division. The typical international division concentrates human resources (with international expertise) into one unit and serves as the central point for all information flow related to international operations, such as international market opportunities or international research and development. At the same time, firms with an international division structure take advantage of economies of scale by keeping manufacturing and related functions within the domestic divisions. Firms may develop international divisions at any stage of their international development. However, an increasing number of firms are recognizing the importance of going global early on. As such, these firms use exporting, licensing and franchising, trading companies, contract manufacturing, and joint ventures as possible modes of international market entry.

The implementation of an international division highlights the importance of coordination and cooperation among domestic and international operations within a firm. Frequent interaction and strategic planning meetings are required to make this structure work effectively. In particular, firms that use an international division structure are often organized domestically on the basis of functions or product divisions, while the international division is organized on the basis of geography. This means that coordination and strategic alignment across domestic divisions and the international division are critical to success. At the same time, lack of coordination between domestic and international operations is commonly the most significant flaw in the international division structure. An example of a firm that has used the international division structure to achieve worldwide success is Abbott Laboratories, a diversified health-care company that develops products that span prevention and diagnosis to treatment and cures. As international sales grew in the late 1960s, the firm added an international division to its structure. This international division structure has benefits and drawbacks for Abbott, as it does for other firms that use it.[75]

Some argue that to offset the natural "isolation" that may result between domestic and international operations in this structure, the international division structure should be used only when a company (1) intends to market only a small assortment of goods or services internationally and (2) when foreign sales account for only a small portion of total sales. When the product assortment increases or the percentage of foreign sales becomes significant, an internationally integrated structure may be more appropriate.

## 9-5c  Internationally Integrated Structures

Finally, companies may choose to integrate international operations and activities throughout their entire organization in their quest to achieve global success. The product division structure, the geographic area structure, and the global matrix structure are three means of doing so. Firms with these varied structures have multiple choices for international market entry similar to international divisions (e.g., exporting, licensing and franchising, trading companies, contract manufacturing, and joint ventures). However, they are the most likely to engage in direct ownership activities internationally.

The product division structure is the form used by the majority of multinational enterprises. This structure lends itself to firms that are diversified, often driven by their current domestic operations. Each division is a self-contained entity with responsibility for its own operations, whether it is based on a country or regional structure. The worldwide headquarters maintains the overall responsibility for the strategic direction of the firm, while each product division is in charge of its implementation. Procter & Gamble has a long-standing tradition of operating in a product division structure, with leading brands like Pampers, Tide, Pantene, Bounty, Charmin, Downy, Crest, and Olay.

The geographic area structure is well suited to firms with a low degree of diversification. Under this domestically influenced functional structure, the world is divided into logical geographical areas based on the firms' operations and the customers' characteristics. Accenture, a global management consulting firm, operates worldwide largely based on a geographic area structure. Each area tends to be relatively self-contained, and integration across areas is typically via the worldwide or the regional headquarters. This structure facilitates local responsiveness, but it is not ideal for reducing global costs and transferring core knowledge across the firm's geographic units. A key issue in geographic area structures, as in almost all multinational corporations, is the need to become more regionally and globally integrated.

The global matrix structure was designed to achieve both global integration and local responsiveness. Asea Brown Boveri (ABB), a Swedish-Swiss engineering multinational, is the best-known firm to implement a global matrix structure. ABB is an international leader in power and automation technologies that enable customers to improve their performance while lowering environmental impact. Global matrix structures theoretically facilitate a simultaneous focus on realizing local responsiveness, cost efficiencies, and knowledge transfers. However, few firms can operate a global matrix well, since the structure is based on, for example, product and geographic divisions simultaneously (or a combination of any two traditional structures). This means that employees belong to two divisions and often report to two managers throughout the hierarchies of the firm. An effectively implemented global matrix structure has the benefit of being global in scope while also being nimble and responsive locally. However, a poorly implemented global matrix structure results in added bureaucracy and indecisiveness in leadership and implementation.

# 9-6 CUSTOMIZATION VERSUS GLOBALIZATION OF INTERNATIONAL MARKETING MIXES

Like domestic marketers, international marketers develop marketing strategies to serve specific target markets. Traditionally, international marketing strategies have customized marketing mixes according to cultural, regional, and national differences. Table 9.7 provides a sample of international issues related to product, distribution, promotion, and price. For example,

Table 9.7 **Marketing Mix Issues Internationally**

| | Sample International Issues |
|---|---|
| **Product Element** | |
| Core Product | Is there a commonality of the customer's needs across countries? What will the product be used for and in what context? |
| Product Adoption | How is awareness created for the product in the various country markets? How and where is the product typically bought? |
| Managing Products | How are truly new products managed in the country markets vis-á-vis existing products or products that have been modified slightly? |
| Branding | Is the brand accepted widely around the world? Does the home country help or hurt the brand perception of the consumer? |
| **Distribution Element** | |
| Marketing Channels | What is the role of the channel intermediaries internationally? Where is value created beyond the domestic borders of the firm? |
| Physical Distribution | Is the movement of products the most efficient from the home country to the foreign market or to a regional warehouse? |
| Retail Stores | What is the availability of different types of retail stores in the various country markets? |
| Retailing Strategy | Where do customers typically shop in the targeted countries—in department stores, specialty stores, online, or through direct selling? |
| **Promotion Element** | |
| Advertising | Some countries' customers prefer firm-specific advertising instead of product-specific advertising. How does this affect advertising? |
| Public Relations | How is public relations used to manage the stakeholders' interests internationally? Are the stakeholders' interests different worldwide? |
| Personal Selling | What product types require personal selling internationally? Does it differ from how those products are sold domestically? |
| Sales Promotion | Is coupon usage a widespread activity in the targeted international markets? What other forms of sales promotion should be used? |
| **Pricing Element** | |
| Core Price | Is price a critical component of the value equation of the product in the targeted country markets? |
| Analysis of Demand | Is the demand curve similar internationally and domestically? Will a change in price drastically change demand? |
| Demand, Cost, and Profit Relationships | What are the fixed and variable costs when marketing the product internationally? Are they similar to the domestic setting? |
| Determination of Price | How do the pricing strategy, environmental forces, business practices, and cultural values affect price? |

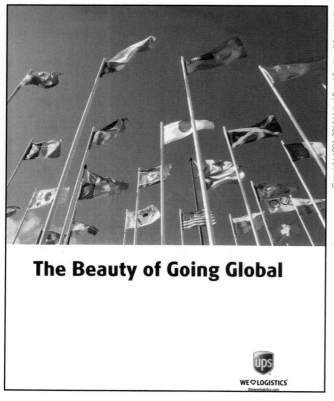

Copyright 1994–2014 United Parcel Service of America, Inc.

**The Beauty of Going Global**

WE ♡ LOGISTICS
thenewlogistics.com

**Globalization**
UPS demonstrates that it is a global firm by depicting flags from various countries waving in the wind.

many developing countries lack the infrastructure needed for expansive distribution networks, which can make it harder to get the product to consumers. Realizing that both similarities and differences exist across countries is a critical first step to developing the appropriate marketing strategy effort targeted to particular international markets. Today, many firms strive to build their marketing strategies around similarities that exist instead of customizing around differences.

For many firms, **globalization** of marketing is the goal; it involves developing marketing strategies as though the entire world (or its major regions) were a single entity: a globalized firm markets standardized products in the same way everywhere. Global brands are emerging that are rapidly losing their associations with individual countries.[76] Nike and Adidas shoes, for example, are standardized worldwide. Other examples of globalized products include electronic communications equipment, Western-style clothing, movies, soft drinks, music, cosmetics, and toothpaste. In this advertisement, UPS demonstrates globalization through its depiction of flags from various countries. UPS is using this advertisement to inform consumers that it is a global logistics firm that reaches across the world.

For many years, organizations have attempted to globalize their marketing mixes as much as possible by employing standardized products, distribution channels, promotion campaigns, and prices for all markets. The economic and competitive payoffs for globalized marketing strategies are certainly great. Brand name, product characteristics, packaging, and labeling are among the easiest marketing mix variables to standardize; media allocation, retail outlets, and price may be more difficult. In the end, the degree of similarity among the various environmental and market conditions determines the feasibility and degree of globalization. A successful globalization strategy often depends on the extent to which a firm is able to implement the idea of "think globally, act locally."[77] Even take-out food lends itself to globalization: McDonald's, KFC, and Taco Bell restaurants satisfy hungry customers in both hemispheres, although menus may be altered slightly to satisfy local tastes. When 7-Eleven opened stores in the United Arab Emirates, it sold its signature Slurpee drinks but also offered more local fare such as hummus, curries, and samosas.[78]

International marketing demands some strategic planning if a firm is to incorporate foreign sales into its overall marketing strategy. International marketing activities often require customized marketing mixes to achieve the firm's goals. Globalization requires a total commitment to the world, regions, or multinational areas as an integral part of the firm's markets; world or regional markets become as important as domestic ones. Global brands exist in an increasingly local world where consumer behavior, economic conditions, and distribution systems differ. Therefore, global brands may shift to local responsibility for marketing strategy implementation.[79] Regardless of the extent to which a firm chooses to globalize its marketing strategy, extensive environmental analysis and marketing research are necessary to understand the needs and desires of the target market(s) and successfully implement the chosen marketing strategy.

A global presence does not automatically result in a global competitive advantage. However, a global presence generates five opportunities for creating value: (1) to adapt to local market differences, (2) to exploit economies of global scale, (3) to exploit economies of global

**globalization** The development of marketing strategies that treat the entire world (or its major regions) as a single entity

# EMERGING **TRENDS IN MARKETING**

## Can Netflix Conquer the World?

Netflix is taking on the world as it becomes available in more countries. With a presence in about 50 countries, it wants to increase this number to 200 in two years. In 2015 the company entered Italy, Spain, Portugal, and Japan. It became one of the first U.S. companies to announce it would expand into Cuba. Netflix also wants to enter China.

The key to Netflix's rapid international expansion is its globalized approach. Because Netflix is an Internet streaming service, it is easily obtained by any household with a strong enough Internet connection. Its products and distribution channels are therefore highly standardized. As more consumers become connected to the Internet worldwide, Netflix is taking advantage of the opportunity to reach them.

However, even companies with a globalization approach face certain challenges that vary by country. For instance, laws in China tend to restrict online streaming. In Cuba the price for its services is $7.99, which consists of half the monthly salary of the average Cuban worker. Payments must be made with credit or debit cards that are not accessible to the majority of Cubans. Netflix may therefore have to customize its payment options. Finally, Netflix's success depends upon how much of the population has sufficient Internet connections. Only about 26 percent of Cubans have Internet access. On the other hand, Japan has one of the fastest connections worldwide.[b]

scope, (4) to mine optimal locations for activities and resources, and (5) to maximize the transfer of knowledge across locations.[80] To exploit these opportunities, marketers need to conduct marketing research and work within the constraints of the international environment and regional trade alliances, markets, and agreements.

# Summary

## 9-1  Define *international marketing*.

International marketing involves developing and performing marketing activities across national boundaries. International markets can provide tremendous opportunities for growth and renewed opportunity for the firm.

## 9-2  Differentiate between the environmental forces that affect international marketing efforts.

A detailed analysis of the environment is essential before a company enters an international market. Environmental aspects of special importance include sociocultural; economic; political, legal, and regulatory; social and ethical; competitive; and technological forces. Because marketing activities are primarily social in purpose, they are influenced by beliefs and values regarding family, religion, education, health, and recreation. Cultural differences may affect marketing negotiations, decision-making behavior, and product adoption and use. A nation's economic stability and trade barriers can affect marketing efforts. Significant trade barriers include import tariffs, quotas, embargoes, and exchange controls. Gross domestic product (GDP) and GDP per capita are common measures of a nation's economic standing. Political and legal forces include a nation's political system, laws, regulatory bodies, special-interest groups, and courts. In the area of ethics, cultural relativism is the concept that morality varies from one culture to another and that business practices are therefore differentially defined as right or wrong by particular cultures. In addition to considering the types of competition and the types of competitive structures that exist in other countries, marketers also need to consider the competitive forces at work and recognize the importance of the global customer who is well informed about product choices from around the world. Advances in technology have greatly facilitated international marketing.

## 9-3  List important international trade agreements.

Various regional trade alliances and specific markets create both opportunities and constraints for companies engaged in international marketing. Important trade agreements include the North American Free Trade Agreement, European Union, Southern Common Market, Asia-Pacific Economic

Cooperation, Association of Southeast Asian Nations, and World Trade Organization.

### 9-4 Identify methods of international market entry.

There are several ways to enter international marketing. Importing (the purchase of products from a foreign source) and exporting (the sale of products to foreign markets) are the easiest and most flexible methods. Marketers may employ a trading company, which links buyers and sellers in different countries but is not involved in manufacturing and does not own assets related to manufacturing. Licensing and franchising are arrangements whereby one firm pays fees to another for the use of its name, expertise, and supplies. Contract manufacturing occurs when a company hires a foreign firm to produce a designated volume of the domestic firm's product to specification, and the final product carries the domestic firm's name. Joint ventures are partnerships between a domestic firm and a foreign firm or government. Strategic alliances are partnerships formed to create competitive advantage on a worldwide basis. Finally, a firm can build its own marketing or production facilities overseas. When companies have direct ownership of facilities in many countries, they may be considered multinational enterprises.

### 9-5 Examine various forms of global organizational structures.

Firms develop their international marketing strategies and manage their marketing mixes by developing and maintaining an organizational structure that best leverages their resources and core competencies. Three basic structures of international organizations include export departments, international divisions, and internationally integrated structures (e.g., product division structures, geographic area structures, and matrix structures).

### 9-6 Describe the use of the marketing mix internationally

Although most firms adjust their marketing mixes for differences in target markets, some firms standardize their marketing efforts worldwide. Traditional full-scale international marketing involvement is based on products customized according to cultural, regional, and national differences. Globalization, however, involves developing marketing strategies as if the entire world (or regions of it) were a single entity; a globalized firm markets standardized products in the same way everywhere. International marketing demands some strategic planning if a firm is to incorporate foreign sales into its overall marketing strategy.

---

**Go to www.cengagebrain.com for resources to help you master the content in this chapter as well as for materials that will expand your marketing knowledge!**

---

## Important Terms

international marketing  258
gross domestic product
    (GDP)  262
import tariff  264
quota  265
embargo  265
exchange controls  265
balance of trade  265
cultural relativism  267
North American Free Trade
    Agreement (NAFTA)  270
European Union (EU)  270

Southern Common Market
    (MERCOSUR)  272
Asia-Pacific Economic Cooperation
    (APEC)  272
Association of Southeast Asian Nations
    (ASEAN)  273
World Trade Organization (WTO)  274
General Agreement on Tariffs
    and Trade (GATT)  274
dumping  274
importing  275
exporting  275

trading company  276
licensing  277
contract manufacturing  277
outsourcing  278
offshoring  278
offshore outsourcing  278
joint venture  278
strategic alliance  278
direct ownership  279
multinational enterprise  279
globalization  284

## Discussion and Review Questions

1. How does international marketing differ from domestic marketing?
2. What factors must marketers consider as they decide whether to engage in international marketing?

3. Why are the largest industrial corporations in the United States so committed to international marketing?
4. Why do you think this chapter focuses on an analysis of the international marketing environment?

5. If you were asked to provide a small tip (or bribe) to have a document approved in a foreign nation where this practice is customary, what would you do?

6. How will NAFTA affect marketing opportunities for U.S. products in North America (the United States, Mexico, and Canada)?

7. What should marketers consider as they decide whether to license or enter into a joint venture in a foreign nation?

8. Discuss the impact of strategic alliances on international marketing strategies.

9. Contrast globalization with customization of marketing strategies. Is one practice better than the other?

10. What are some of the product issues that you need to consider when marketing luxury automobiles in Australia, Brazil, Singapore, South Africa, and Sweden?

# Video Case 9.1

## Alibaba and Global E-Commerce: Should Amazon Be Afraid?

From rural farmers to multimillionaires, millions of people in China are reaping economic opportunities from the growing e-commerce market. One entrepreneur earns $5 million in sales annually from his ladies' handbag e-commerce business—a far cry from his humble origins. Although his success might be the exception to the norm, many Chinese consumers with similar backgrounds have found jobs working in e-commerce.

"We grew up in a rural area which left us few choices. I never thought about my future or had any belief in it," the entrepreneur says.

At the center of this is Alibaba, an online marketplace founded by entrepreneur Jack Ma in 1999. Jack Ma conceived of an online portal that could connect Chinese manufacturers with buyers from other countries. He chose the name Alibaba because it was globally recognized based upon the famous character in the collection *Arabian Nights*. Today this multibillion dollar firm has 500 million registered users. Its sales surpass those of eBay and Amazon combined. Alibaba runs a number of businesses that handle approximately 80 percent of all online shopping in China. Unlike Amazon, it does not own its own merchandise but acts a portal to bring buyers and sellers together.

Alibaba has a number of trading platforms that sell to both business-to-business (B2B) and business-to-consumer (B2C) markets. Its B2C market portal, Taobao, has been termed the Chinese

version of Amazon.com or eBay. Taobao has enabled rural farmers to start their own businesses and created employment opportunities for locals. Because of its influence, entire "Taobao Villages" have sprung up across China. These villages consist of residents who operate in e-commerce. Today there are estimated to be 780 Taobao Villages in China.

This is just the beginning for Alibaba. In 2014 it was listed on the U.S. stock exchange with an initial offering of $25 billion, the largest IPO to date. To emphasize its global intentions, Alibaba opened offices in France, Germany, and Italy. It is also focused on selling more international brands such as Macy's, Apple, and L'Oreal. In its quest to expand into media, Alibaba entered into a licensing agreement with Disney to sell a streaming device that will broadcast movies, television shows, e-books, games, and more.

Although it is listed on the U.S. stock exchange, investing in Alibaba differs from the traditional model due to regulatory and legal barriers. The Chinese government restricts foreign investment in certain areas, meaning that global investors outside of China cannot own shares of Alibaba outright. In reality, investors purchased shares of a shell corporation in the Cayman Islands. Alibaba itself owns all of its non-Chinese assets. Jack Ma has the most power in the company, and some investors are concerned about his tendency to make large decisions or transfer ownership without consulting many other people.

Another issue that Alibaba is coming across as it expands involves counterfeit products. In China counterfeit goods have traditionally been more accepted than in other countries. Its international e-commerce site AliExpress has gained widespread popularity in Russia, the United States, and Brazil, but its rise in popularity has been accompanied by a rise in counterfeit goods sold through the site. Regulators are worried that the site is allowing counterfeits to go straight from Chinese manufacturers to consumers on a global scale. In fact, Kering SA—a French luxury group—filed a lawsuit against Alibaba accusing the firm of knowingly allowing the sale of counterfeit products. Alibaba denies the charges and is working with government bodies to improve counterfeiting controls.

Despite the risks of investing in a firm that they cannot actually own, investors were eager to purchase shares during Alibaba's initial public offering. China is overtaking the United States as the largest e-commerce market, and the opportunities are too good for many investors to pass up. They believe Alibaba has the potential for massive global growth as it is less capital intensive and therefore more flexible than global rivals such as Amazon.com.[81]

### Questions for Discussion

1. What are some of the barriers Alibaba is facing as it expands globally?
2. How has Taobao created economic opportunities for Chinese entrepreneurs that were inaccessible to them before?
3. Why would the sale of counterfeit products through its sites be damaging to Alibaba?

# Case 9.2

## NFL Goes Global: From Soccer to Football?

Soon American football may not be characterized as much with America. Referred to as American football in many countries (in most countries the term "football" is applied to what Americans refer to as soccer), the sport is gaining a loyal following in Australia, the United Kingdom, Mexico, and Canada. In 2005, for instance, a game held in Mexico City's Azteca Stadium attracted more than 103,000 fans. In 2016 the NFL returned to Mexico when the Oakland Raiders played the Houston Texans. The NFL has established a strong presence in the United Kingdom (U.K.) as well through its NLF International Series. As global popularity of the sport increases, the NFL is expanding on a wider basis.

Although Mexico City hosted the first regular season game outside of the United States, the U.K. is where the NFL started its wide-scale expansion. Beginning in 2007, the NFL began hosting regular season games in London each year. In 2015 the NFL announced it would continue hosting its games at London's Wembley Stadium and expand to London's Twickenham Stadium and Tottenham Hotspur. Many believe it is only a matter of time before a team moves there permanently.

One reason football has become so popular in the U.K. is that Sky Sports, the biggest sports television channels in the country, pays the NFL for rights to broadcast 80 live NFL games each season. This has familiarized many British consumers with the game and created a passionate fan base. More than 80 percent of those who attend the London games are

from the U.K., and the NFL has become the sixth most popular sport to watch on Sky Sports.

It is notable that many of the countries with American football fans, such as Australia, Canada, and the United Kingdom, share several similarities with the U.S. culture. However, as the NFL continues to expand throughout Europe and other areas of the world, it is encountering more cultural challenges. For instance, the NFL has expressed an interest in expanding into Germany. This would not be the first time that the NFL would have a presence there. Between 1998 and 2007, the NFL backed NFL Europe, a league created in an attempt to spread American football globally. At one time six of NFL Europe's teams were based in Germany. And while these games were popular among the populace, they did not set well with Germany's local club teams.

Germany's local football club teams saw interest steadily decline as more people chose to watch NLF Europe games. The president of the American Football Association in Germany believes that the NFL will not be able to develop an effective sports presence in the country because of cultural differences. Despite this resistance on the local level, the NFL disagrees and believes Germany offers a lucrative opportunity for expansion.

Another challenge the NFL faces is competing against the world's most popular sport, soccer. While 160 million viewers watch the Super Bowl, 1 billion global viewers watch the World Cup. In many countries, including China, consumers know little about American football. NFL representatives have acknowledged that football is unlikely to replace the global popularity of soccer. These competitive forces could present a strong barrier to the NFL as it expands.

Infrastructure and time differences are also obstacles. Many countries struggle with the infrastructure needed to hold NFL games. At Mexico City's Azteca stadium, for instance, locker rooms, space for broadcasting networks, and technical infrastructure all present challenges. Time differences can be difficult on players, making it harder to hold games in countries far from the United States. In Japan time and cultural differences could be the major reasons why the NFL has not held games there for years, despite the enthusiasm of Japanese fans. Players have indicated that in addition to the time differences, the Japanese diet, hotel rooms, and narrow sidewalks all present difficulties for their large size.

Despite these barriers, the NFL is determined that globalization is the right route. They believe that football may be approaching market saturation in the United States, and a number of concerns—including player misconduct and safety issues—have harmed its reputation among some U.S. consumers. Going global—if successful—will greatly enhance expansion opportunities for the NFL and create loyal groups of fans worldwide.[82]

### Questions for Discussion

1. Why do you think the NFL has an easier time expanding into countries such as the United Kingdom and Canada than countries such as Germany or China?
2. Describe some of the global forces acting as barriers to the NFL as it expands globally.
3. Do you think the NFL will have to customize the games it plays overseas to fit better with the local cultures?

# NOTES

[1] Peter Evans, "World's Poor Open Wallets for Premium Products," *The Wall Street Journal*, January 1, 2015, A1, A12; Mehreen Khan, "Unilever sales beat expectations as prices rise in emerging markets," *The Telegraph*, April 16, 2015, http://www.telegraph.co.uk/finance/newsbysector/epic/ulvr/11541020/Unilever-sales-beat-expectations-as-prices-rise-in-emerging-markets.html (accessed October 5, 2015); "Hindustan Unilever hikes prices of select brands," *Times of India*, September 13, 2013, http://timesofindia.indiatimes.com/business/india-business/Hindustan-Unilever-hikes-prices-of-select-brands/articleshow/22530667.cms (accessed October 5, 2015).

[2] Sara Schonhardt, "Indonesia's Growing Pains," *The Wall Street Journal*, September 28, 2015, B3.

[3] "Where in the World Is Walmart," Walmart, http://corporate.walmart.com/our-story/our-locations (accessed January 5, 2016).

[4] "Export Assistance," Office of the United States Trade Representative, www.ustr.gov/trade-topics/trade-toolbox/export-assistance (accessed September 1, 2015).

[5] Gary A. Knight and S. Tamer Cavusgil, "Innovation, Organizational Capabilities, and the Born-Global Firm," *Journal of International Business Studies* 35, 2 (2004): 124–141.

[6] Vu Trong Kranh, "Vietnam Gets Its First McDonald's," *The Wall Street Journal*, February 11, 2014, B4.

[7] Olga Kravets and Ozlem Sandikci, "Competently Ordinary: New Middle Class Consumers in the Emerging Markets," *Journal of Marketing* 78 (July 2014): 125–140.

[8] Geoffrey James, "20 Epic Fails in Global Branding," *Inc.*, October 29, 2014, http://www.inc.com/geoffrey-james/the-20-worst-brand-translations-of-all-time.html (accessed January 5, 2016).

[9] John Revill and Annie Gasparro, "Cereal Makers Tweak Recipes for Emerging Markets," *The Wall Street Journal*, September 28, 2015, B6.

[10] Xiaoling Guo, "Living in a Global World: Influence of Consumer Global Orientation on Attitudes Toward Global Brands from Developed Versus Emerging Countries," *Journal of International Marketing* 21, 1 (March 2013): 1–22.

[11] Sadrudin A. Ahmed and Alain D'Astous, "Moderating Effects of Nationality on Country-of-Origin Perceptions: English-Speaking Thailand Versus French-Speaking Canada," *Journal of Business Research* 60, 3 (2007): 240–248; George Balabanis and Adamantios Diamantopoulos, "Domestic Country Bias, Country-of-Origin Effects, and Consumer Ethnocentrism: A Multidimensional Unfolding Approach," *Journal of the Academy of Marketing Science* 32, 1 (2004): 80–95; Harri T. Luomala, "Exploring the Role of Food Origin as a Source of Meanings for Consumers and as a Determinant of Consumers' Actual Food Choices," *Journal of Business Research* 60, 2 (2007): 122–129; Durdana Ozretic-Dosen, Vatroslav Skare, and Zoran Krupka, "Assessments of Country of Origin and Brand Cues in Evaluating a Croatian, Western and Eastern European Food Product," *Journal of Business Research* 60, 2 (2007): 130–136.

[12] David A. Griffith, Goksel Yalcinkaya, and Gaia Rubera, "Country-Level Performance of New Experience Products in a Global Rollout: The Moderating Effects of Economic Wealth and National Cul-ture," *Journal of International Marketing* 22, 4 (2014): 1–20.

[13] John Hilsenrath and Brian Blackstone, "Cheaper Chinese Currency Has Global Impact," The Wall Street Journal, April 11, 2015, http://www.wsj.com/articles/cheaper-chinese-currency-has-global-impact-1439336422 (accessed January 6, 2016); Adam Shell, "Currency War: What You Need to Know," *USA Today*, August 13, 2015, 3B.

14 Inti Landauro, "Colombia, Mexico Criticize Rich Countries on Monetary, Fiscal Policies," *The Wall Street Journal*, January 24, 2011, http://online.wsj.com/article/BT-CO-20110124-710562.html (accessed January 20, 2012).

15 International Monetary Fund, http://www.imf.org/external/index.htm (accessed July 1, 2016).

16 Ibid.

17 Stephen A. Samaha, Joshua T. Beck, and Robert W. Palmatier, "The Role of Culture in International Relationship Marketing," *Journal of Marketing* 78 (September 2014): 78–98.

18 James Hookway and Samuel Rubenfeld, "U.S. Temporarily Lifts Trade Restrictions on Myanmar," *The Wall Street Journal*, December 7, 2015, http://www.wsj.com/articles/u-s-temporarily-lifts-trade-restrictions-on-myanmar-1449539262 (accessed January 6, 2016).

19 "Emirates," The Emirates Group, http://www.theemiratesgroup.com/english/our-brands/air-transportation/emirates-airline.aspx (accessed January 6, 2016).

20 American Marketing Association, "Statement of Ethics," http://www.marketingpower.com/AboutAMA/Pages/Statement%20of%20Ethics.aspx (accessed January 5, 2016).

21 Felicia Schwartz, "U.S. and Cuba Renew Diplomatic Relations," *The Wall Street Journal*, July 2, 2015, A8.

22 Central Intelligence Agency, "Guide to Country Comparisons."

23 Charles R. Taylor, George R. Franke, and Michael L. Maynard, "Attitudes toward Direct Marketing and Its Regulation: A Comparison of the United States and Japan," *Journal of Public Policy & Marketing* 19, 2 (2000): 228–237.

24 "Welcome to BASCAP," International Chamber of Commerce, http://www.iccwbo.org/advocacy-codes-and-rules/bascap/ (accessed January 5, 2015).

25 Gillian Wong, "Counterfeits Test Alibaba's Goals," *The Wall Street Journal*, November 11, 2015, B8.

26 Business for Social Responsibility, www.bsr.org (accessed February 5, 2016).

27 Elizabeth Dwoskin, "EU Privacy Law Raises Daunting Prospects for Firms," *The Wall Street Journal*, December 17, 2015, B1, B8.

28 "This Is Systembolaget," https://www.systembolaget.se/English/ (accessed January 5, 2016).

29 Central Intelligence Agency, "Guide to Country Comparisons," World Factbook, https://www.cia.gov/library/publications/the-world-factbook/rankorder/rankorderguide.html (accessed January 8, 2016).

30 Alexandra Wexler, "Mobile Money Gets Easier in Africa," *The Wall Street Journal*, July 17, 2015, B5.

31 Economist staff, "Special Report: The World Economy, *The Economist*, October 4, 2014, pp. 1–18.

32 "The North American Free Trade Agreement (NAFTA)," export.gov, http://export.gov/FTA/nafta/index.asp (accessed January 5, 2016).

33 Central Intelligence Agency.

34 United States Census Bureau, "Trade in Goods with Canada," https://www.census.gov/foreign-trade/balance/c1220.html (accessed February 5, 2016).

35 Statistics Canada, "Table 1 Merchandise trade: Canada's top 10 principal trading partners – Seasonally adjusted, current dollars," December 5, 2014, http://www.statcan.gc.ca/daily-quotidien/141205/t141205b001-eng.htm (accessed January 5, 2016).

36 Central Intelligence Agency.

37 "Trade in Goods with Mexico," U.S. Census Bureau: Foreign Trade, https://www.census.gov/foreign-trade/balance/c2010.html (accessed February 5, 2016).

38 Office of the United States Trade Representative, "CAFTA-DR (Dominican Republic-Central America FTA)," www.ustr.gov/trade-agreements/free-trade-agreements/cafta-dr-dominican-republic-central-america-fta (accessed January 7, 2016).

39 Economist staff, "Crisis revisited," *Economist*, December 13, 2014, p. 17.

40 "Member States of the EU, Europa, http://europa.eu/about-eu/countries/index_en.htm (accessed January 5, 2016); "The History of the European Union," Europa, http://europa.eu/abc/history/index_en.htm (accessed January 5,

2016); "Europe in 12 Lessons," Europa, http://europa.eu/abc/12lessons/lesson_2/index_en.htm (accessed January 5, 2016).

41 Central Intelligence Agency, "The World FactBook: European Union," https://www.cia.gov/library/publications/the-world-factbook/geos/ee.html (accessed January 7, 2016).

42 "About the EU," Europa, http://europa.eu/about-eu/index_en.htm (accessed January 5, 2016).

43 "Special Advertising Section: The European Union and the United States," *Foreign Policy*, January 2013, 1.

44 "Special Advertising Section: The European Union and the United States," *Foreign Policy*, January 2013, 1.

45 "In a Nutshell," MERCOSUR, http://www.mercosur.int/innovaportal/v/3862/2/innova.front/en-pocas-palabras (accessed and translated from Spanish via Chrome on September 2, 2015); Thomas Favaro, "Don't Hold Your Breath for Mercosur's Changes," Forbes, July 27, 2015, http://www.forbes.com/sites/riskmap/2015/07/27/dont-hold-your-breath-for-mercosurs-changes/ (accessed February 5, 2016).

46 Joanna Klonsky, Stephanie Hanson, and Brianna Lee, "Mercosur: South America's Fractious Trade Bloc," Council on Foreign Relations, July 31, 2012, http://www.cfr.org/trade/mercosur-south-americas-fractious-trade-bloc/p12762 (accessed January 5, 2016); "Agri-Food Regional of the South (Mercosur): Brazil, Argentina, Paraguay," Agriculture and Agrifood Canada, January 2011, www.ats.agr.gc.ca/lat/3947-eng.htm (accessed January 5, 2016); TeleSur, "MERCOSUR: Paving the Way for Latin American Integration," December 15, 2014, http://www.telesurtv.net/english/analysis/MERCOSUR-Paving-the-Way-for-Latin-American-Integration-20141213-0025.html (accessed January 5, 2016).

47 Indira A.R. Lakshmanan, "A Breakout Year for Cuban Entrepreneurs," *Bloomberg Businessweek*, August 20, 2015, 14–15

48 "About APEC," Asia-Pacific Economic Cooperation, http://www.apec.org/home.aspx (accessed January 5, 2016).

49 Juro Osawa, "China Steps Up Fight Against Online Music Piracy," *The Wall Street Journal*, August 10, 2015, http://blogs.wsj.com/digits/2015/08/10/china-steps-up-fight-against-online-music-piracy/ (accessed January 6, 2016).

50 Kathy Chu, "China Loses Edge on Labor Costs," *The Wall Street Journal*, December 3, 2015, B1, B4.

51 Kevin Granville, "The Trans-Pacific Partnership Trade Deal Explained," *The New York Times*, May 11, 2015, http://www.nytimes.com/2015/05/12/business/unpacking-the-trans-pacific-partnership-trade-deal.html?_r=0 (accessed February 5, 2016).

52 Paul Davidson, "Trade Deal May Lift Consumers," *The Wall Street Journal*, October 6, 2015, 1B-2B; Office of the United States Trade Representative, "Overview of the Trans-Pacific Partnership," https://ustr.gov/tpp/overview-of-the-TPP (accessed January 6, 2016).

53 Kevin Granville, "The Trans-Pacific Partnership Trade Deal Explained"; Hiroko Tabuchi, "Premier Says Japan Will Join Pacific Free Trade Talks," *The New York Times*, November 11, 2011, http://www.nytimes.com/2011/11/12/world/asia/japan-to-join-talks-on-pacific-trade-pact.html (accessed February 5, 2016); Tom Barkley, "Framework Is Set For New Trade Bloc," *The Wall Street Journal*, November 14, 2011, http://www.wsj.com/articles/SB10001424052970203503204577036553639815214 (accessed February 5, 2016).

54 Simon Kennedy, Isabel Reynolds, and Keiki Ujikane, "A Mega Trade Deal," *Bloomberg Businessweek*, October 12-October 18, 2015, 12–13.

55 Association of Southeast Asian Nations website, http://www.asean.org/ (accessed February 5, 2016).

56 "ASEAN Economic Community: 12 Things to Know," *Asian Development Bank*, December 29, 2015, http://www.adb.org/features/asean-economic-community-12-things-know (accessed January 6, 2016).

57 Association of Southeast Asian Nations website, http://www.asean.org/asean/about-asean/ (accessed January 5, 2016).

58 Simon Long, "Safety in numbers," *The Economist*, The World In 2015 Edition, p. 68.

59 Nick Mead, "OECD: South-East Asian Economic Outlook to Return to Pre-crisis Levels," *The Guardian*, November 18, 2012, http://www.theguardian.com/global-development/datablog/2012/nov/18/oecd-south-east-asia-economic-outlook (accessed February 5, 2016); Kathy Quiano, "ASEAN Summit Starts amid Cloud of Thai-Cambodia Border Row," *CNN*, May 7, 2011, http://www.cnn.com/2011/WORLD/asiapcf/05/07/asia.asean.summit/index.html (accessed February 5, 2016).

60 Shelley Goldberg, "PTT Chemical Public Company to Benefit from ASEAN Growth," *Seeking Alpha*, August 17, 2015, http://seekingalpha.com/article/3445536-ptt-chemical-public-company-to-benefit-from-asean-growth (accessed January 19, 2016)

61 Eric Bellman, "Asia Seeks Integration despite EU's Woes," *The Wall Street Journal*, July 22, 2011, A9.

62 World Trade Organization, "What Is the WTO?," https://www.wto.org/english/thewto_e/whatis_e/whatis_e.htm (accessed September 3, 2015).

63 World Trade Organization, "What Is the WTO?"

64 Tennille Tracy, "WTO Rules Against U.S. Meat Labels," *The Wall Street Journal*, May 19, 2015, A5.

65 Jan Johanson and Finn Wiedersheim-Paul, "The Internationalization of the Firm," *Journal of Management Studies* 12, 3 (1975): 305–322; Jan Johanson and Jan-Erik Vahlne, "The Internationalization Process of the Firm—A Model of Knowledge Development and Increasing Foreign Commitments," *Journal of International Business Studies* 8, 1 (1977): 23–32; S. Tamer Cavusgil and John R. Nevin, "Internal Determinants of Export Marketing Behavior: An Empirical Investigation," *Journal of Marketing Research* 18, 1 (1981): 114–119.

66 Pradeep Tyagi, "Export Behavior of Small Business Firms in Developing Economies: Evidence from the Indian Market," *Marketing Management Journal* 10, 2 (2000): 12–20.

67 Berrin Dosoglu-Guner, "How Do Exporters and Non-Exporters View Their 'Country of Origin' Image Abroad?" *Marketing Management Journal* 10, 2 (2000): 21–27.

68 WTSC Industrial Group website, http://www.wtsc.eu/ (accessed January 6, 2016).

69 Farok J. Contractor and Sumit K. Kundu, "Franchising Versus Company-Run Operations: Model Choice in the Global Hotel Sector," *Journal of International Marketing* 6, 2 (1998): 28–53.

70 James R. Hagerty, "Offshoring Outpaces 'Reshoring'," *The Wall Street Journal*, December 15, 2014, B3.

71 Paul Mozer, "Qualcomm in Venture with Chinese Chip Maker," *The New York Times*, June 23, 2015, http://www.nytimes.com/2015/06/24/business/international/qualcomm-in-venture-with-chinese-chip-maker.html?_r=0 (accessed January 6, 2016).

72 Calum Fuller, "EY and LinkedIn announce strategic alliance," *Accountancy Age*, October 30, 2015, http://www.accountancy-age.com/aa/news/2432737/ey-and-linkedin-announce-strategic-alliance (accessed January 6, 2016).

73 Matt Krantz,"As Europe Reels, 9 U.S. Companies Under Pressure," *The Wall Street Journal*, November 17, 2015, 1B.

74 "Export," Lone Star Distribution, http://lonestardistribution.com/export/ (accessed February 5, 2016).

75 Abbott, "Abbott Global," www.abbott.com/global/url/content/en_US/10.17:17/general_content/General_Content_00054.htm (accessed February 5, 2016).

76 Dana L. Alden, James B. Kelley, Petra Riefler, Julie A. Lee, and Geoffrey N. Soutar, "The Effect of Global Company Animosity on Global Brand Attitudes in Emerging and Developed Markets: Does Perceived Value Matter?" *Journal of International Marketing* 21, 2 (2013): 17–38.

77 Deborah Owens, Timothy Wilkinson, and Bruce Keillor, "A Comparison of Product Attributes in a Cross-Cultural/Cross-National Context," *Marketing Management Journal* 10, 2 (2000): 1–11.

[78] PR Newswire, "First 7-Eleven Store Opens in Middle East," *PR Newswire*, October 13, 2015, http://www.prnewswire.com/news-releases/first-7-eleven-store-opens-in-middle-east-300158789.html (accessed January 6, 2016).

[79] Larry Light, "How organisations manage global brands in an increasingly global world," *Journal of Brand Strategy* 2, 3 (Fall 2013): 228–235.

[80] Anil K. Gupta, Vijay Govindarajan, and Peter Roche, "Converting Global Presence into Global Competitive Advantage," *Academy of Management Executive* 15, 2 (2001): 45–58.

[81] Susanna Kim, "Alibaba: How Did the Chinese Company Gets Its Name?" *ABC News*, September 18, 2014, http://abcnews.go.com/Business/alibaba-chinese-company/story?id=25591454 (accessed January 13, 2016); Leena Rao, "Disney Teams Up With Alibaba to Sell Movies, TV Shows in China," *Fortune*, December 15, 2015, http://fortune.com/2015/12/15/disney-alibaba/ (accessed January 13, 2016); Patrick Frater, "Alibaba Seeks International Expansion Hitches with 'Avengers' in China," *Variety*, May 14, 2015, http://variety.com/2015/biz/asia/alibaba-seeks-international-expansion-1201495896/ (accessed January 13, 2016); Bloomberg News, "Alibaba to Open Offices in Europe as U.S. Expansion Continues," *Bloomberg*, October 13, 2015, http://www.bloomberg.com/news/articles/2015-10-13/alibaba-to-open-offices-in-europe-as-u-s-expansion-continues (accessed January 13, 2016); Paul Mozur, "Alibaba Profit Surges, but a Revenue Gain of 40% Still Misses Forecasts," *The New York Times*, January 29, 2015, http://www.nytimes.com/2015/01/30/business/international/in-alibaba-earnings-revenue-falls-short.html (accessed January 13, 2016); Helen H. Wang, "Why Amazon Should Fear Alibaba," *Forbes*, July 8, 2015, http://www.forbes.com/sites/helenwang/2015/07/08/why-amazon-should-fear-alibaba/ (accessed January 13, 2016); John Watling, "China's Internet Giants Lead in Online Finance," *The Financialist*, February 14, 2014, https://www.thefinancialist.com/

not-just-a-paypal-clone-chinas-internet-giants-chart-their-own-course/ (accessed January 13, 2016); Juro Osawa, Paul Mozur, and Rolfe Winkler, "Alibaba Flexes Muscles Before IPO," *The Wall Street Journal*, April 15, 2015, http://www.wsj.com/news/articles/SB10001424052702303887804579501411932558776 (accessed January 13, 2016); Bloomberg News, "Alibaba's IPO Filing: Everything You Need to Know," *The Wall Street Journal*, May 6, 2014, http://blogs.wsj.com/digits/2014/05/06/alibabas-ipo-filing-everything-you-need-to-know/ (accessed January 13, 2016); Gillian Wong, "Alibaba's Global Ambitions Face Counterfeit Challenge," *The Wall Street Journal*, November 10, 2015, http://www.wsj.com/articles/alibabas-global-ambitions-face-genuine-counterfeit-challenge-1447147654 (accessed January 13, 2016); Steven Davidoff Solomon, "Alibaba Investors Will Buy a Risky Corporate Structure," *The New York Times*, May 6, 2014, http://dealbook.nytimes.com/2014/05/06/i-p-o-revives-debate-over-a-chinese-structure/?_php=true&_type=blogs&_r=1 (accessed January 13, 2016).

[82] Kevin Patra, "NFL evaluating Azteca Stadium for potential '16 game," NFL.com, November 21, 2015, http://www.nfl.com/news/story/0ap3000000584416/article/nfl-evaluating-azteca-stadium-for-potential-16-game (accessed February 5, 2016); Ryan Wilson, "NFL, Tottenham Hotspur agree on 10-year partnership for NFL games," *CBS Sports*, July 8, 2015, http://www.cbssports.com/nfl/eye-on-football/25236443/nfl-tottenham-hotspur-agree-on-10-year-partnership-for-nfl-games (accessed February 5, 2016); AP News, "NFL extends deal to play games at Wembley through 2020," *The Big Story*, October 22, 2015, http://bigstory.ap.org/article/decc44cd-fece478d820723df034e59c7/nfl-extends-deal-play-games-wembley-through-2020 (accessed February 5, 2016); Associated Press, "NFL commissioner says Super Bowl may someday be held in London," *ESPN*, October 15, 2007, http://sports.espn.go.com/espn/wire?section=nfl&id=3065083 (accessed February 5, 2016); Associated Press, "3 NFC, 3

AFC teams named possible 'hosts' in Europe," *ESPN*, January 8, 2007, http://sports.espn.go.com/nfl/news/story?id=2724315 (accessed February 5, 2016); Brandon Zimmerman, "NFL Banking on 'Passion' of U.K. Fans to Make London Expansion a Success," *Sports Business Daily*, August 28, 2013, http://www.sportsbusinessdaily.com/Global/Issues/2013/08/28/Marketing-and-Sponsorship/NFL-London.aspx (accessed February 5, 2016); Associated Press, "NFL looking closely at expanding to 17 games with international flavor," *ESPN*, May 10, 2007, http://sports.espn.go.com/espn/wire?section=nfl&id=2865949 (accessed February 5, 2016); Jason La Canfora, "NFL's move to London could come soon; Jags a target," *CBS Sports*, October 28, 2012, http://www.cbssports.com/nfl/writer/jason-la-canfora/20724077/nfls-move-to-london-could-come-soon-jags-a-target (accessed February 5, 2016); Conor Orr, "NFL continues to explore opportunities in Mexico," NFL.com, August 7, 2015, http://www.nfl.com/news/story/0ap3000000507542/article/nfl-continues-to-explore-opportunities-in-mexico (accessed February 5, 2016); "The NFL's Future in Europe," *MMQB*, July 24, 2015, http://mmqb.si.com/mmqb/2015/07/24/nfl-future-europe (accessed February 5, 2016); Mark Maske, "NFL expands plans for international games, will consider sites beyond London," *The Washington Post*, October 7, 2015, https://www.washingtonpost.com/news/sports/wp/2015/10/07/nfl-expands-plans-for-international-games-will-consider-sites-beyond-london/ (accessed February 5, 2016); Andrew Both, "Super Bowl has ways to go in captivating global audience," *Reuters*, January 24, 2015, http://www.reuters.com/article/us-nfl-international-idUSKBN0KX0KK20150124 (accessed February 5, 2016); "Back to Mexico: Texans-Raiders to play Nov. 21 in Mexico City," NFL.com, February 5, 2016, http://www.nfl.com/news/story/0ap3000000632878/article/back-to-mexico-texansraiders-to-play-nov-21-in-mexico-city (accessed February 5, 2016).

# Feature Notes

[a] Ted Redmond and Yuko Takeo, "Skimming Profits From Pond Scum," *Bloomberg Businessweek*, July 20-July 26, 2015, 31–32; Chisaki Watanabe, "Japan's Isuzu, Euglena to Begin Biodiesel Development With Algae," *Bloomberg*, June 25, 2014, http://www.bloomberg.com/news/articles/2014-06-25/japan-s-isuzu-euglena-to-begin-biodiesel-development-with-algae (accessed July 21, 2015); Durga Madhab Mahapatra, H.N. Chanakya, and T.V. Ramachandra, "Euglena sp. as a suitable source of lipids for potential use as biofuel and sustainable wastewater treatment," *Journal of Applied Psychology* 25, 3 (2013): 855–865; Euglena, "Research and Business Strategy," http://www.euglena.jp/en/labo/research.html (accessed July 21, 2015); Nikkei Inc., "Japan to get Asia's first jet biofuel refinery," *Nikkei Asian Review*, February 22, 2015, http://asia.nikkei.com/Japan-Update/Japan-to-get-Asia-s-first-jet-biofuel-refinery (accessed July 21, 2015).

[b] Emma S Hinchliffe, "On Obama's cue, Netflix launches in Cuba," *USA Today*, February 10, 2015, 1A; Sam Schechner, "Netflix to Expand Into Italy, Portugal, Spain," *The Wall Street Journal*, June 8, 2015, B4; *NPR*, Carrie Khan, "Netflix Streams Its Way to Cuba–Slowly," *NPR*, February 14, 2015, http://www.npr.org/2015/02/14/386323314/netflix-streams-its-way-to-cuba-slowly (accessed October 7, 2015); Trefis Team, "China Makes Sense for Netflix, But It Won't Be Easy," *Trefis Team*, May 26, 2015, http://www.trefis.com/stock/nflx/articles/297718/china-makes-sense-for-netflix-but-it-won%E2%80%99t-be-easy/2015-05-26 (accessed October 7, 2015); Trefis Team, "A Closer Look at Netflix's Foray Into Japan," *Trefis*, February 18, 2015, http://www.trefis.com/stock/nflx/articles/281080/a-closer-look-at-netflix%E2%80%99s-foray-into-japan/2015-02-18 (accessed October 7, 2015).

Bloomua/Shutterstock.com

# chapter 10 Digital Marketing and Social Networking

## OBJECTIVES

**10-1** Define *digital media, digital marketing*, and *electronic marketing*.

**10-2** Summarize the growth and importance of digital marketing.

**10-3** Describe different types of digital media and how they can be used for marketing.

**10-4** Critique the seven different ways consumers use digital media.

**10-5** Describe how digital media affect the four variables of the marketing mix.

**10-6** Identify legal and ethical considerations in digital marketing.

## MARKETING INSIGHTS

### GE: E-Connecting the World

Olga Besnard/Shutterstock.com

There are many opportunities to reach out to consumers through digital marketing channels, but what about a company focusing on the business-to-business market (not end-user consumers)? Should these types of companies, often hi-tech in nature, still try to reach out to the average consumer? General Electric not only says yes but has become an expert in social media marketing targeting consumers.

GE uses social media channels to display branded content, a type of promotion that blends advertising with entertainment. For instance, it developed the "GE Show" on YouTube consisting of episodes about GE technologies that impact our daily lives. Its "badass machines" board on Pinterest has pictures of the large machines GE builds. GE spends about 40 percent of its marketing budget on digital media.

The idea is to attract potential business clients, future hires, and end consumers. While GE does not sell to end consumers directly, it recognizes that its products have a major impact on their lives. GE wants to make its brand relatable and generate excitement about what it is doing.

As such, it is often the first to embrace new social media tools. When the video-service Vine was launched on Twitter, GE immediately launched the "6SecondScience" series in which consumers were encouraged to film their own science experiments. Additionally, GE's global director of digital content has organized "Instawalks" to bring popular Instagram profile holders to tour GE facilities, take photos, and post them onto GE's Instagram account.

GE's efforts have paid off, with 56,000 subscribers on YouTube and 1.3 million Facebook fans. It was nominated for the *Best Fortune 500 Brand on Social Media* for several categories. GE demonstrates how even a business-to-business, hi-tech brand can form strong relationships with end-user consumers.[1]

**Internet of Things**
Accenture and Visa utilize the Internet of Things—a phenomenon in which billions of items will be connected through the Internet—to allow cars to store payment information.

Since the 1990s, the Internet and information technology have dramatically changed the marketing environment and the strategies that are necessary for marketing success. Digital media have created exciting opportunities for companies to target specific markets more effectively, develop new marketing strategies, and gather more information about customers. Using digital media channels, marketers are better able to analyze and address consumer needs. Fueled by changing technology, consumer behavior has changed with Internet-enabled consumer empowerment. This has resulted in a shift in the balance of power between consumer and marketer.[2]

One of the defining characteristics of information technology in the 21st century is accelerating change. Consider that by the end of decade, it is estimated that up to 50 billion things including cars and household items will be connected to the Internet in a phenomenon termed the "Internet of Things."[3] As the advertisement demonstrates, Accenture partnered with Visa to make it possible for a car to store credit credentials that can then be shared across different platforms. Accenture claims that tapping into the Internet of Things to develop connected commerce will make consumers' lives easier.

New systems and applications advance so rapidly that a chapter on this topic has to strain to incorporate the possibilities of the future. When Google first arrived on the scene in 1998, a number of search engines were fighting for dominance. Google, with its fast, easy-to-use format, soon became the number-one search engine. Google has used its dominance to expand into e-mail, smartphones, social networking, and even driver-less vehicles. Google has become so disparate, in fact, that the CEO reorganized the firm so that Google is now a division under the conglomerate Alphabet.[4] However, even a corporate giant like Google faces competition as search engines from other countries gain market share. Baidu, for instance, is often considered to be the Chinese equivalent of Google.

In this chapter, we focus on digital marketing strategies—particularly communication channels such as social networks—and discuss how consumers are changing their information searches and consumption behaviors to fit with these emerging technologies and trends. Most importantly, we analyze how marketers can use new media to their advantage to connect with consumers, gather more information about their target markets, and convert this information into successful marketing strategies.

**digital media** Electronic media that function using digital codes; when we refer to digital media, we are referring to media available via computers, cellular phones, smartphones, and other digital devices that have been released in recent years

## 10-1 DEFINING *DIGITAL MARKETING*

Before we move on, we must first provide a definition of digital media. **Digital media** are electronic media that function using digital codes—when we refer to digital media, we are referring to media available via computers, smart phones, and other smart devices, including wearable technology and televisions that have been released in recent years. A number of terms have been coined to describe marketing activities on the Internet. **Digital marketing** uses all digital media, including the Internet and mobile and interactive channels, to develop communication and exchanges with customers. In this chapter, we focus on how the Internet relates to all aspects of marketing, including strategic planning. Thus, we use the term **electronic marketing**, or **e-marketing**, to refer to the strategic process of distributing, promoting, and pricing products, and discovering the desires of customers using digital media and digital marketing. Although there are differences between the terms, many people use *digital marketing* and *electronic marketing* interchangeably. In addition, we sometimes use the term *e-tailing* to describe online retailing. Our definition of e-marketing goes beyond the Internet and also includes mobile phones, banner ads, digital outdoor marketing, and social networks.

**digital marketing** The use of the telephone, Internet, and nonpersonal media to introduce products to customers, who can then purchase them via mail, telephone, or the Internet

**electronic marketing or e-marketing** The strategic process of distributing, promoting, and pricing products, and discovering the desires of customers using digital media and digital marketing

## 10-2 GROWTH AND BENEFITS OF DIGITAL MARKETING

The phenomenal growth of the Internet has provided unprecedented opportunities for marketers to forge interactive relationships with consumers. As the Internet and digital communication technologies have advanced, they have made it possible to target markets more precisely and reach markets that were previously inaccessible. As the world of digital media continues to develop, e-marketing has developed strategies that include all digital media, including television advertising and other mobile and interactive media that do not use the Internet (advertising media are discussed in detail in Chapter 17). In fact, marketers are using the term *digital marketing* as a catch-all for capturing all digital channels for reaching customers. This area is progressing rapidly, and the digital world is evolving into effective marketing strategy integration.[5]

One of the most important benefits of e-marketing is the ability of marketers and customers to share information. Through websites, social networks, and other digital media, consumers can learn about everything they consume and use in life. As a result, the Internet is changing the way marketers communicate and develop relationships. Today's marketers can use the Internet to form relationships with a variety of stakeholders, including customers, employees, and suppliers. This results in the need to adjust marketing strategies to the digital world. Digital marketing and social media permit innovative forms of communication and co-created content in relationship-based interactions.[6]

For many businesses, engaging in digital and online marketing activities is essential to maintaining competitive advantages. Increasingly, small businesses can use digital media to develop strategies to reach new markets and access inexpensive communication channels. In addition, large companies like Target use online catalogs and company websites to supplement their brick-and-mortar stores. At the other end of the spectrum, companies

Source: Slack

brewbetter | .slack.com

Blue Bottle Coffee uses Slack, an easy-to-use messaging app that integrates with your existing tools and gathers all your communication in one place. It's teamwork made simpler, more pleasant, and more productive.

slack
work on purpose

**New Business Opportunities**
Businesses are using the messaging app Slack to integrate their communication tools and bring all their communication to one place.

Table 10.1  **Characteristics of Online Media**

| Characteristic | Definition | Example |
|---|---|---|
| Addressability | The ability of the marketer to identify customers before they make a purchase | Amazon installs cookies on a user's computer that allow the company to identify the user when he or she returns to the website. |
| Interactivity | The ability of customers to express their needs and wants directly to the firm in response to its marketing communications | Texas Instruments interacts with its customers on its Facebook page by answering concerns and posting updates. |
| Accessibility | The ability for marketers to obtain digital information | Google can use Web searches done through its search engine to learn about customer interests. |
| Connectivity | The ability for consumers to be connected with marketers along with other consumers | Mary Kay offers users the opportunity to sign up for My MK, a system that connects customers with beauty consultants and allows them to develop their own personalized space. |
| Control | The customer's ability to regulate the information they view as well as the rate and exposure to that information | Consumers use Kayak.com to discover the best travel deals. |

like Amazon.com and Alibaba, which have traditionally lacked physical stores and sell products solely online, are challenging traditional brick-and-mortar businesses. Interestingly, however, even online companies seem to be acknowledging that physical stores have their advantages. Amazon opened up its first physical bookstore in Seattle. Physical stores are helpful for interacting with customers to gain more insights, allowing them to check out merchandise in-store and giving employees the ability to encourage them to purchase additional products online.[7] Social networking sites are advancing e-marketing by providing features to aid in commerce, such as the ability to view daily deals or purchase items using Facebook. Finally, some corporate websites and social media sites provide feedback mechanisms through which customers can ask questions, voice complaints, indicate preferences, and otherwise communicate about their needs and desires.

This increase in digital promotions is providing new business opportunities for Internet services. Slack is a messaging app that brings all communication together into one place. This is particularly helpful for businesses because it enables them to engage in real-time messaging. As the advertisement demonstrates, Blue Bottle—a U.S. coffee roaster and retailer in Oakland, California—uses Slack to enhance communication and teamwork.

One of the biggest mistakes a marketer can make when engaging in digital marketing is to treat it like a traditional marketing channel. Digital media offer a whole new dimension to marketing that marketers must consider when concocting their companies' marketing strategies. The quality of the website will have a major impact on whether the customer exhibits loyalty to the site. Website aesthetics, navigational quality, information content, and information quality positively impact the level of a customer's relative loyalty to the e-tailer website.[8] Some of the characteristics that distinguish online media from traditional marketing include addressability, interactivity, accessibility, connectivity, and control, as defined in Table 10.1.

## 10-3 TYPES OF CONSUMER-GENERATED MARKETING AND DIGITAL MEDIA

Although digital and e-marketing have generated exciting opportunities for producers of products to interact with consumers, it is essential to recognize that social media are more consumer-driven than traditional media. Consumer-generated material is having a profound effect on marketing. As the Internet becomes more accessible worldwide, consumers are creating and reading consumer-generated content like never before. Social networks and advances in software technology provide an environment for marketers to utilize consumer-generated content.

Two major trends have caused consumer-generated information to gain importance:

1. The increased tendency of consumers to publish their own thoughts, opinions, reviews, and product discussions through blogs or digital media.
2. Consumers' tendencies to trust other consumers over corporations. Consumers often rely on the recommendations of friends, family, and fellow consumers when making purchasing decisions.

By understanding where online users are likely to express their thoughts and opinions, marketers can use these forums to interact with consumers, address problems, and promote their companies. It is also helpful for targeting certain demographics. For example, young adults aged 16 to 24 favor Instagram, Twitter, Snapchat, Vine, and Tumblr, though many use other sites including blogs, wikis, media-sharing sites, virtual reality gaming, mobile devices, applications and widgets, and more.

## 10-3a Social Networks

Social networks have been integrated into marketing strategies. A **social network** is a website where users can create a profile and interact with other users, post information, and engage in other forms of web-based communication. They are widely used in marketing strategies to develop relationships with customers. Each wave of social network has become increasingly sophisticated. Marketers are thereby using these sites and their popularity with consumers to promote products, handle questions and complaints, and provide information to assist customers in buying decisions. Marketing is evolving from digital into strategic interactive marketing that facilitates two-way communication. Allowing consumers to opt-in or opt-out of programs facilitates communication without intruding on privacy.[9]

Another benefit of social networking is marketers' ability to reach out to new target markets. Snapchat is a mobile photo messaging application that allows users to send photos, messages, or videos to their friends for a certain amount of time. After that time the post is deleted from both the recipient's phone and Snapchat servers. Snapchat is also partnering with television to show sports and professional content. It has grown immensely popular with

**social network** A website where users can create a profile and interact with other users, post information, and engage in other forms of Web-based communication

# EMERGING **TRENDS IN MARKETING**

### Iceland's Cool Play to Drive Tourism

Digital marketing is becoming a crucial marketing tool for promoting global tourism. Take Iceland, for example. Iceland has seen enormous growth in interest after it launched social media campaigns promoting tourism. Its "Ask Guðmundur" campaign uses volunteers named Guðmundur (the most popular name in Iceland) to answer online questions and promote the country's hidden gems. The campaign used the "human element" to demonstrate that Iceland should be visited year-round and not just in the summer. After the launch, Google searches of Iceland increased by 165 percent.

Successful digital marketing campaigns have also generated interest in New Zealand and the United Arab Emirates (UAE). New Zealand partnered with Facebook to launch a five-film web series featuring a couple and their encounters as they drive across New Zealand. The intent of the films is to give tourists a better idea of what they may experience when traveling throughout the island.

Restaurateurs in the UAE's biggest city of Dubai are successfully using Instagram to promote Dubai as a "foodie" hotspot. For instance, Dubai food truck Salt posts photos on Instagram as well as hashtags that help users find its location. It had 82,000 followers after only one year in operation. Despite their differences, countries are using digital marketing to promote a common purpose: to increase global interest in what their countries have to offer.[a]

teenagers and Millennials, profitable but difficult demographics for marketers to reach. When Snapchat featured a live broadcast of the MTV Video Music Awards, firms such as Cover Girl, Taco Bell, and Verizon paid $200,000 per sponsor to advertise on the site.[10] Many countries or regions have their own popular social networking sites as well. For instance, Weibo and RenRen are popular social networking sites in China. More information on how marketers use social networks is provided in later sections of this chapter.

Social networks are building business models for economic success. As Figure 10.1 demonstrates, the majority of social network users are between the ages of 18 and 29, but other age groups are not that far behind. Approximately 65 percent of American adults use social networks. There has been a large increase in older people who use social media sites since 2010.[11] As social networks evolve, both marketers and the owners of social networking sites are realizing the incredible opportunities such networks offer—an influx of advertising dollars for social networking owners and a large reach for the advertiser. As a result, marketers have begun investigating and experimenting with promotion on social networks. The challenge to improve the brand is to expand the range of social media used and to target various stakeholders that should be a part of the dialogue. Therefore, social media should be a part of corporate communication and brand building strategy.[12] The following social networks are among the most popular worldwide.

## Facebook

Facebook is the most popular social networking site in the world. When it was launched in 2004 by Harvard student Mark Zuckerberg and four of his classmates, it was initially limited to Harvard students. In 2006 the site was opened to anyone aged 13 or older. Internet users create Facebook profiles and then search the network for people with whom to connect. The social networking giant has surpassed 1.5 billion users and is still growing. It has also

**Figure 10.1    Social Networking Use by Age and Year**

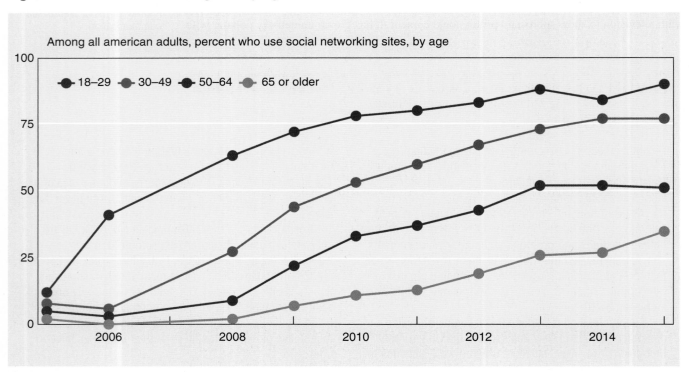

Source: Pew Research Center surveys, 2005–2006, 2008–2015. No data are available for 2007.

acquired a number of companies as it expands into other services, including Instagram, WhatsApp, and Oculus.[13] Facebook estimates that it had a $227 billion global economic impact through job growth, product sales, event planning, and more.[14]

For this reason, many marketers are turning to Facebook to market products, interact with consumers, and take advantage of free publicity. Consumers can become fans of major companies like Avon by clicking on the "like" icon on their Facebook pages. Organizations use Facebook and other digital media sites to give special incentives to customers. Although Facebook is banned in mainland China, Air China has used Facebook to inter-

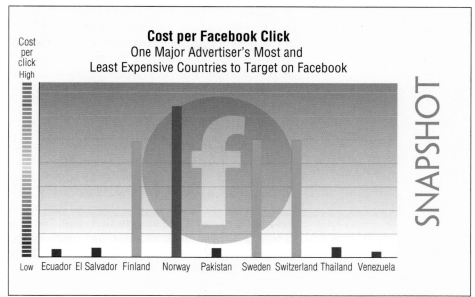

**Cost per Facebook Click**
One Major Advertiser's Most and
Least Expensive Countries to Target on Facebook

Cost per click

High

Low    Ecuador  El Salvador  Finland  Norway  Pakistan  Sweden  Switzerland  Thailand  Venezuela

SNAPSHOT

Source: Nanigans.

act with customers, offer free giveaways, and link users to its booking engine. Air China's digital marketing through the social networking site was so impressive that Facebook awarded it for best use of the social network for international marketing.[15] Advertising on Facebook has also been increasing. Its advertising revenue grew 45 percent in a one-year period, and 78 percent of this growth was in the mobile area.[16]

Additionally, social networking sites are useful for relationship marketing, or the creation of relationships that mutually benefit the marketing business and the customer. A poll revealed that 30 percent of consumers claim social media has some influence on their purchasing decisions. This is leading firms to focus more on the quality of their Facebook interactions rather than simply their quantity. Ritz-Carlton, for instance, spends more time analyzing its social-media conversations and reaching out to non-customers. The emphasis is shifting from simply selling a product or promoting a brand to developing a mutually beneficial relationship in which the brand provides the user with a positive outcome.[17] Thanks to Facebook, companies that are focused upon building and enhancing customer relationships are able to understand who their customers are and how they can meet their needs.

## Twitter

Twitter is a hybrid mix of a social networking site and a micro-blogging site that asks viewers one simple question: "What's happening?" Users can post answers of up to 140 characters, which are then available for their "followers" to read. A limitation of 140 characters may not seem like enough for companies to send an effective message, but some have become experts at using Twitter in their marketing strategies. For instance, American Airlines was ranked as the top airline on Twitter due to its customer engagement and responsiveness.[18] For sports enthusiasts, the National Football League developed a deal with Twitter to feature football video highlights, pictures, and clips on the site. Twitter also sells all of the advertising for the NFL that is tied to tweets.[19]

Like other social networking sites, Twitter is being used to enhance customer service and create publicity about company products. For example, Taco Bell uses Twitter to interact extensively with consumers. In addition to posting announcements and featuring polls on its Twitter site, Taco Bell has been recognized for its humorous tweets and one-liners.[20] Yet approximately 70 percent of companies ignore complaints on Twitter. This failure acts as a missed opportunity to address customer concerns and maintain strong relationships.[21]

Twitter is also expanding into video with its acquisition of the mobile application Vine. In keeping with Twitter's reputation for short, concise postings, Vine allows users to display up to 6 seconds of video and share them with other users. Vine has become highly popular among celebrities and teenagers, with 100 million users. Although most company-sponsored videos are posted on Facebook or YouTube, approximately 4 percent of branded social video content is posted on Vine.[22]

## 10-3b  Blogs and Wikis

Today's marketers must recognize the impact of consumer-generated material like blogs and wikis, as their significance to online consumers has increased a great deal. **Blogs** (short for "weblogs") are web-based journals in which writers can editorialize and interact with other Internet users. It is estimated that 33 percent of Millennials read blogs before they make a purchase.[23] Many bloggers use Twitter and Facebook to announce a new blog post with a link and a photo to encourage users to click on it. The blogging site Tumblr, which allows anyone to post text, hyperlinks, pictures, and other media for free, is particularly popular with younger consumers. The site has approximately 272 million blogs. In 2013 Yahoo! purchased Tumblr for $1.1 billion. Although marketers are eager to reach the younger demographic that uses Tumblr, many are unsure how to market effectively through the site. To make it easier Tumblr set up a network that pairs advertisers with Tumblr artists and bloggers.[24]

Blogs give consumers control, sometimes more control than companies would like. Whether or not the blog's content is factually accurate, bloggers can post whatever opinions they like about a company or its products. Although companies have filed lawsuits against bloggers for defamation, they usually cannot prevent the blog from going viral. Responding to a negative blog posting is a delicate matter. For instance, although companies sometimes force bloggers to remove blogs, readers often create copies of the blog and spread it across the Internet after the original's removal. In other cases, a positive review of a product posted on a popular blog can result in large increases in sales. Thus, blogs can represent a potent threat to corporations as well as an opportunity.

Many businesses use blogs to their advantage. Rather than trying to eliminate blogs that cast their companies in a negative light, some marketers are using such blogs to answer consumer concerns or defend their corporate reputations. Many major corporations have created their own blogs or encourage employees to blog about the company. Bill Marriott, Executive Chairman of Marriott International, maintains a blog called "Marriott on the Move" where he not only discusses the hotel business but posts on a number of insightful business and inspirational topics to engage his readers.[25] As blogging changes the face of media, companies like Marriott are using blogs to build enthusiasm for their products and develop customer relationships.

A **wiki** is a type of software that creates an interface that enables users to add or edit the content of some types of websites. One of the best known is Wikipedia, an online encyclopedia with more than 35 million articles in 290 languages on nearly every subject imaginable.[26] Wikipedia is consistently one of the top 10 most popular sites on the Web. Like all social media, wikis

**blogs** Web-based journals (short for "weblogs") in which writers editorialize and interact with other Internet users

**wiki** Type of software that creates an interface that enables users to add or edit the content of some types of websites

Roman Pyshchyk/Shutterstock.com

**Blogging**
Tumblr is a popular microblogging and social networking site. It receives over 550 million visitors monthly.

have advantages and disadvantages for companies. Wikis on controversial companies like Walmart and Nike often contain negative publicity about the companies. However, some companies have begun to use wikis as internal tools for teams working on a project requiring lots of documentation.[27] Additionally, monitoring wikis provides companies with a better idea of how consumers feel about the company brand.

There is too much at stake financially for marketers to ignore blogs and wikis. Despite this fact, statistics show that only about 30 percent of Fortune 500 companies have a corporate blog.[28] Marketers who want to form better customer relationships and promote their company's products must not underestimate the power of these two tools as new media outlets.

## 10-3c Media-Sharing Sites

Marketers share their corporate messages in more visual ways through media-sharing sites. Media-sharing sites allow marketers to share photos, videos, and podcasts but are more limited in scope in how companies interact with consumers. They tend to be more promotional-oriented. This means that while firms can promote their products through videos or photos, they usually do not interact with consumers through personal messages or responses. At the same time, the popularity of these sites has the potential to reach a global audience of consumers.

Video-sharing sites allow virtually anybody to upload videos, from professional marketers at Fortune 500 corporations to the average Internet user. Some of the most popular video-sharing sites include YouTube, Metacafe.com, and Vimeo. Video-sharing sites give companies the opportunity to upload ads and informational videos about their products. A few videos become viral at any given time, and although many of these gain popularity because they embarrass the subject in some way, others reach viral status because people find them entertaining (viral marketing will be discussed in more detail in Chapter 16). Marketers are seizing upon opportunities to use this viral nature to promote awareness of their companies. For example, Android released a "Friends Furever" video on YouTube showing unlikely pairs of animal friends. The videos only mentioned Android at the end and were more to generate interest and social buzz than talk about specific products. It became the most shared video of the year with more than 6 million video shares.[29]

YouTube offers the opportunity to spread marketing campaigns at a fraction of the cost of other advertising channels. It has proven so popular that video networks have begun to use the online site as a staging ground for their shows.[30] YouTube is also developing stars such as Ipsy founder Michelle Phan. Ipsy provides a beauty subscription service to help women through Phan's beauty tutorials. She has more than 8 million subscribers and more than 1 billion views. Approximately 10,000 amateur beauty bloggers help create videos in the subscription service. The company is not as involved in selling products or advertising but has been valued at $800 million for driving subscriptions.[31] On the other hand, as video becomes more popular, competition is intensifying for YouTube. Facebook and AOL have begun to gain more market share in video advertising, and users seem to be spending more time on Netflix when watching online videos.[32]

A new trend in video marketing is the use of amateur filmmakers. Entrepreneurs have begun to realize that they can use consumer-generated content to their advantage. Consumer-generated videos save companies money because they do not have to hire advertising firms to develop professional advertising campaigns. Snickers awarded an amateur filmmaker $50,000 for his winning video after holding a contest encouraging random people on the Internet to make their own videos for its "You're Not You When You're Hungry" campaign. Such contests enable brands to tap into the creative capacities of their customers and keep them engaged with the brand.[33] Marketers believe consumer videos appear more authentic and create enthusiasm for the product among participants.

Photo-sharing sites allow users to upload and share their photos with the world. Well-known photo-sharing sites include Flickr, Picasa, Shutterfly, Snapfish, and Instagram. Flickr is a popular photo-sharing site on the Internet. A Flickr user can upload images, edit them, classify the images, create photo albums, and share photos or videos with friends without having to

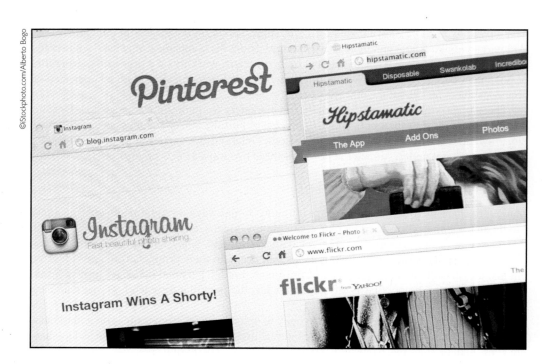

**Social Photo Sharing**
Pinterest, Instagram, Flickr, and Hipstamatic allow users to share photos with a variety of other people on the Internet.

e-mail bulky image files or send photos through the mail. Instagram is the most popular mobile photo-sharing application. Instagram allows users to be creative with their photos by using filters and tints and then sharing them with their friends. Chobani uses Instagram to build communities and suggest new uses for its yogurt products.[34] In 2012 Facebook purchased Instagram for $1 billion with the intention to break into the mobile industry. To compete against Twitter's short-form video service Vine, Facebook now allows marketers to upload 30-second video ads onto Instagram.[35] With more people using mobile apps or accessing the Internet through their smartphones, the use of photo sharing through mobile devices is increasing.

Other sites are emerging that take photo sharing to a new level. Pinterest is a photo-sharing bulletin board that combines photo sharing with elements of bookmarking and social networking. Users can share photos and images with other Internet users, communicating mostly through images that they "pin" to their boards. Other users can "repin" these images to their boards, follow each other, "like" images, and make comments. Marketers have found that an effective way of marketing through Pinterest is to post images conveying a certain emotion that represents their brand.[36] It has become so popular that it has surpassed Google+ in number of users. Because Pinterest users create boards that deal with their interests, marketers also have a chance to develop marketing messages encouraging users to purchase the product or brand that interests them. Pinterest hopes to learn how to influence a customer to proceed from showing interest in a product to having an intent to purchase. This knowledge will be helpful to advertisers marketing through Pinterest's website.[37]

Photo sharing represents an opportunity for companies to market themselves visually by displaying snapshots of company events, company staff, and/or company products. For example, pasta brand Buitoni has purchased advertising through Pinterest and features recipes on its board. Pinterest offers tools for support and consultations to advertisers in the retailing and consumer-packaging industries.[38] Digital marketing companies are also scanning photos and images on photo sharing sites to gather insights about how brands are being displayed or used. These companies hope to offer these insights to big-name companies such as Kraft.[39] The opportunities for marketers to use photo-sharing sites to gather information and promote brands appear limitless.

Podcasting, traditionally used for music and radio broadcasts, is also an important digital marketing tool. **Podcasts** are audio or video files that can be downloaded from the Internet with a subscription that automatically delivers new content to listening devices or personal

**podcast** Audio or video file that can be downloaded from the Internet with a subscription that automatically delivers new content to listening devices or personal computers; podcasts offer the benefit of convenience, giving users the ability to listen to or view content when and where they choose computers. Podcasts offer the benefit of convenience, giving users the ability to listen to or view content when and where they choose. American Public Media's Marketplace is a business news show on the radio that has downloadable podcasts. The advertisement describes three podcasts involving different topics in business news that users can download. If they choose to subscribe, they will automatically get new content once it is uploaded. Companies can use podcasts to demonstrate how to use their products or understand certain features. As podcasting continues to catch on, radio and television networks like CBC Radio, NPR, MSNBC, and PBS are creating podcasts of their shows to profit from this growing trend. Through podcasting, many companies hope to create brand awareness, promote their products, and encourage customer loyalty.

## 10-3d Virtual Gaming Sites

Virtual gaming sites are offering significant opportunities for marketers to connect with consumers in unique ways. Virtual gaming sites include Second Life, Everquest, FarmVille, and the role-playing game World of Warcraft. Many of these games are role-playing games where the gamer takes on or assumes a particular persona, also known as an *avatar*. These games are social in nature, allowing players to compete against, partner with, or do things for other gamers. In Second Life users connect with other users, communicate with one another, purchase goods with virtual Linden dollars (convertible to real dollars on a floating exchange rate), and even own virtual businesses.

**Podcasts**

Consumers interested in business news can subscribe to Marketplace's three new podcasts and get updated content automatically.

Real-world marketers and organizations have been eager to capitalize on the popularity of virtual gaming sites and virtual realities. JCPenney developed an immersive virtual reality experience using the Oculus headset during the holiday season. Children that put on the headset experienced the sensation of flying in a sleigh pulled by Santa's reindeer. Among the presents in the sleigh were well-known brands including Nike and KitchenAid.[40] Facebook has also shown interest in virtual reality possibilities with its purchase of virtual reality startup Oculus Rift. Facebook is investigating ways to use the Oculus VR headsets for social virtual tours and live-chatting. It believes virtual realities will supplant phones to become the biggest computing platform.[41] By interacting with the public virtually, businesses hope to connect with younger generations of consumers in entirely new ways.

## 10-3e Mobile Marketing

Mobile devices, such as smartphones, mobile computing devices, and tablet computers, allow customers to leave their desktops and access digital networks from anywhere. About 91 percent of American adults have a mobile device.[42] Many of these mobile devices are smartphones, which have the ability to access the Internet, download apps, listen to music, take photographs, and more. It is estimated that 90 percent of those who use Facebook access the site through their phones.[43] Figure 10.2 breaks down smartphone ownership by age and activity. Mobile marketing is exploding—marketers worldwide spend about $100 billion on mobile ad spending.[44]

Mobile marketing has proven effective in grabbing consumers' attention. In one study, 45 percent of consumers recalled a full-page ad shown through a smartphone device, compared to 38 percent who saw it on a desktop.[45] Capital One saw its brand recall increase by 16 percent after it began advertising through the mobile social service Instagram.[46] Despite these promising trends, many brands have yet to take advantage of mobile marketing opportunities. Although most major businesses have websites, not all of these websites are easily viewable on mobile devices. It is also important for marketers to understand what types of promotions users prefer and when to show them. For instance, studies show that app users tend to dislike advertisements that show up while the app is in use but do like when brands provide them with information during the processing time of the app.[47]

To avoid being left behind, brands must recognize the importance of mobile marketing. Some of the more common mobile marketing tools include the following:

- *SMS messages:* SMS messages are text messages of 160 characters or less. SMS messages can be used to send coupons to prospective customers.

---

**Figure 10.2    Smartphone Ownership by Age and Activity**

Percent of smartphone owners in each age group who used the following features on their phone at least once over the course of 14 surveys spanning a one-week period.

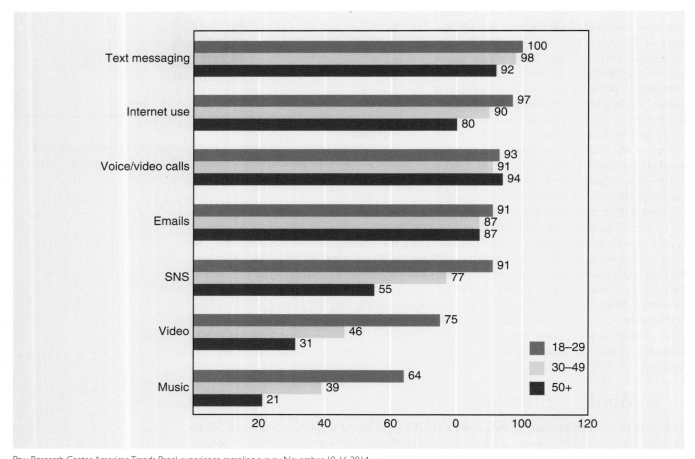

Pew Research Center American Trends Panel experience sampling survey, November 10-16 2014.

Respondents were contacted twice a day over the course of one week (14 total surveys) and asked how they had used their phone in the preceding hour (besides completing the survey). Only those respondents who completed 10 or more surveys over the course of the study period are included in this analysis.

- *Multimedia messages:* Multimedia messaging takes SMS messaging a step further by allowing companies to send video, audio, photos, and other types of media over mobile devices. The MMS market is estimated to be a $20 billion market. Approximately 98 percent of all U.S. cell phones can receive MMS.[48]
- *Mobile advertisements:* Mobile advertisements are visual advertisements that appear on mobile devices. Companies might choose to advertise through search engines, websites, or games accessed on mobile devices. Mobile accounts for over half of digital ad spending.[49]
- *Mobile websites:* Mobile websites are websites designed for mobile devices. Over 50 percent of e-commerce website traffic now comes through mobile devices.[50]
- *Location-based networks:* Location-based networks are built for mobile devices. One of the most popular location-based networks is Foursquare, which lets users check in and share their location with others. It introduced a new advertising network called Pinpoint specifically for marketers. Samsung Galaxy, Olive Garden, and Jaguar Land Rover are examples of companies that have used its new service.[51]
- *Mobile applications:* **Mobile applications**, or "apps," are software programs that run on mobile devices and let users communicate, work, play games, or carry out tasks. Businesses release apps to help consumers access more information about their company or to provide incentives. These are discussed in further detail in the next section.

## 10-3f Applications and Widgets

Applications, or apps, are adding an entirely new layer to the marketing environment. Approximately half of all American adult cell phone users have applications on their mobile devices.[52] The most important feature of apps is the convenience and cost savings they offer to the consumer. Certain apps permit consumers to scan a product's barcode and then compare it with the prices of identical products in other stores or download store discounts. Others are developed for more personal purposes. The Cozi app is marketed toward families as a way to keep schedules and activities organized. The advertisement uses the stress of getting children ready for school to demonstrate how it can simplify the process. The app can be accessed from any computer or mobile device, making it easier for consumers as they go from one place to another throughout the day.

To remain competitive, companies are beginning to use mobile marketing to offer additional incentives to consumers. As Unilever expands into Southeast Asia, it developed a mobile campaign that gives consumers rewards in exchange for providing Unilever with certain information about themselves, such as shopping habits.[53] Another application that marketers are finding useful is the QR scanning app. QR codes are black-and-white squares that sometimes appear in magazines, posters, and storefront displays. Smartphone users that have downloaded the QR scanning application can open their smartphones and scan the code, which contains a hidden message accessible with the app. The QR scanning app recognizes the code and opens the link, video, or image on the phone's screen. Marketers are using QR codes to promote their companies and offer consumer discounts.[54]

Mobile technology is also making inroads in transforming the shopping experience. Not only can shoppers use mobile applications to compare prices or download electronic discounts, but they can also use mobile applications to tally up purchases and pay through their smartphones. Mobile payments are gaining traction, and companies like Google and Apple are working to capitalize on this opportunity.[55] Google Wallet and Apple Pay are mobile apps that allow users to pay with their phones. When the shopper is ready to check out, he or she can tap the phone at the point of sale for the transaction to be registered.[56] Square is a company that provides organizations with smartphone swiping devices for credit cards and tablets that can be used to tally purchases. Bitcoin is a virtual peer-to-peer currency used to make a payment via smartphone. Smaller organizations have begun to accept Bitcoin at some of their stores. The success of digital payment systems in revolutionizing the shopping experience will largely depend upon retailers to adopt this payment system, but companies like Starbucks are already rising to the opportunity.

**mobile applications** Software programs that run on mobile devices and give users access to certain content

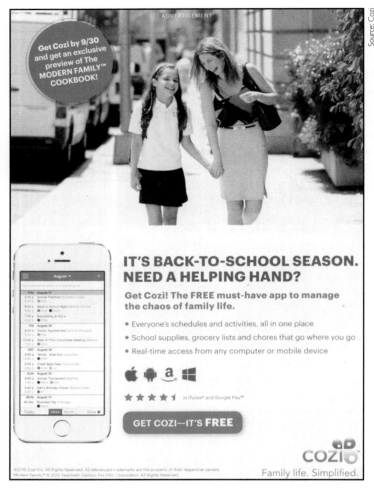

**Mobile applications**
The free Cozi app allows consumers to manage their schedules and
activities to make their lives easier.

**widgets** Small bits of software on a website, desktop, or mobile device that performs a simple purpose, such as providing stock quotes or blog updates

**Widgets** are small bits of software on a website, desktop, or mobile device that perform a simple purpose, such as providing stock quotes or weather updates. Marketers might use widgets to display news headlines, clocks, or games on their webpages.[57] CNBC uses widgets to send alerts and financial news to subscribers. Widgets downloaded to a user's desktop can update the user on the latest company or product information, enhancing relationship marketing between companies and their fans. For instance, Toyota used a widget to place a social-media-driven photo gallery on one of its sites. Approximately 34 percent of users that visited the site clicked on the gallery.[58] Widgets are an innovative digital marketing tool to personalize webpages, alert users to the latest company information, and spread awareness of the company's products.

## 10-4 CHANGING DIGITAL MEDIA BEHAVIORS OF CONSUMERS

Consumers now have a greater ability to regulate the information that they view as well as the rate and sequence of their exposure to that information. The Internet is sometimes referred to as a *pull* medium because users determine which websites they are going to view; the marketer has only limited ability to control the content to which users are exposed, and in what sequence. Today, blogs, wikis, podcasts, and ratings sites such as Yelp and Angie's List are used to publicize, praise, or challenge companies. Digital media require marketers to approach their jobs differently compared to traditional marketing. However, most companies in the United States do not routinely monitor consumers' postings to online social networking sites. In many cases, this represents a missed opportunity to gather information.

On the other hand, some companies are using the power of the consumer to their advantage. While negative ratings and reviews are damaging to a company, positive customer feedback is free publicity that often helps the company more than corporate messages do. Because consumer-generated content appears more authentic than corporate messages, it can go far in increasing a company's credibility. Additionally, while consumers can use digital media to access more information, marketers can also use the same sites to get information on the consumer—often more information than could be garnered through traditional marketing venues. They can examine how consumers are using the Internet to target marketing messages to their audience. Finally, marketers are also using the Internet to track the success of their online marketing campaigns, creating an entirely new way of gathering marketing research.

### 10-4a Online Consumer Behavior

As Internet technology evolves, digital media marketers must constantly adapt to new technologies and changing consumer patterns. Unfortunately, with so many new technologies emerging, the attrition rate for digital media channels is very high, with some dying off each year as new ones emerge. As time passes, digital media are becoming more sophisticated so as to reach consumers in more effective ways. Those that are not able to adapt and change eventually fail.

Forrester Research, a technology and market research company, emphasizes the importance of understanding these changing relationships in the online media world. By grouping online consumers into different segments based on how they utilize digital online media, marketers can gain a better understanding of the online market and how best to proceed.[59]

The Social Technographics Profile developed by Forrester Research groups the online community into seven segments according to how they interact with digital media. It is important to note that these segments do overlap with each other; many online consumers may belong to multiple segments simultaneously. Table 10.2 provides a description of these seven different groups. *Creators* are those consumers who create their own media outlets, such as blogs, podcasts, consumer-generated videos, and wikis.[60] Creators are becoming increasingly important to online marketers as a conduit for addressing consumers directly. These types of consumer-generated media are becoming a major part of companies' public relations strategies. For instance, many marketers are pitching new products or stories to professional reporters and bloggers. Bloggers who post this information can reach online consumers as well as reporters in the mainstream media, who often read blogs for story ideas.[61]

The Technographics profile calls its second group of Internet users *conversationalists*. Conversationalists regularly update their Twitter feeds or status updates on social networking sites. Although they are less involved than creators, conversationalists spend time at least once a week (and often more) on digital media sites posting updates.[62] The third category is *critics*. Critics are people who comment on blogs or post ratings and reviews. If you have ever posted a product review or rated a movie, you have engaged in this activity. Critics need to be an important component in a company's digital marketing strategy, because the majority of online shoppers read ratings and reviews to aid in their purchasing decisions. Consumers often

Table 10.2  **Social Technographics**

| | |
|---|---|
| Creators | Publish a blog<br>Publish personal webpages<br>Upload original video<br>Upload original audio/music<br>Write articles or stories and post them |
| Conversationalists | Update status on social networking sites<br>Post updates on Twitter |
| Critics | Post ratings/reviews of products or services<br>Comment on someone else's blog<br>Contribute to online forums<br>Contribute to/edit articles in a wiki |
| Collectors | Use RSS feeds<br>Add tags to webpages or photos<br>"Vote" for websites online |
| Joiners | Maintain profile on a social networking site<br>Visit social networking sites |
| Spectators | Read blogs<br>Watch video from other users<br>Listen to podcasts<br>Read online forums<br>Read customer ratings/reviews |
| Inactives | None of the activities |

Source: Charlene Li and Josh Bernoff, *Groundswell* (Boston: Harvard Business Press, 2008), p. 43; "Forrester Unveils New Segment of Social Technographics—The Conversationalists," 360 Digital Connections, January 21, 2010, http://blog.360i.com/social-media/forrester-new-segment-social-technographics-conversationalists (accessed December 19, 2013).

visit review websites like Yelp for recommendations on organizations. Yelp is one of the most comprehensive review sites on businesses, with 90 million reviews.[63]

*Collectors* are perhaps the least recognized group of the seven. Collectors gather information and organize content generated by critics and creators. The growing popularity of this segment led to the creation of social news sites like Delicious and Reddit. Want to know the top news stories according to online consumers? Collectors gather this type of information and post their findings to social networking sites like Reddit, where users vote on the sites they like the best. Collectors usually constitute a smaller part of the online population than the other groups; however, they can still have a significant impact on marketing activities.[64] Because collectors are active members in the online community, a company story or site that catches the eye of a collector is likely to be posted and discussed on collector sites and made available to other online users looking for information.

Another Technographics segment, known as *joiners*, is growing rapidly. Anyone who becomes a member of Twitter, Facebook, Pinterest, Google+, or other social networking sites is a joiner.[65] It is not unusual for consumers to be members of several social networking sites at once. Joiners participate in these sites to connect and network with other users, but, as previously discussed, marketers can take significant advantage of these sites to connect with consumers and form customer relationships.

The last two segments are classified as *spectators* and *inactives*. Inactives are online users who do not participate in any digital online media, but as more people begin to use computers as a resource, this number is dwindling. Spectators are the largest group in most countries, and it is not hard to see why. Spectators are those consumers who read what other consumers produce but do not create any content themselves.

Marketers will need to consider what portion of online consumers are creating, conversing, rating, collecting, joining, or simply reading online materials. As with traditional marketing efforts, marketers need to know the best ways to reach their target market. In markets where spectators make up the majority of the online population, companies should post their own corporate messages through blogs and websites promoting their organizations. In a population of joiners, companies could try to connect with their target audience by creating profile pages and inviting consumers to post their thoughts. In areas where a significant portion of the online community consists of creators, marketers should continually monitor what other consumers are saying and incorporate bloggers into their public relations strategies. By knowing how to segment the online population, marketers can better tailor their messages to their target markets.

## 10-5 E-MARKETING STRATEGY

More than one-fourth of the world's population uses the Internet, and this number is growing at a high rate. These trends display a growing need for businesses to use the Internet to reach an increasingly Web-savvy population. As more shoppers go online for purchases, the power of traditional brick-and-mortar businesses is lessening.

This makes it essential for businesses, small and large alike, to learn how to effectively use new social media. Most businesses are finding it necessary to use digital marketing to gain or maintain market share. When Amazon.com first became popular as an online bookstore in the 1990s, the brick-and-mortar bookseller chain Barnes & Noble quickly made online shopping possible through its website, but did not abandon its physical stores. This "brick-and-clicks" model is now standard for businesses from neighborhood family-owned restaurants to national chain retailers. The following sections will examine how businesses are effectively using these social media forums to create effective marketing strategies on the Web.

### 10-5a Product Considerations

In traditional marketing, marketers must anticipate consumer needs and preferences and then tailor their products to meet these needs. The same is true with marketing products using digital media. Digital media provide an opportunity to add a service dimension to traditional products and create new products that could only be accessible on the Internet. The applications available on the iPad, for instance, provide examples of products that are only available in the digital world. The advertisement from *Inc.* magazine directs consumers to a site where they can subscribe to mobile versions of its magazine. Subscribers have the option to purchase digital subscriptions for a variety of tablet and app platforms including the iPad, Nook, Kindle, and Google Play.

The ability to access information for any product can have a major impact on buyer decision making. However, with larger companies now launching their own extensive marketing campaigns, and with the constant sophistication of digital technology, many businesses are finding it necessary to continually upgrade their product offerings to meet consumer needs. In managing a product, it is important to pay attention to consumer-generated brand stories that address quality and performance and impact image.[66] As has been discussed throughout this chapter, the Internet represents a large resource to marketers for learning more about consumer wants and needs.

Some companies now use online advertising campaigns and contests to help develop better products. Companies have also begun selling their products through social networking sites. Facebook developed a new payment service in which users can send money instantly through its app Facebook Messenger. This service is one step toward Facebook being able to compete with e-commerce sites such as Amazon. Snapchat and other social networks are following suit with their payment systems.[67]

**Digital Products**
*Inc.* offers digital content of its magazine that can be viewed on a variety of tablet devices.

## 10-5b **Distribution Considerations**

The role of distribution is to make products available at the right time, at the right place, and in the right quantities. Digital marketing can be viewed as a new distribution channel that helps businesses increase efficiency. The ability to process orders electronically and increase the speed of communications via the Internet reduces inefficiencies, costs, and redundancies while increasing speed throughout the marketing channel. Shipping times and costs have become an important consideration in attracting consumers, prompting many companies to offer consumers low shipping costs or next-day delivery. 1-800-Flowers.com uses local florists to offer same-day delivery options for its floral arrangements and fruit bouquets.[68]

Distribution involves a push-pull dynamic: The firm that provides a product will push to get that product in front of the consumer, while at the same time connectivity aids those channel members that desire to find each other—the pull side of the dynamic. An iPhone application can help consumers find the closest Starbucks, McDonald's, or KFC. On the other hand, a blog or Twitter feed can help a marketer communicate the availability of products and how and when they can be purchased. This process can help push products through the marketing channel to consumers or enable customers to pull products through the marketing channel.

# Entrepreneurship in Marketing

## Instacart: New Way to 'Bring Home the Bacon'

**Founder:** Apoorva Mehta
**Business:** Instacart
**Founded:** 2012, in San Francisco, California
**Success:** Instacart has expanded to 18 metro areas and earned the nickname "the Uber of grocery delivery."

Apoorva Mehta has learned from past mistakes that a successful business depends upon solving a problem the entrepreneur cares about. Mehta hated grocery shopping and wanted to make it more convenient for people without easy access to grocery stores. Instacart, an Internet-based grocery delivery service, was born.

Instacart is based on the sharing-economy concept popularized by Uber and Airbnb. Customers who want their groceries delivered use an app connecting them to a personal shopper. These shoppers are independent contractors who use their own cars for delivery. Minimum base pay is $10 an hour, and shoppers often earn more from tips. On the consumer's side, most deliveries cost $3.99. Instacart will often mark-up groceries, so groceries purchased through Instacart cost more than those purchased in-store.

Instacart has a unique distribution model as it partners with grocery stores, eliminating the need for physical stores of its own. Grocery stores like Instacart because it has helped to increase their volume of customers. For busy and on-the-go consumers, the extra cost is often well worth the convenience.[b]

## 10-5c Promotion Considerations

The majority of this chapter has discussed ways that marketers use digital media to promote products, from creating profiles on social networks to connecting with consumers to inserting brands into virtual social games. Social networking sites also allow marketers to approach promotion in entirely new, creative ways. Marketers who choose to capitalize on these opportunities have the chance to boost their firms' brand exposure. For instance, Walgreens used cinematic pins on Pinterest to promote its lip gloss. These types of pins played short animations when users scrolled on the page. The Walgreen's cinematic pin featured a model wearing large sunglasses blowing kisses as the user scrolled through the page.[69]

Digital media has also created opportunities for business-to-business promotions. As more companies adopt digital marketing strategies, the need for better platforms and digital solutions has grown. Consider IBM's advertisement directed toward marketers that struggle to deliver meaningful experiences for their customers. In its advertisement, IBM claims that its cloud technology helps companies deliver relevant messages to consumers at exactly the right time. By creating better experiences for customers, businesses will be able to create mutually beneficial relationships that could result in more sales and satisfaction.

Digital promotions all attempt to increase brand awareness and market to consumers. As a result of online promotion, consumers are more informed, reading consumer-generated content before making purchasing decisions and increasingly shopping at Internet stores. Consumer consumption patterns are changing radically, and marketers must adapt their promotional efforts to meet these new patterns.

## 10-5d Pricing Considerations

Pricing relates to perceptions of value and is the most flexible element of the marketing mix. Digital media marketing facilitates both price and nonprice competition, because Internet marketing gives consumers access to more information about costs and prices. As consumers become more informed about their options, the demand for low-priced products has grown, leading to the creation of daily deal sites like Groupon, CrowdCut, and LivingSocial. These companies partner with local businesses to offer major discounts to subscribers in order to generate new business. Several marketers are also offering buying incentives like online coupons or free samples to generate consumer demand for their product offerings.

Digital connections can help the customer find the price of the product available from various competitors in an instant. Websites provide price information, and mobile applications can help the customer find the lowest price. Consumers can even bargain with retailers in the store by using a smartphone to show the lowest price available during a transaction. Although this new access to price information benefits the consumer, it also places new pressures on the seller to be competitive and to differentiate products so that customers focus on attributes and benefits other than price.

Until recently, social networks like Facebook and Twitter were mainly used for promotional purposes and customer service. Those who wanted to purchase items were often redirected to the company's website. However, retailers and other organizations are developing e-commerce stores or "buy" options so that consumers will not have to leave the site to purchase items. Pinterest, for example, added a "buy" button on its site so consumers could purchase the product they like without having to leave the site.[70] London-based comic book store Raygun sells through Facebook groups for comic fans as well as through eBay.[71] For the business that wants to compete on price, digital marketing provides unlimited opportunities.

Source: IBM

IBM Marketing Cloud:
## Can you design an experience your customers actually want to have?
There's a new way to engage. IBM Marketing Cloud, just a part of our 400 services, helps you send your customers the right messages through the right channels at the right time. Connect at ibm.com/madewithibm

Smarter personalization is made with IBM.

**B2B Promotion**
IBM markets its cloud-based services to businesses that are having difficulty developing meaningful customer experiences.

## 10-6 ETHICAL AND LEGAL ISSUES

How marketers use technology to gather information—both online and offline—raises numerous legal and ethical issues. The popularity and widespread use of the Internet grew so quickly in the 1990s that global regulatory systems were unable to keep pace. The global regulatory environment is not uniform, with areas such as Europe more concerned above privacy than the United States. Among the issues of concern are personal privacy, fraud, misappropriation of copyrighted intellectual property, as well as the violation of social norms in areas where there is vague or ambiguous legal guidelines. For example, fantasy sports sites such as FanDuel are under close scrutiny to determine whether its gaming activities constitute online gambling. In addition, websites that promote socially questionable activities such as Avid Media—owner of the adultery website Ashley Madison—are highly criticized from an ethical perspective. Even companies in the app-based sharing economy such as Uber, Lyft, and Airbnb are criticized for avoiding traditional regulatory and tax codes with which their competitors must comply.

### 10-6a Privacy

One of the most significant privacy issues involves the use of personal information that companies collect from website visitors in their efforts to foster long-term relationships with customers. Some people fear that the collection of personal information from website users may violate users' privacy, especially when it is done without their knowledge. Google, Facebook, and other Internet firms have also come under fire for privacy issues. This has taken on even greater significance overseas where privacy laws can differ greatly from those in the United States. For instance, Belgium threatened to fine Facebook if it did not stop storing information from users who do not have Facebook accounts.[72] The European Union (EU) also adopted a new regulation that gives consumers in the EU the right to be forgotten. Consumers in the EU who feel that the information about them on the Internet is inaccurate or irrelevant now have the legal right to request for search engines to delist the content.[73] The EU also struck down an American-European agreement allowing data transfer to the United States. This means EU authorities can cancel the Internet transfer of customer data to the United States if they express concern about how the data might be used. While this has important implications for large companies such as Google and Facebook, it could be devastating for smaller Internet firms with operations in the EU that rely heavily on customer data information.[74]

Due to consumer concerns over privacy, the Federal Trade Commission (FTC) is considering developing regulations that would protect consumer privacy by limiting the amount of consumer information that businesses can gather online. Other countries are pursuing similar actions. The European Union passed a law requiring companies to get users' consent before using cookies to track their information. In the United States, some government officials have called for a "do not track" bill, similar to the "do not call" bill for telephones, to allow users to opt out of having their information tracked. Legislators reintroduced a Do Not Track Kids bill that would make it illegal for companies to track children between the ages of 13 and 15 over the Internet or mobile devices without parental permission (currently, marketers are prohibited from gathering information about consumers aged 13 or younger without parental permission). They also desire a system that would erase information that these teenagers found to be embarrassing.[75] Certain laws pertaining to privacy have also taken on new meanings with the increase in digital marketing. For instance, the Federal Video Privacy Protection Act requires that any marketers who wish to disclose or share information about a consumer's video content consumption must obtain separate, independent consent from the consumer. This means that a company cannot share information about videos that users watched on their sites with other parties without permission.[76]

While consumers may welcome such added protections, Web advertisers, who use consumer information to target advertisements to online consumers, see it as a threat. In response to impending legislation, many Web advertisers are attempting self-regulation in order to stay ahead of the game. For instance, the Digital Advertising Alliance (DAA) has adopted privacy guidelines for online advertisers. The DAA has created a "trusted mark" icon that websites adhering to their guidelines can display. However, because it is self-regulatory, not all digital advertisers may choose to participate in its programs.[77] Table 10.3 describes industry best practices for digital marketers to consider before launching digital marketing campaigns. It is important for digital marketers to craft campaigns that comply with FTC rules.

## Table 10.3  Best Practices for Digital Marketing Campaigns

| |
|---|
| 1. Implement privacy during the conceptualization phase of the marketing campaign. |
| 2. Disclose all passive tracking systems used to collect information. |
| 3. Data collection involving third parties should involve clear guidelines regarding how the data will be used and who owns it. Provide ways for users to opt out of tracking or e-mail marketing through visible notices. |
| 4. Screen age of users if appropriate for the campaign. Collecting personal information of children under 13 requires parental consent. If marketing to children is allowed, ensure that the content and language is appropriate for the age range targeted. |
| 5. Ensure that all tracking or data collection activities that occur do not conflict with the company's online privacy policy. |
| 6. Adopt security measures for any data collected from users. User information must be protected, particularly if it is identifiable. |
| 7. Be aware of all legal requirements and industry codes of ethics on digital marketing. |

Source: Adapted from Jesse Brody, "Terms and Conditions," *Marketing News*, November 2014, pp. 34-41; Direct Marketing Association, *Direct Marketing Association's Guidelines for Ethical Business Practice*, January 2014, http://thedma.org/wp-content/uploads/DMA_Guidelines_January_2014.pdf (accessed January 7, 2015).

## 10-6b Online Fraud

**Online fraud** includes any attempt to conduct dishonest activities online. Online fraud includes, among other things, attempts to deceive consumers into releasing personal information. It is becoming a major source of frustration with social networking sites. Cybercriminals are discovering ways to use sites like Facebook and Twitter to carry out fraudulent activities. Hacking attacks—in which criminals break into company computers to steal information—have almost become the norm. Companies including Target, Home Depot, and Sony have experienced wide-scale hacking attacks. Hackers may break into websites and steal users' personal information, enabling them to commit identity theft. In one of the worst cybercrimes to date, three individuals were able to steal data on more than 100 million people from the computers of 11 companies, including J.P. Morgan, Dow Jones & Co., and E*Trade Financial Corp. The men used the stolen information to make more than $100 million.[78] Hackers also used stolen information taken from Home Depot and Target to conduct transactions over Apple Pay, Apple's mobile-payment system, using other people's credit card information.[79]

Organizations and social networking sites alike are developing ways to combat fraudulent activity on digital media sites. For instance, organizations known as brand-protection firms monitor social networks for fraudulent accounts.[80] ForgeRock is an identity and access management software firm. In its advertising, it assures companies that it secures their identities to protect against identity theft. However, the best protection for consumers is to be careful when divulging information online. Privacy advocates advise that the best way to stay out of trouble is to avoid giving out personal information, such as social security numbers or credit card information, unless the site is definitely legitimate.

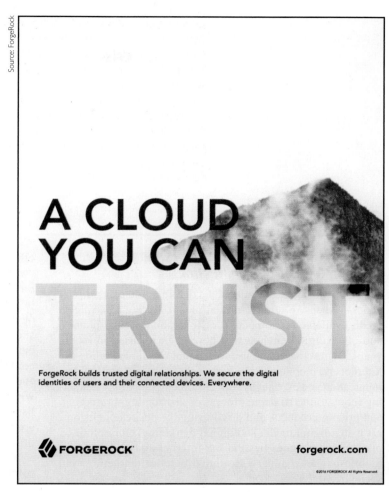

A CLOUD YOU CAN TRUST™

ForgeRock builds trusted digital relationships. We secure the digital identities of users and their connected devices. Everywhere.

**FORGEROCK**

forgerock.com

©2016 FORGEROCK All Rights Reserved.

**Identify Protection**
ForgeRock offers protection services that can be used to secure the identities of users and connect them with their devices.

## 10-6c Intellectual Property

The Internet has also created issues associated with intellectual property, the copyrighted or trademarked ideas and creative materials developed to solve problems, carry out applications, and educate and entertain others. Each year, intellectual property losses in the United States total billions of dollars stemming from the illegal copying of computer programs, movies, compact discs, and books. YouTube has often faced lawsuits on intellectual property infringement. With millions of users uploading content to YouTube, it can be hard for Google to monitor and remove all the videos that may contain copyrighted materials.

The software industry is particularly hard-hit when it comes to the pirating of materials and illegal file sharing. The Business Software Alliance estimates that the global computer software industry loses more than $63 billion a year to illegal theft.[81] Consumers view illegal downloading in different ways, depending on the motivation for the behavior. If the motivation is primarily utilitarian, or for personal gain, then the act is viewed as less ethically acceptable than if it is for a hedonistic reason, or just for fun.[82]

**online fraud** Any attempt to conduct fraudulent activities online, including deceiving consumers into releasing personal information

Consumers rationalize pirating software, video games, and music for a number of reasons. First, many consumers feel they just do not have the money to pay for what they want. Second, because their friends engage in piracy and swap digital content, they feel influenced to engage in this activity. Third, for some, the attraction is the thrill of getting away with it and the slim risk of consequences. Fourth, to some extent, there are people who think they are smarter than others; engaging in piracy allows them to show how tech savvy they are.[83]

As digital media continues to evolve, more legal and ethical issues will certainly arise. As a result, marketers and all other users of digital media should make an effort to learn and abide by ethical practices to ensure that they get the most out of the resources available in this growing medium. Doing so will allow marketers to maximize the tremendous opportunities digital media has to offer.

# Summary

## 10-1  Define *digital media, digital marketing,* and *electronic marketing.*

Digital media are electronic media that function using digital codes—when we refer to digital media, we are referring to media available via computers, cellular phones, smartphones, and other digital devices that have been released in recent years. Digital marketing uses all digital media, including the Internet and mobile and interactive channels, to develop communication and exchanges with customers. Electronic marketing refers to the strategic process of distributing, promoting, and pricing products, and discovering the desires of customers using digital media and digital marketing. Our definition of e-marketing goes beyond the Internet and also includes mobile phones, banner ads, digital outdoor marketing, and social networks.

## 10-2  Summarize the growth and importance of digital marketing.

The phenomenal growth of the Internet has provided unprecedented opportunities for marketers to forge interactive relationships with consumers. As the Internet and digital communication technologies have advanced, they have made it possible to target markets more precisely and reach markets that were previously inaccessible. One of the most important benefits of e-marketing is the ability of marketers and customers to share information. Through websites, social networks, and other digital media, consumers can learn about everything they consume and use in life. As a result, the Internet is changing the way marketers communicate and develop relationships. For many businesses, engaging in digital marketing activities is essential to maintaining competitive advantages.

## 10-3  Describe different types of digital media and how they can be used for marketing.

Many types of digital media can be used as marketing tools. A social network is a website where users can create a profile and interact with other users, post information, and engage in other forms of web-based communication. Blogs (short for "weblogs") are web-based journals in which writers can editorialize and interact with other Internet users. A wiki is a type of software that creates an interface that enables users to add or edit the content of some types of websites. Media-sharing sites allow marketers to share photos, videos, and podcasts but are more limited in scope in how companies interact with consumers. One type of media sharing is podcasts, which are audio or video files that can be downloaded from the Internet with a subscription that automatically delivers new content to listening devices or personal computers. Virtual gaming sites are three-dimensional game sites that are social in nature and often involve role-playing. Advertising over mobile devices is becoming increasingly common. Mobile applications are software programs that run on mobile devices and give users access to certain content. Widgets are small bits of software on a website, desktop, or mobile device that performs a simple purpose such as displaying stock updates.

As a result of these new marketing channels, digital marketing is moving from a niche strategy to becoming a core consideration in the marketing mix. At the same time, digital technologies are largely changing the dynamic between marketer and consumer. Consumers use social networking sites and mobile applications to do everything from playing games to engaging in commerce. The menu of digital media alternatives continues to grow, requiring marketers to make informed decisions about strategic approaches.

## 10-4  Critique the seven different ways consumers use digital media.

It is essential that marketers focus on the changing social behaviors of consumers and how they interact with digital media. Consumers now have a greater ability to regulate the information that they view as well as the rate and sequence of their exposure to that information. This is why the Internet is sometimes referred to as a *pull* medium because users determine which websites they are going to view; the marketer has only limited ability to control the content to which users are exposed, and in what sequence. Marketers must modify their marketing strategies to adapt to the changing behaviors of online consumers.

Forrester Research groups online consumers into seven categories depending upon how they use digital media. Creators are those consumers who create their own media outlets. Conversationalists regularly update their Twitter feeds or status updates on social networking sites. Critics are people who comment on blogs or post ratings and reviews. Collectors gather information and organize content generated by critics and creators. Joiners are those who become members of social networking sites. Spectators are those consumers who read what other consumers produce but do not produce any content themselves. Finally, inactives are online users who do not participate in any digital online media, but this number is decreasing as the popularity of digital media grows. Marketers who want to capitalize on social and digital media marketing will need to consider what portion of online consumers are creating, conversing, rating, collecting, joining, or simply reading online materials.

## 10-5 Describe how digital media affect the four variables of the marketing mix.

The reasons for a digital marketing strategy are many. The low costs of many digital media channels can provide major savings in promotional budgets. Digital marketing is allowing companies to connect with market segments that are harder to reach with traditional media. Despite the challenges involved in such a strategy, digital marketing is opening up new avenues in the relationship between businesses and consumers.

The marketing mix of product, distribution, promotion, and price continues to apply in digital marketing. From a product perspective, digital media provide an opportunity to add a service dimension to traditional products and create new products that could only be accessible on the Internet. Many businesses find it necessary to continually upgrade their product offerings to meet consumer needs. For distribution, the ability to process orders electronically and increase the speed of communications via the Internet reduces inefficiencies, costs, and redundancies while increasing speed throughout the marketing channel. Marketers can promote their products to consumers in new and creative ways using digital media. Finally, from a pricing dimension, digital media facilitate both price and nonprice competition, because Internet marketing gives consumers access to more information about costs and prices.

## 10-6 Identify legal and ethical considerations in digital marketing.

How marketers use technology to gather information—both online and offline—has raised numerous legal and ethical issues. Privacy is one of the most significant issues, involving the use of personal information that companies collect from website visitors in their efforts to foster long-term relationships with customers. Some people fear that the collection of personal information from website users may violate users' privacy, especially when it is done without their knowledge. Another concern is that hackers may break into websites and steal users' personal information, enabling them to commit identity theft.

Online fraud includes any attempt to conduct dishonest activities online. Online fraud includes, among other things, attempts to deceive consumers into releasing personal information. It is becoming a major source of frustration with social networking sites. Cybercriminals are discovering entirely new ways to use sites like Facebook and Twitter to carry out fraudulent activities. The best way for users to combat fraudulent activity is not to give out personal information except on trustworthy sites.

The Internet has also created issues associated with intellectual property, the copyrighted or trademarked ideas and creative materials developed to solve problems, carry out applications, and educate and entertain others. Each year, intellectual property losses in the United States total billions of dollars stemming from the illegal copying of computer programs, movies, compact discs, and books. The software industry is particularly hard-hit when it comes to pirating material and illegal file sharing.

---

**Go to www.cengagebrain.com for resources to help you master the content in this chapter as well as for materials that will expand your marketing knowledge!**

---

# Important Terms

digital media  296
digital marketing  297
electronic marketing (e-marketing)  297
social network  299
blogs  302

wiki  302
podcast  304
mobile applications  307
widget  308
online fraud  315

# Discussion and Review Questions

1. How does digital marketing differ from traditional marketing?
2. Define *interactivity* and explain its significance. How can marketers exploit this characteristic to improve relations with customers?
3. Explain the distinction between push and pull media. What is the significance of control in terms of using websites to market products?
4. Why are social networks becoming an increasingly important marketing tool? Find an example online in which a company has improved the effectiveness of its marketing strategy by using social networks.
5. How has digital media changed consumer behavior? What are the opportunities and challenges that face marketers with this in mind?
6. Describe the different Technographics segments. How can marketers use this segmentation in their strategies?
7. How can marketers exploit the characteristics of the Internet to improve the product element of their marketing mixes?
8. How do the characteristics of digital marketing affect the promotion element of the marketing mix?
9. How have digital media affected the pricing of products? Give examples of the opportunities and challenges presented to marketers in light of these changes.
10. Name and describe the major ethical and legal issues that have developed in response to the Internet. How should policy makers address these issues?

# Video Case 10.1

## Zappos Drives Sales through Relationship Building on Social Media

Zappos was one of the first companies to incorporate social media into its business, and they have established themselves as a leader in its use. Steven Hill, Vice President of Merchandising, explains, "Social media . . . is more about discovering our culture rather than our business." Zappos focuses on building customer relationships through human interaction and emphasizes comments related to service and fun. For example, if a customer experienced a problem with an order or has a question about a product, the Zappos team ensures that these comments are responded to honestly, authentically, and in a timely manner. Sometimes customers will leave fun comments about their experience with the company. Zappos takes these comments just as seriously. Both instances are at the heart of their operations, which is to "deliver happiness."

Zappos does not maintain a specific strategy for marketing on social media, nor do they have a policy for responding to customers. As with any Zappos activity, marketing is guided by the company's core values, including creating "WOW" customer experiences and a culture characterized by fun and a little weirdness. Product Manager Robert Richman explains, "Social media is a communication tool . . . and we want to be available to people wherever they're at." If customers are congregating on Facebook, Zappos makes sure to have a presence there so they can engage them in conversation. In fact, Kenshoo, a digital marketing specialist, has recognized Zappos' Facebook activity for its effectiveness. Over a 2-month period, the company initiated 85,000 visits to their webpage through status updates. Forty-two percent of these updates led to purchases, while the other 58 percent left comments or likes on the webpage.

Rob Siefker, Director of the Customer Loyalty Team, emphasizes the importance of using Twitter. He states, "Most people went on Twitter as a way to interact with friends. Some companies went on there and solely focused on the business or service aspect. For us, part of service is being playful . . . it makes it much more human to the customer . . . it makes it much more personal." Most companies that use social media use it for promotion rather than for truly interacting with customers. This creates a distance between the company and the customer. Mr. Siefker points out that customers "feel when they are being marketed to, and they know there is a reason for it." However, Zappos strives to go beyond using digital media simply for promotion purposes. They want to forge a real connection with customers and describe themselves as a human company, requiring strong interactions between customers and the organization.

The company has been able to achieve rapid growth through their use of values in their marketing activities. They are a large company with a small business feel when it comes to how they treat their customers and how their customers feel about them. This is due in large part to their presence on social media and the way they cross-promote their activities across platforms. For example, if they receive or post a comment on Facebook, they will also share it on Twitter, Google+, YouTube, and Pinterest in order to reach other current or potential customers. While the company focuses mainly on current customers, this activity generates wide-spread effects such as word-of-mouth marketing that brings in new customers. The current customers in this sense serve as brand advocates or brand enthusiasts.

Zappos also generates interest by encouraging customers to share promotions and purchases with friends. One campaign they used on Facebook was to ask people to like their page. It read, "Let's be in a Like-Like relationship." Then they asked users to sign up for their e-mail list. The order in which they made these requests gave people the impression that Zappos was indeed concerned about building relationships. They also have exclusive content for people who opt to become fans. Once deemed a fan, people are able to see special offers, videos, and promotions and share comments about them. Finally, another major campaign Zappos launched was its engagement strategy called "Fan of the Week Contest," where

people were encouraged to take and post photos of themselves with Zappos products. Then users voted on the best photo, and the one with the most votes won. Zappos posted the photo on their website for all to see. Overall, Zappos ensures that they are using social media to build relationships by bringing customers closer to the company. Marketing for Zappos is an authentic and human activity that is not about selling products but building relationships.[84]

### Discussion Questions

1. Describe some ways in which Zappos uses digital media tools.
2. How does Zappos encourage word-of-mouth marketing through digital media?
3. How does Zappos use digital media to create an authentic relationship with consumers?

# Case 10.2

## The Challenges of Intellectual Property in Digital Marketing

Marketing has been forever changed with the advent of social media. Approximately 65 percent of adults claim to use some form of social media. Marketers are well aware of the strong presence on these sites. On average, 60 percent of their time is committed toward digital media activities. The top three social networks used by business-to-business marketers are LinkedIn, Twitter, and Facebook. Additionally, platforms such as Instagram, Pinterest, Vine, and YouTube, which reach the ideal marketing age group of 18–34-year-olds, are a perfect venues for marketers. Starbucks, for example, perpetuates brand awareness by posting images of its products and logo on Instagram, a photo-sharing application. Walmart utilizes YouTube to host its "Associate Stories Video Series," which is a series of interviews with Walmart employees around the globe. These types of activities seem to generate relationships and loyalty.

However, with the growing popularity of digital media also comes the growing tendency to violate the intellectual property of other people. Intellectual property (IP) refers to any creation that is both tangible and intangible and used in commerce. Media such as videos, artwork, music, movies, and writings are often copyrighted, or protected from being used except by the owner's permission. Similarly, trademarks are used to protect brand names and marks from being used by others without permission.

It did not take long for the Internet to impact intellectual property rights. In 1999, the music industry recorded an all-time high in sales with $14.6 billion. A decade later their revenues from music sales totaled $6.3 billion. File-sharing

websites such as Pirate Bay provide a platform for people to pirate, or illegally download, music and movies. The music industry has taken a much larger hit from file sharing because of the simplicity of downloading a 5-minute song compared to a video or movie.

It might seem relatively simple for an organization's marketers to ensure that employees do not place content on social media sites that violate another's copyright or trademark. However, the interactive nature of the Internet complicates this issue. For instance, a direct selling firm with thousands of independent distributors remains responsible for what their distributors post concerning its brand or business. If an independent direct seller unknowingly posts content that is copyrighted or trademarked, the company can be held responsible.

Additionally, many digital marketing campaigns make use of user-generated content, such as videos or postings. This provides a significant advantage to marketers as content developed by other users is generally considered more trustworthy than corporate marketing initiatives. However, marketers must also be careful that users do not post content that infringes on another's intellectual property. For instance, if a user posts something to a popular blog that violates intellectual property law, the blogging company must take down the post immediately or risk being sued.

YouTube has had particular trouble with user-generated content violating copyrights. Millions of consumer-generated videos are uploaded to YouTube, and Google (who owns the site) is hard-pressed to monitor all content to make certain it is original. Viacom, the English Premier League, German performance rights organization GEMA, Kim Kardashian, and Kanye West have all filed lawsuits against YouTube for intellectual property violations (with differing outcomes). Although YouTube is protected somewhat by the Digital Millennium Copyright Act, it must have controls in place to detect potentially copyrighted material and remove any copyrighted material it discovers without permission. A system called Content ID allows rights holders to run it against user uploads on YouTube to detect possible copyrighted materials. Still, as long as illegal uploads and downloads continue, YouTube and other digital media sites are likely to face lawsuits from rights holders who feel their intellectual property has been violated. Most copyright holders tend to sue web platforms and websites that host copyrighted content rather than against users who download the content because suing individual users would not be feasible.

One way companies can protect themselves is through browse wrap agreements, which is the part of the website that informs users about the conditions of using the site.

These agreements should have clear policies regarding intellectual property violations. This demonstrates to outside parties that the organization is committed to warning users against violating intellectual property. However, penalties are not often enforced when users violate the agreement because courts have determined that many of the links for these agreements are not conspicuous enough for users to notice. Recommendations are being made to create a standardized and transparent method for websites to display these browse wrap agreements so they meet all relevant conditions. These recommendations could have significant implications for global public policy on intellectual property over the Internet.[85]

### Discussion Questions

1. How has Internet piracy impacted organizations?
2. Why is it hard for firms to monitor and protect against intellectual property violations over the Internet?
3. What are some ways organizations can guard against intellectual property violations on their websites?

# Strategic Case 4

## Eaton Corporation: Experts at Targeting Different Markets

Eaton Corporation is a power management company based in Cleveland, Ohio. Founded by Joseph Eaton in 1911, this $22.6 billion company originally manufactured truck axels. Today, the company produces more than 900,000 different industrial components and employs 99,000 people globally. It sells products in 175 countries. Eaton's goods and services include electrical components and systems for power quality, distribution, and control; hydraulics components, systems, and services for industrial and mobile equipment; aerospace fuel, hydraulics, and pneumatic systems for commercial and military use; and truck and automotive drivetrain and powertrain systems for performance, fuel economy, and safety. Eaton Corporation has also been one of the most profitable companies, with its stock price surpassing the average of the S&P 500 for the past decade. It has been ranked by *Fortune* magazine as number six in industrial and farm equipment.

Eaton supplies products that help customers reduce their energy consumption, including monitoring software, power management systems, high-efficiency transformers, hydraulic systems, and truck transmissions. These products help customers to increase the energy efficiency of buildings, vehicles, and machinery; conserve natural resources; shrink their carbon footprints; and reduce their environmental impact. Although the company sells mostly to industrial and government users, it also sells products to consumers for

residences and recreation. Eaton's global presence is extensive. The firm is successfully facing political, environmental, and cultural challenges to create a global name for itself. To help in this endeavor, Eaton uses social media sites including Facebook, Twitter, and YouTube to connect with users and spread awareness about its products.

### Business Markets

Eaton's businesses consist of two major sectors: electrical and industrial. Its industrial sector is further split up into hydraulic, aerospace, filtration, and vehicle groups. Eaton's vast array of products targets producer, reseller, and government markets. For instance, in the aerospace industry, Eaton offers components such as fuel and inerting systems, hydraulic systems, and motion control for aircraft. It offers electrical systems, hydraulic systems, fueling, and clutches and brakes for military marine vessels. Eaton also uses many intermediaries such as distributors and retailers to sell products to businesses. Because Eaton's business products entail more risk of purchase, the company employs salespeople and has customer support available for its many different product lines. Eaton also has support staff to handle customer emergencies that happen after hours.

Eaton does not limit its industrial products to large businesses only. It also targets smaller businesses that have need of its products. For instance, in one customer transaction, Eaton provided filter bags to help a family-owned mushroom farm improve its filtration system—which was estimated to increase productivity and led to a savings of $22,000 a year. Eaton's Cooper Lighting division also helped a privately-held California firm improve the efficiency of its outdoor lighting system. By installing more energy-efficient lighting, Eaton helped the firm save 50 percent on energy costs.

Eaton markets to its business customers in a variety of ways. It uses digital media such as its website to describe products, and also has a Success Stories page that describes how Eaton technologies improved their customers' operations. It has a sales force to market its products to business customers and resellers. It also develops advertising campaigns to reach its audience. One of its campaigns even won the Eloqua Markie award for Most Creative Marketing Campaign. In its campaign titled "Things Have Changed," Eaton targeted the IT industry by marketing its expertise in the IT and data center solutions. The campaign used the desk toys of an IT manager to get the message across. The campaign also used social media, direct marketing, and event promotions to enhance its advertising campaign. Eaton clearly demonstrates a strong focus on business and government users of its products.

## Consumer Markets

While the majority of Eaton's products are sold to business markets, some of its products also target end-use consumers. For instance, Eaton markets its Golf Pride® golf club grip to golfers for both club manufacturers and professional/amateur golfers. These products are found at Dick's Sporting Goods stores and other locations. Eaton also sells residential products including solar devices, circuit breakers, spa panels, and in-ceiling speakers. To help consumers learn about the quality of its products, Eaton offers a virtual tour of a house that demonstrates how its products can be used throughout the home.

Most of Eaton's products represent high-involvement products for consumers due to the expense of the product and the costs of installation. Therefore, Eaton must take steps to emphasize the high quality and significance of its products and, if possible, lower the risks of purchase. Eaton realizes that like its business market, customers are more interested in the functionality of its products. For instance, a home owner is more likely to be concerned with whether a circuit breaker works correctly than how it looks. Eaton puts a major emphasis on service to reassure its customers that the company puts their needs first. It emphasizes on its website that it delivers service 24/7 depending on customers' needs. Eaton also offers warranties to reassure customers that defects in the product will be addressed. For instance, it offers a 12-month standard warranty on DC products.

Finally, Eaton continually solicits customer feedback in order to assess customer satisfaction. One of the most important ways the company gets customer opinions is through the Customer Relationship Review (CRR). Each year, Eaton conducts more than 1,000 in-person interviews of customers, including at least one person from every major account. Eaton then generates and distributes an Executive Summary that summarizes the company's strengths and weaknesses. In addition, Eaton creates several smaller and more focused reports for employee use. Eaton considers both business and consumer customers to be important stakeholders.

## Global Business and Social Media

Eaton has had a global presence since 1946, when it acquired a minority interest in U.K. firm Hobourn-Eaton Manufacturing Company Limited. Today its global headquarters are located in Dublin, Ireland. Eaton is a truly multinational company with 55 percent of its revenues coming from outside the United States and 24 percent from developing countries. Eaton sees opportunities for massive growth in the Asia-Pacific region and has 28 manufacturing centers in China. However, with these opportunities come challenges that Eaton must face. For instance, China is experiencing increases in safety laws, land prices and taxes, and minimum wage laws. Eaton is choosing to locate more facilities in China to increase its localization so it can handle these challenges more effectively.

Additionally, both the Chinese and Indian governments have set sustainability goals for their countries, meaning that companies will have to increase their sustainability and sales of eco-friendly products. By investing in energy-efficient operations and selling more sustainable products, Eaton has been meeting these environmental challenges head on.

Another major challenge is ethics and compliance. The more Eaton expands into other countries, the harder it will be to ensure that its facilities, suppliers, and partners are adhering to ethical conduct. By creating more of a localized presence in places like China, Eaton has the ability to increase managerial oversight and emphasize ethical expectations. The firm has a Global Ethics office that encourages global employees to report questions or concerns. Non-English-speaking employees can write e-mails and letters to the Global Ethics office in their native language, and Eaton will translate them.

Finally, Eaton has found that an effective way of communicating with global customers is through the use of digital media. In addition to its highly informational website, Eaton also offers online catalogs and e-newsletters easily distributed with just a click of a button. Eaton maintains an active presence on Facebook, Twitter, and YouTube, allowing the firm to answer customer questions and provide updates. Eaton maintains different product categories on these social media sites to address different target markets. For instance, it has pages that focus on electrical, vehicle, and filtration products. YouTube videos help to demonstrate how Eaton products work, acting as a sort of sales promotional tool.

Eaton has a company-wide commitment to serving the needs of business, consumer, and global markets. It uses different marketing approaches to target its various markets, including advertising and digital media campaigns. Eaton's strong understanding of its customer markets is the key to its reputation and global success.[86]

## Discussion Questions

1. How does Eaton target business and consumer markets? Are there any differences?
2. Describe ways that Eaton is addressing global challenges.
3. How is Eaton using digital marketing to reach its customers?

# NOTES

[1] Molly Soat, "She's Blinding Them With Science," *Marketing News*, February 2015, 51-59; Ted Mann, "GE Touts Its New-Media Cred," *The Wall Street Journal*, December 1, 2014, http://www.wsj.com/articles/ge-touts-its-new-media-cred-1417482888 (accessed September 17, 2015); Wendy Frink, "How 122-Year-Old General Electric Is Killing It on Social Media," *Entrepreneur*, April 8, 2014, http://www.entrepreneur.com/article/232918 (accessed September 17, 2015); The GE Show, http://www.ge.com/thegeshow/healthyhospitals/ (accessed September 17, 2015).

[2] Lauren I. Labrecque, Jonas vor dem Esche, Charla Mathwick, Thomas P. Novak, and Charles F. Hofacker, "Consumer Power: Evolution in the Digital Age," *Journal of Interactive Marketing* 27, 4 (November 2013): 257–269.

[3] Economist staff, "Home, Hacked Home," *The Economist: Special Report on Cyber-Security*, July 12, 2014, pp. 14-15; Economist staff, "Prevention is better than cure," *The Economist: Special Report on Cyber-Security*, July 12, 2014, p. 16.

[4] Harry McCracken, "Inside Mark Zuckerberg's Bold Plan for the Future of Facebook," *Fast Company*, December 2015/January 2016, pp. 86–100, 136.

[5] Piet Levy, "The State of Digital Marketing," *Marketing News*, March 15, 2010, pp. 20–21.

[6] Maria Teresa Pinheiro Melo Borges Tiago and José Manuel Cristóvão Veríssimo, "Digital marketing and social media: Why bother?" *Business Horizons* 57, 6 (November 2014): 703–708.

[7] Elizabeth Weise, "Online Retailers Getting Physical," *USA Today*, November 9, 2015, 6B.

[8] Sanjit Kumar Roy and Gul T. Butaney, "Customer's relative loyalty: an empirical examination," *Journal of Strategic Marketing* 22, 3 (2014): 206–221.

[9] V. Kumar, Xi Zhang, and Anita Luo, "Modeling Customer Opt-In and Opt-Out in a Permission-Based Marketing Context," *Journal of Marketing Research* 51, 4 (August 2014): 403–419.

[10] Adam Kleinberg, "Thinking about Snapchat Advertising? Snap Out of It," *Advertising Age*, August 22, 2014, http://adage.com/article/agency-viewpoint/thinking-snapchat-snap/294667/ (accessed January 8, 2016); Austin Carr, "I Ain't Afraid of No Ghost," *Fast Company*, November 2015, pp. 100–122.

[11] Andrew Perrin, "Social Media Usage: 2005-2015," *Pew Research Center*, October 8, 2015, http://www.pewinternet.org/2015/10/08/social-networking-usage-2005-2015/ (accessed January 7, 2016).

[12] Maria Vernuccio, "Communicating Corporate Brands Through Social Media: An Exploratory Study," *Journal of Business Communication* 51, 3 (July 2014): 211–233.

[13] Harry McCracken, "Inside Mark Zuckerberg's Bold Plan for the Future of Facebook," *Fast Company*, December 2015/January 2016, pp. 86–100, 136.

[14] Reed Albergotti, "Facebook Touts Economic Impact," *The Wall Street Journal*, January 21, 2015, B5.

[15] Clement Tan, "Air China Likes Facebook for Marketing, Despite Ban," *Bloomberg*, January 22, 2015, http://www.bloomberg.com/news/articles/2015-01-22/air-china-likes-facebook-for-marketing-despite-ban (accessed January 8, 2016).

[16] Tom DiChristopher, "Why Facebook's ad revenue can keep growing: revenue," *CNBC*, November 5, 2015, http://www.cnbc.com/2015/11/05/why-facebooks-ad-revenue-can-keep-growing-analyst.html (accessed January 8, 2016).

[17] Jeff Elder, "Facing Reality, Companies Alter Social-Media Strategies," *The Wall Street Journal*, June 23, 2014, B1–B2.

[18] Harriet Baskas, "Which airlines do best on Facebook and Twitter?" *USA Today*, March 20, 2015, http://www.usatoday.com/story/todayinthesky/2015/03/20/airlines-facebook-twitter/25087101/ (accessed January 6, 2016).

[19] Michael Liedtke, "Twitter huddles with NFL to tackle audience challenge," *Yahoo Finance!*, August 10, 2015, http://finance.yahoo.com/news/twitter-huddles-nfl-tackle-audience-130113486.html (accessed January 8, 2016).

[20] Samantha Grossman, "The 13 Sassiest Brands on Twitter," *Time*, February 7, 2014, http://time.com/5151/sassiest-brands-on-twitter-ranked/ (accessed January 14, 2016); "Taco Bell," Twitter, https://twitter.com/tacobell (accessed January 14, 2016).

[21] Belinda Parmar, "50 Companies that Get Twitter—and 50 that Don't," *Harvard Business Review*, April 27, 2015, https://hbr.org/2015/04/the-best-and-worst-corporate-tweeters (accessed January 6, 2016).

[22] Lauren Johnson, "Why Brands are Ditching Twitter's 6-Second Vine App," *AdWeek*, December 6, 2015, http://www.adweek.com/news/technology/why-brands-are-ditching-twitter-s-6-second-vine-app-168433 (accessed January 14, 2016); "Hey Twitter Inc., It's Time to Monetize Vine!" *Motley Fool*, August 2015, http://www.fool.com/investing/general/2015/08/18/hey-twitter-inc-its-time-to-monetize-vine.aspx (accessed January 14, 2016).

[23] Dan Schwbel, "10 New Findings About the Millennial Consumer," *Forbes*, January 20, 2015, http://www.forbes.com/sites/danschawbel/2015/01/20/10-new-findings-about-the-millennial-consumer/#2715e4857a0b9cbb89c28a87 (accessed January 20, 2016).

[24] Tumblr, "About Tumblr," www.tumblr.com/about (accessed January 15, 2016); Mike Shields, "Tumblr Rolls Out Network to Match Top Creators with Brands," *The Wall Street Journal*, January 22, 2015, http://blogs.wsj.com/cmo/2015/01/22/tumblr-rolls-out-network-to-match-top-creators-with-brands/ (accessed January 15, 2016).

[25] Niall Harbison and Lauren Fisher, "40 of the best corporate blogs to inspire you," *Ragan's PR Daily*, September 13, 2012, http://www.prdaily.com/Main/Articles/40_of_the_best_corporate_blogs_to_inspire_you_12645.aspx (accessed January 20, 2016).

[26] Wikipedia, "Wikipedia: About," https://en.wikipedia.org/wiki/Wikipedia:About (accessed January 20, 2016).

[27] Charlene Li and Josh Bernoff, *Groundswell* (Boston: Harvard Business Press, 2008), p. 24.

[28] Ayaz Nanji, "Blog and Social Media Usage by Fortune 500 Companies," *MarketingProfs*, September 12, 2014, http://www.marketingprofs.com/charts/2014/25998/blog-and-social-media-usage-by-fortune-500-companies (accessed January 15, 2016).

[29] Lauren Johnson, "Here are the 10 Brands with the Most-Shared Videos of 2015," *AdWeek*, December 15, 2015, http://www.adweek.com/news/technology/here-are-10-brands-most-shared-videos-2015-168637 (accessed January 20, 2016).

[30] Miguel Helft, "How YouTube Changes Everything," *Fortune*, August 12, 2013, pp. 50–60.

[31] Nicole LaPorte, "Serious Beauty," *Fast Company*, February 2016, pp. 27–28.

[32] Brian Womack and Lucas Shaw, "Rivals are Gaining on YouTube," *Bloomberg Businessweek*, April 28, 2015, 39–40.

[33] David Kiefaber, "Here's the Amateur Snickers Ad that Just Won Its Creator $50,000," *AdWeek*, September 23, 2015 (accessed January 15, 2016).

[34] "Photoset," Instagram, http://blog.business.instagram.com/post/78694901404/how-yogurt-maker-chobani-uses-instagram-to-open (accessed January 15, 2016).

[35] Tribune wire reports, "Instagram expands marketing reach for businesses," *Chicago Tribune*, September 9, 2015, http://www.chicagotribune.com/bluesky/technology/ct-instagram-marketing-business-20150909-story.html (accessed January 8, 2016).

[36] Laura Schlereth, "Marketers' Interest in Pinterest," *Marketing News*, April 30, 2012, pp. 8–9; Pinterest website, http://pinterest.com (accessed January 20, 2016); http://pinterest.com/wholefoods/whole-planet-foundation (accessed January 20, 2016).

[37] Jeff Bercovici, "Social Media's New Mad Men," *Forbes*, November 2014, pp. 71-82.

[38] Mike Shields, "Pinterest Narrows Its Advertising Focus," *The Wall Street Journal*, December 15, 2015, B1–B2.

[39] Douglas MacMillan and Elizabeth Dwoskin, "Smile! Marketers Are Mining Selfies," *The Wall Street Journal*, October 10, 2014, B1–B2.

[40] Laura Northrup, "JCPenney Offers Virtual Reality Flight with Santa, Reindeer, and Product Placements," *Consumerist*, December 14, 2015, http://consumerist.com/2015/12/14/jcpenney-offers-virtual-reality-flight-with-santa-reindeer-and-product-placements/ (accessed January 20, 2016); Adrianne Pasquarelli, "JC Penney Shoppers Visit Santa's Workshop in New Virtual Reality Initiative," *Advertising Age*, December 14, 2015, http://adage.com/article/cmo-strategy/jc-penney-shoppers-visit-santa-s-workshop-virtual-reality-initiative/301721/ (accessed January 15, 2016).

[41] Austin Carr, "Facebook Everywhere," *Fast Company*, July/August 2014, pp. 56-98; Harry McCracken, "Inside Mark Zuckerberg's Bold Plan for the Future of Facebook," *Fast Company*, December 2015/January 2016, pp. 86–100, 136.

[42] Pew Research Center, "Mobile Technology Fact Sheet," www.pewinternet.org/fact-sheets/mobile-technology-fact-sheet/ (accessed January 20, 2016).

[43] Harry McCracken, "Inside Mark Zuckerberg's Bold Plan for the Future of Facebook," *Fast Company*, December 2015/January 2016, pp. 86–100, 136.

[44] eMarketer, "Mobile Ad Spend to Top $100 Billion Worldwide in 2016, 51% of Digital Mar-ket," April 2, 2015, http://www.emarketer.com/Article/Mobile-Ad-Spend-Top-100-Billion-Worldwide-2016-51-of-Digital-Market/1012299 (accessed January 15, 2016).

[45] Lauren Johnson, "Study with Major Brands Compares Ad Recall for Mobile and Desktop Promos," *AdWeek*, July 16, 2015, http://www.adweek.com/news/technology/study-major-brands-compares-ad-recall-mobile-and-desktop-promos-165905 (accessed January 15, 2016).

[46] Lauren Johnson, "How Capital One Used Instagram to Boost Ad Recall by 16 Percent," *AdWeek*, August 11, 2015, http://www.adweek.com/news/technology/how-capital-one-used-instagram-boost-ad-recall-16-percent-166317 (accessed January 15, 2016).

47 Don E. Schultz, Varsha Jain, and Vijay Viswanathan, "Differential Gen Y's World of Apps," *Marketing News*, August 2015, pp. 14–15.

48 James Citron, "2014: The Year the MMS Upswing Arrives and How to Take Advantage of It," *Wired*, January 21, 2014, http://insights.wired.com/profiles/blogs/2014-the-year-the-mms-upswing-arrives-and-how-to-take-advantage#axzz3xLvg3dvO (accessed January 15, 2016).

49 "Mobile to Account for More than Half of Digital Ad Spending in 2015," *eMarketer*, September 1, 2015, http://www.emarketer.com/Article/Mobile-Account-More-than-Half-of-Digital-Ad-Spending-2015/1012930 (accessed January 15, 2016).

50 Jake Jeffries, "10 Incredible Mobile Marketing Stats 2015 [INFOGRAPHIC]," *Social Media Today*, January 13, 2015, http://www.socialmediatoday.com/content/10-incredible-mobile-marketing-stats-2015-infographic (accessed January 15, 2016).

51 Christopher Heine, "Foursquare Unleashes Location Data for Cross-Mobile Ad Targeting," *AdWeek*, April 14, 2015, http://www.adweek.com/news/technology/foursquare-finally-unleashes-location-data-cross-mobile-ad-targeting-164069 (accessed January 19, 2016).

52 "Half of All Adult Cell Phone Owners Have Apps on Their Phones," Pew Internet and American Life Project, November 2, 2011, http://pewinternet.org/~/media/Files/Reports/2011/PIP_Apps-Update-2011.pdf (accessed January 20, 2016).

53 Michelle Yeomans, "Unilever opts for 'mobile marketing platform' to reach south-east Asia," *Cosmetics Design*, September 15, 2015, http://www.cosmeticsdesign-asia.com/Business-Financial/Unilever-opts-for-mobile-marketing-platform-to-reach-south-east-Asia (accessed January 19, 2016).

54 Umika Pidaparthy, "Marketers Embracing QR Codes, for Better or Worse," *CNN Tech*, March 28, 2011, www.cnn.com/2011/TECH/mobile/03/28/qr.codes.marketing/ (accessed January 20, 2016).

55 Ann Zimmerman, "Check Out the Future of Shopping," *The Wall Street Journal*, May 18, 2011, p. D1.

56 "Google Wallet," www.google.com/wallet/what-is-google-wallet.html (accessed January 20, 2016).

57 Vangie Beal, "All about Widgets," Webopedia™, August 31, 2010, www.webopedia.com/DidYouKnow/Internet/2007/widgets.asp (accessed January 20, 2016).

58 Dylan Tweney, "Plyfe's interactive widgets for your site have 46% engagement—and they're free," *Venture Beat*, June 25, 2015, http://venturebeat.com/2015/06/25/plyfes-interactive-widgets-for-your-site-have-46-engagement-and-theyre-free/ (accessed January 19, 2016).

59 Li and Bernoff, *Groundswell*, p. 41.

60 Li and Bernoff, pp. 41–42.

61 David Meerman Scott, *The New Rules of Marketing and PR* (Hoboken, NJ: John Wiley & Sons, Inc., 2009), pp. 195–196.

62 "Forrester Unveils New Segment of Social Technographics—The Conversationalists," *360 Digital Connections*, January 21, 2010, http://blog.360i.com/social-media/forrester-new-seg ment-social-technographics-conversationalists (accessed January 20, 2016).

63 Yelp, "An Introduction to Yelp Metrics as of September 30, 2015," http://www.yelp.com/fact-sheet (accessed January 12, 2016).

64 Li and Bernoff, p. 44.

65 Li and Bernoff, pp. 44–45.

66 Sonja Gensler, Franziska Völckner, Yuping Liu-Thompkins, and Caroline Wiertz, "Managing Brands in the Social Environment," *Journal of Interactive Marketing* 27, 4 (2013): 242–256.

67 Cade Metz, "You Can Now Send Money through Facebook. What's In It For Them?" *Wired*, March 17, 2015, http://www.wired.com/2015/03/can-now-send-money-facebook-whats/ (accessed January 19, 2016).

68 1-800-Flowers.com website, http://www.1800flowers.com/flowers-same-day-delivery?gnavFlag=gnav_close&stateCode=&ddkey=http:FDFlowersControllerCmd (accessed January 19, 2016).

69 Yoree Koh, "Pinterest Bolsters Ads with 'Cinematic Pins'," *The Wall Street Journal*, May 19, 2015, http://blogs.wsj.com/digits/2015/05/19/pinterest-bolsters-ads-with-cinematic-pins/ (accessed January 19, 2016).

70 Mike Shields, "Pinterest Narrows Its Advertising Focus," *The Wall Street Journal*, December 15, 2015, B1–B2.

71 Deepa Seetharaman, "Facebook Advances Bazaar Ambitions," *The Wall Street Journal*, September 3, 2015, www.wsj.com/articles/facebook-advances-bazaar-ambitions-1441323353 (accessed January 19, 2016).

72 Jon Swartz, "Facebook faces fines in Belgium on privacy issue," *USA Today*, November 10, 2015, 5B.

73 Farhad Manjoo, "'Right to be Forgotten' Online Could Spread," *The New York Times*, August 5, 2015, http://www.nytimes.com/2015/08/06/technology/personaltech/right-to-be-forgotten-online-is-poised-to-spread.html (accessed January 12, 2016).

74 Natalia Drozdiak, "EU Regulators Set Grace Period for New Trans-Atlantic Data Pact," *The New York Times*, October 16, 2015, http://www.wsj.com/articles/regulators-want-new-eu-u-s-data-pact-1445016094 (accessed January 12, 2016).

75 Cecilia Kang, "Bill Would Curb Tracking of and Advertising to Children on Internet," *The Washington Post*, November 14, 2013, www.washingtonpost.com/business/technology/bills-would-curb-tracking-of-and-advertising-to-children-on-internet/2013/11/14/dee03382-4d58-11e3-ac54-aa84301ced81_story.html (accessed January 20, 2016); Anne Flaherty, "Senate Chairman Calls for 'Do Not Track' Bill," *Yahoo! News*, April 24, 2013, phys.org/news/2013-04-senate-chairman-track-bill.html (accessed January 20, 2016).

76 Jesse Brody, "Terms and Conditions," *Marketing News*, November 2014, pp. 34–41.

77 Ibid.

78 Nicole Hong, "Massive Cybertheft Scheme Is Alleged," *The Wall Street Journal*, November 11, 2015, A1.

79 Robin Sidel and Daisuke Wakabayashi, "Apple Pay Beset by Low-Tech Fraudsters," *The Wall Street Journal*, March 6, 2015, A1–A2.

80 Sarah Needleman, "Social-Media Con Game," *The Wall Street Journal*, October 12, 2009, http://online.wsj.com/article/SB10001424052748704471504574445502831219412.html (accessed January 20, 2016).

81 BSA Software Alliance, "The Compliance Gap: BSA Global Software Survey," http://globalstudy.bsa.org/2013/ (accessed January 12, 2016).

82 Aubry R. Fowler III, Barry J. Babin, and May K. Este, "Burning for Fun or Money: Illicit Consumer Behavior in a Contemporary Context," presented at the Academy of Marketing Science Annual Conference, May 27, 2005, Tampa, FL.

83 Kevin Shanahan and Mike Hyman, "Motivators and Enablers of SCOURing: A Study of Online Piracy in the US and UK," *Journal of Business Research* 63, 9–10 (2010): 1095–1102.

84 Todd Wasserman, "Zappos Facebook Activity over 2 Months Drives 85,000 Website Visits," *Mashable*, February 6, 2013, http://mashable.com/2013/02/06/zappos-facebook-results (accessed January 20, 2016); Laura Stampler, "Why Zappos Sees Sponsored Posts on Facebook as 'A Necessary Evil,'" *Business Insider*, February 6, 2013, www.businessinsider.com/zappos-on-facebook-and-social-media-2013-2 (accessed January 20, 2016); Mike Schoultz, "Zappos Marketing Strategy . . . What Is Their Difference Maker?" *Digital Spark Marketing*, November 12, 2013, www.digitalsparkmarketing.com/creative-marketing/brand/zappos-marketing-strategy (accessed December 6, 2013); Amy Porterfield, "9 Companies Doing Social Media Right and Why," *Social Media Examiner*, April 12, 2011, www.socialmediaexaminer.com/9-companies-doing-social-media-right-and-why (accessed January 20, 2016).

85 Andrew Perrin, "Social Media Usage: 2005-2015," *Pew Research Center*, October 8, 2015, http://www.pewinternet.org/2015/10/08/social-networking-usage-2005-2015/ (accessed January 20, 2016); Robert Allen, "Digital Marketing Stats from 2015: The Good, the Bad, and the Intriguing," *Smart Insights*, 2015, www.smartinsights.com/internet-marketing-statistics/2015-digital-marketing-stats-the-good-the-bad-and-the-intriguing/ (accessed January 20, 2015); Venable LLP, "When Marketing through Social Media, Legal Risks Can Go Viral," White Paper, www.venable.com/files/Publication/b4f467b9-0666-4b36-b021-351540962d65/Presentation/PublicationAttachment/019f4e5f-d6f8-4eeb-af43-40a4323b9ff1/Social_Media_white_paper.pdf (accessed January 20, 2016); Christina Warren, "How YouTube Fights Copyright Infringement," *Mashable*, February 17, 2012, http://mashable.com/2012/02/17/youtube-content-id-faq (accessed January 20, 2015); Martin U. Müller interview, "German Court Ruling Against YouTube: 'We Don't Want to Sue, We Want a Contract,'" *Der Spiegel*, April 23, 2012, www.spiegel.de/international/business/german-copyright-group-succeeds-in-case-against-youtube-a-829124.html (accessed January 20, 2016); Sam Gustin, "How Google Beat Viacom in the Landmark YouTube Case," *Time*, April 19, 2013, http://business.time.com/2013/04/19/how-google-beat-viacom-in-the-landmark-youtube-copyright-case-again (accessed January 20, 2016); Jon Brodkin, "YouTube's Defeat of Copy-right Owners Is Final in Premier League Case," *ars technica*, http://arstechnica.com/tech-policy/2013/11/youtubes-defeat-of-copyright-owners-is-final-in-premier-league-case (accessed January 20, 2016); The Reliable Source, "Kanye West, Kim Kardashian Sue YouTube Founder for Leaked Proposal Footage," *The Washington Post*, November 4, 2013, www.washingtonpost.com/blogs/reliable-source/wp/2013/11/04/kanye-west-kim-kardashian-sue-youtube-founder-for-leaked-proposal-footage (accessed January 20, 2015); Derek Overbey, "3 Big Brand Social Media Ideas Small Businesses Can Use," *Vertical Response*, November 6, 2013, www.verticalresponse.com/blog/3-big-brand-social-media-ideas-small-businesses-can-use (accessed January 20, 2016); World Intellectual Property Organization, "What Is Intellectual Property?" www.wipo.int/about-ip/en (accessed January 20, 2016); Matt Richtell, "The Napster Decision: The Overview: Appellate Judges Back Limitations on Copying Music," *The New York Times*, February 13, 2001, www.nytimes.com/2001/02/13/business/napster-decision-overview-appellate-judges-back-limitations-copying-music.html?pagewanted=all&src=pm (accessed January 20, 2016); National Paralegal College, "History and Sources of Intellectual Property Law," http://nationalparalegal.edu/public_documents/courseware_asp_files/patents/IntroIP/History.asp (accessed January 20, 2016); International Trademark Association, "Fact Sheets Types of Protection," 2013, www.inta.org/Trademark-Basics/FactSheets/Pages/TrademarksvsGenericTermsFactSheet.aspx (accessed January 20, 2016); David Goldman, "Music's Lost Decade: Sales Cut in Half," *CNN Money*, Feburary 3, 2010, http://money.cnn.com/2010/02/02/news/companies/napster_music_industry (accessed January 20, 2016); Maurizio Borghi, Indranath Gupta, and Eva Hemmungs Wirtén, "Deliverable D26: Reusing Copyrighted Material in User-Generated Content," *Counter© Counterfeiting and Piracy Research* (March 5, 2010); Maurizio Borghi, Maria Lillà Montagnani, and Indranath Gupta, "Deliverable D27: Evaluating Scenarios for Managing Copyright Online," *Counter© Counterfeiting and Piracy Research* (May 30, 2010).

86 Eaton Corporation, "2014 Annual Report," www.eaton.com/ecm/groups/public/@pub/@eaton/@corp/documents/content/pct_1224149.pdf (accessed January 20, 2016); Eaton, "Fast Facts," www.eaton.com/Eaton/OurCompany/AboutUs/CorporateInformation/FastFacts/index.htm (accessed January 20, 2016); Eaton Corporation, "Global Ethics & Compliance," www.eaton.com/Eaton/OurCompany/GlobalEthics (accessed January 20, 2016); Ethisphere Institute, "2013 World's Most Ethical Companies," *Ethisphere*, worldsmostethicalcompanies.ethisphere.com/honorees (accessed January 20, 2016); Eaton website, www.eaton.com/Eaton/index.htm (accessed January 20, 2016); Eaton, "Aerospace," www.eaton.com/Eaton/ProductsServices/Aerospace/index.htm?wtredirect=www.eaton.com/aerospace (accessed January 20, 2016); Eaton, "Success Stories: Mushroom Farming Industry," www.eaton.com/Eaton/OurCompany/SuccessStories/ManufacturingIndustrial/Mushroom-Farming-Industry/index.htm (accessed January 20, 2016); Fortune, "Most Admired: Industrial and Farm Equipment," *Fortune*, archive.fortune.com/magazines/fortune/most-admired/2012/industries/28.html (accessed January 20, 2016); Eaton, "Eaton Receives Eloqua Markie Award for Most Creative Marketing Campaign," November 21, 2012, www.eaton.com/Eaton/OurCompany/NewsEvents/NewsReleases/PCT_403135 (accessed January 20, 2016); Eaton, "Eaton's LED Solutions Allow California Facility to Save More Than 50 Percent on Exterior," September 19, 2013, www.eaton.com/Eaton/OurCompany/NewsEvents/NewsReleases/PCT_508987 (accessed January 20, 2016); Curt Hutchins, *A Transition in Global Markets: Asia-Pacific Is the Future*, 2012, www.amcham-shanghai.org/NR/rdonlyres/73F016E2-0E5F-4BC0-9B99-AC028BD9EA16/17086/CurtHutchins.pdf (accessed January 20, 2016); Anna Clark, "Mega-trends: The Power behind Eaton's Global Green Growth," *Green Biz*, June 19, 2013, www.greenbiz.com/blog/2013/06/19/power-behind-eatons-global-green-growth (accessed January 20, 2016).

## Feature Notes

[a] Christine Birkner, "A Marketable Moniker," *Marketing News*, August 1, 2015, p. 25; Molly Soat, "Selfies of Arabian Nights," *Marketing News*, August 1, 2015, p. 27; Grant Bradley, "Tourism NZ takes to Facebook for new pitch," *New Zealand Herald*, July 27, 2015, http://m.nzherald.co.nz/business/news/article.cfm?c_id=3&objectid=11487580 (accessed August 21, 2015); Emma Hutchings, "Iceland Launches Human Search Engine to Educate Tourists," *PSFK*, April 28, 2015, http://www.psfk.com/2015/04/3d-printers-gabriel-garcia-marquez-think-big-factory.html (accessed August 21, 2015).

[b] Greg Bensinger, "Rebuilding History's Biggest Dot-Com Bust," *The Wall Street Journal*, January 13, 2015, B1-B2; Farhad Manjoo, "Grocery Deliveries in Sharing Economy," *The New York Times*, May 21, 2015, http://www.nytimes.com/2014/05/22/technology/personaltech/online-grocery-start-up-takes-page-from-sharing-services.html?_r=0 (accessed October 5, 2015); Laura Entis, "After Many Strikeouts, a $44 Million Home Run," *Entrepreneur*, July 22, 2014, http://www.entrepreneur.com/article/235796 (accessed October 5, 2015); Hadley Malcolm, "Target starts testing grocery delivery with Instacart," *USA Today*, September 15, 2015, http://www.usatoday.com/story/money/2015/09/15/target-testing-grocery-delivery-with-instacart/72301440/ (accessed October 5, 2015).

# part 5
# Product Decisions

11: Product Concepts, Branding, and Packaging

12: Developing and Managing Products

13: Services Marketing

We are now prepared to analyze the decisions and activities associated with developing and maintaining effective marketing mixes.

**PART 5** explores the product and price ingredients of the marketing mix.

**CHAPTER 11** focuses on basic product concepts and on branding and packaging decisions.

**CHAPTER 12** analyzes various dimensions regarding product management, including line extensions and product modification, new-product development, product deletions, and the management of services as products.

In **CHAPTER 13** we discuss services marketing, including its importance, key characteristics, marketing strategies for services, and the nature of nonprofit marketing.

# chapter 11

## Product Concepts, Branding, and Packaging

### OBJECTIVES

11-1 Explain the concept of a product.

11-2 Discuss how products are classified.

11-3 Explain the concepts of product line and product mix and how they are related.

11-4 Describe the product life cycle and its impact on marketing strategies.

11-5 Discuss the product adoption process.

11-6 Explain the major components of branding, including brand types, branding strategies, and brand protection.

11-7 Describe the major packaging functions, design considerations, and how packaging is used in marketing strategies.

11-8 Identify the functions of labeling and legal issues related to labeling.

# MARKETING INSIGHTS

## Shinola Is "Built in Detroit" and Is No Longer Shoe Polish

Shinola is an old brand given new life and new meaning, thanks to Tom Kartsotis, an experienced entrepreneur with a vision. Kartsotis founded the Fossil Group in 1984 to import and market fashion wristwatches and accessories. After stepping down from Fossil's leadership in 2010, Kartsotis began planning for a new business that would produce stylish wristwatches and other items in American factories. First, he bought the Shinola brand created by a shoe polish firm that went bankrupt in 1960, knowing that the brand was still recognized as an American original. Next, he selected Detroit as his manufacturing center, to take advantage of local resources and to build on the industrial heritage of "built in Detroit."

Kartsotis teamed with a Swiss manufacturer of quality quartz watch movements to design Shinola's Detroit production facility, develop the equipment, and supply some watch parts. Shinola introduced its initial line of upscale fashion wristwatches in 2012. Sales were so strong that the company immediately began expanding. The firm now makes and markets 300,000 watches every year, along with thousands of vintage-style bicycles, leather goods, and apparel items. Because of their high-end price tags, Shinola products are available in luxury stores such as Neiman Marcus as well as in branded boutiques located in hip neighborhoods of major metropolitan centers from coast to coast and beyond.

Shinola is about to introduce a new line of "built in Detroit" stereo speakers, turntables, and headphones. The firm has also applied to trademark potential new products such as Shinola sunglasses and aftershave. "We're always looking for nooks and crannies," Kartsotis explains.[1]

Shinola is an example of an admired but unused brand name reinvented for the modern age. In this chapter, we first define a product and discuss how products are classified. Next, we examine the concepts of product line and product mix. We then explore the stages of the product life cycle and the effect of each life-cycle stage on marketing strategies. Next, we outline the product adoption process. Then, we discuss branding, its value to customers and marketers, brand loyalty, and brand equity. We examine the various types of brands and consider how companies choose and protect brands, the various branding strategies employed, brand extensions, co-branding, and brand licensing. We also look at the role of packaging, the functions of packaging, issues to consider in packaging design, and how the package can be a major element in marketing strategy. We conclude with a discussion of labeling and some related legal issues.

## 11-1  WHAT IS A PRODUCT?

**good** A tangible physical entity

**service** An intangible result of the application of human and mechanical efforts to people or objects

**idea** A concept, philosophy, image, or issue

As defined in Chapter 1, a *product* is a good, a service, or an idea received in an exchange. It can be either tangible or intangible and includes functional, social, and psychological utilities or benefits. A **good** is a tangible physical entity, such as an Apple iPhone or a Subway sandwich. A **service**, in contrast, is intangible. It is the result of the application of human and mechanical efforts to people or objects. Examples of services include a concert performance by Beyoncé, online car insurance, a medical examination, an airline flight, and child day care. German–based Lufthansa, featured in the advertisement, offers transportation services through its global airline. Lufthansa promotes its smooth flying experience with the tagline "air travel engineered around you." The advertisement underscores the service and amenities offered by Lufthansa by showing a relaxed woman interacting with a flight attendant while using her laptop on a flight.

An **idea** is a concept, philosophy, image, or issue. Ideas provide the psychological stimulation that aids in solving problems or adjusting to the environment. Charity: Water, for example, uses traditional marketing and social media activities to raise money to dig wells that bring safe drinking water to 800 million people around the world who lack access to clean water.[2]

It is useful to think of a total product offering as having three interdependent elements: the core product, its supplemental features, and its symbolic or experiential benefits. The core product consists of a product's fundamental utility or main benefit and usually addresses a fundamental need of the consumer. Most consumers, however, appreciate additional features and services. For instance, a basic cell phone allows consumers to make calls, but increasingly consumers expect supplemental features, such as unlimited texting, widely available high-speed Internet access, and apps. Consumers also may seek out symbolic benefits, such as a trendy brand name, when purchasing a phone.

Supplemental features provide added value or attributes that are in addition to the product's core

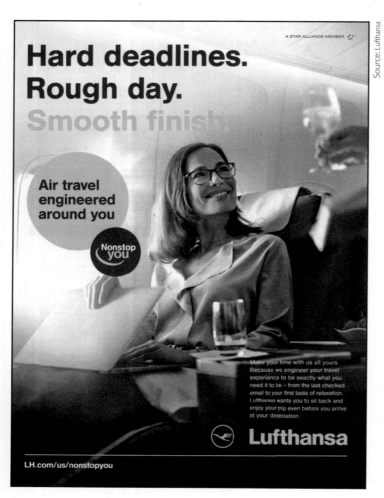

**Hard deadlines.
Rough day.**
Smooth finish.

Air travel
engineered
around you

Nonstop
you

Make your time with us all yours. Because we engineer your travel experience to be exactly what you need it to be – from the last checked email to your first taste of relaxation. Lufthansa wants you to sit back and enjoy your trip even before you arrive at your destination.

A STAR ALLIANCE MEMBER

Source: Lufthansa

**Lufthansa**

LH.com/us/nonstopyou

**Services**
Lufthansa offers transportation services through its airline.

utility or benefit. These features often include perks such as free installation, guarantees, product information, promises of repair or maintenance, delivery, training, or financing. These supplemental attributes are not required to make the core product function effectively, but they help to differentiate one product brand from another and may increase customer loyalty. For instance, Drury Hotels creates customer loyalty through strong customer service and supplemental benefits. In addition to its core product, the hotel's value package offers supplemental product features including free breakfast, free Wi-Fi, free popcorn and soda in the hotel lobby, a snack and beverage social in the evenings, free local and long-distance calls, and a busi-ness center and fitness center. These supplemental benefits differentiate the hotel chain in customers' minds, making them feel as if they are getting a better deal than they would receive at rival hotels.[3]

### Are You Buying Less Music?

| Product | Sales (in millions) | Percent change from previous year |
|---------|---------------------|-----------------------------------|
| Total | 257 | -11% |
| CD | 141 | -15% |
| Digital | 107 | -9% |
| LP/Vinyl | 9 | +50% |

Source: Nielsen 2014 U.S. Music Report.

SNAPSHOT

Finally, customers also receive benefits based on their experiences with the product, which give symbolic meaning to many products (and brands) for buyers. For some consumers, the simple act of shopping gives them pleasure, which lends to its symbolic value and improves their attitudes about the products they consider buying. Some retailers capitalize on this by striving to create a special, personalized experience for customers. Even well-established retail chains are recognizing the importance of an individualized customer experience for gaining a competitive advantage. McDonald's, known for its quick service, is introducing Create Your Taste in some of its stores that allow customers to choose their bread, meat, cheese, and top-pings however they like it. Although customization takes more time and may conflict with McDonald's reputation for quick service, Millennials—McDonald's key target market for this venture—appear to value customization over time.[4]

The atmosphere and décor of a retail store, the variety and depth of product choices, the customer support, and even the sounds and smells all contribute to the experiential element. Thus, when buyers purchase a product, they are really buying the benefits and satisfaction they think the product will provide. A Rolex or Patek Philippe watch is purchased to make a statement that the wearer has high status or has achieved financial success—not just for telling time. Services, in particular, are purchased on the basis of expectations. Expectations, sug-gested by images, promises, and symbols, as well as processes and delivery, help consumers to make judgments about tangible and intangible products. Often symbols and cues are used to make intangible products more tangible, or real, to the consumer. Prudential Insurance, for example, features the Rock of Gibraltar on its logo to symbolize strength and permanency.

## 11-2 CLASSIFYING PRODUCTS

Products fall into one of two general categories. Products purchased to satisfy personal and family needs are **consumer products**. Those bought to use in a firm's operations, to resell, or to make other products are **business products**. Consumers buy products to satisfy their per-sonal wants, whereas business buyers seek to satisfy the goals of their organizations. Product

**consumer products** Products purchased to satisfy personal and family needs

**business products** Products bought to use in a firm's operations, to resell, or to make other products classifications are important because they may influence pricing, distribution, and promotion decisions. In this section, we examine the characteristics of consumer and business products and explore the marketing activities associated with some of these products.

## 11-2a  Consumer Products

The most widely accepted approach to classifying consumer products is based on characteristics of consumer buying behavior. It divides products into four categories: convenience, shopping, specialty, and unsought products. However, not all buyers behave in the same way when purchasing a specific type of product. Thus, a single product might fit into several categories. To minimize complexity, marketers think in terms of how buyers *generally* behave when purchasing a specific item. Examining the four traditional categories of consumer products can provide further insight.

### Convenience Products

**Convenience products** are relatively inexpensive, frequently purchased items for which buyers exert only minimal purchasing effort. They range from bread, soft drinks, and chewing gum to gasoline and newspapers. The buyer spends little time planning the purchase or comparing available brands or sellers. Even a buyer who prefers a specific brand will generally choose a substitute if the preferred brand is not conveniently available. A convenience product is normally marketed through many retail outlets, such as gas stations, drugstores, and supermarkets. Coca-Cola products, for instance, are available in grocery stores, convenience stores, gas stations, restaurants, and airports—among many other outlets. Because sellers experience high inventory turnover, per-unit gross margins can be relatively low. Producers of convenience products, such as Wrigley's chewing gum, expect little promotional effort at the retail level and thus must provide it themselves with advertising and sales promotion. Packaging and displays are also important because many convenience items are available only on a self-service basis at the retail level, and thus the package plays a major role in selling the product.

### Shopping Products

**Shopping products** are items for which buyers are willing to expend considerable effort in planning and making the purchase. Buyers spend considerable time comparing stores and brands with respect to prices, product features, qualities, services, and perhaps warranties. Shoppers may compare products at a number of outlets such as Best Buy, Amazon.com, Lowe's, or Home Depot; they may begin their shopping at the websites of these stores. Appliances, bicycles, furniture, stereos, cameras, and shoes exemplify shopping products. These products are expected to last a fairly long time and are more expensive than convenience products. These products, however, are still within the budgets of most consumers and are purchased less frequently than convenience items. Shopping products are distributed via fewer retail outlets than convenience products.

Because shopping products are purchased less frequently, inventory turnover is lower, and marketing channel members expect to receive higher gross margins to compensate for the lower turnover. In certain situations, both shopping products and convenience products may be marketed in the same location. For instance, retailers such as Target or Walmart carry shopping products like televisions, furniture, and cameras as well as groceries and other convenience products. Take a look at the two advertisements for convenience versus shopping products. Sun Chips are a convenience product made from whole grains that are inexpensive and widely available. The advertisement—which highlights that Sun Chips differ from conventional chips—does not even mention where Sun Chips are sold because they are so widely available. A Cannondale bicycle, on the other hand, is a shopping product. This ad depicts a high-end Supersix Evo road bike and emphasizes its speed and balance of features. Consumers who purchase this product are likely to have conducted research

**convenience products**
Relatively inexpensive, frequently purchased items for which buyers exert minimal purchasing effort

**shopping products** Items for which buyers are willing to expend considerable effort in planning and making purchases

**Convenience versus Shopping Products**
Convenience products such as Sun Chips do not require much shopping effort. However, a consumer might expend considerable effort in deciding on, locating, and purchasing a high-end Cannondale bicycle, such as this Supersix Evo.

and will seek out this specific Cannondale model because of its features and reputation for speed.

A marketer must consider several key issues to market a shopping product effectively, including how to allocate resources, whether personal selling is needed, and cooperation within the supply chain. Although advertising for shopping products often requires a large budget, an even larger percentage of the overall budget is needed if marketers determine that personal selling is required. The producer and the marketing channel members usually expect some cooperation from one another with respect to providing parts and repair services and performing promotional activities. Marketers should consider these issues carefully so that they can choose the best course for promoting these products.

## Specialty Products

**Specialty products** possess one or more unique characteristics, and generally buyers are willing to expend considerable effort to obtain them. On average, this is the most expensive category of products. Buyers conduct research, plan the purchase of a specialty product, know exactly what they want, and will not accept a substitute. Examples of specialty products include fine jewelry or limited-edition collector's items. When searching for specialty products, buyers do not compare alternatives and are unlikely to base their decision on price. They are concerned primarily with finding an outlet that sells the preselected product. The advertisement for Patek Philippe watches underscores the fact that these are specialty products. The advertisement shows a father, wearing the high-end luxury watch, laughing with his son. This is meant to become a family heirloom, hinting that price should be no object. The watch is very expensive and available only at exclusive outlets.

**specialty products** Items with unique characteristics that buyers are willing to expend considerable effort to obtain

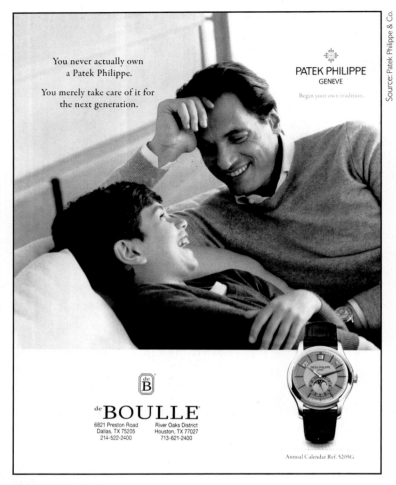

**Specialty Product**
A Swiss-made watch, such as this Patek Philippe model, is a specialty product. It is expensive, exclusive, and is meant to be treasured for a long time.

Marketers will approach their efforts for specialty products differently from convenience or shopping products in several ways. Specialty products are often distributed through a very limited number of retail outlets. Similar to shopping products, they are purchased infrequently, causing lower inventory turnover and thus requiring high gross margins to be profitable.

## Unsought Products

**Unsought products** are those purchased when a sudden problem must be solved, products of which customers are unaware until they see them in a store or online, and products that people do not plan on purchasing. Emergency medical services and automobile repairs are examples of products needed quickly and suddenly to solve a problem. A consumer who is sick or injured has little time to plan to go to an emergency medical center or hospital and will find the closest location to receive service. Likewise, in the event of a broken fan belt in a car, a consumer likely will seek the nearest auto repair facility or call AAA to minimize the length of time before the car is operational again. In such cases, speed of problem resolution is more important than price or other features a buyer might normally consider if there were more time for making a decision.

## 11-2b  **Business Products**

Business products are usually purchased on the basis of an organization's goals and objectives. Generally, the functional aspects of the product are more important than the psychological rewards sometimes associated with consumer products. Business products can be classified into seven categories according to their characteristics and intended uses: installations, accessory equipment, raw materials, component parts, process materials, MRO supplies (maintenance, repair, and operating), and business services.

## Installations

**Installations** include facilities, such as office buildings, factories, and warehouses, and major nonportable equipment such as production lines and very large machines. Normally, installations are expensive and intended to be used for a considerable length of time. Because installations tend to be costly and involve a long-term investment of capital, these purchase decisions often are made by high-level management. Marketers of installations must frequently provide a variety of services, including training, repairs, maintenance assistance, and even aid in financing.

## Accessory Equipment

**Accessory equipment** does not become part of the final physical product but is used in production or office activities. Examples include file cabinets, fractional-horsepower motors, calculators, and tools. Compared with major equipment, accessory items usually are less

**unsought products** Products purchased to solve a sudden problem, products of which customers are unaware, and products that people do not necessarily think of buying

**installations** Facilities and nonportable major equipment

**accessory equipment** Equipment that does not become part of the final physical product but is used in production or office activities expensive, purchased routinely with less negotiation, and are often treated as expense items rather than capital items because they are not expected to last as long. More outlets are required for distributing and selling accessory equipment than for installations, but sellers do not have to provide the multitude of services expected of installations marketers.

## Raw Materials

**Raw materials** are the basic natural materials that actually become part of a physical product. They include minerals, chemicals, agricultural products, and materials from forests and oceans. Corn, for instance, is a raw material that is found in many different products, including food (in many forms), beverages (as corn syrup), and even fuel (as ethanol).

## Component Parts

**Component parts** become part of the physical product and are either finished items ready for assembly or products that need little processing before assembly. Although they become part of a larger product, component parts often can be identified and distinguished easily, even after the product is assembled. Spark plugs, tires, clocks, brakes, and headlights are all component parts of an automobile. Buyers purchase such items according to their own specifications or industry standards, and they expect the parts to be of a specified quality and delivered on time so that production is not slowed or stopped. Producers that are primarily assemblers, such as auto or computer manufacturers, depend heavily on suppliers of component parts. Apple, for example, procures component parts from a number of companies in order to manufacture its iPhones. At least nine of Apple's component part suppliers derive 40 percent or more of their revenues from doing business with Apple, including Cirrus Logic, Pegatron, and Dialog Semiconductor.[5]

## Process Materials

**Process materials** are used directly in the production of other products. Unlike component parts, however, process materials are not readily identifiable. Case in point, a salad dressing manufacturer includes vinegar as an ingredient in dressing. The vinegar is a process material because it is not identifiable or extractable from the other ingredients in the dressing. As with component parts, process materials are purchased according to industry standards or the purchaser's specifications.

## MRO Supplies

**MRO supplies** are maintenance, repair, and operating items that facilitate production and operations, but do not become part of the finished product. Many products that were purchased as consumer products could also be considered MRO supplies to businesses. These might include paper, pencils, cleaning supplies, and paints. MRO supplies are sold through

**raw materials** Basic natural materials that become part of a physical product

**component parts** Items that become part of the physical product and are either finished items ready for assembly or items that need little processing before assembly

**process materials** Materials that are used directly in the production of other products but are not readily identifiable

**MRO supplies** Maintenance, repair, and operating items that facilitate production and operations but do not become part of the finished product

**Business Services**
Although Progressive provides insurance services to both consumers and businesses, the insurance services mentioned in this ad are specifically for businesses.

numerous outlets and are purchased routinely, much like convenience products in the consumer market. To ensure supplies are available when needed, buyers often deal with more than one seller.

## Business Services

**Business services** are the intangible products that many organizations use in their operations. They include financial, legal, marketing research, information technology, and janitorial services. Firms must decide whether to provide these services internally or obtain them from outside the organization. This decision depends on the costs associated with each alternative and how frequently the services are needed. In this advertisement, Progressive promotes how its insurance products provide "coverage that keeps your business moving forward." It targets small businesses with custom coverage for business and commercial auto insurance needs. The ad also employs the Flo trade character from its consumer insurance promotions to reinforce its expertise in insurance products.

# 11-3 **PRODUCT LINE AND PRODUCT MIX**

Marketers must understand the relationships among all the products of their organization to coordinate the marketing of the total group of products. The following concepts help to describe the relationships among an organization's products.

A **product item** is a specific version of a product that can be designated as a distinct offering among an organization's products. An American Eagle Outfitters T-shirt represents a product item. A **product line** is a group of closely related product items that are considered to be a unit because of marketing, technical, or end-use considerations. Birchbox, a monthly subscription service, developed its own product line of cosmetics, called LOC (Love of Color), to market smaller sizes of makeup that consumers can use up quickly and then move on to the latest color or style without feeling like they are wasting product.[6]

Specific product items in a product line, such as different lipstick shades or shampoos for oily and dry hair, usually reflect the desires of different target markets or the varying needs of consumers. Thus, to develop the optimal product line, marketers must understand buyers' goals. Firms with high market share are more likely to expand their product lines aggressively, as are marketers with relatively high prices or limited product lines.[7] This pattern can be seen in many industries—including the computer industry, where companies are likely to expand their product lines when industry barriers are low or perceived market opportunities exist.

A **product mix** is the composite, or total, group of products that an organization makes available to customers. The **width of product mix** is measured by the number of product lines a company offers. Deere & Co. offers multiple product lines for the agricultural industry, including tractors, scrapers, grain harvesting equipment, agricultural management solutions, home and workshop products, and even crop insurance.[8] The **depth of product mix** is the average number of different product items offered in each product line. Procter & Gamble offers a broad product mix, comprised of all the health care, beauty-care, laundry and cleaning, food and beverage, paper, cosmetic, and fragrance products the firm manufactures, some of which are quite deep. Figure 11.1 shows the width and depth of part of Procter & Gamble's product mix. Procter & Gamble is known for using distinctive branding, packaging, segmentation, and consumer advertising to promote individual items in its product lines. Tide, Bold, Gain, Cheer, and Era, for example, are all Procter & Gamble detergents that share the same distribution channels and similar manufacturing facilities, but each is promoted as a distinctive product, adding depth to the product line.

**business services** Intangible products that many organizations use in their operations

**product item** A specific version of a product that can be designated as a distinct offering among a firm's products

**product line** A group of closely related product items viewed as a unit because of marketing, technical, or end-use considerations

**product mix** The composite, or total, group of products that an organization makes available to customers

**width of product mix** The number of product lines a company offers

**depth of product mix** The average number of different products offered in each product line

Figure 11.1    **The Concepts of Product Mix Width and Depth Applied to U.S. Procter & Gamble Products**

| Laundry | Oral Care | Bar Soaps | Deodorants | Shampoos | Tissue/Towel | Health |
|---|---|---|---|---|---|---|
| Dreft 1933 | Crest 1955 | Ivory 1879 | Old Spice 1948 | Pantene 1947 | Charmin 1928 | Pepto-Bismol 1901 |
| Tide 1946 | Scope 1966 | Safeguard 1963 | Secret 1956 | Head & Shoulders 1961 | Puffs 1960 | Vicks 1905 |
| Cheer 1950 | Oral-B 2006 | Olay 1993 | | Herbal Essence 2001 | Bounty 1965 | Prilosec OTC 2003 |
| Downy 1960 | | | | Aussie 2003 | | |
| Bold 1965 | | | | | | |
| Gain 1966 | | | | | | |
| Era 1972 | | | | | | |
| Febreze 2000 | | | | | | |

*Depth* (vertical axis, left)

**Width** (horizontal axis, bottom)

# 11-4 PRODUCT LIFE CYCLES AND MARKETING STRATEGIES

Product life cycles follow a similar trajectory to biological life cycles, progressing from birth to death. As Figure 11.2 shows, a **product life cycle** has four major stages: introduction, growth, maturity, and decline. As a product moves through each cycle, the strategies relating to competition, pricing, distribution, promotion, and market information must be evaluated and possibly adjusted. Astute marketing managers use the life-cycle concept to make sure that strategies relating to the introduction, alteration, and deletion of products are timed and executed properly. By understanding the typical life-cycle pattern, marketers can maintain profitable product mixes.

## 11-4a Introduction

The **introduction stage** of the product life cycle begins at a product's first appearance in the marketplace. Sales start at zero and profits are negative because companies must invest in product development and launch prior to selling. Profits may remain low or below zero because initial revenues will be low while the company covers large expenses for promotion and distribution. Notice in Figure 11.2 how, as sales move upward from zero over time, profits also increase.

Sales may be slow at first because potential buyers must be made aware of a new product's features, uses, and advantages through marketing. Apple, for instance, invited customers into Apple stores to try on and experience the Apple Watch before it was even available for sale. The company also used advertising and personal selling in stores to inform potential buyers and spark desire and excitement for the innovative smartwatch.[9] Efforts to highlight a new product's value can create a foundation for building brand loyalty and customer relationships.[10]

Two difficulties may arise during the introduction stage. First, sellers may lack the resources, technological knowledge, and marketing expertise to launch the product successfully. A large marketing budget is not required to launch a successful product. Marketers can attract attention

**product life cycle** The progression of a product through four stages: introduction, growth, maturity, and decline

**introduction stage** The initial stage of a product's life cycle; its first appearance in the marketplace, when sales start at zero and profits are negative

Figure 11.2    **The Four Stages of the Product Life Cycle**

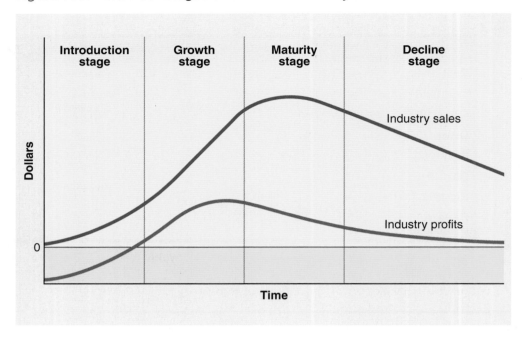

through such techniques as giving away free samples or through media appearances. Websites, such as Retailmenot.com, help firms with lost-cost promotion by listing coupons and samples for thousands of companies—exposing customers to great deals and new brands.[11] Some firms also choose to host online brand communities to promote the new product and predict its success. Apple and eBay have become experts in hosting online brand communities to promote products.[12] Second, the initial product price may have to be high to recoup expensive marketing research or development costs, which can depress sales. Given these difficulties, it is not surprising that many products never last beyond the introduction stage.

Most new products start off slowly and seldom generate enough sales to bring immediate profits. Although new-product success rates vary a great deal between companies and in different industries, it is estimated that only 15 to 25 percent of new products succeed in the marketplace.[13] Even among established and successful companies, new-product success rates are rarely above 50 percent. As buyers learn about the new product and express interest, the firm should constantly monitor the product and marketing strategy for weaknesses and make corrections quickly to prevent the product's early demise. A marketing strategy should be designed to attract the segment that is most interested in, most able, and most willing to buy the product. As sales increase, you can see in Figure 11.2 that eventually the firm reaches the breakeven point, which is when profits match expenses. It is after this point—when competitors enter the market—that the growth stage begins.

## 11-4b Growth

During the **growth stage**, sales rise rapidly and profits reach a peak and then start to decline (see Figure 11.2). The growth stage is critical to a product's survival because competitive reactions to the product's success during this period will affect the product's life expectancy. 3D printers are in the growth stage. Profits begin to decline late in the growth stage as more competitors enter the market, driving prices down and creating the need for heavy promotional expenses. At this point, a typical marketing strategy seeks to strengthen market share and position the product favorably against aggressive competitors by emphasizing product benefits. Marketers should analyze competing brands' product positions relative to their own and adjust

**growth stage** The product life-cycle stage when sales rise rapidly, profits reach a peak, and then they start to decline the marketing mix in response to their findings. Aggressive pricing, including price cuts, is also typical during this stage as a means of gaining market share—even if it means short-term loss of profits. The goal of the marketing strategy in the growth stage is to establish and fortify the product's market position by encouraging adoption and brand loyalty. The advertisement for Silk Almond Milk, for example, strives to encourage adoption of the product by promoting that more people in a taste test found it tastier than milk. The ad pictures an almond-encircled carton spouting almond milk that almost seems to shout the taste comparison results, while the text promotes that almond milk is smooth and tasty. In the case of Silk, promotional effort must help minimize indirect competition from milk as well as direct competition from dairy replacement products.

Firms should seek to fill gaps in geographic market coverage during the growth period. As a product gains market acceptance, new distribution outlets usually become easier to secure. Marketers sometimes move from an exclusive or a selective exposure to a more intensive network of dealers to achieve greater market penetration. Marketers must also make sure the physical distribution system is running efficiently so that customers' orders are processed accurately and delivered on time.

Promotion expenditures in the growth stage may be slightly lower than during the introductory stage, but are still large. As sales continue to increase, promotion costs should drop as a percentage of total sales, which contributes significantly to increased profits. Advertising messages should stress brand benefits.

**Growth Stage**
Silk Almond Milk seeks to strengthen its market share by encouraging greater adoption and use.

## 11-4c  Maturity

During the **maturity stage**, sales peak and start to level off or decline, and profits continue to fall (see Figure 11.2). DVDs are an example of a product in the maturity phase as Internet streaming of entertainment grows in popularity. This stage is characterized by intense competition because many brands are now in the market. Competitors emphasize improvements and differences in their versions of the product. Another example of a product that has many competitors and many variations available on the market is tablets. The advertisement for Amazon's Fire HD8, a product in the maturity stage, touts that the tablet is more durable than the Apple iPad. The advertisement further underscores the comparison to the iPad by pointing out the Fire HD8's ready access to millions of movies, TV episodes, songs, books, and more. Finally, the ad informs that the Fire HD8 starts at $149.99, significantly less than an iPad. Weaker competitors are squeezed out of the market during this stage.

During the maturity phase, the producers who remain in the market are likely to change their promotional and distribution efforts. Advertising and dealer-oriented promotions are typical during this stage of the product life cycle. Marketers also must take into account that as it reaches maturity, buyers' knowledge of the product is likely to be high. Consumers are no longer inexperienced generalists. They have become experienced specialists. Marketers of mature products sometimes expand distribution into global markets, in which case products may have to be adapted to fit differing needs of global customers more precisely. For instance, as Barbie doll sales decline in the United States, Mattel has been trying to increase interest for

**maturity stage** The stage of a product's life cycle when the sales curve peaks and starts to decline, and profits continue to fall

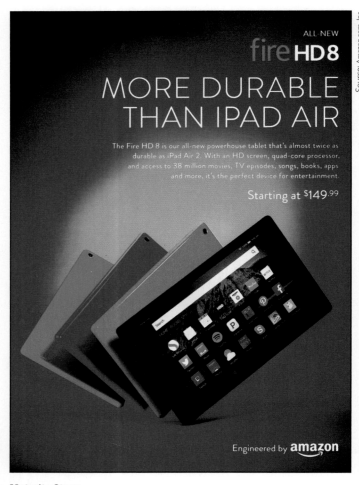

Source: Amazon.com, Inc.

ALL-NEW
fire HD8

MORE DURABLE
THAN IPAD AIR

The Fire HD 8 is our all-new powerhouse tablet that's almost twice as
durable as iPad Air 2. With an HD screen, quad-core processor,
and access to 38 million movies, TV episodes, songs, books, apps
and more, it's the perfect device for entertainment.

Starting at $149.<sup>99</sup>

Engineered by amazon

**Maturity Stage**
Amazon highlights the durability, low price, and access to millions of
movies, TV episodes, songs, and more to help differentiate its Fire HD8
from competitors.

Barbie in China. Because parents have a different view of toys in China than those of the United States, Mattel has had to adapt Barbie to focus more on learning and intellectual pursuits. If the iconic doll fails to take off there, Mattel may have to shift to a decline strategy for Barbie.[14]

Because many products are in the maturity stage of their life cycles, marketers must know how to deal with them and be prepared to adjust their marketing strategies. There are many approaches to altering marketing strategies during the maturity stage. To increase the sales of mature products, marketers may suggest new uses for them. As customers become more experienced and knowledgeable about products during the maturity stage (particularly about business products), the benefits they seek may change as well, necessitating product modifications. Nestlé, for example, reformulated Baby Ruth, Butterfinger, and other chocolate bars so that they would be free of artificial flavors and colors. Because consumers today are increasingly concerned about the safety of artificial ingredients, Nestlé recognized this as an opportunity to differentiate its mature products from rivals. Nestlé hopes its reformulated candy bars will turn critics of artificial ingredients into loyal customers.[15]

During the maturity stage, marketers actively encourage resellers to support the product. Resellers may be offered promotional assistance to lower their inventory costs. In general, marketers go to great lengths to serve resellers and provide incentives for displaying and selling their brand. Maintaining market share during the maturity stage requires promotion expenditures, which can be large if a firm seeks to increase a product's market share through new uses. Advertising messages in this stage may focus on differentiating a brand from the field of competitors, and sales promotion efforts may be aimed at both consumers and resellers.

## 11-4d  Decline

During the **decline stage**, sales fall rapidly (see Figure 11.2). When this happens, the marketer must consider eliminating items from the product line that no longer earn a profit. The marketer also may cut promotion efforts, eliminate marginal distributors, and finally, plan to phase out the product. This can be seen in the decline in demand for most sweetened carbonated beverages such as soda, which has been continuing for decades as consumers turn instead to bottled teas and flavored waters. Companies have responded to this shift in consumer preference by expanding their offerings of juices, waters, and healthier drink options.

In the decline stage, marketers must decide whether to reposition the product to extend its life, or whether it is better to eliminate it. Usually a declining product has lost its distinctiveness because similar competing or superior products have been introduced. Competition engenders increased substitution and brand switching among consumers as they become increasingly insensitive to minor product differences. For these reasons, marketers do little to change a product's style, design, or other attributes during its decline. New technology or social trends, product substitutes, or environmental considerations may also indicate that the time has come to delete the product.

During a product's decline, spending on promotion efforts is usually reduced considerably. Advertising of special offers and sales promotions, such as coupons and premiums, may

**decline stage** The stage of a
product's life cycle when sales
fall rapidly

# EMERGING **TRENDS IN MARKETING**

### Marketing Marvel's Cinematic Universe

Decades ago, when Marvel marketed only comic books, its characters often made guest appearances in each other's extended storylines to enlarge the audience for each character as a brand. Today, as part of Disney, Marvel remains a pioneer in the marketing of a brand ecosystem, a mix-and-match strategy that maximizes the product possibilities within the Marvel Cinematic Universe. This ecosystem is a driving force behind the company's development of movies, television shows, comics, merchandise, and other products based on interconnections between Marvel's characters.

The Marvel Cinematic Universe was launched in 2008 with the release of *Iron Man* and *The Incredible Hulk*, and continued through the years as these and other Marvel characters played pivotal roles in blockbuster Marvel movies like *The Avengers*. Marvel mined its character brands for television programs such as *Jessica Jones* and licensed character brands for tie-in toys. Hasbro, for example, holds the brand license to produce toys based on Marvel's teen superhero Spider-Man, plus the license for Thor and other characters from Marvel's *Avengers* movies.

Although Marvel had previously sold the movie rights for some characters, it has been making deals to bring characters back into its movie empire. Spider-Man, for example, earned plenty of money for other movie studios before his recent return to the Marvel Cinematic Universe. In addition to appearing as a supporting character in *Captain America: Civil War*, Spider-Man will once again be the star of his own Marvel movies, even as he continues to star in his own Marvel comics, in print and in pixels.[a]

slow the rate of decline temporarily. Firms will maintain outlets with strong sales volumes and eliminate unprofitable outlets. An entire marketing channel may be eliminated if it does not contribute adequately to profits. A channel not used previously, such as a factory outlet or Internet retailer, can help liquidate remaining inventory of a product that is being eliminated. As sales decline, the product becomes harder for consumers to find, but loyal buyers will seek out resellers who still carry it. As the product continues to decline, the sales staff at outlets where it is still sold will shift emphasis to more profitable products.

# 11-5 **PRODUCT ADOPTION PROCESS**

Acceptance of new products—especially new-to-the-world products—usually does not happen quickly. It can take a very long time for consumers to become aware of and overcome skepticism about a new product, particularly if it represents a dramatic innovation. Many consumers prefer to wait to adopt a new product until the "second generation," when kinks are more likely to have been worked out. Customers come to accept new products through an adoption process, detailed in Figure 11.3. The stages of the **product adoption process** are as follows:

*Awareness:* The buyer becomes aware of the product.
*Interest:* The buyer seeks information and is receptive to learning about the product.

Figure 11.3  **Product Adoption Process**

**product adoption process** The five-stage process of buyer acceptance of a product: awareness, interest, evaluation, trial, and adoption

*Evaluation:* The buyer considers the product's benefits and decides whether to try it, considering its value versus the competition.

*Trial:* The buyer examines, tests, or tries the product to determine if it meets his or her needs.

*Adoption:* The buyer purchases the product and can be expected to use it again whenever the need for this product arises.[16]

In the first stage, when consumers initially become aware that the product exists, they possess little information and are not yet concerned about obtaining more. Consumers enter the interest stage when they become motivated to learn about the product's features, uses, advantages, disadvantages, price, or location. During the evaluation stage, individuals consider whether the product will address the criteria that are crucial to meeting their specific needs. In the trial stage, consumers use or experience the product for the first time, possibly by purchasing a small quantity, taking advantage of free samples, or borrowing the product from someone else. Individuals move into the adoption stage when they need a product of that general type and choose to purchase the new product on a trial basis. However, entering the adoption stage does not mean that the person will eventually adopt the new product. Rejection may occur at any stage. Both product adoption and product rejection can be temporary or permanent.

When an organization introduces a new product, consumers in the target market enter into and move through the adoption process at different rates. For most products, there is also a group of non-adopters who never begin the process. For business marketers, success in managing production innovation, diffusion, and adoption requires great adaptability and significant effort in understanding customers.[17]

Depending on the length of time it takes them to adopt a new product, consumers tend to fall into one of five major adopter categories: innovators, early adopters, early majority, late majority, and laggards.[18] **Innovators** are the first to adopt a new product because they enjoy trying new products and do not mind taking a risk. **Early adopters** choose new products carefully and are viewed as people who are in-the-know by those in the remaining adopter categories. People in the **early majority** adopt just prior to the average person. They are deliberate and cautious in trying new products. Individuals in the **late majority** are skeptical of new products, but eventually adopt them because of economic necessity or social pressure. **Laggards**, the last to adopt a new product, are oriented toward the past. They are suspicious of new products, and when they finally adopt them, they may already have been replaced by even newer products.

**innovators** First adopters of new products

**early adopters** People who adopt new products early, choose new products carefully, and are viewed as "the people to check with" by later adopters

**early majority** Individuals who adopt a new product just prior to the average person

**late majority** Skeptics who adopt new products when they feel it is necessary

**laggards** The last adopters, who distrust new products

**brand** A name, term, design, symbol, or other feature that identifies one seller's product as distinct from those of other sellers

**brand name** The part of a brand that can be spoken, including letters, words, and numbers

## 11-6 **BRANDING**

Marketers must make many decisions about products, including choices about brands, brand names, brand marks, trademarks, and trade names. A **brand** is a name, term, design, symbol, or any other feature that identifies one marketer's product as distinct from those of other marketers.[19] A brand may identify a single item, a family of items, or all items of that seller. Some have defined a brand as not just the physical good, name, color, logo, or ad campaign, but everything associated with the product, including its symbolism and experiences.[20] Firms that try to shift the image of a brand risk losing market share. Coca-Cola learned this the hard way with its failed New Coke brand. However, simple brand changes have also led to major marketing successes. For example, when MillerCoors temporarily repackaged its Miller Lite beer for a short-term promotion using its original white can design instead of the blue design it had used for the past decade, sales of the mature product increased dramatically. The result prompted MillerCoors to make the retro look permanent, and extended the white label to all Miller Lite cans, bottles, and coasters.[21]

A **brand name** is the part of a brand that can be spoken—including letters, words, and numbers—such as 7UP or V8. A brand name is essential, as it is often a product's only distinguishing characteristic without which a firm could not differentiate its products. To consumers, a brand name is as fundamental as the product itself. Indeed, many brand names have become synonymous with the product, such as Scotch Tape, Xerox copiers, and Kleenex tissues. Marketers must make efforts, through promotional activities, to ensure that such brand names do not become generic terms, which are not protected under the law.

The element of a brand that is comprised of words—often a symbol or design—is a **brand mark**. Examples of brand marks include the McDonald's Golden Arches, Nike's "swoosh," and Apple's silhouette of an apple with a bite missing. A **trademark** is a legal designation indicating that the owner has exclusive use of a brand or a part of a brand and that others are prohibited by law from its use. To protect a brand name or brand mark in the United States, an organization must register it as a trademark with the U.S. Patent and Trademark Office. Finally, a **trade name** is the full and legal name of an organization, such as Ford Motor Company, rather than the name of a specific product.

## 11-6a **Value of Branding**

Both buyers and sellers benefit from branding. Brands help buyers recognize specific products that meet their criteria for quality, which reduces the time needed to identify and purchase products by facilitating identification of products that satisfy consumer needs. Without brands, product selection would be more difficult because buyers would have fewer guideposts indicating quality and product features. For many consumers, purchasing certain brands is a form of self-expression. For instance, clothing brand names, such as The North Face or Ralph Lauren, are important to many consumers because they convey signals about their lifestyle or self-image. Especially when a customer is unable to judge a product's quality, a brand indicates a quality level and image to the customer and reduces a buyer's perceived risk of purchase. Customers want to purchase brands whose quality they trust, such as Coca-Cola, Apple, and Panera. In addition, customers might receive a psychological reward from purchasing and owning a brand that symbolizes high status, such as Aston Martin or Chanel. On the other hand, conspicuous brand usage that is considered to be attention-getting can cause dilution in some

**brand mark** The part of a brand that is not made up of words, such as a symbol or design

**trademark** A legal designation of exclusive use of a brand

**trade name** The full legal name of an organization

## MARKETING DEBATE

### Should the Public Know Who's Funding Research and Advocacy?

**ISSUE: Should marketers have to disclose funding of research and advocacy groups?**

Coca-Cola is among the soft-drink marketers, candy marketers, and other businesses that have been accused of selling foods and beverages that contribute to public-health problems such as obesity. Coca-Cola has, in fact, invested millions of dollars in marketing campaigns to encourage consumers to be more active and exercise regularly.

The company also gave $1.5 million to start the Global Energy Balance Network, a nonprofit advocacy group led by academic experts. This group deemphasized the role of nutrition in obesity and heavily promoted increased physical activity. The connection between the business and the nonprofit was never disclosed—until a major newspaper revealed Coca-Cola's financial support in a published report.

Coca-Cola responded by saying that it had never attempted to hide its support of researchers and nonprofit organizations, and that it wanted to have a positive impact on public-health issues such as obesity. "Coca-Cola has always believed that a healthy diet and regular exercise are essential for a healthy lifestyle," the CEO stated in *The Wall Street Journal*. He vowed to be more open about dealings with researchers and nonprofit groups, and appointed an independent committee to advise on such funding. As the controversy simmered on, the Coca-Cola official in charge of working with the Global Energy Balance Network retired, and the nonprofit group disbanded. So do consumers have the right to know when a company has paid for research or advocacy groups?[b]

cases. Some brand users with a low self–brand connection may have a harder time connecting with the brand. For example, showing-off behaviors such as wearing Gucci sunglasses indoors may be perceived negatively by brand users.[22]

Sellers also benefit from branding because brands are identifiers that make repeat purchasing easier for customers, thereby fostering brand loyalty. Furthermore, branding helps a firm introduce a new product by carrying the name and image of one or more existing products—buyers are more likely to experiment with the new product because of familiarity with products carrying firm's existing brand names. It also facilitates promotional efforts because the promotion of each branded product indirectly promotes all other products bearing the same brand. As consumers become loyal to a specific brand, the company's market share will achieve a level of stability, allowing the firm to use its resources more efficiently.

Branding also involves a cultural dimension in that consumers confer their own social meanings onto them. A brand appeals to customers on an emotional level based on its symbolic image and key associations.[23] For some brands, such as Harley-Davidson and Apple, this can result in an almost cult-like following. These brands may develop communities of loyal customers that communicate through get-togethers, online forums, blogs, podcasts, and other means. They may even help consumers to develop their identity and self-concept and serve as a form of self-expression. In fact, the term *cultural branding* has been used to explain how a brand conveys a powerful myth that consumers find useful in cementing their identities.[24] It is also important for marketers to recognize that brands are not completely within their control because a brand exists independently in the consumer's mind. Every aspect of a brand is subject to a consumer's emotional involvement, interpretation, and memory. By understanding how branding influences purchases, marketers can foster customer loyalty.[25]

## 11-6b **Brand Equity**

A well-managed brand is an asset to an organization. The value of this asset is often referred to as brand equity. **Brand equity** is the marketing and financial value associated with a brand's strength in a market. In addition to actual proprietary brand assets, such as patents and trademarks, four major elements underlie brand equity: brand name awareness, brand loyalty, perceived brand quality, and brand associations (see Figure 11.4).[26]

Being aware of a brand leads to brand familiarity, which results in a level of comfort with the brand. A consumer is more likely to select a familiar brand than an unfamiliar one because the familiar brand is more likely to be viewed as reliable and of an acceptable level of quality. The familiar brand is also likely to be in a customer's consideration set, whereas the unfamiliar brand is not.

**brand equity** The marketing and financial value associated with a brand's strength in a market

Figure 11.4    **Major Elements of Brand Equity**

**Brand loyalty** is a customer's favorable attitude toward a specific brand. If brand loyalty is sufficiently strong, customers will purchase the brand consistently when they need a product in that specific product category. Customer satisfaction with a brand is the most common reason for loyalty to that brand.[27] Companies with the most brand loyalty include JetBlue (airlines), Amazon (online retailer), Ritz-Carlton (luxury hotels), Dunkin' Donuts (coffee and packaged coffee), Shell (gasoline), and Discover (credit cards).[28] Brand loyalty has advantages for the customer as well as the manufacturer and seller. It reduces a buyer's risks and shortens the time spent deciding which product to purchase. The degree of brand loyalty is highly variable among product categories. For instance, it is challenging for a firm to foster brand loyalty for products such as fruits or vegetables, because customers can readily judge their quality by looking at them in the grocery store without referring to a brand. However, when consumers perceive products as being green or sustainable, their attitude toward the brand tends to improve.[29]

The rapid pace of technological transformation also presents challenges for marketers. With new computers, apps, and other digital devices entering the market at an ever more rapid pace, it can be difficult for marketers to sustain a high level of emotional engagement with consumers, and therefore retain their loyalty from year to year. Brand loyalty also varies by country, as different cultures may identify with a certain brand to a greater or lesser degree. Globally, international tech brands Apple, Google, and Microsoft have a higher degree of brand loyalty than brands in other product categories.[30]

There are three degrees of brand loyalty: recognition, preference, and insistence. **Brand recognition** occurs when a customer is aware that the brand exists and views it as an alternative purchase if the preferred brand is unavailable or if the other available brands are unfamiliar. This is the weakest form of brand loyalty. **Brand preference** is a stronger degree of brand loyalty. A customer has a definite preference for one brand over competitive offerings, and will purchase this brand if it is available. However, if the brand is not available, the customer will accept a substitute rather than expending the additional effort required to find and purchase the preferred brand. **Brand insistence** is the strongest and least common level of brand loyalty. A customer will accept no substitute and is willing to spend a great deal of time and effort to acquire that brand. If a brand-insistent customer goes to a store and finds the brand unavailable, he or she will seek the brand elsewhere rather than purchase a substitute. Brand insistence also can apply to service products, such as Hilton Hotels, or sports teams, such as the Dallas Cowboys. Although rare, marketers aspire to achieve brand insistence.

Brand loyalty is an important component of brand equity because it reduces a brand's vulnerability to competitors' actions. It allows an organization to retain existing customers and avoid expending significant resources to gain new ones. Loyal customers help to promote a brand by providing visibility and reassuring potential new customers of the brand's quality. Retailers strive to carry the brands known for their strong

**brand loyalty** A customer's favorable attitude toward a specific brand

**brand recognition** The degree of brand loyalty in which a customer is aware that a brand exists and views the brand as an alternative purchase if their preferred brand is unavailable

**brand preference** The degree of brand loyalty in which a customer prefers one brand over competitive offerings

**brand insistence** The degree of brand loyalty in which a customer strongly prefers a specific brand and will accept no substitute

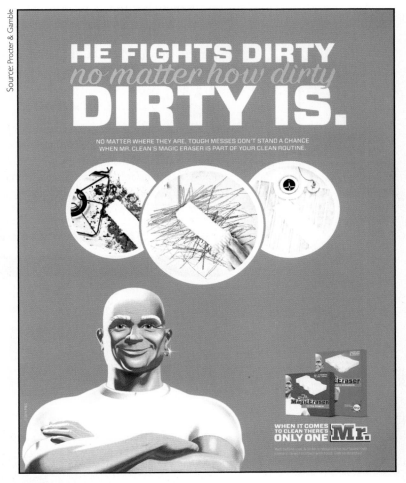

Source: Procter & Gamble

**Trade Character**
The Mr. Clean bald man with an earring is a highly recognizable brand character, even among those who do not use Mr. Clean cleaning products.

customer following to satisfy customers because they expect these brands to be available when and where they shop.

Customers associate a particular brand with a certain level of overall quality. As mentioned, customers frequently use a brand name as a proxy for an actual assessment of a product's quality. In many cases, customers cannot actually judge the quality of the product for themselves and instead must rely on the brand as a quality indicator. A consumer looking to purchase a new car might have never purchased a Toyota or Honda vehicle. However, because the brands rank among the highest in quality, a potential car buyer might give preference to them over other brands.[31]

The set of associations linked to a brand is another key component of brand equity. At times, a marketer works to connect a particular lifestyle or, in some instances, a certain personality type with a specific brand. These types of brand associations contribute significantly to the brand's equity. Brand associations sometimes are facilitated by using trade characters, such as the GEICO Gecko, Mr. Clean, and the Keebler Elves. Placing these trade characters in advertisements and on packaging helps consumers to link the ads and packages with the brands. This practice is particularly effective with younger consumers, which is why many cereals and candies feature licensed characters such as Dora the Explorer.[32] For instance, Mr. Clean usually portrays its bald man with an earring trade character in advertisements for its cleaning products. This advertisement reminds buyers that Mr. Clean "fights dirty no matter how dirty dirty is" and shows messes that its Magic Eraser product cleans up. Consumers immediately recognize that it is an ad for a cleaning product because the trade character is so recognizable.

Although difficult to measure, brand equity represents the value of a brand to an organization—it includes both tangible assets and intangibles such as public perception and consumer loyalty. Table 11.1 lists the top 10 brands with the highest economic value. Any company that owns a brand listed in Table 11.1 would agree that equity is likely to be the greatest single asset in the organization's possession.

## 11-6c  Types of Brands

There are three categories of brands: manufacturer, private distributor, and generic. **Manufacturer brands** are initiated by producers and ensure that producers are identified with their products at the point of purchase—for example, Green Giant, Dell Computer, and Levi's jeans. A manufacturer brand usually requires a producer to become involved in distribution, promotion, and to some extent, pricing decisions.

**manufacturer brands** A brand initiated by producers to ensure that producers are identified with their products at the point of purchase

Table 11.1  **The 10 Most Valuable Brands in the World**

| Rank | Brand | Brand Value ($ Billions) |
|------|-------|--------------------------|
| 1 | Apple | 247.0 |
| 2 | Google | 173.7 |
| 3 | Microsoft | 115.5 |
| 4 | IBM | 94.0 |
| 5 | Visa | 92.0 |
| 6 | AT&T | 89.5 |
| 7 | Verizon | 86.0 |
| 8 | Coca-Cola | 83.8 |
| 9 | McDonald's | 81.2 |
| 10 | Marlboro | 80.4 |

Source: Millward Brown, "BrandZ Top 100 Most Valuable Global Brands, 2015," https://www.millwardbrown.com/BrandZ/2015/Global/2015_BrandZ_Top100_Chart.pdf (accessed February 25, 2016).

**Private distributor brands** (also called *private brands, store brands*, or *dealer brands*) are initiated and owned by resellers—wholesalers or retailers. The major characteristic of private brands is that the manufacturers are not identified on the products. Retailers and wholesalers use private distributor brands to develop more efficient promotion, generate higher gross margins, and change store image. Private distributor brands give retailers or wholesalers freedom to purchase products of a specified quality at the lowest cost without disclosing the identities of the manufacturers. Wholesaler brands include IGA (Independent Grocers' Alliance) and Topmost (General Grocer). Successful private brands are distributed nationally, and many rival the quality of manufacturer brands. Familiar retailer brand names include Target's Archer Farms and Up and Up, Walmart's Great Value, and Whole Foods' 365 Everyday Value. Sometimes retailers with successful private distributor brands start manufacturing their own products to gain more control over product costs, quality, and design in the hope of increasing profits. Sales of private labels have grown considerably as the quality of store brands has increased. Indeed, quality and benefits relative to price is a significant reason many shoppers choose store brands over manufacturer ones. In recent years, store brand sales have grown by 8.8 percent, while the leading national manufacturer brands have seen sales growth of just 0.7 percent.[33]

Some products, on the other hand, are not branded at all, which is often called *generic branding*. **Generic brands** indicate only the product category and do not include the company name or other identifying terms. These items are typically staples that would be marketed using an undifferentiated strategy because they lack special features, such as sugar, salt, or aluminum foil. Generic brands usually are sold at lower prices than comparable branded items and compete on the basis of price and value. The prevalence of generic brands has decreased over time, particularly as the quality and value of private brands have increased.

## 11-6d Selecting a Brand Name

Marketers consider several factors in selecting a brand name. First, the name should be easy for customers (including foreign buyers if the firm intends to market its products in other countries) to say, spell, and recall. Short, one-syllable names, such as Cheer, often satisfy this requirement. Second, the brand name should indicate in some way the product's major benefits and, if possible, should suggest the product's uses and special characteristics. Marketers should always avoid negative or offensive references. Thus, the brand names of household cleaning products such as Ajax dishwashing liquid, Vanish toilet bowl cleaner, Formula 409 multipurpose cleaner, Cascade dishwasher detergent, and Wisk laundry detergent connote strength and effectiveness. On the other hand, Tata Motors was forced to rename its Zica hatchback Tiago because of its similarity to Zika, a dangerous mosquito-borne virus.[34] There is evidence that consumers are more likely to recall and to evaluate favorably names that convey positive attributes or benefits.[35] Third, to set it apart from competing brands, the brand should be distinctive. Further research findings have shown that creating a brand personality that aligns with the products sold and the target market's self-image is important to brand success—if the target market feels aligned with the brand, they are more likely to develop brand loyalty.[36] If a marketer intends to use a brand for a product line, that brand must be compatible with all products in the line. Finally, a brand should be designed to be used and recognized in all types of media. Finding the right brand has become an increasingly challenging task because many obvious names have already been used.

Marketers can devise brand names from single or multiple words—for example, Dodge Nitro. Letters and numbers, alone or in combination, are used to create such brands as the Honda CR-V or Toshiba's KIRAbook 13 computer. Words, numbers, and letters are combined to yield brand names, such as Apple iPhone 6s Plus or BMW's 528i xDrive sedan. To avoid terms that have negative connotations, marketers sometimes use fabricated words that have absolutely no meaning when created—for example, Häagen-Dazs. For marketing in China, U.S. brands strive to use names that translate well and have significant meaning in Chinese, but stay true to their U.S. identities. Thus Starbucks goes by Starry Hope, which is consistent with its U.S. logo. Nike calls itself "Nai ke," which translates to "endurance and perseverance" but sounds like its U.S. name; rival Reebok is called "Rui bu," which means "fast steps."[37]

**private distributor brands**
A brand initiated and owned by a reseller

**generic brands** A brand indicating only the product category

Who actually creates brand names? Brand names are generally created by individuals or a team within the organization. Sometimes a name is suggested by individuals who are close to the development of the product. Some organizations have committees that participate in brand-name creation and approval. Large companies that introduce numerous new products annually are likely to have a department that develops brand names. At times, outside consultants and companies that specialize in brand-name development are used.

## 11-6e  Protecting a Brand

A marketer should also design a brand that can be protected easily through registration. A series of court decisions has created a broad hierarchy of protection based on brand type. From most protectable to least protectable, these brand types are fanciful (Exxon), arbitrary (Dr Pepper), suggestive (Spray 'n Wash), and descriptive (Minute Rice). Generic terms, such as aluminum foil, are not protectable. Surnames and descriptive, geographic, or functional names are difficult to protect.[38] However, research findings show that consumers prefer these descriptive and suggestive brand names and find them easier to recall compared with fanciful and arbitrary brand names.[39] A firm should take steps so that its brands are protected and trademarks are renewed as needed.

To guard its exclusive rights to a brand, a company must ensure that the brand is not likely to be considered an infringement on any brand already registered with the U.S. Patent and Trademark Office. Actually proving that patent infringement has occurred may be complex because infringement is determined by the courts, which base their decisions on whether a brand causes consumers to be confused, mistaken, or deceived about the source of the product. McDonald's is the company probably most famous for aggressively protecting its trademarks against infringement by launching legal charges against a number of companies with *Mc* names. It fears that use of the prefix will give consumers the impression that these companies are associated with or owned by McDonald's.

A marketer should guard against allowing a brand name to become a generic term because these cannot be protected as exclusive brand names. For example, *aspirin, escalator*, and *shredded wheat*—all brand names at one time—eventually were declared generic terms that refer to product classes. Thus, they could no longer be protected. To keep a brand name from becoming a generic term, the firm should spell the name with a capital letter and use it as an adjective to modify the name of the general product class and include the word *brand* after the brand name, as in Kool-Aid Brand Soft Drink Mix or Kleenex Brand Tissues.[40] An organization can deal with this problem directly by advertising that its brand is a trademark and should not be used generically. The firm also can indicate that the brand is a registered trademark by using the symbol ®.

A U.S. firm that tries to protect a brand in a foreign country is likely to encounter additional problems. In many countries, brand registration is not possible. In such places, the first firm to use a brand in such a country automatically has the rights to it. In some instances, U.S. companies actually have had to buy their own brand rights from a firm in a foreign country because the foreign firm was the first user in that country. Consider that in China, "trademark squatters" look for valuable foreign brands and rush to register them as trademarks there. When the actual brand owners attempt to launch their products in China, they are forced to buy back their trademark for huge sums, rebrand their product, or spend considerable time and money fighting the infringement in Chinese courts.[41]

Marketers trying to protect their brands also must contend with brand counterfeiting. In the United States, for instance, one can purchase fake General Motors parts, Cartier and Rolex watches, Louis Vuitton handbags, Walt Disney character dolls, Microsoft software, Warner Brothers clothing, Mont Blanc pens, and a host of other products illegally marketed by manufacturers that do not own the brands. Annual trade losses caused by counterfeit products are estimated at $250 billion. This number is continuing to rise, with estimates placing losses at more than $1 trillion in upcoming years. The most commonly counterfeited products are handbags and wallets, watches and jewelry, and consumer electronics.[42] Counterfeit products not only harm manufacturers, but can also harm consumers when their manufacture is subpar or they are made of harmful ingredients.

## 11-6f **Branding Strategies**

Before establishing branding strategies, a firm must decide whether to brand its products at all. If a company's product is homogeneous and similar to competitors' products, it may be difficult to brand in a way that will result in consumer loyalty. Raw materials and commodities such as coal, carrots, or gravel are hard to brand because of their homogeneity and their physical characteristics.

If a firm chooses to brand its products, it may use individual or family branding, or a combination. **Individual branding** is a policy of naming each product differently. Nestlé S.A., the world's largest food and nutrition company, uses individual branding for many of its 6,000 different brands, such as Nescafé coffee, PowerBar nutritional food, Maggi soups, and Häagen-Dazs ice cream. A major advantage of individual branding is that if an organization introduces a product that fails in the marketplace, the negative images associated with it do not influence consumers' decisions to purchase the company's other products. An individual branding strategy may also facilitate market segmentation when a firm wishes to enter many segments of the same market. Separate, unrelated names can be used, and each brand can be aimed at a specific segment. With individual branding, however, a firm cannot capitalize on the positive image associated with successful products.

When using **family branding**, all of a firm's products are branded with the same name, or part of the name, such as the cereals Kellogg's Frosted Flakes, Kellogg's Rice Krispies, and Kellogg's Corn Flakes. In some cases, a company's name is combined with other words, such as with Arm & Hammer Heavy Duty Detergent, Arm & Hammer Pure Baking Soda, and Arm & Hammer Carpet Deodorizer, which uses the "Arm & Hammer" name followed by a description. Unlike individual branding, family branding means that the promotion of one item with the family brand promotes the firm's other products.

Family branding can be a benefit when consumers have positive associations with brands, or a drawback if something happens to make consumers think negatively of the brand. For example, Johnson's Baby, a brand produced by Johnson & Johnson, was criticized for putting potentially harmful chemicals in some of its products, causing some health-conscious consumers to mistrust all the products carrying the brand name. In response to consumer outrage, Johnson & Johnson reformulated the products, restoring trust in the entire family of products.[43]

An organization is not limited to a single branding strategy. A company that uses primarily individual branding for many of its products also may use family branding for a specific product line. Branding strategy is influenced by the number of products and product lines the company produces, the number and types of competing products available, and the size of the firm.

## 11-6g **Brand Extensions**

A **brand extension** occurs when an organization uses one of its existing brands to brand a new product in a different product category. For example, Tesla—which makes upscale electric cars—introduced a line of battery products for residential and commercial use under the Tesla brand.[44] A brand extension should not be confused with a line extension, which will be discussed in greater detail in Chapter 12. A line extension refers to using an existing brand on a new product in the same product category, such as new flavors or sizes. Victorinox has long been known for its Swiss Army brand of multi-function knives and tools. The advertisement shows that Victorinox has extended the Swiss Army brand and its trademark red color to a number of other product categories including watches, luggage, apparel, and fragrances. The tagline of the ad, "Functionality is part of our family," reminds consumers of the versatility of its renowned Swiss Army knife and strives to attach those qualities to entirely new types of products in the minds of consumers.

If a brand is extended too many times or extended too far outside its original product category, it can be weakened through dilution of its image and symbolic impact. For example, Heineken shoes has been voted as one of the worst brand extensions because shoes do not appear to relate to its iconic beer product.[45] Research has found that a line extension into premium categories can be an effective strategy to revitalize a brand, but the extension needs to

**individual branding** A branding strategy in which each product is given a different name

**family branding** Branding all of a firm's products with the same name or part of the name

**brand extension** An organization uses one of its existing brands to brand a new product in a different product category

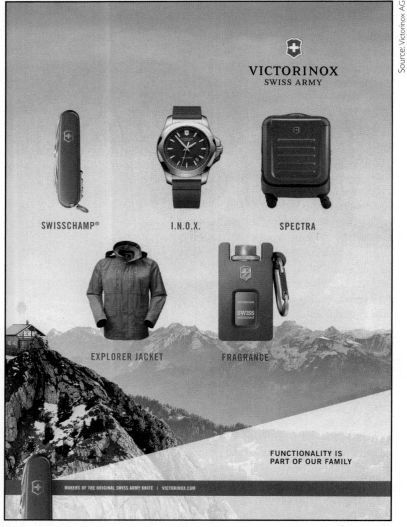

Source: Victorinox AG

**Brand Extensions**
Victorinox extended the Swiss Army brand from its venerable line of multi-tool knives to watches, luggage, clothing, and even fragrances.

be closely linked to the core brand.[46] Successful branding strategies for new product categories depend largely on how they fit with the product categories of the parent brand, as well as how the positioning of the new product is similar to how the parent brand is positioned.[47] Table 11.2 describes brand extensions that failed because they were too dissimilar to their core product.

## 11-6h Co-Branding

**Co-branding** is the use of two or more brands on one product. Marketers employ co-branding to capitalize on the brand equity of multiple brands. For instance, Benjamin Moore partnered with the retailer, Target, to release a co-branded line of paint colors that coordinate with Target's kids' furniture and accessories collection.[48] Co-branding is popular in several processed-food categories and in the credit card industry. The brands used for co-branding can be owned by the same company. Many food items are co-branded initially. Cinnabon has released co-branded items with Kellogg's (cereal) and Pillsbury (Toaster Strudel).

Effective co-branding capitalizes on the trust and confidence customers have in the brands involved. For instance, Harley Davidson successfully teamed up with Best Western to develop a rewards program for motorcycle enthusiasts. At more than 1,200 hotels throughout the United States, motorcycle enthusiasts can receive a free wipe-down motorcycle towel and other benefits. The partnership was so successful that it was extended for three years and expanded to areas outside

### Table 11.2 **Worst Brand Extensions**

| Brand Name | Core Product | Failed Brand Extension |
|---|---|---|
| Smith & Wesson | Firearms | Mountain Bikes |
| Bic | Pens | Bic Underwear |
| Cosmopolitan | Magazine | Yogurt |
| Wrigley | Candy | Life Savers Soda |
| Coors | Beer | Rocky Mountain Spring Water |
| Colgate | Consumer products | Colgate Kitchen Entrees |
| Frito-Lay | Snack foods | Lemonade |
| Harley-Davidson | Motorcycles | Perfume |

**co-branding** Using two or more brands on one product

Source: "Top 25 Biggest Product Flops of All Time," *DailyFinance*, www.dailyfinance.com/photos/top-25-biggest-product-flops-of-all-time (accessed February 26, 2016).

of the United States.[49] The brands should not lose their identities, and it should be clear to customers which brand is the main brand. It is important for marketers to understand before entering a co-branding relationship that when a co-branded product is unsuccessful, both brands are implicated in the failure. To gain customer acceptance, the brands involved must represent a complementary fit in the minds of buyers. Trying to link a brand such as Harley-Davidson with a brand such as Healthy Choice would not achieve co-branding objectives because customers are not likely to perceive these brands as compatible.

### 11-6i Brand Licensing

A popular branding strategy involves **brand licensing**, an agreement in which a company permits another organization to use its brand on other products for a licensing fee. Royalties may be as low as 2 percent of wholesale revenues or higher than 10 percent. The licensee is responsible for all manufacturing, selling, and advertising functions and bears the costs if the licensed product fails. The top U.S. licensing company is Disney Consumer Products, the products arm of the Walt Disney Company, with $45 billion in licensing revenue.[50] Sports is an industry that engages in much licensing, with the NFL, the NCAA, NASCAR, and Major League Baseball, all leaders in the retail sales of licensed sports-related products. The advantages of licensing range from extra revenues and the low cost of brand expansion to generating free publicity, developing a new image, or protecting a trademark. The major disadvantages are a lack of manufacturing control and the risks of making consumers feel bombarded with too many unrelated products bearing the same name.

## 11-7 PACKAGING

Packaging involves the development of a container to hold a product. A package can be a vital part of a product, making it more versatile, safer, and easier to use. It also conveys vital information about the product and is an opportunity to display interesting graphic design elements. Like a brand name, a package can influence customers' attitudes toward a product and their decisions to purchase. Consequently, packaging convenience can be a major factor in purchase. Producers of jellies, sauces, and ketchups package their products in squeezable plastic containers that can be stored upside down, which make dispensing and storing the product more convenient. Package characteristics help to shape buyers' impressions of a product at the time of purchase and during use. In this section, we examine the main functions of packaging and consider several major packaging decisions. We also analyze the role of the package in a marketing strategy.

### 11-7a Packaging Functions

At the most basic level, packaging materials serve the basic purpose of protecting the product and maintaining its functional form. Fluids, like milk or orange juice, require packages that are waterproof and durable to preserve and protect their contents. Packaging should prevent damage that could affect the product's usefulness, which leads to higher costs. Packaging techniques have also been developed to prevent product tampering, as this has been a major problem for many firms. Some packages are also designed to deter shoplifting through the inclusion of antitheft devices.

Another function of packaging is to offer convenience to consumers. For instance, single-serving containers for food and drinks that do not require refrigeration appeal to children, parents, and those with active lifestyles because they are easily portable. Packaging can prevent product waste, make storage easier for retailers and for consumers, and even promote greater consumption. Additionally, packaging can promote a product by communicating its features, uses, benefits, and image. Sometimes a reusable package can make the product more desirable. SC Johnson encourages consumers to reuse their Windex bottles by selling smaller recyclable refill packages. These refills help reduce the waste that comes with purchasing an entirely new

**brand licensing** An agreement whereby a company permits another organization to use its brand on other products for a licensing fee bottle of Windex each time the old one runs out.[51] Finally, packaging can be used to communicate symbolically the quality or premium nature of a product. When Beech-Nut reformulated its baby foods to simplify the ingredients in response to mothers looking for more natural and simpler foods for their babies' first foods, it also redesigned the packaging. The baby food is now packaged in custom canning-jar style glass containers so that consumers can see the quality of the product. The new containers stack easily on the shelf and in transit, and they can be easily reused or recycled.[52] Packaging can also evoke an emotional response.

### 11-7b **Major Packaging Considerations**

Marketers must take many factors into account when designing and producing packages. Obviously, a major consideration is cost. Although a number of different packaging materials, processes, and designs are available, costs can vary greatly. In recent years, buyers have shown a willingness to pay more for improved packaging, but there are limits. Marketers should conduct research to determine exactly how much customers are willing to pay for effective and efficient package designs.

Increasingly, firms are finding that they can cut down on the cost of packaging and be more environmentally-friendly through developing minimalist packaging. Redesigned packaging requires fewer materials, is easier and cheaper to ship because it is lighter, and consumers appreciate the lower carbon footprint. Kraft Foods saved more than a million pounds of packaging a year simply by redesigning the zipper on its bags of pre-grated cheese.[53]

As mentioned previously, developing tamper-resistant packaging is very important for certain products. Although no package is completely tamper-proof, marketers can develop packages that are difficult to contaminate. At a minimum, all packaging must comply with the Food and Drug Administration's packaging regulations. However, packaging should also make any product tampering evident to resellers and consumers. Although effective tamper-resistant packaging may be expensive to develop, when compared to the potential costs of lost sales, loss of consumer confidence and company reputation, and potentially expensive product liability lawsuits, the costs of ensuring consumer safety through safer packaging are relatively small.

Marketers should consider how much consistency is desirable between the package designs of different products produced by an organization. If a firm's products are unrelated or aimed at very different target markets, no consistency may be the best policy. In many cases, however, packaging uniformity may be best, especially if a firm's products are unrelated or aimed at vastly different target markets. To promote an overall company image, a firm may decide that all packages should be similar or should all feature a major design element. This approach is called **family packaging**. It is generally used for lines of products, as with Campbell's soups, Weight Watchers' foods, or Planters Nuts.

A package's promotional role is an important consideration. Through verbal and nonverbal symbols, the package can inform potential buyers about the product's content, features, uses, advantages, and hazards. Pangea Organics, for instance, shows its commitment to natural ingredients and sustainability by packaging its soaps in containers embedded with seeds. Its boxes are made of recycled ingredients that, when buried in the ground, yield a plant such as a basil or a spruce tree. Packaged in sleek grey boxes with pleasing design features, the label on Pangea's soaps clearly display this creative means of promoting the firm's product and commitment to the cause of sustainability.[54]

A firm can create desirable images and associations by its choice of color, design, shape, and texture. Many cosmetics manufacturers, for example, design their packages to create impressions of luxury and exclusivity. A package performs a promotional function when it is designed to be safer or more convenient to use if such characteristics help stimulate demand.

A package designer must consider size, shape, texture, color, and graphics—as well as functionality—to develop a package that has a definite promotional value. Clever design can make a package appear taller or shorter or larger or smaller, depending on the desire of the marketer and expectations of consumers.

**family packaging** Using similar packaging for all of a firm's products or packaging that has one common design element

Marketers often carefully consider what colors to use on packages to attract attention and positively influence customers' emotions. People associate specific colors with certain feelings and experiences. Here are some examples:

- White represents sincerity, simplicity, and purity.
- Yellow is associated with cheerfulness, optimism, and friendliness.
- Red connotes excitement and stimulation.
- Pink is considered soft, nurturing, and feminine.
- Blue is soothing; it is also associated with intelligence, trust, and security.
- Black represents power, status, and sophistication.
- Purple is associated with dignity, quality, and luxury.
- Brown is linked to seriousness, ruggedness, and earthiness.
- Green is associated with nature and sustainability.[55]

When opting for color on packaging, marketers must judge whether a particular color will evoke positive or negative feelings when linked to a specific product. Thus, marketers are not likely to package meat or bread in green materials because customers may associate green with mold. Marketers must also determine whether a specific target market will respond favorably or unfavorably to a color.

Packaging also must meet the needs of resellers. Wholesalers and retailers consider whether a package facilitates transportation, storage, and handling. Resellers may refuse to carry certain products if their packages are cumbersome or require too much shelf space. For instance, concentrated versions of laundry detergents and fabric softeners aid retailers and shoppers alike by offering products in smaller containers that are easier to transport, store, and display.

A final consideration is whether to develop packages that are viewed as environmentally responsible. Nearly one-half of all garbage consists of discarded plastic packaging, such as polystyrene containers, plastic soft-drink bottles, and carryout bags. Plastic packaging material does not biodegrade, and paper requires the destruction of valuable forests. Consequently, many companies have changed to environmentally sensitive packaging that is recycled, lighter weight, and uses fewer materials.

## 11-7c  Packaging and Marketing Strategy

Packaging can be a major component of a marketing strategy. A new cap or closure, a better box or wrapper, or a more convenient container may give a product a competitive advantage. The right type of package for a new product can help it gain market recognition very quickly. Apple Inc. recognizes that packaging is an important element of the customer experience. Apple believes that the experience of opening the package is particularly important to enhancing

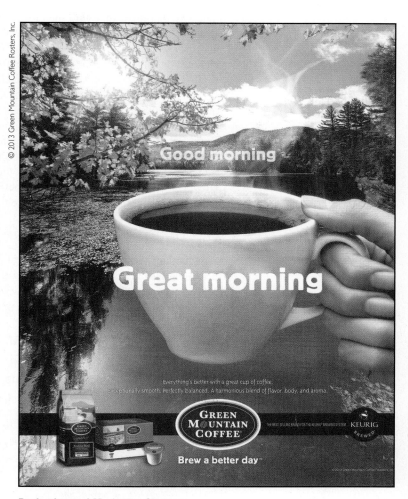

© 2013 Green Mountain Coffee Roasters, Inc.

**Packaging and Marketing Strategy**
Offering a range of packaging options that address the different needs of consumers helps Green Mountain Coffee increase sales and consumer loyalty.

the customer experience. For this reason, the company maintains a secret packaging area where packaging is designed and tested.[56] This advertisement for Green Mountain Coffee emphasizes the quality and satisfaction the product can bring, showing someone holding a cup of coffee against a beautiful landscape. The advertisement also emphasizes the different types of packaging in which the coffee is sold, which underscores the range of options available to consumers. If consumers prefer freshly ground coffee, they can purchase the bags. If they like convenience or variety, Keurig K-Cups allow consumers to brew a single serving of coffee in a matter of seconds.

In the case of existing brands, marketers should reevaluate packages periodically. Marketers should view packaging as a strategic tool, especially for consumer convenience products. When considering the strategic uses of packaging, marketers must also analyze the cost of packaging and package changes. In this section, we will examine several ways to use packaging strategically in marketing efforts.

## Altering the Package

At times, a marketer changes a package or labeling because the existing design is no longer in style, especially when compared with the packaging of competitive products. Nestlé hired global brand and design consultancy Elmwood to redesign the packaging of its Acti-V yogurt. The redesign, which incorporated a packaging shape that communicated the benefits of the product in a way that resonated with the target market, caused sales to substantially increase in Hong Kong.[57] A package may be redesigned because new product features need to be highlighted or because new packaging materials have become available. Cleaning supply company Seventh Generation sells its 4x concentrated laundry detergent in a paper bottle, which encloses a plastic shell. The design is innovative, completely recyclable, and requires fewer materials to make.[58]

An organization may also decide to change a product's packaging to make the product safer or more convenient to use. When Procter & Gamble released its popular Tide Pods product, it did not anticipate that children would mistake the colorful packaging and pods as candy. After a number of children were poisoned by the pods, Procter & Gamble developed a double safety latch for the packaging and redesigned the transparent container to make it opaque. These moves were meant to make the pods look less like candy and harder for children to open. However, continued ingestions led Procter & Gamble and other laundry pod manufacturers to make additional modifications to make the packaging safer.[59]

## Secondary-Use Packaging

A secondary-use package can be reused for purposes other than its initial function. For example, a margarine container can be reused to store leftovers, and a jelly container can serve as a drinking glass. Customers often view secondary-use packaging as adding value to products, in which case its use should stimulate unit sales.

## Category-Consistent Packaging

With category-consistent packaging, the product is packaged in line with the packaging practices associated with a particular product category. Some product categories—for example, mayonnaise, mustard, ketchup, and peanut butter—have traditional package shapes. Other product categories are characterized by recognizable color combinations, such as red and white for soup and red, white, and blue for Ritz-like crackers. When an organization introduces a brand in one of these product categories, marketers will often use traditional package shapes and color combinations to ensure that customers will recognize the new product as being in that specific product category.

## Innovative Packaging

Sometimes a marketer employs a unique cap, design, applicator, or other feature to make a product distinctive. Such packaging can be effective when the innovation makes the product safer, easier to use, or provides better protection. Marketers also use innovative or unique packages that are inconsistent with traditional packaging practices to make the brand stand out from its competitors. Basing their packaging on research findings that wine drinkers tend to decide which product to purchase in the store, not in advance, Stack Wine offers its products in unique single-serve cups. The cups are filled with wine, sealed, and come stacked together in four packs. The unique packaging is eye-catching and practical, designed for parties, camping, or other situations where wine glasses are not readily available. It is also a convenient product for the occasional wine drinker, who may not want to open an entire bottle just to have one glass.[60] Unusual packaging sometimes requires expending considerable resources, not only when designing the package but also on making customers aware of the unique package and why it is an improvement. Researchers suggest that uniquely shaped packages that attract attention are likely to be perceived as containing a higher volume of product than comparable products that generate less attention.[61]

**Innovative Packaging**
Using vacuum-sealed packaging is an innovative way to preserve the freshness of apples with minimal waste.

## Multiple Packaging

Rather than packaging a single unit of a product, marketers sometimes use twin packs, tri-packs, six-packs, or other forms of multiple packaging. For certain types of products, multiple packaging may increase demand because it increases the amount of the product available at the point of consumption (e.g., in one's house). It may also increase consumer acceptance of the product by encouraging the buyer to try the product several times. Multiple packaging can make products easier to handle and store, as in the case of six-packs for soft drinks, and it can facilitate special price offers, such as two-for-one sales. However, multiple packaging does not work well for all types of products. One would not use additional table salt, for example, simply because an extra box is in the pantry.

## Handling-Improved Packaging

A product's packaging may be changed to make it easier to handle in the distribution channel—for example, by altering the outer carton or using special bundling, shrink-wrapping, or pallets. In some cases, the shape of the package itself is changed. An ice cream producer, for instance, may adopt a rectangular-shaped package over a cylindrical one to facilitate handling. In addition, at the retail level, the ice cream producer may be able to get more shelf facings with a rectangular package than with a round one. Outer containers for products are sometimes altered so they will proceed more easily through automated warehousing systems.

# 11-8 **LABELING**

**Labeling** is very closely related with packaging and is used for identification, promotional, informational, and legal purposes. Labels can be small or large relative to the size of the product and carry varying amounts of information. The stickers on a banana or apple, for example, are small and display only the brand name of the fruit, the type, and perhaps a stock-keeping unit number. A label can be part of the package itself or a separate feature attached to the package. The label on a can of Coke is actually part of the can, whereas the label on a two-liter bottle of Coke is separate and can be removed. Information presented on a label may include the

**labeling** Providing identifying, promotional, or other information on package labels brand name and mark, the registered trademark symbol, package size and content, product features, nutritional information, presence of potential allergens, type and style of the product, number of servings, care instructions, directions for use and safety precautions, the name and address of the manufacturer, expiration dates, seals of approval, and other facts.

Labels can facilitate the identification of a product by displaying the brand name in combination with a unique graphic design. For instance, Heinz ketchup and Coca-Cola are both easy to identify on a supermarket shelf because of their iconic labels, which feature the name and recognizable brand marks. By drawing attention to products and their benefits, labels can strengthen an organization's promotional efforts. Labels may contain promotional messages, such as "Thirty percent more at no additional cost." Also, a label might be about a new or improved product feature, such as "New, improved scent."

Several federal laws and regulations specify information that must be included on the labels of certain products. Garments must be labeled with the name of the manufacturer, country of manufacture, fabric content, and cleaning instructions. Labels on nonedible items, such as shampoos and detergents, must include both safety precautions and directions for use. The Nutrition Labeling Act of 1990 requires the FDA to review food labeling and packaging for nutrition content, label format, ingredient labeling, food descriptions, and health messages. Any food product making a nutritional claim must follow standardized nutrition labeling. Food product labels must state the number of servings per container, serving size, number of calories per serving, number of calories derived from fat, number of carbohydrates, and amounts of specific nutrients such as vitamins. Many firms that used to feature the word "Natural" on their product labels are retracting that claim in an effort to protect themselves from lawsuits. Though natural food products are profitable, bringing in more than $40 billion in annual U.S. retail sales, the claim is problematic because there are no regulations for what is natural. General Mills is one of many companies that have been taken to court over its "Natural" claims; it agreed to stop using the term, "100% Natural" on its Nature Valley line because the products include processed and genetically modified ingredients. Until the Food and Drug Administration issues clearer guidelines for what constitutes natural ingredients, it is likely that more companies will change their labels to downplay their "natural" ingredients.[62]

Another concern for many manufacturers are the Federal Trade Commission's (FTC) guidelines regarding "Made in USA" labels, a problem owing to the increasingly global nature of manufacturing. Many countries attach high brand value to American-made brands, including Russia, India, Brazil, and China, giving U.S. firms an even greater incentive to adopt the "Made in USA" label.[63] The FTC requires that "all or virtually all" of a product's components be made in the United States if the label says "Made in USA." The "Made in USA" labeling issue remains complicated, as so many products involve parts sourced, produced, or assembled in places around the globe. Because business shows little sign of becoming less international, the FTC criteria for "Made in USA" are likely to be challenged and may be changed or adapted over time.[64]

PaCondryx/DigitalVision Vectors/Getty Images

**Labeling as Marketing Strategy**
Labeling can be an important part of the marketing strategy. The label can be attached to the packaging to communicate that the product is organic. Labeling can include claims about sustainability as well as other information that is potentially valuable to the buyer.

# Summary

### 11-1 Explain the concept of a product.

A product is a good, a service, an idea, or any combination of the three received in an exchange. It can be either tangible or intangible and includes functional, social, and psychological utilities or benefits. When consumers purchase a product, they are buying the benefits and satisfaction they think the product will provide.

### 11-2 Discuss how products are classified.

Products can be classified on the basis of the buyer's intentions. Consumer products are those purchased to satisfy personal and family needs. Business products are purchased for use in a firm's operations, to resell, or to make other products. Consumer products can be subdivided into convenience, shopping, specialty, and unsought products. Business products can be classified as installations, accessory equipment, raw materials, component parts, process materials, MRO supplies, and business services.

### 11-3 Explain the concepts of product line and product mix and how they are related.

A product item is a specific version of a product that can be designated as a distinct offering among an organization's products. A product line is a group of closely related product items that are considered a unit because of marketing, technical, or end-use considerations. The composite, or total, group of products that an organization makes available to customers is called the product mix. The width of the product mix is measured by the number of product lines the company offers. The depth of the product mix is the average number of different products offered in each product line.

### 11-4 Describe the product life cycle and its impact on marketing strategies.

The product life cycle describes how product items in an industry move through four stages: introduction, growth, maturity, and decline. The sales curve is at zero at introduction, rises at an increasing rate during growth, peaks during the maturity stage, and then declines. Profits peak toward the end of the growth stage of the product life cycle.

### 11-5 Discuss the product adoption process.

When customers accept a new product, they usually do so through a five-stage adoption process. The first stage is awareness, when buyers become aware that a product exists. Interest, the second stage, occurs when buyers seek information and are receptive to learning about the product. The third stage is evaluation—buyers consider the product's benefits and decide whether to try it. The fourth stage is trial, during which buyers examine, test, or try the product to determine if it meets their needs. The last stage is adoption, when buyers purchase the product and use it whenever a need for this general type of product arises.

### 11-6 Explain the major components of branding, including brand types, branding strategies, and brand protection.

A brand is a name, term, design, symbol, or any other feature that identifies one seller's good or service and distinguishes it from those of other sellers. Branding helps buyers to identify and evaluate products, helps sellers to facilitate product introduction and repeat purchasing, and fosters brand loyalty. Brand equity is the marketing and financial value associated with a brand's strength. It represents the value of a brand to an organization. The four major elements underlying brand equity include brand name awareness, brand loyalty, perceived brand quality, and brand associations.

There are three degrees of brand loyalty. Brand recognition occurs when a customer is aware that the brand exists and views it as an alternative purchase if the preferred brand is unavailable or if the other available brands are unfamiliar. Brand preference is a stronger degree of brand loyalty. Brand insistence is the strongest and least common level of brand loyalty.

A manufacturer brand is initiated by a producer. A private distributor brand is initiated and owned by a reseller, sometimes taking on the name of the store or distributor. A generic brand indicates only the product category and does not include the company name or other identifying terms. When selecting a brand name, a marketer should choose one that is easy to say, spell, and recall and that alludes to the product's uses, benefits, or special characteristics. Brand names can be devised from words, letters, numbers, nonsense words, or a combination of these. Companies protect ownership of their brands through registration with the U.S. Patent and Trademark Office.

Individual branding designates a unique name for each of a company's products. Family branding identifies all of a firm's products with a single name. A brand extension is the use of an existing name on a new or improved product in a different product category. Co-branding is the use of two or more brands on one product. Through a licensing agreement and for a licensing fee, a firm may permit another organization to use its brand on other products. Brand licensing enables producers to earn extra revenue, receive low-cost or free publicity, and protect their trademarks.

### 11-7 Describe the major packaging functions, design considerations, and how packaging is used in marketing strategies.

Packaging involves the development of a container and a graphic design for a product. Effective packaging offers protection, economy, safety, and convenience. It can influence a customer's purchase decision by promoting features, uses, benefits, and image. When developing a package, marketers must consider the value to the customer of efficient and effective packaging, offset by the price the customer is willing to pay. Other considerations include how to make the package tamper resistant, whether to use multiple packaging and family packaging, how to design the package as an effective promotional tool, and how best to accommodate resellers. Packaging can be an important part of an overall marketing strategy and can be used to target certain market segments. Modifications in packaging can revive a mature product and extend its product life cycle. Producers alter packages to convey new features or to make them safer or more convenient.

If a package has a secondary use, the product's value to the consumer may increase. Innovative packaging enhances a product's distinctiveness.

## 11-8   Identify the functions of labeling and legal issues related to labeling.

Labeling is closely interrelated with packaging and is used for identification, promotional, and informational and legal purposes. Various federal laws and regulations require that certain products be labeled or marked with warnings, instructions, nutritional information, manufacturer's identification, and perhaps other information.

---

**Go to www.cengagebrain.com for resources to help you master the content in this chapter as well as for materials that will expand your marketing knowledge!**

---

# Important Terms

| | | | |
|---|---|---|---|
| good 330 | MRO supplies 335 | product adoption | brand recognition 345 |
| service 330 | business services 336 | process 341 | brand preference 345 |
| idea 330 | product item 336 | innovators 342 | brand insistence 345 |
| consumer products 331 | product line 336 | early adopters 342 | manufacturer brands 346 |
| business products 331 | product mix 336 | early majority 342 | private distributor |
| convenience products 332 | width of product | late majority 342 | brands 347 |
| shopping products 332 | mix 336 | laggards 342 | generic brands 347 |
| specialty products 333 | depth of product | brand 342 | individual branding 349 |
| unsought products 334 | mix 336 | brand name 342 | family branding 349 |
| installations 334 | product life cycle 337 | brand mark 343 | brand extension 349 |
| accessory equipment 334 | introduction stage 337 | trademark 343 | co-branding 350 |
| raw materials 335 | growth stage 338 | trade name 343 | brand licensing 351 |
| component parts 335 | maturity stage 339 | brand equity 344 | family packaging 352 |
| process materials 335 | decline stage 340 | brand loyalty 345 | labeling 355 |

---

# Discussion and Review Questions

1. Is a personal computer sold at a retail store a consumer product or a business product? Defend your answer.
2. How do convenience products and shopping products differ? What are the distinguishing characteristics of each type of product?
3. How does an organization's product mix relate to its development of a product line? When should an enterprise add depth to its product line rather than width to its product mix?

4. How do industry profits change as a product moves through the four stages of its life cycle?
5. What are the stages in the product adoption process, and how do they affect the commercialization phase?
6. How does branding benefit consumers and marketers?
7. What is brand equity? Identify and explain the major elements of brand equity.
8. What are the three major degrees of brand loyalty?

9. Compare and contrast manufacturer brands, private distributor brands, and generic brands.
10. Identify the factors a marketer should consider in selecting a brand name.
11. What is co-branding? What major issues should be considered when using co-branding?
12. Describe the functions a package can perform. Which function is most important? Why?
13. What are the main factors a marketer should consider when developing a package?
14. In what ways can packaging be used as a strategic tool?
15. What are the major functions of labeling?

# Video Case 11.1

## GaGa: Not Just a Lady

Several years before Lady Gaga made her musical debut, Jim King started a company he named GaGa after his beloved grandmother. King, a Rhode Island television news anchor turned entrepreneur, planned to use his grandmother's recipe for frozen dessert as the basis of his first product. Because the lemony dessert contains more butterfat than sherbet and less butterfat than ice cream, he couldn't legally label it as either. So King came up with the idea of calling the product "SherBetter," using the word play to suggest that it's similar to sherbet, but better.

King wasn't intending to compete with major ice cream firms like Hood, Breyers, and Ben & Jerry's. First, as a tiny start-up business, GaGa couldn't begin to match the marketing resources of the national brands. Second, GaGa's focus would be much narrower than the big brands, because sherbets and sorbets make up only a tiny fraction of the overall market for ice cream products. King determined that GaGa would compete on the basis of high quality, all-natural ingredients, and a fresh, creamy taste. He coined the slogan "Smooth as ice cream, fresh like sherbet" to describe SherBetter's appeal.

After he cooked up batches of SherBetter in his home kitchen, King drove from grocery store to grocery store until he made a sale to his first retail customer, Munroe Dairy. This initial order for 500 pints of lemon Sher-Better was enough to get GaGa off to a solid start. During the first four years of business, the company marketed only one product—the original lemon SherBetter in pint containers. At that time, Stefani Germanotta shot to fame under the stage name of Lady Gaga, giving GaGa's frozen desserts an unexpected but welcome boost in brand awareness and sales.

Four years after founding GaGa, King realized that he could increase sales and increase his brand's visibility in supermarket frozen-food cases by expanding with sufficient products to fill a shelf. Over the next four years, he introduced raspberry, orange, and several other new flavors of SherBetter packed in pint containers. He also launched a line of frozen dessert novelty bars, called "SherBetter on a stick" because they're shaped like ice-cream bars. In addition, he decided to develop a tropical flavor to enhance his product offerings. That led to the introduction of toasted coconut SherBetter, a flavor that tested very well during GaGa's research. As he gained experience, King learned to account for cannibalization of existing products when he launched new products, knowing that overall sales would gain over time.

However, King didn't anticipate that supermarkets would display SherBetter pints and bars in separate freezer sections several doors away from each other. This complicated GaGa's marketing effort, because customers might not know they could buy SherBetter in both bars and pints unless they looked in both frozen-food sections. GaGa simply couldn't afford advertising to promote bars and pints. Instead, King and his wife Michelle, who serves as marketing director, began setting up a table outside the frozen-foods case in different supermarkets and distributing free samples on weekends. They found that when they offered samples, customers responded positively and the store sold a lot of GaGa products that day. This opened the door to repeat purchasing and brand loyalty.

©iStockphoto.com/loooby

One lesson King learned is that the GaGa brand is more memorable than the SherBetter product name. As a result, he changed the product packaging to emphasize the GaGa brand and its playful implications. After hiring professionals to analyze the company's marketing activities, he also learned that he should focus on what makes GaGa's products unique rather than trying to fit into the broader ice cream product category. The basics of high quality, a unique recipe, and a fun brand have helped King acquire distribution in 1,500 supermarkets and grocery stores throughout the Eastern United States.[65]

### Questions for Discussion

1. When GaGa began adding novelty bars in new flavors, what was the effect on the width and depth of its product mix?
2. Why is packaging particularly important for a company like GaGa, which can't afford advertising?
3. Do you think GaGa's SherBetter pints and bars are likely to follow the product life cycle of traditional ice cream products? Explain your answer.

## Case 11.2

## Hilton Worldwide Expands to New Brands and New Markets

As Hilton Worldwide approaches its 100th anniversary, the lodging giant is expanding by adding new brands and opening in new markets to continue its aggressive growth. Based in McLean, Virginia, Hilton has a wide product mix covering multiple brands. Its line of luxury hotels includes two brands, Waldorf Astoria and Conrad. It markets lifestyle hotels under the Canopy by Hilton brand and full-service hotels under four brands: Hilton, Curio Collection by Hilton, Doubletree by Hilton, and Embassy Suites by Hilton. Hilton's hotel brands with limited services include Hilton Garden Inn, Hampton Inn by Hilton, Homewood Suites by Hilton, Home2 Suites by Hilton, and Tru by Hilton.

Hilton is currently opening the doors to the first of more than two dozen Canopy boutique hotels. These are hotels in locations like Reykjavik, Iceland and Bethesda, Maryland, where customers can use mobile devices for convenient check-in, then check out the neighborhood using the hotel's on-site bikes. Canopy hotels have open lobbies to invite lingering, a free gift waiting in every room, and free wine tastings in the evening to encourage mingling.

Another of Hilton's newer brands is Tru, a group of more than 100 mid-priced hotels designed with Millennials in mind. Introducing the brand, Hilton's CEO stated: "We have a very large swath of demand that indexes very young, and we're not serving it." The company's analysis indicates that 40 percent of demand for hotel rooms comes from customers seeking affordable accommodations. Tru is geared to

chrisdorney/Shutterstock.com

travelers in their twenties and thirties who want accommodations with a modern design and a reasonable price, plus opportunities to personalize the experience for individual needs.

Each Tru hotel has flexible public-space areas for customers to enjoy as they choose: Some may want to play foosball, others may do a bit of work, while still others will relax in easy chairs or get a snack from the "grab and go" eatery. Tru's guest rooms are smaller than typical U.S. hotel rooms but carefully set up with amenities preferred by the target market, such as 65-inch TVs and showers rather than bathtubs. Tru will compete in the mid-priced market with rival brands such as Comfort Inn by Choice Hotels and Marriott's Fairfield Inn & Suites.

Meanwhile, the marketing environment continues to evolve, leading to challenges and opportunities for Hilton and its competitors. To achieve economies of scale and build their product portfolios, competitors are buying up hotel brands at a rapid pace. InterContinental Hotels acquired Kimpton Hotels, for instance, to take advantage of growing interest in boutique hotels and to plant its brands in more cities. Marriott International acquired Starwood Hotels, and AccorHotels acquired Fairmont, among other hotel brands. The industry is also feeling competitive pressure from rental services such as Airbnb, which link owners of apartments, condos, and homes with customers who want to rent for a day or longer.

Rather than buy an existing brand, Hilton is developing its own hotel brands from scratch so it can build in the features and services desired by particular target markets, with appropriate pricing. It is also entering new markets, such as Bolivia and Chad, bringing its total to more than 100 countries. With a portfolio of 13 brands covering hundreds of thousands of rooms worldwide, Hilton is well positioned to meet the needs of a wide range of customers in a wide range of locations, now and in the future.[66]

### Questions for Discussion

1. Which branding strategy is Hilton using? Why is this appropriate for Hilton?
2. How does the state of competition among hotels indicate where this category is in the product life cycle?
3. Is Hilton's product mix deep as well as wide? Explain your answer.

# NOTES

[1] Alex Williams, "Shinola Takes Its 'Detroit Cool' Message on the Road," *New York Times*, January 6, 2016, www.nytimes.com/2016/01/07/fashion/shinola-watches-bicycles-leather-goods-expansion.html (accessed February 5, 2016); Kai Ryssdal, "Shinola Has Perfect Timing in Detroit," *Marketplace*, January 20, 2016, www.marketplace.org/2016/01/20/world/shinola (accessed February 5, 2016); J.C. Reindl, "Shinola Stands by 'Built in Detroit,' Edits Swiss Claim, *Detroit Free Press*, December 16, 2015, www.freep.com/story/money/business/michigan/2015/12/16/shinola-stands-by-built-detroit-edits-swiss-claim/77092374/ (accessed February 5, 2016); www.shinola.com (accessed February 5, 2016).

[2] "Team Charity: Water," http://www.charitywater.org/about/ (accessed February 22, 2016); Elise Hu, "How Millennials Are Reshaping Charity and Online Giving," NPR: All Tech Considered, October 13, 2014, http://www.npr.org/blogs/alltechconsidered/2014/10/13/338295367/how-millennials-are-reshaping-charity-and-online-giving (accessed February 22, 2016).

[3] Drury Hotels, https://wwwc.druryhotels.com/about (accessed February 22, 2016); Drury Hotels, "Drury Hotels Receives Record-Setting Tenth Consecutive J.D. Power Award," press release, July 15, 2015, https://wwwc.druryhotels.com/DruryNewsItem.aspx?id=6004137 (accessed February 22, 2016).

[4] Katie Little "McDonald's Tests New Take on Custom Sandwiches," CNBC, April 29, 2015, http://www.cnbc.com/2015/04/29/mcdonalds-tests-new-take-on-custom-sandwiches.html (accessed February 22, 2016); Bruce Horovitz, "McDonald's Expands Custom Sandwich Option," *USA Today,* December 7, 2014, http://www.usatoday.com/story/money/business/2014/12/07/mcdonalds-fast-food-restaurants-create-your-taste-millennials/19943987/ (accessed February 22, 2016).

[5] Adam Satariano and Peter Burrows, "There's a Downside to Making Parts for Apple," September 18, 2014, *Bloomberg Businessweek*, http://www.businessweek.com/articles/2014-09-18/some-apple-suppliers-get-cut-off-must-scramble-for-new-business (accessed February 23, 2016).

[6] Laura Lorenzetti, "Birchbox Is Selling Its Own Makeup Now," *Fortune,* October 14, 2015, http://fortune.com/2015/10/14/birchbox-makeup/ (accessed February 23, 2016).

[7] William P. Putsis Jr and Barry L. Bayus, "An Empirical Analysis of Firms' Product Line Decisions," *Journal of Marketing Research* 38, 1 (2001): 110–118.

[8] John Deere & Co. website, "Agriculture," https://www.deere.com/en_US/industry/agriculture/agriculture.page (accessed February 23, 2016).

[9] Brian X. Chen, "Changing Tactics, Apple Promotes Watch as Luxury Item," *The New York Times*, April 19, 2015, http://www.nytimes.com/2015/04/20/technology/personaltech/changing-tactics-apple-promotes-watch-as-a-luxury-item.html (accessed November 4, 2015).

[10] Michael D. Johnson, Andreas Herrmann, and Frank Huber, "Evolution of Loyalty Intentions," *Journal of Marketing* 70, 2 (2006): 122–132.

[11] RetailMeNot website, Retailmenot.com (accessed February 23, 2016).

[12] Richard L. Gruner, Christian Homburg, and Bryan A. Lukas, "Firm-Hosted Online Brand Communities and New Product Success," *Journal of the Academy of Marketing Science*, 42, 1 (2014): 29–48.

[13] Elaine Watson, "Why Do 85% of New CPG Products Fail within Two Years?" *Food Navigator*, July 31, 2014, http://www.foodnavigator-usa.com/Markets/Why-do-85-of-new-CPG-products-fail-within-two-years (accessed February 23, 2016); Joan Schneider and Julie Hall, "Why Most Product Launches Fail," *Harvard Business Review*, April 2011, https://hbr.org/2011/04/why-most-product-launches-fail (accessed February 23, 2016).

[14] Matt Timms, "Life in Plastic, Not so Fantastic; the Tale of Barbie's Decline" *The New Economy*, January 7, 2015, http://www.theneweconomy.com/home/life-in-plastic-not-so-fantastic-barbies-great-decline (accessed February 24, 2016).

[15] Allison Aubrey, "Chocolate Makeover: Nestle Dumps Artificial Colorings," *NPR: The Salt*, February 19, 2015, http://www.npr.org/blogs/thesalt/2015/02/19/387319835/chocolate-makeover-nestle-dumps-artificial-colorings (accessed February 24, 2016).

[16] Adapted from Everett M. Rogers, *Diffusion of Innovations* (New York: Macmillan, 1962), pp. 81–86.

[17] Arch G. Woodside and Wim Biemans, "Managing Relationships, Networks, and Complexity in Innovation, Diffusion, and Adoption Processes," *Business & Industrial Marketing* 20, 7 (2005): 247–250.

[18] Ibid, 247–250.

[19] "Common Language Marketing Dictionary," American Marketing Association, http://www.marketing-dictionary.org/ama (accessed February 24, 2016).

[20] Warren Church, "Investment in Brand Pays Large Dividends," *Marketing News*, November 15, 2006, p. 21.

[21] John Kell, "Miller Lite Tastes Success Again," *Fortune*, March 4, 2015, http://fortune.com/2015/03/04/miller-lite-new-success/ (accessed February 24, 2016).

22 Rosellina Ferraro, Amna Kirmani, and Ted Matherly, "Look At Me! Look At Me! Conspicuous Brand Usage, Self-Brand Connection, and Dilution," *Journal of Marketing Research*, 50, 4 (2013): 477–488.

23 C. D. Simms and P. Trott, "The Perceptions of the BMW Mini Brand: The Importance of Historical Associations and the Development of a Model," *Journal of Product & Brand Management* 15, 4 (2006): 228–238.

24 Douglas Holt, "Branding as Cultural Activism," *How Brands Become Icons: The Principle of Cultural Branding* (Boston: Harvard Business School Press, 2004), p. 209.

25 Nigel Hollis, "Branding Unmasked," *Marketing Research* (Fall 2005): 24–29.

26 David A. Aaker, "*Managing Brand Equity: Capitalizing on the Value of a Brand Name* (New York: Free Press, 1991), pp. 16–17.

27 Don E. Schulz, "The Loyalty Paradox," *Marketing Management* 14, 5 (2005): 10–11.

28 "2016 Brand Keys Customer Loyalty Engagement Index," Brand Keys, http:// info.brandkeys.com/acton/attachment/94 3/f-0066/1/-/-/-/-/2016%20Customer%20 Loyalty%20Engagement%20Index%20%231%20 brands.pdf (accessed February 24, 2016)).

29 Mitchell C. Olsen, Rebecca J. Slotegraaf, and Sandeep R. Chandukala, "Green Claims and Message Frames: How Green New Products Change Brand Attitude," *Journal of Marketing*, 78, 5 (2014): 119–137.

30 Millward Brown, "BrandZ Top 100 Most Valuable Global Brands, 2015," https://www.millwardbrown .com/BrandZ/2015/Global/2015_BrandZ_Top100_ Chart.pdf (accessed February 24, 2016).

31 "Consumer Reports Names the Best and Worst Cars by Brand," *Consumer Reports*, April 6, 2015, http://www.consumerreports.org/ cro/news/2013/03/consumer-reports-names-the-best-and-worst-cars-by-brand/index.htm (accessed February 24, 2016).

32 Simone M. de Droog, Patti M. Valkenburg, and Moniek Buijzen, "Using Brand Characters to Promote Young Children's Liking of and Purchase Requests for Fruit," *Journal of Health Communication: International Perspectives*, 26, 1 (2010): 79–89.

33 Eddie Yoon, "Store Brands Aren't Just About Price," *Harvard Business Review*, April 15, 2015, https://hbr.org/2015/04/store-brands-arent-just-about-price (accessed February 25, 2016).

34 Alanna Petrof, "Tata's Zica Car Gets a New Name: Tiago," *CNN Money*, February 22, 2016, http://money.cnn.com/2016/02/22/autos/ tata-zica-car-zika-virus-tiago/ (accessed February 17, 2016).

35 Chiranjeev S. Kohli, Katrin R. Harich, and Lance Lethesser, "Creating Brand Identity: A Study of Evaluation of New Brand Names," *Journal of Business Research* 58, 11 (2005): 1506–1515.

36 Richard R. Klink, and Gerard A. Athaide, "Creating Brand Personality with Brand Names," *Marketing Letters* 23, 1 (2012): 109–117.

37 Sophia Yan, "What's in a Brand Name? In China, Everything," CNN Money, September 7, 2015, http://money.cnn.com/2015/09/07/ news/foreign-firms-china-branding/ (accessed February 25, 2016).

38 Dorothy Cohen, "Trademark Strategy," *Journal of Marketing* 50, 1 (1986): 63.

39 Chiranjeev Kohli and Rajneesh Suri, "Brand Names That Work: A Study of the Effectiveness of Different Types of Brand Names," *Marketing Management Journal* 10, 2 (2000): 112–120.

40 International Trademark Association, "Fact Sheets: Types of Protection—Trademarks vs. Generic Terms," www.inta.org/Trademark-Basics/FactSheets/Pages/Trademarksvs-GenericTermsFactSheet.aspx (accessed February 25, 2016).

41 Sophie Brown, "Brand Wars: Battling China's Trademark 'Squatters'," *CNN*, July 17, 2014, http://www.cnn.com/2014/07/17/world/asia/ china-trademark-squatters-penfolds/ (accessed February 25, 2016).

42 "Counterfeit Goods: How to Tell the Real from the Ripoff," *Consumer Reports*, May 28, 2015, http://www.consumerreports.org/cro/ magazine/2015/05/counterfeit-goods-how-to-tell-real-from-ripoff/index.htm (accessed February 25, 2016); Thomas C. Frohlich, Alexander E.M. Hess, and Vince Calio, "9 Most Counterfeited Products in the USA," *USA Today*, March 29, 2014, http://www.usatoday. com/story/money/business/2014/03/29/24-7-wall-st-counterfeited-products/7023233/ (accessed February 25, 2016).

43 Kristina Monllos, "Johnson's Baby Is Sorry Not Sorry in Awkward Reply to Customer Concerns," *Adweek*, July 30, 2014, http://www. adweek.com/adfreak/johnsons-baby-sorry-not-sorry-awkward-reply-customer-concerns-159207

(accessed February 25, 2016); Jane Kay, "Johnson & Johnson Removes Some Chemicals from Baby Shampoo, Other Products," *Scientific American*, May 6, 2013, www.scientificamerican.com/article. cfm?id=johnson-and-johnson-removes-some-chemicals-from-baby-shampoo-other-products (accessed February 25, 2016).

44 Charles Riley, "Tesla's New Product Is a Battery for Your Home," *CNN Money*, May 1, 2015, http://money.cnn.com/2015/05/01/ technology/tesla-powerwall-battery-product/.

45 Robert Klara, "The Worst Brand Extensions of 2013," *Adweek*, January 14, 2014, http://www .adweek.com/news-gallery/advertising-branding/ worst-brand-extensions-2013-154949#heineken-shoes-3 (accessed February 26, 2016).

46 Shantini Munthree, Geoff Bick, and Russell Abratt, "A Framework for Brand Revitalization Through an Upscale Line Extension," *Journal of Product & Brand Management* 15, 3 (2006): 157–167.

47 Kaleel Rahman and Areni Charles S., "Generic, Genuine, or Completely New? Branding Strategies to Leverage New Products," *Journal of Strategic Marketing*, 22, 1 (2014): 3–15.

48 "Target® Colors," Benjamin Moore, http:// store.benjaminmoore.com/storefront/shop-by-color/target-paint-colors/target-colors/ cndShopByColor-cTarget_Paint_Colors-cTarget_Colors_Fall12-p1.html (accessed February 26, 2016).

49 Deena Crawley and McKee Steve, "Twenty Co-Branding Examples," Bloomberg, January 23, 2015, http://www.bloomberg.com/ ss/09/07/0710_cobranded/8.htm (accessed February 26, 2016); PR Newswire, "Best Western and Harley-Davidson Partnership Goes Global," press release, February 20, 2013, http://www.prnews-wire.com/news-releases/best-western-and-harley-davidson-partnership-goes-global-192015471. html (accessed February 26, 2016).

50 "The Top 150 Global Licensors," *License Global*, May 1, 2015, http://www.licensemag. com/license-global/top-150-global-licensors-1 (accessed February 26, 2016).

51 Johnson SC, "Minimizing Packaging," http:// www.scjohnson.com/en/commitment/focus-on/ lesswaste/minimizingpackaging.aspx (accessed February 26, 2016).

52 Mohan Anne Marie, "Beech-Nut Becomes a Disruptive Force in Baby Food," *Pack-World*, June 2, 2014, http://www.pack-world.com/package-design/redesign/

beech-nut-becomes-disruptive-force-baby-food (accessed February 26, 2016).

[53] Hodder Candace, "What Makes Packaging Sustainable?" *The Dieline*, November 13, 2013, www.thedieline.com/blog/2013/11/13/what-makes-a-package-sustainable.html (accessed February 26, 2016).

[54] Pangea Organics, http://www.pangeaorganics.com/ (accessed May 5, 2015).

[55] Lauren I. Labrecque and George R. Milne, "Exciting Red and Competent Blue: The Importance of Color in Marketing," *Journal of the Academy of Marketing Science* 40, 5 (2012): 711–727.

[56] Dooley Roger, "How Your Packaging Improves Customer Experiences," *Forbes*, December 13, 2014, http://www.forbes.com/sites/rogerdooley/2014/10/13/how-your-packaging-improves-customer-experience/ (accessed February 26, 2016).

[57] PR Newswire, "Nestle Packaging Redesign Boosts Yoghurt Sales in Hong Kong," Yahoo! Finance, December 10, 2014, http://finance.yahoo.com/news/nestle-packaging-redesign-boosts-yoghurt-155800699.html (accessed May 5, 2015).

[58] "Laundry Detergent," Seventh Generation, www.seventhgeneration.com/laundry-detergent (accessed February 26, 2016).

[59] Serena Ng, "P&G, Other Laundry Pod Makers Agree to New Safety Standards," The Wall Street Journal, September 4, 2015, http://www.wsj.com/articles/p-g-other-laundry-pod-makers-agree-to-new-safety-standard-1441397456 (accessed November 6, 2015); Christensen Jen,

"Laundry Detergent Pods Are 'Real Risk' to Children," *CNN*, November 10, 2014, http://www.cnn.com/2014/11/10/health/laundry-pod-poisonings/ (accessed February 26, 2016).

[60] Stack Wine website, http://drinkstack.com (accessed February 26, 2016); Ferree Steve, "Take Stack Wine with You for International Picnic Day," *Examinor.com*, June 7, 2015, http://www.examiner.com/article/take-stack-wine-with-you-for-international-picnic-day (accessed February 26, 2016).

[61] Valerie Folkes and Matta Shashi, "The Effect of Package Shape on Consumers' Judgments of Product Volume: Attention as a Mental Contaminant," *Journal of Consumer Research* 31, 2 (2004): 390–401.

[62] Tennille Tracy and Annie Gasparro, "General Mills in Settlement Over '100% Natural' Claim," *The Wall Street Journal*, November 18, 2014, http://www.wsj.com/articles/general-mills-in-settlement-over-100-natural-claim-1416356372 (accessed November 6, 2015); Ferdman Roberto, "The Word 'Natural' Helps Sell $40 Billion Worth of Food in the U.S. Every Year—and the Label Means Nothing," *The Washington Post*, June 24, 2014, http://www.washington-post.com/blogs/wonkblog/wp/2014/06/24/the-word-natural-helps-sell-40-billion-worth-of-food-in-the-u-s-every-year-and-the-label-means-nothing/ (accessed February 26, 2016).

[63] Larry Loffer, "More Consumers Seeking Products Made in the USA," Meters Wagner, May 22, 2014, http://www.wagnermeters.com/wood-moisture-meter/more-consumers-seeking-products-made-in-the-usa/ (accessed February 26, 2016); Felix Gillette, "'Made in

USA' Still Sells," *Bloomberg Businessweek*, October 11, 2012, www.businessweek.com/articles/2012-10-11/made-in-usa-still-sells (accessed February 26, 2016).

[64] "Threading Your Way through the Labeling Requirements under the Textile and Wool Acts," Federal Trade Commission, July 2014, https://www.ftc.gov/tips-advice/business-center/guidance/threading-your-way-through-labeling-requirements-under-textile (accessed February 26, 2016).

[65] Curt Nickisch , "GaGa's for Lady Gaga? Coincidental Celebrity Lifts Local Brands," *WBUR radio (Boston)*, February 29, 2012, www.wbur.org; GaGa website, www.gonegaga.net; "Going Goo Goo for GaGa," *Warwick Online (RI)*, May 12, 2011, www.warwickon-line.com; "GaGa" Cengage video.

[66] Nancy Trejos, "Hilton Announces New Affordable Hotel Brand, Tru," *USA Today*, January 25, 2016, www.usatoday.com/story/travel/hotels/2016/01/25/hilton-tru-new-hotel-brand/79185810 (accessed February 9, 2016); Nancy Trejos, "Hilton Marks a Milestone: Enters 100th Country," *USA Today,* January 21, 2016, www.usatoday.com/story/travel/2016/01/21/hilton-marks-milestone-enters-100th-country/79105564 (accessed February 9, 2016); Abha Bhattarai, "Hilton Tests Guest-Greeting Robots and Noise-Canceling Rooms," *Washington Post,* January 15, 2016, www.washingtonpost.com/business/capitalbusiness/hilton-tests-guest-greeting-robots-and-noise-canceling-rooms/2016/01/15/1eb42e96-b48b-11e5-a76a-0b5145e8679a_story.html (accessed February 9, 2016); www.hiltonworldwide.com.

## Feature Notes

[a] Mannie Holmes, "Spider-Man 'Belongs' in Marvel Universe, Says Kevin Feige," *Variety*, October 1, 2015, http://variety.com/2015/biz/news/marvel-spider-man-kevin-feige-belongs-mcu-1201607393/(accessed February 5, 2016); Anousha Sakoui and Christopher Palmeri, "My Universe Is Bigger than Your Universe," *Bloomberg Businessweek*, April 27, 2015, pp. 19–21; James Cowan, "The Business Insight That Helped Marvel Conquer the Universe," *Canadian Business*, July 22, 2015, www.canadianbusiness.com/innovation/the-business-insight-that-helped-marvel-comics-conquer-the-universe/ (accessed February 5, 2016); Matt Patches, "Why Spider-Man Is Finally Allowed to Join the Avengers' Movie Universe," *Esquire*,

February 10, 2015, www.esquire.com/entertainment/movies/a32685/spider-man-marvel-sony-deal-explained (accessed February 5, 2016); Rachel Abrams and Gregory Schmidt, "Hitching a Toy to a Star Superhero Movies Create Opportunity for Toymakers," *New York Times*, February 13, 2015, www.nytimes.com/2015/02/14/business/superhero-movies-create-opportunity-for-toymakers.html (accessed February 5, 2016).

[b] Michal Addady, "Emails Show Coke Had an Influential Role in Anti-Obesity Group," *Fortune*, November 24, 2015, http://fortune.com/2015/11/24/coke-obesity-group/ (accessed February 5, 2016); Muhtar Kent, "Coca-Cola: We'll Do Better; The Company, Taking to Heart Criticism of How It Deals with Scientific

Research and Childhood Obesity, Vows to Improve Transparency," *Wall Street Journal*, August 19, 2015, www.wsj.com/articles/coca-cola-well-do-better-1440024365?cb=logged0.4340841087445789 (accessed February 5, 2016); Stephanie Strom, "Coca-Cola to Disclose Its Spending on Research Into Soft Drinks and Health," *New York Times*, August 20, 2015, www.nytimes.com/2015/08/21/business/coca-cola-to-disclose-its-spending-on-research-into-soft-drinks-and-health.html (accessed February 5, 2016); "Anti-Obesity Group Funded by Coke Disbanding, *CBS News*, December 1, 2015, www.cbsnews.com/news/anti-obesity-group-funded-by-coke-global-energy-balance-network-disbanding/ (accessed February 5, 2016).

# chapter 12

# Developing and Managing Products

---

## OBJECTIVES

**12-1** Explain how companies manage existing products through line extensions and product modifications.

**12-2** Describe how businesses develop a product idea into a commercial product.

**12-3** Discuss the importance of product differentiation and the elements that differentiate one product from another.

**12-4** Explain how businesses position their products.

**12-5** Discuss how product deletion is used to improve product mixes.

**12-6** Describe organizational structures used for managing products.

# MARKETING INSIGHTS

## Prettie Girls! A One World Vision

A new-product idea came to mind when Houston businessman Trent T. Daniel met toy designer Stacey McBride-Irby in 2010. Both were speakers at a United Negro College Fund event promoting entrepreneurship, and they began chatting about McBride-Irby's background as a designer of African-American Barbie dolls for Mattel. She said she was interested in designing a new line of high-quality, multicultural dolls. As the African-American father of three girls, Daniel was well aware that few dolls on toy-store shelves looked like his daughters—and he sensed a promising marketing opportunity.

Daniel raised $5 million to finance the new venture, and McBride-Irby joined him in founding the One World Dolls Project to market Prettie Girls! The brand is an acronym made up of the initial letters in *p*ositive, *r*espectful, *e*nthusiastic, *t*ruthful, *t*alented, *i*nspiring, and *e*xcellent, personal qualities that the co-founders wanted their dolls to embody.

One World Dolls introduced its first product line in 2013, featuring foot-high teen fashion dolls with a variety of skin tones and facial features. In 2015, it released a second product line named Tween Scene, featuring 16-inch preteen dolls: Lena, an African-American girl; Kimani, an African girl; Hana, an Asian girl; Dhara, a South Asian girl; Valencia, a Hispanic girl, and Alexie, a Caucasian girl.

Now that Prettie Girls! are carried by Walmart and other major U.S. retailers, annual sales have surged beyond $1 million.

The One World Doll Project

One World recently merged with another firm to form Tonner One World, which will continue launching new products to fuel future growth.[1]

To provide products that satisfy target markets and achieve the firm's objectives, a marketer must develop, alter, and maintain an effective product mix—as marketers at Tonner One World do. An organization's product mix may require adjustment for a variety of reasons. Because customers' attitudes and product preferences change over time, their desire for certain products may wane. For instance, Americans' breakfast preferences are shifting from cold cereals, such as Special K and Cheerios, toward healthier and more varied fare like yogurt and snack bars as well as fast-food breakfast items. Cereal makers have responded to the decline in sales of traditional cereals by introducing new products such as cereal-based snack bars as well as reformulating cereals to make them more appealing to more consumers. Kellogg, for example, introduced Special K Chewy Nut Bars and Nutri-Grain Breakfast Biscuits, and plans to stop using artificial colors and flavors by 2018 and to use only cage-free eggs by 2025.[2] In other cases, a company may need to alter its product mix for competitive reasons. A marketer may have to delete a product from the mix because a competitor dominates the market for that product. IBM, for example, sold its personal computer product line to Lenovo because of intense competition in that area. Similarly, a firm may have to introduce a new product or modify an existing one to compete more effectively. A marketer may expand the firm's product mix to take advantage of excess marketing and production capacity.

In this chapter, we examine several ways to improve an organization's product mix. First, we discuss managing existing products through effective line extension and product modification. Next, we examine the stages of new-product development, including idea generation, screening, concept testing, business analysis, product development, test marketing, and commercialization. Then, we go on to discuss the ways companies differentiate their products in the marketplace and follow with a discussion of product positioning and repositioning. Next, we examine the importance of deleting weak products and the methods companies use to eliminate them. Finally, we look at the organizational structures used to manage products.

# 12-1 MANAGING EXISTING PRODUCTS

An organization can benefit by capitalizing on its existing products. By assessing the composition of the current product mix, a marketer can identify weaknesses and gaps. This analysis can then lead to improvement of the product mix through line extensions and product modifications.

## 12-1a Line Extensions

A **line extension** is the development of a product that is closely related to one or more products in the existing product line but designed specifically to meet somewhat different customer needs. For example, in addition to classic Coca-Cola, the Coca-Cola Company markets Diet Coke, Coca-Cola Zero, and caffeine-free Coca-Cola to appeal to customers who have differing needs and wants with regard to Cola drinks. Occasionally, the firm will extend the line when it introduces a new flavor of Coca-Cola, such as black cherry vanilla, or a Coca-Cola product with slightly different ingredients, such as stevia in Coca-Cola Life, to better appeal to a market segment.

Many of the so-called new products introduced each year are in fact line extensions. Line extensions are more common than new products because they are a less-expensive, lower-risk alternative for increasing sales. A line extension may focus on a different market segment or attempt to increase sales within the same market segment by more precisely satisfying the needs of people in that segment. For example, Pfizer introduced Centrum Multigummies multivitamins after recognizing that consumers increasingly like gummy products. The new product extends the Centrum family that already includes tablet, chewable, and liquid forms of vitamins and supplements for men, women, and children.[3] Firms should be careful of which lines they choose to extend and how. The success of a line extension is enhanced if the parent brand has a high-quality brand image and if there is a good fit between the line extension and its parent.[4]

**line extension** Development of a product that is closely related to existing products in the line but is designed specifically to meet different customer needs

Line extensions, when successfully applied, can take market share from competitors. This advertisement for Tidy Cats LightWeight with Glade Tough Odor Solutions cat litter is an extension of Tidy Cat's line of cat litters that features Glade brand scents to freshen a litter that weighs half as much as conventional cat litters. The product in this ad is likely to appeal to cat lovers who want a scented litter to disguise cat litter odors as well as those who don't like lugging twenty pound jugs home from the store. The light-weight product extension may lure new customers away from other heavier brands.

## 12-1b  Product Modifications

**Product modification** means changing one or more characteristics of a product. A product modification differs from a line extension in that the original product does not remain in the line. Automakers, for instance, use product modifications annually when they create new models of the same brand. Makers of running shoes also follow this practice, releasing new shoe models nearly every year and retiring old ones. Once the new models are introduced, the manufacturers stop producing the previous model. Like line extensions, product modifications entail less risk than developing new products.

Product modification can indeed improve a firm's product mix, but only under certain conditions. First, the product must be modifiable. Second, customers must be able to perceive that a modification has been made. Third, the modification should make the product more consistent with customers' desires so it provides greater satisfaction. One drawback to modifying a successful product is that a consumer who had experience with the original version of the product may view a modified version as a riskier purchase. There are three major types of modifications that can be made to products: quality, functional, and aesthetic.

**Line Extension**
Tidy Cats LightWeight with Glade Tough Odor Solutions cat litter is an extension of Tidy Cat's line of cat litters. It is positioned to take away market share from rivals Fresh Step and Arm & Hammer by offering new features.

## Quality Modifications

**Quality modifications** are changes relating to a product's dependability and durability. Usually, the changes are executed by altering the materials or the production process. Look at the advertisement for the Energizer Eco Advanced, an alkaline battery that has undergone quality modifications to make it last longer and be more environmentally friendly due to its recycled content. The ad, which features Energizer's iconic pink bunny exiting a cardboard box that has been recycled into a child's rocket ship, highlights the battery's features to show that the company is "thinking outside the box."

Reducing a product's quality may allow an organization to lower its price and direct the item at a different target market. In contrast, increasing the quality of a product may give a firm an advantage over competing brands. Higher quality may enable a company to charge a higher price by creating customer loyalty and lowering customer sensitivity to price. Case in point, many firms, including Nestlé USA and Hershey Company, are modifying their products

**product modification** Changes in one or more characteristics of a product

**quality modifications** Changes relating to a product's dependability and durability

Source: Energizer Holdings

**Quality Modification**
Quality modification to the Energizer alkaline battery makes it last longer and employs 4 percent recycled content.

to eliminate artificial colors and flavors in response to growing consumer preference for natural and simple ingredients. Nestlé modified its classic candy bars to replace the artificial colors with ones made from annatto, paprika, and cocoa powder.[5] However, higher quality may require the use of more expensive ingredients, components, and processes, which may force the organization to cut costs in other areas. Some firms, such as Caterpillar, are finding ways to increase quality while reducing costs.

## Functional Modifications

Changes that affect a product's versatility, effectiveness, convenience, or safety are called **functional modifications**, and they usually require that the product be redesigned. Product categories that have undergone considerable functional modification include agricultural equipment, appliances, cleaning products, and telecommunications services. Making programs available in 3D on DirectTV is a functional modification. Functional modifications can increase the number of users of a product and thus enlarge its market. For instance, the iPhone is always adding new features. The iPhone 6s has a faster processor, better cameras, faster fingerprint recognition and unlocking, and 3D Touch, the touch screen's ability to detect different touch pressures and respond accordingly.[6] This technology, along with other modifications, makes the iPhone 6s significantly different from previous models. Companies can place a product in a favorable competitive position by providing benefits that competing brands do not offer.

Additionally, functional modifications can help an organization achieve and maintain a progressive image. Finally, functional modifications are sometimes made to reduce the possibility of product liability lawsuits, such as adding a kill switch on a machine in case it malfunctions.

## Aesthetic Modifications

**Aesthetic modifications** change the sensory appeal of a product by altering its taste, texture, sound, smell, or appearance. A buyer making a purchase decision is swayed by sensory inputs, and an aesthetic modification may thus strongly affect purchases. The fashion industry relies heavily on aesthetic modifications from season to season. For example, Louis Vuitton clothing, handbags, and leather goods are leaders in the haute couture industry. In order to maintain its reputation for the utmost level of quality and style, the company performs aesthetic modifications on its products regularly. This ensures that Louis Vuitton maintains its reputation for cutting-edge design and high quality. In addition, aesthetic modifications attempt to minimize the amount of illegal product counterfeiting that occurs through constant change in design.

**functional modifications**
Changes affecting a product's versatility, effectiveness, convenience, or safety

**aesthetic modifications**
Changes relating to the sensory appeal of a product

Aesthetic modifications can help a firm differentiate its product from competing brands and thus gain a sizable market share. The major drawback in using aesthetic modifications is that their value is determined subjectively. Although a firm may strive to improve the product's sensory appeal, some customers actually may find the modified product less attractive.

# 12-2 DEVELOPING NEW PRODUCTS

A firm develops new products as a means of enhancing its product mix and adding depth to a product line. Developing and introducing new products is frequently expensive and risky. However, failure to introduce new products is also risky. Consider the case of Blockbuster, the movie retailer, which failed to innovate with new products in the face of changing consumer shopping habits and the shift to watching movies on demand and streaming movies through outlets such as Netflix. Indeed, Blockbuster turned down an early opportunity to purchase a fledgling Netflix, which would have diversified its product mix.[7] Consumers still watch movies voraciously, but there are very few DVD rental stores left.

The term *new product* can have more than one meaning. A genuinely new product offers innovative benefits. For example, Apple is often considered the most innovative company in the country for releasing such products as the iPod, iPhone, and iPad.[8] The firm benefits from this reputation for developing new products that address consumer needs. However, products that are different and distinctly better are often viewed as new, even if they do not represent a truly new product. For instance, the Colgate Optic White Toothbrush and Whitening Pen features special bristles that help remove tooth stains and comes with a whitening pen for applying a special gel directly on the teeth to make them even whiter; the pen stores inside the toothbrush. Toothbrushes already exist, as do teeth-whitening products. However, consumers who want whiter teeth without expensive dental treatments or hard-to-use strips are likely to view this as a useful new product.[9] This advertisement for Amazon's smart speaker illustrates a product that represents an innovation over existing speakers. The Echo is a voice-controlled speaker that can not only play music but also answer questions, activate smart devices in the home, and look up things on the Internet. The ad shows that the device is always on and "connected to your life," which no competing speaker currently offers. Some popular product innovations of recent decades include cell phones, tablet computers, electric cars, digital video recorders, satellite radio, and drones.

A new product can also be one that a given firm has not marketed previously, although similar products are available from other companies. Android Pay, for example, is not the first digital wallet available, but it is a new product offering from Google. The advertisement for the KitchenAid Spiralizer represents a product that is new to KitchenAid but not totally new to the market. Other companies, such as Paderno and Westmark, market similar spiral slicers. This is the first spiral slicer released by KitchenAid, however, which is underscored by the phrase "fresh ingredients deserve a fresh perspective" written out in the ad. The ad also showcases the potential results of using the product with a colorful array of spiralized

Source: Amazon.com, Inc.

**Product Innovation**
Many product innovations build on products already existing in the marketplace. For instance, this Amazon Echo speaker represents an innovation over existing speakers by responding to voice commands and accessing the Internet.

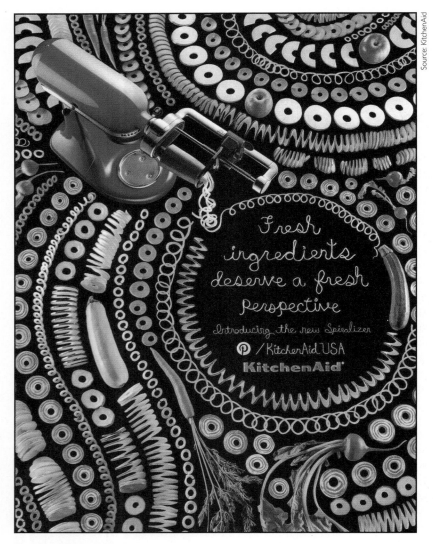

**New Product for a Firm**
The KitchenAid Spiralizer is a new product to the KitchenAid family of products, although similar products have been marketed by other firms.

vegetables that can be used as pasta substitutes or salad garnishes. Finally, a product can be viewed as new when it is brought to one or more markets from another market.

In recent years, a growing number of companies have found success by identifying ways to change how things are done in an industry and then developing products to lead the way. **Disruptive innovation**, first described by Professor Clayton Christensen of Harvard Business School, identifies old technologies that can be exploited in new ways or develops new business models to give customers more than they've come to expect from current products in a specific market. Companies like Google, Netflix, iTunes, Uber and Lyft, and Warby Parker have become successful by recognizing unmet or poorly satisfied needs and developing products to satisfy them. Michael Dubin, for example, founded Dollar Shave Club after recognizing that buying refill cartridges for men's razors was boring, expensive, and often frustrating when retailers keep them locked up. He also realized that most men don't change their cartridges often enough. Dollar Shave Club is a subscription service that sends four or five cartridges every month for as little as $1/month. Its more than 2 million subscribers can also get other skin care products shipped as well. The company's great success has spawned imitators and spurred shaving giant Gillette to launch its own subscription service.[10]

Before a product is introduced, it goes through the seven phases of the **new-product development process** shown in Figure 12.1: (1) idea generation, (2) screening, (3) concept testing, (4) business analysis, (5) product development, (6) test marketing, and (7) commercialization. A product may be dropped at any stage of development. In this section, we look at the process through which products are developed, from idea inception to fully commercialized product.

**disruptive innovation**
Identifies old technologies that can be exploited in new ways or develops new business models to give customers more than they've come to expect from current products in a specific market

**new-product development process** A seven-phase process for introducing products: idea generation, screening, concept testing, business analysis, product development, test marketing, and commercialization

**idea generation** Seeking product ideas to achieve organizational objectives

## 12-2a  Idea Generation

Businesses and other organizations seek product ideas that will help them achieve their objectives. This activity is **idea generation**. The fact that only a few ideas are good enough to be commercially successful underscores the challenge of the task.

Although some organizations get their ideas by chance, firms that are most successful at managing their product mixes usually develop systematic approaches for generating new product ideas. At the heart of innovation is a purposeful, focused effort to identify new ways to serve a market.[11] New product ideas can come from several sources. They may stem from internal sources—marketing managers, researchers, sales personnel, engineers, franchisees, or other organizational personnel. Brainstorming and incentives for good ideas are typical intra-firm devices for stimulating the development of ideas. For instance, the idea for 3M Post-it adhesive-backed notes came from an employee. As a church choir member, he used slips of paper to mark songs in his hymnal. Because the pieces of paper kept falling out, he suggested developing an adhesive-backed note. Over time, employees have become more empowered to express their own product ideas to their supervisors. This collaborative process can be particularly useful to help marketers iron out the details of a new product concept.[12]

New product ideas may also arise from sources outside the firm, such as customers, competitors, advertising agencies, management consultants, and private research organizations. Increasingly, firms are bringing consumers into the product idea development process through online campaigns. The Internet gives marketers the chance to tap into consumer ideas by building online communities and listening to their product needs and wants. These communities provide consumers with a sense of empowerment and allow them to provide insight for new product ideas that can prove invaluable to the firm.[13] The Internet and social media have become very important tools for gathering information from stakeholders, particularly when a firm is targeting younger consumers. Frito-Lay, for example, holds an annual contest inviting consumers to submit their ideas for a new potato chip flavor idea via website, Twitter, Facebook, or text. The winner receives $1 million, and Frito-Lay gets a fresh new flavor.[14] The interactivity of the Internet allows other stakeholders not only to suggest and analyze new product ideas but also interact with one another on evaluating and filtering these ideas.

Many firms offer product development consulting and can be good sources for stimulating new product ideas. For example, Kaleidoscope offers product design, engineering, and development services to companies in the health care, medical, consumer goods, electronics, and high-tech industries.[15] When outsourcing new-product development activities to outside organizations, firms should spell out the specific details of the arrangement and include detailed contractual specifications. Asking customers what they want from products has helped many firms become successful and remain competitive. As more global consumers become interconnected through the Internet, marketers have the chance to tap into consumer ideas by building online communities with them.

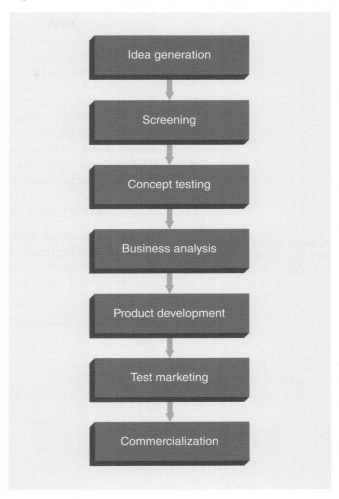

Figure 12.1 **Phases of New-Product Development**

## 12-2b Screening

In the process of **screening**, the ideas with the greatest potential are selected for further review. During screening, product ideas are analyzed to determine if they match the organization's mission, objectives, and resources. A firm's overall abilities to produce and market the product are also analyzed. Other aspects of an idea to be weighed are the nature and wants of buyers and possible environmental changes. At times, a checklist of new-product requirements is used when making screening decisions. This practice encourages evaluators to be systematic and thus reduces the chances of overlooking some pertinent fact. Most new product ideas are rejected during the screening phase.

## 12-2c Concept Testing

To evaluate ideas properly, it may be necessary to test product concepts. In **concept testing**, a small sample of potential buyers is presented with a product idea through a written or oral description (and perhaps a few drawings) to determine their attitudes and initial buying intentions regarding the product. Sonic, for example, maintains a 40-seat dining room at its headquarters

**screening** Selecting the ideas with the greatest potential for further review

**concept testing** Seeking a sample of potential buyers' responses to a product idea for potential new product sampling by employees and focus groups of consumers.[16] For a single product idea, an organization can test one or several concepts of the same product. Concept testing is a low-cost procedure that allows a company to determine customers' initial reactions to a product idea before it invests considerable resources in research and development.

Figure 12.2 shows a concept test for a proposed tick and flea control product. During concept testing, the concept is described briefly, and then a series of questions is presented to a test panel. For a potential food product, a sample may be offered. The questions vary considerably depending on the type of product being tested. Typical questions can include the following: In general, do you find this proposed product attractive? Which benefits are especially attractive to you? Which features are of little or no interest to you? Do you feel that this proposed product would work better for you than the product you currently use? Compared with your current product, what are the primary advantages of the proposed product? If this product were available at an appropriate price, would you buy it? How often would you buy this product? How could the proposed product be improved?

## 12-2d Business Analysis

**business analysis** Evaluating the potential impact of a product idea on the firm's sales, costs, and profits

During the **business analysis** stage, the product idea is evaluated to determine its potential contribution to the firm's sales, costs, and profits. In the course of a business analysis, evaluators ask a variety of questions: Does the product fit in with the organization's existing product mix? Is demand strong enough to justify entering the market, and will this demand endure?

---

Figure 12.2    **Concept Test for a Tick and Flea Control Product**

**Product description**
An insecticide company is considering the development and introduction of a new tick and flea control product for pets. This product would consist of insecticide and a liquid-dispensing brush for applying the insecticide to dogs and cats. The insecticide is in a cartridge that is installed in the handle of the brush. The insecticide is dispensed through the tips of the bristles when they touch the pet's skin (which is where most ticks and fleas are found). The actual dispensing works very much like a felt-tip pen. Only a small amount of insecticide actually is dispensed on the pet because of this unique dispensing feature. Thus, the amount of insecticide that is placed on your pet is minimal compared to conventional methods of applying a tick and flea control product. One application of insecticide will keep your pet free from ticks and fleas for 14 days.

**Please answer the following questions:**

1. In general, how do you feel about using this type of product on your pet?
2. What are the major advantages of this product compared with the existing product that you are currently using to control ticks and fleas on your pet?
3. What characteristics of this product do you especially like?
4. What suggestions do you have for improving this product?
5. If it is available at an appropriate price, how likely are you to buy this product?

   Very likely        Semi-likely        Not likely
6. Assuming that a single purchase would provide 30 applications for an average-size dog or 48 applications for an average-size cat, approximately how much would you pay for this product?

What types of environmental and competitive changes can be expected, and how will these changes affect the product's future sales, costs, and profits?

It is also crucial that a firm determine whether its research, development, engineering, and production capabilities are adequate to develop the product; whether new facilities must be constructed, how quickly they can be built, and how much they will cost; and whether the necessary financing for development and commercialization is on hand or is obtainable based upon terms consistent with a favorable return on investment.

In the business analysis stage, firms seek market information. The results of customer surveys, along with secondary data, supply the specifics needed to estimate potential sales, costs, and profits. For many product ideas in this stage, forecasting sales accurately is difficult. This is especially true for innovative and completely new products. Organizations sometimes employ breakeven analysis to determine how many units they would have to sell to begin making a profit. At times, an organization also uses payback analysis, in which marketers compute the time period required to recover the funds that would be invested in developing the new product. Because breakeven and payback analyses are based on estimates, they are usually viewed as useful but not particularly precise tools.

## 12-2e Product Development

**Product development** is the phase in which the organization determines if it is technically feasible to produce the product and if it can be produced at costs low enough to make the final price reasonable. To test its acceptability, the idea or concept is converted into a prototype, or working model. The prototype should reveal tangible and intangible attributes associated with the product in consumers' minds. The product's design, mechanical features, and intangible aspects must be linked to wants in the marketplace. Through marketing research and concept testing, product attributes that are important to buyers are identified. These characteristics must be communicated to customers through the design of the product.

**product development**
Determining if producing a product is technically feasible and cost-effective

After a prototype is developed, its overall functioning must be assessed. Its performance, safety, convenience, and other functional qualities are tested both in a laboratory and in the

# Entrepreneurship in Marketing

## Jessica Alba's Honest Company Launches Affordable and Safe Beauty and Wellness Products

**Founders:** Jessica Alba, Christopher Gavigan, Brian Lee, and Sean Kane
**Business:** Honest Company
**Founded:** 2011, in Santa Monica, California
**Success:** In five years the Honest Company has obtained a value of $1 billion.

Jessica Alba recognized a problem to be solved by a new product when her baby broke out in hives after wearing an outfit washed in ordinary laundry detergent. A star who shot to fame as a teenager in the lead role of the TV series *Dark Angel*, Alba began to research the ingredients in household products and spoke with members of Congress about banning harmful chemicals. She also set out to establish a company that would make and market baby and beauty products that are safe, effective, affordable, and aesthetically pleasing.

Alba set up the Honest Company with three cofounders: author Christopher Gavigan, who wrote *Healthy Child,*

*Healthy World*, and e-commerce entrepreneurs Brian Lee and Sean Kane. Based on consumer research, the team narrowed its new-product focus to the items most needed by new parents, such as diapers and baby wipes. To start, the company debuted 17 new products, including a line of eco-friendly, fashionable disposable diapers and a line of gentle baby wipes and skin-care lotions. Alba tried every product on her own children and used her star power to connect with potential investors, suppliers, distributors, and customers.

The Honest Company differentiates its products by adding the e-commerce twist of offering home delivery of products such as diapers and wipes for a monthly subscription fee. Explaining this service, Alba says: "Running out of diapers? That's a parent's nightmare." Now most of the firm's revenue comes from subscription orders placed online, and dozens of new products are in the pipeline as the Honest Company continues its growth streak.[a]

field. Functional testing should be rigorous and lengthy enough to test the product thoroughly. Studies have revealed that the form or design of a product can actually influence how consumers view the product's functional performance.[17] Manufacturing issues that come to light at the prototype stage may require adjustments.

A crucial question that arises during product development is how much quality to build into the product. Thus, a major dimension of quality is durability. Higher quality often calls for better materials and more expensive processing, which increase production costs and, ultimately, the product's price. In determining the specific level of quality that is best for a product, a marketer must ascertain approximately what price the target market views as acceptable. In addition, a marketer usually tries to set a quality level consistent with that of the firm's other products. The quality of competing brands is also a consideration.

The development phase of a new product is often a lengthy and expensive process. As a result, only a relatively small number of product ideas are put into development. If the product appears sufficiently successful during this stage to merit test marketing, then, during the latter part of the development stage, marketers begin to make decisions regarding branding, packaging, labeling, pricing, and promotion for use in the test marketing stage.

## 12-2f  Test Marketing

**Test marketing** is a limited introduction of a product in geographic areas chosen to represent the intended market. Fast-food chain Chipotle, for example, test marketed a chorizo (Mexican-style sausage) option for its burrito, bowl, salad, and tacos at its Kansas City locations.[18] The aim of test marketing is to determine the extent to which potential customers will buy the product. Test marketing is not an extension of the development stage, but rather a sample launching of the entire marketing mix. It should be conducted only after the product has gone through development and initial plans have been made regarding the other marketing mix variables. Companies use test marketing to lessen the risk of product failure. The dangers of introducing an untested product include undercutting already profitable products and, should the new product fail, loss of credibility with distributors and customers.

Test marketing provides several benefits. It lets marketers expose a product in a natural marketing environment to measure its sales performance. The company can strive to identify weaknesses in the product or in other parts of the marketing mix. Planet Smoothie, for example, recognized in test marketing that its new Lemon Cayenne Kick smoothie was spicier than its customers preferred, so the firm dialed back the amount of cayenne. On the other hand, Wing Zone found that its new Mango Fire flavor wasn't spicy enough for its patrons, so it ramped up the heat in the final product.[19] A product weakness discovered after a nationwide introduction can be expensive to correct. Moreover, if consumers' early reactions are negative, marketers may be unable to persuade consumers to try the product again. Thus, making adjustments after test marketing can be crucial to the success of a new product. On the other hand, test marketing results may be positive enough to warrant accelerating the product's introduction. Test marketing also allows marketers to experiment with variations in advertising, pricing, and packaging in different test areas and to measure the extent of brand awareness, brand switching, and repeat purchases resulting from these alterations in the marketing mix.

Selection of appropriate test areas is very important because the validity of test marketing results depends heavily on selecting test sites that provide accurate representations of the intended target market. U.S. cities commonly used for test marketing appear in Table 12.1. The criteria used for choosing test cities depend upon the product's attributes, the target market's characteristics, and the firm's objectives and resources.

Test marketing is not without risks. It is expensive, and competitors may try to interfere. A competitor may attempt to "jam" the test program by increasing its own advertising or promotions, lowering prices, and offering special incentives, all to combat consumer recognition and purchase of the new brand. Such tactics can invalidate test results. Sometimes competitors copy the product in the testing stage and rush to introduce a similar product. It is therefore desirable to move to the commercialization phase as soon as possible after successful testing.

**test marketing** A limited introduction of a product in geographic areas chosen to represent the intended market

Table 12.1  **Popular Test Markets in the United States**

| Rank | City |
|------|------|
| 1 | Columbus, Ohio |
| 2 | Peoria, Illinois |
| 3 | Albany, New York |
| 4 | Jacksonville, Florida |
| 5 | Lexington, Kentucky |
| 6 | Des Moines, Iowa |
| 7 | Battle Creek, Michigan |
| 8 | Greensboro, North Carolina |
| 9 | Cleveland, Ohio |
| 10 | Phoenix, Arizona |

Because of these risks, many companies use alternative methods to measure customer preferences. One such method is simulated test marketing. Typically, consumers at shopping centers are asked to view an advertisement for a new product and are given a free sample to take home. These consumers are subsequently interviewed over the phone or through online panels and asked to rate the product. The major advantages of simulated test marketing are greater speed, lower costs, and tighter security, which reduce the flow of information to competitors and reduce jamming. Several marketing research firms, such as ACNielsen Company, offer test marketing services to provide independent assessment of proposed products. Not all products that are test marketed are launched. At times, problems discovered during test marketing cannot be resolved.

## 12-2g Commercialization

During the **commercialization** phase, plans for full-scale manufacturing and marketing must be refined and settled and budgets for the project prepared. Early in the commercialization phase, marketing management analyzes the results of test marketing to find out what changes in the marketing mix are needed before introducing the product. The results of test marketing may tell marketers to change one or more of the product's physical attributes, modify the distribution plans to include more retail outlets, alter promotional efforts, or change the product's price. However, as more and more changes are made based on test marketing findings, the test marketing projections may become less valid.

During the early part of this stage, marketers must not only gear up for large-scale production, but also make decisions about warranties, repairs, and replacement parts. The type of warranty a firm provides can be a critical issue for buyers, especially for expensive, technically complex goods, such as appliances, or frequently used items, such as mattresses. Establishing an effective system for providing repair services and replacement parts is necessary to maintain favorable customer relationships. Although the producer may furnish these services directly to buyers, it is more common for the producer to provide such services through regional service centers. Regardless of how services are provided, it is important to customers that they be performed quickly and correctly.

The product enters the market during the commercialization phase. When introducing a product, a firm may spend enormous sums for advertising, personal selling, and other types of promotion, as well as on manufacturing and equipment costs. Such expenditures may not

**commercialization** Refining and finalizing plans and budgets for full-scale manufacturing and marketing of a product be recovered for several years. Smaller firms may find this process difficult, but even so they may use press releases, blogs, podcasts, and other tools to capture quick feedback as well as to promote the new product. Another low-cost promotional tool is product reviews in newspapers, magazines, or blogs, which can be especially helpful when they are positive and target the same customers.

Products are not usually launched nationwide overnight, but are introduced in stages through a process called a *rollout*. With a rollout, a product is introduced starting in one geographic area or set of areas and gradually expands into adjacent ones. It may take several years to reach national marketing coverage. Sometimes, the test cities are used as initial marketing areas, and the introduction of the product becomes a natural extension of test marketing. A product test marketed in Sacramento, California and Fort Collins, Colorado could be introduced first in those cities. After the stage 1 introduction is complete, stage 2 usually includes market coverage of the states where the test cities are located. In stage 3, marketing efforts might be extended to adjacent states. All remaining states would then be covered in stage 4. Figure 12.3 shows these four stages of commercialization.

Product rollouts do not always occur state by state. Other geographic combinations, such as groups of counties that overlap across state borders, are sometimes used. Products destined for multinational markets may also be rolled out one country or region at a time. Gradual product introduction is desirable for several reasons. First, it reduces the risks of introducing a new product. If the product fails, the firm will experience smaller losses if it introduced the item in only a few geographic areas than if it marketed the product nationally. Second, a company cannot introduce a product nationwide overnight, because a system of wholesalers and retailers to distribute the product cannot be established so quickly. Developing a distribution network can take considerable time. Third, if the product is successful from launch, the number of units needed to satisfy nationwide demand for it may be too large for the firm to produce in a short time. Finally, gradual introduction allows for fine-tuning of the marketing mix to satisfy target customers. As electric charging stations become more prevalent around the nation, Tesla

---

**Figure 12.3    Stages of Expansion into a National Market during Commercialization**

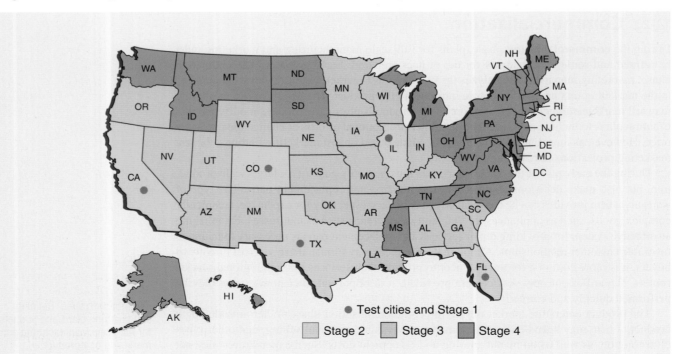

Motors has used a rollout strategy to build demand for its innovative electric vehicles. The rollout strategy has also allowed the company to expand production capacity to accommodate the growing demand.[20]

Despite the good reasons for introducing a product gradually, marketers realize this approach creates problems. A gradual introduction allows competitors to observe what the firm is doing and monitor results just as the firm's own marketers are doing. If competitors see that the newly introduced product is successful, they may quickly enter the same target market with similar products. In addition, as a product is introduced region by region, competitors may expand their marketing efforts to offset promotion of the new product. Marketers should realize that too much delay in launching a product can cause the firm to miss out on seizing market opportunities, creating competitive offerings, and forming cooperative relationships with channel members.[21]

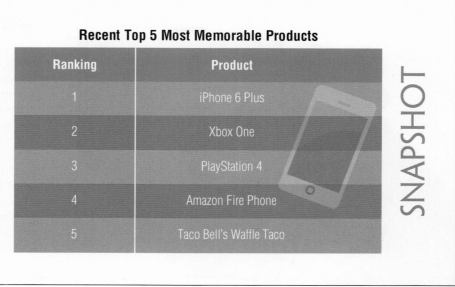

**Recent Top 5 Most Memorable Products**

| Ranking | Product |
|---|---|
| 1 | iPhone 6 Plus |
| 2 | Xbox One |
| 3 | PlayStation 4 |
| 4 | Amazon Fire Phone |
| 5 | Taco Bell's Waffle Taco |

Source: Kristina Monllos, "The 10 Most Memorable New Products of 2014, *Adweek*, http://www.adweek.com/news-gallery/advertising-branding/10-most-memorable-new-products-2014-161886 (accessed February 29, 2016).

## 12-3 PRODUCT DIFFERENTIATION THROUGH QUALITY, DESIGN, AND SUPPORT SERVICES

Some of the most important characteristics of products are the elements that distinguish them from one another. **Product differentiation** is the process of creating and designing products so customers perceive them as different from competing products. Customer perception is critical in differentiating products. Perceived differences might include quality, features, styling, price, or image. In this section, we examine three aspects of product differentiation that companies must consider when creating and offering products for sale: product quality, product design and features, and product support services. These aspects involve the company's attempt to create real differences among products.

### 12-3a Product Quality

**Quality** refers to the overall characteristics of a product that allow it to perform as expected in satisfying customer needs. The words *as expected* are very important to this definition because quality usually means different things to different customers. For some, durability signifies quality. The Craftsman line of tools at Sears is an example of a product with a reputation for durability. Indeed, Sears provides a lifetime guarantee on its tools.

The concept of quality also varies between consumer and business markets. Consumers consider high-quality products to be reliable, durable, and easy to maintain. For business markets, technical suitability, ease of repair, and company reputation are important characteristics. Unlike consumers, most organizations place far less emphasis on price than on product quality.

**product differentiation** Creating and designing products so that customers perceive them as different from competing products

**quality** The overall characteristics of a product that allow it to perform as expected in satisfying customer needs

PRECISION

THE MIDSIZE PICKUP ONLY GMC COULD BUILD.

THE NEW CANYON IS HERE. **GMC**
WE ARE PROFESSIONAL GRADE

**Level of Quality**
GMC demonstrates its quality by comparing the precision of its craftsmanship with that of a fine watch.

One important dimension of quality is **level of quality**, the amount of quality a product possesses. The concept is a relative one because the quality level of one product is difficult to describe unless it is compared to that of other products. The advertisement for the GMC Canyon midsize pickup stresses the product's level of quality, comparing it to the precision of a fine wristwatch. The advertisement hints that such a precisely crafted vehicle could only be built by GMC. To reinforce the idea of quality as measured by precision, the ad makes the photo of the actual product rather small relative to the image of a cut-away of the insides of a wristwatch, showing images of interior parts of the pickup such as the stick shift. The American Customer Satisfaction Index (ACSI) ranks customer satisfaction among a wide variety of businesses in the United States. For instance, Amazon is the highest-ranked online retailer according to the ACSI index.[22] Dissatisfied customers may curtail their overall spending, which could stifle economic growth.

A second important dimension is consistency. **Consistency of quality** refers to the degree to which a product has the same level of quality over time. Consistency means giving consumers the quality they expect every time they purchase the product. As with level of quality, consistency is a relative concept. It implies a quality comparison within the same brand over time.

The consistency of product quality can also be compared across competing products. It is at this stage that consistency becomes critical to a company's success. Companies that can provide quality on a consistent basis have a major competitive advantage over rivals. FedEx, for example, offers reliable delivery schedules and a variety of options, ranking it at the top of consumer shipping companies.[23] No company has ever succeeded by creating and marketing low-quality products that do not satisfy consumers. Many companies have taken major steps, such as implementing total quality management (TQM), to improve the quality of their products and become more competitive.

Higher product quality means firms will have to charge a higher price for the product. Marketers must therefore consider the balance of quality and price carefully in their planning efforts.

**level of quality** The amount of quality a product possesses

**consistency of quality** The degree to which a product has the same level of quality over time

**product design** How a product is conceived, planned, and produced

**styling** The physical appearance of a product

## 12-3b  Product Design and Features

**Product design** refers to how a product is conceived, planned, and produced. Design is a very complex topic because it involves the total sum of all the product's physical characteristics. Many companies are known for the outstanding designs of their products: Apple for electronics and computers, Cuisinart for kitchen appliances, and Merrell for hiking shoes. Good design is one of the best competitive advantages any brand can possess.

One component of design is **styling**, or the physical appearance of the product. The style of a product is one design feature that can allow certain products to sell very rapidly. Good design, however, means more than just appearance—design also encompasses a product's functionality and usefulness. For instance, a pair of jeans may look great, but if they fall apart after three washes, the design was poor. Most consumers seek out products that both look good and function well.

**Product features** are specific design characteristics that allow a product to perform certain tasks. By adding or subtracting features, a company can differentiate its products from those of the competition. Product features can also be used to differentiate products within the same company. For instance, Nike offers a range of shoes designed for purposes from walking, to running, to weightlifting, to cross-training in a gym. In general, the more features a product has, the higher its price and often the higher its perceived quality.

For a brand to have a sustainable competitive advantage, marketers must determine the product designs and features that customers desire. Information from marketing research efforts and databases can help in assessing customers' product design and feature preferences. Being able to meet customers' desires for product design and features at prices they can afford is crucial to a product's long-term success. Marketers must be careful not to misrepresent or overpromise regarding product features or product performance.

## 12-3c  Product Support Services

Many companies differentiate their product offerings by providing support services. Usually referred to as **customer services**, these services include any human or mechanical efforts or activities a company provides that add value to a product. Examples of customer services include delivery and installation, financing arrangements, customer training, warranties and guarantees, repairs, layaway plans, convenient hours of operation, adequate parking, and information through toll-free numbers and websites. Trader Joe's stands out among supermarkets for its stellar customer service. Marketers at Trader Joe's strive to ensure that nothing interrupts the positive experience and to create opportunities for employees to connect with customers. The approach ensures that shoppers find and purchase exactly what they want. To create a more personal environment, the store does not even have loudspeakers. As a result, Trader Joe's customers are highly loyal and sales per square foot frequently are triple that of competitors'.[24]

Whether as a major or minor part of the total product offering, all marketers of goods sell customer services. In the case of markets where all products have essentially the same quality, design, and features, providing good customer service may be the only way a company can

**product features** Specific design characteristics that allow a product to perform certain tasks

**customer services** Human or mechanical efforts or activities that add value to a product

## GOING GREEN

### Bambike: World's Greenest Bicycle

When Filipino-American Bryan Benitez McClelland began volunteering at the Gawad Kalinga community development organization in the Philippines after graduate work at the University of Pennsylvania, he expected to be there only six months. Instead, he stayed on for nearly a decade to create and market the Bambike as the planet's greenest bicycle.

McClelland settled on the idea of making a quality bicycle from local bamboo because he wanted to commercialize an earth-friendly product that would also provide good jobs for people in the community. His research showed that bamboo matures into a strong, tubular material, and helps keep the air clean by absorbing more carbon dioxide than most other plants. It also grows quickly, meaning supplies can be replenished within a short time.

McClelland got design pointers from an expert who builds bamboo bikes in Africa, and continued experimenting with different varieties of bamboo to see which made the most durable frames. Today, Bambike workers can produce up to 30 bamboo frames per month for a target market of middle- and upper-income consumers willing to pay about $1,700 for a good quality bike made from a sustainable resource. One Bambike model is for all-terrain riding, another is for city streets, and a third is for cruising on the beach. All have been tested and meet international standards for sturdy bicycle construction. An offshoot venture, Bambike Ecotours, offers eco-tours of the area via Bambikes, helping the local economy and spreading the word about the world's greenest bike.[b]

differentiate its products. This is especially true in the computer industry. When buying a laptop computer, for example, consumers are likely to shop more for fast delivery, technical support, warranties, and price than for product quality and design, as witnessed by the high volume of "off-the-shelf," non-customized lower-priced laptops sold at retailers such as Best Buy, Costco, Walmart, and Target. Through research, a company can discover the types of services customers want and need. The level of customer service a company provides can profoundly affect customer satisfaction. Additionally, the mere availability of add-on features can enhance the value and quality of a product in the eyes of the consumer.[25]

# 12-4 PRODUCT POSITIONING AND REPOSITIONING

**product positioning** The decisions and activities intended to create and maintain a certain concept of the firm's product, relative to competitive brands, in customers' minds

Once a target market is selected, a firm must consider how to position its product. **Product positioning** refers to the decisions and activities intended to create and maintain a certain concept of the firm's product, relative to competitive brands, in customers' minds. When marketers introduce a product, they try to position it so that it appears to have the characteristics that the target market most desires. This projected image is crucial. For instance, this advertisement for Lindt chocolate positions the confections as a high-end choice for discerning customers. By illustrating a close-up square of chocolate with a chef in the background, Lindt underscores the refined characteristics and high-quality ingredients of the product.

Source: Chocoladefabriken Lindt & Sprüngli AG

**Product Positioning**
Swiss chocolatier Lindt positions its chocolate as very high-end, making it an affordable luxury for those who appreciate fine foods.

## 12-4a Perceptual Mapping

A product's position is the result of customers' perceptions of the product's attributes relative to those of competitive brands. Buyers make numerous purchase decisions on a regular basis. To simplify buying decisions and avoid a continuous reevaluation of numerous products, buyers tend to group, or "position," products in their minds. Rather than allowing customers to position products independently, marketers often try to influence and shape consumers' concepts or perceptions of products through advertising. Marketers sometimes analyze product positions by developing perceptual maps, as shown in Figure 12.4. Perceptual maps are created by questioning a sample of consumers about their perceptions of products, brands, and organizations with respect to two or more dimensions. To develop a perceptual map like the one in Figure 12.4, respondents were asked how they perceive selected pain relievers in regard to price and type of pain for which the products are used. Also, respondents would be asked about their preferences for product features to establish "ideal points" or "ideal clusters," which represent a consensus about what a specific group of customers desire in terms of product features. Then, marketers can compare how their brand is perceived compared with the ideal points.

Figure 12.4    **Hypothetical Perceptual Map for Pain Relievers**

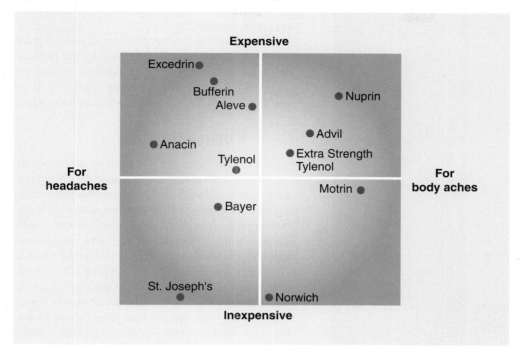

## 12-4b Bases for Positioning

Marketers can use several bases for product positioning. A common basis for positioning products is to use competitors. A firm can position a product to compete head-on with another brand, as PepsiCo has done against Coca-Cola, or to avoid competition, as 7 Up has done relative to Coca-Cola. Head-to-head competition may be a marketer's positioning objective if the product's performance characteristics are at least equal to those of competitive brands and if the product is priced lower. Head-to-head positioning may be appropriate even when the price is higher if the product's performance characteristics are superior. In the Orville Redenbacher's advertisement, marketers choose to position Orville Redenbacher's microwave popcorn head-to-head with Pop Secret microwave popcorn. The ad shows a giant bowl of popcorn with the Orville Redenbacher butter popcorn piled high in the red half of the bowl, but the Pop Secret popcorn barely topping the rim of the blue half of the bowl. This ad indicates, visually and with words, that Orville Redenbacher pops up more than Pop Secret.

Conversely, positioning to avoid competition may be best when the product's performance characteristics do not differ significantly from competing brands. Moreover, positioning a brand to avoid competition may be appropriate when that brand has unique characteristics that are important to some buyers. Prius, for example, does not compete directly with other hybrids. Rather, marketers position it as an eco-friendly hybrid that is also family-friendly. Auto companies are likely to focus on style, fuel efficiency, performance, terms of sale, or safety in their advertisements. Avoiding competition is critical when a firm introduces a brand into a market in which the company already has one or more brands. Marketers usually want to avoid cannibalizing sales of their existing brands, unless the new brand generates substantially larger profits.

A product's position can be based on specific product attributes or features. Apple's iPhone, for instance, is positioned based on product attributes such as its sleek design and compatibility with other Apple products and accessories, such as apps and music through the iTunes' store. Style, shape, construction, and color help create the image and generate appeal. If buyers

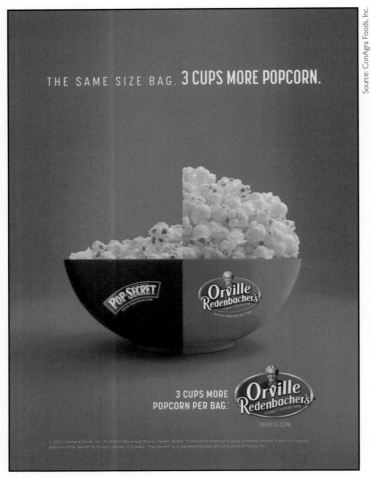

THE SAME SIZE BAG. **3 CUPS MORE POPCORN.**

POP·SECRET

*Orville Redenbacher's*

**3 CUPS MORE POPCORN PER BAG.**

*Orville Redenbacher's*

ORVILLE.COM

**Head-to-Head Positioning**
This advertisement indicates that Orville Redenbacher's popcorn yields more popcorn per bag than Pop Secret.

can easily identify the benefits, they are more likely to purchase the product. When the new product does not offer certain preferred attributes, there is room for another new product.

Other bases for product positioning include price, quality level, and benefits provided by the product. The target market can also be a positioning basis for marketers. This type of positioning relies heavily on promoting to the types of people who use the product.

### 12-4c  Repositioning

Positioning decisions are not only for new products. Evaluating the positions of existing products is important because a brand's market share and profitability may be strengthened by product repositioning. Repositioning requires changes in perception and usually changes in product features. For instance, to boost sales abroad, Nestlé repositioned its Cailler brand as a higher-end brand of Swiss chocolate. The Swiss-made cocoa-rich bars made with the finest ingredients, including local Swiss milk, are labeled in French as well as English, and are now priced about 25 percent more than conventional chocolate bars.[26] When introducing a new product into a product line, one or more existing brands may have to be repositioned to minimize cannibalization of established brands and ensure a favorable position for the new brand.

Repositioning can be accomplished by physically changing the product, its price, or its distribution. Rather than making any of these changes, marketers sometimes reposition a product by changing its image through promotional efforts. Finally, a marketer may reposition a product by aiming it at a different target market.

## 12-5  **PRODUCT DELETION**

Generally, a product cannot satisfy target market customers and contribute to the achievement of the organization's overall goals indefinitely. **Product deletion** is the process of eliminating a product from the product mix, usually because it no longer satisfies a sufficient number of customers. McDonald's, for instance, discontinued its Deluxe Quarter Pounder, six chicken sandwiches, and two snack wraps to streamline its menu in order to simplify ordering and speed up service for customers. The menu changes occurred after the burger chain experienced several quarters of declining revenue.[27] A declining product reduces an organization's profitability and drains resources that could be used to modify other products or develop new ones. A marginal product may require shorter production runs, which can increase per-unit production costs. Finally, when a dying product completely loses favor with customers, the negative feelings may transfer to some of the company's other products.

Most organizations find it difficult to delete a product. A decision to drop a product may be opposed by managers and other employees who believe that the product is necessary to the product mix. Salespeople who still retain loyal customers may be especially upset when a product is dropped. Companies may spend considerable resources and effort to revive a slipping product with a changed marketing mix and thus avoid having to eliminate it.

**product deletion** Eliminating a product from the product mix when it no longer satisfies a sufficient number of customers

Figure 12.5   **Product Deletion Process**

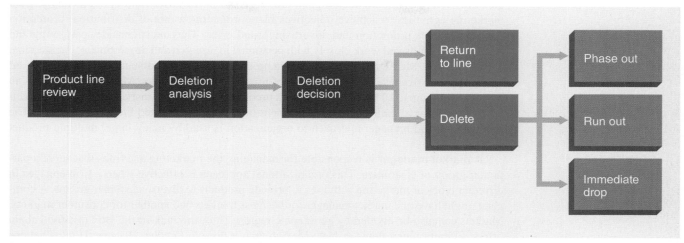

Source: Martin L. Bell, *Marketing: Concepts and Strategy*, 3rd ed., p. 267; Copyright © 1979, Houghton Mifflin Company. Reprinted by permission of Mrs. Martin L. Bell. © Jim R. Bounds/Bloomberg via Getty Images

Some organizations wait to delete products until after they have become heavy financial burdens. A better approach is some form of systematic review in which each product is evaluated periodically to determine its impact on the overall effectiveness of the firm's product mix. This review should analyze the product's contribution to the firm's sales for a given period, as well as estimate future sales, costs, and profits associated with the product. It should also gauge the value of making changes in the marketing strategy to improve the product's performance. A systematic review allows an organization to improve product performance and ascertain when to delete products. General Motors decided to delete the Hummer, Saturn, Saab, and Pontiac brands in order to lower costs, improve reputation, and become more profitable.

There are three basic ways to delete a product: phase it out, run it out, or drop it immediately (see Figure 12.5). A *phase-out* allows the product to decline without a change in the marketing strategy. With this strategy, no attempt is made to give the product new life. A *run-out* exploits any strengths left in the product. Intensifying marketing efforts in core markets or eliminating some marketing expenditures, such as advertising, may cause a sudden temporary jump in profits. This approach is commonly taken for technologically obsolete products, such as older models of computers. Often, the price is reduced to generate a sales spurt. The third alternative, an *immediate drop* of an unprofitable product, is the best strategy when losses are too great to prolong the product's life.

# 12-6 ORGANIZING TO DEVELOP AND MANAGE PRODUCTS

It should be obvious by now that managing products is a complex task. Often, the traditional functional form of an organization does not fit a company's needs. In this case, management must find an organizational approach that accomplishes the tasks necessary to develop and manage products. Alternatives to functional organization include the product or brand manager approach, the market manager approach, and the venture team approach.

A **product manager** is responsible for a product, a product line, or several distinct products that make up an interrelated group within a multiproduct organization. A **brand manager** is responsible for a single brand. Kraft, for example, has one brand manager for Nabisco Oreos,

**product manager** The person within an organization who is responsible for a product, a product line, or several distinct products that make up a group

**brand manager** The person responsible for a single brand

its number-one-selling cookie, and another for Oscar Mayer Lunchables. Both product and brand managers operate cross-functionally to coordinate the activities, information, and strategies involved in marketing an assigned product. Product managers and brand managers plan marketing activities to achieve objectives by coordinating a mix of distribution, promotion (especially sales promotion and advertising), and price. They must consider packaging and branding decisions and work closely with personnel in research and development, engineering, and production. Marketing researchers help product managers understand consumers and find target markets. Because the brand names of luxury brands like Aston Martin and Porsche can be negatively impacted by association with producers' other mass-market brands, brand managers must balance their brands' independent image with associated brands of the firm. The product or brand manager approach to organization is used by many large, multiple-product companies.

A **market manager** is responsible for managing the marketing activities that serve a particular group of customers. This organizational approach is effective when a firm engages in different types of marketing activities to provide products to diverse customer groups. A company might have one market manager for business markets and another for consumer markets. Markets can also be divided by geographic region. Thus, the Jack-in-the-Box fast-food chain offers different menu items in New Mexico than it does in Oregon. Because Hindus believe cows are sacred, and India has a large vegetarian population, McDonald's offers lamb and vegetarian options in lieu of beef burgers at its restaurants in India. The chains recognize that different markets have different preferences. These broad market categories might be broken down into more limited market responsibilities.

A **venture team** creates entirely new products that may be aimed at new markets. Unlike a product or market manager, a venture team is responsible for all aspects of developing a product: research and development, production and engineering, finance and accounting, and marketing. Venture team members are brought together from different functional areas of the organization. In working outside established divisions, venture teams have greater flexibility to apply inventive approaches to develop new products that can take advantage of opportunities in highly segmented markets. Companies are increasingly using such cross-functional teams for product development in an effort to boost product quality. Quality may be positively related to information integration within the team, customers' influence on the product development process, and a quality orientation within the firm. When a new product has demonstrated commercial potential, team members may return to their functional areas, or they may join a new or existing division to manage the product.

**market manager** The person responsible for managing the marketing activities that serve a particular group of customers

**venture team** A cross-functional group that creates entirely new products that may be aimed at new markets

# Summary

### 12-1  Explain how companies manage existing products through line extensions and product modifications.

Organizations must be able to adjust their product mixes to compete effectively and achieve their goals. Using existing products, a product mix can be improved through line extension and through product modification. A line extension is the development of a product closely related to one or more products in the existing line but designed specifically to meet different customer needs. Product modification is the changing of one or more characteristics of a product. This approach can be achieved through quality modifications, functional modifications, and aesthetic modifications.

### 12-2  Describe how businesses develop a product idea into a commercial product.

Before a product is introduced, it goes through a 7-phase new-product development process. In the idea generation phase, new product ideas may come from internal or external sources. In the process of screening, ideas are evaluated to determine whether they are consistent with the firm's overall objectives and resources. Concept testing, the third phase, involves having a small sample of potential customers review a brief description of the product idea to determine their initial perceptions of the proposed product and their early buying intentions. During the business analysis stage, the product idea is evaluated to determine its potential contribution to the firm's sales, costs, and profits. In the product development stage, the organization determines if it is technically feasible to produce the product and if it can be produced at a cost low enough to make the final price reasonable. Test marketing is a limited introduction of a product in areas chosen to represent the intended market. Finally, in the commercialization phase, full-scale production of the product begins and a complete marketing strategy is developed.

### 12-3 Discuss the importance of product differentiation and the elements that differentiate one product from another.

Product differentiation is the process of creating and designing products so that customers perceive them as different from competing products. Product quality, product design and features, and product support services are three aspects of product differentiation that companies consider when creating and marketing products. Product quality includes the overall characteristics of a product that allow it to perform as expected in satisfying customer needs. The level of quality is the amount of quality a product possesses. Consistency of quality is the degree to which a product has the same level of quality over time. Product design refers to how a product is conceived, planned, and produced. Components of product design include styling (the physical appearance of the product) and product features (the specific design characteristics that allow a product to perform certain tasks). Companies often differentiate their products by providing support services, usually called customer services. Customer services are human or mechanical efforts or activities that add value to a product.

### 12-4 Explain how businesses position their products.

Product positioning relates to the decisions and activities that create and maintain a certain concept of the firm's product in customers' minds. Buyers tend to group, or "position," products in their minds to simplify buying decisions. Marketers try to position a new product so that it appears to have all the characteristics that the target market most desires. Positioning plays a role in market segmentation. Organizations can position a product to compete head-to-head with another brand or to avoid competition. Positioning a product away from competitors by focusing on a specific attribute not emphasized by competitors is one strategy. Other bases for positioning include price, quality level, and benefits provided by the product. Repositioning by making physical changes in the product, changing its price or distribution, or changing its image can boost a brand's market share and profitability.

### 12-5 Discuss how product deletion is used to improve product mixes.

Product deletion is the process of eliminating a product that no longer satisfies a sufficient number of customers. Although a firm's personnel may oppose product deletion, weak products are unprofitable, consume too much time and effort, may require shorter production runs, and can create an unfavorable impression of the firm's other products. A product mix should be systematically reviewed to determine when to delete products. Products to be deleted can be phased out, run out, or dropped immediately.

### 12-6 Describe organizational structures used for managing products.

Often, the traditional functional form of organization does not lend itself to the complex task of developing and managing products. Alternative organizational forms include the product or brand manager approach, the market manager approach, and the venture team approach. A product manager is responsible for a product, a product line, or several distinct products that make up an interrelated group within a multiproduct organization. A brand manager is responsible for a single brand. A market manager is responsible for managing the marketing activities that serve a particular group or class of customers. A venture team is sometimes used to create entirely new products that may be aimed at new markets.

---

**Go to www.cengagebrain.com for resources to help you master the content in this chapter as well as materials that will expand your marketing knowledge!**

---

## Important Terms

## Discussion and Review Questions

1. What is a line extension, and how does it differ from a product modification?
2. Compare and contrast the three major approaches to modifying a product.
3. Identify and briefly explain the seven major phases of the new-product development process.
4. Do small companies that manufacture just a few products need to be concerned about developing and managing products? Why or why not?
5. Why is product development a cross-functional activity—involving finance, engineering, manufacturing, and other functional areas—within an organization?
6. What is the major purpose of concept testing, and how is it accomplished?
7. What are the benefits and disadvantages of test marketing?
8. Why can the process of commercialization take a considerable amount of time?
9. What is product differentiation, and how can it be achieved?
10. Explain how the term *quality* has been used to differentiate products in the automobile industry in recent years. What are some makes and models of automobiles that come to mind when you hear the terms *high quality* and *poor quality*?
11. What is product positioning? Under what conditions would head-to-head product positioning be appropriate? When should head-to-head positioning be avoided?
12. What types of problems does a weak product cause in a product mix? Describe the most effective approach for avoiding such problems.
13. What type of organization might use a venture team to develop new products? What are the advantages and disadvantages of such a team?

## Video Case 12.1

### Sriracha Heats Up the Hot Sauce Market

Entrepreneur David Tran cooked up his first batch of hot-pepper sauce in 1975, when he was still living in his native Vietnam. He packaged the sauce in recycled baby-food jars, and family members made customer deliveries by bicycle. When Tran came to America in 1980, he made a living by cooking up batches of his distinctively hot sauce and selling it by the bucketful to Asian restaurants around Chinatown in Los Angeles.

Tran named his company Huy Fong after the freighter that brought him to America. To convey the authenticity of the bright-red sauce made from freshly-crushed jalapeño chili peppers, Tran called it sriracha, which is an actual town in Thailand. He packaged the fiery sauce in a clear squeeze bottle to showcase its "hot" color and quality, added white lettering in English and Chinese, and topped the bottle with a green squirt cap, features that differentiate his product from other sauces. The red rooster sketched on every bottle represents Tran's Chinese zodiac sign.

Although Tabasco and other hot sauces had been popular condiments for years, the fresh quality and unique tang of Tran's sriracha sauce quickly made it a mainstay in restaurants and consumer kitchens through word of mouth only—without advertising or even a sales force. The firm soon needed a larger production facility and, as demand multiplied year after year, it enlarged its production facility a second time.

Now Huy Fong cooks up hundreds of thousands of bottles of its signature sauce every day, using locally grown jalapeño peppers that can be harvested, transported, washed, ground, and stirred into sriracha within just six hours. Because no two crops of peppers are exactly the same, some individual batches may be hotter than others, as Huy Fong warns customers on its website. Annual sales exceed $80 million as Huy Fong's sauces are shipped throughout North America and beyond. Long lines of Sriracha fans wait to tour Huy Fong's production plant in Irwindale, California, where they can watch Tran's sauce being

iStockphoto.com/asiantiger247

made and buy chili-red T-shirts in the Rooster Room gift shop (or online).

When Tran began selling his made-in-America sauce back in 1980, he did not trademark the sriracha name. As a result, his company cannot sue any time another marketer uses the word in a brand name or to describe a particular item. It has also opened the door to competition from sriracha food products made by well-established, deep-pocketed corporations like Tabasco, Heinz, and Kikkoman. When Tran heard that Tabasco was about to launch its own sriracha sauce, his comment was: "My 'rooster killer' jumped into the market."

Despite the sriracha rivalry, Tran believes that widespread use of the word *sriracha* serves as a form of advertising for his product, which is positioned as the pioneer of the category. The entrepreneur also uses the fame of being sriracha's originator to forge partnerships with food marketers that want to add his sauce's flavor to their products.

Pop Gourmet, for example, has a deal to use Huy Fong's sriracha in its popcorn. Neither licensing fees nor royalties are involved, only prominent display of Tran's trademarked rooster on the popcorn's vivid-red packaging. Sriracha popcorn has become Pop Gourmet's best-selling product, and the firm is introducing additional snacks featuring sriracha. Now other marketers have received Tran's permission to use his sauce in their products, reinforcing the product's positioning as the original, most authentic, and best-known of all sriracha sauces.[28]

### Questions for Discussion

1. Because chili peppers are agricultural products, their level of spiciness can fluctuate from crop to crop. What does this mean for consumers' perceptions of the quality of Huy Fong sriracha sauce?
2. If you were to create a perceptual map for sriracha sauces, which four dimensions would you choose? Where would you put Huy Fong's sriracha on this perceptual map, and why?
3. What are the possible benefits and risks of Huy Fong allowing other marketers to use his sauce, and include his brand, when they introduce line extensions?

# Case 12.2

## Quesalupa! Crunchy and All that Cheese from Taco Bell

Remember Doritos Locos Tacos? Introduced in 2012, this one product increased Taco Bell's revenues by a whopping $1 billion during its first year on the market. No wonder the fast-food restaurant company never stops cooking up ideas to change and expand its menu. Taco Bell's research shows that adding new items, even those available for a limited time only, will bring consumers back to its 6,500 outlets again and again. That kind of brand loyalty is especially important in today's competitive marketplace, which is why Taco Bell aims to launch a new product every five weeks. In recent years, the firm has used co-branding for new breakfast items like Cap'n Crunch Delights, a mini-doughnut-cereal available only for a short time. It has also experimented with different ingredients and spices by introducing lunch and dinner items such as spicy, tortilla-wrapped DareDevil Loaded Grillers.

The new-product process at Taco Bell begins with brainstorming, experimentation, and discussion. Top executives scan the overall marketing environment, including social-media sites, seeking inspiration for new flavor sensations or untraditional food combinations that will attract customer interest and fit with Taco Bell's brand personality. Food experts from top suppliers regularly step into the company's test kitchens to whip up innovative creations based on the latest food trends and consumer research. Taco Bell's marketers nibble away, and as the conversation flows, they come away with ideas to shape into specific product concepts. Two Taco Bell restaurants near the company's headquarters also serve as idea generators, by encouraging buyers to creatively customize their food orders. Marketers carefully analyze the frequency of requests for different combinations to gain insights into how consumers' tastes are changing. Although Taco Bell's customers often favor crunchy and cheesy products, the firm is always on the lookout for other ideas that will add a bit of variety to the menu.

Once the company has screened the ideas, tested product concepts, and developed prototypes of new menu

Rob Wilson/Shutterstock.com

items, it puts the best into test marketing. The crunchy, cheese-stuffed Quesalupa, a cross between a quesadilla and chalupa, was tested in 36 Taco Bell restaurants around Toledo, Ohio, the same city where Doritos Locos Tacos were test marketed in 2011 before being launched nationally in 2012. Through test marketing, Taco Bell was able to evaluate customer reaction to the Quesalupa and, just as important, be sure the new product could be prepared to look and taste as it should, every time customers placed an order. The firm also assessed whether it could get sufficient supplies for a large-scale launch, if and when the product was chosen for commercialization. Taco Bell supported its test marketing with Toledo-area ads to encourage product trial.

After months of test marketing in Toledo, Taco Bell determined that customer response was enthusiastic enough to move ahead with a national launch of the Quesalupa. Rather than introduce the new product with a traditional marketing campaign, Taco Bell created a buzz in mass media and social media by trumpeting a big introduction to coincide with the Super Bowl in February 2016—without saying which product was being added to the menu. During the Super Bowl, Taco Bell cleared up the mystery by revealing the Quesalupa in a national ad and five regional ads for targeted markets. This got the launch off to a strong start by bringing consumers into restaurants across the country for a taste and a chance to tell their friends all about the satisfying crunch and the bridges of hot, stringy cheese with taco toppings in the middle.[29]

## Questions for Discussion

1. In terms of product differentiation, why does Taco Bell test market its new products for months before deciding whether to introduce them in a wider area?

2. What are the advantages and disadvantages of Taco Bell introducing a product simultaneously in all outlets nationwide rather than in stages through a rollout?

3. Which product attributes or features does Taco Bell appear to be using to position the Quesalupa, and why?

# NOTES

[1] Laura Furr, "Houston Doll Company to Merge with New York Competitor," *Houston Business Journal*, December 3, 2015, www .bizjournals.com/houston/news/2015/12/03/ houston-doll-company-to-merge-with-new-york. html (accessed February 10, 2016); Joy Sewing, "Pret-tie Girls! Dolls Bring Diversity to Toyland," *Houston Chronicle*, November 30, 2015, www.houstonchronicle.com/life/article/Prettie-Girls-Dolls-bring-diversity-to-toyland-6644552 .php (accessed February 10, 2016); Sarah Rufca, "Pretty Is as Prettie Does," *Houstonia*, September 29, 2015, www.houstoniamag.com/ articles/2015/9/29/pretty-is-as-prettie-does-october-2015 (accessed February 10, 2016); http://oneworlddolls.com.

[2] Anjali Athavaley and Sruthi Ramkrishnan, "Kellogg's Sales Fall as U.S. Consumers Shun Cereals and Snacks," *Reuters*, November 3, 2015, http://www.reuters.com/article/ us-kellogg-results-idUSKCN0SS1I120151103 (accessed March 1, 2016); "Kellogg Company Brands Hit the Hottest Trends with More than 40 New Products," Kellogg Company, press release, June 29, 2015, http://newsroom. kelloggs.com/2015-06-29-Kellogg-Company-brands-hit-the-hottest-trends-with-more-than-40-new-products (accessed March 1, 2016).

[3] Hank Schulz, "Pfizer Throws Hat in Gummy Ring with Centrum Line Extension," *NutraIngredients-USA*, June 9, 2015, http:// www.nutraingredients-usa.com/Markets/Pfizer-throws-hat-in-gummy-ring-with-Centrum-line-extension (accessed March 1, 2016).

[4] Robert E. Carter and David J. Curry, "Perceptions versus Performance When Managing Ex-tensions: New Evidence about the Role of Fit between a Parent Brand and an Extension," *Journal of the Academy of Marketing Science*, www.springerlink. com/content/8030v6q35851821t (accessed March 1, 2016).

[5] Christopher Doering, "Demand for Natural Foods Is Changing Iconic Products," *The Des Moines Register*, April 5, 2015, http:// www.desmoinesregister.com/story/money/ agriculture/2015/04/05/demand-natural-food-ingredients-easter-candy-confection-iconic-brands/25335383/ (accessed March 1, 2016).

[6] Jason Snell, "iPhone 6s and 6s Plus Review: the Best iPhone Ever, by a Wide Margin," *MacWorld*, September 28, 2015, http://www.macworld.com/ article/2986703/smartphones/iphone-6s-and-6s-plus-review-the-best-iphone-ever-by-a-wide-margin.html (accessed March 1, 2016)

[7] Celena Chong, "Blockbuster's CEO Once Passed up a Chance to Buy Netflix for only $50 Million," *Business Insider*, July 17, 2015, http:// www.businessinsider.com/blockbuster-ceo-passed-up-chance-to-buy-netflix-for-50-million-2015-7 (accessed March 1, 2016).

[8] Michael Ringel, Andrew Taylor, and Hadi Zablit, "Innovation in 2015," Boston Consulting Group, December 2, 2015, https://www .bcgperspectives.com/content/articles/growth-lean-manufacturing-innovation-in-2015/ (accessed March 1, 2016).

[9] "Brush. Whiten. Go." Colgate, http://www .colgateopticwhite.com/toothbrushes/whitening-pen-and-toothbrush (accessed March 1, 2016).

[10] Lanre Bakare, "The Best a Man Can Get? Dollar Shave Club, Harry's Lead Shaving's Young Turks," *The Guardian*, October 20, 2015, http://www.theguardian.com/fashion/2015/ oct/20/dollar-shave-club-harrys-shaving-gillette-young-turks-razors (accessed March 2, 2016); Dollar Shave Club, https://www.dollarshave-club.com/ (accessed March 2, 2016).

[11] Christoph Fuchs and Martin Schreier, "Customer Empowerment in New Product Development," *Journal of Product Innovation Management* 28, 1 (2011): 17–31.

[12] Arina Soukhoroukova, Martin Spann, and Bernd Skiera, "Sourcing, Filtering, and Evaluating New Product Ideas: An Empirical Exploration of the Performance of Idea Markets," *Journal of Product Innovation Management* 29, 1 (2012): 100–112.

[13] Christoph Fuchs and Martin Schreier, "Customer Empowerment in New Product

Development," *Journal of Product Innovation Management* 28, 1 (2011): 17–31.

[14] "Frito-Lay Kicks Off 3rd 'Do Us a Flavor' Contest," *Brand Eating*, February 4, 2015, http://www.brandeating.com/2015/02/frito-lay-kicks-off-3rd-do-us-flavor-contest.html (accessed March 2, 2016).

[15] Kaleidoscope, http://kascope.com/ (accessed March 2, 2016).

[16] Charles Passy, "How Fast-Food Chains Cook up New Menu Items," *The Wall Street Journal*, August 24, 2015, http://www.wsj.com/articles/how-fast-food-chains-cook-up-new-menu-items-1440381706?mod=djem_jiewr_MK_domainid (accessed March 2, 2016).

[17] JoAndrea Hoegg and Joseph W. Alba, "Seeing Is Believing (Too Much): The Influence of Product Form on Perceptions of Functional Performance," *Journal of Product Innovation Management* 28, 3 (2011): 346–359.

[18] Jill Wendholt Silva, "Chipotle Uses Kansas City to Test Market Chorizo," *The Kansas City Star*, June 2, 2015, http://www.kansascity.com/living/liv-columns-blogs/chow-town/article22817082.html (accessed March 2, 2016).

[19] Passy, "How Fast-Food Chains Cook up New Menu Items."

[20] Tim Motovalli, "Plug In, Turn On, Pass Gas Station," *The New York Times*, December 27, 2013, www.nytimes.com/2013/12/29/automobiles/plug-in-turn-on-pass-gas-station.html (accessed March 2, 2016).

[21] Roger J. Calantone and C. Anthony Di Benedetto, "The Role of Lean Launch Execution and Launch Timing on New Product Performance," *Journal of the Academy of Marketing*

*Science*, June 2011, http://rd.springer.com/article/10.1007/s11747-011-0258-1 (accessed January 20, 2014).

[22] "ACSI: Retail Customer Satisfaction Falls Back to Long-Term Average," American Customer Satisfaction Index, press release February 23, 2016, https://www.theacsi.org/news-and-resources/press-releases/press-2015/press-release-retail-2015 (accessed March 2, 2016).

[23] "Consumer Shipping Benchmarks by Industry," ACSI, www.theacsi.org/index.php?option=com_content&view=article&id=147&catid=&Itemid=212&i=Consumer+Shipping (accessed March 2, 2016).

[24] Jeanne Bliss, "Trader Joe's Customer Experience Obsession," *1 to 1*, May 24, 2012, www.1to1media.com/weblog/2012/05/trader_joes_customer_experienc.html (accessed March 2, 2016); David DiSalvo, "What Trader Joe's Knows about Making Your Brain Happy," *Forbes*, February 19, 2015, http://www.forbes.com/sites/daviddisalvo/2015/02/19/what-trader-joes-knows-about-making-your-brain-happy/ (accessed March 1, 2016).

[25] Marco Bertini, Elie Ofek, and Dan Ariely, "The Impact of Add-On Features on Consumer Product Evaluations," *Journal of Consumer Research* 36, 1 (2009): 17–28.

[26] Natasha Khan, "Nestle to Reposition Cailler as Premium Chocolate, Brabeck Says," *Bloomberg Business*, March 24, 2015, http://www.bloomberg.com/news/articles/2015-03-24/nestle-to-reposition-cailler-as-premium-chocolate-brabeck-says (accessed March 3, 2016); Cailler, https://cailler.com/us (accessed March 3, 2016).

[27] Tom Huddleston, "McDonald's Drops Seven Sandwiches in 'Menu Simplification'," *Fortune*,

April 28, 2015, http://fortune.com/2015/04/28/mcdonalds-cutting-menu/ (accessed March 3, 2016).

[28] Robert Klara, "How Huy Fong Put Heat in a Bottle and Seared Sriracha into Our Lives," *Adweek*, January 25, 2016, www.adweek.com/news/advertising-branding/how-huy-fong-put-heat-bottle-and-seared-sriracha-our-lives-169131 (accessed February 8, 2016); David Pierson, "With No Trademark, Sriracha Name Is Showing Up Everywhere," *Los Angeles Times*, February 10, 2015, www.latimes.com/business/la-fi-sriracha-trademark-20150211-story.html (accessed February 8, 2016); Elizabeth Segran, "Hot Sauce, USA," *Fast Company*, November 2015, pp. 52–54; www.huyfong.com/ (accessed February 8, 2016).

[29] Jonathan Ringen, "Epic Cheese Pull: How Taco Bell Nailed Its Innovative New Quesalupa," *Fast Company Create*, February 7, 2016, www.fastcocreate.com/3056059/most-innovative-companies/taco-bell-for-combining-corn-beans-meat-and-cheese-into-genius (accessed February 10, 2016); Michelle Castillo, "The Mystery Behind Taco Bell's Super Bowl 50 Ad," *CNBC*, February 5, 2016, www.cnbc.com/2016/02/05/the-mystery-behind-taco-bells-super-bowl-50-ad.html (accessed February 10, 2016); Beth Kowitt, "*Fortune's* 8 Most Extreme Foods of 2015," *Fortune*, January 14, 2016, http://fortune.com/2016/01/14/olive-garden-burger-king-extreme-food (accessed February 10, 2016); Tim Nudd, "Taco Bell Cleverly Crashed These 5 Local Super Bowl Ads With Its Quesalupa," *Adweek*, February 9, 2016, www.adweek.com/adfreak/taco-bell-cleverly-crashed-these-5-local-super-bowl-ads-its-quesalupa-169541 (accessed February 10, 2016).

## Feature Notes

[a] Derek Blasberg, "How Jessica Alba Built a Billion-Dollar Business Empire," *Vanity Fair*, December 1, 2015, www.vanityfair.com/style/2015/11/jessica-alba-honest-company-business-empire (accessed February 11, 2016); Lindsay Blakely, "How Jessica Alba Proved Her Doubters Wrong," *Inc.*, November 2014, www.inc.com/magazine/201411/lindsay-blakely/how-jessica-alba-proved-her-doubters-were-wrong.html (accessed February 11, 2016); Alene Dawson, "Actress-mogul Jessica Alba Expands

Her Honest Company Empire to Include Skin Care and Beauty Products," *Los Angeles Times*, October 27, 2015, www.latimes.com/fashion/alltherage/la-ar-jessica-alba-launches-honest-beauty-20151026-story.html (accessed February 11, 2016).

[b] Erik Ortiz, "Filipino-American Entrepreneur Is Building Bamboo Bikes to Improve the Planet," *NBC News*, February 5, 2016, www.nbcnews.com/news/asian-america/filipino-american-entrepreneur-building-bamboo-bikes-

improve-planet-n507141 (accessed February 11, 2016); J.C. Ansis, "Bambike: Building Bamboo Bicycles, Enriching Lives," *CNN Philippines*, July 24, 2015, http://cnnphilippines.com/business/2015/03/13/story-of-the-filipino-bambike.html (accessed February 11, 2016); "Would You Like to Own a Bike Made of Bamboo?" *The Philippine Star*, September 18, 2015, www.philstar.com/radar/2015/09/18/1501213/would-you-own-bike-made-bamboo (accessed February 11, 2016).

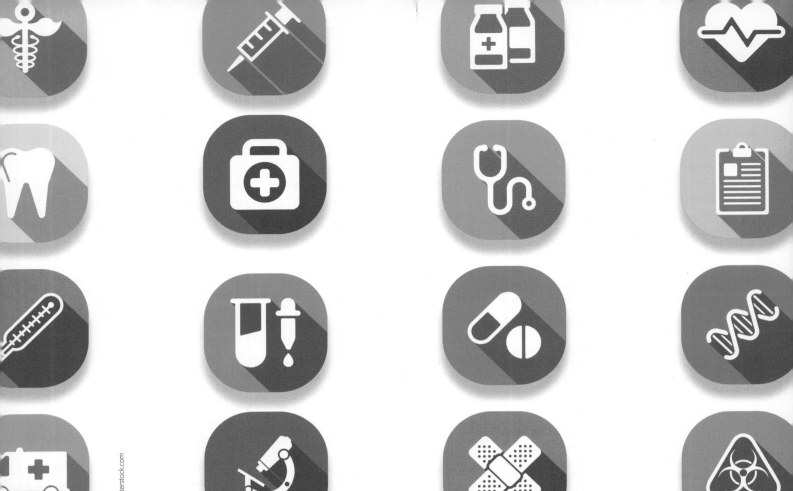

Moofer/Shutterstock.com

# chapter 13     Services Marketing

---

## OBJECTIVES

13-1   Discuss the growth and importance of services.

13-2   Identify the characteristics of services that differentiate them from goods.

13-3   Describe how the characteristics of services influence the development of marketing mixes for services.

13-4   Explain the importance of service quality and explain how to deliver exceptional service quality.

13-5   Discuss the nature of nonprofit marketing.

## MARKETING INSIGHTS

### McDonald's Markets All-Day Breakfast, Finally!

Customers have long clamored for all-day breakfast at McDonald's, repeatedly asking the company to extend ordering hours beyond 10:30 a.m. However, until recently, McDonald's resisted expanding breakfast hours, concerned about the effect on customer service during busy periods later in the day.

McDonald's knew its restaurants had limited space for large, separate grills to keep raw eggs away from burgers during cooking. Also, its restaurants lacked enough toasters to heat buns and muffins simultaneously. As a result, the company and its franchisees were concerned about preparing breakfast items quickly and correctly—every order, every time—during peak lunch and dinner periods.

Recently, McDonald's and its franchisees began testing an all-day breakfast menu, analyzing kitchen utilization and customer requests at different times. They found an egg grill that could be rolled into place when needed, and toasters that could be attached for toasting both buns and muffins. Finally, they recognized that the way to minimize delays during lunch and dinner was to limit the all-day breakfast menu.

McDonald's then began a national rollout of all-day breakfast, tweeting an invitation to thousands of customers who had requested the change. Now restaurants cook breakfast to order after the morning rush, which means customers sometimes wait a little longer for fresh, hot food. Despite the added costs and kitchen complexities, McDonald's enjoyed an increase in sales revenue after implementing all-day breakfast. Looking ahead, it is already planning to expand the number of breakfast items available after 10:30 a.m.[1]

Restaurants like McDonald's offer service products as well as tangible goods. This chapter explores concepts that apply specifically to products that are services. The organizations that market services include for-profit firms (e.g., those offering financial, personal, and professional services) and nonprofit organizations (e.g., educational institutions, churches, charities, and governments).

We begin this chapter with a discussion of the huge importance of service industries in economies, particularly in developed countries like the United States. We then address the unique characteristics of services. Next, we deal with the challenges these characteristics pose in developing and managing marketing mixes for services. We then discuss customers' judgment of service quality and the importance of delivering high-quality services. Finally, we define nonprofit marketing and examine the development of nonprofit marketing strategies.

## 13-1 THE GROWTH AND IMPORTANCE OF SERVICES

All products—whether goods, services, or ideas—are to some extent intangible. We previously defined a service as an intangible product that involves a deed, a performance, or an effort that cannot be physically possessed.[2] Services are usually provided through the application of human and/or mechanical efforts that are directed at people or objects. For example, a service such as education involves the efforts of service providers (teachers) that are directed at people (students), whereas janitorial and interior decorating services direct their efforts at objects. Services can also involve the use of mechanical efforts directed at people (air or public transportation) or objects (freight transportation). A wide variety of services, such as health care and landscaping, involve both human and mechanical efforts. Although many services entail the use of tangibles such as tools and machinery, the primary difference between a service and a good is that a service is dominated by the intangible portion of the total product.

The importance of services in the U.S. economy led the United States to be known as the world's first service economy. In most developed countries, including Germany, Japan, Australia, and Canada, services account for about 70 percent of the gross domestic product (GDP). More than one-half of new businesses in the United States are service businesses, and service employment is expected to continue to grow. A practice that has gained popularity among U.S. businesses as telecommunications technology has improved is **homesourcing**, in which customer-contact jobs, such as at call centers, are outsourced to the homes of workers. Staffing agencies like Rhema Business Solutions are dedicated to providing homesourcing employees to organizations in a variety of industries, including nursing, marketing and sales, advertising, web development, and writing.[3] Companies as diverse as 1-800-FLOWERS, J.Crew, and Office Depot all utilize homesourcing for some tasks.

A major catalyst in the growth of consumer services has been long-term economic growth (slowed by a few recessions) in the United States, which has led to increased prosperity and interest in financial services, travel, entertainment, and personal care. The need for child care, domestic services, online dating services, and other time-saving services has increased during the late 20th and early 21st centuries. Many busy consumers want to minimize or avoid such tasks as meal preparation, house cleaning, yard maintenance, and tax preparation in order to focus on other activities, such as work or family time. Because Americans tend to be health, fitness, and recreation oriented, the demand for services related to exercise and recreation has escalated. Another driver of services is the aging population in the United States, which has spurred expansion of health-care services. Finally, the increasing number and complexity of high-tech goods have spurred demand for support services. Indeed, dramatic changes in information technology have influenced and expanded the services sector in the 21st century. Consider service companies like Google, eBay, and Uber, which use technology to provide

**homesourcing** A practice whereby customer contact jobs are outsourced into workers' homes services that are responsive and well-targeted to customer needs and that have challenged traditional ways of conducting business.

Business services have grown as well. Business services include support and maintenance, consulting, installation, equipment leasing, marketing research, advertising, temporary office personnel, and janitorial services. The growth in business services can be attributed to the increasingly complex, specialized, and competitive business environment.

A way that might help you view services is using the metaphor of a theater. A play features production elements (such as actors, audience, a setting) and a performance. The actors (service workers) create a performance (service) for the audience (customers) in a setting (service environment) where the performance unfolds. Costumes (uniforms), props (devices, music, machines), and the setting (face-to-face or indirect through telephone or Internet) help complete the metaphor.[4] A service provider such as Disney World illustrates the metaphor: Employees wear costumes, there is an entertainment setting, and most service contact with employees involves playing roles and engaging in planned skits.

Services as products should not be confused with the related topic of customer service. Customer service involves any human, mechanical, or electronic activity that adds value to the product. Although customer service is a part of the marketing of goods, service marketers also provide customer services. Many service companies offer service quality guarantees to their customers in an effort to increase value. Hampton Inn, a national chain of mid-price hotels, gives its guests a free night if they are not 100 percent satisfied with their stay (less than one-half of 1 percent of Hampton customers ask for a refund).[5] In some cases, a 100 percent satisfaction guarantee or similar service commitment can motivate employees to provide consistently high-quality service because they are proud to be part of an organization that is so committed to good service.

# 13-2 CHARACTERISTICS OF SERVICES

The issues associated with marketing service products are not exactly the same as those associated with marketing goods. To understand these differences, it is first necessary to understand the distinguishing characteristics of services. Services have six basic characteristics: intangibility, inseparability of production and consumption, perishability, heterogeneity, client-based relationships, and customer contact.[6]

## 13-2a Intangibility

As already noted, the major characteristic that distinguishes a service from a good is intangibility. **Intangibility** means a service is not physical and therefore cannot be touched. It is impossible, for instance, to touch the education that students derive from attending classes—the intangible benefit is becoming more knowledgeable in a chosen field of study. In addition, services cannot be physically possessed. Students cannot physically touch knowledge as they can a smartphone or a car. The level of intangibility of a service increases the overall importance of the brand image when a customer is deciding which to purchase. A customer trying to select an intangible product usually relies more heavily on the brand to act as a cue to the nature and quality of the service.

Figure 13.1 depicts a tangibility continuum from pure goods (tangible) to pure services (intangible). Pure goods, if they exist at all, are rare because practically all marketers of goods also provide customer services. Even a tangible product like sugar must be delivered to the store, priced, and placed on a shelf before a customer can purchase it. Intangible, service-dominant products such as education or health care are clearly service products. Most products fall somewhere in the middle of this continuum. Products such as a restaurant meal or a hotel stay have both tangible and intangible dimensions. Knowing where the product lies on the continuum is important in creating marketing strategies for service-dominant products.

**intangibility** The characteristic that a service is not physical and cannot be perceived by the senses

Figure 13.1    **The Tangibility Continuum**

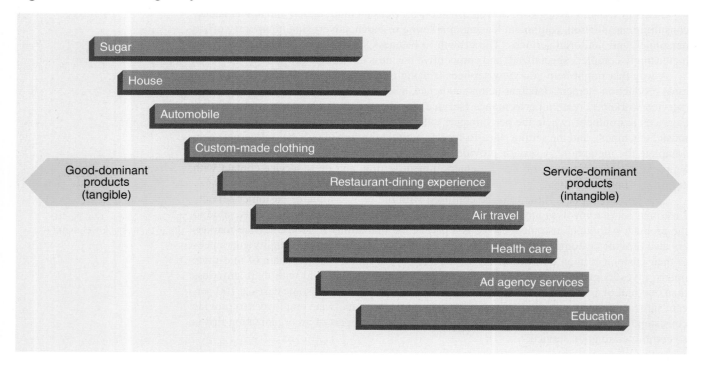

## 13-2b **Inseparability of Production and Consumption**

Another important characteristic of services that creates challenges for marketers is **inseparability**, which refers to the fact that the production of a service cannot be separated from its consumption by customers. For instance, an airline flight is produced and consumed simultaneously—that is, services are produced, sold, and consumed at the same time. In goods marketing, a customer can purchase a good, take it home, and store it until ready for use. The manufacturer of the good may never see an actual customer. Customers, however, often must be present at the production of a service (such as investment consulting or surgery) and cannot take the service home. Indeed, both the service provider and the customer must work together to provide and receive the service's full value. Because of inseparability, customers not only want a specific type of service but expect it to be provided in a specific way by a specific individual. For instance, the production and consumption of a medical exam occur simultaneously, and the patient knows in advance who the physician is and generally understands how the exam will be conducted. Inseparability implies a shared responsibility between the customer and service provider. Training programs for employees in the service sector should stress the importance of the customer in the service experience so that employees understand that the shared responsibility exists.

## 13-2c **Perishability**

Services are characterized by **perishability** because the unused service capacity of one time period cannot be stored for future use. For instance, empty seats on an airline flight today cannot be stored and sold to passengers at a later date. Other examples of service perishability include unsold basketball tickets, unscheduled dentists' appointment times, and empty hotel rooms. Although some goods (e.g., meat, milk, or produce) are perishable, goods generally are less perishable than services. If a pair of jeans has been sitting on a department store shelf for a month, the quality is not affected. Goods marketers can handle the supply–demand problem

**inseparability** The quality of being produced and consumed at the same time

**perishability** The inability of unused service capacity to be stored for future use through production scheduling and inventory techniques. Service marketers do not have the same advantage and face several hurdles in trying to balance supply and demand. They can, however, plan for demand that fluctuates according to day of the week, time of day, or season.

## 13-2d Heterogeneity

Services delivered by people are susceptible to **heterogeneity**, or variation in quality. The quality of manufactured goods is easier to control with standardized procedures, and mistakes are easier to isolate and correct. Because of the nature of human behavior, however, it is very difficult for service providers to maintain a consistent quality of service delivery. This variation in quality can occur from one organization to another, from one service person to another within the same service facility, and from one service facility to another within the same organization. Consequently, the staff people at one bookstore location may be more knowledgeable and therefore more helpful than those at another bookstore owned by the same chain. The quality of the service a single employee provides can vary from customer to customer, day to day, or even hour to hour. Although many service problems are one-time events that cannot be predicted or controlled ahead of time, employee training and the establishment of standard procedures can help increase consistency and reliability. Training should offer ways that will help employees provide quality service consistently to customers, thus mitigating the issue of heterogeneity. Thus, a business that provides services in a cross-cultural environment may want to train its employees to be more sensitive toward people of different countries and cultures.

Heterogeneity usually increases as the degree of labor intensiveness increases. Many services, such as auto repair, education, and hairstyling, rely heavily on human labor. Other services, such as telecommunications, health clubs, and public transportation, are more equipment intensive. People-based services are often prone to fluctuations in quality from one time period to the next. For instance, the fact that a hairstylist gives a customer a good haircut today does not guarantee that customer a haircut of equal quality from the same hairstylist at a later time. Equipment-based services suffer from this problem to a lesser degree than people-based services. For instance, automated teller machines have low inconsistency in the quality of services compared to receiving the same service in-person at a bank, and bar-code scanning has improved the accuracy of service at checkout counters in grocery stores.

**Inseparability of Production and Consumption**
An airline flight is characterized by inseparability. That is, production and consumption occur simultaneously and cannot be separated.

## 13-2e Client-Based Relationships

The success of many services depends on creating and maintaining **client-based relationships**, which are interactions that result in satisfied customers who use a service repeatedly over time.[7] In fact, some service providers such as lawyers, accountants, and financial advisers call their customers *clients* and often develop and maintain close, long-term relationships with them. For such service providers, it is not enough to attract customers. They are successful only to the degree to which they can maintain a group of clients who use their services on an ongoing basis. For example, an accountant may serve a family in his or her area for decades. If the members of this family like the quality of the accountant's services, they are likely to recommend the accountant to other families. If several families repeat this positive word-of-mouth communication, the accountant will likely acquire a long list of satisfied clients.

Social media have made it easier for customers to share information about service companies. On Pinterest, users create separate "pinboards" for different categories, such as a planned wedding or party, and other users can use these boards for ideas and inspiration. Marketers

**heterogeneity** Variation in quality

**client-based relationships** Interactions that result in satisfied customers who use a service repeatedly over time

©Gemenacom/Shutterstock.com

**Heterogeneity**
Do you like to go to the same hair care professional most of the time? If so, it is probably because you want the same quality of hair care, such as a haircut that you have received from this individual in the past.

customer contact The level of interaction between provider and customer needed to deliver the service

are interested in the medium because each "pin" is worth 78 cents in additional revenue and is 100 times more viral than a Twitter tweet—making it a low-cost marketing investment that generates a large return. Pinterest is growing by leaps and bounds and is most popular among young and middle-aged women—the market segment in charge of most household purchasing decisions.[8] Word-of-mouth (or going viral, which is the online equivalent) is a key factor in creating and maintaining client-based relationships. To ensure that it actually occurs, the service provider must take steps to build trust, demonstrate customer commitment, and satisfy customers so well that they become very loyal to the provider and unlikely to switch to competitors.

## 13-2f  Customer Contact

Not all services require a high degree of customer contact, but many do. **Customer contact** refers to the level of interaction between the service provider and the customer necessary to deliver the service. High-contact services include health care, real estate, and legal services. Examples of low-contact services are tax preparation, auto repair, travel reservations, and dry cleaning. Technology has enabled many service-oriented businesses to reduce their level of customer contact. Most airlines, for example, have apps through which fliers can book flights, choose seats, check in, and more on their phone or tablet. Note that high-contact services generally involve actions directed toward people, who must be present during production. A hairstylist's customer, for example, must be physically present at the salon during the styling process. When the customer must be present, the process of production may be just as important as its final outcome. Although it is sometimes possible for the service provider to go to the customer, high-contact services typically require that the customer go to the production facility. Thus, the physical appearance of the facility may be a major component of the customer's overall evaluation of the service. Even in low-contact service situations, the appearance

# EMERGING **TRENDS IN MARKETING**

### How USAA Delivers Services through Mobile Apps

Based in San Antonio, Texas, USAA specializes in delivering financial services to people who are (or were) in the military, and their families. But delivering banking, insurance, and investment services to millions of customers who might be on the move at a moment's notice can be a challenge—especially because USAA has fewer than two dozen financial centers across the United States. That's why the firm uses technology to personalize its services to each individual's needs and preferences.

For example, knowing customers rarely have time for a lengthy phone call or browsing the Internet, USAA offers speedy, secure access to accounts via smart phones equipped with an app for voice recognition, fingerprint recognition, or facial recognition, as customers choose.

This allows customers to skip the frustration of slowly typing a password and instead, use a mobile app to log on with a spoken phrase, the touch of a finger, or simply looking at the phone screen. More than 200,000 customers started using this app within the first 30 days after introduction.

Each customer who visits USAA's website sees a personalized page preloaded with the types of information and transactions that he or she most frequently requests, adding convenience for those in a hurry. And, to encourage younger customers in particular to save more, USAA now has a voice-activated Savings Coach app. With a few words, customers can transfer money from checking to savings, and learn more about the benefits of savings through a game-like app interface.[a]

of the facility is important because the customer likely will need to be present to initiate and finalize the service transaction. Consider customers of auto-repair services. They bring in the vehicle and describe its symptoms but often do not remain during the repair process.

Employees of high-contact service providers represent a very important ingredient in creating satisfied customers. A fundamental precept of customer contact is that satisfied employees lead to satisfied customers. Employee satisfaction is one of the most important factors in providing high service quality to customers. Thus, to minimize potential problems, service organizations must take steps to understand and meet the needs of employees by training them adequately, empowering them to make decisions, and rewarding them for customer-oriented behavior.[9] Southwest Airlines encourages customer loyalty and employee retention through training their staff and broadcasting instances of customer satisfaction and standout customer service through social media channels. Social media can be an inexpensive and effective means of training and engaging employees, as well as spreading awareness of stellar service to customers.[10]

# 13-3 DEVELOPING AND MANAGING MARKETING MIXES FOR SERVICES

The characteristics of services discussed in the previous section create a number of challenges for service marketers (see Table 13.1). These challenges are especially evident in the development and management of marketing mixes for services. Although such mixes contain the four major marketing-mix variables—product, distribution, promotion, and price—the characteristics of services require that marketers consider additional issues.

Table 13.1  **Service Characteristics and Marketing Challenges**

| Service Characteristics | Resulting Marketing Challenges |
|---|---|
| Intangibility | Difficult for customer to evaluate.<br>Customer does not take physical possession.<br>Difficult to advertise and display.<br>Difficult to set and justify prices.<br>Service process is usually not protectable by patents. |
| Inseparability of production and consumption | Service provider cannot mass-produce services.<br>Customer must participate in production.<br>Other consumers affect service outcomes.<br>Services are difficult to distribute. |
| Perishability | Services cannot be stored.<br>Balancing supply and demand is very difficult.<br>Unused capacity is lost forever.<br>Demand may be very time sensitive. |
| Heterogeneity | Service quality is difficult to control.<br>Service delivery is difficult to standardize. |
| Client-based relationships | Success depends on satisfying and keeping customers over the long term.<br>Generating repeat business is challenging.<br>Relationship marketing becomes critical. |
| Customer contact | Service providers are critical to delivery.<br>Requires high levels of service employee training and motivation.<br>Changing a high-contact service into a low-contact service to achieve lower costs is difficult to achieve without reducing customer satisfaction. |

Sources: K. Doublas Hoffman and John E. G. Bateson, *Services Marketing: Concepts, Strategies, and Cases,* 4th ed. (Mason, OH: Cengage Learning, 2011); Valarie A. Zeithaml, A. Parasuraman, and Leonard L. Berry, *Delivering Quality Service: Balancing Customer Perceptions and Expectations* (New York: Free Press, 1990); Leonard L. Berry and A. Parasuraman, *Marketing Services: Competing through Quality* (New York: Free Press, 1991), p. 5.

## 13-3a **Development of Services**

A service offered by an organization is generally a package, or bundle, of services consisting of a core service and one or more supplementary services. A *core service* is the basic service experience or commodity that a customer expects to receive. A *supplementary service* supports the core service and is used to differentiate the service bundle from those of competitors. For example, when a student attends a tutoring session for a class, the core service is the tutoring. Bundled with the core service might be access to outlines with additional information, handouts with practice questions, or online services like a chat room or wiki to address questions that arise outside the designated tutoring time.

As discussed earlier, heterogeneity results in variability in service quality and makes it difficult to standardize services. However, heterogeneity provides one advantage to service marketers: It allows them to customize their services to match the specific needs of individual customers. Customization plays a key role in providing competitive advantage for the service provider. Being able to personalize the service to fit the exact needs of the customer accommodates individual needs, wants, or desires.[11] LensCrafters, depicted in the advertisement, is a firm that offers customized eyeware services that fulfill specific needs for each of its customers. The ad reminds consumers that "one size does not fit all" when it comes to prescription glasses. Not only must the lenses meet the prescription for the vision needs of the individual, but the frame must also be adjusted to fit the individual's unique face. The image of a large blue eye behind an eyeglass lens underscores the importance of high-quality and customized fit.

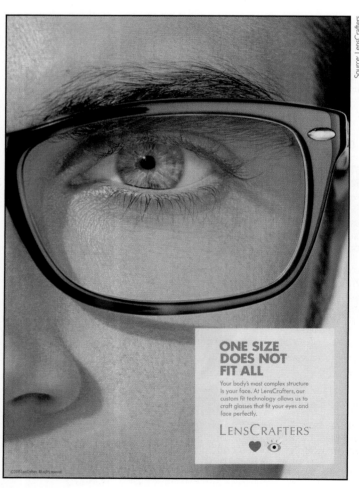

**ONE SIZE
DOES NOT
FIT ALL**

Your body's most complex structure is your face. At LensCrafters, our custom fit technology allows us to craft glasses that fit your eyes and face perfectly.

LENSCRAFTERS

**Customized Services**
LensCrafters is a service firm that offers a tangible product that must be customized for each individual's prescription and face.

Such customized services can be expensive for both provider and customer, and some service marketers therefore face a dilemma: how to provide service at an acceptable level of quality in an efficient and economic manner and still satisfy individual customer needs. To cope with this problem, some service marketers offer standardized packages. Thus, a lawyer may offer a divorce package at a specified price for an uncontested divorce. When service bundles are standardized, the specific actions and activities of the service provider usually are highly specified. Automobile quick-lube providers frequently offer a service bundle for a single price. The specific work to be done on a customer's car is spelled out in detail. Various other equipment-based services are also often standardized into packages. For instance, cable television providers offer several packages, such as "Basic," "Standard," and "Premier."

The characteristic of intangibility makes it difficult for customers to evaluate a service prior to purchase. Intangibility requires service marketers, such as stylists or attorneys, to market promises to customers. The customer must place some degree of trust in the service provider to perform the service in a manner that meets or exceeds those promises. Service marketers should take steps to avoid sending messages that consumers might construe as promises that raise customer expectations beyond what the firm can provide.

To cope with the problem of intangibility, marketers employ tangible cues (such as well-groomed, professional-appearing contact personnel and clean, attractive physical facilities) to assure customers about the quality and professionalism of the service. Most service providers require that at least some of their high-contact employees wear uniforms, which help make the service experience more tangible and serve as physical evidence to signal quality, create consistency, and send cues that suggest a desired image.[12] Consider the professionalism, experience, and competence conveyed by an airline pilot's uniform. Life insurance companies sometimes try to make the quality of their policies more tangible by printing them on premium paper and enclosing them in sheaths or high-quality folders. Because customers often rely on brand names as an indicator of product quality, service marketers at organizations whose names are the same as their service brand names should strive to build a strong national image for their companies. For example, USAA insurance, Ritz Carlton hotels, and Starbucks coffee maintain strong, positive national company images because these names are the brand names of the services they provide.

The inseparability of production and consumption and the level of customer contact also influence the development and management of services. The fact that customers are present and may take part in the production of a service means that other customers can affect the outcome of the service. For instance, a restaurant might give a small discount if children are well-behaved. Service marketers can reduce problems by encouraging customers to share the responsibility of maintaining an environment that allows all participants to receive the intended benefits of the service environment.

## 13-3b Distribution of Services

Marketers deliver services in various ways. In some instances, customers go to a service provider's facility. For instance, most health-care, dry-cleaning, and spa services are delivered at the provider's facilities. Some services are provided at the customer's home or business. Lawn care, air-conditioning and heating repair, and carpet cleaning are examples. Other services are delivered primarily at "arm's length," meaning no face-to-face contact occurs between the customer and the service provider. A number of equipment-based services can be delivered at arm's length, including electric, online, cable television, and telephone services. It can be costly for a firm to install the systems required to deliver high-quality customer service at arm's length, but can be essential in keeping customers satisfied and maintaining market share.

Marketing channels for services usually are short and direct, meaning the producer delivers the service directly to the end user. Credit cards are a service that is frequently offered directly, with customers dealing directly with credit card companies. This advertisement, for example, promotes the Capital One Venture credit card, which offers double airline miles in its reward program. The image in the ad—actress Jennifer Garner pondering which flight to take in an airport—underscores that Capital One's Venture credit card gives consumers rewards and choices, such as using

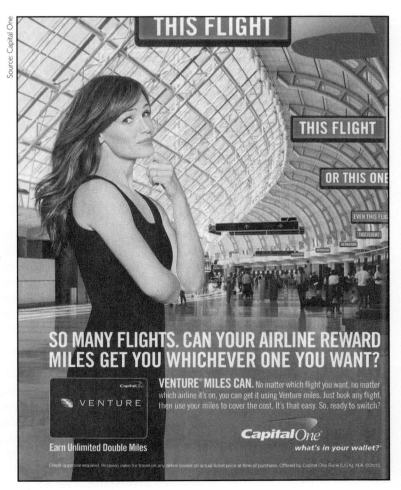

**Direct Marketing Channel**
Most credit card companies provide credit services through direct marketing channels. Credit card holders deal directly with their credit card companies.

their reward miles on any airline and any flight, which may help Capital One stand out in a crowded field of credit cards.

Some services, however, use intermediaries. For example, travel agents facilitate the delivery of airline services, independent insurance agents participate in the marketing of a variety of insurance policies, and financial planners market investment services. The Internet has allowed some service providers to alter marketing and distribution channels. Restaurants are increasingly using third-party intermediaries to deliver hot meals to customers who prefer not (or are unable) to leave their homes or workplaces. A growing number of services, such as Deliver Me Food, Grub Hub, and Eat 24, connect restaurants and customers with website or smartphone ordering and swift delivery. The services are especially popular with corporate and hotel customers.[13] Similarly, Stitch Fix is an online personal shopping service, which ships clothing items to subscribers based on a detailed questionnaire. Personal shopping used to be a high-touch service, but the Internet has allowed Stitch Fix to offer a high-quality service at arm's length.[14]

Service marketers are less concerned with warehousing and transportation than are goods marketers. They are very concerned, however, about inventory management, especially balancing supply and demand for services. The service characteristics of inseparability and level of customer contact contribute to the challenges of demand management. In some instances, service marketers use appointments and reservations as approaches for scheduling delivery of services. Health-care providers, attorneys, accountants, and restaurants often use appointments or reservations to plan and pace delivery of their services. To increase the supply of a service, marketers use multiple service sites and also increase the number of contact service providers at each site.

To make delivery more accessible to customers and increase the supply of a service, as well as reduce labor costs, some service providers have replaced some contact personnel with equipment. In other words, they have changed a high-contact service into a low-contact one. By installing ATMs, banks increased production capacity and reduced customer contact. The transition to more automated services is not always seamless, however. Some customers do not like automated services as they are less personal and would prefer to talk to a staff person. When designing service delivery, marketers must pay attention to the degree of personalization that customers in their target market desire.

## 13-3c Promotion of Services

The intangibility of services results in several promotion-related challenges to service marketers. Because it may not be possible to depict the actual performance of a service in an advertisement or display it in a store, explaining a service to customers can be a difficult task. Promotion of services typically includes tangible cues that symbolize the service. Consider Liberty Mutual Insurance, which features the Statue of Liberty on its logo. This image symbolizes strength and reliability to consumers. Although this symbol has nothing to do with the actual service, it makes it much easier for customers to understand the intangible attributes associated with the service.

To make a service more tangible, promotions for services may show pictures of facilities, equipment, and service personnel. Thus, advertisements for fitness centers may depict the equipment available. Cincinnati-based Fifth Third Bank used an amusing campaign that included short commercials, games, and social media videos to persuade Millennials that its banking app is super fast and reduces their time spent waiting. By showing the target audience how the app can make their banking experience easier and faster, the bank can compete with larger financial institutions that have more branches.[15]

Marketers may also promote their services as a tangible expression of consumers' lifestyles. The advertisement for Air France highlights the five-star service available on its La Première Suite first class, which is targeted at wealthy consumers who expect to be pampered when they fly. The image of a woman lounging on a deeply reclined first-class seat with pillows under a chandelier with berries and champagne beside her highlights the space and luxury first-class flyers can expect when they choose La Première on Air France. The ad emphasizes that the services offered by Air France are an extension of the lifestyle and types of trips taken by target consumers.

Branded marketing can help service firms hone their messages for maximum impact. JP Morgan Chase kept this in mind when it revamped its banking website in part to create a consistent message across all available channels, including its smartphone app. The new website employs a simple, responsive, and personal design to echo the bank's highly used Chase Mobile App. Many of the website's buttons and menus are identical to those used in the app. The website also includes discussions and advice about financial health and stories about neighborhoods. The changes have already resulted in longer stays on the website, allowing Chase to build stronger relationships with its customers.[16] When preparing advertisements, service marketers should be careful to use concrete, specific language to help make services more tangible in customers' minds. Service companies are also careful not to promise too much regarding their services so that customer expectations do not rise to unattainable levels.

Compared with goods marketers, service providers are more likely to promote price, guarantees, performance documentation, availability, and training and certification of contact personnel. It is common, for example, for gyms and yoga or aerobics studios to promote their trainers' degrees and certifications as a way to ensure customers that their trainers are well-qualified to help them reach their fitness goals.

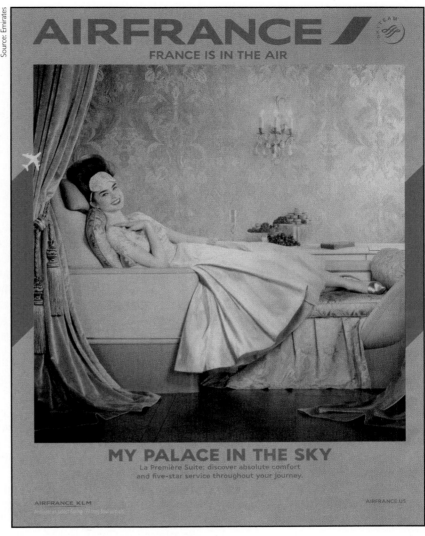

**Services as an Expression of Lifestyles**
Air France targets wealthy consumers and promotes its La Première Suite services as an expression of the luxury they expect.

Through their actions, service contact personnel can be directly or indirectly involved in the personal selling of services. Personal selling may be important because personal influence can help the customer visualize the benefits of a given service. Because service contact personnel may engage in personal selling, some companies invest heavily in training. To recapture lost market share and restore customer trust, United Airlines required its staff to take additional customer service training and instituted a rigorous set of tracking measures to ensure that customers are satisfied. New advertisements emphasize the benefits of flying United, including staff friendliness.[17]

As noted earlier, intangibility makes experiencing a service prior to purchase difficult, if not impossible in some cases. A car can be test-driven, a snack food can be sampled in a supermarket, and a new brand of bar soap can be distributed as a free sample. Some services can also be offered on a trial basis at little or no risk to the customer, but a number of services cannot be sampled before purchase. Promotional programs that encourage trial use of insurance, health care, or auto repair are difficult to design because, even after purchase of such services, assessing their quality may require a considerable length of time. For instance, an individual may purchase auto insurance from the same provider for 10 years before filing a

# Entrepreneurship in Marketing

## Helping Girl Scouts Hone Entrepreneurial Skills

**Founder:** Juliette Gordon Lowe
**Business:** Girl Scouts USA
**Founded:** 1912, in New York City
**Success:** The Girl Scouts Digital Cookie initiative is helping girls learn important entrepreneurial skills at a young age.

Every year, when nearly two million girls set out to sell Thin Mints and other popular cookies, they not only raise money for the nonprofit Girl Scouts, they also gain valuable entrepreneurial marketing skills. A growing number of girls are using the nonprofit's Digital Cookie initiative to sell cookies using websites and mobile apps as a way of supplementing their in-person sales efforts.

Financed by sponsors Dell and Visa, Digital Cookie allows Girl Scouts to build individual websites and then take paid cookie orders online or via mobile app for delivery in person or by mail. The idea is to encourage Scouts' interest in high-tech activities while enhancing cookie

distribution. To help bridge the digital divide between affluent and economically struggling communities, Dell is donating thousands of laptops and tablet computers to Girl Scouts from underprivileged areas. Visa teaches website-building and provides processing for credit- and debit-card payments made through the web or app, streamlining the ordering process for the girls and their customers.

The Digital Cookie encourages girls to develop their entrepreneurial marketing skills with educational yet entertaining games, videos, and quizzes about goal-setting, inventory management, budgeting, business ethics, and other key elements. Participants gain hands-on experience with e-commerce and learn the importance of follow-up service for customer satisfaction. "Girl Scouts is creating the next set of entrepreneurs," explains a Dell executive. "If you catch girls young enough, you can spark the fire."[b]

claim, but the quality of the coverage is based primarily on how the customer is treated and protected when a claim is made.

Because of the heterogeneity and intangibility of services, word-of-mouth communication is particularly important in service promotion. What other people say about a service provider can have a tremendous impact on whether an individual decides to use that provider. Some service marketers attempt to stimulate positive word-of-mouth communication by asking satisfied customers to tell their friends and associates about the service and may even provide incentives to current or new customers. Groupon and Living Social, which offer discounted deals at local businesses in participating cities, offer a free deal to customers who refer friends who then become new customers.

## 13-3d Pricing of Services

Services should be priced with consumer price sensitivity, the nature of the transaction, and its costs in mind.[18] Prices for services can be established on several different bases. The prices of such services as pest-control, dry cleaning, carpet cleaning, and health consultations are usually based on the performance of specific tasks. Other service prices are based on time spent on the task. For example, attorneys, consultants, counselors, piano teachers, and plumbers usually charge by the hour or day.

Some services use demand-based pricing. When demand for a service is high, the price is also high. Conversely, when demand for a service is low, so is the price. The perishability of services means that, when demand is low, the unused capacity cannot be stored and is lost—resulting in forgone revenues for the firm. Every empty seat on an airline flight or in a movie theater represents lost revenue. Some services are time sensitive, meaning that a significant number of customers desire the service around the same time. This point in time is called *peak demand*. A provider of time-sensitive services brings in most of its revenue during peak demand. For an airline, peak demand is usually early and late in the day. For cruise lines, peak demand occurs in the winter for Caribbean cruises and in the summer for Alaskan or European cruises. Customers can receive better deals on services by purchasing during nonpeak times.

Providers of time-sensitive services can use demand-based pricing to manage the problem of balancing supply and demand. They charge top prices during peak demand and lower prices during off-peak demand to encourage more customers to use the service. This is why the price of a matinee movie is generally lower than the same movie shown at a later time. **Off-peak pricing** is the practice of reducing prices of services used during slow periods in order to boost demand. The New York Jets engage in demand-based pricing. The cost of individual seats can rise or fall depending on the opposing team and the expected weather for the football game.[19]

In cases where customers tend to purchase services in a bundle,

**Airlines are charging higher add-on fees**

| Year | Fees (in billions) |
|------|--------------------|
| 2010 | $22.6 |
| 2011 | $32.5 |
| 2012 | $36.1 |
| 2013 | $42.6 |
| 2014 | $49.9 |

SNAPSHOT

Source: IdeaWorks Company and CarTrawler, "Airline ancillary revenue projected to be $49.9 billion worldwide in 2014," http://www.ideaworkscompany.com.

marketers must decide whether to offer the services at one price, price them separately, or use a combination of the two methods. Some service providers offer a one-price option for a specific bundle of services and make add-on services available at additional charges. For instance, telecommunication companies like CenturyLink offer services á la cart or as a standard package, and customers can add services according to their needs for additional fees.

Because of the intangible nature of services, customers sometimes rely heavily on price as an indicator of quality. If customers perceive the available services in a service category as being similar in quality, and if the quality of such services is difficult to judge even after these services are purchased, customers may seek out the lowest-priced provider. For example, many customers search for auto insurance providers with the lowest rates because insurance companies tend to offer packages that are easily comparable between firms. If the quality of different service providers is likely to vary, customers may rely heavily on the price–quality association. For instance, if you have to have an appendectomy, will you choose the surgeon who charges $1,500 or the surgeon who only charges $399?

For certain types of services, market conditions may limit how much can be charged for a specific service, especially if the services in this category are perceived as generic in nature. Thus, the prices charged by a self-serve Laundromat are likely to be limited by the competitive rates for laundry services in a given community. Also, state and local government regulations may reduce price flexibility in some industries, such as for auto insurance, utilities, cable television service, and even housing rentals in rent-controlled communities.

# 13-4 **SERVICE QUALITY**

Delivery of high-quality services is one of the most important and difficult tasks any service organization faces. Because of their characteristics, services are very difficult to evaluate. Hence, customers must look closely at service quality when comparing services. **Service quality** is defined as customers' perceptions of how well a service meets or exceeds their expectations.[20] Research findings by American Express state that 70 percent of American consumers would spend an average of 13 percent more for a product from a company that provides good customer service.[21] Consumers are two times more likely to tell other people about a bad customer service experience than a good one. More than half of the people surveyed admitted to losing their temper with a customer service representative. Finally, 81 percent of participants

**off-peak pricing** The practice of reducing prices of services used during slow periods in order to boost demand

**service quality** Customers' perceptions of how well a service meets or exceeds their expectations in the survey believe that small businesses focus more on customer service than larger companies.[22] A survey by RightNow Technologies revealed that 89 percent of consumers surveyed had switched to a competitor at some point because of a bad customer service experience.[23] Customers, not the organization, evaluate service quality—a critical distinction because it forces service marketers to examine quality from the customer's viewpoint. Thus, it is important for service organizations to determine what customers expect and then develop service products that meet or exceed those expectations.

## 13-4a  Customer Evaluation of Service Quality

The biggest obstacle for customers in evaluating service quality is the intangible nature of the service. How can customers evaluate something they cannot see, feel, taste, smell, or hear? Evaluation of a good is much easier because all goods possess **search qualities**, tangible attributes like color, style, size, feel, or fit that can be evaluated prior to purchase. Trying on a new coat and taking a car for a test drive are examples of how customers evaluate search qualities. Services, on the other hand, have very few search qualities. Instead, they possess experience and credence qualities. **Experience qualities** are attributes, such as taste, satisfaction, or pleasure that can be assessed only during the purchase and consumption of a service.[24] Restaurants and vacations are examples of services high in experience qualities. **Credence qualities** are attributes that customers may be unable to evaluate even after the purchase and consumption of the service. Examples of services high in credence qualities are surgical operations, automobile repairs, and legal representation. Most consumers lack the knowledge or skills to evaluate the quality of these types of services. Consequently, they must place a great deal of faith in the integrity and competence of the service provider.

Despite the difficulties in evaluating quality, service quality may be the only way customers can choose one service over another. For this reason, successful service marketers must understand how consumers judge service quality. Table 13.2 defines five dimensions consumers use

**search qualities** Tangible attributes that can be judged before the purchase of a product

**experience qualities** Attributes that can be assessed only during purchase and consumption of a service

**credence qualities** Attributes that customers may be unable to evaluate even after purchasing and consuming a service

Table 13.2  **Dimensions of Service Quality**

| Dimension | Evaluation Criteria | Examples |
|---|---|---|
| Tangibles: Physical evidence of the service | Appearance of physical facilities<br>Appearance of service personnel<br>Tools or equipment used to provide the service | A clean and professional-looking doctor's office<br>A clean and neatly attired repairperson<br>The freshness of food in a restaurant<br>The equipment used in a medical exam |
| Reliability: Consistency and dependability in performing the service | Accuracy of billing or recordkeeping<br>Performing services when promised | An accurate bank statement<br>A confirmed hotel reservation<br>An airline flight departing and arriving on time |
| Responsiveness: Willingness or readiness of employees to provide the service | Returning customer phone calls<br>Providing prompt service<br>Handling urgent requests | A server refilling a customer's cup of coffee without being asked<br>An ambulance arriving within 3 minutes |
| Assurance: Knowledge/competence of employees and ability to convey trust and confidence | Knowledge and skills of employees<br>Company name and reputation<br>Personal characteristics of employees | A highly trained financial adviser<br>A known and respected service provider<br>A doctor's bedside manner |
| Empathy: Caring and individual attention provided by employees | Listening to customer needs<br>Caring about customers' interests<br>Providing personalized attention | A store employee listening to and trying to understand a customer's complaint<br>A nurse counseling a heart patient |

Sources: Adapted from Leonard L. Berry and A. Parasuraman, *Marketing Services: Competing through Quality* (New York: Free Press, 1991); Valarie A. Zeithaml, A. Parasuraman, and Leonard L. Berry, *Delivering Quality Service: Balancing Customer Perceptions and Expectations* (New York: Free Press, 1990); A. Parasuraman, Leonard L. Berry, and Valarie A. Zeithaml, "An Empirical Examination of Relationships in an Extended Service Quality Model," *Marketing Science Institute Working Paper Series*, Report no. 90–112 (Cambridge, MA: Marketing Science Institute, 1990), p. 29.

when evaluating service quality: tangibles, reliability, responsiveness, assurance, and empathy. Note that all of these dimensions have links to employee performance. Of the five, reliability is the most important in determining customer evaluations of service quality.[25]

Service marketers pay a great deal of attention to the tangibles of service quality. Tangible elements, such as the appearance of facilities and employees, are often the only aspects of a service that can be viewed before purchase and consumption. Therefore, service marketers must ensure that these tangible elements are consistent with the overall image of the service. When it comes to the appearance of service personnel, something that an organization might want to consider is whether service personnel workers have visible tattoos. Research findings indicate that consumers draw conclusions based on visible tattoos that can affect their overall expectations of the service. In general, visible tattoos on white-collar workers, such as those in the medical and financial services sectors, are still viewed as inappropriate and unprofessional. However, attitudes about tattoos are changing as they become more common. More than 12 percent of workers age 30 and younger have a tattoo, meaning the level of acceptance of body modifications in the service industry, even in traditionally buttoned-up industries like accounting, is bound to increase over time.[26]

Except for the tangibles dimension, the criteria customers use to judge service quality are intangible. For instance, how does a customer judge reliability? Because dimensions like reliability cannot be examined with the senses, customers must rely on other ways of judging service. One of the most

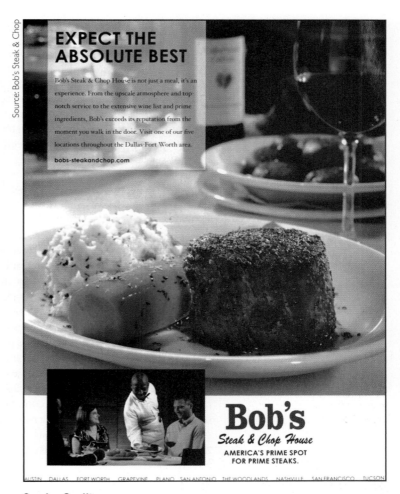

**Service Quality**
Bob's Steak & Chop House offers a high level of service quality to discerning customers.

important factors in customer judgments of service quality is service expectations. Service expectations are influenced by past experiences with the service, word-of-mouth communication from other customers, and the service company's own advertising. For instance, customers are usually eager to try a new restaurant, especially when friends recommend it. These same customers may have also seen advertisements or tweets or Instagram photos from the restaurant. As a result, they have a preconceived idea of what to expect before they visit the restaurant for the first time. When they finally dine there, the quality they experience will change the expectations they have for their next visit. That is why providing consistently high service quality is important. If the quality of a restaurant, or of any service, begins to deteriorate, customers will alter their own expectations and change their word-of-mouth communication to others accordingly. Bob's Steak & Chop House is a restaurant with multiple locations as shown in the advertisement. This advertisement underscores the high level of service quality provided by asking potential diners to "expect the absolute best" and informing them that Bob's isn't just a meal, it's also an experience. The images of a perfectly cooked steak with beautiful sides and a glass of wine as well as a smiling waiter in a black tie help reinforce the expectation of a perfect meal experience. The ad also reminds customers of Bob's reputation for top-notch service, quality ingredients, and extensive wine list.

## 13-4b Delivering Exceptional Service Quality

Providing high-quality service consistently is very difficult. All consumers have experienced examples of poor service: late flight departures and arrivals, inattentive restaurant servers, rude bank employees, and long waits. Obviously, it is impossible for a service organization to ensure exceptional service quality 100 percent of the time. However, an organization can take many steps to increase the likelihood of providing high-quality service. First, though, the service company must consider the four factors that affect service quality: (1) analysis of customer expectations, (2) service quality specifications, (3) employee performance, and (4) management of service expectations (see Figure 13.2).[27]

## 13-4c Analysis of Customer Expectations

Providers need to understand customer expectations when designing a service to meet or exceed those expectations. Only then can they deliver good service. Customers usually have two levels of expectations: desired and acceptable. The desired level of expectations is what the customer really wants. If this level of expectations is provided, the customer will be very satisfied. The acceptable level of expectations is what the customer views as adequate. The difference between these two levels of expectations is called the customer's *zone of tolerance*.[28]

Service companies sometimes use marketing research, such as surveys and focus groups, to discover customer needs and expectations. They can also listen to customers on social media. Analyzing complaints, feedback, and questions on Facebook, Twitter, and other social channels can help a firm identify patterns that may indicate corrective action is needed or suggest market opportunities that a firm can capitalize on. Customer reviews posted to Yelp or local review sites can also yield useful insights. Other service marketers, especially restaurants, may use comment cards on which customers can complain or provide suggestions. Still another approach is to ask employees. Because customer-contact employees interact daily with customers, they are in good positions to know what customers want from the company. Service managers should interact with their employees regularly by asking their opinions on the best way to serve customers.

---

Figure 13.2   **Service Quality Model**

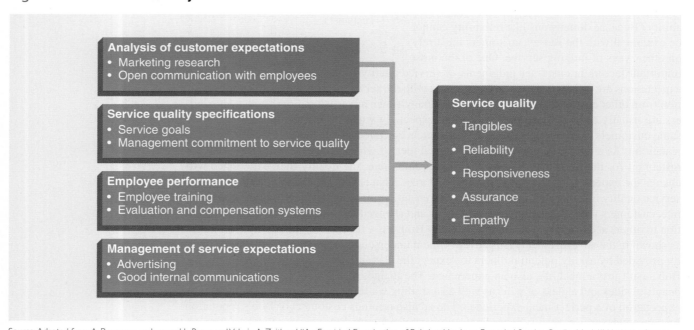

Source: Adapted from A. Parasuraman, Leonard L. Berry, and Valarie A. Zeithaml, "An Empirical Examination of Relationships in an Extended Service Quality Model," *Marketing Science Institute Working Paper Series*, Report no. 90–112, 1990. Reprinted by permission of Marketing Science Institute, and the authors.

## Service Quality Specifications

Once an organization understands its customers' needs, it must establish goals to help ensure good service delivery. These goals, or service specifications, are typically set in terms of employee or machine performance. For example, a bank may require its employees to conform to a dress code. Likewise, the bank may require that all incoming phone calls be answered by the third ring. Specifications like these can be very important in providing quality service as long as they are tied to the needs expressed by customers.

Perhaps the most critical aspect of service quality specifications is managers' commitment to service quality. Service managers who are committed to quality become role models for all employees in the organization. Such commitment motivates customer-contact employees to comply with service specifications. It is crucial that all managers within the organization embrace this commitment, especially frontline managers, who are much closer to customers than higher-level managers.

## Employee Performance

Once an organization sets service quality standards and managers are committed to them, the firm must find ways to ensure that customer-contact employees perform their jobs well. Contact employees in most service industries (bank tellers, flight attendants, servers, sales clerks, etc.) are often the least-trained and lowest-paid members of the organization. Service organizations that excel realize that contact employees are the most important link to the customer, and thus their performance is critical to customer perceptions of service quality. There is a direct relationship between the satisfaction of a company's contact employees, which is manifested in a positive attitude and a good work ethic, and the satisfaction of its customers. Employee and customer satisfaction levels also have a direct relationship with customer retention and loyalty.[29] The way to ensure that employees perform well is to train them effectively so they understand how to do their jobs. Providing information about customers, service specifications, and the organization itself during the training promotes this understanding.

The evaluation and compensation system the organization uses also plays a part in employee performance. Many service employees are evaluated and rewarded on the basis of output measures, such as sales volume (automobile salespeople) or a low error rate (bank tellers). Systems using output measures may overlook other major aspects of job performance, including friendliness, teamwork, effort, and customer satisfaction. These customer-oriented measures of performance might be a better basis for evaluation and reward. In fact, a number of service marketers use customer satisfaction ratings to determine a portion of service employee compensation.

## Management of Service Expectations

Because expectations play such a significant role in customer evaluations of service quality, service companies must set realistic expectations about the service they provide. They can set these expectations through advertising and good internal communication. In their advertisements, service companies make promises about the kind of service they will deliver. As already noted, a service company is forced to make promises because the intangibility of services prevents the organization from showing the benefits in the advertisement. However, the advertiser should not promise more than it can deliver. Doing so will likely mean disappointed customers.

To deliver on promises made, a company needs to have thorough internal communication among its departments, especially management, advertising, and store operations. Assume, for example, that a restaurant's radio advertisements guarantee service within 15 minutes or the meal is free. If top management or the advertising department fails to inform store operations about the 15-minute guarantee, the restaurant will very likely fail to meet its customers' service expectations. Even though customers might appreciate a free meal, the restaurant will lose some credibility as well as revenue. As mentioned earlier, word-of-mouth communication and online viral communication from other customers also shape customer expectations. However, service companies cannot manage this "advertising" directly. The best way to ensure positive word-of-mouth communication is to provide exceptional service quality. It has been estimated that customers tell four times as many people about bad service as they do about good service.

# 13-5 **NONPROFIT MARKETING**

**Nonprofit marketing** refers to marketing activities that are conducted by individuals and organizations to achieve some goal other than ordinary business goals like profit, market share, or return on investment. Nonprofit marketing is divided into two categories: nonprofit-organization marketing and social marketing. Nonprofit-organization marketing is the use of marketing concepts and techniques by organizations whose goals do not include making profits. Social marketing promotes social causes, such as AIDS research or recycling.

**nonprofit marketing** Marketing activities conducted to achieve some goal other than ordinary business goals such as profit, market share, or return on investment

Most of the previously discussed concepts and approaches to service products also apply to nonprofit organizations. Indeed, many nonprofit organizations mainly provide service products. In this section, we examine the concept of nonprofit marketing to determine how it differs from marketing activities in for-profit business organizations. We also explore the marketing objectives of nonprofit organizations and the development of their product strategies.

## 13-5a **How Is Nonprofit Marketing Different?**

Many nonprofit organizations strive for effective marketing activities. Charitable organizations and supporters of social causes are major nonprofit marketers in this country. Political parties, unions, religious sects, and fraternal organizations also perform marketing activities, but they are not considered businesses. Where the chief beneficiary of a business enterprise is one who owns or holds stock in it, in theory, the only beneficiaries of a nonprofit organization are its clients, its members, or the public at large. The Metropolitan Opera in New York City, for example, is run by the nonprofit Metropolitan Opera Association. Many museums and performing arts institutions are run as nonprofits or have a nonprofit arm. Consider this advertisement for the American Cancer Society. The advertisement features a beautiful young woman undergoing chemotherapy for cancer standing with grace and courage. The ad informs consumers that if the society could have a dollar for every act of courage sparked by cancer, it could save many lives. Through the powerful image, the organization hopes to create an emotional reaction among those who view the advertisement, convincing them of the importance of its cause.

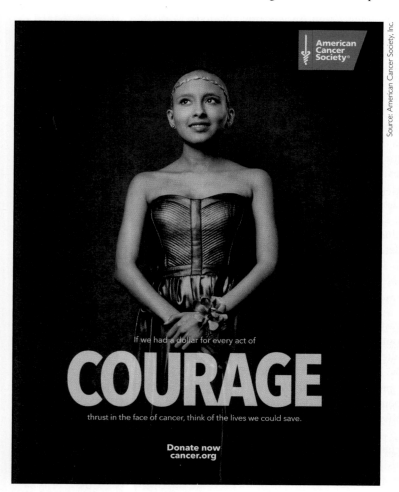

Source: American Cancer Society, Inc.

**Marketing in Nonprofit Organizations**
The American Cancer Society is a nonprofit agency that works to eliminate cancer. Marketing efforts appeal to consumers on an emotional level, encouraging them to donate to the Society.

Nonprofit organizations have greater opportunities for creativity than most for-profit business organizations, but trustees or board members of nonprofit organizations are likely to have difficulty judging the performance of the trained professionals they oversee. It is harder for administrators to evaluate the performance of professors or social workers than it is for sales managers to evaluate the performance of salespeople in a for-profit organization.

Another way nonprofit marketing differs from for-profit marketing is that nonprofit marketing is sometimes quite controversial. Large national nonprofit organizations, such as Greenpeace, the National Rifle Association, and National Association for the Reform of Marijuana Laws, allocate lobbying efforts in their budgets to inform Congress, the White House, and others of their interests and to gain their support. Some nonprofits must devote a large amount to lobbying because their mission is controversial or misunderstood by the general public. However, marketing as a field of study does not attempt to state what an organization's goals should be or debate the issue of nonprofit versus for-profit business goals. Marketing only tries to provide a body of knowledge and concepts to help further an organization's goals. Individuals must decide whether they approve or disapprove of a particular organization's goal orientation. Most marketers would agree that profit and consumer satisfaction are appropriate goals for business enterprises but may disagree about appropriate goals for a nonprofit organization.

## 13-5b Nonprofit Marketing Objectives

The basic aim of nonprofit organizations is to obtain a desired response from a target market. The response could be a change in values, a financial contribution, the donation of services, or some other type of exchange. Nonprofit marketing objectives are shaped by the nature of the exchange and the goals of the organization. These objectives should state the rationale for the organization's existence. An organization that defines its marketing objective as providing a product can be left without a purpose if the product becomes obsolete. However, servicing and adapting to the perceived needs and wants of a target public, or market, enhance an organization's chance to survive and achieve its goals.

## 13-5c Developing Nonprofit Marketing Strategies

Nonprofit organizations develop marketing strategies by defining and analyzing a target market and creating and maintaining a total marketing mix that appeals to that market.

### Target Markets

We must revise the concept of target markets slightly to apply it to nonprofit organizations. Whereas a business seeks out target groups that are potential purchasers of its product, a nonprofit organization may attempt to serve many diverse groups. For our purposes, a **target public** is a collective of individuals who have an interest in or a concern about an organization, a product, or a social cause. The terms *target market* and *target public* are difficult to distinguish from many non-product or social-cause profit organizations. For instance, the target public for ACCION International is anyone interested in supporting international development and relief work. However, the target market for ACCION's advertisements consists of people in developing nations who want microloans to start businesses and spur economic development.[30]

In nonprofit marketing, direct consumers of the product are called **client publics** and indirect consumers are called **general publics**.[31] For example, the client public for a university is its student body, and its general public includes parents, alumni, and trustees. The client public usually receives most of the attention when an organization develops a marketing strategy.

### Developing Marketing Mixes

A marketing strategy directs marketing activities and resources toward achieving organizational goals. The strategy should include a blueprint for making decisions about product, distribution, promotion, and price. These decision variables should be combined in the best way possible to serve the target market.

**target public** A collective of individuals who have an interest in or a concern about an organization, product, or social cause

**client publics** Direct consumers of a product of a nonprofit organization

**general publics** Indirect consumers of a product of a nonprofit organization

In developing the product, nonprofit organizations usually deal with ideas and services. Problems may arise when an organization fails to define what it provides. What product, for example, does the Peace Corps provide? Its services include vocational training, health services, nutritional assistance, and community development. It also markets the ideas of international cooperation and U.S. foreign policy ideals. The product of the Peace Corps is more difficult to define than the average business product. The marketing of ideas and concepts is more abstract than the marketing of tangibles, and much effort is required to present benefits.

Distribution decisions in nonprofit organizations relate to how ideas and services will be made available to clients. If the product is an idea, selecting the right media to communicate the idea will facilitate distribution. By nature, services consist of assistance, convenience, and availability. Availability is thus part of the total service. Making a product like health services available calls for knowledge of such retailing concepts as site location analysis.

Developing a channel of distribution to coordinate and facilitate the flow of nonprofit products to clients is necessary, but in a nonprofit setting, marketers may need to revise the traditional concept of the marketing channel because the independent wholesalers available to a business enterprise do not exist in most nonprofit situations. Instead, a very short channel— nonprofit organization to client—is the norm because production and consumption of ideas and services are often simultaneous.

Making promotional decisions may be the first sign that a nonprofit organization is performing marketing activities. Nonprofit organizations use advertising and publicity to communicate with clients and the public. PACER's National Center for Bullying Prevention utilizes a variety of resources and media to promote its mission. It hosts National Bullying Prevention Month every October, in which thousands of schools participate. It also distributes coloring books to children, sells a CD of anti-bullying songs, and even hosts a fun run. Facebook, CNN, and Yahoo! Kids are multimedia partners of the group.[32] Direct mail continues to be used for fundraising by many social service organizations, such as the Red Cross and Special Olympics. Though direct mail remains important, some organizations have reduced their volume of direct mail in favor of e-mails or other digital communications.

Increasingly, nonprofits are using the Internet to reach fundraising and promotional goals through e-mail, websites, social media, and software that permits online donations. For example, Animal Foundation uses a tool called Charitweet to allow people to make donations through Twitter. Make-A-Wish has a button on its Facebook page to allow Facebook users to "Donate Now."[33] More recently, online crowdfunding sites like GoFundMe, Indiegogo, and Kickstarter have given nonprofits a new channel for targeting many potential donors at once. Crowdfunding enables many people to go online and donate small amounts to a fundraising project. The model works because it allows people to give to a very targeted cause or project and therefore to feel more connected to where their donations go.[34] Mobile forms of marketing help nonprofits raise more money quickly, particularly among younger target publics.

Many nonprofit organizations also use personal selling, although they may call it by another name. Churches and charities rely on personal selling when they send volunteers to recruit new members or request donations. The U.S. Army uses personal selling when its recruiting officers attempt to persuade men and women to enlist. Special events to obtain funds, communicate ideas, or provide services are also effective promotional activities. Amnesty International, for example, has held worldwide concert tours featuring well-known musical artists to raise funds and increase public awareness of political prisoners around the world.

Although product and promotional techniques may require only slight modification when applied to nonprofit organizations, pricing is generally different and decision making is more complex. The different pricing concepts the nonprofit organization faces include pricing in user and donor markets. Two types of monetary pricing exist: *fixed* and *variable*. There may be a fixed fee for users, or the price may vary depending on the user's ability to pay. When a donation-seeking organization will accept a contribution of any size, it is using variable pricing.

The broadest definition of price (valuation) must be used to develop nonprofit marketing strategies. Financial price, an exact dollar value, may or may not be charged for a nonprofit product. Economists recognize giving up alternatives as a cost. **Opportunity cost** is the value of the benefit given up by selecting one alternative over another. According to this traditional economic view of price, if a nonprofit organization persuades someone to donate time to a cause or to change his or her behavior, the alternatives given up are a cost to (or a price paid by) the individual. Volunteers who answer phones for a university counseling service or a suicide hotline, for example, give up the time they could spend studying or doing other things as well as the income they might earn from working at a for-profit business organization.

For other nonprofit organizations, financial price is an important part of the marketing mix. Nonprofit organizations today raise money by increasing the prices of their services or charging for previously free services. They are using marketing research to determine what kinds of products people will pay for. Pricing strategies of nonprofit organizations often stress public and client welfare over equalization of costs and revenues. If additional funds are needed to cover costs, the organization may solicit donations, contributions, or grants.

**opportunity cost** The value of the benefit given up by choosing one alternative over another

# Summary

## 13-1  Discuss the growth and importance of services.

Services are intangible products that involve deeds, performances, or efforts that cannot be physically possessed. They are the result of applying human or mechanical efforts to people or objects. Services are a growing part of the U.S. economy. They have six fundamental characteristics: intangibility, inseparability of production and consumption, perishability, heterogeneity, client-based relationships, and customer contact.

## 13-2  Identify the characteristics of services that differentiate them from goods.

Intangibility means that a service cannot be seen, touched, tasted, or smelled. Inseparability refers to the fact that the production of a service cannot be separated from its consumption by customers. Perishability means unused service capacity of one time period cannot be stored for future use. Heterogeneity is variation in service quality. Client-based relationships are interactions with customers that lead to the repeated use of a service over time. Customer contact is the interaction between providers and customers needed to deliver a service.

## 13-3  Describe how the characteristics of services influence the development of marketing mixes for services.

Core services are the basic service experiences customers expect. Supplementary services are those that relate to and support core services. Because of the characteristics of services, service marketers face several challenges in developing and managing marketing mixes. To address the problem of intangibility, marketers use cues that help assure customers about the quality of their services. The development and management of service products are also influenced by the service characteristics of inseparability and level of customer contact. Some services require that customers come to the service provider's facility, and others are delivered with no face-to-face contact. Marketing channels for services are usually short and direct, but some services employ intermediaries. Service marketers are less concerned with warehousing and transportation than are goods marketers, but inventory management and balancing supply and demand for services are important issues. The intangibility of services poses several promotion-related challenges. Advertisements with tangible cues that symbolize the service and depict facilities, equipment, and personnel help address these challenges. Service providers are likely to promote price, guarantees, performance documentation, availability, and training and certification of contact personnel. Through their actions, service personnel can be involved directly or indirectly in the personal selling of services.

Intangibility makes it difficult to experience a service before purchasing it. Heterogeneity and intangibility make word-of-mouth communication an important means of promotion. The prices of services are based on task performance, time required, or demand. Perishability creates difficulties in balancing supply and demand because unused capacity cannot be stored. The point in time when a significant number of customers desire a service is called peak demand. Demand-based pricing results in higher prices charged for services during peak demand. Off-peak pricing is the practice of reducing prices of services used during slow periods in order to boost demand. When services are offered in a bundle, marketers must decide whether to offer them at one price, price them separately, or use a combination of the two methods. Because services are intangible, customers may rely on price as a sign of quality. For some services, market conditions may dictate the price. For others, state and local government regulations may limit price flexibility.

## 13-4 Explain the importance of service quality and explain how to deliver exceptional service quality.

Service quality is customers' perception of how well a service meets or exceeds their expectations. Although one of the most important aspects of service marketing, service quality is very difficult for customers to evaluate because the nature of services renders benefits impossible to assess before actual purchase and consumption. These benefits include experience qualities, such as taste, satisfaction, or pleasure, and credence qualities, which customers may be unable to evaluate even after consumption. When competing services are very similar, service quality may be the only way for customers to distinguish among them. Service marketers can increase the quality of their services by following the four-step process of understanding customer expectations, setting service specifications, ensuring good employee performance, and managing customers' service expectations.

## 13-5 Discuss the nature of nonprofit marketing.

Nonprofit marketing is marketing aimed at nonbusiness goals, including social causes. It uses most of the same concepts and approaches that apply to business situations. Whereas the chief beneficiary of a business enterprise is whoever owns or holds stock in it, the beneficiary of a nonprofit enterprise should be its clients, its members, or its public at large. The goals of a nonprofit organization reflect its unique philosophy or mission. Some nonprofit organizations have very controversial goals, but many organizations exist to further generally accepted social causes.

The marketing objective of nonprofit organizations is to obtain a desired response from a target market. Developing a nonprofit marketing strategy consists of defining and analyzing a target market and creating and maintaining a marketing mix. In nonprofit marketing, the product is usually an idea or a service. Distribution is aimed at the communication of ideas and the delivery of services. The result is a very short marketing channel. Promotion is very important to nonprofit marketing. Nonprofit organizations use advertising, publicity, and personal selling to communicate with clients and the public. Direct mail remains the primary means of fundraising for social services, but some nonprofits use the Internet for fundraising and promotional activities. Price is more difficult to define in nonprofit marketing because of opportunity costs and the difficulty of quantifying the values exchanged.

> **Go to www.cengagebrain.com for resources to help you master the content in this chapter as well as for materials that will expand your marketing knowledge!**

# Important Terms

| | | |
|---|---|---|
| homesourcing 392 | customer contact 396 | nonprofit marketing 408 |
| intangibility 393 | off-peak pricing 403 | target public 409 |
| inseparability 394 | service quality 403 | client publics 409 |
| perishability 394 | search qualities 404 | general publics 409 |
| heterogeneity 395 | experience qualities 404 | opportunity cost 411 |
| client-based relationships 395 | credence qualities 404 | |

# Discussion and Review Questions

1. How important are services in the U.S. economy?
2. Identify and discuss the major characteristics of services.
3. For each marketing-mix element, which service characteristics are most likely to have an impact? Explain.
4. What is service quality? Why do customers find it difficult to judge service quality?
5. Identify and discuss the five components of service quality. How do customers evaluate these components?
6. What is the significance of tangibles in service marketing?
7. How do search, experience, and credence qualities affect the way customers view and evaluate services?
8. What steps should a service company take to provide exceptional service quality?
9. How does nonprofit marketing differ from marketing in for-profit organizations?
10. What are the differences among clients, publics, and customers? What is the difference between a target public and target market?
11. Discuss the development of a marketing strategy for a university. What marketing decisions must be made as the strategy is developed?

# Video Case 13.1

## Mike Boyle's Services Are Not for Everyone

Everyone wants to be strong, healthy, and fit. But not everyone is in the target market for Mike Boyle Strength and Conditioning (MBSC). With two Massachusetts locations, MBSC offers a variety of services to help athletes at all levels build strength, improve endurance, and enhance performance. Cofounder Mike Boyle developed his approach to athletic training as a result of working as a trainer for various sports teams and with Boston University. He's also trained Olympic athletes, professional athletes, and celebrities.

Over the years, Boyle noticed how many people join a gym with good intentions but then lose their motivation and rarely use the facilities. So when Boyle opened his first gym, he went down a different marketing path. He wants to provide services to customers who expect to actively train, customers who will set personal goals and then come to the gym for regular one-on-one or group training. Boyle recognizes that his business doesn't just provide equipment and space for workouts—it also offers social support and professional guidance, encouraging customers to make progress toward their fitness and performance goals, week after week.

For school athletes in their teens and twenties, MBSC offers services such as middle-school athletic training, high-school performance training, and college break workout sessions. For adults, MSBC offers small-group strength and training services and private or semi-private personal training geared to each customer's individual needs and goals, including weight loss, better stamina, and better mobility. In addition, MBSC provides services to help adults improve capabilities and performance in specific sports, such as golf. Prices vary, depending on the duration of the service programs and whether customers receive private or group training.

As they age, professional athletes who want to continue their high-performance careers see MBSC's services as a way to keep up their strength, speed, and endurance. Even adults who aren't athletes see MBSC as a resource for taking fitness to the next level, learning to prevent injuries, and getting

BraunS/E+/Getty Images

in shape to look their best. Customers also have the option of requesting services such as massage therapy and physical therapy to regain strength and improve agility.

Boyle reaches out to a wider audience with "how to" videos that educate and encourage people who want to know about his training and services. His Facebook page has 23,000 likes, his Twitter account has 27,000 followers, and his YouTube channel has 8,000 subscribers. Boyle maintains a dialogue with customers and prospects by posting notes and videos on his blog and social-media accounts about diverse topics, including effective training techniques and the benefits of school athletics.

Today, MBSC offers services to customers as young as 11 years old, and at the other end of the spectrum, to members in their 80s. A small percentage of customers are professional athletes, and many of his customers are young men and women who want training to supplement their school sports activities. Because he was known for his work with the Boston Bruins hockey team and with Boston University's hockey team, Boyle attracts many varsity hockey players from the Boston area. These days, Boyle has little extra time for the kind of extended workouts he once enjoyed. Still, he makes the rounds of his gyms every day, training in brief, intensive stints and serving as a role model for the ongoing benefits of maintaining strength and conditioning at all ages and for all lifestyles.[35]

### Questions for Discussion

1. In terms of services marketing, why is it important for customers to see Mike Boyle working out and supervising trainers at his gym facilities every day?
2. Mike Boyle only wants to attract customers who will be frequent users of his facilities and training services. What does this suggest about how MBSC manages service expectations?
3. How, specifically, can customers evaluate the search qualities, experience qualities, and credence qualities of MBSC?

# Case 13.2

## American Express Delivers Service with Calls, Tweets, and Apps

Imagine the customer service challenges involved in satisfying 100 million customers worldwide who use their credit, debit, or prepaid cards to make $1 trillion in purchases every year. That's the situation at American Express, the New York-based financial services firm that rings up $34 billion in annual revenues and has 62,000 employees spread around the globe.

Although American Express has been in operation for more than 150 years, it began as a delivery service and did not enter the credit card business until the late 1950s. Since then, the company has expanded to offer a wide range of credit and debit cards for individuals, corporate employees, and small businesses. Its vision is to "make American Express the world's most respected service brand." To do this, it must provide convenient, responsive around-the-clock service to the consumers and executives who carry its cards, as well as to the merchants and small businesses that accept its cards.

Customers usually prefer to call American Express when they have a question or a problem. At the company's call centers, service representatives can view account details such as demographics, purchasing patterns, and payment patterns while they talk with customers. Thanks to sophisticated software, the reps also have access to special codes that indicate whether a customer is likely to remain loyal or leave. All reps are trained to listen carefully and ask questions that will uncover the source of the problem and lead to an acceptable resolution. Instead of reading from a prepared script, reps are encouraged to take as much time as needed to engage customers in conversation. This allows reps to learn more about each individual's underlying needs, identify a suitable solution to the problem at hand, and—if appropriate—recommend other American Express offerings, all with the goal of satisfying customers and earning their long-term loyalty.

©iStockphoto.com/adamdodd

American Express offers customers a number of ways to manage their accounts, check on features and reward benefits, and submit inquiries. Cardholders and merchants can log onto a secure website to access their statements and transaction activity, arrange payments, and request account changes. Online, American Express offers live chat as an option for customers who have a quick question or need immediate assistance while they're at their keyboards. For today's busy lifestyles, the company offers apps for smartphone users to access their account information on the go and to pay for purchases in stores and restaurants. In addition, it maintains a dedicated Twitter account for customer service inquiries, an account that has nearly 45,000 followers.

Because many of American Express's best customers are frequent flyers, the company is opening exclusive VIP lounges in large airports. In addition to lounges in busy U.S. airports such as Las Vegas and Dallas-Fort Worth, the company has customer-only lounges in several overseas airports, including Buenos Aires and Delhi. These luxury lounges offer free food, free Internet access, free concierge service for travel arrangements, and family entertainment areas.

American Express promotes its services and polishes its reputation in traditional advertising media such as television and magazines as well as with posts on its brand-specific social media sites. The company has 6 million Facebook likes, 870,000 Twitter followers, 82,000 YouTube subscribers, and 112,000 Instagram followers. Drawing on its long history as a service business, American Express recently attracted social media attention and positive response by posting a series of historical brand images, such as a 19th century photo of its New York office and a picture of its earliest credit cards. Social media fans appreciated the nostalgic images and shared them with others, resulting in higher brand awareness and favorable word-of-mouth comments.

The company has also received a lot of publicity from its involvement in Small Business Saturday, an annual event it created to encourage shoppers to buy from local and small businesses on the Saturday after Thanksgiving. Launched in

2010, this high-profile event focuses on the "shop small" message, not the American Express brand. The company urges shoppers to buy locally using any payment method, not just its own cards. In 2015, Small Business Saturday resulted in more than $16 billion worth of purchases made at small, independent businesses. The goodwill this event has generated for American Express over the years adds momentum to the company's marketing as it competes for cardholders and for merchant acceptance, day after day.[36]

### Questions for Discussion

1. How is American Express addressing the five dimensions customers use when evaluating service quality? Explain your answer.
2. Why is heterogeneity particularly important to credit card customers?
3. When American Express says its vision is to be "the world's most respected service brand," what are the implications for how it manages service expectations?

# Strategic Case 5

## Nike Runs the Innovation Race Every Day

Nike, the long-time market leader in athletic shoes, apparel, and gear, has been racing into innovation for more than 50 years. Co-founders Phil Knight and Bill Bowerman met at the University of Oregon, where Knight was a student athlete and Bowerman was a veteran coach and trainer. For years, Bowerman had been experimenting with developing homemade running shoes, some of which Knight tested on the track. After Knight graduated, he decided the U.S. market needed an alternative to the high-priced German shoes that many athletes preferred at the time. He formed Blue Ribbon Sports with Bowerman as his partner and became the U.S. distributor for a Japanese sneaker firm, selling shoes from the trunk of his car.

360b/Shutterstock.com

While Knight handled business operations, Bowerman applied his knowledge of running to product development, testing, and improving one type of running shoe after another. The breakthrough came when he created an entirely new design by grafting a waffle-patterned rubber sole to a lightweight, cushioned sneaker. These shoes were the first of Bowerman's innovations to carry the now-iconic swoosh logo, and they burst into the marketplace just as running became a major fitness trend. By 1978, when the company was renamed Nike, after the Greek goddess of victory, it was marketing its shoes on the basis of performance and fashion.

### Athlete Endorsers Add Star Power

CEO Phil Knight believed that endorsements and product input from athletes were the key to attracting consumer attention and building credibility for Nike's quality performance. He raised eyebrows in the 1980s by arranging a $250,000 endorsement deal with a two-time All-American North Carolina basketball player who went on to become NBA Rookie of the Year. It didn't take long for this deal with the now-legendary Michael Jordan to begin paying off in the form of publicity and profits. Nike introduced an entire sneaker line named after Jordan and, later, added Jordan-branded clothing. Today, the Nike Jordan brand rings up annual sales of $2 billion.

Following the strategy Knight pioneered, Nike now markets a number of product lines designed in collaboration with star athletes in key sports. For example, basketball endorsers such as Russell Westbrook and Chris Paul have their own shoe and clothing product lines within the Nike Jordan portfolio, with products influenced by their professional prowess and individual styles. Nike has a lifetime deal with the NBA's Lebron James, reflecting not only his basketball achievements but also his potential influence on sports, fashion, and entertainment in the coming years. Tennis champ Serena Williams has her own Nike shoe and clothing product lines, based on her ideas, aesthetic preferences, and performance requirements.

## Aiming to Achieve Aggressive Growth

Co-founder Phil Knight relinquished the CEO position in 2006 and remained Nike's chairman until 2016. Current CEO Mark Parker heads a $30 billion company that aims to achieve $50 billion in annual sales by 2020 by continuing its track record of innovation in branded goods and services. Nike's brand portfolio includes Converse, Jordan, and Hurley, as well as brands that include the Nike name, such as NIKEiD (personalized versions of Nike products) and Nike+ (apps and online tools for tracking and improving personal athletic performance). The Nike+ product line originally included the FuelBand wristband for performance tracking, but the company dropped the hardware in favor of software as competitors such as FitBit entered the market. Looking ahead, digital services are a priority as Nike seeks to enhance connections with customers by enabling them to chart their progress, compare fitness statistics with friends, and connect with other performance-minded consumers.

In recent years, dozens of high-profile product introductions have fueled Nike's growth and increased brand awareness throughout the 190 countries where it does business. Nike already offers many types of products for men, women, and children, in many variations of sizes, colors, and materials. That's why Nike's CEO works closely with the product-development teams "to edit down our opportunities to the ones that will make the most impact for the company." He challenges Nike marketers to be sure any new offering will represent an improvement, satisfy an actual need, inspire or motivate customers, and enhance the brand.

One lucrative market opportunity the company sees is increasing sales to women. Although Nike currently generates nearly $6 billion in yearly revenue from sales of products for women, this is a small fraction of the revenue generated from its sales of products for men. To appeal to women, Nike is offering new products designed by women athletes, free apps for athletic training, newsletters with advice and tips, and YouTube videos about workouts and motivation. With rivals like Under Armour and Lululemon also targeting women, Nike never stops running the innovation race, always looking for the next hit combination of performance and fashion.[37]

### Questions for Discussion

1. How would you describe Nike's product mix? Why would the CEO talk about editing down opportunities when he's aiming for aggressive growth?
2. What is Nike's branding strategy, and what are the implications for its investment in athlete endorsements?
3. How is Nike using differentiation to distinguish its products in a crowded and competitive marketplace?

# NOTES

[1] Candice Choi, "McDonald's to Test Expanded All-day Breakfast with McGriddle," *Associated Press*, January 28, 2016, http://bigstory.ap.org/article/42e02be767a447baa4f4583fbc1a5626/mcdonalds-test-expanded-all-day-breakfast-mcgriddle (accessed February 12, 2016); Natalie Schachar, "McDonald's Latest Offer: New Burgers, Table Service," *Los Angeles Business Journal*, November 30, 2015, http://labusinessjournal.com/news/2015/nov/30/mcdonalds-latest-offer-new-burgers-table-service/ (accessed February 12, 2016); Julie Jargon, "McDonald's Set to Offer All-Day Breakfast," *Wall Street Journal*, September 1, 2015, www.wsj.com/articles/mcdonalds-set-to-offer-all-day-breakfast-1441134058 (accessed February 12, 2016).

[2] Leonard L. Berry and A. Parasuraman, *Marketing Services: Competing through Quality* (New York: Free Press, 1991), p. 5.

[3] Rhema Homesourcing Business Services, www.facebook.com/Homesourcing (accessed March 4, 2016).

[4] Raymond P. Fisk, Stephen J. Grove, and Joby John, *Interactive Services Marketing* (Boston: Houghton Mifflin, 2008), p. 25.

[5] "100% Hampton Guarantee®," Hampton Inn, http://hamptoninn3.hilton.com/en/about/why-hampton/index.html (accessed March 4, 2016).

[6] The information in this section is based on K. Douglas Hoffman and John E. G. Bateson, *Services Marketing: Concepts, Strategies, and Cases, 4th ed.,* (Mason, OH: Cengage Learning, 2011): 57; Valarie A. Zeithaml, A. Parasuraman, and Leonard L. Berry, *Delivering Quality Service: Balancing Customer Perceptions and Expectations* (New York: Free Press, 1990).

[7] J. Paul Peter and James H. Donnelly, *A Preface to Marketing Management* (Burr Ridge, IL: Irwin/McGraw-Hill, 2011).

[8] "About Pinterest," Pinterest, http://about.pinterest.com (accessed March 4, 2016); Addy Dugdale, "How Much Is a Pinterest Pin Worth? More Than a Tweet," *Fast Company*, November 19, 2013, www.fastcompany.com/3021879/fast-feed/how-much-is-a-pinterest-pin-worth-much-more-than-a-tweet (accessed March 4, 2016).

[9] Michael D. Hartline and O. C. Ferrell, "Service Quality Implementation: The Effects of Organizational Socialization and Managerial Actions of Customer Contact Employee Behavior," *Marketing Science Institute Report*, no. 93–122 (Cambridge, MA: Marketing Science Institute, 1993).

[10] Kare Anderson, "The Priceless Power of Socially Empowered Employees," *Forbes*, August 11, 2013, www.forbes.com/sites/kareanderson/2013/08/11/3000 (accessed March 4, 2016).

[11] Hoffman and Bateson, *Services Marketing: Concepts, Strategies, and Cases, 4th ed.*, pp. 69–70.

[12] Fisk, Grove, and John, *Interactive Services Marketing*, p. 91.

[13] Douglas J. Guth, "Restaurants Take a Chance on Tech-Based Food Delivery," *Crain's*

*Cleveland Business*, March 5, 2016, http://www.crainscleveland.com/article/20160305/NEWS/160309902/restaurants-take-a-chance-on-tech-based-food-delivery (accessed March 8, 2016).

[14] Stitch Fix, https://www.stitchfix.com/ (accessed March 4, 2016).

[15] Adrianne Pasquarelli, "Another Bank Chases Millennials with Games, Ads," *Advertising Age*, January 21, 2016, http://adage.com/article/cmo-strategy/bank-chases-millennials-digital-games-ads/302263/ (accessed March 7, 2016).

[16] Ashley Rodriguez, "Chase Relaunches Website with Focus on Branded Content, Simplicity," *Advertising Age*, July 20, 2015, http://adage.com/article/cmo-strategy/chase-unveils-website-redesign-brings-branded-content-homepage/299542/ (accessed March 8, 2016).

[17] Jane L. Levere, "Old Slogan Returns as United Asserts It Is Customer-Focused," *The New York Times*, September 20, 2013, www.nytimes.com/2013/09/20/business/media/old-slogan-returns-as-united-asserts-it-is-customer-focused.html (accessed March 7, 2016).

[18] Hoffman and Bateson, p. 163.

[19] "Jets Raising Season Ticket Prices by Average of 4 Percent," *CBS New York*, March 1, 2016, http://newyork.cbslocal.com/2016/03/01/jets-raising-season-ticket-prices-metlife-stadium/ (accessed March 7, 2016).

[20] Zeithaml, Parasuraman, and Berry, *Delivering Quality Service*.

[21] "Good Service Is Good Business: American Consumers Willing to Spend More with Companies That Get Service Right, According to American Express Survey," American Express, May 3, 2011, http://about.americanexpress.com/news/pr/2011/csbar.aspx (accessed March 7, 2016).

[22] "Good Service Is Good Business: American Consumers Willing to Spend More with Companies That Get Service Right, According to American Express Survey," American Express, May 3, 2011, http://about.americanexpress.com/news/pr/2011/csbar.aspx (accessed March 7, 2016).

[23] Sabina Stoiciu, "The Importance of Excellent Customer Service & Feedback Surveys," *Business 2 Community*, December 2, 2013, www.business2community.com/customer-experience/importance-excellent-customer-service-feedback-surveys-0698146#!oPm8u (accessed March 7, 2016).

[24] Valarie A. Zeithaml, "How Consumer Evaluation Processes Differ between Goods and Services," in *Marketing of Services*, eds., James H. Donnelly and William R. George (Chicago: American Marketing Association, 1981), pp. 186–190.

[25] A. Parasuraman, Leonard L. Berry, and Valarie A. Zeithaml, "An Empirical Examination of Relationships in an Extended Service Quality Model," *Marketing Science Institute Working Paper Services*, no. 90–112 (Cambridge, MA: Marketing Science Institute, 1990), p. 29.

[26] Steve Evans, "Visible Ink: The Mark of the Future Accountant?" *Accounting, Auditing & Accountability Journal* 25, 7 (2012): 1234–1235.

[27] Valarie A. Zeithaml, Leonard L. Berry, and A. Parasuraman, "Communication and Control Processes in the Delivery of Service Quality," *Journal of Marketing* 52, 2 (1988): 35–48.

[28] Valarie A. Zeithaml, Leonard L. Berry, and A. Parasuraman, "The Nature and Determinants of Customer Expectations of Service," *Journal of the Academy of Marketing Science* 21, 1 (1993): 1–12.

[29] "I'm Happy, You're Happy: Yet More Evidence that Satisfied Employees Make Satisfied, and Loyal, Customers," *Customer Service Psychology Research*, June 3, 2011, http://customerservicepsychology.wordpress.com/2011/06/03/i%e2%80%99m-happy-you%e2%80%99re-happy-yet-more-evidence-that-satisfied-employees-make-satisfied-and-loyal-customers (accessed March 9, 2016).

[30] ACCION International, http://www.accion.org/ (accessed March 10, 2016).

[31] Philip Kotler, *Marketing for Nonprofit Organizations*, 2nd ed. (Englewood Cliffs, NJ: Prentice-Hall, 1982), p. 37.

[32] "Pacer's National Bullying Prevention Center," Pacer, www.pacer.org/bullying/about (accessed March 10, 2016).

[33] Neil Patel, "Top 4 Examples of Effective Social Media Strategies for Nonprofit Organizations," Inc., January 28, 2016, http://www.inc.com/neil-patel/top-4-examples-of-effective-social-media-strategies-for-nonprofit-organizations.html (accessed March 10, 2016).

[34] Jennifer Preston, "In Crowdfunding, New Source of Aid after Catastrophe," *The New York Times*, November 7, 2013, www.nytimes.com/2013/11/08/giving/in-crowdfunding-new-source-of-aid-after-catastrophe.html?_r=0 (accessed March 10, 2016).

[35] Caroline Earle, "Setting the Trend for the Future of Gyms with Boston-Based Strength Coach, Mike Boyle," *BostInno*, February 17, 2014, http://bostinno.streetwise.co/2014/02/17/interview-with-boston-coach-mike-boyle/ (accessed February 12, 2016); Jenni Whalen, "Q&A: Boston Trainer Mike Boyle," *Boston Magazine*, June 13, 2013, www.bostonmagazine.com/health/blog/2013/06/13/mike-boyle/ (accessed February 12, 2016); Cengage Learning, *Mike Boyle Strength and Conditioning* video.

[36] Keith Nelson, Jr., "A record 95 million people shopped at small businesses this past Saturday," *Digital Trends*, December 1, 2015, /www.digitaltrends.com/business/small-business-saturday-2015/ (accessed February 12, 2016); "About American Express: Who We Are," http://about.americanexpress.com/oc/whoweare/ (accessed February 12, 2016); Joe Sharkey, "Airlines' Credit Card Perks Take It on the Chin," *The New York Times*, December 9, 2013, www.nytimes.com/2013/12/10/business/when-airlines-play-hardball-with-favorite-perks.html; Patrick Clark, "Small Business Saturday's $5.7 Billion Shopping Spree," *Bloomberg Businessweek*, December 2, 2013, www.businessweek.com/articles/2013-12-02/small-business-saturdays-5-dot-7-billion-shopping-spree; Erik Schatzker, "Edward Gilligan, President, American Express, Is Interviewed on Bloomberg TV," *Bloomberg*, November 29, 2013, n.p.; Geoff Colvin, "AmEx Customer Service in Action," *Fortune*, April 19, 2012, http://management.fortune.cnn.com/2012/04/19/amex-customer-service-reps; Christopher Heine, "AmEx's Social Data Shows that Nostalgia Is Just Swell," *Adweek*, October 11, 2013, www.adweek.com/news/technology/amexs-social-data-shows-nostalgia-just-swell-153053.

[37] John Kell, "This Is the New Way Nike Is Going After Women," *Fortune*, January 28, 2016, http://fortune.com/2016/01/28/nike-youtube-margot-lily/ (accessed February 16, 2016); Matthew Kish, "A Q&A with Nike CEO Mark Parker, the PBJ's 2015 Executive of the Year," *Portland Business Journal*, January 29, 2016,

www.bizjournals.com/portland/blog/threads_ and_laces/2016/01/a-q-a-with-nike-ceo-mark-parker-the-pbjs-2015.html (accessed February 16, 2016); Jacob Pramuk, "Nike CEO: How We'll Reach $50B in Sales," *CNBC*, October 14, 2015, www.cnbc.com/2015/10/14/nike-ceo-how-well-reach-50b-in-sales.html (accessed February 16, 2016); Matt Townsend, "Nike Exceeds Estimates on New Products, Market-Share Gains," *Bloomberg*, June 25, 2015, www.bloomberg.com/news/articles/2015-06-25/nike-exceeds-profit-estimates-on-new-products-domestic-growth (accessed February 16, 2016); Elaine Low, "Nike Is Ramping Up Its Digital Strategy: What Does That Mean?" *Investor's Business Daily*, February 10, 2016, www.investors.com/news/nike-is-ramping-up-its-digital-strategy-what-does-that-mean (accessed February 16, 2016); Josh Peter, "Phil Knight Sees Finish Line as Nike's Leader," *USA Today*, September 30, 2015, www.usatoday.com/story/sports/2015/09/30/phil-knight-nike-michael-jordan-stepping-down-2016/72885302/ (accessed February 16, 2016); "Bill Bower-man: Nike's Original Innovator," *Nike News*, September 2, 2015, http://news.nike.com/news/bill-bowerman-nike-s-original-innovator (accessed February 16, 2016); "Nike CEO Mark Parker And Serena Williams On Competition: Tennis Great, Serena Williams, and Nike's Leader, Mark Parker, Trade Tales of Collaboration and Competition," *Fast Company*, January 27, 2016, www.fastcompany.com/3055401/nike-ceo-mark-parker-and-serena-williams-on-competition (accessed February 16, 2016); Megan Garber, "How Nike Turned Running Shoes into Fashion," *The Atlantic*, July 6, 2015, www.theatlantic.com/entertainment/archive/2015/07/how-nike-turned-sneakers-into-fashion/397610/ (accessed February 16, 2016).

## Feature Notes

[a] Bailey Reutzel, "Biometrics Find Support from an Unlikely Demographic: Seniors," *American Banker*, May 14, 2015, www.americanbanker.com/news/bank-technology/biometrics-find-support-from-an-unlikely-demographic-seniors-1074341-1.html (accessed February 15, 2016); Mary Wisniewski, "USAA Launches New App to Help Millennials Save," *American Banker*, July 28, 2015, www.americanbanker.com/news/bank-technology/usaa-launches-new-app-to-help-millennials-save-1075714-1. html (accessed February 15, 2016); Penny Crosman, "USAA Strives for Personalization in Its Banking Apps," *American Banker*, June 8, 2015, www.americanbanker.com/news/bank-technology/usaa-strives-for-personalization-in-its-banking-apps-1074740-1.html (accessed February 15, 2016).

[b] Elizabeth Olson, "Girl Scout Cookie Sales Go Digital, with Help from Visa and Dell," *New York Times*, January 3, 2016, www.nytimes.com/2016/01/04/business/media/girl-scout-cookie-sales-go-digital-with-help-from-visa-and-dell.html?ref=technology (accessed February 15, 2016); Michal Addady, "Why Visa and Dell Are Investing $3 Million in the Girl Scouts," *Fortune*, January 4, 2016, http://fortune.com/tag/girl-scouts/ (accessed February 15, 2016); Sheila Shayon, "CES 2016: Girl Scouts Bring Digital Cookie 2.0 and STEM to Las Vegas," *Brand Channel*, January 4, 2016, www.brandchannel.com/2016/01/04/girl-scouts-ces-2016-010416/ (accessed February 15, 2016).

# part 6
## Distribution Decisions

**14:** Marketing Channels and Supply-Chain Management

**15:** Retailing, Direct Marketing, and Wholesaling

Developing products that satisfy customers is important, but it is not enough to guarantee successful marketing strategies. Products must also be available in adequate quantities in accessible locations at the times when customers desire them.

**PART 6** deals with the distribution of products and the marketing channels and institutions that help to make products available.

**CHAPTER 14** discusses supply-chain management, marketing channels, and the decisions and activities associated with the physical distribution of products, such as order processing, materials handling, warehousing, inventory management, and transportation.

**CHAPTER 15** explores retailing and wholesaling, including types of retailers and wholesalers, direct marketing and selling, and strategic retailing issues.

designer491/iStock/Getty Images Plus/Getty Images

# chapter 14

## Marketing Channels and Supply-Chain Management

---

### OBJECTIVES

---

**14-1** Describe the foundations of supply-chain management.

**14-2** Explain the role and significance of marketing channels and supply chains.

**14-3** Identify the intensity of market coverage.

**14-4** Describe strategic issues in marketing channels, including leadership, cooperation, and conflict.

**14-5** Explain physical distribution as being a part of supply-chain management.

**14-6** Describe legal issues in channel management.

## MARKETING INSIGHTS

### Farmgirl Flowers Speeds Blooms from Farm to Vase

When Christina Stembel started Farmgirl Flowers, she had two goals in mind. First, she wanted to eliminate the waste that occurs when florists stock up on blooms so they can fill orders right away, every day. Because florists can't forecast precisely how many and which types of fresh flowers customers will buy, a percentage of the unsold inventory inevitably spoils—and the cost of such waste is passed on to customers in the form of higher prices.

Second, Stembel wanted to buy American. Growing up surrounded by farms in Indiana, she understood the importance of buying local for fresh quality and to support neighbors. She saw that the number of U.S. flower farms was shrinking, due to competition from lower-priced South American flowers. Stembel chose a different approach.

Whereas 80 percent of the flowers sold to U.S. consumers comes from other countries, 100 percent of the flowers sold by Farmgirl Flowers come from U.S. growers.

Farmgirl Flowers uses flowers in season to make long-lasting bouquets that make the trip from farm to vase in short order. Instead of designing dozens of standard bouquets that can be ordered for delivery by local florists—which is how FTD and other national firms do business—Farmgirl Flowers cuts the waste and keeps prices down by offering a "daily arrangement" from locally-grown flowers. It employs delivery people to bring bouquets to customers nearby and ships overnight to customers elsewhere. With $10 million in annual sales, Farmgirl Flowers is growing fast as more customers order "farm to vase" bouquets.[1]

The **distribution** component of the marketing mix focuses on the decisions and activities involved in making products available to customers when and where they want to purchase them. Because of the perishability of its product, Farmgirl must choose its distribution channels and partners carefully to ensure customer satisfaction. Choosing which channels of distribution to use is a major decision in the development of marketing strategies.

In this chapter, we focus on marketing channels and supply-chain management. First, we explore the concept of the supply chain and its various activities. Second, we elaborate on marketing channels and the need for intermediaries and the primary functions they perform. Next, we outline the types and characteristics of marketing channels, discuss how they are selected, and explore how marketers determine the appropriate intensity of market coverage for a product. We then examine the strategic channel issues of leadership, cooperation, and conflict. We also look at the role of physical distribution within the supply chain, including its objectives and basic functions. Finally, we look at several legal issues that affect channel management.

# 14-1 **FOUNDATIONS OF THE SUPPLY CHAIN**

An important function of distribution is to create an effective **supply chain**, which includes all the organizations and activities involved with the flow and transformation of products from raw materials through to the end customer. A distribution system involves firms that are "upstream" in the supply chain (e.g., producers and suppliers) and "downstream" (e.g., wholesalers and retailers) working together to serve customers and generate competitive advantage. Historically, marketing focused solely on certain downstream supply-chain activities. Today, however, marketing professionals are recognizing that they can reduce costs, boost profits, and better serve customers by effectively integrating activities along the entire supply chain. Doing so requires marketing managers to work with other managers in operations, logistics, and supply. **Operations management** is the total set of managerial activities used by an organization to transform resource inputs into goods, services, or both.[2] **Logistics management** involves planning, implementing, and controlling the efficient and effective flow and storage of products and information from the point of origin to consumption to meet customers' needs and wants. The costs of business logistics in the United States are huge, at nearly \$1.5 trillion, about 8.3 percent of the entire U.S. annual gross domestic product (GDP).[3] **Supply management** (e.g., purchasing, procurement, sourcing) in its broadest form refers to the processes that enable the progress of value from raw material to final customer and back to redesign and final disposition.

**Supply-chain management (SCM)** refers to the coordination of all the activities involved with the flow and transformation of supplies, products, and information throughout the supply chain to the ultimate consumer. It integrates the functions of operations management, logistics management, supply management, and marketing channel management so that products are produced and distributed in the right quantities, to the right locations, and at the right times. It includes activities such as manufacturing, research, sales, advertising, and shipping. SCM involves all entities that facilitate product distribution and benefit from cooperative efforts, including suppliers of raw materials and other components to make goods and services, logistics and transportation firms, communication firms, and other firms that indirectly take part in marketing exchanges. The key tasks involved in supply-chain management are outlined in Table 14.1. Supply-chain managers must encourage cooperation between organizations in the supply chain and understand the trade-offs required to achieve optimal levels of efficiency and service.

In an efficient supply chain, upstream firms provide direct or indirect input to make the product, while downstream firms are responsible for delivery of the product and after-market services to the ultimate customers. To ensure quality and customer satisfaction, firms must be involved in the management of every aspect of their supply chain, in close partnership with all involved upstream and downstream organizations.

**distribution** The decisions and activities that make products available to customers when and where they want to purchase them

**supply chain** All the organizations and activities involved with the flow and transformation of products from raw materials through to the end customer

**operations management** The total set of managerial activities used by an organization to transform resource inputs into products, services, or both

**logistics management** Planning, implementing, and controlling the efficient and effective flow and storage of products and information from the point of origin to consumption to meet customers' needs and wants

**supply management** In its broadest form, refers to the processes that enable the progress of value from raw material to final customer and back to redesign and final disposition

**supply-chain management (SCM)** The coordination of all the activities involved with the flow and transformation of supplies, products, and information throughout the supply chain to the ultimate consumer

Table 14.1 **Key Tasks in Supply-Chain Management**

| Marketing Activities | Sample Activities |
|---|---|
| Operations management | Organizational and system-wide coordination of operations and partnerships to meet customers' product needs |
| Supply management | Sourcing of necessary resources, goods, and services from suppliers to support all supply-chain members |
| Logistics management | All activities designed to move the product through the marketing channel to the end user, including warehousing and inventory management |
| Channel management | All activities related to selling, service, and the development of long-term customer relationships |

Supply-chain management should begin with a focus on the customer, who is the ultimate consumer and whose satisfaction should be the goal of all the efforts of channel members. Cooperation between channel members should improve customer satisfaction while also increasing coordination, reducing costs, and increasing profits. When the buyer, the seller, marketing intermediaries, and facilitating agencies work together, the cooperative relationship results in compromise and adjustments that meet customers' needs regarding delivery, scheduling, packaging, or other requirements. Consider that today's technology-savvy consumer expects retailers like Office Depot to offer multiple options for fulfilling orders—in the store, online via desktop computer or smartphone, or shipped to a nearby store—and to be able to deliver their orders quickly—even the very same day. Retailers must adjust their physical distribution strategies in response or risk losing their customers to other retailers who will provide what they want.[4]

Each supply-chain member requires information from other channel members. For instance, suppliers need order and forecast information from the manufacturer. They also may need availability information from their own suppliers. Customer relationship management (CRM) systems exploit the information in supply-chain partners' information systems and make it available for easy reference. CRM systems can help all channel members make better marketing strategy decisions that develop and sustain desirable customer relationships. Companies now offer online programs that integrate business data into a social networking site format. Tibbr and Yammer are two such programs. By inputting all data into a single, easy-to-use online system, businesses can achieve greater efficiencies and improve their CRM.[5]

Demand for innovative goods and services has increased and changed over time. Marketers need to be flexible in order to respond to the fluctuating needs and desires of customers by developing and distributing new products and modifying existing ones. Supply-chain managers can exploit data available through improved information technology to learn about a firm's customers, which helps to improve products in the downstream portion of the supply chain. Customers are also increasingly a knowledge source in developing the right product in the downstream portion of the supply chain. Marketers now understand that managing the entire supply chain is critically important in ensuring that customers get the products when, where, and how they want them. In fact, supply-chain management is one of the industries poised for strong future growth because of the increasing importance of getting the right products where they need to go safely and on time.[6] Amazon has set the gold standard for supply-chain management—offering customers nearly anything they can imagine at low prices, through a user-friendly website that features product reviews and ratings, perks like offering a variety of shipping options, and an easy return policy. Amazon has even moved into selling and distributing everyday items, like toilet paper or cleaning supplies, teaming up with suppliers all over the country to create a seamless distribution system.[7] Many companies have struggled to compete with and adapt to such a large and flexible competitor.

Technology has improved supply-chain management capabilities globally. Advances in information technology, in particular, have created an almost seamless distribution process for matching inventory needs to manufacturer requirements in the upstream portion of the supply chain and to customers' requirements in the downstream portion of the chain. With integrated information sharing among chain members, firms can reduce costs, improve services, and provide increased value to the end customer. Information is a crucial component in operating supply chains efficiently and effectively.

# 14-2 THE ROLE OF MARKETING CHANNELS IN SUPPLY CHAINS

A **marketing channel** (also called a *channel of distribution* or *distribution channel*) is a group of individuals and organizations that direct the flow of products from producers to customers within the supply chain. The major role of marketing channels is to make products available at the right time at the right place in the right quantities. This is accomplished through achieving synergy among operations management, logistics management, and supply management. Providing customer satisfaction should be the driving force behind marketing channel decisions. Buyers' needs and behavior are therefore important concerns of channel members.

Some marketing channels are direct, meaning that the product goes directly from the producer to the customer. For instance, when you order pears online from Harry & David, the product is sent from the manufacturer to the customer. Most channels, however, are indirect and have one or more **marketing intermediaries** that link producers to other intermediaries or to ultimate consumers through contractual arrangements or through the purchase and reselling of products. Marketing intermediaries perform the activities described in Table 14.2. They also play key roles in customer relationship management, not only through their distribution activities but also by maintaining databases and information systems to help all members of the marketing channel maintain effective customer relationships. For example, MercuryGate provides transportation management software to firms to streamline logistics. The company also works directly with shippers and third-party logistics companies and brokers to ensure that its customers have effective and efficient supply chains, using analytics and a robust information database pulled from its many clients. Its methods work—as its clients, such as Walmart and Siemens, are known for their exemplary supply-chain management.[8]

**marketing channel** A group of individuals and organizations that direct the flow of products from producers to customers within the supply chain

**marketing intermediaries** Middlemen that link producers to other intermediaries or ultimate consumers through contractual arrangements or through the purchase and resale of products

Table 14.2 **Marketing Channel Activities Performed by Intermediaries**

| Marketing Activities | Sample Activities |
|---|---|
| Marketing information | Analyze sales data and other information in databases and information systems. Perform or commission marketing research. |
| Marketing management | Establish strategic and tactical plans for developing customer relationships and organizational productivity. |
| Facilitating exchanges | Choose product assortments that match the needs of customers. Cooperate with channel members to develop partnerships. |
| Promotion | Set promotional objectives. Coordinate advertising, personal selling, sales promotion, publicity, and packaging. |
| Price | Establish pricing policies and terms of sales. |
| Physical distribution | Manage transportation, warehousing, materials handling, inventory control, and communication. |

Wholesalers and retailers are examples of intermediaries. Wholesalers buy and resell products to other wholesalers, retailers, and industrial customers. Retailers purchase products and resell them to end consumers. Consider your local supermarket, which probably purchased the Advil on its shelves from a wholesaler. The wholesaler purchased that pain medicine, along with other over-the-counter and prescription drugs, from manufacturers like McNeil Consumer Healthcare. Chapter 15 discusses the functions of wholesalers and retailers in marketing channels in detail.

## 14-2a The Significance of Marketing Channels

Although it is not necessary to make marketing channel decisions before other marketing decisions, they can have a strong influence on the other elements of the marketing mix (i.e., product, promotion, and pricing). Channel decisions are critical because they determine a product's market presence and accessibility. Without marketing channel operations that reach the right customers at the right time, even the best goods and services will not be successful. For example, in spite of spending massive amounts on marketing efforts, Target abandoned the Canadian market after losing a billion dollars in large part due to a poor distribution system. The retail company opened 133 stores in just two years, but Canadian shoppers routinely found empty shelves due to supply-chain issues the company might have identified sooner had it opened just a few stores at a time. Pricing issues and intense competition further hamstrung the U.S. retailer's first foray into a foreign market.[9]

Marketing channel decisions have strategic significance because they generally entail long-term commitments among a variety of firms (e.g., suppliers, logistics providers, and operations firms). Furthermore, it is the least flexible component of the marketing mix. Once a firm commits to a distribution channel, it is difficult to change. Marketing channels serve many functions, including creating utility and facilitating exchange efficiencies. Although some of these functions may be performed by a single channel member, most functions are accomplished through both independent and joint efforts of channel members.

### Marketing Channels Create Utility

Marketing channels create four types of utility: time, place, possession, and form. *Time utility* is having products available when the customer wants them. Services like Netflix allow customers to watch a movie whenever they want. *Place utility* is making products available in locations where customers wish to purchase them. For example, Zappos allows customers to shop for shoes and accessories anywhere they have access to a mobile device and an Internet connection. *Possession utility* means that the customer has access to the product to use or to store for future use. Possession utility can occur through ownership or through arrangements that give the customer the right to use the product, such as a lease or rental agreement. Channel members sometimes create *form utility* by assembling, preparing, or otherwise refining the product to suit individual customer needs.

### Marketing Channels Facilitate Exchange Efficiencies

Even if producers and buyers are located in the same city, there are costs associated with exchanges. Marketing intermediaries can reduce the costs of exchanges by performing certain services or functions efficiently. As Figure 14.1 shows, when four buyers seek products from four producers, 16 separate transactions are possible. If one intermediary serves both producers and buyers, the number of possible transactions is cut in half. Intermediaries are specialists in facilitating exchanges. They provide valuable assistance because of their access to and control over important resources used in the proper functioning of marketing channels. Many firms exist to assist firms with creating supply-chain efficiencies. Take a look at the advertisement for Fidelitone. It shows a man and a woman reviewing a document while informing customers that Fidelitone is paying attention to what matters in your business. Firms like Fidelitone have expert knowledge and have developed distribution networks that can help firms to create supply-chain efficiencies.

Figure 14.1    **Efficiency in Exchanges Provided by an Intermediary**

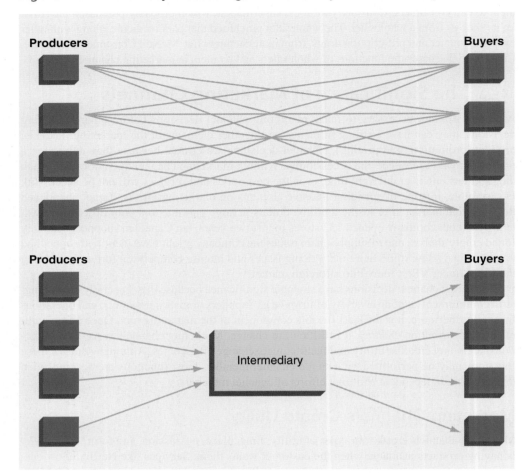

Nevertheless, the media, consumers, public officials, and even other marketers freely criticize intermediaries, especially wholesalers. Critics accuse wholesalers of being inefficient and adding to costs. Buyers often think that making the distribution channel as short as possible will decrease the prices for products, but this is not the case.

Critics who suggest that eliminating wholesalers will lower prices for customers fail to recognize that this would not eliminate the need for the services the wholesalers provide. Although wholesalers can be eliminated, their functions cannot. Other channel members would have to perform those functions, perhaps not as efficiently, and customers still would have to pay for them. In addition, all producers would deal directly with retailers or customers, meaning that every producer would have to keep voluminous records and hire sufficient personnel to deal with a multitude of customers. In the end, customers might end up paying a great deal more for products, because prices would reflect the costs of an inefficient distribution channel. To mitigate criticisms, wholesalers should only perform the marketing activities that are desired, and they must strive to be as efficient and customer-focused as possible.

## 14-2b  Types of Marketing Channels

Because marketing channels that are appropriate for one product may be less suitable for others, many different distribution paths have been developed. The various marketing channels can be classified generally as channels for consumer products and channels for business products.

## Channels for Consumer Products

Figure 14.2 illustrates several channels used in the distribution of consumer products. Channel A depicts the direct movement of products from producer to consumers. For instance, a haircut received at a barber shop moves through channel A because there is no intermediary between the person performing the service and the one receiving it. Direct marketing via the Internet has become a critically important part of some companies' distribution strategies, often as a complement to selling products in traditional retail stores. A firm must evaluate the benefits of going direct versus the transaction costs involved in using intermediaries.

Channel B, which moves goods from the producer to a retailer and then to customers, is a frequent choice of large retailers because it allows them to buy in quantity from manufacturers. Retailers like Target and Walmart sell many items that were purchased directly from producers. New automobiles and new college textbooks are also sold through this type of marketing channel.

Channel C is a common distribution channel for consumer products. It takes goods from the producer to a wholesaler, then to a retailer, and finally to consumers. It is a practical option for producers that sell to hundreds of thousands of customers through thousands of retailers. Some home appliances, hardware, and many convenience goods are marketed through this type of channel. Consider the number of retailers marketing KitchenAid mixers. It would be rather difficult, if not impossible, for KitchenAid to deal directly with each of the many retailers that sell its brand.

Channel D, wherein goods pass from producer, to agents, to wholesalers, to retailers, and finally to consumers, is used frequently for products intended for mass distribution, such as processed foods. Consequently, to place its Wheat Thins crackers in specific retail outlets, supply-chain managers at Nabisco may hire an agent (or a food broker) to sell the crackers to wholesalers. Wholesalers then sell the Wheat Thins to supermarkets, vending-machine operators, and convenience stores.

Contrary to what you might think, a long channel may actually be the most efficient distribution channel for some goods. When several channel intermediaries perform specialized functions, costs are likely to be lower than when one channel member tries to perform them all. Efficiencies arise when firms that specialize in certain elements of producing a product or moving it through the channel are more effective at performing specialized tasks than the manufacturer. This results in added value to customers and reduced costs throughout the distribution channel.

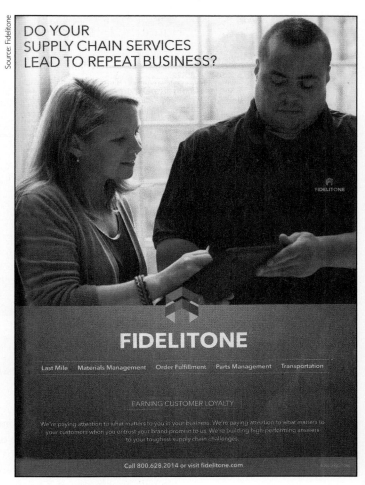

**Supply-Chain Efficiencies**
Logistics firms such as Fidelitone can help businesses to create supply-chain efficiencies, distributing their goods quickly and affordably.

## Channels for Business Products

Figure 14.3 shows four of the most common channels for business products. As with consumer products, manufacturers of business products sometimes work with more than one level of wholesaler.

Channel E illustrates the direct channel for business products. In contrast to consumer goods, business products, especially expensive equipment, are most likely to be sold through direct channels. Business customers prefer to communicate directly with producers, especially

Figure 14.2    **Typical Marketing Channels for Consumer Products**

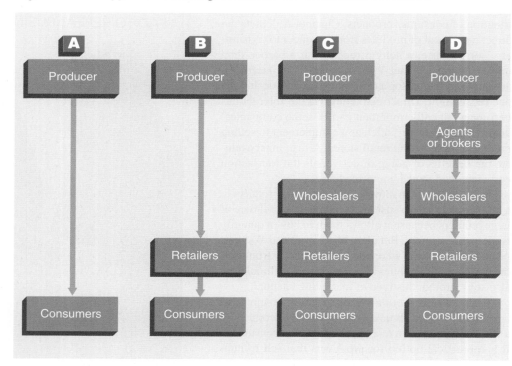

when expensive or technically complex products are involved. For instance, business buyers of Xerox products not only receive devices and equipment, but ongoing maintenance, technical support, and data analytics. Xerox has moved from being a company known for its copiers to a creative powerhouse that delivers a variety of solutions to its clients. Service through direct channels is a big part of Xerox's success. It digitally collects ongoing information from many

# EMERGING **TRENDS IN MARKETING**

## While Some Tourist Seek Adventure, Others Want to Go Shopping

Vacationers often have the urge to splurge—in fact, the main purpose of some trips is to buy products not available or too costly in local stores. Shopping tourism is on the rise as international travelers enjoy the hunt for special brands and special bargains at stores and shopping centers far from home.

For example, the upscale outlet mall Bicester Village in Oxfordshire, England, markets itself as a shopping-tourism destination. Its 130 shops feature designer brands such as Prada, Gucci, and Alexander McQueen, all at discounted prices. Every year, six million bargain-hunters from across the continent and around the world come to Bicester Village. To accommodate these travelers, a new rail line has been opened between London and the mall, which also offers its own luxury bus service to and from London.

Month after month, thousands of Chinese tourists arrive at Bicester Village, part of the wave of newly-affluent Asian consumers who travel to buy status-symbol clothing, leather goods, and beauty products. Prices for imported luxury products are typically higher in Chinese stores than abroad, which is why many tourists from China visit outlet malls, department stores, and specialty stores during their travels. In addition to Europe and the United States, Japan is another top shopping-tourism destination for Chinese consumers. So many visitors from China have descended upon Tokyo stores in recent years, snapping up everything from rice cookers to high-tech toilets, that the Japanese have dubbed the trend "bakugai," meaning "explosive shopping."[a]

Figure 14.3 **Typical Marketing Channels for Business Products**

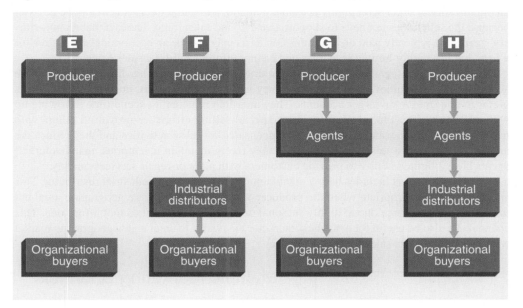

of the products it sells to companies and performs preemptive repairs on machines it senses are about to malfunction. This level of service would be impossible through an intermediary.[10]

In channel F, an industrial distributor facilitates exchanges between the producer and the customer. An **industrial distributor** is an independent business that takes title to products and carries inventories. Industrial distributors usually sell standardized items, such as maintenance supplies, production tools, and small operating equipment. Some industrial distributors carry a wide variety of product lines. Applied Industrial Technologies Inc., for instance, carries millions of products from more than 4,000 manufacturers and works with a wide variety of companies from small janitorial services companies to giant manufacturers such as Boeing.[11] Other industrial distributors specialize in one or a small number of lines. Industrial distributors carry an increasing percentage of business products. Overall, these distributors can be most effective when a product has broad market appeal, is easily stocked and serviced, is sold in small quantities, and is needed on demand to avoid high losses.

Industrial distributors offer sellers several advantages. They can perform the needed selling activities in local markets at a relatively low cost to a manufacturer and reduce a producer's financial burden by providing customers with credit services. Also, because industrial distributors usually maintain close relationships with their customers, they are aware of local needs and can pass on market information to producers. By holding adequate inventories in local markets, industrial distributors reduce producers' capital requirements.

Using industrial distributors has several disadvantages. They may be difficult to manage because they are independent firms. They often stock competing brands, so a producer cannot depend on them to sell its brand aggressively. Furthermore, industrial distributors incur expenses from maintaining inventories and are less likely to handle bulky or slow-selling items, or items that need specialized facilities or extraordinary selling efforts. In some cases, industrial distributors lack the specialized knowledge necessary to sell and service technical products.

The third channel for business products, channel G, employs a *manufacturers' agent*, an independent businessperson who sells complementary products of several producers in assigned territories and is compensated through commissions. Unlike an industrial distributor, a manufacturers' agent does not acquire title to the products and usually does not take possession. Acting as a salesperson on behalf of the producers, a manufacturers' agent has little or no latitude in negotiating prices or sales terms.

**industrial distributor**
An independent business organization that takes title to industrial products and carries inventories

Using manufacturers' agents can benefit an organizational marketer. They usually possess considerable technical and market information and have an established set of customers. For an organizational seller with highly seasonal demand, a manufacturers' agent can be an asset because the seller does not have to support a year-round sales force. The fact that manufacturers' agents are typically paid on a commission basis may also be an economical alternative for a firm that has highly limited resources and cannot afford a full-time sales force.

The use of manufacturers' agents also has drawbacks. The seller has little control over the actions of manufacturers' agents. Because they work on commission, manufacturers' agents prefer to concentrate on larger accounts. They are often reluctant to spend time following up with customers after the sale, putting forth special selling efforts, or providing sellers with market information because they are not compensated for these activities and they reduce the amount of productive selling time. Because they rarely maintain inventories, manufacturers' agents have a limited ability to provide customers with parts or repair services quickly.

Finally, channel H includes both a manufacturers' agent and an industrial distributor. This channel may be appropriate when the producer wishes to cover a large geographic area, but maintains no sales force due to highly seasonal demand or because it cannot afford one. This channel can also be useful for a business marketer that wants to enter a new geographic market without expanding its sales force.

**strategic channel alliance**
An agreement whereby the products of one organization are distributed through the marketing channels of another

**Multichannel Distribution**
Many firms, including Clinique, use multichannel distribution—meaning products are targeted at the same group of consumers via multiple channels. In this case, moisturizer is made available to consumers in department stores and online.

## Multiple Marketing Channels

To reach diverse target markets, manufacturers may use more than one marketing channel simultaneously, with each channel involving a different group of intermediaries. A manufacturer often uses multiple channels when the same product is directed to both consumers and business customers. For example, when Heinz markets ketchup for household use, the product is sold to supermarkets through grocery wholesalers or, in some cases, directly to retailers, whereas ketchup being sold to restaurants or institutions follows a different distribution channel.

A **strategic channel alliance** exists when the products of one firm are distributed through the marketing channels of another. The products of the two firms are often similar with respect to target markets or uses, but they are not direct competitors. A brand of bottled water might be distributed through a marketing channel for soft drinks, or a cereal producer in the United States might form a strategic channel alliance with a European food processor to facilitate international distribution. Such alliances can provide benefits for both the organization that owns the marketing channel and the company whose brand is being distributed through the channel.

Quite often, companies today use multiple channels to reach the same target market. For example, consumers can purchase a Dell computer directly from the company by calling a toll-free number or going through its website as well as indirectly through select retailers such as Best Buy. Likewise, L.L. Bean markets products through its longstanding catalog, its website, and through its own retail stores. In such cases, the firm is using **multichannel distribution**—the use of a variety of marketing channels to ensure maximum distribution. The primary reason for using a multichannel strategy is to reach target customers wherever and whenever they may choose to interact with a company or its products. Some consumers may prefer to shop in a brick-and-mortar store where they can personally compare and sample products, while others prefer the instant gratification of shopping for an item on their smartphone as soon as they recognize a need for the product. Even marketers for cosmetics, such as the Clinique moisturizer featured in the advertisement, employ multichannel distribution. This product—which the ad informs was developed by dermatologists for people with particularly dry skin—is available in department stores, but customers can also purchase it on the producer's website, which is displayed on the advertisement.

Some products can forgo physical distribution altogether. **Digital distribution** involves delivering content through the Internet to a computer or other device. For example, when you watch a TV show on Netflix or Hulu or listen to music on Pandora or Spotify, those networks stream the content to your device so that you can consume them at the same time. In today's high-tech world, it is also possible to rent digital content, such as a textbook, or subscribe to software, such as Office 365, for a specific period of time after downloading them to a computer, tablet, or smartphone. Some services can also be distributed through digital channels such as booking travel services through Expedia.com or Hotels.com.

It is important to recognize that the line between different marketing channels is becoming increasingly blurred. Consider that today's consumer expects to be able to order a product online from, say, Home Depot or Target, and pick up the order at their nearest retail store to avoid paying shipping. Many companies have distribution channels that include physical retail stores as well as Amazon.com or eBay. Younger consumers today have learned to shop online wherever they may be through their smartphones, though they may visit a retail store to assess a product for themselves, and then order it directly from the manufacturer's website or Amazon. Marketers are having to adjust their strategies to respond to the blurred lines between multiple marketing channels by ensuring they are using every channel their target market prefers to use and sending a consistent message across all distribution channels.

## 14-2c Selecting Marketing Channels

Selecting appropriate marketing channels is important because they are difficult to change once chosen. Although the process varies across organizations, channel selection decisions are usually affected significantly by one or more of the following factors: customer characteristics, product attributes, type of organization, competition, marketing environmental forces, and characteristics of intermediaries (see Figure 14.4).

### Customer Characteristics

Marketing managers must consider the characteristics of target market members in channel selection. As we have already seen, the channels that are appropriate for consumers are different from those for business customers. Because of variations in product use, product complexity, consumption levels, and need for services, firms develop different marketing strategies for each group. Business customers often prefer to deal directly with producers (or very knowledgeable channel intermediaries such as industrial distributors), especially for highly technical or expensive products, such as mainframe computers, jet airplanes, or heavy machinery that require strict specifications and technical assistance. Businesses also frequently buy in large quantities.

Consumers, on the other hand, generally buy limited quantities of a product, purchase from retailers, and often do not mind limited customer service. When customers are concentrated in a small geographic area, a direct channel may be best, but when many customers are spread across an entire state or nation, distribution through multiple intermediaries is likely to be more efficient.

**multichannel distribution**
The use of a variety of marketing channels to ensure maximum distribution

**digital distribution** Delivering content through the Internet to a computer or other device

Figure 14.4    **Selecting Marketing Channels**

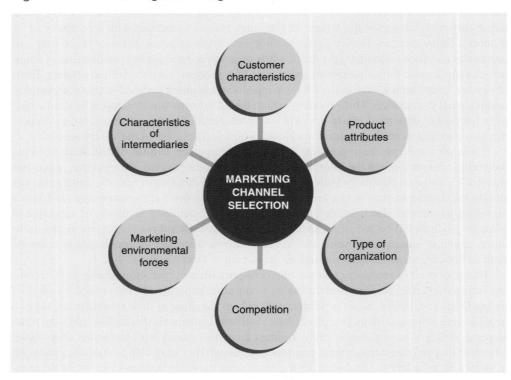

## Product Attributes

The attributes of the product can have a strong influence on the choice of marketing channels. Marketers of complex and expensive products (like automobiles) will likely employ short channels, as will marketers of perishable products (such as dairy and produce). Less-expensive standardized products with long shelf lives, such as soft drinks and canned goods, can go through longer channels with many intermediaries. Fragile products that require special handling are likely to be distributed through short channels to minimize the amount of handling and risk of damage. Firms that desire to convey an exclusive image for their products may wish to limit the number of outlets available.

## Type of Organization

The characteristics of the organization will have a great impact on the distribution channels chosen. Owing to their size, larger firms are in a better position to deal with vendors or other channel members. They are also likely to have more distribution centers, which reduce delivery times to customers. Large companies can also use an extensive product mix as a competitive tool. A smaller company that uses regional or local channel members, on the other hand, might be in a strong position to cater its marketing mix to serve customers in that particular area, compared with a larger and less-flexible organization. However, smaller firms may not have the resources to develop their own sales force, ship their products long distances, maintain a large inventory, or extend credit. In such cases, they might consider including other channel members that have the resources to provide these services to customers.

## Competition

Competition is another important factor for supply-chain managers to consider. The success or failure of a competitor's marketing channel may encourage or dissuade an organization from taking a similar approach. In a highly competitive market, it is important for a company to maintain low costs so it can offer lower prices than its competitors if necessary to maintain a competitive advantage.

## Environmental Forces

Environmental forces can play a role in channel selection. Adverse economic conditions might force an organization to use a low-cost channel, even though it reduces customer satisfaction. In contrast, a growing economy may allow a company to choose a channel that previously had been too costly. The introduction of new technology might cause an organization to add or modify its channel strategy. For instance, many marketers in a variety of industries are finding that it is valuable to maintain online social networking accounts to keep customers up-to-date on new products, offers, and events.

Government regulations can also affect channel selection. As labor and environmental regulations change, an organization may be forced to modify its existing distribution channel structure to comply with new laws. Firms might choose to enact the changes before they are mandated in order to appear proactive. International governmental regulations can complicate the supply chain a great deal, as laws vary from country to country and businesses must make sure they comply with local regulations.

## Characteristics of Intermediaries

When an organization believes that an intermediary is not promoting its products adequately or does not offer the correct mix of services, it may reconsider its channel choices. In these instances, the company may choose another channel member to handle its products, it may select a new intermediary, or it might choose to eliminate intermediaries altogether and perform the functions itself.

# 14-3 **INTENSITY OF MARKET COVERAGE**

In addition to deciding which marketing channels to use to distribute a product, marketers must determine the appropriate intensity of coverage—that is, the number and kinds of outlets in which a product will be sold. This decision depends on the characteristics of the product and the target market. To achieve the desired intensity of market coverage, distribution must correspond to behavior patterns of buyers. In Chapter 11, we divided consumer products into four categories—convenience, shopping, specialty, and unsought—according to how consumers make purchases. In considering products for purchase, consumers take into account such factors as replacement rate, product adjustment (services), duration of consumption, and time required to find the product.[12] These variables directly affect the intensity of market coverage. As shown in Figure 14.5, the three major levels of market coverage are intensive, selective, and exclusive distribution.

## 14-3a Intensive Distribution

**Intensive distribution** uses all available outlets for distributing a product. Intensive distribution is appropriate for products that have a high replacement rate, require almost no service, and are bought based on price cues. Most convenience products like bread, chewing gum, soft drinks, and newspapers are marketed through intensive distribution. Multiple channels may be used to sell through all possible outlets. For example, goods such as soft drinks, snacks, laundry detergent, and pain relievers are available at convenience stores, service stations, supermarkets, discount stores, and other types of retailers. To satisfy consumers seeking to buy these products, they must be available at a store nearby and be obtained with minimal search time. Consumers want to be able to buy these products wherever it is most convenient to them at the lowest price possible while maintaining a reliable level of quality.

**intensive distribution** Using all available outlets to distribute a product

Figure 14.5  **Intensity of Market Coverage**

Sales of low-cost convenience products may be directly related to product availability. In Japan, McDonald's was temporarily forced to stop selling medium- and large-sized french fries due to a potato shortage. The shortage resulted from a labor dispute at ports along the United States' West Coast that interrupted shipments to Japan. The delays caused the company to receive little more than half its shipment during the month of the dispute.[13] Companies like Procter & Gamble that produce consumer packaged items rely on intensive distribution for many of their products (e.g., soaps, detergents, food and juice products, and personal-care products) because consumers want ready availability.

## 14-3b Selective Distribution

**Selective distribution** uses only some available outlets in an area to distribute a product. Selective distribution is appropriate for shopping products, which include durable goods like televisions or computers. Shopping products are more expensive than convenience goods, and consumers are willing to spend more time and possibly visit several retail outlets and websites to compare prices, designs, styles, and other features.

Selective distribution is desirable when a special effort, such as customer service from a channel member, is important to customers. Shopping products require differentiation at the point of purchase. Selective distribution is often used to motivate retailers to provide adequate service. Dealers can offer higher-quality customer service when products are distributed selectively. Consider the advertisement for Nespresso espresso machines and coffees. Nespresso is a moderately high-end brand of coffeemaker that is distributed selectively. Nespresso products are available at specialty stores such as Williams-Sonoma and Sur la Table and at department stores such as Macy's. This advertisement seeks to cultivate a high-end image through the focus on the clean lines of the machine and the fancy coffee shop drinks that customers can create. When shopping for Nespresso products, salespeople will be able to assist customers and will be knowledgeable about the products. Most perfumes and colognes and some cosmetics are marketed using selective distribution in order to maintain a particular image.

**selective distribution** Using only some available outlets in an area to distribute a product

## 14-3c Exclusive Distribution

**Exclusive distribution** uses only one outlet in a relatively large geographic area. This method is suitable for products purchased infrequently, consumed over a long period of time, or that require a high level of customer service or information. It is also used for expensive, high-quality products with high profit margins, such as Porsche, BMW, and other luxury automobiles. It is not appropriate for convenience products and many shopping products because an insufficient number of units would be sold to generate an acceptable level of profits on account of those products' lower profit margins.

Exclusive distribution is often used as an incentive to sellers when only a limited market is available for products. Consider Patek Philippe watches that may sell for $10,000 or more. These watches, like luxury automobiles, are available in only a few select locations. Tourneau, featured in the advertisement, is an exclusive retail outlet that sells new and preowned high-end luxury watches, including Patek Philippe. There are only a few Tourneau outlets, all located in very large cities. Items can retail for tens of thousands of dollars, and the available brands shown in the ad are frequently worn as a status symbol. A producer using exclusive distribution expects dealers to carry a complete inventory, train personnel to ensure a high level of product knowledge and quality customer service, and participate in promotional programs.

Some products are appropriate for exclusive distribution when first introduced, but as competitors enter the market and the product moves through its life cycle, other types of market coverage and distribution channels become necessary. A problem that can arise with exclusive (and selective) distribution is that unauthorized resellers acquire and sell products or counterfeits, violating the agreement between a manufacturer and its exclusive authorized dealers.

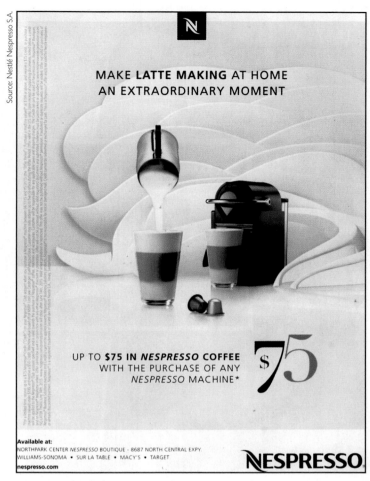

**Selective Distribution**
Nespresso brand espresso makers and coffees are distributed selectively. Salespeople will be knowledgeable and willing to assist a customer in making a selection.

# 14-4 STRATEGIC ISSUES IN MARKETING CHANNELS

To maintain customer satisfaction and an effective supply chain, managers must retain a strategic focus on certain competitive priorities, including developing channel leadership, fostering cooperation between channel members, managing channel conflict, and possibly consolidating marketing channels through channel integration.

## 14-4a Competitive Priorities in Marketing Channels

Increasingly, firms are recognizing that supply chains can be a source of competitive advantage and a strong market orientation because supply-chain decisions cut across all functional areas of business. Building the most effective and efficient supply chain can sustain a business

**exclusive distribution** Using a single outlet in a fairly large geographic area to distribute a product

**Exclusive Distribution**
Tourneau is an exclusive outlet of high-end luxury watches, selling products only in large cities.

and help it to use resources effectively and be more efficient. Many well-known firms, including Amazon, Dell, FedEx, Toyota, and Walmart, owe much of their success to outmaneuvering rivals with unique supply-chain capabilities. Many countries offer firms opportunities to create an effective and efficient supply chain to support the development of competitive national industries. Although developed nations like Germany, the United States, and Canada remain highly competitive manufacturing countries, China has ranked number one on Deloitte's annual survey of global manufacturing competitiveness for years, indicating the country's superior capabilities to produce goods at a low price and efficiently distribute them.[14] India, Mexico, and Taiwan have risen to prominence as well.

To unlock the potential of a supply chain, activities must be coordinated into an effective system. Supply chains driven by firm-established goals focus on the "competitive priorities" of speed, quality, cost, or flexibility as the performance objective. Managers must remember, however, to keep a holistic view of the supply chain so that goals such as "speed" or "cost" do not result in dissatisfied or underpaid workers or other such abuses in factories. This should be a particular concern among firms that use international manufacturers because it can be more difficult to monitor working conditions internationally.

## 14-4b Channel Leadership, Cooperation, and Conflict

Each channel member performs a specific role in the distribution system and agrees (implicitly or explicitly) to accept rights, responsibilities, rewards, and sanctions for nonconformity. Moreover, each channel member holds certain expectations of other channel members. Retailers, for instance, expect wholesalers to maintain adequate inventories and deliver goods on time. Wholesalers expect retailers to honor payment agreements and keep them informed of inventory needs. Manufacturers, wholesalers, and retailers expect shipping companies to deliver products on schedule and at a reasonable cost. Any one organization's failure to meet expectations can disrupt the entire supply chain. When a labor dispute between shipping companies and dockworkers at West Coast ports disrupted vital shipping routes between the United States and Asia, the result was extremely delayed shipments and eventually higher prices as companies scrambled to reroute shipments to less congested but more distant ports. The resulting trade disruptions caused months of channel instability and frustration among supply-chain partners struggling to deal with the situation.[15]

Channel partnerships can facilitate effective supply-chain management when partners agree on objectives, policies, and procedures for physical distribution efforts associated with the supplier's products. Such partnerships eliminate redundancies and assign tasks for maximum system-wide efficiency. Channel cooperation reduces wasted resources, such as time, energy, or materials. A coordinated supply chain can also be more environmentally friendly, a consideration that is increasingly important to many organizations and their stakeholders. In fact, research findings show that companies with environmentally responsible supply chains tend to be more profitable, particularly when a firm's marketing efforts point out the fact that it has a sustainable supply chain.[16] In order to reduce the carbon footprint of the U.S. auto industry's production processes, equipment manufacturers and suppliers partnered with the Environmental Protection Agency to form the Suppliers Partnership for the Environment. It is a forum for companies and their supply-chain partners to share environmental best practices and optimize supply-chain productivity. The result is a more efficient and less polluting supply chain.[17] In this section, we discuss channel member behavior—including leadership, cooperation, and conflict—that marketers must understand to make effective channel decisions.

## Channel Leadership

Many marketing channel decisions are determined through channel member compromise with a better marketing channel as an end goal. Some marketing channels, however, are organized and controlled by a single leader, or **channel captain** (also called *channel leader*). The channel captain may be a producer, wholesaler, or retailer. Channel captains may establish channel policies and coordinate development of the marketing mix. To attain desired objectives, the captain must possess **channel power**, the ability to influence another channel member's goal achievement. The member that becomes the channel captain will accept the responsibilities and exercise the power associated with this role.

When a manufacturer is a channel captain and it determines that it must increase sales volume to achieve production efficiency, it may encourage growth through offering channel members financing, business advice, ordering assistance, advertising services, sales and service training, and support materials. These benefits usually come with requirements related to sales volume, service quality, training, and customer satisfaction.

Retailers may also be channel captains. Walmart, for example, dominates the supply chain for its retail stores by virtue of the magnitude of its resources (especially information management) and a strong, nationwide customer base. To be part of Walmart's supply chain, other channel members must agree to Walmart's rules. Small retailers too may assume leadership roles when they gain strong customer loyalty in local or regional markets. Retailers that are channel captains control many brands and sometimes replace uncooperative producers. Increasingly, leading retailers are concentrating their buying power among fewer suppliers, which makes it easier to coordinate and maintain a high level of quality and transparency along the entire supply chain. These more selective relationships often involve long-term commitments, which enable retailers to place smaller and more frequent orders as needed, rather than waiting for large-volume discounts, or placing large orders and assuming the risks associated with carrying more inventory than needed.

Wholesalers can assume channel leadership roles as well. Wholesaler leaders may form voluntary chains with several retailers, which they supply with bulk buying or management services, and which may also market their own brands. In return, the retailers shift most of their purchasing to the wholesaler leader. The Independent Grocers' Alliance (IGA) is one of the best-known wholesaler leaders in the United States with nearly 5,000 outlets in more than 30 countries.[18] IGA's power is based on its expertise in advertising, pricing, and purchasing knowledge that it makes available to independent business owners. Wholesaler channel leaders may help retailers with store layouts, accounting, and inventory control.

## Channel Cooperation

Because the supply chain is an interrelated system, the success of one firm in the channel depends in part on other member firms. Cooperation enables retailers, wholesalers, suppliers, and logistics providers to speed up inventory replenishment, improve customer service, and cut the costs of bringing products to the consumer.[19] Without cooperation, neither overall channel goals nor individual member goals can be realized. Thus, marketing channel members should make a coordinated effort to satisfy market requirements. Channel cooperation leads to greater trust among channel members and improves the overall functioning of the channel. Cooperation also leads to more satisfying relationships among channel members.

There are several ways to improve channel cooperation. If a marketing channel is viewed as a unified supply chain competing with other systems, individual members will be less likely to take actions that create disadvantages for other members. Channel members should agree

**channel captain** The dominant leader of a marketing channel or a supply channel

**channel power** The ability of one channel member to influence another member's goal achievement

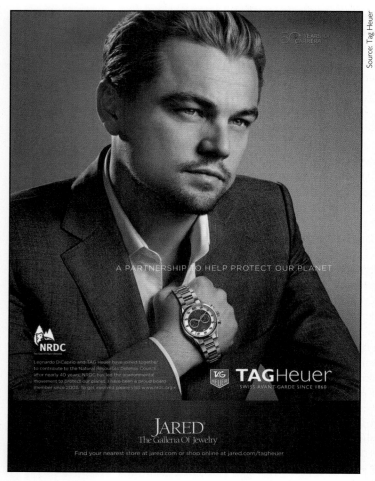

Source: Tag Heuer

**Channel Conflict**

Exclusive brands like Tag Heuer, which previously were only available at authorized retailers, risk channel conflict now that they are also sold online via the company's website.

to direct efforts toward common objectives, and their tasks should be defined precisely so that roles can be structured for maximum effectiveness in working toward achieving objectives. Starting from a common basis allows channel members to set benchmarks for reviewing intermediaries' performance and helps to reduce conflicts as each channel member knows what is expected of it.

## Channel Conflict

Although all channel members work toward the same general goal—distributing products profitably and efficiently—members sometimes may disagree about the best methods for attaining this goal. The Internet has increased the potential for conflict and resentment between manufacturers and intermediaries. When a manufacturer such as Apple or Dell makes its products available through the Internet, it is employing a direct channel that competes with the retailers that also sell its products. Take a look at the advertisement for Tag Heuer watches. This is a very exclusive brand, which is underscored by featuring the famous actor Leonardo DiCaprio as a model. The brand was previously only available via authorized jewelers. Consumers can now purchase the watches directly from the producer via the company's website, creating potential resentment among brick-and-mortar stores if they lose business.

Channel conflicts also arise when intermediaries overemphasize competing products or diversify into product lines traditionally handled by other intermediaries. When a producer that has traditionally used franchised dealers broadens its retailer base to include other types of retail outlets, for example, conflict can arise with the traditional outlets. Sometimes conflict develops because producers strive to increase efficiency by circumventing intermediaries.

If self-interest creates misunderstanding about role expectations, the end result is frustration and conflict for the whole channel. For individual organizations to function together, each channel member must clearly communicate and understand role expectations. For example, using social media to communicate helps supplier-retailer partners achieve common goals, develop relationships, increase customer interaction, and promote the supplier, brand, and competitive environment across the different levels.[20] On the other hand, communication difficulties are a potential form of channel conflict because ineffective communication leads to frustration, misunderstandings, and ill-coordinated strategies, jeopardizing further coordination.

Although there is no single method for resolving conflict, partnerships can be reestablished if two conditions are met. First, the role of each channel member must be clearly defined and followed. Channel members must have a clear understanding of goals and expectations as well as the metrics that different members will use to measure progress and determine incentive rates.[21] To minimize misunderstanding, all members must be able to expect unambiguous performance levels from one another. Second, members of channel partnerships must agree on means of coordinating channels, which requires strong, but not polarizing, leadership. To prevent channel conflict, producers or other channel members may provide competing resellers with different brands, allocate markets among resellers, define policies for direct sales to avoid potential conflict over large accounts, negotiate territorial issues among regional distributors, and provide recognition to certain resellers for their importance in distributing to others.

## 14-4c Channel Integration

Channel members can either combine and control activities or pass them to another channel member. Channel functions may be transferred between intermediaries and producers, even to customers. As mentioned earlier in the chapter, supply-chain functions cannot be eliminated. Unless buyers themselves perform the functions, they must pay for the labor and resources needed to perform them. Various channel stages may be combined, either horizontally or vertically, under the management of a channel captain. Such integration may stabilize supply, reduce costs, and increase channel member coordination.

### Vertical Channel Integration

**Vertical channel integration** combines two or more stages of the channel under one management. This may occur when one member of a marketing channel purchases the operations of another member or simply performs the functions of another member, eliminating the need for that intermediary. In the solar industry, for example, SolarCity, an installer and financier of solar panels, acquired the manufacturing firm Silevo, as well as a solar manufacturing facility previously owned by bankrupt Solyndra, in order to gain new technology and manufacturing capability to begin making its own highly efficient solar panels, bringing many stages of the channel under one roof.[22]

Vertical channel integration represents a more progressive approach to distribution, in which channel members become extensions of one another as they are combined under a single management. Vertically integrated channels can be more effective against competition because of increased bargaining power and the ease of sharing information and responsibilities. At one end of a vertically integrated channel, a manufacturer might provide advertising and training assistance. At the other end, the retailer might buy the manufacturer's products in large quantities and actively promote them.

Integration has been successfully institutionalized in a marketing channel called the **vertical marketing system (VMS)**, in which a single channel member coordinates or manages all activities to maximize efficiencies, resulting in an effective and low-cost distribution system that does not duplicate services. Vertical integration brings most or all stages of the marketing channel under common control or ownership. It can help speed the rate at which goods move through a marketing channel. VMSs account for a large share of retail sales in consumer goods. Most vertical marketing systems take one of three forms: corporate, administered, or contractual.

A *corporate VMS* combines all stages of the marketing channel, from producers to consumers, under a single owner. For example, the Inditex Group, which owns popular clothing retailer Zara, utilizes a corporate VMS to achieve channel efficiencies and maintain a maximum amount of control over the supply chain. Zara's clothing is trendy, requiring the shortest time possible from product development to offering the clothing in stores. Inventory is characterized by very high turnover and frequent changes. Because it has control over all stages of the supply chain, Inditex can maintain an advantage through speed and keeping prices low.[23]

In an *administered VMS*, channel members are independent, but informal coordination achieves a high level of inter-organizational management. Members of an administered VMS may adopt uniform accounting and ordering procedures and cooperate in promotional activities for the benefit of all partners. Although individual channel members maintain autonomy, as in conventional marketing channels, one channel member (such as a producer or large retailer) dominates the administered VMS so that distribution decisions take the whole system into account.

A *contractual VMS* is the most popular type of vertical marketing system. Channel members are linked by legal agreements spelling out each member's rights and obligations. Franchise organizations, such as McDonald's and KFC, are contractual VMSs. Other contractual VMSs include wholesaler-sponsored groups, such as IGA (Independent Grocers' Alliance) stores, in which independent retailers band together under the contractual leadership of a wholesaler.

**vertical channel integration** Combining two or more stages of the marketing channel under one management

**vertical marketing system (VMS)** A marketing channel managed by a single channel member to achieve efficient, low-cost distribution aimed at satisfying target market customers

Retailer-sponsored cooperatives, which own and operate their own wholesalers, are a third type of contractual VMS. Ace Hardware is a retail cooperative of 4,794 stores with revenues of $4.7 billion and strong growth despite competition from so-called big box stores like Home Depot and Lowe's. Each Ace Hardware store contributes to advertising and marketing for the whole group and can capitalize on the well-known brand to build their neighborhood stores.[24]

## Horizontal Channel Integration

Combining organizations at the same level of operation under one management constitutes **horizontal channel integration**. An organization may integrate horizontally by merging with other organizations at the same level in the marketing channel. The owner of a dry-cleaning firm, for example, might buy and combine several other existing dry-cleaning establishments. Likewise, Sherwin-Williams acquired rival paint firm Valspar for $11.3 billion in part to fast-track its move into international markets.[25]

Although horizontal integration permits efficiencies and economies of scale in purchasing, marketing research, advertising, and specialized personnel, it is not always the most effective method of improving distribution. Problems that come with increased size often follow, resulting in decreased flexibility, difficulties coordinating among members, and the need for additional marketing research and large-scale planning. Unless distribution functions for the various units can be performed more efficiently under unified management than under the previously separate managements, horizontal integration will neither reduce costs nor improve the competitive position of the integrating firm.

## 14-5 PHYSICAL DISTRIBUTION IN SUPPLY-CHAIN MANAGEMENT

**horizontal channel integration** Combining organizations at the same level of operation under one management

**physical distribution** Activities used to move products from producers to consumers and other end users

**third-party logistics (3PL) firms** Firms that have special expertise in core physical distribution activities such as warehousing, transportation, inventory management, and information technology and can often perform these activities more efficiently

**Physical distribution**, also known as *logistics*, refers to the activities used to move products from producers to consumers and other end users. These activities include order processing, inventory management, materials handling, warehousing, and transportation. Physical distribution systems must meet the needs of both the supply chain and customers. Distribution activities are thus an important part of supply-chain planning and can require a high level of cooperation among partners.

Within the marketing channel, physical distribution activities may be performed by a producer, wholesaler, or retailer, or they may be outsourced. In the context of distribution, *outsourcing* is the contracting of physical distribution tasks to third parties. **Third-party logistics (3PL) firms** have special expertise in core physical distribution activities such as warehousing, transportation, inventory management, and information technology and can often perform these activities more efficiently. Outsourcing logistics to third-party organizations, such as trucking companies, warehouses, and data-service providers, can reduce marketing channel costs and boost service and customer satisfaction for all supply-chain partners. Indeed, some 86 percent of U.S. Fortune 500 companies outsource logistics and supply-chain functions to 3PLs.[26]

The Internet and technological advancements have revolutionized logistics, allowing many manufacturers to carry out actions and services entirely online, bypassing shipping and warehousing considerations, and transforming physical distribution by facilitating just-in-time delivery, precise inventory visibility, and instant shipment-tracking capabilities. For example, video game and computer software manufacturers such as Microsoft and Sony have increasingly made their products available for download. Emerging technologies such as 3D printing, drones, and driverless vehicles may further advance physical distribution.[27] Technological advances create new challenges for manufacturers, such as how to maintain a high level of customer service when customers never enter a store or meet with a salesperson and how to deal with returns of a product that does not exist in a physical form. However, technology enables companies to avoid expensive mistakes, reduce costs, and generate increased revenues.

Moreover, information technology enhances the transparency of the supply chain, allowing all marketing channel members to track the movement of goods throughout the supply chain and improve their customer service.

Planning an efficient physical distribution system is crucial to developing an effective marketing strategy because it can decrease costs and increase customer satisfaction. When making distribution decisions, speed of delivery, flexibility, and quality of service are often as important to customers as costs. Companies that offer the right goods, in the right place, at the right time, in the right quantity, and with the right support services are able to sell more than competitors that do not. Even when the demand for products is unpredictable, suppliers must be able to respond quickly to inventory needs. In such cases, physical distribution costs may be a minor consideration when compared with service, dependability, and timeliness.

Although physical distribution managers try to minimize the costs associated with order processing, inventory management, materials handling, warehousing, and transportation, decreasing the costs in one area often raises them in another. Figure 14.6 shows the percentage of total costs that physical distribution functions represent. A total-cost approach to physical distribution that takes into account all these different functions enables managers to view physical distribution as a system and shifts the emphasis from lowering the costs of individual activities to minimizing overall costs.

Physical distribution managers must therefore be sensitive to the issue of cost trade-offs. Trade-offs are strategic decisions to combine (and recombine) resources for greatest cost-effectiveness. The goal is not always to find the lowest cost, but rather to find the right balance of costs. Higher costs in one functional area of a distribution system may be necessary to achieve lower costs in another. When distribution managers regard the system as a network of integrated functions, trade-offs become useful tools in implementing a unified, cost-effective distribution strategy.

Another important goal of physical distribution involves **cycle time**, the time needed to complete a process. For instance, reducing cycle time while maintaining or reducing costs and/or maintaining or increasing customer service is a winning combination in supply chains and ultimately results in greater customer satisfaction. Firms should look for ways to reduce cycle time while maintaining or reducing costs and maintaining or improving customer service. Consider Dollar Shave Club, which grew from a tiny business with a highly popular viral video to a large business that ships razor blades to subscribers across the country. To reduce cycle

**cycle time** The time needed to complete a process

Figure 14.6 **Proportional Cost of Each Physical Distribution Function as a Percentage of Total Distribution Costs**

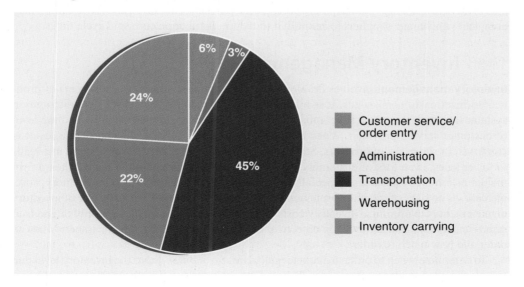

time while maintaining high customer satisfaction and quality, the Venice, California, company turned to a third-party logistics specialist, which allowed it to focus on providing excellent customer service while ensuring on-time deliveries to subscribers.[28] In the rest of this section, we take a closer look at a variety of physical distribution activities, including order processing, inventory management, materials handling, warehousing, and transportation.

## 14-5a Order Processing

**Order processing** is the receipt and transmission of sales order information. Although management sometimes overlooks the importance of these activities, efficient order processing facilitates product flow. Computerized order processing provides a platform for information management, allowing all supply-chain members to increase their productivity. When carried out quickly and accurately, order processing contributes to customer satisfaction, decreased costs and cycle time, and increased profits.

Order processing entails three main tasks: order entry, order handling, and order delivery. Order entry begins when customers or salespeople place purchase orders via customer-service counter, telephone, regular mail, e-mail, or website. Electronic ordering has become the most common. It is less time-consuming than a paper-based ordering system and reduces costs. In some companies, sales representatives receive and enter orders personally and also handle complaints, prepare progress reports, and forward sales order information.

Order handling involves several tasks. Once an order is entered, it is transmitted to a warehouse to verify product availability and, if necessary, to the credit department to set terms and prices and to check the customer's credit rating. If the credit department approves the purchase, warehouse personnel assemble the order. In many warehouses, automated machines carry out this step. If the requested product is not in stock, a production order is sent to the factory, or the customer is offered a substitute.

When the order has been assembled and packed for shipment, the warehouse schedules delivery with an appropriate carrier. If the customer pays for rush service, overnight delivery by an overnight carrier is used. The customer is sent an invoice, inventory records are adjusted, and the order is delivered.

Whether a company uses a manual or an electronic order-processing system depends on which method provides greater speed and accuracy within cost limits. Manual processing suffices for small-volume orders and can be more flexible in certain situations. Most companies, however, use **electronic data interchange (EDI)**, which uses computer technology to integrate order processing with production, inventory, accounting, and transportation. Within the supply chain, EDI functions as an information system that links marketing channel members and outsourcing firms together. It boosts accuracy, reduces paperwork for all members of the supply chain, and allows them to share information on invoices, orders, payments, inquiries, and scheduling. Many companies encourage suppliers to adopt EDI to reduce distribution costs and cycle times.

## 14-5b Inventory Management

**order processing** The receipt and transmission of sales order information

**electronic data interchange (EDI)** A computerized means of integrating order processing with production, inventory, accounting, and transportation

**inventory management** Developing and maintaining adequate assortments of products to meet customers' needs

**Inventory management** involves developing and maintaining adequate assortments of products to meet customers' needs. It is a key component of any effective physical distribution system. Inventory decisions have a major impact on physical distribution costs and the level of customer service provided. When too few products are carried in inventory, the result is *stockouts*, or shortages of products. Stockouts can result in customer dissatisfaction that leads to lower sales, even loss of customers and brand switching. On the other hand, when a firm maintains too many products (especially too many low-turnover products) in inventory, costs increase, as do risks of product obsolescence, pilferage, and damage. The objective of inventory management is to minimize inventory costs while maintaining an adequate supply of goods to satisfy customers. To achieve this objective, marketers focus on two major issues: when to order and how much to order.

To determine when to order, a marketer calculates the *reorder point:* the inventory level that signals the need to place a new order. To calculate the reorder point, the marketer must know the order lead time, the usage rate, and the amount of safety stock required. The *order lead time* refers to the average time lapse between placing the order and receiving it. The *usage rate* is the rate at which a product's inventory is used or sold during a specific time period. *Safety stock* is the amount of extra inventory a firm keeps to guard against stockouts resulting from above-average usage rates and/or longer-than-expected lead times. The reorder point can be calculated using the following formula:

$$\text{Reorder Point} = (\text{Order Lead Time} \times \text{Usage Rate}) + \text{Safety Stock}$$

Thus, if order lead time is 10 days, usage rate is 3 units per day, and safety stock is 20 units, the reorder point is 50 units.

Efficient inventory management with accurate reorder points is crucial for firms that use a **just-in-time (JIT)** approach, in which supplies arrive just as they are needed for use in production or for resale. Companies that use JIT (sometimes referred to as *lean distribution*) can maintain low inventory levels and purchase products and materials in small quantities only when needed. Usually there is no safety stock in a JIT system. Suppliers are expected to provide consistently high-quality products exactly when they are needed. JIT inventory management requires a high level of coordination between producers and suppliers, but it eliminates waste and reduces inventory costs. Toyota was a pioneer of JIT distribution. More recently, Trinity Health, which operates 90 U.S. hospitals, began to apply JIT distribution methods to save an estimated $20 million in inventory-carrying costs and improvements in supply-chain efficiency with the help of 3PL partner XPO Logistics.[29] When a JIT approach is used in a supply chain, suppliers may move operations close to their major customers in order to provide goods as quickly as possible.

## 14-5c **Materials Handling**

**Materials handling**, the physical handling of tangible goods, supplies, and resources, is an important factor in warehouse operations, as well as in transportation from points of production to points of consumption. Efficient procedures and techniques for materials handling minimize inventory management costs, reduce the number of times a good is handled, improve customer service, and increase customer satisfaction. Systems for packaging, labeling, loading, and movement must be coordinated to maximize cost reduction and customer satisfaction.

Increasingly, companies are using **radio frequency identification (RFID)**—which uses radio waves to identify and track materials tagged with special microchips—through every phase of handling. RFID has greatly improved shipment tracking and reduced cycle times. Hundreds of RFID tags can be read at a time, which represents an advantage over barcodes. Firms are discovering that RFID technology has very broad applications, from tracking inventory to paying for goods and services, asset management, and data collection. It is also useful for asset management and data collection. Zara places RFID chips inside the larger security tags of clothing stocked in its retail stores. Because the tags are removed before the customer leaves the store, the RFID tags can be reused and do not violate the consumer's right to privacy by continuing to track the item. Inventory-taking at Zara stores using the RFID technology has decreased from five hours with 40 employees to just two-and-a-half hours with nine employees. When an item is sold, the RFID tag records the time and orders an identical product from the company's stockroom, streamlining the inventory process and facilitating inventory management. Now Zara can do its inventories every six weeks rather than the six months it used to take with employees having to manually scan barcodes.[30] This technology will undoubtedly lead to better inventory management and more satisfied customers.

Product characteristics often determine handling. For example, the characteristics of bulk liquids and gases dictate how they can be moved and stored. Internal packaging is also an important consideration in materials handling. Goods must be packaged correctly to prevent damage or breakage during handling and transportation. Many companies employ packaging consultants during the product design process to help them decide which packaging materials and methods will result in the most efficient handling. Firms that produce food items or other goods that must remain cold may want to consider working with such an organization because

**just-in-time (JIT)** An inventory-management approach in which supplies arrive just when needed for production or resale

**materials handling** Physical handling of tangible goods, supplies, and resources

**radio frequency identification (RFID)** Using radio waves to identify and track materials tagged with special microchips

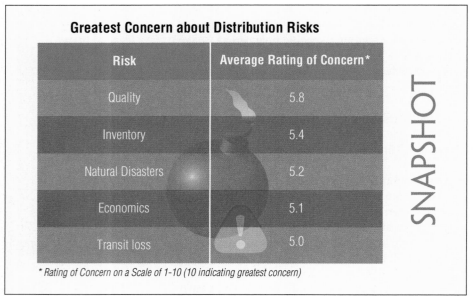

**Greatest Concern about Distribution Risks**

| Risk | Average Rating of Concern* |
|------|----------------------------|
| Quality | 5.8 |
| Inventory | 5.4 |
| Natural Disasters | 5.2 |
| Economics | 5.1 |
| Transit loss | 5.0 |

*\* Rating of Concern on a Scale of 1-10 (10 indicating greatest concern)*

SNAPSHOT

Source: Supply Chain Management Faculty at the University of Tennessee, "Managing Risk in the Global Supply Chain," p. 13, http://globalsupplychaininstitute.utk.edu/publications/documents/Risk.pdf

they feature temperature-controlled warehouses and shipping. Such an operation can help a firm with inventory management by maximizing the shelf life of goods and minimizing loss.

Unit loading and containerization are two common methods used in materials handling. With *unit loading*, one or more boxes are placed on a pallet or skid. These units can then be loaded efficiently by mechanical means, such as forklifts, trucks, or conveyer systems. *Containerization* is the consolidation of many items into a single, large container that is sealed at its point of origin and opened at its destination. Containers are usually 8 feet wide, 8 feet high, and 10 to 40 feet long. Their uniform size means they can be stacked and shipped via train, barge, or ship. Once containers reach their destinations, wheel assemblies can be added to make them suitable for ground transportation by truck. Because individual items are not handled in transit, containerization greatly increases efficiency and security in shipping.

### 14-5d Warehousing

**Warehousing**, the design and operation of facilities for storing and moving goods, is another important physical distribution function. Warehousing provides time utility by enabling firms to compensate for dissimilar production and consumption rates. When mass production creates a greater stock of goods than can be sold immediately, companies warehouse the surplus until customers are ready to buy it. Warehousing also helps to stabilize prices and the availability of seasonal items. The advertisement for Magaya, a logistics software company that provides software for managing inventory in warehouses, highlights the importance of effective inventory management. The image of a worker carrying boxes clearly marked fragile illustrates the importance of effective inventory management systems that minimize product handling and maximize efficient warehouse operations.

Choosing appropriate warehouse facilities is an important strategic consideration because they allow a company to reduce transportation and inventory costs and improve service to customers. The wrong type of warehouse can lead to inefficient physical distribution and added costs. Warehouses fall into two general categories: private and public. In many cases, a combination of private and public facilities provides the most flexible warehousing approach.

Companies operate **private warehouses** for shipping and storing their own products. A firm usually leases or purchases a private warehouse when its warehousing needs in a given geographic market are substantial and stable enough to warrant a long-term commitment to a fixed facility. Private warehouses are also appropriate for firms that require special handling and storage and that want control of warehouse design and operation. Retailers like Sears find it economical to integrate private warehousing with purchasing and distribution for their retail outlets. When sales volumes are fairly stable, ownership and control of a private warehouse may be most convenient and offer cost benefits. Private warehouses, however, face fixed costs, such as insurance, taxes, maintenance, and debt expense. They limit firms' flexibility if they wish to move inventories to different locations. Many private warehouses are being eliminated by direct links between producers and customers, reduced cycle times, and outsourcing to public warehouses.

**warehousing** The design and operation of facilities for storing and moving goods

**private warehouses** Company-operated facilities for storing and shipping products

**Public warehouses** lease storage space and related physical distribution facilities to other companies. They sometimes provide distribution services, such as receiving, unloading, inspecting, filling orders, financing, displaying products, and coordinating shipments. Distribution Unlimited Inc., for example, offers a wide range of such services through its facilities in New York, which contain more than 8 million square feet of warehouse space.[31] Public warehouses are especially useful to firms that have seasonal production or demand, low-volume storage needs, and inventories that must be maintained in many locations. They are also useful for firms that are testing or entering new markets or require additional storage space. Additionally, public warehouses serve as collection points during product-recall programs. Whereas private warehouses have fixed costs, public warehouses offer variable (and possibly lower) costs because users rent space and purchase warehousing services only as needed.

Many public warehouses furnish security for products that are used as collateral for loans, a service provided at either the warehouse or the site of the owner's inventory. *Field public warehouses* are established by public warehouses at the owner's inventory location. The warehouser becomes custodian of the products and issues a receipt that can be used as collateral for a loan. Public warehouses also provide *bonded storage*, a warehousing arrangement in which imported or taxable products are not released until the products' owners pay U.S. customs duties, taxes, or other fees. Bonded warehouses enable firms to defer tax payments on such items until they are delivered to customers.

**Distribution centers** are large facilities used for receiving, warehousing, and redistributing products to stores or customers. They are specially designed for rapid flow of products and are usually one-story buildings with access to transportation networks, such as major highways and/or railway lines. Many distribution centers are automated, with computer-directed robots, forklifts, and hoists that collect and move products to loading docks. Amazon, for example, relies on 90 "fulfillment centers" around the world, each using robots, computer systems, and hundreds of employees to process and fulfill customer orders.[32] Distribution over large geographic areas can be complicated, and having strategically located distribution centers can help a company meet consumer demand. Even Walmart had to build more distribution centers to accommodate a greater number of online sales as it positioned itself to compete directly with Amazon, especially in terms of next-day delivery.[33] Although some public warehouses offer such specialized services, most distribution centers are privately owned. They serve customers in regional markets and, in some cases, function as consolidation points for a company's branch warehouses.

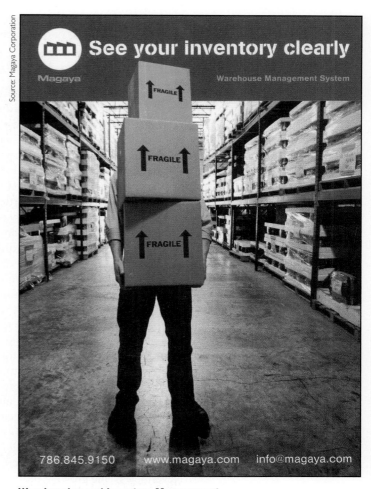

**Warehousing and Inventory Management**
Magaya helps firms manage their warehouse operations efficiently.

## 14-5e **Transportation**

**Transportation**, the movement of products from where they are made to intermediaries and end users, is the most expensive physical distribution function. Transportation costs in the United States reached $907 billion, 62.6 percent of total logistics activities' costs.34 Because product availability and timely deliveries depend on transportation functions, transportation decisions directly affect customer service. In some cases, a firm may choose to build its distribution and marketing strategy around a unique transportation system if that system can ensure on-time

**public warehouses** Storage space and related physical distribution facilities that can be leased by companies

**distribution centers** Large, centralized warehouses that focus on moving rather than storing goods

**transportation** The movement of products from where they are made to intermediaries and end users deliveries and give the firm a competitive edge. Companies may build their own transportation fleets (private carriers) or outsource the transportation function to a common or contract carrier.

## Transportation Modes

The basic transportation modes for moving physical goods are railroads, trucks, waterways, airways, and pipelines. Each has distinct advantages. Many companies adopt physical handling procedures that facilitate the use of two or more modes in combination. Table 14.3 gives more detail on the characteristics of each transportation mode.

Railroads like Union Pacific and Canadian National carry heavy, bulky freight that must be shipped long distances over land. Railroads commonly haul minerals, sand, lumber, chemicals, and farm products, as well as automobiles and low-value manufactured goods. Railroads are especially efficient for transporting full carloads, which can be shipped at lower rates than smaller quantities, because they require less handling. Many companies locate factories or warehouses near rail lines for convenient loading and unloading.

Trucks provide the most flexible schedules and routes of all major transportation modes in the United States, because they can go almost anywhere. Because trucks do not have to conform to a set schedule and can move goods from factory or warehouse to customer, wherever there are roads, they are often used in conjunction with other forms of transport that cannot provide door-to-door deliveries, such as waterways and railroads. Trucks are more expensive and somewhat more vulnerable to bad weather than trains. They are also subject to size and weight restrictions on the loads they carry. Trucks are sometimes criticized for high levels of loss and damage to freight and for delays caused by the re-handling of small shipments.

Waterways are the cheapest method of shipping heavy, low-value, nonperishable goods. Water carriers offer considerable capacity. Powered by tugboats and towboats, barges that travel along intra-coastal canals, inland rivers, and navigation systems can haul at least 10 times the weight of one rail car, and oceangoing vessels can haul thousands of containers. The vast majority of international cargo is transported by water at least part of the way. However, many markets are inaccessible by water transportation and must be supplemented by rail or truck. Droughts and floods also may create difficulties for users of inland waterway transportation. Nevertheless, the growing need to transport goods long distances across the globe will likely increase its use in the future.

Air transportation is the fastest but most expensive form of shipping. It is used most often for perishable goods, for high-value and/or low-bulk items, and for products that require quick delivery over long distances. Some air carriers transport combinations of passengers, freight,

Table 14.3    **Characteristics and Ratings of Transportation Modes by Selection Criteria**

| Selection Criteria | Railroads | Trucks | Pipelines | Waterways | Airplanes |
|---|---|---|---|---|---|
| Cost | Moderate | High | Low | Very low | Very high |
| Speed | Average | Fast | Slow | Very slow | Very fast |
| Dependability | Average | High | High | Average | High |
| Load flexibility | High | Average | Very low | Very high | Low |
| Accessibility | High | Very high | Very limited | Limited | Average |
| Frequency | Low | High | Very high | Very low | Average |
| Products carried | Coal, grain, lumber, paper and pulp products, chemicals | Clothing, computers, books, groceries and produce, livestock | Oil, processed coal, natural gas | Chemicals, bauxite, grain, motor vehicles, agricultural implements | Flowers, food (highly perishable), technical instruments, emergency parts and equipment, overnight mail |

and mail. Despite its expense, air transit can reduce warehousing and packaging costs and losses from theft and damage, thus helping the aggregate cost of the mode. Although air transport accounts for a small minority of total cargo carried, it is an important form of transportation in an increasingly time-sensitive business environment.[35] In fact, the success of many businesses is now based on the availability of overnight air delivery service provided by such organizations as UPS, FedEx, DHL, RPS Air, and the U.S. Postal Service. Many firms offer overnight or same-day shipping to customers.

Pipelines, the most automated transportation mode, usually belong to the shipper and carry the shipper's products. Most pipelines carry petroleum products or chemicals. Slurry pipelines carry pulverized coal, grain, or wood chips suspended in water. Pipelines move products slowly but continuously and at relatively low cost. They are dependable and minimize the problems of product damage and theft. However, contents are subject to as much as 1 percent shrinkage, usually from evaporation—which can result in profit losses. Pipelines also have been a concern to environmentalists, who fear installation and leaks could harm plants and animals.

## Choosing Transportation Modes

Logistics managers select a transportation mode based on the combination of cost, speed, dependability, load flexibility, accessibility, and frequency that is most appropriate for their products and generates the desired level of customer service. Table 14.3 shows relative ratings of each transportation mode by these selection criteria.

Marketers compare alternative transportation modes to determine whether the benefits from a more expensive mode are worth the higher costs. A firm wishing to establish international distribution may consider a large logistics firm for its vast network of global partners. Expeditors International, for instance, has 13,000 associates in 250 locations throughout the world. The company provides tailored solutions and integrated information systems to perform supply-chain management functions at locations around the globe.[36] Look at the MercuryGate advertisement—it is an international logistics company that helps firms identify the optimal modes of transportation for distributing their products around the world. You can see from the advertisement that MercuryGate offers a transportation management system for developing seamless global distribution using all available options, including air, rail, and trucks.

## MARKETING DEBATE

### Online Retailing and the Environment

**ISSUE: Is online retailing good or bad for the environment?**

Consumers are buying more products online than ever before, propelling annual e-commerce purchases beyond $350 billion. What does this mean for the environment? Fewer people driving to individual stores translates into less gasoline used and lower amounts of auto emissions dirtying the air. When e-commerce giants like Amazon buy in huge quantities and receive huge shipments from major suppliers, their suppliers make fewer but larger deliveries. This keeps vehicle emissions lower than if the suppliers had to make many smaller deliveries to a network of retail stores spread across a geographic region. Moreover, when consumers click to buy instead of shopping in person, they don't use plastic and paper bags for individual purchases, which helps save the planet.

On the other hand, the growth in online retailing means an increase in manufacture and disposal of cardboard boxes designed to protect merchandise in transit. Even though cardboard can be recycled, the dramatic increase in shipments requires more trees being turned into more boxes, not a plus for the planet. When consumers buy from multiple online merchants, they receive multiple boxes. From a traffic perspective, more online shopping means more delivery vehicles on the roads, adding to emissions and using up fuel resources as they make dozens of stops every day. And as online retailers race to offer the convenience of same-day delivery, roads will get even more clogged, not an earth-friendly development. So is online retailing good or bad for the environment?[b]

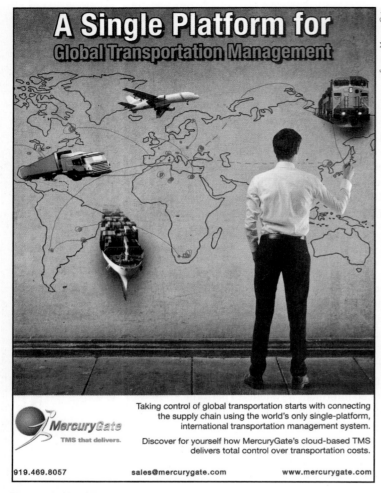

**Transportation Modes**
A logistics company such as MercuryGate can help firms to develop efficient distribution that utilizes available modes of transportation.

## Coordinating Transportation

To take advantage of the benefits offered by various transportation modes and compensate for shortcomings, marketers often combine and coordinate two or more modes. **Intermodal transportation** is easier than ever because of developments within the transportation industry. It combines the flexibility of trucking with the low cost or speed of other forms of transport. Containerization facilitates intermodal transportation by consolidating shipments into sealed containers for transport by *piggyback* (using truck trailers and railway flatcars), *fishyback* (using water carriers), and *birdyback* (using air carriers). As transportation costs have increased and firms seek to find the most efficient methods possible, intermodal shipping has gained popularity.

Specialized outsourcing agencies provide other forms of transport coordination. Known as **freight forwarders**, these firms combine shipments from several organizations into efficient lot sizes. Small loads (less than 500 pounds) are much more expensive to ship than full carloads or truckloads and may make shipping cost-prohibitive for smaller firms. Freight forwarders help such firms by consolidating small loads from various organizations to allow them to qualify collectively for lower rates. Freight forwarders' profits come from the margin between the higher rates firms would have to pay and the lower car-load rates the freight forwarder pays for full loads. Because large shipments also require less handling, freight forwarders can reduce delivery time and the likelihood of shipment damage. Freight forwarders also have the insight to determine the most efficient carriers and routes and are useful for shipping goods to foreign markets, including in foreign markets. Shipping firms such as UPS and FedEx offer freight-forwarding services, as do dedicated freight forwarders such as NRA Global Logistics or Worldwide Express. Some companies may prefer to outsource their shipping to freight forwarders because the forwarders provide door-to-door service.

Another transportation innovation is the development of **megacarriers**, freight transportation companies that offer several shipment methods, including rail, truck, and air service. Prior to the development of megacarriers, transportation companies generally only specialized in one mode. To compete with megacarriers, air carriers have increased their ground-transportation services. As the range of transportation alternatives expands, carriers also put greater emphasis on customer service in order to gain a competitive advantage.

**intermodal transportation** Two or more transportation modes used in combination

**freight forwarders** Organizations that consolidate shipments from several firms into efficient lot sizes

**megacarriers** Freight transportation firms that provide several modes of shipment

## 14-6 LEGAL ISSUES IN CHANNEL MANAGEMENT

The numerous federal, state, and local laws governing distribution channel management in the United States are based on the principle that the public is best served by protecting competition and free trade. Under the authority of such federal legislation as the Sherman Antitrust Act and the Federal Trade Commission Act, courts and regulatory agencies determine under

**Intermodal Transportation**
Containers facilitate intermodal transportation because they can be transported by ships, trains, and trucks.

what circumstances channel management practices violate this underlying principle and must be restricted. Although channel managers are not expected to be legal experts, they should be aware that attempts to control distribution functions might have legal repercussions. When shipping internationally, managers must also be aware of international laws and regulations that might affect their distribution activities. The following practices are among those frequently subject to legal restraint.

## 14-6a Restricted Sales Territories

To tighten control over product distribution, a manufacturer may try to prohibit intermediaries from selling outside of designated sales territories. Intermediaries themselves often favor this practice, because it provides them with exclusive territories where they can minimize competition. Over the years, the courts have adopted conflicting positions in regard to restricted sales territories. Although the courts have deemed restricted sales territories a restraint of trade among intermediaries handling the same brands (except for small or newly established companies), they have also held that exclusive territories can actually promote competition among dealers handling different brands. At present, the producer's intent in establishing restricted territories and the overall effect of doing so on the market must be evaluated for each individual case.

## 14-6b Tying Agreements

When a supplier (usually a manufacturer or franchiser) furnishes a product to a channel member with the stipulation that the channel member must purchase other products as well, it has negotiated a **tying agreement**. Suppliers may institute tying agreements as a means of getting rid of slow-moving inventory, or a franchiser may tie the purchase of equipment and supplies to the sale of franchises, justifying the policy as necessary for quality control and protection of the franchiser's reputation.

A related practice is *full-line forcing*, in which a supplier requires that channel members purchase the supplier's entire line to obtain any of the supplier's products. Manufacturers sometimes use full-line forcing to ensure that intermediaries accept new products and that a suitable range of products is available to customers.

The courts accept tying agreements when the supplier is the only firm able to provide products of a certain quality, when the intermediary is free to carry competing products as well, and when a company has just entered the market. Most other tying agreements are considered illegal.

**tying agreement** An agreement in which a supplier furnishes a product to a channel member with the stipulation that the channel member must purchase other products as well

### 14-6c Exclusive Dealing

When a manufacturer forbids an intermediary to carry products of competing manufacturers, the arrangement is called **exclusive dealing**. Manufacturers receive considerable market protection in an exclusive-dealing arrangement and may cut off shipments to intermediaries that violate the agreement.

The legality of an exclusive-dealing contract is determined by applying three tests. If the exclusive dealing blocks competitors from as much as 15 percent of the market, the sales volume is large, and the producer is considerably larger than the retailer, then the arrangement is considered anticompetitive. If dealers and customers in a given market have access to similar products or if the exclusive-dealing contract strengthens an otherwise weak competitor, the arrangement is allowed.

### 14-6d Refusal to Deal

**exclusive dealing** A situation in which a manufacturer forbids an intermediary from carrying products of competing manufacturers

For nearly a century, courts have held that producers have the right to choose or reject the channel members with which they will do business. Within existing distribution channels, however, suppliers may not legally refuse to deal with wholesalers or dealers merely because these wholesalers or dealers resist policies that are anticompetitive or in restraint of trade. Suppliers are further prohibited from organizing some channel members in refusal-to-deal actions against other members that choose not to comply with illegal policies.

## Summary

### 14-1　Describe the foundations of supply-chain management.

The distribution component of the marketing mix focuses on the decisions and activities involved in making products available to customers when and where they want to purchase them. An important function of distribution is the joint effort of all involved organizations to be part of creating an effective supply chain, which includes all the organizations and activities involved with the flow and transformation of products from raw materials through to the end customer. Operations management is the total set of managerial activities used by an organization to transform resource inputs into goods, services, or both. Logistics management involves planning, implementation, and controlling the efficient and effective flow and storage of goods, services, and information from the point of origin to consumption in order to meet customers' needs and wants. Supply management in its broadest form refers to the processes that enable the progress of value from raw material to final customer and back to redesign and final disposition. Supply-chain management (SCM) refers to the coordination of all the activities involved with the flow and transformation of supplies, products, and information throughout the supply chain to the ultimate consumer. It integrates the functions of operations management, logistics management, supply management, and marketing channel management so that goods and services are produced and distributed in the right quantities, to the right locations, and at the right time. The supply chain includes all entities—shippers and other firms that facilitate distribution, as well as producers, wholesalers, and retailers—that distribute products and benefit from cooperative efforts.

### 14-2　Explain the role and significance of marketing channels and supply chains.

A marketing channel, or channel of distribution, is a group of individuals and organizations that direct the flow of products from producers to customers. The major role of marketing channels is to make products available at the right time, at the right place, and in the right amounts. In most channels of distribution, producers and consumers are linked by marketing intermediaries. The two major types of intermediaries are retailers, which purchase products and resell them to ultimate consumers, and wholesalers, which buy and resell products to other wholesalers, retailers, and business customers.

Marketing channels serve many functions. They create time, place, and possession utilities by making products available when and where customers want them and providing customers with access to product use through sale or rental. Marketing intermediaries facilitate exchange efficiencies, often reducing the costs of exchanges by performing certain services and functions. Although some critics suggest eliminating wholesalers, the functions of the intermediaries in the marketing channel must be performed. As such, eliminating one or more intermediaries results in other organizations in the channel having to do more. Because intermediaries serve both producers and buyers, they reduce the total number of transactions that otherwise would be needed to move products from producer to the end customer.

Channels of distribution are broadly classified as channels for consumer products and channels for business products. Within these two broad categories, different channels are used for different products. Although consumer goods can move directly from producer to consumers, consumer channels that include wholesalers and retailers are usually more economical and knowledge-efficient. Distribution of business products differs from that of consumer products in the types of channels used. A direct distribution channel is common in business marketing. Also used are channels containing industrial distributors, manufacturers' agents, and a combination of agents and distributors. Most producers have multichannel distribution systems that can be adjusted for various target markets.

A strategic channel alliance exists when the products of one firm are distributed through the marketing channels of another. Multichannel distribution—the use of a variety of marketing channels to ensure maximum distribution—is increasingly used to reach target customers wherever and whenever they may choose to interact with a company or its products. Some products use digital distribution to deliver content through the Internet to a computer or other device. It is important to recognize that the line between different marketing channels is becoming increasingly blurred.

Selecting an appropriate marketing channel is a crucial decision for supply-chain managers. To determine which channel is most appropriate, managers must think about customer characteristics, the type of organization, product attributes, competition, environmental forces, and the availability and characteristics of intermediaries. Careful consideration of these factors will assist a supply-chain manager in selecting the correct channel.

## 14-3 Identify the intensity of market coverage.

A marketing channel is managed such that products receive appropriate market coverage. In choosing intensive distribution, producers strive to make a product available to all possible dealers. In selective distribution, only some outlets in an area are chosen to distribute a product. Exclusive distribution usually gives a single dealer rights to sell a product in a large geographic area.

## 14-4 Describe strategic issues in marketing channels, including leadership, cooperation, and conflict.

Each channel member performs a different role in the system and agrees to accept certain rights, responsibilities, rewards, and sanctions for nonconformance. Although many marketing channels are determined by consensus, some are organized and controlled by a single leader, or channel captain. A channel captain may be a producer, wholesaler, or retailer. A marketing channel functions most effectively when members cooperate. When they deviate from their roles, channel conflict can arise.

Integration of marketing channels brings various activities under one channel member's management. Vertical integration combines two or more stages of the channel under one management. The vertical marketing system (VMS) is managed centrally for the mutual benefit of all channel members. Vertical marketing systems may be corporate, administered, or contractual. Horizontal integration combines institutions at the same level of channel operation under a single management.

## 14-5 Explain physical distribution as being a part of supply-chain management.

Physical distribution, or logistics, refers to the activities used to move products from producers to customers and other end users. These activities include order processing, inventory management, materials handling, warehousing, and transportation. An efficient physical distribution system is an important component of an overall marketing strategy because it can decrease costs and increase customer satisfaction. Within the marketing channel, physical distribution activities are often performed by a wholesaler, but they may also be performed by a producer or retailer or outsourced to a third party. Third-party logistics (3PL) firms have special expertise in core physical distribution activities such as warehousing, transportation, inventory management, and information technology and can often perform these activities more efficiently. Efficient physical distribution systems can decrease costs and transit time while increasing customer service.

Order processing is the receipt and transmission of sales order information. It consists of three main tasks—order entry, order handling, and order delivery—that may be done manually but are more often handled through electronic data interchange systems. Inventory management involves developing and maintaining adequate assortments of products to meet customers' needs. Logistics managers must strive to find the optimal level of inventory to satisfy customer needs while keeping costs down. Materials handling, the physical handling of products, is a crucial element in warehousing and transporting products. Radio frequency identification (RFID) uses radio waves to identify and track materials tagged with special microchips through every phase of handling. Warehousing involves the design and operation of facilities for storing and moving goods. Such facilities may be privately owned or public. Transportation, the movement of products from where they are made to where they are purchased and used, is the most expensive physical distribution function. The basic modes of transporting goods include railroads, trucks, waterways, airways, and pipelines.

## 14-6 Describe legal issues in channel management.

Federal, state, and local laws regulate channel management to protect competition and free trade. Courts may prohibit or permit a practice depending on whether it violates this underlying principle. Channel management practices frequently subject to legal restraint include restricted sales territories, tying agreements, exclusive dealing, and refusal to deal. When these practices strengthen weak competitors or increase competition among dealers, they may be permitted. In most other cases, when competition may be weakened considerably, they are deemed illegal.

---

**Go to www.cengagebrain.com for resources to help you master the content in this chapter as well as materials that will expand your marketing knowledge!**

---

# Important Terms

distribution 422
supply chain 422
operations management 422
logistics management 422
supply management 422
supply-chain management 422
marketing channel 424
marketing intermediaries 424
industrial distributor 429
strategic channel alliance 430
multichannel distribution 431
digital distribution 431
intensive distribution 433
selective distribution 434

exclusive distribution 435
channel captain 437
channel power 437
vertical channel integration 439
vertical marketing system
   (VMS) 439
horizontal channel integration 440
physical distribution 440
third-party logistics (3PL) firm 440
cycle time 441
order processing 442
electronic data interchange
   (EDI) 442
inventory management 442

just-in-time (JIT) 443
materials handling 443
radio-frequency identification
   (RFID) 443
warehousing 444
private warehouses 444
public warehouses 445
distribution centers 445
transportation 445
intermodal transportation 448
freight forwarders 448
megacarriers 448
tying agreement 449
exclusive dealing 450

# Discussion and Review Questions

1. Define supply-chain management. Why is it important?
2. Describe the major functions of marketing channels. Why are these functions better accomplished through combined efforts of channel members?
3. List several reasons consumers often blame intermediaries for distribution inefficiencies.
4. Compare and contrast the four major types of marketing channels for consumer products. Through which type of channel is each of the following products most likely to be distributed?
   a. New automobiles
   b. Saltine crackers
   c. Cut-your-own Christmas trees
   d. New textbooks
   e. Sofas
   f. Soft drinks
5. Outline the four most common channels for business products. Describe the products or situations that lead marketers to choose each channel.

6. Describe an industrial distributor. What types of products are marketed through an industrial distributor?
7. Under what conditions is a producer most likely to use more than one marketing channel?
8. Identify and describe the factors that may influence marketing channel selection decisions.
9. Explain the differences among intensive, selective, and exclusive methods of distribution.
10. "Channel cooperation requires that members support the overall channel goals to achieve individual goals." Comment on this statement.
11. Explain the major characteristics of each of the three types of vertical marketing systems (VMSs): corporate, administered, and contractual.
12. Discuss the cost and service trade-offs involved in developing a physical distribution system.
13. What are the main tasks involved in order processing?

14. Explain the trade-offs that inventory managers face when they reorder products or supplies. How is the reorder point computed?

15. Explain the major differences between private and public warehouses. How do they differ from a distribution center?

16. Compare and contrast the five major transportation modes in terms of cost, speed, and dependability.

17. Under what conditions are tying agreements, exclusive dealing, and refusal-to-deal judged illegal?

# Video Case 14.1

## Taza Cultivates Channel Relationships with Chocolate

Taza Chocolate is a small Massachusetts–based manufacturer of stone-ground organic chocolate made in the classic Mexican tradition. Founded in 2006, Taza markets most of its products through U.S. retailers, wholesalers, and distributors. Individual customers around the world can also buy Taza chocolate bars, baking squares, chocolate-covered nuts, and other specialty items directly from the Taza website. If they live in Somerville, Massachusetts, they might even find a Taza employee riding a "chococycle," selling products and distributing samples at an upscale food-truck festival or a weekend market festival.

Taza seeks to make personal connections with all the certified organic growers who supply its ingredients. "Because our process here at the factory is so minimal," says the company's director of sales, "it's really important that we get a very high-quality ingredient. To make sure that we're getting the absolute cream of the [cocoa] crop, we have a direct face-to-face human relationship between us and the actual farmer who's producing those beans."

Dealing directly with suppliers allows Taza to meet its social responsibility goals while ensuring the kind of quality that commands a premium price. "We're a premium brand," explains the director of sales, "and because of the way we do what we do, we have to charge more than your average chocolate bar." A Taza chocolate bar that sells at a retail price of $4.50 carries a wholesale price of about $2.70. The distributor's price, however, is even lower, closer to $2.00.

Distributors buy in the largest quantities, which for Taza means a pallet load rather than a case that a wholesaler would buy. "But wholesale will always be our bread and butter, where we really move the volume and we have good margins," says Taza's director of sales. In the company's experience, distributors are very price-conscious and more interested than wholesalers in promotions and extras.

Taza offers factory tours at its Somerville site, charging a small entrance fee that includes a donation to Sustainable Harvest International. There, visitors can watch the bean-to-bar process from beginning to end, learning about the beans and the stone-ground tradition that differentiates Taza from European chocolates. Visitors enjoy product samples along the way and, at the end of the tour, they can browse through the factory store and buy freshly-made specialties like chipotle chili chocolate and ginger chocolate. On holidays like Halloween and Valentine's Day, Taza hosts special tastings and limited-edition treats to attract customers to its factory store. Its annual beer-and-chocolate pairing event, hosted with the Drink Craft Beer website, is another way to introduce Taza to consumers who appreciate quality foods and drinks.

Taza's marketing communications focus mainly on Facebook, Twitter, blogs, e-mail, and specialty food shows. Also, the company frequently offers samples in upscale and organic food stores in major metropolitan areas. As it does with its growers, Taza seeks to forge personal relationships with its channel partners. "When we send a shipment of chocolate," says the sales director, "sometimes we'll put in a little extra for the people who work there. That always helps because [it's] building that kind of human relationship."

Privately-owned Taza has begun shipping to Canada and a handful of European countries. Its channel arrangements must allow for delivering perishable products that stay fresh and firm, no matter what the weather. As a result, distributors often hold some Taza inventory in refrigerated warehouses to have ready for next-day delivery when retailers place orders.[37]

### Questions for Discussion

1. Which distribution channels does Taza use, and why are they appropriate for this company?

2. In what ways does Taza benefit from selling directly to some consumers? What are some potential problems of selling directly to consumers?

3. In what ways are Taza's distribution efforts influenced by the fact that its products are organic?

# Case 14.2

## Procter & Gamble Tunes Up Channels and Transportation

From Pampers to Puffs, Comet to Crest, Procter & Gamble markets some of the world's best-known brands for household needs, health care, personal care, and baby care. Its portfolio includes 21 brands that bring in more than $1 billion each every year, fueling more than $70 billion in annual sales through stores and online retailers in 180 countries.

Because nearly all of Procter & Gamble's products are convenience goods, the company uses intensive distribution market coverage. Among the retailers that carry its products are supermarkets, drug stores, convenience stores, discount stores, and warehouse clubs. Shelf space is valuable, so not all stores carry the entire product line in any given category. In many stores, Procter & Gamble's branded items compete for shelf space not only with other manufacturers' brands, but also with store brands. And, knowing that warehouse stores have limited backroom storage space, Procter & Gamble makes more frequent deliveries to ensure that its products are always in stock for club members.

Eyeing long-term growth in emerging markets, which already account for nearly 40 percent of its sales, Procter & Gamble is always looking for a distribution edge that will put its products on more shelves. When the company acquired Gillette in 2005, it also obtained access to the marketing channels Gillette had established for its razors, blades, and other accessories. This helped Procter & Gamble gain additional distribution for a wider range of products in India and Brazil, among other nations.

Procter & Gamble is testing new Internet and mobile channels for some of its everyday products. In one Toronto experiment, it teamed with the online retailer Well.ca to create posters of frequently-purchased products like Crest toothpaste and Pampers disposable diapers, along with QR (quick response) codes that can be scanned by consumers with QR apps on their smartphones. The posters were positioned in a busy downtown building adjacent to the subway, where time-pressured commuters could take a minute or two to scan the items they wanted to purchase and arrange delivery from Well.ca at a convenient hour. In another Toronto experiment, Procter & Gamble teamed with Walmart Canada to create

virtual stores inside 50 bus shelters. As consumers waited for a bus, they used their smartphones to scan QR codes for baby products, beauty products, and other merchandise, and set a time for later delivery. Tests such as these help both the manufacturer and retailers to refine future marketing efforts as technology evolves.

In addition, the Internet retailing pioneer Amazon.com has asked Procter & Gamble to help it speed up delivery of products sold online. At Amazon's request, Procter & Gamble has roped off a small, separate area inside seven of its distribution centers, reserving this space just for the use of Amazon. These centers in the United States, Japan, and Germany hold cartons and cartons of bulky products like Pampers disposable diapers and Bounty paper towels while they await delivery to retailers. Instead of trucking these goods to Amazon's distribution centers when needed, Procter & Gamble simply shifts them to the separate Amazon section of the building. There, Amazon employees select individual items to fulfill customer orders and ship the boxes directly from the distribution center to consumers. Not only does this save time, but it also saves money for both Procter & Gamble and Amazon. Amazon also features Tide and other P&G brands on its Amazon Dash buttons, which are physical buttons consumers stick to a cabinet or closet and press to activate automatic online ordering of frequently purchased items.

Efficiency is vital when a marketer like Procter & Gamble distributes products in such massive quantities. In North America alone, the company prepares 800,000 shipments annually for delivery to retailers' warehouses and distribution centers. Shaving even a few dollars per shipment adds up to a significant savings over time. Greener transportation is also helping Procter & Gamble save money while it helps protect the planet. Although the company maintains a small fleet of trucks, most of its products are transported by 80 outside trucking companies. Procter & Gamble is working with the truckers to significantly increase the percentage of shipments transported by vehicles that run on compressed natural gas, making physical distribution greener in environmental and financial terms.[38]

## Questions for Discussion

1. Do you think Procter & Gamble should use a direct channel to sell to consumers? Identify one or more arguments for and against using a direct channel for disposable diapers and paper towels.

2. What issues in channel conflict might arise from Procter & Gamble's special arrangements with Amazon.com?

3. Would you recommend that Procter & Gamble use any mode of transportation other than trucks to transport cartons to retailers? Explain your answer.

# NOTES

[1] Gloria Dawson, "A Start-Up That Aims to Bring Back the Farm-to-Vase Bouquet," *New York Times*, January 9, 2016, www.nytimes.com/2016/01/10/business/a-start-up-that-aims-to-bring-back-the-farm-to-vase-bouquet.html?_r=0 (accessed February 18, 2016); Katy Steinmetz, "Inside the Startups Making It Easier to Buy Flowers," *Time*, February 8, 2016, http://time.com/4117334/valentines-day-flower-delivery-startups/ (accessed February 18, 2016); "Flower Start-Ups Cut Out Red Roses for Valentine's Day," *12 News NBC* (Arizona), February 10, 2016, www.12news.com/news/nation-now/flower-startups-cut-out-red-roses-for-valentines-day/38933431 (accessed February 18, 2016).

[2] Ricky W. Griffin, *Fundamentals of Management* (Mason, OH: South-Western Cengage, 2012), p. 460.

[3] Dan Gilmore, "First Thoughts: State of the Logistics Union 2015," *Supply Chain Digest*, June 25, 2015, http://www.scdigest.com/ASSETS/FIRSTTHOUGHTS/15-06-25.php?cid=9451 (accessed March 11, 2016).

[4] Erica E. Phillips, "Consumers Triggering Major Changes in Retail Supply Chains," *The Wall Street Journal*, May 22, 2015, http://www.wsj.com/articles/consumers-driving-changes-in-retail-supply-chains-1432314236 (accessed March 11, 2016).

[5] Tibbr, "Overview," http://www.tibbr.com/what-is-tibbr/overview/microblogging.php (accessed March 11, 2016); Yammer, "Overview," https://about.yammer.com (accessed March 11, 2016).

[6] Patrick Burnson, "Supply Chain Managers Told to Prepare for Demand Surge in 2014," *Supply Chain Management Review*, November 16, 2013, www.scmr.com/article/supply_chain_managers_told_to_prepare_for_demand_surge_in_2014 (accessed March 11, 2016).

[7] Lisa R. Melsted, "Delivering with Data: How Logistics Companies Are Shipping on Time," *Forbes*, February 16, 2015, http://www.forbes.com/sites/samsungbusiness/2015/02/16/delivering-with-data-how-logistics-companies-are-shipping-on-time/ (accessed March 11, 2016); Christina Ng, "Soap Opera: Amazon Moves In with P&G," *The Wall Street Journal*, October 14, 2013, http://online.wsj.com/news/articles/SB10001424052702304330904579135840230674458? (accessed March 11, 2016).

[8] "Solution Highlights," MercuryGate, www.mercurygate.com/solution_highlights (accessed March 11, 2016); April Joyner, "Best Industries 2012: Supply Chain | 6 Logistics Startups on the Move," *Inc.*, http://www.inc.com/ss/best-industries-2012/april-joyner/supply-chain-management-companies-6-that-fill-a-niche (accessed March 11, 2016).

[9] Jonathan Littman, "Supply-Chain Miseries Doom Target in Canada," *Supply Chain 24/7*, January 17, 2015, http://www.supplychain247.com/article/supply_chain_miseries_doom_target_in_canada (accessed March 11, 2016).

[10] David Zax, "How Xerox Evolved from Copier Company to Creative Powerhouse," *Fast Company*, December 11, 2013, www.fastcompany.com/3023240/most-creative-people/dreaming-together-how-xerox-keeps-big-ideas-flowing (accessed March 14, 2016).

[11] Applied Industrial Technologies, Inc., www.applied.com (accessed March 14, 2016).

[12] Leo Aspinwall, "The Marketing Characteristics of Goods," in *Four Marketing Theories* (Boulder, CO: University of Colorado Press, 1961), pp. 27–32.

[13] Megumi Fujiwaka, "McDonald's Japan Famished by Potato Shortage," The *Wall Street Journal*, December 16, 2014, http://blogs.wsj.com/japanrealtime/2014/12/16/mcdonalds-japan-famished-by-potato-shortage/ (accessed March 15, 2016); David Fickling, "McDonald's Japan Is No Happy Meal," *Crain's Chicago Business*, December 22, 2015, www.chicagobusiness.com/article/20151222/NEWS07/151229950/mcdonalds-japan-is-no-happy-meal (March 15, 2016).

[14] Deloitte, "2016 Global Manufacturing Competitiveness Ranking," http://www2.deloitte.com/global/en/pages/about-deloitte/articles/global-manufacturing-competitiveness-index.html (accessed March 15, 2016).

[15] Jackie Northam, U.S. West Coast Port Dispute Forces Shippers to Find Alternatives," NPR, February 20, 2015, www.npr.org/blogs/thetwo-way/2015/02/20/387305541/u-s-west-coast-port-dispute-forces-shippers-to-find-alternatives (accessed March 15, 2016).

[16] Adam Vaccaro, "Tell Your Customers about Your Responsible Supply Chain," *Inc.*, November 13, 2013, www.inc.com/adam-vaccaro/supply-chain-corporate-social-responsibility.html (accessed March 15, 2016).

[17] Suppliers Partnership for the Environment, www.supplierspartnership.org (accessed March 15, 2016).

[18] IGA website, www.iga.com/about.aspx (accessed March 15, 2016).

[19] Wroe Alderson, *Dynamic Marketing Behavior* (Homewood, IL: Irwin, 1965), p. 239.

[20] Adam Rapp, Lauren Skinner Beitelspacher, Dhruv Grewal, and Douglas E. Hughes, "Understanding Social Media Effects across Seller, Retailer, and Consumer Interactions," *Journal of the Academy of Marketing Science*, *41, 31* (2013): 547–566.

[21] M. Kelly Cunningham, "Reducing Channel Conflict," *Journal of Marketing Development & Competitiveness, 7*, 1 (2013): 78–83.

22 "Katie Fehrenbacher, "SolarCity to Start Making Highly Efficient Solar Panels Later this Moth," *Fortune*, October 2, 2015, http://fortune.com/2015/10/02/solarcity-solar-panel/(accessed March 21, 2016).

23 "Inditex Press Dossier," http://www.inditex.com/en/media/press_dossier (accessed March 21, 2016), p. 6.

24 Clare O'Connor, "How Ace Hardware Turned Corner Stores into a $4.7 Billion Co-op," *Forbes*, March 2, 2015, http://www.forbes.com/sites/clareoconnor/2015/02/11/how-ace-hardware-turned-corner-stores-into-a-4-7-billion-co-op/ (accessed March 21, 2016).

25 "Sherwin Williams to Buy Valspar for $11.3 Billion," *Fortune*, March 20, 2016, http://fortune.com/2016/03/20/sherwin-williams-valspar/ (accessed March 21, 2016).

26 Noel Datko, "Supply Chain Basics: Managing Third Party Logistics and Embracing Technology, *Direct Selling News*, January 1, 2015, http://directsellingnews.com/index.php/view/supply_chain_basics_managing_third_party_logistics_and_embracing_technology#.VVzQQfnnuUk (accessed March 21, 2016).

27 Adam Robinson, "The Future of Logistics: Are 3PL Companies Ready to Adopt These 4 Emerging Technologies?" Cerasis, January 14, 2015, http://cerasis.com/2015/01/14/future-of-logistics/ (accessed March 21, 2016).

28 Adam Lashinsky, "The Cutting Edge of Care," *Fortune*, March 9, 2015, http://fortune.com/2015/03/09/dollar-shave-club/ (accessed March 21, 2016); Darren Dahl, "Riding the Momentum Created by a Cheeky Video" *The Wall Street Journal*, April 11, 2013, www.nytimes.com/2013/04/11/business/smallbusiness/dollar-shave-club-from-viral-video-to-real-business.html (accessed May 22, 2015).

29 Mark B. Solomon, "Hospital Chain Trinity Health, XPO Partner to Take Supply Chain in House," *DC Velocity*, March 9, 2016, http://www.dcvelocity.com/articles/20160309-hospital-chain-trinity-health-xpo-partner-to-take-supply-chain-in-house/ (accessed March 21, 2016).

30 Christopher Bjork, "Zara Builds Its Business around RFID," *The Wall Street Journal*, September 16, 2014, www.wsj.com/articles/at-zara-fast-fashion-meets-smarter-inventory-1410884519?autologin=y (accessed March 21, 2016).

31 Distribution Unlimited Inc., http://distributionunlimited.com/operations.php (accessed March 21, 2016).

32 Marilyn Moritz, "Robots Work Alongside Humans at Amazon Distribution Center," KSAT News, April 17, 2015, www.ksat.com/content/pns/ksat/news/2015/04/17/robots-work-alongside-humans-at-amazon-distribution-center.html (accessed March 21, 2016); Marcus Wohl-sen, "A Rare Peek Inside Amazon's Massive-Wish Fulfilling Machine," *Wired*, June 16, 2014, www.wired.com/2014/06/inside-amazon-warehouse/ (accessed March 21, 2016).

33 Sarah Perez, "Walmart Invests in E-Commerce, Next-Day Delivery Expansions with Two New Fulfillment Centers," *Tech Crunch*, October 15, 2014, http://techcrunch.com/2014/10/15/walmart-invests-in-e-commerce-next-day-delivery-expansions-with-two-new-fulfillment-centers (accessed March 21, 2016).

34 "Supply Chain Graphic of the Week; A Breakdown of 2014 US Logistics Costs," *Supply Chain Digest*, June 24, 2015, http://www.scdigest.com/assets/newsviews/15-06-24-2.php?cid=9443 (accessed March 21, 2016).

35 David Hummels and Georg Schaur, "Time as a Trade Barrier," *National Bureau of Economic Research*, January 2012, No. 17758, papers.nber.org/papers/w17758#fromrss (accessed March 21, 2016).

36 Expeditors International, "Our Company," http://www.expeditors.com/our-company/about-us.asp (accessed March 22, 2016).

37 Alex Pearlman, "Taza Chocolate and Drink Craft Beer Prove that Beer and Chocolate Make a Perfect Pair," *Boston Globe*, February 13, 2012, www.boston.com/lifestyle/blogs/thenextgreatgeneration/2012/02/taza_chocolate_and_drink_craft.html; Rachel Leah Blumenthal, "A Tour of the Taza Chocolate Factory," *CBS Local News* (Boston), October 26, 2011, http://boston.cbslocal.com/2011/10/26/a-tour-of-the-taza-chocolate-factory (accessed December 21, 2013); Ariel Shearer, "Review: Taza Chocolate," *Boston Phoenix*, October 31, 2011, http://thephoenix.com/boston/food/128984-review-taza-chocolate; Courtney Holland, "Sweet Batches of Local Flavor," *Boston Globe*, August 18, 2010, www.boston.com/lifestyle/food/articles/2010/08/18/batch_ice_cream_is_big_on_local_flavor; Kerry J. Byrne, "Festival of Food Trucks," *Boston Herald*, August 6, 2010, http://bostonherald.com/entertainment/food_dining/dining_news/2010/08/festival_food_trucks.

38 Alexander Coolidge, "New P&G CEO to Talk Strategy," *Cincinatti.com,* February 15, 2016, www.cincinnati.com/story/money/2016/02/13/pgs-chief-faces-debut-before-wall-st-skeptics/79875056/ (accessed February 17, 2016); *Procter & Gamble 2015 Annual Report*, pp. 1–7; Jack Neff, "CPG E-Commerce Sales Soared 42% Last Year, Fueled by Amazon," *Advertising Age*, January 29, 2016, http://adage.com/article/ad-age-annual/cpg-e-commerce-sales-soared-42-year-driven-amazon-subscriptions/302405/ (accessed February 17, 2016); Steve Banker, "Procter & Gamble, General Mills, and Frito-Lay Move to Natural Gas Fleets," *Forbes*, November 7, 2013, www.forbes.com/sites/stevebanker/2013/11/07/procter-gamble-general-mills-and-frito-lay-transition-to-natural-gas-fleets; Serena Ng, "Soap Opera: Amazon Moves In with P&G," *The Wall Street Journal*, October 14, 2013, http://online.wsj.com/news/articles/SB10001424052702304330904579135840230674458; Serena Ng, "Procter & Gamble's Profit Rises on Higher Sales," *Wall Street Journal*, October 25, 2013, http://online.wsj.com/news/articles/SB10001424052702304799404579157181457960644; Barney Jopson, "Procter & Gamble: Time to Freshen Up," *Financial Times*, July 28, 2013, www.ft.com/intl/cms/s/0/e1782cc4-e95a-11e2-9f11-00144feabdc0.html; Alicia Androich, "Walmart Canada and P&G Launch Bus Shelter Mobile Store," *Marketing Magazine* (Canada), June 5, 2013, www.marketingmag.ca/news/marketer-news/walmart-canada-and-pg-launch-bus-shelter-mobile-store-80530.

# Feature Notes

[a] Danielle Demetriou, "China's 'Explosive Shopping' Sprees Bring Chaos to Tokyo Roads," *The Telegraph (U.K.)*, February 15, 2016, www.telegraph.co.uk/news/worldnews/asia/japan/12157333/Chinas-explosive-shopping-sprees-bring-chaos-to-Tokyo-roads.html (accessed February 18, 2016); Sarah Jones, "How Can Fashion Brands Leverage Shopping Tourism?" *Luxury Daily*, May 7, 2015, www.luxurydaily.com/how-can-fashion-brands-leverage-shopping-tourism/ (accessed February 18, 2016); Geoffrey Smith, "Why People Are Vacationing at the Mall," *Fortune*, December 6, 2015, http://fortune.com/2015/12/06/vacation-mall-bicester-village/ (accessed February 18, 2016).

[b] Sarah DeWeerdt, "How Green Is Online Shopping?," *Conservation Magazine,* February 17, 2016, www.theguardian.com/environment/2016/feb/17/how-green-is-online-shopping (accessed February 17, 2016); Diane Kukich, "Shop Right," *UDaily (University of Delaware),* February 5, 2016, www.udel.edu/udaily/2016/feb/online-shopping-020516.html (accessed February 17, 2016); Matt Richtel, "E-Commerce: Convenience Built on a Mountain of Card-board," *New York Times,* February 16, 2016, www.nytimes.com/2016/02/16/science/recycling-cardboard-online-shopping-environment.html?_r=0 (accessed February 17, 2016).

# chapter 15

# Retailing, Direct Marketing, and Wholesaling

---

## OBJECTIVES

---

**15-1**  Describe the purpose and function of retailers in the marketing channel.

**15-2**  Identify the major types of retailers.

**15-3**  Explain strategic issues in retailing.

**15-4**  Recognize the various forms of direct marketing, direct selling, and vending.

**15-5**  Describe franchising and its benefits and weaknesses.

**15-6**  Explain the nature and functions of wholesalers.

# MARKETING INSIGHTS

## Gulp! 7-Eleven Slurps up Convenience Store Business

iStockphoto.com/RiverNorthPhotography

With 56,000 stores in 16 countries—including more than 10,500 units in North America—7-Eleven is the market leader among convenience stores. Fueled by acquisitions of regional chains and intent on satisfying customers quickly and conveniently, 7-Eleven now rings up $84 billion in annual sales as it approaches its 90th year in the retail business.

An important marketing priority is differentiating its stores in a marketplace crowded with rivals competing for the attention of on-the-go customers. To set itself apart, 7-Eleven has created a number of products and brands unique to its stores. One is Slurpee, a slushy carbonated beverage introduced in the 1960s. Another is Big Gulp, introduced in the 1970s as a 32-ounce soft-drink cup. This popular product line has been expanded over the years to cover ever-larger sizes, including Double Gulp (a half-gallon container) and Team Gulp (a one-gallon container).

Company research shows that more than half of 7-Eleven's customers drop in to buy a beverage of some sort, such as a soft drink or coffee. Knowing this, the retailer uses its 7Rewards mobile app to encourage loyalty. After six beverage purchases, the seventh beverage is free. The retailer personalizes other rewards based on each customer's individual purchasing patterns, as a way to increase the size of each transaction and build store traffic throughout the day. It is also testing e-commerce pickup lockers. Customers who order from Amazon.com, Walmart.com, or other online sites can have packages delivered by UPS or FedEx to a local 7-Eleven store. Will customers find this convenient, and will they buy something else when picking up a package?[1]

Retailers like 7-Eleven are the most visible and accessible marketing channel members to consumers. They represent an important link in the marketing channel because they are both marketers for and customers of producers and wholesalers. They perform many supply chain functions, such as buying, selling, grading, risk taking, and developing and maintaining information databases about customers. Retailers are in a strategic position to develop relationships with consumers and partnerships with producers and intermediaries in the marketing channel.

In this chapter, we examine the nature of retailing, direct marketing, and wholesaling and their roles in supplying consumers with goods and services. First, we explore the major types of retail stores and consider strategic issues in retailing: location, retail positioning, store image, and category management. Next, we discuss direct marketing, including online retailing, catalog marketing, direct-response marketing, telemarketing, and television home shopping. We also explore direct selling and vending. Then we look at the strengths and weaknesses of franchising, a retailing form that continues to grow in popularity. Finally, we examine the importance of wholesalers in marketing channels, including their functions and classifications.

# 15-1 **RETAILING**

**Retailing** includes all transactions in which the buyer is the ultimate consumer and intends to use the product for personal, family, or household purposes. A **retailer** is an organization that purchases products for the purpose of reselling them to ultimate consumers. Although most retailers' sales are made directly to the consumer, nonretail transactions occur occasionally when retailers sell products to other businesses. Retailing is vital to the U.S. economy. Every time you buy a meal, a smartphone, a movie ticket, or some other product from a retailer, the money you spend flows through the economy to the store's employees, to the government, and to other businesses and consumers. There are 3.8 million retail establishments in the United States, and they employ nearly 29 million people. Retailers contribute $1.2 trillion, or 7.7 percent, directly to the U.S. gross domestic product.[2]

Retailers add value for customers by providing services and assisting in making product selections. They can enhance customers' perceptions of the value of products by making buyers' shopping experiences easier or more convenient, such as providing free delivery or offering a mobile shopping option. Retailers can facilitate comparison shopping, which allows customers to evaluate different options. For instance, car dealerships often cluster in the same general vicinity, as do furniture stores. The Internet also allows consumers to comparison shop easily. Product value is also enhanced when retailers offer services, such as technical advice, delivery, credit, and repair. Finally, retail sales personnel are trained to be able to demonstrate to customers how products can satisfy their needs or solve problems.

Retailers can add significant value to the supply chain, representing a critical link between producers and ultimate consumers by providing the environment in which exchanges occur. Retailers play a major role in creating time, place, possession and, in some cases, form utility. They perform marketing functions that benefit ultimate consumers by making available broad arrays of products that can satisfy their needs.

Historically, retail stores have offered consumers a place to browse and compare merchandise to find just what they need. However, such traditional retailing is evolving to meet changing consumer demographics and buying behavior and is adopting new technologies to improve the shopping experience. Many retailers now engage in **multichannel retailing** by employing multiple distribution channels that complement their brick-and-mortar stores with websites, catalogs, and apps where consumers can research products, read other buyers' reviews, and make actual purchases. The most effective multichannel retail strategies integrate the firm's goals, products, systems, and technologies seamlessly across all platforms so that a customer can research a product through the firm's website at home, find specific information about the product and locate the nearest one through an app on their smartphone while in the car, and check out in a store or online. Regardless of platform, the key to success in retailing is to have a strong customer focus with a retail strategy that provides the level of service, product quality,

**retailing** All transactions in which the buyer intends to consume the product through personal, family, or household use

**retailer** An organization that purchases products for the purpose of reselling them to ultimate consumers

**multichannel retailing** Employing multiple distribution channels that complement their brick-and-mortar stores with websites, catalogs, and apps where consumers can research products, read other buyers' reviews, and make actual purchases and innovation that consumers desire. New store formats, service innovations, and advances in information technology have helped retailers to serve customers better. For example, through Domino's Pizza AnyWare program, regular customers who have set up profiles with the firm can text or tweet a pizza slice emoji, send a message through some smart TVs and automobiles, use the company's app, or call their local Domino's store, and their favorite regular order will be promptly delivered.[3]

Retailing is also increasingly international. In particular, many retailers see significant growth potential in international markets. The market for a product category such as cell phones is mature in North America and Europe. However, demand remains strong in places like India, China, and Brazil. These countries all have large, relatively new middle classes with consumers hungry for goods and services. After recognizing that Indians with increasing discretionary income were buying Coach bags and accessories abroad, the luxury fashion icon partnered with a local firm to open Coach stores in India, one of the largest consumer economies.[4] Many major U.S. retailers have international outlets in order to capitalize on international growth. On the other hand, international retailers, such as Aldi, IKEA, and Zara, have also found receptive markets in the United States.

# 15-2 **MAJOR TYPES OF RETAIL STORES**

Many types of retail stores exist. One way to classify them is by the breadth of products they offer. Two general categories include general-merchandise retailers and specialty retailers.

## 15-2a **General-Merchandise Retailers**

A retail establishment that offers a variety of product lines that are stocked in considerable depth is referred to as a **general-merchandise retailer**. The types of product offerings, mixes of customer services, and operating styles of retailers in this category vary considerably. The primary types of general-merchandise retailers are department stores, discount stores, convenience stores, supermarkets, superstores, hypermarkets, warehouse clubs, and warehouse showrooms (see Table 15.1).

**general-merchandise retailer**
A retail establishment that offers a variety of product lines that are stocked in considerable depth

Table 15.1 **General-Merchandise Retailers**

| Type of Retailer | Description | Examples |
|---|---|---|
| Department store | Large organization offering a wide product mix and organized into separate departments | Macy's, Sears, JCPenney |
| Discount store | Self-service, general-merchandise store offering brand-name and private-brand products at low prices | Walmart, Target, Dollar General |
| Convenience store | Small, self-service store offering narrow product assortment in convenient locations | 7-Eleven |
| Supermarket | Self-service store offering complete line of food products and some non-food products | Kroger, Safeway, Publix |
| Superstore | Giant outlet offering all food and non-food products found in supermarkets, as well as most routinely purchased products | Walmart Supercenters, SuperTarget |
| Hypermarket | Combination supermarket and discount store; larger than a superstore | Carrefour |
| Warehouse club | Large-scale, members-only establishments combining cash-and-carry wholesaling with discount retailing | Sam's Club, Costco |
| Warehouse showroom | Facility in a large, low-cost building with large on-premises inventories and minimal service | IKEA |

## Department Stores

**Department stores** are large retail organizations with at least 25 employees that are characterized by wide product mixes. To facilitate marketing efforts and internal management in these stores, department stores like Macy's, Sears, and Nordstrom's organize related product lines into separate departments such as cosmetics, housewares, apparel, home furnishings, and appliances. This arrangement facilitates marketing and internal management. Often, each department functions as a self-contained business, and buyers for individual departments are fairly autonomous in their decision making.

Department stores are distinctly service-oriented. Their total product may include credit, delivery, personal assistance, merchandise returns, and a pleasant atmosphere. Although some so-called department stores are actually large, departmentalized specialty stores, most department stores are shopping stores. Consumers can compare price, quality, and service at one store with those at competing stores. Along with large discount stores, department stores are often considered retailing leaders in a community and are found in most places with populations of more than 50,000.

At typical department stores, a large proportion of sales come from apparel, accessories, and cosmetics. These stores carry a broad assortment of other products as well, including luggage, electronics, home accessories, and sports equipment. Some department stores offer additional services such as automobile insurance, hair care, income tax preparation, and travel and optical services. In some cases, the department store leases space for these specialized services to other businesses, with proprietors managing their own operations and paying rent to the store. Most department stores also sell products through websites, which can service customers who live in smaller markets where no stores are located or who prefer to shop online or through apps. Macy's app, for example, takes a page from Instagram and lets users take photos of something they like in order to find similar products on Macys.com.[5]

**department stores** Large retail organizations characterized by a wide product mix and organized into separate departments to facilitate marketing efforts and internal management

**discount stores** Self-service, general-merchandise stores that offer brand-name and private-brand products at low prices

## Discount Stores

Department stores have lost sales and market share to discount stores, particularly Walmart and Target, in recent decades. **Discount stores** are self-service, general-merchandise outlets that regularly offer brand-name and private-brand products at low prices. Discounters accept lower profit margins than conventional retailers in exchange for high sales volume. To keep inventory turnover high, they carry a wide but carefully selected assortment of products, from appliances to housewares to clothing. Major discount establishments also offer food products, toys, automotive services, garden supplies, and sports equipment.

Walmart and Target have grown to become not only the largest discount stores in the country, but also some of the largest retailers in the world. Walmart is the world's largest retailer, with revenues over six times higher than Target, which is ranked eleventh in retail sales.[6] Not all discounters are large and international, however. Some, such as Meijer Inc., which has stores in the Midwestern United States, are regional discounters. Most discount stores operate in large (50,000 to 80,000 square feet), no-frills facilities. They usually offer everyday low prices (discussed in Chapter 20), rather than relying on sales events.

Discount retailing developed on a large scale in the early 1950s, when postwar production caught up with strong consumer demand for goods. At first, they were often cash-only operations in warehouse districts, offering goods at savings of 20 to 30 percent over conventional retailers. Facing increased competition from department stores and other discount stores, some

**Department Stores**
Department stores like Macy's offer a wide variety of product lines.

discounters improved store services, atmosphere, and location. Some also raised prices, blurring the distinction between discount store and department store. Consider Target, which has grown more upscale in appearance and offerings over the years. It regularly launches new low-cost clothing lines by popular designers, but it also offers fresh, organic groceries, a pharmacy, and trendy clothing, home goods, and electronics. These adjustments to the firm's strategy are designed to appeal to its customers, who are generally younger and have higher incomes than rival stores such as Walmart.[7]

As conventional discount stores have grown larger and pricier in recent years, low-income and thrifty consumers have turned to extreme-value stores (also known as dollar stores and single-price stores). **Extreme-value stores** are a fraction of the size of conventional discount stores and typically offer very low prices—generally $1 to $10—on smaller size name-brand nonperishable household items. Dollar General, Dollar Tree, and 99¢ Only Stores offer lower per unit prices than discount stores but often charge considerably more when priced per ounce than stores whose customers can afford to stock up on supersized items.

## Convenience Stores

A **convenience store** is a small, self-service store that is open long hours and carries a narrow assortment of products, usually convenience items such as soft drinks and other beverages, snacks, newspapers, tobacco, and gasoline, as well as services such as ATMs. According to the National Association of Convenience Stores, there are more than 152,000 convenience stores in the United States alone, which together boast nearly $700 billion in annual sales.[8] They are typically less than 5,000 square feet, open 24 hours a day and 7 days a week, and stock about 500 items. The convenience store concept was developed in 1927 when Southland Ice in Dallas began stocking basics like milk and eggs along with ice for iceboxes to serve customers who wanted to replenish their supplies. In addition to national chains, there are many family-owned independent convenience stores.

## Supermarkets

**Supermarkets** are large, self-service stores that carry a complete line of food products and some non-food products such as cosmetics and nonprescription drugs. Supermarkets are arranged by department for maximum efficiency in stocking and handling products, but have central checkout facilities. They offer lower prices than smaller neighborhood grocery stores, usually provide free parking, and may also provide services such as check cashing.

Consumers make the majority of all their grocery purchases in supermarkets. However, increased availability of grocery items at discount stores, premium markets, other competitors, and online have eroded supermarkets' market share of the grocery segment. Online grocers, especially in larger cities, have done away with the need to go to grocery stores and have put pressure on supermarkets to increase promotions and marketing efforts and make shopping more convenient. Kroger, Whole Foods, and Costco have partnered with Instacart to provide personal shopping and pick-up or delivery services in 16 metropolitan areas. The service is especially useful to consumers who do not have or want a car or who just don't like shopping. In just a few years, Whole Foods has seen its Instacart sales bloom to $1 million a week.[9] Safeway and Publix supermarket chains offer their own delivery services.

## Superstores

**Superstores**, which originated in Europe, are giant retail outlets that carry not only the food and non-food products ordinarily found in supermarkets, but routinely-purchased consumer products such as housewares, hardware, small appliances, clothing, and personal-care products as well. Superstores combine features of discount stores and supermarkets and generally carry about four times as many items as supermarkets. Superstores also offer additional services, including dry cleaning, automotive repair, check cashing, and bill paying. Examples include Walmart Supercenters, some Kroger stores, SuperTarget stores, and Super Kmart Centers.

**extreme-value stores** Retailers that are a fraction of the size of conventional discount stores and typically offer very low prices on smaller size name-brand nonperishable household items

**convenience store** A small self-service store that is open long hours and carries a narrow assortment of products, usually convenience items

**supermarkets** Large, self-service stores that carry a complete line of food products, along with some nonfood products

**superstores** Giant retail outlets that carry food and non-food products found in supermarkets, as well as most routinely purchased consumer products

To cut handling and inventory costs, superstores use sophisticated operating techniques and often have tall shelving that displays entire assortments of products. Superstores can have an area of as much as 200,000 square feet (compared with 20,000 square feet in traditional supermarkets). Sales volume is typically two to three times that of supermarkets, partly because locations near good transportation networks help generate the in-store traffic needed for profitability.

## Hypermarkets

**Hypermarkets** combine supermarket and discount store shopping in one location. Larger than superstores, they range from 225,000 to 325,000 square feet and offer 45,000 to 60,000 different types of low-priced products. They commonly allocate 40 to 50 percent of their space to grocery products and the remainder to general merchandise, including apparel, appliances, housewares, jewelry, hardware, and automotive supplies. Many also lease space to noncompeting businesses, such as banks, optical shops, and fast-food restaurants. All hypermarkets focus on low prices and vast selections.

Retailers have struggled with making the hypermarket concept successful in the United States. Although Kmart, Walmart, and Carrefour have operated hypermarkets in the United States, most of these stores ultimately closed. Such stores may be too large for time-constrained U.S. shoppers. Hypermarkets have been somewhat more popular in Europe, South America, Mexico, the Middle East, and parts of Asia.

**hypermarkets** Stores that combine supermarket and discount store shopping in one location

**warehouse clubs** Large-scale, members-only establishments that combine features of cash-and-carry wholesaling with discount retailing

**warehouse showrooms** Retail facilities in large, low-cost buildings with large on-premises inventories and minimal services

## Warehouse Clubs

**Warehouse clubs**, a rapidly growing form of mass merchandising, are large-scale, members-only operations that combine cash-and-carry wholesaling with discount retailing. Sometimes called *buying clubs*, warehouse clubs offer the same types of products as discount stores but in a limited range of sizes and styles. Whereas most discount stores carry around 40,000 items, a warehouse club handles only 3,500 to 5,000 products, usually brand leaders. Sam's Club stores, for example, stock about 4,000 items. Costco currently leads the warehouse club industry with sales of more than $113 billion. Sam's Club is second with around $58 billion in store sales.[10] These establishments offer a broad product mix, including food, beverages, books, appliances, housewares, automotive parts, hardware, and furniture.

To keep prices lower than those of supermarkets and discount stores, warehouse clubs offer few services. They also keep advertising to a minimum. Their facilities, frequently located in industrial areas, have concrete floors and aisles wide enough for forklifts. Merchandise is stacked on pallets or displayed on pipe racks. Customers must perform some marketing functions, like transportation of purchases, themselves. Warehouse clubs appeal to price-conscious consumers and small retailers unable to obtain wholesaling services from large distributors.

**Warehouse Clubs**
Costco is a warehouse club that has a wide product mix with limited depth.

## Warehouse Showrooms

**Warehouse showrooms** are retail facilities with five basic characteristics: large, low-cost buildings, warehouse materials-handling technology, vertical merchandise displays, large on-premises inventories, and minimal services. IKEA, a Swedish company that is the world's largest furniture retailer, sells furniture, household goods, and kitchen accessories in warehouse showrooms and through catalogs around the world. These high-volume, low-overhead operations offer few services and retain few personnel. Lower costs are possible at warehouse showrooms because some marketing functions have been shifted to consumers, who must transport, finance, and perhaps store products. Most consumers carry away purchases in the manufacturer's carton, although stores will deliver for a fee.

## 15-2b Specialty Retailers

In contrast to general-merchandise retailers with their broad product mixes, specialty retailers emphasize narrow and deep assortments. Despite their name, specialty retailers do not sell specialty items (except when specialty goods complement the overall product mix). Instead, they offer substantial assortments in a few product lines. We examine three types of specialty retailers: traditional specialty retailers, category killers, and off-price retailers.

### Traditional Specialty Retailers

**Traditional specialty retailers** are stores that carry a narrow product mix with deep product lines. Sometimes called *limited-line retailers*, they may be referred to as *single-line retailers* if they carry unusual depth in one product category. Specialty retailers commonly sell such shopping products as apparel, jewelry, sporting goods, fabrics, computers, and pet supplies. The Limited, Gap, Sunglass Hut, and Foot Locker are examples of retailers offering limited product lines but great depth within those lines.

Because they are usually small, specialty stores may have high costs in proportion to sales, and satisfying customers may require carrying some products with low turnover rates. Successful specialty stores understand their customers and know what products to carry, which reduces the risk of unsold merchandise. Specialty stores usually offer better selections and more sales expertise than department stores, their main competitors. By capitalizing on fashion trends, service, personnel, atmosphere, and location, specialty retailers position themselves strategically to attract customers in specific market segments.

**traditional specialty retailers** Stores that carry a narrow product mix with deep product lines

**category killer** A very large specialty store that concentrates on a major product category and competes on the basis of low prices and product availability

### Category Killers

A more recent kind of specialty retailer is called the **category killer**, which is a very large specialty store that concentrates on a major product category and competes on the basis of low prices and broad product availability. These stores are referred to as category killers because they expand rapidly and gain sizable market shares, taking business away from smaller, higher-cost retail outlets. Examples of category killers include Home Depot and Lowe's (home improvement), Staples (office supply), Barnes & Noble (bookseller), Petco and PetSmart (pet supply), Best Buy (consumer electronics), and Toys 'R' Us (toys).

Just as category killers took business away from traditional specialty retailers by competing largely on price, online retailing has taken market share away from category killers in recent years. One of the original category killers, Toys 'R' Us, now struggles to compete against online retailers, particularly Amazon. To retain a competitive advantage in toys, Toys 'R' Us is working to improve its store experience—brighter lights, faster checkouts, better controlled stock, and more frequent cleanings, and some new stores will include play areas for children to play and interact with products—as well as customer service.[11]

**Category Killer**
Toys 'R' Us is an example of a category killer.

### Off-Price Retailers

**Off-price retailers** are stores that buy manufacturers' seconds, overruns, returns, and off-season production runs at below-wholesale prices for resale to consumers at deep discounts. Unlike true discount stores, which pay regular wholesale prices for goods and usually carry second-line brand names, off-price retailers offer limited lines of national-brand and designer merchandise, usually clothing, shoes, or housewares. Consumers appreciate the ability to purchase name-brand goods at discounted prices, and sales at off-price retailers, such as T.J. Maxx, Marshalls, Stein Mart, and Burlington Coat Factory, have grown. Off-price retailers typically perform well in recessionary times, as consumers who want to own name-brand items search for good value.

Off-price stores charge 20 to 50 percent less than department stores for comparable merchandise but offer few customer services. They often feature community dressing rooms and central checkout counters. Some of these stores do not take returns or allow exchanges. Off-price stores may or may not sell goods with the original labels intact. They turn over their inventory up to a dozen times per year, three times as often as traditional specialty stores. They compete with department stores for many of the same price-conscious customers who are knowledgeable about brand names.

To ensure a regular flow of merchandise into their stores, off-price retailers establish long-term relationships with suppliers that can provide large quantities of goods at reduced prices. Manufacturers may approach retailers with samples, discontinued products, or items that have not sold well. Also, off-price retailers may seek out manufacturers, offering to pay cash for goods produced during the manufacturers' off-season. Although manufacturers benefit from such arrangements, they also risk alienating their specialty and department store customers. Department stores tolerate off-price stores as long as they do not advertise brand names, limit merchandise to last season's or lower-quality items, and are located away from the department stores. When off-price retailers obtain large stocks of in-season, top-quality merchandise, tension builds between department stores and manufacturers.

## 15-3 STRATEGIC ISSUES IN RETAILING

Whereas most business purchases are based on economic planning and necessity, consumer purchases are likely to be influenced by social and psychological factors. Because consumers shop for various reasons—to search for specific items, alleviate boredom, or learn about something new—retailers must do more than simply fill space with merchandise. They must make desired products available, create stimulating shopping environments, and develop marketing strategies that increase store patronage. In this section, we discuss how store location, technology, retail positioning, store image, and category management are used strategically by retailers.

### 15-3a Location of Retail Stores

You have likely heard the phrase "Location, location, location," commonly used in the real estate business. Location is also critical to business success. Making a good location decision is even more important because, once decided, it is the least flexible variable of the marketing mix. Location is an important strategic decision that dictates the limited geographic trading area from which a store draws its customers. Retailers consider various factors when evaluating potential locations, including position of the firm's target market within the trading area, kinds of products being sold, availability of public transportation, customer characteristics, and placement of competitors' stores.

In choosing a location, a retailer evaluates the relative ease of movement to and from the site, including factors such as pedestrian and vehicular traffic, parking, and transportation. Retailers also evaluate the characteristics of the site itself. They research the types of stores in the area and the size, shape, and visibility of the lot or building under consideration. In addition,

**off-price retailers** Stores that buy manufacturers' seconds, overruns, returns, and off-season merchandise for resale to consumers at deep discounts they must scrutinize the rental, leasing, or ownership terms. Retailers should look for compatibility with nearby retailers because stores that complement one another draw more customers with similar product needs for everyone.

Some retailers choose to locate in central business districts, whereas others prefer sites within shopping centers. Some retailers, including Toys 'R' Us, Walmart, Home Depot, and many fast-food restaurants, opt for freestanding structures that are not connected to other buildings, but may be located within planned shopping centers. Sometimes, retailers choose to locate in less orthodox settings where competition will be lower and where consumers have limited other options. Pop-up retailers, which are only located in a space for a short time, and retailers that share space are becoming increasingly common as a means of generating consumer buzz while also cutting down on rental costs for all businesses involved. Pop-ups—inside another retailer, stand alone, or at special events—can help restaurateurs and specialty retailers determine if there is sufficient interest in their concept before investing significant resources in a conventional space. Sharing space can let multiple small retailers save costs or afford a storefront in a more desirable location.[12] For instance, Atlanta's Octane Coffee shares a space with Little Tart Bakeshop, with Little Tart selling its baked goods during the day alongside Octane coffee products, and Octane serving bar snacks and appetizers when the bakeshop closes at 5 P.M.[13]

There are several different types of shopping centers, including neighborhood, community, regional, superregional, lifestyle, power, and outlet centers. **Neighborhood shopping centers**, also called *strip malls*, usually consist of several small convenience and specialty stores, such as small grocery stores, gas stations, and fast-food restaurants. These retailers consider their target markets to be consumers who live within two to three miles of their stores, or 10 minutes' driving time. Because most purchases are based on convenience or personal contact, stores within a neighborhood shopping center generally do not coordinate selling efforts. Generally, product mixes consist of essential products, and depth of the product lines is limited. **Community shopping centers** include one or two department stores and some specialty stores, as well as convenience stores. They draw consumers looking for shopping and specialty products not available in neighborhood shopping centers. Because these offer a wider variety of stores, they serve larger geographic areas and consumers are willing to drive longer distances to community shopping centers to shop. Community shopping centers are planned, and retailer efforts are coordinated to attract shoppers. Special events, such as art exhibits, automobile shows, and sidewalk sales, stimulate traffic. Managers of community shopping centers look for tenants that complement the centers' total assortment of products. Such centers have wide product mixes and deep product lines.

**Regional shopping centers** usually have the largest department stores, widest product mixes, and deepest product lines of all shopping centers. Many shopping malls are regional shopping centers, although some are community shopping centers. With 150,000 or more consumers in their target market, regional shopping centers must have well-coordinated management and marketing activities. Target markets may include consumers traveling from a distance to find products and prices not available in their hometowns. Because of the expense of leasing space in regional shopping centers, tenants are likely to be national chains. Large centers usually advertise, have special events, furnish transportation to some consumer groups (such as seniors), maintain their own security forces, and carefully select the mix of stores. The largest of these centers, sometimes called **superregional shopping centers**, have the widest and deepest product mixes and attract customers from many miles away. Superregional centers often have special attractions beyond stores, such as skating rinks, amusement centers, or upscale restaurants. Mall of America, in the Minneapolis area, is the largest shopping mall in the United States with 520 stores, including Nordstrom and Bloomingdale's, and 50 restaurants. The shopping center also includes a walk-through aquarium, a museum, a seven-acre Nickelodeon theme park, a 14-screen movie theater, hotels, and many special events.[14]

With traditional mall sales declining, some shopping center developers are looking to new formats that differ significantly from traditional shopping centers. A **lifestyle shopping center** is typically an open-air shopping center that features upscale specialty stores, dining,

**neighborhood shopping centers**
A type of shopping center usually consisting of several small convenience and specialty stores

**community shopping centers**
A type of shopping center with one or two department stores, some specialty stores, and convenience stores

**regional shopping centers**
A type of shopping center with the largest department stores, widest product mixes, and deepest product lines of all shopping centers

**superregional shopping centers**
A type of shopping center with the widest and deepest product mixes that attracts customers from many miles away

**lifestyle shopping center**
A type of shopping center that is typically open air and features upscale specialty, dining, and entertainment stores

and entertainment, most usually owned by national chains. Like San Jose's Santana Row, they are often located near affluent neighborhoods and may have fountains, benches, and other amenities that encourage "casual browsing." Some, like Austin's Domain, include offices, hotels, and residences as well. Appealing architectural design is an important aspect of these "mini-cities," which may include urban streets or parks, and is intended to encourage consumer loyalty by creating a sense of place. Some lifestyle centers are designed to resemble traditional "Main Street" shopping centers or may have a central theme evidenced by the architecture.[15]

Some shopping center developers are bypassing the traditional department store anchor and combining off-price stores and small stores with category killers in **power shopping center** formats. These centers may be anchored by popular stores, such as the Gap, Toys 'R' Us, PetSmart, and Home Depot. Power shopping centers can take a variety of formats, all vying for the same retail dollar.

**power shopping center**
A type of shopping center that combines off-price stores with category killers

Factory outlet malls feature discount and factory outlet stores carrying traditional manufacturer brands, such as Polo Ralph Lauren, Nike, and Guess. The advertisement highlights the Banana Republic factory store, which sells last season's Banana Republic fashions at discounted prices. This advertisement displays the low starting price of its products, $17.99, and includes a coupon for an additional 20 percent off. Many outlet centers feature upscale products from last season, discounted for quick sale. Manufacturers own these stores and make a special effort to avoid conflict with traditional retailers of their products. Manufacturers place these stores in noncompetitive locations, often outside of metropolitan areas. Factory outlet centers attract value-conscious customers seeking quality and major brand names. They operate in much the same way as regional shopping centers, but usually draw customers, some of whom may be tourists, from a larger shopping radius. Promotional activity is at the heart of these shopping centers. Craft and antique shows, contests, and special events attract a great deal of traffic.

Source: Banana Republic

**Factory Outlet Mall**
Stores in factory outlet malls feature well-known brands, such as Banana Republic, and offer discounted prices from last season.

### 15-3b  Retail Technology

Today's consumers expect to be able to research and shop for a product wherever and whenever they want—in a mall, subway train, classroom, living room, or anywhere else. Younger shoppers in particular expect retailers to offer convenience, information, and a seamless experience across multiple platforms. Consider Nordstrom's, which is famously guided by its mission to "provide a fabulous customer experience by empowering customers and the employees who serve them." The retailer has made strategic investments into technologies such as point-of-sale systems that allow salespeople to view a customer's requests and needs online, an innovation lab, apps, mobile checkout, support for salespeople texting, a cloud-based men's personalized clothing service, and it

# EMERGING **TRENDS IN MARKETING**

See It on Social Media? Buy It on Social Media

Pinterest began as a virtual bulletin board where users would "pin" images of products they liked or photos of craft projects they had completed. Now it's one of a growing number of social-media sites that are putting "buy" buttons on some posts or images to make purchasing faster and easier, whether consumers are using a smartphone, laptop, or desktop computer.

Twitter, Facebook, and Instagram, as well as Pinterest, see "buy" buttons as a way to keep consumers coming to their sites not just for posting, commenting, and browsing, but also for shopping. This added functionality turns social media into a platform for digital window-shopping, with the option and ability to make a purchase. Click to buy, and up pops a window with payment alternatives such as PayPal so consumers can complete transactions without leaving social media.

Within the first year, Pinterest expanded the availability of "buy" buttons to more than 60 million "pinned" images of items on its site. Because consumers discuss and share pinned images, Pinterest users are likely to be exposed to products they otherwise might not find out about. Spool No. 72, a women's clothing store that posts product images on Pinterest, confirms that "buy" buttons have extended its online reach. Its early results indicate that more than 80 percent of the people who make a Spool No. 72 purchase through a "buy" button are first-time customers. In the long run, how many consumers will use the "buy" button on social media, and how will this affect online retailing? Stay tuned.[a]

began to use social media to build relationships with consumers and generate buzz. The firm's websites and apps are integrated with its inventory management control system so that customers can find an item in a store or online and have it delivered to a third place such as their home or office. Mobile checkout lets a salesperson who has been helping a customer in the store check them out on the spot rather than having to look for a register. All of these efforts contribute to Nordstrom's mission and ensure that customers have a great experience across all of the firm's platforms.[16]

Nowadays, of course, most retailers have websites that, at a minimum, tell shoppers where they are, when their hours are, who they are, and what they sell. Many small retailers' websites also highlight products in current inventory even if they are unable to offer online transactions. For most retailers today, however, a website that customers can use to research products, purchase them, and otherwise interact with the firm is vital. Larger retailers such as Starbucks, Best Buy, and Kohl's are now developing and launching their own apps for customers to carry out those activities on their tablet or smartphone wherever they may be. Starbucks' app, for example, allows customers to pay right from their phone and accumulate loyalty reward points. When implemented well, retailer apps can foster loyalty, repeat purchases, and the customer experience. However, developing a retail app can cost $2 million or more and 80 percent of that per year to maintain it.[17]

Retailers of all sizes can take advantage of technology to improve the store experience for a variety of customers. One way is through the use of *beacons* that can send real-time messages and offers to customers with Bluetooth-enabled smartphones. For example, at Gamestop outlets in Texas, beacons can trigger a customer's access to product details, reviews, and available special offers on games and systems, expediting their product research right in the store.[18] For this technology to work, however, customers must have downloaded the retailer's app onto their smartphones. The inexpensive beacons can activate apps that consumers may not otherwise use once they've downloaded them, thereby advancing a firm's engagement with the customer. Simon Malls has installed nearly 5,000 of the devices in 192 malls and shopping centers around the country to welcome users of its apps and to alert them about special offers in the mall, new fashion trends, and more. Thus far, indications are that beacons do boost retail store sales, and beacon-influenced in-store sales are expected to grow to $44 billion by 2016.[19]

**How do you use your smartphone when you shop?**

| Behavior | Percentage of respondents |
|---|---|
| Take pictures of products | 51% |
| Search for coupons | 49% |
| Compare prices among retailers | 43% |

Source: "Better Homes and Gardens Best New Product Awards Announces 2015 Winners As Voted By More Than 70,000 Consumers," PR Newswire, February 2, 2015, http://www.prnewswire.com/news-releases/better-homes-and-gardens-best-new-product-awards-announces-2015-winners-as-voted-by-more-than-70000-consumers-300028519.html (accessed March 23, 2016).

There are a number of exciting new technologies designed to improve consumers' shopping experience whether they are in the store or at home shopping online. At Neiman Marcus, for example, virtual or smart mirrors can improve the dressing room experience by letting customers view clothing in different colors and compare multiple looks side by side without actually changing outfits or having to leave the dressing room.[20] Virtual fit lets shoppers see how a product, such as eyeglasses, might look on them, using the cameras built into today's computers and smart devices. Self-checkout lets shoppers scan the items in their own shopping cart with their smartphone and pay for the merchandise out of a digital wallet, such as Apple Pay, so they don't have to wait in line. The technology even allows shoppers who subscribe to loyalty programs to get their rewards as they scan their own items.[21]

The reality is that evolving consumer demographics and preferences are spurring retailers to adapt in a variety of ways that are blurring the line between the various types of retailers more than ever before. Consider that most shoppers now research products online and then head to the nearest store to make the actual purchase—a practice sometimes called *webrooming*. For most consumers, there is no clear line between the brick-and-mortar store, the store's website, and its app, and they move back and forth depending on their circumstances and desires.

## 15-3c  Retail Positioning

The large variety of shopping centers and the expansion of product offerings by traditional stores, along with the increased use of retail technology, have all contributed to intense retailing competition. Retail positioning is therefore an important consideration. **Retail positioning** involves identifying an unserved or underserved market segment and reaching it through a strategy that distinguishes the retailer from others in the minds of customers in the market segment. For instance, H&M is positioned as a low-priced fashion-forward retailer. However, in an effort to be associated with fair business practices, the chain announced that prices would increase to allow the retailer to pay its employees a living wage, repositioning itself as a socially responsible retailer—not just a very low-priced one.[22] This is in contrast to a number of discount and specialty store chains that have positioned themselves to appeal to time- and cash-strapped consumers with convenient locations and layouts as well as low prices. This strategy has helped many retailers gain market share at the expense of large department stores.

## 15-3d  Store Image

To attract customers, a retail store must project an image—a functional and psychological picture in the consumer's mind—that appeals to its target market. Store environment, merchandise quality, and service quality are key determinants of store image. **Atmospherics**, the physical elements in a store's design that appeal to consumers' emotions and encourage

**retail positioning** Identifying an unserved or underserved market segment and serving it through a strategy that distinguishes the retailer from others in the minds of consumers in that segment

**atmospherics** The physical elements in a store's design that appeal to consumers' emotions and encourage buying

buying, help to create an image and position a retailer. Retailers can use different elements—music, color, and complexity of layout and merchandise presentation—to influence customer attention, mood, and shopping behavior.

Exterior atmospheric elements include the appearance of the storefront, display windows, store entrances, and degree of traffic congestion. Exterior atmospherics are particularly important to new customers, who tend to base their judgment of an unfamiliar store on its outside appearance and may not ever enter if they feel intimidated by the appearance of the façade or if the location is inconvenient or unhospitable.

Interior atmospheric elements include aesthetic considerations, such as lighting, wall and floor coverings, dressing facilities, and store fixtures. Interior sensory elements contribute significantly to atmosphere. Bars, for example, consider several factors when it comes to atmospherics, including music tempo and volume, lighting, cleanliness, and physical layout. Most bars tend to sell a similar range of products, so they use atmospherics extensively to differentiate themselves and create a unique environment. In order for a bar to be successful and retain customers, it must monitor atmospheric variables and focus on maintaining customer comfort levels, which may vary depending on target audience. Bar patrons tend to be recreationally and socially motivated, rather than task motivated, so the layout must create a sense of flow and spread the crowd to the right places so customers do not feel claustrophobic.[23]

Color can attract shoppers to a retail display. Many fast-food restaurants use bright colors because these have been shown to make customers feel hungrier and eat faster, which increases turnover.[24] For instance, red is associated with impulsivity and hunger, and yellow is associated with feeling good—both of these colors are common in fast-food restaurants. Green, on the other hand, is calming and associated with wellness, so it is more commonly seen in natural foods stores and restaurants.[25] Sound is another important sensory component of atmosphere. A low-end, family dining restaurant might play fast pop music to encourage customers to eat quickly and leave, increasing turnover and sales. A high-end restaurant, on the other hand, will opt to play soft classical music to enhance the experience and encourage patrons to indulge in multiple courses. Retailers may even employ scent, especially food aromas, to attract customers. Most consumers expect the scent of a store to be congruent with the products that are sold there. Thus, Starbucks should smell like its coffee, Panera like its freshly baked bread, and Yankee Candle like its scented candles. Online retailers are not

Sorbis/Shutterstock.com

**Atmospherics**
Atmospherics can greatly influence customers' experiences. The colors, lighting, and spaciousness make this Starbucks coffeehouse attractive and inviting.

exempt from concern over atmospherics. Studies have demonstrated that such elements as the layout of a site and the content of digital ads that appear on that site can affect consumer mood and shopping behavior.[26]

### 15-3e Category Management

**Category management** is a retail strategy of managing groups of similar, often substitutable products produced by different manufacturers. It first developed in the food industry because supermarkets were concerned about competitive behavior among manufacturers. Supermarkets use category management to allocate space for their many product categories, such as cosmetics, cereals, and soups. The strategy is effective for many different types of retailers. The assortment of merchandise a store chooses through category management is strategic and meant to improve sales and enhance customer satisfaction.

Category management is an important part of developing a collaborative supply chain, which enhances value for customers. Successful category management involves collecting and analyzing data on sales and consumers and sharing the information between the retailer and manufacturer. Walmart, for example, has developed strong supplier relationships with many of its manufacturers, like Procter & Gamble. Collaborative supply chains should designate a single source to develop a system for collecting information on demand, consumer behavior, and optimal product allocations. The key is cooperative interaction between the manufacturers of category products and the retailer to create maximum success for all parties in the supply chain.

## 15-4 DIRECT MARKETING, DIRECT SELLING, AND VENDING

Although retailers are the most visible members of the supply chain, many products are sold outside the confines of a retail store. Direct selling and direct marketing account for a huge proportion of the sale of goods globally. Products also may be sold in automatic vending machines, but these account for a very small minority of total retail sales.

### 15-4a Direct Marketing

**Direct marketing** is the use of the telephone, Internet, and nonpersonal media to communicate product and organizational information to customers, who can then purchase products via mail, telephone, or the Internet. Direct marketing is one type of nonstore retailing. Sales through direct marketing activities are significant, accounting for about 8.7 percent of the entire U.S. GDP.[27]

**Nonstore retailing** is the selling of products outside the confines of a retail facility. It is a form of direct marketing that accounts for an increasing percentage of total retail sales, particularly as online retailing becomes more popular. Direct marketing can occur through online retailing, catalog marketing, direct-response marketing, telemarketing, and television home shopping.

### Online Retailing

**Online retailing** makes products available to buyers through Internet connections. Online retailing is a rapidly-growing segment that most retailers now view as vital to their businesses. Forrester Research projects that online retail sales in the United States will climb to nearly $480 billion by 2019, and it reports that 69 percent of the U.S. population regularly buys clothing, consumer electronics, computers, and other goods online.[28] In the United States, Amazon.com—shown in the screen shot—is arguably the best-known online retailer, with net

**category management** A retail strategy of managing groups of similar, often substitutable, products produced by different manufacturers

**direct marketing** The use of the telephone, Internet, and nonpersonal media to introduce products to customers, who can then purchase them via mail, telephone, or the Internet

**nonstore retailing** The selling of products outside the confines of a retail facility

**online retailing** Retailing that makes products available to buyers through computer connections

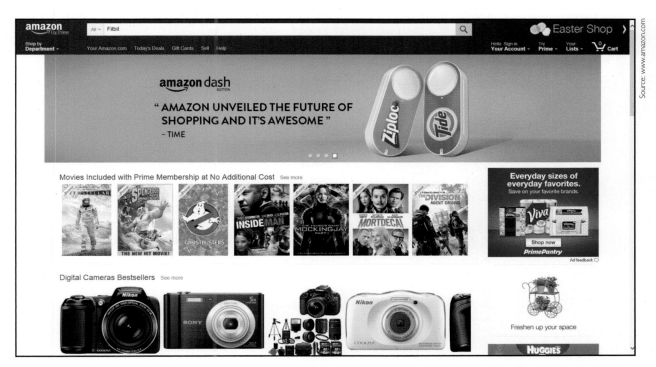

### Online Retailers

While Amazon sells only online, a number of other companies combine online marketing with other forms of retailing.

sales in excess of $70 billion. The company has branched out from selling books and electronics to its own line of tablets and smartphones as well as streaming movies. As shown in the screen shot, Amazon has also introduced Dash buttons that let customers reorder frequently purchased household items like laundry detergent with the touch of a button.

Online retailing satisfies an increasing expectation among consumers to have multiple channels available to obtain the goods and services they desire at their convenience. Consumers can perform a wide variety of shopping-related tasks online, including purchasing virtually anything they wish. They can track down rare collectibles, refill their eyeglass prescriptions, and even purchase high-end jewelry or gourmet food. Retailers frequently offer exclusive online sales, or may reward customers who visit their websites with special in-store coupons and other promotions and discounts. Banks and brokerages offer consumers access to their accounts, where they can perform a wide variety of activities, such as money transfers and stock trading.

With ongoing advances in computer technology and consumers ever more pressed for time, online retailing will continue to escalate. Some firms that were primarily catalog retailers are now primarily online retailers, such as Paul Frederick, which sells men's apparel and accessories online and does not sell in stores.

## Catalog Marketing

In **catalog marketing**, an organization provides a catalog from which customers make selections and place orders by mail, telephone, or the Internet. Catalog marketing began in 1872, when Montgomery Ward issued its first catalog to rural families. There are thousands of catalog marketing companies in the United States, many of which also publish online. Some catalog marketers sell products spread over multiple product lines, while others are more specialized. Take, for example, this catalog cover for the Sharper Image. Sharper Image is a catalog marketer specializing in home electronics, as you can see in the photo of actor Josh Duhamel riding a Hover Board, a product available for sale through the catalog. The catalog cover shows the kinds of electronic "toys" a shopper can find via the catalog or the firm's website.

**catalog marketing** A type of marketing in which an organization provides a catalog from which customers make selections and place orders by mail, telephone, or the Internet

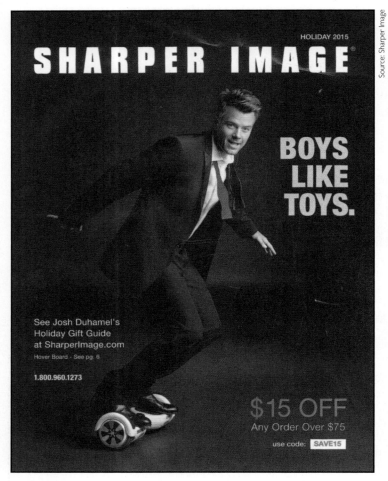

Source: Sharper Image

**Catalog Marketing**
Sharper Image utilizes catalog marketing to sell its electronic toys and home goods.

Many companies, including Land's End, Pottery Barn, and Crate & Barrel, employ a multichannel strategy and sell via catalogs, online, and through retail stores in major metropolitan areas. These retailers generally offer considerable product depth for just a few lines of products. Still other catalog companies specialize in products from a single product line.

The advantages of catalog retailing include efficiency and convenience for customers because they do not have to visit a store. The retailer benefits by being able to locate in remote, low-cost areas, save on expensive store fixtures, and reduce both personal selling and store operating expenses. On the other hand, catalog retailing is inflexible, provides limited service, and is most effective for a selected set of products.

## Direct-Response Marketing

**Direct-response marketing** occurs when a retailer advertises a product and makes it available through mail, telephone, or online orders. Generally, customers use a credit card, but other forms of payment may be permitted. Examples of direct-response marketing include a television commercial offering exercise machines, cosmetics, or household cleaning products available through a toll-free number, and a newspaper or magazine advertisement for a series of children's books available by filling out the form in the ad or calling a toll-free number. Direct-response marketing through television remains a multi-billion dollar industry, although it now competes with the Internet for customers' attention. This marketing method has resulted in many products gaining widespread popularity. Some firms, like Russ Reid, specialize in direct-response marketing and assist firms in developing successful promotions. Direct-response marketing is also conducted by sending letters, samples, brochures, or booklets to prospects on a mailing list and asking that they order the advertised products by mail or telephone. In general, products must be priced above $20 to justify the advertising and distribution costs associated with direct-response marketing.

## Telemarketing

A number of organizations use the telephone to strengthen the effectiveness of traditional marketing methods. **Telemarketing** is the performance of marketing-related activities by telephone. Some organizations use a prescreened list of prospective clients. Telemarketing can help to generate sales leads, improve customer service, speed up payments on past-due accounts, raise funds for nonprofit organizations, and gather marketing data.

However, increasingly restrictive telemarketing laws have made it a less appealing and less popular marketing method. In 2003, the U.S. Congress implemented a national do-not-call registry, which has more than 200 million numbers on it. The Federal Trade Commission (FTC) enforces violations, and companies are subject to fines of up to $16,000 for each call made to numbers on the list.[29] The Federal Communications Commission (FCC) ruled that companies are no longer allowed to call customers using prerecorded marketing calls

**direct-response marketing**
A type of marketing in which a retailer advertises a product and makes it available through mail or telephone orders

**telemarketing** The performance of marketing-related activities by telephone simply because they had done business in the past. The law also requires that an "opt-out" mechanism be embedded in the call for consumers who do not wish to receive the calls. Companies that are still allowed to make telemarketing phone calls must pay for access to the do-not-call registry and must obtain updated numbers from the registry at least every three days. Certain exceptions do apply to no-call lists. For example, charitable, political, and telephone survey organizations are not restricted by the national registry.[30] In spite of regulations, many consumers still find robocalls to be a nuisance, and Congress is seeking further measures to curb them.

## Television Home Shopping

**Television home shopping** presents products to television viewers, encouraging them to order through toll-free numbers and pay with credit cards. The Home Shopping Network originated and popularized this format. The most popular products sold through television home shopping are jewelry, clothing, housewares, and electronics. Most homes in the United States have access to at least one home shopping channel, with the Home Shopping Network and QVC being the largest.

The television home shopping format offers several benefits. Products can be demonstrated easily, and an adequate amount of time can be spent showing the product so viewers are well-informed. The length of time a product is shown depends not only on the time required for performing demonstrations but also on whether the product is selling. Once the calls peak and begin to decline, hosts switch to a new product. Other benefits are that customers can shop at their convenience and from the comfort of their homes. This method is particularly popular among older consumers, who tend to be less comfortable with online shopping and are less mobile to physically go to a store.

**television home shopping** Form of selling in which products are presented to television viewers, who can buy them by calling a toll-free number and paying with a credit card

**direct selling** Marketing products to ultimate consumers through face-to-face sales presentations at home or in the workplace

### 15-4b Direct Selling

**Direct selling** is the marketing of products to ultimate consumers through face-to-face sales presentations at home or in the workplace. For example Cutco, as shown here, is a direct seller of high-quality cutlery. This product is sold through face-to-face selling. The top five global direct selling companies are Amway, Avon, Herbalife, Mary Kay, and Vorwerk.[31] Four of these companies are based in the United States. Direct selling is a highly valuable industry. Amway alone has $10.8 billion in annual sales.[32] Direct selling was once associated with door-to-door sales, but it has evolved into a highly professional industry where most contacts with buyers are prearranged through electronic communication or another means of prior communication. Today, companies identify customers through the mail, telephone, Internet, social networks, or shopping-mall intercepts and then set up appointments with salespeople. Direct selling is most successful in other countries, particularly collective societies like China, where Amway has achieved higher sales than its

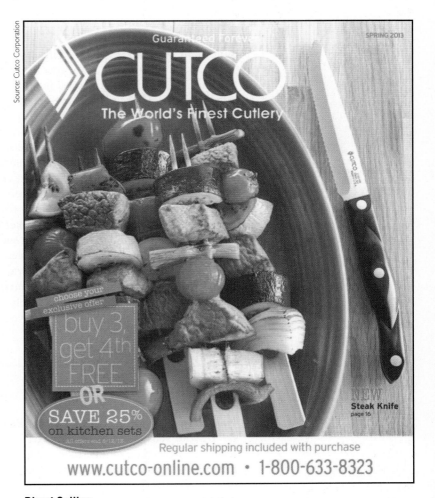

Source: Cutco Corporation

**Direct Selling**
Cutco is a popular brand of cutlery sold through direct selling.

domestic market, the United States. Collective societies prize the one-on-one attention and feeling like they are connecting with the salesperson.

Although the majority of direct selling takes place on an individual, or person-to-person, basis, it sometimes may be carried out in a group, or "party," plan format. With a party plan, a consumer acts as a host and invites friends and associates to view merchandise, often at someone's home. The informal atmosphere helps to overcome customers' reluctance and encourages them to try out and buy products. Tupperware and Mary Kay were the pioneers of this selling technique and remain global leaders.

Direct selling has benefits and limitations. It gives the marketer an opportunity to demonstrate the product in a comfortable environment where it most likely would be used. The seller can give the customer personal attention, and the product can be presented to the customer at a convenient time and location. Product categories that have been highly successful for direct selling include cosmetics and personal-care products, health products, jewelry, accessories, and household products. Personal attention to the customer is the foundation on which many direct sellers have built their businesses. However, because commissions for salespeople are high, around 30 to 50 percent of the sales price, and great effort is required to isolate promising prospects, overall costs of direct selling make it the most expensive form of retailing. Furthermore, some customers view direct selling negatively, owing to unscrupulous and fraudulent practices used by some direct sellers. Some communities even have local ordinances that control or, in some cases, prohibit direct selling. Despite these negative views held by some individuals, direct selling is still alive and well, bringing in annual revenues of more than $34 billion in the United States.[33]

## 15-4c **Automatic Vending**

**Automatic vending** is the use of machines to dispense products. It is one of the most impersonal forms of retailing, and it accounts for a very small minority of all retail sales. Small, standardized, routinely purchased products (e.g., snacks and drinks) are best suited for sale in vending machines because consumers buy them out of convenience. Machines in areas of heavy foot traffic provide efficient and continuous service to consumers. High-volume areas, such as in commercial centers of large cities or in airports, may offer a wide range of automatic vending product options. In some markets, vending machines have taken on cult popularity, particularly among urban-dwelling consumers. In larger cities around the world, customers can find a wide variety of products dispensed via vending machine, even high-end and perishable items. For example, at the Emirates Palace hotel in Abu Dhabi, a vending machine dispenses gold bars, while another distributes mini-bottles of champagne in London. Vending machines around the world have been used to market hot pizza and burritos, cupcakes, fresh salad, and caviar, as well as skin-care products and even cars.[34]

Because vending machines need only a small amount of space and no sales personnel, this retailing method has some advantages over stores. The advantages are partly offset, however, by the high costs of equipment and frequent servicing and repairs. Many machines can now convey status reports via the Internet, helping marketers identify which items are selling and need to be restocked and which may have spoiled and need to be replaced with items with a greater likelihood of selling.

## 15-5 **FRANCHISING**

**automatic vending** The use of machines to dispense products

**franchising** An arrangement in which a supplier (franchiser) grants a dealer (franchisee) the right to sell products in exchange for some type of consideration

**Franchising** is an arrangement in which a supplier, or franchisor, grants a dealer, or franchisee, the right to sell products in exchange for some type of consideration. The franchisor may receive a percentage of total sales in exchange for furnishing equipment, buildings, management know-how, and marketing assistance to the franchisee. The franchisee supplies labor and capital, operates the franchised business, and agrees to abide by the provisions of the franchise agreement. Table 15.2 lists the leading U.S. franchises as well as the types of products they sell and start-up costs.

Table 15.2   **Top U.S. Franchisors and Their Start-Up Costs**

| Rank | Franchise and Description | Start-Up Costs |
|---|---|---|
| 1 | **Jimmy John's Gourmet Sandwiches**<br>Gourmet sandwiches | $323K–544K |
| 2 | **Hampton by Hilton**<br>Mid-priced hotels | $3.8M–14.1M |
| 3 | **Supercuts**<br>Hair salons | $144K–294K |
| 4 | **Servpro**<br>Insurance/disaster restoration and cleaning | $142K–191K |
| 5 | **Subway**<br>Subs, salads | $117K–263K |
| 6 | **McDonald's**<br>Burgers, chicken, salads, beverages | $989K–2.2M |
| 7 | **7-Eleven Inc.**<br>Convenience stores | $38K–1.1M |
| 8 | **Dunkin' Donuts**<br>Coffee, donuts | $217K–1.6M |
| 9 | **Denny's Inc.**<br>Family restaurant | $1.2M–2.1M |
| 10 | **Anytime Fitness**<br>Fitness centers | $63K–418K |

Source: "2016 Franchise 500," *Entrepreneur*, http://www.entrepreneur.com/franchise500 (accessed March 25, 2016).

Because of changes in the international marketplace, shifting employment options in the United States, the large U.S. service economy, and corporate interest in more joint-venture activity, franchising is a very popular retail option. There are more than 782,753 franchise establishments in the United States, which provide 8.8 million jobs across a variety of industries, and generate $892 billion in sales.[35]

Franchising offers several advantages to both the franchisee and the franchisor. It enables a franchisee to start a business with limited capital and benefit from the business experience of others. Generally speaking, franchises have lower failure rates than independent retail establishments and are often more successful because they can build on the established reputation of a national brand. Nationally, about 57 percent of first-time franchise chains fail, and about 61 percent of independent operators are equally unsuccessful.[36] However, franchise failure rates vary greatly depending on the particular franchise. Nationally advertised franchises, such as Subway and Burger King, are often assured of sales as soon as they open because customers already know what to expect. If business problems arise, the franchisee can obtain guidance and advice from the franchisor at little or no cost. Also, the franchisee receives materials to use in local advertising and can benefit from national promotional campaigns sponsored by the franchisor.

Through franchise arrangements, the franchisor gains fast and selective product distribution without incurring the high cost of constructing and operating its own outlets. The franchisor, therefore, has more available capital for expanding production and advertising. It can also ensure, through the franchise agreement, that outlets are maintained and operated according to its own standards. Some franchisors do permit their franchisees to modify their menus, hours, or other operating elements to better match their target market's needs. The franchisor benefits from the fact that the franchisee, being a sole proprietor in most cases, is likely to be very highly motivated to succeed. Success of the franchise means more sales, which translates

Source: Merle Norman Cosmetics

**Franchising**

Merle Norman is a well-known cosmetics franchise, wherein individual stores are owned and managed by the franchisee.

into higher income for the franchisor. This advertisement for Merle Norman Cosmetics touts not only the benefits of using Merle Norman products but also the advantages of becoming a franchisee, including being able to "take control of your destiny." Clearly, this advertisement is targeted at potential franchisees as well as potential customers.

Franchise arrangements also have several drawbacks. The franchisor can dictate many aspects of the business: décor, menu, design of employees' uniforms, types of signs, hours of operation, and numerous details of business operations. In addition, franchisees must pay to use the franchisor's name, products, and assistance. Usually, there is a one-time franchise fee and continuing royalty and advertising fees, often collected as a percentage of sales. Franchisees often must work very hard, putting in 10- to 12-hour days six or seven days a week. In some cases, franchise agreements are not uniform, meaning one franchisee may pay more than another for the same services. Finally, the franchisor gives up a certain amount of control when entering into a franchise agreement with an entrepreneur. Consequently, individual establishments may not be operated exactly according to the franchisor's standards.

## 15-6 WHOLESALING

**Wholesaling** refers to all transactions in which products are bought for resale, making other products, or general business operations. It does not include exchanges with ultimate consumers. A **wholesaler** is an individual or organization that sells products that are bought for resale, making other products, or general business operations. In other words, wholesalers buy products and resell them to reseller, government, and institutional users. For instance, Sysco, the nation's number-one food-service distributor, supplies restaurants, hotels, schools, industrial caterers, and hospitals with everything from frozen and fresh food and paper products to medical and cleaning supplies. Wholesaling activities are not limited to goods. Service companies, such as financial institutions, also use active wholesale networks. There are 419,648 wholesaling establishments in the United States, and more than half of all products sold in this country pass through these firms.[37]

Wholesalers may engage in many supply-chain management activities, which we will discuss. In addition to bearing the primary responsibility for the physical distribution of products from manufacturers to retailers, wholesalers may establish information systems that help producers and retailers manage the supply chain from producer to customer. Many wholesalers use information technology and the Internet to share information among intermediaries, employees, customers, and suppliers and facilitating agencies, such as trucking companies and warehouse firms. Some firms make their databases and marketing information systems available to their supply-chain partners to facilitate order processing, shipping, and product development and to share information about changing market conditions and customer desires. As a result, some wholesalers play a key role in supply-chain management decisions.

**wholesaling** Transactions in which products are bought for resale, for making other products, or for general business operations

**wholesaler** An individual or organization that sells products that are bought for resale, for making other products, or for general business operations

## 15-6a Services Provided by Wholesalers

Wholesalers provide essential services to both producers and retailers. By initiating sales contacts with a producer and selling diverse products to retailers, wholesalers serve as an extension of the producer's sales force. Wholesalers also provide financial assistance. They often pay for transporting goods, reduce a producer's warehousing expenses and inventory investment by holding goods in inventory, extend credit and assume losses from buyers who turn out to be poor credit risks, and can be a source of working capital when they buy a producer's output in cash. Wholesalers also serve as conduits for information within the marketing channel, keeping producers up-to-date on market developments and passing along the manufacturers' promotional plans to other intermediaries. Using wholesalers, therefore, gives producers a distinct advantage because the specialized services wholesalers perform allow producers to concentrate on developing and manufacturing products that match customers' needs and wants.

Wholesalers support retailers by assisting with marketing strategy, especially the distribution component. Wholesalers also help retailers select inventory. They are often specialists on market conditions and experts at negotiating final purchases. In industries in which obtaining supplies is important, skilled buying is indispensable. Effective wholesalers make an effort to understand the businesses of their customers. They also must now understand digital marketing and digital communications. Firms such as Williams Commerce specialize in helping wholesalers to adapt to an increasingly digital environment while maintaining the high level of consumer contact that is sometimes required.[38]

Wholesalers can also reduce a retailer's burden of looking for and coordinating supply sources. If the wholesaler purchases for several different buyers, expenses can be shared by all customers. Furthermore, whereas a manufacturer's salesperson offers retailers only a few products at a time, independent wholesalers always have a wide range of products available. Thus, through partnerships, wholesalers and retailers can forge successful relationships for the benefit of customers.

# Entrepreneurship in Marketing

## Counter Culture Coffee Brews up Wholesale Success

**Founders:** Brett Smith and Fred Houk
**Business:** Counter Culture Coffee
**Founded:** 1995, in Durham, North Carolina
**Success:** Counter Culture Coffee has built successful relationships with retail partners coast-to-coast.

Not every coffee marketer wants to grow up to be a Starbucks-style café business. Counter Culture Coffee, founded in 1995 by two alumni of University of North Carolina graduate programs, has always been a wholesaler of roasted-to-order coffee beans. Cofounder Brett Smith sees a profitable opportunity to market top-quality, full-flavor specialty coffees to wholesale customers such as restaurants, coffee shops, and grocery stores. The goal is to "be the best at one thing—wholesale—and then give retailers the right tools to make great coffee themselves," Smith explains.

Based in Durham, North Carolina, Counter Culture goes to the source by working directly with coffee growers in the Americas and beyond. The company pays above-market prices for the finest quality, sustainably produced beans and constantly adjusts its product line to delete out-of-season beans and add newly ripened varieties. Rather than roast beans and store them until a customer places an order, Counter Culture maintains freshness by roasting when customers order and shipping the same day.

Counter Culture provides more than coffee to its wholesale customers. It will service a customer's coffee machines to ensure the equipment brings out the best in Counter Culture's coffees. It also operates 11 training centers, coast to coast, teaching customers' employees how to brew great coffee and espresso. These centers are open to the public for a few hours each week, providing free tastings and educating consumers about top-quality coffee. Finally, Counter Culture's headquarters has a test kitchen for brewing up new flavor combinations to delight the customers of its wholesale customers.[b]

The distinction between services performed by wholesalers and those provided by other businesses has blurred in recent years. Changes in the competitive nature of business, especially the growth of strong retail chains like Walmart, Home Depot, and Best Buy, are changing supply-chain relationships. In many product categories, such as electronics, furniture, and even food products, retailers have discovered that they can deal directly with producers, performing wholesaling activities themselves at a lower cost. However, when a wholesaler is eliminated from a marketing channel, wholesaling activities still have to be performed by a member of the supply chain, whether a producer, retailer, or facilitating agency. Most retailers rely on computer technology to expedite ordering, track deliveries, and monitor handling of goods. Thus, technology has allowed retailers to take over some wholesaling functions.

## 15-6b **Types of Wholesalers**

Wholesalers are classified according to several criteria: whether a wholesaler is independently owned or owned by a producer, whether it takes title to (owns) the products it handles, the range of services provided, and the breadth and depth of its product lines. Using these criteria, we discuss three general types of wholesaling establishments including merchant wholesalers, agents and brokers, and manufacturers' sales branches and offices.

### Merchant Wholesalers

**Merchant wholesalers** are independently owned businesses that take title to goods, assume risks associated with ownership, and generally buy and resell products to other wholesalers, business customers, or retailers. A producer is likely to rely on merchant wholesalers when selling directly to customers would be economically unfeasible. Merchant wholesalers are also useful for providing market coverage, making sales contacts, storing inventory, handling orders, collecting market information, and furnishing customer support. Some merchant wholesalers are even involved in packaging and developing private brands. Merchant wholesalers go by various names, including *wholesaler*, *jobber*, *distributor*, *assembler*, *exporter*, and *importer*. They fall into two broad categories: full service and limited service (see Figure 15.1).

**Full-Service Wholesalers** **Full-service wholesalers** perform the widest possible range of wholesaling functions. Customers rely on them for product availability, suitable product assortments, breaking large quantities into smaller ones, financial assistance, and technical advice and service. Full-service wholesalers handle either consumer or business products and provide

**merchant wholesalers** Independently owned businesses that take title to goods, assume ownership risks, and buy and resell products to other wholesalers, business customers, or retailers

**full-service wholesalers** Merchant wholesalers that perform the widest range of wholesaling functions

---

**Figure 15.1  Types of Merchant Wholesalers**

**Merchant Wholesaler**
Grainger is a full-service, limited-line wholesaler of electrical equipment and supplies.

numerous marketing services to their customers. Many large grocery wholesalers, for instance, help retailers with store design, site selection, personnel training, financing, merchandising, advertising, coupon redemption, and scanning. Macdonalds Consolidated is a full-service wholesaler of meat, dairy, and produce goods for grocery retailers in North America. Macdonalds offers many services, including communication management, document management, retailer flyers and merchandising, and rebates for valued customers.[39] Although full-service wholesalers often earn higher gross margins than other wholesalers, their operating expenses are also higher because they perform a wider range of functions.

Full-service wholesalers are categorized as general-merchandise, limited-line, and specialty-line wholesalers. **General-merchandise wholesalers** carry a wide product mix but offer limited depth within product lines. They deal in products such as drugs, nonperishable foods, cosmetics, detergents, and tobacco. **Limited-line wholesalers** carry only a few product lines, such as groceries, lighting fixtures, or oil-well drilling equipment, but offer an extensive assortment of products within those lines. AmerisourceBergen Corporation, for example, is a limited-line wholesaler of pharmaceuticals and health products.[40]

General-line wholesalers provide a range of services similar to those of general-merchandise wholesalers. **Specialty-line wholesalers** offer the narrowest range of products, usually a single product line or a few items within a product line. **Rack jobbers** are full-service, specialty-line wholesalers that own and maintain display racks in supermarkets, drugstores, and discount and variety stores. Retailers provide the space, and they set up displays, mark merchandise, stock shelves, and keep billing and inventory records. Rack jobbers specialize in non-food items with high profit margins, such as health and beauty aids, books, magazines, hosiery, and greeting cards.

**Limited-Service Wholesalers** **Limited-service wholesalers** provide fewer marketing services than do full-service wholesalers and specialize in just a few functions. Producers perform the remaining functions or pass them on to customers or other intermediaries. Limited-service wholesalers take title to merchandise but often do not deliver merchandise, grant credit, provide marketing information, store inventory, or plan ahead for customers' future needs. Because they offer restricted services, limited-service wholesalers charge lower rates and have smaller profit margins than full-service wholesalers. The decision about whether to use a limited-service or a full-service wholesaler depends on the structure of the marketing channel and the need to manage the supply chain to create a competitive advantage. Although limited-service wholesalers are less common than other types, they are important in the distribution of products like specialty foods, perishable items, construction materials, and coal.

**general-merchandise wholesalers** Full-service wholesalers with a wide product mix but limited depth within product lines

**limited-line wholesalers** Full-service wholesalers that carry only a few product lines but many products within those lines

**specialty-line wholesalers** Full-service wholesalers that carry only a single product line or a few items within a product line

**rack jobbers** Full-service, specialty-line wholesalers that own and maintain display racks in stores

**limited-service wholesalers** Merchant wholesalers that provide some services and specialize in a few functions

Table 15.3　**Services That Limited-Service Wholesalers Provide**

| | Cash-and-Carry | Truck | Drop Shipper | Mail Order |
|---|---|---|---|---|
| Physical possession of merchandise | Yes | Yes | No | Yes |
| Personal sales calls on customers | No | Yes | No | No |
| Information about market conditions | No | Some | Yes | Yes |
| Advice to customers | No | Some | Yes | No |
| Stocking and maintenance of merchandise in customers' stores | No | No | No | No |
| Credit to customers | No | No | Yes | Some |
| Delivery of merchandise to customers | No | Yes | No | No |

Table 15.3 summarizes the services provided by four typical limited-service wholesalers: cash-and-carry wholesalers, truck wholesalers, drop shippers, and mail-order wholesalers. **Cash-and-carry wholesalers** are intermediaries whose customers—often small businesses—pay cash and furnish transportation. Cash-and-carry wholesalers usually handle a limited line of products with a high turnover rate, such as groceries, building materials, and electrical or office supplies. Many small retailers that other types of wholesalers will not take on because of their small size survive because of cash-and-carry wholesalers. **Truck wholesalers**, sometimes called *truck jobbers*, transport a limited line of products directly to customers for on-the-spot inspection and selection. They are often small operators who own and drive their own trucks. They usually have regular routes, calling on retailers and other institutions to determine their needs. **Drop shippers**, also known as *desk jobbers*, take title to products and negotiate sales but never take actual possession of products. They forward orders from retailers, business buyers, or other wholesalers to manufacturers and arrange for carload shipments of items to be delivered directly from producers to these customers. They assume responsibility for products during the entire transaction, including the costs of any unsold goods. **Mail-order wholesalers** use catalogs instead of a sales force to sell products to retail and business buyers. Wholesale mail-order houses generally feature cosmetics, specialty foods, sporting goods, office supplies, and automotive parts. Mail-order wholesaling enables buyers to choose and order particular catalog items for delivery through various mail carriers. This is a convenient and effective method of selling items to customers in remote areas that other wholesalers might find unprofitable to serve. The Internet has provided an opportunity for mail-order wholesalers to serve a larger number of buyers, selling products over their websites and having the products shipped by the manufacturers.

## Agents and Brokers

Agents and brokers negotiate purchases and expedite sales but do not take title to products (see Figure 15.2 for types of agents and brokers). Sometimes called *functional middlemen*, they perform a limited number of services in exchange for a commission, which generally is based on the product's selling price. **Agents** represent either buyers or sellers on a permanent basis, whereas **brokers** are intermediaries that buyers or sellers employ temporarily.

Although agents and brokers perform even fewer functions than limited-service wholesalers, they are usually specialists in particular products or types of customers and can provide valuable sales expertise. They know their markets well and often form long-lasting associations with customers. Agents and brokers enable manufacturers to expand sales when resources are limited, benefit from the services of a trained sales force, and hold down personal selling costs. Table 15.4 summarizes the services provided by agents and brokers.

**cash-and-carry wholesalers** Limited-service wholesalers whose customers pay cash and furnish transportation

**truck wholesalers** Limited-service wholesalers that transport products directly to customers for inspection and selection

**drop shippers** Limited-service wholesalers that take title to goods and negotiate sales but never actually take possession of products

**mail-order wholesalers** Limited-service wholesalers that sell products through catalogs

**agents** Intermediaries that represent either buyers or sellers on a permanent basis

**brokers** Intermediaries that bring buyers and sellers together temporarily

Figure 15.2   **Types of Agents and Brokers**

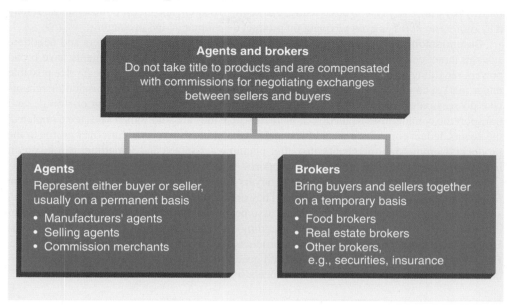

**Manufacturers' agents**, which account for more than half of all agent wholesalers, are independent intermediaries that represent two or more sellers and usually offer complete product lines to customers. They sell and take orders year-round, much as a manufacturer's sales force does. Restricted to a particular territory, a manufacturer's agent handles noncompeting and complementary products. The relationship between the agent and the manufacturer is governed by written contracts that outline territories, selling price, order handling, and terms of sale relating to delivery, service, and warranties. Manufacturers' agents have little or no control over producers' pricing and marketing policies. They do not extend credit and may be unable to provide technical advice. Manufacturers' agents are commonly used in sales of apparel, machinery and equipment, steel, furniture, automotive products, electrical goods, and some food items.

**Selling agents** market either all of a specified product line or a manufacturer's entire output. They perform every wholesaling activity except taking title to products. Selling agents usually assume the sales function for several producers simultaneously, and some firms may use them in place of a marketing department. In fact, selling agents are used most often by small producers or by manufacturers that have difficulty maintaining a marketing department because of such factors as seasonal production. In contrast to manufacturers' agents, selling

**manufacturers' agents**
Independent intermediaries that represent two or more sellers and usually offer customers complete product lines

**selling agents** Intermediaries that market a whole product line or a manufacturer's entire output

Table 15.4   **Services That Agents and Brokers Provide**

|  | Manufacturers' Agents | Selling Agents | Commission Merchants | Brokers |
|---|---|---|---|---|
| Physical possession of merchandise | Some | Some | Yes | No |
| Long-term relationship with buyers or sellers | Yes | Yes | Yes | No |
| Representation of competing product lines | No | No | Yes | Yes |
| Limited geographic territory | Yes | No | No | No |
| Credit to customers | No | Yes | Some | No |
| Delivery of merchandise to customers | Some | Yes | Yes | No |

agents generally have no territorial limits and have complete authority over prices, promotion, and distribution. To avoid conflicts of interest, selling agents represent noncompeting product lines. They play a key role in advertising, marketing research, and credit policies of the sellers they represent, at times even advising on product development and packaging.

**Commission merchants** receive goods on consignment from local sellers and negotiate sales in large, central markets. Sometimes called *factor merchants*, these agents have broad powers regarding prices and terms of sale. They specialize in obtaining the best price possible under market conditions. Most often found in agricultural marketing, commission merchants take possession of truckloads of commodities, arrange for necessary grading or storage, and transport the commodities to auction or markets where they are sold. When sales are completed, the agents deduct commissions and the expense of making the sale and turn over profits to the producer. Commission merchants also offer planning assistance and sometimes extend credit but usually do not provide promotional support.

A broker's primary purpose is to bring buyers and sellers together. Thus, brokers perform fewer functions than other intermediaries. They are not involved in financing or physical possession, have no authority to set prices, and assume almost no risks. Instead, they offer customers specialized knowledge of a particular commodity and a network of established contacts. Brokers are especially useful to sellers of products such as supermarket goods and real estate. Food brokers, for example, connect food and general merchandise to retailer-owned and merchant wholesalers, grocery chains, food processors, and business buyers.

## Manufacturers' Sales Branches and Offices

Sometimes called *manufacturers' wholesalers*, manufacturers' sales branches and offices resemble merchant wholesalers' operations. **Sales branches** are manufacturer-owned intermediaries that sell products and provide support services to the manufacturer's sales force. Situated away from the manufacturing plant, they are usually located where large customers are concentrated and demand is high. They offer credit, deliver goods, give promotional assistance, and furnish other services. Customers include retailers, business buyers, and other wholesalers. Manufacturers of electrical supplies, plumbing supplies, lumber, and automotive parts often have branch operations.

**Sales offices** are manufacturer-owned operations that provide services normally associated with agents. Like sales branches, they are located away from manufacturing plants, but unlike sales branches, they carry no inventory. A manufacturer's sales office (or branch) may sell products that enhance the manufacturer's own product line.

Manufacturers may set up these branches or offices to reach their customers more effectively by performing wholesaling functions themselves. A manufacturer also might set up such a facility when specialized wholesaling services are not available through existing intermediaries. Performing wholesaling and physical distribution activities through a manufacturer's sales branch or office can strengthen supply-chain efficiency. In some situations, though, a manufacturer may bypass its sales office or branches entirely—for example, if the producer decides to serve large retailer customers directly.

**commission merchants** Agents that receive goods on consignment from local sellers and negotiate sales in large, central markets

**sales branches** Manufacturer-owned intermediaries that sell products and provide support services to the manufacturer's sales force

**sales offices** Manufacturer-owned operations that provide services normally associated with agents

# Summary

## 15-1 Describe the purpose and function of retailers in the marketing channel.

Retailing includes all transactions in which buyers intend to consume products through personal, family, or household use. Retailers, organizations that sell products primarily to ultimate consumers, are important links in the marketing channel, because they are both marketers for and customers of wholesalers and producers. Retailers add value, provide services, and assist in making product selections. Many retailers now engage in multichannel retailing by employing multiple distribution channels that complement their brick-and-mortar stores with websites, catalogs, and apps.

## 15-2 Identify the major types of retailers.

Retail stores can be classified according to the breadth of products offered. Two broad categories are general merchandise retailers and specialty retailers. There are several primary types of general-merchandise retailers. Department stores are large retail organizations organized by departments and characterized by wide product mixes in considerable depth. Discount stores are self-service, low-price, general-merchandise outlets. Extreme-value stores are much smaller than conventional discount stores and offer even lower prices on smaller size name-brand nonperishable household items. Convenience stores are small self-service stores that are open long hours and carry a narrow assortment of products, usually convenience items. Supermarkets are large self-service food stores that carry some non-food products. Superstores are giant retail outlets that carry all the products found in supermarkets and most consumer products purchased on a routine basis. Hypermarkets offer supermarket and discount store shopping at one location. Warehouse clubs are large-scale, members-only discount operations. Warehouse and catalog showrooms are low-cost operations characterized by warehouse methods of materials handling and display, large inventories, and minimal services.

Specialty retailers offer substantial assortments in a few product lines. They include traditional specialty retailers, which carry narrow product mixes with deep product lines. Category killers are large specialty stores that concentrate on a major product category and compete on the basis of low prices and enormous product availability. Off-price retailers sell brand-name manufacturers' seconds and product overruns at deep discounts.

## 15-3    Explain strategic issues in retailing.

To increase sales and store patronage, retailers must consider strategic issues. Location determines the trading area from which a store draws its customers and should be evaluated carefully. When evaluating potential sites, retailers take into account a variety of factors, including the location of the firm's target market within the trading area, kinds of products sold, availability of public transportation, customer characteristics, and competitors' locations. Retailers can choose among several types of locations, including freestanding structures, traditional business districts, traditional planned shopping centers (neighborhood, community, regional, and superregional), or nontraditional shopping centers (lifestyle, power, and outlet). As consumer demographics and shopping trends change, retailers are adjusting by exploiting new technologies to improve the store experience and give consumers more shopping platforms. Retail positioning involves identifying an unserved or underserved market segment and serving it through a strategy that distinguishes the retailer from others in those customers' minds. Store image, which various customers perceive differently, derives not only from atmospherics but also from location, products offered, customer services, prices, promotion, and the store's overall reputation. Atmospherics refers to the physical elements of a store's design that can be adjusted to appeal to consumers' emotions and thus induce them to buy. Category management is a retail

strategy of managing groups of similar, often substitutable products produced by different manufacturers.

## 15-4    Recognize the various forms of direct marketing, direct selling, and vending.

Direct marketing is the use of the telephone, Internet, and nonpersonal media to communicate product and organizational information to customers, who can then purchase products via mail, telephone, or the Internet. Direct marketing is a type of nonstore retailing, the selling of goods or services outside the confines of a retail facility. Direct marketing may occur online (online retailing), through a catalog (catalog marketing), advertising (direct-response marketing), telephone (telemarketing), and television (television home shopping). Two other types of nonstore retailing are direct selling and automatic vending. Direct selling is the marketing of products to ultimate consumers through face-to-face sales presentations at home or in the workplace. Automatic vending is the use of machines to dispense products.

## 15-5    Describe franchising and its benefits and weaknesses.

Franchising is an arrangement in which a supplier grants a dealer the right to sell products in exchange for some type of consideration. Franchise arrangements have a number of advantages and disadvantages over traditional business forms, and their use is increasing. There are several advantages for the franchisee. First, franchising enables a franchisee to start a business with limited capital and benefit from the business experience of others. Second, franchises generally have lower failure rates than independent retail establishments and are often more successful because they can build on the franchisor's reputation. Finally, the franchisee receives materials to use in local advertising and can benefit from national promotional campaigns sponsored by the franchisor. In addition, if business problems should arise for the franchise operation, the franchisee can obtain guidance and advice from the franchisor at little or no cost. There are also several advantages for the franchisor. First, the franchisor gains fast and selective product distribution without incurring the high cost of constructing and operating its own outlets. Second, the franchisor has more available capital for expanding production and advertising. Finally, the franchisor benefits from the fact that the franchisee is likely to be highly motivated to succeed—likely resulting in higher income for the franchisor.

There are several disadvantages for the franchisee. The franchisor can dictate many aspects of the business. Franchisees must also pay to use the franchisor's name, products, and assistance; operating a franchise requires hard work and long hours. Another disadvantage is that franchise agreements are not always uniform. Disadvantages for the franchisor include the fact that the franchisor must give up a certain amount of control when entering into an agreement and that individual establishments may not be operated according to standards.

## 15-6 Explain the nature and functions of wholesalers.

Wholesaling consists of all transactions in which products are bought for resale, making other products, or general business operations. Wholesalers are individuals or organizations that facilitate and expedite exchanges that are primarily wholesale transactions. For producers, wholesalers are a source of financial assistance and information. By performing specialized accumulation and allocation functions, they allow producers to concentrate on manufacturing products. Wholesalers provide retailers with buying expertise, wide product lines, efficient distribution, and warehousing and storage.

Merchant wholesalers are independently owned businesses that take title to goods and assume ownership risks. They are either full-service wholesalers, offering the widest possible range of wholesaling functions, or limited-service wholesalers, providing only some marketing services and specializing in a few functions. There are several full-service merchant wholesaler types. General-merchandise wholesalers offer a wide but relatively shallow product mix. Limited-line wholesalers offer extensive assortments within a few product lines. Specialty-line wholesalers carry only a single product line or a few items within a line. Rack jobbers own and service display racks in supermarkets and other stores. Limited-service merchant wholesalers include cash-and-carry wholesalers, which sell to small businesses, require payment in cash, and do not deliver. Truck wholesalers sell a limited line of products from their own trucks directly to customers. Drop shippers own goods and negotiate sales, but never take possession of products. Finally, mail-order wholesalers sell to retail and business buyers through direct-mail catalogs.

Agents and brokers negotiate purchases and expedite sales in exchange for a commission, but they do not take title to products. Usually specializing in certain products, they can provide valuable sales expertise. Whereas agents represent buyers or sellers on a permanent basis, brokers are intermediaries that buyers and sellers employ on a temporary basis to negotiate exchanges. Manufacturers' agents offer customers the complete product lines of two or more sellers. Selling agents market a complete product line or a producer's entire output and perform every wholesaling function except taking title to products. Commission merchants are agents that receive goods on consignment from local sellers and negotiate sales in large, central markets.

Manufacturers' sales branches and offices are owned by manufacturers. Sales branches sell products and provide support services for the manufacturer's sales force in a given location. Sales offices carry no inventory and function much as agents do.

---

**Go to www.cengagebrain.com for resources to help you master the content in this chapter as well as for materials that will expand your marketing knowledge!**

---

# Important Terms

# Discussion and Review Questions

1. What value is added to a product by retailers? What value is added by retailers for producers and ultimate consumers?
2. What are the major differences between discount stores and department stores?
3. In what ways are traditional specialty stores and off-price retailers similar? How do they differ?
4. What major issues should be considered when determining a retail site location?
5. Describe the three major types of traditional shopping centers. Give an example of each type in your area.
6. Discuss the major factors that help to determine a retail store's image. How does atmosphere add value to products sold in a store?
7. How is door-to-door selling a form of retailing? Some consumers believe that direct-response orders bypass the retailer. Is this true?
8. If you were opening a retail business, would you prefer to open an independent store or own a store under a franchise arrangement? Explain your preference.
9. What services do wholesalers provide to producers and retailers?
10. What is the difference between a full-service merchant wholesaler and a limited-service merchant wholesaler?
11. Drop shippers take title to products but do not accept physical possession of them, whereas commission merchants take physical possession of products but do not accept title. Defend the logic of classifying drop shippers as merchant wholesalers and commission merchants as agents.
12. Why are manufacturers' sales offices and branches classified as wholesalers? Which independent wholesalers are replaced by manufacturers' sales branches? By sales offices?

# Video Case 15.1

## L.L.Bean: Open 24/7, Click or Brick

L.L.Bean, based in Freeport, Maine, began life as a one-product firm selling by mail in 1912. Founder Leon Leonwood Bean designed and tested every product he sold, starting with the now-iconic rubber-soled Bean Boot. Today, the catalog business that L.L. Bean began is still going strong, along with a thriving online retail operation and a growing network of retail stores that will total 100 by 2020. In addition, L.L.Bean is expanding its retail presence in Japan and China, where customers are particularly drawn to brand names that represent quality and a distinct personality. The company's outdoorsy image and innovative products, combined with a century-old reputation for standing behind every item, have made its stores popular shopping destinations around the world and around the Web.

Although the award-winning L.L.Bean catalog swelled in size during the 1980s and 1990s, it has slimmed down over the years as the online store has grown. Now, using sophisticated marketing database systems, L.L.Bean manages and updates the mailing lists and customer preferences

John Van Decker/Alamy Stock Photo

for its catalogs. For targeting purposes, L.L.Bean creates 50 different catalogs that are mailed to selected customers across the United States and in 160 countries worldwide. The company's computer-modeling tools indicate which customers are interested in which products so they receive only the specialized catalogs they desire. Still, says the vice president of stores, "what we find is most customers want some sort of touch point," whether they buy online, in a store, by mail, or by phone.

The company's flagship retail store in Freeport, Maine, like its online counterpart, is open 24 hours a day, 7 days a week, throughout the year. Even on major holidays like Thanksgiving and Christmas, when most other stores are closed, the flagship store is open for business. It stocks extra merchandise and hires additional employees for busy buying periods, as does the online store. Day or night, rain or shine, customers can walk the aisles of the gigantic Freeport store to browse an assortment of clothing and footwear for men, women, and children; try out camping gear and other sporting goods; buy home goods like blankets; and check out pet supplies. Every week, the store offers hands-on demonstrations and how-to seminars to educate customers about its products. Customers can pause for a cup of coffee or sit down to a full meal at the in-store café. Thanks to the store's enormous size and entertaining extras, it has become a tourist attraction as well as the center-piece of L.L.Bean's retail empire.

L.L.Bean's online store continues to grow in popularity. In fact, online orders recently surpassed mail and phone orders, a first in the company's history, and the company also offers a mobile app for anytime, anywhere access via cell phone. The web-based store is busy year-round, but especially during the Christmas shopping season, when it receives a virtual blizzard of orders—as many as 120,000 orders in a day. Unlike the physical stores, which have limited space to hold and display inventory for shoppers to buy in person, the online store can offer every product in every size and color. Customers can order via the Web and have purchases sent to their home or office address or shipped to a local L.L.Bean store for pickup.

This latter option is particularly convenient for customers who prefer to pay with cash rather than credit or debit cards.

At the start of L.L.Bean's second century, its dedication to customer satisfaction is as strong as when Leon Leonwood Bean began his mail-order business so many decades ago. "We want to keep . . . the customer happy and keep that cus-tomer coming back to L.L.Bean over and over," explains the vice president of e-commerce. With more than $1.6 billion in annual sales from traditional retailing, catalog sales, and online retailing, L.L. Bean knows that satisfying customers today will help it profit in the years to come.[41]

### Questions for Discussion

1. What forms of direct marketing does L.L.Bean employ? Which additional forms of direct marketing should L.L.Bean consider using?
2. Do you think L.L.Bean's website will ever entirely take the place of its mail-order catalog? Why or why not?
3. What type(s) of location do you think would be most appropriate for future L.L.Bean stores, and why?

# Case 15.2

## Dick's Sporting Goods Scores with Stores within Stores

Dick's Sporting Goods is scoring big points with customers by setting up stores within stores that each feature an exten-sive selection of goods from a particular brand. The Pennsyl-vania–based retailer was founded in 1948 as a bait and tackle shop. Today, the founder's son is CEO, heading up a manage-ment team responsible for 603 large-scale Dick's Sporting Goods stores selling sports equipment, clothing, and shoes for team and individual use. Despite competition from other sporting-goods retailers, including Bass Pro Shops and REI, Dick's continues to grow beyond $6.8 billion in annual sales by putting brand-name merchandise at the core of its strategy for in-store, online, and mobile retailing.

For example, inside some of the larger Dick's stores is a special shop where only Nike-brand products are displayed. Part of the Nike inventory is exclusive to Dick's, which adds to the attraction for customers who prefer that brand. Selected Dick's stores contain a dedicated Under Armour shop or a dedicated North Face shop, again featuring a mix of mer-chandise available nationwide and some items available only at Dick's. These stores-within-a-store not only differentiate Dick's from its rivals, but they also generate higher sales and profits per square foot than other areas of the store.

Not long ago, the retailer teamed up with the National Hockey League to test the sale of league- and team-branded merchandise at Dick's. The NHL operates three flagship spe-cialty stores, and each of the 30 professional hockey teams

also sells its own branded merchandise. However, the NHL decided it needed an experienced retail partner with a national presence to expand the NHL shop concept and reach more hockey fans. Now Dick's is working with the NHL to test ded-icated shops within three Dick's stores. Averaging 400 square feet, each NHL store-within-a-store offers team merchandise geared to the interests and wallets of a wider range of fans. If the dedicated NHL shops do well, Dick's will open dozens more in the coming years.

Dick's also operates 78 Golf Galaxy specialty stores, catering to golf enthusiasts who appreciate the vast selection of golf-related merchandise, including clothing, shoes, and new or used equipment. Customers can take lessons from golf professionals, test clubs in an indoor driving area and a putting green, and use the interactive golf-course simulator to "play" at some of the world's best-known courses. The full-service retailer offers trade-ins, custom fitting, equipment repair, tee-time reservations, and travel arrangements for golf vacations.

In addition, Dick's is opening a series of smaller specialty stores with narrow but deep assortments for specific target markets. For instance, it operates three True Runner specialty stores stocked with footwear, apparel, and accessories for serious runners. These stores use special technology to analyze each runner's arch and gait so salespeople can make personalized suggestions for appropriate shoes. To encourage runners to drop by, True

Runner stores serve as a community hub for running information and provide lockers where customers can leave their belongings while running in the area.

Dick's recently acquired the Field & Stream brand, which has been in existence for more than 140 years. Now the company has begun opening specialty stores under that name to sell equipment and accessories for fishing, camping, and hunting. Dick's sees potential in opening more Field & Stream specialty stores coast to coast, beyond the 19 currently in operation. Field & Stream stores, like True Runner stores, are smaller than Dick's Sporting Goods and—like all of Dick's stores—are staffed by employees who are knowledgeable and can help customers make informed choices.

Recognizing the potential of e-commerce and growing customer interest in mobile access to retail sites, Dick's has upgraded its website retailing technology and streamlined the process of browsing and buying via smartphone. The idea is to give customers more buying options and increase online sales

year after year. Nonetheless, store retailing remains the firm's main focus, because most customers like to see sports equipment in person, seek expert advice, and try products before making a purchase. With that in mind, Dick's has invested in a fourth distribution center to be able to receive, sort, and ship merchandise for up to 750 stores. Looking even further ahead, the retailer's research indicates sufficient long-term demand and profit potential for more than 1,000 Dick's Sporting Goods stores nationwide.[42]

### Questions for Discussion

1. How would you describe the store image of Dick's Sporting Goods?
2. What effect do you think the opening of NHL stores-within-stores will have on the retail positioning of Dick's Sporting Goods?
3. Would you recommend that Dick's Sporting Goods test direct selling through at-home consultants? Explain your answer.

# Strategic Case 6

## IKEA Makes the Most of Its Marketing Channels

The furniture and housewares retailer IKEA has a long history of using multiple marketing channels to reach customers near and far. IKEA's founder, Ingvar Kamprad, was a teenage entrepreneur when he started a mail-order business selling postcards and pencils in Sweden more than 70 years ago. Within a few years, he had expanded into reselling locally-made furniture and, in 1951, he printed the first annual IKEA furniture catalog.

Soon, he opened the first IKEA showroom to allow customers to see and try furniture before making a purchase. By 1955, the company was designing and manufacturing many of its own products to meet customers' needs for stylish yet affordable furniture. IKEA came up with innovative designs for bookcases and other furniture items that are packed flat for shipment to stores and then assembled by buyers at home. This kept costs low and allowed the company to charge low prices.

With the opening of its first store outside Sweden in the early 1960s, IKEA was on its way to becoming a global retailing sensation. Today, 770 million people annually pass through the front doors of 328 IKEA stores in 28 countries. The printed IKEA catalog remains a vital marketing tool, with 38 versions now published in 17 languages. More than 54 million people use IKEA's catalog app every year. In addition, IKEA's websites attract nearly 2 billion online visitors yearly. No matter how consumers like to browse and buy, IKEA wants to accommodate their preferences.

### What's in Store?

Because in-store transactions account for 95 percent of IKEA's sales, the company puts considerable emphasis on brick-and-mortar retailing. Its warehouse-sized stores carry 10,000 items for the home, from measuring cups, mirrors, and mattresses to towels, toys, and tables. Customers can get ideas and inspiration from dozens of sample rooms filled with furnishings and accessories. They can also use in-store computer kiosks, work with employees, or access software from home to design their own kitchens, see which products fit the project and the budget, and view the results in 3D before ordering anything. Staff experts are on hand to provide design advice for customers who are renovating bathrooms, reorganizing closets, or creating a home office.

IKEA complements the merchandise assortment and on-site customer service with optional, fee-based extras such as delivery and installation. The idea is to extend IKEA's reach beyond the do-it-yourselfers who don't mind lugging bulky boxes and assembling furniture to save money. And, to encourage shoppers to linger, each outlet includes a cafeteria serving traditional dishes like Swedish meatballs, local favorites like chicken wings, and specially priced children's meals.

One of IKEA's goals is to increase sales of existing stores by enhancing the customer experience. Through extensive in-home research, the company is constantly learning more about customers' aspirations, irritations, lifestyles, and value perceptions, so its local stores can carry the right mix of products at the right prices for each market. For example, based on in-home visits to local customers, the U.K. stores changed their policy of stocking outdoor furniture only during warm months and began selling such merchandise all year long. Supported by a multimedia marketing campaign, IKEA's U.K. sales of outdoor furniture skyrocketed by 58 percent during the year following this change. The U.K. stores are also testing the sale of solar panel kits, in line with the retailer's commitment to earth-friendly renewable energy.

store in Europe would serve in an entire week. Several couples have even chosen to be married inside one of IKEA's stores in China.

IKEA is also preparing to bring its unique brand of retailing to India, another fast-growing market with great promise. Few large-scale retailers operate in India, and IKEA's fame and novelty have already raised public awareness and anticipation. The most difficult challenge may be navigating all the regulations governing foreign business ownership and the sourcing and shipment of merchandise within India. However, IKEA has the financial strength to wait for profitability as it proceeds with a long-term plan to open 25 stores.

As IKEA blankets the globe with stores, some of its suppliers are opening facilities in nearby areas, to reduce the time and expense of getting products from factory to store. As one example, China-based Liaoyang Ningfeng Woodenware recently created a U.S. subsidiary to manufacture bedroom sets in Virginia for IKEA stores in the United States, Europe, and Asia. The company cited Virginia's abundant raw materials and its well-developed transportation infrastructure as two main reasons for choosing the state for its American division.

### At Home in Asia

Although IKEA has slowed the overall pace of new-store openings in recent years, it sees tremendous growth opportunity in emerging markets such as China, where middle-class incomes are rising and consumers are seeking out foreign brands. The company enjoys a loyal and growing customer base in China, competing on the basis of its dual strengths in European styling and vast selection. Initially, IKEA's prices were higher than those of rival retailers, but once it increased the proportion of merchandise sourced from local suppliers, it was able to reduce costs and prices. Now IKEA rings up more than $1 billion in yearly sales through its stores in China and expects double-digit revenue growth in the future.

IKEA has done its homework, stocking products and setting up displays keyed to the specific needs of customers in each area. For instance, apartment-dwellers in the north of China often set aside part of their balconies for food storage, whereas those in the south use part of their balconies for laundry. Therefore, IKEA's in-store exhibits of balcony organizers include storage units reflecting these regional preferences. Because IKEA's China stores are so much larger than local stores and carry a wider array of merchandise, they are extremely popular shopping destinations. In fact, the Beijing store alone draws more customers on a Saturday than an IKEA

### Apps, Social Media, and the Web

Not every customer wants to spend hours in a store, as IKEA well knows. That's why the company has introduced smartphone apps for tech-savvy customers. One app provides access to IKEA's online catalog, enabling customers to check product listings and view photos and videos of merchandise from home or office or anywhere on the go. This app also allows customers to point a smartphone at a space in a room and see how a piece of IKEA furniture such as a sofa or chair would look if placed there. Customers make more informed buying decisions when they can visualize the furniture's position within a real room—and IKEA benefits from fewer merchandise returns. In addition, customers can use an IKEA app to confirm whether an item is in stock at a particular store, to check store hours and directions, and to receive notices of special deals and events.

IKEA uses social media such as Pinterest, Twitter, Instagram, Facebook, YouTube, and Google+ to connect with local customers in many of its markets. By providing interesting and useful information about decorating and products, the retailer builds brand awareness, polishes its image, and promotes selected products or categories. Its U.S. Facebook page, with nearly 5 million likes, features store news, product photos, and links to nonprofit groups that IKEA supports, such as UNICEF. Its U.S. Twitter account has hundreds of thousands of followers who click to see photos and Vine videos focusing on seasonal merchandise or solutions to common problems like storage and organization.

Although IKEA has traditionally concentrated on brick-and-mortar retailing, it is upgrading its e-commerce technology and its logistics to accommodate customers who like to browse and buy with a click. The retailer now makes 70 percent of its products available for online purchase and delivery in 13 countries. IKEA is investing heavily in e-commerce to support its goal of boosting annual revenues from the current level of $22.4 billion to more than $35 billion by 2020.[43]

### Questions for Discussion

1. Would you recommend that IKEA continue printing and mailing catalogs or should it switch to an online-only catalog? Explain your answer.

2. If you were in charge of choosing IKEA's next U.S. store location, what factors would you consider in making your decision?

3. How much channel power does IKEA possess? What are the implications for the role it plays in the channel?

4. What are the main logistical issues IKEA must address to be able to make 100 percent of its products available for online purchase and delivery?

# NOTES

[1] Taryn Luna, "Tedeschi Food Chain Sold to 7-Eleven," *Boston Globe*, May 18, 2015, www.bostonglobe.com/business/2015/05/18/tedeschi-food-chain-sold-eleven/oUZoZusupv3cNcB010kU8N/story.html (accessed February 22, 2016); Harriet Baskas, "LAX Is First U.S. Airport to Get a 7-Eleven," *USA Today*, June 2, 2015, www.usatoday.com/story/todayinthesky/2015/06/02/los-angeles-airport-7-eleven/28344897/ (accessed February 22, 2016); Loretta Chao, "7-Eleven Expands Locker Space, Hoping to Cash In on E-Commerce Wave," *Wall Street Journal*, November 12, 2015, www.wsj.com/articles/7-eleven-expands-locker-space-hoping-to-cash-in-on-e-commerce-wave-1447326538?cb=logged0.675287766239715 (accessed February 22, 2016); Stephani Overby, "7-Eleven Takes a Big Gulp of Customer Data," *CIO*, October 30, 2015, www.cio.com/article/2993079/analytics/7-eleven-takes-a-big-gulp-of-customer-data.html (accessed February 22, 2016); Erin Rigik, "How 7-Eleven is Taking Convenience to the Next Level," *Convenience Store Decisions*, October 5, 2015, www.cstoredecisions.com/2015/10/05/how-7-eleven-is-taking-convenience-to-the-next-level/ (accessed February 22, 2016).

[2] "Retail's Impact," National Retail Foundation, https://nrf.com/sites/default/files/Documents/retail%20library/Retail%27s%20Impact%20-%20Printable%20Highlights.pdf (accessed March 24, 2016).

[3] "Domino's Anyware," Domino's Pizza, https://anyware.dominos.com/ (accessed March 24, 2016).

[4] Vijaya Rathore, "Fashion Brand Coach Readies India Plan," *ETRetail.com* (from The Economic Times), June 23, 2015, http://retail.economictimes.indiatimes.com/news/apparel-fashion/apparel/fashion-brand-coach-readies-india-plans/47778902 (accessed March 24, 2016).

[5] Lauren Johnson, "Big-Box Stores like Target Think These New Apps Can Beat Amazon," *Adweek*, December 1, 2014, http://www.adweek.com/news/technology/big-box-stores-target-think-these-new-apps-can-defeat-amazon-161648 (accessed March 24, 2016).

[6] "2016 Top 250 Global Powers of Retailing," National Retail Federation, https://nrf.com/news/2016-top-250-global-powers-of-retailing (accessed March 24, 2016).

[7] Phil Wahba, "Why Target's Strategy to Aim Upscale Is Spot-on," *Fortune*, May 20, 2015, http://fortune.com/2015/05/20/target-upscale-walmart/ (accessed March 24, 2016).

[8] "About Us," National Association of Convenience Stores Online, www.nacsonline.com/NACS/About_NACS/Pages/default.aspx (accessed March 24, 2016).

[9] Austin Carr, "Amazon and Instacart, Facing the Heat, Want to Rule Your Kitchen," *Fast Company*, September 2015, http://www.fastcompany.com/3048627/the-new-rivalries-amazon-vs-instacart (accessed March 24, 2016).

[10] "Sam's Club Company Facts," Sam's Club, November 2015, http://www3.samsclub.com/NewsRoom/AboutUs/Facts (accessed March 24, 2016); "Why Become a Member," Costco, http://www.costco.com/membership-information.html (accessed March 24, 2016).

[11] Bryan Pearson, "Run on Fun: Toys 'R' Us Playing Customer Experience to Win against Walmart, Amazon," *Forbes*, April 16, 2015, http://www.forbes.com/sites/bryanpearson/2015/04/16/run-on-fun-toys-r-us-playing-customer-experience-to-win-against-walmart-amazon/ (accessed March 24, 2016).

[12] "Retail Space Sharing Businesses Can Go Together like Coffee and Pastry," *SmallBusiness.com*, April 16, 2015, http://smallbusiness.com/vision/basics-of-retail-space-sharing/ (accessed March 25, 2016).

[13] Susanna Capelouto, "More Storefront 'Roommates' Splitting Space, Customers," All Things Considered, NPR, March 18, 2015, http://www.npr.org/2015/03/18/393870622/more-storefront-roommates-splitting-space-customers (accessed March 25, 2016).

[14] Mall of America website, www.mallofamerica.com (accessed March 25, 2016).

[15] Jeff Hardwick, "The Mall Is Dead. Americans Shop at 'Lifestyle Centers' Now," *New Republic*, March 3, 2015, https://newrepublic.com/article/121203/american-malls-are-changing-their-look-and-their-tactics (accessed March 25, 2016).

[16] Jeanne W. Ross, Cynthia M. Beath, and Ina Sebastian, "Why Nordstrom's Digital Strategy Works (and Yours Probably Doesn't)," *Harvard Business Review*, January 14, 2015, https://hbr.org/2015/01/why-nordstroms-digital-strategy-works-and-yours-probably-doesnt (accessed March 25, 2016).

[17] Krystina Gustafson, "Wait! Before You Build that App, Consider This …," CNBC, March 6, 2015, http://www.cnbc.com/2015/03/06/wait-before-you-build-that-app-consider-this.html (accessed March 25, 2016).

[18] Sara Halzack, "5 New Technologies that may Change How You Shop," *The Washington Post*,

January 14, 2015, http://www.washingtonpost.com/news/business/wp/2015/01/14/5-new-technologies-that-may-change-how-you-shop/ (accessed March 25, 2016).

[19] Sabrina Korber, "Retail's 'Beacon' of Hope: Shopping that's Personal," CNBC, May 26, 2015, http://www.cnbc.com/2015/05/26/retails-newest-brick-and-mortar-bet.html (accessed March 25, 2016).

[20] Sara Halzack, "5 New Technologies that may Change How You Shop."

[21] Ibid.

[22] Kathleen Lee, "It's a Good Thing That H&M Might Soon Cost You More," Daily Life, December 17, 2013, www.dailylife.com.au/dl-fashion/fashion-coverage/its-a-good-thing-that-hm-might-soon-cost-you-more-20131213-2zc4u.html (accessed March 25, 2016).

[23] Rollo A. S. Grayson and Lisa S. McNeill, "Using Atmospheric Elements in Service Retailing: Understanding the Bar Environment," Journal of Services Marketing 23, 7 (2009): 517-527.

[24] Tom Buswell, "Restaurant Colors: Triggering Appetite with the Use of Colors," Send Me the Manager, January 21, 2013, www.sendmethemanager.com/blog/bid/199532/Restaurant-Colors-Triggering-Appetite-With-the-Use-of-Colors (accessed March 25, 2016).

[25] Ibid.

[26] Charles Dennis, J. Brakus, and Eleftherios Alamanos, "The Wallpaper Matters: The Influence of the Content of Digital Ads on Customer In-Store Experience," Journal of Marketing Management, 29, 3/4 (2013): 338–355.

[27] "Facts & Stats" CMO Council, https://www.cmocouncil.org/facts-stats-categories.php?view=all&category=direct-marketing (accessed March 25, 2016).

[28] "Online Retail Sales to Top $480 Billion by 2019," Forrester, April 22, 2015, https://www.forrester.com/Online+Retail+Sales+To+Top+480+Billion+By+2019/-/E-PRE7825 (accessed March 25, 2016).

[29] Do Not Call website, www.donotcall.gov (accessed March 25, 2016).

[30] Ibid.

[31] "2015 DSN Global 100 List," Direct Selling News, April 8, 2015, http://directsellingnews.com/index.php/view/2015_dsn_global_100_list#.VhanQPnnuUk (accessed March 25, 2016).

[32] Ibid.

[33] Direct Selling Association, "What Is Direct Selling?" http://directselling.org/about-direct-selling/ (accessed March 25, 2016).

[34] Christian Storm, "30 Bizarre Vending Machines from around the World," Business Insider, November 10, 2014, http://www.businessinsider.com/most-unique-vending-machines-2014-11?op=1 (March 25, 2016).

[35] "2016 Franchise Business Economic Outlook," International Franchise Association Education Foundation, January 2016, http://emarket.franchise.org/FranchiseOutlook-Jan2016.pdf (accessed March 25, 2016).

[36] "Avoiding Atlantis: Building a Franchise Restaurant That Stays Afloat," PR Newswire, December 5, 2013, www.prnewswire.com/news-releases/avoiding-atlantis-building-a-franchise-restaurant-that-stays-afloat-234620271.html (accessed March 25, 2016).

[37] "Number of Firms, Number of Establishments, Employment, Annual Payroll, and Estimated Receipts by Enterprise Employment Size for the United States, All Industries," Statistics of U.S. Businesses (SUSB) Main, Bureau of the Census, February 9, 2016 release, www.census.gov/econ/susb (accessed March 28, 2016).

[38] "Williams Commerce Report on the Emerging Marketing Tactics Wholesalers Are Pursuing," PR Web, www.prweb.com/releases/2013/12/prweb11379890.htm (accessed March 28, 2016).

[39] Macdonalds Consolidated website, http://macdonaldsconsolidated.ca/ (accessed March 28, 2016).

[40] AmerisourceBergen website, www.amerisourcebergen.com/abc (accessed March 28, 2016).

[41] Randy Hallman, "First-Day Sales Brisk at L.L. Bean in Short Pump Town Center," Richmond Times-Dispatch, November 5, 2015, www.richmond.com/business/local/article_a5b389fa-c721-5577-adcd-79bfb9dae183.html (accessed February 19, 2016) ; "L.L. Bean 2015 Fact Sheet," L.L. Bean http://www.llbean.com/customerService/aboutLLBean/images/FactSheet_2015.pdf (accessed March 23, 2016)); "L.L. Bean Sales Grow Despite Weak Economy," Chicago Sun-Times, March 9, 2012, www.suntimes.com/business/11178636-420/ll-bean-sales-grow-despite-weak-economy.html; Kelli B. Grant, "Walmart Lets Online Shoppers Pay Cash," MarketWatch, March 21, 2012, http://blogs.marketwatch.com/realtimeadvice/2012/03/21/walmart-lets-online-shoppers-pay-cash; Michael

Arndt, "Customer Service Champs: L.L. Bean Follows Its Shoppers to the Web," Bloomberg Businessweek, February 18, 2010, www.businessweek.com/magazine/content/10_09/b4168043788083.htm; Interviews with L.L.Bean employees and the video, "L.L. Bean Employs a Variety of Promotion Methods to Communicate with Customers"; L.L.Bean website, www.llbean.com (accessed January 5, 2014).

[42] Dick's Sporting Goods 2014 Annual Report, pp. 1–7; Teresa F. Lindeman, "Dick's Sporting Goods Tests In-Store NHL-Branded Shops," Pittsburgh Post-Gazette, December 10, 2013, www.post-gazette.com; Tim Schooley, "Exclusive: NHL Branding 'Super Shops' Within Dick's," Pittsburgh Business Times, December 9, 2013, www.bizjournals.com; Shannon Green, "Scoring with Dick's Sporting Goods," Fortune, October 28, 2013, p. 79; Mark Brohan, "Dick's Sporting Goods Is Swinging for the E-Commerce Sales Fences," Internet Retailer, September 25, 2013, www.internetretailer.com; www.dickssportinggoods.com.

[43] Anna Ringstrom, "IKEA's Net Profit Up 5.5 percent, Helped by Online Sales and China," Reuters, December 10, 2015, www.reuters.com/article/us-ikea-results-idUSKBN0TT1EQ20151210 (accessed February 19, 2016); Julia Chatterley and Antonia Matthews, "IKEA CEO: Late to Online Boom But Growth Ahead," CNBC, October 14, 2015, www.cnbc.com/2015/10/14/ikea-ceo-late-to-online-boom-but-growth-ahead.html (accessed February 19, 2016); IKEA Group 2015 Yearly Summary, pp. 1–12; Caroline Baldwin, "IKEA Seeks to Engage Customers with Seamless Shopping Experience," Computer Weekly, January 7, 2014, pp. 9–10; "Chinese Furniture Maker to Open VA Plant," Furniture Today, December 2, 2013, p. 60; Dominic Basulto, "Big Box Solar and the Clean Energy Revolution," Washington Post, October 15, 2013, www.washingtonpost.com/blogs/innovations/wp/2013/10/15/big-box-solar-and-the-clean-energy-revolution; "Why IKEA Encourages Chinese to Literally Make Its Stores Their Own," Advertising Age, December 9, 2013, p. 19; Anna Ringstrom, "One Size Doesn't Fit All: IKEA Goes Local for India, China," Reuters, March 7, 2013, http://in.reuters.com/article/2013/03/07/ikea-expansion-india-china-idINDEE92603L20130307 (accessed January 17, 2014); "All-Year-Round Offer Boosts IKEA Outdoor Furniture 58%," DIY Week (UK), December 13, 2013, p. 5.

# Feature Notes

[a] Sarah Halzack, "Why the Social Media 'Buy Button' Is Still There, Even Though Most Never Use It," *Washington Post*, January 14, 2016, www.washingtonpost.com/news/business/wp/2016/01/14/why-the-social-media-buy-button-is-still-there-even-though-most-never-use-it/ (accessed February 23, 2016); Jim Dallke, "'Contextual Commerce' Is The Future Of Shopping, and It's More Than Just Buy Buttons," ChicagoInno, February 8, 2016, http://chicagoinno.streetwise.co/2016/02/08/mobile-shopping-contextual-commerce-goes-beyond-the-buy-button/ (accessed February 23, 2016); Jayson DeMers, "Is Pinterest's Buy Button Sparking a Social Purchase Revolution?" *Adweek*, Oct. 6, 2015, www.adweek.com/social-times/is-pinterests-buy-button-sparking-a-social-purchase-revolution/627778 (accessed February 23, 2016).

[b] Clint Rainey, "Small Coffee Goes Venti," *Bloomberg Businessweek*, January 7, 2016, www.bloomberg.com/news/articles/2016-01-07/craft-coffee-gets-guzzled-up-by-the-conglomerates (accessed February 19, 2016); Connelly Hardaway, "Counter Culture Coffee opens on Spring Street," *Charleston City Paper (Charleston, S.C.)*, July 23, 2015, www.charlestoncitypaper.com/Eat/archives/2015/07/23/counter-culture-coffee-opens-on-spring-street (accessed February 19, 2016); Lauren Ohnesorge, "Counter Culture Coffee Co-founder Talks New HQ, 'Entrepreneurship Itch,' and Importance of the Word 'Fresh,'" *Triangle Business Journal*, October 7, 2015, www.bizjournals.com/triangle/news/2015/10/07/counter-culture-coffee-co-founder-talks-new-hq.html (accessed February 19, 2016); http://counterculturecoffee.com.

# part 7
## Promotion Decisions

**PART 7** focuses on communication with target market members and other relevant groups. A specific marketing mix cannot satisfy people in a particular target market unless they are aware of the product and know where to find it. Some promotion decisions relate to a specific marketing mix; others are geared toward promoting the entire organization.

**CHAPTER 16** discusses integrated marketing communications. It describes the communication process and the major promotional methods that can be included in promotion mixes.

**CHAPTER 17** analyzes the major steps in developing an advertising campaign. It also explains what public relations is and how it can be used.

**CHAPTER 18** deals with personal selling and sales promotion efforts, exploring the general characteristics of sales promotion and sales promotion techniques.

# chapter 16    Integrated Marketing Communications

## OBJECTIVES

**16-1**   Define integrated marketing communications.

**16-2**   Describe the steps of the communication process.

**16-3**   Recognize the definition and objectives of promotion.

**16-4**   Summarize the four elements of the promotion mix.

**16-5**   Explain the factors that are used to determine a product's promotion mix.

**16-6**   Describe how word-of-mouth communication affects promotion.

**16-7**   Discuss how product placement impacts promotion.

**16-8**   List major criticisms and defenses of promotion.

# MARKETING INSIGHTS

## Relax and Recline: La-Z-Boy's IMC Strategy

La-Z-Boy wants customers to know it sells more than recliners. Approximately 42 percent of La-Z-Boy's sales come from recliners, making the brand almost synonymous with its original product. Until recently La-Z-Boy core products were also associated with men, although women had become the primary decision makers in furniture purchases. La-Z-Boy therefore launched integrated marketing campaigns to reposition its brand.

In 2010 La-Z-Boy partnered with actress Brooke Shields as an endorser. One early advertisement featuring Shields targeted women as well as younger consumers interested in fashionable furniture. The advertisement claimed that "recliners were only the beginning" and listed additional furniture it offers. It also changed its long-running slogan from "Comfort is what we do" to "Live Life Comfortably."

La-Z-Boy's "Live Life Comfortably" campaign used a combination of print, television, and digital advertising to target younger consumers on their level. The campaign highlighted the company's "Urban Collection" of furniture, stressing its stylishness and affordability. Print advertisements appeared in *Martha Stewart Living*, *Real Simple*, and *Traditional Home*, while 30-second television spots were featured on networks such as A&E and OWN.

To make this campaign successful, however, La-Z-Boy could not ignore an essential component of the promotion mix: personal selling. In-store salespeople are critical to La-Z-Boy because they can personally assist consumers in their purchase decisions involving items that are often expensive. Customers also have the option of scheduling appointments with La-Z-Boy designers who will come to the consumer's house and offer advice on design projects. By using a strong mix of celebrity endorsements, advertising, and personal selling, La-Z-Boy has established a strong integrated marketing campaign likely to resonate with a younger, more urban demographic.[1]

Organizations like La-Z-Boy employ a variety of promotional methods to communicate with their target markets. Sometimes the messages are planned in advance. Other times, they may be a response to a dramatic change in the marketing environment. Providing information to customers and other stakeholders is vital to initiating and developing long-term relationships with them.

This chapter looks at the general dimensions of promotion. First, we discuss the nature of integrated marketing communications. Next, we analyze the meaning and process of communication. We then define and examine the role of promotion and explore some of the reasons promotion is used. We consider major promotional methods and the factors that influence marketers' decisions to use particular methods. Next, we explain the positive and negative effects of personal and electronic word-of-mouth communication. Finally, we examine criticisms and benefits of promotion.

## 16-1 THE NATURE OF INTEGRATED MARKETING COMMUNICATIONS

**Integrated marketing communications** refer to the coordination of promotion and other marketing efforts to ensure maximum informational and persuasive impact on customers. Coordinating multiple marketing tools to produce this synergistic effect requires a marketer to employ a broad perspective. A major goal of integrated marketing communications is to send a consistent message to customers. For instance, Domino's Pizza adopted a new ordering option in which its customers could order pies through a pizza emoji (smiley icons used in electronic messaging) sent to Domino's through text message or tweet. To market this new way of ordering, Domino's used a mixture of traditional television advertising and nontraditional digital media. An advertisement featuring an NFL player ordering pizza through Twitter was highly effective. Twitter feeds were also released written entirely in pizza emojis. The integrated marketing campaign was a success, and Domino's emoji ordering was mentioned 599 times on television shows. By the end of the year, 50 percent of Domino's orders in the United States was done digitally.[2]

Because various units both inside and outside most companies have traditionally planned and implemented promotional efforts, customers have not always received consistent messages. Integrated marketing communications allow an organization to coordinate and manage its promotional efforts to transmit consistent messages. Integrated marketing communications also enable synchronization of promotion elements and can improve the efficiency and effectiveness of promotion budgets. Thus, this approach fosters not only long-term customer relationships but also the efficient use of promotional resources.

The concept of integrated marketing communications is increasingly effective for several reasons. Mass media advertising, a very popular promotional method in the past, is used less frequently today because of its high cost and lower effectiveness in reaching some target markets. Marketers can now take advantage of more precisely targeted promotional tools, such as TV, direct mail, the Internet, special-interest magazines, smartphones, mobile applications, social media, sales calls, and outdoor boards. Database marketing and marketing analytics are also allowing marketers to target individual customers more precisely. Until recently, suppliers of marketing communications were specialists. Advertising agencies provided advertising campaigns, sales promotion companies provided sales promotion activities and materials, and public relations organizations engaged in publicity efforts. Today, a number of promotion-related companies provide one-stop shopping for the client seeking advertising, sales promotion, and public relations, thus reducing coordination problems for the sponsoring company. Because the overall cost of marketing communications has risen significantly, marketers demand systematic evaluations of communication efforts and a reasonable return on investment.

The specific communication vehicles employed and the precision with which they are used are changing as both information technology and customer interests become increasingly dynamic. For instance, companies and politicians can hold press conferences where viewers

**Integrated marketing communications** Coordination of promotion and other marketing efforts for maximum informational and persuasive impact on customers can tweet their questions and have them answered on-screen. Some companies are creating their own branded content to exploit the many vehicles through which consumers obtain information. IKEA, for instance, developed branded content featuring its catalog. Poking fun at technology, IKEA created a video that used tech language to rave about the many benefits of its catalog, including its "eternal battery life." A press release was also sent out to proclaim the marvels of the catalog over other technology.[3] Companies are turning toward branded content and other innovative communication media to engage users in ways that they can feel entertained without the pressure of being inundated with marketing messages.

Today, marketers and customers have almost unlimited access to data about each other. Integrating and customizing marketing communications while protecting customer privacy has become a major challenge. Through digital media, companies can provide product information and services that are coordinated with traditional promotional activities. In fact, gathering information about goods and services is one of the main reasons people go online. This has made digital marketing a growing business. Digital channels have become the second most common medium for advertisements after television.[4] College students in particular say they are influenced by Internet ads when buying online or just researching product purchases. The sharing of information and use of technology to facilitate communication between buyers and sellers are essential for successful customer relationship management.

# 16-2 PROMOTION AND THE COMMUNICATION PROCESS

Communication is essentially the transmission of information. For communication to take place, both the sender and receiver of information must share some common ground. They must have a common understanding of the symbols, words, and pictures used to transmit information. An individual transmitting the following message may believe he or she is communicating with you:

在工廠吾人製造化粧品，在商店吾人銷售希望。

However, communication has not taken place if you do not understand the language in which the message is written. Thus, we define **communication** as a sharing of meaning. Implicit in this definition is the notion of transmission of information because sharing necessitates transmission.

As Figure 16.1 shows, communication begins with a source. A **source** is a person, group, or organization with a meaning it attempts to share with an audience. A source could be an electronics salesperson wishing to communicate the attributes of 4D television to a buyer in the store or a TV manufacturer using television ads to inform thousands of consumers about its products. Developing a strategy can enhance the effectiveness of the source's communication. For example, a strategy in which a salesperson attempts to influence a customer's decision by eliminating competitive products from consideration has been found to be effective. A **receiver** is the individual, group, or organization that decodes a coded message, and an *audience* is two or more receivers.

To transmit meaning, a source must convert the meaning into a series of signs or symbols representing ideas or concepts. This is called the **coding process**, or *encoding*. When coding meaning into a message, the source must consider certain characteristics of the receiver or audience. This is especially true for advertising. It is important to encode messages to prevent consumers from avoiding a conscious reception. Costs to the consumer in attention, time, and emotional response can diminish the impact of the message.[5] Therefore, signs or symbols must resonate with the receiver.

**communication** A sharing of meaning through the transmission of information

**source** A person, group, or organization with a meaning it tries to share with a receiver or an audience

**receiver** The individual, group, or organization that decodes a coded message

**coding process** Converting meaning into a series of signs or symbols

Figure 16.1    **The Communication Process**

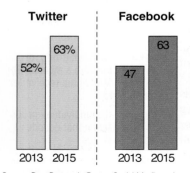

To share meaning, the source should use signs or symbols familiar to the receiver or audience. Research has shown that persuasive messages from a source are more effective when the appeal matches an individual's personality.[6] Marketers that understand this realize the importance of knowing their target market and ensuring that an advertisement or promotion uses language the target market understands and that depicts behaviors acceptable within the culture. With the Hispanic market growing rapidly, marketers are increasingly using Spanish language media in their advertisements.

When coding a meaning, a source needs to use signs or symbols that the receiver or audience uses to refer to the concepts the source intends to convey. Instead of technical jargon, explanatory language that helps consumers understand the message is more likely to result in positive attitudes and purchase intentions. Marketers try to avoid signs or symbols that may have several meanings for an audience. For instance, *soda* as a general term for soft drinks may not work well in national advertisements. Although in some parts of the United States the word means "soft drink," in other regions it may connote bicarbonate of soda, an ice cream drink, or something one mixes with alcoholic beverages.

**communications channel** The medium of transmission that carries the coded message from the source to the receiver

**decoding process** Converting signs or symbols into concepts and ideas

**noise** Anything that reduces a communication's clarity and accuracy

To share a coded meaning with the receiver or audience, a source selects and uses a **communications channel**, the medium of transmission that carries the coded message from the source to the receiver or audience. Transmission media include printed words (newspapers and magazines), broadcast media (television and radio), and digital communication. Figure 16.2 shows how consumers are increasingly getting their news from social media sites.

When a source chooses an inappropriate communication channel, several problems may arise. The coded message may reach some receivers, but possibly the wrong receivers. Dieters who adopt the Weight Watchers diet may hear endorser Oprah Winfrey say that she ate bread every day and lost 26 pounds.[7] This may attract some consumers who are not serious about dieting and who think that it is easy. An advertiser that wants to reach a specific target market would need to take this information into account when choosing an appropriate communications message and channel. While the Weight Watchers diet may be effective in helping people to lose weight, the purpose is not to attract people that want an excuse to eat whatever they want. Thus, finding the right messages that target the right receivers can be a challenging process.

In the **decoding process**, signs or symbols are converted into concepts and ideas. Seldom does a receiver decode exactly the same meaning the source intended. When the result of decoding differs from what was coded, noise exists.

**Noise** is anything that reduces the clarity and accuracy of the communication; it has many sources and may affect any or all parts of the communication process. Noise

Figure 16.2    **Percentage of Users who Get Their News from Facebook or Twitter**

**Twitter**
- 2013: 52%
- 2015: 63%

**Facebook**
- 2013: 47
- 2015: 63

Source: Pew Research Center, Social Media and News Survey, March 13–15 & 20–22, 2015.

sometimes arises within the communications channel itself. Radio or television transmission difficulties, poor or slow Internet connections, and laryngitis are sources of noise. Noise also occurs when a source uses signs or symbols that are unfamiliar to the receiver or have a meaning different from the one intended. Noise may also originate in the receiver; a receiver may be unaware of a coded message when perceptual processes block it out. Those who do not recycle, for instance, can block messages encouraging "green behaviors" such as recycling.

The receiver's response to a decoded message is **feedback** to the source. The source usually expects and normally receives feedback, although perhaps not immediately. During feedback, the receiver or audience provides the original source with a response to the message. Feedback is coded, sent through a communications channel, and decoded by the receiver, the source of the original communication. Thus, communication is a circular process, as indicated in Figure 16.1.

During face-to-face communication, such as personal selling sales promotions, verbal and nonverbal feedback can be immediate. Instant feedback lets communicators adjust messages quickly to improve the effectiveness of their communications. For example, when a salesperson realizes through feedback that a customer does not understand a sales presentation, the salesperson adapts the presentation to make it more meaningful to the customer. This is why face-to-face communication is the most adaptive and flexible, especially compared to digital, web-based, or telephone communications. In interpersonal communication, feedback occurs through talking, touching, smiling, nodding, eye movements, and other body movements and postures.

When mass communication like advertising is used, feedback is often slow and difficult to recognize. Also, it may be several months or even years before the effects of this promotion will be known. Some relevant and timely feedback can occur in the form of sales increases, inquiries about products, or changes in attitude or brand awareness levels.

Each communication channel has a limit on the volume of information it can handle effectively. This limit, called **channel capacity**, is determined by the least efficient component of the communication process. Consider communications that depend on speech. An individual source can speak only so fast, and there is a limit to how much an individual receiver can take in through listening. Beyond that point, additional messages cannot be decoded; thus, meaning cannot be shared. Although a radio announcer can read several hundred words a minute, a 1-minute advertising message should not exceed 150 words, because most announcers cannot articulate words into understandable messages at a rate beyond 150 words per minute.

## 16-3 THE ROLE AND OBJECTIVES OF PROMOTION

**Promotion** is communication that builds and maintains favorable relationships by informing and persuading one or more audiences to view an organization positively and accept its products. Toward this end, many organizations spend considerable resources on promotion to build and enhance relationships with current and potential customers as well as other stakeholders. Case in point, the top ten advertisers in the United States spent more than $15 billion on advertising. Procter & Gamble spends about $2.6 billion on advertising yearly, with more expenditures being spent toward digital marketing channels.[8] Marketers also indirectly facilitate favorable relationships by focusing information about company activities and products on interest groups (such as environmental and consumer groups), current and potential investors, regulatory agencies, and society in general. For instance, some organizations promote responsible use of products criticized by society, such as tobacco, alcohol, and violent movies or video games. Companies sometimes promote programs that help selected groups. For example, Coca-Cola was a founding member of the Special Olympics, a sports organization for people with

**feedback** The receiver's response to a decoded message

**channel capacity** The limit on the volume of information a communication channel can handle effectively

**promotion** Communication to build and maintain relationships by informing and persuading one or more audiences

Figure 16.3    **Information Flows Are Important in Integrated Marketing Communications**

intellectual disabilities. It provides in-kind donations, volunteer hours, financial contributions, and publicity for the organization.[9] Such cause-related marketing links the purchase of products to philanthropic efforts for one or more causes. By contributing to causes that its target markets support, cause-related marketing can help marketers boost sales, increase loyalty, and generate goodwill.

For maximum benefit from promotional efforts, marketers strive for proper planning, implementation, coordination, and control of communications. Effective management of integrated marketing communications is based on information about and feedback from customers and the marketing environment, often obtained from an organization's marketing information system (see Figure 16.3). How successfully marketers use promotion to maintain positive relationships depends to some extent on the quantity and quality of information the organization receives. Because customers derive information and opinions from many different sources, integrated marketing communications planning also takes into account informal methods of communication, such as word of mouth and independent information sources on the Internet. Because promotion is communication that can be managed, we now analyze what this communication is and how it works.

Promotional objectives vary considerably from one organization to another and within organizations over time. Large firms with multiple promotional programs operating simultaneously may have quite varied promotional objectives. For the purpose of analysis, we focus on the eight promotional objectives shown in Table 16.1. Although the list is not exhaustive, one or more of these objectives underlie many promotional programs.

## 16-3a  Create Awareness

A considerable amount of promotion efforts focus on creating awareness. For an organization that is introducing a new product or a line extension, making customers aware of the product is crucial to initiating the product adoption process. A marketer that has invested heavily in product development strives to create product awareness quickly to generate revenues to offset the high costs of product development and introduction. Apple often begins to build awareness about new products months before it releases them. It holds an annual developer conference, where CEO Tim Cook often discusses the features of products that will be released later in the year.[10] The Penske advertisement creates awareness among business readers about the costliness of delays and how Penske can help solve this problem with its logistics services.

Table 16.1  **Possible Objectives of Promotion**

| | |
|---|---|
| Create awareness | Retain loyal customers |
| Stimulate demand | Facilitate reseller support |
| Encourage product trial | Combat competitive promotional efforts |
| Identify prospects | Reduce sales fluctuations |

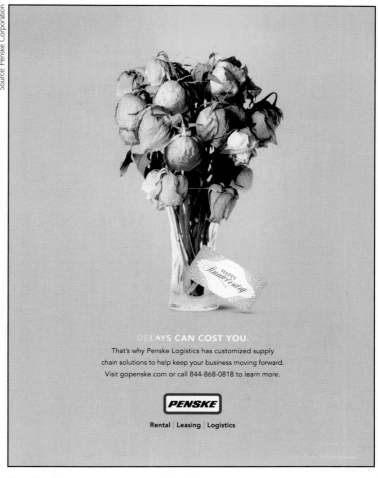

Creating awareness is important for existing products, too. Promotional efforts may aim to increase awareness of brands, product features, image-related issues (such as organizational size or socially responsive behavior), or operational characteristics (such as store hours, locations, and credit availability). Some promotional programs are unsuccessful because marketers fail to generate awareness of critical issues among a significant portion of target market members. Other times, the campaign itself is at fault. Bud Light was criticized for a campaign in which it released 140 labels on its different bottles. In an attempt to portray the beer as the beer of choice for an exciting night, one of the labels claimed that Bud Light would eliminate the word "no" for the night. Critics believed this encouraged the concept of date rape. Bud Light apologized and removed the label.[11]

## 16-3b Stimulate Demand

When an organization is the first to introduce an innovative product, it tries to stimulate **primary demand**—demand for a product category rather than for a specific brand of product—through **pioneer promotion**. Pioneer promotion informs potential customers about the product: what it is, what it does, how it can be used, and where it can be purchased. Because pioneer promotion is used in the introductory stage of the product life cycle, meaning there are no competing brands, it neither emphasizes brand names nor compares brands. This tactic was taken when introducing chia seeds to the food market. Less than a decade ago, the nutritional benefits of chia seeds were relatively unknown. Advertisers therefore had to engage in pioneer advertising to spread awareness of the product category before focusing on specific brands. Today 37 percent of the U.S. population has heard of chia seeds as a food item.[12]

**Creating Awareness**
Penske Logistics uses a depiction of wilting flowers to demonstrate how delays can be costly for businesses. Penske is attempting to create awareness about its services so business customers will remember its brand when looking for logistics solutions.

To build **selective demand**, demand for a specific brand, a marketer employs promotional efforts that point out the strengths and benefits of a specific brand. Consider the advertisement for Mars Drinks. The advertisement depicts a businessman going through a tire run to demonstrate the challenges of the typical workday. The ad promotes its Mars Drinks product as the solution to staying productive and energized during the busy work day. Because the advertisement portrays a specific brand, it builds selective demand for the product. Building selective demand also requires singling out attributes important to potential buyers. Selective demand can be stimulated by differentiating the product from competing brands in the minds of potential buyers. Selective demand can also be stimulated by increasing the number of product uses and promoting them through advertising campaigns, as well as through price discounts, free samples, coupons, consumer contests and games, and sweepstakes. For example, Payless often offers buy-one-get-one free sales promotions to build selective demand for the company. Promotions for large package sizes or multiple-product packages are directed at increasing consumption, which in turn can stimulate demand. In addition, selective demand can be stimulated by encouraging existing customers to use more of the product.

**primary demand** Demand for a product category rather than for a specific brand

**pioneer promotion** Promotion that informs consumers about a new product

**selective demand** Demand for a specific brand

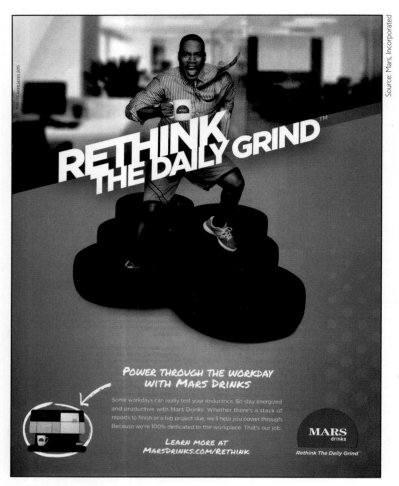

Source: Mars, Incorporated

RETHINK THE DAILY GRIND™

POWER THROUGH THE WORKDAY WITH MARS DRINKS

Some workdays can really test your endurance. So stay energized and productive with Mars Drinks. Whether there's a stack of reports to finish or a big project due, we'll help you power through. Because we're 100% dedicated to the workplace. That's our job.

LEARN MORE AT MARSDRINKS.COM/RETHINK

**MARS** drinks

*Rethink The Daily Grind™*

**Building Selective Demand**
This advertisement builds selective demand by focusing on a specific product—Mars Drinks.

### 16-3c Encourage Product Trial

When attempting to move customers through the product adoption process, a marketer may successfully create awareness and interest, but customers may stall during the evaluation stage. In this case, certain types of promotion—such as free samples, coupons, test drives, or limited free-use offers, contests, and games—are employed to encourage product trial. Texas supermarket chain H.E.B. uses free sampling kiosks and demo kitchens to offer free samples throughout its stores.[13] Whether a marketer's product is the first in a new product category, a new brand in an existing category, or simply an existing brand seeking customers, trial-inducing promotional efforts aim to make product trial convenient and low risk for potential customers.

### 16-3d Identify Prospects

Certain types of promotional efforts aim to identify customers who are interested in the firm's product and are likely potential buyers. A marketer may run a television advertisement encouraging the viewer to visit the company's website and share personal information in order to receive something of value from the company. Customers who respond to such a message usually have higher interest in the product, which makes them likely sales prospects. The organization can respond with phone calls, e-mail, or personal contact by salespeople.

### 16-3e Retain Loyal Customers

Clearly, maintaining long-term customer relationships is a major goal of most marketers. Such relationships are quite valuable. Promotional efforts directed at customer retention can help an organization control its costs, because the costs of retaining customers are usually considerably lower than those of acquiring new ones. Frequent-user programs, such as those sponsored by airlines, car rental agencies, and hotels, aim to reward loyal customers and encourage them to remain loyal. Often airlines provide frequent flyer miles and other benefits for upgrades as well as the use of the company's credit card. Some organizations employ special offers that only their existing customers can use. To retain loyal customers, marketers not only advertise loyalty programs but also use reinforcement advertising, which assures current users that they have made the right brand choice and tells them how to get the most satisfaction from the product.

### 16-3f Facilitate Reseller Support

Reseller support is a two-way street: producers generally want to provide support to resellers to assist in selling their products, and in turn they expect resellers to support their products. When a manufacturer advertises a product to consumers, resellers should view this promotion as a form of strong manufacturer support. In some instances, a producer agrees to pay a certain proportion of retailers' advertising expenses for promoting its products. When a manufacturer is introducing a new consumer brand in a highly competitive product category, it may be difficult to persuade supermarket managers to carry this brand. However, if the manufacturer promotes the new brand with free samples and coupon distribution in the retailer's area, a supermarket manager views these actions as strong support and is much more likely to carry the product. To encourage wholesalers and retailers to increase their inventories of its products, a manufacturer may provide them with special offers and buying allowances. In certain industries, a producer's salesperson may provide support to a wholesaler by working with the wholesaler's customers (retailers) in the presentation and promotion of the products. Strong relationships with resellers are important to a firm's ability to maintain a sustainable competitive advantage. The use of various promotional methods can help an organization achieve this goal.

## 16-3g Combat Competitive Promotional Efforts

At times, a marketer's objective in using promotion is to offset or lessen the effect of a competitor's promotional or marketing programs. This type of promotional activity does not necessarily increase the organization's sales or market share, but it may prevent a sales or market share loss. A combative promotional objective is used most often by firms in extremely competitive consumer markets, such as the fast-food, convenience store, and cable/Internet/phone markets. PepsiCo took a combative promotional approach to Coca-Cola to market its Pepsi loyalty program and Pepsi Pass app. The advertisement mocked the Coca-Cola polar bear and its popular "Share a Coke" campaign.[14] It is not unusual for competitors to respond with a counter-pricing strategy or even match a competitor's pricing.

## 16-3h Reduce Sales Fluctuations

Demand for many products varies from one month to another because of such factors as climate, holidays, and seasons. A business, however, cannot operate at peak efficiency when sales fluctuate rapidly. Changes in sales volume translate into changes in production, inventory levels, personnel needs, and financial resources. When promotional techniques reduce fluctuations by generating sales during slow periods, a firm can use its resources more efficiently.

Promotional techniques are often designed to stimulate sales during sales slumps. Hence, Snapper may offer sales prices on lawn mowers into the fall season to extend the selling season. During peak periods, a marketer may refrain from advertising to prevent stimulating sales to the point at which the firm cannot handle all of the demand. On occasion, a company advertises

Dwight Smith/Shutterstock.com

**Seasonal Demand**
Swimsuit apparel is subject to seasonal demand, with demand peaking in the summer and bottoming out in the fall and winter. To balance demand, marketers might use promotion such as coupons or advertisements that encourage consumers to purchase these products during off-peak periods.

that customers can be better served by coming in on certain days. An Italian restaurant, for example, might distribute coupons that are valid only Monday through Wednesday because on Thursday through Sunday the restaurant is extremely busy.

To achieve the major objectives of promotion discussed here, companies must develop appropriate promotional programs. In the next section, we consider the basic components of such programs: the promotion mix elements.

## 16-4 **THE PROMOTION MIX**

Several promotional methods can be used to communicate with individuals, groups, and organizations. When an organization combines specific methods to manage the integrated marketing communications for a particular product, that combination constitutes the promotion mix for that product. The four possible elements of a **promotion mix** are advertising, personal selling, public relations, and sales promotion (see Figure 16.4). For some products, firms use all four elements; for others, they use only two or three. In this section, we provide an overview of each promotion mix element; they are covered in greater detail in the next two chapters.

### 16-4a **Advertising**

Advertising is a paid nonpersonal communication about an organization and its products transmitted to a target audience through mass media, including television, radio, the Internet, newspapers, magazines, video games, direct mail, outdoor displays, and signs on mass transit vehicles. Advertising is changing as consumers' mass media consumption habits are changing. Companies are striving to maximize their presence and impact through digital media; ads are being designed that cater to smaller, more personalized audiences; and traditional media like newspapers are in a decline due to a drop in readership. Individuals and organizations use advertising to promote goods, services, ideas, issues, and people. Being highly flexible, advertising can reach an extremely large target audience or focus on a small, precisely defined segment. For instance, Sonic's advertising focuses on a large audience of potential fast-food customers, ranging from children to adults, whereas advertising for Gulfstream jets aims at a much smaller and more specialized target market.

**promotion mix** A combination of promotional methods used to promote a specific product

Figure 16.4    **The Four Possible Elements of a Promotion Mix**

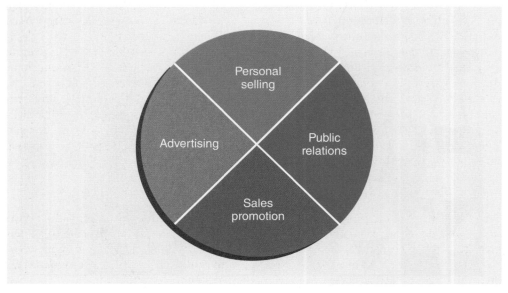

Advertising offers several benefits. It is extremely cost-efficient when it reaches a vast number of people at a low cost per person. For example, the cost of a 4-color, full-page advertisement in the national edition of *Time* magazine costs $352,500. With a circulation of 1.6 million, this makes the cost of reaching roughly a thousand subscribers $220.[15] Advertising also lets the source repeat the message several times. Subway credits its promotional and advertising success to a catchy theme and heavy repetition of its "$5.00 footlong" sub sandwich campaign. Furthermore, advertising a product a certain way can add to the product's value, and the visibility an organization gains from advertising can enhance its image. For instance, incorporating touchable elements that generate positive sensory feedback in print advertising can be a positive persuasive tool.[16] At times, a firm tries to enhance its own or its product's image by including celebrity endorsers in advertisements. ZICO Beverages LLC partnered with actress Jessica Alba to endorse its Zico® Premium Coconut Water™. The advertisement shows Jessica Alba happily holding up her bottle of coconut water. By using Alba as an endorser, ZICO is able to capitalize on her status as a celebrity.

Advertising has disadvantages as well. Even though the cost per person reached may be low, the absolute dollar outlay can be extremely high, especially for commercials during popular television shows and those associated with popular websites. High costs can limit, and sometimes preclude, the use

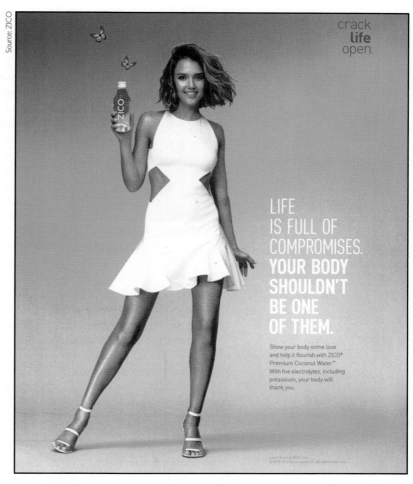

**Celebrity Endorsers**
Jessica Alba endorses coconut water for ZICO Beverages LLC. ZICO is able to capitalize on Alba's popularity as an actress to convince others to give it a try.

of advertising in a promotion mix. Moreover, advertising rarely provides rapid feedback. Measuring its effect on sales is often difficult, and it is ordinarily less persuasive than personal selling. However, advertising can be highly effective in driving sales for products such as fast foods. One research study found that half of McDonald's growth could be explained by variables related to the quality of its advertising.[17] For example, McDonald's breakfast-all-day advertising caused its sales to spike. In most instances, the time available to communicate a message to customers is limited to seconds, because people look at a print advertisement for only a few seconds, and most broadcast commercials are 30 seconds or less. Of course, the use of infomercials can increase exposure time for viewers; however, the format can disengage more sophisticated buyers. Finally, using spokespeople such as celebrities can be challenging as well. When Subway endorser Jared Fogle, well-known for losing vast amounts of weight on the Subway diet, was convicted of sexual misconduct involving underage women, Subway sought to distance itself from its long-time spokesman.[18]

## 16-4b Personal Selling

Personal selling is a paid personal communication that seeks to inform customers and persuade them to purchase products in an exchange situation. The phrase *purchase products* is interpreted broadly to encompass acceptance of ideas and issues. Personal selling is most extensively used in the business-to-business market and also in the business-to-consumer market for high-end products such as homes, cars, electronics, and furniture.

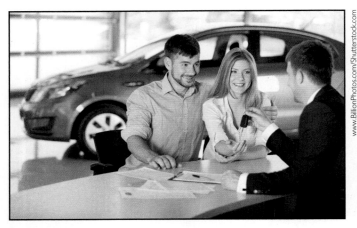

www.BillionPhotos.com/Shutterstock.com

**Personal Selling**
Although expensive, personal selling is especially useful in high-risk transactions such as purchasing a new car.

Personal selling has both advantages and limitations when compared with advertising. Advertising is general communication aimed at a relatively large target audience, whereas personal selling involves more specific communication directed at one or several individuals. Reaching one person through personal selling costs considerably more than through advertising, but personal selling efforts often have greater impact on customers. Personal selling also provides immediate feedback, allowing marketers to adjust their messages to improve communication. Such interaction helps them determine and respond to customers' information needs.

When a salesperson and a customer meet face-to-face, they use several types of interpersonal communication. The predominant communication form is language, both spoken and written. A salesperson and customer frequently use **kinesic communication**, or communication through the movement of head, eyes, arms, hands, legs, or torso. Winking, head nodding, hand gestures, and arm motions are some forms of kinesic communication. A good salesperson can often evaluate a prospect's interest in a product or presentation by noting eye contact and head nodding. **Proxemic communication**, a less obvious form of communication used in personal selling situations, occurs when either person varies the physical distance separating them. When a customer backs away from a salesperson, for example, he or she may be displaying a lack of interest in the product or expressing dislike for the salesperson. Touching, or **tactile communication**, is also a form of communication, although less popular in the United States than in many other countries. Handshaking is a common form of tactile communication both in the United States and elsewhere.

Sales managers need a variety of skills to oversee the sales force. These skills include interpersonal, technical, as well as strategic skills. The importance of these different types of skills depends largely on the level of management.[19] For instance, sales managers need strong leadership skills and must be able to use sales management technology to track and control sales strategies.

## 16-4c Public Relations

Although many promotional activities focus on a firm's customers, other stakeholders—suppliers, employees, stockholders, the media, educators, potential investors, government officials, and society in general—are important to an organization as well. To communicate with customers and stakeholders, a company employs public relations. Public relations is a broad set of communication efforts used to create and maintain favorable relationships between an organization and its stakeholders. Maintaining a positive relationship with one or more stakeholders can affect a firm's current sales and profits, as well as its long-term survival.

Public relations uses a variety of tools, including annual reports, brochures, event sponsorship, and sponsorship of socially responsible programs aimed at protecting the environment or helping disadvantaged individuals. The goal of public relations is to create and enhance a positive image of the organization. Increasingly, marketers are going directly to consumers with their public relations efforts to bypass the traditional media intermediary (newspapers, magazines, and television). Pampered Chef placed content on YouTube that shows consumers how to make certain recipes. This content familiarizes consumers with Pampered Chef and positions the organization as a helper in the kitchen.[20]

Other tools arise from the use of publicity, which is a component of public relations. Publicity is nonpersonal communication in news-story form about an organization or its products, or both, transmitted through a mass medium at no charge. A few examples of publicity-based public relations tools are news releases, press conferences, and feature articles. To generate

**kinesic communication**
Communicating through the movement of head, eyes, arms, hands, legs, or torso

**proxemic communication**
Communicating by varying the physical distance in face-to-face interactions

**tactile communication**
Communicating through touching

publicity, companies sometimes give away products to celebrities in the hope that the celebrities will be seen and photographed with the product, and those photos will stimulate awareness and product trial among their fans. However, to ensure that consumers are not deceived, the Federal Trade Commission requires bloggers, celebrities, and anyone else who receives something of value for endorsing a product to disclose this fact.[21] Ordinarily, public relations efforts are planned and implemented to be consistent with and support other elements of the promotion mix. Public relations efforts may be the responsibility of an individual or of a department within the organization, or the organization may hire an independent public relations agency.

Unpleasant situations and negative events, such as product tampering or an environmental disaster, may generate unfavorable public relations for an organization. For instance, one Krispy Kreme doughnut location in the United Kingdom wanted to promote an event on Wednesdays called Krispy Kreme Klub. Unfortunately, its post on Facebook was abbreviated as KKK Wednesday, sparking outrage from consumers. The company removed the post and issued an apology.[22] To minimize the damaging effects of unfavorable coverage, effective marketers have policies and procedures in place to help manage any public relations problems.

Public relations should not be viewed as a set of tools to be used only during crises. To get the most from public relations, an organization should have someone responsible for public relations either internally or externally and should have an ongoing public relations program.

## 16-4d Sales Promotion

Sales promotion is an activity or material that acts as a direct inducement, offering added value or incentive for the product to resellers, salespeople, or consumers. Examples include free samples, games, rebates, sweepstakes, contests, premiums, and coupons. *Sales promotion* should not be confused with *promotion*; sales promotion is just one part of the comprehensive area of promotion. Marketers spend more on sales promotion than on advertising, and sales promotion appears to be a faster-growing area than advertising. Omaha Steaks, Inc. encourages consumers to purchase its products by releasing advertisements featuring photos of its steaks, the types of food included in its Family Gourmet Feast, and discount information. Omaha Steaks uses a cents-off offer in which the price is drastically reduced, and consumers get the chance to receive four free sausages if they order within a certain time period.

Generally, when companies employ advertising or personal selling, they depend on these activities continuously or cyclically. However, a marketer's use of sales promotion tends to be irregular. Many products are seasonal. Toys may be discounted in January after the holiday selling season to move

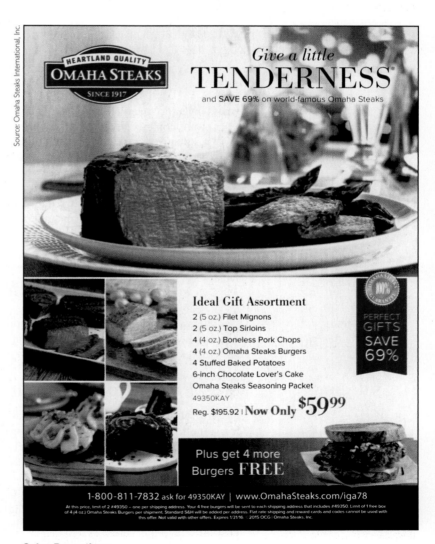

**Sales Promotions**
In addition to attracting customers with its depictions of a quality steak dinner, Omaha Steaks also offers price reductions and free items if customers place an order within a certain time period.

# Entrepreneurship in Marketing

## How to Get "Ginned Up" at Home

**Founders:** Joe and Sarah Maiellano and Jack and Molly Hubbard
**Business:** The Homemade Gin Kit
**Founded:** 2012, in Arlington, VA
**Success:** The Homemade Gin Kit has been featured in over 250 media outlets and is now sold in high-end stores such as Anthropologie and Williams-Sonoma.

Joe and Sarah Maiellano and Jack and Molly Hubbard wanted to open a distillery but could not afford it. Instead, they decided to sell their own do-it-yourself gin kit through an e-commerce site. Priced at $49.95, the kit contains ingredients and tools for making gin. The Homemade Gin Kit outgrew the living room where it originated and expanded to a facility.

The founders knew their success required a strong search engine optimization (SEO) presence. SEO involves affecting a website's visibility in a search engine's search results. The higher the link's location, the more likely an Internet user is to click on it.

The founders turned to traditional public relations tactics to boost its SEO. They sent samples and press releases to bloggers, media, and gift guide curators. Soon the kit appeared in a popular e-newsletter gift guide, and within an 18-month period the Homemade Gin Kit was featured in 250 media outlets. The company has since expanded to high-end gift stores such as Total Wine and Anthropologie.[a]

excess inventory. Marketers frequently rely on sales promotion to improve the effectiveness of other promotion mix elements, especially advertising and personal selling. Coupons appear to be more effective for food marketers. It is estimated that two-thirds of all coupons redeemed are for food offers.[23] The redemption of digital coupons is growing. Mobile devices are a personal technology, so mobile coupons pose an unusual opportunity to reach consumers wherever they go.

An effective promotion mix requires the right combination of components. To see how such a mix is created, we now examine the factors and conditions affecting the selection of promotional methods that an organization uses for a particular product.

# 16-5 SELECTING PROMOTION MIX FACTORS

Marketers vary the composition of promotion mixes for many reasons. Although a promotion mix can include all four elements, frequently, a marketer selects fewer than four. Many firms that market multiple product lines use several promotion mixes simultaneously.

## 16-5a Promotional Resources, Objectives, and Policies

The size of an organization's promotional budget affects the number and relative intensity of promotional methods included in a promotion mix. If a company's promotional budget is extremely limited, the firm is likely to rely on personal selling because it is easier to measure a salesperson's contribution to sales than to measure the sales effectiveness of advertising. Businesses must have sizable promotional budgets to use regional or national advertising. Companies such as Procter & Gamble, Unilever, General Motors, and Coca-Cola are among the leaders in worldwide media spending. Organizations with extensive promotional resources generally include more elements in their promotion mixes, but having more promotional dollars to spend does not necessarily mean using more promotional methods. Researchers have found that resources spent on promotion activities have a positive influence on shareholder value.

An organization's promotional objectives and policies also influence the types of promotion selected. If a company's objective is to create mass awareness of a new convenience good, such as a breakfast cereal, its promotion mix probably leans heavily toward advertising, sales promotion, and possibly public relations. If a company hopes to educate consumers about the features of a durable good, such as a home appliance, its promotion mix may combine a moderate amount of advertising, possibly some sales promotion designed to attract customers to retail stores, and a great deal of personal selling, because this method is an efficient way to inform customers about such products. If a firm's objective is to produce immediate sales of nondurable services, the promotion mix will probably stress advertising and sales promotion. For instance, dry cleaners and carpet-cleaning firms are more likely to use advertising with a coupon or discount rather than personal selling.

## 16-5b  Characteristics of the Target Market

Size, geographic distribution, and demographic characteristics of an organization's target market help dictate the methods to include in a product's promotion mix. To some degree, market size and diversity determine composition of the mix. If the size is limited, the promotion mix will probably emphasize personal selling, which can be very effective for reaching small numbers of people. Organizations selling to industrial markets and firms marketing products through only a few wholesalers frequently make personal selling the major component of their promotion mixes. When a product's market consists of millions of customers, organizations rely on advertising and sales promotion, because these methods reach masses of people at a low cost per person. When the population density is uneven around the country, marketers may utilize regional advertising and target larger markets.

Geographic distribution of a firm's customers also affects the choice of promotional methods. Personal selling is more feasible if a company's customers are concentrated in a small area than if they are dispersed across a vast region. When the company's customers are numerous and dispersed, regional or national advertising may be more practical.

Distribution of a target market's demographic characteristics, such as age, income, or education, may affect the types of promotional techniques a marketer selects, as well as the messages and images employed. According to the U.S. Census Bureau, so-called traditional families—those composed of married couples with children—account for fewer than one-quarter of all U.S. households.[24] To reach the more than three-quarters of households consisting of single parents, unmarried couples, singles, and "empty nesters" (whose children have left home), more companies are modifying the images used in their promotions.

## 16-5c  Characteristics of the Product

Generally, promotion mixes for business products concentrate on personal selling, whereas advertising plays a major role in promoting consumer goods. This generalization should be treated cautiously, however. Marketers of business products use some advertising to promote products. Advertisements for computers, road-building equipment, and aircraft are fairly common, and some sales promotion is also used occasionally to promote business products. Personal selling is used extensively for consumer durables, such as home appliances, automobiles, and houses, whereas consumer convenience items are promoted mainly through advertising and sales promotion. Public relations appears in promotion mixes for both business and consumer products.

Marketers of highly seasonal products often emphasize advertising—and sometimes sales promotion as well—because off-season sales generally will not support an extensive year-round sales force. Although most toy producers have sales forces to sell to resellers, many of these companies depend chiefly on advertising and strong distribution channels to promote their products.

A product's price also influences the composition of the promotion mix. High-priced products call for personal selling, because consumers associate greater risk with the purchase of such products and usually want information from a salesperson. For low-priced convenience

Source: Standard Life PLC

**Potential.** **Delivered.**

Identifying and converting potential can be challenging, especially in volatile markets. It requires conviction, discipline and a focus on the long-term.

At Standard Life Investments, we understand the value of potential.

With expertise across a wide range of asset classes, backed by our distinctive *Focus on Change* investment philosophy, we constantly think ahead and strive to anticipate change before it happens.

This forward-thinking approach helps our clients look to the future with confidence.

Take the long-term view today at us.standardlifeinvestments.com

The value of an investment can fall as well as rise and is not guaranteed. You may get back less than you put in. Past performance is not a guide to future performance.

Equities · Fixed Income · Real Estate · Multi-asset · Private Equity
This communication is for US institutional investors only

**Standard Life Investments**

WORLDWIDE PARTNER

The Ryder Cup logo is a trademark owned by The Professional Golfers' Association of America. This material is not intended as an offer to sell or a solicitation of an offer to buy any security, and does not constitute investment advice. Standard Life Investments (USA) Limited and Standard Life Investments (Corporate Funds) Limited are both registered as an Investment Adviser with the US Securities and Exchange Commission. Standard Life Investments Limited is registered in Scotland (SC123321) at 1 George Street, Edinburgh EH2 2LL. Standard Life Investments Limited and Standard Life Investments (Corporate Funds) Limited are authorized and regulated in the U.K. by the Financial Conduct Authority. © 2015 Standard Life. Images reproduced under licence.

**Portraying Characteristics of Service Products**

Service products, such as Standard Life Investments' financial services, are often portrayed using tangible goods that tell a story about the service. In this advertisement, Standard Life Investments contrasts coal with a diamond to show how Standard Life can take a customer's potential and turn it into something valuable.

items, marketers use advertising rather than personal selling. Research suggests that consumers visiting a store specifically to purchase a product on sale are more likely to have read flyers and purchased other sale-priced products than consumers visiting the same store for other reasons.[25]

Another consideration in creating an effective promotion mix is the stage of the product life cycle. During the introduction stage, advertising is used to create awareness for both business and consumer products. Apple released commercials promoting the ease and convenience of its Apple Watch. It released six different ads showing situations in which people from all walks of life can use the smart watch to manage and transform the messiness of life to achieve their objectives happily and efficiently.[26] For many products, personal selling and sales promotion are also helpful in this stage. In the growth and maturity stages, consumer products require heavy emphasis on advertising, whereas business products often call for a concentration of personal selling and some sales promotion. In the decline stage, marketers usually decrease all promotional activities, especially advertising.

Intensity of market coverage is still another factor affecting the composition of the promotion mix. When products are marketed through intensive distribution, firms depend strongly on advertising and sales promotion. Many convenience products like lotions, cereals, and coffee are promoted through samples, coupons, and refunds. When marketers choose selective distribution, promotion mixes vary considerably. Items handled through exclusive distribution—such as expensive watches, furs, and high-quality furniture—typically require a significant amount of personal selling.

A product's use also affects the combination of promotional methods. Manufacturers of highly personal products, such as laxatives, nonprescription contraceptives, and feminine hygiene products, depend on advertising because many customers do not want to talk with salespeople about these products. Service businesses often use tangible products to promote their intangible services. Standard Life Investments released an advertisement depicting coal on one side of the ad and a diamond on the other to demonstrate how its services can deliver a person's potential from opportunity to value. These tangible elements reassure the audience about the value of Standard Life Investments services.

## 16-5d Costs and Availability of Promotional Methods

Costs of promotional methods are major factors to analyze when developing a promotion mix. National advertising and sales promotion require large expenditures. However, if these efforts succeed in reaching extremely large audiences, the cost per individual reached may be quite small, possibly a few pennies. Some forms of advertising are relatively inexpensive. Many small, local businesses advertise products through local newspapers, magazines, radio and television stations, outdoor displays, Internet ads, and signs on mass transit vehicles.

Another consideration that marketers explore when formulating a promotion mix is the availability of promotional techniques. Despite the tremendous number of media vehicles in the United States, a firm may find that no available advertising medium effectively reaches a certain target market. The problem of media availability becomes more pronounced when marketers advertise in foreign countries. Some media, such as television, simply may not be available, or advertising on television may be illegal. For instance, the advertising of cigarettes on television is banned in many countries. In addition, regulations or standards for media content may be restrictive in varying global outlets. In some countries, advertisers are forbidden to make brand comparisons on television. Other promotional methods also have limitations. Thus, a firm may wish to increase its sales force but be unable to find qualified personnel.

## 16-5e Push and Pull Channel Policies

Another element that marketers consider when planning a promotion mix is whether to use a push policy or a pull policy. With a **push policy**, the producer promotes the product only to the next institution down the marketing channel. In a marketing channel with wholesalers and retailers, the producer promotes to the wholesaler because, in this case, the wholesaler is the channel member just below the producer (see Figure 16.5). Each channel member in turn promotes to the next channel member. A push policy normally stresses personal selling. Sometimes sales promotion and advertising are used in conjunction with personal selling to push the products down through the channel.

As Figure 16.5 shows, a firm that uses a **pull policy** promotes directly to consumers to develop strong consumer demand for its products. It does so primarily through advertising and sales promotion. Because consumers are persuaded to seek the products in retail stores, retailers in turn go to wholesalers or the producers to buy the products. This policy is intended to pull the goods down through the channel by creating demand at the consumer level. Consumers are told that if the stores do not have it, then they should request that the stores begin carrying the product. Push and pull policies are not mutually exclusive. At times, an organization uses both simultaneously.

**push policy** Promoting a product only to the next institution down the marketing channel

**pull policy** Promoting a product directly to consumers to develop strong consumer demand that pulls products through the marketing channel

Figure 16.5    **Comparison of Push and Pull Promotional Strategies**

## 16-6 THE IMPACT OF WORD-OF-MOUTH COMMUNICATIONS ON PROMOTION

When making decisions about the composition of promotion mixes, marketers should recognize that commercial messages, whether from advertising, personal selling, sales promotion, or public relations, are limited in the extent to which they can inform and persuade customers and move them closer to making purchases. Depending on the type of customers and the products involved, buyers to some extent rely on word-of-mouth communication from personal sources, such as family members and friends. **Word-of-mouth communication** is personal, informal exchanges of communication that customers share with one another about products, brands, and companies. Most customers are likely to be influenced by friends and family members when they make purchases. Word-of-mouth communication is very important when people are selecting restaurants and entertainment along with automotive, medical, legal, banking, and personal services like hair care. Research has identified a link between word-of-mouth communication and new-customer acquisition when there is customer involvement and satisfaction.[27] For this reason, organizations should proactively manage their word-of-mouth communications.[28]

Effective marketers who understand the importance of word-of-mouth communication attempt to identify opinion leaders and encourage them to try their products in the hope that they will spread favorable publicity about them. Apple, for example, has long relied on its nearly cult consumer following to spread by word of mouth their satisfaction with Apple products such as MacBooks, iPods, iPhones, and iPads. The impact of consumer-generated communication—communication not made by companies—is powerful and stands strong compared to commercial messages.[29] Firms need to develop proactive management of word-of-mouth communication that considers both the sender and the receiver.[30] Interestingly, women—unlike men—are more likely to share negative word of mouth with those they have strong social ties with rather than those with which they have weak social ties. Overall, consumers are more likely to share negative word-of-mouth information than positive word-of-mouth communication.[31]

In addition, customers are increasingly going online for information and opinions about goods and services as well as about the companies. Electronic word of mouth is communicating about products through websites, blogs, e-mail, social networks, or online forums. Users can go to a number of consumer-oriented websites, such as epinions.com and consumerreview.com. At these sites, they can learn about other consumers' feelings toward and experiences with specific products; some sites even encourage consumers to rate products they have tried. Users can also search within product categories and compare consumers' viewpoints on various brands and models. Not surprisingly, research has identified credibility as the most important attribute of a ratings website and found reducing risk and saving search effort to be the primary motives for using such sites.[32] Buyers can peruse Internet-based newsgroups, forums, and blogs to find word-of-mouth information. A consumer looking for a new cell phone service, for example, might inquire in forums about other participants' experiences and level of satisfaction to gain more information before making a purchase decision. A Nielsen Global Survey of Trust in Advertising found that 83 percent of consumer respondents take action based on recommendations from friends and family, while 70 percent trust the advertising on branded websites.[33] Celebrities who tweet about brands have source credibility if they have a large number of followers. If followers have a social identification with the celebrity, they are more likely to engage in product involvement.[34]

Electronic word of mouth, or word-of-mouth marketing that occurs through the use of Internet technology, is particularly important to consumers staying abreast of trends. Hundreds of blogs (such as TechCrunch, Perez Hilton, and Engadget) play an essential role in propagating electronic word-of-mouth communications about everything from gossip to politics to consumer goods. They provide consumers with information on trends, reviews of products,

**word-of-mouth communication** Personal informal exchanges of communication that customers share with one another about products, brands, and companies and other information on what is new, exciting, and fashionable for consumers. These sites have become so influential in introducing consumers to new products and shaping their views about them that marketers are increasingly monitoring them to identify new trends; some firms have even attempted to influence users' votes on their favorite items. Marketers must increasingly court bloggers, who wield growing influence over consumer perception of companies, goods, and services. Even print advertisements encourage electronic word of mouth. In the advertisement promoting the island of Maui as a vacation destination, the ad not only shows vibrant pictures of the area but also includes a Twitter hashtag and a Web address. By providing these elements, marketers are hoping that visitors to the sites will spread the word to other consumers.

**Buzz marketing** is an attempt to incite publicity and public excitement surrounding a product through a creative event. Event attendance has a positive effect on brand equity.[35] Some marketers are piggybacking off the events of other companies, using long lines for an event or product launch as marketing opportunities. As long lines waited for the newest iPhones outside Apple's London store, a British apple juice brand carried a placard advertising "the latest in apple technology."[36] Buzz marketing can be an effective way of allowing a company to stand out from competing brands. Red Bull is another brand that excels at buzz marketing.

Buzz marketing works best as a part of an integrated marketing communication program that also uses advertising, personal selling, sales promotion, and publicity. However, marketers should also take care that buzz marketing campaigns do not violate any laws or have the potential to be misconstrued and cause undue alarm. For instance, stenciling a brand's name or logo on the sidewalk might be an effective buzz marketing technique but can also be viewed as illegal graffiti by city authorities.

**Viral marketing** is a strategy to get consumers to share a marketer's message, often through e-mail or online video, in a way that spreads dramatically and quickly. The jewelry brand Pandora released an advertisement called "The Unique Connection" in which children were blindfolded and asked to identify their mothers based on their jewelry, facial structure, clothing, and hair. Each child was able to identify his or her mother successfully. The advertisement went viral, with more than 17 million viewings on YouTube.[37] Interestingly, viral marketing appears to be more effective for products that are less utilitarian (practical and functional) in nature. Promoting utilitarian products through social sharing mechanisms such as Facebook may actually be disadvantageous for practical no-frills products.[38]

Word of mouth, no matter how it is transmitted, is not effective in all product categories. It seems to be most effective for new-to-market and more expensive products. Despite the obvious benefits of positive word of mouth, marketers must also recognize the potential dangers of negative word of mouth. This is particularly important in dealing with online platforms that can reach more people and encourage consumers to "gang up" on a company or product.

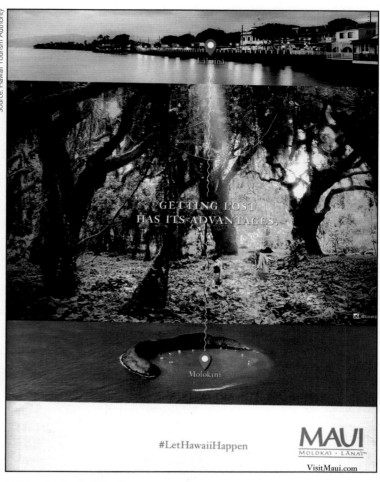

Source: Hawaii Tourism Authority

GETTING LOST HAS ITS ADVANTAGES.

#LetHawaiiHappen

**MAUI**
MOLOKA'I · LĀNA'I™
VisitMaui.com

**Electronic Word of Mouth**
This advertisement for Maui, a Hawaiian island, uses a Twitter hashtag and a Web address to encourage consumers to visit its sites and share the information they learn with others.

**buzz marketing** An attempt to incite publicity and public excitement surrounding a product through a creative event

**viral marketing** A strategy to get consumers to share a marketer's message, often through e-mail or online videos, in a way that spreads dramatically and quickly

# EMERGING **TRENDS IN MARKETING**

## Mattress Direct: Sleep Goes Viral

When we think of products that go viral, mattresses are probably not among them. However, new startups are changing this as they challenge traditional mattress companies. These startups mail the mattress straight to customers, eliminating the need for them to visit showrooms. Many of these mattresses are sold without springs so they can be folded tightly into a shipping box. When the customer opens the box, the mattress expands to its full size.

Recognizing the high impact of social media, mattress companies such as Casper and Leesa are encouraging customers to post videos of them "unboxing" their mattresses online. Customers have found the process of unboxing their mattresses a fun experience they are often willing to share with friends and family. This novelty has led many happy customers to post videos of them unboxing their mattresses onto YouTube.

These mattress startups also give an additional incentive for customers to share their enthusiasm with friends. The videos often include links to referral codes, allowing people who view the video and want the mattresses to purchase them easily. For every new customer a video or review generates, the video generator can receive $50. These startups are proving how the power of word-of-mouth marketing can cause disruption in an established industry.[b]

---

## 16-7 **PRODUCT PLACEMENT AS PROMOTION**

A growing technique for reaching consumers is the selective placement of products within the context of television programs viewed by the target market. **Product placement** is a form of advertising that strategically locates products or product promotions within entertainment media to reach the product's target markets. For instance, the James Bond film *Spectre* featured the vehicles Aston Martin and Land Rover.[39] Apple is considered to be an expert at product placement, and its products are often seen in popular television shows and movies. Such product placement has become more important due to the increasing fragmentation of television viewers who have ever-expanding viewing options and technology that can screen advertisements (e.g., digital video recorders such as TiVo). Researchers have found that 60 to 80 percent of digital video recorder users skip over the commercials when they replay programming.[40]

In-program product placements have been successful in reaching consumers as they are being entertained. Research demonstrates that a TV series can impact consumers' intentions to purchase brands placed in those TV shows. Of course, individual traits, such as consumer sensitivity to social influences, may increase or decrease intentions to purchase a specific brand.[41] As a result, product placement can be found in many of today's most popular shows. For instance, the show "Modern Family" featured a Toyota vehicle, while the Target brand has been featured prominently in episodes of "Jane the Virgin."[42] Reality programming in particular has been a natural fit for product placements, because of the close interchange between the participants and the product (e.g., Sears and *Extreme Makeover Home Edition*; Subway and *The Biggest Loser*; Pepsi and *The X Factor*; Coca-Cola and *American Idol*).

Product placement is not limited to U.S. television shows. The European Parliament approved limited use of product placement, albeit only during certain types of programs and only if consumers were informed at the beginning of the segment that companies had paid to have their products displayed. In general, the notion of product placement has not been favorably viewed in Europe and has been particularly controversial in the United Kingdom. However, legislation has legalized product placement in U.K. television programs.[43]

**product placement** The strategic location of products or product promotions within entertainment media content to reach the product's target market

Supporting the use of product placement are findings that product placement can promote prosocial behavior such as healthy eating habits. For instance, product placements are effective in promoting the consumption of fruits and vegetables among children.[44]

## 16-8 CRITICISMS AND DEFENSES OF PROMOTION

Even though promotional activities can help customers make informed purchasing decisions, social scientists, consumer groups, government agencies, and members of society in general have long criticized promotion. There are two main reasons for such criticism: Promotion does have flaws, and it is a highly visible business activity that pervades our daily lives. Although complaints about too much promotional activity are almost universal, a number of more specific criticisms have been lodged. In this section, we discuss some of the criticisms and defenses of promotion.

### 16-8a Is Promotion Deceptive?

One common criticism of promotion is that it is deceptive and unethical. During the 19th and early 20th centuries, much promotion was blatantly deceptive. Although no longer widespread, some deceptive promotion still occurs. For instance, the Federal Trade Commission filed a lawsuit against dietary supplement maker Sunrise Nutraceuticals, LLC to stop it from advertising that its products could be used to alleviate opiate withdrawal and cure addiction. According to the FTC, these claims were unsubstantiated at best and downright false at worst.[45] Many industries suffer from claims of deception from time to time. One industry that is seemingly constantly bombarded with truthfulness-related claims is the diet products and exercise equipment industry. Some promotions are unintentionally deceiving; for instance, when advertising to children, it is easy to mislead them because they are more naïve than adults and less able to separate fantasy from reality. A promotion may also mislead some receivers, because words can have diverse meanings for different people. However, not all promotion should be condemned because a small portion is flawed. Laws, government regulation, and industry self-regulation have helped decrease deceptive promotion.

### 16-8b Does Promotion Increase Prices?

Promotion is also criticized for raising prices, but in fact it can lower them. The ultimate purpose of promotion is to stimulate demand. If it does, the business should be able to produce and market products in

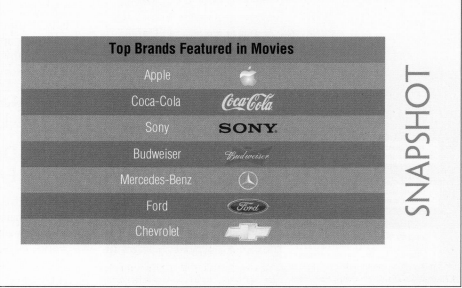

**Top Brands Featured in Movies**

| | |
|---|---|
| Apple | |
| Coca-Cola | |
| Sony | |
| Budweiser | |
| Mercedes-Benz | |
| Ford | |
| Chevrolet | |

SNAPSHOT

Source: Abe Sauer, "Announcing the 2015 Brandcameo Product Placement Awards," *Brandchannel*, February 20, 2015, http://brandchannel.com/2015/02/20/announcing-the-2015-brandcameo-product-placement-awards/ (accessed January 22, 2016); Abe Sauer, "The Envelope, Please: The 2014 Brandcameo Product Placement Awards," *Brandchannel*, http://brandchannel.com/2014/02/27/the-envelope-please-the-2014-brandcameo-product-placement-awards/ (accessed January 22, 2016).

larger quantities and thus reduce per-unit production research and development, overhead, and marketing costs, which can result in lower prices. As demand for flat-screen TVs and MP3 players increased, their prices dropped. When promotion fails to stimulate demand, the price of the promoted product increases because promotion costs must be added to other costs. Promotion also helps keep prices lower by facilitating price competition. When firms advertise prices, their prices tend to remain lower than when they are not promoting prices. Gasoline pricing illustrates how promotion fosters price competition. Service stations with the highest prices seldom have highly visible price signs. In addition, results of an analysis for the long-term economic growth for 64 countries indicated that there is a direct relationship between advertising and economic growth. The research findings indicate that advertising not only is related to economic growth but can also bring about economic growth.[46] A Deloitte study found that for every £1 billion ($1.64 billion) spent on advertising in the United Kingdom, a £6 billion ($9.86 billion) increase in annual GDP occurs.[47] This should help clarify debates over the role of promotion in society.

## 16-8c  Does Promotion Create Needs?

Some critics of promotion claim that it manipulates consumers by persuading them to buy products they do not need, hence creating "artificial" needs. In his theory of motivation, Abraham Maslow (discussed in Chapter 7) indicates that an individual tries to satisfy five levels of needs: physiological needs, such as hunger, thirst, and sex; safety needs; needs for love and affection; needs for self-esteem and respect from others; and self-actualization needs, or the need to realize one's potential. When needs are viewed in this context, it is difficult to demonstrate that promotion creates them. If there were no promotional activities, people would still have needs for food, water, sex, safety, love, affection, self-esteem, respect from others, and self-actualization.

Although promotion may not create needs, it does capitalize on them (which may be why some critics believe promotion creates needs). Many marketers base their appeals on these needs. For instance, several mouthwash, toothpaste, and perfume advertisements associate these products with needs for love, affection, and respect. These advertisers rely on human needs in their messages, but they do not create the needs.

*Source: Sante Fe Natural Tobacco Company*

**100% ADDITIVE-FREE NATURAL TOBACCO**

MADE WITH ORGANIC TOBACCO

NATURAL AMERICAN SPIRIT

No additives in our tobacco does **NOT** mean a safer cigarette.

Organic tobacco does **NOT** mean a safer cigarette.

SURGEON GENERAL'S WARNING: Smoking Causes Lung Cancer, Heart Disease, Emphysema, And May Complicate Pregnancy.

**TRY 1 PACK FOR $2.00***

VISIT NASCIGS.COM OR CALL 1-800-435-5515
PROMO CODE 96451

**CIGARETTES**    *Plus applicable sales tax

Offer for two "1 for $2" Gift Certificates good for any Natural American Spirit cigarette product (excludes RYO pouches and 150g tins). Not to be used in conjunction with any other offer. Offer and website restricted to U.S. smokers 21 years of age and older. Limit one offer per person per 12 month period. Offer void in MA and where prohibited. Other restrictions may apply. Offer expires 06/30/16.

**Marketing Harmful Products**
Natural American Spirit markets its organic tobacco and lack of additives. Although it has a disclaimer stating that this does not mean it is a healthier cigarette, critics believe it is wrong to market the benefits of products that can cause harm.

## 16-8d  Does Promotion Encourage Materialism?

Another frequent criticism of promotion is that it leads to materialism. The purpose of promoting goods is to persuade people to buy them; thus, if promotion works, consumers will want to buy more and more things. Marketers assert that values are instilled in the home and that promotion does not change people into materialistic consumers. However, the behavior of today's children and teenagers contradicts this view; many insist on high-priced, brand name apparel, such as Gucci, Coach, Abercrombie & Fitch, 7 For All Mankind, Jersey Couture, and Ralph Lauren.

## 16-8e Does Promotion Help Customers without Costing Too Much?

Every year, firms spend billions of dollars for promotion. The question is whether promotion helps customers enough to be worth the cost. Consumers do benefit because promotion informs them about product uses, features, advantages, prices, and locations where they can buy the products. Thus, consumers gain more knowledge about available products and can make more intelligent buying decisions. Promotion also informs consumers about services—for instance, health care, educational programs, and day care—as well as about important social, political, and health-related issues. For example, several organizations, such as the California Department of Health Services, inform people about the health hazards associated with tobacco use.

## 16-8f Should Potentially Harmful Products Be Promoted?

Finally, some critics of promotion, including consumer groups and government officials, suggest that certain products should not be promoted at all. Primary targets are products associated with violence and other possibly unhealthy activities, such as handguns, alcohol, and tobacco. Cigarette advertisements, for example, promote smoking, a behavior proven to be harmful and even deadly. Tobacco companies, which spend billions on promotion, have countered criticism of their advertising by pointing out that advertisements for red meat and coffee are not censured, even though these products may also cause health problems. Consider the advertisement for Natural American Spirit. The company uses big letters to emphasize its American origins, organic tobacco, and lack of additives. The image of hands depicted as holding dirt reinforces this sustainability image. It also states in large letters that these benefits do not mean that its products are safer than other cigarettes. Despite these disclaimers, critics believe the marketing of these positive claims could deceive people into believing the cigarettes are safer since they are more eco-friendly. On the other hand, those who defend such promotion assert that, as long as it is legal to sell a product, promoting that product should be allowed.

# Summary

### 16-1 Define integrated marketing communications.

Integrated marketing communications is the coordination of promotion and other marketing efforts to ensure maximum informational and persuasive impact on customers.

### 16-2 Describe the steps of the communication process.

Communication is a sharing of meaning. The communication process involves several steps. First, the source translates meaning into code, a process known as coding or encoding. The source should employ signs or symbols familiar to the receiver or audience. The coded message is sent through a communications channel to the receiver or audience. The receiver or audience then decodes the message and usually supplies feedback to the source. When the decoded message differs from the encoded one, a condition called noise exists.

### 16-3 Recognize the definition and objectives of promotion.

Promotion is communication to build and maintain relationships by informing and persuading one or more audiences.

Although promotional objectives vary from one organization to another and within organizations over time, eight primary objectives underlie many promotional programs. Promotion aims to create awareness of a new product, a new brand, or an existing product; to stimulate primary and selective demand; to encourage product trial through the use of free samples, coupons, limited free-use offers, contests, and games; to identify prospects; to retain loyal customers; to facilitate reseller support; to combat competitive promotional efforts; and to reduce sales fluctuations.

### 16-4 Summarize the four elements of the promotion mix.

The promotion mix for a product may include four major promotional methods: advertising, personal selling, public relations, and sales promotion. Advertising is paid non-personal communication about an organization and its products transmitted to a target audience through a mass medium. Personal selling is paid personal communication that attempts to inform customers and persuade them to purchase products in an exchange situation. Public relations is a broad set of communication efforts used to create and maintain favorable relationships between an organization and its stakeholders. Sales promotion is an activity or material that acts as a direct inducement, offering added value or incentive for the product, to resellers, salespeople, or consumers.

## 16-5 Explain the factors that are used to determine a product's promotion mix.

The promotional methods used in a product's promotion mix are determined by the organization's promotional resources, objectives, and policies; characteristics of the target market; characteristics of the product; and cost and availability of promotional methods. Marketers also consider whether to use a push policy or a pull policy. With a push policy, the producer only promotes the product to the next institution down the marketing channel. Normally, a push policy stresses personal selling. Firms that use a pull policy promote directly to consumers, with the intention of developing strong consumer demand for the products. Once consumers are persuaded to seek the products in retail stores, retailers go to wholesalers or the producer to buy the products.

## 16-6 Describe how word-of-mouth communication affects promotion.

Most customers are likely to be influenced by friends and family members when making purchases. Word-of-mouth communication is personal, informal exchanges of communication that customers share with one another about products, brands, and companies. Customers may also choose to go online to find electronic word of mouth about products or companies. Buzz marketing is an attempt to incite publicity and public excitement surrounding a product through a creative event. Viral marketing is a strategy to get consumers to share a marketer's message, often through e-mail or online videos, in a way that spreads dramatically and quickly.

## 16-7 Discuss how product placement impacts promotion.

Product placement is the strategic location of products or product promotions within television program content to reach the product's target market. In-program product placements have been successful in reaching consumers as they are being entertained rather than in the competitive commercial break time periods.

## 16-8 List major criticisms and defenses of promotion.

Promotional activities can help consumers make informed purchasing decisions, but they have also evoked many criticisms. Promotion has been accused of deception. Although some deceiving or misleading promotions do exist, laws, government regulation, and industry self-regulation minimize deceptive promotion. Promotion has been blamed for increasing prices, but it usually tends to lower them. When demand is high, production and marketing costs decrease, which can result in lower prices. Moreover, promotion helps keep prices lower by facilitating price competition. Other criticisms of promotional activity are that it manipulates consumers into buying products they do not need, that it leads to a more materialistic society, and that consumers do not benefit sufficiently from promotional activity to justify its high cost. Finally, some critics of promotion suggest that potentially harmful products, especially those associated with violence, sex, and unhealthy activities, should not be promoted at all.

---

**Go to www.cengagebrain.com for resources to help you master the content in this chapter as well as for materials that will expand your marketing knowledge!**

---

# Important Terms

integrated marketing
    communications 498
communication 499
source 499
receiver 499
coding process 499
communications channel 500
decoding process 500
noise 500

feedback 501
channel capacity 501
promotion 501
primary demand 503
pioneer promotion 503
selective demand 503
promotion mix 506
kinesic communication 508
proxemic communication 508

tactile communication 508
push policy 513
pull policy 513
word-of-mouth
    communication 514
buzz marketing 515
viral marketing 515
product placement 516

# Discussion and Review Questions

1. What does the term *integrated marketing communications* mean?
2. Define *communication* and describe the communication process. Is it possible to communicate without using all the elements in the communication process? If so, which elements can be omitted?
3. Identify several causes of noise. How can a source reduce noise?
4. What is the major task of promotion? Do firms ever use promotion to accomplish this task and fail? If so, give several examples.
5. Describe the possible objectives of promotion and discuss the circumstances under which each objective might be used.
6. Identify and briefly describe the four promotional methods an organization can use in its promotion mix.
7. What forms of interpersonal communication besides language can be used in personal selling?
8. How do target market characteristics determine which promotional methods to include in a promotion mix?

Assume a company is planning to promote a cereal to both adults and children. Along what major dimensions would these two promotional efforts have to differ from each other?

9. How can a product's characteristics affect the composition of its promotion mix?
10. Evaluate the following statement: "Appropriate advertising media are always available if a company can afford them."
11. Explain the difference between a pull policy and a push policy. Under what conditions should each policy be used?
12. In which ways can word-of-mouth communication influence the effectiveness of a promotion mix for a product?
13. Which criticisms of promotion do you believe are the most valid? Why?
14. Should organizations be allowed to promote offensive, violent, sexual, or unhealthy products that can be legally sold and purchased? Support your answer.

# Video Case 16.1

## Napoletana: Taking a Bite at WOM Promotion

Frank Pepe's Pizzeria Napoletana has opened one of the most recognizable pizzerias in the United States using word of mouth (WOM). After returning from World War I, Frank Pepe initially began with making bread during the week and pizzas on the weekend. After seeing a demand for his product, he utilized his entrepreneurial spirit and focused solely on pizza. Frank Pepe founded Pepe's Pizzeria in 1925, with a heavy influence from his Italian culture, in New Haven, CT.

Frank Pepe developed the New Haven-style thin crust pizza that earned him a reputation as being one of the country's premiere pizzerias. Many people began referring to Frank Pepe as "Old Reliable," which continued to generate positive feedback throughout different communities. Pepe's signature pizza, the White Clam Pizza, was the most notable recipe since the development in the mid-1960s.

Since the beginning, Pepe's has been a family-run business. Frank's wife and children all worked in the original store and after retiring, they passed the business to their children, who still have a stake in the business today. Through the transition between generations, Pepe's has always aimed to deliver a premium product that is consistent and meets customer standards. As people come into the store Pepe's employees engage in personal selling by communicating various menu items.

Current CEO Ken Berry places a high emphasis upon delivering the promise and guarantee of quality within their product every day. As chief executive operator, he sees the challenge of delivering this promise as a duty that helps protect and build the brand, which the Pepe family initially built. He strives to retain brand equity and rely upon feedback from loyal customers as the company continues to grow.

Including the first and flagship store, there are currently nine pizzerias within Connecticut and New York, with additional plans to expand into Boston. With each new store came the difficult task of maintaining the original experience for new, prospective, and loyal customers. When Pepe's began to consistently pursue expansion tactics, some customers appeared dismayed. There were protests and boycotts occurring on opening days, as other happy customers waited in long lines to test the reputation of the premiere pizza.

To ensure customer satisfaction at the new locations, Ken Berry discussed the critical nature of replicating every aspect of the original idea. Everything from the recipes being virtually unchanged to the layout and colors of the stores needed to be congruent to ensure success. He describes Pepe's as an experience that allows customers to step back in time with a handcrafted product.

Another aspect of developing demand for the company in new locations was the advertising tactics used. As Pepe's has always done, it relied upon word of mouth to retain and gain new customers. It places emphasis upon the experience and listens to customer feedback on whether it is delivering a quality product. At times it uses direct mail, which can be an effective form of advertising, and tries to engage with consumers on Twitter and Facebook to remain connected with them. This is sometimes called electronic word of mouth. A major form of promotion comes in the form of free pizza, which is sales promotion. Generally, the week before a grand opening Pepe's will offer free pizza for a week at that location to allow new ovens to be broken in, workers to understand Pepe's culture, and to showcase the confidence that Pepe's has in its product to the local community.

For the public relations side of the company, Pepe's has a donation request option on its website, where customers are welcome to fill out an application to receive primarily gift cards from the company. It also holds a good neighbor night, which allows an organization to hold a fundraiser at any location.

Fifteen percent of proceeds made that night is given to the organization. While Pepe's loses out on some proceeds, these events create quality relationships in the community as well as generating a potentially new customer base. It also donates gift cards to nonprofit organizations for fundraising purposes.

Throughout the years Pepe's has strived to deliver a promise to customers by staying true to the original product. It has maintained its brand equity through its dedication and standards set by customers, family members, and all stakeholders associated with the product. For Pepe's, it is clear that through positive word of mouth, advertising does not always need to be a costly expense.[48]

### Discussion Questions

1. What are the various promotion elements that Pepe's uses to communicate with customers?
2. What role does word of mouth play in Pepe's integrated marketing communications?
3. Evaluate free pizza as a form of sales promotion in Pepe's success.

# Case 16.2

## Because You're Worth It: IMC at L'Oréal

L'Oréal Paris, the French cosmetics division of parent company L'Oréal SA, is an effective architect of integrated marketing communications. It has achieved such status by coordinating a mix of marketing activities through the most appropriate channels and relaying a consistent brand message to customers over several decades. Its success is evidenced by long-term customer relationships, customer loyalty, and influential brand ambassadors over the years. Though L'Oréal Paris has been at times slow to adapt to cultural and demographic changes, it has proven capable of implementing appropriate and synchronized marketing tactics resulting in quick recovery.

L'Oréal's slogan, "Because We're Worth It," is the platform upon which the company's entire marketing strategy is built. Created in 1971, a time when women were seeking to become more empowered, the slogan has remained a powerful force behind the brand. Unlike most company slogans, the L'Oréal slogan has not had significant makeovers due to its simply stated classic message. The slogan has proven resilient in the face of inevitable evolution of brands and consumer tastes. Changes to the company slogan "Because I'm Worth It" have been limited to pronouns. It changed in the 1990s to say "Because You're Worth It," at which point the company launched a global marketing campaign. The slogan has since been translated into 40 languages. In 2010, when nearing its 40th anniversary, the slogan was changed once more to read "Because We're Worth It." The purpose of this change was to refresh its image while remaining loyal to the original message of creating a sense of self-worth and confidence among women.

The company's brand ambassadors have also reinforced the power of the slogan. L'Oréal carefully chooses a wide range of representatives across cultures, ages, and appearances who embody the essence of a strong and empowered woman. Ambassadors such as Aimee Mullins, Beyoncé Knowles, and Jennifer Lopez inspire word-of-mouth communication among customers through advertisements, interviews in which they explain what the brand means to them, and advocacy efforts. Although the slogan's sense of female empowerment may not be as relevant in Europe or America, there is opportunity in Africa and Asia where women's rights are taking hold. L'Oréal's corporate communications team is working to develop more awareness of the brand and greater customer relationships through institutional media relations, corporate social responsibility initiatives, and reputation management. In developing a more global approach, L'Oréal also hires teams of people from multiple countries to research the skin and hair of different people groups.

Although L'Oréal is the largest cosmetics company worldwide, selling an estimated 50 products per second, sales have slipped in recent years. Experts feel that the onset of the digital age and shorter attention spans may be making the slogan less effective and outdated. Despite these concerns, L'Oréal Paris's CEO announced he intends to keep the slogan, and is using it as the basis for digital marketing campaigns. In 2010 the company hired their first chief marketing officer, Marc Speichert, to launch all of the company's brands into the digital realm. Speichert's first contribution was to build a

media team to work closely with a consumer insights team to determine what channels and content are appropriate for their different audiences. Based on this information, the company focused on media and Internet displays, social media, TV and print advertising, search optimization, and videos. Speichert has since been replaced with CMO Marie Gulin.

As of 2012, L'Oréal became one of the biggest advertisers in the United States, having spent more than $2 billion on print and television advertising. It has also seen positive results from search optimization and its former social media partnership with famous beauty blogger Michelle Phan. It also uses social media to connect with employees and potential hires, encouraging employees to participate in social media and share their testimonials. This engagement has resulted in more interactions with fans of L'Oréal's products. L'Oréal is among the top brands recommended by users.

L'Oréal's content marketing is based on three pillars: education, empowerment, and aspiration. In line with these three topics, how-to and do-it-yourself videos have been created informing consumers of various beauty tips. Videos focused on empowerment send the message of the brand's strength and confidence rather than just focusing on cosmetics and beauty, leaving customers with a positive outlook. Finally, aspirational videos are reflections of the company's sponsorships with various awards and fashion events, which infuse the brand with elevated perceptions. Overall, these videos and the entirety of the company's content marketing initiatives work together to tell the story of the firm to consumers, creating value and brand awareness among loyal and new users.[49]

### Questions for Discussion

1. Describe L'Oréal's integrated marketing strategy. What are the strengths? Weaknesses?
2. Describe the function and effectiveness of brand ambassadors. What are some risks associated with choosing a brand ambassador?
3. Why is it important to have a story to tell when developing content marketing?

# NOTES

[1] James R. Hagerty, "Why La-Z-Boy Can't Ditch the Recliner," *The Wall Street Journal*, July 15, 2015, B1; Robert Klara, "Perspective: Sit Back and Relax—La-Z-Boy Shifts from Dude Chair to Mom's Chair," *AdWeek*, August 23, 2012, http://www.adweek.com/news/advertising-branding/perspective-sit-back-and-relax-142941 (accessed July 20, 2015);

La-Z-Boy, "Free In-Home Design," http://www.la-z-boy.com/Design-Center/In-Home-Design/ (accessed July 20, 2015); Tanya Gazdik Irwin, "La-Z-Boy, Brooke Shields Show 'Urban Attitudes'," *MediaPost*, May 8, 2014, http://www.mediapost.com/publications/article/225337/la-z-boy-brooke-shields-show-urban-attitudes.html (accessed July 20, 2015).

[2] Suzanne Vranica, "Advertisements that Hit and Missed This Year," *The Wall Street Journal*, December 28, 2015, B1, B4; Kristina Monllos, "Why Domino's Went Nuts and Wrote Hundreds of Tweets Almost Entirely in Pizza Emojis," *AdWeek*, May 13, 2015, http://www.adweek.com/adfreak/why-dominos-went-nuts-and-wrote-hundreds-tweets-almost-

entirely-pizza-emojis-164732 (accessed January 21, 2016); Bruce Horovitz, "Domino's to roll out tweet-a-pizza," *USA Today*, May 14, 2015, http://www.usatoday.com/story/money/2015/05/12/dominos-pizza-tweet-a-pizza-twitter-tweet-to-order-fast-food-restaurants/27175005/ (accessed January 21, 2016); David Gianatasio, "These Emoji Flash-cards from Domino's Will Teach You How to Talk to Your Kids," *AdWeek*, July 20, 2015, http://www.adweek.com/adfreak/these-emoji-flashcards-dominos-will-teach-you-how-talk-your-kids-165996 (accessed January 21, 2016).

3 Tim Nudd, "Ad of the Day: Ikea Hilari-ously Pitches Its 2015 Catalog as the Coolest Gadget Ever," *AdWeek*, September 3, 2014, http://www.adweek.com/news/advertising-branding/ad-day-ikea-hilariously-pitches-its-2015-catalog-cutting-edge-technology-159846 (accessed January 21, 2016); Jilian Richardson, "10 Campaigns that Should Win at Cannes," *Contently*, June 24, 2015, https://contently.com/strategist/2015/06/24/10-campaigns-that-should-win-best-branded-content-at-cannes/ (accessed January 21, 2016).

4 Jackson Connor, "Digital Advertising Expected to Climb, While Traditional Media May Be in Trouble," *Huffington Post*, http://www.huffingtonpost.com/2015/03/24/digital-advertising-climb-tradional-media-trouble_n_6930958.html (accessed January 21, 2016).

5 Pierre Berthon, Karen Robson, and Leyland Pitt, "The Theory and Practice of Advertising: Counting the Cost to the Consumer," *Journal of Advertising Research* 53 no. 3 (2013): 244–246.

6 Salvador Ruiz and María Sicilia, "The Impact of Cognitive and/or Affective Processing Styles on Consumer Response to Advertising Appeals," *Journal of Business Research* 57 (2004): 657–664.

7 ABC News, "Oprah Winfrey Says She's Lost 26 Pounds, Eats Bread Every Day," January 27, 2016, http://abcnews.go.com/Health/oprah-winfrey-shes-lost-26-pounds-eats-bread/story?id=36539822 (accessed February 16, 2016).

8 Nathalie Tadena, "P&G Cut Traditional Ad Spending by 14% in 2014," *The Wall Street Journal*, March 18, 2015, http://blogs.wsj.com/cmo/2015/03/18/pg-cut-traditional-ad-spending-by-14-in-2014/ (accessed January 22, 2016).

9 Special Olympics, "Coca-Cola Company," http://www.specialolympics.org/Sponsors/Coca-Cola.aspx (accessed January 22, 2016).

10 Adi Robertson, Lizzie Plaugic, and Ariha Setalvad, "The 10 most important things from Apple's iPhone 6S event," *The Verge*, http://www.theverge.com/2015/9/9/9289963/apple-iphone-6s-highlights-announcements-recap (accessed January 22, 2016).

11 Suzanne Vranica, "Advertisements that Hit and Missed this Year," *The Wall Street Journal*, December 28, 2015, B1, B4.

12 Molly Soat, "Chia: From Pets to Protein Powder, the Marketing of the Chia Seed Is a Case Study on How a Superfood Trend Develops," *Marketing News*, January 2015, 42–51.

13 Roger Dooley, "The Smartest Supermarket You've Never Heard Of," *Forbes*, January 28, 2014, http://www.forbes.com/sites/rogerdooley/2014/01/28/h-e-b/ (accessed January 8, 2015).

14 E.J. Schultz, "Pepsi Ads Take Shot at Share-A-Coke, Polar Bears," *Advertising Age*, June 15, 2015, http://adage.com/article/cmo-strategy/post-ej-monday-pepsi-ads-shot-share-a-coke-polar-bears/298985/ (accessed February 8, 2016).

15 Time, Inc., "Advertising Rates," http://www.timemediakit.com/2016-advertising-rates/ (accessed February 8, 2016).

16 Joann Peck and Jennifer Wiggins, "It Just Feels Good: Customers' Affective Response to Touch and Its Influence in Persuasion," *Journal of Marketing* 70, 4 (October 2006): 56–69.

17 Charles Young and Adam Page, "A Model for Predicting Advertising Quality as a Key to Driving Sales Growth," *Journal of Advertising Research* 54, 4 (December 2014): 393–397.

18 Chris Woodyard, "Jared Fogle's Plea Deal Puts Subway Back in Spotlight," *USA Today*, August 19, 2015, http://www.usatoday.com/story/money/2015/08/18/jared-fogel-subway-plea/31951175/ (accessed February 8, 2016).

19 Thomas L. Powers, J'Aime C. Jennings, and Thomas E. DeCarlo, "An Assessment of Needed Sales Management Skills," *Journal of Personal Selling & Sales Management* 34, 3 (Summer 2014): 206–222.

20 Pampered Chef, YouTube, https://www.youtube.com/user/PamperedChefVideo (accessed February 8, 2016).

21 Federal Trade Commission, "The FTC's Endorsement Guides: What People Are Asking," https://www.ftc.gov/tips-advice/business-center/guidance/ftcs-endorsement-guides-what-people-are-asking (accessed February 8, 2016).

22 Ann Fabens-Lassen, "The 5 Worst PR Blunders of 2015," *Contently*, December 23, 2015, https://contently.com/strategist/2015/12/23/the-5-worst-pr-blunders-of-2015/ (accessed February 8, 2016).

23 Inmar, *2014 Coupon Trends: 2013 Year-End Report* (Winston-Salem, North Carolina: Inmar, February 2014).

24 United States Census Bureau, "About Three in Four Parents Living with Children Are Married, Census Bureau Reports," November 25, 2013, http://www.census.gov/newsroom/press-releases/2013/cb13-199.html (accessed February 8, 2016).

25 Rockney G. Walters and Maqbul Jamil, "Exploring the Relationships between Shopping Trip Type, Purchases of Products on Promotion, and Shopping Basket Profit," *Journal of Business Research* 56 (2003): 17–29.

26 Gabriel Beltrone, "Your Life Should Be This Dreamy, Say 6 Beautiful New Ads for the Apple Watch," October 9, 2015, http://www.adweek.com/adfreak/your-life-should-be-dreamy-say-6-beautiful-new-ads-apple-watch-167479 (accessed February 8, 2016).

27 Tomás Bayón, "The Chain from Customer Satisfaction via Word-of-Mouth Referrals to New Customer Acquisition," *Journal of the Academy of Marketing Science* 35 (June 2007): 233–249.

28 Rodolfo Vázquez-Casielles, Leticia Suárez-Álvarez, and Ana-Belén Del Río-Lanza, "The Word of Mouth Dynamic: How Positive (and Negative) WOM Drives Purchase Probability: An Analysis of Interpersonal and Non-Interpersonal Factors," *Journal of Advertising Research* 53, 1 (2013): 43–60.

29 Benjamin Lawrence, Susan Fournier, and Frédéric Brunel, "When Companies Don't Make the Ad: A Multimethod Inquiry into the Differential Effectiveness of Consumer-Generated Advertising," *Journal of Advertising* 42, 4 (October 2013): 292–307.

30 Rodolfo Vázquez-Casielles, Leticia Suárez-Álvarez, and Ana Belén del Río-Lanza, "The Word of Mouth Dynamic: How Positive (and Negative) WOM Drives Purchase Probability: An Analysis of Interpersonal and Non-Interpersonal Factors," *Journal of Advertising Research* 53, no. 1 (2013): 43–60.

31 Yinlong Zhang, Lawrence Feick, and Vikas Mittal, "How Males and Females Differ in Their Likelihood of Transmitting Negative Word of

Mouth," *Journal of Consumer Research* 40 (April 2014): 1097–1108.

[32] Pratibha A. Dabholkar, "Factors Influencing Consumer Choice of a 'Rating Web Site': An Experimental Investigation of an Online Interactive Decision Aid," *Journal of Marketing Theory and Practice* 14 (Fall 2006): 259–273.

[33] Nielsen, "Recommendations from Friends Remain Most Credible Form of Advertising Among Consumers; Branded Websites Are the Second-Highest-Rated Form," September 28, 2015, http://www.nielsen.com/us/en/press-room/2015/recommendations-from-friends-remain-most-credible-form-of-advertising.html (accessed February 8, 2016).

[34] Seung-A Annie Jin and Joe Phua, "Following Celebrities' Tweets About Brands: The Impact of Twitter-Based Electronic Word-of-Mouth on Consumers' Source Credibility Perception, Buying Intention, and Social Identification with Celebrities," *Journal of Advertising* 43, 2 (2014): 181–195.

[35] Lia Zarantonello and Bernd H. Schmitt, "The Impact of Event Marketing on Brand Equity: The Mediating Roles of Brand Experience and Brand Attitude," *International Journal of Advertising* 32, 2 (2013): 255–280.

[36] Simon Zekaria, "Apple's Crowds Draw a Crowd of Guerilla Marketers," *The Wall Street Journal*, September 19, 2014, http://blogs.wsj.com/digits/2014/09/19/apples-crowds-draw-a-crowd-of-guerrilla-marketers/ (accessed February 8, 2016).

[37] Tim Nudd, "The 20 Most Viral Ads of 2015," *AdWeek*, November 19, 2015, http://www.adweek.com/news-gallery/advertising-branding/20-most-viral-ads-2015-168213 (accessed February 8, 2016); Pandora, "The Unique Connection," *YouTube*, https://www.youtube.com/watch?v=DRoqk_z2Lgg (accessed February 8, 2016).

[38] Christian Schulze, Lisa Schöler, and Bernd Skiera, "Not All Fun and Games: Viral Marketing for Utilitarian Products," *Journal of Marketing* 78 (January 2014): 1–19.

[39] Nicholas Barber, "Does Bond's Product Placement Go Too Far?" *BBC*, October 1, 2015, http://www.bbc.com/culture/story/20151001-does-bonds-product-placement-go-too-far (accessed February 8, 2016).

[40] Lynna Goch, "The Place to Be," *Best's Review*, February 2005, 64–65.

[41] Valeria Noguti and Cristel Antonia Russell, "Normative Influences on Product Placement Effects: Alcohol Brands in Television Series and the Influence of Presumed Influence," *Journal of Advertising* 43, 1 (2014): 46–62.

[42] Brian Steinberg, "TV's Old Product-Placement Era Could Be Nearing Its End," http://variety.com/2015/tv/news/tvs-old-product-placement-era-could-be-nearing-its-end-1201423710/ (accessed February 8, 2016).

[43] Lilly Vitorovich, "Product Placement to Be Allowed in U.K. TV Programs," *The Wall Street Journal*, December 21, 2010, B5; Peter Shears, "Product Placement: The UK and the New Rules," *Journal of Production Management* 20 (2014): 59–81.

[44] Karine M. Charry, "Product placement and the promotion of healthy food to pre-adolescents—When popular TV series make carrots look cool," *International Journal of Advertising* 33, 3 (2014): 599–616.

[45] Federal Trade Commission, "FTC Brings Action to Stop Marketer from Making Deceptive Opiate Addiction and Withdrawal Treatment Claims," November 17, 2015, https://www.ftc.gov/news-events/press-releases/2015/11/ftc-brings-action-stop-marketer-making-deceptive-opiate-addiction (accessed February 8, 2016).

[46] Dennis A. Kopf, Ivonne M. Torres, and Carl Enomoto, "Advertising's Unintended Consequence," *Journal of Advertising* 40, 4 (Winter 2011): 5–18.

[47] Charles R. Taylor, "Editorial: On the Economic Effects of Advertising—Evidence That Advertising = Information," *International Journal of Advertising* 32, 3 (2013): 339–342.

[48] Pepe's Pizzeria website, http://www.pepespizzeria.com/ (accessed February 8, 2016); Kara Baskin, "The Fireplace to Stay in Brookline Home; Pepe's Pizzeria Won't Move In," *Boston Globe*, September 18, 2014, http://www.bostonglobe.com/lifestyle/food-dining/2014/09/18/the-fireplace-stay-brookline-home-pepe-pizzeria-won-move/Bz2r5AdCR9jI1dNMH3eVkM/story.html (accessed February 8, 2016); "Good Neighbor Night: Avon Walk for Breast Cancer," http://pepespizzeria.com/pizza/category/pepes-pizza-good-neighbor-nights/ (accessed February 8, 2016).

[49] Christina Passariello and Max Colchester, "L'Oréal's Slogan Proves Timeless," *The Wall Street Journal*, November 15, 2011, B14; Amy Verner, "L'Oréal's 'Because I'm Worth It' Slogan Marks a Milestone," The Globe and Mail, December 2, 2011, www.theglobeandmail.com/life/fashion-and-beauty/beauty/beauty-features/lorals-because-im-worth-it-slogan-marks-a-milestone/article2256825 (accessed February 8, 2016); Kate Shapland, "It Was Worth It: L'Oréal Celebrates 40th Anniversary of Landmark Slogan," *Telegraph.co.uk*, November 16, 2011, http://fashion.telegraph.co.uk/beauty/news-features/TMG8894450/It-was-worth-it-LOreal-celebrates-40th-anniversary-of-landmark-slogan.html (accessed February 8, 2016); Rebecca Leffler, "L'Oréal Fetes 40th Anniversary of 'Because You're Worth It' in Paris," *The Hollywood Reporter*, November 14, 2011, www.hollywoodreporter.com/fash-track/l-oreal-jane-fonda-freida-pinto-261216 (accessed February 8, 2016); L'Oréal, "Corporate Communication," www.loreal.com/who-you-can-be/communication/corporate-communication.aspx (accessed July 26, 2013); L'Oréal USA, "Diversity Is a Priority," www.lorealusa.com/_en/_us/html/our-company/our-teams/research-development.aspx (accessed July 26, 2013); Christina Passariello and Max Colchester, "L'Oréal Slogan Must Prove Worth Anew," *The Wall Street Journal*, November 18, 2011, http://online.wsj.com/news/articles/SB10001424052970204323904577037720293895982 (accessed February 8, 2016); Kristen Comings, "Three Keys to L'Oréal's Content Marketing Strategy," *iMedia Connection*, September 30, 2013, www.imediaconnection.com/content/35113.asp#multiview (accessed February 8, 2016); Giselle Abramovich, "L'Oréal: Ads Matter Less," *Digiday*, October 2, 2012, http://digiday.com/brands/adweek-tracking-the-evolution-of-loreal-marketing (accessed February 8, 2016); Kelly Liyakasa, "L'Oréal CMO: Digital Is Changing Our Content, Creative and Conversation," *Ad Exchanger*, September 13, 2013, www.adexchanger.com/digital-marketing-2/loreal-cmo-digital-is-changing-our-content-creative-and-conversation (accessed February 8, 2016); Jack Neff, "L'Oréal Puts U.S. Digital Media Up for Review," *Ad Age*, August 20, 2013, http://adage.com/article/agency-news/l-oreal-puts-u-s-digital-media-review/243732 (accessed February 8, 2015); Daisy Whitney, "Never Say 'Let's Create a Viral Video,'" *Ad Age*, September 13,

2012, http://adage.com/article/media/create-a-viral-video/237181 (accessed February 8, 2016); Kristen Schweizer, "L'Oreal, Dove Are Among Most Favorited Brands Among Social Media Users," *Bloomberg*, June 23, 3015, http://www.bloomberg.com/news/articles/2015-06-23/l-oreal-dove-are-most-favorited-brands-among-social-media-users (accessed February 8, 2016); Jack Simpson, "How L'Oréal Uses Social Media

to Increase Employee Engagement," *Econsultancy*, October 22, 2015, https://econsultancy.com/blog/67091-how-l-oreal-uses-social-media-to-increase-employee-engagement/ (accessed February 8, 2016); Julie Naughton, "L'Oréal USA, Michelle Phan Part Ways; Em Michelle Phan Heads to Ipsy.com," *WWD*, October 9, 2015, http://wwd.com/beauty-industry-news/beauty/loreal-usa-michelle-phan-part-ways-em-

michelle-phan-heads-to-ipsy-com-10259153/ (accessed February 8, 2016); Jack Neff, "L'Oreal USA Names Marie Gulin to Succeed Speichert as CMO," *Advertising Age*, May 27, 2014, http://adage.com/article/cmo-strategy/l-oreal-usa-names-marie-gulin-cmo/293424/ (accessed February 8, 2016).

## Feature Notes

[a] Molly Soat, "The E-Commerce Elixir," *Marketing News*, October 2014, 10–11; Rachel Nania, "The Homemade Gin Kit: Building a business on booze," *WTOP*, January 9, 2014, http://www.wtop.com/41/3538268/The-Homemade-Gin-Kit-Building-a-business-on-booze (accessed November 13, 2014); Parija Kavilanz, "DIY gin kit: berries included," *CNN Money*, December 20, 2013, http://money.cnn.com/2013/12/20/smallbusiness/gin-kit/

(accessed October 7, 2015); Michael Moroney, "DIY Gin Kit Finds a Home with Spirit Enthusiasts," *Entrepreneur*, August 23, 2014, http://www.entrepreneur.com/article/236381 (accessed October 7, 2015).

[b] Charlie Wells, "The New Mattress Professionals," *The Wall Street Journal*, September 30, 2015, http://www.wsj.com/articles/the-new-mattresses-professionals-1443640077 (accessed October 12, 2015); Erin Griffith,

"Waking up with Casper, an Internet Mattress Company," *Fortune*, September 15, 2015, http://fortune.com/2014/09/15/waking-up-with-casper-an-internet-mattress-company/ (accessed October 12, 2015); Kyle Stock, "New Startups Aren't Keeping Big Mattresses Up at Night," *Bloomberg*, March 12, 2015, http://www.bloomberg.com/news/articles/2015-03-12/new-startups-aren-t-keeping-big-mattress-up-at-night (accessed October 12, 2015).

# chapter 17    Advertising and Public Relations

---

## OBJECTIVES

---

**17-1**   Describe advertising and its different types.

**17-2**   Summarize the eight major steps in developing an advertising campaign.

**17-3**   Identify who is responsible for developing advertising campaigns.

**17-4**   Define *public relations.*

**17-5**   Describe the different tools of public relations.

**17-6**   Analyze how public relations is used and evaluated.

# MARKETING INSIGHTS

## POM Wonderful: Crazy Healthy

Brent Hofacker/Shutterstock.com

Easily recognizable with its hour-glass shaped bottles, POM Wonderful markets pomegranate products as beneficial to your health due to its powerful mix of antioxidants. Antioxidants may be useful in combating a variety of health problems, such as premature aging, cancer, and cardiovascular issues.

This prompted POM Wonderful to market its pomegranate products as having significant health benefits. POM Wonderful released advertising with claims including "Amaze Your Cardiologist" and "Drink to Prostate Health." It maintained that its products could lower the risk of erectile dysfunction, prostate cancer, and heart disease.

These advertising claims came under the scrutiny of the Federal Trade Commission (FTC), which ruled there was not sufficient evidence to support them. It found POM Wonderful guilty of making false efficacy claims—which involves claiming that the product works as advertised—as well as false establishment claims that occur when a company makes claims about products that have not been scientifically proven. The FTC further ruled that in order to make these health claims, two randomized and controlled clinical trials were needed to prove them true.

POM Wonderful appealed the ruling. The U.S. Court of Appeals for the D.C. Circuit upheld the ruling but determined that the FTC's insistence on two clinical trials was excessive. It ruled one trial is enough because it can provide important health information. Additionally, because pomegranate juice is not harmful, it does not need to go through the same stringent requirements as products such as pharmaceuticals. This ruling is significant for the advertising industry as it demonstrates the types of substantiation the FTC requires before making claims that could mislead consumers.[1]

Both large organizations and small companies use conventional and online promotional efforts like advertising to change their corporate images, build brand equity, launch new products, or promote current brands. In this chapter, we explore several dimensions of advertising and public relations. First, we focus on the nature and types of advertising. Next, we examine the major steps in developing an advertising campaign and describe who is responsible for developing such campaigns. We then discuss the nature of public relations and how it is used. We examine various public relations tools and ways to evaluate the effectiveness of public relations. Finally, we focus on how companies deal with unfavorable public relations.

## 17-1  THE NATURE AND TYPES OF ADVERTISING

**advertising** Paid nonpersonal communication about an organization and its products transmitted to a target audience through mass media

Advertising permeates our daily lives. At times, we view it positively; at other times, we feel bombarded and try to avoid it. Some advertising informs, persuades, or entertains us; some bores, annoys, or even offends us. Many companies are taking a different approach to their marketing, even using satire or criticism of their companies as a way to create awareness. Arby's bought two commercials in former television host Jon Stewart's final episode of the "Daily Show" despite the fact that Stewart poked fun at the company's products several times during his show. Rather than acting defensively to Stewart's ridicule, Arby's chose to use his popularity among younger people to reach this demographic.[2]

As mentioned in Chapter 16, **advertising** is a paid form of nonpersonal communication that is transmitted to a target audience through mass media, such as television, radio, the Internet, newspapers, magazines, direct mail, outdoor displays, and signs on mass transit vehicles. Advertising can have a profound impact on how consumers view certain products. One example is locally grown and organic produce. Consumers are likely to view locally grown and organic produce as healthier. Whole Foods and other supermarkets promote locally grown food as being more sustainable since it eliminates emissions from transporting food long distances and supports local farmers. Advertisements even influence how a brand's own sales force views company products. Salesperson perception of brand advertising is positively related to effort and performance because it influences how the salesperson identifies with the brand.[3] Organizations use advertising to reach a variety of audiences ranging from small, specific groups, such as stamp collectors in Idaho, to extremely large groups, such as all athletic-shoe purchasers in the United States.

When asked to name major advertisers, most people immediately mention business organizations. However, many nonbusiness organizations—including governments, churches, universities, and charitable organizations—employ advertising to communicate with stakeholders. Each year, the U.S. government spends hundreds of millions of dollars

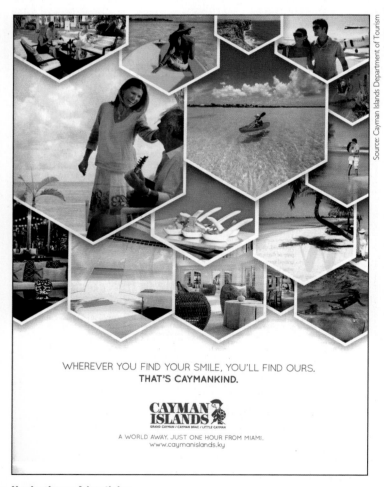

WHEREVER YOU FIND YOUR SMILE, YOU'LL FIND OURS.
**THAT'S CAYMANKIND.**

**CAYMAN ISLANDS**
GRAND CAYMAN / CAYMAN BRAC / LITTLE CAYMAN

A WORLD AWAY. JUST ONE HOUR FROM MIAMI.
www.caymanislands.ky

*Source: Cayman Islands Department of Tourism*

**Nonbusiness Advertising**
This Cayman Islands advertisement is an example of advertising for a nonbusiness purpose. Its intent is to attract tourists to the island chain.

in advertising to advise and influence the behavior of its citizens. Although this chapter analyzes advertising in the context of business organizations, much of the following material applies to all types of organizations. For instance, the advertisement for the Cayman Islands is meant to entice consumers to vacation within the region. It shows photos of people having a good time rather than promoting any particular type of business or product. It is important for cities and states to advertise because tourism generates significant income for their locations.

Advertising is used to promote goods, services, ideas, images, issues, people, and anything else advertisers want to publicize or foster. Depending on what is being promoted, advertising can be classified as institutional or product advertising. **Institutional advertising** promotes organizational images, ideas, and political issues. It can be used to create or maintain an organizational image. Institutional advertisements may deal with broad image issues, such as organizational strengths or the friendliness of employees. Monsanto, for instance, took out an advertisement to describe its supplier diversity. It shows photos of people from different backgrounds to demonstrate its commitment toward inclusion and diversity. Marketers may also aim to create a more favorable view of the organization in the eyes of noncustomer groups, such as shareholders, consumer advocacy groups, potential shareholders, or the general public. When a company promotes its position on a public issue—for instance, a tax increase, sustainability, regulations, or international trade coalitions—institutional advertising is referred to as **advocacy advertising**. Such advertising may be used to promote socially approved behavior, such as recycling or moderation in consuming alcoholic beverages. AT&T, for instance, ran an advertising campaign called "It Can Wait" that showed a terrible car crash in reverse. Its intent was to discourage people from texting and driving.[4] This type of advertising not only has social benefits but also helps build an organization's image.

**Product advertising** promotes the uses, features, and benefits of products. There are two types of product advertising: pioneer and competitive. **Pioneer advertising** focuses on stimulating demand for a product category (rather than a specific brand) by informing potential customers about the product's features, uses, and benefits. Toyota's marketing of its hydrogen-based FCV is an example of pioneer advertising. To help consumers understand the benefits of hydrogen-fuel technology, Toyota announced plans to spend $385 million to subsidize fuel-cell vehicles and hydrogen stations for the 2020 Olympics.[5] Sometimes marketers will begin advertising a product before it hits the market. Apple has had great success using this type of advertising for its iPod and iPad. Product advertising that focuses on products before they are available tends to cause people to think about the product more and evaluate it more positively.[6] Pioneer advertising is also employed when the product is in the introductory stage of the product life cycle, exemplified in the launch of the Samsung Galaxy Gear in the smartwatch

**institutional advertising**
Advertising that promotes organizational images, ideas, and political issues

**advocacy advertising**
Advertising that promotes a company's position on a public issue

**product advertising**
Advertising that promotes the uses, features, and benefits of products

**pioneer advertising**
Advertising that tries to stimulate demand for a product category rather than a specific brand by informing potential buyers about the product

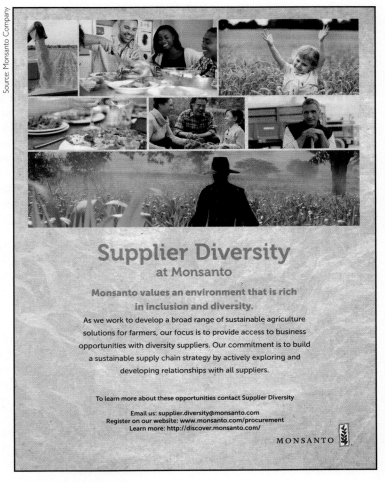

Source: Monsanto Company

**Institutional Advertising**
Monsanto is not directly promoting its product, but is instead describing its supplier diversity in the hopes of building relationships among its various stakeholders.

category. **Competitive advertising** attempts to stimulate demand for a specific brand by promoting the brand's features, uses, and advantages, sometimes through indirect or direct comparisons with competing brands. Cell phone service providers use competitive advertising to position their brands—for example, Verizon against T-Mobile. Advertising effects on sales must reflect competitors' advertising activities. The type of competitive environment will determine the most effective industry approach.

To make direct product comparisons, marketers use a form of competitive advertising called **comparative advertising**, which compares the sponsored brand with one or more identified competing brands on the basis of one or more product characteristics. Surveys show that top creative advertising practitioners view comparative advertising favorably when it clearly identifies the competition.[7] Samsung has used comparative advertising that compares its products' superior features to its rival Apple's. Often, the brands that are promoted through comparative advertisements have low market shares and are compared with competitors that have the highest market shares in the product category. Product categories that commonly use comparative advertising include soft drinks, toothpaste, pain relievers, foods, tires, automobiles, and detergents. Under the provisions of the 1988 Trademark Law Revision Act, marketers using comparative advertisements in the United States must not misrepresent the qualities or characteristics of competing products. Other countries may have laws that are stricter or less strict with regard to comparative advertising. For instance, Brazil has ruled that comparative advertising is acceptable as long as the comparison is fair and truthful. However, determining the fairness of an advertisement can be subjective and can vary in different situations.[8]

Other forms of competitive advertising include reminder and reinforcement advertising. **Reminder advertising** tells customers that an established brand is still around and still offers certain characteristics, uses, and advantages. Clorox, for example, reminds customers about the many advantages of its bleach products, such as their ability to kill germs, whiten clothes, and remove stains. **Reinforcement advertising** assures current users that they have made the right brand choice and tells them how to get the most satisfaction from that brand. Arm & Hammer baking soda does advertisements to remind purchasers to keep using the product for many different purposes. For example, if a box of baking soda is put into the refrigerator to reduce odors, then advertising reminds consumers to change out the baking soda on a periodic basis.

One growing trend among marketers has been the use of **native advertising**, or digital advertising, that matches the appearance and purpose of the content in which it is embedded.

**competitive advertising** Tries to stimulate demand for a specific brand by promoting its features, uses, and advantages relative to competing brands

**comparative advertising** Compares the sponsored brand with one or more identified brands on the basis of one or more product characteristics

**reminder advertising** Advertising used to remind consumers about an established brand's uses, characteristics, and benefits

**reinforcement advertising** Advertising that assures users they chose the right brand and tells them how to get the most satisfaction from it

**native advertising** Digital advertising that matches the appearance and purpose of the content in which it is embedded

# MARKETING DEBATE

## Is Native Advertising Trustworthy?

### ISSUE: How should native advertising be differentiated from content?

Native advertising is advertising that matches the appearance and purpose of the content in which it is embedded. Unlike traditional advertising, native advertising is meant to resemble the content itself. For example, the wedding website The Knot may feature sponsored articles about wedding gowns that consumers can purchase through the website. Consumers are likely to find native advertising useful because the content is likely to follow the publication's topics and style. Native ads have higher brand recall than traditional advertising, and nearly 73 percent of Internet users familiar with native advertising believe it is equally or more effective than non-sponsored ads.

However, because the advertisements are meant to resemble the surrounding content, consumers might not always recognize that an article or advertisement is sponsored. The FTC maintains that advertising must be distinguished from editorial content, but this line becomes blurred when the advertising resembles the content so closely. Self-regulation has been proposed as a solution, and industry guidelines are urging native advertisers to label the native ad as sponsored content to avoid confusion among the audience.[a]

The word "native" refers to the fact that this form of advertising is meant to resemble the content itself. Native advertising differs from content marketing in that it uses a platform outside of its own media. For instance, Netflix used native advertising to promote its "Orange Is the New Black" series on *The New York Times* website. Rather than promoting the show directly, Netflix created a 1,500 word feature article describing the current state of female incarceration in the United States, complete with graphs and other visuals. The native advertisement fits with Netflix's theme of a woman's experience in prison while resembling the form and content of a *New York Times* article.[9] In a world inundated with advertisements, native advertising offers marketers the opportunity to reach consumers in new and innovative ways. It also increases advertising revenue for the sites that host them. For instance, the professional social networking site LinkedIn has opened up a lucrative native advertising platform allowing brands to publish sponsored content. It is estimated that LinkedIn receives 45 percent of its advertising revenue from native advertising.[10] On the other hand, native advertising is potentially misleading when consumers do not realize that a video or post is sponsored by an organization. One survey revealed that two-thirds of respondents felt deceived upon realizing an article or video was sponsored content.[11] To avoid deception and possible legal repercussions, brands should clearly identify sponsored content on digital media sites.

# 17-2 DEVELOPING AN ADVERTISING CAMPAIGN

An **advertising campaign** involves designing a series of advertisements and placing them in various advertising media to reach a particular target audience. As Figure 17.1 shows, the major steps in creating an advertising campaign are (1) identifying and analyzing the target audience, (2) defining the advertising objectives, (3) creating the advertising platform, (4) determining the advertising appropriation, (5) developing the media plan, (6) creating the advertising message, (7) executing the campaign, and (8) evaluating advertising effectiveness. The number of

**advertising campaign** The creation and execution of a series of advertisements to communicate with a particular target audience

---

Figure 17.1 **General Steps in Developing and Implementing an Advertising Campaign**

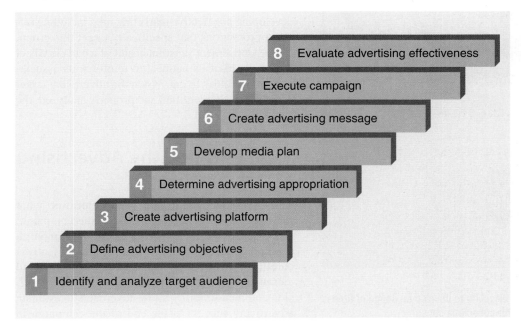

8 Evaluate advertising effectiveness
7 Execute campaign
6 Create advertising message
5 Develop media plan
4 Determine advertising appropriation
3 Create advertising platform
2 Define advertising objectives
1 Identify and analyze target audience

steps and the exact order in which they are carried out may vary according to the organization's resources, the nature of its product, and the type of target audience to be reached. Nevertheless, these general guidelines for developing an advertising campaign are appropriate for all types of organizations.

### 17-2a  Identifying and Analyzing the Target Audience

The **target audience** is the group of people at whom advertisements are aimed. Advertisements for the Dyson vacuum cleaner target more affluent home owners, whereas the Dirt Devil targets lower- to middle-income households. Identifying and analyzing the target audience are critical processes; the information yielded helps determine other steps in developing the campaign. The target audience may include everyone in the firm's target market. Marketers may, however, direct a campaign at only a portion of the target market. Italian company Tod's develops luxury shoes, bags, and other leather goods for those who desire prestige products. Therefore, its advertising focuses on the luxury market.

Advertisers research and analyze advertising targets to establish an information base for a campaign. Information commonly needed includes location and geographic distribution of the target group; the distribution of demographic factors, such as age, income, race, gender, and education; lifestyle information; and consumer attitudes regarding purchase and use of both the advertiser's products and competing products. The exact kinds of information an organization finds useful depend on the type of product being advertised, the characteristics of the target audience, and the type and amount of competition. Additionally, advertisers must be sure to create a campaign that will resonate with the target market. For instance, privacy concerns and irritating ads lead to avoidance, but when online and direct-mail advertising personalizes the information, acceptance of the ad tends to increase.[12] Generally, the more an advertiser knows about the target audience, the more likely the firm is to develop an effective advertising campaign. The advertisement for Quaker oatmeal clearly demonstrates that its target audience is those who seek a healthy breakfast. Knowing the target market for a company helps in developing an effective marketing mix, including relevant promotions that specifically target this group. The advertisement substitutes half of a bicycle wheel with a photo of its oatmeal to reinforce its association with healthy living. When the advertising target is not precisely identified and properly analyzed, the campaign may fail.

**target audience** The group of people at whom advertisements are aimed

**Target Audience**
Quaker Oatmeal associates itself with bicycling to develop an image of fitness and healthy living that targets the health-conscious consumer.

### 17-2b  Defining the Advertising Objectives

The advertiser's next step is to determine what the firm hopes to accomplish with the campaign. Because advertising objectives guide campaign development, advertisers should define objectives carefully. Advertising objectives should be stated clearly, precisely, and in measurable terms. Precision and measurability allow advertisers to evaluate advertising success at the end of the campaign in terms of whether objectives have been met. To provide precision and measurability, advertising objectives should contain benchmarks and indicate how far the advertiser wishes to move from these standards. If the goal is to increase sales, the advertiser should state the current sales level (the benchmark) and the amount of sales increase sought through advertising. An advertising objective should also specify a time frame so that advertisers know exactly how long they have to accomplish the objective. An advertiser with average monthly sales of $450,000 (the benchmark) might set the following objective: "Our primary advertising objective is to increase average monthly sales from $450,000 to $540,000 within 12 months."

If an advertiser defines objectives on the basis of sales, the objectives focus on increasing absolute dollar sales or unit sales, increasing sales by a certain percentage, or increasing the firm's market share. Even though an advertiser's long-run goal is to increase sales, not all campaigns are designed to produce immediate sales. Some campaigns aim to increase product or brand awareness, make consumers' attitudes more favorable, heighten consumers' knowledge of product features, or create awareness of positive, healthy consumer behavior, such as nonsmoking. If the goal is to increase product awareness, the objectives are stated in terms of communication. A specific communication objective might be to increase new product feature awareness, such as increased travel point rewards on a credit card from 0 to 40 percent in the target audience by the end of 6 months.

## 17-2c  Creating the Advertising Platform

Before launching a political campaign, party leaders develop a political platform stating major issues that are the basis of the campaign. Like a political platform, an **advertising platform** consists of the basic issues or selling points that an advertiser wishes to include in the advertising campaign. For instance, Unilever wants to become the company associated with "sustainable living." As such, the end of two of its commercials for its products—laundry brand Persil and Hellman's Mayonnaise—discuss sustainability and responsible sourcing.[13] A single advertisement in an advertising campaign may contain one or several issues from the platform. Although the platform sets forth the basic issues, it does not indicate how to present them.

An advertising platform should consist of issues important to customers. One of the best ways to determine those issues is to survey customers about what they consider most important in the selection and use of the product involved. Selling features must not only be important to customers, but they should also be strongly competitive features of the advertised brand. For instance, Michelob Ultra capitalizes upon its positioning as a "superior light beer." Although research is the most effective method for determining what issues to include in an advertising platform, customer research can be expensive.

Because the advertising platform is a base on which to build the advertising message, marketers should analyze this stage carefully. It has been found that, if the message is viewed as useful, it will create greater brand trust.[14] A campaign can be perfect in terms of selection and analysis of its target audience, statement of its objectives, media strategy, and the form of its message. But the campaign will ultimately fail if the advertisements communicate information that consumers do not deem important when selecting and using the product.

## 17-2d  Determining the Advertising Appropriation

The **advertising appropriation** is the total amount of money a marketer allocates for advertising for a specific time period. Panera Bread Co., for instance, spends about $90 million on advertising per year.[15] Many factors affect a firm's decision about how much to appropriate for advertising. Geographic size of the market and the distribution of buyers within the market have a great bearing on this decision. Both the type of product advertised and the firm's sales volume relative to competitors' sales volumes also play roles in determining what proportion of revenue to spend on advertising. Advertising appropriations for business products are usually quite small relative to product sales, whereas consumer convenience items, such as the cosmetics sold by L'Oréal, generally have large advertising expenditures relative to sales. For instance,

**advertising platform** Basic issues or selling points to be included in an advertising campaign

**advertising appropriation** The advertising budget for a specific time period

Procter & Gamble spends a relatively high percentage of sales to market its product mix of cosmetics, personal care products, appliances, detergents, and pet food. Retailers like Walmart usually have a much lower percent of sales spent on advertising.

Of the many techniques used to determine the advertising appropriation, one of the most logical is the **objective-and-task approach**. Using this approach, marketers determine the objectives a campaign is to achieve and then attempt to list the tasks required to accomplish them. The costs of the tasks are calculated and added to arrive at the total appropriation. This approach has one main problem: Marketers sometimes have trouble accurately estimating the level of effort needed to attain certain objectives. A coffee marketer, for example, may find it extremely difficult to determine how much of an increase in national television advertising is needed to raise a brand's market share from 8 to 10 percent.

In the more widely used **percent-of-sales approach**, marketers simply multiply the firm's past sales, plus a factor for planned sales growth or decline, by a standard percentage based on both what the firm traditionally spends on advertising and the industry average. This approach, too, has a major flaw: It is based on the incorrect assumption that sales create advertising rather than the reverse. A marketer using this approach during declining sales will reduce the amount spent on advertising, but such a reduction may further diminish sales. Though illogical, this technique has been favored because it is easy to implement.

Another way to determine advertising appropriation is the **competition-matching approach**. Marketers following this approach try to match their major competitors' appropriations in absolute dollars or to allocate the same percentage of sales for advertising that their competitors do. Although a marketer should be aware of what competitors spend on advertising, this technique should not be used alone because the firm's competitors probably have different advertising objectives and different resources available for advertising. Many companies and advertising agencies review competitive spending on a quarterly basis, comparing competitors' dollar expenditures on print, radio, and television with their own spending levels. Competitive tracking of this nature occurs at both the national and regional levels.

At times, marketers use the **arbitrary approach**, which usually means a high-level executive in the firm states how much to spend on advertising for a certain period. The arbitrary approach often leads to underspending or overspending. Although hardly a scientific budgeting technique, it is expedient. In general, the corporate culture will drive advertising budget decisions but it is often not based on knowledge that will increase profits. However, budgeting is more complicated than relying on "rules of thumb."[16] One research study found that 61 percent of top advertisers are inefficiently using their advertising budget by overspending an average of 34 percent.[17] It is challenging to know how much to spend and measure advertising effectiveness.

Deciding how large the advertising appropriation should be is critical. If the appropriation is set too low, the campaign cannot achieve its full potential. When too much money is appropriated, overspending results, and financial resources are wasted.

## 17-2e  Developing the Media Plan

Advertisers spend tremendous amounts on advertising media. These amounts have grown rapidly during the past two decades. Figure 17.2 shows the share of advertising revenue allocated to different media categories. Although television and print still comprise a greater share of advertising revenue than digital advertising, this last category is expected to grow rapidly during the next few years. To derive maximum results from media expenditures, marketers must develop effective media plans. A **media plan** sets forth the exact media vehicles to be used (specific magazines, television stations, social media, newspapers, and so forth) and the dates and times the advertisements will appear. Starbucks released a number of magazine and newspapers ads in its media plan for its new menu item, the Latte Macchiato. It also developed a graphic that it posts in stores to describe the differences between its different espresso options.[18] The advertisement provides a side-by-side visual comparison of its Latte Macchiato with its signature Flat White. The plan determines how many people in the target audience will

---

**objective-and-task approach** Budgeting for an advertising campaign by first determining its objectives and then calculating the cost of all the tasks needed to attain them

**percent-of-sales approach** Budgeting for an advertising campaign by multiplying the firm's past and expected sales by a standard percentage

**competition-matching approach** Determining an advertising budget by trying to match competitors' advertising outlays

**arbitrary approach** Budgeting for an advertising campaign as specified by a high-level executive in the firm

**media plan** A plan that specifies the media vehicles to be used and the schedule for running advertisements

Figure 17.2   **Global Percentage Share of Advertising Spend**

Source: Michael Sebastian, "Marketers to Boost Global Ad Spending This Year to $540 Billion," *Advertising Age*, March 24, 2015, http://adage.com/article/media/marketers-boost-global-ad-spending-540-billion/297737/ (accessed February 9, 2016).

be exposed to the message. The method also determines, to some degree, the effects of the message on those specific target markets. Media planning is a complex task requiring thorough analysis of the target audience. Sophisticated computer models have been developed to attempt to maximize the effectiveness of media plans.

To formulate a media plan, the planners select the media for the campaign and prepare a time schedule for each medium. The media planner's primary goal is to reach the largest number of people in the advertising target that the budget will allow. A secondary goal is to achieve the appropriate message reach and frequency for the target audience while staying within budget. *Reach* refers to the percentage of consumers in the target audience actually exposed to a particular advertisement in a stated period. *Frequency* is the number of times these targeted consumers are exposed to the advertisement.

Media planners begin with broad decisions but eventually make very specific ones. They first decide which kinds of media to use: radio, television, newspapers, digital or online advertising, magazines, direct mail, outdoor displays, or signs on mass transit vehicles. Mobile marketing in particular is growing and now consists of more than half of all digital advertising expenditures.[19] Media planners assess different formats and approaches to determine which are most effective. Some media plans are highly focused and use just one medium. Others can be quite complex and dynamic.

Media planners take many factors into account when devising a media plan. They analyze location and demographic characteristics of consumers in the target audience, because people's tastes in media differ according to demographic groups and locations. Media planners also consider the sizes and types of audiences that specific media reach. For instance, *National Geographic* reaches relatively well-educated consumers who are often highly influential decision makers. The magazine has 31 million readers in the United States alone.[20] Many marketers of vehicles, nonprofit organizations, and electronics would consider this an attractive demographic. Declining broadcast television ratings and newspaper and magazine readership have led many companies to explore alternative media, including not only digital

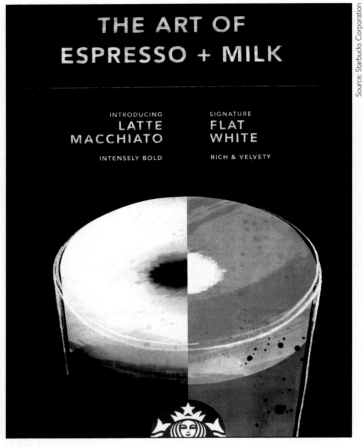

Source: Starbucks Corporation

**Media Plan**
Starbucks took out a number of ads using the Internet, newspapers, magazines, and an in-store graphic describing the differences between its espresso options.

advertising but also ads on cell phones, product placements in video games, and advertisements in nontraditional venues. New media like social networking sites are also attracting advertisers due to their large reach. Research findings have found that, when advertising is a part of a social networking site, consumers need to see the advertising as beneficial, or it may lead them to abandon the site.[21] Advertisers are using social media as a tool for understanding customers and gaining insights.[22] On the other hand, even in this age of digital media, television remains the most successful medium for advertising.[23]

The rise in digital marketing is creating a dramatic shift for advertising agencies. Whereas competition came mostly from other agencies before, today, professional ad agencies face competition from amateur ad makers along with technology companies. For instance, crowdsourcing by organizations like Victor & Spoils is placing the roles of traditional advertising agencies into the hands of creative people worldwide. Digital marketing is not reduced to one medium, but can include platforms such as social networks, e-books, iPads, geotargeting, and mobile apps. Agencies that choose to embrace new advertising media are facing challenges in adapting but are finding increased profits along the way. Big data can open the door to reaching the most desirable customers and have a positive effect on sales.[24] For instance, big data is allowing marketers to break up the Millennial generation into four categories marketers can use to target different products depending on their spending habits.[25] Digital marketing enables firms such as Coca-Cola to find more interactive ways to connect with specific target markets at a reasonable price.

The content of the message sometimes affects media choice. Print media can be used more effectively than broadcast media to present complex issues or numerous details in single advertisements. If an advertiser wants to promote beautiful colors, patterns, or textures, media offering high-quality color reproduction, such as magazines or television, should be used instead of newspapers. For instance, food can be effectively promoted in full-color magazine advertisements but far less effectively in black-and-white media. The UPS advertisement demonstrates how the UPS Store helps small businesses with their printing needs. This particular business requires UPS's assistance with

**Top Ten Advertisers**

| Rank | Company | Expenditure |
|------|---------|-------------|
| 1 | Procter & Gamble | $4.6 billion |
| 2 | AT&T | $3.3 billion |
| 3 | General Motors | $3.1 billion |
| 4 | Comcast Corporation | $3 billion |
| 5 | Verizon Communications | $2.5 billion |
| 6 | Ford Corporation | $2.5 billion |
| 7 | American Express | $2.4 billion |
| 8 | Fiat Chrysler | $2.2 billion |
| 9 | L'Oréal | $2.2 billion |
| 10 | Walt Disney Company | $2.1 billion |

SNAPSHOT

Source: Compiled from Ad Age's annual "200 Leading Advertisers" report. Lara O'Reilly, "These are the 10 companies that spend the most on advertising," *Business Insider*, July 6, 2015, http://www.businessinsider.com/10-biggest-advertising-spenders-in-the-us-2015-7 (accessed February 26, 2016).

printed stickers, postcards, catalogs, and more. By using magazine advertising, the UPS Store is able to emphasize the many bold, colorful stickers it is able to create to meet its client's needs. Decisions are also made in selection for non-English-speaking audiences across multiple media platforms. Advertisers' evaluation of distinct cultural traits and preferences appears to be more important in the case of Spanish-speaking audiences.[26]

The cost of media is an important but troublesome consideration. Planners try to obtain the best coverage possible for each dollar spent. However, there is no accurate way to compare the cost and impact of a television commercial with the cost and impact of a newspaper advertisement. Television marketers are using big data from companies such as TiVo and Nielsen to determine which shows interest their particular target market. By finding out that shows like "Big Cat Diary" on Animal Planet reach a target audience similar to "Good Morning America," marketers are able to select the less costly medium while still reaching their target market.[27] Another common metric is the **cost comparison indicator**, which lets an advertiser compare the costs of several vehicles within a specific medium (such as two magazines) in relation to the number of people each vehicle reaches. The *cost per thousand impressions (CPM)* is the cost comparison indicator for magazines; it shows the cost of exposing 1,000 people to one advertisement.

Figure 17.3 shows the increase in total ad spending worldwide. Emerging media are being used more extensively in light of media fragmentation and decline in traditional media (newspapers and radio). However, although the use of newer forms of media is increasing, many companies continue to spend significant amounts of their marketing dollars advertising in more traditional forums. It is estimated that seven out of 10 consumers still use the Yellow Pages to call businesses, which continues to make it a viable option for some advertisers.[28] Media are selected by weighing the various advantages and disadvantages of each (see Table 17.1).

Like media selection decisions, media scheduling decisions are affected by numerous factors, such as target audience characteristics, product attributes, product seasonality, customer media behavior, and size of the advertising budget. There are three general types of media schedules: continuous, flighting, and pulsing. When a *continuous* schedule is used, advertising runs at a constant level with little variation throughout the campaign period. McDonald's is an example of a company that uses a continuous schedule. With a *flighting* schedule, advertisements run for set periods of time, alternating with periods in which no ads run. For instance, an advertising campaign might have an ad run for 2 weeks, then suspend it for 2 weeks, and then run it again for 2 weeks. Companies like Hallmark, John Deere, and Ray-Ban use a flighting schedule. A *pulsing* schedule combines continuous and flighting schedules: During the entire campaign, a certain portion of advertising runs continuously, and during specific time periods of the campaign, additional advertising is used to intensify the level of communication with the target audience.

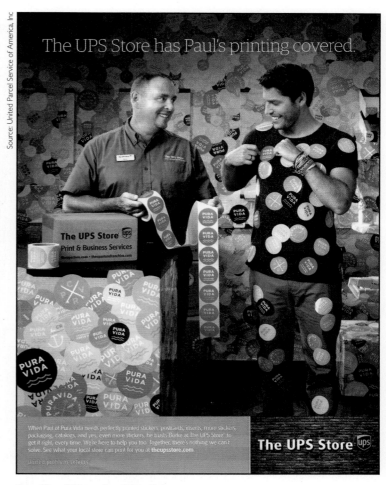

Source: United Parcel Service of America, Inc

**Benefits of Magazine Advertising**
Magazine advertisements allow marketers to show their advertisements using bold colors and patterns. In this advertisement for the UPS Store, colorful stickers cover the entire room—including the client—to demonstrate the company's ability to create customized printing solutions.

**cost comparison indicator**
A means of comparing the costs of advertising vehicles in a specific medium in relation to the number of people reached

Figure 17.3  **Total Media Ad Spending Worldwide, 2014–2019**

Note: Includes digital (desktop/laptop, mobile and other Internet-connected devices), directories, magazines, newspapers, outdoor, radio and TV
Source: eMarketer, September 2015.

## 17-2f  Creating the Advertising Message

The basic content and form of an advertising message are a function of several factors. A product's features, uses, and benefits affect the content of the message. The intensity of the advertising can also have an impact. For instance, push advertising on digital devices refers to advertising that is not requested by the user. Although push advertising might alienate some consumers, younger consumers are more accepting of push advertising if the source is trusted, permission has been given, and the messages are relevant or entertaining.[29] However, research has shown that advertising that pushes too hard to the point that consumers feel uncomfortable may cause consumers to consider the product negatively.[30] With the increase in digital technology, the cost of advertising for marketers is decreasing and advertising is becoming more frequent in venues such as mobile games. Marketers must make sure their advertising is not too intrusive as this could alienate consumers.[31]

Additionally, characteristics of the people in the target audience—gender, age, education, race, income, occupation, lifestyle, life stage, and other attributes—influence both content and form. For instance, gender affects how people respond to advertising claims that use hedging words like *may* and *probably* and pledging words, such as *definitely* and *absolutely*. Researchers have found that women respond negatively to both types of claims, but pledging claims have little effect on men.[32] When Procter & Gamble promotes Crest toothpaste to children, the company emphasizes daily brushing and cavity control, focusing on fun and good flavors like bubblegum. When marketing Crest to adults, P&G focuses on functionality, stressing whitening, enamel protection, breath enhancement, and tartar and plaque control. To communicate

Table 17.1 **Advantages and Disadvantages of Major Media Classes**

| Medium | Advantages | Disadvantages |
|---|---|---|
| Newspapers | Reaches large audience; purchased to be read; geographic flexibility; short lead time; frequent publication; favorable for cooperative advertising; merchandising services | Not selective for socioeconomic groups or target market; short life; limited reproduction capabilities; large advertising volume limits exposure to any one advertisement |
| Magazines | Demographic selectivity; good reproduction; long life; prestige; geographic selectivity when regional issues are available; read in leisurely manner | High costs; 30- to 90-day average lead time; high level of competition; limited reach; communicates less frequently |
| Direct mail | Little wasted circulation; highly selective; circulation controlled by advertiser; few distractions; personal; stimulates actions; use of novelty; relatively easy to measure performance; hidden from competitors | Very expensive; lacks editorial content to attract readers; often thrown away unread as junk mail; criticized as invasion of privacy; consumers must choose to read the ad |
| Radio | Reaches 95 percent of consumers; highly mobile and flexible; very low relative costs; ad can be changed quickly; high level of geographic and demographic selectivity; encourages use of imagination | Lacks visual imagery; short life of message; listeners' attention limited because of other activities; market fragmentation; difficult buying procedures; limited media and audience research |
| Television | Reaches large audiences; high frequency available; dual impact of audio and video; highly visible; high prestige; geographic and demographic selectivity; difficult to ignore | Very expensive; highly perishable message; size of audience not guaranteed; amount of prime time limited; lack of selectivity in target market |
| Internet | Immediate response; potential to reach a precisely targeted audience; ability to track customers and build databases; highly interactive medium | Costs of precise targeting are high; inappropriate ad placement; effects difficult to measure; concerns about security and privacy |
| Yellow Pages | Wide availability; action and product category oriented; low relative costs; ad frequency and longevity; nonintrusive | Market fragmentation; extremely localized; slow updating; lack of creativity; long lead times; requires large space to be noticed |
| Outdoor | Allows for frequent repetition; low cost; message can be placed close to point of sale; geographic selectivity; operable 24 hours a day; high creativity and effectiveness | Message must be short and simple; no demographic selectivity; seldom attracts readers' full attention; criticized as traffic hazard and blight on countryside; much wasted coverage; limited capabilities |

Sources: William F. Arens, *Contemporary Advertising* (Burr Ridge, IL: Irwin/McGraw-Hill, 2011); George E. Belch and Michael Belch, *Advertising and Promotion* (Burr Ridge, IL: Irwin/McGraw-Hill, 2011).

effectively, advertisers use words, symbols, and illustrations that are meaningful, familiar, and appealing to people in the target audience.

Another controversy for advertisers is whether to advertise to children. Many countries have restrictions on advertising to this demographic. Sweden and Norway ban advertising directed at children, and Great Britain limits the advertising of foods high in fat, salt, or sugar on television and radio to children under the age of 16. Many firms in the European Union and the United States are attempting self-regulation, developing codes of conduct regarding this type of advertising.

An advertising campaign's objectives and platform also affect the content and form of its messages. If a firm's advertising objectives involve large sales increases, the message may include hard-hitting, high-impact language, symbols, and messages. Slogans such as Home Depot's basic message, "More saving. More doing", can aid in brand recall. When designing slogans, marketers should make them short, retain them for a long period of time, and provide large marketing budgets to make the slogan memorable.[33] The use of spokescharacters or design elements can also be highly effective. Spokescharacters are visual images that can convey a brand's features, benefits, or brand personality. Flo from Progressive Insurance and the Geico gecko are examples of spokescharacters representing specific brands. The

## GOING GREEN

### Natural Claims for Cigarettes: Blowing Smoke?

Although there is no clear definition of "natural" on product labels, the description has a positive connotation suggesting environmental friendliness and healthier products. It seems fitting that the cigarette brand Natural American Spirit is among the top 10 cigarette brands sold in the United States. Based on the popularity of these claims, several cigarette manufacturers are using the word "natural" in their advertising or labeling. This has garnered the attention of the Food and Drug Administration (FDA).

Unlike the word "organic," there are no clear guidelines to determine whether a product is natural. However, the FDA believes that the words "natural" or

"additive-free" could be misleading to consumers. The claims themselves may not be false, but the positive connotations associated with these products could lead consumers to believe these tobacco products are safer. Santa Fe Natural Tobacco Company, for instance, truthfully marketed their tobacco products as organic. However, because "organic" is perceived to be healthier—whether there is scientific proof for it or not—regulatory pressures forced the company to place large warning signs on its labels to inform consumers that organic tobacco does not mean it is any healthier. On the other hand, the tobacco companies claim that they are in compliance with all regulations and are not being misleading.[b]

spokescharacter can provide a personality and improve brand equity by directly and indirectly enhancing excitement, sincerity, and trust.[34] Keebler uses the elves as spokescharacters for their cookies. Viewers have come to associate these spokescharacters with the company. In the advertisement, Keebler uses the elves to show the 'elfin magic' that goes into making the cookies so tasty. Thus, the advertising platform is the foundation on which campaign messages are built.

Choice of media obviously influences the content and form of the message. Effective outdoor displays and short broadcast spot announcements require concise, simple messages. Magazine and newspaper advertisements can include considerable detail and long explanations. Because several kinds of media offer geographic selectivity, a precise message can be tailored to a particular geographic section of the target audience. Some magazine publishers produce **regional issues**, in which advertisements and editorial content of copies appearing in one geographic area differ from those appearing in other areas. For instance, the AAA Publishing Network publishes 23 regional magazine titles, including *AAA Horizons* (Connecticut, Massachusetts, and Rhode Island), *Go Magazine* (North Carolina and South Carolina), and *Western Journey* (Idaho and Washington).[35] A company advertising with the AAA Publishing Network might decide to use one message in the New England region and another in the rest of the nation. A company may also choose to advertise in only one region. Such geographic selectivity lets a firm use the same message in different regions at different times.

### 17-2g Copy

**Copy** is the verbal portion of an advertisement and may include headlines, subheadlines, body copy, and a signature. Not all advertising contains all of these copy elements. Even handwritten notes on direct-mail advertising that say, "Try this. It works!" seem to increase requests for free samples.[36] The headline is critical because often it is the only part of the copy that people read. It should attract readers' attention and create enough interest to make them want to read the body copy or visit the website. The subheadline, if there is one, links the headline to the body copy and sometimes serves to explain the headline.

Body copy for most advertisements consists of an introductory statement or paragraph, several explanatory paragraphs, and a closing paragraph. Some copywriters have adopted

**regional issues** Versions of a magazine that differ across geographic regions

**copy** The verbal portion of advertisements

guidelines for developing body copy systematically: (1) identify a specific desire or problem, (2) recommend the product as the best way to satisfy that desire or solve that problem, (3) state product benefits and indicate why the product is best for the buyer's particular situation, (4) substantiate advertising claims, and (5) ask the buyer to take action. When substantiating claims, it is important to present the substantiation in a credible manner. The proof of claims should help strengthen both the image of the product and company integrity. A shortcut explanation of what much advertising is designed to accomplish is the AIDA model. Advertising should create *awareness*, produce *interest*, create *desire*, and ultimately result in a purchase (*action*). Typeface selection can help advertisers create a desired impression using fonts that are engaging, reassuring, or very prominent.[37]

The signature identifies the advertisement's sponsor. It may contain several elements, including the firm's trademark, logo, name, and address. The signature should be attractive, legible, distinctive, and easy to identify in a variety of sizes.

Often, because radio listeners are not fully "tuned in" mentally to what they're hearing on the radio, radio copy should be informal and conversational to attract listeners' attention. Radio messages are highly perishable and should consist of short, familiar terms, which increase their impact. The length should not require a rate of speech exceeding approximately 2.5 words per second.

In television copy, the audio material must not overpower the visual material, and vice versa. However, a television message should make optimal use of its visual portion, which can be very effective for product use, applications, and demonstrations. Copy for a television commercial is sometimes initially written in parallel script form. Video is described in the left column and audio in the right. When the parallel script is approved, the copywriter and artist combine copy with visual material by using a **storyboard**, which depicts a series of miniature television screens showing the sequence of major scenes in the commercial. Beneath each screen is a description of the audio portion to be used with that video segment. Technical personnel use the storyboard as a blueprint when producing the commercial.

Source: 2012 Kellogg NA Co

**Spokescharacter**
Keebler uses elves to promote the taste and quality of its cookies.

**storyboard** A blueprint that combines copy and visual material to show the sequence of major scenes in a commercial

**artwork** An advertisement's illustrations and layout

**illustrations** Photos, drawings, graphs, charts, and tables used to spark audience interest in an advertisement

## 17-2h  Artwork

**Artwork** consists of an advertisement's illustrations and layout. **Illustrations** are often photographs but can also be drawings, graphs, charts, and tables. Illustrations are used to draw attention, encourage audiences to read or listen to the copy, communicate an idea quickly, or convey ideas that are difficult to express. Illustrations can be more important in capturing

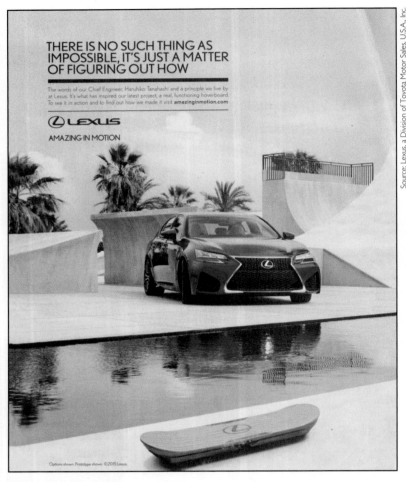

**Source: Lexus, a Division of Toyota Motor Sales, U.S.A., Inc.**

**Components of a Print Ad**
This Lexus advertisement contains components of a print ad, including a headline, subheadline, body copy, signature, and illustration.

attention than text or brand elements, independent of size.[38] They are especially important, because consumers tend to recall the visual portions of advertisements better than the verbal portions. Advertisers use a variety of illustration techniques. They may show the product alone, in a setting, or in use, or show the results of the product's use. For instance, the Lexus advertisement shows a close-up of a Lexus automobile next to a swimming pool. The setting reinforces the elegance of the Lexus brand. Illustrations can also take the form of comparisons, contrasts, diagrams, and testimonials.

The **layout** of an advertisement is the physical arrangement of the illustration and the copy (headline, subheadline, body copy, and signature). These elements can be arranged in many ways. The final layout is the result of several stages of layout preparation. As it moves through these stages, the layout promotes an exchange of ideas among people developing the advertising campaign and provides instructions for production personnel.

## 17-2i Executing the Campaign

Execution of an advertising campaign requires extensive planning and coordination, because many tasks must be completed on time and several people and firms are involved. Production companies, research organizations, media firms, printers, and commercial artists are just a few of the people and firms contributing to a campaign.

Implementation requires detailed schedules to ensure that various phases of the work are done on time. Advertising management personnel must evaluate the quality of the work and take corrective action when necessary. When Target reduced its marketing after the recession hit, the company largely abandoned its Bullseye mascot (a bull terrier with a red circle around its eye) in advertising. However, after years of stagnant marketing, Target decided to take corrective action and reintroduced its mascot. Bullseye now stars in several Target commercials. In an attempt to revamp its marketing, Target spends almost the same on marketing as does its big-box rival Walmart.[39] In some instances, changes are made during the campaign so it meets objectives more effectively. For example, an auto company focusing on gas mileage may need to add more information relative to the competition to achieve its objectives.

## 17-2j Evaluating Advertising Effectiveness

A variety of ways exist to test the effectiveness of advertising. They include measuring achievement of advertising objectives; assessing effectiveness of copy, illustrations, or layouts; and evaluating certain media.

Advertising can be evaluated before, during, and after the campaign. An evaluation performed before the campaign begins is called a **pretest**. A pretest usually attempts to evaluate the effectiveness of one or more elements of the message. To pretest advertisements, marketers

**layout** The physical arrangement of an advertisement's illustration and copy

**pretest** Evaluation of advertisements performed before a campaign begins sometimes use a **consumer jury**, a panel of existing or potential buyers of the advertised product. Jurors judge one or several dimensions of two or more advertisements. Such tests are based on the belief that consumers are more likely than advertising experts to know what influences them. Companies can also solicit the assistance of marketing research firms, such as Information Resources Inc. (IRI), to help assess ads.

To measure advertising effectiveness during a campaign, marketers usually rely on "inquiries" or responses. In a campaign's initial stages, an advertiser may use several advertisements simultaneously, each containing a coupon, form, toll-free phone number, QR code, social media, or website through which potential customers can request information. The advertiser records the number of inquiries or responses returned from each type of advertisement. If an advertiser receives 78,528 inquiries from advertisement A, 37,072 from advertisement B, and 47,932 from advertisement C, advertisement A is judged superior to advertisements B and C. Internet advertisers can also assess how many people "clicked" on an ad to obtain more product information. For the outdoor advertising industry, its independent auditor developed an out-of-home ratings system to determine the audiences likely to see an advertisement. Previous measurement systems used "Daily Effective Circulation," which essentially evolved around traffic counts, not on interested audiences. The industry has modified its rating system to account for new information, including vehicle speed and traffic congestion.[40]

Evaluation of advertising effectiveness after the campaign is called a **posttest**. Advertising objectives often determine what kind of posttest is appropriate. If the objectives' focus is on communication—to increase awareness of product features or brands or to create more favorable customer attitudes—the posttest should measure changes in these dimensions. Advertisers sometimes use consumer surveys or experiments to evaluate a campaign based on communication objectives. These methods are costly, however. In posttests, generalizations can be made about why advertising is failing or why media vehicles are not delivering the desired results.

For campaign objectives stated in terms of sales, advertisers should determine the change in sales or market share attributable to the campaign. Sales of Lincoln's MKZ sedan increased 5.1 percent in an eight-month period and is largely attributed to its advertising campaign featuring actor Matthew McConaughey.[41] However, changes in sales or market share brought about by advertising cannot be measured precisely; many factors independent of advertisements affect a firm's sales and market share. Competitors' actions, regulatory actions, and changes in economic conditions, consumer preferences, and weather are only a few factors that might enhance or diminish a company's sales or market share. By using data about past and current sales and advertising expenditures, advertisers can make gross estimates of the effects of a campaign on sales or market share. Because it is difficult to determine the direct effects of advertising on sales, many advertisers evaluate print advertisements according to how well consumers can remember them. As more advertisers turn to mobile technology, measuring the recall rate of mobile advertisements is becoming increasingly important. Despite this fact, studies suggest that print ads are still the most effective. Recall was approximately 70 percent higher among those who looked at a direct mail ad than a digital one.[42] Researchers have found that ads that play on the theme of social desirability are more memorable when viewed in the presence of other people.

Posttest methods based on memory include recognition and recall tests. Such tests are usually performed by research organizations through surveys. In a **recognition test**, respondents are shown the actual advertisement and asked whether they recognize it. If they do, the interviewer asks additional questions to determine how much of the advertisement each respondent read. When recall is evaluated, respondents are not shown the actual advertisement but instead are asked about what they have seen or heard recently. For Internet advertising, research suggests that the longer a person is exposed to a website containing a banner advertisement, the more likely he or she is to recall the ad.[43]

Recall can be measured through either unaided or aided recall methods. In an **unaided recall test**, respondents identify advertisements they have seen recently but are not shown any clues to help them remember. A similar procedure is used with an **aided recall test**, but respondents are shown a list of products, brands, company names, or trademarks to jog their memories. Research has shown that brand recall is 1.7 times higher among users of a product than non-users.[44]

**consumer jury** A panel of a product's existing or potential buyers who pretest ads

**posttest** Evaluation of advertising effectiveness after the campaign

**recognition test** A posttest in which respondents are shown the actual ad and are asked if they recognize it

**unaided recall test** A posttest in which respondents are asked to identify advertisements they have seen recently but are not given any recall clues

**aided recall test** A posttest that asks respondents to identify recent ads and provides clues to jog their memories

The major justification for using recognition and recall methods is that people are more likely to buy a product if they can remember an advertisement about it than if they cannot. However, recalling an advertisement does not necessarily lead to buying the product or brand advertised. Researchers also use a sophisticated technique called *single-source data* to help evaluate advertisements. With this technique, individuals' behaviors are tracked from television sets to checkout counters. Monitors are placed in preselected homes, and microcomputers record when the television set is on and which station is being viewed. At the supermarket checkout, the individual in the sample household presents an identification card. Checkers then record the purchases by scanner, and data are sent to the research facility. Some single-source data companies provide sample households with scanning equipment for use at home to record purchases after returning from shopping trips. Single-source data supplies information that links exposure to advertisements with purchase behavior.

# 17-3 WHO DEVELOPS THE ADVERTISING CAMPAIGN?

An advertising campaign may be handled by an individual, a few people within a firm, a firm's own advertising department, or an advertising agency. In very small firms, one or two individuals are responsible for advertising (and for many other activities as well). Usually, these individuals depend heavily on local media (TV, radio, and newspaper) for copywriting, artwork, and advice about scheduling media.

In certain large businesses, especially large retail organizations, advertising departments create and implement advertising campaigns. Depending on the size of the advertising program, an advertising department may consist of a few multiskilled individuals or a sizable number of specialists, including copywriters, artists, social media experts, media buyers, and technical production coordinators. Advertising departments sometimes obtain the services of independent research organizations and hire freelance specialists when a particular project requires it.

Many firms employ an advertising agency to develop advertising campaigns. For example, MillerCoors hired the advertising agency 72and-Sunny to revamp its advertising.[45] When an organization uses an advertising agency, the firm and the agency usually develop the advertising campaign jointly. How much each participates in the campaign's total development depends on the working relationship between the firm and the agency. Ordinarily, a firm relies on the agency for copywriting, artwork, technical production, and formulation of the media plan. In addition, advertising agencies, because of their size and number of clients, have the ability to reach celebrities for sponsorship or endorsement. After Mullen Lowe U.S. became the advertising agency for Patrón tequila, it added the tagline "It Doesn't Have to Make Sense to Be

Source: Patrón Spirits International AG

**The Value of Advertising Agencies**
Patrón tequila's advertising agency developed an additional tagline to support its "Simply Perfect" advertising platform.

Perfect." The additional tagline works well in complementing Patrón's "Simply Perfect" advertising platform.[46] In addition to the tagline, the Patrón tequila advertisement displays three of its different colored tequila products against a white background to symbolize their amazing quality.

Advertising agencies assist businesses in several ways. An agency, especially a large one, can supply the services of highly skilled specialists—not only copywriters, artists, and production coordinators, but also media experts, researchers, and legal advisers. Agency personnel often have broad advertising experience and are usually more objective than a firm's employees about the organization's products.

Because an agency traditionally receives most of its compensation from a 15 percent commission paid by the media from which it makes purchases, firms can obtain some agency services at low or moderate costs. If an agency contracts for $400,000 of television time for a firm, it receives a commission of $60,000 from the television station. Although the traditional compensation method for agencies is changing and now includes other factors, media commissions still offset some costs of using an agency. Like advertising, public relations can be a vital element in a promotion mix. We turn to this topic next.

## 17-4 PUBLIC RELATIONS

**Public relations** is a broad set of communication efforts used to create and maintain favorable relationships between an organization and its stakeholders. An organization communicates with various stakeholders, both internal and external, and public relations efforts can be directed toward any and all of them. A firm's stakeholders can include customers, suppliers, employees, shareholders, the media, educators, potential investors, government officials, and society in general. Public relations is also used to respond to negative events. How an organization uses public relations in a crisis often determines how quickly it will recover. Managers spend more resources understanding and responding to negative word of mouth than they do to the promotion of positive word of mouth.[47] Company scandals can often lead to the resignation of top officials such as the CEO or board members. Volkswagen's CEO stepped down after an emissions scandal revealed the company had duped regulators by placing defeat devices into its vehicles.[48] On the other hand, being honest with consumers and responsive to their needs develops a foundation for open communication and trust in the long run.

**public relations** Communication efforts used to create and maintain favorable relations between an organization and its stakeholders

Public relations can be used to promote people, places, ideas, activities, and even countries. It is often used by nonprofit organizations to achieve their goals. Public relations focuses on enhancing the image of the total organization. Assessing public attitudes and creating a favorable image are no less important than direct promotion of the organization's products. Because the public's attitudes toward a firm are likely to affect the sales of its products, it is very important for firms to maintain positive public perceptions. In addition, employee morale is strengthened if the public perceives the firm positively.[49] Although public relations can make people aware of a company's products, brands, or activities, it can also create specific company images, such as innovativeness or dependability. Companies like Keurig Green Mountain, Patagonia, Sustainable Harvest, and Honest Tea have reputations for being socially responsible not only because they engage in socially responsible behavior but also because their actions are reported through news stories and other public relations efforts. By getting the media to report on a firm's accomplishments, public relations helps the company maintain positive public visibility. Some firms use public relations for a single purpose; others use it for several purposes. Table 17.2 describes the top 10 public relations firms.

Table 17.2  **Top 10 Public Relations Firms**

| Rank | PR Agency |
|------|-----------|
| 1 | Edelman |
| 2 | Weber Shandwick |
| 3 | Fleishman-Hillard |
| 4 | Ketchum |
| 5 | MSLGroup |
| 6 | Burson-Marsteller |
| 7 | Hill+Knowlton Strategies |
| 8 | Ogilvy PR |
| 9 | Golin |
| 10 | Havas PR |

Source: The Holmes Report, "Global Top 250 Firms," http://www.holmesreport.com/ranking-and-data/world-pr-report/agency-rankings-2015/top-250 (accessed February 9, 2016).

# 17-5 **PUBLIC RELATIONS TOOLS**

Companies use a variety of public relations tools to convey messages and create images. Public relations professionals prepare written materials and use digital media to deliver brochures, newsletters, company magazines, news releases, blogs, managed social media sites, and annual reports that reach and influence their various stakeholders. Sometimes, organizations use less conventional tools in their public relations campaigns. Burger King paid boxer Floyd Mayweather to allow its mascot, the King, to accompany him as he walked in to one of his boxing matches. Burger King has become known for its buzz marketing stunts, which has led to increased sales among franchisees.[50]

Public relations personnel also create corporate identity materials—such as logos, business cards, stationery, signs, and promotional materials—that make firms immediately recognizable. Speeches are another public relations tool. Because what a company executive says publicly at meetings or to the media can affect the organization's image, the speech must convey the desired message clearly. Event sponsorship, in which a company pays for part or all of a special event, like a benefit concert or a tennis tournament, is another public relations tool. One example is Pizza Hut's sponsorship of ESPN's College GameDay.[51] Sponsoring special events can be an effective means of increasing company or brand recognition with relatively minimal investment. Event sponsorship can gain companies considerable amounts of free media coverage. An organization tries to ensure that its product and the sponsored event target a similar audience and that the two are easily associated in customers' minds. Many companies as well as individuals also assist in their charitable giving. Walmart, for instance, contributes approximately $1.4 billion in cash and in-kind donations.[52] Public relations personnel also organize unique events to "create news" about the company. These may include grand openings with celebrities, prizes, hot-air balloon rides, and other attractions that appeal to a firm's public.

Publicity is a part of public relations. **Publicity** is communication in news-story form about the organization, its products, or both, transmitted through a mass medium at no charge. For instance, each time Apple CEO Tim Cook announces that the company will introduce a new model of the iPhone and iPad, the story is covered in newspapers and television news shows throughout the world for months afterward. Although public relations has a larger, more comprehensive communication function than publicity, publicity is a very important aspect of public relations. Publicity can be used to provide information about goods or services; to announce expansions or contractions, acquisitions, research, or new-product launches; or to enhance a company's image.

The most common publicity-based public relations tool is the **news release**, sometimes called a *press release*, which is usually a single page of type-written copy containing fewer than 300 words and describing a company event or product. A news release gives the firm's or agency's name, address, phone number, and contact person. Companies sometimes use news releases when introducing new products or making significant announcements. Dozens of organizations, including Nike, Starbucks, and clean-energy companies, are partnering to create awareness of the economic benefits of national climate and energy legislation through press releases and other media. As Table 17.3 shows, news releases tackle a multitude of specific issues. A **feature article** is a manuscript of up to 3,000 words prepared for a specific publication. A **captioned photograph** is a photograph with a brief description explaining its contents. Captioned photographs are effective for illustrating new or improved products with highly visible features.

There are several other kinds of publicity-based public relations tools. For example, a **press conference** is a meeting called to announce major news events. Media personnel are invited to a press conference and are usually supplied with various written materials and photographs. Letters to the editor and editorials are sometimes prepared and sent to newspapers and magazines. Videos may be made available to broadcasters in the hope that they will be aired.

**publicity** A news story type of communication about an organization and/or its products transmitted through a mass medium at no charge

**news release** A short piece of copy publicizing an event or a product

**feature article** A manuscript of up to 3,000 words prepared for a specific publication

**captioned photograph** A photograph with a brief description of its contents

**press conference** A meeting used to announce major news events

Table 17.3 **Possible Issues for Publicity Releases**

| | |
|---|---|
| Support of a social cause | New products |
| Improved warranties | New slogan |
| Reports on industry conditions | Research developments |
| New uses for established products | Company's milestones and anniversaries |
| Product endorsements | Employment, production, and sales changes |
| Quality awards | Award of contracts |
| Company name changes | Opening of new markets |
| Interviews with company officials | Improvements in financial position |
| Improved distribution policies | Opening of an exhibit |
| International business efforts | History of a brand |
| Athletic event sponsorship | Winners of company contests |
| Visits by celebrities | Logo changes |
| Reports on new discoveries | Speeches of top management |
| Innovative business practices | Merit awards |
| Economic forecasts | Acquisitions and partnerships |

Publicity-based public relations tools offer several advantages, including credibility, news value, significant word-of-mouth communications, and a perception of media endorsement. The public may consider news coverage more truthful and credible than an advertisement because news media are not paid to provide the information. In addition, stories regarding a new-product introduction or a new environmentally responsible company policy, for example, are handled as news items and are likely to receive notice. Finally, the cost of publicity is low compared with the cost of advertising.[53]

Publicity-based public relations tools have some limitations. Media personnel must judge company messages to be newsworthy if the messages are to be published or broadcast at all. Consequently, messages must be timely, interesting, accurate, and in the public interest. It may take a great deal of time and effort to convince media personnel of the news value of publicity releases, and many communications fail to qualify. Although public relations personnel usually encourage the media to air publicity releases at certain times, they control neither the content nor the timing of the communication. Media personnel alter length and content of publicity releases to fit publishers' or broadcasters' requirements and may even delete the parts of messages that company personnel view as most important. Furthermore, media personnel use publicity releases in time slots or positions most convenient for them. Other outside public relations messages can be picked up during slow news times. Thus, messages sometimes appear in locations or at times that may not reach the firm's target audiences. Although these limitations can be frustrating, properly managed publicity-based public relations tools offer an organization substantial benefits.

## 17-6 EVALUATING PUBLIC RELATIONS EFFECTIVENESS

Because of the potential benefits of good public relations, it is essential that organizations evaluate the effectiveness of their public relations campaigns. Research can be conducted to determine how well a firm is communicating its messages or image to its target audiences. *Environmental monitoring* identifies changes in public opinion affecting an organization. A *public relations audit* is used to assess an organization's image among the public or to evaluate the effect of a specific public relations program. A *communications audit* may include a content analysis of messages, a readability study, or a readership survey. If an organization wants to measure the extent to which stakeholders view it as being socially responsible, it can conduct a *social audit*.

One approach to measuring the effectiveness of publicity-based public relations is to count the number of exposures in the media. To determine which releases are published in print media and how often, an organization can hire a clipping service, a firm that clips and sends news releases to client companies. To measure the effectiveness of television coverage, a firm can enclose a card with its publicity releases requesting that the television station record its name and the dates when the news item is broadcast (although station personnel do not always comply). Some multimedia tracking services exist, but they are quite costly.

Counting the number of media exposures does not reveal how many people have actually read or heard the company's message or what they thought about the message afterward. However, measuring changes in product awareness, knowledge, and attitudes resulting from the publicity campaign helps yield this information. To assess these changes, companies must measure these levels before and after public relations campaigns. Although precise measures are difficult to obtain, a firm's marketers should attempt to assess the impact of public relations efforts on the organization's sales. For example, critics' reviews of films can affect the films' box office performance. Interestingly, negative reviews (publicity) harm revenue more than positive reviews help revenue in the early weeks of a film's release.[54]

## 17-6a Dealing with Unfavorable Public Relations

Thus far, we have discussed public relations as a planned element of the promotion mix. However, companies may have to deal with unexpected and unfavorable publicity resulting from an unsafe product, an accident resulting from product use, controversial actions of employees, or some other negative event or situation. Product recalls or products that could harm consumers can create a crisis and damage a brand. The extent of negative publicity and whether the brand has to publicly take blame will affect the amount of damage.[55] Many companies have experienced unfavorable publicity connected with defective or contaminated products, such as faulty car parts, E.coli in fast food, and industrial compounds in pet foods. Unfavorable coverage can have quick and dramatic effects. Coca-Cola was forced to quickly pull an advertisement it featured in Germany to celebrate Fanta's 75th anniversary in the country. Its marketing referred to the 1940s as "the good old times." Coca-Cola experienced immediate backlash as the 1940s in Germany was marked by the Nazi era.[56]

Negative events that generate public relations can wipe out a company's favorable image and destroy positive customer attitudes established through years of expensive advertising campaigns and other promotional efforts. Target, for instance, suffered reputational damage after hackers hacked into its system and stole credit card information from millions of its customers. Reputation is often considered a valuable company asset. How an organization deals with unfavorable actions and outcomes can have a significant impact on firm valuation. Moreover, today's mass media, including online services and the Internet, disseminate information faster than ever before, and bad news generally receives more media attention than corporate social responsibility.

To protect its image, an organization needs to prevent unfavorable public relations or at least lessen its effect if it occurs. First and foremost, the organization should try to prevent negative incidents and events through safety programs, inspections, training, and effective quality control procedures. Experts insist that sending consistent brand messages and images throughout all communications at all times can help a brand maintain its strength even during a crisis.[57] However, because negative events can strike even the most cautious firms, an organization should have plans in place to handle them when they do occur. Firms need to establish policies and procedures for reducing the adverse impact of news coverage of a crisis or controversy. In most cases, organizations should expedite news coverage of negative events rather than try to discourage or block them. If news coverage is suppressed, rumors and other misinformation may replace facts and create public scrutiny.

An unfavorable event can easily balloon into serious problems or public issues and become very damaging. By being forthright with the press and public and taking prompt action, a firm may be able to convince the public of its honest attempts to deal with the situation, and news personnel may be more willing to help explain complex issues to the public. Dealing effectively with a negative event allows an organization to lessen, if not eliminate, the unfavorable impact on its image. Experts generally advise companies that are dealing with negative publicity to respond quickly and honestly to the situation and to keep the lines of communication with all stakeholders open. Digital media has enhanced the organizational ability to communicate with key stakeholders and develop dialogues on current issues.

# Summary

### 17-1 Describe advertising and its different types.

Advertising is a paid form of nonpersonal communication transmitted to consumers through mass media, such as television, radio, the Internet, newspapers, magazines, direct mail, outdoor displays, and signs on mass transit vehicles. Both business and nonbusiness organizations use advertising. Institutional advertising promotes organizational images, ideas, and political issues. When a company promotes its position on a public issue such as taxation, institutional advertising is referred to as advocacy advertising. Product advertising promotes uses, features, and benefits of products. The two types of product advertising are pioneer advertising, which focuses on stimulating demand for a product category rather than a specific brand, and competitive advertising, which attempts to stimulate demand for a specific brand by indicating the brand's features, uses, and advantages. To make direct product comparisons, marketers use comparative advertising, which compares two or more brands. Two other forms of competitive advertising are reminder advertising, which reminds customers about an established brand's uses, characteristics, and benefits, and reinforcement advertising, which assures current users they have made the right brand choice. A newer form of advertising, native advertising, is digital advertising that matches the appearance and purpose of the content in which it is embedded.

### 17-2 Summarize the eight major steps in developing an advertising campaign.

Although marketers may vary in how they develop advertising campaigns, they should follow a general pattern. First, they must identify and analyze the target audience, the group of people at whom advertisements are aimed. Second, they should establish what they want the campaign to accomplish by defining advertising objectives. Objectives should be clear, precise, and presented in measurable terms. Third, marketers must create the advertising platform, which contains basic issues to be presented in the campaign. Advertising platforms should consist of issues important to consumers. Fourth, advertisers must decide how much money to spend on the campaign; they arrive at this decision through the objective-and-task approach, percent-of-sales approach, competition-matching approach, or arbitrary approach.

Advertisers must then develop a media plan by selecting and scheduling media to use in the campaign. Some factors affecting the media plan are location and demographic characteristics of the target audience, content of the message, and cost of the various media. The basic content and form of the advertising message are affected by product features, uses, and benefits; characteristics of the people in the target audience; the campaign's objectives and platform; and the choice of media. Advertisers use copy and artwork to create the message. The execution of an advertising campaign requires extensive planning and coordination.

Finally, advertisers must devise one or more methods for evaluating advertisement effectiveness. Pretests are evaluations performed before the campaign begins; posttests are conducted after the campaign. Two types of posttests are a recognition test, in which respondents are shown the actual advertisement and asked whether they recognize it, and a recall test. In aided recall tests, respondents are shown a list of products, brands, company names, or trademarks to jog their memories. In unaided tests, no clues are given.

### 17-3 Identify who is responsible for developing advertising campaigns.

Advertising campaigns can be developed by personnel within the firm or in conjunction with advertising agencies. A campaign created by the firm's personnel may be developed by one or more individuals or by an advertising department within the firm. Use of an advertising agency may be advantageous because an agency provides highly skilled, objective specialists with broad experience in advertising at low to moderate costs to the firm.

### 17-4 Define *public relations*.

Public relations is a broad set of communication efforts used to create and maintain favorable relationships between an organization and its stakeholders. Public relations can be used to promote people, places, ideas, activities, and countries, and to create and maintain a positive company image. Some firms use public relations for a single purpose; others use it for several purposes.

## 17-5 Describe the different tools of public relations.

Public relations tools include written materials, such as brochures, newsletters, and annual reports; corporate identity materials, such as business cards and signs; speeches; event sponsorships; and special events. Publicity is communication in news-story form about an organization, its products, or both, transmitted through a mass medium at no charge. Publicity-based public relations tools include news releases, feature articles, captioned photographs, and press conferences. Problems that organizations confront in using publicity-based public relations include reluctance of media personnel to print or air releases and lack of control over timing and content of messages.

## 17-6 Analyze how public relations is used and evaluated.

To evaluate the effectiveness of their public relations programs, companies conduct research to determine how well their messages are reaching their audiences. Environmental monitoring, public relations audits, and counting the number of media exposures are all means of evaluating public relations effectiveness. Organizations should avoid negative public relations by taking steps to prevent negative events that result in unfavorable publicity. To diminish the impact of unfavorable public relations, organizations should institute policies and procedures for dealing with news personnel and the public when negative events occur.

---

**Go to www.cengagebrain.com for resources to help you master the content in this chapter as well as for materials that will expand your marketing knowledge!**

---

# Important Terms

| | | | |
|---|---|---|---|
| advertising 530 | advertising campaign 533 | media plan 536 | recognition test 545 |
| institutional advertising 531 | target audience 534 | cost comparison indicator 539 | unaided recall test 545 |
| advocacy advertising 531 | advertising platform 535 | regional issues 542 | aided recall test 545 |
| product advertising 531 | advertising appropriation 535 | copy 542 | public relations 547 |
| pioneer advertising 531 | objective-and-task approach 536 | storyboard 543 | publicity 548 |
| competitive advertising 532 | percent-of-sales approach 536 | artwork 543 | news release 548 |
| comparative advertising 532 | competition-matching approach 536 | illustrations 543 | feature article 548 |
| reminder advertising 532 | | layout 544 | captioned photograph 548 |
| reinforcement advertising 532 | arbitrary approach 536 | pretest 544 | press conference 548 |
| native advertising 532 | | consumer jury 545 | |
| | | posttest 545 | |

# Discussion and Review Questions

1. What is the difference between institutional and product advertising?
2. What is the difference between competitive advertising and comparative advertising?
3. What are the major steps in creating an advertising campaign?
4. What is a target audience? How does a marketer analyze the target audience after identifying it?
5. Why is it necessary to define advertising objectives?
6. What is an advertising platform, and how is it used?
7. What factors affect the size of an advertising budget? What techniques are used to determine an advertising budget?
8. Describe the steps in developing a media plan.
9. What is the function of copy in an advertising message?

10. Discuss several ways to posttest the effectiveness of advertising.
11. What role does an advertising agency play in developing an advertising campaign?
12. What is public relations? Whom can an organization reach through public relations?
13. How do organizations use public relations tools? Give several examples you have observed recently.
14. Explain the problems and limitations associated with publicity-based public relations.
15. In what ways is the effectiveness of public relations evaluated?
16. What are some sources of negative public relations? How should an organization deal with unfavorable public relations?

# Video Case 17.1

## Scripps Networks Interactive: An Expert at Connecting Advertisers with Programming

Television advertisers have faced challenges in the past several years. People tend to watch fewer television shows at the time of airing or choose to watch them on Internet platforms such as Netflix or Hulu. The use of Digital Video Recorders (DVRs) has also contributed to this challenge as viewers can fast forward through commercials while watching their favorite shows. Scripps Networks Interactive, parent company to Food Network, HGTV, Travel Channel, DIY Network, Cooking Channel, ulive, and Great American Country, has found a way around this issue through product placement and integration, use of social media platforms, and promotion.

Scripps Networks Interactive is unique in that their programming appeals to similar target markets with similar interests. The director of Digital Media and Database Marketing for Scripps Networks Interactive states, "Our programming lends itself so well to speaking to lifestyle and what people are passionate and interested in, and I think our marketing communications strategy is a natural extension of that." This presents a strong opportunity for gaining real results through advertising. At the same time, these promotional initiatives do not always seem like advertising to viewers. One way this is accomplished is through cross-promotional activities across networks. For example, while watching an episode of *Paula's Home Cooking* on the Food Network, viewers would see a commercial for a *Design Star* episode on HGTV featuring Paula Deen. (In 2013 Paula Deen's contract was not renewed.) These marketing promotions appear to be natural extensions of the show rather than advertising that is deemed intrusive.

Product placement and integration works well with the lifestyle content of the company's programming because viewers are interested in the content being provided. In most cases, "our audiences...actually look to our advertisers' products for ideas and as resources," states the Senior Vice President of Interactive Ad Sales Marketing for Scripps. This creates an opportunity for the company to build strong relationships with advertisers. Advertisers seek out Scripps Networks not only for placement in their shows but also for integration into their social media space. The integration of television product placement and social media advertising has been a benefit for both parties. The Senior Vice President of Interactive Ad Sales Marketing explains, "If we tie a specific advertiser to *Iron Chef* or to *Chopped*, then there's opportunities for them to be driven from on-air to say 'check out the recipes from this specific episode online at foodnetwork.com'." Despite the culinary nature of these shows, the advertising platform Scripps attracts other vendors, including automobile manufacturers. Lexus, for example, was featured as the car driven by *Restaurant Impossible's* host Robert Irvine. These clips were then shown on the show's webpage, packaged as a Lexus advertisement.

Scripps has also found a way to integrate product placement into brick and mortar locations as well as on digital space. After Food Network host Guy Fieri won recognition as "The Next Food Network Star," he partnered with TGI Fridays in an endorsement agreement. Fieri hosted a recipe showdown on the Food Network, and TGI Fridays promoted these recipes in their restaurants. Partnerships between chefs and brands have also been developed to create co-branded products. Alex Guarnaschelli, a judge on *Chopped*, was approached by Fisher Nuts to share recipes containing their product. These advertisements were shown on both the Food Network and the Cooking Channel.

Another benefit of this integration is that the company and the advertiser become cooperative marketing partners, where both are working from different directions to promote both the show and the product simultaneously. The General Manager of New Business for the Food Network explains an example of this kind of relationship with Kohl's and *Worst Cooks in America*: "Kohl's is advertising in it—they are sponsoring it. They are putting things on Pinterest or tweeting. We are doing the same thing in the context of the character, so you get both this top-down and bottom-up thing coming together."

Promotions also work well on this platform. A digital marketer for Scripps Networks describes the effectiveness of promotions. "What makes it more than just a giveaway for money is tying in hooks that engage people to not only sign up to a sweepstakes to win a trip...but making it part of the entertainment experience." For example, the Food Network ran a promotion for its show *The Great Food Truck Race*, where people were asked to go to the Facebook page and nominate or vote for their favorite local food truck. The winners would then be featured on the show's website. This event generated buzz and brought attention to the food trucks around the country that were being nominated. The nominees were featured on commercials aired during the show, where they asked viewers to vote for them online. The fans, businesses, and the show were all involved in generating buzz and promoting one another, creating an effect that is advantageous to all parties.[58]

### Questions for Discussion

1. Why is the Food Network such an important venue for many advertisers?
2. Describe some of the ways that Scripps uses product placement on the Food Network.
3. Why do you think even non-food advertisers are attracted to the Food Network?

# Case 17.2

## Greenwashing Harms Companies and Consumers

Sustainability is a multi-billion dollar industry. This includes organic food, electric and hybrid vehicles, energy-efficient light bulbs, and green cleaning products. Consumers have been willing to pay a premium for green and sustainable products even during the Great Recession. This trend, however, is changing due to the phenomenon called greenwashing.

Greenwashing occurs when companies deceptively market products as environmentally friendly. Greenwashing does not have to be completely untrue. For instance, a company might put a label on its product saying that it is "free from chlorofluorocarbons (CFC-free)" as if that is a major accomplishment. CFC-free products are required by law. Greenwashing has decreased consumer trust in the claims that companies are making about their environmentally-friendly products. A survey concluded that consumers' willingness to pay more for green products dropped between 5 and 12 percentage points during a four-year period.

In the past, the Federal Trade Commission (FTC) has cracked down on companies whose advertisements were inaccurate. For instance, the FTC sent warning letters to five providers of environmental certification seals to warn them that they might not be complying with the agency's environmental guidelines. The FTC believes that seals without many details are deceptive because consumers could perceive the product's sustainability differently than what the marketer intended. Further, one study determined that as many as 95 percent of products marketed as green were guilty of at least one form of greenwashing.

The FTC issued a revised set of Green Guides in October of 2012 for businesses to use as they are marketing their products. One of the changes includes advising marketers not to make broad claims about the green attributes of their products. For instance, simply labeling a product as eco-friendly gives the impression that every aspect of the product's production was conducted in an environmentally friendly manner. The product itself may be green, but the way in which it was produced may have created mass amounts of pollution or large amounts of water waste. Although these guidelines do not carry the force of law, they better enable the FTC to pursue companies that violate standards by engaging in deceptive marketing practices.

©iStockphoto.com/bodo23

The European Union (EU) takes these matters so seriously that it requires advertisers to state their carbon emissions on their advertisements. There are also groups such as the Friends of the Earth Europe who engage consumers in taking a stand against companies who make false green claims. Every year the organization hosts a campaign called the Pinocchio Awards, where people can place votes and expose companies involved in greenwashing or other misleading environmental or socially responsible activities. Each year nine companies are nominated in three different categories. The first is Lobbying, which goes to the company that has lobbied the hardest in opposing climate change policies; Greenwashing; and the final category, Local Impacts, awarded to the firm that has had the worst impact on local environments. This tactic puts pressure on companies, not only from the government, but also from consumers to behave in a manner consistent with their claims. It also helps to direct companies away from practices that are harmful to society and the environment.

Greenwashing hurts all businesses in the industry, even those whose claims are accurate and honest. Some companies are taking a unique approach to prove to consumers that they are indeed concerned about their environmental impact. For example, Heineken launched a digital campaign that recognized seven farmers ("Legendary 7") in France, Germany, the United Kingdom, Greece, and the Netherlands for their high-quality, sustainably grown hops and barley used in the company's beer. Consumers who had a mobile app could access the stories behind the farmers, read Heineken's goals toward sustainability, and get a chance to create their own 7elfies they could share on social media. Although this campaign does not contribute directly to profits, it does establish goodwill between the company's brand and the consumer.

Other companies are taking external measures to substantiate their green claims by developing a certification system to help consumers make informed decisions when buying supposedly green products. Partnering with certification organizations such as the Carbon Trust, for example, can validate carbon output claims. However, certification organizations are not always trustworthy either, as demonstrated by the five warning letters the FTC sent to five providers of environmental seals. Some of them charge a fee and do not hold products to rigorous standards. For the time being, the best way for consumers to be informed about eco-friendly products is to do some research before going shopping.[59]

## Questions for Discussion

1. Why does greenwashing have such a negative impact?
2. What are some ways that stakeholders have dissuaded greenwashing?
3. What are some actions organizations are taking to demonstrate a genuine commitment toward sustainability?

# NOTES

[1] Associated Press, "Judge: POM deceptively marketed juice," *CBS News*, May 21, 2012, http://www.cbsnews.com/news/judge-pom-deceptively-marketed-pomegranate-juice/ (accessed June 9, 2015); Andrés Cardenal, "Pom Wonderful's Deceptive Ads: Lessons for Consumers and Investors," *Motley Fool*, May 23, 2015, http://www.fool.com/investing/general/2015/05/23/pom-wonderfuls-deceptive-ads-lessons-for-consumers.aspx (accessed June 9, 2015); "D.C. Circuit: FTC's Two RCT Requirement Violates the First Amendment," Emord & Associates, PC, February 2, 2015, http://emord.com/blawg/d-c-circuit-ftcs-two-rct-requirement-violates-the-first-amendment/ (accessed February 13, 2015); Brent Kendall, "Pom's Ads Mislead Consumers, Court Says," *The Wall Street Journal*, January 1-February 1, 2015, B3; Rich Samp, "The D.C. Circuit's POM Wonderful Decision: Not So Wonderful for FTC's Randomized Clinical Trial Push," *Forbes*, February 4, 2015, http://www.forbes.com/sites/wlf/2015/02/04/the-d-c-circuits-pom-wonderful-decision-not-so-wonderful-for-ftcs-randomized-clinical-trial-push/ (accessed June 9, 2015).

[2] Suzanne Vranica, "Arby's Swallows Pride for Jon Stewart," *The Wall Street Journal*, August 6, 2015, B1, B8.

[3] Douglas E. Hughes, "This ad's for you: The indirect effect of advertising perceptions on salesperson effort and performance," *Journal of the Academy of Marketing Science* 41, 1 (2013): 1–18.

[4] Tim Nudd, "AT&T's Latest 'It Can Wait' Ad Shows a Brutal Crash in Reverse, but There's No Going Back," *AdWeek*, July 20, 2015, http://www.adweek.com/adfreak/atts-latest-it-can-wait-ad-shows-brutal-crash-reverse-theres-no-going-back-166004 (accessed February 10, 2016).

[5] Yuki Hagiwara and Ma Jie, "Tokyo to Get $385 Million Hydrogen Makeover for Olympics," *Bloomberg*, January 20, 2015, http://www.bloomberg.com/news/2015-01-19/tokyo-to-get-385-million-hydrogen-makeover-for-olympics.html (accessed February 11, 2016).

[6] Micael Dahlén, Helge Thorbjørnsen, and Henrik Sjödin, "A Taste of 'Nextopia,'" *Journal of Advertising* 40, 1 (Winter 2011): 33–44.

[7] Fred K. Beard, "Practitioner Views of Comparative Advertising: How Practices Have Changed in Two Decades," *Journal of Advertising Research* 53, 3 (2013): 313–323.

[8] Andrew John Bellingall, "Comparative advertising in Brazil," *Intellectual Property Magazine*, October 2010, pp. 27–30.

[9] Michael Sebastian, "Native Ad Production Values Keep Growing With 'Orange is the New Black' Promo," *Advertising Age*, June 13, 2014, http://adage.com/article/media/york-times-runs-native-ad-orange-black/293713/ (accessed February 11, 2016).

[10] Lucia Moses, "LinkedIn now gets 45 percent of its ad revenue from native advertising," *Digiday*, August 6, 2015, http://digiday.com/publishers/linkedin-native-ads/ (accessed February 11, 2016).

[11] Joe Lazauskas, "Study: Most Readers Have Felt Deceived by Sponsored Content," *Contently*, July 9, 2014, http://contently.com/strategist/2014/07/09/study-sponsored-content-has-a-trust-problem-2/ (accessed February 11, 2016).

[12] Tae Hyun Baek and Mariko Morimoto, "Stay Away from Me," *Journal of Advertising* 41, no. 1 (Spring 2012): 59–76.

[13] Louise Jack, "Why Unilever is Betting Big on Sustainability," *Fast Company*, October 2, 2015, http://www.fastcocreate.com/3051498/behind-the-brand/why-unilever-is-betting-big-on-sustainability (accessed February 11, 2016).

[14] Daniel A. Sheinin, Sajeev Varki, and Christy Ashley, "The Differential Effect of Ad Novelty and Message Usefulness on Brand Judgments," *Journal of Advertising* 40, 3 (Fall 2011): 5–17.

[15] Andrew McMains, "Ad of the Day: Panera Gets Into Lifestyle Branding with Manifesto about Healthy Living," *Ad Week*, June 15, 2015, http://www.adweek.com/news/advertising-branding/ad-day-panera-gets-lifestyle-branding-manifesto-about-healthy-living-165330 (accessed February 10, 2016).

[16] Douglas West, John B. Ford, and Paul W. Farris, "How Corporate Cultures Drive Advertising and Promotion Budgets: Best Practices Combine Heuristics and Algorithmic Tools," *Journal of Advertising Research* (June 2014): 149–162.

[17] Yunjae Cheong, Federico de Gregorio, and Kihan Kim, "Advertising Spending Efficiency Among Top U.S. Advertisers from 1985 to 2012: Overspending or Smart Managing?" *Journal of Advertising* 43, 4 (2014): 344–358.

[18] Jennifer Durando, "Latte Macchiato joining Starbucks menu," *USA Today*, January 5, 2016, http://www.usatoday.com/story/money/nation-now/2016/01/04/latte-macchiato-joining-starbucks-menu/78265942/ (accessed February 19, 2016).

[19] EMarketer, "Mobile to Account for More than Half of Digital Ad Spending in 2015," *eMarketer*, September 1, 2015, http://www.emarketer.com/Article/Mobile-Account-More-than-Half-of-Digital-Ad-Spending-2015/1012930 (accessed February 11, 2016).

[20] Crain Communications Inc., "National Geographic," *AdAge 360° Media Guide*,

http://brandedcontent.adage.com/360/details.php?brand=23 (accessed February 11, 2016).

21 David G. Taylor, Jeffrey E. Lewin, and David Strutton, "Friends, Fans, and Followers: Do Ads Work on Social Networks? How Gender and Age Shape Receptivity," *Journal of Advertising Research* 51, 1 (2011): 258–275.

22 Sonia Dickinson-Delaporte and Gayle Kerr, "Agency-Generated Research of Consumer-Generated Content: The Risks, Best Practices, and Ethics," *Journal of Advertising Research* (December 2014): 469–478.

23 Geoffrey Precourt, "What We Know about TV Today (and Tomorrow)," *Journal of Advertising Research* 53, 1 (2013): 3–4.

24 Gina A. Tran and David Strutton, "What Factors Affect Consumer Acceptance of In-Game Advertisements? Click 'Like' to Manage Digital Content for Players," *Journal of Advertising Research* 53, no. 4 (2013): 455–469.

25 Marty Swant, "Infographic: Marketers Are Spending 500% More on Millennials than All Others Combined," *AdWeek*, November 17, 2015, http://www.adweek.com/news/technology/infographic-marketers-are-spending-500-more-millennials-all-others-combined-168176 (accessed February 11, 2016).

26 Amy Jo Coffey, "The Power of Cultural Factors In Spanish-Language Advertising: Ethnic-Group Traits and Metrics May Predict Advertiser Investment across Media Platforms," *Journal of Advertising Research*, 346–355.

27 Steven Perlberg, "Targeted Ads Are Coming to Your Television," *The Wall Street Journal*, November 21, 2014, B1, B5.

28 DAS Group, "Old Skool: Why Print Yellow Pages Are Still Worth Considering as Part of Your Lead Generation Programs," January 5, 2016, http://www.das-group.com/blog/old-skool-why-print-yellow-pages-are-still-worth-considering-as-part-of-your-lead-generation-programs/ (accessed February 11, 2016).

29 Shintaro Okazaki and Patrick Barwise, "Has the Time Finally Come for the Medium of the Future? Research on Mobile Advertising," 50th Anniversary Supplement, *Journal of Advertising Research* 51, 1 (2011): 59–71.

30 Chingching Chang, "Feeling Ambivalent about Going Green," *Journal of Advertising* 40, 4 (Winter 2011): 19–31.

31 Pierre Berthon, Karen Robson, and Leyland Pitt, "The Theory and Practice of Advertising: Counting the Cost to the Customer," *The Journal of Advertising Research* 53, 3 (2013): 244–246.

32 Ilona A. Berney-Reddish and Charles S. Areni, "Sex Differences in Responses to Probability Markers in Advertising Claims," *Journal of Advertising* 35 (Summer 2006): 7–17.

33 Chiranjeev Kohli, Sunil Thomas, and Rajneesh Suri, "Are You in Good Hands? Slogan Recall: What Really Matters," *Journal of Advertising Research* 53, 1 (2013): 31–42.

34 Judith Anne Garretson Folse, Richard G. Netemeyer, and Scot Burton, "Spokescharacters," *Journal of Advertising* 41, 1 (Spring 2012): 17–32.

35 AAA Publishing Network, "Publishing Network," http://www.aaapublishingnetwork.com/pages.cfm?p=publications_all.cfm (accessed February 11, 2016).

36 Daniel J. Howard and Roger A. Kerin, "The Effects of Personalized Product Recommendations on Advertisement Response Rates: The 'Try This. It Works!' Technique," *Journal of Consumer Psychology* 14, 3 (2004): 271–279.

37 Pamela W. Henderson, Joan L. Giese, and Joseph A. Cote, "Impression Management Using Typeface Design," *Journal of Marketing* 68 (October 2004): 60–72.

38 Rik Pieters and Michel Wedel, "Attention Capture and Transfer in Advertising: Brand, Pictorial, and Text-Size Effects," *Journal of Marketing* 68 (April 2004): 36–50.

39 Hiroko Tabuchi, "Target's Dog Mascot Learns New Tricks in Marketing Blitz," *The New York Times*, December 22, 2015, http://www.nytimes.com/2015/12/23/business/targets-dog-mascot-learns-new-tricks-in-marketing-blitz.html?_r=0 (accessed February 11, 2016).

40 Nathalie Tadena, "What Traffic Congestion, Car Speeds Mean for Outdoor Ads," *The Wall Street Journal*, June 17, 2014, http://blogs.wsj.com/cmo/2014/06/17/measuring-the-other-type-of-on-the-go-ads/ (accessed February 11, 2016).

41 Zach Doell, "Lincoln's Turnaround: 2014 Sales Up—Is It the McConaughey Bump?" *Kelley Blue Book*, http://www.kbb.com/car-news/all-the-latest/lincolns-turnaround-2014-sales-up_is-it-the-mcconaughey-bump/2000011621/ (accessed February 11, 2016).

42 Roger Dooley, "Paper Beats Digital in Many Ways, according to Neuroscience," *Forbes*, September 16, 2015, http://www.forbes.com/sites/rogerdooley/2015/09/16/paper-vs-digital/#14930f761aa2 (accessed February 11, 2016).

43 Peter J. Danaher and Guy W. Mullarkey, "Factors Affecting Online Advertising Recall: A Study of Students," *Journal of Advertising Research* 43 (2003): 252–267.

44 Frank Harrison, "Digging Deeper Down into the Empirical Generalization of Brand Recall: Adding Owned and Earned Media to Paid-Media Touchpoints," *Journal of Advertising Research* 53, no. 2 (June 2013): 181–185.

45 Tripp Mickle, "Can Advertising Revive Light Beer?" *The Wall Street Journal*, October 12, 2015, B1, B4.

46 Steve McClellan, "Patron Unveils First Work from Its New AOR," *MediaPost*, June 9, 2015, http://www.mediapost.com/publications/article/251573/patron-unveils-first-work-from-its-new-aor.html (accessed February 19, 2016); Mullen Lowe U.S. website, http://us.mullenlowe.com/work/patron-it-doesnt-have-to-make-sense-to-be-perfect/ (accessed February 19, 2016).

47 Martin Williams and Francis Buttle, "Managing negative word-of-mouth: an exploratory study," *Journal of Marketing Management* 30, 13/14 (2014): 1423–1447.

48 Russell Hotten, "Volkswagen: The scandal explained," *BBC*, December 10, 2015, http://www.bbc.com/news/business-34324772 (accessed February 11, 2016).

49 George E. Belch and Michael A. Belch, *Advertising and Promotion* (Burr Ridge, IL: Irwin/McGraw-Hill, 2008), p. 570.

50 Craig Giammona, "Long Live the King," *Bloomberg Businessweek*, October 5-October 11, 2015, pp. 23–24.

51 Korri Kezar, "Pizza Hut will be the official pizza sponsor of ESPN College GameDay," *Dallas Business Journal*, http://www.bizjournals.com/dallas/news/2015/09/02/pizza-hut-will-be-the-official-pizza-sponsor-of.html (accessed February 11, 2016).

52 Walmart, "Walmart and the Walmart Foundation Publish FY2015 Giving Report," http://news.walmart.com/news-archive/2015/12/18/walmart-and-the-walmart-foundation-publish-fy2015-giving-report (accessed February 26, 2016).

[53] Belch and Belch, *Advertising and Promotion*, pp. 580–581.

[54] Suman Basuroy, Subimal Chatterjee, and S. Abraham Ravid, "How Critical Are Critical Reviews? The Box Office Effects of Film Critics, Star Power, and Budgets," *Journal of Marketing* (October 2003): 103–117.

[55] Kathleen Cleeren, Harald J. van Heerde, and Marnik G. Dekimpe, "Rising from the Ashes: How Brands and Categories Can Overcome Product-Harm Crises," *Journal of Marketing* 77 (March 2013): 58–77.

[56] Zoe Szathmary, "Coca-Cola pulls 'Nazi' Fanta advertisement which referred to the 1940s as 'the good old times'," *Daily Mail*, March 4, 2015, http://www.dailymail.co.uk/news/article-2979582/Coca-Cola-pulls-Nazi-Fanta-advertisement-referred-1940s-good-old-times.html (accessed February 11, 2016).

[57] Deborah L. Vence, "Stand Guard: In Bad Times, an Ongoing Strategy Keeps Image Intact," *Marketing News*, November 16, 2006, p. 15.

[58] Brian Steinberg, "Food Net's Endorsements Are Woven Inconspicuously Into Its Programming Mix," *Variety*, November 5, 2013, http://variety.com/2013/tv/features/food-net-brand-tie-ins-that-sizzle-but-dont-burn-1200796087/ (accessed February 11, 2016); Carey Polis, "'From Scratch' Goes Behind The Scenes At The Food Network," *The Huffington Post*, October 1, 2013, http://www.huffingtonpost.com/2013/10/01/from-scratch-food-network_n_3984233.html (accessed

February 11, 2016); Stuart Elliot, "Two Media Mainstays Expand Their Video Presence," *The New York Times*, October 2, 2013, http://www.nytimes.com/2013/10/03/business/media/two-media-mainstays-expand-their-video-presence.html (accessed February 11, 2016); John Moulding, "Scripps Network Hails the Impact of Dynamic Advertising Insertion," *Videonet*, October 31, 2013, http://www.v-net.tv/scripps-networks-hails-the-impact-of-dynamic-advertising-insertion/ (accessed February 11, 2016).

[59] O.C. Ferrell and Linda Ferrell, "Are Consumers Being Greenwashed?" http://danielsethics.mgt.unm.edu/pdf/Greenwashing%20DI.pdf (accessed February 11, 2016); FranchiseHelp Holdings LLC, "Green Industry Analysis 2016—Costs and Trends," *Franchise Help*, 2015, https://www.franchisehelp.com/industry-reports/green-industry-report/ (accessed February 11, 2016); Jack Neff, "As More Marketers Go Green, Fewer Consumers Willing to Pay for It," *Advertising Age*, September 24, 2012, http://adage.com/article/news/marketers-green-fewer-consumers-pay/237377 (accessed February 11, 2016); Jack Neff, "Consumers Don't Believe Your Green Ad Claims, Survey Finds," *Advertising Age*, September 16, 2013, http://adage.com/article/news/consumers-green-ad-claims-survey-finds/244172 (accessed February 11, 2016); Federal Trade Commission, "FTC Issues Revised 'Green Guides,'" October 1, 2012, www.ftc.gov/news-events/press-releases/2012/10/

ftc-issues-revised-green-guides (accessed February 11, 2016); Robert Lamb, "Regulating Greenwashing," *How Stuff Works*, http://money.howstuffworks.com/greenwashing.htm (accessed February 11, 2016); Federal Trade Commission, "Guides for the Use of Environmental Marketing Claims ("Environmental Guides" or "Green Guides")," https://www.ftc.gov/enforcement/rules/rulemaking-regulatory-reform-proceedings/guides-use- environmental-marketing-claims (accessed February 11, 2016); Gwendolyn Bounds, "Misleading Claims on 'Green' Labeling," *The Wall Street Journal*, October 26, 2010, http://online.wsj.com/article/SB10001424052702303467004575574521710082414.html (accessed February 11, 2016); Federal Trade Commission, "FTC Issues Revised 'Green Guides,'" October 1, 2012, www.ftc.gov/news-events/press-releases/2012/10/ftc-issues-revised-green-guides (accessed February 11, 2016); Heineken, "New Heineken campaign brings sustainability message closer to consumers," April 28, 2015, http://www.theheinekencompany.com/media/media-releases/press-releases/2015/04/1915885 (accessed February 11, 2016); Federal Trade Commission, "FTC Sends Warning Letters about Green Certification Seals," September 14, 2015, https://www.ftc.gov/news-events/press-releases/2015/09/ftc-sends-warning-letters-about-green-certification-seals (accessed February 11, 2016); "Pinocchio Climate Awards 2015," http://www.pinocchio-awards.org/ (accessed February 11, 2016).

## Feature Notes

[a] Mike Shields, "Publishers Worry that Native Ads Are Vulnerable to Blocking," *The Wall Street Journal*, October 5, 2015, http://www.wsj.com/articles/publishers-worry-that-native-ads-are-vulnerable-to-ad-blocking-1444039200 (accessed October 12, 2015); Lin Grensing-Pophal, "Consumers Coming to Accept Native Advertising Done Right," *EcontentMag.com*, July/August 2014, 8–10; Molly Soat, "The Native Frontier," *Marketing News*, May 2015, 34–43.

[b] Tripp Mickle, "FDA Warns Cigarette Makers on 'Natural' Labels," *The Wall Street Journal*, August 28, 2015, B4; Rob Stein, "FDA Warns Tobacco Companies Advertising 'Natural' Cigarettes," *NPR*, August 27, 2015, http://www.npr.org/sections/health-shots/2015/08/27/435235804/fda-warns-tobacco-companies-advertising-natural-cigarettes (accessed October 12, 2015); Rachel Abrams, "F.D.A. Warns 3 Tobacco Makers about Language Used on Labels," *The New York Times*, August 27, 2015, http://www

.nytimes.com/2015/08/28/business/fda-warns-3-tobacco-makers-about-language-used-on-labels.html?_r=0 (accessed October 12, 2015); "Brown Secures Agreement with American Spirit Cigarettes Maker over Alleged Misleading Marketing of Organic Tobacco Products," *State of California Department of Justice Office of the Attorney General*, March 1, 2010, http://oag.ca.gov/news/press-releases/brown-secures-agreement-american-spirit-cigarettes-maker-over-alleged-misleading (accessed October 12, 2015).

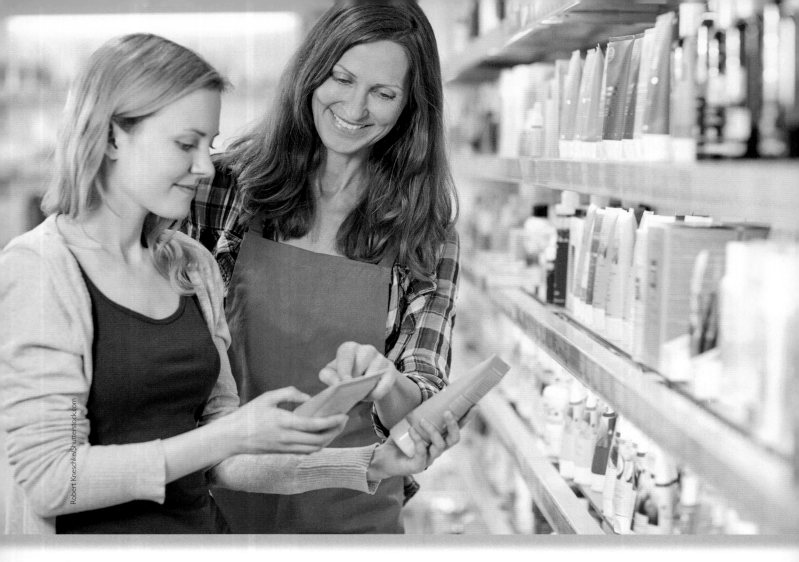

# chapter 18    Personal Selling and Sales Promotion

## OBJECTIVES

18-1    Describe the major goals of personal selling.

18-2    Summarize the seven basic steps in the personal selling process.

18-3    Identify the types of sales force personnel.

18-4    Describe *team selling* and *relationship selling*.

18-5    Discuss eight major decisions in sales force management.

18-6    Describe sales promotion.

18-7    Review consumer sales promotion methods.

18-8    Review trade sales promotion methods.

# MARKETING INSIGHTS

## Who Knew? The Success of Product Sampling

a katz/Shutterstock.com

Free samples are costly forms of sales promotion. For example, a free sample stand in a grocery store may cost food manufacturers hundreds of dollars daily. It is also easy for consumers to misuse free samples, which is why some cosmetics firms no longer offer samples of their more expensive products.

For many companies, however, free sampling is well worth the cost. Approximately 92 percent of consumers claim they would buy a product if they liked it after sampling it. In some cases, free samples have been known to increase sales by 2,000 percent! It is believed that free samples not only allow customers to try out a product risk-free but also activates feelings of reciprocity. In other words, customers who receive a free sample feel an obligation—often subconsciously—to reciprocate by buying the product.

Other sampling techniques also have a psychological impact on whether a customer will buy. For instance, customers are more likely to purchase a product when a salesperson provides the sample. Costco, the sampling guru, takes its sampling program so seriously that it uses a product-demonstration company to run its sampling program. Costco's free samples are credited with creating an exciting shopping experience that gets customers in the door.

Free samples are not just for large companies either. Smaller non-food retailers can also benefit from giving free samples. JadeYoga, a maker of yoga mats, mailed out 500 small mat samples. It received 300 calls as a result of this sampling initiative. Perhaps the most important thing companies should keep in mind is to choose a product that lends itself well to sampling, such as food or perfume.[1]

For many organizations, targeting customers with appropriate personal selling techniques and messages can play a major role in maintaining long-term, satisfying customer relationships, which in turn contribute to company success. Marketing strategy development should involve the sales organization during all stages of development and implementation. Top managers need extensive feedback from the sales force. Managers should strive to make information transparent and jointly analyze sales data. Sales managers should communicate marketing strategy in a language with which salespeople feel comfortable.[2] As we saw in Chapter 16, personal selling and sales promotion are two possible elements in a promotion mix. Personal selling is sometimes a company's sole promotional tool, and it is becoming increasingly professional and sophisticated, with sales personnel acting more as consultants, advisors, and sometimes as partners.

In this chapter, we focus on personal selling and sales promotion. We first consider the purposes of personal selling and then examine its basic steps. Next, we look at types of salespeople and how they are selected. After taking a look at several new types of personal selling, we discuss major sales force management decisions, including setting objectives for the sales force and determining its size; recruiting, selecting, training, compensating, and motivating salespeople; managing sales territories; and controlling and evaluating sales force performance. Then we examine several characteristics of sales promotion, reasons for using sales promotion, and sales promotion methods available for use in a promotion mix.

## 18-1 THE NATURE AND GOALS OF PERSONAL SELLING

**personal selling** Paid personal communication that attempts to inform customers and persuade them to buy products in an exchange situation

**Personal selling** is paid personal communication that attempts to inform customers and persuade them to purchase products in an exchange situation. For instance, a Hewlett-Packard (HP) salesperson describing the benefits of the company's servers, PCs, and printers to a small-business customer is engaging in personal selling. Likewise, a member of the American Marketing Association (AMA) manning a table at an event engages in personal selling to inform interested parties about the benefits of joining the AMA. Personal selling gives marketers the greatest freedom to adjust a message to satisfy customers' information needs. It is the most precise of all promotion methods, enabling marketers to focus on the most promising sales prospects. Personal selling is also the most effective way to form relationships with customers. Personal selling is perhaps most important with business-to-business transactions involving the purchase of expensive products. Because of the high-risk factors involved, personal selling is often necessary to assure prospective customers about the quality of the product and answer any questions.[3] Despite these benefits, personal selling is generally the most expensive element in the promotion mix. The average cost of a sales call for industrial products and business-to-business sales is about $400.[4]

Millions of people earn their living through personal selling. Sales careers can offer high income, a great deal of freedom, a high level of training, and a high degree of job satisfaction. Salespeople who delight customers experience an improvement in customer orientation and job skills.[5] Although the public may harbor negative perceptions of personal selling, unfavorable stereotypes of salespeople are changing, thanks to the efforts of major corporations, professional sales associations, and academic institutions. Personal selling will continue to gain respect as professional sales associations

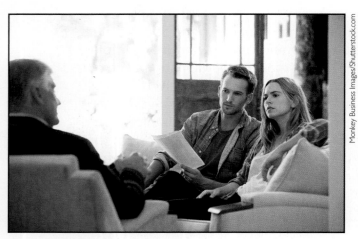

Monkey Business Images/Shutterstock.com

**The Importance of Personal Selling**
Financial advisors engage in personal selling as a way to provide financial advice and form relationships with customers.

develop and enforce ethical codes of conduct.[6] Developing ongoing customer relationships today requires sales personnel with high levels of professionalism as well as technical and interpersonal skills.[7]

Personal selling goals vary from one firm to another. However, they usually involve finding prospects, determining their needs, persuading prospects to buy, following up on the sale, and keeping customers satisfied. Identifying potential buyers interested in the organization's products is critical. Because most potential buyers seek information before making purchases, salespeople can ascertain prospects' informational needs and then provide relevant information. To do so, sales personnel must be well trained regarding both their products and the selling process in general.

Salespeople must be aware of their competitors. They must monitor the development of new products and keep abreast of competitors' sales efforts in their sales territories, how often and when the competition calls on their accounts, and what the competition is saying about their product in relation to its own. Salespeople must emphasize the benefits their products provide, especially when competitors' products do not offer those specific benefits. Salespeople often function as knowledge experts for the firm and provide key information for marketing decisions.[8]

Personal selling is changing today based on new technology, how customers gain information about products, and the way customers make purchase decisions. Customer information sharing through social media, mobile and Web applications, and electronic sales presentations are impacting the nature of personal selling. Technology and social media provide an unprecedented level of transparency and communication between the salesperson and customers.[9] Many firms are using social media technology to reach business customers as well. "Social CRM" (customer relationship management) provides opportunities to manage data in discovering and engaging customers.[10] For instance, the cloud-computing models provided by Salesforce.com that enable firms to manage relationships with their customers can assist in personal selling sales management. Digital technology has become such an important part of our lives that it is not uncommon for salespersons to access their CRM systems through their smartphones. Internal consumer data can help salespeople understand and collaborate with customers in ways that did not exist in the past.

Using websites to manage orders and product information, track inventory, and train salespeople can save companies time and money. Twitter is a relatively new tool that can

# Entrepreneurship in Marketing

## Scentsy: The Sweet Smell of Success

**Founders:** Orville and Heidi Thompson
**Business:** Scentsy
**Founded:** 2004, in Meridian, Idaho
**Success:** Scentsy is the 38th largest direct seller worldwide with revenues of $419 million.

Scentsy is a rags-to-riches story for owners Orville and Heidi Thompson. In 2004 the couple was near bankruptcy after a failed business venture. However, while Orville was manning a booth at a home show, he came across a wickless candle that used a low-watt bulb to melt scented wax candle bars. The Thompsons bought out the inventory of the product's creators and began running the business from their sheep farm. At $700,000 in debt, the couple chose a party plan direct selling model in which individuals host selling parties in their homes to create an exciting selling experience.

Although the Thompsons' first party produced sales of only $75, the second one generated $1,000. Consumers loved the idea of having the scent of a fragrant candle without worrying about the fire danger—Scentsy wax warmers can be kept on all day. Today, Scentsy has 100,000 independent consultants. Scentsy is also developing new product lines such as kitchenware. Through its understanding of the market, it will continue its growth.[a]

be used to post product information and updates, obtain prospects, recruit new salespeople, and communicate with salespeople. Facebook is another valuable tool that can supplement and support face-to-face contacts. On Facebook, salespeople can carry on conversations very similar to traditional face-to-face social networks. Mobile technology and applications provide salespeople with opportunities to offer service and connect with customers. CRM technology enables improved service, marketing and sales processes, and contact and data management and analysis. CRM can help facilitate the delivery of valuable customer experiences and provide the metrics to measure progress and sales successes.[11]

Few businesses survive solely on profits from one-time customers. For long-run survival, most marketers depend on repeat sales and thus need to keep their customers satisfied. In addition, satisfied customers provide favorable word of mouth and other communications, thereby attracting new customers. Although the whole organization is responsible for achieving customer satisfaction, much of the burden falls on salespeople, because they are almost always closer to customers than anyone else in the company and often provide buyers with information and service after the sale. Indeed, a firm's market orientation has a positive influence on salespeople's attitudes, commitment, and influence on customer purchasing intentions.[12] Additionally, collaboration between sales and other marketing areas is positively related to market orientation that puts customers first, which positively impacts organizational performance.[13] Such contact gives salespeople an opportunity to generate additional sales and offers them a good vantage point for evaluating the strengths and weaknesses of the company's products and other marketing-mix components. Their observations help develop and maintain a marketing mix that better satisfies both the firm and its customers. Sales is no longer an isolated function in a global business world. The sales function is becoming part of a cross-functional strategic solution to customer management. This requires salespersons with both managerial and strategic skills.[14]

## 18-2 STEPS OF THE PERSONAL SELLING PROCESS

The specific activities involved in the selling process vary among salespeople, selling situations, and cultures. No two salespeople use exactly the same selling methods. Nonetheless, many salespeople move through a general selling process. This process consists of seven steps, outlined in Figure 18.1: prospecting, preapproach, approach, making the presentation, overcoming objections, closing the sale, and following up.

### 18-2a Prospecting

Developing a database of potential customers is called **prospecting**. Salespeople seek names of prospects from company sales records, trade shows, commercial databases, newspaper announcements (of marriages, births, deaths, and so on), public records, telephone directories, trade association directories, and many other sources. Sales personnel also use responses to traditional and online advertisements that encourage interested persons to send in information request forms. Seminars and meetings targeted at particular types of clients, such as attorneys or accountants, may also produce leads.

Most salespeople prefer to use referrals—recommendations from current customers—to find prospects. For instance, salespeople for Cutco Cutlery, which sells high-quality knives and kitchen cutlery, first make sales calls to their friends and families and then use referrals from them to seek out new prospects. Obtaining referrals requires that the salesperson have a good relationship with the current customer and therefore must have performed well before asking the customer for help. As might be expected, a customer's trust in and satisfaction with a salesperson influence his or her willingness to provide referrals. Research findings show that one referral is as valuable as 12 cold calls.[15] Also, 80 percent of clients are willing to give

**prospecting** Developing a database of potential customers

Figure 18.1    **General Steps in the Personal Selling Process**

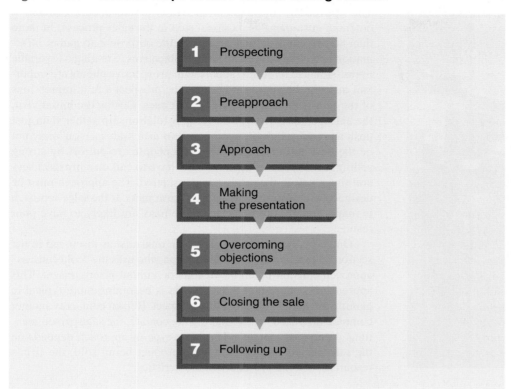

referrals, but only 20 percent are ever asked. Among the advantages of using referrals are more highly qualified sales leads, greater sales rates, and larger initial transactions. Some companies even award discounts off future purchases to customers who refer new prospects to their salespeople. Consistent activity is critical to successful prospecting. Salespeople must actively search the customer base for qualified prospects that fit the target market profile. After developing the prospect list, a salesperson evaluates whether each prospect is able, willing, and authorized to buy the product. Based on this evaluation, prospects are ranked according to desirability or potential.

## 18-2b Preapproach

Before contacting acceptable prospects, a salesperson finds and analyzes information about each prospect's specific product needs, current use of brands, feelings about available brands, and personal characteristics. In short, salespeople need to know what potential buyers and decision makers consider most important and why they need a specific product. The most successful salespeople are thorough in their *preapproach*, which involves identifying key decision makers, reviewing account histories and problems, contacting other clients for information, assessing credit histories and problems, preparing sales presentations, identifying product needs, and obtaining relevant literature. Marketers are increasingly using information technology and customer relationship management systems to comb through databases and thus identify their most profitable products and customers. CRM systems can also help sales departments manage leads, track customers, forecast sales, and assess performance. A salesperson with a lot of information about a prospect is better equipped to develop a presentation that precisely communicates with that prospect.

Adriano Castelli/Shutterstock.com

**Prospecting**
Companies often engage in prospecting at trade shows, which allow representatives to demonstrate the latest company products and collect information on consumers who might be interested in the firm's offerings. Company salespeople can later use this information in the pre-approach and approach steps of the personal selling process.

### 18-2c    Approach

The **approach**—the manner in which a salesperson contacts a potential customer—is a critical step in the sales process. In more than 80 percent of initial sales calls, the purpose is to gather information about the buyer's needs and objectives. Creating a favorable impression and building rapport with prospective clients are important tasks in the approach because the prospect's first impressions of the salesperson are usually lasting ones. During the initial visit, the salesperson strives to develop a relationship rather than just push a product. Indeed, coming across as a "salesperson" may not be the best approach because some people are put off by strong selling tactics. The salesperson may have to call on a prospect several times before the product is considered. The approach must be designed to deliver value to targeted customers. If the sales approach is inappropriate, the salesperson's efforts are likely to have poor results.

One type of approach is based on referrals, as discussed in the section on prospecting. The salesperson who uses the "cold canvass" approach calls on potential customers without prior consent. This approach is decreasing. Social media is becoming more typical in gaining the initial contact with a prospect. Repeat contact is another common approach: When making the contact, the salesperson mentions a previous meeting. The exact type of approach depends on the salesperson's preferences, the product being sold, the firm's resources, and the prospect's characteristics.

### 18-2d    Making the Presentation

During the sales presentation, the salesperson must attract and hold the prospect's attention, stimulate interest, and spark a desire for the product. Salespeople who carefully monitor the selling situation and adapt their presentations to meet the needs of prospects generally have more effective sales performance.[16] Salespeople should match their influencing tactics—such as information exchange, recommendations, threats, promises, ingratiation, and inspirational appeals—to their prospects. Different types of buyers respond to different tactics, but most respond well to information exchange and recommendations, and virtually no prospects respond to threats.[17] The salesperson should have the prospect view, examine, or see the benefits of the product. For some types of goods, it may be possible to touch or hold the product. If possible, the salesperson should demonstrate the product or invite the prospect to use it. If the customer is in a positive mood, suspicion will be eliminated and the presentation will gain strength.[18]

During the presentation, the salesperson must not only talk, but also listen. Listening is half of the communication process and is often the most important part for a salesperson. Research indicates that salesperson listening and cognitive empathy developed through the sales interaction are linked, suggesting that listening positively affects the relationship between the buyer and seller during a sales presentation.[19] Nonverbal modes of communication are especially beneficial in building trust during the presentation.[20] Nonverbal signals provide a deeper understanding. The sales presentation gives the salesperson the greatest opportunity to determine the prospect's specific needs by listening to questions and comments and observing responses. Research findings show that complimenting the buyer on his or her questions adds to incremental sales.[21] Even though the salesperson plans the presentation in advance, she or he must be able to adjust the message to meet the prospect's informational needs. Adapting the message in response to the customer's needs generally enhances performance, particularly in new-task or modified rebuy purchase situations.[22]

**approach** The manner in which a salesperson contacts a potential customer

### 18-2e Overcoming Objections

An effective salesperson usually seeks out a prospect's objections in order to address them. If they are not apparent, the salesperson cannot deal with them, and the prospect may not buy. One of the best ways to overcome objections is to anticipate and counter them before the prospect raises them. However, this approach can be risky, because the salesperson may mention objections that the prospect would not have raised. If possible, the salesperson should handle objections as they arise. They can also be addressed at the end of the presentation.

### 18-2f Closing the Sale

**Closing** is the stage in the personal selling process when the salesperson asks the prospect to buy the product. During the presentation, the salesperson may use a *trial close* by asking questions that assume the prospect will buy. The salesperson might ask the potential customer about financial terms, desired colors or sizes, or delivery arrangements. Reactions to such questions usually indicate how close the prospect is to buying. Properly asked questions may allow prospects to uncover their own problems and identify solutions themselves. One questioning approach uses broad questions *(what, how, why)* to probe or gather information and focused questions *(who, when, where)* to clarify and close the sale. A trial close allows prospects to indicate indirectly that they will buy the product without having to say those sometimes difficult words: "I'll take it."

A salesperson should try to close at several points during the presentation because the prospect may be ready to buy. An attempt to close the sale may result in objections. Thus, closing can uncover hidden objections, which the salesperson can then address. One closing strategy involves asking the potential customer to place a low-risk, trial order.

### 18-2g Following Up

After a successful closing, the salesperson must follow up the sale. In the follow-up stage, the salesperson determines whether the order was delivered on time and installed properly, if installation was required. He or she should contact the customer to learn if any problems or questions regarding the product have arisen. The follow-up stage is also used to determine customers' future product needs.

Following up also aids the salesperson in creating a solid relationship with the customer. New salespeople might find it difficult to understand the reasons for following up on a sale if the customer seems satisfied with the product. However, a large number of customers who stop buying products do so not out of dissatisfaction but because the company neglected to contact them.[23] Thus, the follow-up stage is vital to establishing a strong relationship and creating loyalty on the part of the buyer.

## 18-3 TYPES OF SALESPEOPLE

To develop a sales force, a marketing manager decides what kind of salesperson will sell the firm's products most effectively. Most business organizations use several different kinds of sales personnel. Based on the functions performed, salespeople can be classified into different groups. One salesperson can, and often does, perform multiple functions.

### 18-3a Sales Structure

Most companies have an inside sales force. Inside salespeople support personnel or take orders, follow up on deliveries, and provide technical information. An outside sales force is also important. Usually sales calls outside the firm are more consultative and are built on developing long-term relationships. Using both inside and outside salespersons to manage accounts is very

**closing** The stage in the personal selling process when the salesperson asks the prospect to buy the product

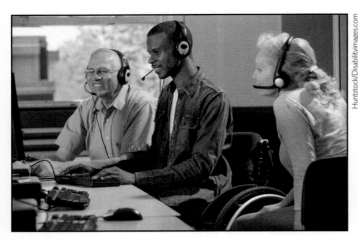

Huntstock/Disabilityimages.com

**Inside Sales**
Inside salespeople are highly important in personal selling. Their responsibilities include supporting personnel, taking orders, following up on deliveries, and providing technical information.

typical. This task is sometimes called *creative selling*. It requires that salespeople recognize potential buyers' needs and give them necessary information. Increasingly, inside salespersons manage the digital approaches to sales and outside salespersons are more face-to-face and relationship-oriented.

## Current-Customer Sales

Sales personnel who concentrate on current customers call on people and organizations that have purchased products from the firm before. These salespeople seek more sales from existing customers by following up on previous sales. Current customers can also be sources of leads for new prospects.

## New-Business Sales

Business organizations depend to some degree on sales to new customers. New-business sales personnel locate prospects and convert them into buyers. Salespeople help generate new business in many organizations, but even more so in organizations that sell real estate, insurance, appliances, automobiles, and business-to-business supplies and services. These organizations depend in large part on new-customer sales.

### 18-3b **Support Personnel**

**Support personnel** facilitate selling but usually are not involved solely with making sales. They engage primarily in marketing industrial products, locating prospects, educating customers, building goodwill, and providing service after the sale. There are many kinds of sales support personnel; the three most common are missionary, trade, and technical salespeople.

## Missionary Salespeople

**Missionary salespeople**, usually employed by manufacturers, assist the producer's customers in selling to their own customers. Missionary salespeople may call on retailers to inform and persuade them to buy the manufacturer's products. When they succeed, retailers purchase products from wholesalers, which are the producer's customers. Manufacturers of medical supplies and pharmaceuticals often use missionary salespeople, called *detail reps*, to promote their products to physicians, hospitals, and pharmacists.

## Trade Salespeople

**Trade salespeople** are not strictly support personnel, because they usually take orders as well. However, they direct much effort toward helping customers—especially retail stores—promote the product. They are likely to restock shelves, obtain more shelf space, set up displays, provide in-store demonstrations, and distribute samples to store customers. Food producers and processors commonly employ trade salespeople.

## Technical Salespeople

**Technical salespeople** give technical assistance to the organization's current customers, advising them on product characteristics and applications, system designs, and installation procedures. Because this job is often highly technical, the salesperson usually has formal training in one of the physical sciences or in engineering. Technical sales personnel often sell technical industrial products, such as computers, heavy equipment, and steel.

**support personnel** Sales staff members who facilitate selling but usually are not involved solely with making sales

**missionary salespeople** Support salespeople, usually employed by a manufacturer, who assist the producer's customers in selling to their own customers

**trade salespeople** Salespeople involved mainly in helping a producer's customers promote a product

**technical salespeople** Support salespeople who give technical assistance to a firm's current customers

When hiring sales personnel, marketers seldom restrict themselves to a single category, because most firms require different types of salespeople. Several factors dictate how many of each type a particular company should have. Product use, characteristics, complexity, and price influence the kind of sales personnel used, as do the number and characteristics of customers. The types of marketing channels and the intensity and type of advertising also affect the composition of a sales force.

# 18-4 TEAM SELLING AND RELATIONSHIP SELLING

Personal selling has become an increasingly complex process due in large part to rapid technological innovation. Most importantly, the focus of personal selling is shifting from selling a specific product to building long-term relationships with customers by finding solutions to their needs, problems, and challenges. As a result, the roles of salespeople are changing. Among the newer philosophies for personal selling are team selling and relationship selling.

## 18-4a Team Selling

Many products, particularly expensive high-tech business products, have become so complex that a single salesperson can no longer be an expert in every aspect of the product and purchase process. **Team selling**, which involves the salesperson joining with people from the firm's financial, engineering, and other functional areas, is appropriate for such products. The salesperson takes the lead in the personal selling process, but other members of the team bring their unique skills, knowledge, and resources to the process to help customers find solutions to their own business challenges. Selling teams may be created to address a particular short-term situation, or they may be formal, ongoing teams. Team selling is advantageous in situations calling for detailed knowledge of new, complex, and dynamic technologies like jet aircraft and medical equipment. It can be difficult, however, for highly competitive salespersons to adapt to a team selling environment.

**team selling** The use of a team of experts from all functional areas of a firm, led by a salesperson, to conduct the personal selling process

**relationship selling** The building of mutually beneficial long-term associations with a customer through regular communications over prolonged periods of time

## 18-4b Relationship Selling

**Relationship selling**, also known as consultative selling, involves building mutually beneficial long-term associations with a customer through regular communications over prolonged periods of time. Like team selling, it is especially used in business-to-business marketing. Relationship selling involves finding solutions to customers' needs by listening to them, gaining a detailed understanding of their organizations, understanding and caring about their needs and challenges, and providing support after the sale.

Sales representatives from organizations have begun to change their sales tactics to focus upon building relationships. Pirch, a retailer that specializes in bathroom and kitchen appliances and fixtures, trains employees on the floor on how to encourage customers to enjoy themselves. Customers can take a cooking class on the store's stoves or don a bathing suit and try out its bath tubs. The philosophy behind this emphasis on experience is for Pirch to develop strong relationships and place customer needs first. Pirch claims this emphasis has led to average sales per square foot of $3,000, higher than Apple stores.[24] Relationships are also built on being able to

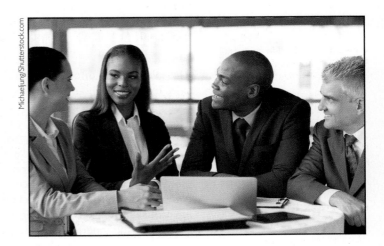

**Team Selling**
Team selling is becoming popular, especially in companies where the selling process is complex and requires a variety of specialized skills.

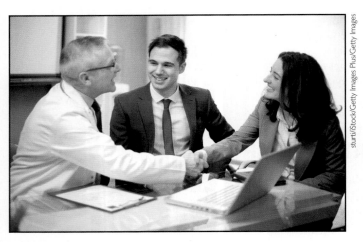

**Relationship selling**
Pharmaceutical companies have begun to change their sales tactics, spending more time listening to doctors and building relationships over simply promoting the benefits of the company's products.

recover when customers are concerned about services. Being proactive in identifying the need for recovery behaviors is a major part of relationship selling.[25] Thus, contacting the customer if delivery time is longer than expected as well as explaining what happened and when the product will be delivered are important.

Relationship selling differs from traditional personal selling due to its adoption of a long-term perspective. Instead of simply focusing on short-term repeat sales, relationship selling involves forming long-term connections that will result in sales throughout the relationship.[26] Relationship selling is well poised to help sellers understand their customers' individual needs. It is particularly important in business-to-business transactions as businesses often require more "individualized solutions" to meet their unique needs than the individual consumer.[27]

Relationship selling has significant implications for the seller. Studies show that firms spend six times longer on finding new customers than in keeping current customers.[28] Thus, relationship selling that generates loyal long-term customers is likely to be extremely profitable for the firm both in repeat sales as well as the money saved in trying to find new customers. Finally, as the personal selling industry becomes increasingly competitive, relationship selling is one way that companies can differentiate themselves from rivals to create competitive advantages.[29]

Relationship selling efforts can be improved through sales automation technology tools that enhance interactive communication.[30] New applications for customer relationship management are also being provided through companies like Salesforce.com, whose cloud-computing model helps companies keep track of the customer life cycle without having to install any software (applications are downloaded). Social networks are being utilized in sales, adding new layers to the selling process. Salesforce CRM, for instance, now allows users to connect with their customers in real time through such networks as Twitter and Facebook. Sales force automation, which involves utilizing information technology to automatically track all stages of the sales process (a part of customer relationship management), has been found to increase salesperson professionalism and responsiveness, customer interaction frequency, and customer relationship quality.[31]

## 18-5 SALES FORCE MANAGEMENT

The sales force is directly responsible for generating one of an organization's primary inputs: sales revenue. Without adequate sales revenue, businesses cannot survive. In addition, a firm's reputation is often determined by the ethical conduct of its sales force. Indeed, a positive ethical climate, one component of corporate culture, has been linked with decreased role stress and turnover intention and improved job attitudes and job performance in sales.[32] Research has demonstrated that a negative ethical climate will trigger higher-performing salespeople to leave a company at a higher rate than those in a company perceived to be ethical.[33] The morale and ultimately the success of a firm's sales force depend in large part on adequate compensation, room for advancement, sufficient training, and management support—all key areas of sales management. Salespeople who are not satisfied with these elements may leave. Evaluating the input of salespeople is an important part of sales force management because of its strong bearing on a firm's success. Empowering leadership that makes salespeople feel like important contributors positively impacts how a sales team spreads knowledge among its customers.[34] Additionally, sales environments that stress creativity appear to place greater

Table 18.1 **Directions for Attracting and Retaining a Top Sales Force**

| Training and development | • On-the-job training<br>• Online individual instruction<br>• Seminars<br>• On-site classroom instruction |
|---|---|
| Compensation | • Make sure pay mix isn't too risky (high commission, low base) for sales role<br>• Mix base salary with commission, bonus, or both<br>• Base bonuses/commission on reaching sales goals rather than on individual sales dollars<br>• Maintain competitive benefits and expense reimbursement practices |
| Work/life autonomy | • Offer flexible hours<br>• Consider telecommuting/work-at-home options |
| Product quality and service | • Ensure goods and services meet customer needs<br>• Provide the appropriate service after the sale |

Source: "Attracting & Retaining a Top Sales Force," *Where Great Workplaces Start*, http://greatworkplace.wordpress.com/ 2010/02/10/ attracting-retaining-a-top-sales-force (accessed February 12, 2016).

significance on the selection and placement of salespeople, sales force training, performance appraisals, and compensation systems.[35] Table 18.1 provides directions on how to attract and retain a top-quality sales force.

We explore eight general areas of sales management: establishing sales force objectives, determining sales force size, recruiting and selecting salespeople, training sales personnel, compensating salespeople, motivating salespeople, managing sales territories, and controlling and evaluating sales force performance.

## 18-5a **Establishing Sales Force Objectives**

To manage a sales force effectively, sales managers must develop sales objectives. Sales objectives tell salespeople what they are expected to accomplish during a specified time period. They give the sales force direction and purpose and serve as standards for evaluating and controlling the performance of sales personnel. Sales objectives should be stated in precise, measurable terms; specify the time period and geographic areas involved; and be achievable.

Sales objectives are usually developed for both the total sales force and individual salespeople. Objectives for the entire force are normally stated in terms of sales volume, market share, or profit. Volume objectives refer to dollar or unit sales. The objective for an electric drill producer's sales force, for instance, might be to sell $18 million worth of drills, or 600,000 drills annually. When sales goals are stated in terms of market share, they usually call for an increase in

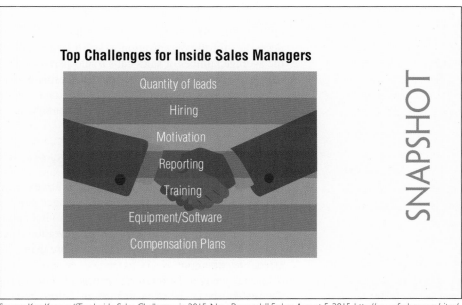

**Top Challenges for Inside Sales Managers**

Quantity of leads

Hiring

Motivation

Reporting

Training

Equipment/Software

Compensation Plans

SNAPSHOT

Source: Ken Krogue, "Top Inside Sales Challenges in 2015: New Research," *Forbes*, August 5, 2015, http://www.forbes.com/sites/ kenkrogue/2015/08/05/top-inside-sales-challenges-in-2015-new-research/#7f3e00eee99c (accessed February 12, 2016).

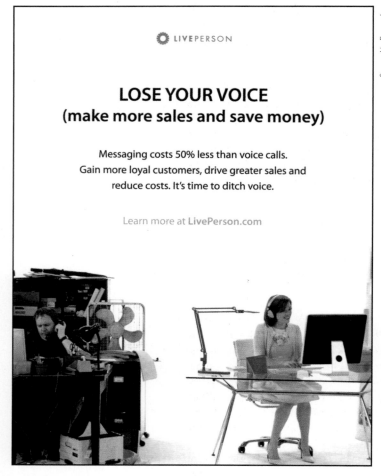

**Sales Force Objectives**
A company using LivePerson's services might choose to measure sales objectives or sales quotas by number of digital messages.

the proportion of the firm's sales relative to the total number of products sold by all businesses in that industry. When sales objectives are based on profit, they are generally stated in terms of dollar amounts or return on investment.

Sales objectives, or quotas, for individual salespeople are commonly stated in terms of dollar or unit sales volume. Other bases used for individual sales objectives include average order size, average number of calls per time period, and ratio of orders to calls. Note the advertisement from LivePerson .com on messaging. LivePerson claims that using messaging rather than phone calls is less costly and more effective at making sales. In this case, a company might measure average number of messages per time period as a way of measuring sales objectives.

## 18-5b Determining Sales Force Size

Sales force size is important, because it influences the company's ability to generate sales and profits. Moreover, size of the sales force affects the compensation methods used, salespeople's morale, and overall sales force management. Sales force size must be adjusted periodically, because a firm's marketing plans change along with markets and forces in the marketing environment. One danger in cutting back the size of the sales force to increase profits is that the sales organization may lose strength and resiliency, preventing it from rebounding when growth occurs or better market conditions prevail.

Several analytical methods can help determine optimal sales force size. One method involves determining how many sales calls per year are necessary for the organization to serve customers effectively and then dividing this total by the average number of sales calls a salesperson makes annually. A second method is based on marginal analysis, in which additional salespeople are added to the sales force until the cost of an additional salesperson equals the additional sales generated by that person. Although marketing managers may use one or several analytical methods, they normally temper decisions with subjective judgments.

## 18-5c Recruiting and Selecting Salespeople

To create and maintain an effective sales force, sales managers must recruit the right type of salespeople. In **recruiting**, the sales manager develops a list of qualified applicants for sales positions. Effective recruiting efforts are a vital part of implementing the strategic sales force plan and can help assure successful organizational performance. The costs of hiring and training a salesperson are soaring, reaching more than $60,000 in some industries. Thus, recruiting errors are expensive.

**recruiting** Developing a list of qualified applicants for sales positions

To ensure that the recruiting process results in a pool of qualified applicants, a sales manager establishes a set of qualifications before beginning to recruit. Although marketers have tried for years to identify a set of traits characterizing effective salespeople, no set of generally accepted characteristics exists yet. Experts agree that good salespeople exhibit optimism, flexibility, self-motivation, good time management skills, empathy, and the ability to network and maintain long-term customer relationships. There also seems to be a connection between high sales performance, motivational leadership, and employees who are coachable and highly competitive.[36] Today, companies are increasingly seeking applicants capable of employing relationship-building and consultative approaches as well as the ability to work effectively in team selling efforts. It is desirable to hire salespeople who are disciplined and adaptive with their time.[37]

Sales managers must determine what set of traits best fits their companies' particular sales tasks. Two activities help establish this set of required attributes. First, the sales manager should prepare a job description listing specific tasks salespeople are to perform. Second, the manager should analyze characteristics of the firm's successful salespeople, as well as those of ineffective sales personnel. From the job description and analysis of traits, the sales manager should be able to develop a set of specific requirements and be aware of potential weaknesses that could lead to failure.

A sales manager generally recruits applicants from several sources: departments within the firm, other firms, employment agencies, educational institutions, respondents to advertisements, websites (like Monster.com), and individuals recommended by current employees. The specific sources depend on the type of salesperson required and the manager's experiences and successes with particular recruiting tactics.

The process of recruiting and selecting salespeople varies considerably from one company to another. Companies intent on reducing sales force turnover are likely to have strict recruiting and selection procedures. Sales management should design a selection procedure that satisfies the company's specific needs. Some organizations use the specialized services of other companies to hire sales personnel. The process should include steps that yield the information required to make accurate selection decisions. However, because each step incurs a certain amount of expense, there should be no more steps than necessary. Stages of the selection process should be sequenced so that the more expensive steps, such as a physical examination, occur near the end. Fewer people will then move through higher-cost stages.

Recruitment should not be sporadic; it should be a continuous activity aimed at reaching the best applicants. The selection process should systematically and effectively match applicants' characteristics and needs with the requirements of specific selling tasks. Finally, the selection process should ensure that new sales personnel are available where and when needed.

## 18-5d **Training Sales Personnel**

Many organizations have formal training programs; others depend on informal, on-the-job training. Some systematic training programs are quite extensive, whereas others are rather short and rudimentary. Whether the training program is complex or simple, developers must consider what to teach, whom to train, and how to train them. On average businesses that are considered to be the "best places to work" train their managers and professionals an average of 78 hours and their hourly and administrative staffers an average of 94 hours.[38]

A sales training program can concentrate on the company, its products, or its selling methods. Training programs often cover all three. Such programs can be aimed at newly hired salespeople, experienced salespeople, or both. The type of leadership is especially important for new salespeople who are just getting familiar with the selling process. Transformational leadership that involves coaching to foster trust and motivation has proven highly effective in training new hires when sales managers observe them making errors during customer interactions. This reduces feelings of helplessness among new salespeople when they encounter difficulties in the process.[39]

Training for experienced company salespeople usually emphasizes product information or the use of new technology, although salespeople must also be informed about new selling techniques and changes in company plans, policies, and procedures. Sales managers should use ethics training to institutionalize an ethical climate, improve employee satisfaction, and help prevent misconduct. Empowering the sales force through comprehensive training increases their effectiveness. The most successful sales forces tend to be those that clearly define the steps of the sales process, spend time each month on managing their sales representatives' networks, and train sales managers on how to manage efficiently.[40] Ordinarily, new sales personnel require comprehensive training, whereas experienced personnel need both refresher courses on established products and training regarding new-product information and technology changes. At the Container Store new full-time store employees are given 263 hours of training. Because retail store employees will be interacting with customers on a consistent basis, the organization believes extensive training will increase employees' personal selling skills and help them form relationships with customers. As the advertisement indicates, the Container Store places great emphasis on its employees' happiness.

Sales training may be done in the field, at educational institutions, in company facilities, and/or online using web-based technology. For many companies, online training saves time and money and helps salespeople learn about new products quickly. Sales managers might even choose to use online platforms from companies such as GoToMeeting to interact with

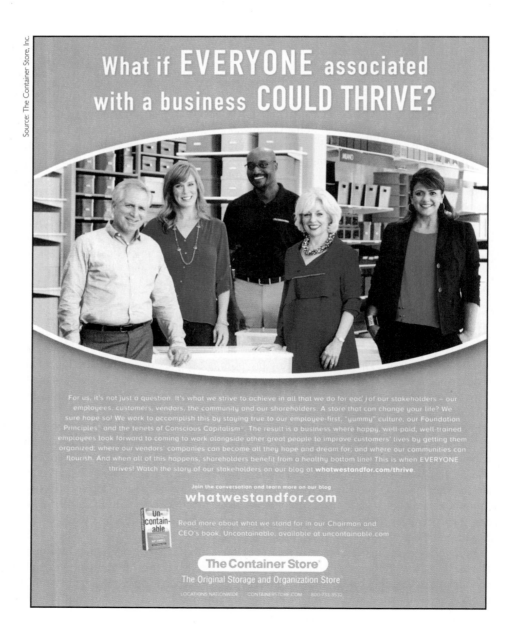

Source: The Container Store, Inc.

**Sales Training**
The Container Store provides 263 hours of training to its retail employees because they are the key to maintaining satisfied customers.

their sales force face-to-face. Others put them into the field immediately, providing formal training only after they have gained some experience. Training programs for new personnel can be as short as several days or as long as three years; some are even longer. Sales training for experienced personnel is often scheduled when sales activities are not too demanding. Because experienced salespeople usually need periodic retraining, a firm's sales management must determine the frequency, sequencing, and duration of these efforts.

Sales managers, as well as other salespeople, often engage in sales training, whether daily on the job or periodically during sales meetings. In addition, a number of outside companies specialize in providing sales training programs. Materials for sales training programs range from videos, texts, online materials, manuals, and cases to programmed learning devices and digital media. Lectures, demonstrations, simulation exercises, role-plays, and on-the-job training can all be effective training methods. Self-directed learning to supplement traditional sales training has the potential to improve sales performance. The choice of methods and materials for a particular sales training program depends on the type and number of trainees, program content and complexity, length and location, size of the training budget, number of trainers, and a trainer's expertise.

## 18-5e Compensating Salespeople

To develop and maintain a highly productive sales force, an organization must formulate and administer a compensation plan that attracts, motivates, and retains the most effective individuals. The plan should give sales management the desired level of control and provide sales personnel with acceptable levels of income, freedom, and incentive. It should be flexible, equitable, easy to administer, and easy to understand. Good compensation programs facilitate and encourage proper treatment of customers. Obviously, it is quite difficult to incorporate all of these requirements into a single program. Figure 18.2 shows the average salaries for sales representatives.

Developers of compensation programs must determine the general level of compensation required and the most desirable method of calculating it. In analyzing the required

Figure 18.2    **Average Salaries for Sales Representatives**

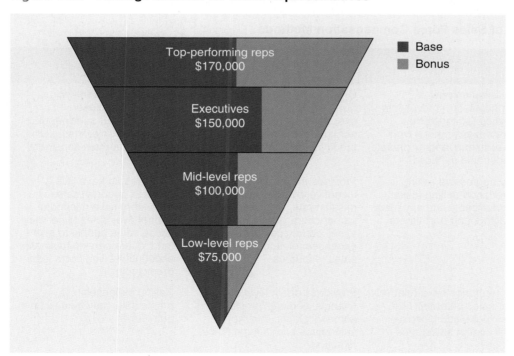

Source: Adapted from Joseph Kornik, "What's It All Worth?" *Sales and Marketing Management*, May 2007, p. 29.

compensation plan, sales management must ascertain a salesperson's value to the company on the basis of the tasks and responsibilities associated with the sales position. Sales managers may consider a number of factors, including salaries of other types of personnel in the firm, competitors' compensation plans, costs of sales force turnover, and non-salary selling expenses. The average low-level salesperson earns $50,000 to $75,000 annually (including commissions and bonuses), whereas a high-level, high-performing salesperson can make hundreds of thousands a year.

Sales compensation programs usually reimburse salespeople for selling expenses, provide some fringe benefits, and deliver the required compensation level. To achieve this, a firm may use one or more of three basic compensation methods: straight salary, straight commission, or a combination of the two. Table 18.2 lists the major characteristics, advantages, and disadvantages of each method. In a **straight salary compensation plan**, salespeople are paid a specified amount per time period, regardless of selling effort. This sum remains the same until they receive a pay increase or decrease. Although this method is easy to administer and affords salespeople financial security, it provides little incentive for them to boost selling efforts. In a **straight commission compensation plan**, salespeople's compensation is determined solely by sales for a given period. A commission may be based on a single percentage of sales or on a sliding scale involving several sales levels and percentage rates (e.g., sales under $500,000 a quarter would receive a smaller commission than sales over $500,000 each quarter). Although this method motivates sales personnel to escalate their selling efforts, it offers them little financial security, and it can be difficult for sales managers to maintain control over the sales force. Many new salespeople indicate a reluctance to accept the risks associated with straight commission. However, more experienced salespeople know this option can provide the greatest income potential. For these reasons, many firms offer a **combination compensation plan** in which salespeople receive a fixed salary plus a commission based on sales volume. Some combination programs require that a salesperson exceed a certain sales level before earning a commission; others offer commissions for any level of sales.

When selecting a compensation method, sales management weighs the advantages and disadvantages listed in the table. Researchers have found that higher commissions are the

**straight salary compensation plan** Paying salespeople a specific amount per time period, regardless of selling effort

**straight commission compensation plan** Paying salespeople according to the amount of their sales in a given time period

**combination compensation plan** Paying salespeople a fixed salary plus a commission based on sales volume

Table 18.2  **Characteristics of Sales Force Compensation Methods**

| Compensation Method | When Especially Useful | Advantages | Disadvantages |
|---|---|---|---|
| Straight salary | Compensating new salespeople; firm moves into new sales territories that require developmental work; sales requiring lengthy presale and post-sale services | Gives salespeople security; gives sales managers control over salespeople; easy to administer; yields more predictable selling expenses | Provides no incentive; necessitates closer supervision of salespeople; during sales declines, selling expenses remain constant |
| Straight commission | Highly aggressive selling is required; non-selling tasks are minimized; company uses contractors and part-timers | Provides maximum amount of incentive; by increasing commission rate, sales managers can encourage salespeople to sell certain items; selling expenses relate directly to sales resources | Salespeople have little financial security; sales managers have minimum control over sales force; may cause sales people to give inadequate service to smaller accounts; selling costs less predictable |
| Combination | Sales territories have relatively similar sales potential; firm wishes to provide incentive but still control sales force activities | Provides certain level of financial security; provides some incentive; can move sales force efforts in profitable direction | Selling expenses less predictable; may be difficult to administer |

Source: Charles Futrell, *Sales Management*, http://people.tamu.edu/~c-futrell/436/sm_home.html (accessed January 17, 2014).

most preferred reward, followed by pay increases. Yet preferences on pay tend to vary, depending upon the industry.[41] The Container Store prefers to pay its sales staff salaries that are 100 percent higher than those offered by rivals instead of basing pay on commission plans.[42]

## 18-5f  Motivating Salespeople

Although financial compensation is an important incentive, additional programs are necessary for motivating sales personnel. The nature of the jobs, job security, and pay are considered to be the most important factors for the college student going into the sales area today.[43] A sales manager should develop a systematic approach for motivating salespeople to be productive. Sales managers act as models for their sales force. When salespeople perceive their managers as being more customer-oriented and adaptive, they are more likely to imitate these positive behaviors.[44] Salespeople who can identify with their sales managers tend to have higher sales performance and customer satisfaction.[45] Effective sales force motivation is achieved through an organized set of activities performed continuously by the company's sales management.

Sales personnel, like other people, join organizations to satisfy personal needs and achieve personal goals. Sales managers must identify those needs and goals and strive to create an organizational climate that allows each salesperson to fulfill them. Enjoyable working conditions, power and authority, job security, and opportunity to excel are effective motivators, as are company efforts to make sales jobs more productive and efficient. Sales managers who are emotionally intelligent tend to have a positive impact on the creativity of their workers.[46] A strong positive corporate culture leads to higher levels of job satisfaction and organizational commitment and lower levels of job stress.[47]

Sales contests and other incentive programs can also be effective motivators. These can motivate salespeople to increase sales or add new accounts, promote special items, achieve greater volume per sales call, and cover territories more thoroughly. However, companies need to understand salespersons' preferences when designing contests in order to make them effective in increasing sales. Some companies find such contests powerful tools for motivating sales personnel to achieve company goals. Managers should be careful to craft sales contests that support a strong customer orientation as well as motivate salespeople. In smaller firms lacking the resources for a formal incentive program, a simple but public "thank you" and the recognition from management at a sales meeting, along with a small-denomination gift card, can be very rewarding.

Salesperson turnover is one of the most critical concerns of organizations. Lower organizational commitment has been found to relate directly to job turnover. Identifying with the organization and performance are tied directly to organizational commitment that reduces turnover.[48] Properly designed incentive programs pay for themselves many times over, and sales managers are relying on incentives more than ever. Recognition programs that acknowledge outstanding performance with symbolic awards, such as plaques, can be very effective when carried out in a peer setting. The most common incentive offered by companies is cash, followed by

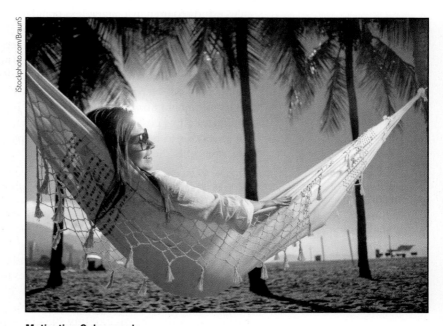

**Motivating Salespeople**
Trips or vacation packages are rewards that a high-performing salesperson might receive for surpassing his or her sales goals.

gift cards and travel.[49] Travel reward programs can confer a high-profile honor, provide a unique experience that makes recipients feel special, and build camaraderie among award-winning salespeople. However, some recipients of travel awards may feel they already travel too much on the job. Limited travel packages might also be a turn-off. In one study, 70 percent of participants claimed they would be more motivated if they had more choices in travel destinations.[50] Cash rewards are easy to administer, are always appreciated by recipients, and appeal to all demographic groups. However, cash has no visible "trophy" value and provides few "bragging rights." The benefits of awarding merchandise are that the items have visible trophy value. In addition, recipients who are allowed to select the merchandise experience a sense of control, and merchandise awards can help build momentum for the sales force. The disadvantages of using merchandise are that employees may have a lower perceived value of the merchandise and the company may experience greater administrative problems. Some companies outsource their incentive programs to companies that specialize in the creation and management of such programs.

## 18-5g **Managing Sales Territories**

The effectiveness of a sales force that must travel to customers is somewhat influenced by management's decisions regarding sales territories. When deciding on territories, sales managers must consider size, geographic shape, routing, and scheduling.

### Creating Sales Territories

Several factors enter into the design of a sales territory's size and geographic shape. First, sales managers must construct territories that allow sales potential to be measured. Sales territories often consist of several geographic units, such as census tracts, cities, counties, or states, for which market data are obtainable. Sales managers usually try to create territories with similar sales potential, or requiring about the same amount of work. If territories have equal sales potential, they will almost always be unequal in geographic size. Salespeople with larger territories have to work longer and harder to generate a certain sales volume. Conversely, if sales territories requiring equal amounts of work are created, sales potential for those territories will often vary. Think about the effort required to sell in New York and Connecticut versus the sales effort required in a larger, less populated area like Montana or Wyoming. If sales personnel are partially or fully compensated through commissions, they will have unequal income potential. Many sales managers try to balance territorial workloads and earning potential by using differential commission rates. At times, sales managers use commercial programs to help them balance sales territories. Although a sales manager seeks equity when developing and maintaining sales territories, some inequities always prevail. A territory's size and geographical shape should also help the sales force provide the best possible customer coverage and minimize selling costs. Customer density and distribution are important factors. It is important for territories to be designed so that salespeople contact customers with the frequency and consistency that feels ideal.[51]

### Routing and Scheduling Salespeople

The geographic size and shape of a sales territory are the most important factors affecting the routing and scheduling of sales calls. Next in importance are the number and distribution of customers within the territory, followed by sales call frequency and duration. Those in charge of routing and scheduling must consider the sequence in which customers are called on, specific roads or transportation schedules to be used, number of calls to be made in a given period, and time of day the calls will occur. In some firms, salespeople plan their own routes and schedules with little or no assistance from the sales manager. In others, the sales manager maintains significant responsibility. No matter who plans the routing and scheduling, the major goals should be to minimize salespeople's non-selling time (time spent traveling and waiting) and maximize their selling time. Sales managers should try to achieve these goals so that a salesperson's travel and lodging costs are held to a minimum.

## 18-5h Controlling and Evaluating Sales Force Performance

To control and evaluate sales force performance properly, sales management needs information. A sales manager cannot observe the field sales force daily and, thus, relies on salespeople's call reports, customer feedback, contracts, and invoices. Call reports identify the customers called on and present detailed information about interactions with those clients. Sales personnel must often file work schedules indicating where they plan to be during specific time periods. Data about a salesperson's interactions with customers and prospects can be included in the company's customer relationship management system. This information provides insights about the salesperson's performance.

Dimensions used to measure a salesperson's performance are determined largely by sales objectives, normally set by the sales manager. If an individual's sales objective is stated in terms of sales volume, that person should be evaluated on the basis of sales volume generated. Even if a salesperson is assigned a major objective, he or she is ordinarily expected to achieve several related objectives as well. Thus, salespeople are often judged along several dimensions. Sales managers evaluate many performance indicators, including average number of calls per day, average sales per customer, actual sales relative to sales potential, number of new-customer orders, average cost per call, and average gross profit per customer. One survey found that 67 percent of sales managers use sales quotas as a form of measurement and 41 percent use winning new accounts.[52]

To evaluate a salesperson, a sales manager may compare one or more of these dimensions with predetermined performance standards. However, sales managers commonly compare a salesperson's performance with that of other employees operating under similar selling conditions or the salesperson's current performance with past performance. Sometimes, management judges factors that have less direct bearing on sales performance, such as personal appearance, product knowledge, and ethical standards. One concern is the tendency to reprimand top sellers less severely than poor performers for engaging in unethical selling practices.

After evaluating salespeople, sales managers take any needed corrective action to improve sales force performance. They may adjust performance standards, provide additional training, or try other motivational methods. Corrective action may demand comprehensive changes in the sales force.

# 18-6 SALES PROMOTION

**Sales promotion** is an activity or material, or both, that acts as a direct inducement, offering added value or incentive for the product, to resellers, salespeople, or consumers. It encompasses all promotional activities and materials other than personal selling, advertising, and public relations. The retailer Payless, for example, often offers buy-one-get-one-free sales on its shoes, a sales promotion tactic known as a bonus or premium. In competitive markets, where products are very similar, sales promotion provides additional inducements that encourage product trial and purchase.

Marketers often use sales promotion to facilitate personal selling, advertising, or both. Companies also employ advertising and personal selling to support sales promotion activities. Marketers frequently use advertising to promote contests, free samples, and premiums. The most effective sales promotion efforts are highly interrelated with other promotional activities. Decisions regarding sales promotion often affect advertising and personal selling decisions, and vice versa.

Sales promotion can increase sales by providing extra purchasing incentives. Many opportunities exist to motivate consumers, resellers, and salespeople to take desired actions. Some kinds of sales promotion are designed specifically to stimulate resellers' demand and effectiveness, some are directed at increasing consumer demand, and some focus on both consumers and resellers. Regardless of the purpose, marketers must ensure that sales promotion objectives

**sales promotion** An activity and/or material intended to induce resellers or salespeople to sell a product or consumers to buy it are consistent with the organization's overall objectives, as well as with its marketing and promotion objectives.

When deciding which sales promotion methods to use, marketers must consider several factors, particularly product characteristics (price, size, weight, costs, durability, uses, features, and hazards) and target market characteristics (age, gender, income, location, density, usage rate, and shopping patterns). How products are distributed and the number and types of resellers may determine the type of method used. The competitive and legal environment may also influence the choice.

The use of sales promotion has increased dramatically over the past 30 years, primarily at the expense of advertising. This shift in how promotional dollars are used has occurred for several reasons. Heightened concerns about value have made customers more responsive to promotional offers, especially price discounts and point-of-purchase displays. Thanks to their size and access to checkout scanner data, retailers have gained considerable power in the supply chain and are demanding greater promotional efforts from manufacturers to boost retail profits. Declines in brand loyalty have produced an environment in which sales promotions aimed at persuading customers to switch brands are more effective. Finally, the stronger emphasis placed on improving short-term performance results calls for greater use of sales promotion methods that yield quick (although perhaps short-lived) sales increases.[53]

In the remainder of this chapter, we examine several consumer and trade sales promotion methods, including what they entail and what goals they can help marketers achieve.

## 18-7 CONSUMER SALES PROMOTION METHODS

**Consumer sales promotion methods** encourage or stimulate consumers to patronize specific retail stores or try particular products. Online sales promotion can create a higher level of product and brand recall.[54] Consumer sales promotion methods initiated by retailers often aim to attract customers to specific locations, whereas those used by manufacturers generally introduce new products or promote established brands. In this section, we discuss coupons, cents-off offers, money refunds and rebates, frequent-user incentives, point-of-purchase displays, demonstrations, free samples, premiums, consumer contests and games, and consumer sweepstakes.

### 18-7a Coupons

**Coupons** reduce a product's price and aim to prompt customers to try new or established products, increase sales volume quickly, attract repeat purchasers, or introduce new package sizes or features. Savings are deducted from the purchase price. Coupons are the most widely used consumer sales promotion technique. Although coupon usage had been spiraling downward for years, the economic downturn started to reverse this trend. However, coupon redemption has once again started to decrease. Although part of the reason is greater spending power, consumers have indicated that a primary reason for not using coupons is they cannot find coupons for what they want to buy.[55] Digital coupons via websites and mobile apps are also becoming popular. Social deal sites like Groupon, Living Social, and Crowd Cut, while not exactly in the coupon area, are encouraging consumers to look for deals or better prices. Bed, Bath & Beyond frequently sends 20-percent off coupons to consumers through the mail. However, these coupons are becoming so common that some analysts believe it could hurt Bed, Bath & Beyond because consumers are so used to getting coupons that they will not shop without them.[56] To take advantage of the new consumer interest in coupons, digital marketing—including mobile, social, and other platforms—is being used for couponing. However, research shows that most Americans still prefer paper coupons over digital.[57]

**consumer sales promotion methods** Sales promotion techniques that encourage consumers to patronize specific stores or try particular products

**coupons** Written price reductions used to encourage consumers to buy a specific product

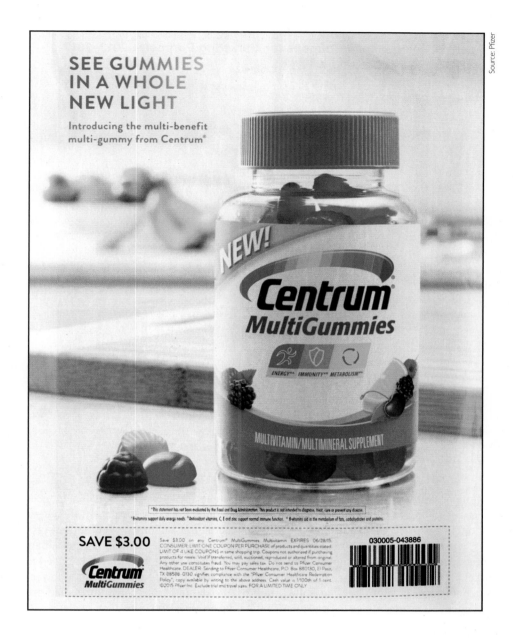

Source: Pfizer

**Print Coupons**
This advertisement features a coupon from Pfizer for Centrum MultiGummies.

For best results, coupons should be easily recognized and state the offer clearly. The nature of the product (seasonal demand for it, life-cycle stage, and frequency of purchase) is the prime consideration in setting up a coupon promotion. Paper coupons are distributed on and inside packages, through freestanding inserts, in print advertising, on the back of cash register receipts, and through direct mail. Electronic coupons are distributed online, via in-store kiosks, through shelf dispensers in stores, and at checkout counters.[58] Figure 18.3 indicates that nearly half of companies in the United States have used mobile coupons, and this number is likely to grow. When deciding on the distribution method for coupons, marketers should consider strategies and objectives, redemption rates, availability, circulation, and exclusivity. This advertisement for Centrum MultiGummies provides a coupon that takes $3.00 off the purchase price. The manufacturer hopes this coupon will increase sales of its product. The coupon distribution and redemption arena has become very competitive. To avoid losing customers, many grocery stores will redeem any coupons offered by competitors. Also, to draw customers to their stores, grocers double and sometimes even triple the value of customers' coupons.

Figure 18.3    **Share of U.S. Companies Using Mobile Coupons for Marketing Purposes, 2013–2017**

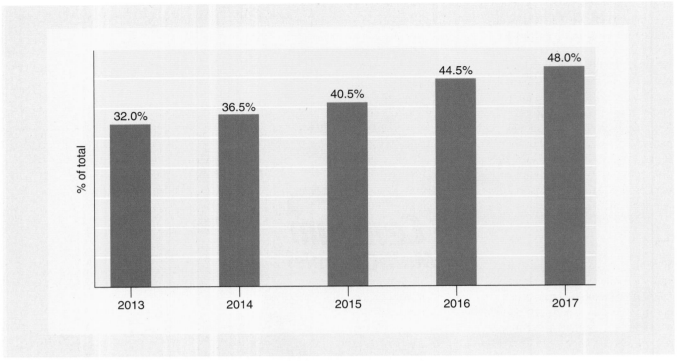

Note: Companies with 100+ employees; includes use of any coupons/codes that are accessed via a mobile device through mobile-optimized websites, mobile apps or SMS for marketing purposes.
Source: eMarketer, May 2015.

Coupons offer several advantages. Print advertisements with coupons are often more effective at generating brand awareness than print ads without coupons. Generally, the larger the coupon's cash offer, the better the recognition generated. Coupons reward current product users, win back former users, and encourage purchases in larger quantities. Because they are returned, coupons also help a manufacturer determine whether it reached the intended target market. The advantages of using electronic coupons over paper coupons include lower cost per redemption, greater targeting ability, improved data-gathering capabilities, and greater experimentation capabilities to determine optimal face values and expiration cycles.[59]

Drawbacks of coupon use include fraud and misredemption, which can be expensive for manufacturers. Coupon fraud—including counterfeit Internet coupons as well as coupons cashed in under false retailer names—costs manufacturers hundreds of millions in losses each year.[60] Another disadvantage, according to some experts, is that coupons are losing their value; because so many manufacturers offer them, consumers have learned not to buy without some incentive, whether that pertains to a coupon, a rebate, or a refund. Furthermore, brand loyalty among heavy coupon users has diminished, and many consumers redeem coupons only for products they normally buy. It is believed that about three-fourths of coupons are redeemed by people already using the brand on the coupon. Thus, coupons have questionable success as an incentive for consumers to try a new brand or product. An additional problem with coupons is that stores often do not have enough of the coupon item in stock. This situation generates ill will toward both the store and the product.

## 18-7b **Cents-Off Offers**

**cents-off offers** Promotions that allow buyers to pay less than the regular price to encourage purchase

With **cents-off offers**, buyers pay a certain amount less than the regular price shown on the label or package. A similar concept includes price discounts on services, which are usually embedded in promotions. Like coupons, this method can serve as a strong incentive for trying new or unfamiliar products and is commonly used in product introductions. It can stimulate product sales or multiple purchases, yield short-lived sales increases, and promote products during off-seasons. It is an easy method to control and is often used for specific purposes. If used on an ongoing basis, however, cents-off offers reduce the price for customers who would buy at the regular price and may also cheapen a product's image. In addition, the method often requires special handling by retailers who are responsible for giving the discount at the point of sale. The advertisement for Waterfall Resort Alaska offers a discount of 30 percent off a two-night package if customers call in soon. The advertisement appears to target those interested in fishing with its photo of a giant king salmon. By encouraging consumers to book their reservations now, Waterfall Resort Alaska is attempting to stimulate immediate sales.

### 18-7c  Money Refunds

With **money refunds**, consumers submit proof of purchase and are mailed a specific amount of money. Usually, manufacturers demand multiple product purchases before consumers qualify for money refunds. Marketers employ money refunds as an alternative to coupons to stimulate sales. Money refunds, used primarily to promote trial use of a product, are relatively low in cost. However, they sometimes generate a low response rate and, thus, have limited impact on sales.

### 18-7d  Rebates

With **rebates**, the consumer is sent a specified amount of money for making a single product purchase. Rebates are

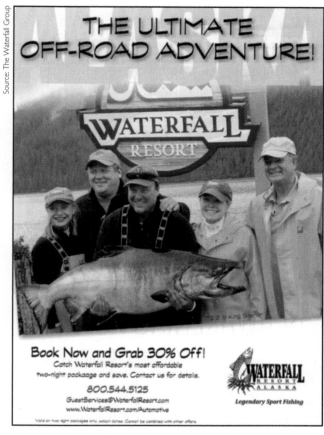

**Price Discounts**
Waterfall Resort Alaska offers a 30 percent discount for consumers who book their reservations during a certain period of time.

generally given on more expensive products than money refunds and are used to encourage customers. Marketers also use rebates to reinforce brand loyalty and encourage product purchase. On larger items, such as cars, rebates are often given at the point of sale. Most rebates, however, especially on smaller items, are given after the sale, usually through a mail-in process. For instance, Discount Tire might provide rebates during specific time periods for customers who purchase new tires, but the customer might have to mail in a form to be eligible for the rebate. Researchers find that these mail-in rebates are most effective in situations where consumers require a reason to purchase an item. On the other hand, rebates for products that provide instant gratification are more effective if provided at the point of purchase.[61]

One problem with money refunds and rebates is that many people perceive the redemption process as being too complicated. To eliminate these complications, many marketers allow customers to apply for a rebate online, which eliminates the need for forms that may confuse customers and frustrate retailers. Consumers might also have negative perceptions of manufacturers' reasons for offering rebates. They may believe the products are untested or have not sold well. If these perceptions are not changed, rebate offers may actually degrade product image and desirability.

### 18-7e  Shopper, Loyalty, and Frequent-User Incentives

Various incentives exist for frequent product users and loyal customers. Organizations such as supermarkets often provide users with loyalty or shopper cards that allow them to track customer purchases while providing periodic discounts to shoppers for continued purchases. Shopper cards tend to have an impact on brand loyalty purchases for secondary brands, but not brands where there is strong brand performance.[62] A key purpose of shopper and frequent-user

**money refunds** Sales promotion techniques that offer consumers a specified amount of money when they mail in a proof of purchase, usually for multiple product purchases

**rebates** Sales promotion techniques in which a consumer receives a specified amount of money for making a single product purchase

## MARKETING DEBATE

### The Advantages of Customer-Loyalty Programs

**ISSUE: Are customer-loyalty programs effective sales promotions for organizations?**

Traditionally, customer loyalty programs are thought to increase profitability. However, a McKinsey study found that for many firms, loyalty programs do not pay off. This means that firms could be giving away incentives to customers without any added benefit. With this in mind, should marketers continue to view customer-loyalty programs as a valid sales promotion tool?

There are some industries where customer-loyalty programs are more effective than others. For instance, companies that sell lower-margin products—such as supermarkets—incur a greater loss by giving away free items. Some consumers have learned to take advantage of the frequent-user system. For reward programs based on volume, it is not unusual for customers to purchase many low-priced products in order to gain the reward.

However, firms can take measures to enhance the effectiveness of their programs. First, customers must perceive the reward as valuable. Many consumers prefer rewards they would not normally purchase for themselves. Therefore, companies should offer rewards that are more pleasurable than functional. Additionally, companies should make loyalty a part of the customer experience. Starbucks has excelled at this. Its customer-loyalty program caused a 26 percent increase in profit.[b]

cards is to encourage continued loyalty. Whole Foods began testing a rewards program at select stores to see if it would make a difference on sales. The program allows shoppers at these stores to earn points and discounts when they shop.[63]

Many firms have similar incentives for rewarding customers who engage in repeat (frequent) purchases. For instance, major airlines offer frequent-flyer programs that reward customers who have flown a specified number of miles with free tickets for additional travel. Frequent-user incentives foster customer loyalty to a specific company or group of cooperating companies. They are favored by service businesses, such as airlines, auto rental agencies, hotels, and local coffee shops. Frequent-user programs not only reward loyal customers but also generate data that can contribute significant information about customers that helps marketers foster desirable customer relationships.

## 18-7f  Point-of-Purchase Materials and Demonstrations

**Point-of-purchase (POP) materials** include outdoor signs, window displays, counter pieces, display racks, and self-service cartons. Innovations in POP displays include sniff-teasers, which give off a product's aroma in the store as consumers walk within a radius of 4 feet, and computerized interactive displays. These items, often supplied by producers, attract attention, inform customers, and encourage retailers to carry particular products. Retailers have also begun experimenting with new forms of POP technology, such as interactive kiosks allowing shoppers to browse through products. A retailer is likely to use point-of-purchase materials if they are attractive, informative, well-constructed, and in harmony with the store's image.

**Demonstrations** are excellent attention-getters. Manufacturers offer them temporarily to encourage trial use and purchase of a product or to show how a product works. Because labor costs can be extremely high, demonstrations are not used widely. They can be highly effective for promoting certain types of products, such as appliances, cosmetics, and cleaning supplies. Even automobiles can be demonstrated, not only by a salesperson but also by the prospective buyer during a test drive. Cosmetics marketers, such as Estée Lauder and Clinique, sometimes offer potential customers "makeovers" to demonstrate product benefits and proper application.

**point-of-purchase (POP) materials** Signs, window displays, display racks, and similar devices used to attract customers

**demonstrations** Sales promotion methods a manufacturer uses temporarily to encourage trial use and purchase of a product or to show how a product works

## 18-7g Free Samples

Marketers use **free samples** to stimulate trial of a product, increase sales volume in the early stages of a product's life cycle, and obtain desirable distribution. Trader Joe's gives out free samples of its coffee, hoping to entice buyers to make a purchase. Sampling is the most expensive sales promotion method because production and distribution—at local events, by mail or door-to-door delivery, online, in stores, and on packages—entail high costs. However, it can also be one of the most effective sales promotion methods. In one survey, 92 percent of respondents said they would purchase a product if they liked it after getting a free sample. Samples eliminate the risk of trying a new product and allow consumers to feel as if they are getting something for free.[64]

Many consumers prefer to get their samples by mail. Other consumers like to sample new food products at supermarkets or try samples of new recipes featuring foods they already like. In designing a free sample, marketers should consider factors like seasonal demand for the product, market characteristics, and prior advertising. Free samples are usually inappropriate for slow-turnover products. Despite high costs, use of sampling is increasing. In a given year, almost three-fourths of consumer products companies may use sampling.

## 18-7h Premiums

**Premiums** are items offered free or at a minimal cost as a bonus for purchasing a product. Like the prize in the Cracker Jack box, premiums are used to attract competitors' customers, introduce different sizes of established products, add variety to other promotional efforts, and stimulate consumer loyalty. Consumers appear to prefer premiums to discounts on products due to the perception that they are receiving something "free."[65] Creativity is essential when using premiums; to stand out and achieve a significant number of redemptions, the premium must match both the target audience and the brand's image. Premiums must also be easily recognizable and desirable. Consumers are more favorable toward a premium when the brand has high equity and there is a good fit between the product and the premium.[66] Premiums are placed on or inside packages and can also be distributed by retailers or through the mail. Examples include a service station giving a free car wash with a fill-up, a free shaving cream with the purchase of a razor, and a free plastic storage box with the purchase of Kraft Cheese Singles.

## 18-7i Consumer Contests

In **consumer contests**, individuals compete for prizes based on their analytical or creative skills. This method can be used to generate retail traffic and frequency of exposure to promotional messages. Contestants are usually more highly involved in consumer contests than in games or sweepstakes, even though total participation may be lower. Contests may also be used in conjunction with other sales promotional methods, such as coupons. During March Madness, Quicken Loans held a consumer contest in which consumers could win the possibility of a $1 billion prize if they successfully picked the winner of every tournament game. After the contest began, brand awareness of Quicken Loans increased 300 percent.[67]

## 18-7j Consumer Games

In **consumer games**, individuals compete for prizes based primarily on chance—often by collecting game pieces like bottle caps or a sticker on a carton of French fries. Because collecting multiple pieces may be necessary to win or increase an individual's chances of winning, the game stimulates repeated business. Development and management of consumer games is often outsourced to an independent public relations firm, which can help marketers navigate federal and state laws that regulate games. Although games may stimulate sales temporarily, there is no evidence to suggest that they affect a company's long-term sales.

**free samples** Samples of a product given out to encourage trial and purchase

**premiums** Items offered free or at a minimal cost as a bonus for purchasing a product

**consumer contests** Sales promotion methods in which individuals compete for prizes based on their analytical or creative skills

**consumer games** Sales promotion methods in which individuals compete for prizes based primarily on chance

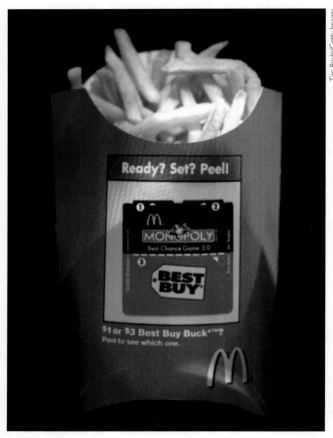

Tim Boyle/Getty Images

**Consumer Games**
McDonald's Monopoly is a popular consumer game that gives customers the opportunity to win prizes with the purchase of McDonald's products.

Marketers considering games should exercise care. Problems or errors may anger customers and could result in a lawsuit. McDonald's wildly popular Monopoly game promotion, in which customers collect Monopoly real estate pieces on drink and French fry packages, has been tarnished by past fraud after a crime ring, including employees of the promotional firm running the game, was convicted of stealing millions of dollars in winning game pieces. McDonald's later reintroduced the Monopoly game with heightened security.

### 18-7k　Sweepstakes

Entrants in a **consumer sweepstakes** submit their names for inclusion in a drawing for prizes. HGTV offered consumers a chance to own a beachfront dream home by entering a sweepstakes through HGTV.com or DIYNetwork.com.[68] Sweepstakes are employed more often than consumer contests and tend to attract a greater number of participants. However, contestants are usually more involved in consumer contests and games than in sweepstakes, even though total participation may be lower. Contests, games, and sweepstakes may be used in conjunction with other sales promotion methods like coupons.

## 18-8　TRADE SALES PROMOTION METHODS

To encourage resellers, especially retailers, to carry their products and promote them effectively, producers use trade sales promotion methods. **Trade sales promotion methods** attempt to persuade wholesalers and retailers to carry a producer's products and market them more aggressively. Marketers use trade sales methods for many reasons, including countering the effect of lower-priced store brands, passing along a discount to a price-sensitive market segment, boosting brand exposure among target consumers, or providing additional incentives to move excess inventory or counteract competitors. These methods include buying allowances, buy-back allowances, scan-back allowances, merchandise allowances, cooperative advertising, dealer listings, free merchandise, dealer loaders, premium or push money, and sales contests.

### 18-8a　Trade Allowances

Many manufacturers offer trade allowances to encourage resellers to carry a product or stock more of it. One such trade allowance is a **buying allowance**, a temporary price reduction offered to resellers for purchasing specified quantities of a product. A soap producer, for example, might give retailers $1 for each case of soap purchased. Such offers provide an incentive for resellers to handle new products, achieve temporary price reductions, or stimulate purchase of items in larger-than-normal quantities. The buying allowance, which takes the form of money, yields profits to resellers and is simple and straightforward. There are no restrictions on how resellers use the money, which increases the method's effectiveness. One drawback of buying allowances is that customers may buy "forward"—that is, buy large amounts that keep them supplied for many months. Another problem is that competitors may match (or beat) the reduced price, which can lower profits for all sellers.

**consumer sweepstakes**
A sales promotion in which entrants submit their names for inclusion in a drawing for prizes

**trade sales promotion methods** Methods intended to persuade wholesalers and retailers to carry a producer's products and market them aggressively

**buying allowance** A temporary price reduction to resellers for purchasing specified quantities of a product

A **buy-back allowance** is a sum of money that a producer gives to a reseller for each unit the reseller buys after an initial promotional deal is over. This method is a secondary incentive in which the total amount of money resellers receive is proportional to their purchases during an initial consumer promotion, such as a coupon offer. Buy-back allowances foster cooperation during an initial sales promotion effort and stimulate repurchase afterward. The main disadvantage of this method is expense.

A **scan-back allowance** is a manufacturer's reward to retailers based on the number of pieces moved through the retailers' scanners during a specific time period. To participate in scan-back programs, retailers are usually expected to pass along savings to consumers through special pricing. Scan-backs are becoming widely used by manufacturers because they link trade spending directly to product movement at the retail level.

A **merchandise allowance** is a manufacturer's agreement to pay resellers certain amounts of money for providing promotional efforts like advertising or point-of-purchase displays. This method is best suited to high-volume, high-profit, easily handled products. A drawback is that some retailers perform activities at a minimally acceptable level simply to obtain allowances. Before paying retailers, manufacturers usually verify their performance. Manufacturers hope that retailers' additional promotional efforts will yield substantial sales increases.

## 18-8b Cooperative Advertising and Dealer Listings

**Cooperative advertising** is an arrangement in which a manufacturer agrees to pay a certain amount of a retailer's media costs for advertising the manufacturer's products. The amount allowed is usually based on the quantities purchased. As with merchandise allowances, a retailer must show proof that advertisements did appear before the manufacturer pays the agreed-upon portion of the advertising costs. These payments give retailers additional funds for advertising. Some retailers exploit cooperative-advertising agreements by crowding too many products into one advertisement. Not all available cooperative-advertising dollars are used. Some retailers cannot afford to advertise, while others can afford it but do not want to advertise. A large proportion of all cooperative-advertising dollars is spent on newspaper advertisements.

**Dealer listings** are advertisements promoting a product and identifying participating retailers that sell the product. Dealer listings can influence retailers to carry the product, build traffic at the retail level, and encourage consumers to buy the product at participating dealers.

## 18-8c Free Merchandise and Gifts

Manufacturers sometimes offer **free merchandise** to resellers that purchase a stated quantity of products. Occasionally, free merchandise is used as payment for allowances provided through other sales promotion methods. To avoid handling and bookkeeping problems, the "free" merchandise usually takes the form of a reduced invoice.

A **dealer loader** is a gift to a retailer that purchases a specified quantity of merchandise. Dealer loaders are often used to obtain special display efforts from retailers by offering essential display parts as premiums. Thus, a manufacturer might design a display that includes a sterling silver tray as a major component and give the tray to the retailer. Marketers use dealer loaders to obtain new distributors and push larger quantities of goods.

## 18-8d Premium Money

**Premium money (push money)** is additional compensation offered by the manufacturer to salespeople as an incentive to push a line of goods. This method is appropriate when personal selling is an important part of the marketing effort; it is not effective for promoting products sold through self-service. Premium money often helps a manufacturer obtain a commitment from the sales force, but it can be very expensive. The use of this incentive must be in compliance with retailers' policies as well as state and local laws.

**buy-back allowance** A sum of money given to a reseller for each unit bought after an initial promotion deal is over

**scan-back allowance** A manufacturer's reward to retailers based on the number of pieces scanned

**merchandise allowance** A manufacturer's agreement to pay resellers certain amounts of money for providing special promotional efforts, such as setting up and maintaining a display

**cooperative advertising** An arrangement in which a manufacturer agrees to pay a certain amount of a retailer's media costs for advertising the manufacturer's products

**dealer listings** Advertisements that promote a product and identify the names of participating retailers that sell the product

**free merchandise** A manufacturer's reward given to resellers that purchase a stated quantity of products

**dealer loader** A gift, often part of a display, given to a retailer that purchases a specified quantity of merchandise

**premium money (push money)** Extra compensation to salespeople for pushing a line of goods

### 18-8e Sales Contest

**sales contest** A sales promotion method used to motivate distributors, retailers, and sales personnel through recognition of outstanding achievements

A **sales contest** is designed to motivate distributors, retailers, and sales personnel by recognizing outstanding achievements. To be effective, this method must be equitable for all individuals involved. One advantage is that it can achieve participation at all distribution levels. Positive effects may be temporary, however, and prizes are usually expensive.

# Summary

### 18-1 Describe the major goals of personal selling.

Personal selling is the process of informing customers and persuading them to purchase products through paid personal communication in an exchange situation. The five general goals of personal selling are finding prospects, determining their needs, persuading prospects to buy, following up on the sale, and keeping customers satisfied.

### 18-2 Summarize the seven basic steps in the personal selling process.

Many salespeople, either consciously or subconsciously, move through a general selling process as they sell products. In prospecting, the salesperson develops a database of potential customers. Before contacting prospects, the salesperson conducts a preapproach that involves finding and analyzing information about prospects and their needs. The approach is the manner in which the salesperson contacts potential customers. During the sales presentation, the salesperson must attract and hold the prospect's attention to stimulate interest and desire for the product. If possible, the salesperson should handle objections as they arise. During the closing, the salesperson asks the prospect to buy the product or products. After a successful closing, the salesperson must follow up on the sale.

### 18-3 Identify the types of sales force personnel.

The sales structure consists of the inside sales force and the outside sales force. The sales function focuses on both selling to current customers and generating new business sales. Sales support personnel facilitate selling, but their duties usually extend beyond making sales. The three types of support personnel are missionary, trade, and technical salespeople.

### 18-4 Describe *team selling* and *relationship selling.*

The roles of salespeople are changing, resulting in an increased focus on team selling and relationship selling. Team selling involves the salesperson joining with people from the firm's financial, engineering, and other functional areas. Relationship selling involves building mutually beneficial long-term associations with a customer through regular communications over prolonged periods of time.

### 18-5 Discuss eight major decisions in sales force management.

Sales force management is an important determinant of a firm's success because the sales force is directly responsible for generating the organization's sales revenue. Major decision areas and activities are establishing sales force objectives; determining sales force size; recruiting, selecting, training, compensating, and motivating salespeople; managing sales territories; and controlling and evaluating sales force performance.

Sales objectives should be stated in precise, measurable terms and specify the time period and geographic areas involved. The size of the sales force must be adjusted occasionally because a firm's marketing plans change along with markets and forces in the marketing environment.

Recruiting and selecting salespeople involve attracting and choosing the right type of salesperson to maintain an effective sales force. When developing a training program, managers must consider a variety of dimensions, such as who should be trained, what should be taught, and how training should occur. Compensation of salespeople involves formulating and administering a compensation plan that attracts, motivates, and retains the right types of salespeople. Motivated salespeople should translate into high productivity. Managing sales territories focuses on such factors as size, shape, routing, and scheduling. To control and evaluate sales force performance, sales managers use information obtained through salespeople's call reports, customer feedback, and invoices.

### 18-6 Describe sales promotion.

Sales promotion is an activity or a material (or both) that acts as a direct inducement, offering added value or incentive for the product to resellers, salespeople, or consumers. Marketers use sales promotion to identify and attract new customers, introduce new products, and increase reseller inventories. Sales promotion techniques fall into two general categories: consumer and trade.

### 18-7 Review consumer sales promotion methods.

Consumer sales promotion methods encourage consumers to patronize specific stores or try a particular product. These sales promotion methods include coupons; cents-off offers;

money refunds and rebates; frequent-user incentives; point-of-purchase displays; demonstrations; free samples and premiums; and consumer contests, games, and sweepstakes.

### 18-8 Review trade sales promotion methods.

Trade sales promotion techniques can motivate resellers to handle a manufacturer's products and market them

aggressively. These sales promotion techniques include buying allowances, buy-back allowances, scan-back allowances, merchandise allowances, cooperative advertising, dealer listings, free merchandise, dealer loaders, premium (or push) money, and sales contests.

---

**Go to www.cengagebrain.com for resources to help you master the content in this chapter as well as for materials that will expand your marketing knowledge!**

---

## Important Terms

personal selling 560
prospecting 562
approach 564
closing 565
support personnel 566
missionary salespeople 566
trade salespeople 566
technical salespeople 566
team selling 567
relationship selling 567
recruiting 570
straight salary compensation plan 574
straight commission compensation plan 574

combination compensation plan 574
sales promotion 577
consumer sales promotion methods 578
coupons 578
cents-off offers 580
money refunds 581
rebates 581
point-of-purchase (POP) materials 582
demonstrations 582
free samples 583
premiums 583
consumer contests 583

consumer games 583
consumer sweepstakes 584
trade sales promotion methods 584
buying allowance 584
buy-back allowance 585
scan-back allowance 585
merchandise allowance 585
cooperative advertising 585
dealer listings 585
free merchandise 585
dealer loader 585
premium money (push money) 585
sales contest 586

## Discussion and Review Questions

1. What is personal selling? How does personal selling differ from other types of promotional activities?
2. What are the primary purposes of personal selling?
3. Identify the steps of the personal selling process. Must a salesperson include all these steps when selling a product to a customer? Why or why not?
4. How does a salesperson find and evaluate prospects? Do you consider any of these methods to be ethically questionable? Explain.
5. Why are support personnel needed in the sales force?
6. Why are team selling and relationship selling becoming more prevalent?
7. Identify several characteristics of effective sales objectives.
8. How should a sales manager establish criteria for selecting sales personnel? What do you think are the general characteristics of a good salesperson?
9. What major issues or questions should management consider when developing a training program for the sales force?
10. Explain the major advantages and disadvantages of the three basic methods of compensating salespeople. In general, which method would you prefer? Why?
11. What major factors should be taken into account when designing the size and shape of a sales territory?
12. How does a sales manager, who cannot be with each salesperson in the field on a daily basis, control the performance of sales personnel?
13. What is sales promotion? Why is it used?
14. For each of the following, identify and describe three techniques and give several examples: (a) consumer sales promotion methods and (b) trade sales promotion methods.
15. What types of sales promotion methods have you observed recently? Comment on their effectiveness.

# Video Case 18.1

## Nederlander Gives Audiences a Reason for a Standing Ovation

The Nederlander Organization is in its 100th year of managing Broadway-type theaters in several states and the United Kingdom. It is a theatrical organization that owns concert venues and Broadway theaters. Nederlander describes itself as a lifestyle company, which puts it in a specific niche with a specific type of customer. Josh Lesnick, President and CEO of Audience Rewards, explains, "I think with something like the arts, customers obviously want a good deal. They want a value-add, but it's really about the experience."

The organization engages in promotional activities for various concerts as well as production of Broadway shows. The success of such activities relies on building and maintaining strong relationships with the many theater owners and ticketing organizations. Nederlander Organization has leveraged these relationships with its Audience Rewards program, a type of sales promotion that has allowed it to build strong relationships with customers by enhancing their experience.

The unique nature of the industry and smaller size of its target market allows Nederlander to create a valuable experience for customers through personal selling and sales promotion activities. Josh Lesnick describes Audience Rewards as similar to a frequent flyer program. Customers can become members for free and are entered into the ticketing system. When they buy tickets and go to shows, they collect points and are able to redeem them for free or discounted tickets and other rewards. The program was developed as an alternative to traditional discounting. "[It is] another way to incentivize customers to go to the theater more, to spend more money, to try out new art."

Nederlander's sales promotion program strongly benefits smaller venues. The theater industry is composed of many small privately-owned theaters, and each show is marketed individually. This can make it difficult and expensive for companies to advertise and promote their shows. Nederlander's Audience Rewards program helps ease this complexity because it works with many theater owners who support and take part in the program. Lesnick explains that it provides "a central platform to market across all the vendors and art."

The Audience Rewards program also depends on outside relationships with major companies who sponsor the rewards for the program. Acquiring such partnerships can be a challenge for most small companies; however, Nederlander's target market is an attractive opportunity for large companies. A market dominated by 30- to 59-year-old females with a high annual income of approximately $200,000 "appeals to our corporate partners because they want to get access to our customers," Lesnick explains. The program has also provided Nederlander with the opportunity to develop new products such as co-branded credit cards and Broadway-wide gift cards. With these new additions, customers and corporate partners are receiving valuable benefits. Customers are not only able to receive free and discounted tickets, but they are also able to redeem their points to participate in special red carpet events and backstage passes to meet performers. Corporate partners receive the benefit of access to a more specific and profitable target market.

Before the institution of the Audience Rewards program, Nederlander was bringing in hundreds of thousands of dollars in ticket sales without the use of technology or innovative customer relationship management techniques. Sean Free, Vice President of Sales and Ticketing, comments on the types of technologies used by businesses for marketing and business strategies. He states that "email blasts, and the retargeting efforts that people are now doing, and following people on the Internet through IP addresses . . . is all very new . . . and Broadway is usually one of the last industries to follow through with the latest technology." Despite the tendency for the industry's slow reaction, Nederlander's implementation of the Audience Rewards program has served as a catalytic innovation for the company. For example, six months before the premier of the Broadway show *Evita*, Nederlander, in conjunction with some of its partners, sent out five million promotional e-mails to over one million members over a 10-day period. Lesnick explains that the e-mails "created a sense of urgency and an incentive to buy early." This "generated in the pre-sale [revenue] of over $1 million . . . which allowed the company to strategically realign their money to make other decisions."

In addition to the many benefits of this program, sales promotion has provided Nederlander Organization with a competitive advantage over other companies. Because this program relies on the relationships and support of the theater owners and outside companies with whom Nederlander has already solidified relationships, it has created a barrier to entry for other theater organizations due to its strong relationship marketing. This loyalty program has proven to be profitable and good for all partners and members involved with the company.[69]

### Questions for Discussion

1. Why do you think more targeted promotional efforts such as personal selling and sales promotion are necessary for Nederlander's specific target market?

2. How does Nederlander's Audience Rewards program result in a competitive advantage?

3. Describe how Nederlander's strong customer relationship management results in increased loyalty to the organization.

# Case 18.2

## Mistine's Mystique: Great Promotional Strategies

Mistine understands the power of promotion in building brand awareness. Owned by Thai firm Better Way, Mistine was launched in 1991 as a direct selling cosmetics firm. The company's adoption of a direct selling model enabled it to become a first mover in the Thai direct selling market. Yet unlike similar firms, Mistine decided to do things differently by becoming the first direct selling company in the world to engage in mass media advertising. Its integrated marketing campaigns have propelled Mistine into one of Thailand's most accepted brands.

Mistine owes its early promotional success to Dr. Amornthep Deerojanawong, co-founder of Better Way. Dr. Deerojanawong began to advertise the company's low-cost but quality cosmetic products through media interviews and seminars. His credibility as a doctor developed trust in Mistine products. To reach a mass audience, however, Mistine had to invest in television advertising. Its first television campaign was meant to spread awareness about the company. With the tagline "Mistine is here!" Mistine's television campaign was widely successful and increased brand awareness from 10 percent to roughly 70 percent. The company markets itself as "The Asian brand for Asian women" as a way to promote the fact that its products are made to complement Asian skin tones.

Mistine continues to engage in heavy advertising, launching campaigns featuring popular actresses, actors, and bands as Mistine brand ambassadors. Many of these celebrities have been featured on Channel 7 or RS Entertainment, Thai television channels with soap operas popular among Mistine's core market. Mistine has become an expert at choosing celebrities that resonate with these target markets. To take advantage of the favorable impression of Korean cosmetics (especially among teenagers), Mistine used a famous Korean band to promote its BB Powder. The company has also created its own Facebook page to extend its worldwide reach.

In addition to its well-known advertisements, Mistine has also garnered publicity for its cause-related marketing campaigns. The firm is adept at linking causes that people care about with its products. For instance, the company featured famous Thai movie actress Petchara Chaowarat to present the company's "Diamond" lipstick collection. By utilizing Chaowarat—considered the "biggest-name actress in Thailand"—to promote the brand, Mistine not only made its

brand appear prestigious but also engaged in cause-related marketing by agreeing to donate part of the lipstick's revenue to the Thailand Association for the Blind (Petchara Chaowarat was struck by blindness during her acting career). This form of public relations allowed Mistine to leave a favorable impression among its target market.

Although customers can find Mistine products in retail stores or order them through the firm's catalog or website, personal selling remains a crucial component to Mistine's integrated marketing strategy. Each day, Mistine salespeople make their rounds to meet customers and prospective customers. This face-to-face interaction enables salespeople to interact with potential customers by presenting product benefits, answering questions, and handling objections. Additionally, it provides Mistine with the opportunity to develop relationships between its sales force and its customers. An advanced computer system tracks sales, and Mistine's fleet of trucks can deliver the products within 1 week of ordering. Mistine's strong distribution system, efficient sales force, and quick delivery services have gained the company many loyal fans—particularly among Thai housewives, factory workers, and teenagers. Additionally, by expanding into different distribution channels Mistine has been able to reach new target markets.

Mistine's effective use of advertising, public relations, and personal selling has provided it with a competitive edge over its rivals. In fact, the company has been so successful that it is expanding into countries such as Myanmar, Indonesia, Ghana, South Africa, and the Democratic Republic of the Congo. As it continues to expand, Mistine will have to change its promotional strategies to account for different cultural values and infrastructures. However, if it can achieve the marketing success that it has in Thailand, then the cosmetics company will be well on its way to becoming a popular global brand.[70]

### Questions for Discussion

1. How has Mistine used different promotional strategies to increase brand awareness?
2. Why is personal selling useful for marketing Mistine products?
3. What has given Mistine its competitive advantage in the Thai direct selling market?

# Strategic Case 7

## Patagonia Climbs into the World of IMC

When it comes to advertising, apparel manufacturer and retailer Patagonia takes a different approach. The headlines of its popular advertisements feature in big, bold letters "Don't Buy This Jacket." Underneath is a photo of a Patagonia jacket made from recycled materials. The copy of the ad describes how much water, carbon dioxide, and waste is expended in manufacturing and transporting the jacket. Patagonia acknowledges that even its eco-conscious products are environmentally damaging.

Patagonia is not trying to put itself out of business with these types of ads. Rather, it is reinforcing its mission of environmental protection and sustainability. Patagonia uses this type of promotion to cause consumers to think about whether they really need a brand-new product. If the answer is yes, then Patagonia encourages them to purchase products that will last them a long time. This is where its own products come in.

### Background

The idea behind Patagonia, headquartered in Ventura, California, started from one man's passion for rock climbing. Outdoor enthusiast Yvon Chouinard loved rock climbing but lacked reusable climbing gear. He began developing his own reusable rock climbing pitons and selling them from out of his car. In 1965 he co-founded Chouinard Equipment. Eventually, the company began selling more eco-friendly chocks to replace pitons. These chocks were designed to eliminate rock damage when climbing. This was the company's first major foray into environmental consciousness.

Chouinard and his wife had begun to sell durable climbing clothing as a way to supplement their hardware business, but by 1972 the clothing had become its own line. They called their clothing line Patagonia to reflect the mysticism of far off lands and adventurous places. Customers appreciated the bright colors and durability of Patagonia clothing. The company decided to align its brand with environmental responsibility and switched to more expensive organic cotton in 1996.

Today, Patagonia sells its gear through its own branded stores, online, and through retailers such as Dick's Sporting Goods and REI. Patagonia has 75 branded stores, profits exceeding $600 million, and 1,200

employees. Patagonia has become known for its environmental consciousness, employee-friendly workplace, and high-quality, long-lasting clothing.

As with all well-known firms, Patagonia's success would not be possible without a carefully integrated promotion mix that educates consumers about what the brand and its products represent. Word-of-mouth communication is highly encouraged, and Patagonia encourages viral marketing through the use of social media including Facebook, YouTube, Twitter, mobile marketing, and its own corporate blog. A strong mix of advertising, public relations, personal selling, and sales promotions is used to keep its brand relevant, both for retailers that sell their products and for customers that buy from them directly.

### Patagonia's "Do Not Buy" Advertising

Patagonia freely admits that advertising is not a high priority in its mission to change the world. The company does not employ an outside ad agency, instead choosing to develop promotions in-house. Much of the advertising that Patagonia does involves advocacy advertising rather than product advertising. For instance, its short film "DamNation" was geared toward demonstrating how removing dams in the United States is important to restoring our rivers. Although this type of promotion promotes a cause rather than a company brand, the advertising's affiliation with the company helps to promote the firm indirectly and give it a reputation for sustainability.

All of Patagonia's advertising reflects the company's mission statement: "Build the best product, cause no unnecessary harm, use business to inspire and implement solutions to the environmental crisis." Encouraging consumers to purchase their products if they do not need them conflicts with Patagonia's mission. As a result, it does the opposite and releases advertisements advising consumers to avoid purchasing what they do not need, even if that means forgoing Patagonia products. Additionally, Patagonia's "Buy Less" campaign encourages consumers to sell their used Patagonia gear on eBay or through Patagonia's website. Patagonia is declaring a war against consumerism.

It might seem that Patagonia's advertising discourages sales. However, its advertising platform of a war against consumerism serves to demonstrate the appeal of its products. Patagonia offers products that last for a lifetime, and by encouraging consumers to purchase less, they are simultaneously encouraging them to make sure that what they do purchase lasts for a long time. Because customers can trust that Patagonia will sell them a high-quality product, they are more likely to become long-term customers of the firm.

### Patagonia's Public Relations Image

Much of the publicity surrounding Patagonia involves its numerous sustainability initiatives in which it participates. For instance, in 1985 Patagonia started giving 1 percent of its total sales to environmental organizations. The organization 1% for the Planet is an alliance of businesses that donate part of its proceeds to environmental organizations to support sustainability and the preservation of the environment. Since it started, Patagonia has made $58 million in grants and in-kind donations.

Patagonia's Common Threads Initiative seeks to get employees and customers involved in the process of environmental responsibility. The company partnered with eBay to allow employees and consumers to sell their used products through eBay's "Common Threads" partner site. Those wishing to sell their products must take the pledge to reduce, reuse, and recycle. The Common Threads Initiative reinforces Patagonia's mission statement and is also an effective public relations tool to get employees and consumers involved in working with the organization.

Patagonia also reaches out to the public through its digital sites. Its blog thecleanestline.com serves as a weblog for customers, employees, and friends of Patagonia to share environmental activism activities and stories of the outdoors. Its Worn Wear program encourages customers to celebrate their stories of their experiences with treasured, well-worn apparel. Patagonia's initiatives and customer relationships have led it to be covered in numerous news and feature articles, from *Fast Company* magazine to *The Wall Street Journal*.

### Personal Selling and Sales Promotions at Patagonia

Patagonia relies heavily on the sales function for its wholesale business. It employs a wholesale management team to build relationships and promote its brand among specialty retailers. As Patagonia expands globally, it is reorganizing and expanding its sales force to meet the needs of stores in different countries. In Europe Patagonia added sales positions and reorganized its sales force into four regions. Sales members are given iPhones and iPads to enhance communication as they travel.

Patagonia also uses personal selling in its retail stores. Retail sales associates are trained to greet customers courteously, assist them in shopping for products, and provide them with accurate information to customer inquiries. They must also honor the company's "ironclad guarantee" for product returns. Sales training for Patagonia employees involves a combination of in-person training and online video.

Additionally, Patagonia offers a number of incentives or inducements to attract customers to its online and physical stores. Because Patagonia products can be expensive, the company mitigates the risk of purchase with liberal return and replacement policies. If the person decides she or he is not happy with the product, the customer may return it to the company to be repaired, replaced, or refunded. Products with wear and tear will be repaired at a reasonable charge. For online purchases Patagonia offers free deliveries for purchases over $75.

Above all, Patagonia wants to ensure that its sales promotions are completely transparent to customers. For this reason, it warns consumers about the authenticity of online coupons offering discounts for Patagonia products. Instead of offering online coupons, Patagonia has a link that will take the customer directly to its discounted product offerings. This eliminates the possibilities of coupon fraud and maintains a transparent, trusting relationship between company and customer.

Patagonia has developed an effective integrated marketing communications mix using advertising, public relations, personal selling, and sales promotion. Its promotion mix serves to establish and maintain long-term relationships with both customers and specialty stores. It also informs stakeholders about the company's avid support for environmental consciousness. Rather than promoting specific products, Patagonia prefers to promote environmental causes and combat the idea of consumerism. Although it might take some unconventional approaches to promotion, Patagonia has developed campaigns that resonate with customers and inspire long-term loyalty.[71]

### Questions for Discussion

1. Describe how Patagonia uses different elements of the promotion mix.
2. Why do you think Patagonia tends to use advocacy advertising instead of product advertising?
3. How do Patagonia's marketing promotion activities serve to reinforce its primary mission?

# NOTES

1 Joe Pinsker, "The Psychology Behind Costco's Free Samples," *The Atlantic*, October 1, 2014, http://www.theatlantic.com/business/archive/2014/10/the-psychology-behind-costcos-free-samples/380969/ (accessed September 15, 2015); Kelly Spors, "Why Giving Things Away for Free Can Boost Sales," *American Express*, October 3, 2014, https://www.americanexpress.com/us/small-business/openforum/articles/free-samples-can-boost-sales/ (accessed September 15, 2015); "Product Sampling," Interactions, http://www.interactionsmarketing.com/our-difference/product-sampling.html (accessed September 15, 2015); Brad Tuttle, "The Power of Freebies: Why Companies Pay to Give Free Samples to Supermarket Customers," *Time*, February 17, 2011, http://business.time.com/2011/02/17/the-power-of-freebies-why-companies-pay-to-give-free-samples-to-supermarket-customers/ (accessed September 15, 2015); Ilan Mochari, "Give it Away Now: Why Free Product Samples Always Pay Off," *Inc.*, http://www.inc.com/ilan-mochari/costco-sampling-free-food-giveaway.html (accessed September 15, 2015); Jeana Delano, "The Power of Product Sampling," *GCI Magazine*, http://www.gcimagazine.com/business/marketing/The-Power-of-Product-Sampling-280537262.html (accessed September 15, 2015); Annabelle Gurwitch, "The Treasure in a Small Package," *The New York Times*, October 17, 2014, http://www.nytimes.com/2014/10/19/fashion/want-a-free-sample-cosmetic-companies-are-onto-you.html (accessed September 15, 2015).

2 Avinash Malshe and Avipreet Sohi, "What Makes Strategy Making across the Sales-Marketing Interface More Successful?" *Journal of the Academy of Marketing Science* 37, 4 (Winter 2009): 400–421.

3 "Advantages of Personal Selling," *KnowThis.com*, www.knowthis.com/principles-of-marketing-tutorials/personal-selling/advantages-of-personal-selling (accessed February 11, 2016).

4 Bob Sullivan, "Lower Cost Per Sales With CRM, Mapping Software, & Call Planning," *Industrial Distribution*, August 12, 2013, http://www.inddist.com/blogs/2013/08/lower-cost-sales-crm-mapping-software-call-planning (accessed January 21, 2015).

5 Donald C. Barnes, Joel E. Collier, Nicole Ponder, and Zachary Williams, "Investigating the Employee's Perspective of Customer Delight," *Journal of Personal Selling & Sales Management* 33, 1 (Winter 2013): 91–104.

6 Jon M. Hawes, Anne K. Rich, and Scott M. Widmier, "Assessing the Development of the Sales Profession," *Journal of Personal Selling & Sales Management* 24 (Winter 2004): 27–37.

7 Dawn R. Deeter-Schmelz and Karen Norman Kennedy, "A Global Perspective on the Current State of Sales Education in the College Curriculum, *Journal of Personal Selling & Sales Management* 31, n1 (Winter 2011): 55–76.

8 Willem Verbeke, Bart Dietz, and Ernst Verwaal, "Drivers of Sales Performance: A Contemporary Meta-Analysis. Have Salespeople Become Knowledge Brokers?" *Journal of the Academy of Marketing Science* 39 (2011): 407–428.

9 Lisa Terry, "Customer Service," *Inbound Logistics*, December 2014, 33–36.

10 Michael Rodriguez and Robert M. Peterson, "Generating Leads via Social CRM: Early Best Practices for B2B Sales," abstract in Concha Allen (ed.), "Special Abstract Section: 2011 National Conference in Sales Management," *Journal of Personal Selling* 31, 4 (Fall 2011): 457–458.

11 Ed Peelena, Kees van Montfort, Rob Beltman, and Arnoud Klerkx, "An Empirical Study into the Foundation of CRM Success," *Journal of Strategic Marketing* 17, 6 (December 2009): 453–471.

12 Eli Jones, Paul Busch, and Peter Dacin, "Firm Market Orientation and Salesperson Customer Orientation: Interpersonal and Intrapersonal Influence on Customer Service and Retention in Business-to-Business Buyer–Seller Relationships," *Journal of Business Research* 56 (2003): 323–340.

13 Kenneth Le Meunier-FitzHugh and Nigel F. Piercy, "Exploring the Relationship between Market Orientation and Sales and Marketing Collaboration," *Journal of Personal Selling & Sales Management* 31, 3 (Summer 2011): 287–296.

14 Kaj Storbacka, Pia Polsa, and Maria Sääksjärvi, "Management Practices in Solution Sales—Multilevel and Cross-Functional Framework," *Journal of Personal Selling & Sales Management* 31, 1 (Winter 2011): 35–54.

15 Julie T. Johnson, Hiram C. Barksdale Jr., and James S. Boles, "Factors Associated with Customer Willingness to Refer Leads to Salespeople," *Journal of Business Research* 56 (2003): 257–263.

16 Ralph W. Giacobbe, Donald W. Jackson, Jr., Lawrence A. Crosby, and Claudia M. Bridges, "A Contingency Approach to Adaptive Selling Behavior and Sales Performance: Selling Situations and Salesperson Characteristics," *Journal of Personal Selling & Sales Management* 26 (Spring 2006): 115–142.

17 Richard G. McFarland, Goutam N. Challagalla, and Tasadduq A. Shervani, "Influence Tactics for Effective Adaptive Selling," *Journal of Marketing* 70 (October 2006): 103–117.

18 Thomas E. DeCarlo and Michael J. Barone, "The Interactive Effects of Sales Presentation, Suspicion, and Positive Mood on Salesperson Evaluations and Purchase Intentions," *Journal of Personal Selling & Sales Management* 33, 1 (Winter 2013): 53–66.

19 Susie Pryor, Avinash Malshe, and Kyle Paradise, "Salesperson Listening in the Extended Sales Relationship: An Exploration of Cognitive, Affective, and Temporal Dimensions," *Journal of Personal Selling & Sales Management* 33, 2 (Spring 2013): 185–196.

20 John Andy Wood, "NLP Revisted: Nonverbal Communications and Signals of Trustworthiness," *Journal of Personal Selling & Sales Management* 26 (Spring 2006): 198–204.

21 John Dunyon, Valerie Gossling, Sarah Willden, and John S. Seiter, "Compliments and Purchasing Behavior in Telephone Sales Interactions," abstract in Dawn R. Deeter-Schmelz (ed.), "Personal Selling & Sales Management Abstracts," *Journal of Personal Selling & Sales Management* 31, 2 (Spring 2011): 186.

22 Stephen S. Porter, Joshua L. Wiener, and Gary L. Frankwick, "The Moderating Effect of Selling Situation on the Adaptive Selling Strategy—Selling Effectiveness Relationship,"

*Journal of Business Research* 56 (2003): 275–281.

23 Tammy Stanley, "Follow-Up: The Success Recipe Salespeople Don't See," *Direct Selling News*, May 2010, http://directsellingnews.com/index.php/view/follow_up_the_success_recipe_salespeople_dont_see#.Vr0hGlLd0cM (accessed February 11, 2016).

24 Dinah Eng, "Does Joy Help You Sell?" *Fortune*, January 1, 2016, p. 30.

25 Gabriel R. Gonzalez, K. Douglas Hoffman, Thomas N. Ingram, and Raymond W. LaForge, "Sales Organization Recovery Management and Relationship Selling: A Conceptual Model and Empirical Test," *Journal of Personal Selling & Sales Management* 30, 3 (Summer 2010): 223–238.

26 Barton A. Weitz and Kevin D. Bradford, "Personal Selling and Sales Management: A Relationship Marketing Perspective," *Journal of the Academy of Marketing Science* 27, 2 (1999): 241–254.

27 Eli Jones, Steven P. Brown, Andris A. Zoltners, and Barton A. Weitz, "The Changing Environment of Selling and Sales Management," *Journal of Personal Selling & Sales Management* 25, 2 (Spring 2005): 105–111.

28 "The Right Questions and Attitudes Can Beef Up Your Sales, Improve Customer Retention," *Selling* (June 2001): 3.

29 Jones et al., 105–111.

30 Gary K. Hunter and William D. Perreault Jr., "Making Sales Technology Effective," *Journal of Marketing* 71 (January 2007): 16–34.

31 Othman Boujena, Johnston J. Wesley, and Dwight R. Merunka, "The Benefits of Sales Force Automation: A Customer's Perspective," *Journal of Personal Selling & Sales Management* 29, 2 (2009): 137–150.

32 Fernando Jaramillo, Jay Prakash Mulki, and Paul Solomon, "The Role of Ethical Climate on Salesperson's Role Stress, Job Attitudes, Turnover Intention, and Job Performance," *Journal of Personal Selling & Sales Management* 26 (Summer 2006): 272–282.

33 Christophe Fournier, John F. Tanner, Jr., Lawrence B. Chonko, and Chris Manolis, "The Moderating Role of Ethical Climate on Salesperson Propensity to Leave," *Journal of Personal Selling & Sales Management* 3, 1 (Winter 2009–2010): 7–22.

34 Bulent Menguc, Seigyoung Auh, and Aypar Uslu, "Customer Knowledge Creation Capability and Performance in Sales Teams," *Journal of the Academy of Marketing Science*, *41*(2013), 19–39.

35 Leonidas A. Zampetakis, "Sales Force Management Practices in Organizations with a Supportive Climate towards Creativity," *Journal of Strategic Marketing* 22 (1), 2014, 59–72.

36 Kirby L. J. Shannahan, Alan J. Bush, and Rachelle J. Shannahan, "Are Your Salespeople Coachable? How Salesperson Coachability, Trait Competitiveness, and Transformational Leadership Enhance Sales Performance," *Journal of the Academy of Marketing Science* 41 (2013): 40–54.

37 Christophe Fournier, William A. Weeks, Christopher P. Blocker, and Lawrence B. Chonko, "Polychronicity and Scheduling's Role in Reducing Role Stress and Enhancing Sales Performance," *Journal of Personal Selling & Sales Management* 33, 2 (Spring 2013): 197–210.

38 Milton Moskowitz, "The best employees in the U.S. say their greatest tool is culture," *Fortune*, March 5, 2015, http://fortune.com/2015/03/05/best-companies-greatest-tool-is-culture/ (accessed February 12, 2016).

39 Jeffrey P. Boichuk, Willy Bolander, Zachary R. Hall, Michael Ahearne, William J. Zahn, and Melissa Nieves, "Learned Helplessness Among Newly Hired Salespeople and the Influence of Leadership," *Journal of Marketing* 78 (January 2014), 95–111.

40 Jason Jordan and Robert Kelly, "Companies with a Formal Sales Process Generate More Revenue," *Harvard Business Review*, January 21, 2015, https://hbr.org/2015/01/companies-with-a-formal-sales-process-generate-more-revenue (accessed January 22, 2015).

41 Tara Burnthorne Lopez, Christopher D. Hopkins, and Mary Anne Raymond, "Reward Preferences of Sales-people: How Do Commissions Rate?" *Journal of Personal Selling & Sales Management* 26 (Fall 2006): 381–390.

42 Jolie Lee, "Container Store pays workers on average $50,000," *USA Today*, October 17, 2014, http://www.usatoday.com/story/money/business/2014/10/17/container-store-salaries-retail/17426865/# (accessed February 12, 2016).

43 Denny Bristow, Douglas Amyx, Stephen B. Castleberry, and James J. Cochran,

"A Cross-Generational Comparison of Motivational Factors in a Sales Career among Gen-X and Gen-Y College Students," *Journal of Personal Selling & Sales Management* 31, 1 (Winter 2011): 35–54.

44 Subhra Chakrabarty, Gene Brown, and Robert E. Widing, "Distinguishing between the Roles of Customer-Oriented Selling and Adaptive Selling in Managing Dysfunctional Conflict in Buyer–Seller Relationships," *Journal of Personal Selling & Sales Management* 33, 3 (Summer 2013): 245–260.

45 Michael Ahearne, Till Haumann, Forian Kraus, and Jan Wieseke, "It's a Matter of Congruence: How Interpersonal Identification between Sales Managers and Salespersons Shapes Sales Success," *Journal of the Academy of Marketing Science* 41 (2013): 625–648.

46 Felicia G. Lassk and C. David Shephard, "Exploring the Relationship between Emotional Intelligence and Salesperson Creativity," *Journal of Personal Selling & Sales Management* 33, 1 (Winter 2013): 25–38.

47 John W. Barnes, Donald W. Jackson, Jr., Michael D. Hutt, and Ajith Kumar, "The Role of Culture Strength in Shaping Salesforce Outcomes," *Journal of Personal Selling & Sales Management* 26 (Summer 2006): 255–270.

48 James B. DeConinck, "The Effects of Leader–Member Exchange and Organizational Identification on Performance and Turnover among Salespeople," *Journal of Personal Selling & Sales Management* 31, no. 1 (Winter 2011): 21–34.

49 Patricia Odell, "Motivating the Masses," *Promo*, September 1, 2005, http://promomagazine.com/research/pitrends/marketing_motivating_masses (accessed April 20, 2011).

50 Anne Hamilton, "Incentive Travel That Pays," *Direct Selling News*, *10*(8), August 2014, 60–61.

51 G. Alexander Hamwi, Brian N. Rutherford, Hiram C. Barksdale, Jr., and Julie T. Johnson, "Ideal Versus Actual Number of Sales Calls: An Application of Disconfirmation Theory," *Journal of Personal Selling & Sales Management*, 33(3), Summer 2013, 307–318.

52 Alix Stuart, "Is Your Sales Team on Track?" *Inc.*, December 2014/January 2015, 76–77.

53 George E. Belch and Michael A. Belch, *Advertising and Promotion* (Burr Ridge, IL: Irwin/McGraw-Hill, 2004), pp. 514–522.

[54] Esmeralda Crespo-Almendros and Salvador Del Barrio-Garcia, "The Quality of Internet-User Recall: A Comparative Analysis by Online Sales-Promotion Types," *Journal of Advertising Research* 54 (1), March 2014, 46–60.

[55] Brad Tuttle, "Why Americans Are Cutting Coupons out of Their Lives," *Time*, February 28, 2013, http://business.time.com/2013/02/28/why-americans-are-cutting-coupons-out-of-their-lives (accessed February 11, 2016).

[56] Sarah Halzack, "The trouble with those 20 pecent off coupons from Bed, Bath & Beyond," *Washington Post*, https://www.washingtonpost.com/news/business/wp/2015/09/30/the-trouble-with-those-20-percent-off-coupons-from-bed-bath-beyond/ (accessed February 12, 2016).

[57] Jiayue Huang, "Americans still prefer their paper coupons," *USA Today*, November 2, 2015, 5B.

[58] Arthur L. Porter, "Direct Mail's Lessons for Electronic Couponers," *Marketing Management Journal* (Spring/Summer 2000): 107–115.

[59] Ibid.

[60] Coupon Information Corporation, http://www.couponinformationcenter.com/ (accessed February 11, 2016).

[61] John T. Gourville and Dilip Soman, "The Consumer Psychology of Mail-in Rebates," *Journal of Product & Brand Management* 20, 2 (2011): 147–157.

[62] Don E. Schultz and Martin P. Block, "Sales promotion influencing consumer brand preferences/purchases," *Journal of Consumer Marketing* 31 (3), 212–217.

[63] Bruce Horovitz, "Whole Foods to test first rewards program," *USA Today*, September 19, 2014, 4B; Whole Foods, "Introducing Whole Foods Market Rewards," http://www.wholefoodsmarket.com/wfm-rewards (accessed February 12, 2016).

[64] Jeana Delano, "The Power of Product Samples," *Global Cosmetic Industry*, November 2014, 46–48.

[65] Katherine Hobson, "A Sales Promotion That Works for Shoes May Not for Chocolate," *The Wall Street Journal*, February 8, 2011, http://blogs.wsj.com/health/2011/02/08/a-sales-promotion-that-works-for-shoes-may-not-for-chocolate (accessed February 11, 2016).

[66] Teresa Montaner, Leslie de Chernatony, and Isabel Buil, "Consumer Response to Gift Promotions," *Journal of Product & Brand Management* 20, 2 (2011): 101–110.

[67] Bruce Horovitz, "Quicken Loans' March game plan pays off," *USA Today*, March 26, 2014, 1B.

[68] HGTV, "HGTV Dream Home Giveaway 2016," http://www.hgtv.com/design/hgtv-dream-home/sweepstakes (accessed February 12, 2016).

[69] Kenneth Jones, "Broadway's Major Producers Join With Regional Presenters for Audience Rewards Program," *Playbill*, June 28, 2007, http://www.playbill.com/news/article/109186-Broadways-Major-Producers-Join-With-Regional-Presenters-for-Audience-Rewards-Program (accessed December 11, 2013); Nederlander Organization–Announcements, "Audience Rewards Hits 1 Million Members," August 25, 2012, http://www.nederlander.com/press_03.html (accessed December 11, 2013); Audience Rewards, "Our History," https://www.audiencerewards.com/redeemcenter/infopage.cfm?id=25 (accessed December 11, 2013).

[70] Adapted from "Mistine: Direct Selling in the Thai Cosmetics Market," in O.C. Ferrell and Michael D. Hartline, *Marketing Strategy*, 6th ed. (Mason, OH: South-Western Cengage Learning, 2014); "Petchara Making an Appearance," *Wise Kwai's Thai Film Journal*, September 29, 2009, http://thaifilmjournal.blogspot.com/2009/09/petchara-making-appearance.html (accessed November 27, 2012).

[71] Drake Baer, "How Patagonia's New CEO Is Increasing Profits While Trying to Save the World," *Fast Company*, February 28, 2014, http://www.fastcompany.com/3026713/lessons-learned/how-patagonias-new-ceo-is-increasing-profits-while-trying-to-save-the-world (accessed July 22, 2015); Meredith Debry Berg, "Why Advertising Is 'Dead Last' Priority at Outerwear Marketer Patagonia," *Advertising Age*, December 17, 2013, http://adage.com/article/cmo-strategy/advertising-dead-priority-patagonia/245712/ (accessed July 22, 2015); eBay, "Join Us in the Common Threads Partnership," http://campaigns.ebay.com/patagonia/join/ (accessed July 22, 2015).

## Feature Notes

[a] Holly Beech, "Scentsy's profits continue to rise sharply," *Idaho Press-Tribune*, October 12, 2011, http://www.idahopress.com/blogs/business_to_business/scentsy-s-profits-continue-to-rise-sharply/article_d88c535e-f43f-11e0-9bf4-001cc4c002e0.html (February 11, 2016); Barbara Seale, "Selling the Sweet Scent of Success," *Direct Selling News*, April 2010, http://directsellingnews.com/index.php/view/scentsy_selling_the_scents_of_success#.Vr0XY1Ld0cM (accessed February 11, 2016); Scentsy website, http://scentsy.net/en-us/ (accessed February 11, 2016); "About Scentsy," https://scentsy.com/about-scentsy-fragrance/fast-facts (accessed February 11, 2016).

[b] Jed Williams and John Swanciger, "Why Small Businesses Should Be Utilizing Customer-Loyalty Programs," *Entrepreneur*, April 25, 2014, http://www.entrepreneur.com/article/233362 (accessed October 9, 2015); Joseph C. Nunes and Xavier Dréze, "Your Loyalty Program Is Betraying You," *Harvard Business Review*, April 2006, https://hbr.org/2006/04/your-loyalty-program-is-betraying-you (accessed October 9, 2015); Marcel Corstjens and Rajiv Lal, "Busting Six Myths About Customer Loyalty Programs," *Harvard Business Review*, February 24, 2014, http://hbswk.hbs.edu/item/busting-six-myths-about-customer-loyalty-programs (accessed October 9, 2015); Marie-Claude Nideau and Marc Singer, "The Secret to Creating Loyalty Programs that Actually Work," *Business Insider*, March 21, 2014, http://www.businessinsider.com/effective-loyalty-programs-2014-3 (accessed October 9, 2015).

# part 8
## Pricing Decisions

**19:**  Pricing Concepts

**20:**  Setting Prices

To provide a satisfying marketing mix, an organization must set a price that is acceptable to the target market.

**PART 8** examines pricing decisions that can have numerous effects on other parts of the marketing mix. For instance, price can influence how customers perceive the product, what types of marketing institutions are used to distribute the product, and how the product is promoted.

**CHAPTER 19** explores the importance of price and looks at some characteristics of price and nonprice competition. It examines fundamental concepts, such as demand, elasticity, marginal analysis, and break-even analysis. The chapter then examines the major factors that affect marketers' pricing decisions.

**CHAPTER 20** discusses six major stages that marketers use to establish prices.

# chapter 19    Pricing Concepts

# MARKETING INSIGHTS

## Smells like a Rat: The Gray Market for Luxury Perfumes

Imagine a 1.7-ounce bottle of luxury perfume that normally sells for $74. Then imagine you can find the same sized bottle at Walmart or Target for only $38.52. This is becoming the reality for the luxury perfume industry. Department stores, normally the major sellers of luxury perfumes such as Dolce & Gabbana's Light Blue fragrance, are losing sales to discounters and drugstores.

The problem is that luxury perfume makers do not sell their products to these retailers. Instead, retailers like Walmart, Target, and CVS are receiving shipments from unauthorized or unofficial resellers for a quick profit.

This type of selling is known as the gray market because these unauthorized resellers use legal means to sell the product. In the case of luxury perfumes, perfume makers often sell through wholesalers and distributors in Europe and Asia. These distributors can then turn around and sell to discount stores with price markdowns of up to 60 percent. Needless to say, discounters and drugstores are capturing an increasingly large share of the $5.9 billion fragrance industry in the United States.

Another problem luxury perfume makers face is showrooming. Showrooming occurs when consumers go into a store such as Bloomingdale's, test the perfume product, and then buy the perfume on Amazon for a fraction of the price. Showrooming is forcing department stores to be on the lookout constantly for competitors trying to undercut their prices. Several are adopting digital displays to quickly change their prices to compete against rivals. Although many consumers feel that purchasing gray market goods or showrooming is unfair, they would rather pay a lower price for premium products.[1]

Many firms, including luxury perfume makers, use pricing as a tool to make their products stand out from those of other firms. However, rival firms may likewise employ pricing as a major competitive tool, potentially leading to price wars. In other industries, firms can be very successful even if they don't have the lowest prices. The best price is not always the lowest price.

In this chapter, we focus first on the nature of price and its importance to marketers. We then consider some characteristics of price and nonprice competition. Next, we discuss several pricing-related concepts, such as demand, elasticity, and break-even analysis. Then we examine in some detail the numerous factors that can influence pricing decisions. Finally, we discuss selected issues related to pricing products for business markets.

## 19-1 THE IMPORTANCE OF PRICE IN MARKETING

**Price** is the value paid for a product in a marketing exchange. Remember that we defined value in Chapter 1 as a customer's subjective assessment of benefits relative to costs in determining the worth of a product. Many factors influence the assessment of value, including time constraints, price levels, perceived quality, and motivations to use available information about prices.[2] In most marketing situations, the price is apparent to both buyer and seller. However, price does not always take the form of money paid. In fact, **barter**, the trading of products, is the oldest form of exchange. Money may or may not be involved. Barter among businesses, because of the relatively large values of the exchanges, usually involves trade credit. Corporate barter amounts to an estimated $20 billion.[3]

Buyers' interest in price stems from their expectations about the usefulness of a product or the satisfaction they may derive from it. Because consumers have limited resources, they must allocate those resources to obtain the products they most desire. They must decide whether the utility gained in an exchange is worth the buying power sacrificed. Almost anything of value—ideas, services, rights, and goods—can be assessed by a price. In our society, financial price is the measurement of value commonly used in exchanges.

As pointed out in Chapter 11, developing a product may be a lengthy process. It takes time to plan promotion and to communicate benefits. Distribution usually requires a long-term commitment to dealers that will handle the product. Price is often the only thing a marketer can change quickly to respond to changes in demand, the actions of competitors, or the marketing environment. Under certain circumstances, however, the price variable may be relatively inflexible.

Price is a key element in the marketing mix because it relates directly to the generation of total revenue. The following equation is an important one for the entire organization:

$$\text{profit} = \text{total revenue} - \text{total costs}$$

$$\text{profit} = (\text{price} \times \text{quantity sold}) - \text{total costs}$$

Price affects an organization's profits in several ways because it is a key component of the profit equation and can be a major determinant of quantities sold. For instance, in recent years, airlines have reduced the price of first-class tickets in order to fill more seats and thereby boost revenue.[4] Furthermore, total costs are influenced by quantities sold. Consider Fossil watches that are priced under $300 versus Rolex watches that can cost tens of thousands of dollars. You would need to sell many more Fossil watches to reach your sales objectives than Rolex watches because of the dramatic difference in price.

Because price has a psychological influence on customers, marketers can use it symbolically. By pricing high, they can emphasize the quality of a product and try to increase the prestige associated with its ownership. By lowering a price, marketers can emphasize a bargain and attract customers who go out of their way to save a small amount of money. Thus, as this chapter details, price can have strong effects on a firm's sales and profitability.

**price** The value paid for a product in a marketing exchange

**barter** The trading of products

## MARKETING DEBATE

### Surge Pricing: Is Uber Expensive?

**ISSUE: Is Uber's surge pricing model fair?**

The laws of supply and demand dictate that prices increase when demand surges. The ride-sharing service company Uber Technologies uses surge-based pricing based on demand. When demand is slow, prices are lower. When demand is high, Uber increases the price to get more of its drivers on the road. The prices charged are therefore based on usage. Uber's pricing strategy is being adopted by organizations like Zappos to reward employees who work during peak times with higher pay. Even Disneyworld has adopted surge pricing for theme park seasonal demand.

However, should surge pricing be used in abnormal situations? During a hostage crisis in Sydney, Australia, as citizens struggled to evacuate, Uber fare prices rose four times their normal rate. The resulting outrage prompted Uber to refund passengers. It maintained that its algorithm automatically determined rates based on demand. However, criticisms of Uber's pricing strategy were far from over. During a Tube strike in England, Uber prices increased 2.9 times their normal rate. Is surge pricing an ethical and legitimate pricing strategy?[a]

## 19-2 PRICE AND NONPRICE COMPETITION

The competitive environment strongly influences the marketing-mix decisions associated with a product. Pricing decisions are often made according to the price or nonprice competitive situation in a particular market.

### 19-2a Price Competition

When choosing to engage in **price competition**, a marketer emphasizes price as an issue and matches or beats competitors' prices. To compete effectively on a price basis, a firm should be the low-cost seller of the product. If all firms producing the same product charge the same price for it, the firm with the lowest costs is the most profitable. Firms that stress low price as a key marketing-mix element tend to market standardized products. A seller competing on price may change prices frequently, or at least must be willing and able to do so. Best Buy, for instance, was

**price competition** Emphasizing price as an issue and matching or beating competitors' prices

**price war** Involves two or more companies engaging in intense price competition, often in an effort to boost market share

having trouble with *showrooming*, a practice where consumers come into their stores, find what they want to purchase, and then go online to purchase it at a lower price. To compete with lower prices from Amazon.com and other online competitors, Best Buy had to adopt a price-matching policy against certain online and local competitors.[5] In a competitive pricing environment, whenever one firm changes its prices, its rivals usually respond quickly and aggressively.

Price competition gives marketers flexibility. They can alter prices in response to changes in their costs or demand for the product. If competitors try to gain market share by cutting prices, a company competing on a price basis can react quickly to such efforts. A major drawback of price competition is that competitors have the flexibility to adjust prices too. If they quickly match or beat a company's price cuts, a price war may ensue. A **price war** involves two or more companies engaging in intense price competition, often in an effort to boost market

**Price Competition**
Best Buy adopted a price-matching policy so it could compete against competitors such as Amazon.com.

share. For instance, electronics retailers are facing a price war in electronics. As we have already mentioned, Best Buy's adoption of a price-matching policy has benefited the firm, but it has required the firm to slash prices drastically when needed to keep up with competitors. The biggest electronics retailers, including Best Buy, Walmart, and Target, all claim that they will match their competitors' prices and free shipping, which is inciting a massive price war. Chronic price wars often benefit consumers in the form of lower prices in the short run, but the constant price cutting is seldom sustainable, so they can substantially weaken organizations by slashing profit margins for everyone.

## 19-2b Nonprice Competition

**nonprice competition**
Emphasizing factors other than price to distinguish a product from competing brands

**Nonprice competition** occurs when a seller decides not to focus on price and instead emphasizes distinctive product features, service, product quality, promotion, packaging, or other factors to distinguish its product from competing brands. Thus, nonprice competition allows a company to increase its brand's unit sales through means other than changing the brand's price. Mars, for example, markets not only Snickers and M&M's but also has an upscale candy line called Ethel's Chocolate. With the tagline "eat chocolate, not preservatives," Ethel's Chocolate competes on the basis of taste, attractive appearance, and hip packaging, and, thus, has little need to engage in price competition.[6] A major advantage of nonprice competition is that a firm can build customer loyalty toward its brand.

Nonprice competition is effective only under certain conditions. A company must be able to distinguish its brand through unique product features, higher product quality, effective promotion, distinctive packaging, and/or excellent customer service. Fabergé commands a premium price due to its status as a luxury brand. Notice the advertisement showing a colorful gem-studded diamond ring. The price of the jewelry is never mentioned in the advertisement. Instead, Farbergé provides a close-up of the ring and its various colors to emphasize its beauty and value. Buyers must not only be able to perceive these distinguishing characteristics but must also deem them important. The distinguishing features that set a particular brand apart from competitors should be difficult, if not impossible, for competitors to imitate. Finally, the firm must extensively promote the brand's distinguishing characteristics to establish its superiority and set it apart from competitors in the minds of buyers.

Even a marketer that is competing on a nonprice basis cannot ignore competitors' prices. The organization must be aware of them and sometimes be prepared to price its brand near or slightly above competing brands. Therefore, price remains a crucial marketing-mix component even in environments that call for nonprice competition.

Source: FABERGÉ

FABERGÉ
THE ART OF COLOUR

**Nonprice Competition**
Fabergé does not mention price anywhere on this advertisement. Rather, it uses nonprice characteristics such as quality, color, and exclusivity to market its jewelry.

## 19-3 DEMAND CURVES AND PRICE ELASTICITY

Another significant factor in pricing decisions is demand. Marketers use marketing research and forecasting techniques to estimate sales potential and determine the relationship between a product's price and the quantity demanded.

### 19-3a The Demand Curve

For most products, the quantity buyers demand goes up as the price goes down, and the quantity demanded goes down as the price goes up. Case in point, prices have fallen precipitously for flat-screen television sets in recent years. This change in price is largely due to strong competition and newer technologies such as 3D and curved screens. In order to compensate, most makers of flat-screen TVs responded by continuing to lower prices. Thus, an inverse relationship exists between price and quantity demanded. As long as the marketing environment and buyers' needs, ability (purchasing power), willingness, and authority to buy remain stable, this fundamental inverse relationship holds.

Figure 19.1 illustrates the effect of price on the quantity demanded. The classic **demand curve** ($D1$) is a graph of the quantity of products a firm expects to sell at various prices if other factors remain constant. It illustrates that, as price falls, quantity demanded usually rises. Demand depends on other factors in the marketing mix, including product quality, promotion, and distribution. An improvement in any of these factors may cause a shift to demand curve $D2$. In such a case, an increased quantity ($Q2$) will be sold at the same price ($P$).

Many types of demand exist, and not all conform to the classic demand curve shown in Figure 19.1. Prestige products, such as selected perfumes and jewelry, tend to sell better at higher prices than at lower ones. This advertisement for Tod's Italian handbags provides

**demand curve** A graph of the quantity of products expected to be sold at various prices if other factors remain constant

Figure 19.1 **Demand Curve Illustrating the Price/Quantity Relationship and Increase in Demand**

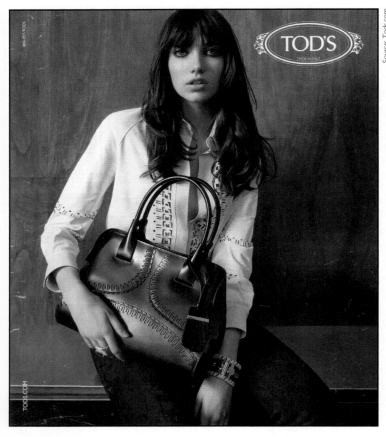

**Prestige Pricing**
Luxury products such as Tod's handbags sell better at higher prices than lower prices because they are considered to be a more exclusive product unavailable to the average consumer.

a close-up of the high-priced handbag to demonstrate its quality and craftsmanship. These products are desirable partly because their expense makes buyers feel elite. If the price fell drastically and many people owned these products, they would lose some of their appeal. The demand curve in Figure 19.2 shows the relationship between price and quantity demanded for prestige products. Quantity demanded is greater, not less, at higher prices. For a certain price range—from $P1$ to $P2$—the quantity demanded ($Q1$) goes up to $Q2$. After a certain point, however, raising the price backfires: If the price goes too high, the quantity demanded goes down. The figure shows that if price is raised from $P2$ to $P3$, quantity demanded goes back down from $Q2$ to $Q1$.

### 19-3b Demand Fluctuations

Changes in buyers' needs, variations in the effectiveness of other marketing-mix variables, the presence of substitutes, and dynamic environmental factors can influence demand. Restaurants and utility companies experience large fluctuations in demand daily. Toy manufacturers, fireworks suppliers, and air-conditioning and heating contractors also face demand fluctuations because of the seasonal nature of their products. However, changes in demand for other products may be less predictable, leading to problems for some companies. Other organizations anticipate demand fluctuations and develop new products and prices to meet consumers' changing needs.

### 19-3c Assessing Price Elasticity of Demand

We have seen how marketers identify the target market's evaluation of price and how they examine demand to learn whether price is related inversely or directly to quantity. The next step is to assess price elasticity of demand. **Price elasticity of demand** provides a measure of the sensitivity of demand to changes in price. It is formally defined as the percentage change in quantity demanded relative to a given percentage change in price (see Figure 19.3).[7] The percentage change in quantity demanded caused by a percentage change in price is much greater for products with elastic demand than for inelastic demand. For a product like electricity, demand is relatively inelastic: When its price increases from $P1$ to $P2$, quantity demanded goes down only a little, from $Q1$ to $Q2$. For products like recreational vehicles, demand is relatively elastic: When price rises sharply, from $P1$ to $P2$, quantity demanded goes down a great deal, from $Q1$ to $Q2$.

If marketers can determine a product's price elasticity of demand, setting a price is much easier. By analyzing total revenues as prices change, marketers can determine whether a product is price elastic. Total revenue is price times quantity. Thus, 10,000 cans of paint sold in one year at a price of $10 per can equals $100,000 of total revenue. If demand is *elastic*, a change in price causes an opposite change in total revenue: An increase in price will decrease total revenue, and a decrease in price will increase total revenue. *Inelastic* demand results in a change in the same direction as total revenue: An increase in price will increase total revenue, and a decrease in price will decrease total revenue. Demand for gasoline, for example, is relatively inelastic—even when prices are close to $4 per gallon—because people must still drive

**price elasticity of demand**
A measure of the sensitivity of demand to changes in price

Figure 19.2    **Demand Curve Illustrating the Relationship between Price and Quantity for Prestige Products**

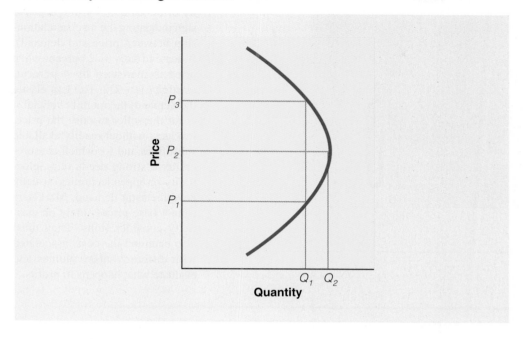

Figure 19.3    **Elasticity of Demand**

to work, run errands, and shop, all of which require fuel for their vehicles. Although higher gasoline prices force more consumers to change some behaviors in an effort to reduce the amount of gasoline they use, most cut spending in other areas instead because they require a certain level of fuel for weekly activities like commuting. The following formula determines the price elasticity of demand:

$$\text{price elasticity of demand} = \frac{\% \text{ change in quantity demanded}}{\% \text{ change in price}}$$

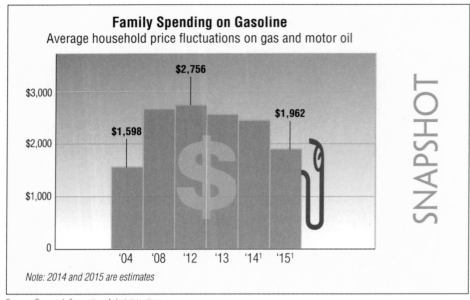

**Family Spending on Gasoline**

Average household price fluctuations on gas and motor oil

$2,756

$1,598

$1,962

$3,000

$2,000

$1,000

0

'04    '08    '12    '13    '14¹    '15¹

*Note: 2014 and 2015 are estimates*

SNAPSHOT

Source: Energy Information Administration

For instance, if demand falls by 8 percent when a seller raises the price by 2 percent, the price elasticity of demand is $-4$ (the negative sign indicating the inverse relationship between price and demand). If demand falls by 2 percent when price is increased by 4 percent, elasticity is $-1/2$. The less elastic the demand, the more beneficial it is for the seller to raise the price. Products without readily available substitutes and for which consumers have strong needs (e.g., electricity or appendectomies) usually have inelastic demand. Marketers cannot base prices solely on elasticity considerations. They must also examine the costs associated with different sales volumes and evaluate what happens to profits.

## 19-4 DEMAND, COST, AND PROFIT RELATIONSHIPS

Understanding the relationship between demand, cost, and profit is imperative. To stay in business, a company must set prices that not only cover its costs but also meet customers' expectations. Consumers are becoming less tolerant of price increases, forcing manufacturers to find new ways to control costs. In the past, many customers who desired premium brands were willing to pay extra for those products. Today, customers pass up certain brand names if they can pay less without sacrificing quality. In this section, we explore two approaches to understanding demand, cost, and profit relationships: marginal analysis and break-even analysis.

### 19-4a Marginal Analysis

**fixed costs** Costs that do not vary with changes in the number of units produced or sold

**average fixed cost** The fixed cost per unit produced

**variable costs** Costs that vary directly with changes in the number of units produced or sold

**average variable cost** The variable cost per unit produced

**total cost** The sum of average fixed and average variable costs times the quantity produced

**average total cost** The sum of the average fixed cost and the average variable cost

**marginal cost (MC)** The extra cost incurred by producing one more unit of a product

Marginal analysis examines what happens to a firm's costs and revenues when production (or sales volume) changes by a single unit. Both production costs and revenues must be evaluated. To determine the costs of production, it is necessary to distinguish among several types of costs. **Fixed costs** do not vary with changes in the number of units produced or sold. Consequently, a paint manufacturer's cost of renting a factory does not change because production increases from one to two shifts a day or because twice as much paint is sold. Rent may go up, but not because the factory has doubled production or revenue. **Average fixed cost** is the fixed cost per unit produced and is calculated by dividing fixed costs by the number of units produced.

**Variable costs** vary directly with changes in the number of units produced or sold. The wages for a second shift and the cost of twice as much paint are extra costs incurred when production is doubled. Variable costs are usually constant per unit; that is, twice as many workers and twice as much material produce twice as many cans of paint. **Average variable cost**, the variable cost per unit produced, is calculated by dividing the variable costs by the number of units produced.

**Total cost** is the sum of average fixed costs and average variable costs times the quantity produced. The **average total cost** is the sum of the average fixed cost and the average variable cost. **Marginal cost (MC)** is the extra cost a firm incurs when it produces one more unit of a product.

Table 19.1 illustrates various costs and their relationships. Notice that average fixed cost declines as output increases. Average variable cost follows a U shape, as does average total cost. Because average total cost continues to fall after average variable cost begins to rise, its lowest point is at a higher level of output than that of average variable cost. Average total cost is lowest at five units at a cost of $22.00, whereas average variable cost is lowest at three units at a cost of $10.67. As Figure 19.4 shows, marginal cost equals average total cost at the latter's lowest level. In Table 19.1, this occurs between five and six units of production. Average total cost decreases as long as marginal cost is less than average total cost and increases when marginal cost rises above average total cost.

### Table 19.1 **Costs and Their Relationships**

| 1 Quantity | 2 Fixed Cost | 3 Average Fixed Cost (2) ÷ (1) | 4 Average Variable Cost | 5 Average Total Cost (3) + (4) | 6 Total Cost (5) × (1) | 7 Marginal Cost |
|---|---|---|---|---|---|---|
| 1 | $40 | $40.00 | $20.00 | $60.00 | $60 | |
| | | | | | | $10 |
| 2 | 40 | 20.00 | 15.00 | 35.00 | 70 | |
| | | | | | | 2 |
| 3 | 40 | 13.33 | 10.67 | 24.00 | 72 | |
| | | | | | | 18 |
| 4 | 40 | 10.00 | 12.50 | 22.50 | 90 | |
| | | | | | | 20 |
| 5 | 40 | 8.00 | 14.00 | 22.00 | 110 | |
| | | | | | | 30 |
| 6 | 40 | 6.67 | 16.67 | 23.33 | 140 | |
| | | | | | | 40 |
| 7 | 40 | 5.71 | 20.00 | 25.71 | 180 | |

### Figure 19.4 **Typical Marginal Cost and Average Total Cost Relationship**

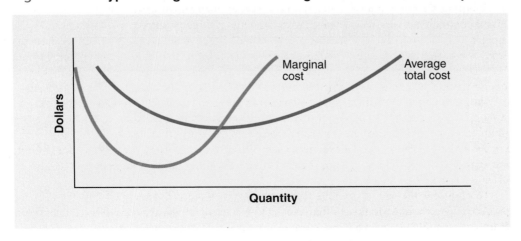

**Marginal revenue (MR)** is the change in total revenue that occurs when a firm sells an additional unit of a product. Figure 19.5 depicts marginal revenue and a demand curve. Most firms in the United States face downward-sloping demand curves for their products; in other words, they must lower their prices to sell additional units. This situation means that each additional unit of product sold provides the firm with less revenue than the previous unit sold. MR then becomes less-than-average revenue, as Figure 19.5 shows. Eventually, MR reaches zero, and the sale of additional units actually hurts the firm.

However, before the firm can determine whether a unit makes a profit, it must know its cost, as well as its revenue, because profit equals revenue minus cost. If MR is a unit's addition to revenue and MC is a unit's addition to cost, MR minus MC tells us whether the unit is profitable. Table 19.2 illustrates the relationships among price, quantity sold, total revenue, marginal revenue, marginal cost, and total cost. It indicates where maximum profits are possible at

**marginal revenue (MR)** The change in total revenue resulting from the sale of an additional unit of a product

**Figure 19.5    Typical Marginal Revenue and Average Revenue Relationship**

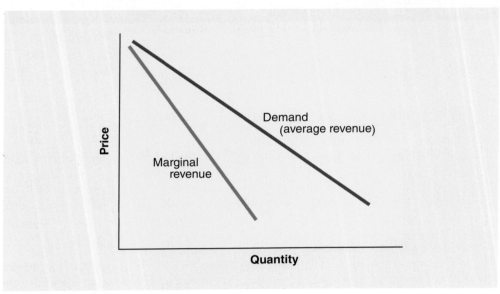

**Table 19.2    Marginal Analysis Method for Determining the Most Profitable Price***

| 1 Price | 2 Quantity Sold | 3 Total Revenue (1) × (2) | 4 Marginal Revenue | 5 Marginal Cost | 6 Total Cost | 7 Profit (3) − (6) |
|---|---|---|---|---|---|---|
| $57 | 1 | $57 | $57 | $60 | $60 | $−3 |
| 50 | 2 | 100 | 43 | 10 | 70 | 30 |
| 38 | 3 | 114 | 14 | 2 | 72 | 42 |
| **33*** | **4** | **132** | **18** | **18** | **90** | **42** |
| 30 | 5 | 150 | 18 | 20 | 110 | 40 |
| 27 | 6 | 162 | 12 | 30 | 140 | 22 |
| 25 | 7 | 175 | 13 | 40 | 180 | −5 |

*Boldface indicates the best price–profit combination.

Figure 19.6    **Combining the Marginal Cost and Marginal Revenue Concepts for Optimal Profit**

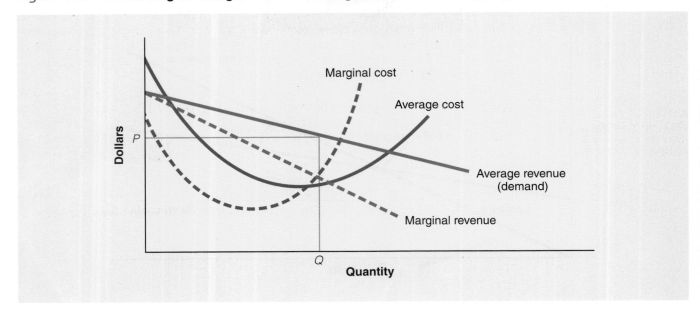

various combinations of price and cost. Notice that the total cost and the marginal cost figures in Table 19.2 are calculated and appear in Table 19.1.

Profit is the highest where MC = MR. In Table 19.2, note that at a quantity of four units, profit is the highest and MR − MC = 0. The best price is $33, and the profit is $42. Up to this point, the additional revenue generated from an extra unit sold exceeds the additional cost of producing it. Beyond this point, the additional cost of producing another unit exceeds the additional revenue generated, and profits decrease. If the price were based on minimum average total cost—$22 (Table 19.1)—it would result in a lower profit of $40 (Table 19.2) for five units priced at $30 versus a profit of $42 for four units priced at $33.

Graphically combining Figures 19.4 and 19.5 into Figure 19.6 shows that any unit for which MR exceeds MC adds to a firm's profits, and any unit for which MC exceeds MR subtracts from profits. The firm should produce at the point where MR equals MC, because this is the most profitable level of production.

This discussion of marginal analysis may give the false impression that pricing can be highly precise. If revenue (demand) and cost (supply) remained constant, prices could be set for maximum profits. In practice, however, cost and revenue change frequently. The competitive tactics of other firms or government action can quickly undermine a company's expectations of revenue, as can changing economic conditions. Thus, marginal analysis is only a model from which to work. Moreover, it offers little help in pricing new products before costs and revenues are established. On the other hand, in setting prices of existing products, especially in competitive situations, most marketers can benefit by understanding the relationship between marginal cost and marginal revenue.

## 19-4b **Break-Even Analysis**

The point at which the costs of producing a product equal the revenue made from selling the product is the **break even point**. If a paint manufacturer has total annual costs of $100,000 and sells $100,000 worth of paint in the same year, the company has broken even.

Figure 19.7 illustrates the relationships among costs, revenue, profits, and losses involved in determining the break even point. Knowing the number of units necessary to break even is important in setting the price. If a product priced at $100 per unit has an average variable cost

**break even point** The point at which the costs of producing a product equal the revenue made from selling the product

Figure 19.7    **Determining the Break Even Point**

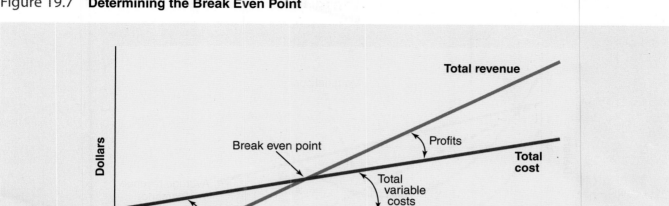

of $60 per unit, the contribution to fixed costs is $40. If total fixed costs are $120,000, the break even point in units is determined as follows:

$$\text{break even point} = \frac{\text{fixed costs}}{\text{per-unit contribution to fixed costs}}$$

$$= \frac{\text{fixed costs}}{\text{price-variable costs}}$$

$$= \frac{\$120,000}{\$40}$$

$$= 3,000 \text{ units}$$

To calculate the break even point in terms of dollar sales volume, the seller multiplies the break even point in units by the price per unit. In the preceding example, the break even point in terms of dollar sales volume is 3,000 (units) times $100, or $300,000.

To use break-even analysis effectively, a marketer should determine the break even point for each of several alternative prices. This determination allows the marketer to compare the effects on total revenue, total costs, and the break even point for each price under consideration. Although this comparative analysis may not tell the marketer exactly what price to charge, it will identify highly undesirable price alternatives that should definitely be avoided.

Break-even analysis is simple and straightforward. It does assume, however, that the quantity demanded is basically fixed (inelastic) and that the major task in setting prices is to recover costs. It focuses more on how to break even than on how to achieve a pricing objective, such as percentage of market share or return on investment. Nonetheless, marketing managers can use this concept to determine whether a product will achieve at least a break-even volume.

## 19-5 **FACTORS THAT AFFECT PRICING DECISIONS**

Pricing decisions can be complex due to the number of factors to consider. Frequently, there is considerable uncertainty about the reactions to price among buyers, channel members, and competitors. Price is also an important consideration in marketing planning, market analysis,

and sales forecasting. It is a major issue when assessing a brand's position relative to competing brands. Most factors that affect pricing decisions can be grouped into one of the eight categories shown in Figure 19.8. In this section, we explore how each of these groups of factors enters into price decision making.

## 19-5a Organizational and Marketing Objectives

Marketers should set prices that are consistent with the organization's goals and mission. For example, a retailer trying to position itself as being value-oriented may wish to set prices that are quite reasonable relative to product quality. In this case, a marketer would not want to set premium prices on products but would strive to price products in line with this overall organizational goal.

Pricing decisions should also be compatible with the firm's marketing objectives. For instance, suppose one of a producer's marketing objectives is a 12 percent increase in unit sales by the end of the following year. Assuming buyers are price sensitive, increasing the price or setting a price above the average market price would not be in line with this objective.

## 19-5b Types of Pricing Objectives

The types of pricing objectives a marketer uses obviously have considerable bearing on the determination of prices. For instance, an organization that uses pricing to increase its market share would likely set the brand's price below those of competing brands of similar quality to attract competitors' customers. Walmart's price objectives are illustrated by its slogan, "Save Money. Live Better." Walmart strives to help consumers save 25 percent or more on organic groceries. A marketer sometimes uses temporary price reductions in the hope of gaining market share. We examine pricing objectives in greater detail in the next chapter.

## 19-5c Costs

Clearly, costs must be an issue when establishing price. A firm may temporarily sell products below cost to match competition, generate cash flow, or even increase market share, but in the long run, it cannot survive by selling its products below cost. Even a firm that has a

Figure 19.8 **Factors That Affect Pricing Decisions**

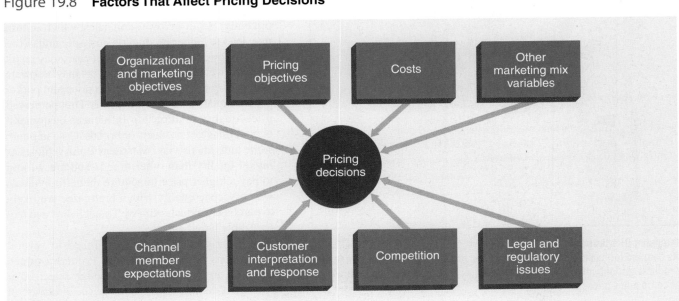

high-volume business cannot survive if each item is sold slightly below its cost. A marketer should be careful to analyze all costs so they can be included in the total cost associated with a product.

To maintain market share and revenue in an increasingly price-sensitive market, many marketers have concentrated on reducing costs. For example, after tumbling behind T-Mobile in market share, Sprint embarked upon a number of cost-cutting measures. These measures included letting go of thousands of employees.[8] Although many companies choose to cut costs by reducing their workforce, such a move should not be taken without careful consideration. Employees that do not lose their jobs are more likely to be dissatisfied, especially if they are required to take on more responsibilities without additional pay. Because employee satisfaction impacts customer satisfaction, lower morale among employees due to cost-cutting measures could negatively affect customers as well. Most of the highest performing companies do not compete solely on the lowest cost.[9]

Labor-saving technologies, a focus on quality, and efficient manufacturing processes have brought productivity gains that translate into reduced costs and lower prices for customers. Smart-building technologies related to the Internet of Things are helping companies save on energy costs. One Silicon Valley energy technology company claims this technology is saving its clients 60–70 percent on lighting and 20–30 percent on air conditioning.[10]

Source: Kashi Company

**Intensive Distribution**
As demand for healthy organic products has grown, Kashi is selling its food products through intensive distribution at grocery stores and supermarkets at competitive prices.

Besides considering the costs associated with a particular product, marketers must take into account the costs the product shares with others in the product line. Products often share some costs, particularly the costs of research and development, production, and distribution. Most marketers view a product's cost as a minimum, or floor, below which the product cannot be priced.

### 19-5d Marketing-Mix Variables

All marketing-mix variables are highly interrelated. Pricing decisions can influence evaluations and activities associated with product, distribution, and promotion variables. A product's price frequently affects the demand for that item, particularly for products with elastic demand. In such cases, a high price may result in lower unit sales, which in turn may lead to higher production costs per unit. Conversely, lower per-unit production costs may result from a lower price. As noted, buyers may associate better product quality with a high price and poorer product quality with a low price. This perceived price–quality relationship influences customers' overall image of products or brands. Case in point, some individuals view Mercedes Benz vehicles as higher quality than other brands and are willing to pay a higher price to acquire them. Individuals who associate quality with a high price are likely to purchase products with well-established and recognizable brand names.

The price of a product is linked to several dimensions of its distribution. Premium-priced products are often marketed through selective or exclusive distribution. Lower-priced products in the same product category may be sold through intensive distribution. Kashi, for instance, has a multitude of distribution outlets to get its products to the consumer. The advertisement shows a bowl of its organic sprouted grain cereal. Kashi positions its cereal as being both environmentally friendly and healthy. At a time when the obesity epidemic is at an all-time high, this advertisement appeals to the increasingly health-conscious consumer. Kashi products can be found at a number of different supermarkets and grocery stores.

An increase in physical distribution costs, such as shipping, may have to be passed on to customers. When fuel prices increase significantly, some distribution companies and airlines pass on these additional costs through surcharges or higher prices. When setting a price, the profit margins of marketing channel members, such as wholesalers and retailers, must also be considered. Channel members must be adequately compensated for the functions they perform.

Price may influence how a product is promoted. Bargain prices often appear in advertisements. Premium prices are less likely to be promoted, though they are sometimes included in advertisements for upscale items like luxury cars or fine jewelry. Higher-priced products are more likely than lower-priced ones to require personal selling. Furthermore, the price structure can affect a salesperson's relationship with customers. A complex pricing structure takes longer to explain to customers, is more likely to confuse potential buyers, and may cause misunderstandings that result in long-term customer dissatisfaction. Anyone who has tried to decipher his or her cell phone bill will empathize with the frustration that complex pricing structures can bring about. Trying to decipher charges for anytime, weekend, daytime, and roaming minutes, not to mention charges for smartphone data usage, can be confusing.

## 19-5e Channel Member Expectations

When making price decisions, a producer must consider what members of the distribution channel expect. A channel member certainly expects to receive a profit for the functions it performs. The amount of profit expected depends on what the intermediary could make if it were handling a competing product instead. Also, the amount of time and the resources required to carry the product influence intermediaries' expectations.

Channel members often expect producers to give discounts for large orders and prompt payment. For example, if POM Wonderful is selling directly to military bases, the government might expect the lowest possible price. At times, resellers expect producers to provide several support activities, such as sales training, service training, repair advisory service, cooperative advertising, sales promotions, and perhaps a program for returning unsold merchandise to the producer. These support activities clearly have associated costs that a producer must consider when determining prices.

## 19-5f Customers' Interpretation and Response

When making pricing decisions, marketers should address a vital question: How will our customers interpret our prices and respond to them? *Interpretation* in this context refers to what the price means or what it communicates to customers. Does the price signal "high quality" or "low quality," or "great deal," "fair price," or "rip-off"? Customer *response* refers to whether the price will move customers closer to purchase of the product and the degree to which the price enhances their satisfaction with the purchase experience and with the product after purchase.

Customers' interpretation of and response to a price are to some degree determined by their assessment of value, or what they receive compared with what they give up to make the purchase. In evaluating what they receive, customers consider product attributes, benefits, advantages, disadvantages, the probability of using the product, and possibly the status associated with the product. In assessing the cost of the product, customers will likely consider its price, the amount of time and effort required to obtain it, and perhaps the resources required to maintain it after purchase.

When interpreting and responding to prices, how do customers determine if the price is too high, too low, or about right? In general, they compare prices with internal or external reference prices. An **internal reference price** is a price developed in the buyer's mind through experience with the product. It reflects a belief that a product should cost approximately a certain amount. To arrive at an internal reference price, consumers may consider one or more values, including what they think the product "ought" to cost, the price usually charged for it, the last price they paid, the highest and lowest amounts they would be willing to pay, the price of the brand they usually buy, the average price of similar products, the expected future price, and the typical discounted price.[11] Researchers have found that less-confident consumers tend to have higher internal reference prices than consumers with greater confidence, and frequent buyers—perhaps because of their experience and confidence—are more likely to judge high prices unfairly.[12] As consumers, our experiences have given each of us internal reference prices for a number of products. For instance, most of us have a reasonable idea of how much to pay for a 12-pack of soft drinks, a loaf of bread, or a cup of coffee.

For the product categories with which we have less experience, we rely more heavily on external reference prices. An **external reference price** is a comparison price provided by others, such as retailers or manufacturers. Some grocery and electronics stores, for example, will show other stores' prices next to their price of a particular good if their price is lower than the competitor's price. This provides a reference point for consumers unfamiliar with the product category. Customers' perceptions of prices are also influenced by their expectations about future price increases, what they paid for the product recently, and what they would like to pay for the product. Other factors affecting customers' perceptions of whether the price is right include time or financial constraints, the costs associated with searching for lower-priced products, and expectations that products will go on sale.

Buyers' perceptions of a product relative to competing products may allow the firm to set a price that differs significantly from rivals' prices. If the product is deemed superior to most of the competition, a premium price may be feasible. However, even products with superior quality can be overpriced. Strong brand loyalty sometimes provides the opportunity to charge a premium price. On the other hand, if buyers view a product less than favorably (though not extremely negatively), a lower price may generate sales.

In the context of price, buyers can be characterized according to their degree of value consciousness, price consciousness, and prestige sensitivity. Marketers who understand these characteristics are better able to set pricing objectives and policies. **Value-conscious** consumers are concerned about both price and quality of a product.[13] During uncertain economic periods, customers become more value and price conscious and tend to limit discretionary spending. Increasingly, department stores are opening discount outlets as a way to capture these price-conscious consumers. For instance, department store Lord & Taylor announced it was opening a chain of off-price retail stores called Find @ Lord & Taylor.[14] These value-conscious consumers may perceive value as quality per unit of price or as not only economic savings but also the additional gains expected from one product over a competitor's brand. The first view is appropriate for

**internal reference price**
A price developed in the buyer's mind through experience with the product

**external reference price**
A comparison price provided by others

**value-conscious** Concerned about price and quality of a product

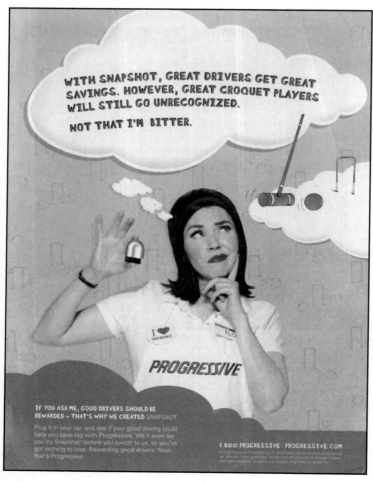

Source: Progressive Insurance

**Price-Conscious Consumers**
Progressive uses its spokesperson Flo to appeal to the price-conscious consumer who wants to be rewarded for being a good driver.

commodities like bottled water, bananas, and gasoline. If a value-conscious consumer perceives the quality of gasoline to be the same for Exxon and Shell, he or she will go to the station with the lower price. For consumers looking not just for economic value but additional gains they expect from one brand over another, a product differentiation value could be associated with benefits and features that are believed to be unique.[15] For instance, a BMW may be considered to be better than a Cadillac.

**Price-conscious** individuals strive to pay low prices. They want the lowest prices, even if the products are not of the highest quality. Amazon.com has long been known for a willingness to sacrifice profit margins in favor of offering the lowest prices. Price-conscious consumers might also shop at extreme-value stores such as Dollar General and 99¢ Only Stores. Commodity markets also tend to compete on price because consumers may not be able to tell the difference between competing products. Progressive, for instance, is constantly using its spokesperson Flo to emphasize the great deals and savings it offers its clients. The advertisement uses humor to describe the great rewards that good drivers can receive by going with Progressive. Because many consumers see insurance as a cost, insurance companies strive hard to offer strong coverage at affordable prices.

**Prestige-sensitive** buyers focus on purchasing products that signify prominence and status. For instance, Audi, known for its luxury cars, developed a limited edition Audi Sport Racing Bike in Japan for $19,650. The higher prices of prestige products convey a sense of exclusivity, creating demand among consumers who value the status associated with the product.[16]

Some consumers vary in their degree of value, price, and prestige consciousness. In some market segments, consumers "trade up" to higher-status products in categories such as automobiles, home appliances, restaurants, and even pet food, yet remain price conscious regarding cleaning and grocery products. This trend has benefited marketers like Starbucks, BMW, Whole Foods, and PETCO, which can charge premium prices for high-quality, prestige products.

## 19-5g Competition

A marketer needs to know competitors' prices so it can adjust its own prices accordingly. This does not mean a company will necessarily match competitors' prices; it may set its price above or below theirs. However, for some organizations, matching competitors'

**price-conscious** Striving to pay low prices

**prestige-sensitive** Drawn to products that signify prominence and status

# EMERGING **TRENDS IN MARKETING**

### Harley-Davidson 'Light': The Econo Model

Harley-Davidson has set its sights on appealing to the younger generation of bikers. Although baby boomers consist of much of Harley-Davidson's market, Harley recognizes it must also acquire younger customers. Doing this requires it to reinvent itself so that young people do not view it as a brand for their parents. However, as the average Harley costs over $30,000, traditional Harley products remain unaffordable for many in the younger generation.

Harley is addressing this problem by creating a stripped-down bike that carries the Harley experience and is affordable for younger people. Its Street bike is designed for smaller, younger riders with a price point of about $7,500. To keep costs low, the Street model does not have

a fuel gauge, tachometer, or clock but will have warning lights that will flash for low fuel or oil pressure. Despite their stripped-down appearance, sales of these smaller bikes have been increasing, while sales for customized Harleys have decreased. This lower-priced model is particularly suitable for more price-conscious consumers in Brazil, South Africa, and India.

Harley-Davidson is also working on an electric bicycle that will appeal to younger, eco-conscious consumers. However, development will still take years to complete, and electric vehicles are currently priced at a 10–20 percent premium, which might deter younger people from adopting them if the price is too high.[b]

prices is an important strategy for survival. Target, for instance, expanded its price-matching policy to 29 retailers including Walmart, Amazon.com, Toys 'R' Us, and Costco to try to convince consumers to shop in Target stores or on its website.[17] When adjusting prices, a marketer must assess how competitors will respond. Will competitors change their prices and, if so, will they raise or lower them? In Chapter 3, we described several types of competitive market structures. The structure that characterizes the industry to which a firm belongs affects the flexibility of price setting. Because of reduced pricing regulation, for instance, firms in the telecommunications industry have moved from a monopolistic market structure to an oligopolistic one, which has resulted in significant price competition for cell phone customers.

When an organization operates as a monopoly and is unregulated, it can set whatever prices the market will bear. However, the company may not price the product at the highest-possible level to avoid government regulation or penetrate a market by using a lower price. If the monopoly is regulated, it normally has less pricing flexibility; the regulatory body lets it set prices that generate a reasonable but not excessive return. A government-owned monopoly may price products below cost to make them accessible to people who otherwise could not afford them. Transit systems, for example, sometimes operate this way. However, government-owned monopolies sometimes charge higher prices to control demand. In some states with state-owned liquor stores, the price of liquor is higher than in states where liquor stores are not owned by a government body.

Source: Discover Financial Services, Inc.

**Oligopolistic Competition**
Capital One uses a 2 percent cash back guarantee on every purchase to convince businesses to adopt its Spark business credit card.

The automotive and airline industries exemplify oligopolies, in which only a few sellers operate and barriers to competitive entry are high. Companies in such industries can raise their prices in the hope that competitors will do the same. When an organization cuts its price to gain a competitive edge, other companies are likely to follow suit. This happens frequently in the credit card industry. Capital One uses price incentives to obtain business clients. Its advertisement informs businesses that using its Spark business credit card allows them to receive 2 percent back on every purchase. This is Capital One's way of attempting to differentiate itself from other major competitors in the industry. However, generally there is very little advantage gained through price cuts in an oligopolistic market structure because competitors will often follow suit.

A market structure characterized by monopolistic competition has numerous sellers with product offerings that are differentiated by physical characteristics, features, quality, and brand images. The distinguishing characteristics of its product may allow a company to set a different price from its competitors. However, firms in a monopolistic competitive market structure are likely to practice nonprice competition, discussed earlier in this chapter.

Under conditions of perfect competition, many sellers exist. Buyers view all sellers' products as the same. All firms sell their products at the going market price, and buyers will not pay more than that. This type of market structure, then, gives a marketer no flexibility in setting prices. Farming, as an industry, has some characteristics of perfect competition. Farmers sell their products at the going market price. At times, for example, corn, soybean, and wheat growers have had bumper crops and have been forced to sell them at depressed market prices. In countries in which farm subsidies are provided, the effects of perfect competition are reduced.

## 19-5h Legal and Regulatory Issues

Legal and regulatory issues also influence pricing decisions. To curb inflation, the federal government can invoke price controls, freeze prices at certain levels, or determine the rates at which firms may increase prices. In some states and many other countries, regulatory agencies set prices on such products as insurance, dairy products, and liquor. Many regulations and laws affect pricing decisions and activities in the United States. Many other nations and trade agreements have similar prohibitions.

The Sherman Antitrust Act prohibits conspiracies to control prices, and in interpreting the act, courts have ruled that price fixing among firms in an industry is illegal. **Price fixing** is an agreement among competing firms to raise, lower, or maintain prices for mutual benefit. To avoid the appearance of price fixing, marketers must develop independent pricing policies and set prices in ways that do not even hint at collusion. Thirty-three Japanese companies pleaded guilty to colluding together on the prices of anti-vibration rubber used in automobiles and ultimately paid a total of $2.4 billion in fines. As a result of their price-fixing conspiracy, U.S. buyers of 25 million vehicles likely overpaid, and trust between Japanese suppliers and U.S. automakers eroded.[18]

Both the Federal Trade Commission Act and the Wheeler-Lea Act prohibit deceptive pricing. **Deceptive pricing** is the use of false or misleading statements or practices to persuade buyers that a product is a better deal than it really is. Michael Kors Holdings recently paid $4.88 million to settle a lawsuit that claimed the marketer of designer accessories used misleading price tags at its outlet stores to deceive shoppers into believing they were getting a bargain on Michael Kors branded items. Although the company denied wrongdoing, it agreed to modify its sales practices to avoid using fabricated "manufacturer's suggested retail prices" to create an illusion of deep discounts on outlet merchandise.[19] In establishing prices, marketers must guard against deceiving customers.

Another law with a strong impact on pricing decisions is the Robinson-Patman Act. For various reasons, marketers may wish to sell the same type of product at different prices. Provisions in the Robinson-Patman Act, as well as those in the Clayton Act, limit the use of such price differentials. **Price discrimination**, the practice of employing price differentials that tend to injure competition by giving one or more buyers a competitive advantage over other buyers, is prohibited by law. Many people are surprised to learn that they may be charged a different price for the same product as somebody else. Companies selling online have used user information on geographic location, platform (PC versus Mac, desktop versus mobile), frequency of purchase, browser history, and/or other characteristics to determine which price to present to an online shopper. Although this practice is not illegal, many Internet shoppers have expressed dismay because they view the practice as unfair.[20] A marketer may use price differentials if they do not hinder competition, result from differences in the costs of selling or transportation to various customers, or arise because the firm has had to cut its price to a particular buyer to meet competitors' prices. Airlines, for example, may charge different customers different prices for the same flights based on the availability of seats at the time of purchase. As a result, flyers sitting in adjacent seats may have paid vastly different fares because one passenger booked weeks ahead, whereas the other booked on the spur of the moment a few days before when only a few seats were still available.

Another practice that can be illegal is predatory pricing. **Predatory pricing**, also called undercutting, involves the intent to set a product's price so low that rival firms cannot compete and therefore withdraw from the marketplace. Determining whether predatory pricing is occurring can be difficult in actual practice and thus actionable charges have been rare. It is not unusual for a company to set a price that is below cost temporarily in order to sell off unsalable products or excess capacity; without the intent to drive out competitors, there is no predatory pricing.

**price fixing** An agreement among competing firms to raise, lower, or maintain prices for mutual benefit

**deceptive pricing** The use of false or misleading statements or practices to persuade buyers that a product is a better deal than it really is

**price discrimination** Employing price differentials that injure competition by giving one or more buyers a competitive advantage

**predatory pricing** Also called undercutting, involves the intent to set a product's price so low that rival firms cannot compete and therefore withdraw from the marketplace

**Counterfeit Products**
Efforts to copy luxury goods result in declining profits for manufacturers and potentially higher prices for consumers of handbags who want authentic products.

A global problem affecting business pricing strategies is the growing market for counterfeit goods. These products are typically bought because of their significantly lower prices. Such low prices should signal that the products are fake and of lower quality, but some bargain shoppers actually seek them out. Counterfeit prescription drugs sold through websites are especially problematic as they seldom contain the promoted drug and may even contain dangerous ingredients. Counterfeit goods are regulated on a country-by-country basis. More sales that are lost to the "gray market" means lower profits and potentially higher prices for the legitimate goods.

## 19-6 PRICING FOR BUSINESS MARKETS

As we saw in Chapter 8, establishing prices for business buyers that purchase products for resale, use those products in their own operations, or produce other products sometimes differs from setting prices for consumers. Differences in the size of purchases, geographic factors, and transportation considerations require sellers to adjust prices. In this section, we discuss several issues unique to the pricing of business products, including discounts, geographic pricing, and transfer pricing.

### 19-6a Price Discounting

Producers commonly provide intermediaries with discounts, or reductions, from list prices. Although many types of discounts exist, they usually fall into one of five categories: trade, quantity, cash, seasonal, and allowance. Table 19.3 summarizes some reasons to use each type of discount and provides examples. Such discounts can be a significant factor in a marketing strategy.

Table 19.3 **Discounts Used for Business Markets**

| Type | Reasons for Use | Examples |
|------|-----------------|----------|
| Trade | To attract and keep effective resellers by compensating them for performing certain functions, such as transportation, warehousing, selling, and providing credit | A college bookstore pays about (functional) one-third less for a new textbook than the retail price a student pays. |
| Quantity | To encourage customers to buy large quantities when making purchases and, in the case of cumulative discounts, to encourage customer loyalty | Large department store chains purchase some women's apparel at lower prices than do individually owned specialty stores. |
| Cash | To reduce expenses associated with accounts receivable and collection by encouraging prompt payment of accounts | Numerous companies serving business markets allow a 2 percent discount if an account is paid within 10 days. |
| Seasonal | To allow a marketer to use resources more efficiently by stimulating sales during off-peak periods | Florida hotels provide companies holding national and regional sales meetings with deeply discounted accommodations during the summer months. |
| Allowance | In the case of a trade-in allowance, to assist the buyer in making the purchase and potentially earning a profit on the resale of used equipment; in the case of a promotional allowance, to ensure that dealers participate in advertising and sales support programs | A farm equipment dealer takes a farmer's used tractor as a trade-in on a new one. Nabisco pays a promotional allowance to a supermarket for setting up and maintaining a large, end-of-aisle display for a 2-week period. |

## Trade Discounts

A reduction off the list price given by a producer to an intermediary for performing certain functions is called a **trade (functional) discount**. A trade discount is usually stated in terms of a percentage or series of percentages off the list price. Intermediaries are given trade discounts as compensation for performing various functions, such as selling, transporting, storing, final processing, and perhaps providing credit services. Although certain trade discounts are often standard practice within an industry, discounts vary considerably among industries. It is important that a manufacturer provide a trade discount large enough to offset the intermediary's costs, plus a reasonable profit, to entice the reseller to carry the product.

## Quantity Discounts

Deductions from list price that reflect the economies of purchasing in large quantities are called **quantity discounts**. Quantity discounts are used in many industries and pass on to the buyer cost savings gained through economies of scale. Quantity discounts can be either cumulative or noncumulative. **Cumulative discounts** are quantity discounts aggregated over a stated time period. Purchases totaling $10,000 in a 3-month period, for example, might entitle the buyer to a 5 percent, or $500, rebate. Such discounts are intended to reflect economies in selling and encourage the buyer to purchase from one seller. **Noncumulative discounts** are one-time reductions in prices based on the number of units purchased, the dollar value of the order, or the product mix purchased. Like cumulative discounts, these discounts should reflect some economies in selling or trade functions.

## Cash Discounts

A **cash discount**, or price reduction, is given to a buyer for prompt payment or cash payment. Accounts receivable are an expense and a collection problem for many organizations. A policy to encourage prompt payment is a popular practice and sometimes a major concern in setting prices. Discounts are based on cash payments or cash paid within a stated time. For instance, "2/10 net 30" means that a 2 percent discount will be allowed if the account is paid within 10 days. If the buyer does not make payment within the 10-day period, the entire balance is due within 30 days without a discount. If the account is not paid within 30 days, interest may be charged.

## Seasonal Discounts

A price reduction to buyers who purchase goods or services out of season is a **seasonal discount**. These discounts let the seller maintain steadier production during the year. Thus, it is usually much cheaper to purchase and install an air-conditioning unit in the winter than it is in the summer. This is because demand for air conditioners is very low during the winter in most parts of the country, and price, therefore, is also lower than in peak-demand season.

## Allowances

Another type of reduction from the list price is an **allowance**, a concession in price to achieve a desired goal. Trade-in allowances, for example, are price reductions granted for turning in a used item when purchasing a new one. Allowances help make the buyer better able to make the new purchase. Another example is a promotional allowance, a price reduction granted to dealers for participating in advertising and sales support programs intended to increase sales of a particular item.

## 19-6b **Geographic Pricing**

**Geographic pricing** involves reductions for transportation costs or other costs associated with the physical distance between buyer and seller. Prices may be quoted as F.O.B. (free-on-board) factory or destination. An **F.O.B. factory** price indicates the price of the merchandise at the

**trade (functional) discount** A reduction off the list price a producer gives to an intermediary for performing certain functions

**quantity discounts** Deductions from the list price for purchasing in large quantities

**cumulative discounts** Quantity discounts aggregated over a stated time period

**noncumulative discounts** One-time price reductions based on the number of units purchased, the dollar value of the order, or the product mix purchased

**cash discount** A price reduction given to buyers for prompt payment or cash payment

**seasonal discount** A price reduction given to buyers for purchasing goods or services out of season

**allowance** A concession in price to achieve a desired goal

**geographic pricing** Reductions for transportation and other costs related to the physical distance between buyer and seller

**F.O.B. factory** The price of merchandise at the factory before shipment factory, before it is loaded onto the carrier, and thus excludes transportation costs. The buyer must pay for shipping. An **F.O.B. destination** price means the producer absorbs the costs of shipping the merchandise to the customer. This policy may be used to attract distant customers. Although F.O.B. pricing is an easy way to price products, it is sometimes difficult to administer, especially when a firm has a wide product mix or when customers are widely dispersed. Because customers will want to know about the most economical method of shipping, the seller must be informed about shipping rates.

To avoid the problems involved in charging different prices to each customer, **uniform geographic pricing**, sometimes called *postage-stamp pricing*, may be used. The same price is charged to all customers regardless of geographic location, and the price is based on average shipping costs for all customers. Paper products and office equipment are often priced on a uniform basis.

**Zone pricing** sets uniform prices for each of several major geographic zones; as the transportation costs across zones increase, so do the prices. For instance, a Florida manufacturer's prices may be higher for buyers on the Pacific coast and in Canada than for buyers in Georgia.

**Base-point pricing** is a geographic pricing policy that includes the price at the factory, plus freight charges from the base point nearest the buyer. This approach to pricing has virtually been abandoned because of its questionable legal status. The policy resulted in all buyers paying freight charges from one location, such as Detroit or Pittsburgh, regardless of where the product was manufactured.

When the seller absorbs all or part of the actual freight costs, it is using **freight absorption pricing**. The seller might choose this method because it wishes to do business with a particular customer or to get more business; more business will cause the average cost to fall and counterbalance the extra freight cost. This strategy is used to improve market penetration and retain a hold in an increasingly competitive market.

## 19-6c **Transfer Pricing**

**Transfer pricing** occurs when one unit in an organization sells a product to another unit. The price is determined by one of the following methods:

- *Actual full cost:* calculated by dividing all fixed and variable expenses for a period into the number of units produced.
- *Standard full cost:* calculated based on what it would cost to produce the goods at full plant capacity.
- *Cost plus investment:* calculated as full cost plus, the cost of a portion of the selling unit's assets used for internal needs.
- *Market-based cost:* calculated at the market price less a small discount to reflect the lack of sales effort and other expenses.

The choice of transfer pricing method depends on the company's management strategy and the nature of the units' interaction. An organization must also ensure that transfer pricing is fair to all units involved in the transactions.

**F.O.B. destination** A price indicating the producer is absorbing shipping costs

**uniform geographic pricing** Charging all customers the same price, regardless of geographic location

**zone pricing** Pricing based on transportation costs within major geographic zones

**base-point pricing** Geographic pricing that combines factory price and freight charges from the base point nearest the buyer

**freight absorption pricing** Absorption of all or part of actual freight costs by the seller

**transfer pricing** Prices charged in sales between an organization's units

# Summary

## 19-1 **Summarize why price is important to the marketing mix.**

Price is the value paid for a product in a marketing exchange. Barter, the trading of products, is the oldest form of exchange. Price is a key element in the marketing mix, because it relates directly to generation of total revenue. The profit factor can be determined mathematically by multiplying price by quantity sold to get total revenue and then subtracting total costs. Price is the only variable in the marketing mix that can be adjusted quickly and easily to respond to changes in the external environment.

## 19-2 Compare price competition with nonprice competition.

A product offering can compete on either a price or a nonprice basis. Price competition emphasizes price as the product differential. Prices fluctuate frequently, and price competition among sellers is aggressive. A price war involves two or more companies engaging in intense price competition. Nonprice competition emphasizes product differentiation through distinctive features, service, product quality, or other factors. Establishing brand loyalty by using nonprice competition works best when the product can be physically differentiated and the customer can recognize these differences.

## 19-3 Explain the importance of demand curves and the price elasticity of demand.

An organization must determine the demand for its product. The classic demand curve is a graph of the quantity of products expected to be sold at various prices if other factors hold constant. It illustrates that, as price falls, the quantity demanded usually increases. However, for prestige products, there is a direct positive relationship between price and quantity demanded: Demand increases as price increases. Next, price elasticity of demand, the percentage change in quantity demanded relative to a given percentage change in price, must be determined. If demand is elastic, a change in price causes an opposite change in total revenue. Inelastic demand results in a parallel change in total revenue when a product's price is changed.

## 19-4 Describe the relationships among demand, costs, and profits.

Analysis of demand, cost, and profit relationships can be accomplished through marginal analysis or break-even analysis. Marginal analysis examines what happens to a firm's costs and revenues when production (or sales volume) is changed by one unit. Marginal analysis combines the demand curve with the firm's costs to develop a price that yields maximum profit. Fixed costs do not vary with changes in the number of units produced or sold; average fixed cost is the fixed cost per unit produced. Variable costs vary directly with changes in the number of units produced or sold. Average variable cost is the variable cost per unit produced. Total cost is the sum of average fixed cost and average variable cost times the quantity produced. The optimal price is the point at which marginal cost (the cost associated with producing one more unit of the product) equals marginal revenue (the change in total revenue that occurs when one additional unit of the product is sold). Marginal analysis is only a model; it offers little help in pricing new products before costs and revenues are established.

Break-even analysis, determining the number of units that must be sold to break even, is important in setting price. The point at which the costs of production equal the revenue from selling the product is the break even point. To use break-even analysis effectively, a marketer should determine the break-even point for each of several alternative prices. This makes it possible to compare the effects on total revenue, total costs, and the break even point for each price under consideration. However, this approach assumes the quantity demanded is basically fixed and the major task is to set prices to recover costs.

## 19-5 Describe eight key factors that may influence marketers' pricing decisions.

Eight factors enter into price decision making: organizational and marketing objectives, pricing objectives, costs, other marketing mix variables, channel member expectations, customer interpretation and response, competition, and legal and regulatory issues. When setting prices, marketers should make decisions consistent with the organization's goals and mission. Pricing objectives heavily influence price-setting decisions. Most marketers view a product's cost as the floor below which a product cannot be priced. Because of the interrelationship among the marketing mix variables, price can affect product, promotion, and distribution decisions. The revenue channel members expect for their functions must also be considered when making price decisions.

Buyers' perceptions of price vary. Some consumer segments are sensitive to price, but others may not be. Thus, before determining price, a marketer needs to be aware of its importance to the target market. Knowledge of the prices charged for competing brands is essential to allow the firm to adjust its prices relative to competitors' prices. Government regulations and legislation also influence pricing decisions, especially with regard to practices such as price fixing, deceptive pricing, and predatory pricing.

## 19-6 Identify seven methods companies can use to price products for business markets.

The categories of discounts include trade, quantity, cash, seasonal, and allowance. A trade discount is a price reduction for performing such functions as storing, transporting, final processing, or providing credit services. If an intermediary purchases in large enough quantities, the producer gives a quantity discount, which can be either cumulative or noncumulative. A cash discount is a price reduction for prompt payment or payment in cash. Buyers who purchase goods or services out of season may be granted a seasonal discount. An allowance, such as a trade-in allowance, is a concession in price to achieve a desired goal.

Geographic pricing involves reductions for transportation costs or other costs associated with the physical distance between buyer and seller. With an F.O.B. factory price, the buyer pays for shipping from the factory. An F.O.B.

destination price means the producer pays for shipping; this is the easiest way to price products, but it is difficult to administer. When the seller charges a fixed average cost for transportation, it is using uniform geographic pricing. Zone prices are uniform within major geographic zones; they increase by zone as transportation costs increase. With base-point pricing, prices are adjusted for shipping expenses incurred by the

seller from the base point nearest the buyer. Freight absorption pricing occurs when a seller absorbs all or part of the freight costs.

Transfer pricing occurs when a unit in an organization sells products to another unit in the organization. Methods used for transfer pricing include actual full cost, standard full cost, cost plus investment, and market-based cost.

---

**Go to www.cengagebrain.com for resources to help you master the content in this chapter as well as for materials that will expand your marketing knowledge!**

---

# Important Terms

price  598
barter  598
price competition  599
price war  599
nonprice competition  600
demand curve  601
price elasticity of demand  602
fixed costs  604
average fixed cost  604
variable costs  604
average variable cost  604
total cost  604
average total cost  604
marginal cost (MC)  604

marginal revenue (MR)  606
break even point  607
internal reference price  612
external reference price  612
value-conscious  612
price-conscious  613
prestige-sensitive  613
price fixing  615
deceptive pricing  615
price discrimination  615
predatory pricing  615
trade (functional) discount  617
quantity discounts  617

cumulative discounts  617
noncumulative discounts  617
cash discount  617
seasonal discount  617
allowance  617
geographic pricing  617
F.O.B. factory  617
F.O.B. destination  618
uniform geographic pricing  618
zone pricing  618
base-point pricing  618
freight absorption pricing  618
transfer pricing  618

# Discussion and Review Questions

1. Why are pricing decisions important to an organization?
2. Compare and contrast price and nonprice competition. Describe the conditions under which each form works best.
3. Why do most demand curves demonstrate an inverse relationship between price and quantity?
4. List the characteristics of products that have inelastic demand, and give several examples of such products.
5. Explain why optimal profits should occur when marginal cost equals marginal revenue.
6. Chambers Company has just gathered estimates for conducting a break-even analysis for a new product. Variable costs are $7 a unit. The additional plant will cost $48,000. The new product will be charged $18,000 a year for its share of general overhead. Advertising

expenditures will be $80,000, and $55,000 will be spent on distribution. If the product sells for $12, what is the break even point in units? What is the break even point in dollar sales volume?

7. In what ways do other marketing-mix variables affect pricing decisions?
8. What types of expectations may channel members have about producers' prices? How might these expectations affect pricing decisions?
9. How do legal and regulatory forces influence pricing decisions?
10. Compare and contrast a trade discount and a quantity discount.
11. What is the reason for using the term *F.O.B.*?
12. What are the major methods used for transfer pricing?

# Video Case 19.1

## Louis Vuitton Bags the Value Shopper

For luxury-goods maker Louis Vuitton, price is a critical part of its marketing strategy. However, unlike most other companies, demand for Louis Vuitton products tends to rise with price increases. This is because its target market focuses on prestige-sensitive buyers—those who purchase products that signify prominence and status. These types of products carry an air of exclusivity because they demonstrate to others that the buyer has enough money to afford them. Louis Vuitton has targeted the elite since its founding in 1854 when it began selling luxury luggage to the rich. Today the company sells leather goods, handbags, trunks, watches, and other accessories.

It would be a mistake, however, to assume that Louis Vuitton products are completely inelastic. While demand for its products may increase as the price increases, this will occur only to a certain level. Afterwards, demand will begin decreasing. Luxury brands like Louis Vuitton also face a constant balancing act. While they can price their products top dollar to attract the elite, this market is relatively small. On the other hand, there are many prestige-conscious customers willing to pay higher prices for Louis Vuitton products but who cannot afford a $50,000 price tag. In order to reach these consumers, it must develop products that are priced lower but still carry enough prestige that consumers will desire their brand. Darla Thomas, a researcher into luxury brands, describes this pricing strategy as "a delicate balance of selling masses to the masses while still remaining exclusive to the rich."

To retain this exclusive image, Louis Vuitton works hard to make its brand seem expensive and somewhat unattainable. Price is a critical factor, and Louis Vuitton often raises prices to try and jumpstart sales by emphasizing its exclusive, top-quality image. For instance, Louis Vuitton raised its prices 13 percent during a time when sales were flatlining to increase demand for its leather and canvas monogrammed bags. It also engages in nonprice competition through promotion, especially when it comes to celebrities endorsing the product. Famous endorsers have included actress Angelina Jolie and athlete Michael Phelps.

Darla Thomas describes Louis Vuitton's product and pricing strategies as similar to a pyramid. "At the top you have the very beautifully made exclusive limited amount of product. They will make anything you want. From there you have the middle range that you can walk into a store and you can buy it . . . And then you have the bottom range where the money comes in."

For many years, developing countries such as China were top markets for luxury brands. As the middle classes increased, so did the desire to demonstrate the ability that they could afford nice products. Darla Thomas uses an example of a Chinese secretary "who wants to put the bag on her desk to show that she can afford a Louis Vuitton bag" as an example of this emerging middle class. These pricing strategies have worked well for Louis Vuitton. With a value of $28.1 billion, Louis Vuitton is one of the most profitable luxury brands with profit margins of 40 percent.

On the other hand, this means that luxury brand makers like Louis Vuitton are highly dependent upon a thriving economy. As economies slow in China, Russia, and Brazil, demand for luxury goods falls. In harder economic times consumers become more value-conscious, desiring quality products at more affordable prices. In recent years, a weaker euro has encouraged consumers from China to come to France and purchase Louis Vuitton products, keeping sales stable. However, desire for Louis Vuitton could be diminishing, prompting the brand to reassess its marketing strategy.

Part of the problem could be that Louis Vuitton has overexpanded. While it only had two stores in 1977, today it has 400. This not only creates costs for Louis Vuitton, but it could also cheapen its image as an exclusive brand. Competition is also intense, with major competitors including Kering, Gucci, and Hermes. Whatever the cause, pricing remains a key component in developing demand. Louis Vuitton is therefore constantly monitoring, reevaluating, and updating its pricing policies to compete with competitors and increase global demand.[21]

### Questions for Discussion

1. Are Louis Vuitton products elastic or inelastic? Why?
2. What type of factors do you think most affect Louis Vuitton's pricing decisions?
3. Generally, what should happen when Louis Vuitton raises its prices? Why is there a limit to how high it can increase its pricing?

# Case 19.2

## CVS: Continuous Value Strategy

In the United States, the industry is dominated by two large firms, Walgreens and CVS. CVS, the second largest pharmacy chain, is constantly competing against Walgreens for market share, especially in its quest to become more of a health-care management company.

One way in which CVS attracts customers is through its pricing strategies. CVS employs price discounts through several methods, including in-store discounts. Retail stores often display discounted prices through the use of shelf signs on individual products. In addition, CVS mails coupons and store-wide purchase discounts to customers and offers a number of online discounts through CVS.com. When customers link their CVS ExtraCare® cards to the company's myWeekly Ad website, they receive weekly sales updates. The Extra-Care® card also gives customers access to personalized coupons in-store and through mobile apps.

CVS provides other consumer sales promotions as well. For instance, customers can save money and get free shipping if they order their prescriptions through the mail with its CVS Caremark Mail Service Pharmacy. Its iSave program also helps consumers save on costs. In this program, CVS has partnered with 270,000 providers in different areas of health-care. Customers who make appointments with these providers and identify themselves as iSave members can save money on these services. CVS's website also offers information on rebates for selected products. Additionally, CVS shows its commitment toward veterans with its Veterans Advantage program. Under this program, veterans can receive 20 percent discounts on products and free shipping on online orders.

CVS's MinuteClinics are also important to consumers because they provide basic care at less cost than going to the doctor. Many people visit MinuteClinics when they are sick or wish to get basic services such as flu shots. The clinics are staffed with certified nurse practitioners and physician assistants qualified in medicine. One major criticism against CVS's MinuteClinics is that customers might choose to go to the clinics when they have extreme illnesses rather than the hospital or doctor's office. However, the CVS Minute-Clinic website contains information that describes their limitations and when consumers should visit their doctors. CVS's MinuteClinics accept most types of insurance and has had more than 18 million patient visits.

CVS assists patients in another important—albeit behind-the-scenes—way. The company has been a tough negotiator when negotiating drug prices with pharmaceutical companies. CVS negotiates drug prices for approximately 65 million people across the nation. Sometimes this has required CVS to take a tough stance and be willing to drop drugs from its insurance unless the drug makers lower the prices. For example, CVS dropped 26 drugs, including Viagra, from its prescription drug insurance in favor of comparable drugs with lower costs. An analysis has revealed that the attempts of drug makers to raise prices have been mitigated by the strong negotiation tactics of companies like CVS and Express Scripts. During a time when some drug makers are raising the prices of medications 50-fold, the use of negotiation is crucial toward keeping prices affordable for consumers.

In 2015 CVS announced it was acquiring Target's in-store pharmacy and clinic. This has raised some concerns that prices could increase for Target pharmacy customers. Whenever two large companies merge, there is less competition in the marketplace. Firms with more control could therefore raise prices. Some believe that the prices will increase for Target pharmacy customers because Target—as a discount store—has traditionally been more focused on keeping prices low than CVS has. However, others believe the merger might result in savings for the customer. One health industry economic analyst suggests that the merger of the two big firms will improve relationships with wholesalers and suppliers of drugs, which could result in cost savings that CVS could then pass on to the customer.

It is clear that pharmacies such as CVS are important in negotiating prices of prescription drugs. The discounts and programs they offer are also important in helping consumers to afford their medications. The cost savings CVS has to offer has made it a popular pharmacy destination for American consumers.[22]

### Questions for Discussion

1. Why is price competition such an issue for CVS as it fights to gain market share?
2. Describe ways CVS uses sales promotion techniques to provide price discounts.
3. Why is it important for CVS to negotiate with pharmaceutical companies on the prices of drugs?

# NOTES

[1] Spencer Soper and Lindsey Rupp, "Stores Try Fixed Prices That Aren't So Fixed," *Bloomberg Businessweek*, July 17, 2015, 22–23; Serena Ng, "Luxury-Perfume Makers Turn to WalMart, Target," *Wall Street Journal*, September 26–27, 2015, B1, B4; *BBC*, Alex Campbell, "The peril of 'showrooming'," *BBC*, April 21, 2013, http://www.bbc.com/news/magazine-22098575 (accessed October 12, 2015); Cameron Wolf, "Designers Can't Stop Walmart and Target From Selling Their Luxury Perfumes," *Racked*, September 28, 2015, http://www.racked.com/2015/9/28/9408993/designer-perfumes-box-stores (accessed October 12, 2015).

[2] Rajneesh Suri and Kent B. Monroe, "The Effects of Time Constraints on Consumers' Judgments of Prices and Products," *Journal of Consumer Research* 30, 1 (2003): 92–104.

[3] Georgann Yara, "Barter business keeps its clients happy," *The Arizona Republic*, December 3, 2015, http://www.azcentral.com/story/money/business/abg/2015/12/03/barter-business-value-card-alliance-keeps-customers-happy/75275198/ (accessed February 12, 2016).

[4] Scott McCartney, "First Class Fares Get Affordable," *The Wall Street Journal*, May 27, 2015, http://www.wsj.com/articles/first-class-fares-get-affordable-1432741041 (accessed February 12, 2016).

[5] Walter Loeb, "Amazon's Pricing Strategy Makes Life Miserable for the Competition," *Forbes*, November 20, 2014, http://www.forbes.com/sites/walterloeb/2014/11/20/amazons-pricing-strategy-makes-life-miserable-for-the-competition/ (accessed February 12, 2016).

[6] "About Ethel M.® Chocolates," www.ethelm.com/about_us/default.aspx (accessed February 12, 2016).

[7] *Dictionary of Marketing Terms*, American Marketing Association, www.marketingpower.com/_layouts/Dictionary.aspx (accessed October 23, 2015).

[8] Edward C. Baig and Eli Blumenthal, "Sprint to cut up to $2.5 billion in costs, layoff workers in next six months," *USA Today*, February 12, 2016, http://www.usatoday.com/story/tech/2015/10/02/sprint-cuts-costs-six-months/73211088/# (accessed February 12, 2016).

[9] Ian Altman, "The Good, the Bad, and the Ugly of Cost Cutting," *Forbes*, March 17, 2015, http://www.forbes.com/sites/ianaltman/2015/03/17/the-good-the-bad-and-the-ugly-of-cost-cutting/2/#756ca90a3b37 (accessed February 12, 2016).

[10] Alan Murray, "For companies, big energy savings are linked to the 'Internet of things'," *Fortune*, September 29, 2015, http://fortune.com/2015/09/29/energy-internet-things/ (accessed February 12, 2016).

[11] Russell S. Winer, *Pricing* (Cambridge, MA: Marketing Science Institute, 2005), p. 20.

[12] Manoj Thomas and Geeta Menon, "When Internal Reference Prices and Price Expectations Diverge: The Role of Confidence," *Journal of Marketing Research* 44, 3 (August 2007): 401–409.

[13] Donald R. Lichtenstein, Nancy M. Ridgway, and Richard G. Netemeyer, "Price Perceptions and Consumer Shopping Behavior: A Field Study," *Journal of Marketing Research*, 30, 2 (1993): 234–245.

[14] Suzanne Kapner, "More Chains Go Off-Price," *The Wall Street Journal*, October 26, 2015, B3.

[15] Gerald E. Smith and Thomas T. Nagle, "A Question of Value," *Marketing Management* 14, 4 (2005): 39–40.

[16] Jun Hongo, "Audi Unveils Ultralight Bicycle with a Car's Price Tag," May 13, 2015, http://blogs.wsj.com/japanrealtime/2015/05/13/audi-unveils-ultralight-bicycle-with-a-cars-price-tag-in-japan/ (accessed February 12, 2016).

[17] Hadley Malcolm, "Target Will now Price Match with 29 Competitors, Including Online Purchases," *USA Today*, September 30, 2015, http://www.usatoday.com/story/money/2015/09/30/target-expands-price-matching-policy-to-29-retailers/73084542/ (accessed February 12, 2016).

[18] Dan Gearino, "Massive Price-Fixing among Auto Parts Manufacturers Hurt U.S. Car Buyers," *The Columbus Dispatch*, March 22, 2015, http://www.dispatch.com/content/stories/business/2015/03/22/a-culture-of-collusion.html (accessed February 12, 2016).

[19] Jonathan Stempel, "Michael Kors Settles US Lawsuit Alleging Deceptive Price Tags," *Business Insider*, June 13, 2015, http://www.businessinsider.com/r-michael-kors-settles-us-lawsuit-alleging-deceptive-price-tags-2015-6 (accessed February 12, 2016).

[20] Christo Wilson, "If You Use a Mac or an Android, E-commerce Sites May Be Charging You More," *The Washington Post*, November 3, 2014, https://www.washingtonpost.com/posteverything/wp/2014/11/03/if-you-use-a-mac-or-an-android-e-commerce-sites-may-be-charging-you-more/ (accessed February 12, 2016).

[21] Jason Chow, "Weak Euro Masks Lingering Woes at LVMH, Kering," *The Wall Street Journal*, July 26, 2015, http://www.wsj.com/articles/low-euro-masks-lingering-woes-at-lvmh-kering-1437942805 (accessed February 15, 2016); "#14 Louis Vuitton," *Forbes*, May 2015, http://www.forbes.com/companies/louis-vuitton/ (accessed February 15, 2016); Christina Passariello, "Louis Vuitton Sports a Richer Price Tag," *The Wall Street Journal*, April 16, 2013, http://www.wsj.com/article_email/SB10001424127887324345804578426902194074008-lMyQjAxMTAzMDEwNzExNDcyWj.html?mod=wsj_valettop_email (accessed February 15, 2016); Lauren Milligan, "Would You Pay 70 Per Cent More for Chanel?" *Vogue*, March 5, 2014, http://www.vogue.co.uk/news/2014/03/05/price-increases-for-luxury-items---chanel-louis-vuitton-bags (accessed February 15, 2016).

[22] Martin Moylan, "As Target pharmacies shift to CVS, will consumers stick around?" *MPR News*, July 29, 2015, http://www.mprnews.org/story/2015/07/29/target-cvs-pharmacy-switch (accessed February 4, 2016); Andrew Pollack, "Drug Goes from $13.50 a Tablet to $750, Overnight," *The New York Times*, September 20, 2015, http://www.nytimes.com/2015/09/21/business/a-huge-overnight-increase-in-a-drugs-price-raises-protests.html?_r=0 (accessed December 4, 2015); CVS Caremark, "Mail Order Direct," https://www2.caremark.com/nlc/mod.htm (accessed February 4, 2016); CVS, "CVS iSave," https://www.cvsisave.com/ (accessed February 4, 2016); Robert Langreth, "Big Pharma's Foe Takes Victory Lap as Drug Prices Increase," *Bloomberg*, September 10, 2015, http://www.bloomberg.com/news/articles/2015-09-10/

big-pharma-s-foe-takes-victory-lap-as-drug-price-increases-slow (accessed February 4, 2016); Randsell Pierson, "CVS urges cost controls for new cholesterol drugs," *Reuters*, February 17, 2015, http://www.reuters.com/article/us-cvs-health-cholesterol-idUSK-BN0LL1CQ20150217 (accessed February 4, 2016); CVS Pharmacy, "Deals," http://www.cvs.com/deals/deals.jsp (accessed February 9, 2016); Robert Langreth, "Good drug deals: CVS, Express Scripts drive hard bargains with manufacturers," *Providence Journal*, September 11, 2015, http://www.providencejournal.com/article/20150911/NEWS/150919716 (accessed February 4, 2016); Trisha Thadani, "CVS drops Viagra, other drugs, from insurance coverage," *USA Today*, August 6, 2015, http://www.usatoday.com/story/news/health/2015/08/06/cvs-drops-viagra/31227269/ (accessed February 4, 2016); CVS, "About Us," MinuteClinic, https://www.cvs.com/minuteclinic/visit/about-us (accessed February 9, 2016); CVS, "Services," MinuteClinic, https://www.cvs.com/minute-clinic/services (accessed February 9, 2016).

## Feature Notes

[a] Claire Zillman, "Zappos is bringing Uber-like surge pay to the workplace," *Fortune*, January 28, 2015, http://fortune.com/2015/01/28/zappos-employee-pay/ (accessed July 13, 2015); Victoria Ward, "Minicab firm Uber doubles prices during Tube strike," *The Telegraph*, July 9, 2015, http://www.telegraph.co.uk/news/uknews/11728226/Minicab-firm-Uber-doubles-prices-during-Tube-strike.html (accessed July 13, 2015); Ed Mazza, "Uber Raises Fares During Sydney Hostage Crisis, Then Offers Free Rides," *The Huffington Post*, December 15, 2014, http://www.huffingtonpost.com/2014/12/15/uber-sydney-surge-pricing_n_6325026.html (accessed July 13, 2015); J. Walker Smith, "The Uber-All Economy," *Marketing News*, June 2015, p. 26.

[b] James R. Hagerty, "Can Harley Spark a Movement?" *The Wall Street Journal*, June 20-21, 2015, B1; Bill Saporito, "This Harley Is Electric." *Time*, June 2014, 48–52; Charles Fleming, "First Times Ride: 2015 Harley-Davidson Street 750," *Los Angeles Times*, July 4, 2014, http://www.latimes.com/business/autos/la-fi-hy-first-times-ride-2015-harley-davidson-street-750-20140616-story.html (accessed July 14, 2015); Kyle Stock, "Is Harley-Davidson Losing Its Diehards?" *Bloomberg*, April 21, 2015, http://www.bloomberg.com/news/articles/2015-04-21/is-harley-davidson-losing-its-diehards- (accessed July 14, 2015).

# chapter 20 Setting Prices

## OBJECTIVES

**20-1** Identify issues related to developing pricing objectives.

**20-2** Discuss the importance of identifying the target market's evaluation of price.

**20-3** Explain how marketers analyze competitors' prices.

**20-4** Describe the bases used for setting prices.

**20-5** Explain the different types of pricing strategies.

**20-6** Describe the selection of a specific price.

# MARKETING INSIGHTS

## Primark Profits from Low Prices and Fast Fashion

Robert Hoetink/Shutterstock.com

Primania has broken out in Boston and is coming to more U.S. cities as Dublin–based retailer Primark transplants its winning combination of fast fashion and affordable prices across the Atlantic Ocean. Owned by Associated British Foods, Primark rings up nearly $8 billion in global sales of clothing and home goods through 300 stores in Ireland, England, Europe, and now North America. The company already sells more clothing than any other merchant in Great Britain, thanks to its legendarily low prices, and it sees the lucrative U.S. market as ripe for profitable expansion.

"We want to be known first and foremost for amazing prices," says the finance director of Primark's parent company. Even by the standards of value-oriented retail competitors such as H&M and Forever 21, Primark's round-number prices are unusually low. The average price of its clothing is about $6—so rock-bottom that the retailer doesn't sell online because of the shipping costs. Primark keeps a tight rein on costs by buying from suppliers in huge quantities, relentlessly streamlining logistics, and constantly deleting the slow sellers while increasing stock of the best sellers. Although its profit margins are slim, it profits from high sales volume and fast inventory turnover.

Primark also saves money by relying more on social media word-of-mouth than expensive advertising to build brand awareness and store traffic. That's where Primania comes in. The retailer encourages customers to upload selfies of themselves wearing their latest Primark purchases, tagged with #Primania, to its website and its Instagram account. Each store showcases Primania posts on LED screens for shoppers to see as they browse, adding to the in-store excitement of finding the latest fashions at remarkably low prices.[1]

Because price has such a profound impact on a firm's bottom line, finding the right pricing strategy is crucial. Marketers must carefully select a pricing strategy that is both profitable for the company and reasonable to the customers. Selecting a pricing strategy is one of the fundamental components of the process of setting prices.

In this chapter, we examine six stages of a process that marketers can use when setting prices. Figure 20.1 illustrates these stages. Stage 1 is the development of a pricing objective that is compatible with the organization's overall marketing objectives. Stage 2 entails assessing the target market's evaluation of price. Stage 3 involves evaluating competitors' prices, which helps determine the role of price in the marketing strategy. Stage 4 requires choosing a basis for setting prices. Stage 5 is the selection of a pricing strategy, or the guidelines for using price in the marketing mix. Stage 6, determining the final price, depends on environmental forces and marketers' understanding and use of a systematic approach to establishing prices. These stages are guidelines that provide a logical sequence for establishing prices, not rigid steps that must be followed in a particular order.

## 20-1 DEVELOPMENT OF PRICING OBJECTIVES

The first step in setting prices is developing **pricing objectives**—goals that describe what a firm wants to achieve through pricing. Developing pricing objectives is an important task because they form the basis for decisions for other stages of the pricing process. Thus, pricing objectives must be stated explicitly and in measurable terms. Objectives should also include a time frame for accomplishing them.

Marketers must ensure that pricing objectives are consistent with the firm's marketing and overall objectives because pricing objectives influence decisions in many functional areas, including finance, accounting, and production. A marketer can use both short- and long-term pricing objectives and can employ one or multiple pricing objectives. For instance, a firm may wish to increase market share by 18 percent over the next three years, achieve a 15 percent return on investment, and promote an image of quality in the marketplace. In this section, we

**pricing objectives** Goals that describe what a firm wants to achieve through pricing

Figure 20.1    **Stages for Establishing Prices**

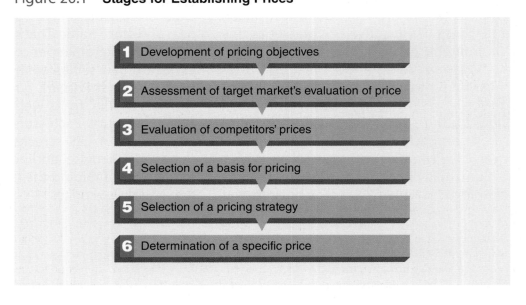

1 Development of pricing objectives

2 Assessment of target market's evaluation of price

3 Evaluation of competitors' prices

4 Selection of a basis for pricing

5 Selection of a pricing strategy

6 Determination of a specific price

Table 20.1   **Pricing Objectives and Typical Actions Taken to Achieve Them**

| Objective | Possible Action |
|---|---|
| Survival | Adjust price levels so the firm can increase sales volume to match organizational expenses. |
| Profit | Identify price and cost levels that allow the firm to maximize profit. |
| Return on investment | Identify price levels that enable the firm to yield targeted ROI. |
| Market share | Adjust price levels so the firm can maintain or increase sales relative to competitors' sales. |
| Cash flow | Set price levels to encourage rapid sales. |
| Status quo | Identify price levels that help stabilize demand and sales. |
| Product quality | Set prices to recover research and development expenditures and establish a high-quality image. |

examine some of the pricing objectives companies might set. Table 20.1 shows the major pricing objectives and typical actions associated with them.

## 20-1a  Survival

Survival is one of the most fundamental pricing objectives. Achieving this objective generally involves temporarily setting prices low, at times below costs, in order to attract more sales. Because price is a flexible ingredient in the marketing mix, survival strategy can be useful in keeping a company afloat by increasing sales volume. Most organizations will tolerate setbacks, such as short-run losses and internal upheaval, if necessary for survival.

## 20-1b  Profit

Although a business may claim that its objective is to maximize profits for its owners, the objective of profit maximization is rarely operational because its achievement is difficult to measure. Therefore, profit objectives tend to be set at levels that the owners and top-level decision makers view as satisfactory and attainable. Specific profit objectives may be stated in terms of either actual dollar amounts or a percentage of sales revenues.

## 20-1c  Return on Investment

Pricing to attain a specified rate of return on the company's investment is a profit-related pricing objective. A return on investment (ROI) pricing objective generally requires some trial and error, as it is unusual for all data and inputs required to determine the necessary ROI to be available when first setting prices. Many pharmaceutical companies use ROI pricing objectives because of the high level of investment in research and development required.

## 20-1d  Market Share

Many firms establish pricing objectives to maintain or increase market share, which is a product's sales in relation to total industry sales. For instance, Sprint slashed prices on its mobile phone service in order to maintain its number-three position in the telecom industry. Although the strategy reduced Sprint's overall revenue by more than 6 percent, it gained new subscribers, which helped the firm maintain traction in the fiercely competitive cell phone market.[2] High relative market shares often translate into high profits for firms. The Profit Impact of Market Strategies (PIMS) studies, conducted annually since the 1960s, have shown that both market share and product quality influence profitability.[3] Thus, marketers often use an increase in market share as a primary pricing objective.

Maintaining or increasing market share need not depend on growth in industry sales. An organization can increase its market share even if sales for the total industry are flat or decreasing. On the other hand, a firm's sales volume can increase while its market share decreases if the overall market grows.

### 20-1e Cash Flow

Some companies set prices so they can recover cash as quickly as possible. Financial managers understandably want to recover quickly the capital spent to develop products. Choosing this pricing objective may have the support of a marketing manager if he or she anticipates a short product life cycle. Although it may be acceptable in some situations, the use of cash flow and recovery as an objective oversimplifies the contribution of price to profits. If this pricing objective results in high prices, competitors with lower prices may gain a large share of the market.

### 20-1f Status Quo

In some cases, an organization is in a favorable position and desires nothing more than to maintain the status quo. Status quo objectives can focus on several dimensions, such as maintaining a certain market share, meeting (but not beating) competitors' prices, achieving price stability, and maintaining a favorable public image. A status quo pricing objective can reduce a firm's risks by helping to stabilize demand for its products. A firm that chooses status quo pricing objectives risks minimizing pricing as a competitive tool, which could lead to a climate of nonprice competition. Professionals such as accountants and attorneys often operate in such an environment.

### 20-1g Product Quality

A company may have the objective of leading its industry in product quality. A high price may signal to customers that the product is of a high quality. Attaining a high level of product quality is generally more expensive for the firm, as the costs of materials, research, and development may be greater. Marmot is a brand associated with quality and performance, even in the coldest climates and activities, as shown in this advertisement. An image of a woman bundled in a Marmot insulated jacket, hat, and ski pants in front of a backdrop of snowy mountains showcases the rugged conditions wearers expect the outerwear brand to perform in. The line at the bottom, "New Dimensions of Warmth," implies that the company cares about the quality of its products and strives to develop new products that perform

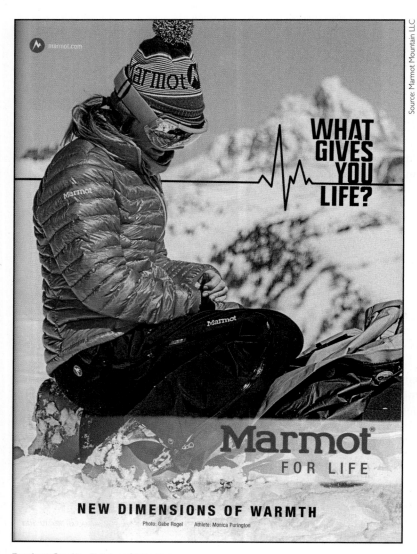

**Product Quality Pricing Objective**
This advertisement emphasizes the high quality of Marmot outerwear, which is something that the company has taken pride in for more than 40 years.

even better. The products and brands that customers perceive to be of high quality are more likely to survive in a competitive marketplace because they trust these products more, even if the prices are higher.

# 20-2 ASSESSMENT OF THE TARGET MARKET'S EVALUATION OF PRICE

After developing pricing objectives, marketers must next assess the target market's evaluation of price. Despite the general assumption that price is a major issue for buyers, the importance of price varies depending on the type of product, target market, and the purchase situation. For instance, buyers are probably more sensitive to gasoline prices than luggage prices. We purchase gasoline regularly and notice fluctuations in price, but because luggage is more likely to be perceived as a long-term investment, we expect to pay more for it. With respect to the type of target market, adults frequently must pay more than children for goods and services, including clothing, meals, and movie tickets, because they consume a larger quantity.

The purchase situation also affects the buyer's view of price. Most moviegoers would never pay, in other situations, the prices charged for soft drinks, popcorn, and candy at concession stands. The markup for popcorn in movie theaters can be up to 1,275 percent.[4] Nevertheless, consumers are willing to pay the markup to enhance their movie experience by enjoying buttery popcorn at the theater. By assessing the target market's evaluation of price, a marketer is in a better position to know how much emphasis to put on price in the overall marketing strategy. Information about the target market's price evaluation may also help a marketer determine how far above the competition the firm can set its prices.

Today, because some consumers seek less-expensive products and the Internet allows consumers to shop more selectively than ever before, some manufacturers and retailers focus on the value of products in their communications with customers. Remember that value is more than just a product's price. It combines price with quality attributes, which customers use to differentiate among competing brands. Generally, consumers want to maximize the value they receive for their money. Consumers may even perceive relatively expensive products, such as organic produce, to have great value if the products have desirable features or characteristics. Consumers are also generally willing to pay a higher price for products that offer convenience and save time. Table 20.2 illustrates this point by showing the unit price difference between basic food products and time-saving food products. Companies that offer both affordable prices and high quality, like Target, have altered consumers' expectations about how much quality they must sacrifice for low prices. Understanding the importance of a product to customers, as well as their expectations about quality and value, helps marketers assess correctly the target market's evaluation of price.

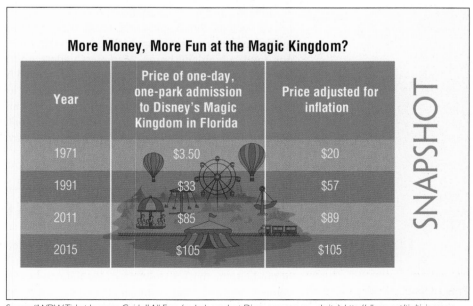

**More Money, More Fun at the Magic Kingdom?**

| Year | Price of one-day, one-park admission to Disney's Magic Kingdom in Florida | Price adjusted for inflation |
|---|---|---|
| 1971 | $3.50 | $20 |
| 1991 | $33 | $57 |
| 2011 | $85 | $89 |
| 2015 | $105 | $105 |

SNAPSHOT

Source: "WDW Ticket Increase Guide," All Ears (an Independent Disney consumer website), http://allears.net/tix/tixincrease.htm (accessed March 30, 2016).

Table 20.2  **Examples of Perceptions of Product Value**

| Basic, Cost-Effective Product | Expensive, Time-Saving Product |
|---|---|
| Whole loose bagels, $0.59 each | Sliced packaged bagels, $0.65 each |
| Whole broccoli, $1.49/lb | Florets broccoli, $3.99/lb |
| Whole carrots, $1.49/lb | Baby carrots, $3.99/lb |
| Whole chicken, $1.49/lb | Cut-up chicken, $1.99/lb |
| Whole feta cheese, $3.23/8 oz | Crumbled feta cheese, $8.65/8 oz |
| Whole Granny Smith apples, $1.99/lb | Sliced Granny Smith apples, $3.97/lb |
| Lean ground chuck (ground), $3.99/lb | Lean ground chuck (patties), $5.99/lb |

Source: "Supermarket Smarts," *Consumer Reports ShopSmart,* www.shopsmartmag.org/files/Supermarket_smarts.pdf (accessed December 28, 2013).

# 20-3 **EVALUATION OF COMPETITORS' PRICES**

In most cases, marketers are in a better position to establish prices when they know the prices charged for competing brands, which is the next step in establishing prices. Identifying competitors' prices should be a regular part of marketing research. Some grocery and department stores even employ comparative shoppers who systematically collect data on prices at competitors' stores. Companies may also purchase price lists from syndicated marketing research services. Even if a marketer has access to competitors' price lists, they may not reflect the actual prices at which competitive products sell because negotiation is involved.

Knowing the prices of competing brands is essential for a marketer. Regardless of its actual costs, a firm does not want to sell its product at a price that is significantly above competitors' prices because the products may not sell as well, or at a price that is significantly below because customers may believe the product is of low quality. Particularly in an industry in which price competition prevails, a marketer needs competitive price information to ensure that a firm's prices are the same as, or slightly lower than, competitors' prices.

In some instances, an organization's prices are designed to be slightly above competitors' prices, such as with Apple brand products, to lend an exclusive image and to signal product quality to consumers. Compare the two advertisements on the next page. One is for Merrick dog food, a high-end brand. Marketers underscore the exclusive image by proclaiming the brand is "guaranteed to make the best dog ever even better" in the advertisement. The other is for Blue brand Freedom dog food, which is priced less than Merrick, though still more than supermarket pet foods. This advertisement features an image of a healthy dog running toward the viewer and highlights what the brand does not contain: gluten-containing grains or artificial flavors and colors that pet owners are increasingly avoiding. Both of these brands emphasize the high quality of their foods.

# 20-4 **SELECTION OF A BASIS FOR PRICING**

The fourth step in establishing prices involves selecting a basis for pricing: cost, demand, and/or competition. Marketers determine the appropriate pricing basis by analyzing the type of product, the market structure of the industry, the brand's market share position relative to competing brands, and customer characteristics. Although we discuss each basis separately in this section, an organization generally considers at least two, or perhaps all three, dimensions. Thus, if a company uses cost as a primary basis for setting prices, its marketers are still aware of and concerned about competitors' prices. If a company uses demand as a basis for pricing, marketers still must consider costs and competitors' prices. Indeed, cost is a factor in every

**Competitor's Prices**
Both Merrick (about $3 a pound) and Blue Freedom (about $2 a pound) pet foods emphasize the quality in their advertisements. Which would you prefer to buy for your pet?

pricing decision because it establishes a price minimum below which the firm will not be able to recoup its production and other costs. Demand, likewise, sets an effective price maximum above which customers are unlikely to buy the product. Setting appropriate prices can be a difficult balance for firms. A high price may reduce demand for the product, but a low price will hurt profit margins and may instill in customers a perception that the product is of low quality. Firms must weigh many different factors when setting prices, including costs, competition, customer buying behavior and price sensitivity, manufacturing capacity, and product life cycles.

## 20-4a Cost-Based Pricing

With **cost-based pricing**, a flat dollar amount or percentage is added to the cost of the product, which means marketers calculate and apply a desired level of profit to the cost of the product and apply it uniformly. Cost-based pricing does not necessarily take into account the economic aspects of supply and demand, nor must it relate to just one pricing strategy or pricing objective. It is a straightforward and easy-to-implement method. Two common forms of cost-based pricing are cost-plus and markup pricing.

### Cost-Plus Pricing

With **cost-plus pricing**, the seller's costs are determined (usually during a project or after a project is completed), and then a specified dollar amount or percentage of the cost is added to the seller's cost to establish the price. When production costs are difficult to predict, cost-plus pricing is appropriate. Projects involving custom-made equipment and commercial construction are often priced using this technique. The government also frequently expects cost-plus pricing from defense contractors. One pitfall for the buyer is that the seller may increase stated costs to

**cost-based pricing** Adding a dollar amount or percentage to the cost of the product

**cost-plus pricing** Adding a specified dollar amount or percentage to the seller's cost gain a larger profit base. Furthermore, some costs, such as overhead, may be difficult to determine. In periods of rapid inflation, cost-plus pricing is popular, especially when the producer must use raw materials that frequently fluctuate in price. In industries in which cost-plus pricing is common and sellers have similar costs, price competition will not be especially intense.

## Markup Pricing

With **markup pricing**, commonly used by retailers, a product's price is derived by adding a predetermined percentage of the cost, called *markup*, to the cost of the product. For instance, most retailers mark up prices by 25 to 50 percent, whereas warehouse clubs, like Costco and Sam's Club, have a lower average markup of around 14 percent.[5] Markups can vary a great deal depending on the product and the situation. Although the percentage markup in a retail store varies from one category of goods to another—35 percent of cost for hardware items and 100 percent of cost for greeting cards, for example—the same percentage is often used to determine the prices on items within a single product category, and the percentage markup may be largely standardized across an industry at the retail level. Using a rigid percentage markup for a specific product category reduces pricing to a routine task that can be performed quickly.

The following example illustrates how percentage markups are determined and distinguishes between two methods of stating a markup. Assume a retailer purchases a can of tuna at 45 cents and adds 15 cents to the cost, making the price 60 cents. There are two ways to look at the markup, as a percentage of cost or as a percentage of selling price:

$$\text{markup as percentage of cost} = \frac{\text{markup}}{\text{cost}}$$
$$= \frac{15}{45}$$
$$= 33.3\%$$

$$\text{markup as percentage of selling price} = \frac{\text{markup}}{\text{selling price}}$$
$$= \frac{15}{60}$$
$$= 25.0\%$$

The markup as a percentage of cost is 33.3 percent, while the markup as a percentage of price is only 25 percent. Obviously, when discussing a percentage markup, it is important to know whether the markup is based on cost or selling price.

Markups normally reflect expectations about operating costs, risks, and stock turnovers. Wholesalers and manufacturers often suggest standard retail markups that are considered profitable. To the extent that retailers use similar markups for the same product category, price competition is reduced. In addition, using rigid markups is convenient and is the major reason retailers favor this method.

## 20-4b **Demand-Based Pricing**

Marketers sometimes base prices on the level of demand for the product. When **demand-based pricing** is used, customers pay a higher price at times when demand for the product is strong and a lower price when demand is weak. Many entertainment venues have implemented demand-based pricing for ticket sales. The Walt Disney Company, for example, introduced demand-based pricing for Disneyland and Disney World, offering cheaper tickets or extra perks on traditionally slow days and more expensive tickets or greater restrictions on traditionally crowded days, such as summer weekends. The goal is to spread out park attendance to relieve crowded conditions that make for less-than-happy experiences.[6] The belief behind this pricing basis is that it is better to take a lower profit margin on a sale than no revenue at all.

**markup pricing** Adding to the cost of the product a predetermined percentage of that cost

**demand-based pricing** Pricing based on the level of demand for the product

Many service industries, including the airline, hotel, bus, car rental, ride sharing, and entertainment venues, use *dynamic pricing* to balance supply and demand. For instance, all tickets for Los Angeles Angels' baseball games are sold using dynamic pricing. Ticket prices are adjusted based on real-time market conditions that include the popularity of opponents.[7] Likewise, in some industries, *yield management* is a strategy of maximizing revenues by making numerous price changes in response to demand, competitors' prices, or environmental conditions. For example, Greyhound, like many firms in the transportation and travel industries, invested in new information technology systems that let it set prices based on real-time analysis and gives customers a better online experience.[8]

To use demand-based pricing, a marketer must be able to estimate the quantity of a product consumers will demand at different times and how demand will be affected by changes in the price. The marketer then chooses the price that generates the highest total revenue. Demand-based pricing is appropriate for industries in which companies have a fixed amount of available resources that are perishable, such as airline seats, hotel rooms, concert seats, and so on. The effectiveness of demand-based pricing depends on the marketer's ability to estimate demand accurately. Compared with cost-based pricing, demand-based pricing places a firm in a better position to reach high profit levels, as long as demand is strong at times and buyers value the product at levels sufficiently above the product's cost.

**Demand-Based Pricing**
Hotels engage in demand-based pricing. When demand at a hotel for a specific night is high, the prices will be higher, and when demand at a hotel is lower on a specific night, the prices will be lower.

# Entrepreneurship in Marketing

## On the Clock at Ziferblat

**Founder:** Ivan Meetin
**Business:** Ziferblat Café
**Founded:** 2011, in Moscow, Russia
**Success:** Ziferblat now has cafés in four different countries.

Customers who grab a cup of espresso and a muffin at the Ziferblat Café in Russia's capital city of Moscow don't pay for what they eat—they pay according to how long they linger in the easy chairs. This innovative restaurant pricing strategy was pioneered by Ivan Meetin, the entrepreneur who founded the Ziferblat concept and is opening new units in Europe and beyond.

Originally, Meetin used a "pay-what-you-can-afford" pricing strategy when he started a small self-serve café in Moscow in 2010. He envisioned it as a community center for staging informal poetry readings and art exhibits. Soon the café became so popular that he moved it to a larger space and switched to a more structured "pay-by-the-minute" pricing approach. To call attention to the pricing, he renamed the café Ziferblat, which is Russian for "clock-face," and added clockfaces to the simple but comfortable décor.

Ziferblat Cafés are already open in London, Liverpool, Prague, Saint Petersburg, and beyond, as Meetin franchises the brand to expand into new markets at a rapid rate. In Manchester, England, for example, franchise owner Colin Shenton has set the price at 5 pence per minute (less than a dime in U.S. currency), capped for customers who stay all day. The café's system is simple: Customers "clock in" with staff members when they enter. They can enjoy as much coffee, cake, Wi-Fi, and conversation as they like, and pay for their total time when they "clock out" at the end of their visit.[a]

### 20-4c Competition-Based Pricing

With **competition-based pricing**, an organization considers costs to be secondary to competitors' prices. This is a common method among producers of relatively homogeneous products, particularly when the target market considers price to be an important purchase consideration. A firm that uses competition-based pricing may choose to set their prices below competitors' or at the same level. Competitors believe that Amazon's competition-based pricing model has been an attempt to gain monopoly control of many retail markets. Amazon uses highly sophisticated analytics to gauge consumer demand and compare its prices to competitors. To stay ahead of the competition, Amazon adjusts its prices millions of times each day to ensure that it undercuts competitors on the most popular items.[9]

## 20-5 SELECTION OF A PRICING STRATEGY

A *pricing strategy* is a course of action designed to achieve pricing objectives, which are set to help marketers solve the practical problems of setting prices. The extent to which a business uses any of the following strategies depends on its pricing and marketing objectives, the markets for its products, the degree of product differentiation, the product's life-cycle stage, and other factors. Generally, pricing strategies help marketers solve the practical problems of establishing prices. Table 20.3 lists the most common pricing strategies, which we discuss in this section.

### 20-5a Differential Pricing

An important issue in pricing decisions is whether to use a single price or different prices for the same product. Using a single price has several benefits. A primary advantage is simplicity. A single price is easily understood by both employees and customers. Since many salespeople and customers dislike negotiating prices, having a single price reduces the risk of a marketer developing an adversarial relationship with customers. The use of a single price does create

**competition-based pricing** Pricing influenced primarily by competitors' prices

Table 20.3   **Common Pricing Strategies**

| Differential Pricing | Psychological Pricing |
|---|---|
| Negotiated pricing | Reference pricing |
| Secondary-market pricing | Bundle pricing |
| Periodic discounting | Multiple-unit pricing |
| Random discounting | Everyday low prices |
|  | Odd-even pricing |
| **New-Product Pricing** | Customary pricing |
| Price skimming | Prestige pricing |
| Penetration pricing |  |
|  | **Professional Pricing** |
| **Product-Line Pricing** |  |
| Captive pricing | **Promotional Pricing** |
| Premium pricing | Price leaders |
| Bait pricing | Special-event pricing |
| Price lining | Comparison discounting |

some challenges, however. If the single price is too high, some potential customers may be unable to afford the product. If it is too low, the organization loses revenue from those customers who would have paid more had the price been higher.

**Differential pricing** means charging different prices to different buyers for the same quality and quantity of product. For example, many movie theaters offer discounted tickets for seniors, and airlines often charge business passengers more because they book at the last minute. The Internet and the collection of large amounts of data about customers based on their online behavior has generated some concern about whether companies may use such data to set discriminatory prices or prices that are unfair to some groups.[10] For differential pricing to be effective, the market must consist of multiple segments with different price sensitivities. When this method is employed, caution should be used to avoid confusing or antagonizing customers. Differential pricing can occur in several ways, including negotiated pricing, secondary-market pricing, periodic discounting, and random discounting.

## Negotiated Pricing

**Negotiated pricing** occurs when the final price is established through bargaining between the seller and the customer. Negotiated pricing occurs in a number of industries and at all levels of distribution. Even when there is a predetermined stated price or a price list, manufacturers, wholesalers, and retailers still may negotiate to establish the final sales price. Consumers commonly negotiate prices for houses, cars, and used equipment. Customers rarely pay the list price on a car, for instance, because they go to a car dealership expecting to negotiate with the seller until they arrive at a price that is satisfactory to both the customer and the seller. Managing personal chemistry between the negotiators is just as important as settling on prices. The negotiation process can help build relationships and increase understanding between different parties in a supply-chain relationship.

## Secondary-Market Pricing

**Secondary-market pricing** means setting one price for the primary target market and a different price for another market. Often the price charged in the secondary market is lower. However, when the costs of serving a secondary market are higher than normal, secondary-market customers may have to pay a higher price. Examples of secondary markets include a geographically-isolated domestic market, a market in a foreign country, and a segment willing to purchase a product during off-peak times (such as "early-bird" diners at restaurants and off-peak hour cell phone users). Secondary markets give an organization an opportunity to use excess capacity and stabilize the allocation of resources.

## Periodic Discounting

**Periodic discounting** is the temporary reduction of prices on a patterned or systematic basis. As a result, many retailers have annual holiday sales, and some apparel stores have regular seasonal sales. From the marketer's point of view, a major problem with periodic discounting is customers can predict when the reductions will occur and may delay their purchases until they can take advantage of the lower prices. Periodic discounting is less effective in an environment where many consumers shop online because they can more easily comparison shop for a better deal even during non-sale times.

## Random Discounting

To alleviate the problem of customers knowing when discounting will occur, some organizations employ **random discounting**—that is, they reduce their prices temporarily on a nonsystematic basis. When price reductions of a product occur randomly, current users of that brand are not able to predict when the reductions will occur. Therefore, they are less likely to delay their purchases in anticipation of buying the product at a lower price. Marketers also use random discounting to attract new customers. Random discounting can also be useful to draw attention to a relatively new product. Many grocery store items, such as a new kind of yogurt

**differential pricing** Charging different prices to different buyers for the same quality and quantity of product

**negotiated pricing** Establishing a final price through bargaining between the seller and the customer

**secondary-market pricing** Setting one price for the primary target market and a different price for another market

**periodic discounting** Temporary reduction of prices on a patterned or systematic basis

**random discounting** Temporary reduction of prices on an unsystematic basis or cereal, will use random discounting. Marketers must be careful not to use random discounting too often, however, because customers will learn to wait for the discounts.

Whether they use periodic discounting or random discounting, retailers often employ tensile pricing when putting products on sale. *Tensile pricing* involves making a broad statement about price reductions, as opposed to detailing specific price discounts. Examples of tensile pricing would be statements like "20 to 50 percent off," "up to 75 percent off," and "save 10 percent or more." Generally, the tensile price that mentions only the maximum reduction (such as "up to 50 percent off") generates the highest customer response.[11]

## 20-5b New-Product Pricing

Setting the base price for a new product is a necessary part of formulating a marketing strategy. Marketers can easily adjust the base price in industries that are not subject to government price controls, and its establishment is one of the most fundamental decisions in the marketing mix. The base price can be set high to recover development costs quickly or provide a reference point for developing discount prices for different market segments. When a marketer sets base prices, he or she considers how quickly competitors are expected to enter the market, whether they will mount a strong campaign on entry, and what effect their entry will have on the development of primary demand. Two strategies used in new-product pricing are price skimming and penetration pricing. Research into the pricing of new digital cameras hints that marketers use a skimming strategy about 20 percent of the time, a penetration strategy about 20 percent of the time, and a straightforward competitive- or market-based strategy most of the time, especially for later entrants to the market.[12]

### Price Skimming

Some consumers are willing to pay a high price for an innovative product, either because of its novelty or because of the prestige or status that ownership confers. **Price skimming** is the strategy of charging the highest possible price for a product during the introduction stage of its life cycle. The seller essentially "skims the cream" off the market, which helps a firm to recover the high costs of R&D more quickly. This approach provides the most flexible introductory base price. Demand tends to be inelastic in the introductory stage of the product life cycle.

Price skimming can provide several benefits. A skimming policy can generate much-needed initial cash flows to help offset development costs. Price skimming protects the marketer from problems that arise when the price is set too low to cover costs. When a firm introduces a product, its production capacity may be limited. A skimming price can help keep demand consistent with the firm's production capabilities. However, price skimming strategies can be dangerous because they may make the product appear more lucrative than it actually is to potential competitors. A firm also risks misjudging demand and facing insufficient sales at the higher price. New-product prices should be based on both the value to the customer and competitive products.

### Penetration Pricing

At the opposite extreme, **penetration pricing** is the strategy of setting a low price for a new product. The main purpose of setting a low price is to build market share quickly to encourage product trial by the target market and discourage competitors from entering the market. This approach is less flexible for a marketer than price skimming, because it is more difficult to raise the price of a product from a penetration price than to lower or discount a skimming price. It is not unusual for a firm to use a penetration price after having skimmed the market with a higher price.

Penetration pricing can be especially beneficial when a marketer suspects that competitors could enter the market easily. If the low price stimulates sales, the firm may be able to order longer production runs, increasing economies of scale and resulting in decreased production

**price skimming** Charging the highest possible price that buyers who most desire the product will pay

**penetration pricing** Setting prices below those of competing brands to penetrate a market and gain a significant market share quickly costs per unit. If penetration pricing allows the marketer to gain a large market share quickly, competitors may be discouraged from entering the market. In addition, because the lower per-unit penetration price results in lower per-unit profit, the market may not appear to be especially lucrative to potential new entrants. A disadvantage of penetration pricing is that it places a firm in a less-flexible pricing position. Again, it is more difficult to raise prices significantly than it is to lower them.

## 20-5c **Product-Line Pricing**

Rather than considering products on an item-by-item basis when determining pricing strategies, some marketers employ product-line pricing. **Product-line pricing** means establishing and adjusting the prices of multiple products within a product line. When marketers use product-line pricing, their goal is to maximize profits for an entire product line rather than to focus on the profitability of an individual product item. Product-line pricing can provide marketers with pricing flexibility. Thus, marketers can set prices so that one product is profitable, whereas another is less profitable but increases market share by virtue of having a low price and, therefore, selling more units.

Before setting prices for a product line, marketers evaluate the relationship among the products in the line. When products in a line are complementary, sales increases in one item raise demand for other items. For instance, desktop printers and toner cartridges are complementary products. However, when products in a line function as substitutes for one another, buyers of one product in the line are unlikely to purchase one of the other products in the same line. In this case, marketers must be sensitive to how a price change for one of the brands may affect the demand not only for that brand but also for the substitute brands. For instance, if decision makers at Procter & Gamble were considering a price change for Tide detergent, they would likely also be concerned about how the price change might influence sales of other detergents, such as Cheer, Bold, and Gain.

When marketers employ product-line pricing, they have several strategies from which to choose. These include captive pricing, premium pricing, bait pricing, and price lining.

## Captive Pricing

When marketers use **captive pricing**, the basic product in a product line is priced low, but the price on the items required to operate or enhance it are higher. A common example of captive pricing is printer ink. The printer is priced quite low to attract sales, but the printer ink replacement cartridges are very expensive. Look at the advertisement for the Gillette FlexBall razor for another example. To promote the innovative razor to men, the advertisement strives to appeal to the adventurous side in men by relating a quote from author Ian Fleming, creator of the James Bond series. The ad also appeals to women who might be looking at the product as a gift by saying "bring out the 007 in him." The FlexBall itself is not very expensive, but the replacement blades are highly specialized and retail for

**product-line pricing** Establishing and adjusting prices of multiple products within a product line

**captive pricing** Pricing the basic product in a product line low, while pricing related items higher

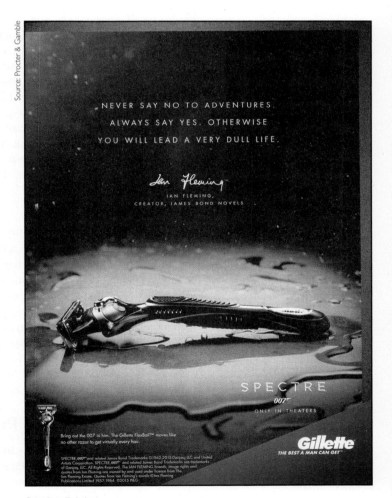

**Captive Pricing**
The Gillette FlexBall razor is an example of a captive pricing strategy because the original razor is sold at a relatively low price, but replacement blades are more expensive. Consumers cannot substitute another brand of blades.

about $4.50 per blade cartridge. Because the razor requires specific replacement cartridges, consumers cannot purchase generic or off-brand replacements to save money.

## Premium Pricing

**Premium pricing** occurs when the highest-quality product, or the most-versatile and most desirable version of a product in a product line, is assigned the highest price. Other products in the line are priced to appeal to price-sensitive shoppers or to those who seek product-specific features. Marketers that use premium pricing often realize a significant portion of their profits from the premium-priced products. Examples of product categories in which premium pricing is common are small kitchen appliances, beer, ice cream, and television cable service. For example, tax software such as Turbo Tax and H&R Block Tax are marketed in multiple versions; the least expensive versions handle the most basic tax preparation and forms, while more expensive versions include more tax forms, state tax forms, planning assistance, and more.

## Bait Pricing

To attract customers, marketers may put a low price on one item in the product line with the intention of selling a higher-priced item in the line. This strategy is known as **bait pricing**. Producers of smartphones and tablets may engage in bait pricing, selling ultra-low-priced models that lure in customers but charging extra for the most desirable features. Additional apps and subscription services can cost owners of these gadgets even more, and customers rarely factor in these costs when calculating the overall expense of the purchase.[13]

As long as a retailer has sufficient quantities of the advertised low-priced model available for sale, this strategy is acceptable. However, it may generate customer resentment if customers go to the store looking for the low-priced model and only find the high-priced model in stock. If this is done intentionally, it is called *bait and switch*. Bait and switch occurs when retailers have no intention of selling the bait product. They use the low price merely to entice customers into the store to sell them higher-priced products. Bait and switch is unethical, and in some states it is even illegal.

## Price Lining

**Price lining** is the strategy of selling goods only at certain predetermined prices that reflect explicit price breaks. For instance, a shop may sell men's ties only at $22 and $37. This strategy is common in clothing and accessory stores. It eliminates minor price differences from the buying decision—both for customers and for managers who buy merchandise to sell in these stores. The basic assumption in price lining is that the demand for various groups or sets of products is inelastic. If the prices are attractive, customers will concentrate their purchases without responding to slight changes in price. Thus, a women's dress shop that carries dresses priced at $85, $55, and $35 may not attract many more sales with a drop to $83, $53, and $33. The "space" between the price of $85 and $55, however, can stir changes in consumer response, with consumers viewing the higher-priced item as higher quality. With price lining, the demand curve looks like a series of steps, as shown in Figure 20.2.

## 20-5d Psychological Pricing

**Psychological pricing** attempts to influence a customer's perception of price to make a product's price more attractive. Psychological pricing strategies encourage purchases based on consumers' emotional responses, rather than on economically rational ones. These strategies are used primarily for consumer products, rather than business products, because most business purchases follow a systematic and rational approach. In this section, we consider several forms of psychological pricing: reference pricing, bundle pricing, multiple-unit pricing, everyday low prices (EDLP), odd-even pricing, customary pricing, and prestige pricing.

**premium pricing** Pricing the highest-quality or most versatile products higher than other models in the product line

**bait pricing** Pricing an item in a product line low with the intention of selling a higher-priced item in the line

**price lining** Setting a limited number of prices for selected groups or lines of merchandise

**psychological pricing** Pricing that attempts to influence a customer's perception of price to make a product's price more attractive

Figure 20.2 **Price Lining**

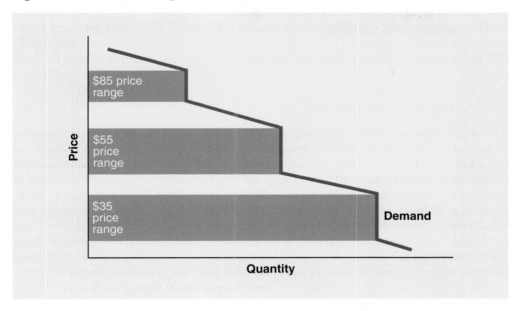

## Reference Pricing

**Reference pricing** means pricing a product at a moderate level and physically positioning it next to a more expensive model or brand in the hope that the customer will use the higher price as a reference price (i.e., a comparison price). Because of the comparison, the customer is expected to view the moderate price more favorably than he or she would if the product were considered alone. Reference pricing is based on the "isolation effect," meaning an alternative is less attractive when viewed by itself than when compared with other alternatives.

## Bundle Pricing

**Bundle pricing** is the packaging together of two or more products, usually of a complementary nature, to be sold for a single price. To be attractive to customers, the single price generally is markedly less than the sum of the prices of the individual products. Being able to buy the bundled combination may be of value to the customer, increasing convenience and reducing the time required to shop. Bundle pricing is common for banking and travel services, computers, and automobiles with option packages. Bundle pricing is also common among products that are used in tandem. Comcast Xfinity, for instance, offers a special rate when consumers bundle television, Internet, and phone service. Bundle pricing can help to increase customer satisfaction. It can also help firms sell slow-moving inventory and increase revenues by bundling it with products with a higher turnover.

## Multiple-Unit Pricing

Many retailers (and especially supermarkets) practice **multiple-unit pricing**, which is setting a single price for two or more units of a product, such as two cans for 99 cents, rather than 50 cents per can. Especially for frequently-purchased products, this strategy can increase sales by encouraging consumers to purchase multiple units when they might otherwise have only purchased one at a time. Customers benefit from the cost savings and convenience this pricing strategy affords. A company may use multiple-unit pricing to attract new customers to its brands and, in some instances, to increase consumption. When customers buy in larger

**reference pricing** Pricing a product at a moderate level and displaying it next to a more expensive model or brand

**bundle pricing** Packaging together two or more complementary products and selling them at a single price

**multiple-unit pricing** Packaging together two or more identical products and selling them at a single price quantities, their consumption of the product may increase as it is more available. Customers who see the single price and who expect eventually to use more than one unit of the product will likely be inclined to purchase multiple units.

Discount stores and especially warehouse clubs, like Sam's Club and Costco, are major users of multiple-unit pricing. For certain products in these stores, customers receive significant per-unit price reductions when they buy packages containing multiple units of the same product.

## Everyday Low Prices (EDLP)

**everyday low prices (EDLP)** Pricing products low on a consistent basis

**odd-even pricing** Ending the price with certain numbers to influence buyers' perceptions of the price or product

To reduce or eliminate the use of frequent short-term price reductions, some organizations use an approach referred to as **everyday low prices (EDLP)**. When EDLPs are used, a marketer sets a low price for its products on a consistent basis, rather than setting higher prices and frequently discounting them. EDLPs, though not deeply discounted, are set low enough to make customers feel confident they are receiving a good deal. EDLPs are employed by retailers, such as Walmart, and by manufacturers, such as Procter & Gamble. A company that uses EDLP benefits from reduced promotional costs, reduced losses from frequent markdowns, and more stable sales. Look at the advertisement for Merona brand clothing, a Target store brand, which features the EDLPs of a variety of fashionable clothing and shoe choices. The advertisement shows the style and the value of this brand of clothing and reminds consumers that they must shop at Target to purchase it.

A major issue with this approach is that customers can have mixed responses. In some instances, customers believe that EDLPs are a marketing gimmick and not truly the good deal that they proclaim. Some retailers have encountered a backlash against EDLP from consumers who enjoy the thrill of hunting down the best sales. For instance, when J.C.Penney opted to stop promotions and coupons in favor of EDLP, some customers stopped shopping there. J.C.Penney marketers discovered the hard way that many consumers want to see the 20 percent off markdown and use coupons because it helps to reinforce the feeling that they are getting a good deal. The company ultimately backtracked on the EDLP policy after seeing sharp declines in sales.[14]

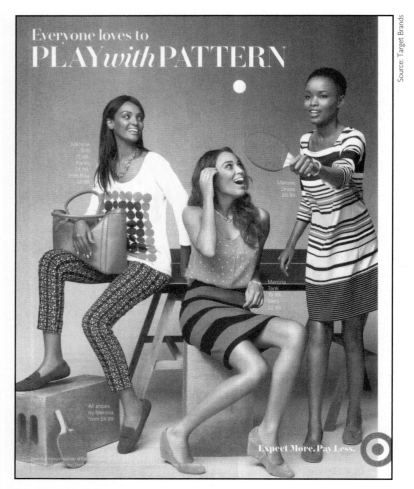

Source: Target Brands

**Everyday Low Prices**
This advertisement for Merona brand clothing features the EDLPs of apparel and shoe styles, emphasizing the value of these fashion-forward items.

## Odd-Even Pricing

**Odd-even pricing** involves ending a price with certain numbers. Through this strategy, marketers try to influence buyers' perceptions of the product. It aligns with the belief among many retailers that consumers respond more positively to odd-number prices, such as $4.99, than to whole-dollar prices, such as $5, for items where customers are looking for value. Odd pricing is the strategy of setting prices using odd numbers that are slightly below whole-dollar amounts. Nine and five are the most popular ending figures for odd-number prices. This strategy assumes more of a product will be sold at $99.95 than at $100. Sellers who use this odd pricing believe that odd numbers increase sales because consumers register the dollar amount, not the cents. Odd-number pricing has been the subject of various psychological studies, but the results have been inconclusive.

Even prices, on the other hand, are often used to give a product an exclusive or upscale image. An even price is believed to influence a customer to view the product as being a high-quality, premium brand. A shirt maker, for example, may print on a premium shirt package a suggested retail price of $42.00 instead of $41.95.

## Customary Pricing

With **customary pricing**, certain goods are priced on the basis of tradition. This is a less common pricing strategy now than it was in the past. An example would be the 25-cent gumballs sold in gumball machines—the price has remained at that level for probably as long as you can remember. In cases of customary pricing, it is usual for the size of the product sold at the customary price to shrink over time to compensate for rising costs of raw materials.

## Prestige Pricing

With **prestige pricing**, prices are set at an artificially high level to convey a quality image. Prestige pricing is used especially when buyers associate a higher price with higher quality.

Maserati is a brand that has successfully used prestige pricing to set prices extremely high to convey an aura of ultra-luxury. The Quattroporte, such as the one depicted in the advertisement, retails for just under $100,000 for a base S sedan, though other models sell for as much as $140,000. The ad features an Italian model wearing a silk dress getting out of a Quattroporte in front of what appears to be an Italian villa to convey a sense of a desirable, luxurious lifestyle—which consumers can seek to emulate through purchasing Maserati vehicles.

Typical product categories that are subject to prestige pricing include perfumes, liquor, jewelry, cars, and some food items. Upscale appliances or furniture capitalizes on the desire of some consumer segments to "trade up" for high-quality products. These consumers are willing to pay extra for a Sub-Zero refrigerator or a Viking commercial range because these products are high quality and project an image that the customers can afford the best.

### 20-5e  Professional Pricing

**Professional pricing** is used by people who have great skill or experience in a particular field. Although costs are considered when setting prices, professionals often believe their fees should not relate directly to the time and/or effort spent in specific cases. Rather, professionals may charge a standard fee regardless of the problems involved in performing the job. Some doctors' and lawyers' fees are prime examples, such as $75 for an office visit, $2,000 for an appendectomy, and $995 for a divorce. Other professionals set prices using different methods. Like other marketers, professionals

**customary pricing**  Pricing on the basis of tradition

**prestige pricing**  Setting prices at an artificially high level to convey prestige or a quality image

**professional pricing**  Fees set by people with great skill or experience in a particular field

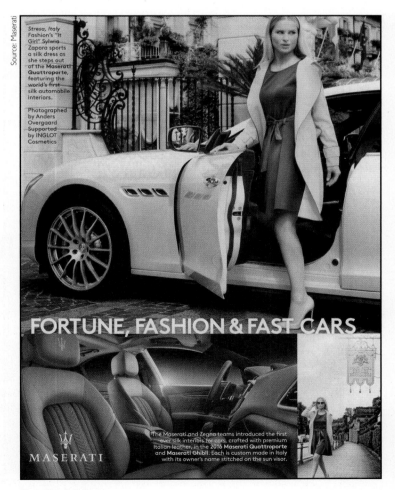

**Prestige Pricing**
Maserati is a premium brand that engages in prestige pricing to convey an image of wealth and luxury.

have costs associated with facilities, labor, insurance, equipment, and supplies. Professionals have an ethical responsibility not to overcharge customers.

## 20-5f Promotional Pricing

Price—as an ingredient in the marketing mix—often is coordinated with promotion. The two variables are sometimes so interrelated that the pricing policy is promotion-oriented. Examples of promotional pricing include price leaders, special-event pricing, and comparison discounting.

### Price Leaders

Sometimes a firm prices a few products below the usual markup, near cost, or below cost, which results in what are known as **price leaders**. This type of pricing is used most often in supermarkets and restaurants to attract customers by offering them especially low prices on a few items, with the expectation that they will purchase other items as well. Management expects that sales of regularly-priced products will more than offset the reduced revenues from the price leaders.

### Special-Event Pricing

To increase sales volume, many organizations coordinate price with advertising or sales promotions for seasonal or special situations. **Special-event pricing** involves advertised sales or price cutting linked to a holiday, season, or event. If the pricing objective is survival, then special sales events may be designed to generate the necessary operating capital. Special-event pricing entails coordination of production, scheduling, storage, and physical distribution. Special-event pricing can be an effective strategy to combat sales lags.

**price leaders** Products priced near or even below cost

**special-event pricing** Advertised sales or price cutting linked to a holiday, a season, or an event

**comparison discounting** Setting a price at a specific level and comparing it with a higher price

### Comparison Discounting

**Comparison discounting** sets the price of a product at a specific level and simultaneously compares it with a higher price. The higher price may be the product's previous price, the price of a competing brand, the product's price at another retail outlet, or a manufacturer's suggested

# EMERGING **TRENDS IN MARKETING**

## Millennial Homebuyers: Are They Looking for Less, for Less?

Smaller homes, with fewer frills and affordable price tags, are attracting first-time buyers from the millennial generation as well as down-sizing seniors from the baby-boom generation. With demand growing, national builders such as D.R. Horton are profiting from marketing new homes that provide the benefits of home ownership valued by both of these markets.

D.R. Horton formed its Express division in 2014 to focus on construction of reasonably-sized, reasonably-priced homes in southern and western states where the population is increasing. Express homes provide the quality associated with the Horton brand, but without the oversized rooms, high-end kitchens, luxury bathrooms, and designer options that can push prices out of reach

for many. Keeping costs in line allows Express to keep new home prices well below the median price of all U.S. homes.

The Express homes are attractive to consumers who are stepping up from rentals as well as to consumers who are trading down from larger homes now that the children are grown or retirement is approaching. As a result, Express accounts for 20 percent of all the homes that D.R. Horton sells in a year and 14 percent of the company's annual revenues. Looking ahead, the company sees Express helping it gain additional market share as more consumers decide they want a modest-sized home they can actually afford, rather than the biggest home that money can buy.[b]

retail price. Customers may find comparative discounting informative, and it can have a significant impact on their purchases.

However, because this pricing strategy on occasion has led to deceptive pricing practices, the Federal Trade Commission has established guidelines for comparison discounting. If the higher price against which the comparison is made is the price formerly charged for the product, the seller must have made the previous price available to customers for a reasonable time period. If sellers present the higher price as the one charged by other retailers in the same trade area, they must be able to demonstrate that this claim is true. When they present the higher price as the manufacturer's suggested retail price, the higher price must be close to the price at which a reasonable proportion of the product was sold. Some manufacturers' suggested retail prices are so high that very few products are actually sold at those prices. In such cases, it is deceptive to use comparison discounting. The Internet has allowed consumers to be more wary of comparison discounting and less susceptible to being fooled, as they can easily compare the listed price for a product with comparable products online.

# 20-6 DETERMINATION OF A SPECIFIC PRICE

A pricing strategy will yield a certain price or range of prices, which is the final step in the pricing process. However, marketers may need to refine this price in order to make it consistent with circumstances (such as a sluggish economy) and with pricing practices in a particular market or industry. Pricing strategies should help in setting a final price. If they are to do so, marketers must establish pricing objectives, have considerable knowledge about target market customers, and determine demand, price elasticity, costs, and competitive factors. Additionally, the way marketers use pricing in the marketing mix will affect the final price.

In the absence of government price controls, pricing remains a flexible and convenient way to adjust the marketing mix. In many situations, marketers can adjust prices quickly—over a few days or even in minutes. Such flexibility is unique to this component of the marketing mix.

# Summary

### 20-1 Identify issues related to developing pricing objectives.

Setting pricing objectives is critical because pricing objectives form a foundation on which the decisions of subsequent stages are based. Organizations may use numerous pricing objectives, including short-term and long-term ones, and different objectives for different products and market segments. Pricing objectives are overall goals that describe the role of price in a firm's long-range plans. There are several major types of pricing objectives. The most fundamental pricing objective is the organization's survival. Price can usually be easily adjusted to increase sales volume or combat competition to help the organization stay alive. Profit objectives, which are usually stated in terms of sales dollar volume or percentage change, are normally set at a satisfactory level rather than at a level designed to maximize profits. A sales growth objective focuses on increasing the profit base by raising sales volume. Pricing for return on investment (ROI) has a specified profit as its objective. A pricing objective to maintain or increase market

share links market position to success. Other types of pricing objectives include cash flow, status quo, and product quality.

### 20-2 Discuss the importance of identifying the target market's evaluation of price.

Assessing the target market's evaluation of price tells the marketer how much emphasis to place on price and may help determine how far above the competition the firm can set its prices. Understanding how important a product is to customers relative to other products, as well as customers' expectations of quality, helps marketers correctly assess the target market's evaluation of price.

### 20-3 Explain how marketers analyze competitors' prices.

A marketer needs to be aware of the prices charged for competing brands. This allows the firm to keep its prices in line with competitors' prices when nonprice competition is used. If a company uses price as a competitive tool, it can price its brand below competing brands.

## 20-4 Describe the bases used for setting prices.

The three major dimensions on which prices can be based are cost, demand, and competition. When using cost-based pricing, the firm determines price by adding a dollar amount or percentage to the cost of the product. Two common cost-based pricing methods are cost-plus and markup pricing. Demand-based pricing is based on the level of demand for the product. To use this method, a marketer must be able to estimate the amounts of a product that buyers will demand at different prices. Demand-based pricing results in a high price when demand for a product is strong and a low price when demand is weak. In the case of competition-based pricing, costs and revenues are secondary to competitors' prices.

## 20-5 Explain the different types of pricing strategies.

A pricing strategy is an approach or a course of action designed to achieve pricing and marketing objectives. Pricing strategies help marketers solve the practical problems of establishing prices. The most common pricing strategies are differential pricing, new-product pricing, product-line pricing, psychological pricing, professional pricing, and promotional pricing.

When marketers employ differential pricing, they charge different buyers different prices for the same quality and quantity of products. For example, with negotiated pricing, the final price is established through bargaining between the seller and the customer. Secondary-market pricing involves setting one price for the primary target market and a different price for another market. Oftentimes the price charged in the secondary market is lower. Marketers employ periodic discounting when they temporarily lower their prices on a patterned or systematic basis because of such reasons as a seasonal change, a model-year change, or a holiday. Random discounting occurs on an unsystematic basis.

Two strategies used in new-product pricing are price skimming and penetration pricing. With price skimming, the organization charges the highest price that buyers who most desire the product will pay. A penetration price is a low price designed to penetrate a market and gain a significant market share quickly.

Product-line pricing establishes and adjusts the prices of multiple products within a product line. This strategy includes captive pricing, in which the marketer prices the basic product in a product line low and prices related items higher. Premium pricing is setting prices on higher-quality or more versatile products higher than those on other models in the product line.

Bait pricing is when the marketer tries to attract customers by pricing an item in the product line low with the intention of selling a higher-priced item in the line. Price lining is when the organization sets a limited number of prices for selected groups or lines of merchandise.

Psychological pricing attempts to influence customers' perceptions of price to make a product's price more attractive. With reference pricing, marketers price a product at a moderate level and position it next to a more expensive model or brand. Bundle pricing is packaging together two or more complementary products and selling them at a single price. With multiple-unit pricing, two or more identical products are packaged together and sold at a single price. To reduce or eliminate use of frequent short-term price reductions, some organizations employ everyday low pricing (EDLP), setting a low price for products on a consistent basis. When employing odd-even pricing, marketers try to influence buyers' perceptions of the price or the product by ending the price with certain numbers. Customary pricing is based on traditional prices. With prestige pricing, prices are set at an artificially high level to convey prestige or a quality image.

Professional pricing is used by people who have great skill or experience in a particular field, therefore allowing them to set the price. This concept carries the idea that professionals have an ethical responsibility not to overcharge customers. As an ingredient in the marketing mix, price is often coordinated with promotion. The two variables are sometimes so closely interrelated that the pricing policy is promotion-oriented. Promotional pricing includes price leaders, special-event pricing, and comparison discounting.

Price leaders are products priced below the usual markup, near cost, or below cost. Special-event pricing involves advertised sales or price cutting linked to a holiday, season, or event. Marketers that use a comparison discounting strategy price a product at a specific level and compare it with a higher price.

## 20-6 Describe the selection of a specific price.

A pricing strategy will yield a certain price or range of prices. Pricing strategies should help in setting a final price. If they are to do so, marketers must establish pricing objectives, have considerable knowledge about target market customers, and determine demand, price elasticity, costs, and competitive factors. Additionally, the way marketers use pricing in the marketing mix will affect the final price. Pricing remains a flexible and convenient way to adjust the marketing mix.

---

**Go to www.cengagebrain.com for resources to help you master the content in this chapter as well as materials that will expand your marketing knowledge!**

## Important Terms

| | | | |
|---|---|---|---|
| pricing objectives  628 | secondary-market | bait pricing  640 | customary pricing  643 |
| cost-based pricing  633 | pricing  637 | price lining  640 | prestige pricing  643 |
| cost-plus pricing  633 | periodic discounting  637 | psychological pricing  640 | professional pricing  643 |
| markup pricing  634 | random discounting  637 | reference pricing  641 | price leaders  644 |
| demand-based pricing  634 | price skimming  638 | bundle pricing  641 | special-event pricing  644 |
| competition-based | penetration pricing  638 | multiple-unit pricing  641 | comparison |
| pricing  636 | product-line pricing  639 | everyday low prices | discounting  644 |
| differential pricing  637 | captive pricing  639 | (EDLP)  642 | |
| negotiated pricing  637 | premium pricing  640 | odd-even pricing  642 | |

## Discussion and Review Questions

1. Identify the six stages in the process of establishing prices.
2. How does a return on an investment pricing objective differ from an objective of increasing market share?
3. Why must marketing objectives and pricing objectives be considered when making pricing decisions?
4. Why should a marketer be aware of competitors' prices?
5. What are the benefits of cost-based pricing?
6. Under what conditions is cost-plus pricing most appropriate?
7. A retailer purchases a can of soup for 24 cents and sells it for 36 cents. Calculate the markup as a percentage of cost and as a percentage of selling price.
8. What is differential pricing? In what ways can it be achieved?
9. For what types of products would price skimming be most appropriate? For what types of products would penetration pricing be more effective?
10. Describe bundle pricing, and give three examples using different industries.
11. What are the advantages and disadvantages of using everyday low prices?
12. Why do customers associate price with quality? When should prestige pricing be used?
13. Are price leaders a realistic approach to pricing? Explain your answer.

# Video Case 20.1

## Warby Parker Puts Affordable Eyewear in Focus

Bringing down the high price of fashion eyeglasses was the goal that four friends set out to achieve when they founded Warby Parker in 2010. The business idea grew out of co-founder Dave Gilboa's personal experience. When he was a graduate student, he lost his glasses while hiking and was so outraged by the high price of replacing them that he squinted for months rather than buy new glasses. Eyeglasses are made from wire, plastic, screws, and glass, yet the retail price is often many times the actual cost of the materials, yielding a hefty profit margin. Adding a designer logo to a pair of frames pushes the final price even higher. Talking with friends, Gilboa learned he wasn't the only person unhappy about having to spend a lot for eyeglasses. So Gilboa teamed up with Neil Blumenthal, Andy Hunt, and Jeff Raider to create a business plan for a new kind of eyewear company,

selling quality eyeglasses directly to customers with a price tag below $100 per pair.

Direct marketing keeps Warby Parker's distribution costs low and avoids the kind of intermediary markups that typically increase the final price. In-house designers develop all frame styles, which means no licensing fees for the right to use famous fashion logos. Customers benefit because Warby Parker passes the savings along in the form of affordable price tags for quality eyewear. The company also has a social conscience: It donates a pair of glasses to someone in need for every pair it sells.

Customers in Warby Parker's target market recognize the value of paying less for glasses by changing their buying behavior. The customer can select up to five eyeglass frames from online inventory and have these choices delivered for a five-day free at-home trial before purchasing a pair. Warby Parker pays the postage both ways, so the customer risks nothing. Frame prices begin at $95 per pair, although optional extras such as progressive lenses will increase the final price. After deciding on a frame, the customer submits a prescription, clicks to finalize the order, and receives new glasses by mail within one to two weeks.

Originally, Warby Parker marketed its eyeglasses only online. Initial sales were so brisk that the startup surpassed its first-year sales objectives by the end of the first three weeks. Six months after its online debut, Warby Parker had already sold 85,000 pairs—and donated an equal amount to people in need. But not everything is online. Customers have always been able to visit the company's New York City headquarters, see frames in person, and try them on before ordering. This proved so popular that after a few years, the co-founders decided to open small showrooms in large cities so more customers could try on frames and consult with staff before ordering.

Now Warby Parker has embarked on an ambitious strategy of opening its own stores in cities where the company's database shows high concentrations of customers. Some of these stores are equipped for optical examinations. Some include photo kiosks so customers can snap fun photos of themselves wearing different frames and post to social media for advice from friends. The photos don't just help customers make buying decisions—they keep the Warby Parker brand in the public eye and help the firm stay in touch with customers who opt to receive communications. What's next for Warby Parker as it shakes up the eyewear industry with direct marketing, retail stores, low prices, fun styles, and social responsibility?[15]

### Questions for Discussion

1. Based on your knowledge of pricing concepts, why does Warby Parker stress that the price tag for frames starts at $95?
2. Given Warby Parker's original idea of selling online to minimize distribution costs and keep prices low, do you agree with its more recent decision to open dozens of stores? Explain your answer.
3. Should Warby Parker charge more for frames purchased in stores than for frames purchased online, to offset the higher cost of rent and store employees? Why or why not?

# Case 20.2

## Under Armour Uses Pricing in the Race for Market Share

Baltimore–based Under Armour is on a mission "to make all athletes better through passion, design, and the relentless pursuit of innovation." Founded by Kevin Plank in 1995, the company made its name with a unique moisture-wicking shirt to keep athletes dry and comfortable during games and workouts. Over the years, it has introduced a wide variety of innovative clothing, accessories, and footwear for specific sports and to support athletic performance in challenging situations, such as in hot, cold, or wet weather conditions. It has raised its public profile through marketing efforts such as outfitting college football teams and U.S. Olympic teams, sponsoring the Under Armour All-American football game, and endorsement deals with outstanding athletes like Olympic medalists Michael Phelps and Lindsey Vonn.

With nearly $5 billion in annual sales, Under Armour is growing quickly and setting its long-term sights on catching up with industry giants such as Nike. Despite high brand awareness, Under Armour has limited financial resources that must be stretched across every product line, whereas Nike and other major competitors possess the financial strength to introduce and promote a multitude of products in multiple categories at one time. Therefore, Kevin Plank, who founded the firm and also serves as CEO, is focusing Under Armour's resources on the specific, high-opportunity markets.

Dean bertoncelj/Shutterstock.com

Since introducing its first athletic shoes in 2006, the company has increased shoe sales at double-digit rates year after year as annual sales of these products surpass $700 million. Under Armour is focused on taking market share from rivals in certain specialized segments. In the market for cleats, Under Armour rocketed to second place only months after launching its first line of football cleats and baseball cleats. The popularity of the firm's NBA-superstar endorser, Stephen Curry, is boosting brand awareness and supercharging purchases of Under Armour's basketball shoes.

Running shoes are a $7 billion market—and Plank sees product-line pricing as the key to growing Under Armour's shoe revenues in this segment. The company initially set premium prices starting at $100 per pair, based on each athletic shoe's innovative features and benefits. But it can't significantly increase market share in running shoes without offering a range of products at a range of prices for buyers with different needs and motivations.

So although Under Armour will continue to offer higher-priced running shoes, it is also introducing new running shoes priced between $70 and $100 per pair. This will attract new customers and lay the foundation for repeat purchasing, because customers who are satisfied with their experience will be more likely to buy from Under Armour again. Just as important, these customers may decide to trade up to more expensive footwear the next time they buy from Under Armour. Thanks to this pricing strategy, Under Armour's share is already inching up. However, the race is far from over. The company still holds less than 5 percent of the market for running shoes, whereas market-leader Nike holds a commanding 57 percent market share.

In combination with pricing, Under Armour is relying on innovative product development for growth. Although the company's initial moisture-wicking clothing products were designed for men, it also sees considerable sales and profit opportunity in the market for women's athletic apparel. Looking ahead, it plans to build the women's line into a $1 billion business and, ultimately, generate enough momentum for sales of the company's women's clothing to surpass sales of men's clothing in the future.

To keep the innovations coming, Under Armour holds an annual "Future Show" competition offering cash prizes and contracts to encourage inventors to submit new product ideas. Two years after an inventor won the competition with a unique zipper that athletes can operate with one hand, his invention was incorporated into thousands of Under Armour jackets and outerwear. Under Armour is currently testing another winner's invention, LED lights embedded in shirts, jackets, and backpacks so athletes can see and be seen in the dark as they jog, compete, or practice. Although the technology might result in prices as high as $250 per product, Under Armour believes sports-minded customers will see the value in these cutting-edge products.[16]

### Questions for Discussion

1. Of the various pricing objectives, which one does Under Armour appear to be pursuing in its marketing of running shoes, and why?
2. When Under Armour prepares to set the price for a new shirt equipped with LED lights, how much emphasis should it place on its evaluation of competitors' prices?
3. Would you recommend that Under Armour use cost-based pricing, demand-based pricing, or competition-based pricing for a new shirt equipped with LED lights? Explain your answer.

## Strategic Case 8

## To Rent or to Own? That Is the Question

Rent or own? That's the question as U.S. consumers in all income brackets consider whether to plunk down money (or borrow money) to make purchases that carry a high price tag. Ownership allows consumers the freedom to use a possession whenever they wish, and to make their own decisions about personalizing it. Still, the purchase price isn't always the only outlay. Car owners, for example, are responsible for insurance, fuel, maintenance, and repairs.

What are the alternatives for consumers who don't want to empty their wallets or pay ongoing costs month after month? A growing number of consumers—Millennials in particular—are flocking to innovators like Rent the Runway for access to pricey goods by renting as needed, rather than paying to own vehicles, designer fashions, or other expensive items.

### Rent to Wear

Rent the Runway, founded in 2009, is a pioneer in fashion rental, with more than five million customers. From their own experiences, co-founders Jennifer Hyman and Jennifer Fleiss know about the high cost of buying special occasion clothes, only to wear them a few times. They envisioned an e-business with a different approach to dressing up without going broke or going out of style. Customers rent daytime, evening, or bridal fashions from the firm's website or at a Rent the Runway showroom in New York, Chicago, Las Vegas, and Washington, D.C. The cost of renting is much lower than the actual purchase price. For example, a $5,000 Naeem Khan dress rents for $800, including prepaid shipping both ways. Rent the Runway also offers an unlimited subscription service for customers who elect to receive new rentals on a regular basis.

Gwynnie Bee, founded by Christine Hunsicker, caters to plus-size women who want more wardrobe choices with the convenience of home delivery. It offers different subscription plans that allow customers to rent one, two, or up to ten pieces of clothing at a time, for as long as they like. When they want to rent something new, customers return clothing in the firm's prepaid packaging and receive another shipment of rented clothing in short order. Gwynnie Bee's slogan, "Clothing without Commitment," sums up the founder's dedication to providing a wide variety of fashion choices so plus-size women can update their wardrobes without having to buy and own.

## Rent for the Road

Car-sharing services like Zipcar and Turo, both facilitated by smartphone apps, are making it quick and easy for consumers to rent wheels for a short time, when and where they please. A pioneer of car sharing, Zipcar has nearly one million members who pay a fee for the right to rent a car, minivan, or earth-friendly hybrid by the hour. Instead of going to a rental office, members pick up a vehicle from a convenient local parking spot and return it locally.

Turo connects consumers who want to rent a car for a limited time with individual car owners willing to let renters use their cars at prices set by the hour, day, or week. This is a more personal experience, because the car owner meets with the rental customer to turn over the keys and, at the end of the rental period, receives the keys back from the customer. No visits to rental offices, no lengthy contracts to sign, just an app to connect with a car owner, followed by a meeting to transfer keys.

Compared with the rental pricing of traditional car-rental companies, or the price of car ownership, the pricing of vehicles rented through services such as Turo and Zipcar are generally lower. These services even offer exotic vehicles for rent, at higher prices, to consumers who want to treat themselves or who need a special set of wheels for a special occasion. Just as important, these car-sharing services generally include basic car-insurance coverage—another money-saving benefit that renters appreciate.

Despite the popular buzz about car sharing, projections indicate that the majority of consumers will still want to own their own vehicles in the future. One study suggests that by 2021, when worldwide car sales are expected to reach 100 million vehicles, car-sharing will mean the loss of only 550,000 vehicle purchases. Already, an estimated 1.5 million consumers are using car-sharing services in North America. As a result, automakers like General Motors and Ford see new marketing opportunity. They are testing their own car-sharing services to introduce their branded vehicles to renters who may, at some point in the future, choose to buy and own.

## Rent a Gadget

Entrepreneur Aarthi Ramamurthy launched Lumoid as a "try before you buy" rental site for expensive fitness-tracking wristbands, headphones, cameras, and other high-tech gadgets, including drones. The idea is to allow consumers to test the gadget at home or at work for two weeks, to be sure that actual performance meets expectations. Before buying headphones that sell for $399, for example, one renter might want to see whether the product feels comfortable when worn during a long workout. Another renter might want to test the same headphones' volume during an airplane flight. Many popular brands of headphones can be rented for two weeks as part of a three-for-$45 offer, so consumers can alternate various headphones during the trial period. At the end of the trial, consumers simply return the rented gear, with no obligation to buy. However, if they do decide to buy through Lumoid, part or all of the rental fee is applied to the purchase price.[17]

## Questions for Discussion

1. How would you expect seasonal fluctuations in demand to affect a rental company's decisions about pricing rented products such as wedding dresses or convertible cars?

2. In terms of pricing principles, why do rental companies often display the retail price alongside the rental price for products they feature?

3. From a marketing perspective, why do Rent the Runway and other rental companies offer a discount to first-time customers?

4. What elements are consumers likely to consider when evaluating the purchase price of a product they want to own compared with the price of renting that product for a limited time?

# NOTES

[1] Sean Farrell, "Primark Trading Picks Up at Start of 2016," *The Guardian (U.K.)*, February 22, 2016, www.theguardian.com/business/2016/feb/22/primark-trading-picks-up-at-start-of-2016 (accessed February 26, 2016); "Faster, Cheaper Fashion," *The Economist*, September 5, 2015, www.economist.com/news/business/21663221-rapidly-rising-super-cheap-irish-clothes-retailer-prepares-conquer-america-rivals-should (accessed February 26, 2016); Heather Long, "Primark: The Retail Sensation That's Cheaper than H&M," *CNN*, October 23, 2015, http://money.cnn.com/2015/10/23/investing/primark-cheap-clothes-coming-to-us/ (accessed February 26, 2016); Joan Verdon, "European Retailer Primark to Open at American Dream Project," *The Bergen Record (N.J.)*, December 15, 2015, www.northjersey.com/news/business/european-retailer-primark-to-open-at-american-dream-project-1.1501222 (accessed February 26, 2016); Hilary Milnes, "On Social, 'Primania' Looks to Fill Primark's E-commerce Void," *Digiday*, December 22, 2015, http://digiday.com/brands/social-primania-looks-fill-primarks-e-commerce-void/ (accessed February 26, 2016).

[2] Geoffrey Smith, "Sprint's Defense of Market Share Comes at a Price," *Fortune*, May 5, 2015, http://fortune.com/2015/05/05/sprints-defense-of-market-share-comes-at-a-price/ (accessed March 29, 2016).

[3] "The Profit Impact of Market Strategies (PIMS) Overview," The Strategic Planning Institute, http://pimsonline.com/about_pims_db.htm (accessed March 29, 2016).

[4] "20 Outrageously Priced Products, and How to Save on Them," *MSN.com*, September 11, 2015, http://www.msn.com/en-us/money/spendingandborrowing/20-outrageously-priced-products-and-how-to-save-on-them/ss-AAebfaz (accessed March 30, 2016).

[5] Amy Livingston, "Is a Warehouse Store (Costco, Sam's Club, BJ's) Worth It? –Costs, Pros, & Cons," *Money Crashers*, June 10, 2015, http://www.moneycrashers.com/warehouse-store-costco-samsclub-bjs-membership-worth-it/ (accessed March 31, 2016).

[6] Ben Fritz, "Disney Parks Consider Off-Peak Prices," *The Wall Street Journal*, October 4, 2015, http://www.wsj.com/articles/disney-parks-consider-higher-prices-during-busy-times-1443960001 (accessed March 31, 2016).

[7] Jody Tillman, "Demand-Based Pricing; How You Can Pay More (or Less) for Disneyland, Angels, Golf, and More," *The Orange County Register*, June 9, 2015, http://www.ocregister.com/articles/pricing-664948-price-prices.html (accessed March 31, 2016).

[8] "Greyhound Modernizes IT Infrastructure to Provide More Pricing Options for Consumers and Optimize Operations," Greyhound, press release, December 9, 2014, https://www.greyhound.com/en/media/2014/12-09-2014 (accessed March 31, 2016).

[9] Bill Snyder, "Report Analyzes Amazon's Dynamic Pricing Strategy," *CIO*, January 16, 2015, http://www.cio.com/article/2870961/consumer-technology/report-analyzes-amazons-dynamic-pricing-strategy.html (accessed March 31, 2016).

[10] Gregory Korte, "White House Report Urges Scrutiny of Pricing Practices," *USA Today*, February 5, 2015, http://www.usatoday.com/story/news/politics/2015/02/05/white-house-report-on-big-data-and-differential-pricing/22919915/ (accessed March 31, 2016).

[11] Joan Lindsay Mulliken and Ross D. Petty, "Marketing Tactics Discouraging Price Search: Deception and Competition," *Journal of Business Research* 64, 1 (2011): 67–73, www.sciencedirect.com/science/article/pii/S0148296309002641 (accessed March 31, 2016).

[12] Martin Spann, Marc Fischer, and Gerard J. Tillis, "Skimming or Penetration? Strategic Dynamic Pricing for New Products," *Marketing Science*, 34, 2 (2015): 235–249; "New USC Marshall Study Challenges Marketing Strategy Assumptions," USC Marshall School of Business news release, March 15, 2015, https://www.marshall.usc.edu/news/releases/2015/new-usc-marshall-study-challenges-marketing-strategy-assumptions (accessed March 31, 2016).

[13] Hilary Osborne, "Parents Buying Tablets for Children Urged to Look Out for Hidden Costs," *The Guardian*, December 25, 2013, www.theguardian.com/technology/2013/dec/25/parents-tablets-children-hidden-costs (accessed March 31, 2016).

[14] Stephanie Clifford and Catherine Rampell, "Sometimes, We Want Prices to Fool Us," *The New York Times*, April 14, 2013, www.nytimes.com/2013/04/14/business/for-penney-a-tough-lesson-in-shopper-psychology.html (accessed March 31, 2016).

[15] Richard Benson, "Warby Parker Is Bringing Affordable Eyewear to the Developing World," *Wired UK*, June 1, 2016, www.wired.co.uk/article/warby-parker-glasses-profit-purpose; Farnoosh Torabi, "Warby Parker: How to Limit Risk When You Try to Double Your Size," *CNBC*, May 3, 2016, www.cnbc.com/2016/05/03/warby-parker-how-to-limit-risk-when-you-try-to-double-your-size.html; Ginia Bellafante, "At Warby Parker, a Sense of Exclusion in a Low Price," *The New York Times*, May 20, 2016, www.nytimes.com/2016/05/22/nyregion/at-warby-parker-a-sense-of-exclusion-in-a-low-price.html; Courtney Rubin, "Smile! Photo Booths Prove You're a Happy Customer," *The New York Times*, October 6, 2015, www.nytimes.com/2015/10/08/fashion/photo-boots-warby-parker-topshop.html; *Innovation Agents: Dave Gilboa, co-founder, Warby Parker*, www.youtube.com/watch?v=jJSKGUPou8w; www.warbyparker.com.

[16] Elaine Low, "Can Stephen Curry Be Under Armour's Michael Jordan?" *Investor's Business Daily*, February 22, 2016, www.investors.com/news/can-stephen-curry-be-under-armours-michael-jordan/ (accessed February 24, 2016); Kevin McCoy, "Under Armour Soars 23% with Stephen Curry," *USA Today*, January 29, 2016, www.usatoday.com/story/money/2016/01/28/under-armour-soars-stephen-curry/79456454/ (accessed February 24, 2016); Sarah Meehan, "Year in Review: Under Armour Stock Price Balloons on New Products, Growth Potential," *Baltimore Business Journal*, December 19, 2013, www.bizjournals.com/baltimore; Sarah Meehan, "For Under Armour, Lower Price Points Lead to Stronger Shoe Sales," *Baltimore Business Journal*, October 29, 2013, www.bizjournals.com/baltimore; Lorraine Mirabella, "Under Armour Profit Up 27 Percent in Third Quarter," *Baltimore Sun*, October 24, 2013, www.baltimoresun.com; www.underarmour.com.

[17] Kerry Hannon, "Rent the Jet, or Island," *The New York Times*, February 14, 2016, p. F2; Lauren A. White, "The Sharing Economy's New Frontier: Everyday Clothing Rental," *CBS News*, January 20, 2016, www.cbsnews.com/news/sharing-economy-gwynnie-bee-everyday-plus-size-clothing-rental/ (accessed February 29, 2016); Phil LeBeau, "Car-Sharing Impact Will Be Limited, Despite a Jump in Shared Mobility Start-Ups, BCG Says," *CNBC*, February 23, 2016, www.cnbc.com/2016/02/23/

car-sharing-impact-will-be-limited-despite-a-jump-in-shared-mobility-start-ups-bcg-says. html (accessed February 29, 2016); Rick Broida, "Rent Private Cars for Cheap with Turo," *CNet*, February 22, 2016, www.cnet.com/how-to/rent-private-cars-for-cheap-with-turo (accessed February 29, 2016); Zoe Henry, "How Rent the Runway Plans to Own Your Closet,"

*Inc.*, November 13, 2015, www.inc.com/zoe-henry/rent-the-runway-2015-company-of-the-year-nominee.html (accessed February 29, 2016); Drew Casey, "Lumoid Pioneers a 'Try Before You Buy' Model of Buying Gadgets," *CNBC*, December 20, 2015, www .cnbc.com/2015/12/17/lumoid-pioneers-a-try-before-you-buy-model-of-buying-gadgets

.html (accessed February 29, 2016); Benny Evangelista, "As Drones Take off, S.F. Startup Lumoid Teaches Flight School," *San Francisco Chronicle*, October 30, 2015, www.sfchronicle. com/business/article/As-drones-take-off-S-F-startup-Lumoid-teaches-6601990.php (accessed February 29, 2016).

## Feature Notes

[a] Gareth May, "Sorry, We Don't Take Money: The Restaurants Offering New Ways to Pay," *The Telegraph (U.K.)*, August 17, 2015, www.telegraph.co.uk/foodanddrink/restaurants/11807524/Sorry-we-dont-take-money-the-restaurants-offering-new-ways-to-pay.html (accessed February 24, 2016); Emily Heward, "Ziferblat: From Poetry Gathering to Global Phenomenon," *Manchester Evening News (U.K.)*, February 13, 2015, www .manchestereveningnews.co.uk/whats-on/food-drink-news/ziferblats-russian-founder-visits-new-8644919 (accessed February 24, 2016);

Henry Meyer and Benjamin D. Katz, "At Ziferblat, It's Pay by the Minute," *Bloomberg*, May 14, 2015, www.bloomberg.com/news/articles/2015-05-14/ziferblat-moscow-pay-by-the-minute-cafe-opens-franchises-abroad (accessed February 24, 2016).

[b] Diana Olick, "Why One Builder Thinks Cheaper Homes Work," *CNBC*, January 25, 2016, www.cnbc.com/2016/01/25/why-one-builder-thinks-cheaper-homes-work.html (accessed February 24, 2016); Prashant Gopal, "Builders' New Niche Has Smaller Homes with Smaller Prices," *Bloomberg News*, December 30,

2015, www.philly.com/philly/news/20151230_Builders__new_niche_has_smaller_homes_with_smaller_prices.html (accessed February 24, 2016); Carole Hawkins, "D.R. Horton Cornering Market on Entry-Level Buyers with Express Homes," *Jacksonville Daily Record*, August 20, 2015, www.jaxdailyrecord.com/showstory. php?Story_id=545989 (accessed February 24, 2016); Brad Hunter, "First-Time Buyers Are Coming Back! (Gradually...)," *Builder Online*, www.builderonline.com/building/first-time-buyers-are-coming-back-gradually_o (accessed February 24, 2016).

# glossary

**accessory equipment** Equipment that does not become part of the final physical product but is used in production or office activities

**advertising** Paid nonpersonal communication about an organization and its products transmitted to a target audience through mass media

**advertising appropriation** The advertising budget for a specific time period

**advertising campaign** The creation and execution of a series of advertisements to communicate with a particular target audience

**advertising platform** Basic issues or selling points to be included in an advertising campaign

**advocacy advertising** Advertising that promotes a company's position on a public issue

**aesthetic modifications** Changes relating to the sensory appeal of a product

**agents** Intermediaries that represent either buyers or sellers on a permanent basis

**aided recall test** A posttest that asks respondents to identify recent ads and provides clues to jog their memories

**allowance** A concession in price to achieve a desired goal

**approach** The manner in which a salesperson contacts a potential customer

**arbitrary approach** Budgeting for an advertising campaign as specified by a high-level executive in the firm

**artwork** An advertisement's illustrations and layout

**Asia-Pacific Economic Cooperation (APEC)** An alliance that promotes open trade and economic and technical cooperation among member nations throughout the world

**Association of Southeast Asian Nations (ASEAN)** An alliance that promotes trade and economic integration among member nations in Southeast Asia

**atmospherics** The physical elements in a store's design that appeal to consumers' emotions and encourage buying

**attitude** An individual's enduring evaluation of feelings about and behavioral tendencies toward an object or idea

**attitude scale** A means of measuring consumer attitudes by gauging the intensity of individuals' reactions to adjectives, phrases, or sentences about an object

**automatic vending** The use of machines to dispense products

**average fixed cost** The fixed cost per unit produced

**average total cost** The sum of the average fixed cost and the average variable cost

**average variable cost** The variable cost per unit produced

**B2B e-commerce sites** Online marketplaces where business buyers and sellers from around the world can exchange information, goods, services, ideas, and payments

**bait pricing** Pricing an item in a product line low with the intention of selling a higher-priced item in the line

**balance of trade** The difference in value between a nation's exports and its imports

**barter** The trading of products

**base-point pricing** Geographic pricing that combines factory price and freight charges from the base point nearest the buyer

**benefit segmentation** The division of a market according to benefits that consumers want from the product

**Better Business Bureau (BBB)** A system of nongovernmental, independent, local regulatory agencies supported by local businesses that helps settle problems between customers and specific business firms

**big data** Massive data files that can be obtained from both structured and unstructured databases

**blogs** Web-based journals (short for "weblogs") in which writers editorialize and interact with other Internet users

**brand** A name, term, design, symbol, or other feature that identifies one seller's product as distinct from those of other sellers

**brand competitors** Firms that market products with similar features and benefits to the same customers at similar prices

**brand equity** The marketing and financial value associated with a brand's strength in a market

**brand extension** An organization uses one of its existing brands to brand a new product in a different product category

**brand insistence** The degree of brand loyalty in which a customer strongly prefers a specific brand and will accept no substitute

**brand licensing** An agreement whereby a company permits another organization to use its brand on other products for a licensing fee

**brand loyalty** A customer's favorable attitude toward a specific brand

**brand manager** The person responsible for a single brand

**brand mark** The part of a brand that is not made up of words, such as a symbol or design

**brand name** The part of a brand that can be spoken, including letters, words, and numbers

**brand preference** The degree of brand loyalty in which a customer prefers one brand over competitive offerings

**brand recognition** The degree of brand loyalty in which a customer is aware that a brand exists and views the brand as an alternative purchase if their preferred brand is unavailable

**breakdown approach** Measuring company sales potential based on a general economic forecast for a specific period and the market potential derived from it

**break even point** The point at which the costs of producing a product equal the revenue made from selling the product

654

**brokers** Intermediaries that bring buyers and sellers together temporarily

**buildup approach** Measuring company sales potential by estimating how much of a product a potential buyer in a specific geographic area will purchase in a given period, multiplying the estimate by the number of potential buyers, and adding the totals of all the geographic areas considered

**bundle pricing** Packaging together two or more complementary products and selling them at a single price

**business analysis** Evaluating the potential impact of a product idea on the firm's sales, costs, and profits

**business (organizational) buying behavior** The purchase behavior of producers, government units, institutions, and resellers

**business cycle** A pattern of economic fluctuations that has four stages: prosperity, recession, depression, and recovery

**business market** Individuals, organizations, or groups that purchase a specific kind of product for resale, direct use in producing other products, or use in general daily operations

**business products** Products bought to use in a firm's operations, to resell, or to make other products

**business services** Intangible products that many organizations use in their operations

**buy-back allowance** A sum of money given to a reseller for each unit bought after an initial promotion deal is over

**buying allowance** A temporary price reduction to resellers for purchasing specified quantities of a product

**buying behavior** The decision processes and actions of people involved in buying and using products

**buying center** The people within an organization who make business purchase decisions

**buying power** Resources, such as money, goods, and services, that can be traded in an exchange

**buzz marketing** An attempt to incite publicity and public excitement surrounding a product through a creative event

**captioned photograph** A photograph with a brief description of its contents

**captive pricing** Pricing the basic product in a product line low, while pricing related items higher

**cash-and-carry wholesalers** Limited-service wholesalers whose customers pay cash and furnish transportation

**cash discount** A price reduction given to buyers for prompt payment or cash payment

**catalog marketing** A type of marketing in which an organization provides a catalog from which customers make selections and place orders by mail, telephone, or the Internet

**category killer** A very large specialty store that concentrates on a major product category and competes on the basis of low prices and product availability

**category management** A retail strategy of managing groups of similar, often substitutable, products produced by different manufacturers

**cause-related marketing** The practice of linking products to a particular social cause on an ongoing or short-term basis

**centralized organization** A structure in which top-level managers delegate little authority to lower levels

**cents-off offers** Promotions that allow buyers to pay less than the regular price to encourage purchase

**channel capacity** The limit on the volume of information a communication channel can handle effectively

**channel captain** The dominant leader of a marketing channel or a supply channel

**channel power** The ability of one channel member to influence another member's goal achievement

**client-based relationships** Interactions that result in satisfied customers who use a service repeatedly over time

**client publics** Direct consumers of a product of a nonprofit organization

**closing** The stage in the personal selling process when the salesperson asks the prospect to buy the product

**co-branding** Using two or more brands on one product

**codes of conduct** Formalized rules and standards that describe what the company expects of its employees

**coding process** Converting meaning into a series of signs or symbols

**cognitive dissonance** A buyer's doubts shortly after a purchase about whether the decision was the right one

**combination compensation plan** Paying salespeople a fixed salary plus a commission based on sales volume

**commercialization** Refining and finalizing plans and budgets for full-scale manufacturing and marketing of a product

**commission merchants** Agents that receive goods on consignment from local sellers and negotiate sales in large, central markets

**communication** A sharing of meaning through the transmission of information

**communications channel** The medium of transmission that carries the coded message from the source to the receiver

**community shopping center** A type of shopping center with one or two department stores, some specialty stores, and convenience stores

**company sales potential** The maximum percentage of market potential that an individual firm within an industry can expect to obtain for a specific product

**comparative advertising** Compares the sponsored brand with one or more identified brands on the basis of one or more product characteristics

**comparison discounting** Setting a price at a specific level and comparing it with a higher price

**competition** Other organizations that market products that are similar to or can be substituted for a marketer's products in the same geographic area

**competition-based pricing** Pricing influenced primarily by competitors' prices

**competition-matching approach** Determining an advertising budget by trying to match competitors' advertising outlays

**competitive advantage** The result of a company matching a core competency to opportunities it has discovered in the marketplace

**competitive advertising** Tries to stimulate demand for a specific brand by promoting its features, uses, and advantages relative to competing brands

**component parts** Items that become part of the physical product and are either finished items ready for assembly or items that need little processing before assembly

**concentrated targeting strategy** A market segmentation strategy in which an organization targets a single market segment using one marketing mix

**concept testing** Seeking a sample of potential buyers' responses to a product idea

**conclusive research** Research designed to verify insights through objective procedures and to help marketers in making decisions

**consideration set** A group of brands within a product category that a buyer views as alternatives for possible purchase

**consistency of quality** The degree to which a product has the same level of quality over time

**consumer buying behavior** The decision processes and purchasing activities of people who purchase products for personal or household use and not for business purposes

**consumer buying decision process** A five-stage purchase decision process that includes problem recognition, information search, evaluation of alternatives, purchase, and postpurchase evaluation

**consumer contests** Sales promotion methods in which individuals compete for prizes based on their analytical or creative skills

**consumer games** Sales promotion methods in which individuals compete for prizes based primarily on chance

**consumer jury** A panel of a product's existing or potential buyers who pretest ads

**consumer market** Purchasers and household members who intend to consume or benefit from the purchased products and do not buy products to make profits

**consumer misbehavior** Behavior that violates generally accepted norms of a particular society

**consumer products** Products purchased to satisfy personal and family needs

**consumer sales promotion methods** Sales promotion techniques that encourage consumers to patronize specific stores or try particular products

**consumer socialization** The process through which a person acquires the knowledge and skills to function as a consumer

**consumer sweepstakes** A sales promotion in which entrants submit their names for inclusion in a drawing for prizes

**consumerism** Organized efforts by individuals, groups, and organizations to protect consumers' rights

**contract manufacturing** The practice of hiring a foreign firm to produce a designated volume of the domestic firm's product or a component of it to specification; the final product carries the domestic firm's name

**convenience products** Relatively inexpensive, frequently purchased items for which buyers exert minimal purchasing effort

**convenience store** A small self-service store that is open long hours and carries a narrow assortment of products, usually convenience items

**cooperative advertising** An arrangement in which a manufacturer agrees to pay a certain amount of a retailer's media costs for advertising the manufacturer's products

**copy** The verbal portion of advertisements

**core competencies** Things a company does extremely well, which sometimes give it an advantage over its competition

**corporate strategy** A strategy that determines the means for utilizing resources in the various functional areas to reach the organization's goals

**cost-based pricing** Adding a dollar amount or percentage to the cost of the product

**cost comparison indicator** A means of comparing the costs of advertising vehicles in a specific medium in relation to the number of people reached

**cost-plus pricing** Adding a specified dollar amount or percentage to the seller's cost

**coupons** Written price reductions used to encourage consumers to buy a specific product

**credence qualities** Attributes that customers may be unable to evaluate even after purchasing and consuming a service

**crowdsourcing** Combines the words *crowd* and *outsourcing* and calls for taking tasks usually performed by a marketer or researcher and outsourcing them to a crowd, or potential market, through an open call

**cultural relativism** The concept that morality varies from one culture to another and that business practices are therefore differentially defined as right or wrong by particular cultures

**culture** The accumulation of values, knowledge, beliefs, customs, objects, and concepts that a society uses to cope with its environment and passes on to future generations

**cumulative discounts** Quantity discounts aggregated over a stated time period

**customary pricing** Pricing on the basis of tradition

**customer advisory boards** Small groups of actual customers who serve as sounding boards for new-product ideas and offer insights into their feelings and attitudes toward a firm's products and other elements of its marketing strategy

**customer contact** The level of interaction between provider and customer needed to deliver the service

**customer forecasting survey** A survey of customers regarding the types and quantities of products they intend to buy during a specific period

**customer lifetime value** A key measurement that forecasts a customer's lifetime economic contribution based on continued relationship marketing efforts

**customer relationship management (CRM)** Using information about customers to create marketing strategies that develop and sustain desirable customer relationships

**customer services** Human or mechanical efforts or activities that add value to a product

**customers** The purchasers of organizations' products; the focal point of all marketing activities

**cycle analysis** An analysis of sales figures for a 3- to 5-year period to ascertain whether sales fluctuate in a consistent, periodic manner

**cycle time** The time needed to complete a process

**database** A collection of information arranged for easy access and retrieval

**dealer listings** Advertisements that promote a product and identify the names of participating retailers that sell the product

**dealer loader** A gift, often part of a display, given to a retailer that purchases a specified quantity of merchandise

**decentralized organization** A structure in which decision-making authority is delegated as far down the chain of command as possible

**deceptive pricing** The use of false or misleading statements or practices to persuade buyers that a product is a better deal than it really is

**decline stage** The stage of a product's life cycle when sales fall rapidly

**decoding process** Converting signs or symbols into concepts and ideas

**Delphi technique** A procedure in which experts create initial forecasts, submit them to the company for averaging, and then refine the forecasts

**demand-based pricing** Pricing based on the level of demand for the product

**demand curve** A graph of the quantity of products expected to be sold at various prices if other factors remain constant

**demonstrations** Sales promotion methods a manufacturer uses temporarily to encourage trial use and purchase of a product or to show how a product works

**department stores** Large retail organizations characterized by a wide product mix and organized into separate departments to facilitate marketing efforts and internal management

**depression** A stage of the business cycle when unemployment is extremely high, wages are very low, total disposable income is at a minimum, and consumers lack confidence in the economy

**depth of product mix** The average number of different products offered in each product line

**derived demand** Demand for business products that stems from demand for consumer products

**descriptive research** Research conducted to clarify the characteristics of certain phenomena to solve a particular problem

**differential pricing** Charging different prices to different buyers for the same quality and quantity of product

**differentiated targeting strategy** A strategy in which an organization targets two or more segments by developing a marketing mix for each segment

**digital distribution** Delivering content through the Internet to a computer or other device

**digital marketing** Uses all digital media, including the Internet and mobile and interactive channels, to develop communication and exchanges with customers

**digital media** Electronic media that function using digital codes; when we refer to digital media, we are referring to media available via computers, cellular phones, smartphones, and other digital devices that have been released in recent years

**direct marketing** The use of the telephone, Internet, and nonpersonal media to introduce products to customers, who can then purchase them via mail, telephone, or the Internet

**direct ownership** A situation in which a company owns subsidiaries or other facilities overseas

**direct-response marketing** A type of marketing in which a retailer advertises a product and makes it available through mail or telephone orders

**direct selling** Marketing products to ultimate consumers through face-to-face sales presentations at home or in the workplace

**discount stores** Self-service, general-merchandise stores that offer brand-name and private-brand products at low prices

**discretionary income** Disposable income available for spending and saving after an individual has purchased the basic necessities of food, clothing, and shelter

**disposable income** After-tax income

**distribution** The decisions and activities that make products available to customers when and where they want to purchase them

**disruptive innovation** Identifies old technologies that can be exploited in new ways or develops new business models to give customers more than they've come to expect from current products in a specific market

**distribution centers** Large, centralized warehouses that focus on moving rather than storing goods

**drop shippers** Limited-service wholesalers that take title to goods and negotiate sales but never actually take possession of products

**dumping** Selling products at unfairly low prices

**early adopters** People who adopt new products early, choose new products carefully, and are viewed as "the people to check with" by later adopters

**early majority** Individuals who adopt a new product just prior to the average person

**electronic data interchange (EDI)** A computerized means of integrating order processing with production, inventory, accounting, and transportation

**electronic marketing (e-marketing)** The strategic process of distributing, promoting, and pricing products, and discovering the desires of customers using digital media and digital marketing

**embargo** A government's suspension of trade in a particular product or with a given country

**environmental analysis** The process of assessing and interpreting the information gathered through environmental scanning

**environmental scanning** The process of collecting information about forces in the marketing environment

**ethical issue** An identifiable problem, situation, or opportunity requiring a choice among several actions that must be evaluated as right or wrong, ethical or unethical

**European Union (EU)** An alliance that promotes trade among its member countries in Europe

**evaluative criteria** Objective and subjective product characteristics that are important to a buyer

**everyday low prices (EDLP)** Pricing products low on a consistent basis

**exchange controls** Government restrictions on the amount of a particular currency that can be bought or sold

**exchanges** The provision or transfer of goods, services, or ideas in return for something of value

**exclusive dealing** A situation in which a manufacturer forbids an intermediary from carrying products of competing manufacturers

**exclusive distribution** Using a single outlet in a fairly large geographic area to distribute a product

**executive judgment** A sales forecasting method based on the intuition of one or more executives

**experience qualities** Attributes that can be assessed only during purchase and consumption of a service

**experimental research** Research that allows marketers to make causal inferences about relationships

**expert forecasting survey** Sales forecasts prepared by experts outside the firm, such as economists, management consultants, advertising executives, or college professors

**exploratory research** Research conducted to gather more information about a problem or to make a tentative hypothesis more specific

**exporting** The sale of products to foreign markets

**extended decision making** A consumer decision-making process employed when purchasing unfamiliar, expensive, or infrequently bought products

**external reference price** A comparison price provided by others

**external search** An information search in which buyers seek information from sources other than their memories

**family branding** Branding all of a firm's products with the same name or part of the name

**family packaging** Using similar packaging for all of a firm's products or packaging that has one common design element

**feature article** A manuscript of up to 3,000 words prepared for a specific publication

**Federal Trade Commission (FTC)** An agency that regulates a variety of business practices and curbs false advertising, misleading pricing, and deceptive packaging and labeling

**feedback** The receiver's response to a decoded message

**first-mover advantage** The ability of an innovative company to achieve long-term competitive advantages by being the first to offer a certain product in the marketplace

**fixed costs** Costs that do not vary with changes in the number of units produced or sold

**F.O.B. destination** A price indicating the producer is absorbing shipping costs

**F.O.B. factory** The price of merchandise at the factory before shipment

**focus group** An interview that is often conducted informally, without a structured questionnaire, in small groups of 8 to 12 people, to observe interaction when members are exposed to an idea or a concept

**franchising** An arrangement in which a supplier (franchiser) grants a dealer (franchisee) the right to sell products in exchange for some type of consideration

**free merchandise** A manufacturer's reward given to resellers that purchase a stated quantity of products

**free samples** Samples of a product given out to encourage trial and purchase

**freight absorption pricing** Absorption of all or part of actual freight costs by the seller

**freight forwarders** Organizations that consolidate shipments from several firms into efficient lot sizes

**full-service wholesalers** Merchant wholesalers that perform the widest range of wholesaling functions

**functional modifications** Changes affecting a product's versatility, effectiveness, convenience, or safety

**General Agreement on Tariffs and Trade (GATT)** An agreement among nations to reduce worldwide tariffs and increase international trade

**general-merchandise retailer** A retail establishment that offers a variety of product lines that are stocked in considerable depth

**general-merchandise wholesalers** Full-service wholesalers with a wide product mix but limited depth within product lines

**general publics** Indirect consumers of a product of a nonprofit organization

**generic brand** A brand indicating only the product category

**generic competitors** Firms that provide very different products that solve the same problem or satisfy the same basic customer need

**geodemographic segmentation** A method of market segmentation that clusters people in zip code areas and smaller neighborhood units based on lifestyle and demographic information

**geographic pricing** Reductions for transportation and other costs related to the physical distance between buyer and seller

**globalization** The development of marketing strategies that treat the entire world (or its major regions) as a single entity

**good** A tangible physical entity

**government markets** Federal, state, county, or local governments that buy goods and services to support their internal operations and provide products to their constituencies

**green marketing** A strategic process involving stakeholder assessment to create meaningful long-term relationships with customers while maintaining, supporting, and enhancing the natural environment

**gross domestic product (GDP)** The market value of a nation's total output of goods and services for a given period; an overall measure of economic standing

**growth stage** The product life-cycle stage when sales rise rapidly, profits reach a peak, and then they start to decline

**heterogeneity** Variation in quality

**heterogeneous market** A market made up of individuals or organizations with diverse needs for products in a specific product class

**homesourcing** A practice whereby customer contact jobs are outsourced into workers' homes

**homogeneous market** A market in which a large proportion of customers have similar needs for a product

**horizontal channel integration** Combining organizations at the same level of operation under one management

**hypermarkets** Stores that combine supermarket and discount store shopping in one location

**hypothesis** An informed guess or assumption about a certain problem or set of circumstances

**idea** A concept, philosophy, image, or issue

**idea generation** Seeking product ideas to achieve organizational objectives

**illustrations** Photos, drawings, graphs, charts, and tables used to spark audience interest in an advertisement

**import tariff** A duty levied by a nation on goods bought outside its borders and brought into the country

**importing** The purchase of products from a foreign source

**impulse buying** An unplanned buying behavior resulting from a powerful urge to buy something immediately

**income** For an individual, the amount of money received through wages, rents, investments, pensions, and subsidy payments for a given period

**individual branding** A branding strategy in which each product is given a different name

**industrial distributor** An independent business organization that takes title to industrial products and carries inventories

**inelastic demand** Demand that is not significantly altered by a price increase or decrease

**information inputs** Sensations received through sight, taste, hearing, smell, and touch

**in-home (door-to-door) interview** A personal interview that takes place in the respondent's home

**innovators** First adopters of new products

**inseparability** The quality of being produced and consumed at the same time

**installations** Facilities and nonportable major equipment

**institutional advertising** Advertising that promotes organizational images, ideas, and political issues

**institutional markets** Organizations with charitable, educational, community, or other nonbusiness goals

**intangibility** The characteristic that a service is not physical and cannot be perceived by the senses

**integrated marketing communications** Coordination of promotion and other marketing efforts for maximum informational and persuasive impact on customers

**intensive distribution** Using all available outlets to distribute a product

**intermodal transportation** Two or more transportation modes used in combination

**internal reference price** A price developed in the buyer's mind through experience with the product

**internal search** An information search in which buyers search their memories for information about products that might solve their problem

**international marketing** Developing and performing marketing activities across national boundaries

**introduction stage** The initial stage of a product's life cycle; its first appearance in the marketplace, when sales start at zero and profits are negative

**inventory management** Developing and maintaining adequate assortments of products to meet customers' needs

**joint demand** Demand involving the use of two or more items in combination to produce a product

**joint venture** A partnership between a domestic firm and a foreign firm or government

**just-in-time (JIT)** An inventory-management approach in which supplies arrive just when needed for production or resale

**kinesic communication** Communicating through the movement of head, eyes, arms, hands, legs, or torso

**labeling** Providing identifying, promotional, or other information on package labels

**laggards** The last adopters, who distrust new products

**late majority** Skeptics who adopt new products when they feel it is necessary

**late-mover advantage** The ability of later market entrants to achieve long-term competitive advantages by not being the first to offer a certain product in a marketplace

**layout** The physical arrangement of an advertisement's illustration and copy

**learning** Changes in an individual's thought processes and behavior caused by information and experience

**level of involvement** An individual's degree of interest in a product and the importance of the product for that person

**level of quality** The amount of quality a product possesses

**licensing** An alternative to direct investment that requires a licensee to pay commissions or royalties on sales or supplies used in manufacturing

**lifestyle** An individual's pattern of living expressed through activities, interests, and opinions

**lifestyle shopping center** A type of shopping center that is typically open air and features upscale specialty, dining, and entertainment stores

**limited decision making** A consumer decision-making process used when purchasing products occasionally or needing information about an unfamiliar brand in a familiar product category

**limited-line wholesalers** Full-service wholesalers that carry only a few product lines but many products within those lines

**limited-service wholesalers** Merchant wholesalers that provide some services and specialize in a few functions

**line extension** Development of a product that is closely related to existing products in the line but is designed specifically to meet different customer needs

**logistics management** Planning, implementing, and controlling the efficient and effective flow and storage of products and information from the point of origin to consumption to meet customers' needs and wants

**mail-order wholesalers** Limited-service wholesalers that sell products through catalogs

**mail survey** A research method in which respondents answer a questionnaire sent through the mail

**manufacturer brand** A brand initiated by producers to ensure that producers are identified with their products at the point of purchase

**manufacturers' agents** Independent intermediaries that represent two or more sellers and usually offer customers complete product lines

**marginal cost (MC)** The extra cost incurred by producing one more unit of a product

**marginal revenue (MR)** The change in total revenue resulting from the sale of an additional unit of a product

**market** A group of individuals and/or organizations that have needs for products in a product class and have the ability, willingness, and authority to purchase those products

**market density** The number of potential customers within a unit of land area

**market growth/market share matrix** A helpful business tool, based on the philosophy that a product's market growth rate and its market share are important considerations in determining its marketing strategy

**market manager** The person responsible for managing the marketing activities that serve a particular group of customers

**market opportunity** A combination of circumstances and timing that permits an organization to take action to reach a particular target market

**market orientation** An organizationwide commitment to researching and responding to customer needs

**market potential** The total amount of a product that customers will purchase within a specified period at a specific level of industry-wide marketing activity

**market segment** Individuals, groups, or organizations sharing one or more similar characteristics that cause them to have similar product needs

**market segmentation** The process of dividing a total market into groups with relatively similar product needs to design a marketing mix that matches those needs

**market share** The percentage of a market that actually buys a specific product from a particular company

**market test** Making a product available to buyers in one or more test areas and measuring purchases and consumer responses to marketing efforts

**marketing** The process of creating, distributing, promoting, and pricing goods, services, and ideas to facilitate satisfying exchange relationships with customers and to develop and maintain favorable relationships with stakeholders in a dynamic environment

**marketing analytics** Use of and methods to measure and interpret the effectiveness of a firm's marketing activities

**marketing channel** A group of individuals and organizations that direct the flow of products from producers to customers within the supply chain

**marketing citizenship** The adoption of a strategic focus for fulfilling the economic, legal, ethical, and philanthropic social responsibilities expected by stakeholders

**marketing concept** A managerial philosophy that an organization should try to satisfy customers' needs through a coordinated set of activities that also allows the organization to achieve its goals

**marketing cost analysis** Analysis of costs to determine which are associated with specific marketing efforts

**marketing decision support system (MDSS)** Customized computer software that aids marketing managers in decision making

**marketing environment** The competitive, economic, political, legal and regulatory, technological, and sociocultural forces that surround the customer and affect the marketing mix

**marketing ethics** Principles and standards that define acceptable marketing conduct as determined by various stakeholders

**marketing implementation** The process of putting marketing strategies into action

**marketing information system (MIS)** A framework for managing and structuring information gathered regularly from sources inside and outside the organization

**marketing intermediaries** Middlemen that link producers to other intermediaries or ultimate consumers through contractual arrangements or through the purchase and resale of products

**marketing mix** Four marketing activities—product, pricing, distribution, and promotion—that a firm can control to meet the needs of customers within its target market

**marketing objective** A statement of what is to be accomplished through marketing activities

**marketing plan** A written document that specifies the activities to be performed to implement and control the organization's marketing strategies

**marketing research** The systematic design, collection, interpretation, and reporting of information to help marketers solve specific marketing problems or take advantage of marketing opportunities

**marketing strategy** A plan of action for identifying and analyzing a target market and developing a marketing mix to meet the needs of that market

**markup pricing** Adding to the cost of the product a predetermined percentage of that cost

**Maslow's hierarchy of needs** The five levels of needs that humans seek to satisfy, from most to least important

**materials handling** Physical handling of tangible goods, supplies, and resources

**maturity stage** The stage of a product's life cycle when the sales curve peaks and starts to decline, and profits continue to fall

**media plan** A plan that specifies the media vehicles to be used and the schedule for running advertisements

**megacarriers** Freight transportation firms that provide several modes of shipment

**merchandise allowance** A manufacturer's agreement to pay resellers certain amounts of money for providing special promotional efforts, such as setting up and maintaining a display

**merchant wholesalers** Independently owned businesses that take title to goods, assume ownership risks, and buy and resell products to other wholesalers, business customers, or retailers

**micromarketing** An approach to market segmentation in which organizations focus precise marketing efforts on very small geographic markets

**mission statement** A long-term view, or vision, of what the organization wants to become

**missionary salespeople** Support salespeople, usually employed by a manufacturer, who assist the producer's customers in selling to their own customers

**mobile applications** software programs that run on mobile devices and give users access to certain content

**modified rebuy purchase** A new-task purchase that is changed on subsequent orders or when the requirements of a straight rebuy purchase are modified

**money refunds** Sales promotion techniques that offer consumers a specified amount of money when they mail in a proof of purchase, usually for multiple product purchases

**monopolistic competition** A competitive structure in which a firm has many potential competitors and tries to develop a marketing strategy to differentiate its product

**monopoly** A competitive structure in which an organization offers a product that has no close substitutes, making that organization the sole source of supply

**motive** An internal energizing force that directs a person's behavior toward satisfying needs or achieving goals

**MRO supplies** Maintenance, repair, and operating items that facilitate production and operations but do not become part of the finished product

**multichannel distribution** The use of a variety of marketing channels to ensure maximum distribution

**multichannel retailing** Employing multiple distribution channels that complement their brick-and-mortar stores with websites, catalogs, and apps where consumers can research products, read other buyers' reviews, and make actual purchases

**multinational enterprise** A firm that has operations or subsidiaries in many countries

**multiple sourcing** An organization's decision to use several suppliers

**multiple-unit pricing** Packaging together two or more identical products and selling them at a single price

**National Advertising Review Board (NARB)** A self-regulatory unit that considers challenges to issues raised by the National Advertising Division (an arm of the Council of Better Business Bureaus) about an advertisement

**native advertising** Digital advertising that matches the appearance and purpose of the content in which it is embedded

**negotiated pricing** Establishing a final price through bargaining between seller and customer

**neighborhood shopping center** A type of shopping center usually consisting of several small convenience and specialty stores

**new-product development process** A seven-phase process for introducing products: idea generation, screening, concept testing, business analysis, product development, test-marketing, and commercialization

**new-task purchase** An organization's initial purchase of an item to be used to perform a new job or solve a new problem

**news release** A short piece of copy publicizing an event or a product

**noise** Anything that reduces a communication's clarity and accuracy

**noncumulative discounts** One-time price reductions based on the number of units purchased, the dollar value of the order, or the product mix purchased

**nonprice competition** Emphasizing factors other than price to distinguish a product from competing brands

**nonprobability sampling** A sampling technique in which there is no way to calculate the likelihood that a specific element of the population being studied will be chosen

**nonprofit marketing** Marketing activities conducted to achieve some goal other than ordinary business goals such as profit, market share, or return on investment

**nonstore retailing** The selling of products outside the confines of a retail facility

**North American Free Trade Agreement (NAFTA)** An alliance that merges Canada, Mexico, and the United States into a single market

**North American Industry Classification System (NAICS)** An industry classification system that generates comparable statistics among the United States, Canada, and Mexico

**objective-and-task approach** Budgeting for an advertising campaign by first determining its objectives and then calculating the cost of all the tasks needed to attain them

**odd-even pricing** Ending the price with certain numbers to influence buyers' perceptions of the price or product

**off-peak pricing** The practice of reducing prices of services used during slow periods in order to boost demand

**off-price retailers** Stores that buy manufacturers' seconds, overruns, returns, and off-season merchandise for resale to consumers at deep discounts

**offshore outsourcing** The practice of contracting with an organization to perform some or all business functions in a country other than the country in which the product or service will be sold

**offshoring** The practice of moving a business process that was done domestically at the local factory to a foreign country, regardless of whether the production accomplished in the foreign country is performed by the local company (e.g., in a wholly owned subsidiary) or a third party (e.g., subcontractor)

**oligopoly** A competitive structure in which a few sellers control the supply of a large proportion of a product

**online fraud** Any attempt to conduct fraudulent activities online, including deceiving consumers into releasing personal information

**online retailing** Retailing that makes products available to buyers through computer connections

**online survey** A research method in which respondents answer a questionnaire via e-mail or on a website

**on-site computer interview** A variation of the shopping mall intercept interview in which respondents complete a self-administered questionnaire displayed on a computer monitor

**operations management** The total set of managerial activities used by an organization to transform resource inputs into products, services, or both

**opinion leader** A member of an informal group who provides information about a specific topic to other group members

**opportunity cost** The value of the benefit given up by choosing one alternative over another

**order processing** The receipt and transmission of sales order information

**organizational (corporate) culture** A set of values, beliefs, goals, norms, and rituals that members of an organization share

**outsourcing** The practice of contracting noncore operations with an organization that specializes in that operation

**patronage motives** Motives that influence where a person purchases products on a regular basis

**penetration pricing** Setting prices below those of competing brands to penetrate a market and gain a significant market share quickly

**percent-of-sales approach** Budgeting for an advertising campaign by multiplying the firm's past and expected sales by a standard percentage

**perception** The process of selecting, organizing, and interpreting information inputs to produce meaning

**performance standard** An expected level of performance against which actual performance can be compared

**periodic discounting** Temporary reduction of prices on a patterned or systematic basis

**perishability** The inability of unused service capacity to be stored for future use

**personal interview survey** A research method in which participants respond to survey questions face-to-face

**personal selling** Paid personal communication that attempts to inform customers and persuade them to buy products in an exchange situation

**personality** A set of internal traits and distinct behavioral tendencies that result in consistent patterns of behavior in certain situations

**physical distribution** Activities used to move products from producers to consumers and other end users

**pioneer advertising** Advertising that tries to stimulate demand for a product category rather than a specific brand by informing potential buyers about the product

**pioneer promotion** Promotion that informs consumers about a new product

**podcast** Audio or video file that can be downloaded from the Internet with a subscription that automatically delivers new content to listening devices or personal computers; podcasts offer the benefit of convenience, giving users the ability to listen to or view content when and where they choose

**point-of-purchase (POP) materials** Signs, window displays, display racks, and similar devices used to attract customers

**population** All the elements, units, or individuals of interest to researchers for a specific study

**posttest** Evaluation of advertising effectiveness after the campaign

**power shopping center** A type of shopping center that combines off-price stores with category killers

**predatory pricing** Also called undercutting, involves the intent to set a product's price so low that rival firms cannot compete and therefore withdraw from the marketplace

**premium money (push money)** Extra compensation to salespeople for pushing a line of goods

**premium pricing** Pricing the highest-quality or most versatile products higher than other models in the product line

**premiums** Items offered free or at a minimal cost as a bonus for purchasing a product

**press conference** A meeting used to announce major news events

**prestige pricing** Setting prices at an artificially high level to convey prestige or a quality image

**prestige sensitive** Drawn to products that signify prominence and status

**pretest** Evaluation of advertisements performed before a campaign begins

**price** The value paid for a product in a marketing exchange

**price competition** Emphasizing price as an issue and matching or beating competitors' prices

**price conscious** Striving to pay low prices

**price discrimination** Employing price differentials that injure competition by giving one or more buyers a competitive advantage

**price elasticity of demand** A measure of the sensitivity of demand to changes in price

**price fixing** An agreement among competing firms to raise, lower, or maintain prices for mutual benefit

**price leaders** Products priced near or even below cost

**price lining** Setting a limited number of prices for selected groups or lines of merchandise

**price skimming** Charging the highest possible price that buyers who most desire the product will pay

**price war** A price war involves two or more companies engaging in intense price competition, often in an effort to boost market share

**pricing objectives** Goals that describe what a firm wants to achieve through pricing

**primary data** Data observed and recorded or collected directly from respondents

**primary demand** Demand for a product category rather than for a specific brand

**private distributor brand** A brand initiated and owned by a reseller

**private warehouses** Company-operated facilities for storing and shipping products

**probability sampling** A type of sampling in which every element in the population being studied has a known chance of being selected for study

**process materials** Materials that are used directly in the production of other products but are not readily identifiable

**producer markets** Individuals and business organizations that purchase products to make profits by using them to produce other products or using them in their operations

**product** A good, a service, or an idea

**product adoption process** The five-stage process of buyer acceptance of a product: awareness, interest, evaluation, trial, and adoption

**product advertising** Advertising that promotes the uses, features, and benefits of products

**product competitors** Firms that compete in the same product class but market products with different features, benefits, and prices

**product deletion** Eliminating a product from the product mix when it no longer satisfies a sufficient number of customers

**product design** How a product is conceived, planned, and produced

**product development** Determining if producing a product is technically feasible and cost-effective

**product differentiation** Creating and designing products so that customers perceive them as different from competing products

**product features** Specific design characteristics that allow a product to perform certain tasks

**product item** A specific version of a product that can be designated as a distinct offering among a firm's products

**product life cycle** The progression of a product through four stages: introduction, growth, maturity, and decline

**product line** A group of closely related product items viewed as a unit because of marketing, technical, or end-use considerations

**product-line pricing** Establishing and adjusting prices of multiple products within a product line

**product manager** The person within an organization who is responsible for a product, a product line, or several distinct products that make up a group

**product mix** The composite, or total, group of products that an organization makes available to customers

**product modifications** Changes in one or more characteristics of a product

**product placement** The strategic location of products or product promotions within entertainment media content to reach the product's target market

**product positioning** The decisions and activities intended to create and maintain a certain concept of the firm's product, relative to competitive brands, in customers' minds

**professional pricing** Fees set by people with great skill or experience in a particular field

**product specifications** Written statements describing a product's necessary characteristics, standards of quality, and other information essential to identifying the best supplier for the needed product

**promotion** Communication to build and maintain relationships by informing and persuading one or more audiences

**promotion mix** A combination of promotional methods used to promote a specific product

**prospecting** Developing a database of potential customers

**prosperity** A stage of the business cycle characterized by low unemployment and relatively high total income, which together ensure high buying power (provided the inflation rate stays low)

**proxemic communication** Communicating by varying the physical distance in face-to-face interactions

**psychological influences** Factors that in part determine people's general behavior, thus influencing their behavior as consumers

**psychological pricing** Pricing that attempts to influence a customer's perception of price to make a product's price more attractive

**public relations** Communication efforts used to create and maintain favorable relations between an organization and its stakeholders

**public warehouses** Storage space and related physical distribution facilities that can be leased by companies

**publicity** A news story type of communication about an organization and/or its products transmitted through a mass medium at no charge

**pull policy** Promoting a product directly to consumers to develop strong consumer demand that pulls products through the marketing channel

**pure competition** A market structure characterized by an extremely large number of sellers, none strong enough to significantly influence price or supply

**push policy** Promoting a product only to the next institution down the marketing channel

**quality** The overall characteristics of a product that allow it to perform as expected in satisfying customer needs

**quality modifications** Changes relating to a product's dependability and durability

**quantity discounts** Deductions from the list price for purchasing in large quantities

**quota** A limit on the amount of goods an importing country will accept for certain product categories in a specific period of time

**quota sampling** A nonprobability sampling technique in which researchers divide the population into groups and then arbitrarily choose participants from each group

**rack jobbers** Full-service, specialty-line wholesalers that own and maintain display racks in stores

**radio frequency identification (RFID)** Using radio waves to identify and track materials tagged with special microchips

**random discounting** Temporary reduction of prices on an unsystematic basis

**random factor analysis** An analysis attempting to attribute erratic sales variations to random, nonrecurrent events

**random sampling** A form of probability sampling in which all units in a population have an equal chance of appearing in the sample, and the various events that can occur have an equal or known chance of taking place

**raw materials** Basic natural materials that become part of a physical product

**rebates** Sales promotion techniques in which a consumer receives a specified amount of money for making a single product purchase

**receiver** The individual, group, or organization that decodes a coded message

**recession** A stage of the business cycle during which unemployment rises and total buying power declines, stifling both consumer and business spending

**reciprocity** An arrangement unique to business marketing in which two organizations agree to buy from each other

**recognition test** A posttest in which respondents are shown the actual ad and are asked if they recognize it

**recovery** A stage of the business cycle in which the economy moves from recession or depression toward prosperity

**recruiting** Developing a list of qualified applicants for sales positions

**reference group** A group that a person identifies with so strongly that he or she adopts the values, attitudes, and behavior of group members

**reference pricing** Pricing a product at a moderate level and displaying it next to a more expensive model or brand

**regional issues** Versions of a magazine that differ across geographic regions

**regional shopping center** A type of shopping center with the largest department stores, widest product mixes, and deepest product lines of all shopping centers

**regression analysis** A method of predicting sales based on finding a relationship between past sales and one or more independent variables, such as population or income

**reinforcement advertising** Advertising that assures users they chose the right brand and tells them how to get the most satisfaction from it

**relationship marketing** Establishing long-term, mutually satisfying buyer–seller relationships

**relationship selling** The building of mutually beneficial long-term associations with a customer through regular communications over prolonged periods of time

**reliability** A condition that exists when a research technique produces almost identical results in repeated trials

**reminder advertising** Advertising used to remind consumers about an established brand's uses, characteristics, and benefits

**research design** An overall plan for obtaining the information needed to address a research problem or issue

**reseller markets** Intermediaries that buy finished goods and resell them for a profit

**retail positioning** Identifying an unserved or underserved market segment and serving it through a strategy that distinguishes the retailer from others in the minds of consumers in that segment

**retailer** An organization that purchases products for the purpose of reselling them to ultimate consumers

**retailing** All transactions in which the buyer intends to consume the product through personal, family, or household use

**roles** Actions and activities that a person in a particular position is supposed to perform based on expectations of the individual and surrounding persons

**routinized response behavior** A consumer decision-making process used when buying frequently purchased, low-cost items that require very little search-and-decision effort

**sales analysis** Analysis of sales figures to evaluate a firm's performance

**sales branches** Manufacturer-owned intermediaries that sell products and provide support services to the manufacturer's sales force

**sales contest** A sales promotion method used to motivate distributors, retailers, and sales personnel through recognition of outstanding achievements

**sales force forecasting survey** A survey of a firm's sales force regarding anticipated sales in their territories for a specified period

**sales forecast** The amount of a product a company expects to sell during a specific period at a specified level of marketing activities

**sales offices** Manufacturer-owned operations that provide services normally associated with agents

**sales promotion** An activity and/or material intended to induce resellers or salespeople to sell a product or consumers to buy it

**sample** A limited number of units chosen to represent the characteristics of a total population

**sampling** The process of selecting representative units from a total population

**scan-back allowance** A manufacturer's reward to retailers based on the number of pieces scanned

**screening** Selecting the ideas with the greatest potential for further review

**search qualities** Tangible attributes that can be judged before the purchase of a product

**seasonal analysis** An analysis of daily, weekly, or monthly sales figures to evaluate the degree to which seasonal factors influence sales

**seasonal discount** A price reduction given to buyers for purchasing goods or services out of season

**secondary data** Data compiled both inside and outside the organization for some purpose other than the current investigation

**secondary-market pricing** Setting one price for the primary target market and a different price for another market

**segmentation variables** Characteristics of individuals, groups, or organizations used to divide a market into segments

**selective demand** Demand for a specific brand

**selective distortion** An individual's changing or twisting of information that is inconsistent with personal feelings or beliefs

**selective distribution** Using only some available outlets in an area to distribute a product

**selective exposure** The process by which some inputs are selected to reach awareness and others are not

**selective retention** Remembering information inputs that support personal feelings and beliefs and forgetting inputs that do not

**self-concept** A perception or view of oneself

**selling agents** Intermediaries that market a whole product line or a manufacturer's entire output

**service** An intangible result of the application of human and mechanical efforts to people or objects

**service quality** Customers' perceptions of how well a service meets or exceeds their expectations

**shopping mall intercept interview** A research method that involves interviewing a percentage of individuals passing by "intercept" points in a mall

**shopping products** Items for which buyers are willing to expend considerable effort in planning and making purchases

**Single-source data** Information provided by a single marketing research firm

**situational influences** Influences that result from circumstances, time, and location that affect the consumer buying decision process

**social class** An open group of individuals with similar social rank

**social influences** The forces other people exert on one's buying behavior

**social network** A website where users can create a profile and interact with other users, post information, and engage in other forms of Web-based communication

**social responsibility** An organization's obligation to maximize its positive impact and minimize its negative impact on society

**sociocultural forces** The influences in a society and its culture(s) that change people's attitudes, beliefs, norms, customs, and lifestyles

**sole sourcing** An organization's decision to use only one supplier

**source** A person, group, or organization with a meaning it tries to share with a receiver or an audience

**Southern Common Market (Mercosur)** An alliance that promotes the free circulation of goods, services, and production factors, and has a common external tariff and commercial policy among member nations in South America

**special-event pricing** Advertised sales or price cutting linked to a holiday, a season, or an event

**specialty products** Items with unique characteristics that buyers are willing to expend considerable effort to obtain

**specialty-line Wholesalers** Full-service wholesalers that carry only a single product line or a few items within a product line

**stakeholders** Constituents who have a "stake," or claim, in some aspect of a company's products, operations, markets, industry, and outcomes

**statistical interpretation** Analysis of what is typical and what deviates from the average

**storyboard** A blueprint that combines copy and visual material to show the sequence of major scenes in a commercial

**straight commission compensation plan** Paying salespeople according to the amount of their sales in a given time period

**straight rebuy purchase** A routine purchase of the same products under approximately the same terms of sale by a business buyer

**straight salary compensation plan** Paying salespeople a specific amount per time period, regardless of selling effort

**strategic alliance** A partnership that is formed to create a competitive advantage on a worldwide basis

**strategic business unit (SBU)** A division, product line, or other profit center within the parent company

**strategic channel alliance** An agreement whereby the products of one organization are distributed through the marketing channels of another

**strategic marketing management** The process of planning, implementing, and evaluating the performance of marketing activities and strategies, both effectively and efficiently

**strategic performance evaluation** Establishing performance standards, measuring actual performance, comparing actual performance with established standards, and modifying the marketing strategy, if needed

**strategic philanthropy** The synergistic use of organizational core competencies and resources to address key stakeholders' interests and achieve both organizational and social benefits

**strategic planning** The process of establishing an organizational mission and formulating goals, corporate strategy, marketing objectives, and marketing strategy

**strategic windows** Temporary periods of optimal fit between the key requirements of a market and the particular capabilities of a company competing in that market

**stratified sampling** A type of probability sampling in which the population is divided into groups with a common attribute and a random sample is chosen within each group

**styling** The physical appearance of a product

**subculture** A group of individuals whose characteristics, values, and behavioral patterns are similar within the group and different from those of people in the surrounding culture

**supermarkets** Large, self-service stores that carry a complete line of food products, along with some nonfood products

**superregional shopping center** A type of shopping center with the widest and deepest product mixes that attracts customers from many miles away

**superstores** Giant retail outlets that carry food and nonfood products found in supermarkets, as well as most routinely purchased consumer products

**supply chain** All the activities associated with the flow and transformation of products from raw materials through to the end customer

**supply-chain management** A set of approaches used to integrate the functions of operations management, logistics management, supply management, and marketing channel management so products are produced and distributed in the right quantities, to the right locations, and at the right time

**supply management** In its broadest form, refers to the processes that enable the progress of value from raw material to final customer and back to redesign and final disposition

**support personnel** Sales staff members who facilitate selling but usually are not involved solely with making sales

**sustainability** The potential for the long-term well-being of the natural environment, including all biological entities, as well as the interaction among nature and individuals, organizations, and business strategies

**sustainable competitive advantage** An advantage that the competition cannot copy

**SWOT analysis** Assessment of an organization's strengths, weaknesses, opportunities, and threats

**tactile communication** Communicating through touching

**target audience** The group of people at whom advertisements are aimed

**target market** A specific group of customers on whom an organization focuses its marketing efforts

**target public** A collective of individuals who have an interest in or concern about an organization, product, or social cause

**team selling** The use of a team of experts from all functional areas of a firm, led by a salesperson, to conduct the personal selling process

**technical salespeople** Support salespeople who give technical assistance to a firm's current customers

**technology** The application of knowledge and tools to solve problems and perform tasks more efficiently

**telemarketing** The performance of marketing-related activities by telephone

**telephone depth interview** An interview that combines the traditional focus group's ability to probe with the confidentiality provided by telephone surveys

**telephone survey** A research method in which respondents' answers to a questionnaire are recorded by an interviewer on the phone

**television home shopping** A form of selling in which products are presented to television viewers, who can buy them by calling a toll-free number and paying with a credit card

**test marketing** A limited introduction of a product in geographic areas chosen to represent the intended market

**third-party logistics (3PL) firms** Firms that have special expertise in core physical distribution activities such as warehousing, transportation, inventory management, and information technology and can often perform these activities more efficiently

**time series analysis** A forecasting method that uses historical sales data to discover patterns in the firm's sales over time and generally involves trend, cycle, seasonal, and random factor analyses

**total budget competitors** Firms that compete for the limited financial resources of the same customers

**total cost** The sum of average fixed and average variable costs times the quantity produced

**trade (functional) discount** A reduction off the list price a producer gives to an intermediary for performing certain functions

**trade name** The full legal name of an organization

**trade sales promotion methods** Methods intended to persuade wholesalers and retailers to carry a producer's products and market them aggressively

**trade salespeople** Salespeople involved mainly in helping a producer's customers promote a product

**trademark** A legal designation of exclusive use of a brand

**trading company** A company that links buyers and sellers in different countries

**traditional specialty retailers** Stores that carry a narrow product mix with deep product lines

**transfer pricing** Prices charged in sales between an organization's units

**transportation** The movement of products from where they are made to intermediaries and end users

**trend analysis** An analysis that focuses on aggregate sales data over a period of many years to determine general trends in annual sales

**truck wholesalers** Limited-service wholesalers that transport products directly to customers for inspection and selection

**tying agreement** An agreement in which a supplier furnishes a product to a channel member with the stipulation that the channel member must purchase other products as well

**unaided recall test** A posttest in which respondents are asked to identify advertisements they have seen recently but are not given any recall clues

**undifferentiated targeting strategy** A strategy in which an organization designs a single marketing mix and directs it at the entire market for a particular product

**uniform geographic pricing** Charging all customers the same price, regardless of geographic location

**unsought products** Products purchased to solve a sudden problem, products of which customers are unaware, and products that people do not necessarily think of buying

**validity** A condition that exists when a research method measures what it is supposed to measure

**value** A customer's subjective assessment of benefits relative to costs in determining the worth of a product

**value analysis** An evaluation of each component of a potential purchase

**value conscious** Concerned about price and quality of a product

**variable costs** Costs that vary directly with changes in the number of units produced or sold

**vendor analysis** A formal, systematic evaluation of current and potential vendors

**venture team** A cross-functional group that creates entirely new products that may be aimed at new markets

**vertical channel integration** Combining two or more stages of the marketing channel under one management

**vertical marketing system (VMS)** A marketing channel managed by a single channel member to achieve efficient, low-cost distribution aimed at satisfying target market customers

**viral marketing** A strategy to get consumers to share a marketer's message, often through e-mail or online videos, in a way that spreads dramatically and quickly

**warehouse clubs** Large-scale, members-only establishments that combine features of cash-and-carry wholesaling with discount retailing

**warehouse showrooms** Retail facilities in large, low-cost buildings with large on-premises inventories and minimal services

**warehousing** The design and operation of facilities for storing and moving goods

**wealth** The accumulation of past income, natural resources, and financial resources

**wholesaler** An individual or organization that sells products that are bought for resale, for making other products, or for general business operations

**wholesaling** Transactions in which products are bought for resale, for making other products, or for general business operations

**widget** Small bits of software on a website, desktop, or mobile device that performs a simple purpose, such as providing stock quotes or blog updates

**width of product mix** The number of product lines a company offers

**wiki** Type of software that creates an interface that enables users to add or edit the content of some types of websites

**willingness to spend** An inclination to buy because of expected satisfaction from a product, influenced by the ability to buy and numerous psychological and social forces

**word-of-mouth communication** Personal informal exchanges of communication that customers share with one another about products, brands, and companies

**World Trade Organization (WTO)** An entity that promotes free trade among member nations by eliminating trade barriers and educating individuals, companies, and governments about trade rules around the world

**zone pricing** Pricing based on transportation costs within major geographic zones

# name index

# organization index

# subject index